# ¿Qué tal?

## An Introductory Course

**ENTH EDITION**

**Thalia Dorwick**

**Ana María Pérez-Gironés**
*Wesleyan University*

**Marty Knorre**

**William R. Glass**

**Hildebrando Villarreal**
*California State University, Los Angeles*

### CONTRIBUTING WRITERS:

**Manuel Cortés-Castañeda**
*Eastern Kentucky University*

**Becky S. Jaimes**
*Austin Community College*

**Talía Loaiza**
*Austin Community College*

**Jane Johnson**
*University of Texas, Austin*

McGraw Hill

Boston   Burr Ridge, IL   Dubuque, IA   Madison, WI   New York   San Francisco   St. Louis
Bangkok   Bogotá   Caracas   Kuala Lumpur   Lisbon   London   Madrid   Mexico City
Milan   Montreal   New Delhi   Santiago   Seoul   Singapore   Sydney   Taipei   Toronto

*The McGraw-Hill Companies*

 **Higher Education**

This is an book.

*¿Qué tal?*
*An Introductory Course*

1 2 3 4 5 6 7 8 9 0 DOW DOW 0 9 8 7 6

ISBN-13: 978-007-304850-5 (Student Edition)
ISBN-10: 0-07-304850-X

ISBN-13: 978-007-320799-5 (Instructor's Edition)
ISBN-10: 0-07-320799-3

Vice president and Editor-in-chief: *Emily G. Barrosse*
Publisher: *William R. Glass*
Senior sponsoring editor: *Christa Harris*
Director of development: *Scott Tinetti*
Development editor: *Pennie Nichols*
Executive marketing manager: *Nick Agnew*
Production editor: *Mel Valentín*
Lead production supervisor: *Randy Hurst*
Senior supplements producer: *Louis Swaim*
Design manager/cover designer: *Violeta Diaz*
Interior designer: *Linda Robertson*
Photo editor: *Alexandra Ambrose*
Photo researcher: *Susan Friedman*
Art editor: *Robin Mouat*
Compositor: *TechBooks/GTS Companies, York, PA*
Typeface: *10/12 Palatino*
Printer and binder: *Donnelley—Willard*

Cover image: Carlos Planck, *La Danza*, 1969. Collection of Annie Orban. Courtesy of Mosto & Rojas Arte, Buenos Aires, Argentina.

LIBRARY OF CONGRESS CATALOGING-IN-PUBLICATION DATA

Que tal? : an introductory course / Thalia Dorwick . . . [et al.].—7th ed.
    p. cm.
  Includes index.
    ISBN   0-07-304850-X (alk. paper : instructor's ed.)
    1. Spanish language—Textbooks for foreign speakers—English. I. Dorwick, Thalia, 1944–

PC4129.E5Q4 2006
468.2'421—dc22

2005058008

http://www.mhhe.com

# De compras 79

# En casa 105

**CAPÍTULO 7**

# De vacaciones  181

**CAPÍTULO 8**

# Los días festivos  207

*Contents*

*" . . . to help students develop proficiency in the four language skills essential to truly communicative language learning . . . "*

from the preface to *¿Qué tal?*, first edition, 1983

Welcome to the seventh edition of *¿Qué tal? An Introductory Course.* It has been more than twenty years since the publication of the first edition, and the coauthors are grateful to the instructors and students who have responded so positively to the goals and approach of *¿Qué tal?*

In those years, much has changed and much has remained constant in *¿Qué tal? ¿Qué tal?* has remained true to the goals of the first edition, as cited above. The approach, however, has evolved and kept pace with technological advances and our increasing knowledge of how languages are learned. The ancillary package for the first edition of *¿Qué tal?* was excellent for its time but seems small in comparison to the plethora of materials available to instructors and students today. Particularly noteworthy are the wide variety of new technologies that enhance language learning in ways not yet dreamed of twenty years ago.

In addition to these new technologies, instructors will find in the seventh edition those features that they have come to know and trust over the years as well as many new features. These features include:

## A Design that Promotes Learning and Teaching

- More than 500 new color illustrations and photographs bring an exciting new visual appeal to the program and enhance the pedagogy of the text. Beautiful drawings illustrate vocabulary words in each chapter, allowing students to make important connections between the Spanish word and the conceptual meaning. Many activities are also enlivened through lively illustrations that review vocabulary and grammar and promote real communication.

- The flow of presentations and activities within the chapter has been carefully crafted to keep students on task and focused. Activities do not break over the front and back of pages, thus eliminating the need for students and instructors to "flip" pages while completing activities.

- Sentence-formation and cloze passage activities are now pedagogically improved through the use of special

shading and color that highlight key elements of the activity and keep students focused on the tasks they are performing.

## Student-Friendly Grammar Features

- Paradigms and charts within grammar presentations have been enhanced by the use of a colored font that directs students' attention to key aspects of the grammar point, such as spelling changes in stem-changing verbs and agreement of adjectives.

- New timelines place major grammar tenses on a continuum from Past ←→ Present ←→ Future and help students understand the "big picture" as they move through the sequence of tenses presented throughout the text.

- **Autoprueba** quizzes allow students to do quick self-assessments of their understanding of key grammar points in every chapter, before they begin the exercises and activities.

- New drawings illustrate many new verb infinitives, encouraging students to learn meaning through visual association.

- Interactive **Flash Grammar** tutorials on the CD-ROM and the *Online Learning Center* Website allow students to "see" core grammar structures. The tutorials are enriched by interactive paradigms and sample sentences.

## An Introduction to Literary Masterpieces and Musical Traditions

- New to this edition, the **Voces de...** (country) page features literature and music from the country or countries of focus in the chapter. The **Literatura** section profiles renowned authors from these countries, accompanied by a brief extract from one of their works. These brief extracts—just a "taste" of some **obras maestras**—will enrich students' appreciation of the literary heritage of the Spanish-speaking world and hopefully motivate some students to continue reading when their Spanish language skills are better developed. The **Música** section presents the rich diversity of musical traditions and styles from the featured country or countries.

## An All-New Video Program That Brings Language and Hispanic Cultures to Life

- The **Entrevista cultural** segments introduce students to a Spanish-speaker from a different country in each chapter, providing a unique glimpse into their lives and their culture. Accompanying activities in the new **Videoteca** section of each chapter both prepare students for viewing and assess comprehension.

- The **Entre amigos** episodes present four students from different countries (Spain, Mexico, Venezuela, and Cuba) who tell entertaining stories as they meet and talk at a university in Mexico. These entertaining vignettes also review vocabulary themes and grammatical structures in each chapter, bringing the language to life. Taken together, both video segments provide an opportunity for students to hear authentic Spanish spoken by real Spanish speakers who interact with each other, rather than actors speaking for the camera.

- The popular video episodes from the previous edition of *¿Qué tal?* continue to be available on the *Video Program,* and can still be used, chapter-by-chapter, with the seventh edition.

## Diverse Cultural Content

- Each chapter focuses on one area of the Spanish-speaking world. A large photo on the chapter opening pages introduces students to the chapter's themes as well as to the country of focus, and provides an engaging starting point for conversation.

- Special cultural features, including the **Nota cultural** and the **En los Estados Unidos y el Canadá** boxes, give quick and interesting glimpses into Hispanic cultures.

- The new **Voces de...** and **Videoteca** section in each chapter, as well as the **Enfoque cultural** section, highlight the country of focus through video segments, texts, and photos.

While much is new to this edition of *¿Qué tal?,* you will continue to find the many hallmarks that make it the book of choice for hundreds of instructors across the country. These hallmark features include:

- the user-friendly **Paso** structure that facilitates lesson planning and helps students stay focused

- an abundance of classroom-tested practice material, ranging from form-focused activities to communicative activities that promote real conversation

- vocabulary, grammar, and culture that work together as interactive units, unifying this important aspect of language learning

- an emphasis on the meaningful use of Spanish

- a positive portrayal of contemporary Hispanic cultures

- print and media supplementary materials that are carefully coordinated with the core text

The pages that follow provide a more detailed overview of changes to this edition in a section called "What's New in the Seventh Edition?" The next section, "A Guided Tour," explains and shows the organization and features of *¿Qué tal?* (useful to both instructors and students!), followed by a comprehensive discussion of supplementary materials. The Preface closes with the acknowledgment of the many instructors and students who helped shape this new edition.

# WHAT'S NEW TO THE SEVENTH EDITION?

## New Art

Instructors will immediately notice the new art in this edition of *¿Qué tal?* While the art of previous editions has always been well received, we felt it was time for a change. The artists were carefully guided so that the art would be both pedagogically sound and visually beautiful. The result of the art is a visually enhanced seventh edition that satisfies the needs of today's sophisticated students and instructors, both pedagogically and visually.

## Chapter Themes

The positive response from instructors using earlier editions confirmed that the chapter themes found in *¿Qué tal?* provide engaging and relevant content for exploration and discussion. Theme vocabulary for all chapters has, of course, been updated to reflect changes in the areas of technology, recreational activities, and so forth. The vocabulary lists in **Capítulos 7** and **16** have been reorganized for easier practice and study. The vocabulary of **Capítulo 14** has been modified to focus more on the natural world, and the vocabulary of **Capítulo 18** now reflects travel vocabulary students are likely to use in today's traveling environment.

## New Chapter Opening Page

We have redesigned the chapter opening page. The result is an introduction to the chapter that is more engaging and more purposeful to the instructor and the student. Spending class time on the chapter opener will provide a useful introduction to the chapter for the student and set the stage for a more successful experience with the chapter content. (A visual presentation of the new Chapter Opener is provided in the Guided Tour presented in this Preface.)

## Capítulo preliminar: Primeros pasos

Responding to reviewer feedback, the authors have carefully recrafted and shortened the **Capítulo preliminar.** Its purpose remains the same: to introduce students to the sounds of Spanish and to a variety of high-frequency language that will ease their transition into the course. In addition, this special chapter continues to introduce students to the geographic and cultural diversity of the Spanish-speaking world. However, the amount of material has been considerably reduced, resulting in two **pasos** rather than three. The material that has been eliminated from the preliminary chapter has been integrated into other chapters of *¿Qué tal?*

## User-Friendly Activities

In addition to being carefully ordered from form-focused to more open-ended, communicative tasks, the activities are now also carefully placed on the pages so that students and instructors will not need to flip pages as they complete an activity. Additional models provide more support and materials, and elicit more student interaction. Many activities focus even more on reviewing and recycling vocabulary and structure from previous chapters.

## Notas culturales

Many of the **Notas culturales** have been replaced with new **Notas** or revised. Instructors will find that the **Notas culturales** consistently reflect some aspect of the chapter theme and focus on high-interest topics. In addition, the *Instructor's Edition* now features a series of follow-up questions for each **Nota,** providing instructors with ready-made activities to use in class.

## Voces de... (country)

Instructors familiar with the previous editions of *¿Qué tal?* will notice a new feature: the new **Voces de...** page. Found between **Pasos 2** and **3, Voces de...** highlights two cultural aspects of the country or countries of focus: literature and music.

- **Literatura de...** This section, developed in response to instructor's requests for more country-specific literature and culture, features an important author from the chapter's country of focus and includes an excerpt from one of that author's works. A short biographical note provides information on the author's life. The intent of this section is to raise students' awareness of the amazingly rich literary tradition of the Spanish-speaking world, as well as give them a "taste" of some **obras maestras.**

  While these brief readings will be challenging for most students, some at least will profit from and be motivated by reading them . . . and perhaps a few will become Spanish majors in part because they were "touched" by one or more selections. While choosing these excerpts was not an easy task for the *¿Qué tal?* author team, all of us—whether we are linguists or literary specialists—remembered and reconnected with our early enthusiasm for Spanish literature as we tried to read the excerpts through the eyes of today's students.

- The purpose of the **Música** section of the **Voces de...** page is to introduce students to the rich diversity of music in the Spanish-speaking world. The section features musical traditions of the featured country or countries. Magazine-style short reading passages provide information on traditional instruments, musical styles and genres, famous musicians, traditional dances, and so on. These brief reading passages are accompanied by photos or drawings.

## Videoteca

The **Videoteca** page found in every chapter is completely new. It has two sections.

- **Entrevista cultural,** a video-based interview with a native speaker from the country of focus. Each interview, directly related to the chapter theme, reflects the native speakers' interests, professions, studies, or background. Student viewers of the interview benefit from the country-specific cultural information in it and also from the link to the chapter's vocabulary and, at times, grammar. When two countries are covered, there is a corresponding interview with a native speaker from each country.

- **Entre amigos,** a video-based feature that follows the entertaining discussions of a group of four college students. These students reflect the geographic and cultural diversity of the Spanish-speaking world.

Rubén is from Spain, Miguel from Mexico, Karina from Venezuela, and Tané from Cuba. In these segments, the four students informally discuss chapter-related topics that affect their daily lives. The language is natural and nonscripted, resulting in spontaneous discussions that reflect the interests and concerns of today's Spanish-speaking young adults, in an environment that encourages cross-cultural comparison.

## Un poco de todo

The **Un poco de todo** review sections are again part of the **Paso 3** of each chapter, the final step in the presentation and practice of the new grammar structures. This edition features twelve new engaging cloze paragraphs that present cultural information as they review the grammatical and lexical material from both the corresponding chapter and previous chapters. Each **Un poco de todo** cloze paragraph is identified as a **Lengua y cultura** activity to underscore the recycling of vocabulary and structures and highlight the activity's cultural focus. This cultural focus is directly related to the theme of the chapter or the chapter's country of focus. Thus, culture and language are naturally integrated in the **Un poco de todo** sections of every chapter.

The seventh edition of *¿Qué tal?* features a uniquely clear and user-friendly **paso** organization. Each of its eighteen regular chapters is divided into four **pasos,** highlighted with color tabs for easy reference, with the **Voces de...** cultural feature in the middle. Thus, each regular chapter has the following structure.

> Paso 1: Vocabulario
> Paso 2: Gramática
> Voces de...
> Paso 3: Gramática
> Paso 4: Un paso más

## Paso 1: Vocabulario

This section presents and practices the chapter's thematic vocabulary. The lexical lists in these sections are read on the Listening Comprehension Audio CD and are signaled by a headphone icon. Each new lexical list is followed by a **Conversación** section that practices the new vocabulary in context.

## Pasos 2 and 3: Gramática

These sections present one to two grammar points each. Each grammar point is introduced by a minidialogue, a cartoon or drawing, realia, or a brief reading that presents the grammar topic in context. Grammar explanations, in English, appear in the left-hand column of the two-column design; paradigms and sample sentences appear in the right-hand column. Each grammar presentation is followed by a series of contextualized exercises and activities that progress from more controlled (**Práctica**) to more open-ended (**Conversación**).

## Voces de...

The cultures of the Spanish-speaking world are an integral part of every section of *¿Qué tal?,* but literature and music take central stage in the **Voces de...** section of each chapter. Located between **Pasos 2** and **3, Voces de...** has two parts: **Literatura** and **Música. Literatura** introduces an important writer from the featured country with a brief biography of him or her and a fragment of an important work. **Música** highlights one or more of the musical traditions of the chapter's country of focus.

## Paso 4: Un paso más

This section integrates the vocabulary and grammar from the first three **pasos** in a rich and stimulating selection of skill-building activities: **Videoteca** (video comprehension

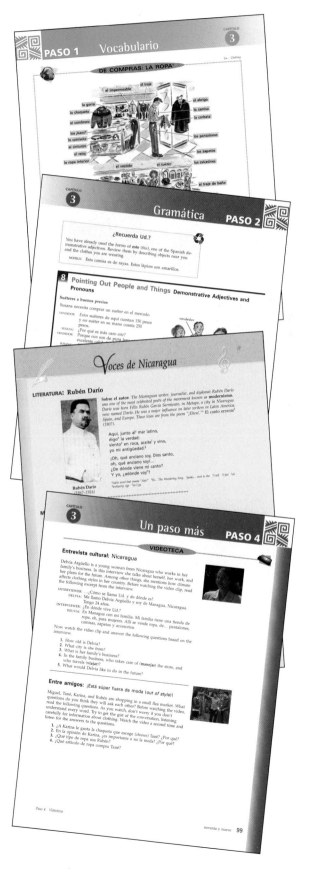

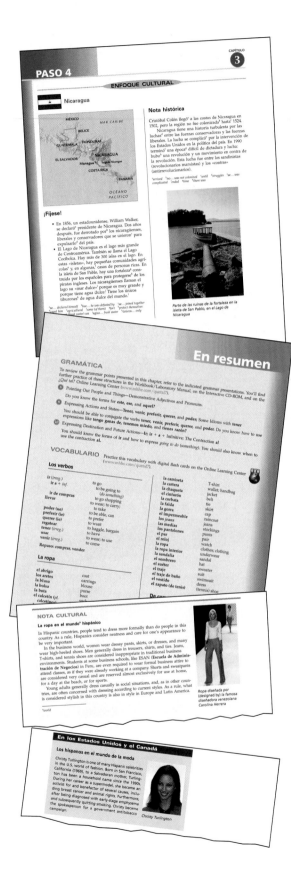

and discussion questions); **Enfoque cultural** (brief readings, photos, and a map that present historical and cultural information about the chapter's country or countries of focus); **A leer** (readings and pre-reading strategies); **A escribir** (brief writing assignments based on the chapter theme); and **A conversar** (chapter-culminating communicative activities). The **A leer** and **A escribir** sections are found in odd-numbered chapters; **A conversar** activities are found in even-numbered chapters.

## En resumen

This end-of-chapter grammar and vocabulary summary consists of two sections: **Gramática** and **Vocabulario.** The **Gramática** section provides students with a quick overview of the major grammar points within the chapter as well as a reminder of what they should know for assessment purposes. The **Vocabulario** section includes all important words and expressions from the chapter that are considered active.

## Additional features

- **Un poco de todo: Lengua y cultura** activities, found in **Paso 3: Gramática,** combine and review grammar presented in the chapter as well as important grammar from previous chapters. Major topics that are continuously spiraled in this section include **ser** and **estar,** preterite and imperfect, gender and gender agreement, and indicative and subjunctive.

- **Nota cultural** features highlight an aspect of Hispanic cultures throughout the world.

- **En los Estados Unidos y el Canadá** are brief sections that focus on U.S. and Canadian Hispanics and institutions. Key words and phrases are highlighted in these sections in order to facilitate comprehension.

- **Nota comunicativa** sections provide additional information about communication in Spanish.

- **Vocabulario útil** boxes give additional vocabulary that may be necessary to work through a chapter's activities.

- **Autoprueba** boxes that follow grammar presentations provide students with the opportunity to quickly check their understanding of a specific grammar point.

For more information on these and other features of *¿Qué tal?,* please visit the text-specific website at **www.mhhe.com/quetal7.**

As with all previous editions of *¿Qué tal?*, the seventh edition is based on the highly successful *Puntos de partida* first-year Spanish text. Responding to the wishes of many instructors across the country, *¿Qué tal?* retains the methodology and functionality of the *Puntos* program but in a shorter version, which can be ideal for classes meeting three or fewer times per week.

In order to create *¿Qué tal?* from *Puntos,* the coauthors reduced the amount of activities and exercises in the *Puntos* main text and supplements as well as the actual number of grammar points presented in *Puntos.* Additional points are subsumed within related structures or within other parts of the text (Instructor's Edition annotations, **Nota comunicativa** features, and so on).

The *Puntos* grammar points that were modified or removed for the sixth edition of *¿Qué tal?* are:

- Asking Yes/No Questions
- Relative Pronouns
- **Hace... que** + *present* and *preterite*
- Summary of the Subjunctive
- Stressed Possessives
- Hypothetical Situations

With one to three grammar points per chapter, we feel *¿Qué tal?* to be a very manageable book for you and your students. Above all, we believe *¿Qué tal?* to be a *flexible* program, one that can be adapted to suit different teaching and learning styles.

# SUPPLEMENTARY MATERIALS FOR THE SEVENTH EDITION

The supplements listed here may accompany the seventh edition of *¿Qué tal?*. Please contact your local McGraw-Hill Higher Education representative for details concerning policies, prices, and availability, as some restrictions may apply.

***Workbook / Laboratory Manual*** and ***Audio Program,*** by Alice A. Arana (formerly of Fullerton College), Oswaldo Arana (formerly of California State University, Fullerton), and María Sabló-Yates (Delta College). The two volumes of the Workbook / Laboratory Manual provide a wealth of activities, both aural and written, that reinforce chapter content. Audio Program CDs are free to adopting institutions and are also available for student purchase upon request. An Audioscript is also available for instructors.

- The *Online Workbook/Laboratory Manual,* developed in collaboration with Quia™, offers an online version of this printed supplement. Increasingly popular, this online version of the printed material offers such benefits for the student as an integrated *Laboratory Audio Program,* self-scoring activities, and instant feedback. Benefits for the instructor include a gradebook that automatically scores, tracks, and records student grades and provides the opportunity to review individual and class performance. Other benefits include customizable activities and features and instant access to grades and performance.

- The *Online Learning Center* Website provides students with a wealth of exercises and activities specially created for use with *¿Qué tal?*. The *Online Learning Center* consists of two general areas: the free content and the premium content. *Free content* includes additional vocabulary and grammar practice quizzes, cultural activities, chapter overviews, and more. All students have access to free content through the *¿Qué tal?* Website (www.mhhe.com/quetal7). *Premium content* includes the *Laboratory Audio Program,* the **Enfoque cultural** video footage, and the **Flash Grammar Tutorials.** Students have access to the premium content through the *Online Learning Center* passcode that is packaged free with every new student text. Students that purchase a used text may purchase a passcode separately at a nominal price if they wish to access this premium content.

- The *Interactive CD-ROM* is an exciting, multimedia supplement that offers additional vocabulary and grammar practice activities, vocabulary games, review activities, interactive grammar tutorials, video-based activities, speaking activities that simulate conversations with native speakers, cultural activities, reading and writing activities, a "talking" dictionary, and much more. This highly popular interactive supplement has been revised and upgraded for the seventh edition and includes new activities and features not available on earlier versions.

- The *Video on CD* provides students with access to the entire *¿Qué tal? Video Program.* Available for purchase, this set of two CD-ROMs includes every video segment from the *Video Program,* as well as follow-up activities for every segment. Instructors who find they do not have the time to show the *Video Program* in class will be pleased to know that it is available to students in this format, providing students with a wealth of authentic and natural linguistic and cultural input.

The *Instructor's Manual and Resource Kit* offers an extensive introduction to teaching techniques, general guidelines for instructors, suggestions for lesson planning in semester and quarter schedules, and additional pre- and post-viewing activities for the video. Also included are a wide variety of interactive and communicative games for practicing vocabulary and grammar. We are very grateful to Linda H. Colville of Citrus College for creating these games.

The *Testing Program* reflects the revisions in the student text for the seventh edition. It also includes sections for testing reading and listening comprehension, as well as tests for oral proficiency and sections designed to test cultural material presented in the program.

- A new *Video Program* accompanies the seventh edition of *¿Qué tal?.* It includes two new video segments for every chapter: The **Entrevista cultural** segment and the **Entre amigos** segment. In addition, the highly popular **Minidramas** vignettes, the **En contexto** functional segments, and the **Conozca...** cultural footage have been retained from the previous edition, resulting in a *Video Program* of approximately five hours in length. This rich resource offers instructors a wide variety of video material of differing types that correspond directly to every chapter of the textbook.

- The *Adopter's Audio CD Program,* provided free to adopting institutions, contains all of the audio CDs from the *Laboratory Audio Program* as well as the *Textbook Listening CD.* It also contains an *Audioscript.* Adopting institutions may use this *Adopter's Audio CD Program* in their Language Laboratory. In addition, institutions may make copies of these materials for students, provided that students are only charged for the cost of blank tapes or CDs.

A set of **Overhead Transparencies,** most in full color, contains drawings from the text and supplementary drawings for use with vocabulary and grammar presentation. An electronic online version of the Transparencies is available to instructors on the *¿Qué tal?* Online Learning Center Website.

- The *Institutional CD-ROM* package consists of twenty copies of the *Interactive CD-ROM.* This package is made available for purchase by departments and laboratories.

# ACKNOWLEDGMENTS

The suggestions, advice, and work of the following friends and colleagues are gratefully acknowledged by the authors of the seventh edition.

- Dr. Bill VanPatten (University of Illinois, Chicago), whose creativity has been an inspiration to us and from whom we have learned so very much about language teaching and how students learn.

- María Sabló-Yates, whose extensive research provides the basis for many of the **Enfoque cultural** sections.

- Dr. Manuel Cortés-Castañeda (Eastern Kentucky University), whose engaging and creative **A conversar** activities provide wonderful chapter-culminating communicative tasks and projects.

- Dr. Gail Fenderson (Brock University), whose work on the revised **En los Estados Unidos y el Canadá** sections has expanded our knowledge of the Hispanic community in Canada.

- Dr. Lynne Lemley (University of Texas, Austin), who created the engaging new cultural cloze passages that appear in the **Un poco de todo** sections.

- Dr. Jane Johnson (University of Texas, Austin), who created the activities that accompany the new **Entrevista cultural** video segments.

- Becky S. Jaimes and Talía Loaiza (both of Austin Community College), whose **Notas culturales** offer students a series of outstanding cultural readings on a wide range of high-interest topics.

- Dr. A. Raymond Elliott (University of Texas, Arlington) whose contributions to the Instructor's Edition and Instructor's Manual and Resource Kit have served to make those supplements even more invaluable teaching resources.

- Laura Chastain (El Salvador), whose invaluable contributions to the text range from language usage to suggestions for realia.

- Ruth Ordás and Dr. Theodore V. Higgs, whose contributions to previous editions are still evident in the seventh edition.

In addition, the publishers wish to acknowledge the suggestions received from the following instructors and professional friends across the country. The appearance of their names in this list does not necessarily constitute their endorsement of the text or its methodology.

## Instructor Focus Group Participants

We thank our instructor focus group participants, who graciously gave us their detailed feedback and suggestions. Their honesty and constructive criticism have greatly enhanced the seventh edition.

Juan Bernal,
*San Diego City College*
Ezequiel Cárdenas,
*Cuyamaca College*
Margaret Eomurian,
*Houston Community College*
Raquel N. González,
*University of Michigan, Ann Arbor*
María Grana,
*Houston Community College*
Yolanda Guerrero,
*Grossmont College*

Carmen M. Hernández,
*Grossmont College*
Judy Hittle,
*Indiana University Northwest*
Casilde Isabelli,
*University of Nevada, Reno*
Joseph P. Kelliher,
*Cuyamaca College*
Ruth Fátima Konopka,
*Grossmont College*
José Manuel Lacorte,
*University of Maryland*

Eva Mendieta,
*Indiana University Northwest*
Judith Minarick,
*Grossmont College*
Lizette Moon,
*Houston Community College*
Nora Olmos,
*Houston Community College*
Nancy Pinnick,
*Indiana University Northwest*

Janet Sandarg,
*Augusta State University*
Jacquelyn Sandone,
*University of Missouri– Columbia*
Edda Temoche-Weldele,
*Grossmont College*
Omaida Westlake,
*Grossmont College*
Carlos H. Villacis,
*Houston Community College*

## Special Consultants

We are especially indebted to the many instructors who completed intense "how does this work in the classroom?" reviews of the text. Their comments and the comments of their students were truly the informing voice of this edition, helping us fine-tune every aspect of the text to ensure that everything "works." These consultants also provided the **Bright Idea** annotations for the *Instructor's Edition.*

Yvette Aparicio,
*Grinnell College*

Ellen Brennan,
*Indiana University–Purdue University Indianapolis*

Obdulia Castro,
*University of Colorado, Boulder*

Arleen Chiclana,
*University of North Florida*

Stephen Clark,
*Northern Arizona University*

Elisabeth Combier,
*North Georgia College and State University*

Kathy Dwyer Navajas,
*University of Florida at Gainesville*

Delia Escalante,
*Phoenix College*

Celia Esplugas,
*West Chester University of Pennsylvania*

Charles Grove,
*West Chester University of Pennsylvania*

Marilen Loyola,
*University of Wisconsin, Madison*

April Marshall,
*New York University*

Delia Montesinos,
*University of Texas, Austin*

Sherrie Nunn,
*University of Florida at Gainesville*

Lynne Overesch-Maister,
*Johnson County Community College*

Tina Peña,
*Tulsa Community College*

Marcia Picallo,
*County College of Morris*

Stacy Powell,
*Auburn University*

Silvia Ramírez,
*University of Texas, Austin*

Jeffrey T. Reeder,
*Sonoma State University*

Jaime Sánchez,
*Volunteer State University*

Emily Scida,
*University of Virginia, Charlottesville*

Louis Silvers,
*Monroe Community College*

Bretton White,
*University of Wisconsin, Madison*

María José Zubieta,
*New York University*

## Reviewers

We are grateful to the following reviewers, whose insight and suggestions have helped shape the seventh edition.

Esther Aguilar,
*San Diego State University*

Serge Ainsa,
*Yavapai College, Prescott*

Enrica J. Ardemagni,
*Indiana University–Purdue University Indianapolis*

Bobbie L. Arndt,
*Pennsylvania State University, Altoona*

Haydee Ayala-Richards,
*Shippensburg University of Pennysylvania*

Angela Bagués,
*Shippensburg University of Pennsylvania*

Nancy J. Barclay,
*Lake Tahoe Community College*

Brenda Calderon,
*Oral Roberts University*

Stephen Clark,
*Northern Arizona University*

Daria Cohen,
*Princeton University*

Linda H. Colville,
*Citrus College*

Brian Cope,
*University of California, Irvine*

Roselyn Costantino,
*Pennsylvania State University, Altoona*

Kit Decker,
*Piedmont Virginia Community College*

Danion L. Doman,
*Truman State University*

Hector F. Espitia,
*Grand Valley State University*

Rafael Falcón,
*Goshen College*

Alla N. Fil,
*New York University*

Laura A. Fox,
*Grand Valley State University*

Khédija Gadhoum,
*Grand Valley State University*

Martha Goldberg,
*California Polytechnic State University*

Andrew Steven Gordon,
*Mesa State College*

Antonio Gragera,
*Southwest Texas State University*

Betty Gudz,
*Sierra College*

Ellen Haynes,
*University of Colorado, Boulder*

Candy Henry,
*Westmoreland Community College, Youngwood*

Carmen M. Hernández,
*Grossmont College*

Todd Anthony Hernández,
*University of Kansas*

María Cecilia Herrera,
*University of Wisconsin, Oshkosh*

Ann M. Hilberry,
*University of Michigan*

Danielle Holden,
*Oakton Community College*

Valerie Y. Job,
*South Plains College,*
*Levelland*
Hilda M. Kachmar,
*Southern Methodist*
*University*
Paula A. Kellar,
*Pennsylvania State*
*University, Altoona*
Marilyn Kiss,
*Wagner College*
Sara Smith Laird,
*Texas Lutheran*
*University*
Paul Larson,
*Baylor University*
Leticia P. López,
*San Diego Mesa College*
María López Morgan,
*Okaloosa-Walton*
*Community College*
Monica Malamud,
*Cañada College*
Jude Thomas Manzo,
*San Antonio College*
Patricia A. Marshall,
*Wesleyan University*

Lisa M. McCallum,
*Auburn University*
Bette J. McLaud,
*Onondaga Community*
*College*
María-Teresa Moinette,
*University of Central*
*Oklahoma*
Kathryn A. Mussett,
*Pennsylvania State*
*University, Altoona*
Eunice D. Myers,
*Wichita State University*
Duane C. Nelson,
*Cloud County*
*Community College*
Michelle Renee Orecchio,
*University of Michigan*
Jorge Pérez,
*University of California,*
*Santa Barbara*
Oralia Preble-Niemi,
*University of Tennessee,*
*Chattanooga*
Jessica J. Ramírez,
*Grand Valley State*
*University*

Tracy Rasmussen,
*Lake Tahoe Community*
*College*
Kathleen Regan,
*University of Portland*
Duane Rhoades,
*University of Wyoming*
Zaira Rivera Casellas,
*University of the*
*Sacred Heart, San*
*Juan*
Claudia Sahagún,
*Broward Community*
*College*
Maritza Salgueiro-
Carlisle,
*Bakersfield College*
Jaime Sánchez,
*Volunteer State*
*Community College*
Carmen Schlig,
*Georgia State*
*University*
Charles C. Schroeder,
*North Iowa Area*
*Community College–*
*Mason City*

Georgia Seminet,
*Texas A&M University,*
*Commerce*
Philippe P. Seminet,
*Texas A&M University,*
*Commerce*
Mary-Lee Sullivan,
*Binghamton University*
Fausto Vergara,
*Houston Community*
*College*
Deborah Walker,
*Muscatine Community*
*College*
Alex Whitman,
*Lower Columbia College*
Gloria Williams,
*Lincoln University*
Joy S. Woolf,
*Westminster College*
Jiyoung Yoon,
*University of North Texas*
Francisco Zabaleta,
*San Diego State University*
Patricia Zuker,
*University of California,*
*San Diego*

Many other individuals deserve our thanks and appreciation for their help and support. Among them are the people who, in addition to the authors, read the seventh edition at various stages of development to ensure its linguistic and cultural authenticity and pedagogical accuracy: Alice A. Arana (United States), Oswaldo Arana (Peru), Laura Chastain (El Salvador), and María Sabló-Yates (Panama).

Special thanks are also due to Margaret Metz who arranged and conducted the instructor focus groups and coordinated the contributions of our Special Consultants. Margaret's participation made it possible for us to incorporate such a vast amount of feedback from instructors, and we are very grateful for her help.

Within the McGraw-Hill family, we would like to acknowledge the contributions of the following individuals: Linda Toy and the McGraw-Hill production group, especially Violeta Díaz for her inspired work on the design of the seventh edition, Mel Valentín for his invaluable assistance as Production Editor, and Randy Hurst and Louis Swaim for their work on various aspects of production. We would also like to thank Amanda Peabody for her helpful editorial assistance. Special thanks are due to Eirik Børve, who originally brought some of us together, and to Nick Agnew and the McGraw-Hill marketing and sales staff for their constant support and efforts. We especially thank Christa Harris, our Sponsoring Editor, who helped us keep our sights and efforts focused on the main goals of this edition. We are especially appreciative of the work of Pennie Nichols, who adroitly wove together the feedback and contributions from many sources into a coherent whole.

The only reasons for publishing a new textbook or to revise an existing one are to help the profession evolve in meaningful ways and to make the task of daily classroom instruction easier and more enjoyable for experienced instructors and teaching assistants alike. Language teaching has changed in important ways since the publication of the first edition of *¿Qué tal?*. We are delighted to have been—and to continue to be—agents of that evolution. And we are grateful to McGraw-Hill for its continuing support of our ideas.

# ¿Qué tal?

## An Introductory Course

# Primeros pasos°

Primeros... *First steps*

*Santiago, Chile*

*San Juan, Puerto Rico*

As you study Spanish in *¿Qué tal?*, you will also learn about the ethnic, racial, and cultural diversity of the Spanish-speaking world.

**¿Qué tal?** means *Hi, how are you doing?* in Spanish. This textbook, called *¿Qué tal?*, will help you begin to learn Spanish and get ready to communicate with Spanish speakers in this country and elsewhere in the Spanish-speaking world.

To speak a language involves much more than just learning its grammar and vocabulary; to know a language is to know the people who speak it. For this reason *¿Qué tal?* will provide you with cultural information to help you understand and appreciate the traditions and values of Spanish-speaking people all over the world.

Are you ready for the adventure of learning Spanish? **Pues, ¡adelante!** (*Well, let's go!*)

**Resources:** Available resources for subsequent chapters are listed in the "Chapter-by-Chapter" section of the Instructor's Manual.

**For Students**
- Workbook/Laboratory Manual and Laboratory Audio Program
- Quia™ Online Workbook/Online Laboratory Manual
- Video on CD
- Interactive CD-ROM
- *¿Qué tal?* Online Learning Center (**www.mhhe.com/quetal7**)

**For Instructors**
- *Instructor's Manual and Resource Kit,* "Chapter-by-Chapter" Supplementary Materials
- Overhead Transparencies 1–6
- Testing Program
- Test Generator
- Video Program
- Audioscript
- *¿Qué tal?* Online Learning Center (**www.mhhe.com/quetal7**)

**Multimedia**
- The multimedia materials that accompany this and subsequent chapters are referenced in the Student Edition with icons to help you identify when and where to incorporate them.
- The *Instructor's Manual and Resource Kit* (IM) provides suggestions for using the multimedia materials in the classroom.

## PRIMER PASO
- Saludos y expresiones de cortesía
- El alfabeto español
- ¿Cómo es usted?

## SEGUNDO PASO
- Los números 0–30; *hay*
- Gustos y preferencias
- ¿Qué hora es?

## PRONUNCIACIÓN
- Las vocales: *a, e, i, o, u*

## CULTURA
- **Nota cultural:** Spanish in the United States and in the World
- **A leer:** La geografía del mundo hispánico
- **Videoteca**
  **Entre amigos:** ¡Encantada!

**Notes**
- Every chapter begins with a photo that introduces the theme of the chapter and places it within the context of the students' knowledge of their own culture *vis-à-vis* the Hispanic cultures.
- Point out the chapter-opener photos. Have students talk about the ethnic makeup of their own campus. Encourage them to consider whether the proportion of students of diverse backgrounds is ideal. Ask what opportunities the campus offers for language learners to meet and talk to heritage speakers from this country and to native speakers from here and abroad. Request and offer information about available Spanish clubs and Spanish "houses" or "tables" where participants speak only Spanish.
- The table on the chapter opener introduces the main cultural content, vocabulary themes, and grammar points of the chapter. This is intended to serve as an advance organizer for the chapter and, in later chapters, to help students recognize material they may have seen before.

### Saludos° y expresiones de cortesía

*Greetings*

Here are some words, phrases, and expressions that will enable you to meet and greet others appropriately in Spanish.

**1.   Sevilla, España**

| 1. | MANOLO: | ¡Hola, Maricarmen! |
|---|---|---|
| | MARICARMEN: | ¿Qué tal, Manolo? ¿Cómo estás? |
| | MANOLO: | Muy bien. ¿Y tú? |
| | MARICARMEN: | Regular. Nos vemos, ¿eh? |
| | MANOLO: | Hasta mañana. |

| 2. | ELISA VELASCO: | Buenas tardes, señor Gómez. |
|---|---|---|
| | MARTÍN GÓMEZ: | Muy buenas, señora Velasco. ¿Cómo está? |
| | ELISA VELASCO: | Bien, gracias. ¿Y usted? |
| | MARTÍN GÓMEZ: | Muy bien, gracias. Hasta luego. |
| | ELISA VELASCO: | Adiós. |

**2.   Quito, Ecuador**

**¿Qué tal?, ¿Cómo estás?,** and **¿Y tú?** are expressions used in informal situations with people you know well, on a first-name basis.

   **¿Cómo está?** and **¿Y usted?** are used to address someone with whom you have a formal relationship.

| 3. | LUPE: | Buenos días, profesor. |
|---|---|---|
| | PROFESOR: | Buenos días. ¿Cómo te llamas? |
| | LUPE: | Me llamo Lupe Carrasco. |
| | PROFESOR: | Mucho gusto, Lupe. |
| | LUPE: | Igualmente. |

**3.   La Ciudad de México, México**

---

*1. MANOLO: Hi, Maricarmen!* MARICARMEN: *How's it going, Manolo? How are you?* MANOLO: *Very well. And you?* MARICARMEN: *OK. See you around, OK?* MANOLO: *See you tomorrow.*
*2. ELISA VELASCO: Good afternoon, Mr. Gómez.* MARTÍN GÓMEZ: *Afternoon, Mrs. Velasco. How are you?* ELISA VELASCO: *Fine, thank you. And you?* MARTÍN GÓMEZ: *Very well, thanks. See you later.* ELISA VELASCO: *Bye.*
*3. LUPE: Good morning, professor.* PROFESOR: *Good morning. What's your name?* LUPE: *My name is Lupe Carrasco.* PROFESOR: *Nice to meet you, Lupe.* LUPE: *Likewise.*

**¿Cómo se llama usted?** is used in formal situations. **¿Cómo te llamas?** is used in informal situations—for example, with other students. The phrases **mucho gusto** and **igualmente** are used by both men and women when meeting for the first time. In response to **mucho gusto,** a woman can also say **encantada;** a man can say **encantado.**

4. MIGUEL: Hola, me llamo Miguel René. ¿Y tú? ¿Cómo te llamas?
   KARINA: Me llamo Karina. Mucho gusto.
   MIGUEL: Mucho gusto, Karina. Y, ¿de dónde eres?
   KARINA: Yo soy de Venezuela. ¿Y tú?
   MIGUEL: Yo soy de México.

4. La Ciudad de México, México

**¿De dónde eres?** is used in informal situations to ask where someone is from. In formal situations the expression used is **¿De dónde es usted?** To reply to either question, the phrase (**Yo**) **Soy de** _____ is used.

## NOTA COMUNICATIVA

### Otros saludos y expresiones de cortesía

| | |
|---|---|
| **buenos días** | good morning (*used until the midday meal*) |
| **buenas tardes** | good afternoon (*used until the evening meal*) |
| **buenas noches** | good evening; good night (*used after the evening meal*) |
| **señor (Sr.)** | Mr., sir |
| **señora (Sra.)** | Mrs., ma'am |
| **señorita (Srta.)** | Miss |
| **gracias** | thanks, thank you |
| muchas gracias | thank you very much |
| **de nada, no** | you're welcome |
| hay de qué | |
| **por favor** | please (*also used to get someone's attention*) |
| **perdón** | pardon me; excuse me (*to ask forgiveness or to get someone's attention*) |
| **con permiso** | pardon me; excuse me (*to request permission to pass by or through a group of people*) |

**OJO** * There is no Spanish equivalent for *Ms.* Use **Sra.** or **Srta.,** as appropriate.

*Watch out, Careful. **¡OJO!** (sometimes just **OJO**) will be used throughout ¿Qué tal? to alert you to pay special attention to the information that follows.*

4. MIGUEL: *Hello, my name is Miguel René. And you? What's your name?* KARINA: *My name is Karina. Nice to meet you.* MIGUEL: *Nice to meet you, Karina. And where are you from?* KARINA: *I'm from Venezuela. And you?* MIGUEL: *I'm from Mexico.*

**Con. A: Answers**
*Possible answers:* **1.** *Muy buenas. (Buenas tardes.) (Muy buenas tardes.)* **2.** *Hasta luego. (Adiós.) (Hasta mañana.)* **3.** *Bien (Muy bien, Regular), gracias. ¿Y tú?* **4.** *Hola. (¿Qué tal?)* **5.** *Bien (Muy bien), gracias. ¿Y usted?* **6.** *Buenas noches. (Muy buenas.) (Adiós.) (Hasta mañana.)* **7.** *De nada. (No hay de qué.)* **8.** *Hasta mañana. (Hasta luego.) (Adiós.)* **9.** *(Me llamo)* _____. **10.** *Encantado/a. (Igualmente.)* **11.** *Soy de* _____.

**Con. A: Suggestion**
Conduct a rapid response drill with students' books closed. See "Teaching Techniques," IM.

**Con. A: Note**
More than one answer is possible for some items.

**Con. C: Answers**
*Possible answers:* **1.** *Con permiso. (Perdón.)* **2.** *Perdón.* **3.** *Perdón.* **4.** *Con permiso. (Por favor.)* **5.** *Perdón.* **6.** *Perdón.*

**Con. D: Suggestion**
Model an interview with two or three students before asking others to form pairs and follow your example.

## ■ Conversación

**A. Cortesía.** How many different ways can you respond to the following greetings and phrases?

1. Buenas tardes.
2. Adiós.
3. ¿Qué tal?
4. Hola.
5. ¿Cómo está?
6. Buenas noches.
7. Muchas gracias.
8. Hasta mañana.
9. ¿Cómo se llama usted?
10. Mucho gusto.
11. ¿De dónde eres?

**B. Situaciones.** If the following people met or passed each other at the times given, what might they say to each other? Role-play the situations with a classmate.

1. Mr. Santana and Miss Pérez, at 5:00 P.M.
2. Mrs. Ortega and Pablo, at 10:00 A.M.
3. Ms. Hernández and Olivia, at 11:00 P.M.
4. you and a classmate, just before your Spanish class
5. you and your Spanish professor, at 11 A.M.
6. you and your cousin, at 10 P.M.
7. you and the president of your university, at 4 P.M.

**C. Más** (*More*) **situaciones.** Are the people in these drawings saying **por favor, con permiso,** or **perdón?** ¡OJO! More than one response is possible for some items.

Resources: Transparency 4

**Con. D: Notes**
• For use of *Pasos* organization in this and subsequent activities, see "Using *Pasos* Activities," IM.
• The word *paso* in the headers *Paso 1* and *Paso 2* means "step."
• The word *paso* in the place name *El Paso* refers to a pass or a passageway.

**D. Entrevista** (*Interview*)

PASO (*Step*) 1 Turn to a person sitting next to you and do the following.

- Greet him or her appropriately, that is, with informal forms.
- Ask where he or she is from.
- Find out his or her name.
- Ask how he or she is.
- Conclude the exchange.

PASO 2 Now have a similar conversation with your instructor, using the appropriate forms (formal or informal, according to your instructor's preference).

# El alfabeto español

There are twenty-nine letters in the Spanish alphabet (**el alfabeto** or **el abecedario**)—three more than in the English alphabet. The three additional letters are the **ch,** the **ll,** and the **ñ.** The letters **k** and **w** appear only in words borrowed from other languages.

In 1994, the **Real Academia Española** (*Royal Spanish Academy*), which establishes many of the guidelines for the use of Spanish throughout the world, decided to adopt the universal Latin order when alphabetizing. In that order, **ch** and **ll** are not considered separate letters. Thus, in dictionaries and other alphabetized materials published since 1994, you will not find separate listings for the letters **ch** and **ll.** They are, however, still considered separate letters by the **Real Academia** and are part of the Spanish alphabet.*

| LETTERS | NAMES OF LETTERS | EXAMPLES | | |
|---|---|---|---|---|
| a | a | Antonio | Ana | (la) Argentina |
| b | be | Benito | Blanca | Bolivia |
| c | ce | Carlos | Cecilia | Cáceres |
| ch | che | Pancho | Chabela | La Mancha |
| d | de | Domingo | Dolores | Durango |
| e | e | Eduardo | Elena | (el) Ecuador |
| f | efe | Felipe | Francisca | Florida |
| g | ge | Gerardo | Gloria | Guatemala |
| h | hache | Héctor | Hortensia | Honduras |
| i | i | Ignacio | Inés | Ibiza |
| j | jota | José | Juana | Jalisco |
| k | ca (ka) | (Karl) | (Kati) | (Kansas) |
| l | ele | Luis | Lola | Lima |
| ll | elle | Guillermo | Estrella | Sevilla |
| m | eme | Manuel | María | México |
| n | ene | Nicolás | Nati | Nicaragua |
| ñ | eñe | Íñigo | Begoña | España |
| o | o | Octavio | Olivia | Oviedo |
| p | pe | Pablo | Pilar | Panamá |
| q | cu | Enrique | Raquel | Quito |
| r | ere | Álvaro | Rosa | (el) Perú |
| s | ese | Salvador | Sara | San Juan |
| t | te | Tomás | Teresa | Toledo |
| u | u | Agustín | Lucía | (el) Uruguay |
| v | ve *or* uve | Víctor | Victoria | Venezuela |
| w | doble ve, ve doble, *or* uve doble | Oswaldo | (Wilma) | (Washington) |
| x | equis | Xavier | Ximena | Extremadura |
| y | i griega | Pelayo | Yolanda | (el) Paraguay |
| z | ceta (zeta) | Gonzalo | Esperanza | Zaragoza |

*The **ch** is pronounced with the same sound as in English cherry or chair, as in Spanish **nachos** or **muchacho.** The **ll** is pronounced as a type of y sound. Spanish examples of this sound that you may already know are **tortilla** and **Sevilla.** The grouping **rr** is not considered a separate letter by the **Real Academia.**

**Suggestions**

Point out that . . .

- the *ch* and the *ll* represent sounds not represented by any other letter in Spanish. This is not the case with the two-letter grouping *rr,* whose sound is also represented by the single *r* when it appears at the beginning of a word or when preceded by the letters *n, l,* or *s.* This distinction explains why the *rr* is not considered a separate letter.
- *ce, ci* produce an [s] sound; *ca, co, cu* produce a [k] sound.
- *ga, go, gu* produce a [g] sound; *ge, gi* are pronounced like Spanish *j.*
- *r* at the beginning of a word is pronounced like the trilled (double) *r.*
- the letter *v* is pronounced like the Spanish *b;* to distinguish *b* and *v,* Spanish speakers sometimes call the letter *b* be grande or be de burro, and the letter *v* ve chica or ve de vaca. In Spain the *v* is called uve.
- the letter *x* is sometimes pronounced like [ks], sometimes like [s], and sometimes like the Spanish *j* (*México, Texas*).
- in Castilian Spanish *ce, ci,* and *z* produce an English *th* sound [Θ].
- in most dialects of Spanish, there is no difference in the pronunciation of the letters *ll* and *y;* however, from one area to another the dialectal variation in *ll/y* is great. Teach the pronunciation of your own dialect and allow for variation. When possible, point out dialectal variation such as the lateral pronunciation of the *ll* in northern Peninsular Spanish or the strong palatal fricative from Argentina [zh].

**Heritage Speakers**

- Invite a sus estudiantes hispanohablantes a pronunciar estas palabras. Pregúnteles a los otros estudiantes si ellos oyen alguna diferencia entre el modo en que los hispanohablantes pronuncian los sonidos, especialmente la *j* y la *ll.*
- Anime a los estudiantes hispanohablantes a que les pidan a varios parientes y conocidos que pronuncien estas palabras mientras ellos graban sus voces. Luego pueden tocar sus grabaciones en clase y comentar sobre las diferencias en la pronunciación de personas de varios países de habla hispana.

**Prác. A: Note**

*Pronunciación* sections appear in this chapter as well as in the *Paso 1* sections of *Capítulos 1–3*. See the Workbook/Laboratory Manual for additional pronunciation practice with specific sounds and letters. Vowel sounds are presented in *Primeros pasos: Segundo paso*. This activity is intended only for immediate practice with sounds and letters that may be strange to some students.

**Prác. A: Answers**

**1.** c **2.** e **3.** i **4.** a **5.** f **6.** h **7.** b **8.** g **9.** d

**Prác. B: Suggestions**

• Introduce the phrase *¿Cómo se deletrea… ?*
• Explain that *acentuada* means "stressed" and that in Spanish the stressed vowel in some words must carry a written accent mark so that the word can be read correctly. Accent marks are presented in *Capítulos 2* and *3*.

**Prác. B: Follow-Up**

• Have students think of other U.S. place names of Hispanic origin and spell them aloud in Spanish as other students pronounce them.

## ▪ Práctica

**A. ¡Pronuncie!** The letters and combinations of letters listed below represent the Spanish sounds that are the most different from English. Pay particular attention to their pronunciation. Can you match the Spanish letters with their equivalent pronunciation?

| EXAMPLES/SPELLING | PRONUNCIATION |
|---|---|
| 1. mucho: **ch** | **a.** like the *g* in English *garden* |
| 2. Geraldo: **ge** (also: **gi**) Jiménez: **j** | **b.** similar to *tt* of *butter* when pronounced very quickly |
| 3. hola: **h** | **c.** like *ch* in English *cheese* |
| 4. gusto: **gu** (also: **ga, go**) | **d.** like Spanish **b** |
| 5. me llamo: **ll** | **e.** similar to a "strong" English *h* |
| 6. señor: **ñ** | **f.** like *y* in English *yes* or like the *li* sound in *million* |
| 7. profesora: **r** | **g.** a trilled sound, several Spanish *r*'s in a row |
| 8. Ramón: **r** (to start a word) Monterrey: **rr** | **h.** similar to the *ny* sound in *canyon* |
| 9. nos vemos: **v** | **i.** never pronounced |

**B. ¿Cómo se deletrea… ?** (*How do you spell . . . ?*)

PASO 1 Pronounce these U.S. place names in Spanish. Then spell the names aloud in Spanish. All of them are of Hispanic origin: **Toledo, Los Ángeles, Texas, Montana, Colorado, El Paso, Florida, Las Vegas, Amarillo, San Francisco.**

PASO 2 Spell your own name aloud in Spanish, and listen as your classmates spell their names. Try to remember as many of their names as you can.

MODELO: Me llamo María: **M** (eme) **a** (a) **r** (ere) **í** (i acentuada) **a** (a).

**Heritage Speakers**

Pídales a los estudiantes hispanohablantes que recopilen una lista de lugares latinoamericanos o españoles que ellos conocen y que les lean sus listas a sus compañeros monolingües.

## NOTA COMUNICATIVA

### Los cognados

As you begin your study of Spanish, you will probably notice that many Spanish and English words are similar or identical in form and meaning. These related words are called *cognates* (**los cognados**). You will see them used in **Primeros pasos** and throughout *¿Qué tal?* At this early stage of language learning, it's useful to begin recognizing cognates and how they are pronounced in Spanish. Here are some examples of Spanish words that are cognates of English words. These cognates and others will help you enrich your Spanish vocabulary and develop your language proficiency!

| SOME ADJECTIVES | | | SOME NOUNS | | |
|---|---|---|---|---|---|
| cruel | inteligente | pesimista | banco | estudiante | oficina |
| elegante | interesante | responsable | bar | examen | parque |
| flexible | optimista | sentimental | café | hotel | teléfono |
| importante | paciente | terrible | diccionario | museo | televisión |

## ¿Cómo es usted?°

¿Cómo... *What are you like?*

You can use these forms of the verb **ser**
(*to be*) to describe yourself and others.

| (yo) | **soy** | I am |
|---|---|---|
| (tú) | **eres** | you (*familiar*) are |
| (usted) | **es** | you (*formal*) are |
| (él, ella) | **es** | he/she is |

—¿Cómo es usted?
—Bueno…° Yo soy moderna, independiente,
    sofisticada…

*Well…*

**Suggestions**
• Introduce the forms of *ser* in brief sentences using the adjectives just presented in the *Nota*.
• Make sure students connect the *eres/es* forms with informal/formal concepts already discussed for greetings.
• Interview students in the classroom, asking them to indicate whether the following statements are *cierto* (true) or *falso* (false).

1. *Sponge Bob es muy elegante.*
2. *El presidente de los Estados Unidos no es muy importante.*
3. *Oprah Winfrey es muy inteligente.*
4. *El programa de televisión «Survivor» es muy interesante.*

Have students provide corrections for the statements they feel are false.

**Con: Note**
Students have not learned adjective/noun agreement. If possible, avoid having students produce sentences that require gender agreement by using adjectives and nouns that are the same for masculine and feminine. Gender is taught in *Gramática 1* (*Capítulo 1*) and *Gramática 4* (*Capítulo 2*).

## ■ Conversación

**Descripciones**

PASO 1  Form complete sentences with the cognates given. Use **no** when
necessary.

| **1.** Yo (no) soy… | **2.** El presidente | **3.** Jennifer López |
|---|---|---|
| estudiante. | (no) es… | (no) es… |
| cruel. | importante. | elegante. |
| responsable. | inteligente. | introvertida. |
| optimista. | pesimista. | romántica. |
| paciente. | flexible. | sentimental. |
| | extrovertido. | egoísta. |

PASO 2  Now think of people you might describe with the following
additional cognates. Use **es** to express *is*.

MODELO:  eficiente → La profesora es eficiente.

| **1.** arrogante | **4.** idealista | **7.** liberal | **10.** rebelde |
|---|---|---|---|
| **2.** egoísta | **5.** impaciente | **8.** materialista | |
| **3.** emocional | **6.** independiente | **9.** realista | |

## PRONUNCIACIÓN

You have probably already noted that there is a very close relationship
between the way Spanish is written and the way it is pronounced. This
makes it relatively easy to learn the basics of Spanish spelling and
pronunciation.

    Many Spanish sounds, however, do not have an exact equivalent in
English, so you should not trust English to be your guide to Spanish
pronunciation. Even words that are spelled the same in both languages
are usually pronounced quite differently. It is important to become so
familiar with Spanish sounds that you can pronounce them automatically,
right from the beginning of your study of the language.

**Note**
Point out the different pronunciations of the English vowel *a: far, fat, fate, fail, sofa;* also point out the silent letter *e: make, mate, crate.*

**Suggestion**
Emphasize diphthongized pronunciation of the English *a* and *o* in *ate, make, same, oh, gold,* and *note.* Pronounce each word slowly, calling attention to the movement of your lips. Contrast with Spanish *me, te, de, lo, no.*

## Las vocales (*Vowels*): *a, e, i, o, u*

Unlike English vowels, which can have many different pronunciations or may be silent, Spanish vowels are always pronounced, and they are almost always pronounced in the same way. Spanish vowels are always short and tense. They are never drawn out with a *u* or *i* glide as in English: **lo** ≠ *low;* **de** ≠ *day.*

**OJO**

The *uh* sound or schwa (which is how most unstressed vowels are pronounced in English: *canal, waited, atom*) does not exist in Spanish.

*a:* pronounced like the *a* in *father,* but short and tense
*e:* pronounced like the *e* in *they,* but without the *i* glide
*i:* pronounced like the *i* in *machine,* but short and tense*
*o:* pronounced like the *o* in *home,* but without the *u* glide
*u:* pronounced like the *u* in *rule,* but short and tense

**A. Sílabas.**   Pronounce the following Spanish syllables, being careful to pronounce each vowel with a short, tense sound.

1. ma fa la ta pa
2. me fe le te pe
3. mi fi li ti pi
4. mo fo lo to po

5. mu fu lu tu pu
6. mi fe la tu do
7. su mi te so la
8. se tu no ya li

**B. Palabras** (*Words*).   Repeat the following words after your instructor.

1. hasta tal nada mañana natural normal fascinante
2. me qué Pérez Elena rebelde excelente elegante
3. sí señorita permiso terrible imposible tímido Ibiza
4. yo con como noches profesor señor generoso
5. uno usted tú mucho Perú Lupe Úrsula

**C. Naciones**

PASO 1   Here is part of a rental car ad in Spanish. Say aloud the names of the countries where you can find this company's offices. Can you recognize all of the countries?

PASO 2   Find the following information in the ad.

1. How many cars does the agency have available?
2. How many offices does the agency have?
3. What Spanish word expresses the English word *immediately*?

———————————————

*The word **y** (and) is also pronounced like the letter **i.***

**Heritage Speakers**
• Los hispanohablantes de los Estados Unidos usan palabras adaptadas del inglés en el habla cotidiana. Muchas veces los hispanohablantes de países latinoamericanos o de España no conocen estas palabras, lo cual puede impedir la comprensión. Algunas de estas palabras son *elevador*

## NOTA CULTURAL

en vez de *ascensor*, *aplicación* en vez de *solicitud*, *bonche* en vez de *montón*, *grados* en vez de *notas*, *lonche* en vez de *almuerzo*, entre otras.

### Spanish in the United States and in the World

Although no one knows exactly how many languages are spoken around the world, linguists estimate that there are between 3,000 and 6,000. Spanish, with 425 million native speakers, is among the top five languages. It is the official language spoken in Spain, in Mexico, in all of South America (except Brazil and the Guianas), in most of Central America, in Cuba, in Puerto Rico, in the Dominican Republic, and in Ecuatorial Guinea (in Africa)—in approximately twenty-one countries in all. It is also spoken by a great number of people in the United States and Canada.

Like all languages spoken by large numbers of people, modern Spanish varies from region to region. The Spanish of Madrid is different from that spoken in Mexico City, Buenos Aires, or Los Angeles. Although these differences are most noticeable in pronunciation ("accent"), they are also found in vocabulary and special expressions used in different geographical areas. Despite these differences, misunderstandings among native speakers are rare, since the majority of structures and vocabulary are common to the many varieties of each language.

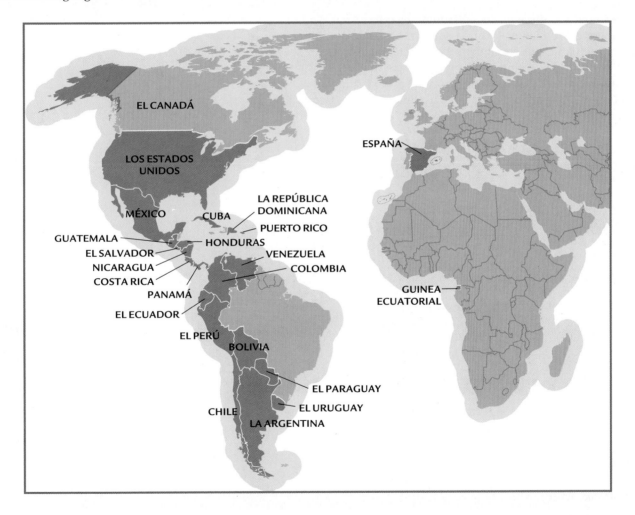

• Anime a los estudiantes hispanohablantes a que les pregunten a sus parientes y conocidos de origen hispánico los nombres por los cuales se refieren a sí mismos, nombres tales como *nica* o *boricua*. Luego invítelos a compartir esta información con sus compañeros de clase.

Resources: Transparency 5

Comprensión
1. How many native Spanish speakers are there in the world? In the United States?
2. Where are the larger Hispanic communities in the United States?

You don't need to go abroad to encounter people who speak Spanish on a daily basis. The Spanish language and people of Hispanic descent have been an integral part of U.S. and Canadian life for centuries. In fact, the United States has the fifth largest Spanish-speaking population in the world!

There is also great regional diversity among U.S. Hispanics. Many people of Mexican descent inhabit the southwestern part of the United States, including populations as far north as Colorado. Large groups of Puerto Ricans can be found in New York, while Florida is host to a large Cuban and Central American population. More recent immigrants include Nicaraguans and Salvadorans, who have established large communities in many U.S. cities, among them San Francisco and Los Angeles.

As you will discover in subsequent chapters of *¿Qué tal?*, the Spanish language and people of Hispanic descent have been and will continue to be an integral part of the fabric of this country. Take special note of **En los Estados Unidos y el Canadá,** a routinely occurring section of *¿Qué tal?* that profiles Hispanics in these two countries.

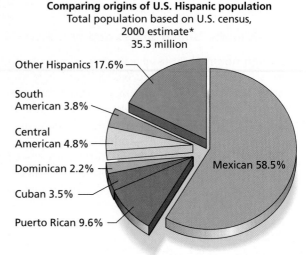

**Comparing origins of U.S. Hispanic population**
Total population based on U.S. census, 2000 estimate*
35.3 million

Other Hispanics 17.6%
South American 3.8%
Central American 4.8%
Dominican 2.2%
Cuban 3.5%
Puerto Rican 9.6%
Mexican 58.5%

*Source: Census Bureau. The Hispanic Population: Information from the 2000 Census.

*Mural en la Pequeña Habana, el barrio cubano de (of) Miami*

**Note**
The following are the 10 states in the United States with the highest Hispanic population, according to the U.S. Census Bureau.

| STATE | TOTAL NUMBER OF HISPANICS | % OF STATE POPULATION |
|---|---|---|
| California | 10,966,556 | 32.4 |
| Texas | 6,669,666 | 32.0 |
| New York | 2,867,583 | 15.1 |
| Florida | 2,682,715 | 16.8 |
| Illinois | 1,530,262 | 12.3 |
| Arizona | 1,295,617 | 25.3 |
| New Jersey | 1,117,191 | 13.3 |
| New Mexico | 765,386 | 42.1 |
| Colorado | 735,601 | 17.1 |
| Nevada | 393,970 | 19.7 |

**Suggestions**
• Point out that mural art has been popularized by Hispanic artists. Mural projects were initiated in the U.S. by Mexican muralists and other artists.
• Have students study the mural and tell what aspects are distinctly Hispanic.

**Need more practice?**

■ Workbook/Laboratory Manual
■ Interactive CD-ROM
■ Online Learning Center (www.mhhe.com/quetal7)

**Follow-Up**
• Use the place names on the map (p. 9) to continue pronunciation practice. Write the names of the countries on the board as students say them, then use the list as a basis for choral repetition drill.
• Have students discuss, research, and make pie charts that illustrate the ethnic makeup of their community.

**Multimedia: Internet**
Have students find information on the Internet about murals in the United States. They can also search for community programs that foster mural-making, for example, the Precita Eyes Mural Arts Center in San Francisco.

## Los números 0–30; *hay*

### Canción infantil

Dos y dos son cuatro,
cuatro y dos son seis,
seis y dos son ocho,
y ocho dieciséis.

### Los números 0–30

| | | | | | |
|---|---|---|---|---|---|
| 0 | cero | | | | |
| 1 | uno | 11 | once | 21 | veintiuno |
| 2 | dos | 12 | doce | 22 | veintidós |
| 3 | tres | 13 | trece | 23 | veintitrés |
| 4 | cuatro | 14 | catorce | 24 | veinticuatro |
| 5 | cinco | 15 | quince | 25 | veinticinco |
| 6 | seis | 16 | dieciséis* | 26 | veintiséis |
| 7 | siete | 17 | diecisiete | 27 | veintisiete |
| 8 | ocho | 18 | dieciocho | 28 | veintiocho |
| 9 | nueve | 19 | diecinueve | 29 | veintinueve |
| 10 | diez | 20 | veint**e** | 30 | treint**a** |

**Suggestions**
• Practice the *Canción infantil.*
• Practice the numbers 0–10: count forward; count by twos in evens and odds; count backwards from 10–0.
• Practice the numbers 11–20: evens 0–20.
• Practice the numbers 21–30: odds 0–30.

• Count from 0 to 30 by threes; by fives; by tens.
• Point out the written accents on 16, 21 (shortened masculine form), 22, 23, 26; final -*e* of *veinte* and final -*a* of *treinta*.

The number *one* has several forms in Spanish. **Uno** is the form used in counting. The forms **un** and **una** are used before nouns. How will you know which one to use? It depends on the gender of the noun.

In **Capítulo 1,** you will learn that all Spanish nouns are either masculine or feminine in gender. For example, the noun **señor** is masculine (*m.*) in gender, and the noun **señora** is feminine (*f.*) in gender. (As you will learn, Spanish nouns that are not sex-linked also have gender.) Here is how the word *one* is expressed with these nouns: **un señor, una señora.** Also note that the number **veintiuno** becomes **veintiún** before masculine nouns and **veintiuna** before feminine nouns: **veintiún señores, veintiuna señoras.** Do learn how to use **un** and **uno** with nouns now, but don't worry about the concept of gender for the moment.

**noun** = a word that denotes a person, place, thing, or idea

**OJO**

**uno**, dos, tres,... veinti**uno**, veinti**dós**,... *but*
**un** señor, veinti**ún** señores
**una** señora, veinti**una** señoras

• Write numbers on the board and identify them (sometimes incorrectly). Students indicate their comprehension with *sí* or *no.* Encourage them to correct your "mistakes."
• Say these pairs of numbers; have students repeat the larger one: *dos / doce; once / uno; treinta / veinte; tres / trece; cuatro / catorce; quince / cinco; diez / once.*

**Heritage Speakers**
Pregúnteles a los estudiantes hispano-hablantes qué canciones infantiles aprendieron de niño y anímelos a cantar alguna.

---

*A children's song* Two and two are four, four and two are six, six and two are eight, and eight (makes) sixteen.

*The numbers 16 to 19 and 21 to 29 can be written as one word (**dieciséis... veintiuno...** ) or as three (**diez y seis... veinte y uno...** ).

**Suggestions**
- Point out that *hay* means both *there is* and *there are*.
- Model the question form. *¿Hay _____?* with rising intonation.

♻ **Reciclado**
Using magazine or newspaper ads or photos, ask *¿Hay _____?* questions with previous cognate vocabulary.

| **hay** = there is / there are |

**Prác. A: Suggestion**
Have students read aloud, practicing pronunciation.

**Prác. A: Variation**
Use this or a similar activity for in-class dictation. See "Teaching Techniques: Dictation," IM.

**Prác. B: Variations**
- Do as a pair activity in which one partner reads the equation and the other provides the answer.
- Write additional problems on large flash cards. Have students read the problems aloud and give answers.
- Teach *¿Cuántos son?* Give additional problems orally.

**Prác. B: Follow-Up**
- *Un problema para Einstein:* $10 - 5 + 7 - 4 + 12 - 15 + 9 - 11 + 17 - 14 + 16 = ?$ (Answer: 22)
- Explain that $\times$ = *por*. Have students read and solve these equations orally.
  1. $2 \times 2 = ?$     5. $4 \times 4 = ?$
  2. $2 \times 6 = ?$     6. $11 \times 0 = ?$
  3. $18 \times 1 = ?$     7. $3 \times 8 = ?$
  4. $3 \times 7 = ?$     8. $2 \times 15 = ?$

**Heritage Speakers**
Recuérdeles a los estudiantes hispano-hablantes que la forma *hay* es impersonal y que no cambia: *Hay un hombre; Hay dos libros.* Recuérdeles que lo mismo ocurre en los tiempos pasados: cuando expresan *there was/were*, *había* y *hubo* no cambian al aparecer ante un sustantivo plural: *Había muchos libros; Hubo varios problemas.*

**Hay**

Use the word **hay** to express both *there is* and *there are* in Spanish. **No hay** means *there is not* and *there are not*. **¿Hay. . . ?** asks *Is there. . . ?* or *Are there. . . ?*

—¿Cuántos estudiantes **hay** en la clase? — *How many students are there in the class?*
—**(Hay)** Treinta. — *(There are) Thirty.*

—**¿Hay** pandas en el zoo? — *Are there any pandas at the zoo?*
—**Hay** veinte osos, pero **no hay** pandas. — *There are twenty bears, but there aren't any pandas.*

## ■ Práctica

**A. Los números.**   Practique los números según (*according to*) el modelo.

MODELO:   1 señor → Hay un señor.

1. 4 señoras
2. 12 pianos
3. 1 café (*m.*)
4. 21 cafés (*m.*)
5. 14 días
6. 1 clase (*f.*)
7. 21 ideas (*f.*)
8. 11 personas
9. 15 estudiantes
10. 13 teléfonos
11. 28 naciones
12. 5 guitarras
13. 1 león (*m.*)
14. 30 señores
15. 20 oficinas

**B. Problemas de matemáticas.**   Do the following simple mathematical equations in Spanish. *Note:* + (**y**), − (**menos**), = (**son**).

MODELOS:   $2 + 2 = 4$ → Dos y dos son cuatro.
  $4 - 2 = 2$ → Cuatro menos dos son dos.

1. $2 + 4 = ?$
2. $8 + 17 = ?$
3. $11 + 1 = ?$
4. $3 + 18 = ?$
5. $9 + 6 = ?$
6. $5 + 4 = ?$
7. $1 + 13 = ?$
8. $15 - 2 = ?$
9. $9 - 9 = ?$
10. $13 - 8 = ?$
11. $14 + 12 = ?$
12. $23 - 13 = ?$
13. $1 + 4 = ?$
14. $1 - 1 + 3 = ?$
15. $8 - 7 = ?$
16. $13 - 9 = ?$
17. $2 + 3 + 10 = ?$
18. $28 - 6 = ?$
19. $30 - 17 = ?$
20. $28 - 5 = ?$
21. $19 - 7 = ?$

## ■ Conversación

**Preguntas** (*Questions*)

1. ¿Cuántos (*How many*) estudiantes hay en la clase de español? ¿Cuántos estudiantes hay en clase hoy (*today*)? ¿Hay tres profesores o un profesor / una profesora?
2. ¿Cuántos días hay en una semana (*week*)? ¿Hay seis? (No, no hay… ) ¿Cuántos días hay en un fin de semana (*weekend*)? ¿Cuántos días hay en el mes de febrero? ¿en el mes de junio? ¿Cuántos meses hay en un año?
3. Hay muchos edificios (*many buildings*) en una universidad. En esta (*this*) universidad, ¿hay una cafetería? (Sí, hay… / No, no hay… ) ¿un teatro? ¿un laboratorio de lenguas (*languages*)? ¿un bar? ¿una clínica? ¿un hospital? ¿un museo? ¿muchos estudiantes? ¿muchos profesores?

## Gustos° y preferencias

*Likes*

¿Te gusta el fútbol? → • Sí, me gusta mucho el fútbol.
  • No, no me gusta el fútbol.

| | |
|---|---|
| To indicate you like something: | **Me gusta _____.** |
| To indicate you don't like something: | **No me gusta _____.** |
| To ask a classmate if he or she likes something: | **¿Te gusta _____?** |
| To ask your instructor the same question: | **¿Le gusta _____?** |

In the following conversations, you will use the word **el** to mean *the* with masculine nouns and the word **la** with feminine nouns. Don't try to memorize which nouns are masculine and which are feminine. Just get used to using the words **el** and **la** before nouns.

You will also be using a number of Spanish verbs in the infinitive form, which always ends in **-r.** Here are some examples: **estudiar** = *to study;* **comer** = *to eat.* Try to guess the meaning of the infinitives used in these activities from context. If someone asks you, for instance, **¿Te gusta** *beber* **Coca-Cola?,** it is a safe guess that **beber** means *to drink.*

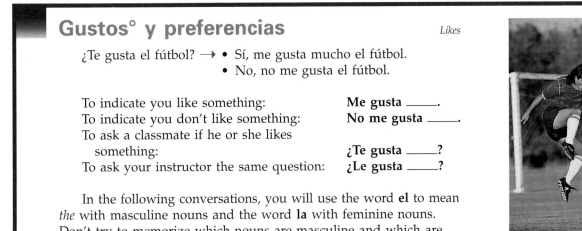

*En español,* ***fútbol*** *=* soccer y ***fútbol*** ***americano*** = football

**verb** = a word that describes an action or a state of being

*Do you like soccer?* → • *Yes, I like soccer very much.* • *No, I don't like soccer.*

## Vocabulario útil*

el café, el té, la limonada, la
  cerveza (beer)
la música moderna, la música
  clásica, el rap, la música
  *country*
la pizza, la pasta, la comida
  (*food*) mexicana, la comida de
  la cafetería
el actor _____, la actriz _____
el/la cantante (singer) _____
  (¡OJO! The word cantante is
  used for both men *and* women.)
el cine (movies), el teatro, la
  ópera, el arte abstracto, el
  fútbol

**Notes**

• The *Vocabulario útil* boxes and sections
  occur throughout *¿Qué tal?* when additional
  vocabulary is needed to complete an
  activity. Similar boxes provide useful
  phrases, expressions, and verbs: *Frases
  útiles, Expresiones útiles, Verbos útiles.*

• Students need not memorize this
  vocabulary. It is provided to help them
  complete activities in the text.

• When *Vocabulario útil* features appear,
  model new vocabulary for students in
  the context of brief sentences, if possible,
  before letting them continue the activity.

• In Latin America, rap is sometimes called
  *el cotorreo* (*cotorrear* means to talk
  without saying anything interesting)
  or *la música rap.*

**Con. A: Extension**
Use other names of
currently famous people
and cognates for sports
and games: *el béisbol, el
vólibol, el basquetbol, hacer jogging, jugar
al bingo, practicar deportes,* and so on.

**Con. B: Follow-Up**
**Paso 1.** Have students expand each interview
to three sentences by adding rejoinders like
*a mí* and *también: A mí me gusta tocar el
violín también.*

Preliminary Exercise
Ask the following questions. *¿Qué le gusta más, el fútbol o el
fútbol americano? ¿el tenis o el vólibol?* (Teach meaning of
*más.*) *¿Qué le gusta a* (name of classmate)*?* Do not emphasize
or expect students to produce the *a* + name phrase.

## ■ Conversación

### A. Gustos y preferencias

PASO 1   Make a list of six things you like and six things you don't like,
following the model. If you wish, you may choose items from the **Vocabulario
útil** box. All words are provided with the appropriate definite article, **el** or **la,**
the Spanish equivalent of *the,* depending on the gender of the noun.

MODELO:   Me gusta *la clase de español.* No me gusta *la clase de matemáticas.*

1. Me gusta _____. No me gusta _____.   3. _____   5. _____
2. Me gusta _____. No me gusta _____.   4. _____   6. _____

PASO 2   Now ask a classmate if he or she shares your likes and
dislikes.

MODELO:   ¿Te gusta la clase de español? ¿y la clase de
          matemáticas?

### B. Más gustos y preferencias

PASO 1   Here are some useful verbs and nouns for talking about what you
like. For each item, combine a verb (shaded) with a noun to form a
sentence that is true for you. Can you use context to guess the meaning of
verbs you don't know?

MODELO:   Me gusta _____. → Me gusta *estudiar inglés.*

1. beber    café   té   limonada   chocolate
2. comer    pizza   enchiladas   hamburguesas   pasta   ensalada
3. estudiar  español   matemáticas   historia   computación (*computer
                                                            science*)
4. hablar   español   con mis amigos (*with my friends*)   por teléfono
                                                            (*on the phone*)
5. jugar    al tenis   al fútbol   al fútbol americano   al béisbol
            al basquetbol
6. tocar    la guitarra   el piano   el violín

PASO 2   Ask a classmate about his or her likes using your own preferences
as a guide.

MODELO:   ¿Te gusta *comer enchiladas?*

PASO 3   Now ask your professor if he or she likes certain things.
¡OJO! Remember to address your professor in a formal manner if that is his
or her preference.

MODELO:   ¿Le gusta *jugar al tenis?*

---

*The material in **Vocabulario útil** lists is not active; that is, it is not part of what you need to focus on
learning at this point. You may use these words and phrases to complete exercises or to help you converse
in Spanish, if you need them.*

# ¿Qué hora es?

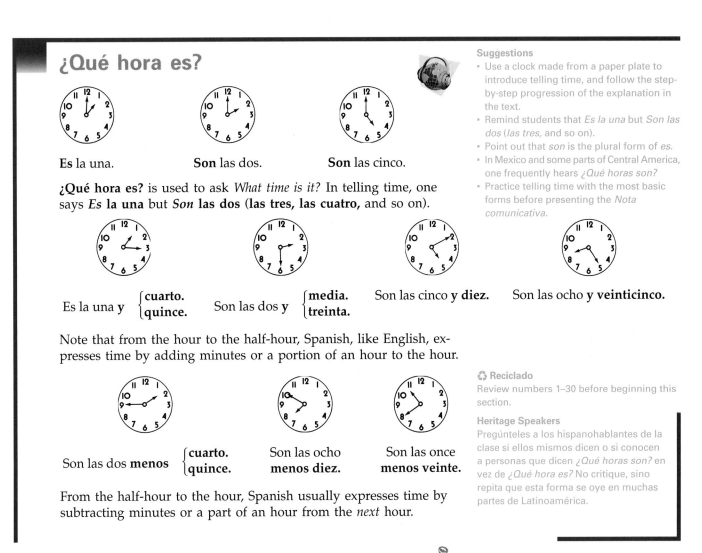

Es la una.  Son las dos.  Son las cinco.

**¿Qué hora es?** is used to ask *What time is it?* In telling time, one says *Es* **la una** but *Son* **las dos** (**las tres, las cuatro,** and so on).

Es la una y $\begin{cases}\textbf{cuarto.}\\\textbf{quince.}\end{cases}$  Son las dos y $\begin{cases}\textbf{media.}\\\textbf{treinta.}\end{cases}$  Son las cinco y **diez.**  Son las ocho y **veinticinco.**

Note that from the hour to the half-hour, Spanish, like English, expresses time by adding minutes or a portion of an hour to the hour.

Son las dos **menos** $\begin{cases}\textbf{cuarto.}\\\textbf{quince.}\end{cases}$  Son las ocho **menos diez.**  Son las once **menos veinte.**

From the half-hour to the hour, Spanish usually expresses time by subtracting minutes or a part of an hour from the *next* hour.

## NOTA COMUNICATIVA

**Para expresar° la hora**  *Para... To express*

| | |
|---|---|
| **de la mañana** | A.M., in the morning |
| **de la tarde** | P.M., in the afternoon (and early evening) |
| **de la noche** | P.M., in the evening |
| **en punto** | exactly, on the dot, sharp |
| **¿a qué hora... ?** | (at) what time . . . ? |
| **a la una** (**las dos,** . . .) | at 1:00 (2:00, . . . ) |

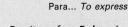 Don't confuse **Es la... / Son las...** with **A la(s)...** The first two are used for telling time, the third for telling *at* what time something happens (at what time class starts, at what time one arrives, and so on).

Son las cuatro de la tarde **en punto.**  *It's exactly 4:00 P.M.*
**¿A qué hora** es la clase de español?  *(At) What time is Spanish class?*
Hay una recepción **a las once** de la mañana.  *There is a reception at 11:00 A.M.*

**Prác. A: Suggestion**

You might present the items in this order: *Son las nueve y media (treinta) de la mañana.* **(6)** *Son las dos (en punto) de la tarde.* **(2)** *Son las seis y dieciséis de la tarde.* **(8)** *Son las doce menos veinte de la noche.* **(1)** *Son las cinco y cuarto (quince) de la noche (mañana).* **(5)** *Son las diez y veintidós de la noche.* **(3)** *Son las dos y diecinueve de la tarde.* **(4)** *Es la una y cinco de la noche (mañana).* **(7)**

**Prác. A: Follow-Up**

Have students respond *sí* or *no* to the following statements. Vary the time as needed for your students. This is an opportunity to review the infinitives from *Conversación B* (p. 14). Pantomime as needed to convey meanings.

## ■ Práctica

**A. ¡Atención!** Listen as your instructor says a time of day. Find the clock or watch face that corresponds to the time you heard and say its number in Spanish. (Note the sun or the moon that accompanies each clock; these indicate whether the time shown is day or night.)

**1.**      **2.**      **3.**      **4.**      **5.**      **6.**      **7.**      **8.**

**Resources: Transparency 6**

1. *Son las once de la noche. Es hora de estudiar.*
2. *Son las siete de la mañana. Es hora de hablar español.*
3. *Son las ocho de la mañana. Es hora de beber café en la cafetería.*
4. *Son las seis y media de la tarde. Es hora de comer en un restaurante elegante.*

**B. ¿Qué hora es?** Express the time in full sentences in Spanish.

| | | | |
|---|---|---|---|
| **1.** 1:00 P.M. | **4.** 1:30 | **7.** 4:15 | **9.** 9:10 on the dot |
| **2.** 6:00 P.M. | **5.** 3:15 | **8.** 11:45 exactly | **10.** 9:50 sharp |
| **3.** 11:00 A.M. | **6.** 6:45 | | |

**Prác. B: Note**

This activity helps students prepare for *Conversación A.*

**Prác. B: Suggestions**

- Ask students at what time they like to . . . *tocar (un instrumento musical), comer, estudiar (español), practicar deportes,* and so on.
- Introduce the interrogative *¿cuándo?*
- Emphasize that students must include the phrase *a la(s)*: *Me gusta (comer) a las (doce en punto).*

## ■ Conversación

**Con. A: Variation**

Expand the exchange in *Paso 2* with *a mí* and *también: A mí me gusta estudiar español a las ocho de la noche también.*

**A. Entrevista**

PASO 1   Ask a classmate at what time the following events or activities take place. He or she will answer according to the cue.

    MODELO:    la clase de español (10:00 A.M.) →
            ESTUDIANTE 1: ¿A qué hora es la clase de español?
            ESTUDIANTE 2: A las diez de la mañana… ¡en punto!

**Resources: Desenlace**

In the *Primeros pasos* segment of "Chapter-by-Chapter Supplementary Materials" in the IM, you will find a chapter-culminating activity. You can use this activity to consolidate and review the vocabulary and grammar skills the students have acquired.

1. la clase de francés (1:45 P.M.)
2. la sesión de laboratorio (3:10 P.M.)
3. la excursión (8:45 A.M.)
4. el concierto (7:30 P.M.)

PASO 2   Now ask at what time your partner likes to perform these activities. He or she should provide the necessary information.

    MODELO:    cenar (*to have dinner*) →
            ESTUDIANTE 1: ¿A qué hora te gusta cenar?
            ESTUDIANTE 2: Me gusta cenar a las ocho de la noche.

1. almorzar (*to have lunch*)
2. mirar (*to watch*) la televisión
3. ir (*to go*) al (*to the*) laboratorio de lenguas
4. ir al cine

**B. Situaciones.** How might the following people greet each other if they met at the indicated time? With a classmate, create brief dialogues.

    MODELO:    Jorge y María, a las once de la noche →
            JORGE: Buenas noches, María.
            MARÍA: Hola, Jorge. ¿Cómo estás?
            JORGE: Bien, gracias. ¿Y tú?
            MARÍA: ¡Muy bien!

1. el profesor Martínez y Gloria, a las diez de la mañana
2. la Sra. López y la Srta. Luna, a las cuatro y media de la tarde
3. usted y su (*your*) profesor(a) de español, en la clase de español

**Need more practice?**

- Workbook/Laboratory Manual
- Interactive CD-ROM
- Online Learning Center (www.mhhe.com/quetal7)

**A LEER**

**ESTRATEGIA: Guessing Meaning from Context**

You will recognize the meaning of a number of cognates in the following reading about the geography of the Hispanic world. In addition, you should be able to guess the meaning of the underlined words from the context (the words that surround them); they are the names of geographical features. The photo captions will also be helpful.

Note also that a series of headings divides the reading into brief parts. It is always a good idea to scan such headings before starting to read, in order to get a sense of a reading's overall content.

**Suggestions**
- Before students begin the reading, review the definite and indefinite articles with them (for recognition). Emphasize *un* → *el* and *una* → *la*. Present the plural definite articles (*los, las*).
- Point out that students should guess the underlined words from context, and discuss the first such word (*pampas*) with them.
- Have students point out or underline words in the text that they recognize as cognates. This practice will be useful in future *A leer* sections, where they will have to understand the meaning of a sentence by referring to the whole context.
- Point out other morphological endings that students can recognize very easily.

# La geografía del mundo[a] hispánico

## Introducción
La geografía del mundo hispánico es impresionante y muy variada. En algunas[b] regiones hay de todo.[c]

## En las Américas
En la Argentina hay <u>pampas</u> extensas en el sur[d] y la <u>cordillera</u> de los Andes en el oeste. En partes de Venezuela, Colombia y el Ecuador, hay regiones tropicales de densa <u>selva</u>. En el Brasil está[e] el famoso <u>Río</u> Amazonas. En el centro de México y también[f] en El Salvador, Nicaragua y Colombia, hay <u>volcanes</u> activos. A veces[g] producen erupciones catastróficas. El Perú y Bolivia comparten[h] el enorme <u>Lago</u> Titicaca, situado en una <u>meseta</u> entre los dos países.[i]

*La <u>cordillera</u> de los Andes, Chile*

*La <u>isla</u> de Caja de Muertos, Puerto Rico*

## En las naciones del Caribe
Cuba, Puerto Rico y la República Dominicana son tres <u>islas</u> situadas en el <u>Mar</u> Caribe. Las bellas playas[j] del Mar Caribe y de la <u>península</u> de Yucatán son populares entre[k] los turistas de todo el mundo.

[a]*world* [b]*some* [c]*de... a bit of everything* [d]*south* [e]*is* [f]*also* [g]*A... Sometimes* [h]*share* [i]*naciones* [j]*bellas... beautiful beaches* [k]*among*

| | | | |
|---|---|---|---|
| *-ción* = -tion | *-tad* = -ty | *-tud* = -tude | *-ista* = -ist |
| acción, legalización | facultad, libertad | multitud, longitud | artista, dentista, oculista |
| *-gión* = -gion | *-dad* = -ty | *-mente* = -ly | *-able* = -able/-ible |
| religión, región | universidad, ciudad | rápidamente, constantemente | responsable, condenable |

### En la Península Ibérica

España comparte[l] la Península Ibérica con Portugal. También tiene[m] una geografía variada. En el norte están los Pirineos, la <u>cordillera</u> que separa a España del[n] resto de Europa. Madrid, la capital del país, está situada en la <u>meseta</u> central. En las <u>costas</u> del sur y del este hay playas tan bonitas como las de[o] Latinoamérica y del Caribe.

Una <u>selva</u> tropical en Colombia

La <u>ciudad</u> de Montevideo, Uruguay

Una <u>meseta</u> de La Mancha, España

### ¿Y las <u>ciudades</u>?

Es importante mencionar también la gran[p] diversidad de las ciudades del mundo hispánico. En la Argentina está la gran ciudad de Buenos Aires. Muchos consideran a Buenos Aires «el París» o «la Nueva York» de Sudamérica. En Venezuela está Caracas, y en el Perú está Lima, la capital, y Cuzco, una ciudad antigua de origen indio.

### Conclusión

En fin,[q] el mundo hispánico es diverso respecto a la geografía. ¿Y Norteamérica?  ■

[l]*shares*  [m]*it has*  [n]*from the*  [o]*tan… as pretty as those of*  [p]*great*  [q]*En… In short*

**Suggestions**
* Have students bring images from magazines, books, and the Internet that illustrate different aspects of Hispanic geography. You might assign specific topics to students or groups, and have them give brief oral presentations based on their findings.
* Ask students to give examples of geographical features from the Hispanic world that are not found in the reading. Accept answers in English, and give the Spanish equivalents if you know them.

## Comprensión

**A. Ejemplos** (*Examples*). Demonstrate your understanding of the words underlined in the reading and other words from the reading by giving an example of a similar geographical feature found in this country or close to it. Then give an example from the Spanish-speaking world.

MODELO: un río → *the Mississippi*, el Río Orinoco

1. un lago
2. una cordillera
3. un río
4. una isla
5. una playa
6. una costa
7. un mar
8. un volcán
9. una península

**B. Descripciones.** Write short sentences with the following words, based on the information provided in **A leer** or on your own knowledge of world geography.

MODELOS: una ciudad → Buenos Aires es una ciudad de la Argentina.
un lago → En el Canadá hay lagos.

1. una ciudad
2. una capital
3. un lago
4. un volcán
5. una playa
6. una isla
7. una nación
8. una península
9. un río
10. un mar

## VIDEOTECA

## Entre amigos: ¡Encantada!

You will watch a video clip of four college students who meet each other for the first time. What questions do you think they will ask each other? Before watching the video, read the following questions. As you watch, don't worry if you don't understand every word. Try to get the gist of the conversation, listening carefully for names and where people are from. Watch the video a second time and listen for the answers to the questions.

1. ¿De dónde es Miguel?
2. ¿Cuántos años tiene (*How old is*) Tané, la señorita de Cuba?
3. ¿De dónde es Rubén?
4. ¿Cómo se llama la señorita de Venezuela?
5. ¿Cuántos años tiene Rubén?

# En resumen

**Note**
Students are *not* expected to know every word they have used in *Primeros pasos.* Only active vocabulary is listed here.

**Suggestion**
Use the material from the inside front cover to familiarize students with frequently used classroom commands and other useful phrases.

## VOCABULARIO
Practice this vocabulary with digital flash cards on the Online Learning Center (www.mhhe.com/quetal7).

Although you have used and heard many words in this preliminary chapter of *¿Qué tal?*, the following words are the ones considered to be active vocabulary. Be sure that you know all of them, including the meaning of all of the words in group titles, before beginning **Capítulo 1.**

### Saludos y expresiones de cortesía

Buenos días. Buenas tardes. Buenas noches.
   Muy buenas.
Hola. ¿Qué tal? ¿Cómo está(s)?
Regular. (Muy) Bien.
¿Y tú? ¿Y usted?
Adiós. Hasta mañana. Hasta luego. Nos vemos.

¿Cómo te llamas? ¿Cómo se llama usted?
   Me llamo _____.

¿De dónde eres? ¿De dónde es usted?
   (Yo) Soy de _____.

señor (Sr.), señora (Sra.), señorita (Srta.)

(Muchas) Gracias.
De nada. No hay de qué.
Por favor. Perdón. Con permiso.
Mucho gusto. Igualmente. Encantado/a.

### ¿Cómo es usted?

soy, eres, es

### Los números 0–30

| | |
|---|---|
| cero | |
| uno | once |
| dos | doce |
| tres | trece |
| cuatro | catorce |
| cinco | quince |
| seis | dieciséis |
| siete | diecisiete |
| ocho | dieciocho |
| nueve | diecinueve |
| diez | veinte |
| | treinta |

**Bright Idea Suggestion**
Give students a phrase or question. They should respond with an appropriate rejoinder. For example:
   *¿Qué tal? → Muy bien.*
   *Gracias. → De nada.*
   *Hola. → Muy buenas.*
and so on.

Bright Idea annotations have been provided by Spanish instructors who are using the *Puntos de partida / ¿Qué tal?* family of textbooks. Look for these wonderful ideas from your colleagues across the country in every chapter.

### Gustos y preferencias

¿Te gusta _____? ¿Le gusta _____?

(Sí,) Me gusta _____. (No,) No me gusta _____.

### ¿Qué hora es?

es la... , son las...
y/menos cuarto (quince)
y media (treinta)
en punto
de la mañana (tarde, noche)
¿a qué hora... ?, a la(s)...

**Heritage Speakers**
Anime a los hispanohablantes a presentar diálogos en clase usando los saludos y expresiones de cortesía.

### Palabras interrogativas

| | |
|---|---|
| ¿cómo? | how?; what? |
| ¿dónde? | where? |
| ¿qué? | what? |

### Palabras adicionales

| | |
|---|---|
| sí | yes |
| no | no |
| hay | there is/are |
| no hay | there is not / are not |
| hoy | today |
| mañana | tomorrow |
| y | and |
| o | or |
| a | to; at (*with time*) |
| de | of; from |
| en | in; on; at |
| pero | but |
| también | also |

**Refrán**

«Antes hoy que mañana.»

Write the *refrán* on the board and help students with the meaning of *antes* (before). Then have them brainstorm possible English equivalents (*Don't put off until tomorrow what you can do today*). Point out that there are many sayings in English and Spanish about today and tomorrow.

# En la universidad

**CAPÍTULO 1**

## CULTURA

- **Nota cultural:** Las universidades del mundo hispánico
- **En los Estados Unidos y el Canadá:** Jaime Escalante: Profesor de matemáticas
- **Voces** de los Estados Unidos
    **Literatura:** Sandra Cisneros
    **Música:** El tejano
- **Videoteca**
    **Entrevista cultural:** Los Estados Unidos
    **Entre amigos:** ¿Qué clases tomas?
- **Enfoque cultural:** Los hispanos en los Estados Unidos
- **A leer:** Las universidades hispánicas

## VOCABULARIO

- En la clase
- Las materias

## PRONUNCIACIÓN

- Diphthongs and Linking

## GRAMÁTICA

1. Singular Nouns: Gender and Articles
2. Nouns and Articles: Plural Forms
3. Subject Pronouns: Present Tense of **-ar** Verbs; Negation

*Unos estudiantes universitarios que hablan de (who are talking about) las clases*

♻ **Reciclado**
Encourage students to generate cognate adjectives by asking:

• *¿Cómo son los estudiantes de _____ (name of university)?*

• *¿Son inteligentes? ¿elegantes? ¿idealistas? ¿interesantes? ¿pesimistas? ¿responsables? ¿serios? ¿extrovertidos?*

You can also call on individual students to provide additional adjectives describing the students at your university.

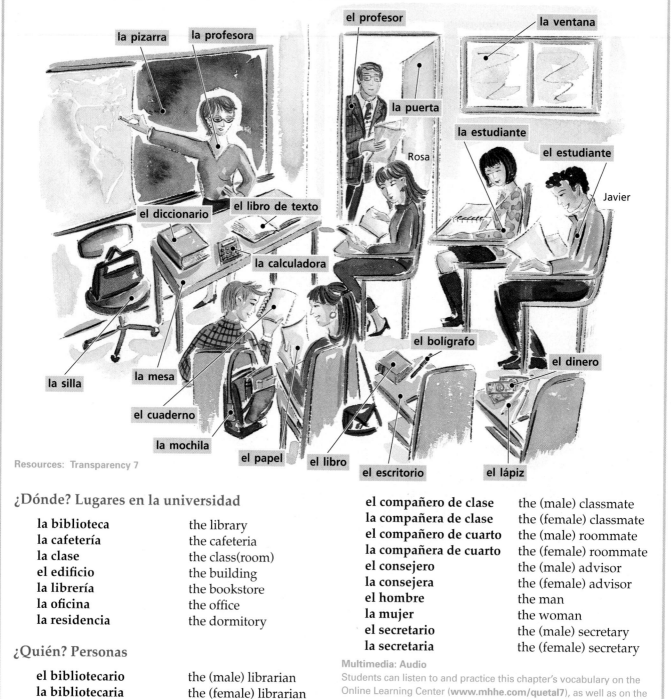

**Paso 1: Vocabulario**
See the "Chapter-by-Chapter Supplementary Materials" in the IM for a model for vocabulary presentation, as well as additional teaching suggestions, notes, activities, and other resources for *Paso 1.*

la pizarra  la profesora  el profesor  la ventana

la puerta

Rosa

la estudiante  el estudiante

el diccionario  el libro de texto

Javier

la calculadora

el bolígrafo

el dinero

la silla  la mesa

el cuaderno

la mochila

**Resources:** Transparency 7

el papel  el libro  el escritorio  el lápiz

## ¿Dónde? Lugares en la universidad

| | |
|---|---|
| la biblioteca | the library |
| la cafetería | the cafeteria |
| la clase | the class(room) |
| el edificio | the building |
| la librería | the bookstore |
| la oficina | the office |
| la residencia | the dormitory |

## ¿Quién? Personas

| | |
|---|---|
| el bibliotecario | the (male) librarian |
| la bibliotecaria | the (female) librarian |

| | |
|---|---|
| el compañero de clase | the (male) classmate |
| la compañera de clase | the (female) classmate |
| el compañero de cuarto | the (male) roommate |
| la compañera de cuarto | the (female) roommate |
| el consejero | the (male) advisor |
| la consejera | the (female) advisor |
| el hombre | the man |
| la mujer | the woman |
| el secretario | the (male) secretary |
| la secretaria | the (female) secretary |

**Multimedia: Audio**
Students can listen to and practice this chapter's vocabulary on the Online Learning Center (**www.mhhe.com/quetal7**), as well as on the Textbook Audio CD, part of the Laboratory Audio Program.

## ■ Conversación

**A. ¿Dónde están ahora** (*are they now*)**?** First, tell where these people are. Then identify the numbered people and things: 1 = **la consejera,** 2 = **la estudiante,** and so on. Refer to the drawing and lists on page 22 as much as you need to.

Resources: Transparency 8

**1.** Están en _____.

**2.** Están en _____.

**3.** Están en _____.

MATRÍCULA I TRIMESTRE

**4.** Están en _____.

**B. Identificaciones.** ¿Es hombre o mujer?

MODELO: ¿La consejera? → Es mujer.

1. ¿El profesor?
2. ¿La estudiante?
3. ¿El secretario?
4. ¿El estudiante?
5. ¿La bibliotecaria?
6. ¿El compañero de cuarto?

**Nota cultural: Comprensión**
1. Where is the oldest university in the Americas? (*¿Dónde está la universidad más antigua de las Américas?*)
2. What is the name of the first university in Peru? (*¿Cómo se llama la primera universidad del Perú?*)

## NOTA CULTURAL

### Las universidades del mundoª hispánico

Universities have a long history in the Spanish-speaking world. The very first university in the western hemisphere was **la Universidad de Santo Domingo,** founded in 1538 in what is now the Dominican Republic. Other early universities in this hemisphere include **la Real y Pontificia Universidad de América** (Mexico City, 1553) and **la Universidad de San Marcos** (Lima, Peru, 1551). Early Spanish colonial cities were meticulously designed and planned, and it is no accident that these universities were established in three of the most important cities. The Spaniards already had almost 300 years of experience with university-level education. **La Universidad de Salamanca,** one of the oldest universities in the world, was founded in 1220 in Salamanca, Spain.

---

ªworld

*Esta estatua de Fray Luis de León está en la Universidad de Salamanca. La Universidad, que* (which) *data del año 1220* (mil doscientos veinte), *es una de las más antiguas* (oldest) *del mundo.*

## LAS MATERIAS°

Las... (School) Subjects

The names for most of these subject areas are cognates. See if you can recognize their meaning without looking at the English equivalent. You should learn in particular the names of subject areas that are of interest to you.

| | |
|---|---|
| **la administración de empresas** | business |
| **las comunicaciones** | communications |
| **la economía** | economics |
| **el español** | Spanish |
| **la filosofía** | philosophy |
| **la literatura** | literature |
| **las matemáticas** | mathematics |
| **la sociología** | sociology |
| **las ciencias** | sciences |
| **las humanidades** | humanities |
| **las lenguas (extranjeras)** | (foreign) languages |

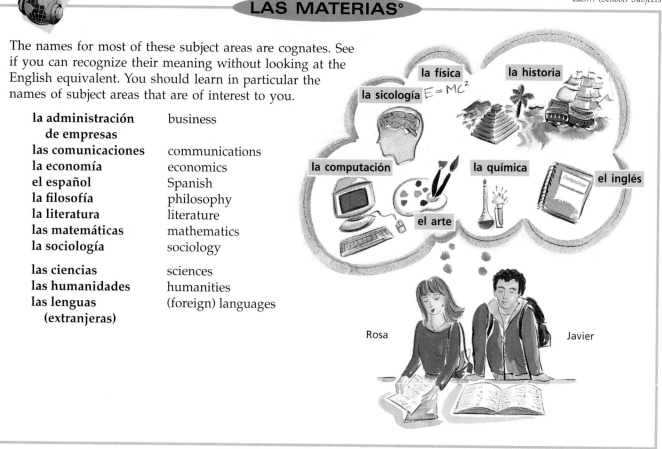

## ■ Conversación

**A. Asociaciones.** ¿Con qué materia(s) asocia usted las siguientes (*following*) cosas (*things*) y las siguientes personas?

1. el nitrógeno, el hidrógeno
2. la doctora Joyce Brothers, el doctor Sigmund Freud
3. NBC, CBS
4. Sócrates, Nietzsche
5. Mark Twain, Toni Morrison, J. K. Rowling
6. Frida Kahlo, Pablo Picasso
7. Microsoft, IBM
8. la civilización azteca, una guerra (*war*) civil

**B. ¿Qué estudia usted?** (*What are you studying?*) The right-hand column lists a number of university subjects. Tell about your academic interests by creating sentences using one word or phrase from each column. You can tell what you *are* studying (**Estudio...**), *want* to study (**Deseo estudiar...**), *need* to study (**Necesito estudiar...**), and *like* to study (**Me gusta estudiar...**). Using the word **no** makes the sentence negative.

(No) Estudio _____.
(No) Deseo estudiar _____.
(No) Necesito estudiar _____.
(No) Me gusta estudiar _____.

**+**

español, francés, inglés
arte, filosofía, literatura, música
ciencias políticas, historia
antropología, sicología, sociología
biología, física, química
matemáticas, computación
¿ ?

## NOTA COMUNICATIVA

### Palabras interrogativas

You have already used a number of interrogative words and phrases to get information. Those and some other useful ones are listed here. You will learn more in later chapters.

| | | | |
|---|---|---|---|
| **¿a qué hora?** | ¿A qué hora es la clase? | **¿cuántos?, ¿cuántas?** | ¿Cuántos días hay en una semana? ¿Cuántas naciones hay en Sudamérica? |
| **¿cómo?** | ¿Cómo estás? ¿Cómo es Gloria Estefan? ¿Cómo te llamas? | **¿dónde?** | ¿Dónde está España? |
| **¿cuál?*** | ¿Cuál es la capital de Colombia? | **¿qué?*** | ¿Qué es un hospital? ¿Qué es esto (*this*)? ¿Qué hora es? |
| **¿cuándo?** | ¿Cuándo es la fiesta? | | |
| **¿cuánto?** | ¿Cuánto (*How much*) es? | **¿quién?** | ¿Quién es el presidente? |

Note that in Spanish the voice falls at the end of questions that begin with interrogative words.

¿Qué es un tren? ¿Cómo estás?

**interrogative** = a word, phrase, or sentence used to ask a question

---

*Use **¿qué?** to mean what? when you are asking for a definition or an explanation. Use **¿cuál?** to mean what? in all other circumstances. See also **Gramática 28** in **Capítulo 9.**

**Con. C: Reciclado**
Use the drawings as a springboard for questions that reenter all of the *Primeros pasos* material. Encourage students to listen to questions for meaning only and to respond with one word or phrase. Top drawing: *¿Quién es el hombre? ¿Quién es la mujer? ¿Cuántos niños* (pantomime) *hay?,* and so on.

**Con. C: Suggestion**
Have students form questions about the drawings. Then have them answer questions asked by others, inventing details. Coach them to keep the sequence of questions going.

**Con. C: Answers**
*Possible answers:* **1.** *¿Cuál es la capital de Colombia? ¿Dónde está Buenos Aires?* **2.** *¿A qué hora es el programa sobre México? ¿Qué hay en la televisión hoy?* **3.** *¿Dónde está el diccionario?* **4.** *¿Qué es esto?* **5.** *¿Cómo estás?* **6.** *¿Quién es?* **7.** *¿Cuándo es la fiesta? ¿Cuántas personas hay en la fiesta?*

**Con. D: Extension**
Make a handout that requires students to interview their classmates. Examples may include:

*¿Quién...*
 *estudia biología, italiano... ?*
 *no estudia los fines de semana?*
 *estudia solamente por la noche / por la mañana?*
 *estudia en la biblioteca, en la cafetería, en la residencia estudiantil?*

Have students report what they found out about their classmates to the entire class.

**Refrán**

«Estudiante que no estudia, en nada bueno se ocupa.»

Write the *refrán* on the board. Have students guess the meaning of *nada* and *se ocupa*. What are some similar sayings in English? (*Idle hands, idle minds.*)

**Need more practice?**
- Workbook/Laboratory Manual
- Interactive CD-ROM
- Online Learning Center
 (www.mhhe.com/quetal7)

**C. Preguntas** (*Questions*). What questions are being asked by the indicated people? More than one answer is possible for some items. Select questions from the following list or create your own questions.

PREGUNTAS

¿A qué hora es el programa sobre (*about*) México?
¿Cómo estás?
¿Cuál es la capital de Colombia?
¿Cuándo es la fiesta?
¿Cuántas personas hay en la fiesta?

¿Dónde está Buenos Aires?
¿Dónde está el diccionario?
¿Qué es esto (*this*)?
¿Qué hay en la televisión hoy?
¿Quién es?

Resources: Transparency 9

**D. Entrevista.** Work with a classmate and use the following questions to interview each other. Find out as much as possible about each other's classes and schedules. Follow up your answers by returning the question or asking for more information.

MODELO: ESTUDIANTE 1: ¿Qué estudias este semestre/trimestre (*this term*)?
ESTUDIANTE 2: Estudio matemáticas, historia, literatura y español. Y tú, ¿qué estudias?

1. ¿Qué estudias este semestre/trimestre?
2. ¿Cuántas horas estudias por semana (*per week*)?
3. ¿Cuándo estudias, por (*in*) la mañana, por la tarde o por la noche?
4. ¿Dónde te gusta estudiar?
5. ¿Quién es tu profesor favorito (profesora favorita)? (Mi profesor... )
6. ¿Cuál es tu clase favorita? (Mi clase... )

## PRONUNCIACIÓN: DIPHTHONGS AND LINKING

Two successive weak vowels (**i, u**) or a combination of a strong vowel (**a, e,** or **o**) and a weak vowel (**i** or **u**) are pronounced as a single syllable in Spanish, forming a *diphthong* (**un diptongo**): L**ui**s, s**ie**te, c**ua**derno.

When words are combined to form phrases, clauses, and sentences, they are linked together in pronunciation. In spoken Spanish, it is usually impossible to hear the word boundaries—that is, where one word ends and another begins.

> **diphthong** = a combination of two vowel sounds in one syllable

**A. Vocales.** Más práctica con las vocales.

| | | | |
|---|---|---|---|
| 1. hablar | regular | reservar | compañera |
| 2. trece | clase | papel | general |
| 3. pizarra | oficina | bolígrafo | libro |
| 4. hombre | profesor | dólares | los |
| 5. universidad | gusto | lugar | mujer |

**B. Diptongos.** Practique las siguientes palabras.

| | | | | |
|---|---|---|---|---|
| 1. historia | secretaria | gracias | estudiante | materia |
| 2. bien | Oviedo | siete | ciencias | diez |
| 3. secretario | biblioteca | adiós | diccionario | Antonio |
| 4. cuaderno | Eduardo | el Ecuador | Guatemala | Managua |
| 5. bueno | nueve | luego | pueblo | Venezuela |

**C. Frases y oraciones** (*sentences*). Practice saying each phrase or sentence as if it were one long word, pronounced without a pause.

1. el papel y el lápiz
2. la profesora y la estudiante
3. las ciencias y las matemáticas
4. la historia y la sicología
5. la secretaria y el profesor
6. el inglés y el español
7. la clase en la biblioteca
8. el libro en la librería
9. Es la una y media.
10. Hay siete estudiantes en la oficina.
11. No estoy muy bien.
12. No hay un consejero en la clase.
13. Hay siete edificios en la universidad.
14. Estudio historia y comercio.
15. Deseo estudiar computación y matemáticas.
16. Necesito un diccionario y una mochila.

**Notes**
- The letter *y* is pronounced like the vowel *i* when standing alone (*y* means *and*) or when ending a word (¡*ay!, hay*).
- Hint for remembering weak vowels: *u* and *i* are weak.

**Preliminary Exercise**
Pronounce these English and Spanish words in random order. Have students identify each as *español* or *inglés*.

| English | Spanish |
|---|---|
| Ray | *rey* |
| lay | *ley* |
| eye | *hay* |
| soy | *soy* |

**A: Suggestion**
Review the pronunciation of single vowel sounds before beginning the activity.

**A: Note**
*Hombre* should not be pronounced as *hambre* (hunger); *dólares* should not sound like *dolores* (pains).

**B: Follow-Up**
Have students sound out the vowels and diphthongs first; then add consonant sounds.

1. *la civilización india*
2. *los negocios internacionales*
3. *una bibliotecaria italiana*
4. *una especialidad fascinante*
5. *los tiempos verbales*

**C: Suggestion**
Before students attempt to pronounce the phrases, do the activity as a dictation, and emphasize the linking effect.

**Heritage Speakers**
Escriba la siguiente canción en la pizarra para que los estudiantes la copien. Pídales que graben las voces de hispanohablantes a quienes conocen mientras leen la selección. Luego toque las grabaciones en clase para que los estudiantes oigan la variedad de acentos.

*¡Al Uruguay, guay!*
*Yo no voy, voy*
*porque temo naufragar.*
*Mándeme a París*
*si es que le da igual.*

## 1  Identifying People, Places, Things, and Ideas
### Singular Nouns: Gender and Articles*

En *la clase* del *profesor* Durán: *El primer* día

| | |
|---|---|
| PROFESOR DURÁN: | Aquí está *el programa* del *curso*. Son necesarios *el libro* de *texto* y *un diccionario*. También hay *una lista* de *novelas* y *libros* de *poesía*. |
| ESTUDIANTE 1: | ¡Es *una lista* infinita! |
| ESTUDIANTE 2: | Sí, y *los libros* cuestan demasiado. |
| ESTUDIANTE 1: | No, *el problema* no es *el precio* de *los libros*. ¡Es *el tiempo* para leer *los libros*! |

**Notes**
- The *minidiálogo* introduces material that appears in both *Gramática 1* and *2*. Continue to use the previous guidelines for the presentation of the *minidiálogos*.
- Remind students that the English equivalent for *minidiálogos* is always provided at the foot of the page.
- Spanish equivalents for English grammatical terms will be given throughout this text.

**Comprensión**

Elija (*Choose*) las palabras o frases correctas según (*according to*) el diálogo.

**Follow-Up**
1. ¿Dónde están las personas del diálogo?
2. ¿Quiénes son?
3. ¿Hay profesor o profesora en esta clase?

1. La clase del profesor Durán es de (literatura/filosofía).
2. En el curso del profesor Durán (es necesario / no es necesario) leer (*to read*) mucho.
3. En un curso de literatura (es lógico / no es lógico) usar un diccionario.

To name people, places, things, or ideas, you need to be able to use nouns. In Spanish, all *nouns* (**los sustantivos**) have either masculine or feminine *gender* (**el género**). This is a purely grammatical feature of nouns; it does not mean that Spanish speakers perceive things or ideas as having male or female attributes.

Since the gender of all nouns must be memorized, it is best to learn the definite article along with the noun; that is, learn **el lápiz** rather than just **lápiz**. The definite article will be given with nouns in vocabulary lists in this book.

> **article** = a determiner that sets off a noun
>
> **definite article** = an article that indicates a specific noun
>
> **indefinite article** = an article that indicates an unspecified noun

| | Masculine Nouns | | Feminine Nouns | |
|---|---|---|---|---|
| **Definite Articles** | el hombre | *the man* | la mujer | *the woman* |
| | el libro | *the book* | la mesa | *the table* |
| **Indefinite Articles** | un hombre | *a (one) man* | una mujer | *a (one) woman* |
| | un libro | *a (one) book* | una mesa | *a (one) table* |

*The grammar sections of ¿Qué tal? are numbered consecutively throughout the book. If you need to review a particular grammar point, the index will refer you to its page number.

**In Professor Durán's class: The first day** PROFESSOR DURÁN: *Here's the course syllabus. The textbook and a dictionary are required. There is also a list of novels and poetry books.* STUDENT 1: *It's a really long list!* STUDENT 2: *Yes, and the books cost too much.* STUDENT 1: *No, the problem isn't the price of the books. It's the time to read the books!*

## Gender

**A.** Nouns that refer to male beings and most other nouns that end in **-o** are *masculine* (**masculino**) in gender.

**sustantivos masculinos:** hombre, libro

**B.** Nouns that refer to female beings and most other nouns that end in **-a, -ción, -tad,** and **-dad** are *feminine* (**femenino**) in gender.

**sustantivos femeninos:** mujer, mesa, nación, libertad, universidad

**C.** Nouns that have other endings and that do not refer to either male or female beings may be masculine or feminine. The gender of these words must be memorized.

el lápiz, la clase, la tarde, la noche

**D.** Many nouns that refer to people indicate gender . . .

1. by changing the last vowel.

OR

el compañero → la compañera
el bibliotecario → la bibliotecaria

2. by adding **-a** to the last consonant of the masculine form to make it feminine.

un profesor → una profesora

**E.** Many other nouns that refer to people have a single form for both masculine and feminine genders. Gender is indicated by an article.

However, a few nouns that end in **-e** also have a feminine form that ends in **-a.**

**el** estudiante → **la** estudiante
(*the male student*) (*the female student*)
**el** cliente → **la** cliente
(*the male client*) (*the female client*)

el presidente → la presidenta
(*the male president*) (*the female president*)
el dependiente → la dependienta
(*the male clerk*) (*the female clerk*)

**OJO** A common exception to the normal rules of gender is the word **el día,** which is masculine in gender. Many words ending in **-ma** are also masculine: **el problema, el programa, el sistema,** and so on. Watch for these exceptions as you continue your study of Spanish.

## Articles

**A.** In English, there is only one *definite article* (**el artículo definido**): *the.* In Spanish, the definite article for masculine singular nouns is **el**; for feminine singular nouns it is **la.**

definite article: *the*

m. sing. → **el**
f. sing. → **la**

**B.** In English, the singular *indefinite article* (**el artículo indefinido**) is *a* or *an.* In Spanish, the indefinite article, like the definite article, must agree with the gender of the noun: **un** for masculine nouns, **una** for feminine nouns. **Un** and **una** can mean *one* as well as *a* or *an.* Context determines meaning.

indefinite article: *a, an*

m. sing. → **un**
f. sing. → **una**

**Suggestion**

Have students try the *Autoprueba* before they begin the *Práctica* section.

**Prác. A: Follow-Up**

Have students give the feminine or masculine counterparts for the following words (ask for articles with answers).

1. *el hombre*        4. *un cliente*
2. *la compañera*     5. *una presidenta*
3. *el secretario*    6. *un turista*

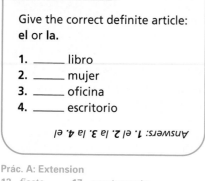

**AUTOPRUEBA***

Give the correct definite article: **el** or **la**.

1. _____ libro
2. _____ mujer
3. _____ oficina
4. _____ escritorio

*Answers: 1. el 2. la 3. la 4. el*

## ■ Práctica

### A. Artículos

PASO 1   Dé (*Give*) el artículo definido apropiado (**el, la**).

1. escritorio   el
2. biblioteca   la
3. bolígrafo   el
4. mochila   la
5. hombre   el
6. diccionario   el
7. universidad   la
8. dinero   el
9. mujer   la
10. nación   la
11. bibliotecario   el
12. calculadora   la

PASO 2   Ahora (*Now*) dé el artículo indefinido apropiado (**un, una**).

1. día   un
2. mañana   una
3. problema   un
4. lápiz   un
5. clase   una
6. noche   una
7. papel   un
8. condición   una
9. programa   un

**Prác. A: Extension**

13. *fiesta*      17. *apartamento*
14. *clase*       18. *cuarto*
15. *puerta*      19. *lengua*
16. *amigo*       20. *física*

**Prác. B: Variation**

Vary *Paso 1* of this activity by using the following model to form the sentences: *estudiante/librería → El estudiante está en la librería.*

### B. Escenas de la universidad

**Prác. B: Extension**

Have students continue the activity with the words from *Práctica A.*

PASO 1   Haga una oración (*Form a sentence*) con las palabras indicadas.

MODELO:   estudiante / librería → Hay un estudiante en la librería.

1. consejero / oficina
2. profesora / clase
3. lápiz / mesa
4. cuaderno / escritorio
5. libro / mochila
6. bolígrafo / silla
7. palabra / papel
8. oficina / residencia
9. compañero / biblioteca

PASO 2   Now create new sentences by changing one of the words in each item in **Paso 1**. If you do this with a partner, try to come up with as many variations as possible.

MODELO:   Hay un estudiante en *la residencia*. (Hay *una profesora* en la librería.)

**Need more practice?**

■ Workbook/Laboratory Manual
■ Interactive CD-ROM
■ Online Learning Center (www.mhhe.com/quetal7)

**Con. A: Extension**

10. *librería*
11. *profesor*
12. *historia*

## ■ Conversación

**Con. A: Suggestion**

Use place and person names from your campus and city as cues.

### A. Definiciones.
Con un compañero / una compañera, defina estas palabras en español según el modelo.

MODELO:   biblioteca / edificio → ESTUDIANTE 1: ¿La biblioteca?
ESTUDIANTE 2: Es un edificio.

1. cliente / persona
2. bolígrafo / cosa
3. residencia / edificio
4. dependiente / ¿ ?
5. hotel (*m.*) / ¿ ?
6. calculadora / ¿ ?
7. computación / ¿ ?
8. inglés / ¿ ?
9. ¿ ?

**Categorías**

**cosa**
**edificio**
**materia**
**persona**

13. *cuaderno*
14. *libro*
15. *dinero*
16. *compañera de clase*
17. *física*
18. *manual* (m.) *de laboratorio*
19. *laboratorio de lenguas*
20. *profesor / la profesora* (name)

### B. Asociaciones.
Identifique una cosa y una persona que usted asocia con los siguientes lugares.

MODELO:   la clase → una silla, un profesor

1. la biblioteca   2. la librería   3. una oficina   4. la residencia

**Con. B: Note**

*Clase* means both *class* and *classroom*. The context of the sentence differentiates them.

**Con. B: Extension**

5. *el laboratorio de lenguas*
6. *la capital de los Estados Unidos* (*del Canadá*)
7. *la universidad*
8. *Puerto Rico*

---

*****Autoprueba** *means* Self-quiz. *These self-quizzes appear at the end of* **Gramática** *explanations and will help you determine if you understand the basics of the grammar point.*

**Con. B: Follow-Up**

Have students compare their lists. What items are similar? What items are different?

Note
Review the *minidiálogo* that precedes *Gramática 1* before presenting the material in this section.

## 2  Identifying People, Places, Things, and Ideas
### Nouns and Articles: Plural Forms

- You can find many nouns in this ad. Can you guess the meaning of most of them?
- Some of the nouns in this ad are plural. Can you tell how to make nouns plural in Spanish, based on these nouns?
- Look for the Spanish equivalent of the following words.

  adult        preparation        program        course

- **Idioma** is another word for *language*, and it is a false cognate. It never means *idiom*.
- Using the vocabulary in the ad, guess what **en el extranjero** means.

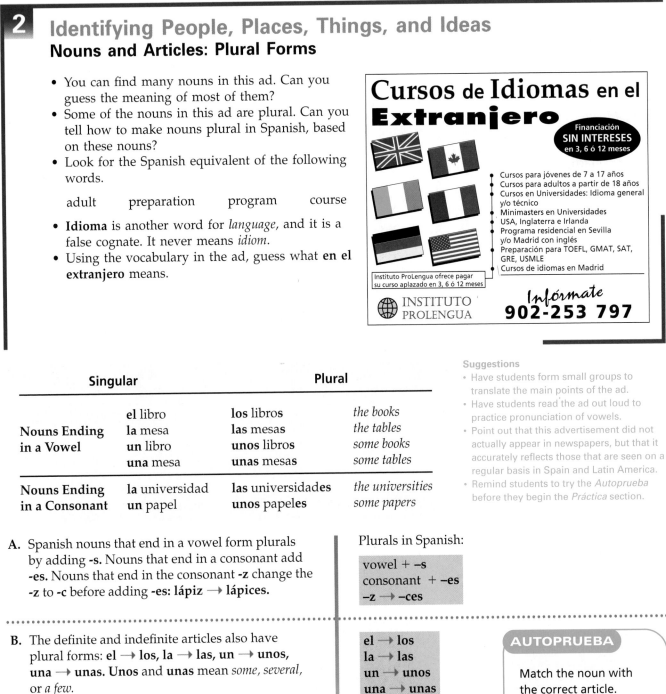

**Cursos de Idiomas en el Extranjero**

Financiación **SIN INTERESES** en 3, 6 ó 12 meses

- Cursos para jóvenes de 7 a 17 años
- Cursos para adultos a partir de 18 años
- Cursos en Universidades: Idioma general y/o técnico
- Minimasters en Universidades USA, Inglaterra e Irlanda
- Programa residencial en Sevilla y/o Madrid con inglés
- Preparación para TOEFL, GMAT, SAT, GRE, USMLE
- Cursos de idiomas en Madrid

Instituto ProLengua ofrece pagar su curso aplazado en 3, 6 ó 12 meses

**INSTITUTO PROLENGUA**

*Infórmate*
**902-253 797**

**Suggestions**
- Have students form small groups to translate the main points of the ad.
- Have students read the ad out loud to practice pronunciation of vowels.
- Point out that this advertisement did not actually appear in newspapers, but that it accurately reflects those that are seen on a regular basis in Spain and Latin America.
- Remind students to try the *Autoprueba* before they begin the *Práctica* section.

| | Singular | Plural | |
|---|---|---|---|
| **Nouns Ending in a Vowel** | **el** libro | **los** libros | *the books* |
| | **la** mesa | **las** mesas | *the tables* |
| | **un** libro | **unos** libros | *some books* |
| | **una** mesa | **unas** mesas | *some tables* |
| **Nouns Ending in a Consonant** | **la** universidad | **las** universidad**es** | *the universities* |
| | **un** papel | **unos** papel**es** | *some papers* |

**A.** Spanish nouns that end in a vowel form plurals by adding **-s.** Nouns that end in a consonant add **-es.** Nouns that end in the consonant **-z** change the **-z** to **-c** before adding **-es: lápiz → lápices.**

Plurals in Spanish:

vowel + **–s**
consonant + **–es**
**–z → –ces**

**B.** The definite and indefinite articles also have plural forms: **el → los, la → las, un → unos, una → unas. Unos** and **unas** mean *some, several,* or *a few.*

**el → los**
**la → las**
**un → unos**
**una → unas**

**AUTOPRUEBA**

Match the noun with the correct article.

1. libros        a. el
2. hombre        b. las
3. librería      c. los
4. profesoras    d. una

*Answers: 1. c 2. a 3. d 4. b*

**C.** In Spanish, the masculine plural form of a noun is used to refer to a group that includes both males and females.

**los** amig**os**
*the friends* (both male and female)

**unos** extranjer**os**
*some foreigners* (both male and female)

**Prác. A: Follow-Up**
Have students give the plural of the following.

1. *Juana, una estudiante; Juana y Elena...*
2. *Ramón, un extranjero; Ramón y Ricardo...*
3. *Ramón, un extranjero; Ramón y Raquel...*
4. *David, un amigo; David y Cecilia...*
5. *David, un amigo; David y Roberto...*

---

### Palabras útiles

la computadora
el experimento
la planta
el teléfono

**Need more practice?**

- Workbook/Laboratory Manual
- Interactive CD-ROM
- Online Learning Center
  (www.mhhe.com/quetal7)

**Con. A: Suggestions**
- Encourage students to speak further about people, places, things, and ideas by asking questions such as: *¿Quién es?* (*¿Quiénes son?*) *¿Qué es? ¿Cuántos/as _____ hay? ¿Dónde está(n)?*
- Introduce *muchos/as.*

♻ **Reciclado**
Review numbers and questions with the practice of singular and plural forms by asking questions such as: *¿Cuántos/as estudiantes / mesas / sillas / libros hay en la clase?* Remind students to use *hay* in their answers.

---

### Palabras útiles

**Con. B: Answers**
*Partial answers: En el dibujo A, hay un escritorio y una cama. En el dibujo B, también hay un escritorio y una cama. En el dibujo A, hay sólo un cuadro. En el dibujo B hay dos cuadros. En el escritorio del dibujo A, hay una lámpara. En el escritorio del dibujo B, no hay lámpara.*

**la alfombra** (rug)
**la almohada** (pillow)
**la cama** (bed)
**el cuadro** (picture)
**el espejo** (mirror)
**la lámpara** (lamp)
**el monitor**

♻ **Reciclado**
Have students form pairs to review cognates presented in the explanations and activities in *Primeros pasos* and scan the realia and drawings in that chapter and in *Capítulo 1.* Then invite them to give as many nouns as they can that fit into the following categories.

1. *lugares de la universidad*
2. *cosas en una librería*
3. *personas en una librería*
4. *problemas de los estudiantes*

---

## ■ Práctica

**A. Singular → plural.**   Dé la forma plural.

1. la mesa
2. el papel
3. el amigo
4. la oficina
5. un cuaderno
6. un lápiz
7. una universidad
8. un bolígrafo

**B. Plural → singular.**   Dé la forma singular.

1. los profesores
2. las calculadoras
3. las bibliotecarias
4. los estudiantes
5. unos hombres
6. unas tardes
7. unas residencias
8. unas sillas
9. unos escritorios

## ■ Conversación

**A. Identificaciones.**   Identifique las personas, las cosas y los lugares.

MODELO:  Hay _____ en _____. → Hay *unos estudiantes* en *la clase.*

1.　　　　　　　　　　　2.

**B. ¡Ojo alerta!** (*Eagle eye!*)* ¿Cuáles son las semejanzas (*similarities*) y las diferencias entre los dos cuartos? Hay por lo menos (*at least*) seis diferencias. Después de identificar (*After identifying*) las diferencias, indique qué hay en su propio (*your own*) cuarto.

MODELOS:  En el dibujo A, hay _____. En el dibujo B, hay sólo (*only*) _____.
En el escritorio del dibujo A, hay _____.
En mi cuarto hay _____. En mi escritorio hay _____.

Ⓐ　　　　　　　　　　　Ⓑ

---

*In Spanish, activities like this one are often called ¡Ojo alerta!*

**Resources: Transparencies 10, 11**

# Voces de los Estados Unidos

## LITERATURA: Sandra Cisneros

**Sobre** (About) **la autora:** *Sandra Cisneros was born in Chicago. She is one of the most prominent Hispanic female writers in the United States. She writes in English, but her prose and poetry are infused with the Hispanic-American experience. She now lives and writes in San Antonio, Texas. The following is from the novel* Caramelo *(2002).*

Outside, roaring like the ocean, Chicago traffic from the Northwest and Congress Expressways. Inside, another roar; in Spanish from the kitchen radio, in English from TV cartoons, and in a mix of the two from her boys begging for, —*Un nikle* for Italian lemonade. But Aunty Licha doesn't hear anything. Under her breath Aunty is bargaining,

—*Virgen Purísima,* if we even make it to Laredo, even that, I'll say three rosaries . . .

**Sandra Cisneros**
**(1954– )**

**Literatura: Notes**
• Sandra Cisneros is the daughter of a Mexican father and a Chicana mother. She is the only daughter of seven children.
• Cisneros' poetry and prose bridge the gap between Anglo and Hispanic cultures.
• *Caramelo* is a multigenerational story of a Mexican-American family. The novel is textured with humor and passion. The protagonist, Lala Reyes, is the granddaughter of a woman from a family of famous shawl makers. Lala becomes the inheritor of one of the most beautiful *rebozos* or shawls, the striped *caramelo* one.

## MÚSICA: El tejano

El tejano, un género[a] musical mexico-americano, tradicionalmente se toca[b] con el acordeón y el bajo sexto.[c] Esta[d] música tradicional es especialmente popular en el suroeste[e] de los Estados Unidos.

[a]*genre, type*  [b]*se... is played*  [c]*bajo... type of guitar*  [d]*This*
[e]*southwest*

**Música: Suggestions**
• Ask students if they are familiar with *tejano* music. If so, find out if any of them listen to Selena, Los Lonely Boys, or other *tejano* groups. Bring or have students bring music by *tejano* musicians to play in class.
• Point out that the movie *Selena* was the launch pad for Jennifer López's acting and singing career. Ask students to name and describe the music of other crossover Hispanic musicians and singers (for example, Jon Secada, Ricky Martin, Gloria Estefan, Marc Anthony, Enrique Iglesias, Shakira, Christina Aguilera).

La joven estrella[f] Selena (1971–1995 [mil novecientos setenta y uno a mil novecientos noventa y cinco]), que cantaba[g] en inglés y español, popularizó[h] el tejano fuera de[i] la comunidad mexicoamericana.

[f]*joven... young star*  [g]*que... who sang*  [h]*popularized*  [i]*fuera... outside of*

Los Lonely Boys, un conjunto[j] popular que canta principalmente en inglés, representa la nueva onda[k] del tejano. Su[l] música, rock «texicano», es una fusión de diferentes estilos.[m]

[j]*band*  [k]*nueva... new wave*  [l]*Their*  [m]*styles*

# PASO 3    Gramática

CAPÍTULO
**1**

Paso 3: Gramática
See the "Chapter-by-Chapter Supplementary Materials" in the IM for additional teaching suggestions, notes, activities, and other resources for *Paso 3*.

## 3   Expressing Actions   Subject Pronouns; Present Tense of *-ar* Verbs; Negation

### Diego *habla* de su vida con su amiga Lupe

**Note**
The *minidiálogo* between Diego and Lupe introduces material that will appear in *Gramática 3*. You may prefer to focus on subject pronouns alone before introducing the *minidiálogo*. Continue to use the previous guidelines for *minidiálogo* presentation.

**Suggestion**
Model Lupe's possible responses to Diego's questions; encourage student repetition and expansion. Translate unfamiliar vocabulary on the board as you proceed.

1. *Yo no pago mucho en cuentas de teléfono. ¿Trabajas?*
2. *Ahora no trabajo. ¿Qué te gusta hacer en tu tiempo libre* (translate)*?*

Imagine que usted es Lupe y conteste las preguntas de Diego. Use **no** si es necesario.

DIEGO: *Yo hablo* con mi familia con frecuencia. Por eso *pago* mucho en cuentas de teléfono. ¿Y tú?

LUPE: [...]

DIEGO: *Necesito* dinero para *comprar* libros. Por eso *enseño* inglés a un estudiante de matemáticas. ¿Y tú?

LUPE: [...]

DIEGO: En mi tiempo libre *escucho* música. También *toco* la guitarra. En las fiestas *bailo* mucho y *tomo* cerveza con mis amigos. Los fines de semana, *busco* libros de antropología en las librerías. ¿Y tú?

LUPE: [...]

### Comprensión: ¿Cierto o falso?

1. Diego no habla mucho con su familia.    falso
2. Es estudiante de ciencias.    falso
3. No le gusta la música.    falso
4. Es una persona introvertida y solitaria.    falso
5. Enseña francés.    falso

## Subject Pronouns

**subject** = the person or thing that performs the action

**pronoun** = a word that takes the place of a noun or represents a person

3. *Yo también bailo en las fiestas. Pero no busco libros de antropología. Busco libros de arte moderno.*

**Follow-Up**
Ask students if these statements are true for them (*¿sí o no?*)

1. *Hablo francés* (*inglés*).
2. *Hablamos español* (*francés*) *en esta clase.* (Suggestion: Introduce *un poco*.)
3. *Bailamos en esta clase.*
4. *Bailo muy mal* (*muy bien*).

| Subject Pronouns | | | |
|---|---|---|---|
| **Singular** | | **Plural** | |
| **yo** | I | **nosotros / nosotras** | we |
| **tú** | you (*fam.*) | **vosotros / vosotras** | you (*fam. Sp.*) |
| **usted (Ud.)*** | you (*form.*) | **ustedes (Uds.)*** | you (*form.*) |
| **él** | he | **ellos** | they (*m, m. + f.*) |
| **ella** | she | **ellas** | they (*f.*) |

*Diego talks about his life with his friend Lupe*   Imagine that you are Lupe and answer Diego's questions. Use no if necessary.
DIEGO: *I speak often with my family. That's why I pay a lot in telephone bills. And you?* LUPE: [...]
DIEGO: *I need money to buy books. That's why I teach English to a math student. And you?* LUPE: [...]
DIEGO: *In my spare time I listen to music. I also play the guitar. At parties I dance a lot and drink beer with my friends. On weekends, I look for anthropology books in bookstores. And you?* LUPE: [...]

***Usted** and **ustedes** are frequently abbreviated in writing as **Ud.** or **Vd.**, and **Uds.** or **Vds.**, respectively.*

**A.** *Subject pronouns* (**Los pronombres personales**) can represent the person that performs the action in a sentence.

In Spanish, several subject pronouns have masculine and feminine forms. The masculine plural form is used to refer to a group of males as well as to a group of males and females.

Mark → *he*
Martha → *she*
Mark and Paul → *they*
Mark and Martha → *they*
Martha and Emily → *they*

Marcos → **él**
Marta → **ella**
Marcos y Pablo → **ellos** (*all male*)
Marcos y Marta → **ellos** (*male and female*)
Marta y Emilia → **ellas** (*all female*)

**B.** Spanish has different words for *you*. In general, **tú** is used to refer to a close friend or a member of your family, while **usted** is used with people with whom the speaker has a more formal or distant relationship. The situations in which **tú** and **usted** are used also vary among different countries and regions.

**tú** → close friend, family member

**usted (Ud.)** → formal or distant relationship

**C.** In Latin America and in the United States and Canada, the plural for both **usted** and **tú** is **ustedes.** In Spain, however, **vosotros/vosotras** is the plural of **tú,** while **ustedes** is used as the plural of **usted** exclusively.

**Latin America, North America**

tú
usted (Ud.) } ustedes (Uds.)

**Spain**

tú → vosotros/vosotras
usted (Ud.) → ustedes (Uds.)

**D.** Subject pronouns are not used as frequently in Spanish as they are in English and may usually be omitted. You will learn more about the uses of Spanish subject pronouns in **Capítulo 2.**

## Present Tense of *-ar* Verbs

Past ------------------- **PRESENT** ------------------- Future
present

**A.** The *infinitive* (**el infinitivo**) of a verb indicates the action or state of being, with no reference to who or what performs the action or when it is done (present, past, or future). In Spanish all infinitives end in **-ar, -er,** or **-ir.** Infinitives in English are indicated by *to*: *to* speak, *to* eat, *to* live.

-ar: habl**ar**   *to speak*
-er: com**er**   *to eat*
-ir: viv**ir**   *to live*

| **infinitive** = a verb form expressing action or condition without reference to person, tense, or number |
| --- |

| **tense** = the form of a verb indicating time: present, past, or future |
| --- |

**Suggestions**
• Model the pronunciation of each infinitive several times. Then use the *yo* form of each in a brief, simple sentence about yourself, repeating several times and pantomiming if necessary.

**B.** To *conjugate* (**conjugar**) a verb means to give the various forms of the verb with their corresponding subjects: *I speak, you speak, she speaks,* and so on. All regular Spanish verbs are conjugated by adding *personal endings* (**las terminaciones personales**) that reflect the subject doing the action. These are added to the *stem* (**la raíz** or **el radical**), which is the infinitive minus the infinitive ending.

| Infinitive | | Stem |
|---|---|---|
| hablar | → | habl- |
| comer | → | com- |
| vivir | → | viv- |

• Have students generate all forms of one verb, after you give the subject pronouns.
• Transform the base sentence into a simple *Ud.* question directed to a student, coaching him or her to answer using the *yo* form. Example: *bailar → Me gusta bailar. Bailo muy bien. Y Ud., ¿baila bien?*

**C.** The right-hand column shows the personal endings that are added to the stem of all regular **-ar** verbs to form the *present tense* (**el presente**).

Regular **-ar** verb endings in the present tense:
**o, -as, -a, -amos, -áis, -an**

• Have students generate all forms of one verb, after you give the subject pronouns.
• Ask students *¿Cómo se dice* I/we dance, I/we sing, I/we buy . . . ?
• Emphasize *tocar* (music), and those infinitives that include prepositions in their meaning.
• Offer the following optional verbs: *caminar, fumar, hablar por teléfono, mirar (la televisión).*

**hablar (*to speak; to talk*): habl-**

| | Singular | | | | Plural | |
|---|---|---|---|---|---|---|
| (yo) | hablo | *I speak* | (nosotros) (nosotras) | | hablamos | *we speak* |
| (tú) | hablas | *you speak* | (vosotros) (vosotras) | | habláis | *you speak* |
| (Ud.) (él) (ella) | habla | *you speak* *he speaks* *she speaks* | (Uds.) (ellos) (ellas) | | hablan | *you speak* *they (m.) speak* *they (f.) speak* |

**D.** Some important **-ar** verbs in this chapter include those in the drawings and list on the right.

bailar

cantar

escuchar

tocar

| | |
|---|---|
| buscar | *to look for* |
| comprar | *to buy* |
| desear | *to want* |
| enseñar | *to teach* |
| estudiar | *to study* |
| hablar | *to speak; to talk* |
| necesitar | *to need* |
| pagar | *to pay (for)* |
| practicar | *to practice* |
| regresar | *to return* (to a place) |
| tomar | *to take; to drink* |
| trabajar | *to work* |

**Heritage Speakers**
• Pídales a los estudiantes hispanohablantes que expliquen la diferencia entre *regresar, volver* y *devolver.* También explique que para expresar *to return a phone call* es preferible decir *devolver una llamada* o *volver a llamar,* no *llamar atrás.*
• Anime a los estudiantes hispanohablantes a formar parejas con estudiantes monolingües para que hagan y contesten preguntas con estos verbos. Por ejemplo: *¿Cuándo regresas de la universidad? → Regreso a las seis.*

**OJO** Note that in Spanish the meaning of the English word *for* is included in the verbs **buscar** (*to look for*) and **pagar** (*to pay for*); *to* is included in **escuchar** (*to listen to*).

# PASO 3

**tú:** buscar, hablar, pagar, tomar
**Ud./él/ella:** cantar, necesitar, regresar, enseñar
**nosotros:** comprar, pagar, estudiar, escuchar
**vosotros:** desear, regresar, cantar, bailar
**Uds./ellos/ellas:** practicar, tomar, desear, tocar

**Preliminary Exercise**
Explain the purpose of a rapid response drill. Have students give the corresponding forms.
*yo: bailar, estudiar, tocar, escuchar*

**E.** As in English, when two Spanish verbs are used in sequence and there is no change of subject, the second verb is usually in the infinitive form.

**Necesito llamar** a mi familia.
*I need to call my family.*

**Me gusta bailar.**
*I like to dance.*

**F.** In both English and Spanish, conjugated verb forms also indicate the *time* or *tense* (**el tiempo**) of the action: *I speak* (present), *I spoke* (past).

Some English equivalents of the present tense forms of Spanish verbs are shown at the right.

**hablo** {
*I speak* — Simple present tense

*I am speaking* — Present progressive (indicates an action in progress)

*I will speak* — Near future action

## Negation

In Spanish the word **no** is placed before the conjugated verb to make a negative sentence.

El estudiante **no** habla español.
*The student doesn't speak Spanish.*

No, **no** necesito dinero.
*No, I don't need money.*

**Suggestion**
Point out that the second *no* = the English *not*.

## ■ Práctica

**Prác. A: Notes**
• See the IM for a discussion of input activities such as this one.
• Generally, the subject pronoun is not used before the verb in a sentence except for clarity or emphasis. The conjugated verb informs the listener as to the identity of the subject.

**A. Mis compañeros y yo**

**PASO 1** **¡Anticipemos!*** Read the following statements and tell whether they are true for you and your classmates and for your classroom environment. If any statement is not true for you or your class, make it negative or change it in another way to make it correct.

MODELO: Toco el piano → Sí, toco el piano.
(No, no toco el piano. Toco la guitarra.)

1. Necesito más (*more*) dinero.
2. Trabajo en la biblioteca.
3. Tomo ocho clases este semestre/trimestre.
4. En clase, cantamos en francés.
5. Deseamos practicar español.
6. Tomamos café en clase.
7. El profesor / La profesora enseña italiano.
8. El profesor / La profesora habla muy bien el alemán (*German*).

**Prác. A: Follow-Up**
**Paso 1.** Convert students' statements into questions addressed to other students: *¿Necesita más dinero (Jim)? ¿(Jim) cree que tomamos cerveza en clase?*

**PASO 2** Now turn to the person next to you and restate each sentence as a question, using **tú** forms of the verbs in all cases. Your partner will indicate whether the sentences are true for him or her.

MODELO: ¿Tocas el piano? → Sí, toco el piano. (No, no toco el piano.)

**Prác. A: Suggestions**
• Paso 2. Encourage students to create their own questions.
• Encourage student partners to write a summary of their similarities and differences, using the *nosotros* forms: (*Nosotros*) *Necesitamos mucho dinero y no tomamos café en clase.*

**Prác. A: Answers**
*Paso 2* 1. ¿Necesitas…?
2. ¿Trabajas… ? 3. ¿Tomas… ? 4. En clase, ¿cantas… ? 5. ¿Deseas… ? 6. ¿Tomas… ?
7. ¿Enseñas… ? 8. ¿Hablas…?

___

*****¡Anticipemos!** (*Lets look ahead!*) identifies activities or **pasos** that allow you to see words and structures in context before you begin to use them actively.

**Prác. B: Suggestion**
Have students explain their answers in simple sentences, for example, 1. *Falso. Marcos está en el apartamento con los estudiantes.* Students might disagree about and discuss items of this kind. For example, another student might say: *¡Sí! Hay profesores en las fiestas de los estudiantes,* and so on.

**Prác. B: Follow-Up**
Do orally or as dictation.

*Cambie por el plural.*
1. *Él no desea tomar una cerveza.*
2. *Ud. baila con un estudiante.*

**Need more practice?**

- Workbook/Laboratory Manual
- Interactive CD-ROM
- Online Learning Center (www.mhhe.com/quetal7)

3. *¿Compro el lápiz mañana?*
4. *Hablas con la dependienta.*
5. *¿Hay sólo una extranjera en la clase?*

*Cambie por el singular.*
6. *Ellas no buscan el dinero.*
7. *¿Enseñan Uds. sólo dos clases de español?*
8. *Necesitamos unos libros de texto.*
9. *Las mujeres estudian sicología.*
10. *¿Pagan Uds. sólo 30 pesos?*

**Nota comunicativa: Preliminary Exercises**
Have students use the cues to form sentences.

- *¿Cómo están Uds.?*

  1. *yo / muy bien*
  2. *tú / bien*
  3. *el profesor (la profesora) / muy bien*
  4. *nosotros / no / enfermo* (pantomime)
  5. *Julio / mal*
  6. *Uds. / bien / también*

- *¿Dónde están las siguientes ciudades?*

  1. *Amarillo, Los Ángeles, San Agustín, Toledo, Santa Fe, Reno*
  2. *Managua, Guadalajara, Buenos Aires, La Habana, Quito, La Paz, Bogotá*

**Nota comunicativa: Suggestions**
- Point out the irregular *yo* form and the accents on other forms.
- Emphasize the use of *estar* for (1) condition or state of health, (2) location. Students have used *estar* to express both concepts since *Primeros pasos.*
- At this time, avoid explaining differences between *ser* and *estar.* If students ask, just tell them more than one verb expresses *to be* in Spanish.

**Prác. B: Answers**
1. *cantan* 2. *bailan* 3. *toca* 4. *escuchan* 5. *busca* 6. *habla* 7. *desea* 8. *bailar* 9. *baila* 10. *necesitan*
**Comprensión** 1. *falso* 2. *falso* 3. *cierto* 4. *cierto*

**B. En una fiesta.** The following paragraphs describe a party. First scan the paragraphs to get a general sense of their meaning. Then complete the paragraphs with the correct form of the numbered infinitives.

Esta noche[a] hay una fiesta en el apartamento de Marcos y Julio. Todos[b] los estudiantes (cantar[1]) y (bailar[2]). Una persona (tocar[3]) la guitarra y otras personas (escuchar[4]) la música.

Jaime (buscar[5]) una Coca-Cola. Marta (hablar[6]) con un amigo. María José (desear[7]) enseñarles a todos[c] un baile[d] de Colombia. Todas las estudiantes desean (bailar[8]) con el estudiante mexicano—¡él (bailar[9]) muy bien!

La fiesta es estupenda, pero todos (necesitar[10]) regresar a casa[e] o a su[f] cuarto temprano.[g] ¡Hay clases mañana!

[a]Esta... *Tonight*  [b]*All*  [c]enseñarles... *to teach everyone*  [d]*dance*  [e]a... *home*  [f]*their*  [g]*early*

## Comprensión: ¿Cierto o falso?

1. Marcos es profesor de español.
2. A Jaime le gusta el café.
3. María José es de Colombia.
4. Los estudiantes desean bailar.

**Prác. B: Note**
The majority of the items in comprehension activities of this kind are inferential; that is, students need to apply their knowledge of the paragraph to the individual items in order to decide if an item is *cierto* or *falso.*

## ■ Conversación

### NOTA COMUNICATIVA

#### The Verb *estar*

**Estar** is another Spanish **-ar** verb. It means *to be,* and you have already used forms of it to ask how others are feeling or to tell where things are located. Here is the complete present tense conjugation of **estar.** Note that the **yo** form is irregular. The other forms take regular **-ar** endings, and some have a shift in the stress pattern (indicated by the accented **á**).

| | | | |
|---|---|---|---|
| yo | **estoy** | nosotros/as | **estamos** |
| tú | **estás** | vosotros/as | **estáis** |
| Ud., él, ella | **está** | Uds., ellos, ellas | **están** |

You will learn the uses of the verb **estar,** along with those of **ser** (the other Spanish verb that means *to be*) gradually, over the next several chapters. In the following questions, **estar** is used to inquire about location or feelings.  ♻ Reciclado
Emphasize interrogative words, presented in *Primeros pasos.*

1. ¿Cómo está Ud. en este momento (*right now*)?
2. ¿Cómo están sus (*your*) compañeros? (Mis compañeros... )
3. ¿Dónde está Ud. en este momento?

**A. ¿Qué hacen?** (*What are they doing?*)
Tell where these people are and what they are doing. Note that the definite article is used with titles when you are talking about a person: **el señor, la señora, la señorita, el profesor, la profesora.**

MODELO:   La Sra. Martínez _____. →
La Sra. Martínez está en la oficina. Busca un documento, trabaja…

> **Frases útiles**
>
> **hablar por teléfono**
> **preparar la lección**
> **pronunciar las palabras**
> **tomar apuntes** (to take notes)
> **trabajar en la caja** (at the register)
> **usar una computadora**

Resources: Transparency 12

1.  Estas (*These*) personas _____.
    La profesora Gil _____.
    Casi (*Almost*) todos los estudiantes _____.
    Un estudiante _____.

2.  Estas personas están _____.
    El Sr. Miranda _____.
    La bibliotecaria _____.
    El estudiante _____.

3.  Estas personas _____.
    El cliente _____.
    La dependienta _____.

**B. Entrevista.**   Use the following questions as a guide to interview a classmate, and take notes on what he or she says. (Write down what your partner says using the **él/ella** form of the verbs.) Your instructor may want you to hand in your notes so that he or she can get to know the students in the class better.

> **Frases útiles**
>
> **por** (in) **la mañana**
> **por la tarde**
> **por la noche**

MODELO:   ESTUDIANTE 1: Karen, ¿estudias filosofía?
ESTUDIANTE 2: No, no estudio filosofía. Estudio música.
ESTUDIANTE 1: (escribe [*writes*]): Karen no estudia filosofía. Estudia música.

1.  ¿Estudias mucho o poco (*a little*)? ¿Dónde estudias, en casa, en la residencia o en la biblioteca? ¿Cuándo estudias, por la mañana, por la tarde o por la noche?
2.  ¿Cantas bien o mal (*poorly*)? ¿Tocas un instrumento musical? ¿Cuál es? (el piano, la guitarra, el violín… )
3.  ¿Trabajas? ¿Dónde? ¿Cuántas horas a la semana (*per week*) trabajas? ¿Trabajas todos los días de la semana? ¿hasta muy tarde (*late*)?
4.  ¿Quiénes pagan los libros de texto, tú o los profesores? ¿Qué más necesitas pagar? ¿Diccionarios? ¿el alquiler (*rent*)? ¿la matrícula (*tuition*)? ¿ ?

**Con. C: Note**

*Escuchar* means *to listen to*: The Spanish verb does not need a preposition in front of the object. Note, however, that the personal *a* is used with animate nouns.

I listen to my mother. →
*Escucho a mi madre.*

### Vocabulario útil

**descansar** (to rest)
**escuchar**
**fumar** (to smoke)
**mirar** (to watch)
  **una película** (a movie)
  **la tele** (TV)
**tocar**
  **la batería** (drums)
  **la guitarra**
  **el piano**
**tomar**
  **cerveza**
  **refrescos** (soft drinks)
  **vino**

**Con. C: Variations**

• Describe the scene shown in the illustration and have students draw what they hear in your description.
• Have several students draw on board what other classmates describe for them.

**Con. C: Answers**

*Possible answers: Paso 1* Felipe toca la batería. José toca la guitarra. Juan toma cerveza. Nora habla por teléfono. Pedro no escucha la música.

## C. ¿Qué pasa (*What's happening*) en la fiesta?

PASO 1  With a classmate, describe what's going on in the following scene.

MODELO:  Pilar y Ana bailan en la fiesta.

Resources: Transparency 13

PASO 2  Now compare the scene above with parties *you* go to. Use the **nosotros** form of verbs to describe what you and your friends do at these parties.

MODELO:  Mis amigos y yo bailamos en las fiestas.

## En los Estados Unidos y el Canadá

### Jaime Escalante: Profesor de matemáticas

Jaime Escalante was born in La Paz, Bolivia, where he was a math and physics teacher for fourteen years. He emigrated to California in 1964 when he was 33. Since he did not speak English, he took menial jobs while he learned the language and went to college to become an accredited teacher. He started teaching in 1974 at Garfield High School, in East Los Angeles, where the students were mostly low-income Hispanics. In 1982, with Escalante's help, his students did so well on an advanced placement calculus test that the Educational Testing Service thought they had cheated and asked them to retake the test. The 1988 film *Stand and Deliver* portrays Escalante and his students' efforts. He was later awarded the United States Presidential Medal and the Andrés Bello award by the Organization of American States.

*Jaime Escalante*

**En los Estados Unidos y el Canadá: Comprensión** (Note: Accept one-word answers if you use the Spanish questions, as students cannot produce past tenses at this point.)

1. What subjects did Mr. Escalante teach? (*¿Qué materias enseñó el Sr. Escalante?*)
2. What is the name of the school where Mr. Escalante taught? (*¿Cómo se llama la escuela donde enseñó el Sr. Escalante?*)

**Follow-Up**

Have students discuss exceptional teachers that they have had or know of. What impact can such teachers have on individual students, a class, a school, and/or the community?

## UN POCO DE TODO

**Lengua y cultura: La universidad perfecta.** Complete Ángela's letter to her cousin about her search for the perfect college. Give the correct form of the verbs in parentheses, as suggested by context. When two possibilities are given in parentheses, select the correct word.

**M**i querida Carmen:

Mi amiga Luisa y yo buscamos la universidad perfecta para nosotras. Deseamos ser (compañeras / consejeras[1]) de cuarto.

Mañana (*nosotras: visitar*[2]) la Universidad de Texas en Austin. ¡(Ser[3]) muy grande[a]! Hay veinticuatro grupos sociales para estudiantes hispanos y (un/una[4]) biblioteca especial. (El/La[5]) colección latinoamericana es muy grande. (Los/Las[6]) materias más populares son (el/la[7]) administración de empresas, (el/la[8]) ingeniería, (los/las[9]) humanidades y (los/las[10]) comunicaciones. Muchos estudiantes (estudiar[11]) en (el/la[12]) Instituto de Estudios[b] Latinoamericanos y en (el/la[13]) Centro para Estudios Mexicoamericanos. La matrícula no es cara,[c] pero el problema es que no me gusta (el/la[14]) idea de estudiar en (un/una[15]) universidad muy grande.

(*Yo: Desear*[16]) estudiar en (un/una[17]) universidad menos grande, como Stanford. Tiene[d] nueve grupos sociales para estudiantes hispanos y (un/una[18]) casa especial para estudiantes de español. Se llama la Casa Zapata y es (un/una[19]) residencia. (Los/Las[20]) estudiantes (practicar[21]) español y participan en celebraciones hispanas. Las (mochilas/materias[22]) más populares de Stanford son la biología, (el/la[23]) economía, la sicología, (el/la[24]) inglés y (los/las[25]) ciencias políticas. Luisa y yo (visitar[26]) Stanford en dos semanas.[e] Pero la matrícula… ¡Los estudiantes (pagar[27]) mucho (dinero/papel[28]) para estudiar en Stanford!

Te hablo[f] por teléfono pronto.[g]
Con cariño,
Ángela

[a]*big* [b]*Studies* [c]*expensive* [d]*It has* [e]*weeks* [f]*Te… I'll speak to you* [g]*soon*

*La* Benson Latin American Collection (*en la Universidad de Texas en Austin*) *es una colección comprensiva de libros, documentos, revistas* (magazines) *y periódicos* (newspapers) *relacionados con* (related to) *Latinoamérica.*

**Comprensión.** Which of these statements do you agree with after reading Ángela's letter? Change incorrect statements to make them true.

1. Luisa y Ángela son amigas.
2. Ángela desea estudiar en una universidad muy grande.
3. En el Instituto de Estudios Latinoamericanos hay pocos (*few*) estudiantes.
4. La Casa Zapata es una biblioteca importante.

**Lengua y cultura: Answers**
1. *compañeras* 2. *visitamos* 3. *Es* 4. *una* 5. *La* 6. *Las* 7. *la* 8. *la* 9. *las* 10. *las* 11. *estudian* 12. *el* 13. *el* 14. *la* 15. *una* 16. *Deseo* 17. *una* 18. *una* 19. *una* 20. *Los* 21. *practican* 22. *materias* 23. *la* 24. *el* 25. *las* 26. *visitamos* 27. *pagan* 28. *dinero* **Comprensión** 1. *cierto* 2. *falso: Ángela no desea estudiar en una universidad muy grande.* 3. *falso. Hay muchos estudiantes en el Instituto.* 4. *falso: Es una residencia.*

**Bright Idea Suggestion**
Have students indicate what they felt was most important when they were looking for a university.

¿los profesores?
¿la fama de la universidad?
¿las «fraternidades»?
¿los grupos sociales?
¿Existe una universidad perfecta?

**Reciclado**
Remind students that some subject pronouns reflect gender. For example, *él/ella, nosotros/nosotras, vosotros/vosotras, ellos/ellas.* Gender, however, is not evident with *yo, tú, Ud.,* and *Uds.*

**Resources: Desenlace**
In the *Capítulo 1* segment of "Chapter-by-Chapter Supplementary Materials" in the IM, you will find a chapter-culminating activity. You can use this activity to consolidate and review the vocabulary and grammar skills the students have acquired.

**Resources for Review and Testing Preparation**
- Workbook/Laboratory Manual
- Interactive CD-ROM
- Online Learning Center (www.mhhe.com/quetal7)

## VIDEOTECA

### Entrevista cultural: Los Estados Unidos

Carlos Rivera is a university professor from San Antonio, Texas. In this interview, Professor Rivera talks about where he lives now and his experiences as a professor. Before watching the video clip, read the following excerpt from the interview.

INTERVIEWER: ¿Cuántas clases enseña Ud.?

PROF. RIVERA: Este semestre, enseño tres clases. Una clase de literatura contemporánea de los Estados Unidos, una clase de literatura chicana y una clase de composición.

Now watch the video clip and answer the following questions based on the interview.

1. Where does Professor Rivera live now?
2. What subject does Professor Rivera teach?
3. How many classes is Professor Rivera teaching this semester?
4. Does he have a favorite class? If so, what is it?
5. Why does Professor Rivera like his job?

### Entre amigos: ¿Qué clases tomas?

Miguel, Tané, Rubén, and Karina are getting to know each other. What questions do you think they will ask each other? Before watching the video, read the following questions. As you watch, don't worry if you don't understand every word. Try to get the gist of the conversation, listening carefully for information about classes. Watch the video a second time and listen for the answers to the questions.

1. ¿De dónde es Rubén?
2. ¿Qué clases toma Rubén? (¡**OJO**! Rubén usa un sinónimo para «la computación».)
3. ¿Qué hace Miguel (*What does Miguel do*) los fines de semana?

## ENFOQUE CULTURAL

### Los hispanos en los Estados Unidos

### ¡Fíjese!ª

- En 2001 (dos mil uno) habíaᵇ veintiún hispanos en el Congreso de los Estados Unidos. ¿Cuántos hay ahora? (www.house.gov)
- De los más deᶜ 35 millones de hispanos en los Estados Unidos, la mayoríáᵈ habla español (mucho o poco).
- Las palabras **hispano** eᵉ **hispánico** se refieren alᶠ idioma y a la cultura, no a la razaᵍ o grupo étnico.

ªCheck it out!   ᵇthere were   ᶜDe... Of the more than   ᵈmajority   ᵉy
ᶠse... refer to the   ᵍrace

### Personas famosas: César Chávez

La contribución de César Chávez (1927–1993 [mil novecientos veintisiete a mil novecientos noventa y tres]) al movimiento de los trabajadores agrícolasª es enorme. La educación de Chávez, hijo de campesinos migrantes,ᵇ sólo llega al séptimo grado.ᶜ

En 1962 (mil novecientos sesenta y dos), Chávez organiza a los campesinos que cosechan uvas.ᵈ Como resultado de las huelgasᵉ y el boicoteo de las uvas de mesa,ᶠ los campesinos reciben contratos más favorables para ellos; el United Farm Workers se estableceᵍ como sindicatoʰ oficial.

En 2003 (dos mil tres), el servicio postal de los Estados Unidos honra a Chávez con un selloⁱ especial.

Hoy en día,ʲ la vida,ᵏ los sacrificios y los ideales de Chávez sirven deˡ inspiración a muchas personas.

ªtrabajadores... agricultural workers   ᵇhijo... son of migrant farm workers   ᶜllega... reaches the seventh grade   ᵈque... who harvest grapes   ᵉstrikes   ᶠuvas... table grapes   ᵍse... is established   ʰunion   ⁱstamp   ʲHoy... Nowadays   ᵏlife   ˡsirven... serve as an

El sello estadounidense (U.S.) con la imagen de César Chávez

**Follow-Up**
After students read the ¡Fíjese! section, ask: ¿Conocen a un político hispano en _____ (name of your state)? Point out that since 2003 Hispanics are the largest minority group in the United States.

**Notes**
- Datos esenciales about all countries presented in Enfoque cultural can be found on the end papers of ¿Qué tal?
- El idioma means la lengua.
- Students can read an excerpt of the novel Caramelo by the Mexican-American writer Sandra Cisneros in Voces de los Estados Unidos: Literatura.
- Students can read about the musical tradition of el tejano in Voces de los Estados Unidos: Música.
- See the Workbook/Laboratory Manual for focused practice with the material in Enfoque cultural.

**Heritage Speakers**
- Latino/a e hispano/a en español no significan «U.S. Hispanic / Latino», sino una persona de un país donde se habla español. Hispanoamericano/a y latinoamericano/a sólo se usan para referirse a personas de Latinoamérica.
- Pídales a los estudiantes hispanohablantes que investiguen más a fondo la vida y labor de César Chávez. Luego pueden preparar y presentarle a la clase un informe oral.

Learn more about Hispanics in the United States with the Video, Interactive CD-ROM, and the Online Learning Center (www.mhhe.com/quetal7).

## PASO FINAL

> **Sobre** (About) **la lectura…**
> This reading was written by the authors of *¿Qué tal?* for students of Spanish like you. Later on in this text, you will have the chance to read more "authentic" selections.

### A LEER

### ESTRATEGIA: More on Guessing Meaning from Context

As you learned in **La geografía del mundo hispánico (Primeros pasos),** you can often guess the meaning of unfamiliar words from the context (the words that surround them) and by using your knowledge about the topic in general. Making "educated guesses" about words in this way will be an important part of your reading skills in Spanish.

What is the meaning of the underlined words in these sentences?

1. En una lista alfabetizada, la palabra **grande** aparece <u>antes de</u> **grotesco.**
2. El edificio no es moderno; es <u>viejo.</u>
3. Me gusta estudiar español, pero detesto la biología. En general, <u>odio</u> las ciencias como materia.

Some words are underlined in the following reading (and in the readings in subsequent chapters). Try to guess their meaning from context.

Like the passages in **Primeros pasos** and some others in subsequent chapters, this reading contains section subheadings. Scanning these subheadings in advance will help you make predictions about the reading's content, which will also help to facilitate your overall comprehension. Another useful way to manage longer passages is to read section by section. At this point, don't try to understand every word. Your main objective should be to understand the general content of the passage.

## Las universidades hispánicas

### Introducción
En el mundo hispánico —y en los Estados Unidos y el Canadá— hay universidades grandes[a] y <u>pequeñas;</u> públicas, religiosas y privadas; modernas y antiguas. Pero el concepto de «vida[b] universitaria» es diferente.

### El *campus*
Por ejemplo, en los países[c] hispánicos la universidad no es un centro de actividad social. No hay muchas residencias estudiantiles. En general, los estudiantes <u>viven</u> en pensiones[d] o en casas particulares[e] y <u>llegan</u> a la universidad en coche o en autobús. En algunas[f] universidades hay un *campus* similar a los de[g] las universidades de los Estados Unidos y el Canadá. En estos casos se habla[h] de la «ciudad[i] universitaria». Otras universidades ocupan sólo un edificio grande, o posiblemente varios edificios, pero no hay zonas verdes.[j]

*Estudiantes de medicina en Caracas, Venezuela*

[a]*large* [b]*life* [c]*naciones* [d]*boardinghouses* [e]*private* [f]*some* [g]*los… those of* [h]*se… one speaks* [i]*city* [j]*green*

## Los <u>deportes</u>

Otra diferencia es que en la mayoría de las universidades hispánicas los deportes no son muy importantes. Si los estudiantes desean practicar un deporte —el tenis, el fútbol o el béisbol— hay clubes deportivos, pero estos[k] no forman parte de la universidad.

## Las diversiones[l]

Como se puede ver,[m] la forma y la organización de la universidad son diferentes en las dos culturas. Pero los estudiantes estudian y se divierten[n] en todas partes.[o] A los estudiantes hispanos, así como[p] a los estadounidenses* y canadienses[q], les gusta mucho toda clase de música: la música clásica, la música con raíces[r] tradicionales y la música moderna —la nacional[s] y la <u>importada</u>. Y hay para todos: Usher, Alicia Keys, Green Day... Otras diversiones preferidas por los estudiantes son las discotecas y los cafés. Hay cafés ideales para hablar con los amigos. También hay exposiciones de arte, <u>obras</u> de teatro y películas[t] interesantes.

## Conclusión

Los días favoritos de muchos jóvenes[u] hispánicos son los fines de semana. ¿Realmente son muy distintos los estudiantes hispanos? ■

[k]*they* (lit. *these*)  [l]*Las... Entertainment*  [m]*Como... As you can see*  [n]*se... have a good time*  [o]*en... everywhere*  [p]*Así... like*  [q]*estadounidenses... people from the United States and Canada*  [r]*roots*  [s]*la... (music) from their own country*  [t]*movies*  [u]*young people*

## Comprensión

**A. ¿Cierto o falso?**   Indique si las siguientes oraciones son ciertas o falsas.

1. En los países hispánicos, la mayoría de los estudiantes vive en residencias.
2. En las universidades hispánicas, los deportes ocupan un lugar esencial en el programa de estudios del estudiante.
3. En una universidad hispánica, no hay mucho tiempo para asistir a (*time for attending*) conciertos y exposiciones de arte.
4. No hay mucha diferencia entre (*between*) una universidad hispánica y una universidad norteamericana con respecto al *campus*.
5. La música es una diversión para los estudiantes en todas partes.
6. Hay grandes jardines (*gardens*) y zonas verdes en las universidades hispánicas.

**B. ¿Qué universidad?**   Indique si las siguientes oraciones son de un estudiante de la Universidad de Sevilla o de un estudiante de la Universidad de Michigan... ¡o de los dos!

|  | SEVILLA | MICHIGAN | LOS DOS |
|---|---|---|---|
| 1. «Me gusta jugar al Frisbee en el *campus*.» | ☐ | ☐ | ☐ |
| 2. «La casa es muy cómoda (*comfortable*) y tengo derecho a usar la cocina (*I have kitchen privileges*).» | ☐ | ☐ | ☐ |
| 3. «Después de (*After*) mi clase, ¿qué tal si tomamos un café?» | ☐ | ☐ | ☐ |
| 4. «El sábado (*Saturday*) hay un partido de basquetbol. ¿Deseas ir (*to go*)?» | ☐ | ☐ | ☐ |
| 5. «Me gusta hablar con mis amigos entre clases en los jardines de la universidad.» | ☐ | ☐ | ☐ |

**A leer: Suggestions**
- Ask students what aspects of campus life are important to them. *¿Son importantes las actividades sociales en la universidad? ¿Y los deportes? ¿Qué más es importante?*
- Have students describe the photo, using as many words from the *Vocabulario* list as possible. Elicit some sentences using questions.

**Comprensión A: Suggestion**
For items 1–3, have students substitute *los Estados Unidos* (*el Canadá*) and *de/en los Estados Unidos* (*del / en el Canadá*), for *hispánico/a(s)*, and respond *cierto* or *falso* to the new statement. Then, have them restate each sentence with themselves (*yo*) as the subject (*Yo vivo en una residencia*) and also respond *cierto* or *falso*.

**Comprensión A: Answers**
1. *falso* 2. *falso* 3. *falso* 4. *falso* 5. *cierto* 6. *falso*

**Comprensión B: Answers**
1. *Michigan* 2. *Sevilla* 3. *los dos* 4. *Michigan* 5. *Michigan*

**Heritage Speakers**
Pídales a los estudiantes hispanoamericanos que hagan una lista de las actividades extraacadémicas que se realizan en la típica universidad iberoamericana: actividades deportivas, publicaciones, derechos humanos, etcétera. Puede pedirles que preparen y presenten un informe oral acerca de estas actividades.

*Although, technically, **norteamericano** refers to all North Americans (people from Canada, the United States, and Mexico), the term is sometimes used to refer solely to people from the United States of America. In this book, **estadounidenses** will refer to people from the United States and **norteamericanos** to North Americans.

# PASO 4

**A escribir A: Suggestions**
• Go over the assignment orally in class to be sure that students understand the meaning of all words and phrases. Assign the preparation of answers in writing as homework. The following day, use one student's answers as a model to form two coherent paragraphs, writing the sentences on the board. Then have students write paragraphs for the next day.
• Have students make similar tables to compare individuals in the class, using *alojamiento, diversiones, comidas* (*¿cafetería?*), and so on, as the headings.

**A escribir B: Suggestions**
• If students created charts comparing individuals, collate and analyze the results on the board. Ask: Can you account for any differences based on age? gender? national origin? and so on. After discussing the comments as a class, have students write a brief report on the findings.
• For additional writing practice, see the *Mi diario* activity in the Workbook/Laboratory Manual.

**Multimedia: Internet**
After students have finished the *A escribir* section, have them visit the website for *la Universidad Iberoamericana* in Mexico City. Then have students write a brief description of the *Universidad Iberoamericana* campus, based on the interactive map (*mapa del plantel*).

## A ESCRIBIR

**A. Una comparación.**   Compare su propia (*your own*) universidad con una universidad hispánica, completando (*by completing*) la siguiente tabla con información de la lectura.

|  | La universidad hispánica | Mi universidad |
|---|---|---|
| **Alojamiento** (*Housing*) | pensiones, casas particulares |  |
| El *campus* |  |  |
| **Deportes** |  |  |
| **Diversiones** | música, discotecas, cafés, películas, exposiciones de arte |  |

## B. Mi universidad

PASO 1   In light of what you now know about some differences and similarities between universities in this country and in Hispanic countries, what information do you think would be important to share with a Hispanic student planning on studying at *your* university?
First, use the following questions to organize your ideas.

1. ¿Es grande o pequeña la universidad? (Mi universidad... )
2. ¿Es pública o privada?
3. ¿Cuántas residencias hay en el *campus*?
4. ¿Cuántas cafeterías hay? ¿En qué edificios están las cafeterías?
5. En general, ¿viven los estudiantes en residencias, en apartamentos o con su (*their*) familia?
6. ¿Cuántas bibliotecas hay? ¿Hay bibliotecas especializadas? ¿Hay computadoras para los estudiantes en las bibliotecas?
7. ¿Dónde vive Ud.? (Yo vivo... )
8. ¿Cómo llega Ud. al *campus*? ¿En coche o en autobús? ¿O camina Ud.? (*Or do you walk?*)
9. ¿En que edificios del *campus* estudia Ud.?
10. ¿Qué materia le gusta más?

PASO 2   Now use your answers to form two paragraphs: 1–6 for the first paragraph and 7–10 for the second paragraph. Remember that you are describing your university and your university life to a student from a Spanish-speaking country.

**Mi universidad...**

**Suggestions**
• Have students create word puzzles that they can exchange and solve.
• Have students play charades, using nouns from the list, for example, *profesor* (the student stands and pantomimes teaching the class).

## GRAMÁTICA

To review the grammar points presented in this chapter, refer to the indicated grammar presentations. You'll find further practice of these structures in the Workbook/Laboratory Manual, on the Interactive CD-ROM, and on the *¿Qué tal?* Online Learning Center (www.mhhe.com/quetal7).

**1** Identifying People, Places, Things, and Ideas—Singular Nouns: Gender and Articles

Do you understand the gender of nouns and how to use the articles **el, la, un,** and **una?**

**2** Identifying People, Places, Things, and Ideas—Nouns and Articles: Plural Forms

Do you know how to make nouns plural and use the articles **los, las, unos,** and **unas?**

**3** Expressing Actions—Subject Pronouns: Present Tense of **-ar** Verbs; Negation

You should be able to use subject pronouns, conjugate regular **-ar** verbs in the present tense, and form negative sentences.

• Have students draw pictures on the board depicting the vocabulary and have their classmates describe what is happening in Spanish.
• Have students guess who is talking based on the following context clues.

## VOCABULARIO

Practice this vocabulary with digital flash cards on the Online Learning Center (www.mhhe.com/quetal7).

### Los verbos

| | |
|---|---|
| **bailar** | to dance |
| **buscar** | to look for |
| **cantar** | to sing |
| **comprar** | to buy |
| **desear** | to want |
| **enseñar** | to teach |
| **escuchar** | to listen (to) |
| **estar** (*irreg.*) | to be |
| **estudiar** | to study |
| **hablar** | to speak; to talk |
|    **hablar por teléfono** | to talk on the phone |
| **necesitar** | to need |
| **pagar** | to pay (for) |
| **practicar** | to practice |
| **regresar** | to return (*to a place*) |
|    **regresar a casa** | to go home |
| **tocar** | to play (*a musical instrument*) |
| **tomar** | to take; to drink |
| **trabajar** | to work |

### Los lugares

| | |
|---|---|
| **el apartamento** | apartment |
| **la biblioteca** | library |
| **la cafetería** | cafeteria |
| **la clase** | class (room) |
| **el cuarto** | room |
| **el edificio** | building |
| **la fiesta** | party |
| **la librería** | bookstore |
| **la oficina** | office |
| **la residencia** | dormitory |
| **la universidad** | university |

### Las personas

| | |
|---|---|
| **el/la amigo/a** | friend |
| **el/la bibliotecario/a** | librarian |
| **el/la cliente** | client |
| **el/la compañero/a (de clase)** | classmate |
| **el/la compañero/a de cuarto** | roommate |
| **el/la consejero/a** | advisor |
| **el/la dependiente/a** | clerk |
| **el/la estudiante** | student |
| **el/la extranjero/a** | foreigner |
| **el hombre** | man |
| **la mujer** | woman |
| **el/la profesor(a)** | professor |
| **el/la secretario/a** | secretary |

**1.** *Trabajo en la escuela. Hablo con muchos estudiantes sobre los cursos que toman y sobre sus planes para sus estudios en la universidad.* (consejero/a)

**2.** *Soy de Colombia pero ahora vivo en los Estados Unidos.* (extranjero/a)

**3.** *Enseño español y matemáticas y tengo muchos estudiantes en la universidad.* (profesor[a])

**4.** *Trabajo en JCPenney y hablo con muchos clientes todos los días.* (dependiente/a)

• Encourage students to develop various strategies for learning vocabulary, such as flash cards or tri-fold lists. For flash cards, they write English on one side and Spanish on the reverse. For tri-fold lists, they write Spanish in one column (far left) and English in a column in the far right. They fold the sheet to see only English or only Spanish. Have students share other strategies they have used that work for them.

## Las cosas

| | |
|---|---|
| el bolígrafo | pen |
| la calculadora | calculator |
| el cuaderno | notebook |
| el diccionario | dictionary |
| el dinero | money |
| el escritorio | desk |
| el lápiz (*pl.* lápices) | pencil |
| el libro (de texto) | (text)book |
| la mesa | table |
| la mochila | backpack |
| el papel | paper |
| la pizarra | chalkboard |
| la puerta | door |
| la silla | chair |
| la ventana | window |

## Las materias

| | |
|---|---|
| la administración de empresas | business administration |
| las ciencias | science |
| la computación | computer science |
| la física | physics |
| las lenguas extranjeras | foreign languages |
| la química | chemistry |
| la sicología | psychology |

**Cognados:** el arte, las comunicaciones, la economía, la filosofía, la historia, las humanidades, la literatura, las matemáticas, la sociología

## Las lenguas (extranjeras)

| | |
|---|---|
| el alemán | German |
| el español | Spanish |
| el francés | French |
| el inglés | English |
| el italiano | Italian |

## Otros sustantivos

| | |
|---|---|
| el café | coffee |
| la cerveza | beer |
| la cosa | thing |

♲ **Reciclado**
Point out words learned in fixed expressions in *Primeros pasos* or used passively as cognates.

| | |
|---|---|
| el día | day |
| el lugar | place |
| la materia | (school) subject |
| la matrícula | tuition |

## Palabras interrogativas

| | |
|---|---|
| ¿cuál? | what?; which? |
| ¿cuándo? | when? |
| ¿cuánto? | how much? |
| ¿cuántos/as? | how many? |
| ¿quién? | who?; whom? |

**Repaso** (*Review*): ¿a qué hora?, ¿cómo?, ¿dónde?, ¿qué?

## ¿Cuándo?

| | |
|---|---|
| ahora | now |
| con frecuencia | frequently |
| el fin de semana | weekend |
| por la mañana (tarde, noche) | in the morning (afternoon, evening) |
| tarde/temprano | late/early |
| todos los días | every day |

## Pronombres personales

yo, tú, usted (Ud.), él/ella, nosotros/nosotras, vosotros/vosotras, ustedes (Uds.), ellos/ellas

## Palabras adicionales

| | |
|---|---|
| aquí | here |
| con | with |
| en casa | at home |
| mal | poorly |
| más | more |
| mucho | much; a lot |
| muy | very |
| poco | little |
| por eso | therefore |
| sólo | only |

**Suggestions**
- Have students use the adverbs from *¿Cuándo?* and the verbs from *Los verbos* to make a chart that plots when and how often they do some things.
- Have students indicate whether or not they have the following things.

| | |
|---|---|
| cuaderno | mochila |
| lápiz | papel |
| calculadora | bolígrafo |
| diccionario | dinero |

# La familia

## CULTURA

• **Nota cultural:** Los apellidos hispánicos
• **En los Estados Unidos y el Canadá:** Los Sheen: Una familia de actores
• **Voces** de México
    **Literatura:** Rosario Castellanos
    **Música:** El corrido
• **Videoteca**
    **Entrevista cultural:** México
    **Entre amigos:** ¿Cuántos hermanos tienes?
• **Enfoque cultural:** México

## VOCABULARIO

• La familia y los parientes
• Los números 31–100
• Adjetivos

## PRONUNCIACIÓN

• Stress and Written Accent Marks (Part 1)

## GRAMÁTICA

**4** Adjectives: Gender, Number, and Position

**5** Present Tense of **ser;** Summary of Uses

**6** Possessive Adjectives (Unstressed)

**7** Present Tense of **-er** and **-ir** Verbs; More About Subject Pronouns

*Una familia mexicana en el Parque Ecológico de Xochimilco, en la Ciudad de México*

# PASO 1 Vocabulario

### LA FAMILIA Y LOS PARIENTES°

**Paso 1: Vocabulario**
See the "Chapter-by-Chapter Supplementary Materials" in the IM for a model for vocabulary presentation, as well as additional teaching suggestions, notes, activities, and other resources for *Paso 1*.

♻ **Reciclado**
Have your students describe what particular family members like or do not like.

*¿A su padre le gusta mirar la televisión?*
*¿A su madre le gusta bailar?*

**Notes**
• Point out that *parientes* is a false cognate.
• Point out the use of the masculine plural form—*el abuelo y la abuela* becomes *los abuelos,* and so on.

**Resources: Transparencies 14–16**

**Heritage Speakers**
• El concepto de la familia para los hispanos no solamente incluye a la familia nuclear sino también a la familia extendida. Cuando llega un nuevo miembro a la familia, como el marido de una hermana, el concepto de la familia crece para incluir a consuegros, cuñados, los concuños o concuñados, etcétera.
• Pregúnteles a los hispanohablantes de la clase qué términos de cariño se usan en sus familias.

**Refrán**

«Más vale pájaro en mano que cien volando.»

Write the *refrán* on the board. Have students guess the meaning of *mano* and *volando*. What is a similar saying in English? (*A bird in the hand is worth two in the bush.*)

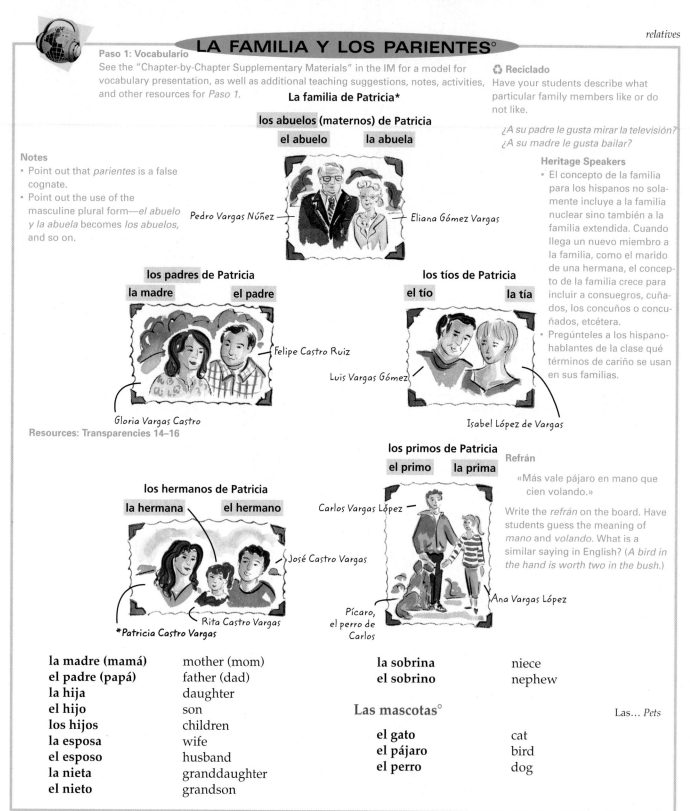

La familia de Patricia*

los abuelos (maternos) de Patricia
el abuelo    la abuela
Pedro Vargas Núñez — Eliana Gómez Vargas

los padres de Patricia
la madre    el padre
Felipe Castro Ruiz
Gloria Vargas Castro

los tíos de Patricia
el tío    la tía
Luis Vargas Gómez
Isabel López de Vargas

los primos de Patricia
el primo    la prima
Carlos Vargas López
Ana Vargas López

los hermanos de Patricia
la hermana    el hermano
José Castro Vargas
Rita Castro Vargas
*Patricia Castro Vargas
Pícaro, el perro de Carlos

| | | | |
|---|---|---|---|
| la madre (mamá) | mother (mom) | la sobrina | niece |
| el padre (papá) | father (dad) | el sobrino | nephew |
| la hija | daughter | | |
| el hijo | son | **Las mascotas°** | Las… *Pets* |
| los hijos | children | el gato | cat |
| la esposa | wife | el pájaro | bird |
| el esposo | husband | el perro | dog |
| la nieta | granddaughter | | |
| el nieto | grandson | | |

**Multimedia: Audio**
Students can listen to and practice this chapter's vocabulary on the Online Learning Center (**www.mhhe.com/quetal7**), as well as on the Textbook Audio CD, part of the Laboratory Audio Program.

## Vocabulario útil

| | |
|---|---|
| el padrastro / la madrastra | stepfather / stepmother |
| el hijastro / la hijastra | stepson / stepdaughter |
| el hermanastro / la hermanastra | stepbrother / stepsister |
| el medio hermano / la media hermana | half-brother / half-sister |
| el suegro / la suegra | father-in-law / mother-in-law |
| el yerno / la nuera | son-in-law / daughter-in-law |
| el cuñado / la cuñada | brother-in-law / sister-in-law |
| ...(ya) murió | . . . has (already) died |

## ■ Conversación

**A. ¿Cierto o falso?** Look at the drawings of the family that appear on page 50. Decide whether each of the following statements is true (**cierto**) or false (**falso**) according to the drawings. Correct the false statements.

1. José es el hermano de Ana.
2. Eliana es la abuela de Patricia.
3. Ana es la sobrina de Felipe y Gloria.
4. Patricia y José son primos.
5. Gloria es la tía de José.
6. Carlos es el sobrino de Isabel.
7. Pedro es el padre de Luis y Gloria.
8. Isabel y Gloria son las esposas de Luis y Felipe, respectivamente.

**Con. A: Answers**
1. *falso; Es el primo de Ana.* 2. *cierto* 3. *cierto* 4. *falso; Son hermanos.* 5. *falso; Es la madre de José.* 6. *falso; Es el hijo de Isabel.* 7. *cierto* 8. *cierto*

**B. ¿Quién es?**

PASO 1   Complete las oraciones lógicamente.

1. La madre de mi (*my*) padre es mi <u>abuela</u>.
2. El hijo de mi tío es mi <u>primo</u>.
3. La hermana de mi padre es mi <u>tía</u>.
4. El esposo de mi abuela es mi <u>abuelo</u>.

**Con. B: Answers**
*Paso 2* 1. *Es la hija de mi tío/a.* 2. *Es el hijo de mi hermano/a.* 3. *Es el hermano de mi madre/ padre.* 4. *Es el padre de mi madre/padre.*

PASO 2   Ahora defina estas (*these*) personas, según (*according to*) el mismo (*same*) modelo.

1. prima
2. sobrino
3. tío
4. abuelo

**C. Entrevista.** Find out as much as you can about the family of a classmate using the following dialogue as a guide. Use **tengo** (*I have*) and **tienes** (*you have*), as indicated. Use **¿cuántos?** with male relations and **¿cuántas?** with females.

MODELO:   E1:*¿Cuántos hermanos tienes?
    E2: Bueno (*Well*), tengo seis hermanos y una hermana.
    E1: ¿Y cuántos primos?
    E2: ¡Uf! Tengo un montón (*bunch*). Más de (*More than*) veinte.

---

*From this point on in the text,* ESTUDIANTE 1 *and* ESTUDIANTE 2 *will be abbreviated as* E1 *and* E2, *respectively.*

**Con. A: Suggestions**
- Introduce your own or a fictitious family with a family tree on the board or on an overhead transparency. Start with the recognizable cognates *padre* (*papá*) and *madre* (*mamá*); do two family members at a time, assigning names and defining relationships as you go along; students just listen during this phase. Use family photographs to personalize this activity even more.
- After several generations are on the board, go back to check comprehension, asking questions with alternatives: *¿Quién es él, mi abuelo o mi padre?*
- Model the names or integrate them in the tree on the board. Ask students if they have a brother, grandmother, and so on. You may also introduce related vocabulary such as: *soltero/a, casado/a, la familia nuclear,* and *la familia extendida.*
- To follow up, have students use your presentation as a guide when presenting their own family members to the class.

**Con. B: Suggestions**
- Do as listening comprehension activity, with students providing completion.
- Have students identify the members of each group: *los hijos → el hijo y la hija.*

  1. *los abuelos*
  2. *los padres*
  3. *los hermanos*
  4. *los nietos*
  5. *los tíos*
  6. *los sobrinos*

**Con. C: Suggestion**
Model dialogue with several students before allowing class to work in pairs. Model options for a small family.

## LOS NÚMEROS 31–100

♻ **Reciclado**
- Review numbers 1–30 with counting drills and math games.
- Remind students of the -e ending in *veinte* vs. the -a in *treinta, cuarenta, cincuenta,* and so on.

Continúe la secuencia:

treinta y uno, treinta y dos…
ochenta y cuatro, ochenta y cinco…

| | | | |
|---|---|---|---|
| 31 | treinta y uno | 40 | cuarenta |
| 32 | treinta y dos | 50 | cincuenta |
| 33 | treinta y tres | 60 | sesenta |
| 34 | treinta y cuatro | 70 | setenta |
| 35 | treinta y cinco | 80 | ochenta |
| 36 | treinta y seis | 90 | noventa |
| 37 | treinta y siete | 100 | cien, ciento |
| 38 | treinta y ocho | | |
| 39 | treinta y nueve | | |

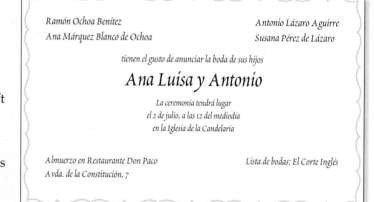

cincuenta y cinco

setenta y ocho

treinta y nueve

cuarenta y cinco

cuarenta y siete

ochenta y cinco

El abuelito Pedro tiene 85 años.

La abuelita Eliana tiene 78 años.

Beginning with 31, Spanish numbers are *not* written in a combined form; **treinta y uno,**\* **cuarenta y dos, sesenta y tres,** and so on, must be three separate words.

**Cien** is used before nouns and in counting.

**cien** casas

noventa y ocho, noventa y nueve, **cien**

*a (one) hundred houses*

*ninety-eight, ninety-nine, one hundred*

**Nota cultural: Comprensión**
1. Have students say what their full names would be if they were Latin American or Spanish.
2. Have students name the bride's and groom's *apellidos.*

**Nota cultural: Follow-Up**
Have students discuss what the advantages and disadvantages of using two last names are.

**Nota cultural: Suggestion**
Point out that this is a very traditional wedding invitation in which the groom's and bride's parents appear as the announcers of their children's wedding.

■ **Conversación**

**A. Problemas de matemáticas.** Recuerde: + **y,** − **menos,** = **son.**

**1.** 30 + 50 = ?  **2.** 45 + 45 = ?  **3.** 32 + 58 = ?  **4.** 77 + 23 = ?

## NOTA CULTURAL

### Los apellidos hispánicos

In most Hispanic countries, people are given two last names (**apellidos**). The custom is demonstrated in this wedding invitation. The names of the bride's parents are in the top left corner: Ramón Ochoa Benítez and Ana Márquez Blanco de Ochoa. Their daughter's name, before her marriage, is Ana Luisa Ochoa Márquez. Her first last name (Ochoa) is her father's first last name, and her second last name (Márquez) is her mother's first last name. The groom's parents are in the top right corner. What do you think his full name (with both last names) is? If you said Antonio Lázaro Pérez, you are correct. Some Spanish-speaking women take their husband's first last name as their new second last name, dropping the second last name they had before marriage. Ana Luisa Ochoa Márquez's name will change to Ana Luisa Ochoa de Lázaro.

> *Ramón Ochoa Benítez*
> *Ana Márquez Blanco de Ochoa*
>
> *Antonio Lázaro Aguirre*
> *Susana Pérez de Lázaro*
>
> *tienen el gusto de anunciar la boda de sus hijos*
>
> ## *Ana Luisa y Antonio*
>
> *La ceremonia tendrá lugar*
> *el 2 de julio, a las 12 del mediodía*
> *en la Iglesia de la Candelaria*
>
> *Almuerzo en Restaurante Don Paco*
> *Avda. de la Constitución, 7*
>
> *Lista de bodas: El Corte Inglés*

---

\**Remember that when* **uno** *is part of a compound number (***treinta y uno,** *and so on), it becomes* **un** *before a masculine noun and* **una** *before a feminine noun:* **setenta y un coches; cincuenta y una mesas.**

Con. B: Note
Point out that two last names are used in the Mexican phone book.

Con. B: Variation
Do as a dictation, with several students working at the board.

## B. Los números de teléfono

**PASO 1** Here is part of a page from an Hispanic telephone book. What can you tell about the names? (See the **Nota cultural** on page 52.)

**PASO 2** With a classmate, practice giving telephone numbers at random from the list. Your partner will listen and identify the person. **¡OJO!** In many Hispanic countries phone numbers are said differently than in this country. Follow the model.

MODELO: 4–15–00–46 →

E1: Es el *cuatro-quince-cero cero-cuarenta y seis.*

E2: Es el número de *A. Lázaro Aguirre.*

**PASO 3** Now give your classmate your phone number and get his or hers.

MODELO: Mi número es el…

| | |
|---|---|
| LAZARO AGUIRRE, A. –Schez Pacheco, 17 | 415 0046 |
| LAZCANO DEL MORAL, A. –E. Larreta, 14 | 215 8194 |
| LAZCANO DEL MORAL, A. –Ibiza, 8 | 274 6868 |
| LEAL ANTON, J. –Pozo, 8 | 222 3894 |
| LIEBANA RODRIGUEZ, A. | |
|   Guadarrama, 10 | 463 2593 |
| LOPEZ BARTOLOME, J. –Palma, 69 | 232 2027 |
| LOPEZ CABRA, J. –E. Solana, 118 | 407 5086 |
| LOPEZ CABRA, J. –L. Van, 5 | 776 4602 |
| LOPEZ GONZALEZ, J. A. –Ibiza, 27 | 409 2552 |
| LOPEZ GUTIERREZ, J. A. –S. Cameros, 7 | 478 8494 |
| LOPEZ LOPEZ, J. –Alamedilla, 21 | 227 3570 |
| LOPEZ MARIN, V. –Illescas, 53 | 218 6630 |
| LOPEZ MARIN, V. –N. Rey, 7 | 463 6873 |
| LOPEZ MARIN, V. –Valmojado, 289 | 717 2823 |
| LOPEZ NUÑEZ, J. –Pl. Pinazo, s/n | 796 0035 |
| LOPEZ NUÑEZ, J. –Rocafort, Bl. 321 | 796 5387 |
| LOPEZ RODRIGUEZ, C. –Pl. Jesus, 7 | 429 3278 |
| LOPEZ RODRIGUEZ, J. –Pl. Angel, 15 | 239 4323 |
| LOPEZ RODRIGUEZ, M. E. | |
|   B. Murillo, 104 | 233 4239 |
| LOPEZ TRAPERO, A. –Cam. Ingenieros, 1 | 462 5392 |
| LOPEZ VAZQUEZ, J. –A. TorreJón, 17 | 433 4646 |
| LOPEZ VEGA, J. –M. Santa Ana, 5 | 231 2131 |
| LORENTE VILLARREAL, G. –Gandia, 7 | 252 2758 |
| LORENZO MARTINEZ, A. –Moscareta, 5 | 479 6622 |
| LORENZO MARTINEZ, A. –P. Laborde, 21 | 778 2800 |
| LORENZO MARTINEZ, A. | |
|   Av. S. Diego, 116 | 477 1040 |
| LOSADA MIRON, M. –Padilla, 31 | 276 9373 |
| LOSADA MIRON, M. –Padilla, 31 | 431 7461 |
| LOZANO GUILLEN, E. | |
|   Juan H. Mendoza, 5 | 250 3884 |
| LOZANO PIERA, F. J. –Pinguino, 8 | 466 3205 |
| LUDEÑA FLORES, G. –Lope Rueda, 56 | 273 3735 |
| LUENGO CHAMORRO, J. | |
|   Gral Ricardos, 99 | 471 4906 |
| LUQUE CASTILLO, J. –Pto Arlaban, 121 | 478 5253 |
| LUQUE CASTILLO, L. –Cardeñosa, 15 | 477 6644 |

**Nota comunicativa: Suggestions**
• Introduce singular forms of *tener.* (Review them if you introduced them in the context of the family tree.)
• Model age dialogue with several students, asking about the ages of some of their relatives.

**Heritage Speakers**
Pregúnteles a los hispanohablantes qué apellidos tienen. Si son estudiantes de la segunda o tercera generación, ¿siguen usando este sistema?

**Con. C: Answers**
*Possible answers:* 1. *noventa y cinco* 2. *un* 3. *abuelo, ochenta* 4. *sobrino, dos* 5. *veinticinco* 6. *veinte* 7. *veintiún* 8. *cien*

## NOTA COMUNICATIVA

### Expressing Age

NORA: ¿Cuántos años tienes, abuela?

ABUELA: Setenta y tres, Nora.

NORA: ¿Y cuántos años tiene el abuelo?

ABUELA: Setenta y cinco, mi amor (*love*). Y ahora, dime (*tell me*), ¿cuántos años tienes tú?

NORA: Tengo cuatro.

In Spanish, age is expressed with the phrase **tener _____ años** (literally, *to have . . . years*). You have now seen all the singular forms of **tener** (*to have*): **tengo, tienes, tiene.**

## C. ¡Seamos (*Let's be*) lógicos! Complete las oraciones lógicamente.

1. Un hombre que (*who*) tiene _____ años es muy viejo (*old*).
2. Un niño (*small child*) que tiene sólo _____ año es muy joven (*young*).
3. La persona más vieja (*oldest*) de mi familia es mi _____.
   Tiene _____ años.
4. La persona más joven (*youngest*) de mi familia es mi _____.
   Tiene _____ años.
5. En mi opinión, es ideal tener_____ años.
6. Si (*If*) una persona tiene _____ años, ya (*already*) es adulta.
7. Para (*In order to*) tomar cerveza en este estado (*this state*) o en esta provincia es necesario tener _____ años.
8. Para mí (*For me*), ¡la idea de tener _____ años es inconcebible (*inconceivable*)!

# PASO 1

**Suggestions**
• Present adjectives in pairs or semantic groups (as organized in the box), using magazine images, names of famous people, and people in class.
• Suggestions for negative adjectives: *feo* (Frankenstein, *un gorila*); *gordo* (Pavarotti, Dom DeLuise), *malo* (Dennis the Menace, Darth Vader), *tonto* (Jim Carrey, Steve Martin).
• Do several pairs; then check comprehension, offering students alternatives: *¿Es guapo o feo Enrique Iglesias?*

## ADJETIVOS

| | |
|---|---|
| **guapo** | handsome; good-looking |
| **bonito** | pretty |
| **feo** | ugly |
| **grande** | large, big |
| **pequeño** | small |
| **casado** | married |
| **soltero** | single |
| **simpático** | nice, likeable |
| **antipático** | unpleasant |
| **corto** | short (*in length*) |
| **largo** | long |
| **bueno** | good |
| **malo** | bad |
| **listo** | smart; clever |
| **tonto** | silly, foolish |
| **trabajador** | hardworking |
| **perezoso** | lazy |
| **rico** | rich |
| **pobre** | poor |
| **delgado** | thin, slender |
| **gordo** | fat |

alto · bajo · Pepe · Juan · rubio · moreno · Luisito · Esteban · joven · viejo · don Paco · Jaime · nuevo · viejo

To describe a masculine singular noun, use **alt*o*, baj*o***, and so on; use **alt*a*, baj*a***, and so on for feminine singular nouns.

Resources: Transparencies 17, 18

## ■ Conversación

**Con. A: Suggestion**
Have students make similar comparisons of classmates and people they know.

**A. Preguntas** (*Questions*). Conteste según los dibujos (*drawings*).

1. Einstein es listo. ¿Y el chimpancé, en comparación con Einstein?

2. Roberto es trabajador. ¿Y José?

3. Pepe es bajo. ¿Y Pablo?

4. Jaime es bueno y simpático. También es guapo. ¿Y Memo?

5. Ramón Ramírez es casado. ¿Y Paco Pereda?

6. El libro es viejo. ¿Y el lápiz?

**Con. A: Answers**
1. *Es tonto.* 2. *Es perezoso.* 3. *Es alto.* 4. *Es malo, antipático y feo.* 5. *Es soltero.* 6. *Es nuevo.*

**B. ¿Cómo es?** Describe a famous personality, using as many adjectives as possible so that your classmates can guess who the person is. Don't forget to use cognate adjectives that you have seen in **Primeros pasos** and **Capítulo 1.**

MODELO: Es un hombre importante; controla una gran compañía de *software.* Es muy trabajador y muy rico. (*Bill Gates*)

Notes
• Stress and accent marks are presented in this chapter and in *Capítulo 3.*
• If you emphasize correct spelling and pronunciation on graded material, cover these sections on written accents carefully. Once you have introduced "Stress and Written Accent Marks (Part 2)," you can practice using accents through short dictations.

**Need more practice?**

- Workbook/Laboratory Manual
- Interactive CD-ROM
- Online Learning Center (www.mhhe.com/quetal7)

## PRONUNCIACIÓN: Stress and Written Accent Marks (Part 1)

Some Spanish words have *written accent marks* over one of the vowels. That mark is called **el acento (ortográfico).** It means that the syllable containing the accented vowel is stressed when the word is pronounced, as in the word **bolígrafo (bo-LÍ-gra-fo),** for example.

Although all Spanish words of more than one syllable have a stressed vowel, most words do not have a written accent mark. Most words have the spoken stress exactly where native speakers of Spanish would predict it. These two simple rules tell you which syllable is accented when a word does not have a written accent.

> In this chapter you will learn predictable patterns of stress. In the next chapter, you will learn when the written accent mark is needed.

- Words that end in a vowel, or **-n**, or **-s** are stressed on the next-to-last syllable.

  **co**-sa    **gra**-cias    e-**xa**-men    **e**-res    i-ta-**lia**-no    **len**-guas

- Words that end in any other consonant are stressed on the last syllable.

  us-**ted**    na-tu-**ral**    es-pa-**ñol**    pro-fe-**sor**    doc-**tor**    es-**tar**

**A. Sílabas.** The following words have been separated into syllables for you. Read them aloud, paying careful attention to where the spoken stress should fall.

**1.** Stress on the next-to-last syllable

| | | |
|---|---|---|
| chi-no | si-lla | li-te-ra-tu-ra |
| ar-te | Car-men | cien-cias |
| cla-se | li-bro | o-ri-gen |
| me-sa | con-se-je-ra | com-pu-ta-do-ra |

**2.** Stress on the last syllable

| | | |
|---|---|---|
| se-ñor | co-lor | sen-ti-men-tal |
| mu-jer | po-pu-lar | lu-gar |
| fa-vor | li-ber-tad | u-ni-ver-si-dad |
| ac-tor | ge-ne-ral | con-trol |

**B. Vocales.** Indicate the stressed vowel in each of the following words.

**1.** mo-chi-la
**2.** me-nos
**3.** re-gu-lar
**4.** i-gual-men-te
**5.** E-cua-dor
**6.** e-le-gan-te
**7.** li-be-ral
**8.** hu-ma-ni-dad

## 4 Describing Adjectives: Gender, Number, and Position

### Un poema sencillo

Amigo
Fiel
Amable
Simpático
¡Lo admiro!

Amiga
Fiel
Amable
Simpática
¡La admiro!

According to their form, which of the adjectives below can be used to describe each person? Which can refer to you?

Marta:
Mario:  fiel    amable    simpática    simpático

*Adjectives* (**Los adjetivos**) are words used to talk about nouns or pronouns. Adjectives may describe or tell how many there are.

You have been using adjectives to describe people since **Primeros pasos.** In this section, you will learn more about describing the people and things around you.

> **adjective** = a word used to describe a noun or pronoun

*large* desk       *few* desks
*tall* woman       *several* women

## Adjectives with *ser*

In Spanish, forms of **ser** are used with adjectives that describe basic, inherent qualities or characteristics of the nouns or pronouns they modify. **Ser** establishes the "norm," that is, what is considered basic reality: *snow is cold, water is wet.*

Tú **eres amable.**
*You're nice. (You're a nice person.)*

El diccionario **es barato.**
*The dictionary is inexpensive.*

---

***A simple poem***   *Friend Loyal Kind Nice I admire him/her!*

**Note**
Gender agreement with adjectives has been used by students since *Primeros pasos*. Handling of this grammar section will depend on how much you have stressed agreement.

## Forms of Adjectives

Spanish adjectives agree in gender and number with the noun or pronoun they modify. Each adjective has more than one form.

**A.** Adjectives that end in **-o (alto)** have four forms, showing gender and number.*

| | Masculine | Feminine |
|---|---|---|
| **Singular** | amigo alto | amiga alta |
| **Plural** | amigos altos | amigas altas |

**B.** Adjectives that end in **-e (amable)** or in most consonants (**fiel**) have only two forms, a singular and a plural form. The plural of adjectives is formed in the same way as that of nouns.

[Práctica A–B]

| | Masculine | Feminine |
|---|---|---|
| **Singular** | amigo amable | amiga amable |
| | amigo fiel | amiga fiel |
| **Plural** | amigos amables | amigas amables |
| | amigos fieles | amigas fieles |

> Notes in brackets, like [**Práctica A–B**] here, let you know that you are now ready to do all of the indicated activities, in this case, **Práctica A–B** (page 59). Then, after you read grammar point C (the next one in this section), you will be prepared to do **Práctica C** on page 59, as the bracketed reference in C indicates.

**Suggestions**
- Emphasize the concept of agreement.
- Point out that adjectives must agree with the gender of the noun they modify grammatically: *Pepe es una persona muy simpática.*
- Remind students that adjectives must also agree with the noun they modify in number.

*Mi profesor es inteligente. / Mis profesores son inteligentes.*

**C.** Most adjectives of nationality have four forms.

The names of many languages—which are masculine in gender—are the same as the masculine singular form of the corresponding adjective of nationality: **el español, el inglés, el alemán, el francés,** and so on.

[Práctica C]

| | Masculine | Feminine |
|---|---|---|
| **Singular** | el doctor | la doctora |
| | mexicano | mexicana |
| | español | española |
| | alemán | alemana |
| | inglés | inglesa |
| **Plural** | los doctores | las doctoras |
| | mexicanos | mexicanas |
| | españoles | españolas |
| | alemanes | alemanas |
| | ingleses | inglesas |

 Note that in Spanish the names of languages and adjectives of nationality are not capitalized, but the names of countries are: **español, española,** but **España.**

- Point out that adjectives of nationality can also be used as nouns: *el español* = the Spaniard, *los ingleses* = the English people, and so on.

## Placement of Adjectives

As you have probably noticed, adjectives do not always precede the noun in Spanish as they do in English. Note the following rules for adjective placement.

**A.** Adjectives of quantity, like numbers, *precede* the noun, as do the interrogatives **¿cuánto/a?** and **¿cuántos/as?**

Hay **muchas** sillas y **dos** escritorios.
*There are many chairs and two desks.*

**¿Cuánto** dinero necesitas?
*How much money do you need?*

---

*Adjectives that end in **-dor, -ón, -án,** and **-ín** also have four forms: **trabajador, trabajadora, trabajadores, trabajadoras.**

Emphasis D: Suggestions
Ask students the following questions.

• ¿Cómo se dice en inglés? una ciudad grande / una gran ciudad; un estado grande / un gran estado
• ¿Cómo se dice en español? a large university / a great university; a large book / a great book

**OJO** | **Otro/a** by itself means *another* or *other*. The indefinite article is never used with **otro/a**. | Busco **otro** coche. / *I'm looking for another car.*

---

**B.** Adjectives that describe the qualities of a noun and distinguish it from others generally *follow* the noun. Adjectives of nationality are included in this category.

un perro **bueno**
un dependiente **trabajador**
una mujer **delgada** y **morena**
un hombre **español**

---

**C.** The adjectives **bueno** and **malo** may *precede or follow* the noun they modify. When they precede a masculine singular noun, they shorten to **buen** and **mal**, respectively.

[Conversación]

un **buen** perro / un perro **bueno**
una **buena** perra / una perra **buena**
un **mal** día / un día **malo**
una **mala** noche / una noche **mala**

---

**D.** The adjective **grande** may also *precede or follow* the noun. When it precedes a singular noun—masculine or feminine—it shortens to **gran** and means *great* or *impressive*. When it follows the noun, it means *large* or *big*.

[Conversación]

Nueva York es una ciudad **grande**.
*New York is a large city.*

Nueva York es una **gran** ciudad.
*New York is a great (impressive) city.*

## Forms of *this/these*

**A.** The demonstrative adjective *this/these* has four forms in Spanish.* Learn to recognize them when you see them.

| est**e** | hijo | *this son* |
| est**a** | hija | *this daughter* |
| est**os** | hijos | *these sons* |
| est**as** | hijas | *these daughters* |

---

**B.** You have already seen the neuter demonstrative **esto.** It refers to something that is as yet unidentified.

¿**Qué es esto?**
*What is this?*

Suggestion
Remind students to try the *Autoprueba.*

**AUTOPRUEBA**

Give the correct adjective endings.

1. una casa viej_____
2. los tíos español_____
3. un primo alt_____
4. un sobrino guap_____
5. las hermanas rubi_____
6. buen_____ amigos

Answers: 1. vieja 2. españoles 3. alto 4. guapo 5. rubias 6. buenos

Preliminary Exercise

Ask students specific questions about their university.

¿Cómo son los profesores de su universidad?
¿Son buenas las residencias?

¿Es deliciosa la comida de la cafetería?
¿Son baratos los libros de la librería?
¿Hay muchas actividades sociales?

*You will learn all forms of the Spanish demonstrative adjectives (this, that, these, those) in **Gramática 8.**

Prác. A: Preliminary Exercise
Have students describe the following things. Cue students with questions and adjectives.

## ■ Práctica

**A. La familia de José Miguel.** The following incomplete sentences describe some members of the family of José Miguel Martín Velasco, a student from Quito, Ecuador. Scan the adjectives to see which ones can complete the statement. Pay close attention to the form of each adjective.

1. El tío Miguel es _____. (<u>trabajador</u> / <u>alto</u> / nueva / <u>grande</u> / fea / <u>amable</u>)
2. Los abuelos son _____. (rubio / antipático / <u>inteligentes</u> / <u>viejos</u> / <u>religiosos</u> / sinceras)
3. La madre de José Miguel es _____. (rubio / <u>elegante</u> / <u>sentimental</u> / buenas / casadas / <u>simpática</u>)
4. Las primas son _____. (<u>solteras</u> / <u>morenas</u> / lógica / bajos / mala)

**B. ¡Dolores es igual!** Cambie (*Change*) Diego → Dolores.

Diego es un buen estudiante. Es listo y trabajador y estudia mucho. Es estadounidense de origen mexicano, y por eso habla español. Desea ser profesor de antropología. Diego es moreno, guapo y atlético. Le gustan las fiestas grandes y tiene buenos amigos en la universidad. Tiene parientes estadounidenses y mexicanos. Diego tiene 20 años.

1. *¿Su famila?* → (*No*) *Es una familia grande.* (*interesante, importante, amable, intelectual*)
2. *¿Los perros?* → (*No*) *Son valientes.* (*fiel, impaciente, inteligente, importante*)
3. *¿Su universidad?* → (*No*) *Es nueva.* (*viejo, grande, pequeño, bueno, famoso, malo*)

Prác. A: Suggestion
Have students correct the form of the adjectives when inappropriate forms are provided.

Prác. B: Follow-Up
• Have students respond *cierto* or *falso*.

   1. *A Diego no le gusta estudiar.* (*falso*)
   2. *Diego es de Sudamérica.* (*falso*)
   3. *Le gustan los deportes* (pantomine). (*cierto*)
   4. *No habla español porque es estadounidense.* (*falso*)

• Have students change *Diego* to *Dolores* and change the text when possible to describe her as being the opposite of Diego. Then, change the subject of the paragraph to *Diego y Dolores.* ¡**OJO**! Help students make changes they do not yet know how to make, for example, *es* → *son*, *le gustan* → *les gustan* and *tiene* → *tienen*.

Prác. C: Extension
Name famous people (imagine that they are all alive). Have students tell what language they speak and what their nationality is or where they are from. Examples: *Pablo Picasso, Napoleón, Antonio Banderas, Beethoven, Enrique Iglesias, Marc Anthony, María Callas y Renata Tebaldi, Pancho Villa, Juan y Eva Perón.*

---

## NOTA COMUNICATIVA

### Más nacionalidades de Latinoamérica

| CENTROAMÉRICA | | SUDAMÉRICA | |
|---|---|---|---|
| costarricense | nicaragüense | argentino/a | ecuatoriano/a |
| guatemalteco/a | panameño/a | boliviano/a | paraguayo/a |
| hondureño/a | salvadoreño/a | brasileño/a | peruano/a |
| | | chileno/a | uruguayo/a |
| | | colombiano/a | venezolano/a |

---

**C. Nacionalidades.** Tell what nationality the following persons could be and in which country from the box they might live. For number 2, select an adjective (**Nota comunicativa**) and supply a country.

1. Monique habla francés; es __*francesa*__ y vive (*she lives*) en __*Francia*__.
2. José habla español; es __answers will vary.__ y vive en __answers will vary__.
3. Greta y Hans hablan alemán; son __*alemanes*__ y viven en __*Alemania*__.
4. Gilberto habla portugués; es __*brasileño*__ y vive en __*el Brasil*__.
5. Gina y Sofía hablan italiano; son __*italianas*__ y viven en __*Italia*__.
6. Winston habla inglés; es __*inglés*__ y vive en __*Inglaterra*__.
7. Hai (*m.*) y Han (*m.*) hablan chino; son __*chinos*__ y viven en __*China*__.

### Naciones

**Alemania** (Germany)
**el Brasil**
**China**
**Francia**
**Inglaterra** (England)
**Italia**

**Need more practice?**

- Workbook/Laboratory Manual
- Interactive CD-ROM
- Online Learning Center (www.mhhe.com/quetal7)

## ■ Conversación

**A. Descripciones.** Describa a su familia, haciendo oraciones completas con estas palabras o las palabras de **Vocabulario útil.**

MODELO: Mi familia no es grande. Es pequeña. Mi padre tiene 50 años.

| Mi familia<br>Mi padre/madre<br>Mi ¿ ? (otro pariente)<br>Mi perro/gato | **+** | (no) es | **+** | interesante<br>amable<br>grande<br>intelectual<br>nuevo | bueno<br>famoso<br>importante<br>(im)paciente<br>pequeño | fiel<br>viejo<br>malo<br>¿ ? |

### Vocabulario útil

Here are some additional adjectives. You should be able to guess the meaning of some of them.

| | | | |
|---|---|---|---|
| **agresivo/a** | ¿ ? | **difícil** | difficult |
| **amistoso/a** | friendly | **encantador(a)** | delightful |
| **animado/a** | lively | **fácil** | easy |
| **atrevido/a** | daring | **sensible** | sensitive |
| **cariñoso/a** | affectionate | **sentimental** | ¿ ? |
| **chistoso/a** | amusing | **tolerante** | ¿ ? |
| **comprensivo/a** | understanding | **travieso/a** | mischievous |

**B. Asociaciones.** With several classmates, talk about people or things you associate with the following phrases. Use the model as a guide. To express agreement or disagreement, use **(No) Estoy de acuerdo.**

MODELO: un gran hombre →
    E1: Creo que (*I believe that*) el presidente es un gran hombre.
    E2: No estoy de acuerdo.

1. un mal restaurante
2. un buen programa de televisión
3. una gran mujer, un gran hombre
4. un buen libro (¿una novela?), un libro horrible
5. un buen coche

### ¿Recuerda Ud.?

Before beginning **Gramática 5,** review the forms and uses of **ser** that you have already learned by answering these questions.

1. ¿Es Ud. estudiante o profesor(a)?
2. ¿Cómo es Ud.? ¿Es una persona sentimental? ¿inteligente? ¿paciente? ¿elegante?
3. ¿Qué hora es? ¿A qué hora es la clase de español?
4. ¿Qué es un hospital? ¿Es una persona? ¿una cosa? ¿un edificio?

## CAPÍTULO 2

# PASO 2

♻ **Reciclado**
Before teaching the conjugation of *ser*, review subject pronouns. Review the differences between *tú* and *Ud.* Have students tell you the difference between *nosotros/as* and *vosotros/as*. Ask where *vosotros* is used most.

## 5 Expressing *to be* Present Tense of *ser;* Summary of Uses

**Note**
Explain that *Manolo* is a nickname for *Manuel.*

### Presentaciones

Manolo Durán y Lola Benítez *son* esposos. Manolo habla de quiénes *son.*

—Hola. Me llamo Manolo Durán.

- *Soy* profesor en la universidad.
- *Soy* alto y moreno.
- *Soy* de Sevilla, España.

**Comprensión: ¿Cierto o falso?**

1. *Manolo y Lola son profesores.* (*cierto*)
2. *Lola es de Sevilla.* (*falso*)
3. *Manolo es alto.* (*cierto*)

—¿Y Lola Benítez, mi esposa? Complete la descripción de ella.

*Es* _____ (profesión).
*Es* _____ y _____ (descripción).
*Es* de _____ (origen).

Málaga, España
bonita
profesora
delgada

**Answers**
*Es profesora. Es bonita y delgada. Es de Málaga, España.*

**Follow-Up**
Ask the following questions about the *minidiálogo.*

1. *¿Qué es Manolo? ¿Es estudiante o profesor?* (*profesor*)
2. *¿De dónde es?* (*de Sevilla, España*)
3. *¿Quién es Lola?* (*la esposa de Manolo*)
4. *¿Cómo es Lola? ¿Y Manolo?* (*Lola es bonita y delgada. Manolo es alto y moreno.*)

**Variation**
Have students practice the *minidiálogo* in small groups, using information about themselves (Manolo's introduction) and about an important person in their lives (Lola's introduction).

♻ **Reciclado**
Students have already used forms of *estar* in *¿Cómo está(s)?* and for telling location. There is no need to go into more detail about *estar* at this time.

### ser (*to be*)

| | | | |
|---|---|---|---|
| yo | soy | nosotros/as | somos |
| tú | eres | vosotros/as | sois |
| Ud.<br>él<br>ella | es | Uds.<br>ellos<br>ellas | son |

There are two Spanish verbs that mean *to be:* **ser** and **estar.** They are not interchangeable; the meaning that the speaker wishes to convey determines their use. In this chapter, you will review the uses of **ser** that you already know and learn some new ones. Remember to use **estar** to express location and to ask how someone is feeling. You will learn more about the uses of **estar** in **Capítulo 5.**

Some basic language functions of **ser** are presented here. You have used or seen all of them already in this and previous chapters.

## To Identify

To *identify* people and things

[Práctica A]

▨ Remember that the notes in brackets refer you to activities that practice the grammar point.

**Yo** soy **estudiante.**
**Alicia y yo** somos **amigas.**
**La doctora Ramos** es **profesora.**
**Esto** es **un libro.**

♻ **Reciclado**
Review *ser* for telling time (from *Primeros pasos*). Telling time is not explicitly listed or reviewed in this section. You may wish to add it to your presentation or discussion.

## To Describe

To *describe* people and things*

**Suggestions**

♻• Most uses of *ser* in this section are a review of material formally presented or used in *Primeros pasos*. Other uses of *ser* will appear in the later chapters: in *Capítulo 3,* to tell what something is made of; in *Capítulo 5,* in contrast with *estar;* in *Capítulo 8,* to mean *to take place.*

Soy **sentimental.**
*I'm sentimental (a sentimental person).*

El coche es **muy viejo.**
*The car is very old.*

## Origin

With **de,** to express *origin*

[Práctica B–C]

• Point out that the indefinite article is not used after *ser* before unmodified (undescribed) nouns of profession. *Ella es profesora.*

Somos **de los Estados Unidos,** pero nuestros padres son **de la Argentina. ¿De dónde** es Ud.?
*We're from the United States, but our parents are from Argentina. Where are you from?*

## Generalization

To express *generalizations* (only **es**)

[Conversación B]

Es **importante** estudiar, pero no es **necesario** estudiar todos los días.
*It's important to study, but it's not necessary to study every day.*

Here are two basic language functions of **ser** that you have not yet practiced.

## Possession

With **de,** to express *possession*

[Práctica D]

Note that there is no **'s** in Spanish.

**OJO** The masculine singular article **el** contracts with the preposition **de** to form **del.** No other article contracts with **de.**

Es el perro **de Carla.**
*It's Carla's dog.*

Son las gatas **de Jorge.**
*They're Jorge's (female) cats.*

de + el → del

Es la casa **del** profesor.
*It's the (male) professor's house.*

Es la casa **de la** profesora.
*It's the (female) professor's house.*

**Suggestions**
• Practice possessive phrases to emphasize that there is no *'s* in Spanish: *Es el libro de Anita. Son los lápices de la profesora.*
• Point out the difference between *el* (article) and *él* (subject pronoun). Emphasize that *de* does not contract with *él.*

## Destination

With **para,** to tell for whom or what something *is intended*

[Conversación A]

*¿Romeo y Julieta?* Es **para** la clase de inglés.
*Romeo and Juliet? It's for English class.*

—¿**Para** quién son los regalos?
—(Son) **Para** mi nieto.
*Who are the presents for?*
*(They're) For my grandson.*

---

*You practiced this language function of **ser** in **Gramática 4** in this chapter.

**♻ Prác. A: Reciclado**
Review classroom vocabulary and practice *ser* + noun. Hold up or point to classroom objects, asking *¿Qué es esto?* Elicit plural forms by holding up two books, pencils, and so on.

**Prác. A: Suggestions**
- Do as listening activity. Have students assume that you are Gloria or Felipe. Adjust items 1, 2, and 6 as needed.
- Ask personalized questions based on statements.

*¿Tiene Ud. esposo/a?*
*¿Tiene abuelos/as?*
*¿Cuántos?*
*¿Tiene primos?*

*¿De quién es sobrino?*
*¿Es Ud. tío/a?*
and so on.

**Suggestion**
Remind students to try the *Autoprueba*.

## ■ Práctica

**A. ¡Anticipemos! Los parientes de Gloria.** Look back at the family drawings on page 50. Then tell whether the following statements are true (**cierto**) or false (**falso**) from Gloria's standpoint. Correct the false statements.

1. Felipe y yo somos hermanos.
2. Pedro es mi esposo.
3. Pedro y Eliana son mis (*my*) padres.
4. Carlos es mi sobrino.
5. Mi hermano es el esposo de Isabel.
6. El padre de Felipe no es abuelo todavía (*yet*).
7. Mi familia no es muy grande.

### AUTOPRUEBA

Give the correct forms of **ser**.

1. yo _____
2. Ud. _____
3. tú _____
4. Pedro _____
5. Inés y yo _____
6. ellos _____

*Answers: 1. soy 2. es 3. eres 4. es 5. somos 6. son*

## B. Nacionalidades

PASO 1  ¿De dónde son, según los nombres, apellidos y ciudades?

MODELO:  João Gonçalves, Lisboa →
João Gonçalves es de Portugal.

**Prác. B: Suggestion**
Model the pronunciation of names and countries.

1. John Doe, Nueva York
2. Karl Lotze, Berlín
3. Graziana Lazzarino, Roma
4. María Gómez, Ciudad Juárez
5. Claudette Moreau, París
6. Timothy Windsor, Londres

PASO 2  Ahora, ¿de dónde es Ud.? ¿De este estado / esta provincia? ¿de una metrópoli? ¿de un área rural? ¿Es Ud. de una ciudad que tiene un nombre hispano? ¿Es de otro país (*country*)?

### Naciones

**Alemania**
**los Estados Unidos**
**Francia**
**Inglaterra**
**Italia**
**México**
**Portugal**

**Prác. B: Extension**
- Review names of languages (*francés, español, italiano, inglés, alemán*). Have students expand by telling where people are from and what language they speak.
- Name real or fictitious people from countries listed, asking *¿De dónde es _____?*
- Imagine that you are a friend of persons listed in *Práctica B*. Tell where both of you are from: *John y yo somos de _____. Hablamos _____.*

## C. Personas extranjeras

PASO 1  ¿Quiénes son, de dónde son y dónde trabajan ahora?

MODELO:  Teresa: actriz / de Madrid / en Cleveland →
Teresa es actriz. Es de Madrid. Ahora trabaja en Cleveland.

1. Carlos Miguel: médico (*doctor*) / de Cuba / en Milwaukee
2. Maripili: profesora / de Burgos / en Miami
3. Mariela: dependienta / de Buenos Aires / en Nueva York
4. Juan: dentista* / de Lima / en Los Ángeles

PASO 2  Ahora hable sobre un amigo o pariente según el **Paso 1**.

**D. ¡Seamos lógicos!**  ¿De quién son estas cosas? Con un compañero/una compañera, haga y conteste preguntas (*ask and answer questions*) según el modelo. Las respuestas pueden variar (*can vary*).

**Prác. D: Suggestion**
Have students give simple explanations using *porque, por eso*.

MODELO:  E1: ¿De quién es el perro?
E2: Es de...

¿De quién es/son... ?

1. la casa en Beverly Hills
2. la casa en Viena
3. la camioneta (*station wagon*)
4. el perro
5. las fotos de la Argentina
6. las mochilas con todos los libros

### Personas

**la actriz**
**el estudiante extranjero**
**las estudiantes**
**la familia con diez hijos**
**el niño**
**los Sres. Schmidt**

**Need more practice?**
- Workbook/Laboratory Manual
- Interactive CD-ROM
- Online Learning Center (www.mhhe.com/quetal7)

---

*A number of professions end in **-ista** in both masculine and feminine forms. The article indicates gender: **el/la dentista, el/la artista,** and so on.*

# PASO 2

## ■ Conversación

**NOTA COMUNICATIVA**

**Explaining Your Reasons**

♻ **Nota comunicativa: Reciclado**
*Por eso* (expression with *por*) was active in *Capítulo 1*.

In conversation, it is often necessary to explain a decision, tell why someone did something, and so on. Here are some simple words that speakers use to offer explanations.

**porque** because      **para** in order to

—¿Por qué necesitamos un televisor nuevo?
—Pues... **para** mirar el partido de fútbol...
  ¡Es el campeonato!

*Why do we need a new TV set?*
*Well . . . (in order) to watch the soccer game . . .*
  *It's the championship!*

—¿Por qué trabajas tanto?
—¡**Porque** necesitamos el dinero!

*Why do you work so much?*
*Because we need the money!*

Note the differences between **porque** (one word, no accent) and the interrogative **¿por qué?** (two words, accent on **qué**), which means *why?*

**Bright Idea Suggestion**
Ask the class as a whole questions like the following. Have them explain why using *porque.*

*¿Quién necesita un televisor nuevo / un carro nuevo / más dinero?*
*¿Por qué?*

**A. El regalo** (*gift*) **ideal.** Look at Diego's list of gifts and what his family members like. With a partner, decide who receives each gift and why. The first one is done for you.

MODELO:   **1.** una novela de Stephen King →
  E1: ¿Para quién es la novela de Stephen King?
  E2: Es para la prima.
  E1: ¿Por qué?
  E2: Porque le gustan las novelas de horror.

### REGALOS

**2.** la calculadora
**3.** los libros de literatura clásica
**4.** los discos compactos de Andrés Segovia
**5.** el televisor
**6.** el radio
**7.** el dinero

### MIEMBROS DE LA FAMILIA

**a.** el padre: Le gusta escuchar las noticias (*news*).
**b.** los abuelos: Les gusta mucho la música de guitarra clásica.
**c.** la madre: Le gusta mirar programas cómicos.
**d.** el hermano: Le gustan mucho las historias viejas.
**e.** la hermana: Desea estudiar en otro estado.
**f.** el primo: Le gustan las matemáticas.
**g.** la prima: Le gustan las novelas de horror.

**Con. A: Follow-Up**
*¿Qué son buenos/malos regalos para las madres? ¿Y para los padres?*
*¿Qué les regala Ud. a sus hermanos?*

**B. ¿Qué opina Ud.?** Exprese opiniones originales, afirmativas o negativas, con estas palabras.

MODELO:   Es importante hablar español en la clase de español.

(No) Es importante
(No) Es muy práctico
(No) Es necesario
(No) Es tonto (*foolish*)
(No) Es fascinante
(No) Es una lata (*pain, drag*)
(No) Es posible

**+**

mirar la televisión todos los días
hablar español en la clase
tener muchas mascotas
llegar (*to arrive*) a clase puntualmente
tomar cerveza en clase
hablar con los animales / las plantas
tomar mucho café y fumar cigarrillos
trabajar dieciocho horas al día
tener muchos hermanos
estar en las fiestas familiares

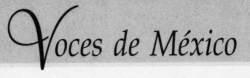
## LITERATURA: Rosario Castellanos

**Sobre la autora:** *Rosario Castellanos was born in Mexico City in 1925 but spent much of her childhood in Chiapas, a region in the south of Mexico with a large indigenous population. She returned to the province of Chiapas as an adult to work with Indian theater groups and the Indigenous Institute of San Cristóbal. Castellanos wrote in many forms, from poetry to journalism. The following lines are from "Economía doméstica," a poem in her most famous collection of poetry,* Poesía no eres tú *(1972).*

He aquí la regla de oro,[a] el secreto del orden:

tener un sitio[b] para cada[c] cosa
y tener
cada cosa en su[d] sitio. Así arreglé[e] mi casa.

[a]*He... Here is the golden rule* [b]*place* [c]*each* [d]*its* [e]*Así... That's how I organized*

**Rosario Castellanos**
**(1925–1974)**

## MÚSICA: El corrido

El corrido es una canción[a] que narra[b] eventos importantes o históricos, sean[c] heroicos o escandalosos, de valentía[d] o crueldad. Las canciones, acompañadas de guitarra y acordeón, son cortas para que el cantante,[e] tradicionalmente del sexo masculino, pueda cantarlas a todo pulmón.[f] El grupo mexicano Los Tigres del Norte canta muchos corridos tradicionales.

[a]*song* [b]*narrates* [c]*whether they be* [d]*bravery* [e]*para... so that the singer* [f]*pueda... can sing them at the top of his lungs*

### Literatura: Notes

• Rosario Castellanos was named Ambassador of Mexico in Israel from 1971 to 1974. While in Tel Aviv, Israel, Castellanos died in a freak household accident. As a writer who often addressed the inequity women suffered and her own problems as a woman and a Mexican, she might have found irony in her place of burial: the rotunda of Illustrious Men, in Mexico City.
• Prizes that Castellanos received include *Premio Chiapas* 1958 for *Balún Canán, Premio Xavier Villaurrutia* 1961 for *Ciudad real, Premio Sor Juana Inés de la Cruz* 1962 for *Oficio de tinieblas, Premio Carlos Trouyet de Letras* 1967, *Premio Elías Sourasky de Letras* 1972.

Estos versos son del corrido «Romance[g] de Román Castillo».

¿Dónde vas,[h] Román Castillo?
¿Dónde vas? ¡Pobre de ti[i]!
Ya no busques más querellas,[j]
Por nuestras[k] damas de aquí....

[ . . . ]

Tú eres noble, eres bravo,
Hombre de gran corazón;[l]
Pero que tu amor no manche
Nunca mi reputación.[m]

[g]*Song* [h]*¿Dónde... Where are you going* [i]*de... you* [j]*Ya... Don't look for any more fights* [k]*Por... Because of our* [l]*heart* [m]*que... may your love never stain my reputation*

### Música: Notes

• Many traditional *corridos* are about historical figures from the Mexican Revolutions. One revolutionary-era *corrido* students are probably familiar with is "*La Cucaracha.*" "*La Cucaracha,*" a *corrido* from the state of Chihuahua, was the marching tune for Pancho Vila's followers.
• The lyrics to and historical background for many *corridos* are available on the Internet.
• *Corridos* are the standard genre of songs played by Mariachi groups. You can read more about Mariachis on page 329 (*Capítulo 13*).

**PASO 3** Gramática

CAPÍTULO
**2**

Paso 3: Gramática
See the "Chapter-by-Chapter Supplementary Materials" in the IM for additional teaching suggestions, notes, activities, and other resources for *Paso 3*.

## 6 Expressing Possession Possessive Adjectives (Unstressed)

*La familia de Carlos IV* (**cuarto**)

Aquí está la familia de Carlos IV, un rey español del siglo XVIII. En el cuadro están *su* esposa, *sus* hijos… ¿Y *sus* padres y *sus* abuelos? ¿Quiénes son las personas a la izquierda del rey?

**¿Y Ud.?**

¿Tiene Ud. una foto reciente de su familia? ¿Quiénes están en la foto?

*La familia de Carlos IV, por el pintor español Francisco Goya y Lucientes*

Possessive adjectives are words that tell to whom or to what something belongs: *my* (book), *his* (sweater). You have already seen and used several possessive adjectives in Spanish. Here is the complete set.

**possessive adjective** = adjective that shows who owns or has something

**Suggestions**
- Remind students that *nuestro* and *vuestro*, like most *-o* adjectives, have four forms: *nuestro, nuestra, nuestros, nuestras; vuestro, vuestra, vuestros, vuestras.*
- Emphasize that possessive adjectives must agree with the noun they modify, that the choice between *mi/mis, tu/tus, su/sus,* and so on, depends on the number of the following noun, not on the number of the possessor(s).
- Have students identify the possessive forms that are the same for two different grammatical persons (*Ud.* and *él/ella*). Point out that the ambiguity of *su*(s) (*su hijo* = your/his/her/their son) can be clarified using *el hijo de él / de ella,* and so on.

♻ **Reciclado**
Have students describe people they know using adjectives from this chapter and *Primeros pasos* (*Mis tíos son ricos.*).

### Possessive Adjectives

| *my* | **mi** hijo/hija<br>**mis** hijos/hijas | *our* | **nuestro** hijo<br>**nuestros** hijos | **nuestra** hija<br>**nuestras** hijas |
|---|---|---|---|---|
| *your (fam.)* | **tu** hijo/hija<br>**tus** hijos/hijas | *your (fam.)* | **vuestro** hijo<br>**vuestros** hijos | **vuestra** hija<br>**vuestras** hijas |
| *your (form.),*<br>*his, her, its* | **su** hijo/hija<br>**sus** hijos/hijas | *your (form.),*<br>*their* | **su** hijo/hija<br>**sus** hijos/hijas | |

In Spanish, the ending of a possessive adjective agrees in form with the person or thing possessed, not with the owner or possessor. Note that these possessive adjectives are placed before the noun.

Son { mis / tus / sus } hermanos.

The possessive adjectives **mi(s), tu(s),** and **su(s)** show agreement in number only. **Nuestro/a/ os/as** and **vuestro/a/os/as,** like all adjectives that end in **-o,** show agreement in both number and gender.

Es { nuestra / vuestra / su } familia.

---

*Another set of possessives are called the *stressed possessive adjectives.* They can be used as nouns. For information on them, see Appendix 2, Using Adjectives as Nouns.

**Carlos IV's family** *Here is the family of Carlos IV, an 18th-century Spanish king. In the painting are his wife, his children . . . And his parents and grandparents? Who are the people to the left of the king?*

The forms **vuestro/a/os/as** are used extensively in Spain, but are not common in Latin America.

**Su(s)** can have several different equivalents in English: *your* (*sing.*), *his*, *her*, *its*, *your* [*pl.*], and *their*. Usually its meaning will be clear in context. When the meaning of **su[s]** is not clear, **de** and a pronoun are used instead to indicate the possessor.

**Prác. A: Preliminary Exercises**
• Have students give the forms orally.

1. *Dé la forma singular: nuestras abuelas, sus universidades, tus amigos, vuestros consejeros.*
2. *Dé la forma plural: nuestro profesor, nuestra clase, vuestro compañero, vuestra actividad, tu familia, su perro.*

el padre
la madre
los abuelos
las tías
} de él (de ella, de Ud., de ellos, de ellas, de Uds.)

¿Son jóvenes los hijos **de él**?
*Are his children young?*

¿Dónde vive el abuelo **de ellas**?
*Where does their grandfather live?*

**Suggestion**
Remind students to try the *Autoprueba*.

■ **Práctica**   • Have students relate possessives to their respective subject pronouns: *mi → yo* (*sus, tus, mi, nuestras, vuestros, su, tu*)

**A. Posesiones.** Which nouns can these possessive adjectives modify without changing form?

1. su:   <u>problema</u>   primos   <u>dinero</u>   tías   escritorios   <u>familia</u>
2. tus:   perro   idea   <u>hijos</u>   <u>profesoras</u>   abuelo   examen
3. mi:   <u>ventana</u>   médicos   <u>cuarto</u>   <u>coche</u>   <u>abuela</u>   gatos
4. sus:   <u>animales</u>   oficina   <u>nietas</u>   padre   hermana   abuelo
5. nuestras:   guitarra   libro   <u>materias</u>   lápiz   <u>sobrinas</u>   tía
6. nuestros:   <u>gustos</u>   <u>consejeros</u>   <u>parientes</u>   puerta   clase   residencia

**B. ¿Cómo es la familia de David?**

PASO 1   Mire (*Look at*) la familia de David en el dibujo. Complete las oraciones según el modelo.

MODELO:   familia / pequeño →   Resources: Transparency 19
Su familia es pequeña.

1. hijo pequeño / guapo
2. perro / feo
3. hija / rubio
4. padre / viejo
5. esposa / bonito

David

PASO 2   Imagine que Ud. es David y cambie las respuestas (*answers*).

MODELO:   familia / pequeño →
Mi familia es pequeña.

PASO 3   Imagine que Ud. es la esposa de David y hable por (*speak for*) Ud. y por su esposo. Cambie sólo las respuestas del 1 al 3.

MODELO:   familia / pequeño →
Nuestra familia es pequeña.

**Prác. B: Answers**
*Paso 1*   1. *Su hijo pequeño es guapo.* 2. *Su perro es feo.* 3. *Su hija es rubia.* 4. *Su padre es viejo.*
5. *Su esposa es bonita.* *Paso 2*   1. *Mi hijo pequeño es guapo.* 2. *Mi perro es feo.* 3. *Mi hija es rubia.* 4. *Mi padre es viejo.* 5. *Mi esposa es bonita.* *Paso 3*   1. *Nuestro hijo pequeño es guapo.*
2. *Nuestro perro es feo.* 3. *Nuestra hija es rubia.*

**AUTOPRUEBA**

Give the correct possessive adjective.

1. la casa de nosotros = _____ casa
2. los perros de Juan = _____ perros
3. la clase de Luisa = _____ clase

*Answers: 1. nuestra 2. sus 3. su*

**Prác. B: Variation**
Have students work in pairs to think of famous families, like presidents' families or those from TV programs, and to describe each member to the rest of the class until their classmates guess them correctly.

**Need more practice?**

■ Workbook/Laboratory Manual
■ Interactive CD-ROM
■ Online Learning Center (www.mhhe.com/quetal7)

# PASO 3

**Con. A: Suggestion**
Remind students to use *tu* forms with classmates. Students will need to use *su* forms, however, to report information to the class about someone else (his/her/their).

**Con. B: Follow-Up**
Ask students what they associate with the following phrases: *su perro/gato, sus padres, la casa del presidente de los Estados Unidos / del primer ministro del Canadá, la casa del profesor / de la profesora.*

**Con. B: Extension**

6. *nuestra cafetería*
7. *nuestro libro de español*
8. *nuestro presidente*
9. *nuestros estudiantes*
10. *nuestros profesores*
11. *nuestro equipo de fútbol*

♻ **¿Recuerda Ud.?: Suggestion**
Have students conjugate the following verbs chorally.

| | |
|---|---|
| *bailar* | *desear* |
| *buscar* | *enseñar* |
| *cantar* | *pagar* |

## ■ Conversación

**A. Entrevista.** Take turns asking and answering questions about your families. Talk about what family members are like, their ages, some things they do, and so on. Use the model as a guide. Take notes on what your partner says. Then report the information to the class.

MODELO: tu abuela →
 E1: Mi abuela es alta. ¿Y tu abuela? ¿Es alta?
 E2: Bueno, no. Mi abuela es baja.
 E1: ¿Cuántos años tiene?…

1. tu familia en general
2. tus padres
3. tus abuelos
4. tus hermanos / hijos
5. tu esposo/a / compañero/a de cuarto

**B. Asociaciones.** Working with several classmates, see how many words you can associate with the following phrases. Everyone in the group must agree with the associations decided on. Remember to use the words and phrases you know to agree or disagree with the suggestions of others.

MODELO: nuestro país →
 Nuestro país es _____. (En nuestro país hay _____. En nuestro país uno puede [*can*] _____.)

1. nuestro país
2. nuestra clase de español
3. nuestra universidad (librería)
4. nuestra ciudad (nuestro estado / nuestra provincia)
5. el centro de nuestra ciudad

### ¿Recuerda Ud.?

The personal endings used with **-ar** verbs share some characteristics of those used with **-er** and **-ir** verbs, which you will learn in the next section. Review the present tense endings of **-ar** verbs by telling which subject pronoun(s) you associate with each of these endings.

1. **-amos**   2. **-as**   3. **-áis**   4. **-an**   5. **-o**   6. **-a**

**Note**
*Gustar* appears in this narration. Students will learn more about the verb *gustar* and other verbs like *gustar* in *Capítulo 7*.

**7** **Expressing Actions** Present Tense of *-er* and *-ir* Verbs; More About Subject Pronouns

♻ **Reciclado**
• Review subject pronouns and have students indicate the difference between *tú/vosotros* and *Ud./Uds.*
• Have students recite chorally regular *-ar* verb endings.

**Diego se presenta**

Hola. Me llamo Diego González. Soy estudiante de UCLA, pero este año *asisto* a la Universidad Nacional Autónoma de México. *Vivo* con mi tía Matilde en la Ciudad de México. *Como* pizza con frecuencia y *bebo* cerveza en las fiestas. Me gusta la ropa de moda; por eso *recibo* varios catálogos. *Leo* muchos libros de antropología para mi especialización. También *escribo* muchas cartas a mi familia. *Creo* que una educación universitaria es muy importante. Por eso estudio y *aprendo* mucho. ¡Pero *comprendo* también que es muy importante estar con los amigos y con la familia!

**¿Y Ud.?**

¿Es Diego un estudiante típico? ¿Cómo es Ud.? Adapte las oraciones de Diego a su conveniencia.

Past -------------------- **PRESENT** -------------------- Future
present

## Verbs That End in *-er* and *-ir*

**A.** The present tense of **-er** and **-ir** verbs is formed by adding personal endings to the stem of the verb (the infinitive minus its **-er/-ir** ending). The personal endings for **-er** and **-ir** verbs are the same except for the first and second person plural.

| **comer** (*to eat*) | | **vivir** (*to live*) | |
|---|---|---|---|
| como | comemos | vivo | vivimos |
| comes | coméis | vives | vivís |
| come | comen | vive | viven |

**B.** These are the frequently used **-er** and **-ir** verbs you will find in this chapter.

| | *-er* verbs | | *-ir* verbs | |
|---|---|---|---|---|
| | **aprender** | *to learn* | **abrir** | *to open* |
| | **comprender** | *to understand* | **asistir (a)** | *to attend,* |
| | **creer (en)** | *to think; to* | | *go to* |
| | | *believe* (*in*) | | *(a class,* |
| | **deber** (*+ inf.*) | *should, must,* | | *function)* |
| | | *ought to* (*do* | **recibir** | *to receive* |
| | | *something*) | **vivir** | *to live* |
| | **vender** | *to sell* | | |

**Suggestion**
• Point out that *asistir* is a false cognate.

*Diego introduces himself* Hello. My name is Diego González. I'm a student at UCLA, but this year I attend the **Universidad Nacional Autónoma de México.** I live with my aunt Matilde in Mexico City. I eat pizza frequently and I drink beer at parties. I like fashionable clothes; that's why I receive various catalogues. I read lots of anthropology books for my major. I also write a lot of letters to my family. I think that a university education is very important. That's why I study and learn a lot. But I also understand that it's very important to be with friends and family!

Remember that the Spanish present tense has a number of present tense equivalents in English. It can also be used to express future meaning.

**como** = *I eat, I am eating, I will eat*

## Use and Omission of Subject Pronouns

In English, a verb must have an expressed subject (a noun or pronoun): **she** *says,* **the train** *arrives.* In Spanish, however, as you have probably noticed, an expressed subject is not required. Verbs are accompanied by a subject pronoun only for clarification, emphasis, or contrast.

- *Clarification:* When the context does not make the subject clear, the subject pronoun is expressed. This happens most frequently with third person singular and plural verb forms.
- *Emphasis:* Subject pronouns are used in Spanish to emphasize the subject when in English you would stress it with your voice.
- *Contrast:* Contrast is a special case of emphasis. Subject pronouns are used to contrast the actions of two individuals or groups.

**Ud.** / **él** / **ella** vende
**Uds.** / **ellos** / **ellas** venden

—¿Quién debe pagar?    *Who should pay?*
—¡**Tú** debes pagar!    *You should pay!*

**Ellos** leen mucho; **nosotros** leemos poco.
*They read a lot; we read little.*

### AUTOPRUEBA

Give the correct verb forms.

1. Elena (comer) _____
2. yo (beber) _____
3. nosotros (leer) _____
4. José (escribir) _____
5. Uds. (vivir) _____
6. tú (abrir) _____

*Answers: 1. come 2. bebo 3. leemos 4. escribe 5. viven 6. abres*

## ■ Práctica

### A. En la clase de español

PASO 1  **¡Anticipemos!** Read the following statements and tell whether they are true for your classroom environment. If any statement is not true for you or your class, make it negative or change it in another way to make it correct.

MODELO:  Bebo café en clase. →
Sí, bebo café en clase.
(No, no bebo café en clase. Bebo café en casa.)

1. Debo estudiar más para esta clase.
2. Leo todas (*all*) las partes de las lecciones.
3. Comprendo bien cuando mi profesor(a) habla español.
4. Asisto al laboratorio con frecuencia.
5. Debemos abrir más los libros en clase.
6. Escribimos mucho en esta clase.
7. Aprendemos a hablar español en esta clase.*
8. Vendemos nuestros libros al final del año.

PASO 2  Now turn to the person next to you and rephrase each sentence, using **tú** forms of the verbs. Your partner will indicate whether the sentences are true for him or her.

MODELO:  Debes estudiar más para esta clase, ¿verdad (*right*)? →
Sí, debo estudiar más.
(No, no debo estudiar más.)
(No. Debo estudiar más para la clase de matemáticas.)

*Note: **aprender** + **a** + *infinitive* = *to learn how to* (do something)

**B. Diego habla de su padre.** Complete este párrafo con la forma correcta de los verbos entre paréntesis.

Mi padre (vender¹) coches y trabaja mucho. Mis hermanos y yo (aprender²) mucho de papá. Según mi padre, los jóvenes (deber³) (asistir⁴) a clase todos los días, porque es su obligación. Papá también (creer⁵) que no es necesario mirar la televisión por la noche. Es más interesante (leer⁶) el periódico,ª una revistaᵇ o un buen libro. Por eso nosotros (leer⁷) o (escribir⁸) por la noche y no miramos la televisión mucho. Yo admiro mucho a* mi papá y (creer⁹) que él (comprender¹⁰) la importancia de la educación.

ªnewspaper   ᵇmagazine

### Comprensión: ¿Cierto o falso?

1. Diego y sus hermanos venden coches.
2. Diego mira mucho la televisión.
3. El padre de Diego probablemente lee mucho.

**C. Un sábado (*Saturday*) en Sevilla.** In this activity you will take the part of Manolo, who lives with his family in Sevilla. Using all the cues given, form complete sentences about a Saturday at home with your family. Make any changes and add words when necessary. When the subject pronoun is in parentheses, do not use it in the sentence.

MODELO:   (nosotros) beber / café / por / mañana →
            Bebemos café por la mañana.

1. yo / leer / periódico
2. mi hija, Marta / mirar / televisión
3. también / (ella) escribir / composición / en inglés
4. no / (ella) comprender / todo / instrucciones
5. (ella) deber / usar / diccionario
6. mi esposa, Lola / abrir / y / leer / cartas
7. ¡hoy / (nosotros) recibir / carta / de / tío Ricardo!
8. (él) ser de / España / pero / ahora / vivir / en México
9. ¡ay! / ser / dos / de / tarde
10. ¡(nosotros) deber / comer / ahora!
11. (nosotros) comer / a / dos / todo / días
12. hoy / un / amigos / comer / con / nosotros / y / llegar (*to arrive*) / diez minutos

**Need more practice?**

■ Workbook/Laboratory Manual
■ Interactive CD-ROM
■ Online Learning Center (www.mhhe.com/quetal7)

*Note the use of **a** here. In this context, the word **a** has no equivalent in English. It is used in Spanish before a direct object that is a specific person. You will learn more about this use of **a** in **Capítulo 6.** Until then, the exercises and activities in ¿Qué tal? will indicate when to use it.*

**Nota comunicativa: Suggestion**
Have students use *casi nunca* and *nunca* at the beginning of a sentence only, to avoid the double negative. Students will learn the double negative in *Gramática 18*.

■ **Conversación**

## NOTA COMUNICATIVA

**Telling How Frequently You Do Things**

Use the following words and phrases to tell how often you perform an activity. Some of them will already be familiar to you.

♻ **Reciclado**
*Todos los días* and *con frecuencia* were presented in *Capítulo 1*.

| | | | |
|---|---|---|---|
| **todos los días, siempre** | every day, always | **una vez a la semana** | once a week |
| **con frecuencia** | frequently | **casi nunca** | almost never |
| **a veces** | at times | **nunca** | never |

Hablo con mis amigos **todos los días.** Hablo con mis padres **una vez a la semana. Casi nunca** hablo con mis abuelos. Y **nunca** hablo con mis tíos que viven en Italia.

For now, use the expressions **casi nunca** and **nunca** only at the beginning of a sentence. You will learn more about how to use them in **Gramática 18.**

**Con.: Extension**
Have students add three original items before doing *Paso 2*.

**Con.: Follow-Up**
• Have students interview their partner to obtain more specific information about the items in *Paso 2*. Examples: *¿Cuál es tu pizzería favorita? ¿Qué recibes por correo, cartas o revistas?* and so on. Remind students to use *tu(s)* in this activity.
• Have students prepare a brief *informe oral* about their partner or about the similarities and differences between themselves and their partner, using all the information they have learned about him/her.

**¿Con qué frecuencia?**

PASO 1  How frequently do you do the following things?

| | CON FRECUENCIA | A VECES | CASI NUNCA | NUNCA |
|---|---|---|---|---|
| 1. Asisto al laboratorio de lenguas (o uso los discos compactos). | ☐ | ☐ | ☐ | ☐ |
| 2. Recibo cartas. | ☐ | ☐ | ☐ | ☐ |
| 3. Escribo poemas. | ☐ | ☐ | ☐ | ☐ |
| 4. Leo novelas románticas. | ☐ | ☐ | ☐ | ☐ |
| 5. Como en una pizzería. | ☐ | ☐ | ☐ | ☐ |
| 6. Recibo y leo catálogos. | ☐ | ☐ | ☐ | ☐ |
| 7. Aprendo palabras nuevas en español. | ☐ | ☐ | ☐ | ☐ |
| 8. Asisto a todas las clases. | ☐ | ☐ | ☐ | ☐ |
| 9. Compro regalos para los amigos. | ☐ | ☐ | ☐ | ☐ |
| 10. Vendo los libros al final del semestre/trimestre. | ☐ | ☐ | ☐ | ☐ |

PASO 2  Now compare your answers with those of a classmate. Then answer the following questions. (*Note:* **los/las dos** = *both* [*of us*]; **ninguno/a** = *neither*)

| | YO | MI COMPAÑERO/A | LOS/LAS DOS | NINGUNO/A |
|---|---|---|---|---|
| 1. ¿Quién es muy estudioso/a? | ☐ | ☐ | ☐ | ☐ |
| 2. ¿Quién necesita mucho dinero? | ☐ | ☐ | ☐ | ☐ |
| 3. ¿Quién lee mucho? | ☐ | ☐ | ☐ | ☐ |
| 4. ¿Quién come mucha pizza? | ☐ | ☐ | ☐ | ☐ |
| 5. ¿Quién compra muchas cosas? | ☐ | ☐ | ☐ | ☐ |
| 6. ¿Quién es muy romántico/a? | ☐ | ☐ | ☐ | ☐ |
| 7. ¿Quién recibe mucho por correo (*by mail*)? | ☐ | ☐ | ☐ | ☐ |

1. What are Martin Sheen's Hispanic first and last names? (*¿Cuáles son el nombre y el apellido hispánicos de Martin Sheen?*)
2. How many children does Martin Sheen have? (*¿Cuántos hijos tiene Martin Sheen?*)
3. What is his wife's name? (*¿Cómo se llama su esposa?*)

## En los Estados Unidos y el Canadá

### Los Sheen: Una familia de actores

Two generations of Sheens have made names for themselves in film and television. Martin Sheen, the father, was born Ramón Estévez in Dayton, Ohio (1940– ), to a Spanish father and an Irish mother. Martin explains that he felt he needed to change his Hispanic name in order to successfully pursue an acting career in the 1950s. In his heart, however, he says he is still Ramón. Martin's acting career spans several decades and includes important movies such

*Charlie Sheen, Martin Sheen y Emilio Estévez*

as *Apocalypse Now.* Most recently, he stars in the television series "The West Wing," winner of more than fifty Emmys, including four for Outstanding Drama Series.

Martin and his wife of more than 40 years, Janet Sheen, have four children—Emilio (1962– ), Ramón (1963– ), Carlos (1965– ), and Renée (1967– )—all of whom have pursued acting careers. Emilio, who uses his father's original last name, Estévez, and Carlos, who is known as Charlie Sheen, are the most famous actors of the Sheen children.

Resources: Transparency 20
Transparency 20 provides additional practice with family vocabulary and with adjectives and the verb *ser*.

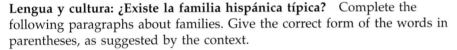

## UN POCO DE TODO

**Lengua y cultura: ¿Existe la familia hispánica típica?** Complete the following paragraphs about families. Give the correct form of the words in parentheses, as suggested by the context.

**M**uchas personas (creer[1]) que (todo[2]) las familias (hispánico[3]) son (grande[4]). Pero el concepto de la familia (ser[5]) diferente ahora, sobre todo[a] en las ciudades (grande[6]).

(Ser[7]) cierto que la familia rural (típico[8]) es grande, pero es así[b] en casi (todo[9]) las sociedades rurales del mundo.[c] Muchos hijos (trabajar[10]) la tierra[d] con sus padres. Por eso es bueno y (necesario[11]) tener muchos niños.

Pero en los grandes centros (urbano[12]) las familias con sólo dos o tres hijos (ser[13]) más comunes. Es difícil[e] tener (mucho[14]) hijos en una sociedad (industrializado[15]). Y cuando los padres (trabajar[16]) fuera de[f] casa, ellos (pagar[17]) mucho para cuidar a[g] los niños. Esto pasa especialmente en las familias de la clase media.[h]

Pero es realmente difícil (hablar[18]) de una familia (hispánico[19]) típica. ¿Hay una familia (norteamericano[20]) típica?

[a]sobre… *especially* [b]es… *that's the way it is* [c]*world* [d]*land* [e]*difficult* [f]fuera… *outside of the* [g]cuidar… *care for* [h]*middle*

La familia, *por Fernando Botero, de Colombia*

Resources: Desenlace
In the *Capítulo 2* segment of "Chapter-by-Chapter Supplementary Materials" in the IM, you will find a chapter-culminating activity. You can use this activity to consolidate and review the vocabulary and grammar skills students have acquired.

**Resources for Review and Testing Preparation**
■ Workbook/Laboratory Manual
■ Interactive CD-ROM
■ Online Learning Center (www.mhhe.com/quetal7)

**Comprensión: ¿Cierto o falso?** Corrija (*Correct*) las oraciones falsas.

1. Todas las familias hispánicas son iguales.
2. Las familias rurales son grandes en casi todas partes del mundo.
3. Las familias rurales necesitan muchos niños.
4. Por lo general (*Generally*), las familias urbanas son más pequeñas.
5. Las madres urbanas típicamente cuidan a los hijos durante el día.

Lengua y cultura: Answers
1. creen 2. todas 3. hispánicas 4. grandes 5. es 6. grandes 7. Es 8. típica 9. todas 10. trabajan 11. necesario 12. urbanos 13. son 14. muchos 15. industrializada 16. trabajan 17. pagan 18. hablar 19. hispánica 20. norteamericana **Comprensión** 1. falso: Todas las familias hispánicas no son iguales. 2. cierto 3. cierto 4. cierto 5. falso: Muchas madres trabajan fuera de casa.

# PASO 4    Un paso más

**Paso 4: Un paso más**
- The *Paso 4: Un paso más* sections are optional.
- See the "Chapter-by-Chapter Supplementary Materials" in the IM for additional teaching suggestions, notes, activities, and other resources for *Paso 4*.

**VIDEOTECA**

**Entrevista cultural: Suggestions**
- Before showing the video, have students role-play the part of grandparents. What kinds of things would they say about their grandchildren? For students who are grandparents, have them tell how many grandchildren they have, their ages, and what they are like. Use questions to elicit and/or extend descriptions.

  *¿Cuántos nietos tiene Ud.?*
  *¿Cómo se llama(n)?*
  *¿Cuántos años tiene(n)?*
  *¿Cómo es/son?*

- Show the video and allow students one to two minutes to work on the questions. Encourage them to answer in Spanish if possible. You might want to ask the questions in Spanish when you review the answers as a class.
  1. *¿De qué ciudad es Dolores?*
  2. *¿Cómo describe a su familia?*
  3. *¿Cuántos nietos tiene Dolores?*
  4. *¿Cómo son sus nietos en general?*
  5. *¿Cuáles son algunos de los intereses particulares de sus nietos?*

Have volunteers answer the questions.

- Have volunteers role-play Dolores and the interviewer

## Entrevista cultural: México

Dolores Suárez is from Mexico. In this interview, she talks about her family. Like many grandparents, she is proud of her grandchildren. Before watching the video clip, read the following excerpt from the interview.

INTERVIEWER: ¿Cómo se llama Ud. y de dónde es?
DOLORES: Me llamo Dolores Suárez. Soy de aquí, del Distrito Federal.[a]
INTERVIEWER: ¿Cómo es su familia, Sra. Dolores?
DOLORES: Pues es una familia muy bonita porque es una familia muy numerosa. Tengo seis hijos y tengo ocho nietos. Entonces eh,[b] somos muy unidos y por eso es muy bonito.

[a]Distrito… *what Mexicans call Mexico City*   [b]Entonces… *Well then*

Now watch the video clip and answer the following questions based on the interview.

**Entrevista cultural: Answers**
**1.** del Distrito Federal **2.** Es bonita y numerosa. **3.** ocho **4.** Son preciosos e inteligentes. **5.** el arte y la ciencia

1. What city is Dolores from?
2. How does she describe her family?
3. How many grandchildren does Dolores have?
4. How does she describe her grandchildren in general?
5. What are some of the specific interests of her grandchildren?

## Entre amigos: ¿Cuántos hermanos tienes?

Miguel, Tané, Karina, and Rubén are talking about their families. What questions do you think they will ask each other? Before watching the video, read the following questions. As you watch, don't worry if you don't understand every word. Try to get the gist of the conversation, listening carefully for information about their family members. Watch the video a second time and listen for the answers to the questions.

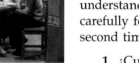

1. ¿Cuántas hermanas tiene Karina?
2. ¿Cuántos hermanos tiene Rubén?
3. ¿Cómo son los hermanos de Rubén?
4. ¿Vive Karina con sus padres o vive sola (*alone*)?

**Entre amigos: Answers**
**1.** dos **2.** cinco **3.** divertidos y muy guapos **4.** Vive sola.

**Entre amigos: Suggestions**
- Before viewing the video, review the questions with the students and ask them similar questions.

  *¿Cuántos hermanos tiene Ud.?*
  *¿Cómo son sus hermanos?*
  *¿Vive Ud. con su familia o vive solo/a?*

Have students answer or work in small groups to ask and answer these questions.

- After viewing the video, have volunteers read and answer the questions.

Suggestions
• Bring or have students bring images of some of the murals by these artists to class. Have students compare the three artists.

## ENFOQUE CULTURAL

## México

### ¡Fíjese!

- México tiene 31 estados y el Distrito Federal.
- La población de México es aproximadamente: 30% (por ciento) indígena, 9% blanca,[a] 60% mestiza (que se refiere a las personas de padres de razas indígena y blanca) y 1% de otros orígenes.
- Los indígenas mexicanos pertenecen a[b] grupos diversos: aztecas, mayas, zapotecas, mixtecas, olmecas y otros. La influencia de estas culturas indígenas contribuye a la diversidad y la riqueza de la cultura mexicana actual.[c]
- La ciudad de México ocupa el lugar del antiguo[d] Lago Texcoco. En el centro del lago estaba[e] Tenochtitlán, la capital del imperio azteca. Tenochtitlán era[f] una de las ciudades más grandes del mundo en el siglo XVI.[g]
- La Universidad Nacional Autónoma de México es una de las universidades más antiguas[h] de las Américas: es del año[i] 1551 (mil quinientos cincuenta y uno).

[a]*white* [b]*pertenecen… belong to* [c]*current* [d]*old, ancient* [e]*was* [f]*was* [g]*siglo… 16th century* [h]*más… oldest* [i]*es… it dates from the year*

Notes
• Students can read an excerpt of the poem *"Economía doméstica"* by Mexico's Rosario Castellanos in *Voces de México: Literatura.*
• Students can read about Mexico's musical tradition of *corridos* in *Voces de México: Música.*
• See the Workbook/Laboratory Manual for focused practice with the material in *Enfoque cultural.*

Heritage Speakers
Pregúnteles a los hispanohablantes de la clase si conocen el Distrito Federal, Tenochtitlán o Teotihuacán, o si han oído hablar de la Universidad Autónoma de México. Si alguien contesta que sí, pídale que dé una breve descripción del lugar.

• Point out that Rivera and Orozco created murals with social and political commentary. Siqueiros did not. What can they say about Rivera's and Orozco's personal opinions by studying the murals? Have students compare the social commentary of the two artists.

### Personas famosas: Los grandes muralistas mexicanos

El muralismo es el estilo de pintura[a] que decora las paredes[b] de edificios públicos. Con su obra,[c] los muralistas desean enseñar la historia y la cultura de su país, y con frecuencia sus murales representan sus ideales políticos también.

Los tres grandes muralistas mexicanos son Diego Rivera (1886–1957 [mil ochocientos ochenta y seis a mil novecientos cincuenta y siete]), José Clemente Orozco (1883–1949 [mil ochocientos ochenta y tres a mil novecientos cuarenta y nueve]) y David Alfaro Siqueiros (1898–1974 [mil ochocientos noventa y ocho a mil novecientos setenta y cuatro]). Hay muchos murales de estos tres grandes muralistas por todo México.

[a]*painting* [b]*walls* [c]*work*

*El mural* The Epic of American Civilization *por Orozco, en Dartmouth College*

Learn more about Mexico with the Video, Interactive CD-ROM, and the Online Learning Center (www.mhhe.com/quetal7).

## PASO FINAL

## A CONVERSAR

### La familia y los amigos

PASO 1   Using the verbs and adjectives you have learned, write five sentences describing what your family members and friends do or what they are like.

MODELO:   Mi padre trabaja mucho. Mi amigo John es perezoso.

PASO 2   Work with a partner to find out which of your family members and friends do the same thing or fit the same description. Use **¿Quién de tu familia... ?** (*Who in your family . . . ?*) and **¿Cuál de tus amigos... ?** (*Which of your friends . . . ?*) to get the information. If your answer to a question is *no one* or *none*, use **Nadie en mi familia es...** (*No one in my family is . . .* ) or **Ninguno de mis amigos es...** (*Not one of my friends is . . .* ).

MODELOS:   E1: Mi padre trabaja mucho. ¿Quién de tu familia trabaja mucho?

E2: Mi tía Anita trabaja mucho. (o: Nadie en mi familia trabaja mucho.) Pero mi amigo John es perezoso. ¿Cuál de tus amigos es perezoso?

E1: Mi amiga Raquel es perezosa. (o: Ninguno de mis amigos es perezoso.)

PASO 3   Ask follow-up questions about information you learned.

MODELO:   E1: ¿Dónde trabaja tu tía Anita?

E2: Trabaja en un hospital.

PASO 4   Compare notes with the rest of the class. Talk about your family and friends and what you learned about your partner's family and friends.

MODELO:   La tía de Jorge, Anita, trabaja en un hospital. Ella trabaja mucho...

Tamalada (*Making Tamales*), *por Carmen Lomas Garza* (*estadounidense*)

## GRAMÁTICA

To review the grammar points presented in this chapter, refer to the indicated grammar presentations. You'll find further practice of these structures in the Workbook/Laboratory Manual, on the Interactive CD-ROM, and on the *¿Qué tal?* Online Learning Center (www.mhhe.com/quetal7).

**4** Describing—Adjectives: Gender, Number, and Position

You should know how to place adjectives as well as how to make adjectives like **alto, inteligente, español,** and **inglés** agree with the nouns they describe.

**5** Expressing *to be*—Present Tense of **ser;** Summary of Uses

Can you conjugate and use the irregular verb **ser** in the present tense?

**6** Expressing Possession—Possessive Adjectives (Unstressed)

You should be able to recognize and use the possessive adjectives **mi, tu, su, nuestro,** and **vuestro.**

**7** Expressing Actions—Present Tense of **-er** and **-ir** Verbs; More About Subject Pronouns

Can you conjugate verbs like **comer** and **escribir** in the present tense? Do you know how to use subject pronouns and when to omit them?

## VOCABULARIO

Practice this vocabulary with digital flash cards on the Online Learning Center (www.mhhe.com/quetal7).

### Los verbos

| | |
|---|---|
| abrir | to open |
| aprender | to learn |
| asistir (a) | to attend, go to (*a class, function*) |
| beber | to drink |
| comer | to eat |
| comprender | to understand |
| creer (en) | to think; to believe (in) |
| deber (+ *inf.*) | should, must, ought to (*do something*) |
| escribir | to write |
| leer | to read |
| mirar | to look at, watch |
|   mirar la televisión |   to watch television |
| recibir | to receive |
| ser (*irreg.*) | to be |
| vender | to sell |
| vivir | to live |

### La familia y los parientes

| | |
|---|---|
| el/la abuelo/a | grandfather/grandmother |
| los abuelos | grandparents |
| el/la esposo/a | husband/wife |
| el/la hermano/a | brother/sister |
| el/la hijo/a | son/daughter |
| los hijos | children |
| la madre (mamá) | mother (mom) |
| el/la nieto/a | grandson/granddaughter |
| el/la niño/a | small child; boy/girl |
| el padre (papá) | father (dad) |
| los padres | parents |
| el/la pariente | relative |
| el/la primo/a | cousin |
| el/la sobrino/a | nephew/niece |
| el/la tío/a | uncle/aunt |

### Las mascotas

| | |
|---|---|
| el gato | cat |
| la mascota | pet |
| el pájaro | bird |
| el perro | dog |

## Otros sustantivos

| | |
|---|---|
| la carta | letter |
| la casa | house, home |
| la ciudad | city |
| el coche | car |
| el estado | state |
| el/la médico/a | (medical) doctor |
| el país | country |
| el periódico | newspaper |
| el regalo | present, gift |
| la revista | magazine |

## Los adjetivos

| | |
|---|---|
| alto/a | tall |
| amable | kind; nice |
| antipático/a | unpleasant |
| bajo/a | short (in height) |
| bonito/a | pretty |
| buen, bueno/a | good |
| casado/a | married |
| corto/a | short (in length) |
| delgado/a | thin, slender |
| este/a | this |
| estos/as | these |
| feo/a | ugly |
| fiel | faithful |
| gordo/a | fat |
| gran, grande | large, big; great |
| guapo/a | handsome; good-looking |
| inteligente | intelligent |
| joven | young |
| largo/a | long |
| listo/a | smart; clever |
| mal, malo/a | bad |
| moreno/a | brunet(te) |
| mucho/a | a lot (of) |
| muchos/as | many |
| necesario/a | necessary |
| nuevo/a | new |
| otro/a | other, another |
| pequeño/a | small |
| perezoso/a | lazy |
| pobre | poor |
| posible | possible |
| rico/a | rich |
| rubio/a | blond(e) |
| simpático/a | nice, likeable |
| soltero/a | single (not married) |
| todo/a | all; every |
| tonto/a | silly, foolish |
| trabajador(a) | hardworking |
| viejo/a | old |

**Suggestions**
- Have students make and exchange word puzzles.
- Play Hangman, using family words and adjectives.
- Have students group the adjectives in different ways (opposites, negative/positive).

**Note**
The following vocabulary items are used in direction lines in *Capítulo 2* and in subsequent chapters, but they are not assumed to be "active" until they are listed in *Vocabulario: Cambie* (*Ud.*), *Conteste* (*Ud.*), *Corrija* (*Ud.*), *el dibujo, la pregunta, la respuesta.*

**Heritage Speakers**
En México, la palabra *huevón* se usa como sinónimo de *perezoso* aunque se considera una grosería en muchos países latinoamericanos. Aunque se oye la palabra *huevón* en la conversación común y corriente, se recomienda el uso de *perezoso.*

## Los adjetivos de nacionalidad

| | |
|---|---|
| alemán/alemana | German |
| español(a) | Spanish |
| estadounidense | U.S. (adj.) |
| francés/francesa | French |
| inglés/inglesa | English |

Cognado: mexicano/a

## Los adjetivos posesivos

| | |
|---|---|
| mi(s) | my |
| tu(s) | your (fam. sing.) |
| nuestro/a(s) | our |
| vuestro/a(s) | your (fam. pl. Sp.) |
| su(s) | his, hers, its, your (form. sing.); their, your (form. pl.) |

## Los números 31–100

treinta, cuarenta, cincuenta, sesenta, setenta, ochenta, noventa, cien (ciento)

## ¿Con qué frecuencia... ?

| | |
|---|---|
| a veces | sometimes, at times |
| casi nunca | almost never |
| nunca | never |
| siempre | always |
| una vez a la semana | once a week |

Repaso: con frecuencia, todos los días

## Palabras adicionales

| | |
|---|---|
| bueno… | well . . . |
| casi | almost |
| ¿de quién? | whose? |
| del | of the, from the |
| esto | this |
| (no) estoy de acuerdo | I (don't) agree |
| para | (intended) for; in order to |
| ¿por qué? | why? |
| porque | because |
| que | that; who |
| según | according to |
| si | if |
| tener (irreg.)… años | to be . . . years old |

Repaso: ¿de dónde es Ud.?

# De compras°

°**De...** *Shopping*

## CULTURA
• **Nota cultural:** La ropa en el mundo hispánico
• **En los Estados Unidos y el Canadá:** Los hispanos en el mundo de la moda
• **Voces** de Nicaragua
    **Literatura:** Rubén Darío
    **Música:** Los garífuna
• **Videoteca**
    **Entrevista cultural:** Nicaragua
    **Entre amigos:** ¡Está súper fuera de moda!
• **Enfoque cultural:** Nicaragua
• **A leer:** La psicología de los colores

## VOCABULARIO
• De compras: La ropa
• ¿De qué color es?
• Más allá del número 100

## PRONUNCIACIÓN
• Stress and Written Accent Marks (Part 2)

## GRAMÁTICA
8  Demonstrative Adjectives and Pronouns

9  **Tener, venir, preferir, querer,** and **poder;** Some Idioms with **tener**

10  **Ir; ir** + **a** + Infinitive; The Contraction **al**

*De compras en Plaza Inter, un centro comercial en Managua, Nicaragua*

**DE COMPRAS: LA ROPA°**

*La... Clothing*

**Paso 1: Vocabulario**
See the "Chapter-by-Chapter Supplementary Materials" in the IM for a model for vocabulary presentation, as well as additional teaching suggestions, notes, activities, and other resources for *Paso 1*.

**Notes**
• In many Hispanic countries, store hours in the morning are similar to those in the United States and Canada; however, some shops close in the early afternoon until 4 P.M. and generally reopen until 9 or 10 P.M. All stores are generally closed on Sundays and holidays.
• Some Spanish speakers use the singular *el pantalón* to talk about pants.

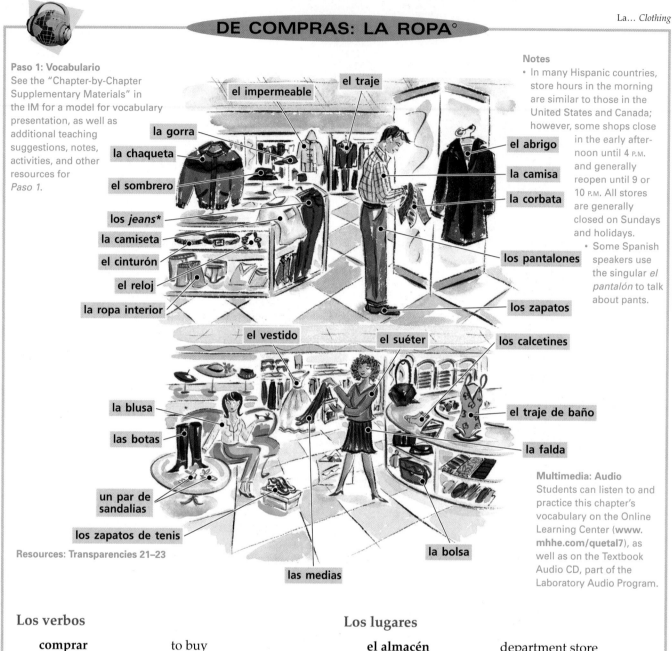

el impermeable · el traje · la gorra · la chaqueta · el sombrero · los *jeans*\* · la camiseta · el cinturón · el reloj · la ropa interior · el abrigo · la camisa · la corbata · los pantalones · los zapatos · el vestido · el suéter · los calcetines · la blusa · las botas · un par de sandalias · los zapatos de tenis · las medias · el traje de baño · la falda · la bolsa

**Multimedia: Audio**
Students can listen to and practice this chapter's vocabulary on the Online Learning Center (**www.mhhe.com/quetal7**), as well as on the Textbook Audio CD, part of the Laboratory Audio Program.

**Resources: Transparencies 21–23**

## Los verbos

| | |
|---|---|
| **comprar** | to buy |
| **llevar** | to wear; to carry; to take |
| **regatear** | to haggle, bargain |
| **usar** | to wear; to use |
| **vender** | to sell |
| **venden de todo** | they sell (have) everything |

## Los lugares

| | |
|---|---|
| **el almacén** | department store |
| **el centro** | downtown |
| **el centro comercial** | shopping mall |
| **el mercado** | market(place) |
| **la tienda** | shop, store |

**Heritage Speakers**
Pregúnteles a sus estudiantes hispano-hablantes si usan el Internet para comprar cosas de países hispánicos. ¿Cuál es su sitio web hispánico favorito?

\**The influx of U.S. goods to Latin America and Spain has affected common language. Jeans is one example of an English word that is commonly used in Spanish-speaking countries.*

Write the *refrán* on the board and have students guess the meaning of the word *caber* (to fit). Then ask what they think the saying means. Are there similar sayings in English? (*You get what you pay for.*)

## ¿Cuánto cuesta?

| | |
|---|---|
| la ganga | bargain |
| el precio | price |
| el precio fijo | fixed (set) price |
| las rebajas | sales, reductions |
| barato/a | inexpensive |
| caro/a | expensive |

## Otras palabras y expresiones útiles

| | |
|---|---|
| la cartera | wallet; handbag* |
| es de (algodón, lana, seda)† | it is made of (cotton, wool, silk) |
| ¡Es de última moda! | It's the latest style! |

Con. A: Extension
Have students give the appropriate clothing (*la ropa apropiada*) for the following.

## ■ Conversación

### A. La ropa

¿para los yuppies?
¿los cantantes country-western?
¿los líderes militares?
¿los detectives?

PASO 1 ¿Qué ropa llevan estas personas? ¿los personajes bíblicos (write Biblical names on board, for example, *Noé, Moisés, Rebekah*)?

Resources: Transparency 24

♻ Con. A: Reciclado
Review use of the definite article with titles.

1. El Sr. Rivera lleva _____.
2. La Srta. Alonso lleva _____. El perro lleva _____.
3. Sara lleva _____.
4. Alfredo lleva _____. Necesita comprar _____.

**Con A: Answers**
*Paso 1* 1. El Sr. Rivera lleva un traje, zapatos, calcetines, una corbata y una camisa. 2. La Srta. Alonso lleva pantalones, una chaqueta y zapatos. El perro lleva un suéter. 3. Sara lleva una falda, una blusa, medias y zapatos. 4. Alfredo lleva una camiseta, una chaqueta, jeans y zapatos de tenis. Necesita comprar ropa nueva. (Different answers are possible.)
*Paso 2* Possible answers: El Sr. Rivera trabaja hoy. Sara va a una fiesta. Alfredo (La Srta. Alonso, Sara) no trabaja en este momento.

PASO 2 De estas personas, ¿quién trabaja hoy? ¿Quién va a (*is going to*) una fiesta? ¿Quién no trabaja en este momento?

### B. Asociaciones. Complete las oraciones lógicamente con palabras de **De compras: La ropa.** *Some answers will vary.*

1. Un _____almacén_____ es una tienda grande.
2. No es posible _____regatear_____ cuando hay precios fijos.
3. En la librería, _____venden_____ de todo: textos y otros libros, cuadernos, lápices, discos compactos. Hay grandes _____rebajas_____ al final del semestre/trimestre, en los cuales (*in which*) todo es muy barato.
4. Siempre hay *boutiques* en los _____centros comerciales_____.
5. El _____centro_____ de una ciudad es la parte céntrica.
6. Estos artículos de ropa no son para hombres: _____faldas/blusas/vestidos_____.
7. Estos artículos de ropa son para hombres y mujeres: _____camisetas_____.
8. La ropa de _____seda_____ (material) es muy elegante.
9. La ropa de _____algodón_____ es muy práctica.

**Con. B: Follow-Up**
Have students answer the following questions.

1. ¿Dónde compra Ud. la ropa generalmente, en una tienda o en un almacén?
2. En esta ciudad, ¿hay tiendas o mercados donde regateen los clientes? ¿donde haya buenas rebajas?
3. ¿Lleva Ud. _____ hoy?
4. ¿Necesita Ud. comprar ropa nueva? ¿Qué necesita comprar? ¿Qué tipo de ropa compra con más frecuencia?

*In some South American Spanish-speaking countries, speakers use* la cartera *to refer to a purse.*
†*Note another use of* **ser** + **de:** *to tell what material something is made of.*

**Heritage Speakers**
Pídales a sus estudiantes hispanohablantes que describan la ropa que llevan hoy mismo.

*Paso 1 Vocabulario*

# PASO 1

**Con. D: Notes**

• Point out that there are many tag questions in English, e.g., *won't you?, doesn't he?, will they?,* and so on. Spanish tag questions are invariable, i.e., they don't change regardless of the number or gender of the subject.

---

### Vocabulario útil

The preposition **para** can be used to express *in order to,* followed by an infinitive.

**Para ir** al centro, me gusta llevar pantalones, una camiseta y sandalias.
(*In order*) *To go downtown, I like to wear pants, a T-shirt, and sandals.*

### Vocabulario útil

Tag phrases can turn statements into questions. They are the equivalent of English *right?, don't they?, do I?, do you?,* and so on, at the end of a sentence.

Venden de todo aquí, **¿no?**
(**¿verdad?**)
No necesito impermeable hoy, **¿verdad?**

---

**C. ¿Qué lleva Ud.?**   Para hablar de Ud. y de la ropa, complete estas oraciones lógicamente.

1. Para ir a la universidad, me gusta llevar _____.
2. Para ir a las fiestas con los amigos, me gusta usar _____.
3. Para pasar un día en la playa (*beach*), me gusta llevar _____.
4. Cuando estoy en casa todo el día, llevo _____.
5. Nunca uso _____.
6. _____ es un artículo / son artículos de ropa absolutamente necesario(s) para mí.

**D. Entrevista.**   Using **¿no?** and **¿verdad?** (*right?*), ask a classmate questions based on the following statements. He or she will answer based on general information—or as truthfully as possible—if the question is about aspects of his or her life.

MODELO:   E1: Estudias en la biblioteca por la noche, ¿verdad? (¿no?)
　　　　　E2: No. Estudio en la biblioteca por la mañana. (No, no estudio en la biblioteca. Me gusta estudiar en casa.)

1. En un almacén hay precios fijos.
2. Regateamos mucho en este país.
3. No hay muchos mercados en esta ciudad.
4. Los *jeans* Gap son muy baratos.
5. Es necesario llevar traje y corbata a clase.
6. Eres una persona muy independiente.
7. Tienes una familia muy grande.
8. No hay examen (*test*) mañana.

• *¿Verdad?* is found after affirmative or negative statements; *¿no?* is usually found only after affirmative statements. Note that the inverted question mark comes immediately before the tag question, not at the beginning of the statement.

---

## NOTA CULTURAL

**Nota cultural: Follow-Up**
Have students discuss the different "messages" clothing can communicate.

### La ropa en el mundoª hispánico

In Hispanic countries, people tend to dress more formally than do people in this country. As a rule, Hispanics consider neatness and care for one's appearance to be very important.

In the business world, women wear dressy pants, skirts, or dresses, and many wear high-heeled shoes. Men generally dress in trousers, shirts, and ties. Jeans, T-shirts, and tennis shoes are considered inappropriate in traditional business environments. Students at some business schools, like ESAN (**Escuela de Administración de Negocios**) in Peru, are even required to wear formal business attire to attend classes, as if they were already working at a company. Shorts and sweatpants are considered very casual and are reserved almost exclusively for use at home, for a day at the beach, or for sports.

Young adults generally dress casually in social situations, and, as in other countries, are often concerned with dressing according to current styles. As a rule, what is considered stylish in this country is also in style in Europe and Latin America.

*Ropa diseñada por (designed by) la famosa diseñadora venezolana Carolina Herrera*

---

ª*world*   **Nota cultural: Comprensión**

1. Who are generally more formal, people from the Hispanic world or people from the United States/Canada? (*En general, ¿quiénes son más formales, los hispanos o los estadounidenses / canadienses?*)
2. What do Hispanic students wear to class, a T-shirt and jeans or a shirt and pants? (*¿Qué llevan los estudiantes hispanos a clase, una camiseta y jeans o una camisa y pantalones?*)
3. What do students from ESAN wear to class? (*¿Qué llevan los estudiantes de ESAN para ir a clase?*)

¿DE QUÉ COLOR ES?

Here are colors you can use to describe clothing and other objects.

**Refrán**

«Amor y dolor son del mismo color.»

After writing the *refrán* on the board, have students guess the meaning of the words *amor* and *dolor*. Ask students if they think *color* refers to an actual color or something else, and if there are any similar sayings in English. (*There's a fine line between love and hate.*)

Resources: Transparency 25

- rosado
- anaranjado
- blanco
- amarillo
- negro
- verde
- rojo
- gris
- morado
- azul
- (de) color café*

**OJO** Remember that colors, like all adjectives, must agree in gender and number with the nouns they modify. Note, however, that some colors only have one form for masculine and feminine nouns.

el traje **azul**, la camisa **azul**

Con. A: Note
Gonzalo Endara Crow (1936–1996) is a *naif* artist. His paintings are also described as part of a style called magical realism. Ask students what *naif* (primitivistic) and magical realism elements they can see in this painting. (This is probably best discussed in English.)

Con. A: Suggestion
Write Endara Crow's birth-death years on the board (1936–1996), and say the numbers in Spanish to preview *Más allá del número 100* (page 84).

## ■ Conversación

**A. Muchos colores.** ¿Cuántos colores hay en este cuadro (*painting*) de Gonzalo Endara Crow? ¿Cuáles son?

**B. Asociaciones.** ¿Qué colores asocia Ud. con... ?

1. el dinero   verde
2. la una de la mañana   negro
3. una mañana bonita   azul
4. una mañana fea   gris
5. el demonio   rojo
6. los Estados Unidos / el Canadá   rojo, blanco y azul / rojo y blanco
7. una jirafa   amarillo y negro
8. un pingüino   negro y blanco
9. un limón   amarillo
10. una naranja   anaranjado
11. un elefante   gris
12. las flores (*flowers*)   rosado

*Después de* (After) *la noche,* por el pintor ecuatoriano Gonzalo Endara Crow

Con. B: Suggestion
Have students tell the color of things in your classroom, especially the clothing their classmates are wearing. Give an example: *El bolígrafo de Anita es amarillo. Roberto lleva calcetines azules, una camisa de cuadros* (draw on board) *morados y azules,* jeans…

*The expression **(de) color café** is invariable: **el sombrero (de) color café, la falda (de) color café, los pantalones (de) color café.**

**Con C: Answers**

*Possible answers: En el dibujo A, hay un traje azul con corbata roja y camisa blanca, pero en el dibujo B hay un traje (de) color café con un suéter. En el dibujo A hay un vestido*

---

### Palabras útiles

**de rayas** (striped) **multicolor**

---

*amarillo, pero en el dibujo B hay un vestido blanco y rojo (de rayas). En el dibujo A hay una camisa rosada y un suéter azul, pero en el dibujo B hay una camisa verde y un suéter de rayas. En el dibujo A hay dos pares de zapatos: un par de zapatos (de) color café para hombres a cincuenta pesos y un par de zapatos morados para mujeres, pero en el dibujo B hay sólo un par de zapatos; son zapatos rojos para mujeres. En el dibujo B hay una corbata a cuarenta dólares. En el dibujo A hay una bolsa azul, pero en el dibujo B hay una bolsa (de) color café.*

**Con C: Expansion**

Have students describe the differences between these department stores: JC Penney's, Saks Fifth Avenue, Macy's, and WalMart.

**Con. C: Note**

Point out that the adjective *alerta* is used to modify both masculine and feminine nouns.

**C. ¡Ojo alerta! ¿Escaparates (*Window displays*) idénticos?** These window displays are almost alike . . . but not quite! Work with a partner to find at least eight differences between them.

MODELO: En el dibujo A hay _____, pero en el dibujo B hay _____.

Resources: Transparency 26

**A.**

**B.**

---

MÁS ALLÁ DEL° NÚMERO 100

*Más... Beyond the*

Continúe la secuencia:

    noventa y nueve, cien, ciento uno...
    mil, dos mil...
    un millón, dos millones...

| | | | |
|---|---|---|---|
| **100** | cien, ciento | **700** | setecientos/as |
| **101** | ciento uno/una | **800** | ochocientos/as |
| **200** | doscientos/as | **900** | novecientos/as |
| **300** | trescientos/as | **1.000*** | mil |
| **400** | cuatrocientos/as | **2.000** | dos mil |
| **500** | quinientos/as | **1.000.000** | un millón |
| **600** | seiscientos/as | **2.000.000** | dos millones |

¡CIENTO SETENTA Y NUEVE DÓLARES!

- **Ciento** is used in combination with numbers from 1 to 99 to express the numbers 101 through 199: **ciento uno, ciento dos, ciento setenta y nueve,** and so on. **Cien** is used in counting and before numbers greater than 100: **cien mil, cien millones.**
- When the numbers 200 through 900 modify a noun, they must agree in gender: **cuatrocientas niñas, doscientas dos casas.**
- **Mil** means *one thousand* or *a thousand*. It does not have a plural form in counting, but **millón** does. When directly followed by a noun, **millón** (**dos millones,** and so on) must be followed by **de.**

    3.000 habitantes                  tres mil habitantes
    14.000.000 **de** habitantes      catorce millones **de** habitantes

- Note how years are expressed in Spanish.

    1899   mil ochocientos noventa y nueve       2005   dos mil cinco

---

*In many parts of the Spanish-speaking world, a period in numerals is used where English uses a comma, and a comma is used to indicate the decimal where English uses a period: **$1.500; $1.000.000; $10,45; 65,9%.***

## ■ Conversación

**A. ¿Cuánto pesan?** (*How much do they weigh?*)

PASO 1   Estos son los animales terrestres más grandes. ¿Cuánto pesan en kilos? ¡OJO! Use el artículo masculino, menos para (*except for*) **jirafa.**

> **Note**
> MODELO:   El elefante pesa cinco mil kilos. To convert kilograms to pounds, use the following formula: *kilogram* × *2.2* = *lbs.*

PASO 2   Pregúntele (*Ask*) a un compañero / una compañera  aproximadamente cuánto pesan en libras las siguientes cosas.

1. su perro/gato
2. su mochila con los libros para hoy
3. su coche
4. su libro de español
5. el animal más grande del mundo (*world*)

**B. ¿Cuánto es?**   Diga (*Say*) los precios.

1. 7.345 euros
2. $100
3. 5.710 quetzales
4. 670 bolívares
5. $1.000.000
6. 528 nuevos pesos
7. 836 bolívares
8. 101 euros
9. $4.000.000,00
10. 6.000.000 quetzales

> **el dólar (los Estados Unidos, el Canadá, Puerto Rico)**
> **el nuevo peso (México)**
> **el bolívar (Venezuela)**
> **el euro (España)**
> **el quetzal (Guatemala)**

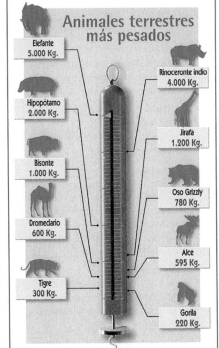

**Animales terrestres más pesados**

Elefante 5.000 Kg.

Rinoceronte indio 4.000 Kg.

Hipopótamo 2.000 Kg.

Jirafa 1.200 Kg.

Bisonte 1.000 Kg.

Oso Grizzly 780 Kg.

Dromedario 600 Kg.

Alce 595 Kg.

Tigre 300 Kg.

Gorila 220 Kg.

De los animales terrestres, el elefante, con sus 5.000 kilos de peso medio entre todas sus especies, es sin duda el mamífero más pesado. El hipopótamo y el rinoceronte son los siguientes en la lista, y el hombre, ni aparece.

**Need more practice?**

- Workbook/Laboratory Manual
- Interactive CD-ROM
- Online Learning Center (www.mhhe.com/quetal7)

## PRONUNCIACIÓN: Stress and Written Accent Marks (Part 2)

### ¿Recuerda Ud.?

Most Spanish words do not need a written accent mark because their pronunciation is completely predictable by native speakers. Here are the two basic rules.

- A word that ends in a vowel, **-n,** or **-s** is stressed on the next-to-last syllable.
- A word that ends in any other consonant is stressed on the last syllable.

The written accent mark is used in the following situations.

- A written accent mark is needed when a word does not follow the two basic rules presented. Look at the words in this group.

ta-bú       ca-fé       a-le-mán       na-ción       in-glés       es-tás

**Note**
Students are not accustomed to separating syllables in English. Syllable division in English is not as necessary as it is in Spanish. Also, English syllables are not as obvious as Spanish syllables.

**Suggestion**
Point out that accent marks are added or deleted to preserve the original stress pattern when words are made plural.

Accent deleted: *nación → naciones; francés → franceses.*
Accent added: *joven → jóvenes; examen → exámenes.*

**Heritage Speakers**
Anime a los hispanohablantes a modelar la pronunciación de las palabras que se usan en esta sección para practicar la colocación de los acentos escritos. Invite a los anglo-parlantes a imitar su pronunciación, repitiendo las palabras que oyen.

**Preliminary Exercises**
• Write pairs of words on the board that vary only in stress. Read one word of each pair of words aloud at random. Students decide which word you said.

| | | | |
|---|---|---|---|
| hable | hablé | espere | esperé |
| doblo | dobló | paso | pasó |
| baje | bajé | pase | pasé |
| bajo | bajó | papa | papá |

• Have students identify the stressed syllable.

*¿Última o penúltima?*

| esta | español | inglés |
|---|---|---|
| está | Pérez | chimpancé |

*¿Penúltima o antepenúltima?*

| política | Italia | teléfono |
|---|---|---|
| delgado | estados | Toledo |
| simpático | | |

*¿Última, penúltima o antepenúltima?*

| busco | clásico | clasifico |
|---|---|---|
| buscó | lógico | clasificó |
| típico | | |

• *¿Diptongo o no?*

| María | estudia | geo (¡OJO!) |
|---|---|---|
| baila | patio | geografía |
| día | tío | |

**A: Follow-Up**
• Give students a *dictado* that includes sentences such as:

1. *José es rico.*
2. *Ramón es romántico.*
3. *El Sr. Gómez es simpático.*
4. *David es perezoso y antipático.*
5. *Joaquín es alto y guapo.*
6. *El Sr. Pérez es bajo y viejo.*

• Have several students write the dictation on the board while the rest of the class works at their seats. Correct errors on the board, paying special attention to accents and why they are needed or not needed.

**B: Answers**
1. *exámenes* (written accent mark) 2. *lápiz* (written accent mark) 3. *necesitar* (ends in consonant) 4. *perezoso* (ends in vowel) 5. *actitud* (ends in consonant) 6. *acciones* (ends in -s) 7. *dólares* (written accent mark) 8. *francés* (written accent mark) 9. *están* (written accent mark) 10. *hombre* (ends in vowel) 11. *peso* (ends in vowel) 12. *mujer* (ends in consonant) 13. *plástico* (written accent mark) 14. *María* (written accent mark) 15. *Rodríguez* (written accent mark) 16. *Patricia* (ends in diphthong)

The preceding words end in a vowel, **-n,** or **-s,** so one would predict that they would be stressed on the next-to-last syllable. But the written accent mark shows that they are in fact accented on the last syllable.

• Now look at the words in this group.

| lá-piz | dó-lar | ál-bum | á-gil | dó-cil |
|---|---|---|---|---|

These words end in a consonant (other than **-n** or **-s**), so one would predict that they would be stressed on the last syllable. But the written accent mark shows that they are in fact accented on the next-to-last syllable.

• All words that are stressed on the third-to-last syllable must have a written accent mark.

| bo-lí-gra-fo | ma-trí-cu-la | ma-te-má-ti-cas |
|---|---|---|

• When a stressed weak vowel (**i** or **u**) is directly preceded or followed by a strong vowel (**a, e,** or **o**), it will have a written accent mark. This pattern is very frequent in words that end in **-ía.**

| Ma-rí-a | po-li-cí-a | as-tro-no-mí-a |
|---|---|---|
| dí-a | bio-lo-gí-a | |

• Contrast the pronunciation of those words with the following words in which the vowels **i** and **a** *do* form a diphthong.

| Patricia | Francia | infancia | distancia |
|---|---|---|---|

• Some one-syllable words have accents to distinguish them from other words that sound like them. For example:

| él (*he*)/el (*the*) | tú (*you*)/tu (*your*) |
|---|---|
| sí (*yes*)/si (*if*) | mí (*me*)/mi (*my*) |

• Interrogative and exclamatory words have a written accent on the stressed vowel. For example:

¿quién?          ¡Qué ganga! (*What a bargain!*)
¿dónde?

**A. Sílabas.** The following words have been separated into syllables for you. Read them aloud, paying careful attention to where the spoken stress should fall. Don't worry about the meaning of words you haven't heard before. The rules you have learned will help you pronounce them correctly.

| | | | |
|---|---|---|---|
| **1.** a-quí | pa-pá | a-diós | bus-qué |
| **2.** prác-ti-co | mur-cié-la-go | te-lé-fo-no | ar-chi-pié-la-go |
| **3.** Ji-mé-nez | Ro-drí-guez | Pé-rez | Gó-mez |
| **4.** si-co-lo-gí-a | so-cio-lo-gí-a | sa-bi-du-rí-a | e-ner-gí-a |
| **5.** his-to-ria | te-ra-pia | Pre-to-ria | me-mo-ria |

**B. Reglas** (*Rules*). Indicate the stressed vowel of each word in the following list. Give the rule that determines the stress of each word.

| | | | |
|---|---|---|---|
| **1.** exámenes | **5.** actitud | **9.** están | **13.** plástico |
| **2.** lápiz | **6.** acciones | **10.** hombre | **14.** María |
| **3.** necesitar | **7.** dólares | **11.** peso | **15.** Rodríguez |
| **4.** perezoso | **8.** francés | **12.** mujer | **16.** Patricia |

Paso 2: Gramática
See the "Chapter-by-Chapter Supplementary Materials" in the IM for additional teaching suggestions, notes, activities, and other resources for *Paso 2*.

## ¿Recuerda Ud.?

You have already used the forms of **este** (*this*), one of the Spanish demonstrative adjectives. Review them by describing objects near you and the clothes you are wearing.

MODELO: Esta camisa es de rayas. Estos lápices son amarillos.

**Suggestions**
• Have students act out the *minidiálogo* and try to define the italicized words before checking the translation below.
• Ask students to explain the difference between a demonstrative adjective and a demonstrative pronoun. Give them these examples in English, then ask them to provide others.

*This* car is John's. vs. *This* (*one*) is John's.
*That* cat is white. vs. *That* (*one*) is white.

## 8  Pointing Out People and Things  Demonstrative Adjectives and Pronouns

### Suéteres a buenos precios

**Bright Idea Suggestion**
Have three students stand in three distinct areas of the room, perhaps placing one student just outside the classroom door. Stand at one end with one student. Then as you indicate the student closest to you, say, *"Este/a estudiante se llama* [name of student]." Then point to the student who is farther away, but not farthest away, from you and say, *"Ese/a estudiante se llama* [name of student]."

Susana necesita comprar un suéter en el mercado.

Resources: Transparency 27

| | |
|---|---|
| VENDEDOR: | *Estos* suéteres de aquí cuestan 150 pesos y *ese* suéter en su mano cuesta 250 pesos. |
| SUSANA: | ¿Por qué es más caro *este*? |
| VENDEDOR: | Porque *esos* son de pura lana virgen, de excelente calidad. |
| SUSANA: | ¿Y *aquellos* suéteres de rayas? |
| VENDEDOR: | *Aquellos* cuestan cien pesos solamente; son acrílicos. |

vendedor

Jorge

Susana

Finally point to the student who is farthest away and say *"Aquel* (*Aquella*) *estudiante se llama* [name of student]."

### Comprensión: ¿Quién habla, Susana, Jorge o el vendedor?

1. Me gustan estos suéteres de rayas, y sólo cuestan cien pesos.    Jorge
2. Señores, miren (*look at*) estos suéteres en mi mesa. Cuestan 150 pesos.    el vendedor
3. Voy a (*I am going to*) comprar este suéter. Me gusta la ropa de lana.    Susana
4. Este suéter acrílico es más barato que aquel suéter de lana.    Jorge

## Demonstrative Adjectives

### Demonstrative Adjectives

| | Singular | | | Plural | |
|---|---|---|---|---|---|
| *this* | este abrigo | esta gorra | *these* | estos abrigos | estas gorras |
| *that* | ese abrigo<br>aquel abrigo<br>(allí) | esa gorra<br>aquella gorra<br>(allí) | *those* | esos abrigos<br>aquellos abrigos<br>(allí) | esas gorras<br>aquellas gorras<br>(allí) |

---

*Sweaters at good prices*    Susana needs to buy a sweater in the market. SALESMAN: *These sweaters here cost 150 pesos and that sweater in your hand costs 250 pesos.* SUSANA: *Why is this one more expensive?* SALESMAN: *Because those are of pure virgin wool, of excellent quality.* SUSANA: *What about those striped sweaters over there?* SALESMAN: *Those cost only one hundred pesos; they are acrylic.*

# PASO 2

 Note that the final -e in the singular forms **este** and **ese** becomes an -o in the plural forms: **estos, esos**.

*Demonstrative adjectives* (**Los adjetivos demostrativos**) are used to indicate a specific noun or nouns. In Spanish, demonstrative adjectives precede the nouns they modify. They also agree in number and gender with the nouns.

In the chart on page 87, **allí** ([*over*] *there*) is provided as a clue that **aquel, aquella, aquellos,** and **aquellas** refer to a more remote location. However, it is not obligatory to use the word **allí** when using forms of **aquel.**

> **demonstrative adjective** = adjective used in place of a definite article to indicate a particular person, place, thing, or idea

There are two ways to say *that/those* in Spanish. Forms of **ese** refer to nouns that are not close to the speaker in space or in time. Forms of **aquel** refer to nouns that are even farther away.

**Este** niño es mi hijo. **Ese** joven es mi hijo también.
  Y **aquel** señor allí es mi esposo.
*This boy is my son. That young man is also my son.*
  *And that man over there is my husband.*

## Demonstrative Pronouns*

- *Demonstrative pronouns* (**Los pronombres demostrativos**) are used to point out or indicate people, places, or things when omitting the noun they refer to (remember that pronouns replace nouns). *Demonstrative pronouns* are the same as *demonstrative adjectives*, except that the noun is not used. In English, the demonstrative pronouns are *this (one), that (one), these,* and *those.*

- In Spanish, demonstrative pronouns agree in gender and number with the noun they are replacing, as in the preceding example.

- Use the neuter demonstratives **esto, eso,** and **aquello** to refer to as yet unidentified objects or to a whole idea, concept, or situation.

—¿Te gusta aquella casa?
*Do you like that house?*

—¿Cuál?
*Which one?*

—**Aquella,** con las ventanas grandes.
***That one,** with the big windows.*

—¡Ah, **aquella** me gusta mucho!
*Oh, I like **that one** a lot!*

**♻ Suggestion**
In order to practice demonstrative adjectives, use real objects in the classroom: *este lápiz, esa pizarra, estos cuadernos.* You may also bring or have students bring in photographs or magazine clippings of buildings, houses, or city scenes to use in small group activities or to display in the classroom. Students can then describe the scenes.

*Esta casa es bonita.*
*Esta ciudad es moderna.*
*Estos edificios son enormes.*

¿Qué es **esto**?   **Eso** es todo.   ¡**Aquello** es terrible!
*What is this?*   *That's it. That's all.*   *That's terrible!*

**Note**
Students will not be exposed to the accented form of the demonstrative pronoun in *¿Qué tal?* unless they appear in a piece of realia that is reproduced as originally published. You may wish to make students aware of these accented forms.

**AUTOPRUEBA**

Match each word with the corresponding meaning in English.

1. _____ estas
2. _____ aquellos
3. _____ ese
4. _____ esas
5. _____ este

a. that
b. those (over there)
c. these
d. this
e. those

Answers: 1. c 2. b 3. a 4. e 5. d

*Some Spanish speakers prefer to use accents on these forms: **este coche y ése, aquella casa y ésta.** However, it is acceptable in modern Spanish, per the **Real Academia Española** in Madrid, to omit the accent on these forms when context makes the meaning clear and no ambiguity is possible. To learn more about these forms, consult Appendix 2, Using Adjectives As Nouns.*

**Prác. A: Follow-Up**
Have students point out things in class using the demonstratives. Students must repeat the appropriate form of demonstrative to doublecheck comprehension, for example, *Esa ventana es grande.* → *¿Esta/Esa/Aquella ventana?* → *Sí, esa.*

## ■ Práctica

**A. Comparaciones.** Restate the sentences, changing forms of **este** to **ese** and adding **también,** following the model. Then restate a second time changing the forms of **este** to **aquel.**

MODELO: Este abrigo es muy grande. →
Ese abrigo también es muy grande.
Aquel abrigo también es muy grande.

1. Esta falda es muy pequeña.
2. Estos pantalones son muy largos.
3. Este libro es muy bueno.
4. Estas corbatas son muy feas.

**B. Situaciones.** Find an appropriate response for each situation.

1. Aquí hay un regalo para Ud.
2. Ocurre un accidente en la cafetería: Ud. tiene tomate en su camisa favorita.
3. No hay clases mañana.
4. La matrícula cuesta más este semestre/ trimestre.
5. Ud. tiene una A en su examen de español.

> **Posibilidades**
>
> **¡Eso es un desastre!**
> **¿Qué es esto?**
> **¡Eso es magnífico!**
> **¡Eso es terrible!**

♻ **Prác. A: Reciclado**
Ask personalized questions regarding items in the classroom. Use possessive pronouns as well as demonstratives. Have students respond with the correct statements: *¿Es ese mi lápiz, _____?* → *No, este es el lápiz de _____. ¿Son estos libros de los estudiantes de filosofía?* → *No, son nuestros libros.* Emphasize the *de* + noun in case of ambiguity.

**Prác. B: Variation**
Have students provide similar cues to other students, who then react appropriately.

**Need more practice?**

- Workbook/Laboratory Manual
- Interactive CD-ROM
- Online Learning Center (www.mhhe.com/quetal7)

**Con: Suggestion**
Ask the following questions.

## ■ Conversación

1. *¿Qué va a hacer Ud. esta noche? ¿Y este fin de semana?*
2. *¿Cómo es esta universidad? ¿Cómo es esta clase? Y este libro, ¿cómo es?*
3. *¿Cómo es esta ciudad? ¿Y este estado?*

### Una tarde en un patio mexicano

Resources: Transparency 28

PASO 1 Write brief descriptions of the following people and pets without identifying their location in the drawing.

MODELO: Lleva una falda y zapatos azules…

PASO 2 Now take turns with a partner reading a description. Your partner will guess who you're talking about. You should use demonstratives (**este/ese/aquel**) to identify the person.

MODELO: E1: Lleva una falda y zapatos azules…
E2: Es esta mujer.

PASO 3 Now work with your partner to invent information about the people. Include names, where they're from, and their relationship to others in the drawing.

MODELO: Esta mujer se llama María. Es de Cuernavaca. Es la hermana de aquel hombre…

4. *¿Cómo se llama el decano (new word) de esta facultad? ¿el rector (new word) de esta universidad? ¿el presidente / primer ministro de este país?*
5. *¿Cuántos estados (¿Cuántas provincias) hay en este país?*
6. *¿Tiene Ud. muchos exámenes esta semana? ¿Tiene que estudiar mucho esta noche?*

# PASO 2

## **9** Expressing Actions and States *Tener, venir, preferir, querer,* and *poder;* Some Idioms with *tener*

**Una gorra para José Miguel**

Elisa acompaña a\* su hijo José Miguel para buscar una gorra.

| | |
|---|---|
| ELISA: | ¿Qué gorra *prefieres*, José Miguel? |
| JOSÉ MIGUEL: | *Prefiero* la gris. |
| ELISA: | ¡Pero ya *tienes* una gris, y es casi idéntica! |
| JOSÉ MIGUEL: | Pues, no *quiero* esas otras gorras. ¿*Podemos* mirar en la tienda anterior otra vez? |
| ELISA: | ¿Otra vez? Bueno, si realmente insistes… |

**Comprensión: ¿Sí o no?**

1. José Miguel quiere comprar una corbata.   no
2. Él prefiere la gorra azul.   no
3. No puede decidir entre las gorras.   no
4. Elisa tiene mucha paciencia.   sí

---

### *Tener, venir, preferir, querer,* **and** *poder*

**Suggestion**
Model infinitives and talk through conjugations, using the forms in complete sentences and questions.

**tener** (*to have*)

| | |
|---|---|
| tengo | tenemos |
| tienes | tenéis |
| tiene | tienen |

**venir** (*to come*)

| | |
|---|---|
| vengo | venimos |
| vienes | venís |
| viene | vienen |

**preferir** (*to prefer*)

| | |
|---|---|
| prefiero | preferimos |
| prefieres | preferís |
| prefiere | prefieren |

**querer** (*to want*)

| | |
|---|---|
| quiero | queremos |
| quieres | queréis |
| quiere | quieren |

**poder** (*to be able, can*)

| | |
|---|---|
| puedo | podemos |
| puedes | podéis |
| puede | pueden |

**Bright Idea Suggestion**
Point out to students that a helpful way to remember which forms have a stem change is to remember the "boot" shape shown in the paradigms. Forms inside the boot show a stem change; those outside do not. There are two exceptions in this chart—the *yo* forms of *tener* and *venir*—but they are included in the boot, as they have an irregularity.

- The **yo** forms of **tener** and **venir** are irregular.

- In other forms of **tener** and **venir**, and in **preferir** and **querer,** the stressed stem vowel **e** becomes **ie.**

- Similarly, the stem vowel **o** in **poder** becomes **ue** when stressed.

- In vocabulary lists these changes are shown in parentheses after the infinitive: **poder (ue).** Verbs of this type are called *stem-changing verbs.* You will learn more verbs of this type in **Gramática 10.**

Irregularities:

tener: yo tengo, tú **tie**nes (e → ie)…

venir: yo vengo, tú **vie**nes (e → ie)…

preferir, querer: (e → ie)

poder: (o → ue)

 The **nosotros** and **vosotros** forms of these verbs do not have changes in the stem vowel because it is not stressed.

---

*A cap for José Miguel*   Elisa accompanies her son José Miguel to look for a cap. ELISA: *Which cap do you prefer, José Miguel?* JOSÉ MIGUEL: *I prefer the gray one.* ELISA: *But you already have a gray one, and it's almost identical!* JOSÉ MIGUEL: *Well, I don't want those other caps. Can we look in the previous store again?* ELISA: *Again? Well, if you really insist . . .*

\**Remember that the word* **a** *is necessary before a direct object that is a specific person. You will learn more about this use of* **a** *in* **Capítulo 6.**

## Some Idioms with *tener*

**A.** Many ideas expressed in English with the verb *to be* are expressed in Spanish with *idioms* (**los modismos**) using **tener**. You have already used one **tener** idiom: **tener... años**. At the right are some additional ones. Note that they describe a condition or state that a person can experience.

> **idiom** = an expression whose meaning cannot be inferred from the meanings of the words that make it up

Idiomatic expressions are often different from one language to another. For example, in English, *to pull Mary's leg* usually means *to tease her*, not *to grab her leg and pull it*. In Spanish, *to pull Mary's leg* is **tomarle el pelo a Mary** (literally, *to take hold of Mary's hair*).

**Suggestions**
- Point out that there is generally no word-to-word correspondence of idioms between the two languages.
- Tell students some complete sentences about yourself that model the idioms.
- Give students these optional phrases: *mucha prisa, mucho miedo, mucho sueño.*

**Note**
Students will learn *tener calor/frío* in *Capítulo 5* with weather and *tener hambre/sed* in *Capítulo 6* with foods.

**Heritage Speakers**
Pregúnteles a sus estudiantes hispanohablantes si se les ocurren otras expresiones con *tener*, como *tener ánimo, tener fama* y *tener suerte*.

tener miedo (de)

tener prisa

tener razón

no tener razón

tener sueño

**B.** Other **tener** idioms include **tener ganas de** (*to feel like*) and **tener que** (*to have to*). The infinitive is always used after these two idiomatic expressions.

> Note that the English translation of one of these examples results in a verb ending in *-ing*, not the infinitive.

Tengo ganas de **comer.**
*I feel like eating.*

¿No tiene Ud. que **leer** este capítulo?
*Don't you have to read this chapter?*

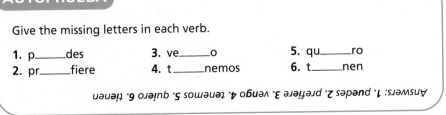

**AUTOPRUEBA**

Give the missing letters in each verb.

1. p_____des
2. pr_____fiere
3. ve_____o
4. t_____nemos
5. qu_____ro
6. t_____nen

*Answers: 1. puedes 2. prefiere 3. vengo 4. tenemos 5. quiero 6. tienen*

**Need more practice?**

- Workbook/Laboratory Manual
- Interactive CD-ROM
- Online Learning Center (www.mhhe.com/quetal7)

## ■ Práctica

### A. ¡Sara tiene mucha tarea (homework)!

PASO 1  Haga (*Form*) oraciones con las palabras indicadas. Añada (*Add*) palabras si es necesario.

MODELO: Sara / tener / que / estudiar / mucho / hoy → Sara tiene que estudiar mucho hoy.

1. Sara / tener / muchos exámenes
2. (ella) venir / a / universidad / todos los días
3. hoy / trabajar / hasta / nueve / de / noche
4. preferir / estudiar / en / biblioteca
5. querer / leer / más / pero / no poder
6. por eso / regresar / a / casa
7. tener / ganas de / leer / más
8. pero / unos amigos / venir a mirar / televisión
9. Sara / decidir / mirar / televisión / con ellos

PASO 2  Now retell the same sequence of events, first as if they had happened to you, using **yo** as the subject of all but sentence number 8, then as if they had happened to you and your roommate, using **nosotros/as.**

### B. Situaciones.

Expand the situations in these sentences by using an appropriate idiom with **tener.** There is often more than one possible answer.

MODELO: Tengo un examen mañana. Por eso... →
Por eso tengo que estudiar mucho.

1. ¿Cuántos años? ¿Cuarenta? No, yo...  tengo _____ años.
2. Un perro grande y feo vive en esa casa. Por eso yo...  tengo miedo
3. ¿Ya son las tres de la mañana? Ah, por eso yo...  tengo sueño
4. No, dos y dos no son cinco. Son cuatro. Tú...  no tienes razón
5. Son las tres menos cuarto y tengo que estar en el centro a las tres. Yo...  tengo prisa.
6. Cuando hay un terremoto (*earthquake*), todos...  tienen (tenemos) miedo.
7. ¿Los exámenes de esa clase? ¡Esos son siempre muy fáciles (*easy*)! Yo no...  tengo que estudiar.
8. Sí, la capital de la Argentina es Buenos Aires. Tú...  tienes razón.

## ■ Conversación

## NOTA COMUNICATIVA

### Using *mucho* and *poco*

In the first chapters of *¿Qué tal?*, you have used the words **mucho** and **poco** as both adjectives and adverbs. *Adverbs* (**Los adverbios**) are words that modify verbs, adjectives, or other adverbs: *quickly, very smart, very quickly.* In Spanish and in English, adverbs are invariable in form. However, in Spanish adjectives agree in number and gender with the word they modify.

> **adverb** = a word that modifies a verb, adjective, or another adverb

ADVERB

Rosario estudia **mucho** hoy.
Julio come **poco.**

*Rosario is studying a lot today.*
*Julio doesn't eat much.*

ADJECTIVE

Rosario tiene **mucha** ropa. Sobre todo tiene **muchos** zapatos.
Julio come **poca** carne. Come **pocos** postres.

*Rosario has a lot of clothes. She especially has a lot of shoes.*
*Julio doesn't eat much meat. He eats few desserts.*

Con. A: Suggestions
• Have students work in groups to compare notes. Then assign different areas of the board where all groups make a short list of their conclusions. Compare all of the lists. Emphasize note taking.

## A. Preferencias

PASO 1   Working with a classmate, try to predict the choices your instructor will make in each of the following cases.

MODELO:   El profesor / La profesora tiene… muchos / pocos libros →
muchos libros

1. El profesor / La profesora tiene…
mucha ropa / poca ropa          sólo un coche / varios coches
2. Prefiere…
los gatos / los perros          la ropa elegante / la ropa informal
3. Quiere comprar…
un coche deportivo (*sports car*), por ejemplo, un Porsche / una
camioneta (*station wagon*)
un abrigo / un impermeable
4. Viene a la universidad…
todos los días / sólo tres veces a la semana
en coche / en autobús / en bicicleta / a pie (*on foot*)
5. Esta noche tiene muchas ganas de…
mirar la televisión / leer    comer en un restaurante / comer en casa
6. Su color favorito es… verde / rojo / amarillo
7. Prefiere usar… botas / zapatos / sandalias

PASO 2   Now, using tag questions, ask your instructor questions to find out if you are correct.

MODELO:   muchos libros →
Ud. tiene muchos libros, ¿verdad?

## B. Estereotipos.

Draw some conclusions about Isabel based on this scene. Think about things that she has, needs to or has to do or buy, likes, and so on. When you have finished, compare your predictions with a classmate's. Did you both reach the same conclusions?

MODELO:   Isabel tiene cuatro gatos. Tiene que…

Resources:
Transparency
29

• After students have used items to ask you questions, reverse the situation, using the same items or different ones.

Con. A: Follow-Up
Use the following categories to ask students about their preferences. Have them answer *No tengo preferencia* when they do not have a preference. Have students add two or three options of their own invention.

MODELOS:   ¿Prefiere los gatos o los perros?
¿Le gusta más bailar o cantar?

1. *Los animales: ¿los gatos siameses o los persas? ¿los perros pastores alemanes o los perros de lanas (draw on board)?*
2. *El color de la ropa informal: ¿el color negro o el blanco? ¿el rojo o el azul?*
3. *La ropa informal: ¿las camisas de algodón o las de seda? ¿los jeans de algodón o los pantalones de lana?*
4. *La ropa de mujeres: ¿las faldas largas o las minifaldas? ¿los pantalones largos o los pantalones cortos?*
5. *La ropa de hombres: ¿las camisas de cuadros o las de rayas (draw on board)? ¿las camisas de un solo (pantomine) color? ¿chaqueta y pantalón o un traje formal?*
6. *Las actividades en casa: ¿mirar la televisión o leer una novela? ¿escribir cartas o hablar con unos amigos?*

Con. B: Suggestion
Coach students to help them invent a situation for or a story about the drawing. Caution them to stay within the limits of the language they know. Offer brief model sentences: *Isabel no estudia mucho.*

Con. B: Follow-Up
Ask the following questions.

*¿Es Ud. como Isabel?*
*¿Qué problemas tienen Isabel y Ud. en común?*
*¿Cómo es su cuarto?*
*¿Vive Ud. solo/a?*

### Palabras útiles

**los aretes** (earrings)
**el juguete** (toy)
**los muebles** (furniture)
**el sofá**

**hablar por teléfono**
**tener** (*irreg.*) **alergia a** (to be allergic to)

Heritage Speakers
En algunos dialectos del español del suroeste de los Estados Unidos, se oye decir *muncho* por *mucho.* Aunque *muncho* es parte del habla cotidiana, *mucho* es la forma preferida.

*Paso 2   Gramática*

## LITERATURA: Rubén Darío

**Rubén Darío**
*(1867–1916)*

**Sobre el autor:** *The Nicaraguan writer, journalist, and diplomat Rubén Darío was one of the most celebrated poets of the movement known as* **modernismo.** *Darío was born Félix Rubén García Sarmiento, in Metapa, a city in Nicaragua now named Darío. He was a major influence on later writers in Latin America, Spain, and Europe. These lines are from the poem "¡Eheu!,"*[a] *El canto errante*[b] *(1907).*

Aquí, junto al[c] mar latino,
digo[d] la verdad:
siento[e] en roca, aceite[f] y vino,
yo mi antigüedad.[g]

¡Oh, qué anciano soy, Dios santo,
oh, qué anciano soy!...
¿De dónde viene mi canto?
Y yo, ¿adónde voy[h]?

[a]*Latin word that means "Alas!"*  [b]*El… The Wandering Song*  [c]*junto… next to the*  [d]*I tell*  [e]*I feel*  [f]*oil*  [g]*antiquity, age*  [h]*do I go*

**Literatura: Notes**
- Rubén Darío was raised by an aunt. He began writing at a very young age, and by 11 years old he was known as the "boy poet." He chose the name Darío from a family name.
- Darío attributed the success of his poetic innovations to having learned to think in French and write in Spanish. For some, Darío's style was the result of a brilliant synthesis of the French, Spanish, and American spirits.
- Darío was a world traveler. He traveled extensively from 1882 on, primarily in South America and Europe.

## MÚSICA: Los garífuna

**Música: Notes**
- There are about 500,000 Garífuna in areas of Mexico, Belize, Guatemala, and Nicaragua.
- The Garífuna are descendents of the Kalipuna tribe of South America, who invaded St. Vincent Island and conquered the Arawak tribe. The Arawak men were killed and the women were taken as wives. The descendents became known as the Garífuna, which means "cassava-eating people." The Spaniards called them Caribs, a name derived from "cannibal" and also the origin of the name later given to the area. In 1635, Nigerian slaves escaped from a shipwreck on St. Vincent Island. After some years of struggle between the slaves and the Caribs or Garifuna, these groups eventually intermarried. Their descendents are called Black Caribs.

La punta es la música tradicional de los garífuna, un grupo afro-indígena de las costas de Nicaragua, Honduras y Belice. Su música es esencial en sus ritos[a] y tradiciones. Los instrumentos tradicionales son el garawón[b] y otros instrumentos de percusión. Típicamente hay competencias[c] entre parejas[d] que bailan. Como muchos otros géneros[e] de música caribeña, se basa[f] en la llamada y respuesta.[g]

[a]*rituals*  [b]*traditional drum of Central America*  [c]*competitions*  [d]*entre… between couples*  [e]*Como… Like many other genres, types*  [f]*se… it is based*  [g]*llamada… call and response (in music, a succession of phrases in which the second phrase is a response to the first, and so on; the "communication" is between two different musicians, between a musician and a singer or dancer, or between two or more singers)*

Todos los años[h] en mayo[i] en Bluefields en la costa atlántica de Nicaragua, se celebra[j] el festival Palo de Mayo.[k] El festival es una tradición que refleja[l] la confluencia[m] de tradiciones europeas y africanas. De Europa vienen las fiestas del *maypole,* y de África, las celebraciones en honor a Mayaya, diosa[n] de la fertilidad. Antes bailaban las damas y caballeros[o] alrededor del[p] palo de mayo a la música del vals,[q] la polka y la mazurca. Ahora comparsas[r] del pueblo[s] garífuna bailan al ritmo[t] de sus garawones.

[h]*Todos… Every year*  [i]*May*  [j]*se… is celebrated*  [k]*Palo… Maypole*  [l]*reflects*  [m]*coming together*  [n]*goddess*  [o]*Antes… Before ladies and noblemen used to dance*  [p]*alrededor… around the*  [q]*waltz*  [r]*dance troupes*  [s]*people*  [t]*rhythm*

Paso 3: Gramática
See the "Chapter-by-Chapter Supplementary Materials" in the IM for additional teaching
suggestions, notes, activities, and other resources for *Paso 3*.

## 10 Expressing Destination and Future Actions *Ir; ir + a +* Infinitive; The Contraction *al*

**¿Adónde *vas*?**

Rosa y Casandra son compañeras de cuarto.

CASANDRA: ¿Adónde *vas*?
ROSA: *Voy al* centro.
CASANDRA: ¿Qué *vas a* hacer en el centro?
ROSA: *Voy a* comprar un vestido para la fiesta de Javier. ¿No *vas a ir* a su fiesta este fin de semana?
CASANDRA: ¡Claro que *voy*!

**Comprensión: ¿Sí o no?**

1. Rosa va a estudiar.    no
2. Rosa va a hacer (*give*) una fiesta.    no
3. Casandra va a asistir a la fiesta.    sí

**Notes**
• *Ir* and *venir* are used somewhat differently than their English equivalents. *Venir* means *to come to* (*where the speaker is*). *Ir* refers to some place other than where the speaker is. The speaker of *¿Vienes a mi casa?* is at his/her house when asking the question. Otherwise, he/she would ask *¿Vas a mi casa?*
• *¡Ya voy!* means *I'm coming*, not *I'm going*.

**Ir** is the irregular Spanish verb used to express *to go*.

**Follow-Up**
Ask students: *¿Qué voy a hacer yo mañana / esta tarde / noche?*
Then give them sentences about things you may or may not do.
*Voy a bailar en una fiesta esta noche.*
Students guess if your sentences are true (*Es verdad*) or false (*No es cierto*).

The first person plural of **ir, vamos** (*we go, are going, do go*), is also used to express *let's go*.

| ir (*to go*) | |
|---|---|
| **voy** | **vamos** |
| **vas** | **vais** |
| **va** | **van** |

**Vamos** a clase ahora mismo.
*Let's go to class right now.*

## *Ir* + *a* + Infinitive

**Ir** + **a** + infinitive is used to describe actions or events in the near future.

**Van a venir** a la fiesta esta noche.
*They're going to come to the party tonight.*

**Heritage Speakers**
Los hispanohablantes tienden a usar la expresión *ir a* + infinitivo en vez del futuro. Por ejemplo, es más común oír *va a llamar* en vez de *llamará*. Pregúnteles a los hispanohablantes de la clase en qué situaciones usan el futuro en vez de *ir a* + infinitivo.

*Where are you going?* Rosa and Casandra are roommates. CASANDRA: *Where are you going?* ROSA: *I'm going downtown.* CASANDRA: *What are you going to do downtown?* ROSA: *I'm going to buy a dress for Javier's party. Aren't you going to go to his party this weekend?* CASANDRA: *Of course I'm going!*

## The Contraction *al*

Suggestion
Point out the difference between *el* (article) and *él* (subject pronoun). Remind students that *de* + *él* and *a* + *él* do not contract.

In **Capítulo 2** you learned about the contraction **del (de + el → del).** The only other contraction in Spanish is **al (a + el → al). ¡OJO!** Both **del** and **al** are obligatory contractions.

**a + el → al**

Voy **al** centro comercial.
*I'm going to the mall.*

Vamos **a la** tienda.
*We're going to the store.*

**Preliminary Exercise**
Have students give the Spanish equivalents.

1. I'm going to the market.
2. He's going to the bookstore.
3. My mother's going downtown.
4. You're going to read.
5. We're going to be sleepy.
6. You and Mrs. Robinson are going to eat.

**Prác. B: Variation**
Personalize the sequence, having students do all items with *yo* forms; then change the details as necessary.

**Prác. B: Follow-Up**
Make statements that are true for students right now, varying the information according to individuals in your class. Using the follow-up question, students will tell what they will do in the future.

1. *Este semestre / trimestre Ud. toma clases muy fáciles. ¿Y el próximo semestre?*
2. *Ud. vive ahora en una residencia. ¿Y el próximo semestre?*
3. *Ahora _____ es el presidente / primer ministro. ¿Y en cuatro años?*
4. *Ud. lleva ropa muy vieja hoy. ¿Y mañana?*
5. *Ud. tiene problemas económicos ahora. ¿Y en cinco años?*
6. *Este año Ud. escucha música rap. ¿Y en diez años?*

**AUTOPRUEBA**

Give the subject pronouns for these forms of **ir.**

**1.** va   **2.** vamos   **3.** voy   **4.** van   **5.** vas

Answers: **1.** *Ud., él/ella* **2.** *nosotros/as* **3.** *yo* **4.** *Uds., ellos/as* **5.** *tú*

## ■ Práctica

**A. ¿Adónde van de compras?** Haga oraciones completas usando **ir.** Recuerde: **a + el → al.**

MODELO: Marta / el centro → Marta *va al* centro.

1. nosotros / una *boutique*
2. Francisco / el almacén Goya
3. Juan y Raúl / el centro comercial
4. tú / un mercado
5. Ud. / una tienda pequeña
6. yo / ¿ ?

**Prác. A: Answers**
1. *Nosotros vamos a una* boutique.
2. *Francisco va al almacén Goya.* **3.** *Juan y Raúl van al centro comercial.* **4.** *Tú vas a un mercado.* **5.** *Ud. va a una tienda pequeña.* **6.** *Yo voy…*

**B. ¡Vamos de compras!** Describa el día, desde el punto de vista (*from the point of view*) de Lola, la esposa de Manolo. Use **ir + a +** el infinitivo, según el modelo.

**Prác. B: Note**
Students may need extra help with item 7. *¿Vas a ir de… ?*

MODELO: Manolo compra un regalo para su madre. →
Manolo *va a comprar* un regalo para su madre.

1. Llegamos al centro a las diez de la mañana.
2. Mi hija Marta quiere comer algo (*something*).
3. Compro unos chocolates para Marta.
4. Manolo busca una blusa de seda.
5. No compras esta blusa azul, ¿verdad?
6. Buscamos algo más barato.
7. ¿Vas de compras mañana también?

**Prác. B: Answers**
1. *Vamos a llegar al centro a las diez de la mañana.* **2.** *Mi hija Marta va a querer comer algo.* **3.** *Voy a comprar unos chocolates para Marta.* **4.** *Manolo va a buscar una blusa de seda.* **5.** *No vas a comprar esta blusa azul, ¿verdad?* **6.** *Vamos a buscar algo más barato.* **7.** *¿Vas a ir de compras mañana también?*

**Need more practice?**

■ Workbook/Laboratory Manual
■ Interactive CD-ROM
■ Online Learning Center
(www.mhhe.com/quetal7)

## ■ Conversación

**A. ¿Adónde va Ud. si... ?** ¿Cuántas oraciones puede hacer?

MODELO: Me gusta leer novelas. Por eso voy a una librería.

Me gusta **+** 

leer novelas.
ir de compras —¡y no regateo!
buscar gangas y regatear.
hablar con mis amigos.
comer en restaurantes elegantes.
mirar programas de detectives.

**+** Por eso voy a _____.

**B. Entrevista: El fin de semana**

PASO 1 Interview a classmate about his or her plans for the weekend. "Personalize" the interview with additional questions. For example, if your partner is going to read a novel, ask **¿Qué novela?** or **¿Quién es el autor?**

¿Vas a... ?

1. ir de compras
2. leer una novela
3. asistir a un concierto
4. estudiar para un examen
5. ir a una fiesta
6. escribir una carta
7. ir a bailar
8. escribir los ejercicios para la clase de español
9. practicar un deporte (*sport*)
10. mirar mucho la televisión
11. comprar ropa en un centro comercial
12. escuchar cintas (*tapes*) o CDs en español

PASO 2 En el **Paso 1,** los números pares (2, 4, 6,... ) son actividades pasivas o tranquilas. Los números impares (1, 3, 5,... ) son más activas. ¿Cómo es su compañero/a? ¿Es activo/a? ¿O prefiere la tranquilidad?

## En los Estados Unidos y el Canadá

### Los hispanos en el mundo de la moda

Christy Turlington is one of many Hispanic celebrities in the U.S. world of fashion. Born in San Francisco, California (1969), to a Salvadoran mother, Turlington has been a household name since the 1990s. During her career as a supermodel, she became an activist for and benefactor of several causes, including breast cancer and animal rights. Furthermore, after being diagnosed with early-stage emphysema and subsequently quitting smoking, Christy became the spokesperson for a government antitobacco campaign.

*Christy Turlington*

**Reciclado**
- Do a quick review of verb endings for *-ar*, *-er*, and *-ir* regular verbs.
- Review chorally the conjugations of irregular verbs such as *ir*, *poder*, and *tener*.
- Review adjective-noun agreement rules and the four possible forms for adjectives ending in *-o*.

Un mercado en Chincheros, Perú

**Resources for Review and Testing Preparation**

- Workbook/Laboratory Manual
- Interactive CD-ROM
- Online Learning Center (www.mhhe.com/quetal7)

**Lengua y cultura: Answers**
1. *las* 2. *gran* 3. *ir* 4. *elegantes* 5. *los* 6. *fijos*
7. *pequeñas* 8. *formar* 9. *cree* 10. *otros* 11. *va*
12. *puede* 13. *debe* 14. *los* 15. *tiene* 16. *que*
17. *informal* 18. *grandes* 19. *debe* 20. *a*
*Comprensión* 1. falso: *Hay una gran variedad de tiendas.* 2. falso: *Los precios son fijos en los almacenes.* 3. falso: *Es posible comprar papel.* 4. falso: *El precio es alto al principio.*

**Resources: Desenlace**
In the *Capítulo 3* segment of "Chapter-by-Chapter Supplementary Materials" in the IM, you will find a chapter-culminating activity. You can use this activity to consolidate and review the vocabulary and grammar skills students have acquired.

## UN POCO DE TODO

**Lengua y cultura: Pero, ¿no se puede** (can't one) **regatear?** Complete the following paragraph with the correct form of the words in parentheses, as suggested by the context. When two possibilities are given in parentheses, select the correct word.

¿A Ud. le gusta ir de compras? ¿Le gusta regatear? En (los/las[1]) ciudades hispánicas, hay una (grande[2]) variedad de tiendas para (ir[3]) de compras. Hay almacenes, centros comerciales y *boutiques* (elegante[4]), como en (los/las[5]) Estados Unidos y el Canadá, donde los precios son siempre (fijo[6]).

También hay tiendas (pequeño[7]) que venden un solo[a] producto. Por ejemplo,[b] en una zapatería sólo hay zapatos. En español el sufijo **-ería** se usa[c] para (formar[8]) el nombre de la tienda. ¿Dónde (creer[9]) Ud. que venden papel y (otro[10]) artículos de escritorio? ¿A qué tienda (ir[11]) a ir Ud. a comprar fruta?

Si Ud. (poder[12]) pagar el precio que piden,[d] (deber[13]) comprar los recuerdos[e] en (los/las[14]) almacenes o *boutiques*. Pero si (tener[15]) ganas o necesidad de regatear, tiene (de/que[16]) ir a un mercado: un conjunto[f] de tiendas o locales[g] donde el ambiente[h] es más (informal[17]) que[i] en los (grande[18]) almacenes. Ud. no (deber[19]) pagar el primer[j] precio que menciona el vendedor.[k] ¡Casi siempre va (a/de[20]) ser muy alto!

[a]*single* [b]*Por... For example* [c]*se... is used* [d]*they ask* [e]*souvenirs* [f]*group* [g]*stalls* [h]*atmosphere* [i]*than* [j]*first* [k]*seller*

**Comprensión: ¿Cierto o falso?** Corrija las oraciones falsas.

1. En el mundo hispánico, todas las tiendas son similares.
2. Uno puede regatear en un almacén hispánico.
3. Es posible comprar limones en una papelería.
4. En un mercado, el vendedor siempre ofrece un precio bajo al principio (*beginning*).

**Follow-Up**
- Have students give the names of stores. Write an example on the board.

  *La tienda donde se venden zapatos se llama... → una zapatería*
  *fruta → frutería*
  *carne* (new word) *→ carnicería*
  *papel → papelería*
  *pan* (new word) *→ panadería*
  *perfume → perfumería*
  *¿y animales? ¡OJO! → tienda de animales*

- Have students write similar paragraphs, comparing shopping experiences in different towns and cities, or in different kinds of stores and shopping areas.

Paso 4: Un paso más
• The *Paso 4: Un paso más* sections are optional.
• See the "Chapter-by-Chapter Supplementary

**VIDEOTECA**

Materials" in the IM for additional teaching suggestions, notes, activities, and other resources for *Paso 4*.

## Entrevista cultural: Nicaragua

Delvia Argüello is a young woman from Nicaragua who works in her family's business. In this interview she talks about herself, her work, and her plans for the future. Among other things, she mentions how climate affects clothing styles in her country. Before watching the video clip, read the following excerpt from the interview.

**Entrevista cultural: Suggestions**
• Before showing the video, have students play the role of a clothing store clerk. Ask them questions about their store and what they sell.

INTERVIEWER:  …¿Cómo se llama Ud. y de dónde es?

DELVIA:  Me llamo Delvia Argüello y soy de Managua, Nicaragua. Tengo 24 años.

INTERVIEWER:  ¿En dónde vive Ud.?

DELVIA:  En Managua con mi familia. Mi familia tiene una tienda de ropa, eh, para mujeres. Allí se vende ropa, de… pantalones, camisas, zapatos y accesorios.

*¿Dónde está la tienda?*
*¿Qué tipo de ropa venden?*
*¿Qué días y cuántas horas trabaja?*

• Show the video and allow students one to two minutes to work on the questions. Encourage them to answer in Spanish if possible. You might want to ask the questions in Spanish when you review the answers as a class.

Now watch the video clip and answer the following questions based on the interview.

**Entrevista cultural: Answers**
1. *24* 2. *Managua* 3. *una tienda de ropa* 4. *Delvia y su madre manejan la tienda y su padre viaja.* 5. *Quiere abrir una tienda de ropa (para novias).*

1.  How old is Delvia?
2.  What city is she from?
3.  What is her family's business?
4.  In the family business, who takes care of (**manejar**) the store, and who travels (**viajar**)?
5.  What would Delvia like to do in the future?

1. *¿Cuántos años tiene Delvia?*
2. *¿De qué ciudad es?*
3. *¿Cuál es el negocio de su familia?*

## Entre amigos: ¡Está súper fuera de moda (*out of style*)!

Miguel, Tané, Karina, and Rubén are shopping in a small flea market. What questions do you think they will ask each other? Before watching the video, read the following questions. As you watch, don't worry if you don't understand every word. Try to get the gist of the conversation, listening carefully for information about clothing. Watch the video a second time and listen for the answers to the questions.

4. *En el negocio de la familia, ¿quién maneja la tienda y quién viaja?* (explain)
5. *A Delvia, ¿qué le gustaría hacer en el futuro?*

Have volunteers answer the questions.

1.  ¿A Karina le gusta la chaqueta que escoge (*chooses*) Tané? ¿Por qué?
2.  En la opinión de Karina, ¿es importante o no la moda? ¿Por qué?
3.  ¿Qué tipo de ropa usa Rubén?
4.  ¿Qué artículo de ropa compra Tané?

• Have volunteers role-play Delvia and the interviewer.

**Entre amigos: Suggestions**
• Before viewing the video, review the questions with the students and ask them similar questions.

*En su opinión, ¿es importante o no la moda? ¿Por qué?*
*¿Qué tipo de ropa usa Ud. para ir a clase? ¿para asistir a una fiesta? ¿para trabajar?*

Have students answer or work in small groups to ask and answer these questions.

• After viewing the video, have volunteers read and answer the questions.

**Entre amigos: Answers**
1. *No, porque está fuera de moda.* 2. *Sí, porque la apariencia es importante.* 3. *pantalones vaqueros, camisa y sombrero* 4. *una chaqueta*

## Nicaragua

**Notes**
• *El Lago de Nicaragua* has freshwater sharks and fish we associate with oceans and seas because, scientists believe, the lake was once part of the Pacific Ocean. The lake probably separated from the ocean after seismic or volcanic activity. The saltwater creatures that were trapped in the lake adapted as the water turned fresh to become freshwater creatures.

## ENFOQUE CULTURAL

## Nota histórica

Cristóbal Colón llegó[a] a las costas de Nicaragua en 1502, pero la región no fue colonizada[b] hasta[c] 1524.

Nicaragua tiene una historia turbulenta por las luchas[d] entre las fuerzas conservadoras y las fuerzas liberales. La lucha se complicó[e] por la intervención de los Estados Unidos en la política del país. En 1990 terminó[f] una época[g] difícil de dictadura y lucha: hubo[h] una revolución y un movimiento en contra de la revolución. Esta lucha fue entre los sandinistas (revolucionarios marxistas) y los «contras» (antirrevolucionarios).

[a]*arrived*  [b]*no… was not colonized*  [c]*until*  [d]*struggles*  [e]*se… was complicated*  [f]*ended*  [g]*time*  [h]*there was*

• The Nicaraguan priest, poet, and author Ernesto Cardenal was born on the coast of *el Lago de Nicaragua* in the city of Granada in 1925. He is a major poet not only in Nicaragua but in the Spanish-speaking world. A Christian-Marxist, Cardenal is known as a spokesperson for justice and self-determination in Latin America. He has served as the Minister of Culture of Nicaragua, and currently codirects *la Casa de Los Tres Mundos*, a literary and cultural organization.

## ¡Fíjese!

• En 1856, un estadounidense, William Walker, se declaró[a] presidente de Nicaragua. Dos años después, fue derrotado por[b] los nicaragüenses, liberales y conservadores que se unieron[c] para expulsarlo[d] del país.

• El Lago de Nicaragua es el lago más grande de Centroamérica. También se llama el Lago Cocibolca. Hay más de 300 islas en el lago. En estas «isletas», hay pequeñas comunidades agrícolas[e] y, en algunas,[f] casas de personas ricas. En la isleta de San Pablo, hay una fortaleza[g] construida por los españoles para protegerse[h] de los piratas ingleses. Los nicaragüenses llaman el lago su «mar dulce»[i] porque es muy grande y porque tiene agua dulce.[j] Tiene los únicos tiburones[k] de agua dulce del mundo.[l]

[a]*se… declared himself*  [b]*fue… he was defeated by*  [c]*se… joined together*  [d]*expel him*  [e]*agricultural*  [f]*some (of them)*  [g]*fort*  [h]*protect themselves*  [i]*mar… sweet (fresh water) sea*  [j]*agua… fresh water*  [k]*únicos… only sharks*  [l]*world*

*Parte de las ruinas de la fortaleza en la isleta de San Pablo, en el Lago de Nicaragua*

• Violeta Barrios de Chamorro was president of Nicaragua from 1990 to 1997. She was the first female president of that country.
• Students can read part of an excerpt of the poem "¡Eheu!" by Nicaragua's Rubén Darío in *Voces de Nicaragua: Literatura.*
• Students can read about the music of the *garífuna* in *Voces de Nicaragua: Música.*
• See the Workbook/Laboratory Manual for focused practice with the material in *Enfoque cultural.*

Learn more about Nicaragua with the Video, Interactive CD-ROM, and the Online Learning Center (www.mhhe.com/quetal7).

**Multimedia: Internet**
Have students look up additional information about Nicaragua's history, government, people, culture, geography, tourism, and media on the Internet. You might assign specific topics and have students give brief oral reports about Nicaragua.

*Capítulo 3 • De compras*

PASO FINAL

## A LEER

### ESTRATEGIA: Using Visual Clues to Predict Content

In **Capítulo 1** you learned that you can use section subheadings to help you better understand a passage. Another useful strategy is to use photographs and other visual clues (charts, drawings, graphic images, and so on) that accompany the reading as tools to help you predict the content of the passage. A successful reader is able to make predictions about content in advance, and then confirms or rejects these predictions while reading.

Before reading the article that follows, look at the titles above each paragraph. What predictions can you make based on the visual presentation of these paragraph titles?

**Sobre la lectura...** This reading is adapted from an article that appeared in *Quo*, a magazine published in Spain that is comparable to *Vanity Fair, Details,* and other glossy general interest magazines. *Quo* publishes articles about topics ranging from diet and health to fashion to politics.

Suggestions
• Do the *Estrategia* in class before assigning the reading.
• Have students read the title of the article and jot down their ideas about the psychological effects of colors. In their opinion, are there any colors that make them feel relaxed, tense, aggressive, or uncomfortable?
• Have students brainstorm and list some images they think would help illustrate the article, based on their predictions. After reading, ask which images would work and which would not.

## *La psicología de los colores*

«Está demostrado[a] que los colores percibidos[b] por la vista[c] <u>provocan</u> una reacción psicológica sobre nuestro estado de ánimo[d]», asegura Carlos Obelleiro, <u>experto</u> en la utilización de color. Y de un buen estado de ánimo depende mucho la salud física. Según expertos en psicología de los colores, cada uno indica una actitud en quien lo lleva puesto.[e]

### Rojo
Es el color que produce mayor impacto visual. Actúa como un estimulante psíquico, pero activa la <u>agresividad</u> y si alguien lo lleva puede incomodar a los demás.[f]

### Amarillo
Está íntimamente relacionado con la autoestima[g] y <u>estimula</u> la creatividad, pero puede resultar agresivo para gente emocionalmente <u>frágil</u>.

### Azul
Favorece la calma y la concentración en trabajos que exigen[h] esfuerzo[i] mental. Tranquiliza, pero puede dar imagen de frialdad.[j] Cuanto más oscuro es,[k] más idea da[l] de eficiencia y autoridad.

### Verde
Es el color más relajante y suele[m] provocar una sensación de <u>equilibrio</u> y de tranquilidad personal.

### Blanco
Aunque[n] es muy higiénico, puede resultar muy severo y dar la impresión de que la persona que lo lleva quiere crear una barrera.[o]

### Rosado
Es la más pura expresión de la <u>feminidad</u>. Utilizado en decoración actúa como relajante, pero en exceso causa debilitamiento.[p]

### Negro
Es elegante, pero puede resultar amenazador[q] y, como el blanco, crear barreras entre la persona que lo lleva y el resto de la gente.

### Violeta
Es el color de la introversión. Puede transmitir la sensación de que quien lo viste[r] quiere estar solo, sin intromisiones.[s]

### Gris
Se trata del único color totalmente <u>neutro</u>, con lo que no tiene apenas[t] propiedades psicológicas. A veces puede indicar falta[u] de confianza en uno mismo. ■

[a]Está... *It has been shown* [b]*perceived* [c]*sight* [d]estado... *state of mind* [e]quien... *the person who wears it* [f]incomodar... *make others uncomfortable* [g]*self-esteem* [h]*demand* [i]*effort* [j]*coldness* [k]Cuanto... *The darker it is* [l]*it gives* [m]*it tends to* [n]*Although* [o]crear... *to create a barrier* [p]*debilitation, weakness* [q]*threatening* [r]quien... *the person who wears it* [s]sin... *without intrusions* [t]*hardly any* [u]*a lack*

# PASO 4

## Comprensión

A. **¿Qué color?**  Identify the color (or colors!) that corresponds to each psychological trait below, according to the reading.

1. Este color no se asocia con la extroversión, sino lo contrario (*but rather the opposite*).
2. A veces este color se asocia con la frigidez.
3. Estos dos colores dan la impresión de crear obstáculos.
4. Este color provoca reacciones muy agresivas.
5. Este color provoca la creatividad.
6. Este color es un estimulante psíquico.
7. Este color tiene muy poco estímulo psíquico.
8. Estos colores son relajantes.
9. Este color puede expresar eficiencia.

B. **¿Qué color recomienda Ud.** (*do you recommend*)?  Which color do you recommend a person use in order to make the following impressions or provoke the following reactions?

1. Una persona desea crear una impresión de control y poder (*power*).
2. Una persona quiere expresar su confianza en sí misma (*confidence in him- or herself*).
3. Una persona no quiere producir ningún (*any*) impacto.
4. Una persona quiere tener un lugar muy tranquilo y relajante en su casa.

## A ESCRIBIR

A. **Mi ropa favorita.**  In a brief paragraph, write a description of your favorite article of clothing. Use the questions that follow to organize your thoughts. Your instructor can help you with words or constructions that are unfamiliar to you.

¿De qué material es?
¿Por qué le gusta?
¿De qué color es?
¿Cómo se siente (*do you feel*) cuando lleva este artículo de ropa? (Me siento… tranquilo/a, enérgico/a, etcétera.)
¿Provoca el color algunas (*any*) reacciones como las reacciones descritas (*described*) en la lectura? ¿Cuáles?

B. **El inventario.**  Take an inventory of the clothing you have and express it in Spanish.

• What items do you have? How many of each? What colors?
• Do you have clothes that you wear almost every week? What items are they? Why do you wear them often?
• How many things do you have in your closet and drawers that you no longer wear or do not need? What are they?

You can describe your clothing inventory in paragraph form or create a table or list to show the things you have.

## GRAMÁTICA

To review the grammar points presented in this chapter, refer to the indicated grammar presentations. You'll find further practice of these structures in the Workbook/Laboratory Manual, on the Interactive CD-ROM, and on the *¿Qué tal?* Online Learning Center (www.mhhe.com/quetal7).

**8** Pointing Out People and Things—Demonstrative Adjectives and Pronouns.

Do you know the forms for **este, ese,** and **aquel?**

**9** Expressing Actions and States—**Tener, venir, preferir, querer,** and **poder;** Some Idioms with **tener**

You should be able to conjugate the verbs **tener, venir, preferir, querer,** and **poder.** Do you know how to use expressions like **tengo ganas de, tenemos miedo,** and **tienes razón?**

**10** Expressing Destination and Future Actions—**Ir; ir + a +** Infinitive; The Contraction **al**

You should know the forms of **ir** and how to express *going to do (something).* You should also know when to use the contraction **al.**

## VOCABULARIO

Practice this vocabulary with digital flash cards on the Online Learning Center (www.mhhe.com/quetal7).

### Los verbos

| | |
|---|---|
| **ir** (*irreg.*) | to go |
| **ir a** + *inf.* | to be going to (*do something*) |
| **ir de compras** | to go shopping |
| **llevar** | to wear; to carry; to take |
| **poder (ue)** | to be able, can |
| **preferir (ie)** | to prefer |
| **querer (ie)** | to want |
| **regatear** | to haggle, bargain |
| **tener** (*irreg.*) | to have |
| **usar** | to wear; to use |
| **venir** (*irreg.*) | to come |

*Repaso:* comprar, vender

### La ropa

| | |
|---|---|
| **el abrigo** | coat |
| **los aretes** | earrings |
| **la blusa** | blouse |
| **la bolsa** | purse |
| **la bota** | boot |
| **el calcetín** (*pl.* calcetines) | sock socks |
| **la camisa** | shirt |
| **la camiseta** | T-shirt |
| **la cartera** | wallet; handbag |
| **la chaqueta** | jacket |
| **el cinturón** | belt |
| **la corbata** | tie |
| **la falda** | skirt |
| **la gorra** | cap |
| **el impermeable** | raincoat |
| **los** *jeans* | jeans |
| **las medias** | stockings |
| **los pantalones** | pants |
| **el par** | pair |
| **el reloj** | watch |
| **la ropa** | clothes; clothing |
| **la ropa interior** | underwear |
| **la sandalia** | sandal |
| **el sombrero** | hat |
| **el suéter** | sweater |
| **el traje** | suit |
| **el traje de baño** | swimsuit |
| **el vestido** | dress |
| **el zapato (de tenis)** | (tennis) shoe |

### De compras

| | |
|---|---|
| **la ganga** | bargain |
| **el precio (fijo)** | (fixed, set) price |
| **las rebajas** | sales, reductions |

| | |
|---|---|
| de todo | everything |
| de última moda | the latest style |
| ¿cuánto cuesta? | how much does it cost? |
| ¿cuánto es? | how much is it? |

## Los materiales

| | |
|---|---|
| es de... | it is made of . . . |
| algodón (*m.*) | cotton |
| lana | wool |
| seda | silk |

## Los lugares

| | |
|---|---|
| el almacén | department store |
| el centro | downtown |
| el centro comercial | shopping mall |
| el mercado | market(place) |
| la tienda | shop, store |

## Los colores

| | |
|---|---|
| amarillo/a | yellow |
| anaranjado/a | orange |
| azul | blue |
| blanco/a | white |
| (de) color café | brown |
| gris | gray |
| morado/a | purple |
| negro/a | black |
| rojo/a | red |
| rosado/a | pink |
| verde | green |

## Otros sustantivos

| | |
|---|---|
| la cinta | tape |
| el ejercicio | exercise |
| el examen | exam, test |

## Los adjetivos

| | |
|---|---|
| barato/a | inexpensive |
| caro/a | expensive |
| poco/a | little |

**Repaso: mucho/a**

**Heritage Speakers**

Es muy probable que los hispanohablantes de su clase usen otras palabras para hablar de la ropa. Por ejemplo, en algunos países

## Más allá del número 100

| | |
|---|---|
| doscientos/as | |
| trescientos/as | |
| cuatrocientos/as | |
| quinientos/as | |
| seiscientos/as | |
| setecientos/as | |
| ochocientos/as | |
| novecientos/as | |
| mil | |
| un millón (de) | |

**Repaso: cien(to)**

## Formas demostrativas

| | |
|---|---|
| aquel, aquella, aquellos/as | that, those (over there) |
| ese/a, esos/as | that, those |
| eso, aquello | that, that (over there) |

**Repaso: este/a, esto, estos/as**

## Palabras adicionales

| | |
|---|---|
| ¿adónde? | where (to)? |
| al | to the |
| algo | something |
| allí | (over) there |
| tener (*irreg.*)... | |
| ganas de + *inf.* | to feel like (*doing something*) |
| miedo (de) | to be afraid (of) |
| prisa | to be in a hurry |
| que + *inf.* | to have to (*do something*) |
| razón | to be right |
| sueño | to be sleepy |
| no tener (*irreg.*) razón | to be wrong |
| ¿no?, ¿verdad? | right?, don't they (you, . . . ?) |

**Repaso: mucho (*adv.*), poco (*adv.*)**

# En casa°

°**En…** *At home*

# CAPÍTULO 4

## CULTURA
• **Nota cultural:** Las casas en el mundo hispánico
• **En los Estados Unidos y el Canadá:** Las misiones de California
• **Voces** de Costa Rica
  **Literatura:** Carmen Naranjo
  **Música:** La marimba y el punto guanacaste
• **Videoteca**
  **Entrevista cultural:** Costa Rica
  **Entre amigos:** Quiero cambiar los muebles.
• **Enfoque cultural:** Costa Rica

## VOCABULARIO
• ¿Qué día es hoy?
• Los muebles, los cuartos y otras partes de la casa
• ¿Cuándo? Las preposiciones

## GRAMÁTICA
11 **Hacer, oír, poner, salir, traer,** and **ver**
12 Present Tense of Stem-Changing Verbs
13 Reflexive Pronouns

*Una casa en San José, Costa Rica*

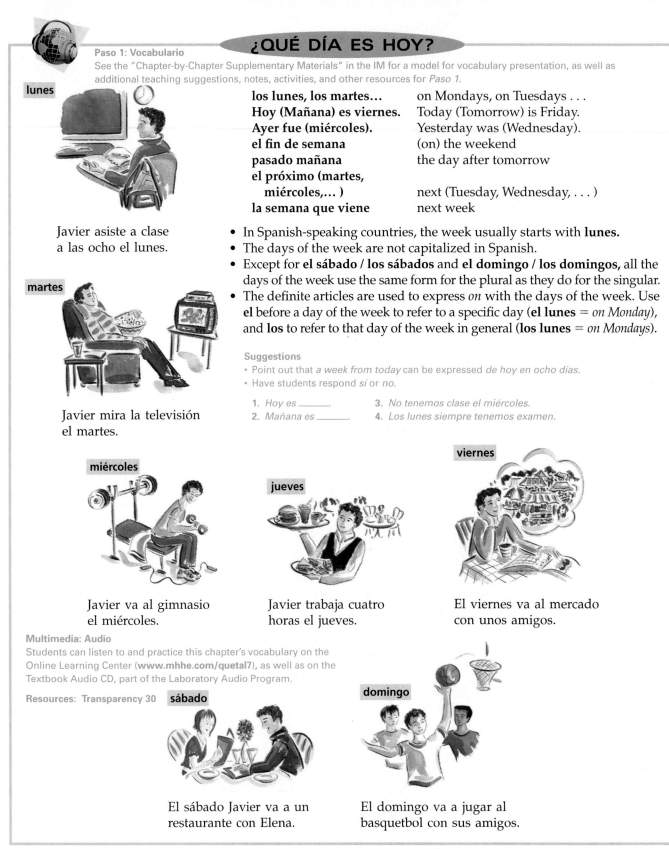

## ¿QUÉ DÍA ES HOY?

**Paso 1: Vocabulario**
See the "Chapter-by-Chapter Supplementary Materials" in the IM for a model for vocabulary presentation, as well as additional teaching suggestions, notes, activities, and other resources for *Paso 1.*

**lunes**

| | |
|---|---|
| **los lunes, los martes…** | on Mondays, on Tuesdays . . . |
| **Hoy (Mañana) es viernes.** | Today (Tomorrow) is Friday. |
| **Ayer fue (miércoles).** | Yesterday was (Wednesday). |
| **el fin de semana** | (on) the weekend |
| **pasado mañana** | the day after tomorrow |
| **el próximo (martes, miércoles,… )** | next (Tuesday, Wednesday, . . . ) |
| **la semana que viene** | next week |

Javier asiste a clase
a las ocho el lunes.

- In Spanish-speaking countries, the week usually starts with **lunes.**
- The days of the week are not capitalized in Spanish.
- Except for **el sábado / los sábados** and **el domingo / los domingos,** all the days of the week use the same form for the plural as they do for the singular.
- The definite articles are used to express *on* with the days of the week. Use **el** before a day of the week to refer to a specific day (**el lunes** = *on Monday*), and **los** to refer to that day of the week in general (**los lunes** = *on Mondays*).

**martes**

**Suggestions**
- Point out that *a week from today* can be expressed *de hoy en ocho días.*
- Have students respond *sí* or *no.*

1. *Hoy es _____.*
2. *Mañana es _____.*
3. *No tenemos clase el miércoles.*
4. *Los lunes siempre tenemos examen.*

Javier mira la televisión
el martes.

**miércoles**

**jueves**

**viernes**

Javier va al gimnasio
el miércoles.

Javier trabaja cuatro
horas el jueves.

El viernes va al mercado
con unos amigos.

**Multimedia: Audio**
Students can listen to and practice this chapter's vocabulary on the Online Learning Center (**www.mhhe.com/quetal7**), as well as on the Textbook Audio CD, part of the Laboratory Audio Program.

**Resources: Transparency 30**

**sábado**

**domingo**

El sábado Javier va a un
restaurante con Elena.

El domingo va a jugar al
basquetbol con sus amigos.

**Con. A: Note**
Stress the use in item 1 of *ayer*, which students should understand in context. *Fue* and other forms of the preterite are introduced in *Capítulo 7*.

**Con. A: Reciclado**
Remind students of the meaning of *de la mañana* (*tarde, noche*) and contrast it with *por la mañana* (*tarde, noche*).

## ■ Conversación

**A. Entrevista.** Con un compañero / una compañera, haga y conteste las siguientes (*following*) preguntas.

1. ¿Qué día es hoy? ¿Qué día es mañana? Si hoy es sábado, ¿qué día es mañana? Si hoy es jueves, ¿qué día es mañana? ¿Qué día fue ayer?
2. ¿Qué días de la semana tenemos clase? ¿Qué días no?
3. ¿Estudias mucho durante (*during*) el fin de semana? ¿y los domingos por la noche?
4. ¿Qué te gusta hacer (*to do*) los viernes por la tarde? ¿Te gusta salir (*to go out*) con los amigos los sábados por la noche?

**B. Mi semana.** Indique una cosa que Ud. quiere, puede o tiene que hacer cada (*each*) día de esta semana.

MODELO: El lunes tengo que (puedo, quiero) ir al laboratorio de lenguas.

---

**Palabras útiles**

**descansar** (to rest)
**dormir** (to sleep) **hasta muy tarde**
**ir** (*irreg.*) **al bar (al parque, al museo, a…)**
**ir** (*irreg.*) **al cine (movies)**
**jugar** (to play) **al tenis (al golf, al vólibol, al…)**

---

**Con. B: Reciclado**
Put on the board a list of all verbs students know, plus cognate verbs, and encourage them to use as many as they can in sentences with days of the week.

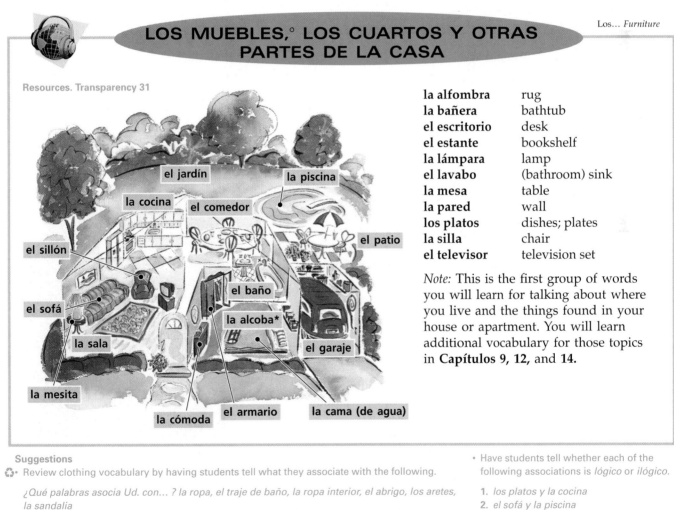

**LOS MUEBLES,° LOS CUARTOS Y OTRAS PARTES DE LA CASA**

Los… *Furniture*

Resources. Transparency 31

el jardín · la piscina · la cocina · el comedor · el patio · el sillón · el baño · el sofá · la alcoba* · la sala · el garaje · la mesita · la cómoda · el armario · la cama (de agua)

| | |
|---|---|
| la alfombra | rug |
| la bañera | bathtub |
| el escritorio | desk |
| el estante | bookshelf |
| la lámpara | lamp |
| el lavabo | (bathroom) sink |
| la mesa | table |
| la pared | wall |
| los platos | dishes; plates |
| la silla | chair |
| el televisor | television set |

*Note:* This is the first group of words you will learn for talking about where you live and the things found in your house or apartment. You will learn additional vocabulary for those topics in **Capítulos 9, 12,** and **14.**

**Suggestions**
• Review clothing vocabulary by having students tell what they associate with the following.

  *¿Qué palabras asocia Ud. con… ?* la ropa, el traje de baño, la ropa interior, el abrigo, los aretes, la sandalia

• Have students tell whether each of the following associations is *lógico* or *ilógico.*

1. *los platos y la cocina*
2. *el sofá y la piscina*
3. *el garaje y el coche*
4. *la alcoba y el armario*
5. *la cama y el comedor*

---

*Other frequently used words for bedroom include **el dormitorio** and **la habitación.***

Refrán

«Mientras en casa estoy, rey me soy.»

## ■ Conversación

**A. ¿Qué hay en esta casa?** Con un compañero / una compañera, identifique las partes de esta casa y diga lo que (*what*) hay en cada cuarto.

MODELO: 7 →

E1: El número 7 es el patio de la casa.
E2: ¿Qué hay en el patio? ¿Hay una piscina?
E3: No, sólo hay plantas.

**B. Asociaciones**

PASO 1 ¿Qué muebles o partes de la casa asocia Ud. con las siguientes
actividades?

1. estudiar para un examen
2. dormir la siesta (*taking a nap*) por la tarde
3. pasar una noche en casa con la familia
4. celebrar con una comida (*meal*) especial
5. tomar el sol (*sunbathing*)
6. hablar de temas (*topics*) serios con los amigos (padres, hijos)

PASO 2 Ahora compare sus asociaciones con las (*those*) de otros
estudiantes. ¿Tienen todos las mismas costumbres (*same customs*)?

## NOTA CULTURAL

### Las casas del mundo hispánico

There is no such thing as a typical Hispanic house. Often, the style of
housing depends on geographic location. For example, in hot regions
such as southern Spain, many houses are built around a central interior
patio. These patios are filled with plants, and some even have a fountain.

The population in Hispanic countries tends to be centered in urban
areas. Due to population density in cities, many people live in apart-
ments, like people in larger cities in this country.

Here are some more details about Hispanic houses.

- While the Spanish word **hogar** literally means *home,* the word **casa** is
  often used to mean *home.*

  Voy a casa.    *I'm going home.*    Estoy en casa.    *I'm at home.*

- In Spain, people use the word **piso** or **apartamento** to refer to an
  apartment; in some Hispanic countries, the word **departamento** is
  used.

- In big Latin American cities and especially with reference to more
  modern homes, a small front yard with ornamental plants and/or
  small trees is called **un jardín.** Large backyards are uncommon
  (except in rural areas and small towns) because the lots where houses
  are built are rather small. If a house has a back area, it is generally
  referred to as **el patio.** This area, usually paved, adjoins the house
  and is commonly enclosed by the walls of neighboring buildings.

*El patio interior de una casa, en
Sevilla, España*

## ¿CUÁNDO? • LAS PREPOSICIONES

Resources: Transparency 34

**Antes de** la fiesta, Rosa
prepara la comida.

**Durante** la fiesta,
Rosa baila.

**Después de** la fiesta,
Rosa limpia la sala.

*Prepositions* (**Las preposiciones**) express relationships in time and space.

The book is *on* the table.          The homework is *for* tomorrow.

Some common prepositions you have already used include **a, con, de, en,
para,** and **por.** Here are some prepositions that express time relationships.

| | | | |
|---|---|---|---|
| **antes de** *before* | **después de** *After* | **durante** *during* | **hasta** *until* |

The infinitive is the only verb form that can follow a preposition.

¿Adónde vas **después de estudiar**?          *Where are you going after studying*
*(after you study)?*

> **preposition** = a word or phrase
> that specifies the relationship,
> usually spatial or temporal, of
> one word to another

**Note**
The concept of the infinitive following
prepositions was seen in *Capítulo 3: para +*
infinitive.

♻ **Con. B: Reciclado**
Review telling time. Write the following
times on the board.

9:15 A.M.          7:45 P.M.
1:10 P.M.          3:30 A.M.

Then ask students: *¿Cómo se dice... ?* As
students interview each other for *Conversa-*
*ción B,* encourage them to ask partners for
specific times of day (*¿A qué hora es tu*
*programa favorito?*).

**Con. B: Follow-Up**
Use the information in this activity to create
a descriptive table of students' habits. Have
students try to characterize themselves as a
class (*¿trabajadores? ¿estudiosos?*).

## ▪ Conversación

**A. ¿Antes o después?** Complete las oraciones con **antes de** o **después de.**

Possible answers
1. Voy a la clase de español ____después de____ preparar la lección.
2. Los viernes siempre descanso ____antes de____ salir para una fiesta.
3. Me gusta investigar un tema ____antes de____ escribir una composición.
4. Prefiero comer fuera (*to eat out*) ____después de (antes de)____ ir al cine.
5. Tengo que estudiar mucho ____antes de____ tomar un examen

**B. Entrevista.** Con un compañero / una compañera, haga y conteste las
siguientes preguntas.

1. ¿Estudias durante tu programa favorito de televisión? ¿Qué más
   haces (*do you do*) cuando estudias?
2. ¿Hablas por teléfono antes o después de estudiar? ¿Dónde hablas por
   teléfono, en la sala o en tu cuarto?
3. ¿Hasta qué hora estudias, generalmente? ¿Estudias después de
   medianoche (*midnight*)?
4. ¿Trabajas durante las vacaciones? ¿Cuántas horas? ¿Trabajas por la
   noche hasta muy tarde?

**Note**

Beginning in this chapter,
the sounds of Spanish
consonants are systemati-
cally presented and practiced in the Workbook/
Laboratory Manual. The

letters *b* and *v* are presented
in *Capítulo 4* of the ancillary.

**Need more practice?**
▪ Workbook/Laboratory Manual
▪ Interactive CD-ROM
▪ Online Learning Center
(www.mhhe.com/quetal7)

# PASO 2    Gramática

CAPÍTULO 4

Paso 2: Gramática
See the "Chapter-by-Chapter Supplementary Materials" in the IM for additional teaching suggestions, notes, activities, and other resources for *Paso 2*.

## 11  Expressing Actions *Hacer, oír, poner, salir, traer,* and *ver*

**Los jóvenes de hoy**

**Follow-Up**
Ask students if they experience differences in opinion (conflicts) about how the rooms or house should be kept.

«¡Estos muchachos sólo quieren *salir*! No *ponen* sus cosas en orden en sus cuartos… Los jóvenes de hoy día no *hacen* nada bien; no son responsables… ¡Hasta quieren *traer* muchachas a sus cuartos!»

**¿Y Ud.?**

¿Son estos comentarios típicos de las personas mayores (*older adults*) de su país?
¿Cree Ud. que tienen razón?
¿Tienen los jóvenes algunos (*any*) estereotipos sobre (*about*) las personas mayores?

♻ **Reciclado**
Review the form of *tener* and *venir,* which have the *-g-* in the first person singular form, as do some of the verbs presented in this section.

| hacer<br>(*to do;<br>to make*) | | oír<br>(*to hear*) | | poner<br>(*to put;<br>to place*) | | salir<br>(*to leave;<br>to go out*) | | traer<br>(*to bring*) | | ver<br>(*to see*) | |
|---|---|---|---|---|---|---|---|---|---|---|---|
| hago | hacemos | oigo | oímos | pongo | ponemos | salgo | salimos | traigo | traemos | veo | vemos |
| haces | hacéis | oyes | oís | pones | ponéis | sales | salís | traes | traéis | ves | veis |
| hace | hacen | oye | oyen | pone | ponen | sale | salen | trae | traen | ve | ven |

• **hacer**

Some common idioms with **hacer:**

**hacer ejercicio** (*to exercise*)
**hacer un viaje** (*to take a trip*)
**hacer una pregunta** (*to ask a question*)

¿Por qué no **haces** la tarea?
*Why aren't you doing the homework?*

Quieren **hacer un viaje** al Perú.
*They want to take a trip to Peru.*

Los niños siempre **hacen muchas preguntas.**
*Children always ask a lot of questions.*

• **oír**

The command forms of **oír** are used to attract someone's attention in the same way that English uses *Listen!* or *Hey!*

**oye** (tú)    **oiga** (Ud.)    **oigan** (Uds.)

**Heritage Speakers**
Anime a los estudiantes hispanohablantes a hablar de las diferencias de generaciones en los países de habla española. ¿Son parecidas a las diferencias generacionales que existen en este país?

**Oye,** Juan, ¿vas a la fiesta?
*Hey, Juan, are you going to the party?*

**¡Oigan!** ¡Silencio, por favor!
*Listen! Silence, please!*

No **oigo** bien por el ruido.

---

*Today's young people*  *These boys only want to go out! They don't put things in order in their rooms . . . Today's young people don't do anything right; they are not responsible people . . . They even want to bring girls to their rooms!*

- **poner**

  Many Spanish speakers use **poner** with appliances to express *to turn on*.

  Voy a **poner** el televisor.
  *I'm going to turn on the TV.*

  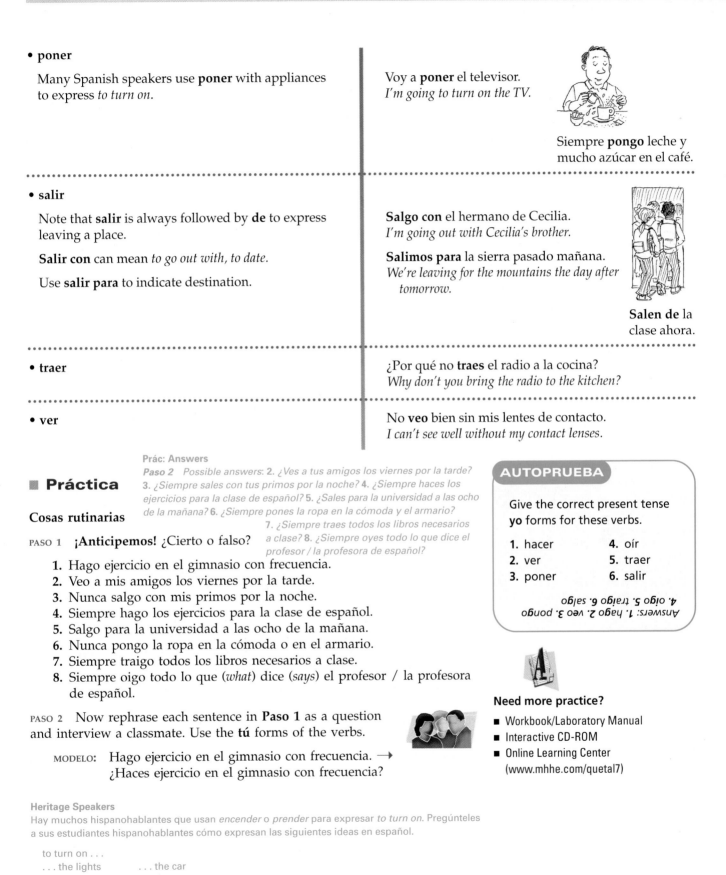

  Siempre **pongo** leche y mucho azúcar en el café.

- **salir**

  Note that **salir** is always followed by **de** to express leaving a place.

  **Salir con** can mean *to go out with, to date*.

  Use **salir para** to indicate destination.

  **Salgo con** el hermano de Cecilia.
  *I'm going out with Cecilia's brother.*

  **Salimos para** la sierra pasado mañana.
  *We're leaving for the mountains the day after tomorrow.*

  **Salen de** la clase ahora.

- **traer**

  ¿Por qué no **traes** el radio a la cocina?
  *Why don't you bring the radio to the kitchen?*

- **ver**

  No **veo** bien sin mis lentes de contacto.
  *I can't see well without my contact lenses.*

Prác: Answers
*Paso 2* Possible answers: **2.** ¿Ves a tus amigos los viernes por la tarde?
**3.** ¿Siempre sales con tus primos por la noche? **4.** ¿Siempre haces los ejercicios para la clase de español? **5.** ¿Sales para la universidad a las ocho de la mañana? **6.** ¿Siempre pones la ropa en la cómoda y el armario?
**7.** ¿Siempre traes todos los libros necesarios a clase? **8.** ¿Siempre oyes todo lo que dice el profesor / la profesora de español?

## ■ Práctica

### Cosas rutinarias

PASO 1  **¡Anticipemos! ¿Cierto o falso?**

1. Hago ejercicio en el gimnasio con frecuencia.
2. Veo a mis amigos los viernes por la tarde.
3. Nunca salgo con mis primos por la noche.
4. Siempre hago los ejercicios para la clase de español.
5. Salgo para la universidad a las ocho de la mañana.
6. Nunca pongo la ropa en la cómoda o en el armario.
7. Siempre traigo todos los libros necesarios a clase.
8. Siempre oigo todo lo que (*what*) dice (*says*) el profesor / la profesora de español.

PASO 2  Now rephrase each sentence in **Paso 1** as a question and interview a classmate. Use the **tú** forms of the verbs.

MODELO:  Hago ejercicio en el gimnasio con frecuencia. →
¿Haces ejercicio en el gimnasio con frecuencia?

**AUTOPRUEBA**

Give the correct present tense **yo** forms for these verbs.

1. hacer        4. oír
2. ver          5. traer
3. poner        6. salir

Answers: 1. hago 2. veo 3. pongo 4. oigo 5. traigo 6. salgo

**Need more practice?**

- Workbook/Laboratory Manual
- Interactive CD-ROM
- Online Learning Center (www.mhhe.com/quetal7)

**Heritage Speakers**
Hay muchos hispanohablantes que usan *encender* o *prender* para expresar *to turn on*. Pregúnteles a sus estudiantes hispanohablantes cómo expresan las siguientes ideas en español.

to turn on . . .
. . . the lights        . . . the car
. . . the television    . . . the water
. . . the oven

*Paso 2  Gramática*

# PASO 2

## ■ Conversación

**Frases útiles**

hacer (*irreg.*) **un viaje / una
pregunta**
oír (*irreg.*) **al profesor / a la
profesora\***
poner (*irreg.*) **el televisor / el
estéreo**
salir (*irreg.*) **con / de / para...**
traer (*irreg.*) **el libro a
clase**
ver (*irreg.*) **mi
programa favorito**

**Con. A: Answers**
*Possible answers:* **1.** ...*hago un viaje a
Colorado.* **2.** ...*traigo el libro a clase.*
**3.** ...*salgo para la biblioteca.* **4.** ...*pongo el
estéreo.* **5.** ...*no oigo al profesor.* **6.** ...*salgo
para la residencia.* **7.** ...*ponemos el estéreo.*
**8.** ...*hago una pregunta.*

**Con. A: Follow-Up**
Have students give the Spanish equivalents
for the following sentences.

1. I'm going to turn on the TV. I want to turn
on the radio.
2. She's going out with her boyfriend
(*novio*). He wants to go out with
Margarita.
3. She's leaving for Rome tomorrow. I'm
leaving for Bogotá on Friday.
4. We have to take a trip. They should ask a
question.

♻ **Con. A: Reciclado**
Help students review clothing vocabulary.
Write on the board:

*La ropa. Voy a hacer un viaje y en mi ma-
leta voy a poner...*

Divide the class into small groups and have
students take turns adding the name of an
item to the list of clothing they will pack.
Each student must name all the items previously mentioned by others before adding
his or her own.

**A. Consecuencias lógicas.** Con un compañero / una compañera, indique
una acción lógica para cada situación, usando (*using*) las **Frases útiles**.

MODELO: No tengo tarea. Por eso... → pongo el televisor.

1. Me gusta esquiar en las montañas. Por eso...
2. En la clase de español usamos este libro todos los días. Por eso...
3. Mis compañeros de cuarto hacen mucho ruido en la sala. Por eso...
4. El televisor no funciona. Por eso...
5. Hay mucho ruido en la clase. Por eso...
6. Estoy en la biblioteca y ¡no puedo estudiar más! Por eso...
7. Queremos bailar y necesitamos música. Por eso...
8. No comprendo la lección. Por eso...

**B. Entrevista.** Con un compañero / una compañera, haga y conteste las
siguientes preguntas.

1. ¿Qué pones en el armario? ¿en la cómoda? ¿en el cajón (*drawer*) del
escritorio?
2. Generalmente, ¿qué traes a clase todos los días? ¿Crees que traes más
cosas que tus compañeros o menos? ¿Sales a veces para la clase sin
tu libro de texto? ¿Qué traen tus profesores a clase?
3. ¿Qué haces los jueves por la noche? ¿Cuándo sales con los amigos?
¿Adónde van cuando salen juntos (*together*)?
4. ¿Pones el televisor con frecuencia cuando estás en casa? ¿Qué
programa(s) ves todos los días? ¿Pones el radio con frecuencia?
¿Prefieres oír las noticias por radio o verlas (*to see them*) en la televisión? ¿Cuál es la estación de radio que más escuchas? ¿el canal de
televisión que más miras? ¿Por qué te gusta tanto (*so much*)?
5. ¿Te gusta hacer ejercicio? ¿Haces ejercicios aeróbicos? ¿Dónde haces
ejercicio? ¿En casa? ¿en el gimnasio? ¿en la piscina?

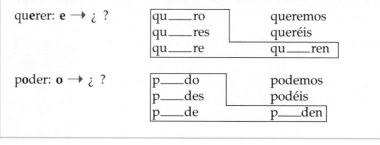

## ¿Recuerda Ud.?

The change in the stem vowels of **querer** and **poder** (**e** and **o**, respectively) follows the same pattern as that of the verbs presented in the
next section. Review the forms of **querer** and **poder** before beginning
that section.

querer: **e** → ¿ ?

| qu__ro | queremos |
| qu__res | queréis |
| qu__re | qu__ren |

poder: **o** → ¿ ?

| p__do | podemos |
| p__des | podéis |
| p__de | p__den |

---

*\*Remember that the word **a** is necessary in front of a human direct object. You will study this usage of **a** in*
**Capítulo 6.** *For now, you can answer following the pattern of the **Frases útiles**.*

CAPÍTULO
4  Follow-Up
Ask students the following questions after reading the *minidiálogo*.

*¿Piensan preparar una fiesta de sorpresa esta semana?*
*¿A qué hora vuelven Uds. de clase?*

# PASO 2

## 12 Expressing Actions Present Tense of Stem-Changing Verbs

**Una fiesta para Marisa**

Hoy es el cumpleaños de Marisa. Gracia y Catalina preparan una pequeña sorpresa para su compañera de cuarto.

GRACIA: ¿A qué hora *vuelve* Marisa?
CATALINA: No estoy segura pero *pienso* que *vuelve* a las cinco.
GRACIA: ¡No *podemos* estar listas a las cinco!
CATALINA: ¡Con calma! La sala está arreglada ahora y la comida casi está lista. A las cinco, *empieza* a llegar la gente y cuando Marisa abra la puerta, gritamos: «¡Sorpresa!» Entonces *sirvo* el champán y traigo la comida. Ya verás. Una sorpresa pequeña pero perfecta.

**Comprensión: ¿Cierto o falso?**

1. Gracia y Catalina empiezan a preparar una fiesta muy grande para Marisa.  *falso*
2. Marisa vuelve a casa por la noche.  *falso*
3. Marisa sirve la comida.  *falso*
4. Catalina piensa que necesitan más tiempo (*time*).  *falso*

Past ------------------- **PRESENT** ------------------- Future
present

| e → ie<br>**pensar (ie)**<br>(*to think*) | | o (u) → ue<br>**volver (ue)**<br>(*to return*) | | e → i<br>**pedir (i)**<br>(*to ask for; to order*) | |
|---|---|---|---|---|---|
| pienso | pensamos | vuelvo | volvemos | pido | pedimos |
| piensas | pensáis | vuelves | volvéis | pides | pedís |
| piensa | piensa | vuelve | vuelve | pide | piden |

♻ **Reciclado**
Review *querer* and *poder*, pointing out the diphthongization of the stem vowel in stressed positions, except for the *nosotros* and *vosotros* forms.

---

***A party for Marisa***   *Today is Marisa's birthday. Gracia and Catalina are preparing a small surprise for their roommate.* GRACIA: *When is Marisa getting back?* CATALINA: *I'm not sure but I think she returns at five.* GRACIA: *We can't be ready by five!* CATALINA: *Calm down! The living room is straightened up now and the food is almost ready. At five, people will begin to arrive, and when Marisa opens the door, we'll shout "Surprise!" Then I'll serve champagne and bring the food. You'll see. A small surprise, but perfect.*

# PASO 2

**Note**
The expression *pensar de* is used in Spanish to indicates one's opinion of someone or something: *¿Qué piensas de esta situación?*

**A.** You have already learned five *stem-changing verbs* (**los verbos que cambian el radical**).

**querer    preferir    tener    venir    poder**

In these verbs the stem vowels **e** and **o** become **ie** and **ue**, respectively, in stressed syllables. There is also another group of stem-changing verbs in which the stem vowel **e** becomes **i** in stressed syllables. The stem vowels are stressed in all present tense forms of these verbs except **nosotros** and **vosotros**. All three classes of stem-changing verbs follow this regular "boot" pattern in the present tense.

**B.** Some stem-changing verbs practiced in this chapter include the following.

**Emphasis A: Suggestion**
Write one of the verb paradigms on the board and draw a boot around the stem-changing verbs to help illustrate the pattern.

Stem vowel changes:

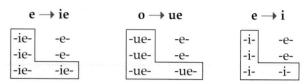

e → ie    o → ue    e → i

| -ie- | -e- |
| -ie- | -e- |
| -ie- | -ie- |

| -ue- | -e- |
| -ue- | -e- |
| -ue- | -ue- |

| -i- | -e- |
| -i- | -e- |
| -i- | -i- |

**Nosotros** and **vosotros** forms do not have a stem vowel change.

In vocabulary lists, the stem change will always be shown in parentheses after the infinitive: **volver (ue)**.

**Emphasis B: Suggestions**
• Model infinitives you have not yet presented, creating a brief conversational exchange with each.
• Emphasize the spelling differences between *perder* and *pedir*.
• Model verbs with infinitives to emphasize the use of prepositions with some, and not with others: *empezar a* + infinitive; *volver a* + infinitive; *pensar* + infinitive.
• Tell students that *volver* means *to return (to a place)*. Point out that the verb *devolver* means *to return (something)*. *Devolver* will become active vocabulary in *Capítulo 16*.

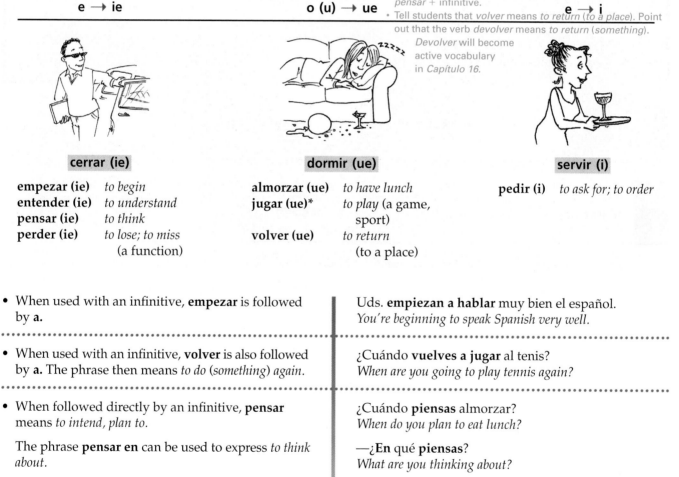

e → ie                o (u) → ue                e → i

**cerrar (ie)**       **dormir (ue)**       **servir (i)**

**empezar (ie)**   *to begin*          **almorzar (ue)**   *to have lunch*          **pedir (i)**   *to ask for; to order*
**entender (ie)**  *to understand*     **jugar (ue)***     *to play* (a game,
**pensar (ie)**    *to think*                              sport)
**perder (ie)**    *to lose; to miss*  **volver (ue)**     *to return*
                   *(a function)*                          *(to a place)*

• When used with an infinitive, **empezar** is followed by **a**.

Uds. **empiezan a hablar** muy bien el español.
*You're beginning to speak Spanish very well.*

• When used with an infinitive, **volver** is also followed by **a**. The phrase then means *to do (something) again*.

¿Cuándo **vuelves a jugar** al tenis?
*When are you going to play tennis again?*

• When followed directly by an infinitive, **pensar** means *to intend, plan to*.

The phrase **pensar en** can be used to express *to think about*.

¿Cuándo **piensas** almorzar?
*When do you plan to eat lunch?*

—¿**En** qué **piensas**?
*What are you thinking about?*

—**Pienso en** las cosas que tengo que hacer el domingo.
*I'm thinking about the things I have to do on Sunday.*

***Jugar** is the only **u** → **ue** stem-changing verb in Spanish. **Jugar** is usually followed by **al** when used with the name of a sport: **Juego al tenis.** Some Spanish speakers, however, omit the **al**.

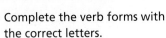
## ■ Práctica

**A. ¿Dónde están Jacobo y Margarita?** Tell in what part of Jacobo and Margarita's house the following things are happening. More than one answer is possible in some cases.

MODELO: Jacobo y Margarita empiezan a preparar el desayuno (*breakfast*). → Están en la cocina.

1. Jacobo sirve el desayuno.
2. Margarita cierra la revista y pone el televisor.
3. Los dos almuerzan con un amigo del barrio (*neighborhood*).
4. Los dos juegan al ajedrez (*chess*), y Jacobo pierde. No entiende bien el juego.
5. Margarita piensa en las cosas que tiene que hacer hoy.
6. Jacobo vuelve a casa después de ir al supermercado.
7. Margarita duerme la siesta.
8. Jacobo pide una pizza por teléfono.

**B. Una tarde típica en casa.** ¿Cuáles son las actividades de todos? Haga oraciones completas con una palabra o frase de cada grupo. Use sólo los sujetos que son apropiados para Ud.

| yo<br>mi padre/madre<br>mi esposo/a<br>los niños<br>mi amigo/a (*nombre*) y yo<br>el perro/gato<br>mi compañero/a | **+** | (no) | almorzar<br>volver<br>preferir<br>perder<br>pensar<br>entender<br>jugar<br>pedir<br>dormir<br>¿ ? | **+** | descansar, dormir<br>en un sillón / en la cocina<br>toda la tarde / la siesta<br>su pelota (*ball*) / sus llaves (*keys*) / su mochila<br>tarde / temprano a casa<br>en el patio / en la piscina / afuera (*outside*)<br>al golf / tenis / vólibol / ¿ ?<br>las películas (*movies*) viejas / recientes<br>el ajedrez / la lección<br>¿ ? |

♻ **Prác. B: Reciclado**
• Use the activity to review names of family members.
• Use the verb *servir* to review classroom objects.

## ■ Conversación

*¿Para qué sirve el lápiz? (Sirve para escribir.)*

**¿Qué piensas hacer esta semana?** Other objects that can be used in this pattern: *el bolígrafo, el cuaderno, el libro, la computadora.*

PASO 1 Organice la semana que viene. Indique lo que Ud. va a hacer **por la mañana, por la tarde** y **por la noche** cada día (de lunes a domingo). Puede usar las **Frases útiles,** pero invente por lo menos tres actividades que no están en la lista.

PASO 2 **Entrevista.** Ahora, hable con un compañero / una compañera de sus horarios (*schedules*) esta semana, basándose (*based*) en el **Paso 1.**

MODELO: E1: ¿Qué piensas hacer el domingo por la tarde?
E2: Pienso ver un poco la televisión y dormir una siesta. Y tú, ¿qué haces el domingo?
E1: El domingo juego al tenis con mi amigo Alex.

**Con: Follow-Up**
Students report the actions that they have in common.

*Jim y yo pensamos ir al cine el domingo por la tarde.*

*Paso 2 Gramática*

**Need more practice?**
■ Workbook/Laboratory Manual
■ Interactive CD-ROM
■ Online Learning Center (www.mhhe.com/quetal7)

**Frases útiles**

**almorzar (ue) en un restaurante con** _____
**dormir (ue) una siesta**
**empezar (ie) un proyecto para** _____
**hacer (*irreg.*) ejercicio**
**hacer (*irreg.*) la tarea de** _____
**jugar (ue) al tenis/golf/ basquetbol con** _____
**servir (i) una comida (*meal*) para mis amigos**
**ver (*irreg.*) la televisión**
**volver (ue) a ver a** _____

# Voces de Costa Rica

## LITERATURA: Carmen Naranjo

**Carmen Naranjo**
*(1929– )*

**Sobre la autora:** *Carmen Naranjo was born in Cartago, Costa Rica. She was a student of philology, and she has done graduate studies at the* **Universidad Nacional Autónoma de México** *as well as at the University of Iowa, Iowa City. She is a prolific writer of novels, stories, essays, and poetry. The following poem is from* En esta tierra redonda[a] y plana[b] *(XLVII) (2001).*

Ayer te busqué[c]
en ese asiento vacío[d]
del avión
en ese asiento vacío
del parque
en ese asiento vacío
del vestíbulo
en ese asiento vacío
del taxi
en ese asiento vacío
del comedor
en ese asiento vacío
de mi cuarto.
Hoy te seguiré buscando.[e]

[a]*round*  [b]*flat*  [c]*te... I looked for you*  [d]*asiento... empty seat*  [e]*te... I will continue to look for you*

**Literatura: Notes**

- Naranjo, a member of the *Asociación Costarricense de Escritoras*, is considered one of the most important literary figures, a pioneer of internal discourse, in Costa Rica and Central America. She denounces and challenges social, political, religious, intellectual, and sexual order institutions. She has dedicated much time, energy, and ink to the fight for equality for women.
- She has served on international boards and organizations, including *la Asociación Mundial de Escritores y Periodistas, la Organización de Estados Americanos,* and UNICEF.
- She has received the *Aquileo J. Echeverría* prize two times: in 1966 for her novel *Los perros no ladraron* and in 1971 for her novel *Responso por el niño Juan Manuel.* In 1977 she received *el Orden Alfonso X el Sabio* from the Spanish government and in 1986 *el Premio Nacional de Cultura Magón.*

**Música: Suggestions**

- Point out to students that they will read about marimbas in other chapters. The marimba is a popular instrument in many Spanish-speaking countries. There are great variations in the physical style of the instrument, including the material from which it is made. The playing style can vary greatly as well. In Costa Rica marimbas are often painted with bright colors, and the music is quiet and restrained.

- Many traditional instruments in Costa Rica and other Spanish-speaking countries were developed from materials grown or available in the area. Have students research different "natural" instruments. You might have some students look for different instruments made from gourds, bamboo, and so on.

## MÚSICA: La marimba y el punto guanacaste

En Costa Rica, como en muchos países latinoamericanos, la marimba es un instrumento de la música tradicional y folklórica. Hay muchas variaciones de este instrumento: doble o sencilla,[a] de materiales naturales, como calabazas[b] y madera,[c] o de metales o plástico. La marimba costarricense es sencilla, de materiales naturales y a veces pintada[d] de colores vivos.[e] La música de marimba costarricense se distingue[f] por ser suave[g] y serena.[h]

[a]*single (row of keys)*  [b]*gourds*  [c]*wood*  [d]*painted*  [e]*lively*  [f]*se... is unique*  [g]*por... for being soft*  [h]*restrained*

De la región de Guanacaste viene el baile nacional, punto guanacaste. La música del punto guanacaste se toca con marimbas de calabaza y guitarra.

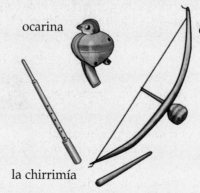

ocarina

el quijongo

la chirrimía

La música indígena de Costa Rica se toca con instrumentos tradicionales como el quijongo,[i] la ocarina[j] y la chirimía.[k]

[i]*single-string bow with gourd resonator*  [j]*potato-shaped wind instrument*  [k]*clarinet-type wind instrument*

**Paso 3: Gramática**
See the "Chapter-by-Chapter Supplementary Materials" in the IM for additional teaching suggestions, notes, activities, and other resources for *Paso 3*.

**Suggestion**
Point out the sequencing adverbs used in the presentation: *primero, luego, por fin.*

## 13 Expressing *-self/-selves* Reflexive Pronouns

**Follow-Up**
Have students respond *cierto* or *falso* based on their own situations.

### La rutina diaria de Andrés

La rutina de Andrés empieza a las siete y media.

1. *Me despierto temprano.*
2. *Me levanto a las seis.*
3. *El sábado me levanto a las siete.*
4. *Prefiero bañarme por la mañana.*
5. *Me gusta acostarme a las diez.*
6. *El sábado me acuesto a las doce.*

**Resources: Transparency 35**

**1.**     **2.**     **3.**     **4.**

(1) *Me despierto* a las siete y media y *me levanto* en seguida. Primero, (2) *me ducho* y luego (3) *me cepillo* los dientes. (4) *Me peino*, (5) *me pongo* la bata y (6) voy al cuarto a *vestirme*. Por fin, (7) salgo para mis clases. No tomo nada antes de salir para la universidad porque, por lo general, ¡tengo prisa!

**5.**     **6.**     **7.**

♻ **Reciclado**
Review the phrases students know with the verb *llamarse: me llamo, te llamas, se llama.*

**¿Y Ud.?** ¿Cómo es la rutina diaria de Ud.?

1. Yo me levanto a las _____.
2. Me ducho por la (mañana/noche).
3. Me visto en (el baño/mi cuarto).
4. Me peino (antes de/después de) vestirme.
5. Antes de salir para las clases, (tomo/no tomo) el desayuno.

## Uses of Reflexive Pronouns

### bañarse (*to take a bath*)

| | | | | | |
|---|---|---|---|---|---|
| (yo) | **me** baño | *I take a bath* | (nosotros) | **nos** bañamos | *we take baths* |
| (tú) | **te** bañas | *you take a bath* | (vosotros) | **os** bañáis | *you take baths* |
| (Ud.) | | *you take a bath* | (Uds.) | | *you take baths* |
| (él) | **se** baña | *he takes a bath* | (ellos) | **se** bañan | *they take baths* |
| (ella) | | *she takes a bath* | (ellas) | | *they take baths* |

**Suggestion**
Contrast *I bathe the kids* with *I bathe (myself)* (*I take a bath*). In the first sentence, the subject and object are different; in the second they are the same person (the object pronoun reflects the subject).

---

***Andrés's daily routine*** *Andrés's routine begins at seven-thirty. (1) I wake up at seven-thirty and I get up right away. First, (2) I take a shower and then (3) I brush my teeth. (4) I comb my hair, (5) I put on my robe, and (6) I go to my room to get dressed. Finally, (7) I leave for my classes. I don't eat or drink anything before leaving for the university because I'm generally in a hurry!*

**Refrán**

«Camarón que se duerme, se lo lleva el corriente.»

Write the *refrán* on the board. Give students the meaning of *camarón* (shrimp), and have them guess what *corriente* means (current). Have students guess the meaning of this saying, and ask them if they know similar or related sayings in English. (*You snooze, you lose. The early bird gets the worm.*)

**A.** The pronoun **se** at the end of an infinitive indicates that the verb is used reflexively. The reflexive pronoun in Spanish reflects the subject doing something to or for himself, herself, or itself. When the verb is conjugated, the reflexive pronoun that corresponds to the subject must be used.

**bañarse** = to take a bath (to bathe oneself)
**me baño** = I take a bath (bathe myself)

Many English verbs that describe parts of one's daily routine—to get up, to take a bath, and so on—are expressed in Spanish with a reflexive construction.

**Emphasis A: Suggestion**
Refer students to the vocabulary list to see the -se at the end of reflexive verbs.

### Reflexive Pronouns

| | | | |
|---|---|---|---|
| **me** | myself | **nos** | ourselves |
| **te** | yourself (*fam. sing.*) | **os** | yourselves (*fam. pl. Sp.*) |
| **se** | himself, herself, itself; yourself (*form. sing.*) | **se** | themselves; yourselves (*form. pl.*) |

**B.** Here are some reflexive verbs you will find useful as you talk about daily routines. Note that some of these verbs are also stem-changing.

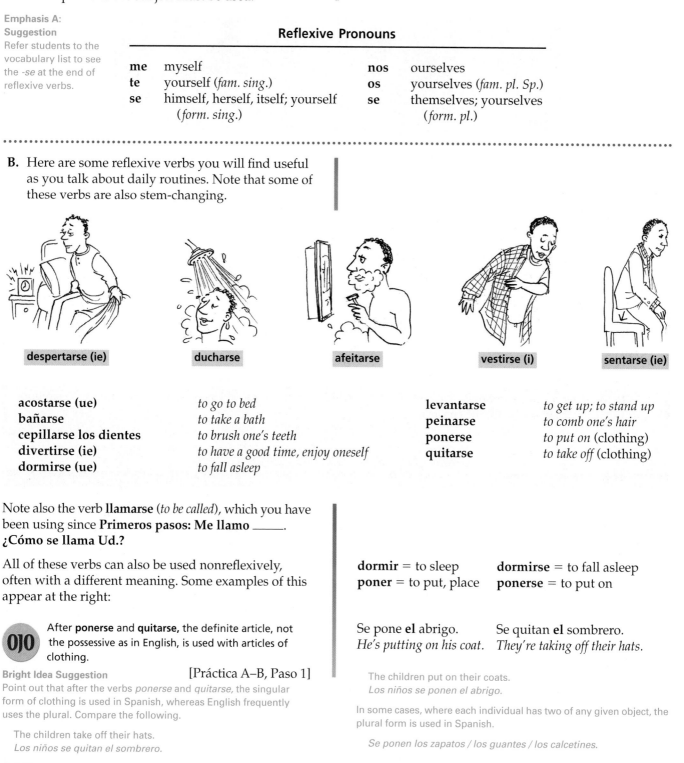

**despertarse (ie)**  **ducharse**  **afeitarse**  **vestirse (i)**  **sentarse (ie)**

| | | | | |
|---|---|---|---|---|
| **acostarse (ue)** | *to go to bed* | **levantarse** | *to get up; to stand up* |
| **bañarse** | *to take a bath* | **peinarse** | *to comb one's hair* |
| **cepillarse los dientes** | *to brush one's teeth* | **ponerse** | *to put on (clothing)* |
| **divertirse (ie)** | *to have a good time, enjoy oneself* | **quitarse** | *to take off (clothing)* |
| **dormirse (ue)** | *to fall asleep* | | |

Note also the verb **llamarse** (*to be called*), which you have been using since **Primeros pasos: Me llamo _____.** **¿Cómo se llama Ud.?**

All of these verbs can also be used nonreflexively, often with a different meaning. Some examples of this appear at the right:

**OJO** After **ponerse** and **quitarse,** the definite article, not the possessive as in English, is used with articles of clothing.

**Bright Idea Suggestion**
Point out that after the verbs *ponerse* and *quitarse,* the singular form of clothing is used in Spanish, whereas English frequently uses the plural. Compare the following.

The children take off their hats.
*Los niños se quitan el sombrero.*

[Práctica A–B, Paso 1]

**dormir** = to sleep  **dormirse** = to fall asleep
**poner** = to put, place  **ponerse** = to put on

Se pone **el** abrigo.  Se quitan **el** sombrero.
*He's putting on his coat.*  *They're taking off their hats.*

The children put on their coats.
*Los niños se ponen el abrigo.*

In some cases, where each individual has two of any given object, the plural form is used in Spanish.

*Se ponen los zapatos / los guantes / los calcetines.*

## Placement of Reflexive Pronouns

Reflexive pronouns are placed before a conjugated verb. In a negative sentence, they are placed in between the word **no** and the conjugated verb: **No** *se* **bañan.** When a conjugated verb is followed by an infinitive, the pronouns may either precede the conjugated verb or be attached to the infinitive.

[Práctica B, Paso 2]

**Me** tengo que levantar temprano.
Tengo que levantar**me** temprano.
*I have to get up early.*

**Prác. A: Variation**
Have students correct the sentences to express what they actually do.

■ **Práctica**

**A. ¡Anticipemos! Su rutina diaria** ¿Hace Ud. lo mismo (*the same thing*) todos los días? Indique si hace las siguientes cosas los lunes o los sábados. ¿Tiene Ud. una rutina diferente los sábados? ¿Prefiere el sábado o el lunes? ¿Por qué?

**1.** Me levanto antes de las ocho.
**2.** Siempre me baño o me ducho.
**3.** Siempre me afeito.
**4.** Me pongo un traje / un vestido / una falda.
**5.** Me quito los zapatos después de llegar a casa.
**6.** Me acuesto antes de las once de la noche.

**B. Mi rutina diaria**

PASO 1 ¿Qué acostumbra Ud. a hacer en un día típico? Use las siguientes frases para describir su rutina diaria. Añada (*Add*) otras ideas si quiere. Use las palabras de la **Nota comunicativa** en sus oraciones.

MODELO: despertarse / a (hora) → Me despierto a las siete (de la mañana). Luego,…

**1.** despertarse / a (hora)
**2.** levantarse / a (hora)
**3.** (no) ducharse o bañarse / por la mañana
**4.** vestirse / antes o después de tomar algo
**5.** ir / a / universidad / y / asistir / a (número) clases
**6.** sentarse / en (lugar) / para estudiar
**7.** volver / a / casa o apartamento o residencia / a (hora)
**8.** comer / con (persona[s]) o solo/a (*alone*)
**9.** acostarse / tarde o temprano
**10.** dormirse / a (hora)

PASO 2 Use las oraciones del **Paso 1** para indicar lo que Ud. va a hacer mañana. Añada información si puede.

MODELO: despertarse / a (hora) → Primero, voy a despertarme (me voy a despertar) a las diez. ¡Es sábado! Luego…

### NOTA COMUNICATIVA

**Sequence Expressions**

These phrases will help you indicate the sequence of events.

**primero** first      **luego** then, afterward
**después** later      **finalmente** finally
**entonces** then, next **por fin** finally

**Primero,** me ducho y me visto. **Entonces,** tomo un café y leo el periódico. **Luego,** salgo para el trabajo.

**Need more practice?**

■ Workbook/Laboratory Manual
■ Interactive CD-ROM
■ Online Learning Center
  (www.mhhe.com/quetal7)

**Con: Suggestions**
- **Paso 1.** Have students add two questions of their own.
- **Paso 2.** Have students compare a classmate's routine with their own: *Jim se levanta a las siete, pero yo me levanto a las ocho,* or *Jim y yo nos levantamos a las ocho,* and so on.

**Con: Follow-Up**
Have students explain in what room or part of the house they do the following activities. They should also tell what furniture they use. Have them work in pairs or trios to elaborate on their answers and ask for extra information. Remind them to use the appropriate reflexive pronouns with infinitives, for example: *Tengo que levantarme, Queremos divertirnos,* and so on. Emphasize that when two verbs appear in sequence, the reflexive object pronouns can be placed before the conjugated verb or come after and be attached to the infinitive. Students will learn more about object pronoun placement in *Capítulos 6, 7,* and *8.*

MODELO: *estudiar →*

*Cuando estudio, prefiero estar (por lo general estoy) en la alcoba. Uso el escritorio, una silla, los libros y la computadora.*

1. *estudiar*
2. *dormir la siesta*
3. *quitarse los zapatos*
4. *bañarse o ducharse*
5. *despertarse*
6. *tomar el desayuno*
7. *sentarse a almorzar*
8. *vestirse*
9. *divertirse*
10. *acostarse*

## ■ Conversación

### Entrevista: ¿Cómo es tu rutina diaria?

PASO 1   Con un compañero / una compañera, haga y conteste preguntas sobre su rutina diaria. Anote (*Jot down*) las respuestas de su compañero/a.

1. Los días de la semana (*weekdays*), ¿te levantas temprano? ¿antes de las siete de la mañana? ¿A qué hora te levantas los sábados?
2. ¿Te bañas o te duchas? ¿Cuándo lo haces (*do you do it*), por la mañana o por la noche?
3. ¿Te afeitas todos los días? ¿Usas una afeitadora eléctrica? ¿Prefieres no afeitarte los fines de semana?
4. Por lo general, ¿te vistes con elegancia o informalmente? ¿Qué ropa te pones cuando quieres estar elegante? ¿cuando quieres estar muy cómodo/a (*comfortable*)? ¿Qué te pones para ir a la universidad?
5. ¿A qué hora vuelves a casa, generalmente? ¿Qué haces cuando regresas? ¿Te quitas los zapatos? ¿Te pones ropa más cómoda? ¿Estudias? ¿Miras la televisión? ¿Preparas la cena (*dinner*)?
6. ¿A qué hora te acuestas? ¿Cuál es la última (*last*) cosa que haces antes de acostarte? ¿Cuál es la última cosa o persona en que piensas antes de dormirte?

PASO 2   Ahora, describa la rutina de su compañero/a a la clase, usando las respuestas del **Paso 1.** ¿Cuántos estudiantes de la clase tienen rutinas parecidas (*similar*)?

## En los Estados Unidos y el Canadá

### Las misiones de California

The twenty-one **misiones** in California along what was called **el Camino Real** (*the Royal Highway*) were founded between 1769 and 1817 as outposts for bringing the Catholic religion to new lands. The indigenous people of California whose territories were colonized by these first Spanish settlements were deeply impacted. Some groups eventually became known by the name of a nearby **misión**—for example, the **diegueños (Misión de San Diego),** the **luiseños (Misión de San Luis Obispo),** and the **gabrielinos (Misión de San Gabriel).** Many of these missions later became important cities, including San Diego, San Francisco, and Santa Barbara.

**En los Estados Unidos y el Canadá: Comprensión**
1. How many missions are there in California? (*¿Cuántas misiones hay en California?*)
2. What does *luiseño* mean? (*¿Qué significa* luiseño*?*)

*La Misión San Juan Capistrano en San Juan Capistrano, California*

## UN POCO DE TODO

**Lengua y cultura: Una visita a una familia «tica».**   Complete the following letter with the correct forms of the words in parentheses, as suggested by the context. When two possibilities are given in parentheses, select the correct word. In addition to reviewing vocabulary from previous chapters, you will decide when to use **ser** or **estar** in situations that you have already learned. You will learn more about **ser** and **estar** in **Capítulo 5.**

**Suggestion**
Point out that Costa Ricans often use the diminutives -ico/-tico and the nickname for their nationality is *ticos.* Have students think of nicknames given to people of different areas in this country, for example, *Hoosiers,* which is used to refer to people from Indiana.

**M**elissa, una estudiante de los Estados Unidos, está en Costa Rica por seis semanas con una familia «tica», es decir, costarricense. Este es uno de los primero mensajes electrónicos[a] que les manda[b] a sus amigos estadounidenses.

¡Hola a todos!

Por fin (*yo:* ir[1]) a contestar[c] todos (su/sus[2]) mensajes. Perdón por no escribir antes. Siempre (*yo:* estar[3]) ocupada con muchas actividades con mi familia de acá[d] y con mis clases.

En casa de los Arriaga, mi familia tica (las personas de Costa Rica [llamarse[4]] ticos y costarricenses), (*yo:* divertirse[5]) mucho porque todos son superamables. En general, todos los ticos (ser[6]) muy simpáticos con las personas (extranjero[7]). Siempre (*ellos:* venir[8]) a hablar conmigo[e] cuando (*yo:* estar/ser[9]) con mi familia y me[f] (hacer[10]) muchas preguntas sobre[g] los Estados Unidos. Muchos estadounidenses que visitan (este[11]) país no (tener[12]) ganas (de/en[13]) volver a casa.

La casa de mi familia (costarricense[14]), como[h] muchas otras casas de San José, es más pequeña que[i] (nuestro[15]) casas en Chicago. Está pintada de un azul claro[j] muy bonito; por aquí hay muchas otras casas pintadas de (unas/unos[16]) colores pastel que yo no (ver[17]) mucho en Illinois. Los ticos (tener[18]) las casas abiertas al aire libre[k] todo el día, porque la temperatura casi nunca (llegar[19])[l] a los 80° (grados). Por (eso/ese[20]), los ticos casi no tienen aire acondicionado. ¡Es (muy/mucho[21]) agradable!

Costa Rica es famosa por (su/sus[22]) parques nacionales y por la ecología. Los parques incluyen un 25 por ciento del país y (un/una[23]) variedad de volcanes, selvas[m] (tropical[24]) y playas. (*Yo:* Ir[25]) a visitar varios parques durante mi visita. También la familia Arriaga me quiere llevar a Sarchí, (un/una[26]) pueblo cerca de[n] San José. En Sarchí, uno (poder[27]) comprar muchas artesanías de Costa Rica. El pueblo también es famoso por (su/sus[28]) carretas[o] de brillantes colores.

Bueno, con esto, voy a despedirme[p] porque tengo (a/que[29]) (ducharse[30]). Si yo no (vestirse[31]) pronto, voy a (salir[32]) tarde para las clases.

Un abrazo muy fuerte,
Melissa.

[a]mensajes... *e-mails* [b]les... *she sends* [c]*answer* [d]*aquí* [e]*with me* [f]*of me* [g]*about* [h]*like* [i]*than* [j]*light* [k]*abiertas... open to fresh air* [l]*to get up to* [m]*jungles* [n]*cerca... close to* [o]*wooden carts* [p]*say good-bye*

**Comprensión: ¿Hay evidencia o no?** Decide whether there is evidence in Melissa's letter to support the following statements. For each statement, say **Sí, hay evidencia de esto** or **No, no hay evidencia de esto.** Change statements for which there is no evidence in the letter so that they will contain information that is included in the letter.

1. Melissa les escribe muchos mensajes a sus amigas estadounidenses.
2. Melissa toma clases en la universidad.
3. A Melissa le gusta mucho estar en Costa Rica.
4. Los ticos tienen cierta curiosidad acerca de (*about*) los estadounidenses.
5. Melissa prefiere las casas de los Estados Unidos.
6. Los ticos no tienen mucha necesidad del aire acondicionado.

**Resources: Transparency 36**
Transparency 36 provides additional practice with stem-changing verbs.

El Parque Nacional Cahuita, en Costa Rica

**Lengua y cultura: Answers**
1. *voy* 2. *sus* 3. *estoy* 4. *se llaman* 5. *me divierto* 6. *son* 7. *extranjeras* 8. *vienen* 9. *estoy* 10. *hacen* 11. *este* 12. *tienen* 13. *de* 14. *costarricense* 15. *nuestras* 16. *unos* 17. *veo* 18. *tienen* 19. *llega* 20. *eso* 21. *muy* 22. *sus* 23. *una* 24. *tropicales* 25. *Voy* 26. *un* 27. *puede* 28. *sus* 29. *que* 30. *ducharme* 31. *me visto* 32. *salir* **Comprensión** 1. *No, no hay evidencia de esto. Marisa no les escribe muchos mensajes a sus amigas estadounidenses.* 2. *Sí, hay evidencia de esto.* 3. *Sí, hay evidencia de esto.* 4. *Sí, hay evidencia de esto.* 5. *No, no hay evidencia de esto. Marisa piensa que las casas de Costa Rica son bonitas.* 6. *Sí, hay evidencia de esto.*

**Resources: Desenlace**
In the *Capítulo 4* section of "Chapter-by-Chapter Supplementary Materials" in the IM, you will find a chapter-culminating activity. You can use this activity to consolidate and review the vocabulary and grammar skills students have acquired.

**Heritage Speakers**
Invite a sus estudiantes hispanohablantes a inventar diálogos basados en los dibujos para presentar a la clase. Luego, los otros estudiantes pueden hacerles preguntas sobre los diálogos.

**Resources for Review and Testing Preparation**

- Workbook/Laboratory Manual
- Interactive CD-ROM
- Online Learning Center (www.mhhe.com/quetal7)

# PASO 4 Un paso más

**Paso 4: Un paso más**
• The *Paso 4: Un paso más* sections are optional.
• See the "Chapter-by-Chapter Supplementary Materials" in the IM for additional teaching suggestions, notes, activities, and other resources for *Paso 4*.

**Entrevista cultural: Suggestions**

• Before showing the video, ask students questions about where they work. If they do not work during the school year, ask if they work during the summer.

*¿Dónde trabaja Ud.?*
*¿Cuántas horas por semana trabaja?*
*¿Cuáles son sus responsabilidades en el trabajo?*

• Show the video and allow students one to two minutes to work on the questions. Encourage them to answer in Spanish if possible. You might want to ask the questions in Spanish when you review the answers as a class.

1. *¿En qué ciudad trabaja Alexander?*
2. *¿Qué hace para sus clientes?*
3. *¿Qué diferencias hay entre una casa «típica» en la ciudad y una fuera de la ciudad?*
4. *¿Cómo describe la diferencia entre un apartamento amueblado y un apartamento sin muebles? ¿Qué muebles menciona?*
5. *¿Tiene Alexander su propia casa?*

Have volunteers answer the questions.

• Have volunteers role-play Alexander and the interviewer.

**Entrevista cultural: Answers**
**1.** *San José* **2.** *mostrarles casas* **3.** *En la ciudad hay muchos apartamentos y condominios. Fuera de la ciudad hay más casas particulares con patio.* **4.** *Un apartamento amueblado tiene de todo, por ejemplo, refrigerador, cocina y camas. Un apartamento sin muebles no tiene nada de eso.* **5.** *no*

## VIDEOTECA

### Entrevista cultural: Costa Rica

Alexander Burbón is a Costa Rican who works in real estate. In this interview he talks about his country and his work. One topic he discusses is the "typical" Costa Rican home. Before watching the video clip, read the following excerpt from the interview.

INTERVIEWER: ¿Cómo te llamas tú y en dónde trabajas?

ALEXANDER: Mi nombre es Alexander Burbón y trabajo en Costa Rica en una compañía de bienes raíces[a] que queda[b] en San José, en la capital. Eh, los bienes raíces, básicamente lo que yo hago es ir y mostrarles casas a personas que las quieren comprar o alquilar.[c] Y entonces, luego, los ayudo con los trámites[d] para comprar o para alquilar.

[a]bienes... *real estate* [b]está [c]*rent* [d]*details*

Now watch the video clip and answer the following questions based on the interview.

1. In what city does Alexander work?
2. What does he do for his clients?
3. What differences are there between a "typical" home in the city and outside the city?
4. How does he describe the difference between a furnished and unfurnished apartment? What items does he mention?
5. Does Alexander own his home?

### Entre amigos: Quiero cambiar los muebles.

Rubén is waiting for Karina when Tané arrives. Tané is going shopping for furniture. What questions do you think they will ask each other? Before watching the video, read the following questions. As you watch, don't worry if you don't understand every word. Try to get the gist of the conversation, listening carefully for information about their plans for the day. Watch the video a second time and listen for the answers to the questions.

1. ¿Por qué espera Rubén a Karina?
2. ¿Trabaja Rubén mucho o poco? ¿Cuándo estudia?
3. ¿Por qué está cansada (*tired*) Karina?
4. ¿Adónde va Rubén?

**Entre amigos: Suggestions**
• Before viewing the video, review the questions with the students and ask them related questions. *¿Trabaja Ud. mucho? ¿Cuándo estudia? ¿Qué muebles tiene Ud. en su cuarto/casa? ¿Desea Ud. comprar muebles nuevos?* Have volunteers describe the furniture they have and tell what furniture they would like to buy.

Have students answer or work in small groups to ask and answer these questions.
• After viewing the video, have volunteers read and answer the questions.

**Entre amigos: Answers**
**1.** *Karina le trae un libro.* **2.** *Trabaja mucho. Estudia entre clases.* **3.** *No durmió (give preterite form) anoche.* **4.** *Va a trabajar.*

ENFOQUE CULTURAL

### Costa Rica

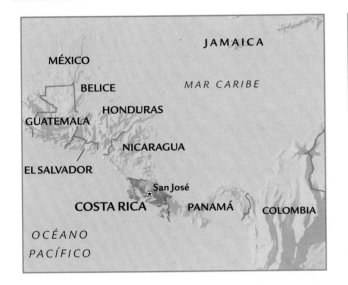

## ¡Fíjese!

- El ecoturismo es importante para la economía de Costa Rica y para la preservación de la biodiversidad y la belleza[a] natural que existe en el país. El ecoturismo tiene como propósito[b] controlar la entrada[c] de turistas en regiones protegidas[d] y, a la vez,[e] obtener fondos[f] para continuar con la protección de las regiones naturales. Aproximadamente un treinta por ciento (%) del territorio costarricense está cubierto de selvas o bosques.[g] En total, más de un cuarto[h] del territorio del país ha sido destinado[i] para la preservación.

- Costa Rica es una de las primeras democracias de las Américas. En 1821, convocaron[j] las primeras elecciones. Costa Rica tiene tres ramas[k] gubernamentales: ejecutiva (un presidente y dos vicepresidentes), legislativa y judicial. Es notable que Costa Rica no tiene un esfuerzo militar[l] permanente. Muchos consideran que Costa Rica es «la Suiza[m] de las Américas» porque es un país «amistoso»[n] que se mantiene neutro durante conflictos entre naciones. A menudo[o] los líderes de Costa Rica intervienen para negociar la paz[p] durante un conflicto internacional.

[a]*beauty* [b]*purpose* [c]*entrance* [d]*protected* [e]*a… at the same time* [f]*funds* [g]*está… is covered with jungles or forests* [h]*fourth* [i]*ha… has been set aside* [j]*they held* [k]*branches* [l]*esfuerzo… military force* [m]*Switzerland* [n]*friendly* [o]*A… Often* [p]*peace*

## Personas famosas: Óscar Arias Sánchez

Óscar Arias Sánchez (1941– ), presidente de Costa Rica de 1986 a 1990, asistió a[a] la Universidad de Costa Rica, a Boston University y a otras universidades en Inglaterra.[b] En 1987, Arias recibió[c] el Premio Nóbel de la Paz[d] por sus esfuerzos[e] por aliviar las tensiones entre el gobierno sandinista de Nicaragua y los Estados Unidos. El acuerdo de paz[f] de Arias se firmó[g] en 1986. Desde 1990, se encarga de[h] la Fundación Arias para la paz y el progreso humano.

[a]*asistió… attended* [b]*England* [c]*received* [d]*Premio… Nobel Peace Prize* [e]*efforts* [f]*acuerdo… peace agreement* [g]*se… was signed* [h]*se… he has been running*

*Óscar Arias Sánchez*

**Notes**

- Costa Rica was not developed as a Spanish colony to the same extent that other Central American countries were. A number of factors caused this. Costa Rica was geographically distant from Guatemala, the seat of Spanish government, and it did not have extensive mineral resources, nor the abundant indigenous work force to develop those that did exist. As a result, the few settlers that arrived turned to agriculture.
- Costa Rica currently has a parliamentary democracy and an advanced social welfare system.
- Students can read "XLVII," a poem by Costa Rica's Carmen Naranjo in *Voces de Costa Rica: Literatura.*

Learn more about Costa Rica with the Video, the Interactive CD-ROM, and the Online Learning Center (www.mhhe.com/quetal7).

- Students can read about Costa Rica's *marimba* and *punto guanacaste* traditions in *Voces de Costa Rica: Música.*
- See the Workbook/Laboratory Manual for focused practice with the material in *Enfoque cultural.*

PASO 4

## PASO FINAL

 **A CONVERSAR**

**Compartiendo° casa**                                    *Sharing*

Imagine that you and two classmates live in the same house. There's only one bedroom, one living room, and one kitchen. While you all get along, you don't always want to do the same things together. Try to come up with a plan for sharing the house.

PASO 1   Working individually, write three sentences for each room, describing what you do in that room and at what time.

> MODELO:   la sala → Leo el periódico por la mañana antes de ir a clase (a eso de [*around*] las siete y media). Miro la televisión por la noche, después de hacer la tarea (a eso de las nueve). Me gusta leer una novela antes de dormir (a eso de las once).

PASO 2   Take turns telling what you do and when in the three rooms. If there is a conflict of time or activity, try to reach a compromise.

> MODELO:   E1: Me ducho por la mañana antes de desayunar, a eso de las seis y media.
> E2: Yo también me ducho a eso de las seis y media.
> E1: Está bien. Yo puedo ducharme primero, a las seis.

PASO 3   As a group, create schedules for the three rooms. Use a separate sheet of paper to create a schedule for each room similar to the one below for Juan, María, and Esteban.

MODELO:

| Hora | El baño | La sala | La cocina |
|------|---------|---------|-----------|
| 6:00 | Juan: ducharse | María: leer el periódico | |
| 6:30 | María: ducharse | | Esteban y Juan: desayunar |
| 7:00 | | | María: desayunar |

**Variation**
Have students try to find the perfect house-mates by first interviewing as many class-mates as possible about their routines. If two potential roommates find each other, they should look for a third together.

**Suggestion**
For writing practice, see the *Mi diario* activity in each chapter of the Workbook/ Laboratory Manual.

**Suggestions**
• Have students play Hangman using different groups of words.
• Play password with the house vocabulary. The cues may not include the target word or any form of it. You can divide the class into two teams, and while one member takes a turn giving a cue the other team members try to guess the word.

## GRAMÁTICA

To review the grammar points presented in this chapter, refer to the indicated grammar presentations. You'll find further practice of these structures in the Workbook/Laboratory Manual, on the Interactive CD-ROM, and on the *¿Qué tal?* Online Learning Center (www.mhhe.com/quetal7).

**11** Expressing Actions—**Hacer, oír, poner, salir, traer,** and **ver**

Do you know the forms of **hacer, oír, poner, salir, traer,** and **ver** and how to use them?

**12** Expressing Actions—Present Tense of Stem-Changing Verbs

Do you know the forms of verbs like **pensar (ie), volver (ue),** and **pedir (i)?**

**13** Expressing -*self*/-*selves*—Reflexive Pronouns

You should be able to talk about your daily routine using reflexive verbs like **levantarse, bañarse,** and **afeitarse.**

## VOCABULARIO

Practice this vocabulary with digital flash cards on the Online Learning Center (www.mhhe.com/quetal7).

### Los verbos

| | |
|---|---|
| **almorzar (ue)** | to have lunch |
| **cerrar (ie)** | to close |
| **contestar** | to answer |
| **descansar** | to rest |
| **dormir (ue)** | to sleep |
|   **dormir la siesta** | to take a nap |
| **empezar (ie)** | to begin |
|   **empezar a** + *inf.* | to begin to (*do something*) |
| **entender (ie)** | to understand |
| **hacer** (*irreg.*) | to do; to make |
|   **hacer ejercicio** | to exercise |
|   **hacer un viaje** | to take a trip |
|   **hacer una pregunta** | to ask a question |
| **jugar (ue) (al)** | to play (*a game, sport*) |
| **oír** (*irreg.*) | to hear |
| **pedir (i)** | to ask for; to order |
| **pensar (ie) (en)** | to think (about); to intend, plan to |
| **perder (ie)** | to lose; to miss (*a function*) |
| **poner** (*irreg.*) | to put; to place; to turn on (*appliances*) |
| **salir** (*irreg.*) **(de)/ (para)/(con)** | to leave (*a place*); to leave (for/to) (*a place*); to go out (with) |
| **servir (i)** | to serve |
| **traer** (*irreg.*) | to bring |
| **ver** (*irreg.*) | to see |

| | |
|---|---|
| **volver (ue)** | to return (*to a place*) |
|   **volver a** + *inf.* | to (*do something*) again |

### Los verbos reflexivos

| | |
|---|---|
| **acostarse (ue)** | to go to bed |
| **afeitarse** | to shave |
| **bañarse** | to take a bath |
| **cepillarse los dientes** | to brush one's teeth |
| **despertarse (ie)** | to wake up |
| **divertirse (ie)** | to have a good time, enjoy oneself |
| **dormirse (ue)** | to fall asleep |
| **ducharse** | to take a shower |
| **levantarse** | to get up; to stand up |
| **llamarse** | to be called |
| **peinarse** | to comb one's hair |
| **ponerse** (*irreg.*) | to put on (*clothing*) |
| **quitarse** | to take off (*clothing*) |
| **sentarse (ie)** | to sit down |
| **vestirse (i)** | to get dressed |

### Los cuartos y otras partes de una casa

| | |
|---|---|
| **la alcoba** | bedroom |
| **el baño** | bathroom |
| **la cocina** | kitchen |
| **el comedor** | dining room |
| **el jardín** | yard |

• Write the following on the board.

*Ayer fue _____.*
*Hoy es _____. _____ voy a _____.*
*Pero antes, tengo que _____.*
*Después voy a _____.*
*Por lo general, _____ todos los _____.*

Have students complete these sentences in writing, using vocabulary to fill the blanks. Then ask them to share sentences and correct them with a partner. Have several students read their sentences aloud.

| la pared | wall |
|---|---|
| el patio | patio; yard |
| la piscina | swimming pool |
| la sala | living room |

Cognado: el garaje

## Los muebles y otras cosas de una casa

| la alfombra | rug |
|---|---|
| el armario | closet |
| la bañera | bathtub |
| la cama (de agua) | (water) bed |
| la cómoda | bureau; dresser |
| el estante | bookshelf |
| la lámpara | lamp |
| el lavabo | (bathroom) sink |
| la mesita | end table |
| los muebles | furniture |
| los platos | dishes; plates |
| el sillón | armchair |
| el sofá | sofa |
| el televisor | television set |

Repaso: el escritorio, la mesa, la silla

## Otros sustantivos

| el ajedrez | chess |
|---|---|
| el cine | movies; movie theater |
| el desayuno | breakfast |
| el/la muchacho/a | boy / girl |
| la película | movie |
| el ruido | noise |
| la rutina diaria | daily routine |
| la tarea | homework |

## Los adjetivos

| cada (*inv.*)* | each, every |
|---|---|
| cómodo/a | comfortable |
| siguiente | following |

## Las preposiciones

| antes de | before |
|---|---|
| después de | after |
| durante | during |
| hasta | until |
| por | during; for |
| sin | without |

Repaso: a, con, de, en, para, por (in)

## ¿Cuándo?

**Los días de la semana**
  lunes
  martes
  miércoles
  jueves
  viernes
  sábado
  domingo

| ayer fue (miércoles) | yesterday was (Wednesday) |
|---|---|
| pasado mañana | the day after tomorrow |
| el próximo (martes) | next (Tuesday) |
| la semana que viene | next week |

Repaso: el fin de semana, hoy, mañana

## Palabras adicionales

| lo que | what |
|---|---|
| luego | then; afterwards |
| por fin | finally |
| por lo general | generally |
| primero | first |

• Have students write a paragraph about an activity that they perform routinely. Ask them to use as many of the new prepositions as possible and to:

1. tell when they perform this activity,
2. where they perform it, and
3. what steps they take and in what order.

*The abbreviation inv. means invariable in form. The adjective **cada** is used with masculine and feminine nouns **(cada libro, cada mesa),** and it is never used in the plural.*

**Suggestions**
• Point out the chapter-opener photo. Have students talk about the climate in their area and their ideas about climate in Spanish-speaking countries. Encourage them to describe the scene in the photo, and compare it to their own experience and/or ideas.

# Las estaciones y el tiempo°

Ask students: *¿Qué tiempo hace en el sitio que se ve en la foto? Hace sol, ¿verdad? Pero, ¿creen que hace frío?* (pantomime)

°**Las...** *The seasons and the weather*

# CAPÍTULO

# 5

• Have students tell their ideas about Guatemala, including information on geography, politics, economy, culture, music, and cuisine. When you finish the chapter, return to the lists and ask students what ideas they would change and/or add.

## CULTURA

- **Nota cultural:** El Niño
- **En los Estados Unidos y el Canadá:** Alfredo Jaar: América y su expresión artística
- **Voces** de Guatemala
  **Literatura:** Miguel Ángel Asturias
  **Música:** La marimba y la banda cívica
- **Videoteca**
  **Entrevista cultural:** Guatemala
  **Entre amigos:** ¡A mí me encanta el verano!
- **Enfoque cultural:** Guatemala
- **A leer:** Todos juntos en los trópicos

## VOCABULARIO

- ¿Qué tiempo hace hoy?
- Los meses y las estaciones del año
- ¿Dónde está? Las preposiciones

## GRAMÁTICA

14 Present Progressive: **estar** + **-ndo**

15 Summary of the Uses of **ser** and **estar**

16 Comparisons

*Unos catamaranes en el lago Atitlán, en Guatemala*

♻ **Reciclado**
Review clothing and parts of the house. Ask questions that relate weather to those topics.

**1.** *¿Qué deben llevar las personas en este clima?*

**2.** *¿Qué llevan Uds. cuando hace calor? ¿Y cuando hace frío?*

**3.** *¿Dónde prefiere Ud. estar (en su casa) cuando hace frío? ¿cuando hace calor?*

¿Qué... What's the weather like today?

*Resources: Transparency 37*

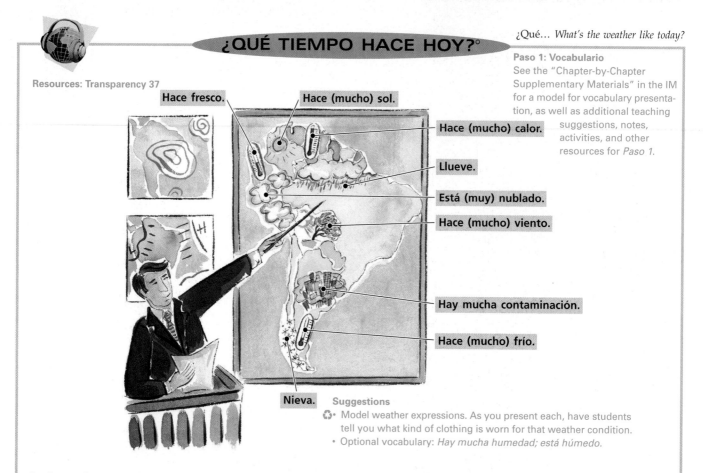

**¿QUÉ TIEMPO HACE HOY?**

- Hace fresco.
- Hace (mucho) sol.
- Hace (mucho) calor.
- Llueve.
- Está (muy) nublado.
- Hace (mucho) viento.
- Hay mucha contaminación.
- Hace (mucho) frío.
- Nieva.

**Suggestions**
- Model weather expressions. As you present each, have students tell you what kind of clothing is worn for that weather condition.
- Optional vocabulary: *Hay mucha humedad; está húmedo.*

In Spanish, many weather conditions are expressed with **hace.** The adjective **mucho** is used with the nouns **frío, calor, viento,** and **sol** to express *very.*

> **Hace (muy) buen/mal tiempo.**   It's (very) good/bad weather. The weather is (very) good/bad.

*Pronunciation hint:* Remember that, in most parts of the Spanish-speaking world, **ll** is pronounced exactly like **y: llueve.**

### ■ Conversación

**A. El tiempo y la ropa.**   Diga qué tiempo hace, según la ropa de cada persona.

MODELO:   Miami: Todos llevan traje de baño y sandalias. →
Hace calor. (Hace buen tiempo.)

1. San Diego: María lleva pantalones cortos y una camiseta.
2. Madison: Juan lleva suéter, pero no lleva chaqueta.
3. Toronto: Roberto lleva suéter y chaqueta.
4. San Miguel de Allende, México: Ramón lleva impermeable y botas y también tiene paraguas (*umbrella*).
5. Buenos Aires, Argentina: Todos llevan abrigo, botas y sombrero.

**B. Consejos** (*Advice*) **para Joaquín.** Joaquín es de Valencia, España. El clima (*climate*) allí es mediterráneo: hace mucho sol y las temperaturas son moderadas. No hay mucha contaminación.

PASO 1 Joaquín tiene una lista de lugares que desea visitar en los Estados Unidos. Con un compañero / una compañera, ayúdelo (*help him*) con información sobre el clima. Como Joaquín no sabe (*As Joaquín doesn't know*) en qué estación va a viajar (*travel*), es bueno ofrecerle información sobre el clima de todo el año (*year*).

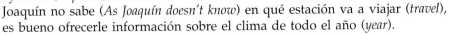

1. Seattle, Washington
2. Los Ángeles, California
3. Phoenix, Arizona
4. Buffalo, Nueva York
5. las islas hawaianas
6. Chicago, Illinois

PASO 2 Es obvio que la lista de Joaquín no está completa. ¿Qué otros tres lugares cree Ud. que debe visitar? ¿Qué clima hace allí?

**C. El tiempo y las actividades.** Haga oraciones completas, indicando una actividad apropiada para cada situación.

cuando llueve
cuando hace buen/mal tiempo
cuando hace calor
cuando hace frío
cuando nieva
cuando hay mucha contaminación

**+**

me quedo (*I stay*) en cama/casa
juego al basquetbol/vólibol con mis amigos
almuerzo afuera (*outside*) / en el parque
me divierto en el parque / en la playa (*beach*) con mis amigos
no salgo de casa
vuelvo a casa y trabajo o estudio

## NOTA COMUNICATIVA

### More *tener* Idioms

More conditions expressed in Spanish with **tener** idioms—not with *to be*, as in English—include the following.

| | |
|---|---|
| **tener (mucho) calor** | to be (very) warm, hot |
| **tener (mucho) frío** | to be (very) cold |

These expressions are used to describe people or animals only. To be comfortable—neither hot nor cold—is expressed with **estar bien.**

**D. ¿Tienen frío o calor? ¿Están bien?** Describe the following weather conditions, and tell how the people depicted are feeling.

1.  2.  3.  4.  5.  6.  7.

**Con. B: Follow-Up**
Ask students the following questions.

1. ¿Llueve mucho en Inglaterra? ¿en el desierto Sahara?
2. ¿Nieva mucho en el Brasil? ¿en Minnesota?
3. ¿Hace mucho frío en Siberia? ¿en el Ecuador?
4. ¿Hace mucho sol en la Florida? ¿en España?
5. ¿Hace calor en Panamá? ¿en Alaska?

**Con. C: Suggestion**
Ask students if they do the following things when it is hot.

*Cuando hace calor...*

1. ¿bebe Ud. agua, refrescos (new word) o cerveza? ¿o jugo de fruta?
2. ¿prefiere estar en casa o afuera?
3. ¿prefiere estar en el parque o en la playa?
4. ¿juega al tenis (al golf, etcétera) o duerme?

**Nota comunicativa: Suggestions**
• With *tener* + noun expressions, *very* is expressed with *mucho/a*: tener mucho frío/calor; tener muchas ganas.
• Point out that *tener* means *to feel* in these idioms.
• Point out that *to have a cold* in Spanish is *tener catarro* or *tener gripe*.

**Con. D: Preliminary Exercise**
Ask students the following questions before beginning the activity.

1. ¿Qué tiempo hace hoy?
2. Imagine que hoy es un día fatal. ¿Qué tiempo hace hoy?
3. Hoy es un día estupendo. ¿Qué tiempo hace hoy?

**Con. D: Answers**
*Possible answers:* **1.** *Nieva y hace frío. El niño tiene mucho frío.* **2.** *Hace mucho sol y calor. El hombre tiene mucho calor.* **3.** *Hace mucho viento. El hombre no está bien.* **4.** *Llueve mucho. La mujer tiene frío.* **5.** *Hay mucha contaminación. El hombre no está bien.* **6.** *Hace buen tiempo. Las personas están muy bien.* **7.** *Hace fresco por la noche. Las personas están bien.*

**Resources:** Transparency 38

# PASO 1

## LOS MESES Y LAS ESTACIONES DEL AÑO

**♻Reciclado**
Review numbers and years with the following questions.

*¿En qué año estamos?*
*¿En qué año nació Ud.?*
*¿En qué año nació su padre*
*(madre, abuela, etcétera)?*
*¿En qué año piensa graduarse?*

**Suggestions**
• Model months of the year, linking them to seasons.

*Los meses de otoño son*
*septiembre, octubre y*
*noviembre, ¿verdad?*

*Los meses de verano son mayo,*
*junio y julio, ¿no?*
and so on.

Then ask students what the weather is like in each season:

*En muchas partes de este país hace frío*
*en enero, ¿cierto o falso?*
*También nieva mucho en julio, ¿cierto*
*o falso?*

• Point out that September has two accepted spellings: *septiembre* and *setiembre*.
• Remind students that months are not capitalized in Spanish.

**Refrán**

«Febrerillo, mes loquillo.»

Write the *refrán* on the board. Point out that *-illo* is a Spanish diminutive. Ask students why they think the diminutive is used here and why February would be a "crazy" month.

**Resources: Transparency 39**

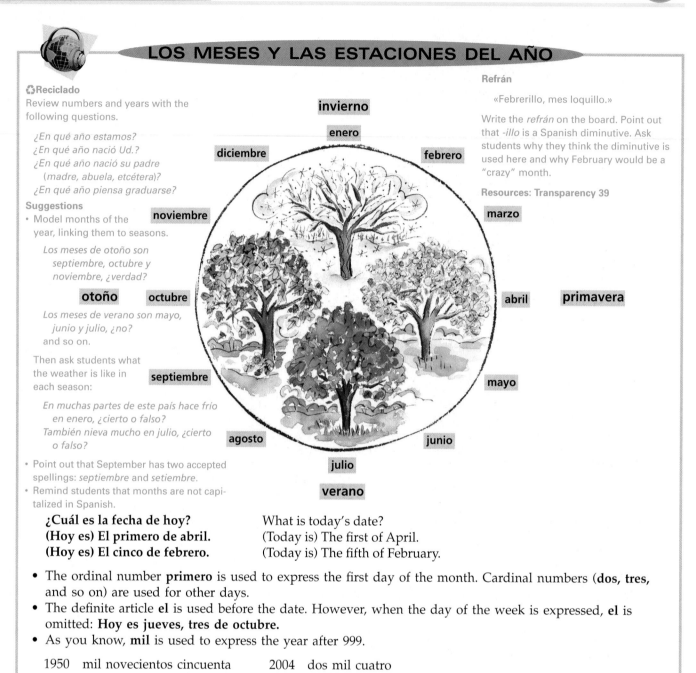

invierno
enero
diciembre
febrero
noviembre
marzo
otoño    octubre
abril    primavera
septiembre
mayo
agosto    junio
julio
verano

| **¿Cuál es la fecha de hoy?** | What is today's date? |
| **(Hoy es) El primero de abril.** | (Today is) The first of April. |
| **(Hoy es) El cinco de febrero.** | (Today is) The fifth of February. |

• The ordinal number **primero** is used to express the first day of the month. Cardinal numbers (**dos, tres,** and so on) are used for other days.
• The definite article **el** is used before the date. However, when the day of the week is expressed, **el** is omitted: **Hoy es jueves, tres de octubre.**
• As you know, **mil** is used to express the year after 999.

1950   mil novecientos cincuenta          2004   dos mil cuatro

**Con. A: Answers**
1. *El doce es lunes.* 2. *El primero es jueves.*
3. *El veinte es martes.* 4. *El dieciséis (diez y seis) es viernes.* 5. *El once es domingo.* 6. *El cuatro es domingo.* 7. *El veintinueve (veinte y nueve) es jueves.*

## ■ Conversación

A. **El mes de noviembre.** Mire este calendario para el mes de noviembre. ¿Qué día de la semana es el 12 (1, 20, 16, 11, 4, 29) de noviembre?

MODELO: ¿Qué día de la semana es el 5 de noviembre? → El 5 es lunes.

## B. Fechas

PASO 1  Exprese estas fechas en español. ¿En qué estación caen (*do they fall*)?

1. March 7
2. August 24
3. December 1
4. June 5

5. September 19, 1997
6. May 30, 1842
7. January 31, 1660
8. July 4, 1776

PASO 2  ¿Cuándo se celebran? ¿Y en qué día de la semana caen (*do they fall*) este año?

1. el Día de la Raza (*Columbus Day*)   el 12 de octubre
2. el Día del Año Nuevo   el primero de enero
3. el Día de los Enamorados (de San Valentín)   el 14 de febrero
4. el Día de la Independencia de los Estados Unidos   el 4 de julio
5. el Día de los Inocentes (*Fools*), en los Estados Unidos   el primero de abril
6. la Navidad (*Christmas*)   el 25 de diciembre
7. su cumpleaños (*birthday*)   *Answers vary.*
8. el cumpleaños de su novio/a (*boy/girlfriend*), esposo/a, mejor (*best*) amigo/a...   *Answers vary.*

**Con. B: Notes**

• Point out that the Hispanic *Día de los Inocentes* (December 28) is a religious holiday (Catholic) commemorating the day King Herod had all babies slaughtered in Bethlehem.

• Friday the 13th is considered to be a day of bad luck in this country. In Spanish-speaking countries, however, it's *martes trece*.

 Note that the word **se** before a verb changes the verb's meaning slightly. **¿Cuándo se celebran?** = *When are they celebrated?* You will see this construction throughout *¿Qué tal?* Learn to recognize it, for it is frequently used in Spanish.

**Heritage Speakers**

Pregúnteles a los hispanohablantes de su clase qué días festivos celebran. Pídales que describan las celebraciones.

---

## NOTA CULTURAL

### El Niño

**Nota cultural: Comprensión**
1. With what celebration or religious figure is the name of the El Niño phenomenon associated? (*¿Con qué celebración o figura religiosa se asocia el nombre del fenómeno El Niño?*)

Most people have heard of El Niño, a weather phenomenon that is often associated with devastating climatic events. But why is it called El Niño?

The name El Niño dates from the end of the nineteenth century, when Peruvian fishermen noticed the periodic appearance of an abnormally warm ocean current off the coast of Peru. This warm current made its appearance around Christmas time. The name *El Niño* is a reference to the Christ Child, or El Niño Jesús, whose birth is celebrated by Christians at Christmas. At the time the name only referred to the current. Nowadays, it is used to refer to the meteorological phenomenon as a whole. Torrential rains, flooding, and landslides can occur from the southwestern United States to Peru, whereas in Australia, Indonesia, and southeast Africa, the opposite may happen: severe droughts and the potential for destructive fires.   2. What climate conditions are associated with El Niño? (*¿Qué condiciones climáticas se asocian con El Niño?*)

*Destrucción causada* (caused) *en California por* (by) *El Niño*

## C. Entrevista: ¡Feliz (*Happy*) cumpleaños!

Entreviste a un compañero / una compañera de clase acerca de (*about*) su cumpleaños. Use las siguientes preguntas.

1. ¿Cuál es la fecha de tu cumpleaños? ¿Cuál es tu signo del horóscopo?
2. ¿En qué estación es tu cumpleaños?
3. Generalmente, ¿qué tiempo hace en tu ciudad el día de tu cumpleaños?
4. ¿Cómo celebras tu cumpleaños? (por lo menos tres actividades)
5. ¿Con quién(es) prefieres celebrar tu cumpleaños?

| Los signos del horóscopo | |
|---|---|
| Aries | Libra |
| Tauro | Escorpión |
| Géminis | Sagitario |
| Cáncer | Capricornio |
| Leo | Acuario |
| Virgo | Piscis |

**Con. C: Note**

Point out the difference between *la fecha de cumpleaños* and *la fecha de nacimiento*.

**Suggestion**
Have students locate their country, city, or university using these prepositions. Write model sentences on the board.

*España está al lado de Portugal en la Península Ibérica. Está al sur de Francia y al norte de África.*

## ¿DÓNDE ESTÁ? • LAS PREPOSICIONES

La silla está **a la derecha de** la puerta.

Teresa está **entre** Carmen y Pablito.

El libro está **encima de** la mesa.

La mochila está **debajo de** la mesa.

| | |
|---|---|
| **cerca de** | close to |
| **lejos de** | far from |
| **encima de** | on top of |
| **debajo de** | below |
| **al lado de** | alongside of |
| **entre** | between, among |
| **delante de** | in front of |
| **detrás de** | behind |
| **a la izquierda de** | to the left of |
| **a la derecha de** | to the right of |
| **al este/oeste/** | to the east/west/ |
| **norte/sur de** | north/south of |

Resources: Transparency 40

*Nueva York está al norte de Miami. México está al sur de los Estados Unidos.*

**Bright Idea Suggestion**
Teach students the following rhyme with hand signals.

*Izquierda, derecha, delante, detrás,*
*cerca, lejos y algo más,*
*abajo, arriba, debajo, encima,*
*y ahora, señores, se acaba la rima.*

## ■ Conversación

**OJO** Note that **mí** has a written accent, but **ti** does not. This is to distinguish the object of a preposition (**mí**) from the possessive adjective (**mi**).

## NOTA COMUNICATIVA

### Los pronombres preposicionales

In Spanish, the pronouns that serve as objects of prepositions are identical in form to the subject pronouns, except for **mí** and **ti**.

| | |
|---|---|
| Julio está delante de **mí**. | *Julio is in front of me.* |
| María está detrás de **ti**. | *María is behind you.* |
| Me siento a la izquierda de **ella**. | *I sit on her left.* |

**Mí** and **ti** combine with the preposition **con** to form **conmigo** (*with me*) and **contigo** (*with you*), respectively.

| | |
|---|---|
| ¿Vienes **conmigo**? | *Are you coming with me?* |
| Sí, voy **contigo**. | *Yes, I'll go with you.* |

**Heritage Speakers**
Invite a los hispanohablantes a explicar la diferencia entre *delante de* y *enfrente de*. Pídales que den ejemplos de las dos expresiones.

Con. A: Variation

Play Ten Questions. Think of a person or object in the classroom. Students are allowed ten yes/no questions to locate and identify the person or object, for example, *¿Está lejos de la puerta?* Follow up with students thinking of the object or person.

**A. ¿Quién?/¿Qué es?** Describa a una persona o una cosa en la sala de clase, sin nombrarla (*without naming him/her/it*), usando (*using*) las preposiciones y los pronombres preposicionales. Su compañero/a debe adivinar (*guess*) quién o qué es la persona o cosa descrita.

MODELO: E1: Está a la derecha de nosotros ahora, pero a veces se sienta detrás de mí. Siempre llega a clase contigo.

E2: Es Antonio.

**B. Entrevista: ¿De dónde eres?** Find out as much information as you can about the location of each others' hometown or state, or about the country you are from. You should also tell what the weather is like, and ask if the other person would like to go there with you.

MODELO: E1: ¿De dónde eres?

E2: Soy de Tylertown.

E1: ¿Dónde está Tylertown?

E2: Está cerca de…

**C. ¿De qué país se habla?**

PASO 1 Escuche la descripción que da (*gives*) su profesor(a) de un país de Sudamérica. ¿Puede Ud. identificar el país?

PASO 2 Ahora describa un país de Sudamérica. Sus compañeros de clase van a identificarlo. Siga (*Follow*) el modelo, usando (*using*) todas las frases que sean (*are*) apropiadas.

MODELO: Este país está al norte/sur/este/oeste de _____.
También está cerca de _____.
Pero está lejos de _____. Está entre _____ y _____. ¿Cómo se llama?

Con. C: Suggestion

Use the following description as a model for describing other countries: *Este país está al sur de los Estados Unidos. También está cerca de Panamá. Pero está lejos de la Argentina. ¿Cómo se llama?* (*Colombia*)

Con. C: Variation

Have students give information about the location of their hometown or state, or about

the country you are from, as well as about the weather there.

MODELO: *Soy de Sevilla. Está en el sur de España, cerca de África. En el verano hace mucho calor, pero nunca hace mucho frío. Por lo general, no llueve mucho, pero llueve en el otoño, el invierno y parte de la primavera. Casi nunca llueve en verano.*

PASO 3 A la derecha hay una lista de los nombres de las capitales de varios países de Sudamérica. Sin mirar el mapa, empareje (*match*) los nombres con el país correspondiente.

MODELO: _____ es la capital de _____.

| Capitales | |
|---|---|
| Asunción | La Paz |
| Bogotá | Lima |
| Brasilia | Montevideo |
| Buenos Aires | Quito |
| Caracas | Santiago |

Multimedia: Internet

Have students search the Internet for more information about South America's geography, climate, people, economy, transportation, and military. You might assign different countries and have students give brief oral presentations about the geography and climate of their assigned country.

**Need more practice?**

- Workbook/Laboratory Manual
- Interactive CD-ROM
- Online Learning Center (www.mhhe.com/quetal7)

Note

See the Workbook/Laboratory Manual for presentation and practice of the letters *r* and *rr*.

**Paso 2: Gramática**
See the "Chapter-by-Chapter Supplementary Materials" in the IM for additional
teaching suggestions, notes, activities, and other resources for *Paso 2*.

**Suggestions**
• Use the visuals given here to teach the concept of the progressive; students
should be able to produce progressive forms by following the models you giv

## 14 ¿Qué están haciendo? Present Progressive: *estar* + *-ndo*

• Emphasize that the Spanish progressive is used only for describing
actions actually in progress. Ask which of the following sentences would
be expressed with progressive forms in Spanish.

¿Qué *están haciendo* en Quito, Ecuador?

Hoy es sábado y José Miguel y su madre Elisa no están en la universidad
o en el trabajo. ¿Qué *están haciendo*?

José Miguel juega al tenis y levanta pesas con frecuencia. Ahora no *está
jugando* al tenis. Tampoco *está levantando* pesas. ¿Qué *está
haciendo*?
Está _____.

1. They are reading the newspaper nov
2. Mary is typing all her homework this
year.

Elisa es periodista. Por eso escribe
mucho y habla mucho por teléfono. Pero ahora, no *está escribiendo*.
Tampoco *está hablando* por teléfono. ¿Qué *está haciendo*?
Está _____.

**Follow-Up**
After covering the presentation device,
ask students the following question.

*¿Cuáles son algunas actividades que
Ud. puede hacer pero que no está
haciendo en este momento?*

Coach students, based on activities they
mentioned in the previous class discussion.

*Carlos, ¿está Ud. mirando la televisión
en este momento?*

**¿Y Ud.?**

¿Qué está haciendo Ud. en este momento?

3. I'm speaking English right now.
4. We're going to San Francisco
next summer.

1. ¿Está estudiando en casa? ¿en clase? ¿en la cafetería?
2. ¿Está leyendo? ¿Está mirando la tele al mismo tiempo (*at the same
time*)?
3. ¿Está escuchando al profesor / a la profesora?

```
Past -------------------- PRESENT -------------------- Future
                            present
                       present progressive
```

## Uses of the Progressive

In Spanish, you can use special verb forms to describe
an action in progress— that is, something actually
happening at the time it is being described. These
Spanish forms, called **el progresivo,** correspond in
form to the English *progressive: I am walking, we are
driving, she is studying.* But their use is not identical.
Compare the Spanish and English verb forms in the
sentences on the next page.

> **progressive** = a verb form that
> expresses continuing action

*What are they doing in Quito, Ecuador?* Today is Saturday, and José Miguel and his mother Elisa
aren't at the university or at work. What are they doing? José Miguel often plays tennis and lifts weights.
Now he isn't playing tennis. He isn't lifting weights either. What's he doing? He's _____. Elisa is a journalist. That's why she writes a great deal and talks on the phone a lot. But now she isn't writing. She isn't
talking on the phone either. What's she doing? She's _____.

In Spanish, the present progressive is used primarily to describe an action that is actually *in progress*, as in the first example. The simple Spanish present is used in other cases where English would use the present progressive: to tell what is going to happen (the second sentence), and to tell what someone is doing over a period of time but not necessarily at this very moment (the third sentence).

1. Ramón **está comiendo** ahora mismo.
   *Ramón is eating right now.*

2. **Compramos** la casa mañana.
   *We're buying the house tomorrow.*

3. Adelaida **estudia** química este semestre.
   *Adelaida is studying chemistry this semester.*

## Formation of the Present Progressive

**A.** The Spanish present progressive is formed with **estar** plus the *present participle* (**el gerundio**).

The present participle is formed by adding **-ando** to the stem of **-ar** verbs and **-iendo** to the stem of **-er** and **-ir** verbs.*

The present participle never varies; it always ends in **-o.**

**estar** + present participle

| | | |
|---|---|---|
| tomar → | **tomando** | *taking; drinking* |
| comprender → | **comprendiendo** | *understanding* |
| abrir → | **abriendo** | *opening* |

**OJO** Unaccented **i** represents the sound [y] in the participle ending **-iendo: comiendo, viviendo.** Unaccented **i** between two vowels becomes the letter **y:**

leer: le + iendo → le**y**endo
oír: o + iendo → o**y**endo

**B.** The stem vowel in the present participle of **-ir** stem-changing verbs also shows a change. From this point on in *¿Qué tal?*, both stem changes for **-ir** verbs will be given with infinitives in vocabulary lists.

| | | |
|---|---|---|
| preferir (ie, i) → | prefiriendo | *preferring* |
| pedir (i, i) → | pidiendo | *asking* |
| dormir (ue, u) → | d**u**rmiendo | *sleeping* |

## Using Pronouns with the Present Progressive

Reflexive pronouns may be attached to a present participle or precede the conjugated form of **estar.** Note the use of a written accent mark when pronouns are attached to the present participle.

Pablo **se** está bañando.
Pablo está bañándo**se.** } *Pablo is taking a bath.*

**Heritage Speakers**
Los tiempos progresivos también pueden formarse combinando el gerundio con los verbos *andar, continuar, ir, seguir* y *venir* (véase los ejemplos). Invite a los estudiantes hispanohablantes a dar algunos ejemplos de estas construcciones. ¿Se puede usar el verbo *estar* en las mismas construcciones?

*Carlos anda buscando su abrigo.*
*Estos días vamos entendiéndolo mejor.*
*Sigue lloviendo.*
*Lorena siempre viene quejándose de algo.*

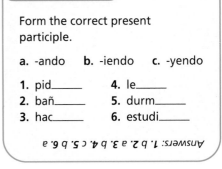

**AUTOPRUEBA**

Form the correct present participle.

**a.** -ando   **b.** -iendo   **c.** -yendo

1. pid_____    4. le_____
2. bañ_____    5. durm_____
3. hac_____    6. estudi_____

Answers: 1. b 2. a 3. b 4. c 5. b 6. a

*Ir, poder,* and **venir** *have irregular present participles:* **yendo, pudiendo, viniendo.** *These three verbs, however, are seldom used in the progressive.*

**Heritage Speakers**

Los tiempos progresivos se usan para expresar acciones en curso, sean del presente o del pasado. El verbo *estar* puede conjugarse en cualquier tiempo verbal (*estoy / estaba / estuve / estaré / estaría comiendo*), pero el presente progresivo y el imperfecto progresivo ocurren con mayor frecuencia. Invite a los hispanohablantes a explicar la diferencia entre *Están viendo las noticias* y *Estarán viendo las noticias.*

**Prác. A: Follow-Up**

Ask students the following personal questions.

*Generalmente, ¿qué está haciendo Ud. / su familia a las seis de la mañana?*
*¿a las ocho de la mañana?*
*¿a las siete y media de la tarde?*
*¿a las nueve y media de la noche?*

**Prác. A: Answers**

*Paso 1* **1.** *por la mañana* **2.** *por la tarde* **3.** *más tarde* **4.** *por la tarde* **5.** *por la mañana* **6.** *por la mañana* **7.** *más tarde* **8.** *por la tarde* **9.** *más tarde* **10.** *por la tarde* **Paso 2** *Possible answers:* POR LA MAÑANA: *Son las seis de la mañana. Los gemelos están durmiendo. El padre está duchándose. La hija está levantándose. La madre está leyendo el periódico.* MÁS TARDE *Son las ocho de la mañana. Los gemelos están comiendo (tomando el desayuno). El padre está trabajando. La madre está vistiéndose. La hija está saliendo para la escuela.* POR LA TARDE: *Son las siete y media de la tarde. El padre está preparando la cena. Los gemelos están jugando con el perro. La hija está haciendo la tarea. La madre está quitándose la ropa después de trabajar.*

■ **Práctica**

### A. En casa con la familia Duarte

PASO 1  The Duarte family leads a busy life. Each set of drawings shows what the parents, the teen-age daughter, and the twins (**los gemelos**) are doing at a particular time of their day. Read the following sentences and tell to which set each statement refers.

MODELO:  Se está duchando. → por la mañana

1. Está levantándose.
2. Está haciendo la tarea.
3. Se está vistiendo.
4. Está preparando la cena (*dinner*).
5. Está leyendo el periódico.
6. Están durmiendo.
7. Está trabajando.
8. Están jugando con el perro.
9. Están comiendo.
10. Está quitándose la blusa.

Resources: Transparency 41

**Por la mañana**

**Más tarde**

**Por la tarde**

PASO 2  Now tell what is happening at each time of day.

MODELO:  Son las seis de la mañana. Los niños están…

**B. ¿Qué están haciendo?** Diga qué están haciendo las siguientes personas, usando una palabra o frase de cada columna y la forma progresiva. Si Ud. no sabe (*know*) qué están haciendo esas personas, ¡use su imaginación!

**Prác. B: Suggestion**
Encourage students to be creative and to use verbs and phrases other than those on the list.

MODELO: (Yo) Estoy escribiendo la tarea.

| | | | | |
|---|---|---|---|---|
| yo<br>mi mejor amigo/a<br>mis padres<br>los Bills de Buffalo / los Bulls de Chicago<br>el rector / la rectora (*president*) de la universidad<br>el presidente de los Estados Unidos<br>el profesor / la profesora de español<br>_____ (un compañero / una compañera de la clase de español que está ausente hoy)<br>mi consejero/a | **+** | jugar (al)<br>dormir(se)<br>leer<br>descansar<br>viajar (*to travel*)<br>escuchar<br>trabajar<br>practicar<br>hacer<br>escribir<br>¿ ? | **+** | fútbol/basquetbol<br>un libro / una novela<br>la radio<br>a los estudiantes / a sus consejeros<br>la tarea<br>un informe<br>ejercicio físico<br>¿ ? |

**Need more practice?**

- Workbook/Laboratory Manual
- Interactive CD-ROM
- Online Learning Center (www.mhhe.com/quetal7)

## ▓ Conversación

**Entrevista**

1. ¿Pasas (*Do you spend*) más tiempo leyendo o mirando la televisión? ¿tocando o escuchando música? ¿trabajando o estudiando? ¿estudiando o descansando?
2. ¿Cómo te diviertes más, mirando la tele o bailando en una fiesta? ¿practicando un deporte o leyendo una buena novela? ¿haciendo un *picnic* o preparando una cena (*dinner*) elegante en casa? ¿mirando una película en casa o en el cine?

**Con: Note**
This activity shows how the present participle functions with other verbs, just as in the English sentence *Did you spend more time reading or watching TV?* Past participles can also function as nouns in English, but not in Spanish; only the infinitive functions as a noun in Spanish.

- subject: I like **reading.** = *Me gusta leer.*
- object of a preposition: I insist on **traveling** today. = *Insisto en viajar hoy.*

Students do not have to know these linguistic facts, yet they certainly can profit from knowing this information. For now, remind students that Spanish cannot use a present participle after a preposition, only an infinitive.

**Con: Suggestion**
Have students work in pairs and then report comparisons to the class.

*Fred pasa más tiempo leyendo y yo paso más tiempo mirando la tele.*
*Fred y yo pasamos más tiempo leyendo.*

### ¿Recuerda Ud.?

You have been using forms of **ser** and **estar** since **Primeros pasos,** the preliminary chapter of *¿Qué tal?* The following section will help you consolidate everything you know so far about these two verbs, both of which express *to be* in Spanish. You will learn a bit more about them as well.

Before you begin, think in particular about the following questions: **¿Cómo está Ud.? ¿Cómo es Ud.?** What do these questions tell you about the difference between **ser** and **estar?**

## 15 ¿*Ser* o *estar?* Summary of the Uses of *ser* and *estar*

**Una conversación por larga distancia**

Aquí hay un lado de la conversación entre una esposa que *está* en un viaje de negocios y su esposo, que *está* en casa. Habla el esposo. ¿Qué contesta la esposa?

Aló. [...¹] ¿Cómo *estás*, mi amor? [...²] ¿Dónde *estás* ahora? [...³] ¿Qué hora *es* allí? [...⁴] ¡Huy!, *es* muy tarde. Y el hotel, ¿cómo *es*? [...⁵] Oye, ¿qué *estás* haciendo ahora? [...⁶] Ay, pobrita, lo siento. *Estás* muy ocupada. ¿Con quién *estás* citada mañana? [...⁷] ¿Quién *es* el dueño de la compañía? [...⁸] Ah, él *es* de Cuba, ¿verdad? [...⁹] Bueno, ¿qué tiempo hace allí? [...¹⁰] Muy bien, mi vida. Hasta luego, ¿eh? [...¹¹] Adiós.

**Suggestions**
- Have students reenact the conversation as if they were talking on the phone. Have students sit back-to-back, if possible. Emphasize that they don't have to memorize the whole conversation on the phone between the two spouses.

### Comprensión

Aquí está el otro lado de la conversación... pero las respuestas no están en orden. Ponga las respuestas en el orden apropiado.

- Assume the identity of a famous person (actor, artist, singer, athlete, and so on). Have students ask you yes/no questions in order to determine your identity. They may ask about your place of origin, your personality traits, your nationality, your profession, and so on. Model questions to get them started.

a. __5__ Es muy moderno. Me gusta mucho.
b. __9__ Sí, pero vive en Nueva York ahora.
c. __4__ Son las once y media.
d. __1__ Hola, querido (*dear*). ¿Qué tal?
e. __8__ Es el Sr. Cortina.
f. __6__ Pues, todavía (*still*) tengo que trabajar.
g. __11__ Sí, hasta pronto.
h. __3__ Estoy en Nueva York.
i. __2__ Un poco cansada (*tired*), pero estoy bien.
j. __10__ Pues, hace buen tiempo, pero está un poco nublado.
k. __7__ Con un señor de Computec, una nueva compañía de computadoras.

1. ¿Es Ud. hombre? (*mujer/niño/animal*)
2. ¿Es Ud. viejo? (*joven/guapo/rubio/moreno*)
3. ¿Es de los Estados Unidos? (*del Canadá / de México*)
4. ¿Es casado? (*soltero/viudo*)
5. ¿Está en (*lugar*) hoy?
6. ¿Está muy ocupado con su vida estos días? (*contento*)
7. ¿Está en (*programa de televisión / película*)?

**Follow-Up**
Ask the following questions.

1. ¿Quiénes son las dos personas?
2. ¿Dónde están?
3. ¿Qué están haciendo en este momento?
4. ¿Es una situación normal? ¿Es agradable para los esposos?
5. ¿A la esposa le gusta viajar?

---

*A long-distance conversation*   *Here is one side of a conversation between a wife who is on a business trip and her husband, who is at home. The husband is speaking. What does the wife answer? Hello . . . How are you, dear? . . . Where are you now? . . . What time is it there? . . . Boy, it's very late. And how's the hotel? . . . Hey, what are you doing now? . . . You poor thing, I'm sorry. You're very busy. Who are you meeting with tomorrow? . . . Who's the owner of the company? . . . Ah, he's from Cuba, isn't he? . . . Well, what's the weather like? . . . Very well, sweetheart. See you later, OK? . . . Good-bye.*

## Summary of the Uses of *ser*

**Suggestion**
Have students identify which verb would be used with the following.

*con la hora*
*con participios presentes*
*con generalizaciones*
*para expresar posesión*
*para expresar locación*
*para expresar nacionalidad*
*para indicar el material*

- To *identify* people and things

  Ella **es doctora.**
  Tikal **es una ciudad maya.**

- To express *nationality;* with **de** to express *origin*

  **Son cubanos.**
  **Son de La Habana.**

- With **de** to tell of what *material* something is made.

  Este bolígrafo **es de plástico.**

- With **de** to express *possession*

  **Es de Carlota.**

- With **para** to tell *for whom something is intended*

  El regalo **es para Sara.**

- To tell *time*

  **Son las once.**
  **Es la una y media.**

- With *adjectives* that describe *basic, inherent characteristics*

  Ramona **es inteligente.**

- To form many *generalizations*

  **Es necesario** llegar temprano.
  **Es importante** estudiar.

## Summary of the Uses of *estar*

- To tell *location*

  El libro **está en la mesa.**

- To describe *health*

  **Estoy** muy **bien,** gracias.

- With *adjectives* that describe *conditions*

  **Estoy** muy **ocupada.**

- In a number of *fixed expressions*

  **(No) Estoy de acuerdo. Está bien.**

- With *present participles* to form the *progressive tense*

  **Estoy estudiando** ahora mismo.

## *Ser* and *estar* with Adjectives

**A. Ser** is used with adjectives that describe the fundamental qualities of a person, place, or thing.

**Emphasis A: Suggestion**
Point out that *ser* + adjective represents the norm; *estar* + adjective represents a change from the norm.

♻ **Reciclado**
- Review adjective–noun placement with students.
- Have students provide the four forms for adjectives ending in *-o*.
- Have students explain forms for adjectives of nationality such as *francés, inglés, portugués,* and *irlandés.*

Esa mujer es muy **baja.**
*That woman is very short.*

Sus calcetines son **morados.**
*His socks are purple.*

Este sillón es **cómodo.**
*This armchair is comfortable.*

Sus padres son **cariñosos.**
*Their parents are affectionate people.*

# PASO 2

**Emphasis B: Suggestion**
Point out that *estar* is used to express an unexpected quality.

*¡Qué fría está el agua!*

To express what is expected, *ser* is used.

*El agua es fría.* (The speaker expects the water to be cold.)

**B. Estar** is used with adjectives to express conditions or observations that are true at a given moment but that do not describe inherent qualities of the noun. The following adjectives are generally used with **estar.**

| | | | |
|---|---|---|---|
| **abierto/a** | open | **limpio/a** | clean |
| **aburrido/a** | bored | **loco/a** | crazy |
| **alegre** | happy | **nervioso/a** | nervous |
| **cansado/a** | tired | **ocupado/a** | busy |
| **cerrado/a** | closed | **ordenado/a** | neat |
| **congelado/a** | frozen; very cold | **preocupado/a** | worried |
| **contento/a** | content, happy | **seguro/a** | sure, certain |
| **desordenado/a** | messy | **sucio/a** | dirty |
| **enfermo/a** | sick | **triste** | sad |
| **furioso/a** | furious, angry | | |

**Emphasis B: Suggestion**
Offer the following additional vocabulary: *de buen humor, de mal humor, enojado/a, enfadado/a, roto/a.*

**Resources: Transparency 42**
Transparency 42 provides additional adjective expressions with *estar,* as well as some *tener* expressions.

**C.** Many adjectives can be used with either **ser** or **estar,** depending on what the speaker intends to communicate. In general, when *to be* implies *looks, feels,* or *appears,* **estar** is used. Compare the following pairs of sentences.

Daniel **es** guapo.
*Daniel is handsome. (He is a handsome person.)*

Daniel **está** muy guapo esta noche.
*Daniel looks very nice (handsome) tonight.*

—¿Cómo **es** Amalia?
*What is Amalia like (as a person)?*
—**Es** simpática.
*She's nice.*

—¿Cómo **está** Amalia?
*How is Amalia (feeling)?*
—**Está** enferma todavía.
*She's still sick.*

**Emphasis C: Suggestion**
Point out that to express how something looks, tastes, feels, or appears, *estar* is used. Contrast pairs of sentences and meanings found in this section.

**Emphasis C: Note**
Point out that *Daniel está muy guapo esta noche* does not imply that he is by nature ugly, but rather comments on his appearance at a given point in time (he is especially handsome) or expresses the surprise of the speaker at how handsome he is tonight.

## AUTOPRUEBA

**¿Ser o estar?**

| | SER | ESTAR |
|---|---|---|
| **1.** to describe a health condition | ☐ | ☐ |
| **2.** to tell time | ☐ | ☐ |
| **3.** to describe inherent qualities | ☐ | ☐ |
| **4.** to tell where a thing or person is located | ☐ | ☐ |

*Answers: 1. estar 2. ser 3. ser 4. estar*

## ■ Práctica

**Prác. A: Suggestion**
Have students justify the use of *ser* or *estar* in each case.

**Prác. A: Follow-Up**
• Think or have students think of an object or a person without saying who or what it is. Have students ask questions to guess.

*¿Dónde está?*
*¿Cómo es?*
*¿De qué color es?*
*¿De dónde es?*

• Have students bring in magazine clippings and ask questions with *ser* and *estar* about the images.

**A. Un regalo especial.** Hay algo nuevo en el comedor. Es una computadora. ¿Qué puede Ud. decir de ella (*say about it*)? Haga oraciones completas con **es** o **está.**

La computadora es/está…

1. en la mesa del comedor.   está
2. un regalo de cumpleaños.   es
3. para mi compañero de cuarto.   es
4. de la tienda Computec.   es
5. en una caja (*box*) verde.   está
6. de los padres de mi compañero.   es
7. un regalo muy caro pero estupendo.   es
8. de metal y plástico gris.   es
9. una Dell, el último (*latest*) modelo.   es
10. muy fácil (*easy*) de usar.   es

**CAPÍTULO**

**5**

Prác. B: Follow-Up
• Have students talk about inherent traits of the house and its inhabitants by making sentences with *ser: La casa es grande.*
• Have students imagine what the following people are doing at 6:30 in the afternoon.

1. *Ud.*
2. *su profesor(a)*
3. *dos compañeros de clase*
4. *sus padres (hijos)*
5. *los españoles*

**PASO 2**

## B. Una tarde terrible

PASO 1  Describa lo que pasa hoy por la tarde en esta casa, cambiando por antónimos las palabras indicadas.

Resources: Transparency 43

1. No hace *buen* tiempo; hace <u>mal tiempo</u>.
2. El bebé no está *bien*; está <u>mal</u>.
3. El gato no está *limpio*; está <u>sucio</u>.
4. El esposo no está *tranquilo*; está <u>nervioso</u> por el bebé.
5. El garaje no está *cerrado*; está <u>abierto</u>.
6. Los niños no están *ocupados*; están <u>aburridos</u>.
7. La esposa no está *contenta*; está <u>triste</u> por (*about*) el tiempo.
8. El baño no está *ordenado*; está <u>desordenado</u>.

PASO 2  Ahora imagine que son las seis y media de la tarde. Exprese lo que están haciendo los miembros de la familia en este momento. Use su imaginación y diga también lo que generalmente hacen estas personas a esa hora.

MODELO:  Hoy, a las seis y media, la madre está conduciendo su coche a casa. Generalmente prepara la comida a esa hora.

> **Palabras útiles**
>
> **cenar** (to have dinner)
> **conducir (conduzco)** (to drive)
> **ladrar** (to bark)
> **llorar** (to cry)

**Need more practice?**
■ Workbook/Laboratory Manual
■ Interactive CD-ROM
■ Online Learning Center (www.mhhe.com/quetal7)

Prác. B: Note
The purpose of this activity is to give students practice with the "new" adjectives presented in the preceding section. No *ser* vs. *estar* decisions are called for.

## ■ Conversación

**A. Ana y Estela.**  Describa este dibujo de un cuarto típico de la residencia. Conteste las preguntas e invente los detalles necesarios.

1. ¿Quiénes son las dos compañeras de cuarto?
2. ¿De dónde son? ¿Cómo son?
3. ¿Dónde están en este momento?
4. ¿Qué hay en el cuarto?
5. ¿En qué condición está el cuarto?
6. ¿Son ordenadas o desordenadas las dos?

Con. A: Extension
Bring or have students bring magazine ads and clippings to class. Have students describe what they see and invent background stories. Use questions similar to those in *Conversación A* to get students going.

Resources: Transparency 44

Ana          Estela

> **Palabras útiles**
>
> **el cajón** (drawer)
> **el cartel** (poster)
> **la foto**

Heritage Speakers
En Latinoamérica, es más común usar el verbo *manejar* o *guiar* para expresar *to drive,* pero en España se dice *conducir.* Pregúnteles a los hispanohablantes de la clase qué término prefieren usar.

# PASO 2

**B. Sentimientos.** Complete the following sentences by telling how you feel in the situations described. Then ask questions of other students in the class to find at least one person who completed a given sentence the way you did.

MODELO: Cuando saco (*I get*) una «A» en un examen, estoy *alegre.* →
¿Cómo te sientes (*do you feel*) cuando sacas una «A» en un examen?

1. Cuando el profesor / la profesora da (*assigns*) una tarea difícil (fácil), estoy _____.
2. Cuando tengo mucho trabajo, estoy _____.
3. En otoño generalmente estoy _____ porque _____.
4. En verano estoy _____ porque _____.
5. Cuando llueve (nieva), estoy _____ porque _____.
6. Los lunes por la mañana estoy _____.
7. Los viernes por la noche estoy _____.
8. Cuando me acuesto muy tarde, estoy _____ al día siguiente (*the next day*).
9. Cuando otra persona habla y habla y habla, estoy _____.
10. Cuando estoy con mi familia, estoy _____.
11. Cuando estoy de vacaciones, estoy _____.
12. Cuando tengo problemas con mi coche, estoy _____.
13. Cuando voy al dentista, estoy _____.

## En los Estados Unidos y el Canadá

### Alfredo Jaar: América y su expresión artística

Upon arriving in the United States, Chilean artist Alfredo Jaar was surprised to learn that English speakers generally don't think of Canadians, Mexicans, Colombians, and so forth as "Americans." It bothered him that he was perceived as "Hispanic" or "Latin" but not as "American." "This country has co-opted the word *America,*" he claimed.

So, Jaar used his artistic talents in an effort to enlighten people in the United States about the true meaning of the word *America.* He created a computerized animation that appeared on a sign board above New York City's Times Square in April 1987. The computer animation depicted a lighted map of the United States with the statement "This is not America" written across it. Slowly the word *America* grew larger and larger until it filled

*El arte electrónico de Alfredo Jaar*

the entire sign. At the same time, the letter *R* transformed itself into a map of North and South America. This use of *America* is the meaning used in Spanish, the meaning that Jaar had known.

The message that Jaar was trying to send was that *America* does not belong only to the United States. Another thirty-three nations say that they are a part of America and that their approximately 500 million inhabitants are also Americans.

Jaar was also trying to combat the stereotype that all Hispanics are alike and that all the inhabitants of South America are Hispanics. For one thing, many inhabitants of South America are Brazilians, and thus of Portuguese rather than of Spanish heritage. In addition, there are many indigenous peoples throughout the Americas that have traditions, cultures, and languages that precede Columbus's arrival in this hemisphere.

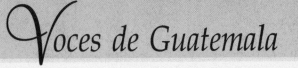

# *Voces de Guatemala*

## LITERATURA: Miguel Ángel Asturias

**Sobre el autor:** *Miguel Ángel Asturias was born near Guatemala City. One of the more important themes in his creative works is the indigenous peoples of Guatemala. In 1967, he was awarded the Nobel Prize for Literature. He spent many of his adult years in France, where he was buried in 1974. The following excerpt is from the poem "Letanías del desterrado[a]," published in* Páginas de lumbre de Miguel Ángel Asturias *(1999).*

**Miguel Ángel Asturias**
*(1899–1974)*

Y, tú, desterrado:

Estar de paso,[b] siempre de paso,
tener la tierra como posada,[c]
contemplar cielos que no son nuestros,
vivir con gente[d] que no es la nuestra,
cantar canciones que no son nuestras,
reír con risa[e] que no es la nuestra,
estrechar manos[f] que no son nuestras,
llorar con llanto[g] que no es el nuestro,
tener amores que no son nuestros,
probar[h] comida que no es la nuestra,
rezar a dioses[i] que no son nuestros,
oír un nombre que no es el nuestro,
pensar en cosas que no son nuestras,
usar moneda[j] que no es la nuestra,
sentir caminos[k] que no son nuestros...

**Literatura: Notes**

- Miguel Ángel Asturias spent much of his life in exile due to his outspoken opposition to the dictatorship in Guatemala. For many years his writing was not published or circulated in Guatemala. Although this poem, *"Letanías del desterrado,"* was not published for many years, it circulated orally and was important to many Guatemalan exiles.
- Asturias studied law at *la Universidad de San Carlos.* His thesis for that degree was "The Social Problem of the Indian."
- Asturias wrote his most famous novel, *El Señor Presidente,* during his stay in Paris (1923–1933). The novel criticized the social conditions to which an insensitive dictator condemns his people. This was a politically sensitive topic, especially in Guatemala, whose ruler was the dictator Jorge Ubico. Asturias could not bring his manuscript with him when he returned to Guatemala and didn't publish the original version for 13 years. In 1944, Ubico fell, and the new president, Professor Juan José Arévalo, appointed Asturias cultural attaché to the Guatemalan Embassy in Mexico, where *El Señor Presidente* was published for the first time.

♻ **Literatura: Reciclado**

Review possessive adjectives and point out the different forms of *nuestro* used in the poem.

[a]*exile* [b]*de... passing through* [c]*boardinghouse* [d]*people* [e]*reír... to laugh with laughter* [f]*estrechar... to shake hands* [g]*llorar... to cry with tears* [h]*to taste/try* [i]*rezar... to pray to gods* [j]*currency* [k]*roads*

## MÚSICA: La marimba y la banda cívica

**Música: Notes**

- The marimba is used in several Spanish-speaking countries, and there are many physical varieties of the marimba, as well as a variety of playing styles. Physically, the marimba can have one or two rows of keys. The traditional marimbas are made from natural products like gourds, bamboo, and wood. Modern versions can be made of metal and plastic.
- The marimba is used for many different kinds of music, from waltzes to polka to music with African roots.

La marimba, el instrumento musical nacional de Guatemala, es de origen africano, y originalmente se hacía[a] con calabazas.[b] Es un instrumento importante en casi todas las ocasiones sociales en Guatemala, desde[c] las fiestas populares hasta las celebraciones formales.

Muchas ciudades tienen una banda, estilo militar, en que predominan los tambores[d] y los cobres.[e] Los músicos tocan en procesiones y otras festividades religiosas solemnes, como, por ejemplo, la Semana Santa,[f] y también en los funerales.

[a]*se... it was made* [b]*gourds* [c]*from*

[d]*drums* [e]*brass instruments* [f]*Semana... Holy Week*

**Paso 3: Gramática**
See the "Chapter-by-Chapter Supplementary Materials" in the IM for additional teaching suggestions, notes, activities, and other resources for *Paso 3*.

## 16 Describing Comparisons

**Dos ciudades**

Follow-Up
Have students compare their university with another.

*¿Cuál es más grande?*
*¿Es tan cara su universidad como _____ (la otra)?*
*Los estudiantes de esta universidad, ¿estudian tanto como los estudiantes de la otra (universidad)?*

*México, D.F. (Distrito Federal)*

*El barrio de Santa Cruz, Sevilla, España*

Ricardo, el tío de Lola Benítez, hace comparaciones entre la Ciudad de México, o el D.F. (Distrito Federal), y Sevilla.

«De verdad, me gustan las dos ciudades.

- La Ciudad de México es *más* grande *que* Sevilla.
- Tiene *más* edificios altos *que* Sevilla.
- En el D.F. no hace *tanto* calor *como* en Sevilla.

Pero…

- Sevilla es *tan* bonita *como* la Ciudad de México.
- No tiene *tantos* habitantes *como* el D.F.
- Sin embargo, los sevillanos son *tan* simpáticos *como* los mexicanos.

En total, ¡me gusta Sevilla *tanto como* la Ciudad de México!»

**¿Y Ud.?**

Describa su ciudad o pueblo.

Mi ciudad/pueblo…

- (no) es tan grande como Chicago
- es más/menos cosmopolita que Quebec

Me gusta _____ (nombre de mi ciudad/pueblo)…

- más que _____ (nombre de otra ciudad)
- menos que _____ (nombre de otra ciudad)
- tanto como _____ (nombre de otra ciudad)

Bright Idea Follow-Up
Have students compare their city with New York, Chicago, Toronto, or Montreal.

*¿Cuál es más grande/pequeña?*
*¿Cuál tiene edificios más altos?*
*¿Cuál es más bonita?*
*¿Cuál es más/menos cosmopolita?*

Multimedia: Internet
Have students search the Internet for more information on attractions and tourism in Mexico City or Seville. You might assign specific topics and have students give brief oral presentations based on their findings.

Heritage Speakers
Pídales a los estudiantes hispanohablantes que busquen información sobre la historia de la Ciudad de México o de Sevilla en la biblioteca y en el Internet. Anímelos a escribir varios párrafos acerca de la ciudad que escojan.

| Equal Comparisons | | Unequal Comparisons |
|---|---|---|
| tan _____ como | **With Adjectives or Adverbs** | más/menos _____ que |
| tanto/a/os/as _____ como | **With Nouns** | |
| _____ tanto como | **With Verbs** | _____ más/menos que |

---

**Two cities**   *Ricardo, Lola Benítez's uncle, makes comparisons between Mexico City, or* **el D.F.** *(Federal District), and Seville. Really, I like both cities.* • *Mexico City is bigger than Seville.* • *It has more tall buildings than Seville.* • *It is not as hot in Mexico City as it is in Seville. But . . .* • *Seville is as beautiful as Mexico City.* • *It doesn't have as many inhabitants as Mexico City.* • *Nevertheless, the people from Seville are as nice as those from Mexico City. All told, I like Seville as much as Mexico City!*

**Suggestions**
• Point out the plural forms of irregular comparisons.

• Explain that *más grande* and *más pequeño* refer to size. *Mayor* and *menor* generally refer to age.

• Use model sentences to emphasize the exception, for example: *No tengo más que un hijo* (only one).

In English the *comparative* (**el comparativo**) is formed in a variety of ways. Equal comparisons are expressed with the word *as.* Unequal comparisons are expressed with the adverbs *more* or *less,* or by adding *-er* to the end of the adjective.

as cold as
as many as

more intelligent,
less important
tall**er**, smart**er**

> **comparative** = form of or structure with adjectives and adverbs used to compare nouns or actions

## Comparison of Adjectives

| | | |
|---|---|---|
| EQUAL COMPARISONS | **tan** + *adjective* + **como** | Enrique es **tan** trabajador **como** Amalia. *Enrique is as hardworking as Amalia.* |
| UNEQUAL COMPARISONS (REGULAR) | **más** + *adjective* + **que** <br> **menos** + *adjective* + **que** | Alicia es **más** perezosa **que** Marta. *Alicia is lazier than Marta.* <br><br> Julio es **menos** listo **que** Jaime. *Julio is not as bright as Jaime.* |
| UNEQUAL COMPARATIVES WITH IRREGULAR FORMS | bueno/a → mejor | Estos coches son **buenos,** pero esos son **mejores.** *These cars are good, but those are better.* |
| | malo/a → peor | Mi lámpara es **peor que** esta. *My lamp is worse than this one.* |
| | mayor (*older*) | Mi hermana es **mayor que** yo. *My sister is older than I (am).* |
| | menor (*younger*) | Mis primos son **menores que** yo. *My cousins are younger than I (am).* |

## Comparison of Nouns

| | | |
|---|---|---|
| EQUAL COMPARISONS | **tanto/a/os/as** + *noun* + **como** | Alicia tiene **tantas** bolsas **como** Pati. *Alicia has as many purses as Pati (does).* |
| | **Tanto** must agree in gender and number with the noun it modifies. | Pablo tiene **tanto** dinero **como** Sergio. *Pablo has as much money as Sergio (does).* |
| UNEQUAL COMPARISONS | **más/menos** + *noun* + **que** | Alicia tiene **más/menos** bolsas **que** Susana. *Alicia has more/fewer purses than Susana (does).* |
| The preposition **de** is used when the comparison is followed by a number. | **más/menos de** + *noun* | Alicia tiene **más de** cinco bolsas. *Alicia has more than five purses.* |

[Práctica A–C]

## Comparison of Verbs

| EQUAL COMPARISONS | **tanto como** | Yo estudio **tanto como** mi hermano mayor. *I study as much as my older brother (does).* |
|---|---|---|
| Note that **tanto** is invariable in this usage. | | |
| UNEQUAL COMPARISONS | **más/menos que** | Yo duermo **más que** mi hermano menor. *I sleep more than my younger brother (does).* |

## Comparison of Adverbs

| EQUAL COMPARISONS | **tan** + *adverb* + **como** | Yo juego al tenis **tan** bien **como** mi hermano. *I play tennis as well as my brother (does).* |
|---|---|---|
| UNEQUAL COMPARISONS | **más/menos** + *adverb* + **que** | Yo como **más** rápido **que** mi padre. *I eat faster than my father (does).* |
| | **mejor/peor que** | Yo juego al tenis **peor que** mi hermana. *I play tennis worse than my sister (does).* |

[Práctica D]

Prác. A: Suggestion
Have students substitute other people to create sentences that are true.

*No soy tan guapo como Antonio Banderas, pero soy tan guapo como mi hermano mayor.*

## ■ Práctica

**A. ¿Es Ud. sincero/a?**   Conteste las preguntas lógicamente.

¿Es Ud.... ?   **1.** tan guapo/a como Antonio Banderas / Jennifer López
**2.** tan rico como Bill Gates
**3.** tan fiel como su mejor amigo/a
**4.** tan inteligente como Einstein
**5.** tan honesto/a como su padre/madre (novio/a... )

¿Tiene Ud.... ?   **1.** tantos tíos como tías
**2.** tantos amigos como amigas
**3.** tanto talento como Carlos Santana
**4.** tanta sabiduría (*knowledge*) como su profesor(a)

**B. Alfredo y Gloria.**   Compare la casa y las posesiones de Alfredo y Gloria.

MODELOS:   La casa de Alfredo tiene tantas alcobas como la casa de Gloria. Sin embargo, Gloria tiene más camas que Alfredo.

| | cuartos en total | baños | alcobas | camas | coches | bicicletas | dinero en el banco |
|---|---|---|---|---|---|---|---|
| Alfredo | 8 | 2 | 3 | 3 | 3 | 2 | $500.000 |
| Gloria | 6 | 1 | 3 | 5 | 1 | 2 | $5.000 |

**Prác. C: Extension**
6. *Los exámenes de matemáticas son más fáciles que los exámenes de español.*
7. *El dinero es tan importante como la salud* (new word).
8. *Los amigos son tan importantes como la familia.*

**C. Opiniones.** Cambie las siguientes oraciones para expresar su opinión personal. Si está de acuerdo con la oración, diga **Estoy de acuerdo.**

MODELO: El invierno es *tan divertido* como el verano. →
El invierno es *más/menos divertido* que el verano.
Estoy de acuerdo.

1. Mi casa (apartamento/residencia) es *tan grande* como la casa de Bill Gates.
2. El fútbol (*soccer*) es *tan popular* como el fútbol americano.
3. Las artes son *tan importantes* como las ciencias.
4. Los estudios son *menos importantes* que los deportes.
5. La comida (*food*) de la cafeteria es *tan buena* como la de mi mamá/papá (esposo/a, compañero/a... ).

**D. Más opiniones.** Cambie, indicando su opinión personal: **tanto como** → **más/menos que,** o vice versa. O, si es apropiado, diga **Estoy de acuerdo.**

1. Los profesores trabajan más que los estudiantes.
2. Me divierto tanto con mis amigos como con mis parientes.
3. Los niños duermen tanto como los adultos.
4. Aquí llueve más en primavera que en invierno.
5. Necesito más el dinero que la amistad (*friendship*).

**Prác. C: Suggestions**
• Have students create their own sentences about their university and have others tell whether they agree or not. Those that disagree should change the sentence so that it is true for them.

*Nuestra universidad es tan buena como la Universidad de Texas.* →
*No, nuestra universidad es mejor que la Universidad de Texas.*

• *¿Cómo se dice?* Ask students how the following are said in Spanish.

1. I enjoy myself more/less than my roommate.
2. I work as much as she does.
3. She watches TV as much as all of us.
4. We eat more/less than she does.

**Need more practice?**
■ Workbook/Laboratory Manual
■ Interactive CD-ROM
■ Online Learning Center (www.mhhe.com/quetal7)

## ■ Conversación

**A. La familia de Lucía y Miguel**

PASO 1 Mire el dibujo e identifique a los miembros de esta familia. Luego compárelos (*compare them*) con otro pariente. **¡OJO!** Lucía y Miguel tienen tres hijos: Amalia, Ramón y Sancho. Laura y Javier son los padres de Miguel.

MODELO: Amalia es la hermana de Sancho. Ella es menor que Sancho, pero es más alta que él.

Amalia (19) Ramón (24) Sancho (20) Laura (75) Javier (80) Lucía (43) Miguel (45) Sarita (25) Ramoncito (1)

Resources: Transparency 45

PASO 2 **Su familia.** Now compare the members of your own family, making ten comparative statements.

MODELOS: Mi hermana Mary es mayor que yo, pero yo soy más alto/a que ella.

Mi abuela es mayor que mi abuelo; sin embargo ella es más activa que él.

PASO 3 Now read your sentences from **Paso 2** to a classmate. Then ask him or her questions about your comparisons and see if he or she remembers the details of your family.

MODELO: ¿Qué miembro de mi familia es mayor que yo?

♻ **Con. A: Reciclado**
Have students bring a picture of their family to class and introduce and compare members as in *Conversación A.*

# PASO 3

Heritage Speakers
Invite a los estudiantes hispanohablantes que han vivido en un país latinoamericano a escribir unos párrafos comparando y contrastando su rutina diaria en este país con la que tenían en el país latinoamericano donde vivían. ¿Cómo es diferente su rutina diaria ahora?

**Con. B: Follow-Up**

- Have students use the items as a guide to ask a partner about the same information. As follow-up homework, have students write a comparison of their activities with their partner's.
- Have students report their findings to the class. Tally answers and end the activity with some generalizations provided by students, for example, *Por lo general, nos acostamos más tarde en el verano que en el invierno...*

## B. La rutina diaria... en invierno y en verano

PASO 1 ¿Es diferente nuestra rutina diaria en las diferentes estaciones? Complete las siguientes oraciones sobre su rutina.

EN INVIERNO...

1. me levanto a _____ (hora)
2. almuerzo en _____
3. me divierto con mis amigos / mi familia en _____
4. estudio _____ horas todos los días
5. estoy / me quedo en _____ (lugar) por la noche
6. me acuesto a _____

EN VERANO...

me levanto a _____
almuerzo en _____
me divierto con mis amigos / mi familia en _____
(no) estudio _____ horas todos los días
estoy / me quedo en _____ por la noche
me acuesto a _____

PASO 2 Compare sus actividades en invierno y en verano, según los modelos.

MODELO: En invierno me levanto más temprano/tarde que en verano.
(En invierno me levanto a la misma hora que en verano.)
(En invierno me levanto tan temprano como en verano.)

### Palabras útiles

el gimnasio
el parque

afuera

♻ Reciclado

To review *ser, estar,* and *tener* phrases used in this chapter, have students ask and answer questions about the figures in Transparency 45.

## UN POCO DE TODO

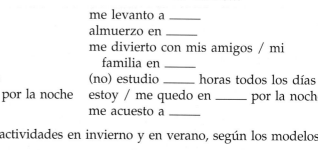

*En la playa Mar del Plata, en el mes de diciembre, en la Argentina*

**Resources: Desenlace**

In the *Capítulo 5* section of "Chapter-by-Chapter Supplementary Materials" in the IM, you will find a chapter-culminating activity. You can use this activity to consolidate and review the vocabulary and grammar skills students have acquired.

## Resources for Review and Testing Preparation

- Workbook/Laboratory Manual
- Interactive CD-ROM
- Online Learning Center (www.mhhe.com/quetal7)

**Lengua y cultura: Dos hemisferios.** Complete the following paragraphs with the correct forms of the words in parentheses, as suggested by the context. When two possibilities are given in parentheses, select the correct word.

¿**S**abe Ud.[a] algo de las diferencias entre los hemisferios del norte y del sur? Hay (mucho[1]) diferencias entre el clima del hemisferio norte y el del hemisferio sur. Cuando (ser/estar[2]) invierno en este país, por ejemplo, (ser/estar[3]) verano en la Argentina, en Bolivia, en Chile... Cuando yo (salir[4]) para la universidad en febrero, con frecuencia tengo que (llevar[5]) abrigo y botas. En (los/las[6]) países del hemisferio sur, una persona (poder[7]) asistir (a/de[8]) un concierto en febrero llevando sólo pantalones (corto[9]), camiseta y sandalias. En muchas partes de este país, (antes de / durante[10]) las vacaciones en diciembre, casi siempre (hacer[11]) frío y a veces (nevar[12]). En (grande[13]) parte de Sudamérica, al otro lado del ecuador, hace calor y (muy/mucho[14]) sol durante (ese[15]) mes. A veces en enero hay fotos, en los periódicos, de personas que (tomar[16]) el sol y nadan[b] en las playas sudamericanas.

Tengo un amigo que (ir[17]) a (hacer/tomar[18]) un viaje a Buenos Aires. Él me dice[c] que allí la Navidad[d] (ser/estar[19]) una fiesta de verano y que todos (llevar[20]) ropa como la que[e] llevamos nosotros en julio. Parece[f] increíble, ¿verdad?

[a]¿Sabe... *Do you know* [b]*are swimming* [c]*Él... He tells me* [d]*Christmas* [e]*la... that which* [f]*It seems*

## Comprensión: ¿Probable o improbable?

1. Los estudiantes argentinos van a la playa en julio.
2. Muchas personas sudamericanas hacen viajes de vacaciones en enero.
3. Hace frío en Santiago (Chile) en diciembre.

**Lengua y cultura: Answers**

1. *muchas* 2. *es* 3. *es* 4. *salgo* 5. *llevar* 6. *los* 7. *puede* 8. *a* 9. *cortos* 10. *durante* 11. *hace* 12. *nieva* 13. *gran* 14. *mucho* 15. *ese* 16. *toman* 17. *va* 18. *hacer* 19. *es* 20. *llevan* **Comprensión** 1. *improbable* 2. *probable* 3. *improbable*

# Un paso más   PASO 4

Paso 4: Un paso más
• The *Paso 4: Un paso más* sections are optional.
• See the "Chapter-by-Chapter Supplementary Materials" in the IM for additional teaching suggestions, notes, activities, and other resources for *Paso 4*.

### VIDEOTECA

## Entrevista cultural: Guatemala

Débora David is a meteorologist from Guatemala. In this interview she describes the climate in her country. Before watching the interview, read the following excerpt.

INTERVIEWER: ...Y ¿cómo es el clima en Guatemala?

DÉBORA: Bueno, este...[a] Guatemala está en la América Central y... y tiene un clima templado, moderado, ni tanto frío ni tanto calor. Yo creo que por eso se le llama «el país de la eterna primavera».

INTERVIEWER: Y ¿hay temporadas[b] de mal tiempo en Guatemala?

DÉBORA: Sí sí sí, tenemos temporadas de mal tiempo, este..., cuando vienen las lluvias, eh, también a raíz de eso[c] los huracanes ¿no? que han pegado[d] lo que es las costas de Guatemala, eh, pero normalmente el clima en Guatemala es superagradable así como también toda América Central.

[a]Este *is a filler word, like the English* uh *or* um.   [b]estaciones   [c]a... por eso   [d]han... *have hit*

Now watch the video and answer the following questions based on the interview.

1. Where does Débora work?
2. Basically, what is the climate like in Guatemala?
3. What is the most severe weather problem in Guatemala?
4. What is considered bad weather?
5. When does the bad weather come?

## Entre amigos: ¡A mí me encanta (*I love*) el verano!

Tané, Karina, Miguel, and Rubén are talking about birthdays, seasons, and different times of the year. What questions do you think they will ask each other? Before watching the video, read the following questions. As you watch, don't worry if you don't understand every word. Try to get the gist of the conversation, listening carefully for information about seasons and times of the year. Watch the video a second time and listen for the answers to the questions.

1. ¿Cuándo es el cumpleaños de Karina?
2. ¿Adónde va Tané este verano, y qué va a hacer allí?
3. ¿Qué planes tiene Rubén para el verano?
4. ¿Qué estación del año prefiere Miguel, y por qué?
5. ¿Por qué le gusta el verano a Karina?

**Entrevista cultural: Suggestions**
• Before showing the video, ask students questions about climate in your area and in other areas they are familiar with.

*¿Cómo es el clima en esta región?*
*¿Qué tiempo hace típicamente en el verano? ¿en el invierno?*

• Show the video and allow students one to two minutes to work on the questions. Encourage them to answer in Spanish if possible. You might want to ask the questions in Spanish when you review the answers as a class.

1. *¿Dónde trabaja Débora?*
2. *En general, ¿cómo es el clima en Guatemala?*
3. *¿Cuál es el problema climático más severo de Guatemala?*
4. *¿Qué tiempo hace cuando hace mal tiempo en Guatemala?*
5. *¿Cuándo hace mal tiempo en Guatemala?*

Have volunteers answer the questions.

• Have volunteers role-play Débora and the interviewer.

**Entrevista cultural: Answers**
*Possible answers:* **1.** *en un canal de televisión* **2.** *Es templado, moderado y superagradable.* **3.** *los huracanes* **4.** *Llueve cuando hace mal tiempo.* **5.** *Hace mal tiempo en febrero y marzo.*

**Entre amigos: Suggestions**
• Before viewing the video, review the questions with students and ask them similar questions.

*¿Cuándo es su cumpleaños?*
*¿Qué planes tiene Ud. para el verano?*
*¿Qué estación prefiere Ud.? ¿Por qué?*

Have students answer or work in small groups to ask and answer these questions.

• After viewing the video, have volunteers read and answer the questions.

**Entre amigos: Answers**
*Possible answers:* **1.** *Es el 10 de noviembre.* **2.** *a Cuba, a visitar a su familia y amigos* **3.** *Va a trabajar.* **4.** *Prefiere la primavera porque todo es verde, hay flores, el clima es rico y no hay mucha lluvia.* **5.** *por las vacaciones*

# PASO 4

## ENFOQUE CULTURAL

### Guatemala

MAR CARIBE

MÉXICO · BELICE · HONDURAS · GUATEMALA · Ciudad de Guatemala · NICARAGUA · EL SALVADOR · COSTA RICA · PANAMÁ · OCÉANO PACÍFICO

### ¡Fíjese!

Más del cincuenta por ciento de los habitantes de Guatemala son descendientes de los antiguos[a] mayas. Esta civilización antigua tenía[b] un sistema de escritura jeroglífica que usaban[c] para documentar su historia, sus costumbres[d] religiosas y su mitología. El calendario maya, base del famoso calendario azteca, era[e] el calendario más exacto de su época. Los mayas también tenían un sistema político y social muy desarrollado.[f] Tikal, en Guatemala, fue[g] una de las ciudades mayas más importantes y también una de las más grandes. Las ruinas de Tikal son muestra[h] de la grandeza de la civilización maya. Hoy día,[i] son un lugar turístico muy visitado.

[a]ancient  [b]had  [c]they used  [d]customs  [e]was  [f]developed  [g]was  [h]an example  [i]Hoy… Nowadays

Learn more about Guatemala with the Video, Interactive CD-ROM, and the Online Learning Center (www.mhhe.com/quetal7).

## Personas famosas: Rigoberta Menchú

Al período entre los años 1978 y 1985 en Guatemala se le llama[a] con frecuencia «La violencia». Durante este tiempo el ejército guatemalteco[b] empieza una campaña[c] violenta contra la población indígena[d] del oeste del país.

Rigoberta Menchú, mujer de la región indígena y de lengua[e] quiché (un grupo étnico de la familia de los mayas) pierde a sus padres y dos hermanos, todos asesinados por el ejército. Menchú describe esta tragedia durante «La violencia» en su famosa autobiografía *Yo, Rigoberta Menchú*.

El trabajo de Menchú a favor de los derechos humanos[f] y del pluralismo étnico de Guatemala le otorgó[g] el Premio Nóbel de la Paz en 1992, exactamente quinientos años después de la llegada[h] de Cristóbal Colón a América.

[a]Al… *The period between 1978 and 1985 in Guatemala is called*  [b]ejército… *Guatemalan army*  [c]*campaign*  [d]población… *indigenous population*  [e]*language*  [f]a… *on behalf of human rights*  [g]le… *won her*  [h]*arrival*

*Tikal, Guatemala*

## PASO FINAL

### A LEER

### ESTRATEGIA: Forming a General Idea About Content

Before starting a reading, it is a good idea to try to form a general sense of the content. The more you know about the reading before you begin to read, the easier it will seem to you. Here are some things you can do to prepare yourself for reading. You have already applied some of these strategies to the readings thus far in *¿Qué tal?*

1. Make sure you understand the title. Think about what it suggests to you and what you already know about the topic. Do the same with any subtitles in the reading.
2. Look at the drawings, photos, or other visual clues that accompany the reading. What do they indicate about the content?
3. Read the comprehension questions before starting to read the selection. They will direct you to the kind of information you should be looking for.

You should be able to determine the general message of the reading if you apply the preceding strategies.

- **The title.** The reading, **"Todos juntos en los trópicos,"** contains a key word in the title: **trópicos.** It is a cognate. Can you guess what it means?
- **The art.** The reading is accompanied by a photograph and caption. What additional information do these tell you about the reading?
- **The comprehension questions.** Scan the questions in **Comprensión.** What additional clues do they give you about the content of the passage?

**Suggestions**
- Do the *Estrategia* in class the day you assign the reading as homework for the next class period. Note that the strategy is applied point by point to the reading.
  Stress that this reading is authentic, with a few words changed to accommodate beginning students. If students can do the comprehension activities, they have understood enough. Emphasize the importance of this accomplishment at this stage of their language learning.
- Ask students questions about what they know about the tropics.

  *¿Conoce Ud. (new expression) una región en los trópicos?*
  *¿Cómo es?*
  *¿Qué tipos de flores se encuentran allí?*
  *¿Qué animales están en las regiones tropicales?*
  *¿Qué países tienen regiones tropicales?*
  *¿Hay personas que vivan allí?*
  *¿Hay regiones tropicales en este país?*

**Sobre la lectura…** This reading is taken from the magazine *Muy interesante*, which generally contains articles about popular science and related topics. Knowing the source of a passage can also help you formulate hypotheses about the reading before you begin to read.

## *Todos juntos en los trópicos*

Los trópicos son las regiones biológicamente más diversas del planeta y cuentan con[a] el triple de <u>especies</u> que en cualquier otra zona. Pero, ¿por qué? Los biólogos no han sido capaces[b] de dar una respuesta unívoca.[c] Es más, las diferentes teorías que se han propuesto[d] tienen todos sus puntos débiles.[e]

En resumen, existen tres <u>razones</u> expuestas para esta riqueza.[f] La primera teoría fue diseñada[g] hace 20 años[h] por Michael Rosenzweigh, de Arizona. Según él, en los trópicos hay más especies, sencillamente[i] porque se cuenta con más espacio geográfico <u>habitable</u>.

*No hay una teoría única para explicar la exuberancia natural que se produce en los trópicos.*

[a]cuentan… tienen   [b]no… *have not been able*   [c]respuesta… *unambiguous answer*   [d]que… *that have been proposed*   [e]puntos… *weak points*   [f]expuestas… *given for this wealth*   [g]fue… *was outlined*   [h]hace… *20 years ago*   [i]*simply*

*La biodiversidad de los trópicos se demuestra (is demonstrated) en la gran variedad de especies que viven en estas regiones. Las ranas (frogs) son parte de esta biodiversidad.*

La segunda es de los últimos años 80 y fue diseñada por George Stevens, de Nuevo México: las especies tropicales son esclavas[j] de sus condiciones térmicas;[k] por eso no pueden colonizar nuevos territorios menos cálidos[l] y se concentran como un gueto[m] en el trópico.

La tercera es una teoría histórica y explica que los trópicos fueron[n] las áreas de la Tierra que escaparon al efecto destructor del aumento[o] de las regiones heladas[p] durante las glaciaciones.

Ninguna de las tres ha sido confirmada.[q] ∎

[j]*slaves* [k]*thermal* [l]*hot* [m]*ghetto* [n]*were* [o]*increase* [p]*frozen* [q]*ha… has been confirmed*

## Comprensión

**A. ¿Se menciona o no?** ¿Cuáles de los siguientes temas se mencionan en la lectura?

|  | SÍ | NO |
|---|---|---|
| **1.** Información sobre la gente (*people*) indígena de los trópicos. | ☐ | ☑ |
| **2.** Teorías que explican (*explain*) la biodiversidad de los trópicos. | ☑ | ☐ |
| **3.** Información sobre la deforestación de los trópicos. | ☐ | ☑ |
| **4.** Teorías que explican la climatología de los trópicos. | ☐ | ☑ |
| **5.** La contaminación de algunas regiones de los trópicos. | ☐ | ☑ |

**B. Resumen.** En inglés, escriba un breve resumen de las tres teorías presentadas en la lectura. Compare su resumen con el de otro estudiante. ¿Cuál de las teorías parece más factible (*feasible*)?

## A ESCRIBIR

**A. La biodiversidad local.** La lectura comenta la gran biodiversidad de los trópicos, y propone teorías que explican este fenómeno. Escriba un breve ensayo (*essay*) que comente cómo es el clima donde Ud. vive y qué animales y plantas habitan la zona. Use las siguientes preguntas para empezar y consulte un diccionario bilingüe si es necesario.

¿Cómo es la biodiversidad en la región donde Ud. vive?
¿Hay muchos animales y plantas indígenas?
¿Cuál es la relación entre el clima de la región y la flora y la fauna?

**B. Las selvas latinoamericanas.** Busque información sobre las selvas en Latinoamérica. Use las siguientes preguntas como guía para empezar una introducción. Luego dé más detalles sobre la selva de un país específico.

¿Qué países tienen selvas tropicales?
¿Cómo se llaman las selvas?
¿Qué grupos indígenas viven en las selvas?
¿Qué tiempo hace en las selvas y cuáles son las estaciones?

## Suggestions

• Ask students if the following activities are typical on their campus when it's bad weather.

1. *Cuando hace frío, juegan al basquetbol en el gimnasio.*
2. *Cuando nieva, pasan la tarde en la sala de la residencia estudiantil.*
3. *Cuando nieva, hacen muñecos de nieve* (draw on the board).

4. *Cuando llueve, no salen de la residencia.*
5. *Cuando hace mucho calor, duermen todo el día.*

## GRAMÁTICA

To review the grammar points presented in this chapter, refer to the indicated grammar presentations. You'll find further practice of these structures in the Workbook/Laboratory Manual, on the Interactive CD-ROM, and on the *¿Qué tal?* Online Learning Center (www.mhhe.com/quetal7).

**14** ¿Qué están haciendo?— Present Progressive: **estar** + **-ndo**

Do you know how to form and when to use the present progressive in Spanish?

**15** ¿**Ser** o **estar**?— Summary of the Uses of **ser** and **estar**

Should you use **ser** or **estar** to describe inherent qualities, to describe health and physical conditions, to express time, to form the present progressive?

**16** Describing—Comparisons

Do you know how to compare things and people?

• Ask students what they prefer.

*¿Prefiere Ud.... ?*

1. *¿los días cortos del invierno o los días largos del verano?*
2. *¿el tiempo del otoño o el de la primavera?*
3. *¿las actividades de verano o las de invierno?*

## VOCABULARIO

Practice this vocabulary with digital flash cards on the Online Learning Center (www.mhhe.com/quetal7).

### Los verbos

| | |
|---|---|
| celebrar | to celebrate |
| pasar | to spend (*time*); to happen |
| quedarse | to stay, remain (*in a place*) |

### ¿Qué tiempo hace?

| | |
|---|---|
| está (muy) nublado | it's (very) cloudy, overcast |
| hace... | it's . . . |
| (muy) buen/mal tiempo | (very) good/bad weather |
| (mucho) calor | (very) hot |
| fresco | cool |
| (mucho) frío | (very) cold |
| (mucho) sol | (very) sunny |
| (mucho) viento | (very) windy |
| hay (mucha) contaminación | there's (lots of) pollution |
| llover (ue) | to rain |
| llueve | it's raining |
| nevar (ie) | to snow |
| nieva | it's snowing |

• Have students answer the following questions.

1. *¿Dónde prefiere Ud. vivir, donde hace calor o donde hace fresco?*
2. *¿Le gusta vivir donde llueve mucho? ¿donde nieva mucho?*
3. *Describa la diferencia entre el clima de Michigan y el de Texas.*
4. *¿Prefiere Ud. vivir en un lugar con cuatro estaciones o con solamente una?*
5. *¿En qué partes de este país hay solamente una estación?*

### Los meses del año

| | |
|---|---|
| ¿Cuál es la fecha de hoy? | What's today's date? |
| el primero de | the first of (*month*) |

| | |
|---|---|
| enero | julio |
| febrero | agosto |
| marzo | septiembre |
| abril | octubre |
| mayo | noviembre |
| junio | diciembre |

### Las estaciones del año

| | |
|---|---|
| la primavera | spring |
| el verano | summer |
| el otoño | fall, autumn |
| el invierno | winter |

### Los lugares

| | |
|---|---|
| la capital | capital city |
| la isla | island |
| el parque | park |
| la playa | beach |

## Otros sustantivos

| | |
|---|---|
| el año | year |
| el clima | climate |
| el cumpleaños | birthday |
| la estación | season |
| el mes | month |
| el/la novio/a | boyfriend/girlfriend |
| la respuesta | answer |
| el tiempo | weather |

## Los adjetivos

| | |
|---|---|
| abierto/a | open |
| aburrido/a | bored |
| alegre | happy |
| cansado/a | tired |
| cariñoso/a | affectionate |
| cerrado/a | closed |
| congelado/a | frozen; very cold |
| contento/a | content, happy |
| desordenado/a | messy |
| difícil | hard, difficult |
| enfermo/a | sick |
| fácil | easy |
| furioso/a | furious, angry |
| limpio/a | clean |
| loco/a | crazy |
| nervioso/a | nervous |
| ocupado/a | busy |
| ordenado/a | neat |
| preocupado/a | worried |
| querido/a | dear |
| seguro/a | sure, certain |
| sucio/a | dirty |
| triste | sad |

**Suggestions**

- Divide the class into two teams. Call out the name of a month and have representatives from each team take turns mentioning a word or phrase related to that month. Other members of the team can offer suggestions if their representative falters. When all related terms have been suggested, call out another month.
- Play charades in Spanish, using nouns adjectives, and comparisons from the *Vocabulario* list.
- Using a map or a globe, have students compare geographical locations. Prompt them with questions.

  *¿Qué ciudad está más al norte, Nueva York o Quito?*

  Have them answer in full sentences.

- Place a common classroom item in different places in the classroom (behind the door, underneath a desk, and so on) and have students describe its location.

## Las comparaciones

| | |
|---|---|
| más/menos... que | more/less . . . than |
| tan... como | as . . . as |
| tanto como | as much as |
| tanto/a(s)... como | as much/many . . . as |
| mayor | older |
| mejor | better; best |
| menor | younger |
| peor | worse |

## Las preposiciones

| | |
|---|---|
| a la derecha de | to the right of |
| a la izquierda de | to the left of |
| al lado de | alongside of |
| cerca de | close to |
| debajo de | below |
| delante de | in front of |
| detrás de | behind |
| encima de | on top of |
| entre | between, among |
| lejos de | far from |

## Los puntos cardinales

el norte, el sur, el este, el oeste

## Palabras adicionales

| | |
|---|---|
| afuera | outdoors |
| conmigo | with me |
| contigo | with you (*fam.*) |
| esta noche | tonight |
| estar (*irreg.*) bien | to be comfortable (*temperature*) |
| mí (*obj. of prep.*) | me |
| sin embargo | however |
| tener (*irreg.*) (mucho) calor | to be (very) warm, hot |
| tener (*irreg.*) (mucho) frío | to be (very) cold |
| ti (*obj. of prep.*) | you |
| todavía | still |

# ¿Qué le gusta comer?

## CULTURA

## VOCABULARIO

## GRAMÁTICA

*Un mercado en la Ciudad de Panamá*

Paso 1: Vocabulario
See the "Chapter-by-Chapter Supplementary Materials" in the IM for a model for vocabulary presentation, as well as additional teaching suggestions, notes, activities, and other resources for *Paso 1*.

*La… Food*

## LA COMIDA°

**Resources: Transparency 46–49**
Transparencies 47–49 include additional vocabulary and provide more practice with meals (47), food groups (48), and menus (49).

**Las comidas** (*Meals*)

**el desayuno**
(*breakfast*)

el jugo (de fruta)
el cereal
la leche
la mantequilla
el té
el pan tostado
el huevo
el café

**Suggestion**
Use magazine clippings or other visuals to present words from the vocabulary. Model pronunciation and ask *sí/no* questions.

**el almuerzo**
(*lunch*)

**Heritage Speakers**
• En muchos países latinoamericanos, se puede hacer las compras en supermercados modernos o en mercados al aire libre. Pídales a sus estudiantes hispanohablantes que comparen y contrasten los dos tipos de mercado.
• Recuerde que en algunos dialectos del español la palabra *almorzar* significa *comer a media mañana* y es parecida a la expresión en inglés *to have brunch*.

el sándwich
la manzana
el queso
la cerveza
el agua mineral*
el tomate
la lechuga
la ensalada
la hamburguesa
la sopa

**la cena**
(*dinner, supper*)

**Multimedia: Audio**
Students can listen to and practice this chapter's vocabulary on the Online Learning Center (**www.mhhe.com/quetal7**), as well as on the Textbook Audio CD, part of the Laboratory Audio Program.

**Refrán**

«La manzana podrida, pierde a su compañía.»

Write the *refrán* on the board. Students will need help with the word *podrida* (rotten). Ask what rotten apple saying we have in English (*One rotten apple spoils the whole bushel.*), and have them brainstorm other apple sayings. (*You are the apple of my eye. Don't upset the apple cart. An apple a day keeps the doctor away. As American as apple pie. The apple doesn't fall far from the tree.*)

el pastel
el vino blanco
el vino tinto
las zanahorias
el bistec
las arvejas
el pescado
el pan
la patata / la papa†
el pollo (asado)

*The noun **agua** (water) is feminine, but the masculine articles are used with it in the singular: **el agua**. This occurs with all feminine nouns that begin with a stressed **a** sound, for example, **el (un) ama de casa** (homemaker).

†In Latin America, many Spanish speakers use **la papa,** not **la patata,** to refer to potatoes.

*Capítulo 6 • ¿Qué le gusta comer?*

**Heritage Speakers**

Algunos mexicanos y mexicoamericanos dicen *guajolote* en vez de *pavo*. Pregúnteles a los hispanohablantes de la clase qué otras variaciones usan para referirse a la comida.

| Otra bebida | | Otros pescados y mariscos | |
|---|---|---|---|
| el refresco | soft drink | el atún | tuna |
| | | los camarones | shrimp |
| **Otras frutas** | | la langosta | lobster |
| la banana | banana | el salmón | salmon |
| la naranja | orange | | |
| | | **Otros postres** | |
| **Otras verduras** | | el flan | (baked) custard |
| el champiñón | mushroom | la galleta | cookie |
| los espárragos | asparagus | el helado | ice cream |
| los frijoles | beans | | |
| | | **Otras comidas** | |
| **Otras carnes** | | el arroz | rice |
| la chuleta (de cerdo) | (pork) chop | el yogur | yogurt |
| el jamón | ham | | |
| el pavo | turkey | **Otras expresiones** | |
| la salchicha | sausage; hot dog | desayunar | to have (eat) breakfast |
| | | almorzar (ue) | to have (eat) lunch |
| | | cenar | to have (eat) dinner, supper |

**Con. A: Suggestion**

Remind students that *tomar* also means *to drink* and is synonymous with *beber*.

## ■ Conversación

**Con. A: Follow-Up**
Have students give alternative menus for the types of meals listed.

**A. ¿Qué quiere tomar?** Match the following descriptions of meals with a category.

1. __c__ una sopa fría, langosta, espárragos, una ensalada de lechuga y tomate, todo con vino blanco y, para terminar, un pastel
2. __d__ jugo de fruta, huevos con jamón, pan tostado y café
3. __a__ pollo asado, arroz, arvejas, agua mineral y, para terminar, una manzana
4. __b__ una hamburguesa con patatas fritas, un refresco y un helado

a. un menú ligero (*light*) para una dieta
b. una comida rápida
c. una cena elegante
d. un desayuno estilo norteamericano

**B. Definiciones.** ¿Qué es?

1. un plato (*dish*) de lechuga y tomate    la ensalada
2. una bebida alcohólica blanca o roja    el vino
3. un líquido caliente (*hot*) que se toma* con cuchara (*spoon*)    la sopa
4. una verdura anaranjada    la zanahoria
5. la carne típica para la barbacoa en este país    el bistec

**Con. B: Variation**
Do the activity once, according to the directions. Then, with books closed, give the names of food items and have students give the corresponding definitions, following the model of items in *Conversación B*.

6. una comida muy común en la China y en el Japón    el arroz
7. la comida favorita de los ratones (*mice*)    el queso
8. una verdura frita que se come con las hamburguesas    la patata / la papa
9. una fruta roja o verde    la manzana
10. una fruta amarilla de las zonas tropicales    la banana

**Con. B: Note**
The *se* + verb structure is not stressed for active use in *¿Qué tal?*, but it is used, as appropriate, in readings and in direction lines.

*Remember that placing **se** before a verb form can change its English equivalent slightly: **usa** (he/she/it uses) → **se usa** (is used).

# PASO 1

**Nota cultural: Comprensión**
1. What are some foods originally from America? (*¿Qué comidas son originalmente de América?*)
2. Where are the following ingredients for a taco originally from? (*¿De dónde son originalmente los siguientes ingredientes para un taco?*) *¿el tomate?* (*América*) *¿la carne de res* (new word)*?* (*Europa*) *¿el pollo?* (*Europa*) *¿la tortilla?* (*América*)

---

## NOTA COMUNICATIVA

### More *tener* Idioms

Use these **tener** idioms to talk about foods and eating.

| | |
|---|---|
| **tener (mucha) hambre** | to be (very) hungry |
| **tener (mucha) sed** | to be (very) thirsty |

---

**C. Entrevista. Consejos** (*Advice*) **a la hora de comer.**   ¿Qué debe comer o beber su compañero/a en las siguientes situaciones? Déle consejos según el modelo.

MODELO:   E1: Tengo mucha hambre.
          E2: Debes comer un bistec con patatas fritas.

1. Quiero comer algo ligero porque no tengo hambre.
2. Quiero comer algo fuerte (*heavy*) porque tengo mucha hambre.
3. Tengo un poco de sed y quiero tomar algo antes de la comida.
4. Quiero comer algo antes del plato principal (*main course*).
5. Quiero comer algo después del plato principal.
6. Estoy a dieta (*on a diet*).
7. Estoy de vacaciones en Maine (o Boston).
8. Después de levantarme, no estoy completamente despierto/a (*awake*).

---

## NOTA CULTURAL

### La comida del mundo hispánico

Often when we think of dishes from the Spanish-speaking world, what comes to mind are rice, beans, spicy **chiles,** corn or flour **tortillas,** and **burritos.** That, however, is a misconception. Corn and flour tortillas and burritos are unknown in many Spanish-speaking countries. Many Hispanic cuisines are not spicy at all, and if you are in Spain and order **una tortilla,** you will be served a wedge of potato omelette!

*Una tortilla española*

The cuisines of Spanish-speaking countries are as diverse as their inhabitants. With the arrival of the Spaniards in the Americas, indigenous cuisines were influenced by European foods that did not exist there before, such as beef and chicken. Likewise, European cuisines were influenced by the introduction of foods from the Americas, such as the tomato, the potato, and chocolate. Later, immigration from countries such as Ireland, Germany, Italy, China, and Japan further influenced American cuisines.*

*Unas tortillas mexicanas*

*Remember that, in this context, American *refers to all the countries in North, Central, and South America.*

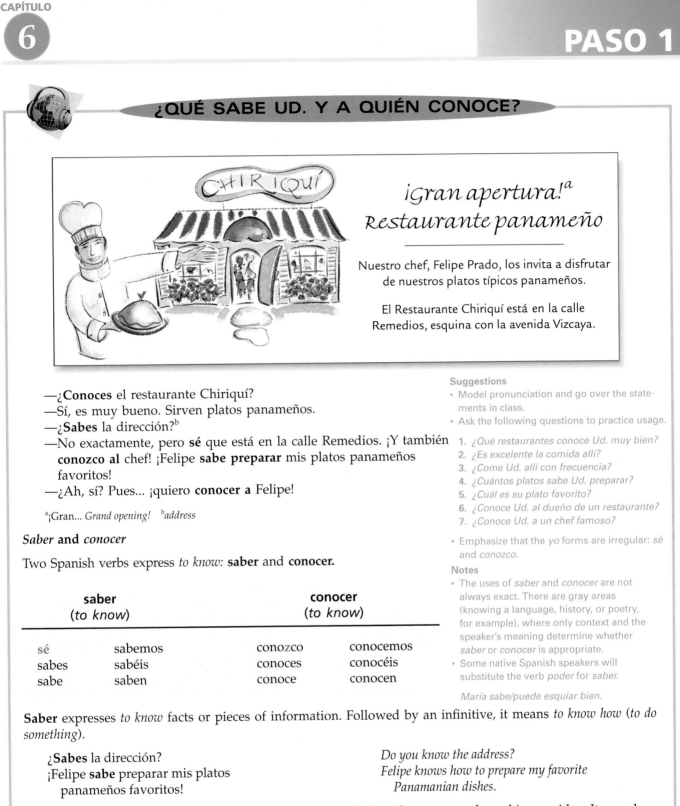

## ¿QUÉ SABE UD. Y A QUIÉN CONOCE?

### ¡Gran apertura!ᵃ Restaurante panameño

Nuestro chef, Felipe Prado, los invita a disfrutar de nuestros platos típicos panameños.

El Restaurante Chiriquí está en la calle Remedios, esquina con la avenida Vizcaya.

—¿**Conoces** el restaurante Chiriquí?
—Sí, es muy bueno. Sirven platos panameños.
—¿**Sabes** la dirección?ᵇ
—No exactamente, pero **sé** que está en la calle Remedios. ¡Y también **conozco al** chef! ¡Felipe **sabe preparar** mis platos panameños favoritos!
—¿Ah, sí? Pues... ¡quiero **conocer a** Felipe!

ᵃ¡Gran... *Grand opening!*   ᵇ*address*

### *Saber* and *conocer*

Two Spanish verbs express *to know:* **saber** and **conocer.**

| saber (to know) | | conocer (to know) | |
|---|---|---|---|
| sé | sabemos | conozco | conocemos |
| sabes | sabéis | conoces | conocéis |
| sabe | saben | conoce | conocen |

**Saber** expresses *to know* facts or pieces of information. Followed by an infinitive, it means *to know how* (*to do something*).

| ¿**Sabes** la dirección? | *Do you know the address?* |
|---|---|
| ¡Felipe **sabe** preparar mis platos panameños favoritos! | *Felipe knows how to prepare my favorite Panamanian dishes.* |

**Conocer** is used to express *to know* or *be acquainted* (*familiar*) *with* a person, place, thing, or idea. It can also mean *to meet.*

| ¿**Conoces** el restaurante Chiriquí? | *Do you know (Are you familiar with) the restaurant Chiriquí?* |
|---|---|
| Sí... ¡Y también **conozco** al chef! | *Yes . . . And I also know the chef!* |
| ¡Quiero **conocer** a Felipe! | *I want to meet Felipe!* |

**Refrán**

«Unos saben lo que hacen, y otros hacen lo que saben.»

Ask students which phrase from this *refrán* describes them best, the first or the second.

**Heritage Speakers**
Note que la *a* personal no se usa con complementos directos cuando estos se refieren a personas indefinidas o cuya existencia se desconoce. Invite a los hispanohablantes a explicar la diferencia entre las siguientes oraciones.

## The Personal *a*

Note (on page 159) the use of the word **a** before the nouns **chef** and **Felipe** in the brief dialogue and in the last two examples. In Spanish, the word **a** immediately precedes the direct object* of a sentence when the direct object refers to a specific person or persons. This **a,** called the **a personal,** has no equivalent in English.[†] Remember that **a** contracts with the article **el: a + el = al.**

 The personal **a** is used before the interrogative words **¿quién?** and **¿quiénes?** when they function as direct objects.

**¿A quién** llamas?
*Who(m) are you calling?*

 The verbs **buscar** (*to look for*), **escuchar** (*to listen to*), **esperar** (*to wait for; to expect*), and **mirar** (*to look at*) include the sense of the English prepositions *for, to,* and *at*. These verbs take direct objects in Spanish (not prepositional phrases, as in English).

**Busco mi abrigo.**
*I'm looking for my overcoat.*

**Espero a mi hijo.**
*I'm waiting for my son.*

*Carlos busca un consejero que lo pueda ayudar.*
*Carlos conoce a un consejero que lo puede ayudar.*

Sin embargo, los pronombres *alguien, nadie, alguno* y *ninguno* siempre requieren el uso de la *a* personal.

---

**Con. A: Follow-Up**

- Ask students the following questions to check comprehension.

  *¿Conocen Lola y Manolo el restaurante nuevo?*
  *¿Saben qué tipo de comida se sirve allí?*
  *¿Saben el número de teléfono de Virginia?*

- Have students list three things they know how to do. Then have them work in groups of three to four to state what they know how to do and to find out if others in their group also know how to do it.

  MODELO: *Yo sé tocar el acordeón. Y tú, Alex, ¿sabes tocar el acordeón?*

Discuss the results. *¿Qué sabe hacer más gente? ¿A cuántas personas conoce Ud. que (hacen... )?*

**Need more practice?**

- Workbook/Laboratory Manual
- Interactive CD-ROM
- Online Learning Center (www.mhhe.com/quetal7)

## ■ Conversación

**A. ¿Dónde cenamos?** Lola y Manolo quieren cenar fuera. Pero, ¿dónde? Complete el diálogo con la forma correcta de **saber** o **conocer.**

LOLA: ¿(Sabes/Conoces[1]) adónde quieres ir a cenar?

MANOLO: No (sé/conozco[2]). ¿Y tú?

LOLA: No. Pero hay un restaurante nuevo en la calle Betis. Creo que se llama Guadalquivir. ¿(Sabes/Conoces[3]) el restaurante?

MANOLO: No, pero (sé/conozco[4]) que tiene mucha fama. Es el restaurante favorito de Virginia. Ella (sabe/conoce[5]) al dueño.[a]

LOLA: ¿(Sabes/Conoces[6]) qué tipo de comida tienen?

MANOLO: No (sé/conozco[7]). Pero podemos llamar a Virginia. ¿(Sabes/Conoces[8]) su teléfono?

LOLA: Está en mi guía telefónica. Y pregúntale[b] a Virginia si ella (sabe/conoce[9]) si aceptan reservas con anticipación[c] o no.

[a]*owner* [b]*ask* [c]*con... in advance*

## B. Entrevista

1. ¿Qué restaurantes conoces en esta ciudad? ¿Cuál es tu restaurante favorito? ¿Por qué? ¿Es buena la comida allí? ¿Qué tipo de comida sirven? ¿Te gusta el ambiente (*atmosphere*)? ¿Comes allí con frecuencia?

2. ¿Conoces a alguna persona famosa? ¿Quién es? ¿Cómo es? ¿Qué detalles sabes de la vida de esta persona?

3. ¿Qué platos sabes preparar? ¿Tacos? ¿enchiladas? ¿pollo frito? ¿Te gusta cocinar (*to cook*)? ¿Siempre usas ingredientes frescos?

4. ¿Esperas a tus amigos para ir a la universidad / después de la clase? ¿A quién buscas cuando necesitas ayuda (*help*) con el español? ¿Dónde buscas a tus amigos por la noche / cuando es hora de comer?

---

*The direct object (**el complemento directo**) *is the part of the sentence that indicates to whom or to what the action of the verb is directed or upon whom or upon what it acts. In the sentence* I saw John, *the direct object is* John. *The direct object is explained in more detail in* **Gramática 17** *of this chapter.*

[†]*The personal* **a** *is not generally used with* **tener: Tengo cuatro hijos.**

**Note**
See the Workbook/Laboratory Manual for presentation and practice of the letters *d* and *t*.

Paso 2: Gramática
See the "Chapter-by-Chapter Supplementary Materials" in the IM for additional
teaching suggestions, notes, activities, and other resources for *Paso 2*.

## 17 Expressing *what* or *whom* Direct Object Pronouns

**De compras en el supermercado**

**LA MODERNA MARKET**
930-932 State Street • New Haven, CT • (203) 776-2333

• **TODA CLASE
DE CARNES
FRESCAS**

• **VEGETALES
FRESCOS**
• **GROCERY**

• **LÍNEA COMPLETA
DE PRODUCTOS
MEXICANOS**
La Moderna • La Morena
• La Costeña • Nestle

Solicite Nuestra Propia Longaniza y Cesina
**ATENDEMOS PEDIDOS PARA NEGOCIOS**

Indique cuáles de estas afirmaciones son verdaderas para Ud.

1. la carne
   - ☐ *La* como todos los días. Por eso tengo que comprar*la* con frecuencia.
   - ☐ *La* como de vez en cuando (*once in a while*). Por eso no *la* compro a menudo (*often*).
   - ☐ Nunca *la* como. No necesito comprar*la*.

2. el café
   - ☐ *Lo* bebo todos los días. Por eso tengo que comprar*lo* con frecuencia.
   - ☐ *Lo* bebo de vez en cuando. Por eso no *lo* compro a menudo.
   - ☐ Nunca *lo* bebo. No necesito comprar*lo*.

3. los huevos
   - ☐ *Los* como todos los días. Por eso tengo que comprar*los* con frecuencia.
   - ☐ *Los* como de vez en cuando. Por eso no *los* compro a menudo.
   - ☐ Nunca *los* como. No necesito comprar*los*.

4. las bananas
   - ☐ *Las* como todos los días. Por eso tengo que comprar*las* con frecuencia.
   - ☐ *Las* como de vez en cuando. Por eso no *las* compro a menudo.
   - ☐ Nunca *las* como. No necesito comprar*las*.

5. el agua
   - ☐ *La* tomo todos los días. Por eso tengo que comprar*la* con frecuencia.
   - ☐ *La* tomo de vez en cuando. Por eso no *la* compro a menudo.
   - ☐ Nunca *la* tomo. No necesito comprar*la*.

**Extension**
Give students cues for additional sentences; for example, *el pollo: Lo como todos los días...*

**Suggestions**
- Introduce third person direct object pronouns first. Put a number of objects on the desk (*un libro, una flor, un coche* [toy car]) and model sentences with a noun-to-pronoun transformation: *Miro el libro.* → *Lo miro.*
- Follow a similar sequence with feminine singular nouns, then plural masculine and feminine nouns.
- After presenting third person object pronouns with visuals, expand their use to include the meaning of *you.* Have students stand up as appropriate.

  *Yo lo/la veo* (*a Ud., Roberto,* and so on).
  *¿Ud. me ve* (*a mí*)? → *Sí, profesor(a), lo/la veo.*

- Point out that, like the subject pronoun *ellos,* the direct object pronoun *los* can refer to either a masculine group or a combination of masculine and feminine nouns.
- Point out that like direct object nouns, direct object pronouns answer the question *what?* or *whom?* after the verb.
- Point out that many verbs commonly used with reflexive pronouns can also be used with direct object nouns and pronouns when the action of the verb is directed at someone other than the subject of the sentence. The meaning of the verb will change slightly. Provide the following examples.

  *Generalmente me despierto a las ocho. La radio **me** despierta.* (I generally wake up at eight. The radio wakes me.)
  *En un restaurante, el camarero **nos** sienta.* (In a restaurant, the waiter seats us.)

Have students note these verbs as well: *afeitar, acostar,* and *bañar.*

# PASO 2

## Direct Object Pronouns

| | | | | |
|---|---|---|---|---|
| me | me | | nos | us |
| te | you (*fam. sing.*) | | os | you (*fam. pl.*) |
| lo* | you (*form. sing.*), him, it (*m.*) | | los | you (*form. pl.*), them (*m., m. + f.*) |
| la | you (*form. sing.*), her, it (*f.*) | | las | you (*form. pl.*), them (*f.*) |

**A.** Like direct object nouns, *direct object pronouns* (**los pronombres del complemento directo**) are the first recipient of the action of the verb. Direct object pronouns are placed before a conjugated verb and after the word **no** when it appears. Third person direct object pronouns are used only when the direct object noun has already been mentioned.
[Práctica A]

¿El menú? Diego no **lo** necesita.
*The menu? Diego doesn't need it.*

¿Dónde están el pastel y el helado? **Los** necesito ahora.
*Where are the cake and the ice cream? I need them now.*

Ellos **me** ayudan.
*They're helping me.*

> **direct object** = the noun or pronoun that receives the action of a verb

**B.** The direct object pronouns may be attached to an infinitive or a present participle.
[Práctica B–C]

**Las** tengo que leer.
Tengo que leer**las**.
} *I have to read them.*

**Lo** estoy comiendo.
Estoy comiéndo**lo**.
} *I am eating it.*

**C.** Note that the direct object pronoun **lo** can refer to actions, situations, or ideas in general. When used in this way, **lo** expresses English *it* or *that.*

**Lo** comprende muy bien.
*He understands it (that) very well.*

No **lo** creo.
*I don't believe it (that).*

**Lo** sé.
*I know (it).*

♻ **Reciclado**
Review clothing vocabulary. Have students answer the following questions using direct object pronouns. Write a model answer on the board.

*Ud. hace la maleta* (You are packing) *para un viaje a Acapulco. ¿Necesita las siguientes cosas?*
 el traje de baño
 las sandalias
 las gafas de sol
 el libro de español
 el libro de sicología
 los pantalones cortos
 las camisetas
 la crema bronceadora
 el reloj
*Claro que* [no] *lo necesito.*

**AUTOPRUEBA**

Match the direct object pronouns with the nouns and subject pronouns.

1. _____ los
2. _____ la
3. _____ te
4. _____ lo
5. _____ las
6. _____ nos

a. Ana
b. tú
c. Pedro y Carolina
d. María y yo
e. Jorge
f. Elena y Rosa

*Answers: 1. c 2. a 3. b 4. e 5. f 6. d*

**Heritage Speakers**
En España y en algunos países de Latinoamérica, a veces se usa *le* en vez de *lo.* Este fenómeno se llama *leísmo.* Por ejemplo, *Raquel lo/le conoció en Sevilla. Ella lo/le vio en el tren.* Aunque la mayoría de los españoles prefiere usar *le* en estos casos, la Real Academia Española y la mayoría de los latinoamericanos prefieren el uso de *lo.*

---

*In Spain and in some other parts of the Spanish-speaking world, **le** is frequently used instead of **lo** for the direct object pronoun him. This usage, called **el leísmo,** will not be followed in ¿Qué tal?*

### ■ Práctica

#### A. ¿Qué comen los vegetarianos?

PASO 1  Aquí hay una lista de diferentes comidas. ¿Van a formar parte de la dieta de un vegetariano? Conteste según los modelos.

> MODELOS:  el bistec → No *lo* va a comer.
> la banana → *La* va a comer.

1. las patatas
2. el arroz
3. las chuletas de cerdo
4. el pollo
5. las zanahorias
6. las manzanas
7. los camarones
8. el pan
9. los champiñones
10. los frijoles
11. la ensalada

PASO 2  Si hay un estudiante vegetariano / una estudiante vegetariana en la clase, pídale que verifique (*ask him or her to verify*) las respuestas de Ud.

#### B. La cena de Lola y Manolo.
La siguiente descripción de la cena de Lola y Manolo es muy repetitiva. Combine las oraciones, cambiando los nombres de complemento directo por pronombres cuando sea (*whenever it is*) necesario.

> MODELO:  El camarero (*waiter*) trae un menú. Lola lee *el menú*. →
> El camarero trae un menú y Lola *lo* lee.

1. El camarero trae una botella de vino tinto. Pone *la botella* en la mesa.
2. El camarero trae las copas (*glasses*) de vino. Pone *las copas* delante de Lola y Manolo.
3. Lola quiere la especialidad de la casa. Va a pedir *la especialidad de la casa*.
4. Manolo prefiere el pescado fresco (*fresh*). Pide *el pescado fresco*.
5. Lola quiere una ensalada también. Por eso pide *una ensalada*.
6. El camerero trae la comida. Sirve *la comida*.
7. Manolo necesita otra servilleta (*napkin*). Pide *otra servilleta*.
8. «¿La cuenta (*bill*)? El dueño está preparando *la cuenta* para Uds.»
9. Manolo quiere pagar con tarjeta (*card*) de crédito. Pero no trae *su tarjeta*.
10. Por fin, Lola toma la cuenta. Paga *la cuenta*.

---

### NOTA COMUNICATIVA

#### Talking About What You Have Just Done

To talk about what you have *just* done, use the phrase **acabar + de** with an infinitive.

**Acabo de llegar** con Beto.

*I just arrived with Beto.*

**Acabas de celebrar** tu cumpleaños, ¿verdad?

*You just celebrated your birthday, didn't you?*

Note that the infinitive follows **de.** Remember that the infinitive is the only verb form that can follow a preposition in Spanish.

# PASO 2

**Prác. C: Preliminary Exercise**
Have students answer questions using *acabar de.*

**Need more practice?**

- Workbook/Laboratory Manual
- Interactive CD-ROM
- Online Learning Center
  (www.mhhe.com/quetal7)

**Prác. C: Answers**
*Possible answers:* **1.** *Acabo de escribirlas.
(Las acabo de escribir.)* **2.** *Acabo de
comprarlo. (Lo acabo de comprar.)* **3.** *Acabo
de pagarlos. (Los acabo de pagar.)* **4.** *Acabo
de prepararla. (La acabo de preparar.)*
**5.** *Acabo de pedirla. (La acabo de pedir.)*
**6.** *Acabo de ayudarte. (Te acabo de ayudar.)*

---

**Palabras útiles**

**nuestros padres (compañeros,
consejeros, amigos… )**

---

---

**Palabras y frases útiles**

**la cafeína
las calorías
el colesterol
la grasa** (fat)

**estar** (*irreg.*) **a dieta
ser** (*irreg.*) **alérgico/a a
ser** (*irreg.*) **bueno/a para la salud**
  (health)

**lo/la/los/las detesto
me da asco** (it makes me sick) **/
  me dan asco** (they make me
  sick)
**me pone** (it makes me)
  **nervioso/a**

---

*¿Quiere comer?* →
*Acabo de comer.*

| | |
|---|---|
| 1. *ver la televisión* | 4. *desayunar* |
| 2. *leer* | 5. *almorzar* |
| 3. *ir al centro* | 6. *cenar* |

**C. ¡Acabo de hacerlo!**   Imagine that a friend is pressuring you to do the
following things. With a classmate, tell him or her that you just did
each one, using either of the forms in the model.

MODELO:   E1: ¿Por qué no estudias la lección? →
          E2: Acabo de estudiar*la.* (*La* acabo de estudiar.)

1. ¿Por qué no escribes las composiciones para tus clases?
2. ¿Vas a comprar el periódico hoy?
3. ¿Por qué no pagas los cafés?
4. ¿Vas a preparar la comida para la fiesta?
5. ¿Puedes pedir la cuenta?
6. ¿Quieres ayudarme con la lección?

**Prác. C: Variation**
Have students work in groups of two
or three to make suggestions to each
other. Students should respond to
suggestions by saying they have just
done it.

*¿Quiere Ud. comer?* →
*No, acabo de comer.*
*¿Quiere Ud. mirar la televisión?* →
*No, acabo de mirarla.*

## ■ **Conversación**

**A. ¿Quién ayuda?**   Todos necesitamos ayuda en diferentes circunstancias.
¿Quién los ayuda a Uds. con lo siguiente? Use **nos** en sus respuestas.

MODELO:   con las cuentas → Nuestros padres *nos* ayudan con las
          cuentas.

1. con las cuentas
2. con la tarea
3. con la matrícula
4. con el horario de clases
5. con los problemas personales

**B. Una encuesta sobre la comida.**   Hágales (*Ask*) preguntas a sus
compañeros de clase para saber si toman las comidas o bebidas
indicadas y con qué frecuencia. Deben explicar por qué toman o *no*
toman cierta cosa.

MODELO:   la carne → E1: ¿Comes carne?
                     E2: No, no *la* como casi nunca porque tiene mucho
                         colesterol.

| | |
|---|---|
| 1. la carne | 7. el café |
| 2. los mariscos | 8. los dulces (*sweets; candy*) |
| 3. el yogur | 9. el alcohol |
| 4. la pizza | 10. el atún |
| 5. las hamburguesas | 11. los espárragos |
| 6. el pollo | 12. el hígado (*liver*) |

♻ **Prác. C: Reciclado**
Have students tell what they have just done before leaving these places:

  *¿Qué acaba de hacer Ud. cuando sale de… ?*

1. *¿un mercado?*
2. *¿una discoteca?*
3. *¿un restaurante?*
4. *¿una librería?*
5. *¿el laboratorio de lenguas?*
6. *¿una clase de literatura inglesa?*
7. *¿un bar?*

---

*Capítulo 6 • ¿Qué le gusta comer?*

Follow-Up

Ask the following questions to personalize information and to check comprehension of the *minidiálogo*.

## 18 Expressing Negation · Indefinite and Negative Words

1. ¿Tienen Uds. ganas de comer algo ahora mismo? ¿Qué?

2. ¿Quién no tiene dinero nunca?

3. ¿A alguien le gusta ir de compras para comprar comida?

4. ¿A quién nunca le gusta ir de compras?

### En la cocina de Diego y Antonio

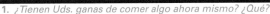

Diego llega a casa y tiene hambre.

DIEGO: Quiero comer *algo*, pero *no* hay *nada* de comer en esta casa. Y *no* tengo ganas de ir de compras. Y además, ¡*no* tengo *ni* un centavo!

ANTONIO: ¡Ay! *Siempre* eres así. Tú *nunca* tienes ganas de ir de compras. Y lo del dinero… ¡esa ya es otra historia!

### Comprensión: ¿Quién… ?

1. tiene hambre   Diego
2. nunca tiene dinero   Diego
3. critica a su amigo   Antonio
4. no quiere ir de compras   Diego

Here is a list of the most common indefinite and negative words in Spanish. You have been using many of them since the first chapters of *¿Qué tal?*

♻ Reciclado

Remind students that the personal *a* is used before *alguien, nadie, alguno*, and *ninguno* when they refer to people and function as a direct object. Note that the personal *a* is omitted after *hay* and *tener*.

| | |
|---|---|
| **algo** | something, anything |
| **alguien** | someone, anyone |
| **algún (alguno/a/os/as)** | some, any |
| **siempre** | always |
| **también** | also |

| | |
|---|---|
| **nada** | nothing, not anything |
| **nadie** | no one, nobody, not anybody |
| **ningún (ninguno/a)** | no, none, not any |
| **nunca, jamás** | never |
| **tampoco** | neither, not either |

*Pronunciation hint:* Remember to pronounce the **d** in **nada** and **nadie** as a fricative, that is, like a *th* sound: **na đa, na đie.**

Suggestion

Offer optional vocabulary: *o… o…* and *ni… ni…*

## The Double Negative

When a negative word comes after the main verb, Spanish requires that another negative word—usually **no**—be placed before the verb. When a negative word precedes the verb, **no** is not used.

Heritage Speakers

En algunos dialectos del español del suroeste de los Estados Unidos, a veces se oye decir *nadien* o *naidien* por *nadie*. Estas formas se usan en el habla popular de algunos grupos, pero la forma *nadie* es la preferida. Pregúnteles a los estudiantes hispanohablantes si han oído este vocablo alguna vez o si ellos mismos lo usan entre amigos.

¿**No** estudia **nadie**?
¿**Nadie** estudia?  *Isn't anyone studying?*

**No** estás en clase **nunca**.
**Nunca** estás en clase.  *You're never in class.*

**No** quieren cenar aquí **tampoco**.
**Tampoco** quieren cenar aquí.  *They don't want to have dinner here, either.*

---

*In Diego and Antonio's kitchen*   Diego arrives home and he's hungry. DIEGO: *I want to eat something, but there's nothing to eat in this house. And I don't feel like going shopping. And furthermore, I don't have a cent!* ANTONIO: *Ah! You're always like that. You never feel like going shopping. And that bit about the money . . . , that's another story!*

# PASO 2

**Note**
The plural forms *ningunos/as* are rarely used. As in the example, indefinite questions with plural *algunos/as* frequently require singular *ningún/ninguna* in the negative answers. The exceptions would be nouns usually used in plural in Spanish, for example, *pantalones, medias, vacaciones,* and so on.

## *Alguno* and *ninguno*

**Alguno** and **ninguno** are adjectives. Unlike **nadie** and **nada** (nouns) or **nunca, jamás,** and **tampoco** (adverbs), **alguno** and **ninguno** must agree with the noun they modify.

**Alguno** and **ninguno** shorten to **algún** and **ningún,** respectively, before a masculine singular noun—just as **uno** shortens to **un, bueno** to **buen,** and **malo** to **mal.**

The plural forms **ningunos** and **ningunas** are rarely used.

—¿Hay **algunos** recados para mí hoy?
*Are there any messages for me today?*
—Lo siento, pero hoy no hay **ningún** recado para Ud.
*I'm sorry, but there are no messages for you today.*
    (*There is not a single message for you today.*)

**AUTOPRUEBA**

Give the corresponding negative word.

1. siempre          4. alguna
2. también          5. algo
3. alguien

*Answers: 1. nunca 2. tampoco 3. nadie 4. ninguna 5. nada*

Resources: Transparency 50

■ **Práctica**

**Prác. A: Suggestion**
Use items from *Práctica A* as an inductive activity to present and practice the double negative.

♻ **Prác. A: Reciclado**
Recycle words about houses and rooms. Ask students about things that they do or do not have in their rooms or houses.

*¿Tiene un baño privado?*

Also ask questions about their routines.

*¿Come con frecuencia en la cocina?*
*¿Cocina todos los días?*

**Need more practice?**

- Workbook/Laboratory Manual
- Interactive CD-ROM
- Online Learning Center
  (www.mhhe.com/quetal7)

**A. ¡Anticipemos! ¿Qué pasa esta noche en casa?** Tell whether the following statements about what is happening at this house are true (**cierto**) or false (**falso**). Then create as many additional sentences as you can about what is happening, following the model of the sentences.

1. No hay nadie en el baño.   falso
2. En la cocina, alguien está preparando la cena.   falso
3. No hay ninguna persona en el patio.   cierto
4. Hay algo en la mesa del comedor.   cierto
5. Algunos amigos se están divirtiendo en la sala.   cierto
6. Hay algunos platos en la mesa del comedor.   falso
7. No hay ningún niño en la casa.   falso

**B. ¡Por eso no come nadie allí!** Exprese negativamente, usando la negativa doble.

MODELO: Hay alguien en el restaurante. → *No hay nadie en el restaurante.*

1. Hay algo interesante en el menú.
2. Tienen algunos platos típicos.
3. El profesor cena allí también.
4. Mis amigos siempre almuerzan allí.
5. Preparan algo especial para grupos grandes.
6. Siempre hacen platos nuevos.
7. Y también sirven paella, mi plato favorito.

**Prác. B: Note**
Alert students that item 2 requires the singular form, *ninguno: No tienen ningún plato...*

## ■ Conversación

**Preguntas**

1. ¿Vamos a vivir en la luna (*moon*) algún día? ¿Vamos a viajar (*travel*) a otros planetas? ¿Vamos a vivir allí algún día? ¿Vamos a establecer contacto con seres (*beings*) de otros planetas algún día?

2. ¿Algunos de los estudiantes de esta universidad son de países extranjeros? ¿De dónde son? ¿Algunos de sus amigos son de habla española (*Spanish-speaking*)? ¿De dónde son?

3. En esta clase, ¿quién...

| | |
|---|---|
| siempre tiene algunas buenas ideas? | nunca contesta ninguna pregunta? |
| nunca les pregunta nada a sus compañeros? | va a ser muy rico algún día? |
| | nunca tiene tiempo para divertirse? |
| tiene algunos amigos españoles? | nunca mira la televisión? |
| siempre lo entiende todo? | no practica ningún deporte? |
| | siempre invita a los otros a comer? |

## En los Estados Unidos y el Canadá*

### Goya Foods, Inc.

**Necesita Tenerlos**

En Norteamérica muchos conocen **la marca Goya**: hay frijoles, arroz, condimentos, bebidas, café, productos de coco,[a] jugos de frutas tropicales y muchos **productos** más que son **fundamentales para las cocinas caribeña, mexicana, centroamericana y sudamericana.**

En los años 30 Prudencio Unanue, **un emigrante vasco del norte de España, funda[b] la compañía Goya.** Unanue y su esposa puertorriqueña llegan a Nueva York en 1916 y fundan Unanue Inc. en Manhattan en 1935, una compañía **especializada en importaciones de productos españoles** como olivas, aceite de oliva[c] y sardinas enlatadas.[d] En 1936 la compañía adopta el nombre de Goya. Desde 1974

la oficina principal está en Nueva Jersey. Hoy tiene **centros de procesamiento y distribución** en diversos estados, además de Puerto Rico, la República Dominicana y España.

La compañía Goya **está todavía en manos de[e] la familia Unanue:** los hijos de Prudencio y seis miembros de la tercera[f] generación. Goya es la primera compañía propiedad de hispanos representada en el Museo Nacional de Historia Americana del Instituto Smithsonian, en Washington, D.C., donde hay una colección de sus anuncios y envases.[g]

[a]*coconut* [b]*founds, starts* [c]*aceite... olive oil* [d]*canned* [e]*está... still belongs to* [f]*third* [g]*anuncios... ads and containers*

*From this point on in ¿Qué tal?, the **En los Estados Unidos y el Canadá** sections will be written in Spanish. Important words will be in boldface type. Scanning those words before you begin to read will help you get the gist of the passage.*

## LITERATURA: Carlos Guillermo Wilson

**Carlos Guillermo Wilson** *(1941– )*

**Sobre el autor:** *Carlos Guillermo Wilson es originario de Panamá. Actualmente enseña literatura en* San Diego State University *en California. Su poesía y sus cuentos tratan con frecuencia los temas de la raza y el prejuicio racial. El siguiente poema es del cuento «Los mosquitos de orixá Changó[a]»**

Desarraigado[b]

Abuelita africana,
¿no me reconoces?

Mi lengua es cervantina
Mi letanía[c] es cristiana
Mi danza es flamenca
Mi raza es mulata

Abuelita africana,
¿por qué no me reconoces?

[a]orixá… *the ancient deity Changó, a god representing man's virility*   [b]*Uprooted*   [c]*litany (religious rite)*

**Literatura: Notes**
- Carlos Guillermo Wilson has published two novels, *Chombo* (1981) and *Los nietos de Felicidad Dolores* (1991), and several collections of short stories and poems.
- *Los nietos de Felicidad Dolores* is about the 500-year journey (1492–199[?]) through identity conflicts, racial discrimination, and injustice of the African slaves and their descendents in the Antilles and Latin Americ[a]
- Wilson himself is a descendent of French-speaking great-grandparents from the island of St. Lucia and English-speaking maternal grandparents from Barbados and Jamaica. The latter moved to Panama where they were contracted to work on the Panama Canal.
- Wilson studied in Panama and in the United States and holds a doctora[te] in Hispanic Language and Literature from UCLA. He writes extensivel[y] on African American issues in Latin America and the Caribbea[n]

**Música: Notes**
- The musical duels were a common practice among calypso musicians. To win, the musicians not only had to be musical, but be able to think quickly.

## MÚSICA: El calipso

El calipso es una de las formas musicales más populares de Panamá. El calipso tuvo su origen[a] en Trinidad entre los esclavos[b] africanos. Llegó[c] a Panamá con los muchos obreros[d] contratados[e] para la construcción del Canal de Panamá. Desde[f] los tiempos de la esclavitud[g] en Trinidad, los duelos de improvisación[h] entre los cantantes[i] del calipso han sido[j] populares. Estos duelos se parecen a[k] los duelos del estilo musical *rap* de este país.

[a]tuvo… *originated*   [b]*slaves*   [c]*It came*   [d]*workers*   [e]*contracted*   [f]*Since*   [g]*slavery*   [h]duelos… *extemporization, improvisation duels*   [i]*singers*   [j]han… *have been*   [k]se… *resemble*

- Walter Gavitt Ferguson (1919- ) is a well-known *calipsero* who began playing and singing when he was 24 years old, and continues to give concerts today. He was called *Míster Gavitt* by his friends and fans, and was considered the Master of Calypso, especially in the "dueling"

competitions. He was mentally quick, and had a great sense of humor. Although *Míster Gavitt* sometimes sings in Spanish, he sings mostly in English or Creole English. One of his most memorable songs is "Me no wanna glamour gal."

Para tocar el calipso, se puede usar casi cualquier[l] instrumento. Con frecuencia se usan instrumentos hechos[m] en casa, de bambú o de bidones.[n] La música del calipso es menos importante que su letra,[o] que con frecuencia es improvisada y satírica. Ofrece una crítica de la política y la vida social.

[l]*any*   [m]*made*   [n]*(oil) drums*   [o]*lyrics*

Julio Mou, descendiente de padres chinos y arquitecto de profesión, es ahora uno de los compositores de música del calipso más conocidos[p] en Panamá. Aquí está Julio (a la izquierda) con el acordeonista Juancín Henríquez.

[p]*well-known*

*Publication of the Afro-Latin/American Research Association (PALARA), #1, 1997: 138–142.*

Paso 3: Gramática
See the "Chapter-by-Chapter Supplementary Materials" in the IM for additional
teaching suggestions, notes, activities, and other resources for *Paso 3*.

## ¿Recuerda Ud.?

In **Gramática 19,** you will learn to form one type of command. In Spanish, the formal commands are based on the first person singular of the present tense. To review what you already know about irregular first person present tense forms, give the **yo** form of the following infinitives.

**1.** salir    **2.** tener    **3.** conocer    **4.** pedir    **5.** hacer    **6.** dormir    **7.** perder    **8.** traer

## 19 Influencing Others Formal Commands

**Receta para guacamole**

En español, los mandatos se usan con frecuencia en las recetas. Estos verbos se usan en forma de mandato en esta receta. ¿Puede encontrarlos?

| | |
|---|---|
| **añadir** | to add |
| **cortar** | to cut |
| **mezclar** | to mix |
| **servir (i, i)** | to serve |

**Suggestion**
Help students formulate recipes for simple foods, such as a salad or a sandwich.

**Answers** *Corte, Añada, Mezcle, sírvalo*

ᵃ*avocado*  ᵇ*diente… clove of garlic*  ᶜ*crushed*  ᵈ*fresh*  ᵉ*pieces*  ᶠ*corn*

**Heritage Speakers**
Pídales a los hispanohablantes que le expliquen al resto de la clase las diferencias entre la comida auténtica de Latinoamérica y España, y la comida latinoamericana y española que se consume en este país.

*El guacamole*

*Ingredientes:*
1 aguacateᵃ
1 diente de ajo,ᵇ prensadoᶜ
1 tomate
jugo de un limón
sal
un poco de cilantro frescoᵈ

*Cómo se prepara*
*Corte* el aguacate y el tomate en trozosᵉ pequeños. *Añada* el jugo del limón, el ajo, el cilantro y la sal a su gusto. *Mezcle* bien todos los ingredientes y *sírvalo* con tortillas fritas de maíz.ᶠ

```
Past ------------------- PRESENT --------------------- Future
                         present
                         present progressive
                         formal commands
```

## Formal Command Forms

In *¿Qué tal?* you have seen formal commands in the direction lines of activities since the beginning of the text: **haga, complete, conteste,** and so on.

Commands (imperatives) are verb forms used to tell someone to do something. In Spanish, *formal commands* (**los mandatos formales**) are used with people whom you address as **Ud.** or **Uds.** Here are some of the basic forms.

**Note**
Optional material: If you wish to present informal commands now, see the *¿Qué tal?* Online Learning Center for this chapter for a presentation of informal commands at this point. These commands will be presented in *Capítulo 12* of the textbook.

| | hablar | comer | escribir | volver | poner |
|---|---|---|---|---|---|
| **Ud.** | hable | coma | escriba | vuelva | ponga |
| **Uds.** | hablen | coman | escriban | vuelvan | pongan |
| **English** | *speak* | *eat* | *write* | *come back* | *put, place* |

> **command or imperative** = a verb form used to tell someone to do something

# PASO 3

Emphasis A: Suggestions
• Explain that formal command forms use the "opposite" vowel.

-ar → -e; -er/-ir → -a

• Present the regular command forms.
• Use the following rapid response drill.

*¿Cuál es el mandato formal (Ud.) de _____?*

| | | |
|---|---|---|
| cierro | prefiero | duermo |
| pienso | sirvo | |
| vuelvo | pido | |

**A.** Most formal command forms can be derived from the **yo** form of the present tense.

    **-ar: -o** → **-e**      **-er/-ir: -o** → **-a**
            **-en**                      **-an**

hablo → habl**e**
como → com**a**
escribo → escrib**a**

• Present commands with spelling changes, including these verbs.

| | |
|---|---|
| buscar | llegar |
| practicar | pagar |
| tocar | almorzar |
| jugar | empezar |

**B.** Formal commands of stem-changing verbs will show the stem change.

p**ie**nse Ud.
v**ue**lva Ud.
p**i**da Ud.

**C.** Verbs ending in **-car**, **-gar**, and **-zar** have a spelling change to preserve the **-c-**, **-g-**, and **-z-** sounds.

c → qu      buscar: bus**que** Ud.
g → gu      pagar: pa**gue** Ud.
z → c       empezar: emp**iece** Ud.

**D.** Verbs that have irregular **yo** forms in the present tense will reflect the irregularity in the **Ud./Uds.** commands.

**Preliminary Exercises**
• Have students give the singular formal command of the following verbs.

| | | | |
|---|---|---|---|
| ir | estar | levantarse | ser |
| comer | bailar | volver | |

• Have students give the plural formal command of the following verbs.

| | | | |
|---|---|---|---|
| saber | esperar | acostarse | tener |
| conocer | jugar | dormir | |

| | |
|---|---|
| conocer: cono**z**co | → cono**z**ca Ud. |
| decir* (*to say, tell*): di**g**o | → di**g**a Ud. |
| hacer: ha**g**o | → ha**g**a Ud. |
| oír: oi**g**o | → oi**g**a Ud. |
| poner: pon**g**o | → pon**g**a Ud. |
| salir: sal**g**o | → sal**g**a Ud. |
| tener: ten**g**o | → ten**g**a Ud. |
| traer: trai**g**o | → trai**g**a Ud. |
| venir: ven**g**o | → ven**g**a Ud. |
| ver: v**e**o | → v**e**a Ud. |

**E.** A few verbs have irregular **Ud./Uds.** command forms.

• Ask students.
*¿Dónde se pone el pronombre de complemento directo lo, delante o detrás de estos verbos?*

| | | |
|---|---|---|
| no coma | estudie | no paguen |
| mire | no compren | haga |

| | |
|---|---|
| dar* (*to give*) | → **dé** Ud. |
| estar | → **esté** Ud. |
| ir | → **vaya** Ud. |
| saber | → **sepa** Ud. |
| ser | → **sea** Ud. |

## Position of Pronouns with Formal Commands

• Direct object pronouns and reflexive pronouns must follow affirmative commands and be attached to them. In order to maintain the original stress of the verb form, an accent mark is added to the stressed vowel if the original command has two or more syllables.

Pída**lo** Ud.        *Order it.*
Siénte**se**, por favor.    *Sit down, please.*

**Suggestion**
Stress the use of written accents in command forms with attached direct object and reflexive pronouns.

• Direct object and reflexive pronouns must precede negative commands.

**No lo** pida Ud.      *Don't order it.*
**No se** siente.        *Don't sit down.*

**Heritage Speakers**
En algunos dialectos del español que se hablan tanto en los países de habla hispana como en los Estados Unidos, a veces se oye decir *siéntensen*, *acuéstensen* o *vístansen* para la tercera persona plural (*Uds.*). Aunque haya personas que usen estas formas en el habla popular, las formas preferidas son *siéntense*, *acuéstense* y *vístanse*.

*Decir and dar are used primarily with indirect objects. Both of these verbs and indirect object pronouns will be formally introduced in* **Capítulo 7.**

## ■ Práctica

**A. Profesor(a) por un día.** Imagine que Ud. es el profesor / la profesora hoy. ¿Qué mandatos debe dar a la clase?

MODELOS: hablar español → Hablen Uds. español.
hablar inglés → No hablen Uds. inglés.

1. llegar a tiempo
2. leer la lección
3. escribir una composición
4. abrir los libros
5. estar en clase mañana
6. traer los libros a clase
7. estudiar los verbos nuevos
8. ¿ ?

**Prác. A: Suggestion**
Have students offer commands about what you should or should not do in class. Remind them to add *por favor* for politeness, and perhaps a begging tone to convince you to be nice to them.

**B. ¡Pobre Sr. Casiano!**

PASO 1 El Sr. Casiano no se siente (*feel*) bien. Lea la descripción que él da de algunas de sus actividades.

«Trabajo[1] muchísimo[a] —¡me gusta trabajar! En la oficina, soy[2] impaciente y critico[3b] bastante[c] a los otros. En mi vida personal, a veces soy[4] un poco impulsivo. Fumo[5d] bastante y también bebo[6] cerveza y otras bebidas alcohólicas, a veces sin moderación… Almuerzo[7] y ceno[8] fuerte, y casi nunca desayuno.[9] Por la noche, con frecuencia salgo[10] con los amigos —me gusta ir a las discotecas— y vuelvo[11] tarde a casa.»

[a]*a great deal* [b]*critico → criticar* [c]*a good deal* [d]*Fumo → fumar*

PASO 2 ¿Qué *no* debe hacer el Sr. Casiano para estar mejor? Aconséjele (*Advise him*) sobre lo que no debe hacer. Use los verbos indicados en azul o cualquier (*any*) otro, según los modelos.

MODELOS: Trabajo → Sr. Casiano, no trabaje tanto.
soy → Sr. Casiano, no sea tan impaciente.

**C. Situaciones.** El Sr. Casiano quiere adelgazar (*to lose weight*). ¿Debe o no debe comer o beber las siguientes cosas? Con otro/a estudiante, haga y conteste preguntas según los modelos:

MODELOS: ensalada → E1: ¿Ensalada?　　postres → E1: ¿Postres?
　　　　　　E2: Cóma*la*.　　　　　　　　　　　E2: No *los* coma.

1. alcohol (*m.*)
2. verduras
3. pan
4. dulces
5. leche
6. hamburguesas con queso
7. frutas frescas
8. refrescos dietéticos
9. pollo
10. carne
11. pizza
12. jugo de fruta

**Prác. C: Follow-Up**
Give students the following situation and have them provide appropriate commands.

*Luisa y Carlos llegan a su primer día de escuela en la clase del primer año. La maestra les explica las reglas de conducta, especialmente la conducta prohibida. ¿Qué mandatos les da?*

Offer students the following suggestions.
*no comer en el salón de clase*
*no hablar cuando habla la maestra*
*no pegar (to hit) a los amiguitos*
*no traer animales a clase*
*no escribir en las paredes*
*no llegar tarde*

*¿Qué otros mandatos, afirmativos o negativos, recuerdan Uds. de la escuela primaria?*

**Prác. B: Answers**
*Paso 2* Possible answers: 1. No trabaje tanto. 2. No sea tan impaciente. 3. No critique a los otros. 4. No sea tan impulsivo. 5. No fume tanto. 6. No beba bebidas alcohólicas. 7. No almuerce y 8. no cene tan fuerte. 9. Desayune todos los días. 10. No salga tanto con los amigos. 11. No vuelva tarde a casa.

**Prác. B: Variation**
Have students give advice to *los Sres. Casiano.*

**Prác. C: Answers**
*Possible answers:* 1. No lo beba. 2. Cómalas. 3. No lo coma. 4. No los coma. 5. No la beba. 6. No las coma. 7. Cómalas. 8. Bébalos. 9. Cómalo. 10. No la coma. 11. No la coma. 12. Bébalo.

**Prác. C: Preliminary Exercises**
• Have students give the negative command for each of these affirmative commands.

1. *Cómprelo.*
2. *Estúdielas.*
3. *Mírelo.*
4. *Llámeme.*
5. *Apréndalo.*
6. *Escríbame.*

• Have students give the affirmative command for each of these negative commands.

1. *No lo coma.*　　4. *No lo sirva.*
2. *No lo lea.*　　　5. *No lo traiga.*
3. *No lo haga.*

**Prác. D: Answers**
1. *Despiértense más temprano.* 2. *Levántense más temprano.* 3. *Báñense más.* 4. *Quítense esa ropa sucia.* 5. *Pónganse ropa limpia.* 6. *Vístanse mejor.*
7. *Estudien más.* 8. *No se diviertan todas las noches con los amigos.* 9. *Vayan más a la biblioteca.* 10. *No se acuesten tan tarde.* 11. *Ayuden con los quehacere.*

**D. ¡Estoy harto de Uds. dos!** (*I'm fed up with you two!*)  Imagine que Ud. acaba de volver de clase y la casa es un desastre. Está enojado/a (*angry*) y empieza a gritarles (*yell*) mandatos a sus compañeros de casa sobre su apariencia física y sus hábitos.

MODELO:  afeitarse → ¡Aféitense!

1. despertarse más temprano
2. levantarse más temprano
3. bañarse más
4. quitarse esa ropa sucia
5. ponerse ropa limpia
6. vestirse mejor
7. estudiar más
8. no divertirse todas las noches con los amigos
9. ir más a la biblioteca
10. no acostarse tan tarde
11. ayudar con los quehaceres
12. ¿ ?

**Prác. D: Variation**
Have students give advice (*Uds.* commands) to the roommates.

## NOTA COMUNICATIVA

### El subjuntivo

Except for the command form, all verb forms that you have learned thus far in *¿Qué tal?* have been part of the *indicative mood* (**el modo indicativo**). In both English and Spanish, the indicative is used to state facts and to ask questions. It objectively expresses most real-world actions or states of being.

Both English and Spanish have another verb system called the *subjunctive mood* (**el modo subjuntivo**), which will be introduced in **Capítulo 12.** The **Ud./Uds.** command forms that you have just learned are part of the subjunctive system. From this point on in *¿Qué tal?* you will see the subjunctive used where it is natural to use it. What follows is a brief introduction to the subjunctive that will make it easy for you to recognize it when you see it.

Here are some examples of the forms of the subjunctive. The **Ud./Uds.** forms (identical to the **Ud./Uds.** command forms) are highlighted.

| HABLAR | | COMER | | SERVIR | | SALIR | |
|---|---|---|---|---|---|---|---|
| hable | hablemos | coma | comamos | sirva | sirvamos | salga | salgamos |
| hables | habléis | comas | comáis | sirvas | sirváis | salgas | salgáis |
| hable | hablen | coma | coman | sirva | sirvan | salga | salgan |

The subjunctive is used to express more subjective or conceptualized states, in contrast to the indicative, which reports facts, information that is objectively true. Here are just a few of the situations in which the subjunctive is used in Spanish.

- to express what the speaker wants others to do (I want you to . . .)
- to express emotional reactions (I'm glad that . . .)
- to express probability or uncertainty (It's likely that . . .)

**Nota comunicativa: Suggestion**
Conjugate the present subjunctive of *bailar* and *comer* on the board. Start with *Quiero que* (*tú/él/ella...* ). Point out that if the subject of both clauses is the same, the second verb is often used in the infinitive.

♻ **Prác. D: Reciclado**
- Have students give the negative command for each of the following affirmative commands with reflexives.

  1. *Acuéstese.*   3. *Lávese.*
  2. *Aféitese.*   4. *Siéntese.*

- Have students give the affirmative command for each of the following negative commands with reflexives.

  1. *No se bañe.*   3. *No se quite los zapatos.*
  2. *No se levante.*   4. *No se ponga la chaqueta.*

**Nota comunicativa: Notes**
- This introduction to the subjunctive will familiarize students with its forms and uses. At this point, students will only be expected to passively recognize these forms and understand why/how they are used. More detailed explanations of and subsequent practice with the subjunctive are provided in *Capítulo 12*. From this point on, however, instructor's annotations may use the subjunctive so that students receive meaningful input.
- See the *¿Qué tal? Instructor's Manual* or Online Learning Center for this chapter for more detailed presentation and practice with the subjunctive in noun clauses at this point in the text.

**CAPÍTULO**

**6**

Prác. E: Preliminary Exercises
• Have students tell whether these verbs are subjunctive or indicative:

*cene, cena / vaya, va / hago, haga / pido, pida / lleve, llevo / me visto, me vista*

**PASO 3**

**E. El cumpleaños de María.** Fíjese en (*Notice*) los verbos subrayados (*underlined*) en los siguientes diálogos. Diga en inglés por qué razón están subrayados. (Use la lista de la **Nota comunicativa.**)

Prác. E: Note
This activity deals with recognition of forms and conceptualization of the subjunctive only.

### En el parque

RAÚL: Como hoy es tu cumpleaños, quiero invitarte a cenar. ¿En qué restaurante quieres que <u>cenemos</u>?

MARÍA: Prefiero que tú me[a] <u>prepares</u> una de tus espléndidas cenas.

RAÚL: ¡Con mucho gusto!

Prác. E: Answers
*cenemos:* to express what the speaker wants others to do; *prepares:* to express what the speaker wants others to do; *esté:* to express probability; *llame:* to express what the speaker wants others to do.

### En casa de María

MADRE: (*Hablando por teléfono.*) No, lo siento,[b] pero María no está en casa.

LUISA: ¿Es posible que <u>esté</u> en la biblioteca?

MADRE: No. Sé que ella y Raúl están cenando en casa de él.

LUISA: Ah, sí. Bueno, ¿puede pedirle a ella que <u>llame</u> a Luisa cuando regrese?

Prác. E: Suggestions

MADRE: Sí, cómo no,[c] Luisa. Adiós.

LUISA: Hasta luego.

• Have students read for the general idea of the dialogues. They should pay close attention to the forms of the underlined verbs and begin thinking about why some are in the indicative and some in the subjunctive.

[a]*for me*  [b]*lo… I'm sorry*  [c]*cómo… of course*

• Note also the use of the subjunctive in the phrase *cuando regrese*. This use of the subjunctive was not previewed for students in the *Nota comunicativa;* if students notice it, you may wish to explain it, especially since this use of the subjunctive is very high frequency.

## ■ Conversación

**En la oficina del consejero.** Imagine that you are a guidance counselor. Students consult you with all kinds of questions, some trivial and some important. Offer advice to them in the form of affirmative or negative commands. Working with a partner, how many different commands can you invent for each situation?

MODELO: Primero, hábleme de su horario.
Y, por favor, incluya las comidas y…

1. EVELIA: No me gusta tomar clases por la mañana. Siempre estoy muy cansada durante esas clases y además (*besides*) a esa hora tengo hambre. Pienso constantemente en el almuerzo… y no puedo concentrarme en las explicaciones.

2. FABIÁN: En mi clase de cálculo, ¡no entiendo nada! No puedo hacer los ejercicios y durante la clase tengo miedo de hacer preguntas, porque no quiero parecer (*seem*) tonto.

3. FAUSTO: Fui (*I went*) a México el verano pasado y me gustó (*I liked it*) mucho. Quiero volver a México este verano. Ahora que lo conozco mejor, quiero ir en mi coche y no en autobús como el verano pasado. Desgraciadamente (*Unfortunately*) no tengo dinero para hacer el viaje.

4. RAMÓN: Siempre llego tarde a las clases. Como tengo tanta prisa, no traigo los libros ni los papeles que necesito. Hoy no desayuné pero, ¡ni eso (*not even that*) me ayudó (*helped*)!

• Have students complete the sentence with the correct *Uds.* forms of the subjunctive of the verbs that follow.

*Yo deseo que Uds… estudiar / bailar / comprarme regalos / llegar a tiempo a clase / divertirse*

Prác. E: Follow-Up
Ask students the following *sí/no* questions.

1. *¿María quiere ir a un restaurante? ¿Quiere cocinar?*

2. *Y Raúl, ¿quiere hacer algo para María? ¿Quiere María que Raúl haga algo para ella?*

3. *¿Quiere María que Raúl la invite a un restaurante? ¿Quiere que él cocine para ella?*

### Need more practice?

■ Workbook/Laboratory Manual
■ Interactive CD-ROM
■ Online Learning Center (www.mhhe.com/quetal7)

4. *La amiga de María, ¿quiere hablar con la madre de María? ¿Sabe la amiga dónde está María? Y la madre, ¿sabe dónde está María?*

5. *La amiga, ¿quiere ir a casa de Raúl para hablar con María? ¿Quiere que María la llame?*

6. *¿Quiere la amiga que María la llame durante la cena con Raúl? ¿cuándo María vuelva a casa?*

Con: Follow-Up
• Have students give affirmative and negative commands in response to the following statements.

1. *Estoy cansado/a.*
2. *Tengo sed.*
3. *Tengo hambre.*
4. *No puedo dormir.*
5. *No entiendo el ejercicio.*
6. *Necesito más dinero.*
7. *Mis padres/hijos quieren saber cómo estoy.*
8. *No puedo encontrar mi libro de español.*

• Have students write commands that they would like to give to the following persons:

1. *el presidente / el primer ministro*
2. *los candidatos para _____*
3. *Jay Leno, David Letterman (or any other television personality)*
4. *sus amigos*
5. *el profesor / la profesora*

# PASO 3

## UN POCO DE TODO

**Lengua y cultura: La cocina** (*cooking*) **panameña.** Complete the following passages with the correct forms of the words in parentheses, as suggested by the context. When two possibilities are given in parentheses, select the correct word. **¡OJO!** As you conjugate verbs in this activity, note that you will make formal commands with some infinitives.

¿Creen Uds. que la comida panameña es similar a la[a] de México? ¿(*Uds.:* Creer[1]) que los tacos y las tortillas (ser / estar[2]) parte de la comida de los panameños? Si creen que sí,[b] entonces[c] no (*Uds.:* saber / conocer[3]) (algo / nada[4]) de la comida de (esto[5]) nación. (*Uds.:* Empezar[6]) (a / de[7]) leer esta lectura, porque van a aprender mucho.

Hoy en día, Panamá tiene muy (bueno[8]) relaciones con los Estados Unidos y el Canadá, especialmente por[d] la (grande[9]) importancia para Norteamérica que tiene su canal. En Panamá, observamos mucho la influencia de los Estados Unidos. Muchos panameños (saber / conocer[10]) inglés perfectamente y (lo/la[11]) hablan con frecuencia.

La influencia (extranjero[12]) en la comida de la cosmopolita ciudad de Panamá es muy visible. Hay (mucho[13]) restaurantes que (servir[14]) comida italiana, china, (francés[15]), estadounidense y otras de otros países también.

Los panameños no (perder[16]) su identidad nacional, y frecuentemente (preferir[17]) servir la comida tradicional. En la comida tradicional panameña hay muchos platos de mariscos y pescados, especialmente el ceviche. Las personas vegetarianas no (tener[18]) problema con la comida tradicional porque hay una variedad de platos (preparado[19]) con verduras y arroz. El arroz es un ingrediente importante en la comida de Panamá. Generalmente cuando los turistas (preguntar[20]) «¿Cuál es el plato nacional de Panamá?», los panameños (contestar[21]): «Es el arroz con pollo. (*Uds.:* Pedirlo[22]). Les va a gustar».

[a]*la... that* [b]*Si... If you think so* [c]*then* [d]*because of*

*El arroz con pollo, un plato panameño típico*

**Comprensión: La cocina panameña.** Conteste las siguientes preguntas.

1. ¿Por qué tiene Panamá muy buenas relaciones con los Estados Unidos y el Canadá?
2. ¿Cómo se sabe que la ciudad de Panamá es cosmopolita?
3. ¿Cuál es el plato que representa mejor la cocina panameña?
4. ¿Qué ingredientes son muy comunes en la comida de Panamá? ¿Cómo se puede explicar esto?

**Paso 4: Un paso más**
- The *Paso 4: Un paso más* sections are optional.
- See the "Chapter-by-Chapter Supplementary Materials" in the IM for additional teaching suggestions, notes, activities, and other resources for *Paso 4*.

## VIDEOTECA

## Entrevista cultural: Panamá

Maír Citón Moreno es dueño de un restaurante en su país, Panamá. En esta entrevista habla de los platos que se sirven en su restaurante. También habla de los ingredientes más comunes y de su plato favorito. Antes de ver el vídeo, lea el siguiente fragmento de la entrevista.

ENTREVISTADORA: ¿Qué tipo de restaurante es, y qué tipo de comida se sirve?

MAÍR: Es un restaurante exclusivamente de comida típica panameña y en base al maíz[a] y el arroz.

ENTREVISTADORA: ¿Cuáles son los platillos más típicos de Panamá?

MAÍR: Los platillos más típicos de Panamá serían[b] el arroz de frijoles de palo,[c] el sancocho de gallina,[d] los tamales, las tortillas asadas, entre otros.

[a]en… *corn-based*   [b]*would be*   [c]frijoles… *palo beans*   [d]sancocho… *dish with chicken, yucca, plantain, and other ingredients*

Ahora vea el vídeo y conteste las siguientes preguntas basándose en la entrevista.

1. ¿Dónde vive y trabaja Maír?
2. ¿Qué tipo de comida se sirve en el restaurante de Maír?
3. ¿Cuáles son los ingredientes básicos de la cocina panameña?
4. ¿Cuáles son unos ingredientes tropicales y unos tipos de carne que se mencionan en la entrevista?
5. ¿Cuál es el plato favorito de Maír?

## Entre amigos: ¿Quién cocina en tu casa?

Tané prepara la comida para una fiesta. Karina, Rubén y Miguel van a ayudarla a cocinar. En su opinión, ¿qué preguntas van a hacerse (*ask each other*)? Antes de mirar el vídeo, lea las preguntas a continuación (*that follow*). Mientras mire el vídeo, trate de entender la conversación en general y fíjese en la información sobre la comida. Luego mire el vídeo una segunda (*second*) vez, fijándose en la información que necesita para contestar las preguntas.

1. ¿Qué prepara Tané?
2. ¿Quién cocina en casa de Tané?
3. ¿Sabe cocinar Rubén? ¿Por qué sí o por qué no?
4. Según Miguel, ¿cómo se prepara el pozole, un plato mexicano muy conocido (*well-known*)?

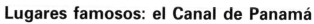
## ENFOQUE CULTURAL

### Panamá

**Notes**
- Vasco Núñez de Balboa explored the Isthmus of Panama in 1513 and discovered that it was only a short distance from the Atlantic Ocean to the Pacific Ocean. He founded the first settlements on the north coast.
- Gold from Peru traveled across Panama during Spanish colonial times, as did prospectors headed for the California gold fields in 1849.

## ¡Fíjese!

- Panamá es una palabra indígena que significa «tierra de muchos peces[a]».
- La Carretera[b] Panamericana, el sistema de carreteras que va de Alaska a la Argentina, se interrumpe[c] en la densa e[d] impenetrable selva[e] panameña de Darién. Para llegar a Sudamérica es necesario tomar un barco[f] hasta Colombia, donde continúa la carretera.
- La Sra. Mireya Moscoso ganó[g] las elecciones presidenciales de 1998. La viuda[h] de otro presidente, doña Mireya es la primera mujer panameña en asumir el cargo.[i]

[a]*fish*  [b]*Highway*  [c]*se… breaks off, is interrupted*  [d]*y*  [e]*jungle*  [f]*boat*
[g]*won*  [h]*widow*  [i]*post*

- General Manuel Noriega ousted the Panamanian president in 1985 and became acting head of government. After Noriega was indicted for drug activities and other illegal acts, the U.S. Army invaded Panama and brought Noriega to Miami for trial. He was convicted in 1992.
- Students can read *"Desarraigado"* by Panama's Carlos Guillermo Wilson in *Voces de Panamá: Literatura.*

- Students can read about Panama's musical tradition *el calipso* in *Voces de Panamá: Música.*
- See the Workbook/Laboratory Manual for focused practice with the material in *Enfoque cultural.*

Learn more about Panama with the Video, the Interactive CD-ROM, and the Online Learning Center (www.mhhe.com/quetal7).

**Multimedia: Internet**
Have students search the Internet for more information about traveling to Panama. Students will be able to find pages about Panamanian food, education, culture, newspapers, and more. Some pages are in both English and Spanish. Remind students to look for images of the Panama Canal as well.

## Lugares famosos: el Canal de Panamá

El Canal de Panamá, construido a través del[a] istmo entre los dos continentes americanos, comunica los océanos Atlántico y Pacífico. Mide[b] aproximadamente 80 kilómetros (50 millas) de largo, 12,5 metros (41 pies[c]) de ancho[d] y 200 metros (más de 63 pies) de profundidad. Su construcción facilita la comunicación marítima entre las costas este y oeste de los continentes. Antes de la existencia del canal, los barcos tenían que darle la vuelta a[e] América del Sur para ir de una costa a otra. Hoy, el viaje por el Canal de Panamá toma aproximadamente ocho horas, pues[f] es necesario pasar por un número de esclusas.[g]

La idea de construir un canal a través del istmo data de 1534, cuando el emperador español Carlos V (Quinto) la propone. Más tarde, en 1881, el ingeniero francés Fernando de Lesseps también sugiere un proyecto similar. Pero el canal no se construye hasta el siglo XX, por los Estados Unidos. Esto ocasiona[h] la presencia de los Estados Unidos en la vida de Panamá. Como resultado, hay un uso extendido del inglés en el país, se usa el dólar y ha habido[i] una gran intervención en la política del país.

El canal se inaugura en 1914 y es administrado por los Estados Unidos hasta 1999. Desde el primero de enero del año 2000, la República de Panamá está a cargo de[j] su gran canal.

[a]*construido… built across the*  [b]*It measures*  [c]*feet*  [d]*de… in width*
[e]*tenían… had to go around*  [f]*because*  [g]*canal locks*  [h]*brings about*
[i]*ha… there has been*  [j]*a… in control of*

*Una esclusa del Canal de Panamá*

## PASO FINAL

## A CONVERSAR

### El menú del día

PASO 1 En grupos de tres o cuatro estudiantes, lean el siguiente menú del restaurante 'El toro bravo'. Basándose en el menú, ¿qué tipo de restaurante es? ¿Creen que es un restaurante con un ambiente elegante y caro o un restaurante con un ambiente relajado y precios módicos (*moderate*)? El menú que Uds. leen es el menú del día, es decir (*that is*), las especialidades del día. En su opinión, ¿qué otras cosas sirven en este restaurante?

### *Restaurante 'El toro bravo'*
#### Menú del día: €12,60

#### De entrada:

Ensalada mixta
(lechuga, tomate, zanahoria, cebolla[a] y aceitunas[b] verdes con salsa vinagreta)

Sopa de cebolla con queso fundido[c]

Espárragos con jamón serrano[d]

#### De plato principal:

Paella de mariscos
(arroz, camarones, almejas,[e] pescado, salchicha[f])

Pollo asado con patatas al horno

Verduras asadas con cous-cous
(pimiento verde, cebolla, berenjena,[g] broculí, champiñones)

#### De postre:

Ensalada de frutas
(fresas,[h] melón, manzana, naranja)

Flan

Varios helados

**Menú: Point out**
On January 1, 2002, the *euro* replaced the *peseta* as the standard monetary denomination for Spain. Eleven other European Union member countries also adopted the common currency on that date. At the time of publication, 1 *euro* equaled approximately 160 *pesetas*. The price in this menu is read as *doce euros sesenta* (*céntimos* [*Sp.*]).

[a]*onion*   [b]*olives*   [c]*melted*   [d]jamón... *type of cured Spanish ham*   [e]*clams*   [f]*sausage*   [g]*eggplant*   [h]*strawberries*

**Follow-Up**
Have the waiters move to a different group
of clients and begin a new role play.

**Suggestion**
For writing practice, see the *Mi diario*
activity in each chapter of the Workbook/
Laboratory Manual.

PASO 2   Ahora, imaginen que Uds. están en el restaurante. Uno/a de Uds. es camarero/a y los demás (*the rest*) son clientes que desean cenar. Antes de improvisar una escena, revisen (*look over*) las expresiones a continuación y piensen en el tipo de personaje que van a representar (un camarero difícil o un camarero simpático, una clienta exigente [*demanding*] o una clienta paciente, etcétera).

| Clientes | Camarero/a |
| --- | --- |
| ¿Qué recomienda (de plato principal / de postre)? | ¿Qué le(s)* traigo (hoy / de beber)? |
| ¿Qué hay en (la sopa de cebolla)? | ¿Ya saben lo que desean tomar? |
| Quiero (la paella de mariscos), por favor. | ¿Y qué quiere de (entrada [*first course*] / plato principal / postre)? |
| Para mí, (los espárragos), por favor. | ¿Y para Ud.? |
| ¿Hay (tomates) en (la ensalada mixta)? | Lo siento mucho (*I'm very sorry*). No hay más (flan) hoy. |
| Por favor, preparen (los espárragos) sin (jamón). | Le(s)* recomiendo (la sopa de cebolla). |
| | La especialidad de la casa es (la paella). |
| | Lo siento; no podemos preparar (los espárragos) sin (jamón). |
| | Muy bien. Le* preparamos (los espárragos) sin (jamón). |

PASO 3   Improvisen una escena entre los clientes y el camarero / la camarera. La escena debe incluir saludos, preguntas y respuestas sobre los platos, recomendaciones y sugerencias, el orden. Después de practicar la escena, represéntenla para la clase.

---

*Le and les are *indirect object pronouns*. Their equivalents in English are (*to / for*) *you* (*sing.*) and *you* (*pl.*), respectively. You will learn more about indirect object pronouns in **Capítulo 7.** For now, you can just use them in the phrases indicated.

## GRAMÁTICA

To review the grammar points presented in this chapter, refer to the indicated grammar presentations. You'll find further practice of these structures in the Workbook/Laboratory Manual, on the Interactive CD-ROM, and on the *¿Qué tal?* Online Learning Center (www.mhhe.com/quetal7).

**17** Expressing *what* or *whom*—Direct Object Pronouns

Do you know how to avoid repetition by using direct object pronouns?

**18** Expressing Negation—Indefinite and Negative Words

Do you know how to use the double negative in Spanish?

**19** Influencing Others—Formal Commands

You should know how to use commands to order in restaurants and to have someone do something for you.

## VOCABULARIO

Practice this vocabulary with digital flash cards on the Online Learning Center (www.mhhe.com/quetal7).

### Los verbos

| | |
|---|---|
| **acabar de** + *inf.* | to have just (*done something*) |
| **ayudar** | to help |
| **cenar** | to have (eat) dinner, supper |
| **cocinar** | to cook |
| **conocer (zc)*** | to know, be acquainted with |
| **desayunar** | to have (eat) breakfast |
| **esperar** | to wait (for); to expect |
| **invitar** | to invite |
| **llamar** | to call |
| **preguntar** | to ask (a question) |
| **preparar** | to prepare |
| **saber** (*irreg.*) | to know |
| **saber** + *inf.* | to know how to (*do something*) |

**Repaso: almorzar (ue) (c)***

### La comida

| | |
|---|---|
| **el arroz** | rice |
| **las arvejas** | peas |
| **el atún** | tuna |
| **el bistec** | steak |
| **los camarones** | shrimp |
| **la carne** | meat |

| | |
|---|---|
| **el champiñón** | mushroom |
| **la chuleta (de cerdo)** | (pork) chop |
| **los dulces** | sweets; candy |
| **los espárragos** | asparagus |
| **el flan** | (baked) custard |
| **los frijoles** | beans |
| **la galleta** | cookie |
| **el helado** | ice cream |
| **el huevo** | egg |
| **el jamón** | ham |
| **la langosta** | lobster |
| **la lechuga** | lettuce |
| **la mantequilla** | butter |
| **la manzana** | apple |
| **los mariscos** | shellfish |
| **la naranja** | orange |
| **el pan** | bread |
| **el pan tostado** | toast |
| **la papa** | potato |
| **el pastel** | cake; pie |
| **la patata (frita)** | (French fried) potato |
| **el pavo** | turkey |
| **el pescado** | fish |
| **el pollo (asado)** | (roast) chicken |
| **el postre** | dessert |
| **el queso** | cheese |
| **la salchicha** | sausage; hot dog |

*\*From this chapter on, the spelling changes for verbs in the subjunctive and formal commands such as* **-c-** → **-qu-**, **-g-** → **-gu-**, **-z-** → **-c-**, *as well as verbs with* **-zc-** *and* **-g-** *changes in the present tense* **yo** *form, will be indicated in parentheses in the vocabulary lists.*

**Suggestions**
· Have students respond *cierto* or *falso*.

1. *El bistec viene del cerdo.*
2. *El bistec es más caro que la hamburguesa.*
3. *Son populares los sándwiches de jamón.*

· Have students complete the following sentences.

1. *Los niños beben _____.*
2. *Se comen _____ y _____ en McDonald's.*
3. *Con el desayuno se bebe _____.*

4. *Los conejos (draw on the board) comen _____.*
5. *Un almuerzo sencillo incluye sopa y _____.*
6. *Generalmente se come _____ para el desayuno.*
7. *Los Óreos son un tipo de _____.*

| | |
|---|---|
| la sopa | soup |
| las verduras | vegetables |
| la zanahoria | carrot |

**Cognados:** la banana, el cereal, la ensalada, la fruta, la hamburguesa, el salmón, el sándwich, el tomate, el yogur

## Las bebidas

| | |
|---|---|
| el agua (mineral) | (mineral) water |
| el jugo (de fruta) | (fruit) juice |
| la leche | milk |
| el refresco | soft drink |
| el vino (blanco, tinto) | (white, red) wine |

**Cognado:** el té
**Repaso:** el café, la cerveza

## Las comidas

| | |
|---|---|
| el almuerzo | lunch |
| la cena | dinner, supper |

**Repaso:** el desayuno

## En un restaurante

| | |
|---|---|
| el/la camarero/a | waiter/waitress |
| la cuenta | check, bill |
| el plato | dish; course |

**Cognado:** el menú

## Otros sustantivos

| | |
|---|---|
| la bebida | drink, beverage |
| la comida | food; meal |

| | |
|---|---|
| el consejo | (piece of) advice |
| el detalle | detail |
| el/la dueño/a | owner |
| la tarjeta de crédito | credit card |

## Los adjetivos

| | |
|---|---|
| fresco/a | fresh |
| frito/a | fried |
| fuerte | heavy (*meal, food*); strong |
| ligero/a | light, not heavy |
| rápido/a | fast |

## Palabras indefinidas y negativas

| | |
|---|---|
| alguien | someone, anyone |
| algún (alguno/a/os/as) | some, any |
| jamás | never |
| nada | nothing, not anything |
| nadie | no one, nobody, not anybody |
| ningún (ninguno/a) | no, none, not any |
| tampoco | neither, not either |

**Repaso:** algo, nunca, siempre, también

## Palabras adicionales

| | |
|---|---|
| estar (*irreg.*) a dieta | to be on a diet |
| tener (*irreg.*) (mucha) hambre | to be (very) hungry |
| tener (*irreg.*) (mucha) sed | to be (very) thirsty |

· Ask questions about foods.

1. *¿Cuál tiene más cafeína, el café o el té? ¿Cuál prefiere Ud.? ¿Cuándo lo toma, por la mañana o por la noche?*
2. *¿Bebe Ud. mucha cerveza? ¿mucho vino? ¿Qué tipo de vino prefiere, el vino tinto o el vino blanco?*
3. *¿Come Ud. carne? ¿Qué tipo de carne prefiere, el bistec, la hamburguesa, el jamón o las chuletas de cerdo? ¿Le gusta comer sándwiches?*
4. *¿Come Ud. muchas ensaladas? ¿Come la ensalada antes o después del plato principal?*
5. *En su opinión, ¿cuál es más picante, la comida india o la comida mexicana? ¿la china? ¿la tailandesa? ¿Cuál es más popular en este país?*

· Remind students that *conocer* is irregular in the *yo* form: *conozco*.
· Have students state the following ideas in Spanish.

1. I know the truth.
2. She knows the president.
3. They know how to dance.
4. Do you know New York? (Are you familiar with it?)
5. We don't know the answer.
6. Everyone wants to meet the new students.

# CAPÍTULO 7

# De vacaciones

*Una playa de Roatán, una isla en la Bahía (Bay) de Honduras*

**Paso 1: Vocabulario**
See the "Chapter-by-Chapter Supplementary Materials" in the IM for a model for vocabulary presentation, as well as additional teaching suggestions, notes, activities, and other resources for *Paso 1*.

**DE VIAJE**

**Suggestions**

- Point out the meanings of the verbs *bajar* and *subir*: *bajar* = to go down vs. *bajar de* = to get out of (a vehicle) and *subir* = to go up vs. *subir a* = to get in/on (a vehicle).
- Have students name items and activities they associate with the following. *¿Qué asocia Ud. con… un avión, una asistente de vuelo, el equipaje, la sala de espera, la sección de fumar, las maletas, un boleto?*

Resources: Transparency 51

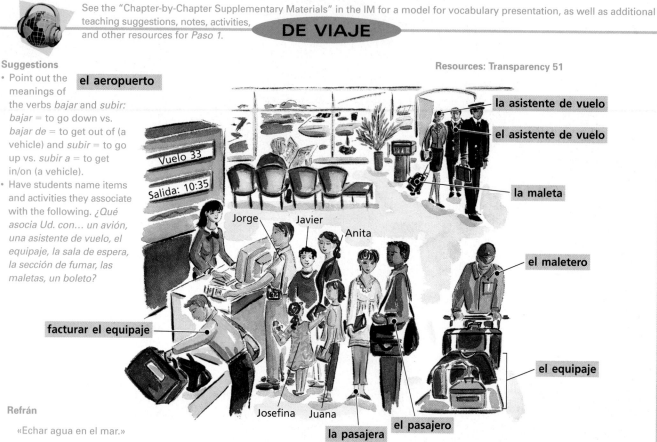

el aeropuerto
la asistente de vuelo
el asistente de vuelo
la maleta
el maletero
el equipaje
facturar el equipaje
Jorge Javier Anita
Josefina Juana
la pasajera
el pasajero

**Refrán**

«Echar agua en el mar.»

Write the *refrán* on the board. Give students the meaning of *echar* (to throw), then have them guess the meaning of the saying. A similar saying in English is *To carry coals to Newcastle* (a needless task).

## Modos de transporte

| | |
|---|---|
| **el barco** | boat, ship |
| **la cabina** | cabin (*on a ship*) |
| **la estación** | station |
| **de autobuses** | bus |
| **del tren** | train |
| **el puerto** | port |
| **la sala de espera** | waiting room |
| **la sección de (no)** | (non)smoking |
| **fumar** | section |
| **el vuelo** | flight |
| **ir** (*irreg.*) **en…** | to go/travel by . . . |
| **autobús** | bus |
| **avión** | plane |
| **barco** | boat, ship |
| **tren** | train |

## El viaje

| | |
|---|---|
| **la agencia de viajes** | travel agency |
| **el/la agente de viajes** | travel agent |
| **el asiento** | seat |
| **el billete/el boleto/ el pasaje*** | ticket |
| **de ida** | one-way |
| **de ida y vuelta** | round-trip |
| **la demora** | delay |
| **la llegada** | arrival |
| **la salida** | departure |
| **bajar (de)** | to get down (from); to get off (of) (*a vehicle*) |
| **estar** (*irreg.*) **atrasado/a** | to be late |
| **guardar (un puesto)** | to save (a place [*in line*]) |
| **hacer** (*irreg.*) **cola** | to stand in line |

**Multimedia: Audio**
Students can listen to and practice this chapter's vocabulary on the Online Learning Center (**www.mhhe.com/quetal7**), as well as on the Textbook Audio CD, part of the Laboratory Audio Program.

*\*Throughout Spanish America, **el boleto** is the word used for a ticket for travel. **El billete** is commonly used in Spain. **El pasaje** is used throughout the Spanish-speaking world. The words **la entrada** and **la localidad** are used to refer to tickets for movies, plays, or similar functions.*

| hacer (*irreg.*) escalas/paradas | to make stops | pasar por el control de la seguridad | to go/pass through security (check) |
| hacer (*irreg.*) la(s) maleta(s) | to pack one's suitcase(s) | subir (a) | to go up; to get on (*a vehicle*) |
| hacer (*irreg.*) un viaje | to take a trip | viajar | to travel |

## ■ Conversación

**A. Un viaje en avión.** Imagine que Ud. va a hacer un viaje en avión. El vuelo sale a las siete de la mañana. Usando los números del 1 al 9, indique en qué orden van a pasar las siguientes cosas.

a. __8__ Subo al avión.
b. __5__ Voy a la sala de espera.
c. __3__ Hago cola para comprar el boleto y facturar el equipaje.
d. __2__ Llego al aeropuerto a tiempo (*on time*) y bajo del taxi.
e. __7__ Por fin se anuncia la salida del vuelo.
f. __1__ Estoy atrasado/a. Salgo para el aeropuerto en taxi.
g. __9__ La asistente me indica el asiento en clase turística.
h. __4__ Pido un asiento de ventanilla (*window seat*).
i. __6__ Hay demora. Por eso todos tenemos que esperar el vuelo.

**B. ¡Seamos (*Let's be*) lógicos!** ¿Qué va a hacer Ud. en estas situaciones?

1. Ud. no tiene mucho dinero. ¿Qué clase de pasaje va a comprar?
   **(a.)** clase turística   **b.** primera clase   **c.** clase de negocios (*business*)

2. Ud. es una persona muy nerviosa y tiene miedo de viajar en avión. Necesita ir desde Nueva York a Madrid. ¿Qué pide Ud.?
   **(a.)** una cabina en un barco   **b.** un vuelo sin escalas

3. Ud. viaja en tren y tiene muchas maletas. Pesan (*They weigh*) mucho y no puede cargarlas (*carry them*). ¿Qué hace Ud.?
   **a.** Compro boletos.   **b.** Guardo un asiento.   **(c.)** Facturo el equipaje.

**C. En el aeropuerto.** ¿Cuántas cosas y acciones puede Ud. identificar o describir en este dibujo? Trabaje con un compañero / una compañera.

## DE VACACIONES

Resources: Transparencies 52, 53

las montañas

el *camping*

la playa

el mar

la camioneta

Josefina

la tienda (de campaña)

hacer (*irreg.*) camping

Juana

nadar — Javier

Anita

tomar el sol

Jorge

sacar (qu) fotos

| el mar | sea |
| el océano | ocean |
| **ir** (*irreg.*) / **estar** (*irreg.*) **de vacaciones** | to go/ be on vacation |

## ■ Conversación

**A. ¿Qué hace Ud.? ¿Cierto o falso?** Lea las siguientes oraciones e indique si son ciertas o falsas para Ud.

1. Cuando estoy de vacaciones, tomo el sol.
2. Prefiero ir de vacaciones a las montañas.
3. Duermo muy bien en una tienda de campaña.
4. Saco muchas fotos cuando estoy de vacaciones.
5. Es fácil viajar a playas bonitas desde (*from*) aquí.

**B. Entrevista**

1. Por lo general, ¿cuándo tomas tus vacaciones? ¿En invierno? ¿en verano? En las vacaciones, ¿te gusta viajar o prefieres no salir de tu ciudad? ¿Te gusta ir de vacaciones con tu familia? ¿Prefieres ir solo/a (*alone*), con un amigo / una amiga o con un grupo de personas? ¿Prefieres viajar sólo a lugares en este país o te gustaría (*would you like*) viajar por otros países del mundo (*world*)?
2. De los medios de transporte mencionados en **De viaje** (página 182), ¿cuáles conoces por experiencia? ¿Cuál es el más rápido? ¿el más económico? ¿Cuáles hacen más escalas o hacen paradas con más frecuencia? ¿Cómo prefieres viajar? ¿Prefieres un asiento de ventanilla o un asiento de pasillo? ¿la clase turística o primera clase?

Nota comunicativa: Suggestion
Ask students the following questions to practice the impersonal *se*.

1. ¿Qué lengua se habla en Francia? ¿en México? ¿en el Brasil? ¿en Alemania? ¿en Inglaterra? ¿en los Estados Unidos? ¿en el Canadá?
2. ¿Cuáles son las diferentes maneras de viajar? (*Se viaja en...* avión, coche, tren, autobús, bicicleta.)

## NOTA COMUNICATIVA

### Other Uses of *se* (For Recognition)

It is likely that you have often seen and heard the phrase shown in the photo that accompanies this box: **Se habla español.** (*Spanish is spoken* [*here*]). Here are some additional examples of this use of **se** with Spanish verbs. Note how the meaning of the verb changes slightly.

**Se venden** billetes aquí.    *Tickets are sold here.*

Aquí no **se fuma.**    *You don't (One doesn't) smoke here. Smoking is forbidden here.*

Be alert to this use of **se** when you see it because it will occur with some frequency in readings and in direction lines in *¿Qué tal?* The activities in this text will not require you to use this grammar point on your own, however.

*Nueva York*

Con. C: Answers
*Possible answers:* **1.** *en el aeropuerto* **2.** *en casa* **3.** *en el aeropuerto* **4.** *en la agencia de viajes* **5.** *en el aeropuerto* **6.** *en el avión* **7.** *en el avión* **8.** *en la playa*

**C.** **¿Dónde se hace esto?**   Indique el lugar (o los lugares) donde se hacen las siguientes actividades.

Note
See the Workbook/Laboratory Manual for presentation and practice of the letters *g,* *gu,* and *j.*

1. Se factura el equipaje.
2. Se hacen las maletas.
3. Se compran los pasajes y se anuncian los vuelos.
4. Se hace una reservación.
5. Se espera en la sala de espera.
6. Se pide una bebida.
7. Se mira una película.
8. Se nada y se toma el sol.

**Lugares**

en casa
en el aeropuerto
en el avión
en la agencia de viajes
en la playa

## NOTA CULTURAL

### Los nuevos tipos de turismo en el mundo hispánico

**El turista** de hoy ya no es el turista tradicional y fácil de complacer.[a] Por eso hay nuevas industrias para satisfacer su interés en **la ecología, la agricultura** o **la aventura: el ecoturismo, el agroturismo y el aventurismo.** Los países hispánicos ofrecen ricas oportunidades para disfrutar de[b] estas nuevas formas de hacer turismo.

El ecoturismo consiste en **viajar a lugares no explotados por el ser humano.**[c] El ecoturista puede visitar **las selvas tropicales** de Centroamérica y la Amazonia. También puede explorar la Patagonia (en el sur de la Argentina y Chile) y las Islas Galápagos (el Ecuador).

El agroturismo implica **viajes a lugares rurales** donde el turista se queda en casas rurales renovadas. Algunas excursiones son informativas o educativas, con visitas a **granjas y campos de cultivo.**[d] Otras son simplemente parte de un programa para renovar casas y pueblos rurales. España ofrece varias oportunidades al agroturista por todo el país, especialmente en el País Vasco y en las Islas Baleares. La isla Chiloé de Chile también tiene una organización agroturística.

El aventurista, o sea[e] el turista que busca **viajes emocionantes, a veces peligrosos,**[f] también tiene amplias oportunidades en los países hispánicos. En los Andes, la Patagonia y las montañas de España, puede practicar **el alpinismo, el ciclismo de montaña, la navegación en rápidos, el esquí, el** *snowboard* y otros deportes **extremos.**

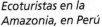

*Ecoturistas en la Amazonia, en Perú*

[a]*please* [b]*disfrutar... enjoying* [c]*por... by humans* [d]*granjas... farms and croplands* [e]*o... or in other words* [f]*dangerous*

Nota cultural: Comprensión

1. ¿Qué es el ecoturismo? ¿En qué países hispanos hay mucho ecoturismo?
2. ¿Cuál es la diferencia entre el agroturismo y el ecoturismo?
3. ¿Cuáles son algunos de los deportes emocionantes que se mencionan?

4. ¿Qué significan las siguientes palabras?

• el alpinismo
• el ciclismo de montaña
• la navegación en rápidos

**Paso 2: Gramática**
See the "Chapter-by-Chapter Supplementary Materials" in the IM for additional teaching suggestions, notes, activities, and other resources for *Paso 2.*

**¿Recuerda Ud.?: Note**
The direct object pronouns from the exchange are in **boldface.**
—*Roberto, ¿tienes los boletos?*
—*No, no **los** tengo, pero mi agente de viajes ya **los** tiene listos.*
—*Si quieres, **te** acompaño a la agencia.*
—*Sí, ¡qué buena idea! Casi nunca **te** veo. Podemos pasar por la plaza a tomar un café también.*
—*Perfecto.*

---

## ¿Recuerda Ud.?

In **Gramática 17, Capítulo 6,** you learned how to use direct object pronouns to avoid repetition. Can you identify the direct object pronouns in the following exchange? To what or to whom do these pronouns refer?

—Roberto, ¿tienes los boletos?
—No, no los tengo, pero mi agente de viajes los tiene listos (*ready*).
—Si quieres, te acompaño a la agencia.
—Sí, ¡qué buena idea! Casi nunca te veo. Podemos pasar por la plaza a tomar un café también.
—Perfecto.

---

## 20   Expressing *to whom* or *for whom*   Indirect Object Pronouns; *dar* and *decir*

**Las vacaciones de primavera**

Javier habla con sus padres de sus planes para las vacaciones de primavera. *Les* pide un poco de dinero para su pasaje de avión.

JAVIER: …así que mis amigos y yo ya tenemos todas las reservaciones. Pero tengo muy poco dinero para el viaje. Yo nunca *les* pido dinero a Uds. durante el semestre y trabajo mucho. Por esta vez, ¿*me* pueden *dar* un poco de dinero para el pasaje de avión?

MADRE: Siempre *le digo* a tu padre que eres muy trabajador y sé que nunca *nos* pides dinero.

PADRE: Es verdad. *Te* podemos *dar* un cheque para el pasaje y para la comida durante el viaje.

**Comprensión**

1. ¿Qué les pide Javier a sus padres?   *Les pide dinero.*
2. ¿Qué le dice la madre al padre de Javier?   *Le dice que Javier es muy trabajador y que nunca les pide dinero.*
3. ¿Qué le dan los padres a Javier?   *Le dan un cheque.*

**Follow-Up**
Ask the following question to introduce the concept of indirect objects.

*¿Qué palabras en cada oración indican las personas afectadas por las acciones de los verbos?*

Emphasize the meaning of the indirect object pronouns.

   me = to me
   le = to him/her/you (form. sing.)
   les = to them/you (form. pl.)

---

*Spring vacation (break)*   *Javier talks to his parents about his plans for spring break. He asks them for a little money for his airplane ticket.* JAVIER: *. . . so, my friends and I already have all of the reservations. But I don't have much money for the trip. I never ask you for money during the semester and I work very hard. Just this once, can you give me a little money for the airplane ticket?* MOTHER: *I always tell your father that you are very hardworking and I know you never ask us for money.* FATHER: *It's true. We can give you a check for the airplane ticket and for food during the trip.*

**CAPÍTULO**

**7**

Emphasis A: Suggestion
Illustrate the concept of the indirect object by suggesting that a student has asked you to get another student's attention for him/her. Tap the student: I tapped John for Tom. Ask: Who is directly affected? Students should answer: John, the direct object. Ask: Who was indirectly affected (second recipient of the action)? Students should answer: Tom, the indirect object.

**PASO 2**

# Indirect Object Pronouns

| me | to/for me | nos | to/for us |
|---|---|---|---|
| te | to/for you (*fam. sing.*) | os | to/for you (*fam. pl.*) |
| le | to/for you (*form. sing.*), him, her, it | les | to/for you (*form. pl.*), them |

Note that indirect object pronouns have the same form as direct object pronouns, except in the third person: **le, les.**

> **indirect object** = noun or pronoun that indicates for whom an action is performed

**Bright Idea Suggestion**
Have students use these two questions to identify and distinguish direct and indirect objects.
To identify the direct object, they should ask: *verb* what/whom?

**A.** Indirect object nouns and pronouns are the second recipient of the action of the verb. They usually answer the questions *to whom?* or *for whom?* in relation to the verb. The word *to* is frequently omitted in English.

Indicate the direct and indirect objects in the following sentences.

> **1.** I'm giving her the present tomorrow.
> **2.** Could you tell me the answer now?
> **3.** El profesor nos va a hacer algunas preguntas.
> **4.** ¿No me compras una revista ahora?

**B.** Like direct object pronouns, *indirect object pronouns* (**los pronombres del complemento indirecto**) are placed immediately before a conjugated verb. They may also be attached to an infinitive or a present participle.

To identify the indirect object they should ask: *verb* to/for what/whom?

*I bought them the cheapest tickets.* → *I bought what?* (direct object = tickets) *I bought for whom?* (indirect object = them)

No, no **te** presto el coche.
*No, I won't lend you the car.*

Voy a guardar**te** el asiento.
**Te** voy a guardar el asiento.
*I'll save your seat for you.*

**Le** estoy escribiendo una carta **a Marisol.**
Estoy escribiéndo**le** una carta **a Marisol.**
*I'm writing Marisol a letter.*

**C.** Since **le** and **les** have several different equivalents, their meaning is often clarified or emphasized with the preposition **a** followed by a pronoun (object of a preposition).

Voy a mandar**le** un telegrama **a Ud. (a él, a ella).**
*I'm going to send you (him, her) a telegram.*

**Les** hago una comida **a Uds. (a ellos, a ellas).**
*I'm making you (them) a meal.*

**D.** It is common for a Spanish sentence to contain both the indirect object noun and the indirect object pronoun, especially with third person forms.

Vamos a decir**le** la verdad **a Juan.**
*Let's tell Juan the truth.*

¿**Les** guardo los asientos **a Jorge y Marta?**
*Shall I save the seats for Jorge and Marta?*

**E.** As with direct object pronouns, indirect object pronouns are attached to the affirmative command form and precede the negative command form.

Sírva**nos** un café, por favor.
*Serve us some coffee, please.*

No **me** dé su número de teléfono ahora.
*Don't give me your phone number now.*

**Refrán**

«Quien algo quiere, algo le cuesta.»

Write the *refrán* on the board and point out that a similar saying in English is often used when talking about exercise (*No pain, no gain.*). Another similar saying is *There's no free lunch.* Ask if students recognize the indirect object pronoun in the Spanish saying.

**F.** Here are some verbs frequently used with indirect objects.

| | | | |
|---|---|---|---|
| **escribir** | *to write* | **preguntar** | *to ask* (a question) |
| **explicar (qu)** | *to explain* | **prestar** | *to lend* |
| **hablar** | *to speak* | **prometer** | *to promise* |
| **mandar** | *to send* | **recomendar (ie)** | *to recommend* |
| **mostrar (ue)** | *to show* | **regalar** | *to give* (as a gift) |
| **ofrecer (zc)** | *to offer* | **servir (i, i)** | *to serve* |
| **pedir (i, i)** | *to ask for* | | |

## Dar and *decir*

**dar**
*(to give)*

| | |
|---|---|
| d**oy** | damos |
| das | dais |
| da | dan |

**decir**
*(to say; to tell)*

| | |
|---|---|
| di**go** | decimos |
| dices | decís |
| dice | dicen |

Javier les **dice** a sus padres que necesita dinero.

Su padre le **da** un cheque.

• **Dar** and **decir** are almost always used with indirect object pronouns in Spanish.

**OJO**

In Spanish there are two verbs for *to give*: **dar** (*to give* [in general]) and **regalar** (*to give as a gift*). Also, do not confuse **decir** (*to say* or *to tell*) with **hablar** (*to speak*).

¿Cuándo **me das** el dinero?
*When will you give me the money?*

¿Por qué no **le dice** Ud. la verdad, señor?
*Why don't you tell him/her the truth, sir?*

• **Dar** and **decir** also have irregular formal command forms. There is a written accent on **dé** to distinguish it from the preposition **de**.

Formal commands of **dar** and **decir**:

dar → **dé, den**
decir → **diga, digan**

## ■ Práctica

**A. De vuelta a Honduras.** Your friends the Padillas, from Honduras, need help arranging for and getting on their flight back home. Explain how you will help them, using the cues as a guide.

MODELO:   confirmar el vuelo → *Les confirmo el vuelo.*

1. llamar un taxi
2. bajar (*to carry down*) las maletas
3. guardar el equipaje
4. facturar el equipaje
5. guardar el puesto en la cola
6. guardar el asiento en la sala de espera
7. comprar una revista
8. por fin decir adiós

**Prác. B: Follow-Up**
Follow up the activity with these questions.

1. ¿A quién le manda Ud. flores? ¿Quién le manda flores a Ud.?
2. ¿A quién le escribe Ud. cartas? ¿Qué tipo de cartas escribe Ud.? ¿Cartas políticas? ¿amistosas? ¿románticas? ¿Quién le escribe cartas a Ud.?
3. ¿Les va a comprar algo a sus padres/hijos este año? ¿a su mejor amigo/a? ¿a su profesor(a)?

**B. ¿Qué hacen estas personas?** Complete las siguientes oraciones con un verbo lógico y un pronombre de complemento indirecto.

MODELO: El vicepresidente __le ofrece__ consejos al presidente.

1. Romeo __le da__ flores (*flowers*) a Julieta.
2. Snoopy __le da__ besos (*kisses*) a Lucy... ¡Y a ella no le gusta!
3. Eva __le ofrece__ una manzana a Adán.
4. Los bancos __les prestan__ dinero a las personas que quieren comprar una casa.
5. Los asistentes de vuelo __les sirven__ bebidas a los pasajeros.
6. Yo siempre __les digo__ la verdad a todos.

> **Verbos útiles**
>
> **dar** (*irreg.*)
> **decir** (*irreg.*)
> **ofrecer (zc)**
> **prestar**
> **servir (i, i)**

**C. En un restaurante.** Imagine that your four-year-old cousin Benjamín has never eaten in a restaurant before. Explain to him what will happen, filling in the blanks with the appropriate indirect object pronoun.

Primero el camarero __te__¹ indica una mesa desocupada.ª Luego tú __le__² pides el menú al camarero. También __le__³ haces preguntas sobre los platos y las especialidades de la casa y __le__⁴ dices tus preferencias. El camarero __te__⁵ trae la comida. Por fin tu papá __le__⁶ pide la cuenta al camarero. Si tú quieres pagar, __le__⁷ pides dinero a tu papá y __le__⁸ das el dinero al camarero.

ªvacant

**Prác. C: Follow-Up**
Ask questions about the story and have students answer as if they were Benjamín.

**Need more practice?**
- Workbook/Laboratory Manual
- Interactive CD-ROM
- Online Learning Center (www.mhhe.com/quetal7)

■ **Conversación**

**Entrevista: ¿Quién... ?** Read through the following items and think about people whom you associate with the indicated action. Then, working with a partner, ask and answer questions to find out information about each topic.

MODELO: darle consejos →
E1: ¿A quién le das consejos?
E2: Con frecuencia le doy consejos a mi compañero de cuarto. ¡Él los necesita!
E1: ¿Quién te da consejos a ti?
E2: Mis abuelos me dan muchos consejos.

1. darle consejos
2. pedirle ayuda con los estudios
3. prestarle la ropa
4. mandarle flores
5. decirle secretos
6. hacerle favores
7. escribirle tarjetas postales (*postcards*)
8. ofrecerle bebidas
9. mostrarle fotos de las vacaciones
10. servirle la comida

**Con: Suggestions**
- Ask some questions based on the cues before assigning the activity to pairs.

  *¿A quién le da consejos?*
  *¿De quién acepta consejos?*
  *¿A quién le pide ayuda con el español?*
  *¿A quién le da ayuda?*, and so on.

- Have students report to the class at least two interesting things they learned about their partner.

- Have students pass around a small object (ball, toy, book, pen). As they do it, have them provide a sentence about what they did or about what they are about to do. Their sentences should include both direct and indirect objects.

  *Voy a darle la pelota a Jim. / Le doy la pelota a Jim.*

  Other useful verbs that you might write on the board are *tirar, pasar, llevar.*

**Note**
Students have been using the *gustar* construction since *Primeros pasos*.

1. *A las personas de los Estados Unidos / del Canadá, ¿les gusta ir a la playa? ¿Qué playas les gusta visitar? ¿Les gusta viajar en avión?*
2. *Y a Ud., ¿le gustan más las playas o las montañas? ¿Adónde le gustaría viajar este verano?*

---

## ¿Recuerda Ud.?

In **Primeros pasos** you started to use forms of **gustar** to express your likes and dislikes. Review what you know by answering the following questions. Then, changing their form as needed, use the forms of **gustar** to interview your instructor.

1. ¿Te gusta el café (el vino, el té… )?
2. ¿Te gusta jugar al béisbol (al golf, al vólibol, al… )?
3. ¿Te gusta viajar en avión (fumar, viajar en tren… )?
4. ¿Qué te gusta más, estudiar o ir a fiestas (trabajar o descansar, cocinar o comer)?

**Note**
Spanish constructions with *gustar* are similar to some English ones.

*The very idea disgusts me.*
*Snakes frighten me.*

---

## 21 Expressing Likes and Dislikes *Gustar*

**Los chilenos viajeros**

Según el anuncio, a muchos chilenos *les gusta* viajar a otros países. Lea el anuncio y luego indique si las oraciones son ciertas o falsas.

1. A los chilenos *les gusta* viajar sólo en este hemisferio.   falso
2. A los chilenos *les gustan* mucho las playas.   cierto
3. Sólo *les gusta* viajar en países de habla española.   falso
4. No *les gustaría* el precio del viaje.   falso

¿Y Ud.?

¿A Ud. le gusta viajar? ¿Le gustan los viajes en avión? ¿Cuál de estos lugares le gustaría visitar?

---

## Constructions with *gustar*

| Spanish | Literal Equivalent | English Phrasing |
|---|---|---|
| **Me gusta la playa.** | The beach is pleasing to me. | *I like the beach.* |
| **No le gustan sus cursos.** | His courses are not pleasing to him. | *He doesn't like his courses.* |
| **Nos gusta leer.** | Reading is pleasing to us. | *We like to read.* |

You have been using the verb **gustar** since the beginning of *¿Qué tal?* to express likes and dislikes. However, **gustar** does not literally mean *to like*, but rather *to be pleasing.*

Me gusta viajar.
*Traveling is pleasing to me.* (*I like traveling.*)

Note that an infinitive is viewed as a singular subject in Spanish.

---

*Capítulo 7 • De vacaciones*

| encantar | interesar |
|----------|-----------|
| faltar | parecer |
| importar | quedar |

**A. Gustar** is always used with an indirect object pronoun: Someone or something is pleasing *to* someone else. The verb must agree with the subject of the sentence—that is, the person or thing that is pleasing.

Me **gusta** la comida mexicana.
*Mexican food is pleasing to me. (I like Mexican food.)*

Me **gustan** los viajes aventureros.
*Adventurous trips are pleasing to me. (I like adventurous trips.)*

**B.** When the person pleased is a noun, a phrase with **a** + a *noun* must be used in addition to the indirect object pronoun. The prepositional phrase usually appears before the indirect object pronoun, but it can also appear after the verb.

**A David** no **le** gustan los aviones.
No le gustan los aviones a **David.**
*David doesn't like airplanes.*

**C.** A phrase with **a** + a *pronoun* is often used for clarification or emphasis. The prepositional phrase can appear before the indirect object pronoun or after the verb.

Remember that **mí** (with an accent) and **ti** (no accent) are used as the object of a preposition in Spanish. Subject pronouns are used for all other persons.

 Remember that the indirect object pronoun *must* be used with **gustar** even when the prepositional phrase **a** + *noun* or *pronoun* is used.

[Práctica A]

CLARIFICATION

¿Le gusta **a Ud.** viajar?
*Do you like to travel?*

EMPHASIS

**A mí** me gusta viajar en avión, pero **a mi esposo** le gusta viajar en coche. **Y a ti,** ¿cómo te gusta viajar?

*I like to travel by plane, but my husband likes to travel by car. And how do **you** like to travel?*

## Would Like / Wouldn't Like

What one *would* or *would not* like to do is expressed with the form **gustaría**\*+*infinitive* and the appropriate indirect objects.

[Práctica B]

**A mí me gustaría** viajar a Colombia.
*I would like to travel to Colombia.*

**Nos gustaría** hacer *camping* este verano.
*We would like to go camping this summer.*

**Preliminary Exercises**

• To make sure the *gustar* construction is clearly understood, have students give the Spanish for the following sentences, then have them give literal equivalents in English of the Spanish construction, for example:

I like the car. → *Me gusta el coche.* → The car is pleasing to me.

1. We/He/You/I like(s) the car.
2. I/We/She/They like(s) to read.
3. She likes the soup/chicken/coffee.
4. He likes tomatoes/tacos/movies/to go to the movies. (¡OJO! Use the definite articles.)

• Have students give the Spanish equivalents of these sentences to stress the redundancy of the indirect object pronoun and noun.

1. My father likes to travel.
2. My mother likes trains.
3. The boys like the beach.
4. María likes to swim.

**AUTOPRUEBA**

Complete each verb with **-a** or **-an.**

1. Me gust_____ las playas de México.
2. Les gust_____ esquiar en las montañas.
3. No nos gust_____ viajar con mi padre.
4. ¿Te gust_____ este restaurante?
5. A Julio le gust_____ mucho las fotos de mi viaje.

*Answers: 1. gustan 2. gustan 3. gusta 4. gusta 5. gustan.*

\**This is one of the forms of the conditional of* **gustar.** *You will study all of the forms of the conditional in* **Gramática 45.**

**Note**

*Gustaría* will be used only with infinitives until all forms of the conditional are presented (*Capítulo 18*).

**Prác. A: Suggestion**
*Paso 2.* Model exchanges of several kinds for students.

**Prác. A: Answers**

*Paso 1* **1.** *(No) Me gusta el vino.* **2.** *(No) Me gustan los niños pequeños.* **3.** *(No) Me gusta la música clásica.* **4.** *(No) Me gusta Ricky Martin.* **5.** *(No) Me gusta el invierno.* **6.** *(No) Me gusta hacer cola.* **7.** *(No) Me gusta el chocolate.* **8.** *(No) Me gustan las películas de terror.* **9.** *(No) Me gustan las clases que empiezan a las ocho de la mañana.* **10.** *(No) Me gusta cocinar.* **11.** *(No) Me gusta la gramática.* **12.** *(No) Me gustan las clases de este semestre/trimestre.* **13.** *(No) Me gustan los vuelos con muchas escalas.* **14.** *(No) Me gusta bailar en las discotecas.* **15.** *(No) Me gusta el béisbol.* **16.** *(No) Me gusta el fútbol.*

**Prác. A: Extension**

**Paso 2.** Have students add two or three things that they like or dislike to the list in *Paso 1.*

### Reacciones

**A mí también.** (So do I.)
**A mí tampoco.** (I don't either. [Neither do I.])
**Pues a mí, sí.** (Well, I do.)
**Pues a mí, no.** (Well, I don't.)

**Prác. B: Answers**

*Paso 1* **1.** *A mi padre le gusta el océano. Le gustaría ir a la playa.* **2.** *A mis hermanos pequeños les gusta nadar. También les gustaría ir a la playa.* **3.** *A mi hermano Ernesto le gusta hacer camping. Le gustaría ir a las montañas.* **4.** *A mis abuelos les gusta descansar. Les gustaría quedarse en casa.* **5.** *A mi madre le gusta la tranquilidad. Le gustaría visitar un pueblecito en la costa.* **6.** *A mi hermana Elena le gustan las discotecas. Le gustaría pasar las vacaciones en una ciudad grande.* **7.** *A ti te gustan los sitios que prefiere la familia Soto. Te gustaría visitar a la familia.* **8.** *Al perro no le gusta quedarse en casa. Le gustaría ir con la familia.* **9.** *A la tía Ramona le gustan las visitas de la familia. Le gustaría recibirlos en su casa.* **10.** *A mí me gusta(n)... Me gustaría...* **Paso 2** **1.** *A Elena.* **2.** *Al padre y a los hermanos pequeños.* **3.** *Los abuelos.* **4.** *A la madre.* **5.** *Ernesto.* **6.** *La tía Ramona.*

**Need more practice?**

- Workbook/Laboratory Manual
- Interactive CD-ROM
- Online Learning Center (www.mhhe.com/quetal7)

---

—Me gusta el café. —No me gusta el café.
—A mí también. —A mí tampoco.
—Pues a mí, no. —Pues a mí, sí.

## ■ Práctica

### A. Gustos y preferencias

PASO 1 Use the models as a guide to tell whether or not you like the following.

MODELOS: ¿el café? → (No) Me gusta el café.
¿los pasteles? → (No) Me gustan los pasteles.

1. ¿el vino?
2. ¿los niños pequeños?
3. ¿la música clásica?
4. ¿Ricky Martin?
5. ¿el invierno?
6. ¿hacer cola?
7. ¿el chocolate?
8. ¿las películas de terror?
9. ¿las clases que empiezan a las ocho de la mañana?
10. ¿cocinar?
11. ¿la gramática?
12. ¿las clases de este semestre/trimestre?
13. ¿los vuelos con muchas escalas?
14. ¿bailar en las discotecas?
15. ¿el béisbol?
16. ¿el fútbol?

 PASO 2 Share your reactions with a classmate. He or she will respond with one of the reactions. How do your likes and dislikes compare?

### B. ¿Adónde vamos este verano?

PASO 1 The members of the Soto family all prefer different vacation activities and, of course, would like to go to different places this summer. Imagine that you are one of the Sotos and describe the family's various preferences, following the model.

MODELO: padre / nadar: ir a la playa →
A mi padre *le gusta* nadar. *Le gustaría* ir a la playa.

1. padre / el océano: ir a la playa
2. hermanos pequeños / nadar: también ir a la playa
3. hermano Ernesto / hacer *camping:* ir a las montañas
4. abuelos / descansar: quedarse en casa
5. madre / la tranquilidad: visitar un pueblecito (*small town*) en la costa
6. hermana Elena / discotecas: pasar las vacaciones en una ciudad grande
7. ti / los sitios que prefiere la familia Soto: visitar a la familia
8. el perro / no / quedarse en casa: ir con la familia
9. la tía Ramona / las visitas de la familia: recibirlos en su casa
10. mí/¿ ?

PASO 2 Now, remembering what you have learned about the vacation preferences of your imaginary family, answer the following questions.

1. ¿A quién le gustaría ir a Nueva York?
2. ¿A quién le gustaría viajar a Acapulco?
3. ¿Quién no quiere salir de casa?
4. ¿A quién le gustaría ir a Cabo San Lucas, un pueblo de Baja California, en México?
5. ¿Quién quiere ir a Colorado?
6. ¿Quién quiere recibir a la familia en su casa?

**Prác. B: Note**
These sentences require the redundant use of the indirect object pronoun and noun.

## ■ Conversación

**A. ¿Conoce bien a sus compañeros de clase?**  Piense en una persona de la clase que Ud. conoce. En su opinión, ¿a esa persona le gustan o no las siguientes cosas? Apunte: **Sí, le gusta(n)** o **No, no le gusta(n).** Luego, entreviste a su compañero/a para verificar sus respuestas.

1. la música clásica
2. el color negro
3. viajar en coche
4. la comida mexicana
5. tener clases por la mañana
6. estudiar otras lenguas
7. las películas trágicas
8. las casas viejas

**Resources: Transparency 54**
This transparency provides additional practice with *gustar* and can also be used as a springboard for talking about what someone else likes.

### NOTA COMUNICATIVA

#### More About Expressing Likes and Dislikes

Here are some ways to express intense likes and dislikes.

- Use the phrases **mucho/muchísimo** or **(para) nada.**

| | |
|---|---|
| **Me gusta mucho/muchísimo.** | *I like it a lot / a whole lot.* |
| **No me gusta (para) nada.** | *I don't like it at all.* |

- To express *love* and *hate* in reference to likes and dislikes, you can use **encantar** and **odiar.**

**Encantar** is used just like **gustar.**

| | |
|---|---|
| **Me encanta** el chocolate. | *I love chocolate.* |
| **Les encanta** viajar, ¿verdad? | *They love traveling, right?* |

**Odiar,** on the other hand, functions like a transitive verb (one that can take a direct object).

| | |
|---|---|
| **Odio** el apio. | *I hate celery.* |
| Mi madre **odia** viajar sola. | *My mother hates traveling alone.* |

- To express interest in something, use **interesar.** This verb is also used like **gustar** and **encantar.**

| | |
|---|---|
| **Me interesa** la comida salvadoreña. | *I'm interested in Salvadoran food.* |

**Nota comunicativa: Note**
*Odiar* is not like *gustar:* (*Yo*) *Odio el café* / (*A mí*) *Me gusta el café.*

**Nota comunicativa: Suggestion**
Ask students to make lists of their favorite and least favorite things and categorize them as:

*Cosas que odio, cosas que no me gustan*
*Cosas que me interesan*
*Cosas que me gustan mucho*
*Cosas que me encantan*

Then ask them to compare their lists with those of a partner.

*A mí me encanta la música rock, pero Juan la odia.*

**B. ¿Qué te gusta? ¿Qué odias?**  Almost every situation has aspects that one likes or dislikes, even hates. Pick at least two of the following situations and tell what you like or don't like about them. Add as many details as you can, using **me gustaría** when possible.

MODELO: en la playa →
Me gusta mucho el agua, pero no me gusta el sol. Por eso no me gusta pasar todo el día en la playa. Me encanta nadar pero odio la arena (*sand*). Por eso me gustaría más ir a nadar en una piscina.

**Situaciones**

| | |
|---|---|
| en un almacén grande | en clase |
| en un autobús | en el coche |
| en un avión | en una discoteca |
| en la biblioteca | en una fiesta |
| en una cafetería | en un parque |
| en casa con mis amigos | en la playa |
| en casa con mis padres/hijos | en un tren |

*Paso 2   Gramática*

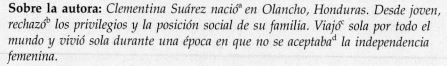

# *Voces de Honduras y El Salvador*

## LITERATURA: Clementina Suárez

**Clementina Suárez**
*(1902–1991)*

**Literatura: Notes**

- Clementina Suárez was a rebel in her era. Not only did she travel alone extensively at a time when it was frowned upon for a woman of her position to do so, but she also lived alone most of her life. She was married and divorced two times. But what was seen as scandalous were her many love affairs with writers and artists and the two children she had out of wedlock. She purportedly read her poetry once in see-through clothing.

**Sobre la autora:** *Clementina Suárez nació[a] en Olancho, Honduras. Desde joven, rechazó[b] los privilegios y la posición social de su familia. Viajó[c] sola por todo el mundo y vivió sola durante una época en que no se aceptaba[d] la independencia femenina.*

### *Canto a la encontrada[e] patria y su héroe*

No puedo llegar...
Porque jamás me he ido.[f]
Eres una Patria construida
en lo interior.
Caminas[g] dentro de mí
como un abierto[h] río.
Vienes desde muy atrás[i]
rebelde y vegetal,
todo en ti es nuevo y viejo
tierra para la infancia
y para inmortalizar el tiempo.

- The scandal she invoked should not overshadow her artistic endeavors. Suárez was an energetic supporter and promoter of the arts. She opened some of the first art galleries in Central America. In Mexico she opened a gallery to display the work of Central American artists, including that of Salvadorian José Mejía Vides (her second husband) and Costa Rican Francisco Amighetti.
- Additionally, she served as cultural attaché to El Salvador and worked in Honduras's Ministry of Education.
- Tragically, Clementina Suárez was murdered in December 1991. Her murderer remains at large.

[a]*was born* [b]*she rejected* [c]*She traveled* [d]*no... people didn't accept* [e]*found* [f]*jamás... I have never left* [g]*You walk* [h]*free-flowing* [i]*desde... from long ago*

## MÚSICA: Yolocamba I Ta y el folklore

**Música: Notes**

- The name Yolocamba I Ta is from the indigenous languages of El Salvador, *el chorti* and *la lenca*.
- Many of the songs of Yolocamba I Ta fall within the tradition of *el canto nuevo* or *la nueva canción,* a Latin American musical movement, especially strong in Chile, that celebrates all things that are authentically Latin America, and rejects political and cultural oppression. Students will read more about *el canto nuevo* in *Capítulo 15, Voces de Chile: Música.*

El nombre indígena del grupo Yolocamba I Ta significa «la rebelión de la siembra[a]». Por unos treinta años, el grupo ha interpretado[b] ritmos nativos de El Salvador que enfocan en la realidad[c] histórico-social de su país y promueven[d] la paz[e] y la justicia. En 1975, los hermanos Franklin y Roberto Quezada, junto con[f] otros estudiantes, fundaron[g] este grupo para difundir[h] la música popular salvadoreña. Por[i] sus canciones de protesta, sufrieron[j] persecución política, y por muchos años vivieron[k] en México.

[a]*harvest* [b]*ha... has been performing* [c]*reality* [d]*promote* [e]*peace* [f]*junto... along with* [g]*formed* [h]*spread* [i]*Because of* [j]*they suffered* [k]*they lived*

La suaca, música y danza folklóricas típicas de El Salvador, representa las bodas[l] de los años 30 del siglo pasado,[m] en las que[n] varias parejas[o] de indígenas se casaban[p] en una boda colectiva.

[l]*weddings* [m]*siglo... last century* [n]*las... which* [o]*varias... several couples* [p]*se... would get married*

- Yolocamba I Ta combines traditional and indigenous rhythms, instruments, and styles, as well those that are considered classical and modern. Their tunes include the sounds of traditional marimbas as well as electric guitars.
- *La suaca* is a descendent of the Spanish dance *la jota aragonesa.*
- The collective weddings, which are represented in the *suaca* dance, were part of the effort to christianize the indigenous people of El Salvador.

Paso 3: Gramática
See the "Chapter-by-Chapter Supplementary Materials" in the IM for additional teaching suggestions, notes, activities, and other resources for *Paso 3*.

## 22 Talking About the Past (1) Preterite of Regular Verbs and of *dar*, *hacer*, *ir*, and *ser*

### Elisa habla de su viaje a Puerto Rico

Elisa es reportera. Recientemente *fue* a Puerto Rico para escribir un artículo.

«Recientemente *fui* a Puerto Rico para escribir un artículo sobre esa isla. *Hice* el viaje en avión. El vuelo *fue* largo, pues el avión *hizo* escala en Miami. *Pasé* una semana entera en la Isla. *Hablé* con muchas personas de la industria turística y *visité* los lugares más interesantes de Puerto Rico. También *comí* mucha comida típica de la Isla. Además, *tomé* el sol en las preciosas playas puertorriqueñas y *nadé* en el mar Caribe. Me *divertí* mucho. ¡Mi viaje *fue* casi como unas vacaciones!»

### Comprensión: ¿Cierto o falso?

1. Elisa fue a Puerto Rico para pasar sus vacaciones.    falso
2. El avión hizo escala en los Estados Unidos.    cierto
3. Elisa no visitó ningún lugar importante de Puerto Rico.    falso
4. Elisa también pasó tiempo cerca del océano.    cierto

In previous chapters of *¿Qué tal?*, you have talked about a number of your activities, but always in the present tense. In this section, you will begin to work with the forms of the preterite, one of the tenses that will allow you to talk about the past. To talk about all aspects of the past in Spanish, you need to know how to use two *simple tenses* (tenses formed without an auxiliary or "helping" verb): the preterite and the imperfect. In this chapter, you will learn the regular forms of the preterite and those of four irregular verbs: **dar, hacer, ir,** and **ser.** In this chapter and in **Capítulos 8, 9, 10,** and **11,** you will learn more about preterite forms and their uses as well as about the imperfect and the ways in which it is used alone and with the preterite.

The *preterite* (**el pretérito**) has several equivalents in English. For example, **hablé** can mean *I spoke* or *I did speak*. The preterite is used to report finished, completed actions or states of being in the past. If the action or state of being is viewed as completed—no matter how long it lasted or took to complete—it will be expressed with the preterite.

```
PAST -------------------- Present -------------------- Future
preterite                     present
                       present progressive
                         formal commands
```

♻ **Reciclado**
Follow up the narration by having students respond to the following questions, using direct object pronouns.

*Elisa Velasco, ¿visitó lugares interesantes en Puerto Rico?*

*¿Entrevistó* (write on board) *a muchas personas?*

*¿Comió comida típica?*

*¿Visitó las playas puertorriqueñas?*

*¿Hizo el viaje en avión?*

*¿Pasó una semana en Puerto Rico?*

*¿Tomó el sol en las playas?*

**Note**
There will be opportunities to practice the preterite and the imperfect in *Capítulos 7–10*, and throughout the rest of the text.

**Heritage Speakers**
Anime a un(a) estudiante hispanohablante a leer en voz alta la narración de Elisa.

*Elisa talks about her trip to Puerto Rico*    Elisa is a reporter. She recently went to Puerto Rico to write an article. "Recently I went to Puerto Rico to write an article about that island. I made the trip by plane. The flight was long because the plane made a stop in Miami. I spent a whole week on the Island. I spoke with many people in the tourist industry and I visited the most interesting places in Puerto Rico. I also ate lots of typical food from the Island. Furthermore, I sunbathed on beautiful Puerto Rican beaches and swam in the Caribbean Sea. I had lots of fun. My trip was almost like a vacation!"

# PASO 3

## Preterite of Regular Verbs

| hablar | | comer | | vivir | |
|---|---|---|---|---|---|
| hablé | *I spoke (did speak)* | comí | *I ate (did eat)* | viví | *I lived (did live)* |
| hablaste | *you spoke* | comiste | *you ate* | viviste | *you lived* |
| habló | *you/he/she spoke* | comió | *you/he/she ate* | vivió | *you/he/she lived* |
| hablamos | *we spoke* | comimos | *we ate* | vivimos | *we lived* |
| hablasteis | *you spoke* | comisteis | *you ate* | vivisteis | *you lived* |
| hablaron | *you/they spoke* | comieron | *you/they ate* | vivieron | *you/they lived* |

- Note that, in the preterite, the **nosotros** forms of regular -**ar** and -**ir** verbs are the same as the present tense forms. Context usually helps determine meaning.

Hoy **hablamos** con la profesora Benítez.
*Today we're speaking with Professor Benítez.*

Ayer **hablamos** con el director de la facultad.
*Yesterday we spoke with the head of the department.*

- Note the accent marks on the first and third person singular of the preterite tense. These accent marks are dropped in the conjugation of **ver: vi, vio.**

ver:  vi      vimos
      viste   visteis
      vio     vieron

- Verbs that end in -**car**, -**gar**, and -**zar** show a spelling change in the first person singular (**yo**) of the preterite. (This is the same change you have already learned to make in formal commands.)

-car → **qu**    **buscar**
                 busqué      buscamos
                 buscaste    buscasteis
                 buscó       buscaron

-gar → **gu**    **pagar**
                 pagué       pagamos
                 pagaste     pagasteis
                 pagó        pagaron

-zar → **c**     **empezar**
                 empecé      empezaron
                 empezaste   empezasteis
                 empezó      empezaron

**Heritage Speakers**
- En algunos dialectos del español, hay una tendencia a añadirle una -*s* al final de la segunda persona del singular (*tú*) del pretérito, por ejemplo, *hablaste → hablastes, comiste → comistes, viviste → vivistes*. Aunque se oyen estas formas, es preferible no añadir la -*s* al final.
- En algunos dialectos del español, a veces se oye *vide, vidiste, vido, ...* en vez de *vi, viste, vio...* Aunque se oyen estas formas, las que se presentan aquí son las preferidas.

- -**Ar** and -**er** stem-changing verbs show no stem change in the preterite.
  -**Ir** stem-changing verbs do show a change.*

despertar (ie): **desperté, despertaste,...**
volver (ue): **volví, volviste,...**

- An unstressed -**i**- between two vowels becomes -**y**-. Also, note the accent on the **í** in the **tú, nosotros,** and **vosotros** forms.

| **creer** | | **leer** | |
|---|---|---|---|
| creí | creímos | leí | leímos |
| creíste | creísteis | leíste | leísteis |
| creyó | creyeron | leyó | leyeron |

---

*You will learn more about and practice the preterite of stem-changing verbs in **Capítulo 8.***

**Suggestions**
• Present some sentences using the preterite of *ser* and *ir* to show that context clarifies the meaning.

• Remind students that single-syllable forms such as the *yo* and *Ud.* forms of *dar* and *ver* do not require an accent: *di, dio; vi, vio.*

# Irregular Preterite Forms

| **dar** | | **hacer** | | **ir/ser** | |
|---|---|---|---|---|---|
| di | dimos | hice | hicimos | fui | fuimos |
| diste | disteis | hiciste | hicisteis | fuiste | fuisteis |
| dio | dieron | hizo | hicieron | fue | fueron |

• The preterite endings for **dar** are the same as those used for regular **-er/-ir** verbs in the preterite, except that the accent marks are dropped.

• **Hizo** is spelled with a **z** to keep the [s] sound of the infinitive.

$$\text{hic-} + \text{-o} \rightarrow \text{hizo}$$

• **Ir** and **ser** have identical forms in the preterite. Context will make the meaning clear.

**Fui** a la playa el verano pasado.
*I went to the beach last summer.*

**Fui** agente de viajes.
*I was a travel agent.*

**Resources: Transparency 55**
This transparency includes practice with daily routines in the preterite.

## AUTOPRUEBA

Give the correct preterite forms.

1. (nosotros) buscar
2. (mi papá) volver
3. (yo) despertarme
4. (Ud.) ver
5. (ellas) leer
6. (tú) ser

*Answers: 1. buscamos 2. volvió 3. me desperté 4. vio 5. leyeron 6. fuiste*

**Suggestions**
• Say the following verbs and have students give the corresponding subject pronoun. Singular forms:

| | | |
|---|---|---|
| *pregunté* | *bajó* | *ayudaste* |
| *fumé* | *llamé* | *anunció* |
| *mandaste* | *bebió* | *aprendí* |
| *comiste* | *nadé* | *ayudó* |

Plural forms:

| | | |
|---|---|---|
| *escuchamos* | *terminaron* | *mirasteis* |
| *estudiamos* | *bailaron* | *regresaron* |
| *pagamos* | *bebieron* | *comimos* |
| *aprendisteis* | | |

• Say the following verbs and have students tell whether each could be present, past, or both.

| | | |
|---|---|---|
| *miró* | *mandé* | *escuché* |
| *escucha* | *escribimos* | *fumaste* |
| *bebió* | *ayudamos* | *vive* |
| *volvió* | *creo* | *empiezan* |
| *leyó* | *pagáis* | *buscaste* |

• Say the following verbs and have students tell whether each is a command or a form of the preterite.

| | | |
|---|---|---|
| *estudie* | *estudié* | *fumé* |
| *fumen* | *ayudé* | *busque* |
| *leyó* | *hablé* | *pagué* |
| *lleve* | *decidí* | |

## Práctica

**A. ¡Anticipemos! ¿Qué hizo Ud. el verano pasado?** Indique las oraciones que son ciertas para Ud., contestando con **sí** o **no.**

El verano pasado…

1. tomé una clase en la universidad.
2. asistí a un concierto.
3. trabajé mucho.
4. hice *camping* con algunos amigos / mi familia.
5. viví con mis padres / mis hijos.
6. me quedé en este pueblo / esta ciudad.
7. fui a una playa.
8. hice una excursión a otro país.
9. fui a muchas fiestas.
10. no hice nada especial.

**Prác. A: Variation**
Have students work in pairs and report each other's actions to the class.

**Need more practice?**

- Workbook/Laboratory Manual
- Interactive CD-ROM
- Online Learning Center
  (www.mhhe.com/quetal7)

### B. El día de tres compañeras

PASO 1   Teresa, Evangelina y Liliana comparten (*share*) un apartamento. Ayer Teresa y Evangelina fueron a la universidad mientras Liliana se quedó en casa. Describa lo que hicieron, según la perspectiva de cada una.

MODELO:   (nosotras) levantarse / a / siete y media →
Nos levantamos a las siete y media.

TERESA Y EVANGELINA

1. (nosotras) salir / de / apartamento / a / nueve
2. llegar / biblioteca / a / diez
3. estudiar / toda la mañana / para / examen
4. escribir / muchos ejercicios
5. almorzar / con / amigos / en / cafetería
6. ir / a / laboratorio / a / una
7. hacer / todos los experimentos / de / manual (*m.*)
8. tomar / examen / a / cuatro
9. ¡examen / ser / horrible!
10. regresar / a casa / después de / examen
11. ayudar / Liliana / a / preparar / cena
12. cenar / todas juntas / a / siete

LILIANA

1. (yo) quedarse / en casa / todo el día
2. ver / televisión / por / mañana
3. llamar / mi / padres / a / once
4. tomar / café / con / vecinos (*neighbors*)
5. estudiar / para / examen / de / historia / y / escribir / composición / para / clase / sociología
6. ir / a / garaje / para / dejar / muebles / viejo / allí
7. ir / a / supermercado / y / comprar / comida
8. empezar / a / preparar / cena / a / cinco

PASO 2   ¿Quién lo dijo (*said*), Evangelina o Liliana?

1. Mis compañeras no pasaron mucho tiempo en casa hoy.
2. ¡El examen fue desastroso!
3. Estudié mucho hoy.
4. Me gustó mucho el programa de «Oprah» hoy.
5. ¿Saben? Hablé con mis padres hoy y…

PASO 3   Ahora vuelva a contar (*tell*) cómo fue el día de Liliana, pero desde el punto de vista de sus compañeras de cuarto. Luego diga cómo fue el día de Teresa y Evangelina según Liliana.

### ■ Conversación

#### A. Entrevista

1. ¿Qué le(s) diste a tu mejor amigo/a (tu esposo/a, tu novio/a, tus hijos) para su cumpleaños el año pasado? ¿Qué te regaló a ti esa persona para tu cumpleaños? ¿Alguien te mandó flores el año pasado? ¿Le mandaste flores a alguien? ¿Te gusta que te traigan chocolates? ¿otras cosas?

2. ¿Dónde y a qué hora comiste ayer? ¿Con quién(es) comiste? ¿Te gustaron todos los platos que comiste? Si comiste fuera, ¿quién pagó?

3. ¿Cuándo decidiste estudiar español? ¿Cuándo lo empezaste a estudiar? ¿Vas a seguir (*continue*) con el español el semestre/trimestre que viene?

4. ¿Qué hiciste ayer? ¿Adónde fuiste? ¿Con quién(es)? ¿Ayudaste a alguien a hacer algo? ¿Te llamó alguien? ¿Llamaste a alguien? ¿Te invitaron a hacer algo especial algunos amigos?

**B. El viernes por la tarde...**  The following drawings depict what Julián did last Friday night. Match the phrases with the individual drawings in the sequence. Then narrate what Julián did using verbs in the preterite. Use words and phrases like **primero, luego, después,** and **finalmente** to indicate sequence.

Resources: Transparency 56

**Con. A: Follow-Up**
Have students write questions about personal habits and life events they can then use to interview classmates. Write the following verbs on the board to give them ideas: *despertarse, regresar, pagar, enamorarse* (to fall in love), *sacar una nota* (grade).

**Con. B: Notes**
• Students learned adverbs and phrases to express sequence of events in the *Nota comunicativa* of *Capítulo 4* (page 119).

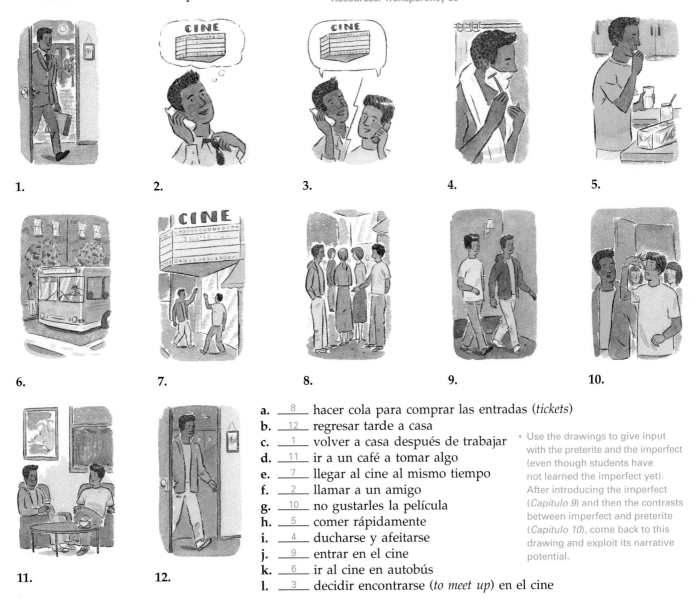

1.  2.  3.  4.  5.

6.  7.  8.  9.  10.

11.  12.

a. __8__ hacer cola para comprar las entradas (*tickets*)
b. __12__ regresar tarde a casa
c. __1__ volver a casa después de trabajar
d. __11__ ir a un café a tomar algo
e. __7__ llegar al cine al mismo tiempo
f. __2__ llamar a un amigo
g. __10__ no gustarles la película
h. __5__ comer rápidamente
i. __4__ ducharse y afeitarse
j. __9__ entrar en el cine
k. __6__ ir al cine en autobús
l. __3__ decidir encontrarse (*to meet up*) en el cine

• Use the drawings to give input with the preterite and the imperfect (even though students have not learned the imperfect yet). After introducing the imperfect (*Capítulo 9*) and then the contrasts between imperfect and preterite (*Capítulo 10*), come back to this drawing and exploit its narrative potential.

**Con. B: Suggestion**
Read the following whole paragraph out loud. Then repeat, phrase by phrase. Have students retell the story line by line.

*Anoche Miguel volvió a casa a las siete. Preparó la comida y cenó rápidamente. Estudió para su examen de filosofía hasta las ocho y después habló por teléfono con una compañera de clase. Y a las nueve en punto llegaron sus padres.*

**En los Estados Unidos y el Canadá: Suggestion**
Have students visit NASA's website for more information about the astronauts.

**En los Estados Unidos y el Canadá: Comprensión**
1. ¿Cuándo empezó Ochoa a trabajar para la NASA?
2. ¿Cuándo hizo su misión más reciente?

## En los Estados Unidos y el Canadá

### Ellen Ochoa: Una viajera[a] espacial

La Dra. Ellen L. Ochoa, de California (1958– ), es **la primera mujer hispana astronauta** de los Estados Unidos; trabaja en la NASA desde 1990. Se graduó con **un doctorado**[b] en **ingeniería eléctrica** de la Universidad de Stanford. Pasó **más de 975 horas viajando en el espacio,** la misión más reciente en el año 2002. Entre sus muchos honores está el de ser[c] miembro de la Comisión Presidencial para la Celebración de Mujeres en la Historia Americana.

La Dra. Ochoa no es la única persona hispana en la NASA. Hay **otros cinco astronautas hispanos** en misiones espaciales: el argentino Frank Caldeiro, el costarricense[d] Franklin Chang-Díaz, los españoles Pedro Duque y Michael López-Alegría y el peruano Carlos Noriega.

*Ellen Ochoa*

[a]*traveler*  [b]*Ph.D.*  [c]*el… that of being*  [d]*Costa Rican*

**Lengua y cultura: Answers**
1. *Les* 2. *algo* 3. *la* 4. *la* 5. *conocen* 6. *Está* 7. *es* 8. *es* 9. *más* 10. *incaicos* 11. *visitarla* 12. *Les* 13. *es* 14. *ir* 15. *mejores* 16. *comprar* 17. *muchos* 18. *países* 19. *Sé* 20. *les* **Comprensión** 1. *falso: Machu Picchu está en el Perú.* 2. *cierto* 3. *cierto* 4. *falso: Los turistas de todo el mundo conocen Machu Picchu.*

## UN POCO DE TODO

*Las ruinas incaicas de Machu Picchu*

**Resources for Review and Testing Preparation**

- Workbook/Laboratory Manual
- Interactive CD-ROM
- Online Learning Center
  (www.mhhe.com/quetal7)

**Lengua y cultura: Machu Picchu, la ciudad perdida** (*lost*) **de los incas.**
Complete the following vacation suggestion with the correct form of the words in parentheses, as suggested by the context. When two possibilities are given in parentheses, select the correct word.

Los países de Centro y Sudamérica ofrecen una gran variedad de posibilidades para el viajero. Si a Uds. les interesa un viaje menos típico, deben planear una aventura en el mundo hispánico.

(Les/Los[1]) quiero decir (algo/nada[2]) sobre (el/la[3]) ciudad de Machu Picchu. ¿Ya (lo/la[4]) (saber/conocer[5]) Uds.? (Ser/Estar[6]) situada en los Andes, a unos ochenta kilómetros[a] de la ciudad de Cuzco, Perú. Machu Picchu (ser/estar[7]) conocida[b] como la ciudad escondida[c] de los incas. Se dice que (ser/estar[8]) una de las manifestaciones (más/tan[9]) importantes de la arquitectura incaica. Era[d] refugio y a la vez[e] ciudad de vacaciones de los reyes[f] (incaico[10]).

Uds. deben (visitarlo/visitarla[11]). (Le/Les[12]) gustaría porque (ser/estar[13]) un sitio inolvidable.[g] Es mejor (ir/van[14]) a Machu Picchu en primavera o verano —son las (mejor[15]) estaciones para visitar este lugar. Pero es necesario (comprar/compran[16]) los boletos con anticipación,[h] porque (mucho[17]) turistas de todos los (país[18]) del mundo visitan este sitio extraordinario. ¡(Yo: Saber/Conocer[19]) que a Uds. (los/les[20]) va a gustar el viaje!

[a]*ochenta… 50 millas*  [b]*known*  [c]*hidden*  [d]*It was*  [e]*a… at the same time*  [f]*kings*  [g]*unforgettable*  [h]*con… ahead of time*

**Comprensión: ¿Cierto o falso?** Corrija las oraciones falsas.

1. Machu Picchu está en Chile.
2. Fue un lugar importante en el pasado.
3. Todavía es una atracción turística de gran interés.
4. Sólo los turistas latinoamericanos conocen Machu Picchu.

**Resources: Desenlace**
In the *Capítulo 7* segment of "Chapter-by-Chapter Supplementary Materials" in the IM, you will find a chapter-culminating activity. You can use this activity to consolidate and review the vocabulary and grammar skills students have acquired.

*Capítulo 7* • *De vacaciones*

CAPÍTULO

**7**

Paso 4: Un paso más
• The *Paso 4: Un paso más* sections are optional.

# Un paso más    PASO 4

• See the "Chapter-by-Chapter Supplementary Materials" in the IM for additional teaching suggestions, notes, activities, and other resources for *Paso 4.*

## VIDEOTECA

## Entrevista cultural: Honduras

Heidi Luna es una agente de viajes hondureña. Aquí habla de los destinos favoritos de sus clientes y también menciona sus propios planes para viajar. Antes de ver el vídeo, lea el siguiente fragmento de la entrevista.

HEIDI:  …La mayoría de nuestros clientes nos busca para que los ayudemos en viajes especiales o en vacaciones especiales. Es muy divertido poder ayudarlos.

Ahora vea el vídeo y conteste las siguientes preguntas basándose en la entrevista.

1. ¿Qué destinos latinoamericanos menciona Heidi como los preferidos de sus clientes? ¿Qué destinos norteamericanos menciona?
2. ¿Adónde piensa viajar Heidi? ¿Por qué?

## Entrevista cultural: El Salvador

Rubén Guillén es de El Salvador. En la entrevista, explica por qué le encanta ser guía turístico. Antes de ver el vídeo, lea el siguiente fragmento de la entrevista.

RUBÉN:  Bueno, yo soy guía turístico y trabajo precisamente en un hotel de la capital y me encargo de[a] organizar excursiones y viajes hacia las diferentes playas y lugares turísticos de nuestro país. Eso, exactamente.

[a]me… *I'm in charge of*

Ahora vea el vídeo y conteste las siguientes preguntas basándose en la entrevista.

1. ¿Dónde trabaja Rubén?
2. Según Rubén, ¿cuáles son algunas de las ventajas de su trabajo?

## Entre amigos: El verano pasado, me fui al Canadá

Rubén, Tané, Miguel y Karina pasan una tarde en el Parque Ecológico de Xochimilco. Hablan de las vacaciones. En su opinión, ¿qué preguntas van a hacerse? Antes de mirar el vídeo, lea las preguntas a continuación. Mientras mire el vídeo, trate de entender la conversación en general y fíjese en la información sobre las vacaciones. Luego mire el vídeo una segunda vez, fijándose en la información que necesita para contestar las preguntas.

1. A Karina, ¿qué le gusta hacer durante las vacaciones? ¿Y a Tané?
2. ¿Adónde fue Tané el verano pasado? ¿Y Miguel?
3. ¿Qué hizo Rubén el verano pasado?

**Entre amigos: Answers**
*Possible answers:* 1. *A Karina le gusta bailar, nadar y correr. A Tané le gusta patinar, relajarse, estar tranquila y nadar.* 2. *Tané fue a Tepotzlán y Miguel fue al Canadá.* 3. *Trabajó.*

**Entrevistas culturales: Suggestions**

*¿Qué destinos turísticos conoce Ud.?
¿Adónde piensa viajar este año?*

• Before showing the video clips, ask students questions about their experiences with travel agents and/or traveling.

• Tell students they will be listening to a travel agent from Honduras (Heidi) and a tourist guide from El Salvador (Rubén). Have them predict what type of information they may hear.

• Show the video clips and allow students one to two minutes to work on the questions for each one. Have volunteers answer the questions.

• Have volunteers role-play the parts of Heidi and Rubén with their respective interviewers.

**Entrevista cultural: Honduras: Answers**
*Possible answers:* 1. *Los destinos latinoamericanos que menciona son Sudamérica y México, y los destinos norteamericanos que menciona son Miami y Orlando, en la Florida.* 2. *Piensa viajar a Toronto, Canadá, para pasar unas vacaciones.*

**Entrevista cultural: El Salvador: Answers**

*Possible answers:*
1. *Trabaja en un hotel como guía turístico.*
2. *Puede conocer todo su país y a muchas personas de varios países.*

**Entre amigos: Suggestions**
• Before viewing the video, review the questions with the students and ask them similar questions: *¿Qué le gusta a Ud. hacer durante las vacaciones? ¿Adónde fue de vacaciones el verano pasado? ¿Qué hizo allí?* Have students answer or work in small groups to ask and answer these questions.
• After viewing the video, have volunteers read and answer the questions.

Notes
• In the early 1960s, there were more Peace Corps volunteers in Honduras than in any other country. Presently there are approximately 200 volunteers in the country.
• Students can read the poem *"Canto a la encontrada patria y su héroe"* by Honduras's Clementina Suárez in *Voces de Honduras y El Salvador: Literatura.*
• Students can read about El Salvador's folkloric music and the musical group Yolocamba I Ta in *Voces de Honduras y El Salvador: Música.*
• See the Workbook/Laboratory Manual for focused practice with the material in *Enfoque cultural.*

## ENFOQUE CULTURAL

### Honduras y El Salvador

### ¡Fíjese!

- El centro ceremonial maya de Copán, en Honduras, es hoy un parque nacional que contiene una colección de ruinas mayas superadas[a] sólo por las ruinas de Tikal en Guatemala.
- La moneda de Honduras, el lempira, lleva el nombre de un cacique[b] indígena que luchó contra[c] los españoles.
- El nombre indígena de la capital de Honduras, Tegucigalpa, significa «cerros de plata».[d] Honduras recibió su nombre español por la profundidad[e] de sus aguas costeras.[f] El nombre indígena de El Salvador era[g] Cuzcatlán, que significa «tierra de joyas[h] y cosas preciosas».
- Las erupciones del Volcán de Izalco en El Salvador fueron constantes entre los años 1770 y 1966, por casi dos siglos.[i] Este volcán se conoce con el nombre de «el faro[j] del Pacífico», porque estuvo encendido[k] por muchos años y sirvió de[l] guía a los navegantes.

[a]*exceeded (in quality)* [b]*chief* [c]luchó... *fought against* [d]cerros... *silver hills* [e]*depth* [f]*coastal* [g]*was* [h]*jewels* [i]*centuries* [j]*lighthouse* [k]estuvo... *it was lit up* [l]sirvió... *served as a*

### Personas famosas: El Arzobispo[a] Óscar Arnulfo Romero

El 24 de marzo de 1980 un héroe de El Salvador fue asesinado mientras oficiaba una misa.[b] En vida,[c] el arzobispo Óscar Arnulfo Romero (1917–1980) fue la conciencia de su país. Criticó a los líderes políticos por su violencia e injusticia, y trabajó para mejorar[d] las condiciones económicas y sociales del país. Por eso, fue nominado para el premio Nóbel de la Paz[e] en 1979.

[a]*Archbishop* [b]oficiaba... *he was celebrating a Mass* [c]*life* [d]*improve* [e]premio... *Nobel Peace Prize*

*El Volcán de Izalco, El Salvador*

Multimedia: Internet
Have students search the Internet for more information on Honduras and El Salvador. You might assign specific topics, such as the life and social ideas of Archbishop Óscar Romero, and have students give brief oral presentations based on their findings.

Learn more about Honduras and El Salvador with the Video, the Interactive CD-ROM, and the Online Learning Center (www.mhhe.com/quetal7).

PASO FINAL

## A LEER

### ESTRATEGIA: Identifying the Source of a Passage

If you pick up a copy of the *New England Journal of Medicine,* what sort of articles do you expect to find? For whom are they written and for what purpose? Would you anticipate finding similar articles in *People* magazine? You can often make useful predictions about an article—the article's content, its narrative style, the target audience, the author's purpose, and so on—if you know something about the magazine or journal from which it comes. The article you are about to read was first published in *Nexos,* a Spanish-language in-flight magazine published by American Airlines for its Spanish-speaking customers. Knowing this, which of the following topics do you think might be treated in a given issue of this magazine?

1. the Incas and Machu Picchu
2. how to install a ceiling fan
3. a walking tour of Boston
4. Miami by night

All but number 2 might logically appear in *Nexos.* Keeping in mind the source of a reading will often help you to predict its content.

> **Sobre la lectura...** *Nexos* is for the reader who is interested in all aspects of travel, different cultures and customs, and similar issues. The following article was taken from a section called **"Destinos"** (*Destinations*). This particular article deals with El Salvador.

> **Suggestion**
> Do the *Estrategia* in class the day you assign the reading as homework. Bring in titles of articles from several different magazines and have students match each article with the magazine it came from. This will further demonstrate how readers associate certain types of features with specific magazines.

## *El Salvador: Un tesoro<sup>a</sup> al alcance de la mano<sup>b</sup>*

En sus 20.742 kilómetros cuadrados, el territorio salvadoreño ofrece al visitante una rica mezcla de cultura y <u>entretenimiento</u> bajo la premisa de la inmediatez.<sup>c</sup> En la ciudad se encuentra una amplia oferta <u>hotelera</u>. Por su seguridad y facilidad de desplazamiento,<sup>d</sup> hospédese<sup>e</sup> cerca de centros comerciales, como Metrocentro, Galerías y la Zona Rosa. En esta última,<sup>f</sup> visite el Museo de Antropología David J. Guzmán y el <u>recién inaugurado</u> Museo de Arte (MARTE), que ofrece un itinerario por<sup>g</sup> los momentos clave<sup>h</sup> del arte salvadoreño. Al sur de la ciudad, a un costado del Parque Cuscatlán, hallará<sup>i</sup> el Museo Tin Marín y su <u>santuario</u> de mariposas.<sup>j</sup>

El Salvador, antiguamente llamado en náhuatl<sup>k</sup> «Cuzcatlán» o «Tierra de Riquezas o Preseas<sup>l</sup>», fue conquistado<sup>m</sup> en 1524 por el capitán español Pedro de Alvarado. La influencia colonial se aprecia en la arquitectura del Palacio y el Teatro Nacional, en el centro histórico de San Salvador.

Visite el Mercado de Artesanías de la Avenida Manuel Enrique Araujo, en donde venden bellas artesanías.

Las playas salvadoreñas son un imán,<sup>n</sup> especialmente las<sup>o</sup> del Puerto de La Libertad y la Costa del Sol.

Fresco gracias a su exuberante vegetación, Los Planes de Renderos es el sitio ideal afuera<sup>p</sup> de la ciudad para degustar<sup>q</sup> el platillo nacional: las pupusas, que son tortillas de maíz rellenas de frijoles molidos,<sup>r</sup> queso derretido<sup>s</sup> y chicharrón.<sup>t</sup>

*El Palacio Nacional, en San Salvador*

<sup>a</sup>*treasure* <sup>b</sup>*al... within easy reach* <sup>c</sup>*bajo... all within reach; easily accessible* <sup>d</sup>*facilidad... moving around easily (in the city)* <sup>e</sup>*(you should) stay* <sup>f</sup>*esta... the latter* <sup>g</sup>*through* <sup>h</sup>*key* <sup>i</sup>*you will find* <sup>j</sup>*butterflies* <sup>k</sup>*Nahuatl, indigenous language of the Aztecs* <sup>l</sup>*Treasures* <sup>m</sup>*fue... was conquered* <sup>n</sup>*magnet* <sup>o</sup>*those* <sup>p</sup>*outside* <sup>q</sup>*trying, sampling* <sup>r</sup>*tortillas... corn tortillas filled with refried beans* <sup>s</sup>*melted* <sup>t</sup>*pork flavorings*

# PASO 4

La vida nocturna <u>capitalina</u> caracteriza a los restaurantes y bares de la calle San Antonio Abad. Si desea bailar, escoja una discoteca de la Zona Rosa.

Su visita no debe concluir sin un vistazo[u] a Joya de Cerén, en San Juan Opico, La Libertad, 35 kilómetros al occidente de San Salvador. Este poblado maya, enterrado[v] bajo las <u>cenizas</u> volcánicas hace 1.400 años[w] y declarado Patrimonio de la Humanidad por la UNESCO en 1993, da cuenta de[x] cómo transcurría[y] la vida cotidiana[z] en una aldea[aa] indígena.

Tampoco se vaya sin recorrer[bb] los pueblos de La Ruta de la Paz[cc]: Perquín, Arambala, Villa Rosario, Joateca, Cacaopera, Corinto y Guatajiagua en Morazán, 170 kilómetros al noreste de San Salvador. Ahí podrá deleitarse[dd] en las aguas del río Sapo y la cascada[ee] de Olomina, además de explorar las cuevas del cerro El Pericón.[ff]

[u]*glimpse* [v]*buried* [w]*hace... 1400 years ago* [x]*da... shows* [y]*used to be* [z]*daily* [aa]pueblo pequeño [bb]*Tampoco... You shouldn't go without visiting* [cc]*pueblos... towns of The Road of Peace* [dd]*Ahí... There you can have fun* [ee]*waterfall* [ff]cuevas... *caves of El Pericón hill*

## Comprensión

**A. ¿Adónde les gustaría ir?** A base del (*Based on the*) artículo, identifique un lugar de interés para los siguientes turistas norteamericanos.

1. la profesora Martínez, arqueóloga dedicada al estudio de las culturas indígenas
2. el Sr. Nelson, propietario de una tienda de artefactos importados
3. María Rosa, pintora y artista

**B. El título.** Lea otra vez el título del artículo. ¿Por qué se titula así esta lectura? Es decir, ¿cuál es el mensaje (el tema principal) del artículo?

1. Hay pocas atracciones turísticas en El Salvador.
2. El Salvador es tan grande que es difícil visitar y ver todos los sitios de interés.
3. El Salvador tiene mucho que ofrecer al turista y todo está accesible.

 **A ESCRIBIR**

**De vacaciones en El Salvador.** Prepare un breve informe sobre dos de los lugares mencionados en el artículo. Consulte recursos (*resources*) en la biblioteca o en el Internet para hacer su investigación. Use los siguientes pasos como guía.

PASO 1 Escoja los lugares que van a ser el enfoque (*focus*) de su investigación.

PASO 2 Piense en el tipo de información que quiere incluir.

PASO 3 Vaya a la biblioteca o consulte sitios del Internet para hacer su informe.

PASO 4 Escriba una breve composición para presentar a la clase.

## GRAMÁTICA

To review the grammar points presented in this chapter, refer to the indicated grammar presentations. You'll find further practice of these structures in the Workbook/Laboratory Manual, on the Interactive CD-ROM, and on the *¿Qué tal?* Online Learning Center (www.mhhe.com/quetal7).

**20** Expressing *to whom* or *for whom*—Indirect Object Pronouns; **dar** and **decir**

Do you know how to use indirect object pronouns to express *to whom* or *for whom*?

**21** Expressing Likes and Dislikes—**Gustar**

Do you know how to talk about things you and others like and like to do?

**22** Talking About the Past (1)—Preterite of Regular Verbs and of **dar, hacer, ir,** and **ser**

You should know how to conjugate regular preterite verbs. Can you use the irregular verbs **dar, hacer, ir,** and **ser** in the preterite as well?

## VOCABULARIO

Practice this vocabulary with digital flash cards on the Online Learning Center (www.mhhe.com/quetal7).

### Los verbos

| | |
|---|---|
| **anunciar** | to announce |
| **contar (ue)** | to tell |
| **dar** (*irreg.*) | to give |
| **decir** (*irreg.*) | to say; to tell |
| **encantar** | to like very much, love |
| **explicar (qu)** | to explain |
| **fumar** | to smoke |
| **gustar** | to be pleasing |
| **interesar** | to be interesting |
| **mandar** | to send |
| **mostrar (ue)** | to show |
| **odiar** | to hate |
| **ofrecer (zc)** | to offer |
| **prestar** | to lend |
| **prometer** | to promise |
| **recomendar (ie)** | to recommend |
| **regalar** | to give (*as a gift*) |

### De viaje

| | |
|---|---|
| **el aeropuerto** | airport |
| **la agencia de viajes** | travel agency |
| **el/la agente de viajes** | travel agent |
| **el asiento** | seat |
| **el/la asistente de vuelo** | flight attendant |
| **el autobús** | bus |

| | |
|---|---|
| **el avión** | airplane |
| **el barco** | boat, ship |
| **el billete** | ticket |
|   **de ida** | one-way |
|   **de ida y vuelta** | round-trip |
| **el boleto** | ticket |
|   **de ida** | one-way |
|   **de ida y vuelta** | round-trip |
| **la cabina** | cabin (*on a ship*) |
| **la clase turística** | tourist class |
| **la demora** | delay |
| **el equipaje** | baggage, luggage |
| **la estación** | station |
|   **de autobuses** | bus |
|   **del tren** | train |
| **la llegada** | arrival |
| **la maleta** | suitcase |
| **el maletero** | porter |
| **el modo (de transporte)** | means (of transportation) |
| **el pasaje** | passage; ticket |
| **el/la pasajero/a** | passenger |
| **la primera clase** | first class |
| **el puerto** | port |
| **la sala de espera** | waiting room |
| **la salida** | departure |
| **la sección de (no) fumar** | (non)smoking section |
| **la tarjeta (postal)** | (post)card |
| **el tren** | train |

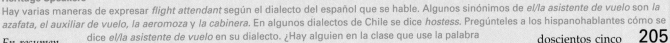

**Suggestion**

• Read the following sentences as a *dictado* or as listening comprehension. In either case, have students correct false statements.

1. *Si hay una demora, el avión llega temprano.*
2. *Los pasajeros hacen las maletas después de hacer un viaje.*
3. *El avión está atrasado; no tenemos que esperarlo.*

4. *Hay muchas personas en la sala de espera; no hay ningún asiento desocupado.*
5. *El asistente de vuelo nos sirve la comida durante el vuelo.*
6. *Cuando se hace cola, generalmente es necesario esperar un poco.*
7. *No quiero subir las maletas al avión; voy a facturarlas.*
8. *El maletero es un objeto en que se pone la ropa.*

| | |
|---|---|
| **el viaje** | trip |
| **el vuelo** | flight |
| **bajar (de)** | to get down (from); to get off (of) (*a vehicle*) |
| **facturar** | to check (*baggage*) |
| **guardar (un puesto)** | to save (a place) (*in line*) |
| **hacer** (*irreg.*) **cola** | to stand in line |
| **hacer** (*irreg.*) **escalas** | to make stops |
| **hacer** (*irreg.*) **la(s) maleta(s)** | to pack one's suitcase(s) |
| **hacer** (*irreg.*) **paradas** | to make stops |
| **ir** (*irreg.*) **en…** | to go/travel by . . . |
| autobús | bus |
| avión | plane |
| barco | boat, ship |
| tren | train |
| **pasar por el control de la seguridad** | to go/pass through security (check) |
| **subir (a)** | to go up; to get on (*a vehicle*) |
| **viajar** | to travel |

**Repaso: hacer** (*irreg.*) **un viaje**

## De vacaciones

| | |
|---|---|
| **la camioneta** | station wagon |
| **el** *camping* | campground |
| **la foto(grafía)** | photo(graph) |
| **el mar** | sea |
| **la montaña** | mountain |
| **el océano** | ocean |

| | |
|---|---|
| **la tienda (de campaña)** | tent |

**Repaso: la playa**

| | |
|---|---|
| **estar** (*irreg.*) **de vacaciones** | to be on vacation |
| **hacer** (*irreg.*) **camping** | to go camping |
| **ir** (*irreg.*) **de vacaciones** | to go on vacation |
| **nadar** | to swim |
| **sacar (qu)** | to take (*photos*) |
| **tomar el sol** | to sunbathe |

## Otros sustantivos

| | |
|---|---|
| **la flor** | flower |
| **el mundo** | world |

## Los adjetivos

| | |
|---|---|
| **atrasado/a** (*with* estar) | late |
| **solo/a** | alone |

## Palabras adicionales

| | |
|---|---|
| **a tiempo** | on time |
| **de viaje** | on a trip |
| **desde** | from |
| **me gustaría…** | I would (really) like . . . |
| **muchísimo** | an awful lot |

9. *Los billetes sólo pueden ser de ida y vuelta.*
10. *Al final de un vuelo, se baja del avión; no se sube.*

• Ask the following questions to personalize and contextualize vocabulary.

1. *Cuando Ud. viaja en avión, ¿es importante que haga buen tiempo? ¿Le molesta mucho cuando hay demora?*
2. *Cuando mi esposo/a (hijo/a) viaja solo/a, yo siempre le pido que me llame cuando llegue a su destino. ¿Llama Ud. siempre a sus padres (su esposo/a) cuando llega a su destino?*

• Read the following definitions and have students give the corresponding words.

1. *La persona que nos ayuda con el equipaje en la estación de trenes.*
2. *La cosa que se compra antes de hacer un viaje.*
3. *El antónimo de subir a.*
4. *Se va allí cuando se hace un viaje en avión.*
5. *Se va allí cuando se hace un viaje en tren.*
6. *La persona que nos ayuda durante un vuelo.*

Show students an image of a scene that includes vocabulary items. Put the image away and have students write as many sentences as possible describing the scene. They should use words from *Vocabulario*. Have students read or write their sentences on the board in order to compare descriptions.

# Los días festivos°

°**Los...** *Holidays*

*Una muchacha cubana reza (prays) en una iglesia (church) en Santiago, Cuba, durante las Navidades*

## CULTURA

- **Nota cultural:** Días festivos importantes del mundo hispánico
- **En los Estados Unidos y el Canadá:** El Día de César Chávez
- **Voces** de Cuba
  **Literatura:** José Martí
  **Música:** El son
- **Videoteca**
  **Entrevista cultural:** Cuba
  **Entre amigos:** ¡Comemos «las uvas de la suerte»!
- **Enfoque cultural:** Cuba

## VOCABULARIO

- La fiesta de Javier
- Emociones y condiciones

## GRAMÁTICA

## LA FIESTA DE JAVIER

**Paso 1: Vocabulario**
See the "Chapter-by-Chapter Supplementary Materials" in the IM for a model for vocabulary presentation, as well as additional teaching suggestions, notes, activities, and other resources for *Paso 1*.

Resources: Transparency 57

la sorpresa

¡Qué sorpresa!

pasarlo mal

¡Es para ti!

divertirse (ie, i) / pasarlo bien

regalar

Fiesta de sorpresa para Javier
¡Se gradúa y cumple 21 años!
¿Dónde es la fiesta?
¡La fiesta es en casa de Javier!

cumplir años

FELICITACIONES!

los entremeses

los refrescos

| | | | |
|---|---|---|---|
| **celebrar** | to celebrate | **reunirse (me reúno) (con)** | to get together (with) |
| **cumplir años** | to have a birthday | **ser** (*irreg.*) + **en** + *place* | to take place at/in (*place*) |
| **dar** (*irreg.*)/**hacer** (*irreg.*) **una fiesta** | to give/have a party | —¿**Dónde es** la fiesta? | Where is the party? |
| **faltar (a)** | to be absent (from), not attend | —(**Es**) **En** casa de Javier. | (It's) At Javier's house. |
| **gastar (dinero)** | to spend (money) | **gracias por** | thanks for |

**Suggestions**
• Model vocabulary in short sentences and questions, for example: *Cuando hago una fiesta en mi casa, siempre sirvo entremeses y refrescos. ¿Qué entremeses le gustan a Ud.? ¿En qué tipo de fiesta se divierte Ud. más?*
• Ask students the following questions about the class.

   *De tus amigos, ¿quién… ?*

1. *¿falta a clase con frecuencia?*
2. *¿nunca falta a clase?*
3. *¿nunca se divierte?*
4. *¿siempre lo pasa bien?*

• When introducing *ser* + *en* + place, review the difference between *ser* (to take place) and *estar* (to be located).
• Bring greeting cards in Spanish to class and have students read the different kinds of expressions used. Students may wish to find examples of Spanish-language virtual greeting cards on the Internet and send them to classmates and friends. Encourage them to design greeting cards of their own and include appropriate sentiments in Spanish.

**Bright Idea Suggestion**
Emphasize that *ser* is used to tell where an event takes place. For example, *El baile (El*

*examen, El partido) es en el gimnasio.* Have students explain the difference between the following phrases.

   *¿Dónde es el examen?*
   *¿Dónde está el examen?*

**Multimedia: Audio**
Students can listen to and practice this chapter's vocabulary on the Online Learning Center (**www.mhhe.com/quetal7**), as well as on the Textbook Audio CD, part of the Laboratory Audio Program.

## Vocabulario útil*

| | |
|---|---|
| **el Día de Año Nuevo** | New Year's Day |
| **el Día de los Reyes Magos** | Day of the Magi (Three Kings) (January 6) |
| **el Día de San Patricio** | Saint Patrick's Day (March 17) |
| **la Pascua (judía)** | Passover |
| **la Pascua (Florida)** | Easter |
| **las vacaciones de primavera** | spring break |
| **el Cinco de Mayo** | Cinco de Mayo (*Mexican awareness celebration in some parts of the United States*) |
| **el Día del Canadá** | Canada Day (July 1) |
| **el Cuatro de Julio (el Día de la Independencia [estadounidense])** | Fourth of July ([*U.S.*] Independence Day) |
| **el Día de la Raza** | Columbus Day (*Hispanic awareness day in some parts of the United States*) (October 12) |
| **el Día de todos los Santos** | All Saints' Day (November 1) |
| **el Día de los Muertos** | Day of the Dead (November 2) |
| **el Día de Acción de Gracias** | Thanksgiving |
| **la Nochebuena** | Christmas Eve |
| **la Noche Vieja** | New Year's Eve |
| **el cumpleaños** | birthday |
| **el día del santo** | saint's day (*the saint for whom one is named*) |
| **la quinceañera** | young woman's fifteenth birthday party |

la Navidad

el Día de San Valentín
(de los Enamorados)

la Fiesta de las Luces

**Suggestions**
• Have students tell what holidays they associate with the following.

| | |
|---|---|
| *los irlandeses* | *el champán* |
| *los regalos* | *las flores* |
| *los dulces* | |

• Have students respond to the following statements with *cierto* or *falso*.

1. *Hoy es el cumpleaños de _____; vamos a darle una fiesta.*
2. *La Noche Vieja se celebra en octubre.*
3. *La Nochebuena viene después de la Navidad.*

## ■ Conversación

**A. Definiciones.** ¿Qué palabra o frase corresponde a estas definiciones?

1. el día en que se celebra el nacimiento (*birth*) de Jesús
2. algo que alguien no sabe o no espera
3. algo de comer y algo de beber que se sirven en las fiestas (dos respuestas)
4. el día en que algunos hispanos visitan el cementerio para honrar la memoria de los difuntos (*deceased*)
5. la fiesta en que se celebra el hecho (*fact*) de que una muchacha cumple quince años
6. el día en que todo el mundo (*everybody*) debe llevar ropa verde
7. la noche en que se celebra el final del año
8. palabra que se dice para mostrar una reacción muy favorable, por ejemplo, cuando un amigo cumple años
9. una fiesta de ocho días, muy importante para los judíos (*Jewish people*)

♻ **Reciclado**
Use a calendar and present the holidays month-by-month. Emphasize and explain holidays of importance to Hispanics: *el Cinco de Mayo, el Día de los Reyes Magos.* If you know when your saint's day is, point it out and explain its relevance. At the end, review by asking questions with months and seasons such as *¿Qué día festivo se celebra en febrero? ¿en octubre? ¿en el invierno?*, and so on.

**Con. A: Suggestion**
Have students give a definition of a holiday that is not already defined in the list.

**Con. A: Answers**
1. *la Navidad* 2. *una sorpresa* 3. *los refrescos y los entremeses* 4. *el Día de los Muertos* 5. *la quinceañera* 6. *el Día de San Patricio* 7. *la Noche Vieja* 8. *¡Felicitaciones!* 9. *la Fiesta de las Luces*

*All of the items on this list are not considered active vocabulary for this chapter. Just learn the holidays and celebrations that are relevant to you.*

# PASO 1

CAPÍTULO
8

Nota cultural: Comprensión
1. ¿Cuáles son las fiestas religiosas mencionadas?
2. En España, ¿de quién(es) reciben regalos de Navidad los niños?
3. ¿Qué fiesta marca una transición en la vida de las muchachas?

## NOTA CULTURAL

### Días festivos importantes del mundo hispánico

Algunas fiestas se celebran **en casi todos los países hispánicos.**

**La Nochebuena** En esta fiesta los hispanos cristianos siguen principalmente sus **tradiciones católicas.** Celebran la víspera[a] de la Navidad con **una gran cena.** Esta **celebración familiar** puede incluir también a amigos y vecinos.[b] Muchas familias van a la Misa del Gallo,[c] un **servicio religioso** que se celebra a medianoche. Es posible que la fiesta de Nochebuena termine muy tarde con música y baile. A veces, los niños reciben **la visita de Papá Noel,** otro nombre para Santa Claus, quien les deja regalos.

*Una quinceañera mexicana*

**La Noche Vieja** Como en este país, la Noche Vieja es una ocasión para **grandes celebraciones,** tanto entre familia como en lugares públicos. En España y otros países algunos practican la tradición de comer una uva[d] por cada una de las doce campanadas[e] de medianoche.

**El Día de los Reyes Magos** En España y otros países, muchas personas (especialmente los católicos) celebran **el 6 de enero,** el día de los Reyes Magos, también conocido como la Epifanía. Los tres Reyes son los encargados[f] de traer regalos. Muchos niños ponen sus zapatos en la ventana o balcón antes de acostarse la noche del 5 de enero. Los Reyes llegan en camellos durante la noche y llenan los zapatos con regalos y dulces.

**El Día de la Independencia** Todos los países latinoamericanos celebran el día de **la declaración de su independencia de España.** Por ejemplo, México celebra su independencia el 16 de septiembre, Bolivia el 6 de agosto, el Paraguay el 15 de mayo y El Salvador el 15 de septiembre.

**La quinceañera** **Las muchachas que cumplen quince años** celebran ese día especial que marca su paso de niña a mujer con **una gran fiesta entre la familia y los amigos.** La muchacha se viste de largo[g] y, con sus invitados, asiste a una misa especial para ella. Luego hay una cena y una fiesta con música para bailar.

[a]*eve* [b]*neighbors* [c]*Misa... Midnight Mass* [d]*grape* [e]*strokes* [f]*los... in charge* [g]*se... dresses up (in a gown)*

### Vocabulario útil

**el árbol** (tree)
**el corazón** (heart)
**la corona** (wreath)
**el desfile** (parade)
**la fiesta del barrio** (neighborhood [block] party)
**los fuegos artificiales** (fireworks)
**el globo** (balloon)

**Con. B: Follow-Up**
Have students describe the holidays in brief paragraphs. Then have them read their paragraphs to the class without identifying the holiday.

**Con. B: Reciclado**
Note the review of clothing and food vocabulary.

### B. Hablando de fiestas

PASO 1 ¿Cuáles de estas fiestas le gustan a Ud.? ¿Cuáles no le gustan? Explique por qué. Compare sus respuestas con las (*those*) de sus compañeros de clase.

MODELO: el Cuatro de Julio → Me gusta mucho el Cuatro de Julio porque vemos fuegos artificiales en el parque y...

1. el Cuatro de Julio
2. el Día de Acción de Gracias
3. el Día de San Patricio
4. la Noche Vieja
5. el Día de la Raza
6. el Día de los Enamorados

PASO 2 Ahora piense en su fiesta favorita. Puede ser una de la lista del **Paso 1** o una del **Vocabulario útil** de la página 209. Piense en cómo celebra Ud. esa fiesta, para explicárselo (*explain it*) luego a un compañero / una compañera de clase. Debe pensar en lo siguiente.

• los preparativos que Ud. hace de antemano (*beforehand*)
• la ropa especial que lleva
• las comidas o bebidas especiales que compra o prepara
• el lugar donde se celebra
• los adornos especiales que hay

Suggestions
• Offer the following optional vocabulary: *enojado/a, llegar a ser, acordarse de, enojarse, hacerse*
• Point out that the following adjectives are frequently used with *ponerse* (to become): *alegre, rojo/a, triste, contento/a.*
• *To become* can also be expressed with reflexive forms: *enojarse, enrojecerse, alegrarse, entristecerse,* and so on.
• Contrast the following words: *olvidar, olvidarse de, recordar.*

## EMOCIONES Y CONDICIONES

Resources: Transparency 58

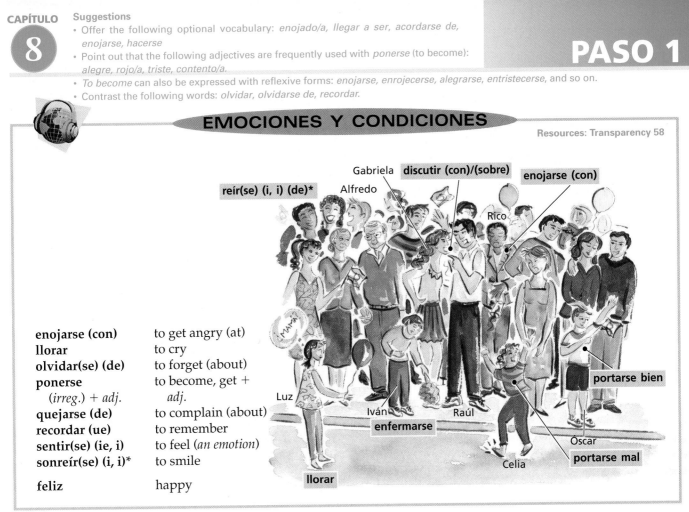

| | |
|---|---|
| **enojarse (con)** | to get angry (at) |
| **llorar** | to cry |
| **olvidar(se) (de)** | to forget (about) |
| **ponerse** | to become, get + |
| (*irreg.*) + *adj.* | *adj.* |
| **quejarse (de)** | to complain (about) |
| **recordar (ue)** | to remember |
| **sentir(se) (ie, i)** | to feel (*an emotion*) |
| **sonreír(se) (i, i)\*** | to smile |
| **feliz** | happy |

Nota comunicativa: Suggestion
Ask students questions.

1. ¿Es Ud. perezosísimo/a?
2. ¿Hay una persona rica en su familia? ¿Quién es? ¿Hay una persona riquísima? ¿alta? ¿altísima? ¿interesante? ¿interesantísima? ¿simpática? ¿simpatiquísima?

## NOTA COMUNICATIVA

### Being Emphatic

To emphasize the quality described by an adjective or an adverb, speakers of Spanish often add **-ísimo/a/os/as** (adjectives) or **-ísimo** (adverbs) to it. This change adds the idea *extremely* (*exceptionally; very, very; super*) to the quality expressed. You have already used one emphatic adverb of this type: **Me gusta muchísimo.**

Estos entremeses son **dificilísimos** de preparar.
Durante la época navideña, los niños son **buenísimos.**

*These hors d'œuvres are very, very hard to prepare.*
*At Christmastime, kids are extremely good.*

• If the word ends in a consonant, **-ísimo** is added to the singular form: **difícil → dificilísimo** (and any accents on the word stem are dropped).
• If the word ends in a vowel, the final vowel is dropped before adding **-ísimo: bueno → buenísimo** (and any accents on the word stem are dropped).
• Spelling changes occur when the final consonant of an adjective is **c, g,** or **z: riquísimo, larguísimo, felicísimo.**

---

*The verbs **reír** and **sonreír** are* **e → i** *stem-changing verbs, but due to the double vowels, accents are required for all present tense forms:* (son)**río**, (son)**ríes**, (son)**ríe**, (son)**reímos**, (son)**reís**, (son)**ríen**.

# PASO 1

Con. A: Suggestions
• Do this activity as listening comprehension only.
• Offer the following optional vocabulary: *de buen/mal humor impaciente*.

**Bright Idea Suggestion**
Give students sentences with *muy, muy* and have them reword the sentences using *-ísimo* endings.

## Palabras útiles

**avergonzado/a** (*embarrassed*)
**contento/a**
**feliz/triste**
**furioso/a**
**nervioso/a**
**serio/a**

MODELO: *Lupe está muy, muy contenta porque va a una fiesta de Noche Vieja.* → *Lupe está contentísima porque va a una fiesta de Noche Vieja.*

**Con. A: Answers**
*Possible answers:* **1.** *Me pongo felicísimo/a [contentísimo/a].* **2.** *Me pongo tristísimo/a [furiosísimo/a]. Lloro.* **3.** *Me pongo nerviosísimo/a. Les ofrezco más refrescos y entremeses.* **4.** *Me pongo muy nervioso/a y avergonzado/a.* **5.** *Me pongo muy contento/a. Me río. (Me pongo muy triste. Lloro.)* **6.** *Me pongo muy triste.* **7.** *Me pongo avergonzado/a.* **8.** *Me pongo muy serio/a.* **9.** *Me pongo triste.* **10.** *Me pongo nervioso/a.* **11.** *Me enojo.* **12.** *Me pongo furioso/a.* **13.** *Me pongo nerviosísimo/a.* **14.** *Me enojo y me quejo.*

**Con. B: Suggestion**

Have students write down a description of a negative aspect of a holiday, for them in particular or for people in general, for example:

*La Navidad es una fiesta demasiado comercializada.*

*No me gusta el Día de Acción de Gracias… ¡porque no me gusta comer pavo ni calabaza!*

The descriptions should be anonymous. Have students hand in their ideas. Redistribute the descriptions to other students, and have them write responses to the negative aspect of the holiday in the form of advice or recommendations for having a better time or improving the situation. Return the complaint and the advice to the original author of the negative description.

Alternatively, read the negative descriptions to the class, and have students give advice orally.

**Need more practice?**

- Workbook/Laboratory Manual
- Interactive CD-ROM
- Online Learning Center (www.mhhe.com/quetal7)

**Note**
See the Workbook/Laboratory Manual for presentation and practice of the letters *c* and *qu*.

## ■ Conversación

**A. Reacciones.** ¿Cómo reacciona o cómo se pone Ud. en estas situaciones? Use estos adjetivos o cualquier otro, y también los verbos que describen las reacciones emocionales. No se olvide de usar las formas enfáticas cuando sea (*whenever it is*) apropiado.

1. Es Navidad y alguien le hace a Ud. un regalo carísimo.
2. Es su cumpleaños y sus padres/hijos no le regalaron nada.
3. Ud. da una fiesta en su casa pero los invitados no se divierten. Nadie se ríe ni sonríe.
4. Hay un examen importante hoy, pero Ud. no estudió anoche.
5. Ud. acaba de terminar un examen difícil/fácil y cree que lo hizo bien/mal.
6. En un examen de química, Ud. no puede recordar una fórmula muy importante.
7. Ud. cuenta un chiste (*joke*) pero nadie se ríe.
8. Un amigo tiene un problema grave (*serious*) y necesita su ayuda.
9. Llueve todo el día.
10. Ud. no sabe la respuesta, pero el profesor le pide que hable.
11. Ud. sabe la respuesta y levanta la mano, pero el profesor no le presta atención.
12. Ud. quiere bañarse y no hay agua caliente.
13. Ud. está solo/a en casa y oye un ruido.
14. Ud. le pide a alguien que no fume, pero la persona sigue fumando.

**B. ¿Son buenos todos los días festivos?** Los días festivos pueden ser difíciles para muchas personas. Para Ud., ¿son ciertas o falsas las siguientes oraciones? Cambie las oraciones falsas para que sean (*so that they are*) ciertas. Luego compare sus respuestas con las de sus compañeros de clase.

EN LAS FIESTAS DE FAMILIA

1. Toda o casi toda mi familia, incluyendo a mis tíos, primos, abuelos, etcétera, se reúne por lo menos (*at least*) una vez al año.
2. Las fiestas de familia me gustan muchísimo.
3. Hay un pariente que siempre se queja de algo.
4. Uno de mis parientes siempre me hace preguntas indiscretas.
5. Alguien siempre bebe/come demasiado (*too much*) y luego se enferma.
6. A todos les gustan los regalos que reciben.
7. Todos lo pasan bien en las fiestas de familia.

LOS DÍAS FESTIVOS EN GENERAL

8. La Navidad / La Fiesta de las Luces es esencialmente una excusa para gastar dinero.
9. La época de fiestas en noviembre y diciembre es triste y deprimente (*depressing*) para mí.
10. Sólo las personas que practican una religión deben tener vacaciones en los días de fiestas religiosas.
11. Las vacaciones de primavera son para divertirse muchísimo. De hecho (*In fact*), son las mejores vacaciones del año.
12. Debería haber (*There should be*) más días festivos… por lo menos uno al mes.

Paso 2: Gramática
See the "Chapter-by-Chapter Supplementary Materials" in the IM for additional teaching suggestions, notes, activities, and other resources for *Paso 2*.

Variation
To follow up the questions about the art, have students think of the last party they or their family hosted and answer the questions.

## 23 Talking About the Past (2)   Irregular Preterites

**La fiesta de la Noche Vieja**

Conteste las siguientes preguntas sobre esta fiesta.

1. ¿Quién *estuvo* hablando por teléfono?   Marina
2. ¿Quién *dio* la fiesta?   Sofía y Paco
3. ¿Quién no *pudo* ir a la fiesta?   Jorge
4. ¿Quién *puso* su copa de champán en el televisor?   Ernesto
5. ¿Quién *hizo* mucho ruido?   Sultán
6. ¿Quiénes no *quisieron* beber más?   Patricia y Esteban
7. ¿Quiénes *vinieron* con sus niñas?   Gema y Javier
8. ¿Quiénes le *trajeron* un regalo al anfitrión (*host*)?   Gema y Javier

**¿Y Ud.?**

Resources: Transparency 59

¿Estuvo alguna vez en una fiesta como esta? ( …estuve… ) ¿Tuvo que salir temprano o se quedó hasta después de la medianoche (*midnight*)? ( …tuve… ) ¿Le trajo algo al anfitrión / a la anfitriona? ( …traje… )

Suggestions
• Point out that the first and third persons singular of irregular forms have no accent on the -e or -o. Students should not confuse these with the present indicative *él/ella/Ud.* or *yo* forms, respectively.

• Emphasize and model verbs that change meaning in the preterite.

| PAST -------------------- | Present -------------------- Future |
|---|---|
| preterite | **present** |
| | **present progressive** |
| | **formal commands** |

• You have already learned the irregular preterite forms of **dar, hacer, ir,** and **ser.** The following verbs are also irregular in the preterite. Note that the first and third person singular endings, which are the only irregular ones, are unstressed, in contrast to the stressed endings of regular preterite forms.

| estar | |
|---|---|
| estuve | estuvimos |
| estuviste | estuvisteis |
| estuvo | estuvieron |

Bright Idea Suggestion
Have students brainstorm ways to organize the verbs or offer the following groups.

| -u- | tener | poner | -i- | hacer | venir |
|---|---|---|---|---|---|
| | estar | saber | | querer | |
| | poder | | -j- | decir | -ucir verbs |
| | | | | traer | |

| | | |
|---|---|---|
| estar: | estuv- | -e |
| poder: | pud- | -iste |
| poner: | pus- | -o |
| querer: | quis- | -imos |
| saber: | sup- | -isteis |
| tener: | tuv- | -ieron |
| venir: | vin- | |

• When the preterite verb stem ends in **-j-,** the **-i-** of the third person plural ending is omitted: **dijeron, trajeron.**

| | |
|---|---|
| decir: | **dij-** |
| traer: | **traj-** |

-e, -iste, -o, -imos, -isteis, **-eron**

• The preterite of **hay (haber)** is **hubo** (*there was/were*).

**Hubo** un accidente ayer en el centro.
*There was an accident yesterday downtown.*

# PASO 2

## Changes in Meaning

Several of the following Spanish verbs have an English equivalent in the preterite tense that is different from that of the infinitive.

| | Infinitive Meaning | Preterite Meaning |
|---|---|---|
| **saber** | to know (*facts, information*) | to find out, learn |
| | Ya lo sé. *I already know it.* | Lo **supe** ayer. *I found it out (learned it) yesterday.* |
| **conocer** | to know, be familiar with (*people, places*) | to meet (*for the first time*) |
| | Ya la conozco. *I already know her.* | La **conocí** ayer. *I met her yesterday.* |
| **querer** | to want | to try |
| | Quiero hacerlo hoy. *I want to do it today.* | **Quise** hacerlo ayer. *I tried to do it yesterday.* |
| **no querer** | not to want | to refuse |
| | No quiero hacerlo hoy. *I don't want to do it today.* | **No quise** hacerlo anteayer. *I refused to do it the day before yesterday.* |
| **poder** | to be able to (*do something*) | to succeed (*in doing something*) |
| | Puedo leerlo *I can (am able to) read it.* | **Pude** leerlo ayer. *I could (and did) read it yesterday.* |
| **no poder** | not to be able, capable (*of doing something*) | to fail (*in doing something*) |
| | No puedo leerlo. *I can't (am not able to) read it.* | **No pude** leerlo anteayer. *I couldn't (did not) read it the day before yesterday.* |

Prác. A: Follow-Up
Have students add one action that they did and one that they didn't do.

Prác. A: Bright idea Suggestion
Point out that *sino* is used after a negative clause. For example, *No tengo un lápiz sino un bolígrafo.*

■ **Práctica**

**A. ¡Anticipemos! La última Noche Vieja.** Piense en lo que Ud. hizo la Noche Vieja del año pasado e indique si las siguientes oraciones son ciertas o falsas para Ud.

1. Fui a una fiesta en casa de un amigo / una amiga.
2. Di una fiesta en mi casa.
3. No estuve con mis amigos, sino (*but rather*) con la familia.
4. Quise ir a una fiesta, pero no pude.
5. Les dije «¡Feliz Año Nuevo!» a muchas personas.
6. Conocí a algunas personas.
7. Tuve que preparar la comida de esa noche.
8. Me puse ropa elegante esa noche.
9. Pude quedarme despierto/a (*awake*) hasta la medianoche.
10. No quise bailar. Me sentía (*I felt*) mal.

**AUTOPRUEBA**

Give the correct irregular preterite forms.

1. (yo) saber
2. (ellos) tener
3. (tú) venir
4. (él) poner
5. (nosotros) querer
6. (Ud.) poder

*Answers: 1. supe 2. tuvieron 3. viniste 4. puso 5. quisimos 6. pudo*

**Refrán**

«Quien quiso, hizo.»

Give students this *refrán* and have them try to think of sayings in English that have similar connotations. (*Where there's a will, there's a way.*)

**B. Una Nochebuena en casa de los Ramírez.** Describa lo que pasó en casa de los Ramírez, haciendo el papel (*playing the role*) de uno de los hijos. Haga oraciones en el pretérito según las indicaciones, usando el sujeto pronominal cuando sea necesario.

1. todos / estar / en casa / abuelos / antes de / nueve
2. (nosotros) poner / mucho / regalos / debajo / árbol
3. tíos y primos / venir / con / comida y bebidas
4. yo / tener / que / ayudar / a / preparar / comida
5. haber / cena / especial / para / todos
6. más tarde / alguno / amigos / venir / a / cantar / villancicos (*carols*)
7. niños / ir / a / alcoba / a / diez / y / acostarse
8. niños / querer / dormir / pero / no / poder
9. a / medianoche / todos / decir / «¡Feliz Navidad!»
10. al día siguiente / todos / decir / que / fiesta / estar / estupendo

## ■ Conversación

**A. ¡Un viaje de sueños (*dream*)!** Conteste las siguientes preguntas sobre un viaje de sueños. Debe inventar una historia muy extraordinaria o fantástica. Puede ser de un viaje que a Ud. le gustaría hacer, de un viaje hecho (*taken*) por un amigo o de un viaje totalmente imaginario. ¡Sea creativo/a! Luego cuénteles su historia a sus compañeros de clase. ¿Quién inventó la mejor historia?

1. ¿Adónde fue de viaje? ¿Cómo fue (modo de transporte)? ¿Con quién(es) fue?
2. ¿Cuánto tiempo estuvo allí? ¿Dónde se alojó (*did you stay*)?
3. ¿A qué persona famosa o interesante conoció allí? ¿Qué le dijo a esa persona cuando la conoció? ¿Supo algo interesante de esa persona?
4. ¿Qué cosa divertida (*enjoyable*) hizo durante el viaje? ¿Qué no pudo hacer?
5. ¿Qué recuerdos (*souvenirs*) trajo a casa?

Con. A: Suggestion
Paso 2. Have the other students ask the narrator questions to get as much additional information as they can.

**B. Entrevista**

1. ¿En qué mes conociste al profesor / a la profesora de español? ¿A quién(es) más conociste ese mismo (*same*) día? ¿Tuviste que hablar español el primer día de clase? ¿Qué les dijiste a tus amigos después de esa primera clase? ¿Qué les vas a decir hoy?
2. El año pasado, ¿dónde pasaste la Nochebuena? ¿el Día de Acción de Gracias? ¿Dónde estuviste durante las vacaciones de primavera? ¿Ya hiciste planes para estas ocasiones este año? ¿Dónde piensas estar?
3. ¿Alguien te dio una fiesta de cumpleaños este año? (¿O le diste una fiesta a alguien?) ¿Fue una fiesta de sorpresa? ¿Dónde fue? ¿Qué te trajeron tus amigos? ¿Qué te regalaron tus parientes? ¿Alguien te hizo un pastel? ¿Qué te dijeron todos? ¿Y qué les dijiste tú? ¿Quieres que te den otra fiesta para tu próximo cumpleaños?

♻ Con B: Reciclado
Remind students of emphatic forms using -ísimo that they can use for this activity.

Prác. B: Extension
• Have students respond *cierto, falso,* or *no se sabe.*
1. *Hubo muy poca gente (new word) en la fiesta. (falso)*
2. *Sólo vinieron miembros de la familia. (falso)*
3. *Todos comieron bien... ¡y mucho! (no se sabe)*
4. *Los niños abrieron sus regalos antes de las doce. (falso)*

• Have students tell what happened on Christmas Day at the Ramírez house, inventing more details.

**Need more practice?**
■ Workbook/Laboratory Manual
■ Interactive CD-ROM
■ Online Learning Center (www.mhhe.com/quetal7)

Prác. B: Variation
Have students use the activity items as a guide for describing their own Christmas (or other holiday) celebrations.

Prác. B: Answers
1. *Todos estuvimos (estuvieron) en casa de los abuelos antes de las nueve.* 2. *Pusimos muchos regalos debajo del árbol.* 3. *Mis (Los) tíos y primos vinieron con comida y bebidas.* 4. *Yo tuve que ayudar a preparar la comida.* 5. *Hubo una cena especial para todos.* 6. *Más tarde algunos (de mis) amigos vinieron a cantar villancicos.* 7. *Los niños fueron a la alcoba a las diez y se acostaron.* 8. *Los niños quisieron dormir pero no pudieron.* 9. *A la medianoche todos dijimos (dijeron) «¡Feliz Navidad!».* 10. *Al día siguiente todos dijimos (dijeron) que la fiesta estuvo estupenda.*

Con. B: Follow-Up
Ask students the following question after completing item *1*.

*Ahora que Ud. conoce bien al profesor / a la profesora, ¿cree que ese día presentó una clase típica?*

## 24 Talking About the Past (3) Preterite of Stem-Changing Verbs

### La quinceañera de Lupe Carrasco

Imagine los detalles de la fiesta de Lupe cuando cumplió quince años.

**1.** Lupe *se vistió* con

☑ un vestido blanco muy elegante.
☐ una camiseta y *jeans*.
☐ el vestido de novia (*wedding gown*) de su abuela.

**2.** Cortando el pastel de cumpleaños, Lupe

☐ *empezó* a llorar.     ☐ *rió* mucho.
☑ *sonrió* para una foto.

**Follow-Up**
Follow up the sentences about Lupe's *quinceañera* with questions about the party.

*¿A qué hora llegaron / se fueron los invitados?*
*¿Con quién bailó Lupe?*

And so on.

**3.** Lupe *pidió* un deseo (*wish*) al cortar el pastel. Ella

☐ les dijo a todos su deseo.
☐ *prefirió* guardarlo en secreto.

**4.** En la fiesta *sirvieron*

☐ champán y refrescos.     ☐ sólo té y café.
☐ refrescos.

**5.** Todos *se divirtieron* mucho en la fiesta.
Los invitados *se despidieron* (*said goodbye*) a la(s) _____.

### ¿Y Ud.?

¿Recuerda qué hizo cuando cumplió quince años? ¿Pidió muchos regalos? ( …pedí… ) ¿Se divirtió? ( …me divertí… ) ¿Cómo se sintió? ( …me sentí… )

**Emphasis A:**
**Suggestion**
Have students give the third person singular and plural (preterite) of the following verbs.

| PAST ---------------------- Present -------------------- Future |
|---|
| preterite |
| present |
| present progressive |
| formal commands |

**A.** In **Capítulo 7** you learned that the **-ar** and **-er** stem-changing verbs have no stem change in the preterite (or in the present participle).

**1.** (*ue*): contar, recordar, encontrar, jugar, volver, llover (third person singular only)
**2.** (*ie*): empezar, recomendar, cerrar, despertarse, nevar (third person singular only)

| recordar (ue) | | perder (ie) | |
|---|---|---|---|
| recordé | recordamos | perdí | perdimos |
| recordaste | recordasteis | perdiste | perdisteis |
| recordó | recordaron | perdió | perdieron |
| | recordando | | perdiendo |

**B.** The **-ir** stem-changing verbs do have a stem change in the preterite, but only in the third person singular and plural, where the stem vowels **e** and **o** change to **i** and **u**, respectively. This is the same change that occurs in the present participle of **-ir** stem-changing verbs.

| pedir (i, i) | | dormir (ue, u) | |
|---|---|---|---|
| pedí | pedimos | dormí | dormimos |
| pediste | pedisteis | dormiste | dormisteis |
| pidió | pidieron | durmió | durmieron |
| | pidiendo | | durmiendo |

**C.** Here are some **-ir** stem-changing verbs. You already know or have seen many of them. The reflexive meaning, if different from the nonreflexive meaning, is in parentheses.

**OJO** Note the simplification:
ri-ió → rió; ri-ieron → rieron
son-ri-ió → sonrió; son-ri-ieron → sonrieron

¡Adiós!

**despedirse (i, i) (de)**

| | |
|---|---|
| **conseguir (i, i) (g)** | *to get, obtain* |
| **conseguir** + *inf.* | *to succeed in (doing something)* |
| **divertir(se) (ie, i)** | *to entertain (to have a good time)* |
| **dormir(se) (ue, u)** | *to sleep (to fall asleep)* |
| **morirse (ue, u)** | *to die* |
| **pedir (i, i)** | *to ask for; to order* |

| | |
|---|---|
| **preferir (ie, i)** | *to prefer* |
| **reír(se) (i, i)** | *to laugh* |
| **sentir(se) (ie, i)** | *to feel (an emotion)* |
| **servir (i, i)** | *to serve* |
| **sonreír(se) (i, i)** | *to smile* |
| **sugerir (ie, i)** | *to suggest* |
| **vestir(se) (i, i)** | *to dress (to get dressed)* |

---

**AUTOPRUEBA**

Complete the verbs with preterite stems.

1. nos div____rtimos
2. se d____rmieron
3. tú s____rviste

4. se v____stió
5. yo sug____rí
6. Uds. p____dieron

*Answers: 1. divertimos 2. durmieron 3. serviste 4. vistió 5. sugerí 6. pidieron*

---

**Preliminary Exercises**
• Have students give the third person singular and plural (preterite) of the following verbs.

1. (ue, u) *dormir, morir, dormirse*
2. (i, i) *pedir, repetir, despedir*
3. (ie, i) *preferir, sentir, sentirse, divertirse, sugerir*

• Have students do the following chain drill to practice the preterite forms.

*Todos pasaron un día fatal ayer.*

1. *Dormimos muy mal anoche.* (*yo, todos, Irma, tú, Ud., vosotros*)
2. *No recordaste traer los ejercicios.* (*Raúl, nosotros, Ud., ellos, vosotros*)
3. *Raúl perdió las llaves (keys) del coche.* (*tú, Horacio y Estela, yo, Ud., vosotras*)
4. *Pedimos mariscos pero no había (they were out of them).* (*yo, Jacinto, tú, Uds., vosotros*)
5. *Todos se rieron mucho de Nati.* (*nosotros, Esteban, yo, Uds., vosotras*)

**Prác. A: Suggestion**
Have students add statements about other topics.

*¿Pasó algo muy interesante en la clase? ¿y en el país?*

## ■ **Práctica**

**A. ¡Anticipemos! ¿Quién lo hizo?** ¿Ocurrieron algunas de estas cosas en clase la semana pasada? Conteste con el nombre de la persona apropiada. Si nadie lo hizo, conteste con **Nadie...**

1. _____ se vistió de una manera muy elegante.
2. _____ se vistió de una manera rara (*strange*).
3. _____ se durmió en clase.
4. _____ le pidió al profesor / a la profesora más tarea.
5. _____ se sintió muy contento/a.
6. _____ se divirtió muchísimo, riendo y sonriendo.
7. _____ no sonrió ni siquiera (*not even*) una vez.
8. _____ sugirió tener la clase afuera.
9. _____ prefirió no contestar ninguna pregunta.

# PASO 2

## Prác. B: Suggestion
Have students read through each sequence first before beginning the activity.

## Prác. B: Follow-Up
Ask the following questions after completing the activity.

1. ¿Dónde almorzó Ud. ayer? ¿Qué pidió? ¿Quién se lo sirvió? ¿Quién pagó la cuenta? ¿Cuánto dejó Ud. de propina (new word)? La última vez que cenó en un restaurante, ¿qué pidió? ¿Prefiere Ud.

### Need more practice?

- Workbook/Laboratory Manual
- Interactive CD-ROM
- Online Learning Center (www.mhhe.com/quetal7)

que otra persona pague en un restaurante elegante?

2. ¿A qué hora se acostó Ud. anoche? ¿Cuántas horas durmió? ¿Durmió bien? ¿Se sintió descansado/a cuando se despertó? ¿Cómo se vistió esta mañana, elegante o informalmente?

3. ¿Qué película o programa de televisión lo/la divirtió más el año pasado? ¿Se rió Ud. mucho cuando vio... ? ¿Les gustó también a sus amigos? ¿Qué película quiere ver este mes?

## Prác. B: Answers
1. se sentó, vino, pidió, recordó, pidió, sirvió, quiso, dijo, pedí, contestó 2. se acostó, se durmió, Durmió, se despertó, Se vistió, salió, vio, sonrieron, se hablaron 3. me vestí, fui, me divertí, volví, decidió, vio, se divirtió, Perdió, sintió

## Con: Suggestion
Have students ask you questions first as a model for the interviews. You might provide outrageous answers to set up a fun activity.

**B. Historias breves.** Cuente las siguientes historias breves en el pretérito. Luego continúelas, si puede.

1. **En un restaurante:** Juan (sentarse) a la mesa. Cuando (venir) el camarero, le (pedir) una cerveza. El camarero no (recordar) lo que Juan (pedir) y le (servir) una Coca-Cola. Juan no (querer) beber la Coca-Cola. Le (decir) al camarero: «Perdón, señor. Le (pedir: yo) una cerveza.» El camarero le (contestar): «_____.»

2. **Un día típico:** Rosa (acostarse) temprano y (dormirse) en seguida.ᵃ (Dormir) bien y (despertarse) temprano. (Vestirse) y (salir) para la universidad. En el autobús (ver) a su amigo José y los dos (sonreír) pero no (hablarseᵇ). A las nueve _____.

3. **Dos noches diferentes:** Yo (vestirse), (ir) a una fiesta, (divertirse) mucho y (volver) tarde a casa. Mi compañero de cuarto (decidir) quedarse en casa y (ver) la televisión toda la noche. No (divertirse) nada. (Perder) una fiesta excelente y lo (sentir) mucho. Yo _____.

ᵃen… *immediately* ᵇ*to talk to each other*

## ■ Conversación

### Una entrevista indiscreta

PASO 1   Lea las siguientes preguntas y piense en cómo va a contestarlas. Debe contestar algunas preguntas con información falsa.

1. ¿A qué hora se durmió anoche?
2. En alguna ocasión, ¿perdió Ud. mucho dinero? ¿Lo encontró (*did you find*) por fin?
3. ¿Cuánto dejó de propina (*tip*) la última vez que comió en un restaurante?
4. Alguna vez, ¿se despidió Ud. de alguien tardísimo?
5. ¿Se rió alguna vez al oír una noticia (*piece of news*) trágica?
6. ¿Con qué programa de televisión se divirtió mucho el año pasado / la semana pasada… pero se avergüenza (*you're ashamed*) de admitirlo?

PASO 2   Use las preguntas para entrevistar a un compañero / una compañera de clase. Luego cuénteles a todos algunas de las respuestas de su compañero/a. La clase va a decidir si la información es cierta o falsa.

MODELO:   E1: ¿A qué hora te dormiste anoche?
          E2: Me dormí a las tres de la mañana y me levanté a las siete.
          E1: Alicia se durmió a las tres y se levantó a las siete.
       CLASE: No es cierto.
          E2: ¡Sí, es cierto! (Tienes razón. / No es cierto.)

# Voces de Cuba

**Note**
José Martí was a prolific writer and poet. He is often credited with initiating the fight for Cuba's independence from Spain. He died in one of the first battles of independence. He often wrote about liberty. You can find many of his thoughts on the Internet. The following is one that is often quoted.

## LITERATURA: José Martí

**Sobre el autor:** *José Martí nació en la Habana, Cuba, pero se exilió a los 17 años por su oposición a la dominación colonial de España. Martí se considera uno de los grandes escritores del mundo hispano. Murió en una de las primeras batallas por la independencia de Cuba del dominio español.*

### XXXIX tomado de *Versos sencillos* (1891)

Cultivo una rosa blanca
en junio como enero
para el amigo sincero
que me da su mano franca.[a]

Y para el cruel que me arranca[b]
el corazón[c] con que vivo,
cardo[d] ni ortiga[e] cultivo;
cultivo la rosa blanca.

[a]*mano... open (sincere) hand* [b]*uproots, tears out* [c]*heart* [d]*thistle* [e]*nettle*

**José Martí**
**(1853–1895)**

*El hombre ama la libertad, aunque no sepa que la ama, y anda empujado de ella y huyendo de donde no la hay.*

**Heritage Speakers**
Anime a sus estudiantes hispanohablantes a recitar un poema breve que saben de memoria.

## MÚSICA: El son

El son, que se desarrolló[a] en las comunidades rurales del este de Cuba, es uno de los estilos[b] de música cubana más viejos. Muchos lo consideran como el abuelo de todas las otras formas musicales caribeñas. El uso de las «inspiraciones», o sea,[c] llamada y respuesta,[d] revela[e] su origen africano.

[a]*se... developed* [b]*styles* [c]*o... in other words* [d]*llamada... call and response (a performance style in which one performer listens to another performer sing or play a few bars of music, then responds with his or her own voice or instrument)* [e]*shows*

**Notes**
• One reason that the rhythm of the African drums took root in Cuba and influenced the music so strongly is that the slave owners of Cuba, unlike most slave owners elsewhere, allowed their African slaves to play their drums.
• Other popular Cuban music with strong African influence includes: *la rumba, el mambo,* and *la salsa.*
• The word *batá* literally means "speak" in the Yoruba language, which was spoken by the African slaves. The three drums of the *batá* are played as one instrument. The largest, *el iyá* (mother), improvises to follow the steps of the dancer(s) and carries on the "conversation" with *el itólele*, the mid-sized drum. *El okónkolo*, the smallest of the three drums, emphasizes the main beats.
• Students can look up information about Septeto Santiaguero's CDs and concerts on the Internet.

Septeto Santiaguero es un conjunto cubano sonero[f] muy conocido que da conciertos por toda Latinoamérica y Europa. Su nombre «septeto» se refiere a la instrumentación de siete instrumentos, y «santiaguero» se refiere a su origen de la ciudad de Santiago, Cuba. Los instrumentos principales de este septeto son: la guitarra, el tres,[g] el bongó,[h] los claves,[i] las maracas, el contrabajo[j] y la trompeta.

[f]*conjunto... "son" band* [g]*type of guitar* [h]*bongo drum* [i]*two sticks used together as a percussion instrument* [j]*double bass*

Los tambores[k] batá son tres: el iyá, el itólele y el okónkolo. Los batá, muy presentes en la música popular de Cuba como el son, tienen su origen en la santería[l] y las ceremonias religiosas de los afrocubanos.

[k]*drums* [l]*syncretic religion that combines West African religious practices with Catholic traditions and that is primarily practiced in Caribbean nations*

*Voces de Cuba*

## 25 Expressing Direct and Indirect Objects Together **Double** Object Pronouns

Paso 3: Gramática
See the "Chapter-by-Chapter Supplementary Materials" in the IM for additional teaching suggestions, notes, activities, and other resources for *Paso 3*.

Resources: Transparency 61

**Berta habla de la fiesta que Anita hizo para sus amigos.**

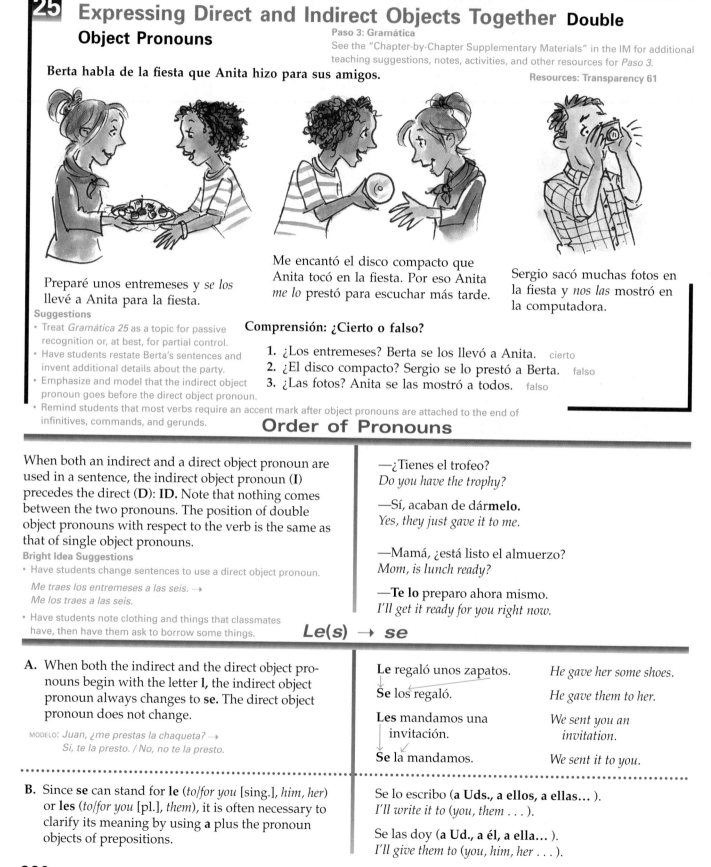

Preparé unos entremeses y *se los* llevé a Anita para la fiesta.

Me encantó el disco compacto que Anita tocó en la fiesta. Por eso Anita *me lo* prestó para escuchar más tarde.

Sergio sacó muchas fotos en la fiesta y *nos las* mostró en la computadora.

**Suggestions**

• Treat *Gramática 25* as a topic for passive recognition or, at best, for partial control.
• Have students restate Berta's sentences and invent additional details about the party.
• Emphasize and model that the indirect object pronoun goes before the direct object pronoun.
• Remind students that most verbs require an accent mark after object pronouns are attached to the end of infinitives, commands, and gerunds.

**Comprensión: ¿Cierto o falso?**

1. ¿Los entremeses? Berta se los llevó a Anita.   cierto
2. ¿El disco compacto? Sergio se lo prestó a Berta.   falso
3. ¿Las fotos? Anita se las mostró a todos.   falso

## Order of Pronouns

When both an indirect and a direct object pronoun are used in a sentence, the indirect object pronoun (**I**) precedes the direct (**D**): **ID**. Note that nothing comes between the two pronouns. The position of double object pronouns with respect to the verb is the same as that of single object pronouns.

**Bright Idea Suggestions**

• Have students change sentences to use a direct object pronoun.

  *Me traes los entremeses a las seis.* →
  *Me los traes a las seis.*

• Have students note clothing and things that classmates have, then have them ask to borrow some things.

—¿Tienes el trofeo?
*Do you have the trophy?*

—Sí, acaban de dár**melo**.
*Yes, they just gave it to me.*

—Mamá, ¿está listo el almuerzo?
*Mom, is lunch ready?*

—**Te lo** preparo ahora mismo.
*I'll get it ready for you right now.*

## Le(s) → se

**A.** When both the indirect and the direct object pronouns begin with the letter **l**, the indirect object pronoun always changes to **se**. The direct object pronoun does not change.

MODELO: *Juan, ¿me prestas la chaqueta?* →
  *Sí, te la presto. / No, no te la presto.*

| | |
|---|---|
| **Le** regaló unos zapatos. | *He gave her some shoes.* |
| **Se** los regaló. | *He gave them to her.* |
| **Les** mandamos una invitación. | *We sent you an invitation.* |
| **Se** la mandamos. | *We sent it to you.* |

**B.** Since **se** can stand for **le** (*to/for you* [sing.], *him, her*) or **les** (*to/for you* [pl.], *them*), it is often necessary to clarify its meaning by using **a** plus the pronoun objects of prepositions.

Se lo escribo (**a Uds., a ellos, a ellas…**).
*I'll write it to (you, them . . .).*

Se las doy (**a Ud., a él, a ella…**).
*I'll give them to (you, him, her . . .).*

## AUTOPRUEBA

Match each sentence with the correct double object pronouns.

1. Le dieron el libro. → _____ _____ dieron.
2. Le sirvieron la paella. → _____ _____ sirvieron.
3. Le di las direcciones. → _____ _____ di.
4. Les trajo los boletos. → _____ _____ trajo.

a. Se las
b. Se los
c. Se lo
d. Se la

*Answers: 1. c 2. d 3. a 4. b*

## ■ Práctica

**A. ¡Anticipemos! Lo que se oye en casa.** ¿A qué se refieren las siguientes oraciones? Fíjese en (*Note*) los pronombres y en el sentido (*meaning*) de la oración.

1. _e_ No **lo** prendan (*switch on*). Prefiero que los niños lean o que jueguen.
2. _b_ ¿Me **la** pasas? Gracias.
3. _f_ Tengo muchas ganas de comprárme**los** todos. Me encanta esa música.
4. _a_ ¿Por qué no se **las** mandas a los abuelos? Les van a gustar muchísimo.
5. _c_ Tengo que reservárte**los** hoy mismo, porque se va a terminar (*expire*) la oferta especial de Aeroméxico.
6. _d_ Yo se **la** organicé a Lupe para su cumpleaños. Antonio y Diego le hicieron un pastel.

a. unas fotos
b. la ensalada
c. unos billetes de avión para Guadalajara
d. la fiesta
e. el televisor
f. los discos compactos de Luis Miguel

**B. En la mesa.** Imagine que Ud. acaba de comer pero todavía tiene hambre. Pida más comida, según el modelo. Fíjese en el uso del tiempo presente como sustituto para el mandato.

MODELO: ensalada → ¿Hay más *ensalada?* ¿Me *la* pasas, por favor?

1. pan 2. tortillas 3. tomates 4. fruta 5. vino 6. jamón

**C. En el aeropuerto.** Cambie los sustantivos a pronombres para evitar (*avoid*) la repetición.

1. ¿La hora de la salida? Acaban de decirnos la hora de la salida.
2. ¿El horario? Sí, léame el horario, por favor.
3. ¿Los boletos? No, no tiene que darle los boletos aquí.
4. ¿El equipaje? Claro que le guardo el equipaje.
5. ¿Los pasajes? Ya te compré los pasajes.
6. ¿El puesto? No te preocupes. Te puedo guardar el puesto.
7. ¿La clase turística? Sí, les recomiendo la clase turística, señores.
8. ¿La cena? La asistente de vuelo nos va a servir la cena en el avión.

**Prác. A: Follow-Up**
Have students convert all the sentences to commands.

♻ **Prác. B: Reciclado**
Note review of food vocabulary.

**Prác. B: Answers**
1. ¿Hay más pan? ¿Me lo pasas, por favor?
2. ¿Hay más tortillas? ¿Me las pasas, por favor? 3. ¿Hay más tomates? ¿Me los pasas, por favor? 4. ¿Hay más fruta? ¿Me la pasas, por favor? 5. ¿Hay más vino? ¿Me lo pasas, por favor? 6. ¿Hay más jamón? ¿Me lo pasas, por favor?

♻ **Prác. C: Note**
Note review of travel vocabulary.

**Prác. C: Answers**
1. *Acaban de decírnosla. (Nos la acaban de decir.)* 2. *Sí, léamelo, por favor.* 3. *No, no tiene que dárselos (se los tiene que dar) aquí.* 4. *Claro que se lo guardo.* 5. *Ya te los compré.* 6. *Te lo puedo guardar. (Puedo guardártelo.)* 7. *Sí, se la recomiendo, señores.* 8. *La asistente de vuelo nos la va a servir (va a servírnosla) en el avión.*

**Need more practice?**

■ Workbook/Laboratory Manual
■ Interactive CD-ROM
■ Online Learning Center (www.mhhe.com/quetal7)

## ■ Conversación

### A. Regalos especiales

PASO 1  The drawings in **Grupo A** show the presents that a number of people have just received. They were given by the people in **Grupo B.** Can you match the presents with the giver? Make as many logical guesses as you can.

GRUPO A

Carlos y Juanita

GRUPO B

Raúl

PASO 2  Now compare your matches with those of a partner.

MODELO: ¿Quién le regaló (mandó, dio) la computadora a Maritere? Se la regaló (mandó, dio) _____.

### B. ¿Quién le regaló eso?

PASO 1  Haga una lista de los cinco mejores regalos que Ud. ha recibido (*have received*) en su vida. Si no sabe cómo expresar algo, pregúnteselo a su profesor(a).

En los Estados Unidos y el Canadá: Comprensión: ¿Cierto o falso?
1. *El Día de César Chávez es un día festivo nacional.*

PASO 2  Ahora déle a un compañero / una compañera su lista. Él/Ella le va a preguntar: **¿Quién te regaló _____?** Use pronombres en su respuesta. **¡OJO!** Fíjese en estas formas plurales (**ellos**): **regalaron, dieron, mandaron.**

MODELO: E1: ¿Quién te regaló los aretes?
E2: Mis padres me los regalaron.

2. *Se celebra el Día de César Chávez en primavera.*

## En los Estados Unidos y el Canadá

### El Día de César Chávez

Desde el año 2000, el líder sindical[a] mexicoamericano César Chávez (1927–1993) tiene **un día festivo en su honor en el estado de California.** El lunes o el viernes alrededor del[b] 31 de marzo, los colegios y otros organismos[c] pueden cerrar para honrar[d] a **Chávez** y **el movimiento en defensa de los trabajadores agrícolas**[e] que él defendió.

*César Chávez*

«[César Chávez] debe ser honrado porque su trabajo formó la América en la que hoy vivimos. Su vida nos dio a todos **el coraje**[f] y **la esperanza**[g] de que podemos hacer una diferencia. En su vida, nos enseñó que es importante **llevar una vida moral y responsable.**»

[a]*union* [b]*alrededor... around the* [c]*institutions* [d]*honor* [e]*trabajadores... farm workers* [f]*courage* [g]*hope*

## UN POCO DE TODO

**Lengua y cultura: Más días festivos.** Complete the following paragraphs with the correct form of the words in parentheses, as suggested by the context. When two possibilities are given in parentheses, select the correct word. Use the preterite of the infinitives in italics.

Los días festivos son muy importantes en el mundo hispano, pero varían mucho de país en país y de pueblo en pueblo.

### La fiesta de la Virgen de Guadalupe

En (alguno¹) países hispánicos (los/las²) días de varios santos (ser/estar³) fiestas nacionales. El día 12 (de/del⁴) diciembre los mexicanos (conmemorar⁵) a la santa patrona de México, la Virgen de Guadalupe. (Mucho⁶) mexicoamericanos celebran (este⁷) fiesta también. Se cree que la Virgen María se le (aparecer⁸) (a/de⁹) Juan, (un/una¹⁰) humilde pastor,ᵃ en el pueblo (a/de¹¹) Guadalupe. La Virgen (dejar¹²)ᵇ su imagen en un rebozoᶜ que todavía se puede (ver¹³) en su Basílicaᵈ en la Ciudad de México.

ᵃshepherd  ᵇto leave  ᶜshawl  ᵈlarge church

### La fiesta de San Fermín

No (todo¹⁴) las fiestas hispánicas (ser/estar¹⁵) religiosas. Esta fiesta de Pamplona (España) lleva (el/la¹⁶) nombre de un santo y (ser/estar¹⁷) de origen religioso, pero es esencialmente secular. Durante diez días —entre (el/la¹⁸) 7 y (el/la¹⁹) 14 de julio— se interrumpe la rutina diaria (del / de la²⁰) ciudad. (Llegar²¹) personas de todas partes de España e inclusiveᵃ de (otro²²) países para beber, cantar, bailar... y (pasarlo²³) (bien/bueno²⁴). Todas las mañanas algunos torosᵇ (correr²⁵) sueltosᶜ por la calleᵈ de la Estafeta, en dirección (al / a la²⁶) plaza de toros.ᵉ (Alguno²⁷) personas atrevidasᶠ (correr²⁸) delante de ellos. No (haber²⁹) dudaᵍ de que (este³⁰) demostración de valorʰ (ser/estar³¹) bastante peligrosa.ⁱ Luego por (el/la³²) tarde se celebra una corridaʲ en la famosa plaza de toros que (describir³³) Ernest Hemingway en (su³⁴) novela *The Sun Also Rises*. En Pamplona todavía (ser/estar³⁵) posible (hablar³⁶) con personas que (saber/conocer³⁷) a este famoso escritor estadounidense.

ᵃeven  ᵇbulls  ᶜcorrer... to run free  ᵈstreet  ᵉplaza... bullring  ᶠdaring  ᵍdoubt  ʰcourage
ⁱbastante... quite dangerous  ʲbullfight

### Comprensión: ¿Cierto o falso?   Corrija las oraciones falsas.

1. Todas las fiestas hispánicas son religiosas.
2. Sólo los mexicanos celebran la fiesta de la Virgen de Guadalupe.
3. La fiesta de San Fermín es esencial para los niños.
4. Algunos españoles todavía recuerdan a Hemingway.

*Una bandera* (banner) *típica durante la fiesta de la Virgen de Guadalupe*

**Resources for Review and Testing Preparation**

- Workbook/Laboratory Manual
- Interactive CD-ROM
- Online Learning Center (www.mhhe.com/quetal7)

*Comprensión* **1.** *falso: No todas las fiestas hispánicas son religiosas.* **2.** *falso: Algunos mexicoamericanos también celebran esta fiesta.* **3.** *falso: La fiesta de San Fermín es esencialmente para los adultos.* **4.** *cierto*

**Multimedia: Internet**
Have students search the Internet for images and websites relating to the celebration of the *Virgen de Guadalupe* and to the running of the bulls or the *Fiesta de San Fermín*. You might have groups develop visual and oral presentations about these festivals.

**Follow-Up**
Ask the following questions to follow up the activity.

*¿Qué fiestas religiosas se celebran en los Estados Unidos y el Canadá en general?*
*¿Cuáles celebra su familia?*
*¿Y las fiestas que no son religiosas?*
*¿Qué fiestas se celebran en los países hispanohablantes que no se celebran en este país?*

**Lengua y cultura: Answers**
**1.** *algunos* **2.** *los* **3.** *son* **4.** *de* **5.** *conmemoran* **6.** *Muchos* **7.** *esta* **8.** *apareció* **9.** *a* **10.** *un* **11.** *de* **12.** *dejó* **13.** *ver* **14.** *todas* **15.** *son* **16.** *el* **17.** *es* **18.** *el* **19.** *el* **20.** *de la* **21.** *Llegan* **22.** *otros* **23.** *pasarlo* **24.** *bien* **25.** *corren* **26.** *a la* **27.** *Algunas* **28.** *corren* **29.** *hay* **30.** *esta* **31.** *es* **32.** *la* **33.** *describió* **34.** *su* **35.** *es* **36.** *hablar* **37.** *conocieron*

**Resources: Desenlace**
In the *Capítulo 8* segment of "Chapter-by-Chapter Supplementary Materials" in the IM, you will find a chapter-culminating activity. You can use this activity to consolidate and review the vocabulary and grammar skills students have acquired.

# PASO 4    Un paso más

## Entrevista cultural: Cuba

Rocío García nació en Cuba pero ahora vive y trabaja en México. En esta entrevista, Rocío describe su trabajo. También habla de unas costumbres cubanas. Antes de ver el vídeo, lea el siguiente fragmento de la entrevista.

ENTREVISTADORA: Rocío, ¿en dónde trabajas?

ROCÍO: Trabajo en una tienda que vende artículos típicos de fiesta, como son globos, serpentinas[a]… Y tiene una sección especial para artículos típicos de fiestas mexicanas, que es en la que nos encontramos.

ENTREVISTADORA: ¿Cómo se celebran los cumpleaños en Cuba?

ROCÍO: En Cuba hacemos una gran fiesta. Hay payasos,[b] globos, *cake*, piñatas, refrescos —todo para que los niños la pasen bien. Y jugamos mucho con ellos para que disfruten[c] ese día.

[a]*streamers*    [b]*clowns*    [c]*they enjoy*

Ahora vea el vídeo y conteste las siguientes preguntas basándose en la entrevista.

1. ¿Dónde trabaja Rocío?
2. ¿Qué se vende allí?
3. ¿Cómo son las fiestas de cumpleaños en Cuba?
4. ¿Cómo se celebra la Navidad en Cuba?
5. ¿Cuál es el día festivo preferido de Rocío?

## Entre amigos: ¡Comemos «las uvas de la suerte (*the lucky grapes*)»!

Rubén, Miguel, Tané y Karina preparan las decoraciones para una fiesta, y hablan de las tradiciones navideñas (*Christmas traditions*) de sus países. En su opinión, ¿de qué van a hablar? Antes de mirar el vídeo, lea las preguntas a continuación. Mientras mire el vídeo, trate de entender la conversación en general y fíjese en la información sobre los días festivos. Luego mire el vídeo una segunda vez, fijándose en la información que necesita para contestar las preguntas.

1. ¿Qué van a hacer Miguel y Rubén con los adornos (*decorations*)?
2. ¿Qué hacen en España durante los días de Navidad?
3. ¿Cuándo comen «las uvas de la suerte» en España?
4. ¿Qué hacen en Venezuela para la Navidad?
5. ¿Y qué hacen en Cuba para la Navidad?

## ENFOQUE CULTURAL

Cuba

José Martí
The Buena Vista Social Club
Fidel Castro

Radio Martí
*los marielitos*
Theodore Roosevelt
Elián González

Iván Hernández
*la Bahía de Guantánamo*
Fulgencio Batista
the USS Maine

LOS ESTADOS UNIDOS
(Florida)
GOLFO DE
MÉXICO

OCÉANO
ATLÁNTICO

*Estrecho de Florida*

ISLAS BAHAMAS

La Habana

CUBA

• Camagüey

• Santiago

MAR CARIBE

HAITÍ

### ¡Fíjese!

- Cuba obtuvo[a] su independencia de España en 1898, tras[b] la guerra de Cuba.[c] Los Estados Unidos ayudó a Cuba en esta guerra.

- Después de la revolución socialista cubana en 1959, hubo un éxodo de cubanos a los Estados Unidos. La mayor parte de ellos se estableció en Florida, con la esperanza[d] de volver muy pronto a su isla. Pero empezó el milenio y todavía[e] Fidel Castro, el primer líder de la revolución, gobierna a Cuba.

- Los días festivos oficiales de Cuba incluyen el Aniversario del triunfo de la Revolución o el Día de la Liberación (1º de enero), el Día Internacional de los Trabajadores (1º de mayo), las Celebraciones por el Día de la Rebeldía Nacional (25–27 de julio) y el Inicio de las guerras de Independencia (10 de octubre). Al tomar[f] el control del poder de Cuba, Castro declaró el país oficialmente ateo[g] y prohibió que practicantes religiosos participaran en el gobierno. En 1992, Castro levantó esa prohibición. En 1997, un poco antes de la visita del Papa Juan Pablo II a Cuba, la Navidad, que por casi cuarenta años no fue un día festivo oficial, fue celebrada[h] pública y oficialmente.

- El régimen de Castro ha reducido[i] el analfabetismo[j] a menos de 5 por ciento y ha reformado el sistema educativo con resultados admirables.

Pero la situación económica del país es difícil. Con la caída[k] de la Unión Soviética, Cuba perdió fondos de apoyo[l] indispensables. El embargo económico de los Estados Unidos también sigue afectando las condiciones de vida[m] de los cubanos.

[a]*obtained* [b]*after* [c]*guerra… Spanish-American War* [d]*hope* [e]*still* [f]*Al… Upon taking* [g]*atheist* [h]*celebrated* [i]*ha… has reduced* [j]*illiteracy* [k]*fall* [l]*fondos… economic assistance* [m]*condiciones… living conditions*

### Personas famosas: Nicolás Guillén

Nicolás Guillén (1902–1989), poeta cubano de origen africano y europeo, es quizás[a] el poeta que mejor refleja la influencia africana en la cultura hispana. El lenguaje, los mitos[b] y las leyendas afro-cubanos aparecen en su obra. Sus temas incluyen la injusticia social y una crítica al colonialismo.

[a]*perhaps* [b]*myths*

*Nicolás Guillén*
*(1902–1989)*

Learn more about Cuba with the Video, the Interactive CD-ROM, and the Online Learning Center (www.mhhe.com/quetal7).

# PASO 4

## A CONVERSAR

### ¿Cómo celebraron Uds. los días festivos?

PASO 1  En una hoja de papel aparte, prepare un cuadro (*grid*) como el siguiente. Primero, escoja cuatro de los días festivos de la lista en la página 209. Luego escríbalos en el cuadro. Deje espacios en blanco para escribir el nombre de una persona y sus respuestas breves a tres preguntas.

MODELO:

| día festivo | el Día de San Patricio | la Noche Vieja | el cumpleaños | el Cinco de Mayo |
|---|---|---|---|---|
| **persona** | | | | |
| **actividades** | | | | |

**Suggestion**
Remind students that there are expressions and verbs throughout the chapter that they may wish to use in their questions and responses. Refer them to lists on pages 208 and 211, as well as the end-of-chapter list.

**Follow-Up**
Ask students how they themselves spent the holidays on their charts.

*¿Qué hizo Ud. en* (name of holiday)*?*
*¿Recibió regalos? ¿Le regaló algo a otra persona? ¿Hizo una fiesta? ¿Sirvió algún plato especial?*, and so on.

**Suggestion**
For writing practice, see the *Mi diario* activity in each chapter of the Workbook/Laboratory Manual.

PASO 2  Apunte (*Jot down*) tres preguntas que Ud. puede hacerles a sus compañeros sobre cómo celebraron estos días festivos el año pasado.

MODELO:  El año pasado, ¿qué hiciste en la Noche Vieja? ¿Te reuniste con amigos en algún lugar especial? ¿Lo pasaste bien o mal?

PASO 3  Formen parejas para hacer y contestar las tres preguntas sobre el primer día festivo en el cuadro. Después de hacer y contestar esas tres preguntas, formen parejas con otras personas para hacer y contestar las preguntas del siguiente día festivo. En total, van a formar cuatro parejas diferentes para hacer y contestar las preguntas sobre los cuatro días festivos. Escriban los nombres de sus compañeros y sus respuestas debajo del día festivo correspondiente para recordar con quiénes hablaron y qué dijeron.

MODELO:  la Noche Vieja →
Felipe: Salió con su novia. Se reunieron con unos amigos en un bar. Lo pasaron muy bien.

PASO 4  Escoja uno de los días festivos y cuéntele a la clase cómo lo celebró la persona que contestó sus preguntas.

## GRAMÁTICA

To review the grammar points presented in this chapter, refer to the indicated grammar presentations. You'll find further practice of these structures in the Workbook/Laboratory Manual, on the Interactive CD-ROM, and on the *¿Qué tal?* Online Learning Center (www.mhhe.com/quetal7).

**23** Talking About the Past (2)—Irregular Preterites

Do you know how to conjugate the verbs that are irregular in the preterite? How does the preterite change the meaning of **saber, conocer, querer,** and **poder?**

**24** Talking About the Past (3)—Preterite of Stem-Changing Verbs

You should know the stem-changing patterns for **-ir** verbs like **pedir, sentir,** and **dormir.**

**25** Expressing Direct and Indirect Objects Together—Double Object Pronouns

Do you know in which order the direct and indirect object pronouns occur when they are used together in Spanish? You should also know where to place the pronouns and when an accent is required on the verb forms.

## VOCABULARIO

Practice this vocabulary with digital flash cards on the Online Learning Center (www.mhhe.com/quetal7).

### Los verbos

| | |
|---|---|
| **conseguir (i, i) (g)** | to get, obtain |
| **conseguir** + *inf.* | to succeed in (*doing something*) |
| **despedirse (i, i) (de)** | to say good-bye (to), take leave (of) |
| **encontrar (ue)** | to find |
| **morirse (ue, u)** | to die |
| **reaccionar** | to react |
| **sugerir (ie, i)** | to suggest |

### Los días festivos y las fiestas

| | |
|---|---|
| **el anfitrión / la anfitriona** | host, hostess |
| **el chiste** | joke |
| **el deseo** | wish |
| **el día festivo** | holiday |
| **los entremeses** | hors d'œvres |
| **el/la invitado/a** | guest |
| **el pastel de cumpleaños** | birthday cake |
| **la sorpresa** | surprise |

**Repaso: el cumpleaños, el dinero, el refresco**

| | |
|---|---|
| **cumplir años** | to have a birthday |
| **dar** (*irreg.*) **una fiesta** | to give a party |
| **faltar (a)** | to be absent (from), not attend |
| **gastar** | to spend (*money*) |
| **hacer** (*irreg.*) **una fiesta** | to have a party |
| **pasarlo bien/mal** | to have a good/bad time |
| **reunirse (me reúno) (con)** | to get together (with) |

**Repaso: celebrar, divertirse (ie, i), regalar**

### Emociones y condiciones

| | |
|---|---|
| **discutir (con)/(sobre)** | to argue (with)/(about) |
| **enfermarse** | to become sick |
| **enojarse (con)** | to get angry (at) |
| **llorar** | to cry |
| **olvidarse (de)** | to forget (about) |
| **ponerse** (*irreg.*) + *adj.* | to become, get + *adj.* |
| **portarse bien/mal** | to behave well/badly |
| **quejarse (de)** | to complain (about) |
| **recordar (ue)** | to remember |
| **reír(se) (i, i) (de)** | to laugh (about) |
| **sentirse (ie, i)** | to feel (*an emotion*) |
| **sonreír(se) (i, i)** | to smile |

## Los sustantivos

| | |
|---|---|
| el hecho | fact, event |
| la medianoche | midnight |
| la noticia | piece of news |

## Los adjetivos

| | |
|---|---|
| avergonzado/a | embarrassed |
| feliz (*pl.* felices) | happy |
| raro/a | strange |

## Algunos días festivos

| | |
|---|---|
| la Navidad | Christmas |
| la Noche Vieja | New Year's Eve |
| la Nochebuena | Christmas Eve |
| la Pascua (Florida) | Easter |

## Palabras adicionales

| | |
|---|---|
| ¡felicitaciones! | congratulations! |
| gracias por | thanks for |
| por lo menos | at least |
| ser (*irreg.*) en + *place* | to take place at/in (*place*) |
| ya | already |

**Suggestions**

- Give a series of situations or problems and have students react quickly by expressing how they would feel. For example:

  *un examen difícil → Me pongo nervioso.*
  *un chiste cómico → Me río.*

- Play a game of word associations with words from the *Vocabulario.* Continue round-robin associations for at least ten turns for each word. For example, *entremeses → sándwiches → fiestas → cumpleaños,* and so on.

- Have students respond *probable* or *improbable.*

  1. *Ud. se siente triste si los amigos se olviden de su cumpleaños.*
  2. *Ud. se ríe si su novio/a sale con otra persona.*
  3. *El profesor se enoja si los estudiantes se portan bien.*

- Ask students:

  *¿En qué días festivos mandamos tarjetas?*

  1. *¿la Navidad?*
  2. *¿el Cuatro de Julio?*
  3. *¿el Día de San Valentín?*
  4. *¿el cumpleaños?*

  *¿Qué colores asociamos con estos días festivos?*

  5. *la Pascua (Florida)*
  6. *la Navidad*
  7. *el Cuatro de Julio*
  8. *el Día de San Patricio*

- Ask students the following questions.

  1. *¿Se ríe Ud. con frecuencia? ¿fácilmente? ¿Sonríe fácilmente? Dé un ejemplo de una situación en que Ud. sonríe. ¿Sonríe cuando está nervioso/a? ¿Cuándo no se debe sonreír? ¿Cuándo es necesario sonreír?*
  2. *¿Cuándo fue la última vez que Ud. se sintió muy feliz? ¿Qué pasó ese día?*
  3. *¿Llora Ud. mucho? ¿Quiénes lloran más, los niños o los adultos? ¿las mujeres o los hombres? ¿En qué situaciones es común que lloren las personas? ¿Es bueno que los hombres no lloren con frecuencia? Cuando alguien llora, ¿qué indica?*
  4. *¿Se enoja Ud. fácilmente? ¿Discute con frecuencia con alguien? ¿Se pone contento/a fácilmente? ¿nervioso/a? ¿Cuándo se pone Ud. nervioso/a? ¿Durante un examen? ¿cuando habla español? ¿durante una entrevista?*
  5. *¿Tiene Ud. hoy todas las cosas necesarias para la clase? ¿Se olvidó de traer algo? ¿Se olvidó alguna vez de un examen?*
  6. *¿Recuerda Ud. fácilmente los nombres? ¿los números? ¿los números de teléfono? ¿el vocabulario nuevo? ¿Qué números es muy necesario recordar?*

# El tiempo libre

*Fuegos artificiales* (Fireworks) *al final de un festival de teatro, en la Plaza de Bolívar en Bogotá, Colombia*

## PASATIEMPOS, DIVERSIONES Y AFICIONES°

**Paso 1: Vocabulario**
See the "Chapter-by-Chapter Supplementary Materials" in the IM for a model for vocabulary presentation, as well as additional teaching suggestions, notes, activities, and other resources for *Paso 1.*

**Multimedia: Audio**
Students can listen to and practice this chapter's vocabulary on the Online Learning Center (www. mhhe. com/quetal7), as well as on the Textbook Audio CD, part of the Laboratory Audio Program.

**Resources:**
**Transparencies 63–66**
Transparencies 64–66 provide additional vocabulary and practice with *pasatiempos.*

Nina
**ir (irreg.) al cine/ a ver una película**
**visitar un museo**
Sara
**pasear en bicicleta**
Eva
Irene
**correr**
Emilio
**patinar en línea**
**dar (irreg.) un paseo**
Rita
Felipe
Julio
**hacer (irreg.) un picnic**
Leona
**jugar (ue) (gu) a las cartas**
Andrés
**montar a caballo**

## Los pasatiempos

| | |
|---|---|
| **los ratos libres** | spare (free) time |
| **dar** (*irreg.*)/**hacer** (*irreg.*) **una fiesta** | to give a party |
| **hacer** (*irreg.*) *camping* | to go camping |
| **hacer** (*irreg.*) **planes para** + *inf.* | to make plans to (*do something*) |
| **ir** (*irreg.*)... | to go . . . |
| **a una discoteca / a un bar** | to a disco / to a bar |
| **al teatro / a un concierto** | to the theater / to a concert |
| **jugar (ue) (gu) al ajedrez** | to play chess |
| **tomar el sol** | to sunbathe |
| **aburrirse** | to get bored |
| **ser** (*irreg.*) **aburrido/a, divertido/a** | to be boring, fun |

## Los deportes

| | |
|---|---|
| **el ciclismo** | bicycling |
| **el fútbol** | soccer |
| **el fútbol americano** | football |
| **el/la jugador(a)** | player |
| **la natación** | swimming |
| **esquiar (esquío)** | to ski |
| **nadar** | to swim |
| **patinar** | to skate |

**Cognados: el basquetbol, el béisbol, el golf, el hockey, el tenis, el vólibol**

| | |
|---|---|
| **entrenar** | to practice, train |
| **ganar** | to win |
| **jugar (ue) (gu) al** + *sport* | to play (*a sport*) |
| **perder (ie)** | to lose |
| **practicar (qu)** | to participate (*in a sport*) |
| **ser** (*irreg.*) **aficionado/a (a)** | to be a fan (of) |

## ■ Conversación

**A.** **¿Cómo pasan estas personas su tiempo libre?**

PASO 1  ¿Qué cree Ud. que hacen las siguientes personas para divertirse en un sábado típico? Use su imaginación pero manténgase (*keep yourself*) entre los límites de lo posible.

1. una persona rica que vive en Nueva York
2. un grupo de amigos que trabajan en una fábrica (*factory*) de Detroit
3. un matrimonio joven con poco dinero y dos niños pequeños

PASO 2  ¿Cómo se divierten los jóvenes españoles? Este recorte (*clipping*) de una revista española indica el tiempo medio (*average*) que los jóvenes españoles dedican a sus aficiones. ¿Puede explicar en español lo que significan los términos **Tomar copas** y **prensa**? ¿A qué tipos de «**Juegos**» cree Ud. que se refiere el recorte?

PASO 3  Indique el número de minutos que Ud. les dedica a estas aficiones cada día. ¿Qué diferencia hay entre Ud. y los jóvenes españoles?

**B.** **¿Cierto o falso?**  Corrija (*Correct*) las oraciones falsas según su opinión.

1. Ver un partido (*match, game*) de fútbol en la televisión es más aburrido que ir al cine.
2. Lo paso mejor con mi familia que con mis amigos.
3. Las actividades educativas me gustan más que las deportivas (*sporting*).
4. Odio el béisbol tanto como el fútbol.

| TIEMPO QUE DEDICAN A SUS AFICIONES | |
|---|---|
| (Media de minutos diarios) | |
| Ver la televisión | **120** |
| Tomar copas | **60** |
| Pasear | **22** |
| Leer libros | **15** |
| Escuchar música | **15** |
| Oír la radio | **8** |
| Hacer deporte | **9** |
| Practicar *hobbies* | **8** |
| Leer la prensa | **6** |
| «Juegos» | **4** |

**Nota cultural: Comprensión**
1. *¿Qué deporte atrae a más televidentes en el mundo hispano para sus grandes eventos, el fútbol or el fútbol americano?*
2. *¿En qué países del mundo hispano es popular el béisbol?*

## NOTA CULTURAL

3. *¿Quién ganó la medalla de oro de basquetbol durante los Juegos Olímpicos de 2004?*
4. *¿Quiénes son algunos de los jugadores hispanos que juegan en la NBA?*

### El fútbol, el béisbol y el basquetbol

Sin duda,[a] el deporte más popular en los países hispánicos es **el fútbol.*** La Copa Mundial de fútbol es el evento deportivo más popular del mundo. Este **torneo internacional** ocurre cada cuatro años y tiene más **espectadores** que cualquier[b] otro evento deportivo. Por ejemplo, en 2002, más de un billón de televidentes miraron el partido final de la Copa Mundial mientras el mismo año, 132 millones miraron el *Super Bowl* de los Estados Unidos. Como es un deporte tan popular, en todas las ciudades hispanas hay muchos **campos**[c] de **fútbol.** Los niños y los adultos van a jugar siempre que pueden.[d]

*Un partido de la Copa Mundial entre el Brasil y Honduras*

**El béisbol** también es muy popular, sobre todo en el Caribe. Hay muchos hispanos en **las ligas profesionales** de los Estados Unidos. El puertorriqueño Roberto Clemente fue el primer jugador hispano elegido al *Baseball Hall of Fame* en 1973.

Otro deporte muy popular es **el basquetbol** o **el baloncesto.** En los Juegos Olímpicos de verano de 2004, la Argentina se llevó la medalla de oro[e] después de derrotar[f] a Italia. En la Asociación Nacional de Basquetbol (*NBA*) de los Estados Unidos hay varios jugadores hispanos, entre ellos Emanuel Ginobili, Eduardo Nájera, Pau Gasol y Felipe Arroyo.

---

[a]*doubt*  [b]*any*  [c]*fields*  [d]siempre... *whenever they can*  [e]se... *took the gold medal*  [f]*defeating*

---

*Remember that* **fútbol** *is soccer, not U.S.-style football.*

# PASO 1

♻ **Reciclado**

Recycle house vocabulary with the following question.

*¿Qué quehaceres domésticos asocia Ud. con la cocina? ¿el garaje? ¿la alcoba? ¿la sala? ¿el baño?*

## LOS QUEHACERES DOMÉSTICOS°

Resources: Transparency 67

### Algunos aparatos domésticos

| | |
|---|---|
| **la cafetera** | coffeemaker |
| **el horno de microondas** | microwave oven |
| **la tostadora** | toaster |

### Los quehaceres domésticos

| | |
|---|---|
| **dejar (en... )** | to leave behind (in [*a place*]) |
| **lavar (los platos, la ropa)** | to wash (the dishes, the clothes) |
| **limpiar la casa (entera)** | to clean the (whole) house |
| **poner** (*irreg.*) **la mesa** | to set the table |
| **quitar la mesa** | to clear the table |
| **sacudir los muebles** | to dust the furniture |

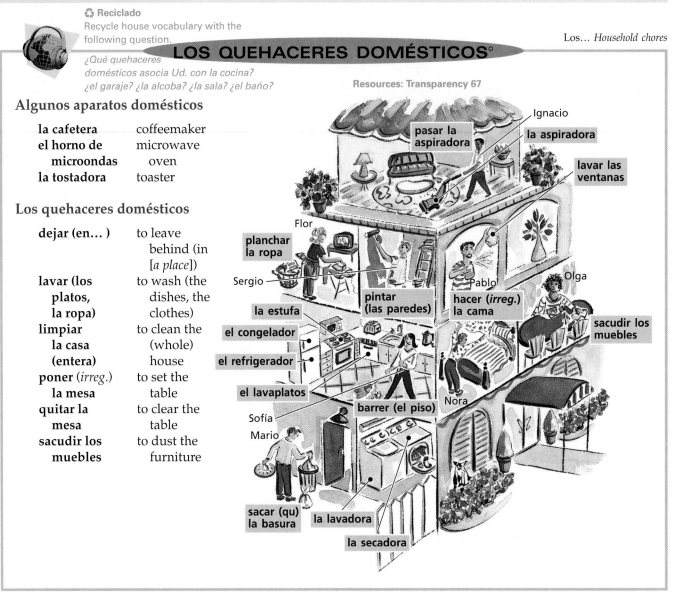

## Vocabulario útil

Here are some alternative phrases related to household chores and appliances that are used in some parts of the Spanish-speaking world. This vocabulary is for your information only and will not be actively practiced in *¿Qué tal?*

**hacer** (*irreg.*) **la cama** → **tender (ie) la cama**
**lavar los platos** → **fregar (ie) (gu) los platos**
**sacar (qu) la basura** → **tirar la basura**
**sacudir los muebles** → **quitar el polvo** (literally, *to remove the dust*)

**el congelador** → **la nevera**
**la estufa** → **la cocina** (**el horno** is generally used for *oven*)
**el refrigerador** → **el frigorífico, la refrigeradora**

**Bright Idea Suggestion**

Ask students what chores they like or do not like to do.

*¿A quién le gusta...? ¿planchar la ropa? ¿limpiar la casa? ¿lavar las ventanas?*

Con. A: Suggestion
Have students come up with all logical and possible parts of the house where the action can take place.

# ■ Conversación

**A. Los quehaceres.** ¿En qué cuarto o parte de la casa se hacen las siguientes actividades? Hay más de una respuesta en muchos casos.

1. Se hace la cama en ___la alcoba___.
2. Se saca la basura de ___la cocina___ y se deja en ___el garaje / el patio___.
3. Se sacude los muebles de ___Answers will vary___.
4. Uno se baña en ___el cuarto de baño___. Pero es mejor que uno bañe al perro en ___el patio / el garaje___.
5. Se barre el piso de ___la cocina___.
6. Se pasa la aspiradora en ___la sala / el comedor / las alcobas___.
7. Se lava y se seca la ropa en ___Answers will vary___. La ropa se plancha en ___Answers will vary___.
8. Se usa la cafetera en ___la cocina___.

## NOTA COMUNICATIVA

### Talking About Obligation

You already know several ways to express the obligation to carry out particular activities.

| **Tengo que** | | *I have to* | |
|---|---|---|---|
| **Necesito** | barrer el suelo. | *I need to* | *sweep the floor.* |
| **Debo** | | *I should* | |

Of the three, **tener que** + *infinitive* expresses the strongest sense of obligation.

The concept *to be someone's turn or responsibility* (to do something) is expressed in Spanish with the verb **tocar** plus an indirect object.

—¿**A quién le toca** lavar los platos esta noche?
—**A mí me toca** solamente sacar la basura. Creo que **a papá le toca** lavar los platos.

*Whose turn is it to wash the dishes tonight?*
*I only have to take out the garbage. I think it's Dad's turn to wash the dishes.*

Con. B: Follow-Up
Paso 1. Have students total their score and give them the following scale for interpreting it.

**B. ¿A quién le toca?**

PASO 1 ¿Mantiene Ud. su casa en orden? ¿Con qué frecuencia hace Ud. los siguientes quehaceres? Complete el siguiente formulario. Si Ud. vive en una residencia estudiantil, imagine que vive en una casa o en un apartamento.

1. _____ lavar las ventanas
2. _____ hacer las camas
3. _____ poner la mesa
4. _____ preparar la comida
5. _____ sacudir los muebles
6. _____ lavar los platos
7. _____ limpiar la casa entera
8. _____ sacar la basura
9. _____ pasar la aspiradora
10. _____ limpiar la estufa
11. _____ planchar la ropa
12. _____ barrer el piso

_____ TOTAL

INTERPRETACIONES

*0–8 puntos: ¡Cuidado (new word)! Ud. es descuidado/a (new word). ¿Estudia*

> 0 = **nunca**
> 1 = **a veces**
> 2 = **frecuentemente**
> 3 = **todos los días**

*demasiado (new word)? Por favor, ¡limpie su casa! ¡No lo deje para mañana!*
*9–17 puntos: Ud. puede vivir en su casa, pero no debe invitar a otras personas sin limpiarla bien primero.*
*18–27 puntos: Su casa, aunque no está*

PASO 2 Ahora hable con un compañero / una compañera sobre sus hábitos domésticos. Básense en el formulario del **Paso 1.** Luego hablen de los quehaceres domésticos para hoy, mañana o esta semana.

*perfecta, está limpia. Es un modelo para todos.*

MODELO: lavar las ventanas →
E1: ¿Con qué frecuencia lavas las ventanas?
E2: Nunca las lavo.
E1: ¿Qué te toca hacer en casa hoy (manana, esta semana)?

*28–36 puntos: ¡Ud. es una maravilla y tieneuna casa muy, muy limpia! Pero, ¿pasa Ud. demasiado tiempo limpiando? ¡Váyase al aire libre de vez en cuando!*

**Need more practice?**

- Workbook/Laboratory Manual
- Interactive CD-ROM
- Online Learning Center (www.mhhe.com/quetal7)

Note
See the Workbook/Laboratory Manual for presentation and practice of the letters *p* and *t*.

**Paso 2: Gramática**
See the "Chapter-by-Chapter Supplementary Materials" in the IM for additional teaching suggestions, notes, activities, and other resources for *Paso 2*.

**Follow-Up**
Ask students the following questions to follow up the *minidiálogo*.

*Cuando Ud. era pequeño/a…*

1. ¿creía en Santa Claus?
2. ¿iba a ceremonias religiosas con su familia?
3. ¿jugaba a algún deporte con sus padres? ¿con sus hermanos?
4. ¿siempre hacía sus quehaceres?

**Suggestion**
Ask students what modern sports are related or similar to this Aztec sport.

*¿Con qué deportes modernos se puede relacionar el antiguo deporte azteca?*

---

### ¿Recuerda Ud.?

In **Capítulos 7** and **8,** you learned the forms and some uses of the preterite. Before you learn the other simple past tense, you might want to review the forms of the preterite in those chapters. The verbs in the following sentences are in the preterite. Can you identify any words in the sentences that emphasize the completed nature of the actions expressed by the verbs?

1. Me levanté a las seis esta mañana.
2. Ayer fui al cine con un amigo.
3. Pinté las paredes de la cocina la semana pasada.

---

## 26 Descriptions and Habitual Actions in the Past Imperfect of Regular and Irregular Verbs

**En su clase de antropología, Diego habla de los aztecas**

Diego, un estudiante de California que estudia en México, da un informe sobre los aztecas.

«Los aztecas construyeron grandes pirámides para sus dioses. En lo alto de cada pirámide *había* un templo donde *tenían* lugar las ceremonias y *se ofrecían* los sacrificios. Las pirámides *tenían* muchísimos escalones, y *era* necesario subirlos todos para llegar a los templos.

Cerca de muchas pirámides *había* un terreno como el de una cancha de basquetbol. Allí *se celebraban* partidos que *eran* parte de una ceremonia. Los participantes *jugaban* con una pelota de goma dura, que sólo *podían* mover con las caderas y las rodillas… »

**Comprensión: ¿Cierto o falso?**

1. Los aztecas creían en un solo dios.    falso
2. Las pirámides aztecas tenían una función religiosa.    cierto
3. Los aztecas practicaban un deporte similar al basquetbol.    cierto

---

**Resources: Transparency 68**
Transparency 68 provides examples of uses of the imperfect.

**Multimedia: Internet**
Have students search the Internet for more information on the former Aztec civilization as well as information on other early Latin American civilizations. Encourage them to look for images of the cities and for information about rituals and the famous Aztec calendar. You might assign specific topics and have students develop brief oral presentations based on their findings.

---

*In his anthropology class, Diego talks about the Aztecs*    *Diego, a student from California who is studying in Mexico, is giving a report on the Aztecs. "The Aztecs constructed large pyramids for their gods. At the top of each pyramid there was a temple where ceremonies took place and sacrifices were offered. The pyramids had many, many steps, and it was necessary to climb them all in order to get to the temples.*

*"Close to many pyramids there was an area of land like that of a basketball court. Ceremonial matches were celebrated there. The participants played with a ball made of hard rubber that they could only move with their hips and knees . . . "*

You have already learned to use the *preterite* (**el pretérito**) to express events in the past. The *imperfect* (**el imperfecto**) is the second simple past tense in Spanish. In contrast to the preterite, which is used when you view actions or states of being as begun or completed in the past, the imperfect tense is used when you view past actions or states of being as habitual or as "in progress." The imperfect is also used for describing the past.

The imperfect has several English equivalents. For example, **hablaba,** the first person singular of **hablar,** can mean *I spoke, I was speaking, I used to speak,* or *I would speak* (when *would* implies a repeated action). Most of these English equivalents indicate that the action was still in progress or was habitual, except for *I spoke,* which can correspond to either the preterite or the imperfect.

**Suggestions**
• Point out that the imperfect is the second of two simple past tenses. This section presents and practices only the imperfect. *Gramática 29* in *Capítulo 10* contrasts the two tenses, but some activities before that section will combine the two tenses in controlled situations.
• Use the regular imperfect forms of *trabajar, beber,* and *vivir* in conversational exchanges with students.
• Emphasize that *would* can imply both conditional and habitual actions in the past. Only the latter (habit) is expressed by the imperfect.

```
PAST------------------- Present --------------------Future
preterite                        present
imperfect                   present progressive
                              formal commands
```

## Forms of the Imperfect

| hablar | | comer | | vivir | |
|---|---|---|---|---|---|
| hablaba | hablábamos | comía | comíamos | vivía | vivíamos |
| hablabas | hablabais | comías | comíais | vivías | vivíais |
| hablaba | hablaban | comía | comían | vivía | vivían |

• Stem-changing verbs do not show a change in the imperfect. The imperfect of **hay** is **había** (*there was, there were, there used to be*).

*Pronunciation Hint:* Remember that the pronunciation of a **b** between vowels, such as in the imperfect ending **-aba,** is pronounced as a fricative [ƀ] sound.

In the other imperfect forms, it is important not to pronounce the ending **-ía** as a diphthong, but to pronounce the **i** and the **a** in separate syllables (the accent mark over the **í** helps remind you of this).

Imperfect of stem-changing verbs = no change

almorzar (ue) → almorzaba
perder (ie) → perdía
pedir (i, i) → pedía

Imperfect of **hay** = **había**

• Point out that the *yo* form is identical to the *Ud./él/ella* form. Context will often make the meaning clear, but the subject pronouns are more frequently used with the imperfect forms in order to clarify meaning.
• Point out that there are no stem changes in the imperfect.
• Present and model the irregular forms of *ir, ser,* and *ver.*

• Only three verbs are irregular in the imperfect: **ir, ser,** and **ver.**

| ir | | ser | | ver | |
|---|---|---|---|---|---|
| iba | íbamos | era | éramos | veía | veíamos |
| ibas | ibais | eras | erais | veías | veíais |
| iba | iban | era | eran | veía | veían |

**Heritage Speakers**
• Algunos hispanohablantes usan la forma plural de *haber* (*habían*) en el habla popular cuando el sustantivo que la sigue es plural. Por ejemplo, es común oír *Habían muchas personas* en vez de *Había muchas personas.* Sin embargo, la forma singular *había* es la forma aceptada para expresar *there was/were.*
• En algunos dialectos rurales del español, hay hispanohablantes que dicen *traíba* o *comiba* en vez de *traía* o *comía,* que son las formas aceptadas en el uso formal.

*Paso 2 Gramática*

# PASO 2

**Suggestions**
• Emphasize that the preterite and imperfect are both equally "past" tenses. Their use depends on which aspect of a past action the user focuses on (beginning/completion aspect or the ongoing/habitual aspect of an action).

## Uses of the Imperfect

Note the following uses of the imperfect. If you have a clear sense of when and where the imperfect is used, understanding where the preterite is used will be easier. When talking about the past, the preterite *is* used when the imperfect *isn't*. That is an oversimplification of the uses of these two past tenses, but at the same time it is a general rule of thumb that will help you out at first. • *Have students give the Spanish for some expressions: I always used to stay . . . Every summer we used to go . . . , and so on. Vary the subjects in your sentences.*

The imperfect has the following uses.

• To describe *repeated habitual actions* in the past

• Emphasize the English "cues" associated with the imperfect: used to, would (habitual action), every day (month, and so on), was/were _____-ing.
• Point out: *mientras* and *mientras que* indicate simultaneous actions.

Siempre **nos quedábamos** en aquel hotel.
*We always stayed (used to stay, would stay) at that hotel.*

Todos los veranos **iban** a la costa.
*Every summer they went (used to go, would go) to the coast.*

• To describe an *action that was in progress* (*when something else happened*)

**Pedía la cena.**
*She was ordering dinner.*

• To describe two *simultaneous past actions in progress*, with **mientras**

Tú **leías mientras** Juan **escribía** la carta.
*You were reading while Juan was writing the letter.*

• To describe ongoing *physical, mental,* or *emotional states* in the past

• Point out that in the imperfect, unlike in the preterite, *saber, conocer, querer,* and *poder* retain the base meaning of their infinitives. See *Gramática 29* for more details.

**Estaban** muy distraídos.
*They were very distracted.*

La **quería** muchísimo.
*He loved her a lot.*

• To tell *time* in the past and to *express age* with **tener**

**OJO** Just as in the present, the singular form of the verb **ser** is used with one o'clock, the plural form from two o'clock on.

**Era** la una. / **Eran** las dos.
*It was one o'clock. / It was two o'clock.*

**Tenía** 18 años.
*She was 18 years old.*

• To form a *past progressive:* imperfect of **estar** + *present participle**

Note that the simple imperfect—**cenábamos, estudiabas**—could also be used in the example sentences to express the ongoing actions. The use of the progressive emphasizes that the action was actually in progress.

**Estábamos cenando** a las diez.
*We were having dinner at ten.*

¿No **estabas estudiando**?
*Weren't you studying?*

• Contrast an action in progress and the past progressive. Reenter the contrast between the simple present tense and the present progressive.
• Point out that the imperfect is used to project into the future from a specific point in the past. Contrast: *Va a ser una noche de lluvia. Sabíamos que iba a ser una noche de lluvia.*

*\*A progressive tense can also be formed with the preterite of **estar: Estuvieron cenando hasta las doce.** The use of the progressive with the preterite of **estar,** however, is relatively infrequent, and it will not be practiced in ¿Qué tal?*

**Prác. A: Extension**
Have students add two to three original
sentences about their childhood.

**Prác. A: Follow-Up**
Poll students to see which descriptions were
true for them.

## ■ Práctica

### A. ¡Anticipemos! Mi niñez (*childhood*)

PASO 1  Indique si las siguientes oraciones eran ciertas o falsas para Ud.
cuando tenía 10 años.

|   |   | C | F |
|---|---|---|---|
| **1.** | Estaba en el cuarto grado (*fourth grade*). | ☐ | ☐ |
| **2.** | Me acostaba a las nueve todas las noches. | ☐ | ☐ |
| **3.** | Los sábados me levantaba temprano para mirar los dibujos animados (*cartoons*). | ☐ | ☐ |
| **4.** | Mis padres me pagaban por los quehaceres que hacía: cortar el césped (*cutting the grass*), lavar los platos… | ☐ | ☐ |
| **5.** | Me gustaba acompañar a mi madre/padre al supermercado. | ☐ | ☐ |
| **6.** | Le pegaba (*I hit*) a mi hermano/a con frecuencia. | ☐ | ☐ |
| **7.** | Tocaba un instrumento musical en la orquesta de la escuela. | ☐ | ☐ |
| **8.** | Mis héroes eran personajes (*characters*) de los dibujos animados como Superman y Kim Possible. | ☐ | ☐ |

PASO 2  Ahora corrija las oraciones que son falsas para Ud.

MODELO:  2. Es falso. Me acostaba a las diez, no a las nueve.

### B. Cuando Tina era niña…  Describa la vida de Tina cuando tenía 6 años, haciendo oraciones según las indicaciones.

De niña, la vida de Tina era muy diferente.

1. todos los días / asistir / a / escuela primaria
2. por / mañana / aprender / a / leer / y / escribir / en / pizarra
3. a / diez / beber / leche / y / dormir / un poco
4. ir / a / casa / para / almorzar / y / regresar / a / escuela
5. estudiar / geografía / y / hacer / dibujos
6. jugar / con / compañeros / en / patio / de / escuela
7. camino de (*on the way*) casa / comprar / dulces / y / se los / comer
8. frecuentemente / pasar / por / casa / de / abuelos
9. cenar / con / padres / y / ayudar / a / lavar / platos
10. mirar / tele / un rato / y / acostarse / a / ocho

**AUTOPRUEBA**

Give the correct imperfect
ending for each verb.

1. yo habl_____
2. Uds. er_____
3. nosotros com_____
4. Pedro ib_____
5. tú ten_____

*Answers: 1. hablaba 2. eran
3. comíamos 4. iba 5. tenías*

**Prác. B: Suggestion**
Ask students:

*¿Qué cosas no hacía Ud. que Tina sí hacía?
¿Qué cosas no hacía Tina que Ud. sí hacía?*

**Prác. B: Extension**
Have students create a new paragraph,
using the same cues but this time to
describe Tina and her sister.

*La vida de Tina y su hermanita Mariana
era muy diferente de niñas. Todos los
días asistían…*

**Prác. B: Follow-Up**
Ask students the following questions.

1. *¿Cantaba/Jugaba Ud. mucho en la primaria?*
2. *De niño/a, ¿bebía mucha leche/Coca-Cola? ¿Dormía la siesta? ¿De qué hora a qué hora?*
3. *¿Veía Ud. programas interesantes en la televisión cuando era niño/a? ¿Cuáles le gustaban más?*
4. *¿A qué hora se acostaba Ud. cuando tenía 3 (7, 12) años? ¿Le gustaba acostarse tan temprano/tarde? ¿Leía Ud. a veces en la cama?*

**Prác. B: Answers**
1. *Todos los días asistía a la escuela primaria.* 2. *Por la mañana aprendía a leer y escribía en la pizarra.* 3. *A las diez bebía leche y dormía un poco.* 4. *Iba a casa para almorzar y regresaba a la escuela.* 5. *Estudiaba geografía y hacía dibujos.* 6. *Jugaba con sus compañeros en el patio de la escuela.* 7. *Camino de casa, compraba dulces y se los comía.* 8. *Frecuentemente pasaba por la casa de los abuelos.* 9. *Cenaba con sus padres y los ayudaba a lavar los platos.* 10. *Miraba la tele un rato y se acostaba a las ocho.*

# PASO 2

**CAPÍTULO**

**9**

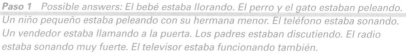

### Palabras útiles

**el timbre** (doorbell)

**discutir** (to argue)
**ladrar** (to bark)
**pelear** (to fight)
**sonar (ue)*** (to ring; to sound)

Resources: Transparency 69

## C. El trabajo de niñera (*baby-sitter*)

PASO 1   El trabajo de niñera puede ser muy pesado (*difficult*), pero cuando los niños son traviesos (*mischievous*), también puede ser peligroso (*dangerous*). ¿Qué estaba pasando cuando la niñera perdió por fin la paciencia? Describa todas las acciones que pueda, usando **estaba(n) + -ndo.**

MODELO:   Cuando la niñera perdió la paciencia… →
el bebé estaba llorando.

Cuando la niñera perdió la paciencia…

PASO 2   De joven (*As a youth*), ¿trabajaba Ud. de niñero/a? ¿Tuvo alguna vez una mala experiencia? Complete la siguiente oración, si puede, usando un verbo en el pretérito.

MODELO:   Una vez, cuando yo estaba (leyendo, mirando la tele, hablando con un amigo / una amiga… ), el niño / la niña…

### Need more practice?

- Workbook/Laboratory Manual
- Interactive CD-ROM
- Online Learning Center (www.mhhe.com/quetal7)

## ■ Conversación

**Entrevista. ¡Qué cambio!**   Hágale las siguientes preguntas a un compañero / una compañera de clase. Él/Ella va a pensar en las costumbres que tenía a los 14 años, es decir, cuando estaba en el noveno (*ninth*) o décimo (*tenth*) grado.

1. ¿Qué te gustaba comer? ¿Y ahora?
2. ¿Qué programa de televisión no te perdías nunca? ¿Y ahora?
3. ¿Qué te gustaba leer? ¿Y ahora?
4. ¿Qué hacías los sábados por la noche? ¿Y ahora?
5. ¿Qué deportes te gustaba practicar? ¿Y ahora?
6. ¿Con quién discutías mucho? ¿Y ahora?
7. ¿A quién te gustaba molestar (*to annoy*)? ¿Y ahora?

---

*Although **sonar** is a stem-changing verb (**o → ue**), remember that the stem of present participles does not change with **-ar** verbs (**sonando**).*

**Multimedia: Internet**
Have students search the Internet for information on Hispanic musicians. Encourage them to look for music clips, as well as official websites for the artist or for his or her fan club.

## ¿Recuerda Ud.?

Before beginning **Gramática 27,** review comparisons, which were introduced in **Capítulo 5.** How would you say the following in Spanish?

1. I work as much as you do.
2. I work more/less than you do.
3. Bill Gates has more money than I have.

4. My housemate has fewer things than I do.
5. I have as many friends as you do.
6. My computer is worse/better than this one.

## 27 Expressing Extremes · Superlatives

**Follow-Up**
After reviewing *¡El número uno!,* have students give superlatives in other categories: *la comida, los quehaceres domésticos, las marcas* (give examples of brand names) *de ropa, las tiendas.*

### ¡El número uno!

*Jennifer López*

*Enrique Iglesias*

*Ricky Martin*

♻ **Reciclado**
Review the comparative forms and structures before presenting the superlatives.

*¿Cómo se dice?*

1. taller than John
2. bigger than an apple
3. better than Susie
4. easier than Spanish
5. older than my grandmother

¿Está Ud. de acuerdo con las opiniones expresadas en estas oraciones?

1. Jennifer López es *la* mujer *más bella* (*beautiful*) *del* mundo.
2. Enrique Iglesias es *el mejor* cantante (*singer*) *de* su familia.
3. Ricky Martin es *el* puertorriqueño *más conocido* (*well-known*) *de* hoy.

### ¿Y Ud.?

Ahora le toca a Ud. formular su propia (*own*) opinión.

1. El/La cantante hispánico/a más popular del momento es _____.
2. La mejor actriz del momento es _____.
3. La música popular más interesante es _____.

**Suggestions**
• Emphasize the importance of the definite article. Remind students to use *de,* not *en* (for the English *in*).
• Ask students the following questions.

*¿Es Jennifer López más bonita que Britney Spears?*
*¿Es Enrique Iglesias más guapo que Ricky Martin?*
*¿Es Ricky Martin más joven que Jennifer López?*

The *superlative* (**el superlativo**) is formed in English by adding *-est* to adjectives or by using expressions such as *the most* and *the least* with the adjective. In Spanish, this concept is expressed in the same way as the comparative but is always accompanied by the definite article. In this construction **mejor** and **peor** tend to precede the noun; other adjectives follow. *In* or *at* is expressed with **de.**

 **OJO** The superlative forms **-ísimo/a/os/as** cannot be used with this type of superlative construction.

el/la/los/las + *noun* + **más/menos** + *adjective* + **de**

El basquetbol es **el deporte más interesante del** mundo.
*Basketball is the most interesting sport in the world.*

el/la/los/las + **mejor(es)/peor(es)** + *noun* + **de**

Son **los mejores** refrigeradores **de** aquella tienda.
*They are the best refrigerators at that store.*

> **superlative** = adjective or adverb phrase used to compare three or more nouns or actions

# PASO 2

**Prác. A: Bright Idea Suggestion**
Have students guess the meaning of *poliomielitis*. Can they also guess the meaning of the following words?

CAPÍTULO
9

hepatitis          meningitis
bronquitis         laringitis
amigdalitis (tonsillitis)

## ■ Práctica

### AUTOPRUEBA

Unscramble the words to express a superlative idea.

1. Es... ciudad más el grande la parque de
2. Son... clase los difíciles de niños la más
3. Visité... del los mundo museos mejores
4. Vi... peor año película la del

*Answers: 1. Es el parque más grande de la ciudad. 2. Son los niños más difíciles de la clase. 3. Visité los mejores museos del mundo. 4. Vi la peor película del año.*

**A. ¡Anticipemos! ¿Está Ud. de acuerdo o no?**

PASO 1  Indique si Ud. está de acuerdo o no con las siguientes oraciones.

|  | SÍ | NO |
|---|---|---|
| 1. El descubrimiento (*discovery*) científico más importante del siglo XX fue la vacuna (*vaccine*) contra la poliomielitis. | ☐ | ☐ |
| 2. La persona más influyente (*influential*) del mundo es el presidente de los Estados Unidos. | ☐ | ☐ |
| 3. El problema más serio del mundo es la deforestación de la región del Amazonas. | ☐ | ☐ |
| 4. El día festivo más divertido del año es la Noche Vieja. | ☐ | ☐ |
| 5. La mejor novela del mundo es *Don Quijote de la Mancha.* | ☐ | ☐ |
| 6. El animal menos inteligente de todos es el avestruz (*ostrich*). | ☐ | ☐ |
| 7. El peor mes del año es enero. | ☐ | ☐ |
| 8. La ciudad más contaminada de los Estados Unidos es Los Ángeles. | ☐ | ☐ |

PASO 2  Para cada oración que no refleja su opinión, invente otra oración.

MODELO:   4. No estoy de acuerdo. Creo que el día festivo más divertido del año es el Cuatro de Julio.

**B. Superlativos.**   Expand the information in these sentences based on the model. Then, if you can, restate each sentence with true information at the beginning.

MODELO:   Es una estudiante muy *trabajadora*. (la clase) →
Es *la* estudiante *más trabajadora de la clase.* →
*Carlota* es la estudiante más trabajadora de la clase.

1. Es un día festivo muy *divertido*. (el año)
2. Es una clase muy *interesante*. (todas mis clases)
3. Es una persona muy *inteligente*. (todos mis amigos)
4. Es una ciudad muy *grande*. (los Estados Unidos / el Canadá)
5. Es un estado muy *pequeño* / una provincia muy *pequeña*. (los Estados Unidos / el Canadá)
6. Es un metro muy *rápido*. (el mundo)
7. Es una residencia muy *ruidosa* (*noisy*). (la universidad)
8. Es una montaña muy *alta*. (el mundo)

**Prác. B: Extension**
9. *El Presidente Reagan fue un presidente viejo.*
10. *El Presidente Kennedy fue un presidente joven.*
11. *Rip Van Winkle fue un hombre perezoso.*
12. *El chihuahua es un perro pequeño.*

**Prác. B: Suggestion**
Have students imagine that Rodolfo, a big exaggerator, visits their house during the Christmas holidays. Have them invent things he might say.

*¿Qué va a decir Rodolfo sobre los siguientes aspectos del día de Navidad en su casa?*

1. *¿su árbol de Navidad? (grande, elegante)*
2. *¿los platos? (ricos, muchos)*
3. *¿sus hermanitos? (felices)*
4. *¿los regalos? (caros, bonitos, muchos)*

**Prác. B: Answers**
1. _____ *es el día festivo más divertido del año.* 2. _____ *es la clase más interesante de todas mis clases.* 3. _____ *es la persona más inteligente de todos mis amigos.* 4. *Nueva York es la ciudad más grande de los Estados Unidos./Toronto es la ciudad más grande del Canadá.* 5. *Rhode Island es el estado más pequeño de los Estados Unidos. / Prince Edward Island es la provincia más pequeña del Canadá.* 6. *El metro de Guangzhou (China) es el metro más rápido del mundo.* 7. _____ *es la residencia más ruidosa de la universidad.* 8. *Everest es la montaña más alta del mundo.*

## Need more practice?

- Workbook/Laboratory Manual
- Interactive CD-ROM
- Online Learning Center (www.mhhe.com/quetal7)

Con: Note

This activity integrates the superlative and absolute superlative forms.

## ■ Conversación

**Entrevista.** With another student, ask and answer questions based on the following phrases. Then report your opinions to the class. Report any disagreements as well.

MODELO: E1: Shakira es la mujer más guapa del mundo.
E2: Estoy de acuerdo / No estoy de acuerdo. Para mí Salma Hayek es la más guapa.

1. la persona más guapa del mundo
2. la noticia más seria de esta semana
3. un libro interesantísimo y otro pesadísimo (*very boring*)
4. el mejor restaurante de la ciudad y el peor
5. el cuarto más importante de la casa y el menos importante
6. un plato riquísimo y otro malísimo
7. un programa de televisión interesantísimo y otro pesadísimo
8. un lugar tranquilísimo, otro animadísimo y otro peligrosísimo (*very dangerous*)
9. la canción (*song*) más bonita del año y la más fea
10. la mejor película/canción del año y la peor

Con: Follow-Up

Have students work in small groups to describe the following, using superlatives.

1. Alaska
2. Rhode Island

3. John F. Kennedy
4. *el monte Everest*
5. *el río Amazonas*
6. *esta universidad*
7. *la comida de la residencia / cafetería estudiantil*

Suggest additional items about people, places, and things on your campus that students like to discuss.

En los Estados Unidos y el Canadá: Comprensión

1. *¿Qué significa la palabra* peletero*?*
2. *¿Qué porcentaje de los jugadores de la Liga Mayor de Béisbol es hispano o de origen hispano?*
3. *¿Qué países hispanohablantes tienen sus propias ligas? ¿Cree Ud. que esto tiene algún impacto en las ligas profesionales de este país? Explique.*

## En los Estados Unidos y el Canadá

### Peloteros hispanos

Si a Ud. le gusta el béisbol, seguro que conoce los nombres de muchos **beisbolistas, o peloteros, de origen hispano.** Sólo tiene que mirar las listas de los jugadores de los Yanquis de Nueva York, los Azulejos[a] de Toronto, los Expos de Montreal, los Medias Rojas de Boston o los Rancheros de Texas, sólo por nombrar algunos de los equipos[b] más famosos, para ver cuántos nombres hispanos hay. El 30 por ciento de todos los jugadores de la Liga Mayor de Béisbol (LMB) y el 50 por ciento de los jugadores de las ligas menores son hispanos o de origen hispano.

Varios países hispanos tienen sus **propias**[c] **ligas de béisbol** y «exportan» a jugadores de béisbol a los Estados Unidos y al Canadá. Esos países hispanos son principalmente los **países caribeños:** Puerto Rico, la República Dominicana, Cuba y Venezuela, además de[d] México. Por ejemplo, al principio[e] del año 2004, setenta y tres peloteros de los treinta equipos principales **habían nacido** en[f] la República Dominicana.

¿Cuántos beisbolistas reconoce Ud. de esta lista? ¿Puede añadir otros nombres?

**Estadounidenses de nacimiento:** Alex Rodríguez (A-Rod) y Nomar Garcíaparra

**Dominicanos:** Sammy Sosa, Alfonso Soriano, Tony Batista y Vladimir Guerrero

*Alex Rodríguez (A-Rod) durante un partido contra los Azulejos de Toronto*

**Cubanos:** Rafael Palmeiro y José Canseco

**Mexicanos:** Erubiel Durazo y Juan Castro

**Puertorriqueños:** Jorge Posada y Carlos Delgado

**Panameño:** Mariano Rivera

[a]*Blue Jays* [b]*teams* [c]*own* [d]*además... in addition to* [e]*al... at the beginning* [f]*habían... were from*

# Voces de Colombia

## LITERATURA: Gabriel García Márquez

**Literatura: Notes**
• García Márquez was raised by his grand-parents and a series of aunts. His grand-mother would narrate stories to him when he was young. She didn't dis-tinguish between the stories that were true and those that were not only not true but fantastical and magical.

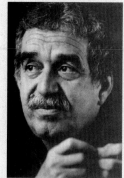

**Gabriel García Márquez**
**(1928– )**

**Sobre el autor:** *Gabriel José García Márquez nació en Aracataca, en el norte de Colombia. Empezó su vida profesional como periodista. Vivió casi toda su vida de adulto fuera de Colombia, en Europa y México. Recibió el Premio Nóbel de Literatura en 1982 por su novela* Cien años de soledad. *Sus novelas y cuentos combinan lo fantástico y lo real, un estilo que se llama el realismo mágico. El siguiente fragmento es de* Cien años de soledad *(1967).*

Muchos años después, frente al pelotón de fusilamiento,[a] el coronel Aureliano Buendía había de[b] recordar aquella tarde remota en que su padre lo llevó a conocer el hielo.[c] Macondo era entonces una aldea[d] de veinte casas de barro[e] y cañabrava[f] construidas a la orilla[g] de un río de aguas diáfanas que se precipitaban por un lecho[h] de piedras pulidas,[i] blancas y enormes como huevos prehistóricos.

[a]*pelotón… firing squad* [b]*había… would* [c]*ice* [d]*village* [e]*mud* [f]*cane* [g]*bank* [h]*bed* [i]*piedras… polished rocks*
• Ask students who have read short stories or novels by García Márquez to talk to the class about them, perhaps describing incidents of magical realism.
• A number of films have been made of García Márquez's short stories and novels, most recently of *El coronel no tiene quien le escriba*. This last film, directed by the Mexican director Arturo Ripstein, won the Latin American Cinema Award at the Sundance Film Festival 2000 as well as other prizes. You may wish to show this film to the class.

## MÚSICA: El vallenato

• Have students research the history of magical real-ism from its beginnings in the works of Alejo Carpentier in Cuba to the present.

**Música: Notes**
• Originally, *el vallenato* was the music of the agrarian communities in northern Colombia.

el acordeón

la caja

la guacharaca

El vallenato, de raíces[a] africanas, nació hace unos cien años[b] en Valledupar, un pueblo en el norte de Colombia. Tiene cuatro ritmos básicos: el son (el ritmo más lento), el paseo (el ritmo intermedio), el merengue (un ritmo más alegre y acelerado) y la puya (el ritmo más rápido de los cuatro). La letra[c] de esta música generalmente trata[d] el amor[e] por una mujer o por la tierra[f] y sus costumbres.[g]

El vallenato se toca con tres instrumentos básicos: el acordeón, la caja[h] y la guacharaca,[i] pero estos pueden ir acompañados[j] de otros instrumentos.

[h]*type of drum* [i]*wooden percussion stick* [j]*ir… be accompanied*

[a]*roots* [b]*nació… was born about one hundred years ago* [c]*lyrics* [d]*deal with* [e]*love* [f]*land* [g]*customs*

• The rhythmic pattern of *el vallenato*, called *el son*, should not be confused with the Cuban *son*.
• The *guacharaca* is a rasping instrument, traditionally made from a cane (called *cañabrava*), which is given successive notches. The sound is produced by scraping a percussion stick along the notches.

Carlos Vives es el «embajador universal» del vallenato y es muy popular dentro y fuera de[k] Colombia. En 1993, causó gran sensación[l] con su música, que toma mucho de la tradición del vallenato. El estilo de Vives combina el vallenato con ritmos pop, rock, cumbia[m] y son.

[k]*dentro… in and outside of* [l]*causó… he made a big splash* [m]*another popular, traditional Colombian music style*

• The word *guacharaca* is an indigenous word, claimed by more than one group. There is also a plant and a bird called *guacharaca*.
• Students can look up Carlos Vives's homepage, where they can listen to audio clips of some of his songs.

**Paso 3: Gramática**
See the "Chapter-by-Chapter Supplementary Materials" in the IM for additional
teaching suggestions, notes, activities, and other resources for *Paso 3*.

## 28 Getting Information **Summary of Interrogative Words**

Este es un anuncio de un restaurante de Connecticut.

1. ¿*Cómo* se llama el restaurante?   El Pavo real
2. ¿En *qué* ciudad de Connecticut está?   New Haven
3. ¿*Cuáles* son las especialidades de este restaurante?   los mariscos

¿Y Ud.?

¿Cuántas preguntas más puede Ud. hacer sobre este restaurante, basándose en el anuncio?

**Follow-Up**
After reviewing the ad, have students work in pairs to make plans to go to the restaurant. Only one student is allowed to look at the printed information. The other student should ask questions to get information.

**El Pavo real**
RESTAURANTE • CLUB DE BAILE

**32 Garvey St., New Haven, CT**

El lugar más amplio y más lujoso de CT.

**Comida Colombiana con Especialidad en Mariscos**

*Venga y deléitese con nuestros sabrosos platos*
ABIERTO TODOS LOS DÍAS DESDE LAS 11:30 A.M. - 2:00 A.M

**VIERNES, 6 DE OCTUBRE**
• PRESENTANDO LA SENSACIÓN DEL MERENGUE •   CANTANDO
**ORQUESTA MALA FE**   TODOS SUS ÉXITOS

♻ **Reciclado**
Remind students that *ser en + place* is used to express *to take place at* (*place*). Model the expression in some communicative exchanges with a student: *¿Dónde es su primera clase los lunes? ¿Dónde es el partido de fútbol?*

| | | | |
|---|---|---|---|
| **¿Cómo?** | How? | **¿Dónde?** | Where? |
| **¿Cuándo?** | When? | **¿De dónde?** | From where? |
| **¿A qué hora?** | At what time? | **¿Adónde?** | Where (to)? |
| **¿Qué?** | What? Which? | **¿Cuánto/a?** | How much? |
| **¿Cuál(es)?** | What? Which one(s)? | **¿Cuántos/as?** | How many? |
| **¿Por qué?** | Why? | **¿Quién(es)?** | Who? |
| | | **¿De quién(es)?** | Whose? |

**Note**
Students have actively used all of the interrogatives in this section. Treat this section as a summary, using it to emphasize variations of the interrogative forms, for example, *¿dónde?* vs. *¿de dónde?* vs. *¿adónde?*

**Refrán**

«Quien de refranes no sabe, ¿qué es lo que sabe?»

Read this *refrán* to the students. Have them identify the question word in the sentence. Point out that *quien* in this case is not a question word but a relative pronoun; *qué* is the only question word. Have students explain the meaning of this saying.

You have been using interrogative words to ask questions and get information since the beginning of *¿Qué tal?* The chart shows all of the interrogatives you have learned so far. Be sure that you know what they mean and how they are used. If you are not certain, the index and end-of-book vocabularies will help you find where they are first introduced. Only the specific uses of **¿qué?** and **¿cuál?** represent new information.

## Using ¿qué? and ¿cuál?

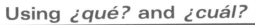

• **¿Qué?** asks for a definition or an explanation.

**¿Qué** es esto?
*What is this?*

**¿Qué** quieres?
*What do you want?*

**¿Qué** tocas?
*What (instrument) do you play?*

**Suggestions**
• Point out the plural forms of *¿cuál?* and *¿quién?* Point out the difference in meaning in English between *¿cuánto/a?* and *¿cuántos/as?*
• Point out that *¿Cómo?* is used to request repetition or clarification in communicative exchanges.

**Bright Idea Suggestion**
Point out the difference between *¿qué?* and *¿cuál?* by using contrastive sentences.

*¿Qué es su hermano? (Es profesor.)*
*¿Cuál es su hermano? (Es el muchacho que lleva la camisa roja.)*

• **¿Qué?** can be directly followed by a noun.

**¿Qué traje** necesitas?
*What (Which) suit do you need?*

**¿Qué playa** te gusta más?
*What (Which) beach do you like most?*

**¿Qué instrumento** musical tocas?
*What (Which) musical instrument do you play?*

• **¿Cuál(es)?** expresses *what?* or *which?* in all other cases.

 The **¿cuál(es)?** + *noun* structure is not used by most speakers of Spanish: *¿Cuál de los dos libros quieres?* (Which of the two books do you want?) BUT *¿Qué libro quieres?* (Which [What] book do you want?)

**¿Cuál** es la clase más grande?
*What (Which) is the biggest class?*

**¿Cuáles** son tus actrices favoritas?
*What (Which) are your favorite actresses?*

**¿Cuál** es la capital del Uruguay?
*What is the capital of Uruguay?*

**¿Cuál** es tu teléfono?
*What is your phone number?*

**Note**
In Latin America, *¿cuál?* and *¿cuáles?* may be used as adjectives, for example, *¿Cuál libro quieres?* In Spain, they are used only as pronouns.

**Need more practice?**

■ Workbook/Laboratory Manual
■ Interactive CD-ROM
■ Online Learning Center (www.mhhe.com/quetal7)

## ■ Práctica

**¿Qué o cuál(es)?**

1. ¿ _Qué_ es esto? —Un lavaplatos.
2. ¿ _Qué_ son los Juegos Olímpicos? —Son un conjunto (*group*) de competiciones deportivas.
3. ¿ _Cuál_ es el quehacer que más te gusta? —Lavar los platos.
4. ¿ _Qué_ bicicleta vas a usar? —La de mi hermana.
5. ¿ _Cuáles_ son los cines más modernos? —Los del centro.
6. ¿ _Qué_ vídeo debo sacar? —El nuevo de Salma Hayek.
7. ¿ _Qué_ es una cafetera? —Es un aparato que se usa para preparar el café.
8. ¿ _Cuál_ es tu padre? —En la foto, es el hombre a la izquierda del coche.

## ■ Conversación

**Entrevista: Datos** (*Information*) **personales.** Primero, forme preguntas para averiguar datos (*find out facts*) de un compañero / una compañera de clase. Se puede usar más de una palabra interrogativa para conseguir la información. (Debe usar las formas de **tú**.) Luego, entreviste a su compañero/a usando las preguntas.

MODELO: su dirección (*address*) → ¿Cuál es tu dirección? (¿Dónde vives?)

1. su teléfono
2. su dirección
3. su cumpleaños
4. la ciudad en que nació (*he/she was born*)
5. su número de seguro (*security*) social
6. la persona en que más confía (*he/she trusts*)
7. su tienda favorita
8. la fecha de su próximo examen

CAPÍTULO

9
Resources: Transparency 70
This transparency provides practice using the preterite and
the imperfect without requiring students to discriminate
between the two. It also provides practice with sequencing
events. The transparency can be used for review before
presenting *Gramática 29*.

PASO 3

○ **Bright Idea Suggestion**
Review the verb endings for the preterite. Have students provide conjugations chorally of the following verbs.

bañarse     comer
acostarse    dormir
salir

## UN POCO DE TODO

**Lengua y cultura: Diversiones familiares en Colombia.** Complete the following passages with the correct forms of the words in parentheses, as suggested by the context. When two possibilities are given in parentheses, select the correct word. **¡OJO!** As you conjugate verbs in this activity, put the infinitives preceded by *I* in the imperfect.

**M**ayra y Joaquín son dos colombianos que llegaron recientemente a los Estados Unidos. Los dos (ser / estar[1]) de Cartagena, una gran ciudad colombiana y puerto[a] que (ser / estar[2]) en el mar Caribe. De niña, Mayra (*I:* vivir[3]) en la parte más antigua de la ciudad, el Centro Amurallado[b] colonial. En cambio,[c] la familia de Joaquín (*I:* tener[4]) un apartamento en Bocagrande, el sector más moderno de Cartagena. La manera de (divertirse[5]) cada uno[d] en su país los fines de semana era diferente.

En Cartagena, Mayra y su familia (*I:* ir[6]) con mucha frecuencia a la playa de La Boquilla* los fines de semana y (*I:* pasar[7]) todo el día (*pres. part.:* nadar[8]). Por la noche iban a un restaurante a (comer[9]) mariscos y a (*I:* bailar[10]) la cumbia. Por su parte, a Joaquín (se / le[11]) (*I:* gustar[12]) pasear por las fortalezas y las viejas y enormes murallas[e] de la ciudad. ¿(Saber / Conocer[13]) Uds. que (alguno[14]) de (ese[15]) murallas miden veinte metros de ancho[f] por veinte metros de alto? ¡(Ser / Estar[16]) realmente impresionantes!

Joaquín y Mayra (ser / estar[17]) de acuerdo en que, al visitar[g] Cartagena, es necesario ir también al centro comercial Las Bóvedas[†] y a la isla Barú.[‡] Allí, en las aguas del Parque Natural Corales del Rosario, (son / hay[18]) unos bancos de coral[h] muy bonitos. ¡Qué chévere![i]

*Las Bóvedas en Cartagena, Colombia*

[a]port  [b]*Centro… Walled Center*  [c]*En… On the other hand*  [d]*cada… each of them*  [e]*walls*  [f]*de… wide*  [g]*al… when one visits*  [h]*bancos… coral reefs*  [i]*¡Qué… How cool!*

**Comprensión: Ahora y entonces.** Conteste las preguntas en español.

1. ¿De qué ciudad son Mayra y Joaquín? ¿De qué partes de esa ciudad son?
2. ¿Qué sabe Ud. de la vida de ellos?
3. ¿Cómo pasaba Mayra los fines de semana en Cartagena?
4. Y Joaquín, ¿qué hacía él los fines de semana?

**Lengua y cultura: Answers**
1. *son* 2. *está* 3. *vivía* 4. *tenía* 5. *divertirse* 6. *iban* 7. *pasaban* 8. *nadando* 9. *comer* 10. *bailar* 11. *le* 12. *gustaba* 13. *Saben* 14. *algunas* 15. *esas* 16. *Son* 17. *están* 18. *hay* **Comprensión** *Possible answers:* 1. *Son de Cartagena. Mayra es del Centro Amurallado y Joaquín es de Bocagrande.* 2. *Son dos colombianos que llegaron recientemente a los Estados Unidos.* 3. *Iba con su familia a la playa y a un restaurante a comer mariscos.* 4. *Iba a las fortalezas y murallas.*

○ **Reciclado**
Review verbs with spelling changes in the preterite. Have students indicate where these changes occur in the verb paradigm (*yo* forms).

| INFINITIVE | CHANGE | FORMS |
|---|---|---|
| -car | c → qu | yo busqué, toqué |
| -gar | g → gu | yo llegué, pagué |
| -zar | z → c | yo almorcé, empecé |

**Resources: Desenlace**
In the *Capítulo 9* segment of "Chapter-by-Chapter Supplementary Materials" in the IM, you will find a chapter-culminating activity. You can use this activity to consolidate and review the vocabulary and grammar skills students have acquired.

**Resources for Review and Testing Preparation**

- Workbook/Laboratory Manual
- Interactive CD-ROM
- Online Learning Center (www.mhhe.com/quetal7)

*La Boquilla, a fishing village outside Cartagena, has a long secluded beach with restaurants and bars.*

[†]*Las Bóvedas (The Vaults) were barracks and storerooms built by the Spanish into the outer walls of the old city. Twenty-two of the dungeonlike rooms have been turned into small, upscale shops.*

[‡]*Barú Island, approximately ten minutes by motorboat from Cartagena, offers white sand beaches, crystal clear water, and big coral reefs.*

**VIDEOTECA**

## Entrevista cultural: Colombia

Mauricio Tautiba es un colombiano apasionado de los deportes. Él habla en la entrevista de su equipo y de sus esperanzas para el futuro. Antes de ver el vídeo, lea el siguiente fragmento de la entrevista.

ENTREVISTADORA: Me dicen que juegas fútbol.* ¿Es cierto?
MAURICIO: Sí, juego fútbol, eh, inclusive juego en una liga todos los fines de semana.
ENTREVISTADORA: Y ¿es bueno tu equipo?
MAURICIO: Sí, muy bueno. La temporada[a] pasada ganamos casi todos los partidos, pero desafortunadamente no fuimos campeones.

[a]*season*

Ahora vea el vídeo y conteste las siguientes preguntas basándose en la entrevista.

1. ¿A qué deporte se dedica Mauricio?
2. ¿Con qué frecuencia lo practica y juega?
3. ¿Qué otros deportes practica?
4. ¿Juega bien o mal el equipo de Mauricio?
5. ¿Qué espera hacer Mauricio en el futuro?

## Entre amigos: ¿Sabes bailar salsa?

Rubén, Karina, Miguel y Tané hacen planes para el fin de semana. Quieren ir a un club que se llama Mamá Rumba. En su opinión, ¿de qué van a hablar? Antes de mirar el vídeo, lea las preguntas a continuación. Mientras mire el vídeo, trate de entender la conversación en general y fíjese en la información sobre los planes de los amigos para el fin de semana. Luego mire el vídeo una segunda vez, fijándose en la información que necesita para contestar las preguntas.

1. Según Karina, ¿qué tipo de lugar es Mama Rumba?
2. ¿Le gusta a Miguel ir a Mama Rumba? ¿Por qué?
3. ¿Sabe bailar salsa Rubén?
4. ¿Por qué no debe preocuparse (*worry*) Rubén?
5. ¿Qué van a hacer los amigos el domingo?

*Some Spanish speakers omit the **al** after **jugar** when talking about playing sports:* **jugar fútbol** *vs.* **jugar al fútbol.**

## Colombia

## ¡Fíjese!

• Colombia obtuvo su independencia de España en 1819, bajo la dirección de Simón Bolívar. Bolívar fue declarado el primer presidente de la independiente República de la Gran Colombia.

• Colombia produce más oro que cualquier[a] otro país sudamericano y tiene los yacimientos[b] de platino[c] más grandes del mundo. Las esmeraldas también son un producto minero importante.

• Aunque el café es reconocido[d] como el producto agrícola principal de exportación de Colombia, en los años noventa lo sobrepasó[e] el petróleo como primer producto de exportación.

• Aproximadamente un 14 por ciento de la población colombiana es de origen africano.

• Las misteriosas estatuas de piedra de San Agustín fueron creadas por una cultura indígena de la cual[f] se sabe muy poco. Se cree que las estatuas son del siglo VI (sexto) antes de Cristo. Una de las estatuas representa un pájaro con una serpiente en el pico,[g] imagen muy similar a la de una leyenda azteca.

[a]*any* [b]*deposits* [c]*platinum* [d]*recognized* [e]*surpassed* [f]*de… of which* [g]*beak*

## Personas famosas: Juanes

Juanes es un fenómeno colombiano en el mundo de la música. Nacido[a] en Medellín, Colombia, Juanes fundó el grupo Ekhymosis a los 14 años. El grupo se desintegró después de doce años y Juanes empezó su carrera como solista con el álbum *Fíjate bien*.[b] En los últimos años, Juanes ha ganado[c] varios premios[d] latinoamericanos e internacionales, entre ellos nueve Grammy Latinos, cinco Premios MTV y seis Premios Lo Nuestro. En 2002 tenía siete nominaciones en los Grammy Latino y salió de las ceremonias en Los Ángeles con tres Grammys: Mejor Canción Rock, Mejor Nuevo Artista y Mejor Solista Vocal para Álbum en Rock. En su gira[e] por Colombia en la primavera de 2003, dedicó su concierto en Bogotá a las víctimas de la violencia y a los que tratan de proteger[f] los derechos[g] y la vida de los colombianos.

[a]*Born* [b]*Fíjate… Pay close attention* [c]*ha… has won* [d]*prizes* [e]*tour* [f]*tratan… try to protect* [g]*rights*

*Estatuas de piedra, de San Agustín*

Learn more about Colombia with the Video, the Interactive CD-ROM, and the Online Learning Center (www.mhhe.com/quetal7).

# PASO 4

**Sobre la lectura...** Este artículo apareció en la revista *Quo*, una publicación española que trata temas populares, como la tecnología, la salud, la vida cotidiana (*daily*) y las relaciones entre los sexos. La lectura relata un fenómeno cultural reciente en España, el creciente (*growing*) número de empresas (*businesses*) de servicios «veinticuatro horas».

**Suggestions**
- Do the *Estrategia* as an in-class activity the day before you cover the reading.
- Work with students to decode underlined words, and have students write sentences using them.

## PASO FINAL

 **A LEER**

**ESTRATEGIA: Recognizing Derivative Adjectives**

In previous chapters of *¿Qué tal?*, you learned to recognize cognates, word endings, and new words that are related to familiar words. In this chapter, you will learn about derivative adjectives, a large group of adjectives derived from verbs. These adjectives end in **-ado/a** or **-ido/a.** You can often guess their meaning if you know the related verb. For example: **conocer** (*to know*) → **conocido** (*known, famous*); **preparar** (*to prepare*) → **preparado** (*prepared*).

In the following reading there are several **-do** adjectives. Try to guess their meaning based on the related verb and the context.

## *Noctámbulos*

Las ciudades españolas se están adaptando con rapidez a la llamada «sociedad de las veinticuatro horas». Cualquier[a] necesidad puede ser cubierta[b] a cualquiera hora. Esto es algo que en países como Estados Unidos, Holanda o Canadá hace tiempo que es[c] una realidad, pero en España es ahora cuando se está produciendo el *boom* de las empresas de servicios veinticuatro horas. Es lo que llamamos la «sociedad de las veinticuatro horas». Ya no sólo basta con[d] poder comer de madrugada,[e] bien sea en un restaurante o pidiendo que nos lleven la comida a casa. Por eso la oferta se está ampliando notablemente. En los «*work center*» se puede realizar todo tipo de trabajos a cualquier hora, desde una simple fotocopia a una presentación completa en «PowerPoint».

[a]*Any* [b]*covered, taken care of* [c]*hace... for some time has been* [d]*Ya... It's no longer enough* [e]*de... late at night*

*Un gimnasio que está abierto las veinticuatro horas, en Barcelona, España*

*Una cerrajería* (locksmith) *que ayuda a sus clientes a cualquier hora del día, en Madrid, España*

Pero no son los únicos servicios que podemos encontrar de noche. Ya hay gimnasios <u>abiertos</u> hasta la madrugada y videoclubes nocturnos que incluyen cajeros expendedores[f] de películas que funcionan las veinticuatro horas. Pero, por supuesto, también podemos <u>hacer la compra</u> de madrugada en un supermercado. De hecho,[g] en una encuesta[h] realizada en Reino Unido[i] más de un millón de personas declaró que sólo podía hacer la compra a partir de[j] las diez de la noche. En plena era de las comunicaciones[k] no podíamos dejar de mencionar los cibercafés, que en algunos casos abren hasta bien entrada la madrugada.[l]

En total, entre un 10 y un 20 por ciento de la población activa, en función de los distintos sectores de producción, realiza toda o parte de su jornada laboral[m] por la noche. En España, son casi 2 millones de personas las que trabajan de noche, sin olvidarnos de quienes optan por el ocio:[n] el 63 por ciento de los jóvenes dedican su tiempo libre a salir de noche, porcentaje que se va reduciendo con la edad.

[f]cajeros... *dispensing machines*  [g]De... *In fact*  [h]*survey*  [i]Reino... *United Kingdom*  [j]a... *después de*  [k]En... *At the height of the communications age*  [l]hasta... *well into the early morning*  [m]jornada... *work day*  [n]*leisure*

## Comprensión

**A. ¿Cierto o falso?**   Prepárese para explicar sus respuestas.

1. La sociedad española está cambiando para aceptar un horario mucho más flexible y adaptable.
2. La variedad de empresas que abren las veinticuatro horas en España está limitada.
3. También hay servicios para los que salen a divertirse hasta bien entrada la madrugada.

**B. Palabras relacionadas**

PASO 1   ¿De qué verbos se derivan los siguientes adjetivos del artículo?

1. llamada _____ llamar _____
2. realizada _____ realizar _____
3. entrada _____ entrar _____

PASO 2   Hay dos formas derivadas irregulares en la lectura. ¿Puede identificar los verbos de que se derivan estas palabras?

1. cubierta _____ cubrir _____
2. abriertos _____ abrir _____

 **A ESCRIBIR**

**A. ¿Y Ud.?**   ¿Qué servicios de las veinticuatro horas necesita o usa Ud.? ¿Cuáles son algunos de los servicios disponibles (*available*) para los estudiantes de esta universidad? ¿Tiene su comunidad muchos servicios abiertos las veinticuatro horas o hasta muy tarde? Describa brevemente los servicios de su universidad y/o comunidad y explique cuáles usa Ud. y por qué.

**B. La sociedad de las 24 horas.**   La llamada «sociedad de las veinticuatro horas» es bastante común en este país. Esto se ve en los horarios de muchos restaurantes, gimnasios, tiendas, talleres y otras empresas. De hecho, hay una cadena (*chain*) de clubes de salud que se llama *24 Hour Fitness.* ¿Cree Ud. que este cambio social es bueno o malo? ¿Por qué? Escriba una breve composición de 150 palabras que presente las ventajas (*advantages*) y desventajas de este fenómeno. Dé ejemplos específicos.

**Suggestions**
- Bring or have students bring clippings that illustrate items and activities from the *Vocabulario*. Use these to review (have students describe, play word games, and so on).
- Have students name activities they associate with the following places. *¿Qué se hace en… ?*

1. *el estadio*
2. *el campo* (new word)
3. *el gimnasio*
4. *la piscina*
5. *el cine*
6. *el teatro*

## GRAMÁTICA

To review the grammar points presented in this chapter, refer to the indicated grammar presentations. You'll find further practice of these structures in the Workbook/Laboratory Manual, on the Interactive CD-ROM, and on the *¿Qué tal?* Online Learning Center (www.mhhe.com/quetal7).

**26** Descriptions and Habitual Actions in the Past—Imperfect of Regular and Irregular Verbs

You should know the imperfect forms of all verbs. What are the three verbs that are irregular in the imperfect?

**27** Expressing Extremes—Superlatives

Do you know how to express that something is *the best* or *the most*?

**28** Getting Information—Summary of Interrogative Words

You should know how to form questions with question words and how to express English *what?* with **¿qué?** or **¿cuál?**

## VOCABULARIO

Practice this vocabulary with digital flash cards on the Online Learning Center (www.mhhe.com/quetal7).

### Los verbos

| | |
|---|---|
| aburrirse | to get bored |
| dejar (en) | to leave (behind) (in [*a place*]) |
| pegar (gu) | to hit |
| pelear | to fight |
| sonar (ue) | to ring; to sound |
| jugar (ue) (gu) a las cartas | to play cards |
| ser (*irreg.*) aburrido/a/ divertido/a | to be boring/fun |
| visitar un museo | to visit a museum |

**Repaso: dar** (*irreg.*) / **hacer** (*irreg.*) **una fiesta, hacer** (*irreg.*) *camping*, **jugar** (ue) (gu) **al ajedrez, tomar el sol**

### Pasatiempos, diversiones y aficiones

| | |
|---|---|
| la afición | pastime, fun activity, hobby |
| el deporte | sport |
| la diversión | entertainment, amusement |
| el pasatiempo | pastime, hobby |
| los ratos libres | spare (free) time |
| dar (*irreg.*) un paseo | to take a walk |
| hacer (*irreg.*) un *picnic* | to have a picnic |
| hacer (*irreg.*) planes para + *inf.* | to make plans to (*do something*) |
| ir (*irreg.*)… | to go … |
| al cine / a ver una película | to the movies / to see a movie |
| a una discoteca / a un bar | to a disco / to a bar |
| al teatro / a un concierto | to the theater / to a concert |

### Los deportes

| | |
|---|---|
| el ciclismo | bicycling |
| el fútbol | soccer |
| el fútbol americano | football |
| el/la jugador(a) | player |
| la natación | swimming |
| el partido | match, game |

**Cognados: el basquetbol, el béisbol, el golf, el hockey, el tenis, el vólibol**

| | |
|---|---|
| correr | to run; to jog |
| entrenar | to practice, train |
| esquiar (esquío) | to ski |
| ganar | to win |
| montar a caballo | to ride a horse |
| pasear en bicicleta | to ride a bicycle |
| patinar | to skate |
| patinar en línea | to rollerblade |

**♻ Reciclado**

Note the recycling of vocabulary items that are listed in a new context in addition to those items that are explicitly listed as *Repaso*.

*En resumen*

| | |
|---|---|
| el ajedrez | la pared |
| la cama | la película |
| la casa | los platos |
| el cine | la ropa |
| la mesa | la ventana |
| los muebles | |

**ser** (*irreg.*) **aficionado/a (a)**     to be a fan (of)

**Repaso: jugar (ue) (gu) (al)** (*sport*)**, nadar, perder (ie), practicar (qu)**

## Algunos aparatos domésticos

| | |
|---|---|
| la aspiradora | vacuum cleaner |
| la cafetera | coffeemaker |
| el congelador | freezer |
| la estufa | stove |
| el horno de microondas | microwave oven |
| la lavadora | washing machine |
| el lavaplatos | dishwasher |
| el refrigerador | refrigerator |
| la secadora | clothes dryer |
| la tostadora | toaster |

## Los quehaceres domésticos

| | |
|---|---|
| barrer (el piso) | to sweep (the floor) |
| hacer (*irreg.*) la cama | to make the bed |
| lavar (las ventanas, los platos, la ropa) | to wash (the windows, the dishes, the clothes) |
| limpiar la casa (entera) | to clean the (whole) house |
| pasar la aspiradora | to vacuum |
| pintar (las paredes) | to paint (the walls) |
| planchar la ropa | to iron clothing |
| poner (*irreg.*) la mesa | to set the table |
| quitar la mesa | to clear the table |

| | |
|---|---|
| sacar (qu) la basura | to take out the trash |
| sacudir los muebles | to dust the furniture |

## Otros sustantivos

| | |
|---|---|
| el aparato doméstico | home appliance |
| la costumbre | custom, habit |
| la dirección | address |
| la escuela | school |
| el grado | grade, year (*in school*) |
| el/la niñero/a | baby-sitter |
| la niñez | childhood |
| el quehacer doméstico | household chore |

## Adjetivos

| | |
|---|---|
| deportivo/a | sporting, sports (*adj.*); sports-loving |
| pesado/a | boring; difficult |

## Palabras adicionales

| | |
|---|---|
| de joven | as a youth |
| de niño/a | as a child |
| mientras | while |
| tocarle (qu) a uno | to be someone's turn |

**Repaso: ¿a qué hora?, ¿adónde?, ¿cómo?, ¿cuál(es)?, ¿cuándo?, ¿cuánto/a?, ¿cuántos/as?, ¿de dónde?, ¿de quién(es)?, ¿dónde?, ¿por qué?, ¿qué?, ¿quién(es)?**

**Suggestions**
• Have students respond *cierto* or *falso* to the following statements.

1. *El béisbol requiere la participación de varias personas.*
2. *El ejercicio es importante para la salud mental.*
3. *Para una persona que le gusta estar entre mucha gente, la natación es el deporte favorito.*

• Have students answer the following questions.

1. *¿Dónde se puede escuchar música, en un concierto o en un museo?*
2. *¿Cuál es una actividad cultural, hacer camping o ir al teatro?*
3. *¿Dónde se puede ver a su actor favorito, en un bar o en el cine?*

• Have students complete these sentences with the correct activity, based on the noun at the beginning of the sentence.

1. *La secadora sirve para _____.*
2. *La plancha sirve para _____.*
3. *En la cocina se puede _____.*
4. *La lavadora sirve para _____.*

• Ask students these questions.

1. *¿Ud. hace la cama todos los días? Si tiene prisa por la mañana, ¿hace la cama o la deja sin hacer? Cuando visita la casa de su familia, ¿su mamá (abuela) le hace la cama?*
2. *¿Cuándo limpia Ud. la casa, durante el fin de semana? ¿La limpia entera o sólo una parte? ¿Alguien lo/la ayuda a limpiarla?*
3. *¿Qué prefiere Ud., sacudir los muebles o pasar la aspiradora? ¿lavar la ropa o*

*barrer el piso? ¿quitar la mesa o lavar los platos?... Yo odio* (fill in what you dislike)*. ¿Quién también odia _____?*

• Have students make single statements about something they used to do when they were younger (*de joven / de niño/a*). Have them make their statements in a round-robin format, without repeating anything someone else has already said.
• Have students describe three to four activities that they think someone famous used to do as a child. They should not name the person they describe. The class should try to guess the identity.

**Heritage Speakers**
En algunos dialectos del español que se habla en los Estados Unidos, a veces se usa la palabra *grado* en vez de *nota* o *calificación,* por la influencia del inglés.

# La salud°

°**La...** *Health*

*Un farmacéutico y su cliente, en una farmacia en Venezuela*

## CULTURA

- **Nota cultural:** La medicina en los países hispanos
- **En los Estados Unidos y el Canadá:** Edward James Olmos: Actor y activista de la comunidad
- **Voces de Venezuela**
    Literatura: Rómulo Gallegos
    Música: El joropo
- **Videoteca**
    Entrevista cultural: Venezuela
    Entre amigos: ¡Yo sí hago ejercicio!
- **Enfoque cultural:** Venezuela

## VOCABULARIO

- La salud y el bienestar
- En el consultorio

## GRAMÁTICA

29 Using the Preterite and the Imperfect

30 Reciprocal Actions with Reflexive Pronouns

# PASO 1   Vocabulario

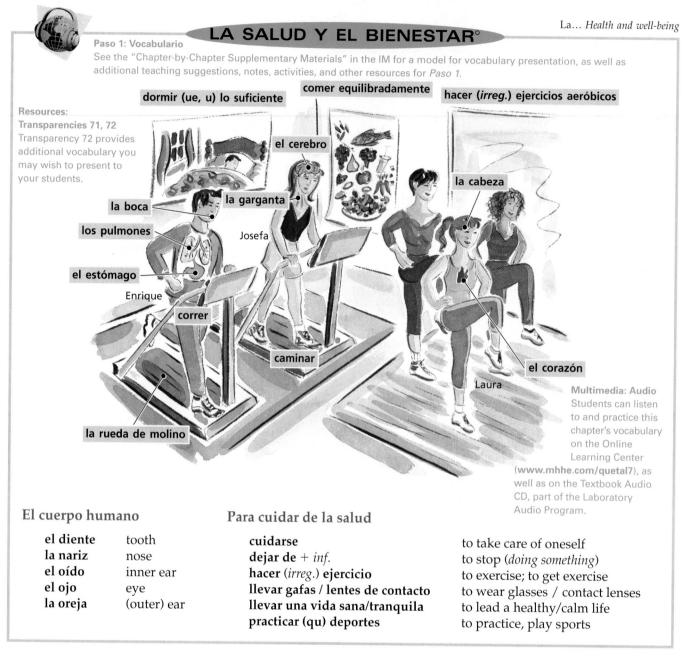

**LA SALUD Y EL BIENESTAR°**

*La… Health and well-being*

Paso 1: Vocabulario
See the "Chapter-by-Chapter Supplementary Materials" in the IM for a model for vocabulary presentation, as well as additional teaching suggestions, notes, activities, and other resources for *Paso 1*.

**dormir (ue, u) lo suficiente**

**comer equilibradamente**

**hacer (irreg.) ejercicios aeróbicos**

Resources:
**Transparencies 71, 72**
Transparency 72 provides additional vocabulary you may wish to present to your students.

el cerebro

la boca

la garganta

los pulmones

Josefa

el estómago

Enrique

correr

caminar

la cabeza

el corazón

Laura

la rueda de molino

**Multimedia: Audio**
Students can listen to and practice this chapter's vocabulary on the Online Learning Center (**www.mhhe.com/quetal7**), as well as on the Textbook Audio CD, part of the Laboratory Audio Program.

## El cuerpo humano

| | |
|---|---|
| **el diente** | tooth |
| **la nariz** | nose |
| **el oído** | inner ear |
| **el ojo** | eye |
| **la oreja** | (outer) ear |

## Para cuidar de la salud

| | |
|---|---|
| **cuidarse** | to take care of oneself |
| **dejar de** + *inf.* | to stop (*doing something*) |
| **hacer** (*irreg.*) **ejercicio** | to exercise; to get exercise |
| **llevar gafas / lentes de contacto** | to wear glasses / contact lenses |
| **llevar una vida sana/tranquila** | to lead a healthy/calm life |
| **practicar (qu) deportes** | to practice, play sports |

**Suggestions**
• Offer optional vocabulary.

| LA CARA Y EL CUERPO: | ACTIVIDADES: |
|---|---|
| la barbilla | hacer footing |
| las cejas | jugar a los bolos (al |
| el frente | tenis, al ráquetbol) |
| la mejilla | levantar pesas |
| las muelas | montar en bicicleta |
| el pecho | nadar |
| las pestañas | |

• Ask students the following questions to check comprehension and personalize.

1. ¿Hace Ud. algún ejercicio físico? ¿Camina? ¿Corre? ¿Juega al ráquetbol? ¿No hace nada?

## ■ Conversación

**A. Asociaciones**   ¿Qué partes del cuerpo humano asocia Ud. con las siguientes palabras? A veces hay más de una respuesta posible.

| | | |
|---|---|---|
| 1. un ataque | 5. pensar | 9. la música |
| 2. comer | 6. la digestión | 10. el perfume |
| 3. cantar | 7. el amor | 11. un beso (*kiss*) |
| 4. las gafas | 8. fumar | 12. una flor |

2. *En su opinión, ¿qué tipo de ejercicio es el mejor de todos? ¿Por qué?*
3. *¿Lleva Ud. una vida sana? ¿Qué hace Ud. para cuidarse? ¿Come equilibradamente? ¿Duerme lo suficiente? ¿Practica algún deporte?*

• Point out that *sano/a* (healthy) is a false cognate.

**B. Más asociaciones.** ¿Qué palabras asocia Ud. con las siguientes partes del cuerpo? *Possible answers*

**1.** los ojos *ver*  **3.** la boca *hablar*  **5.** el estómago *tener hambre*

**2.** los dientes *comer*  **4.** el oído *oír*  **6.** la nariz *respirar*

## C. Hablando de la salud

PASO 1 ¿Qué significan para Ud. las siguientes oraciones?

MODELO: Se debe comer equilibradamente. →
Eso quiere decir (*means*) que es necesario comer muchas verduras, que… También significa que no debemos comer muchos dulces o…

**1.** Se debe dormir lo suficiente todas las noches.
**2.** Hay que hacer ejercicio.
**3.** Es necesario llevar una vida tranquila.
**4.** En general, uno debe cuidarse mucho.
**5.** Es importante llevar una vida sana.

PASO 2 ¿Lleva Ud. una vida sana? Dígale a un compañero / una compañera cómo vive, usando frases del **Paso 1** y del **Vocabulario.**

MODELO: Creo que llevo una vida sana porque como una dieta equilibrada. No como muchos dulces, excepto en los días festivos como la Navidad…

PASO 3 Ahora cambie su narración para describir lo que hacía de niño/a. ¿Qué hacía y qué *no* hacía Ud.? Debe organizar las ideas lógicamente.

MODELO: De niño, no llevaba una vida muy sana. Comía muchos dulces. También odiaba las frutas y verduras…

---

### Palabras y frases útiles

Eso quiere decir…
Esto significa que…
También…

---

---

## NOTA CULTURAL

### La medicina en los países hispanos

Los hispanos pueden **consultar a otros profesionales de la salud,** además de los médicos, especialmente **en relación con enfermedades** que no son graves. La gente consulta a los **farmacéuticos** con frecuencia, pues estos son profesionales con un riguroso entrenamiento universitario en farmacología. Además, **hay farmacias en cada barrio,** lo cual hace que haya[a] una relación bien establecida entre los farmacéuticos y sus clientes.

En las ciudades y pueblos hispanos siempre hay algunas farmacias abiertas a todas las horas del día. Se establecen horarios de turnos, y la farmacia que está abierta a horas en que las otras están cerradas se llama **farmacia de guardia.** Se puede saber cuáles son las farmacias de guardia a través del periódico o simplemente yendo a la farmacia más cercana, donde siempre hay una lista de todas las farmacias.

Otros profesionales al cuidado de la salud muy solicitados son los **practicantes,** que son enfermeros o estudiantes de medicina con varios años de estudio, que están capacitados[b] para poner inyecciones o hacer visitas a domicilio para **tratamientos sencillos.**

Finalmente, se debe mencionar la relativa popularidad de **remedios tradicionales,** como la homeopatía. Aunque hay expertos homeópatas con años de entrenamiento, también existe un repertorio popular de **reme-**
**dios naturales** básicos para enfermedades o molestias[c] cotidianas, conocimientos[d] que se transmiten de generación a generación.

FARMACIAS 4º turno
Abiertas de Sábado a Viernes de 8 a 22 hs.

---

[a]lo… *which creates*  [b]*trained*  [c]*nuisances*  [d]*knowledge*

**EN EL CONSULTORIO°** · *doctor's office*

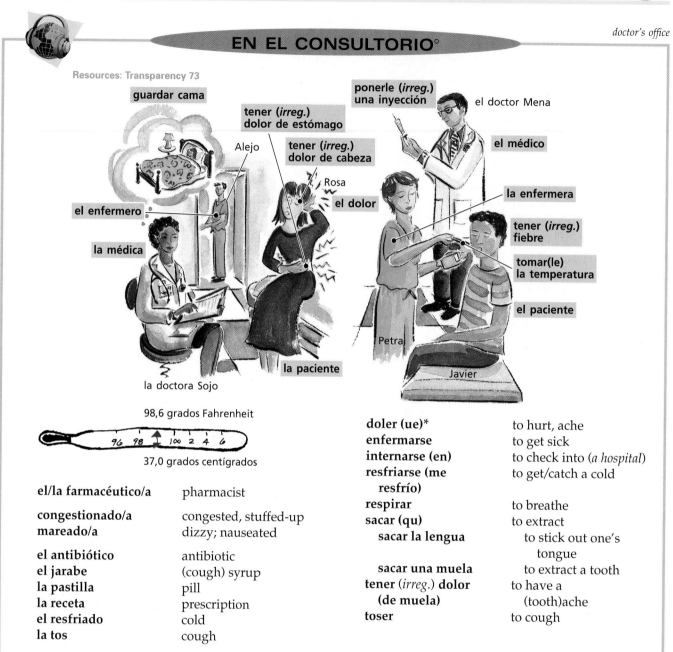

Resources: Transparency 73

guardar cama

tener (*irreg.*) dolor de estómago

Alejo

tener (*irreg.*) dolor de cabeza

ponerle (*irreg.*) una inyección — el doctor Mena

el médico

Rosa

el dolor

la enfermera

tener (*irreg.*) fiebre

el enfermero

la médica

tomar(le) la temperatura

el paciente

la doctora Sojo

la paciente

Petra

Javier

98,6 grados Fahrenheit

96 98 100 2 4 6

37,0 grados centígrados

| el/la farmacéutico/a | pharmacist |
|---|---|
| congestionado/a | congested, stuffed-up |
| mareado/a | dizzy; nauseated |
| el antibiótico | antibiotic |
| el jarabe | (cough) syrup |
| la pastilla | pill |
| la receta | prescription |
| el resfriado | cold |
| la tos | cough |

| doler (ue)* | to hurt, ache |
|---|---|
| enfermarse | to get sick |
| internarse (en) | to check into (*a hospital*) |
| resfriarse (me resfrío) | to get/catch a cold |
| respirar | to breathe |
| sacar (qu) | to extract |
| sacar la lengua | to stick out one's tongue |
| sacar una muela | to extract a tooth |
| tener (*irreg.*) dolor (de muela) | to have a (tooth)ache |
| toser | to cough |

## ■ Conversación

**A. Estudio de palabras.**   Complete las siguientes oraciones con una palabra de la misma (*same*) familia que la palabra en letras cursivas (*italics*).

1. Si me *resfrío,* tengo ___un resfriado___.
2. La *respiración* ocurre cuando alguien ___respira___.
3. Si me ___enfermo___, estoy *enfermo/a.* Un(a) ___enfermero/a___ me toma la temperatura.
4. Cuando alguien *tose,* se oye una ___tos___.
5. Si me *duele* el estómago, tengo un ___dolor___ de estómago.

———————————

*Doler *is used like *gustar: Me duele la cabeza. Me duelen los ojos.*

«De médico, poeta y loco, todos tenemos un poco.»

Write this *refrán* on the board and poll students to find out if they all agree, and why.

**B. Situaciones.** Describa Ud. la situación de estas personas. ¿Dónde y con quiénes están? ¿Qué síntomas tienen? ¿Qué van a hacer?

Resources: Transparency 74

1.

2.

3. (illustration)

1. Anamari está muy bien de salud. Nunca le duele(n) _____. Nunca tiene _____. Siempre _____. Más tarde, ella va a _____.
2. Martín tiene _____. Debe _____. El dentista va a _____. Después, Martín va a _____.
3. A Inés le duele(n) _____. Tiene _____. El médico y la enfermera van a _____. Luego, Inés tiene que _____.

---

## NOTA COMUNICATIVA

**The Good News . . . The Bad News . . .**

To describe general qualities or characteristics of something, use **lo** with the masculine singular form of an adjective.

**lo bueno / lo malo   lo más importante   lo mejor / lo peor   lo mismo**

This structure has a number of English equivalents, especially in colloquial speech.

**lo bueno** = the good thing/part/news, what's good

---

**C. Ventajas y desventajas.** (*Advantages and Disadvantages.*) Casi todas las cosas tienen un aspecto bueno y otro malo.

PASO 1   ¿Qué es lo bueno y lo malo (o lo peor y lo mejor) de las siguientes situaciones?

1. tener un resfriado
2. ir a una universidad cerca/lejos del hogar familiar (*family home*)
3. tener hijos cuando uno es joven (entre 18 y 25 años)
4. ser muy rico
5. ir a un consultorio médico
6. ir al consultorio de un dentista

PASO 2   Compare sus respuestas con las de sus compañeros. ¿Dijeron algo que Ud. no consideró?

**Note**
See the Workbook/Laboratory Manual for presentation and practice of the letters *s, z, ce,* and *ci.*

Paso 2: Gramática
See the "Chapter-by-Chapter Supplementary Materials" in the IM for additional teaching suggestions, notes, activities, and other resources for *Paso 2*.

Resources: Transparency 70 from *Capítulo 9* can be used to review preterite and imperfect forms.

## ¿Recuerda Ud.?

Throughout the last chapters of *¿Qué tal?*, beginning with **Capítulo 7**, you have been using first the preterite and then the imperfect in appropriate contexts. Do you remember which tense you used to do each of the following?

1. to tell what you did yesterday
2. to tell what you used to do when you were in grade school
3. to explain the situation or condition that caused you to do something
4. to tell what someone did as the result of a situation
5. to talk about the way things used to be
6. to describe an action that was in progress

If you understand those uses of the preterite and the imperfect, the following summary of their uses will not contain much that is new information for you.

## 29 Narrating in the Past — Using the Preterite and the Imperfect

Follow-Up
After reviewing the *minidiálogo,* ask students the following questions to check comprehension.

¿Quién estaba enferma?
¿Qué síntomas tenía?
¿Por qué se sintió mejor rápidamente?

### En el consultorio de la Dra. Méndez

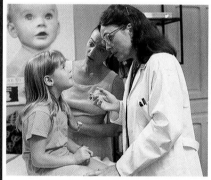

**Answers**
1. *empezó, notó, tomé*
2. *Estaba, tosía, se quejaba, dolían, tenía*

Marta, la hija de Lola y Manolo, se siente mal y su madre la lleva al consultorio de la Dra. Méndez.

DRA. MÉNDEZ: ¿Cuándo *empezó* a sentirse mal su hija?
LOLA: Ayer por la tarde. *Estaba* congestionada, *tosía* mucho y *se quejaba* de que le *dolían* el cuerpo y la cabeza.
DRA. MÉNDEZ: ¿Y le *notó* algo de fiebre?
LOLA: Sí. Por la noche le *tomé* la temperatura y *tenía* treinta y ocho grados.
DRA. MÉNDEZ: A ver… Tal vez necesito ponerle una inyección…
MARTA: Eh… bueno… ¡Creo que ahora me encuentro un poco mejor!

### Comprensión

In the preceding dialogue, locate all of the verbs that do the following.

1. indicate actions
2. indicate conditions or descriptions

When speaking about the past in English, you choose different past tense forms to use, depending on the context: *I wrote letters, I was writing letters, I used to write letters,* and so on. Similarly, you can use either the preterite or the imperfect in many Spanish sentences, depending on the meaning you wish to convey. Often the question is: How do you view the action or state of being?

**Bright Idea Suggestion**
On the board or a transparency, write a brief paragraph about a health incident. Have students note the verbs, then list them. Have students work on the board or transparency to put the verbs in categories (imperfect/preterite), then talk about the different reasons the verbs require preterite or imperfect.

*In Dr. Méndez's office*  Marta, Lola and Manolo's daughter, feels sick, and her mother takes her to Dr. Méndez's office. DR. MÉNDEZ: When did your daughter begin to feel ill? LOLA: Yesterday afternoon. She was stuffed up, she was coughing a lot, and she was complaining that her body and head were hurting. DR. MÉNDEZ: And did you note any fever? LOLA: Yes. At night I took her temperature and it was thirty-eight degrees. DR. MÉNDEZ: Let's see . . . Perhaps I'll need to give her a shot . . . MARTA: Um . . . well . . . I think I feel a little bit better now!

| PAST ----------------- Present ----------------- Future |
|---|
| preterite | **present** |
| imperfect | **present progressive** |
| | **formal commands** |

**Suggestions**
· Offer students these examples.

Two preterite actions occurring either sequentially or simultaneously in the past.

*Me puse los zapatos y me levanté.*
*Elena se fue cuando yo entré.*

Two ongoing actions occurring simultaneously in the past.

*Hacía mi tarea mientras veía las noticias.*

One ongoing action in the past when another interrupts.

*Yo estudiaba cuando llegó Juan.*

| **Preterite** | **Imperfect** |
|---|---|
| • beginning/end of past action | • habitual/repeated action |
| • completed action | • progress of a past action |
| • series of completed actions | • background details |
| • interrup**ting** action | • interrup**ted** action |
| • the action on the "stage" | • the backdrop (setup) of the "stage" |

## Beginning/End vs. Habitual

Use the preterite to . . .

• tell about the beginning or the end of a past action.

· Model the difference in meaning of *pensó* (he thought, it occurred to him) and *pensaba* (he was of the opinion, planned/intended to). Use *creer* forms in a similar contrast.

El sábado pasado, el partido de fútbol **empezó** a la una. **Terminó** a las cuatro. El entrenador **habló** a las cinco.
*Last Saturday, the soccer game began at one. It ended at four. The coach spoke (began to speak) at five.*

Use the imperfect to . . .

• talk about the habitual nature of an action (something you always did).

· Offer students these additional examples.

*Carlos fue al médico ayer. / Carlos siempre iba al médico cuando se resfriaba.*

*Juanita estuvo (became) nerviosa. / Juanita estaba (was) nerviosa.*

**Había** un partido todos los sábados. Muchas personas **jugaban** todas las semanas.
*There was a game every Saturday. Many people played every week.*

## Completed vs. Ongoing

Use the preterite to . . .

• express an action that is viewed as completed.

El partido **duró** tres horas. **Ganaron** Los Lobos, de Villalegre.
*The game lasted three hours. The Lobos of Villalegre won.*

Use the imperfect to . . .

• tell what was happening when another action took place and tell about simultaneous events (with **mientras** = *while*).

Yo no vi el final del partido. **Estaba** en la cocina cuando **terminó.**
*I didn't see the end of the game. I was in the kitchen when it ended.*
Mientras mi amigo **veía** el partido, **hablaba** con su novia.
*While my friend was watching the game, he was talking with his girlfriend.*

# PASO 2

Resources: Transparency 56 from *Capítulo 7* (page 199) can be used to practice preterite vs. imperfect.

## Series of Completed Actions vs. Background

Use the preterite to . . .

- express a series of completed actions.

**Heritage Speakers**

Anime a los hispanohablantes a explicar la diferencia entre los siguientes pares de oraciones.

Durante el partido, los jugadores **corrieron, saltaron** y **gritaron.**
*During the game, the players ran, jumped, and shouted.*

Use the imperfect to . . .

- give background details of many kinds: time, location, weather, mood, age, physical and mental characteristics.

    *Juan me dijo que le dolía la cabeza.* [indefinite period of time, perhaps continuing into present]

    *Juan me dijo que le dolió la cabeza.* [a specific time period that is now over]

    *No sé cuánto costó.* [implies someone made a purchase, but speaker does not know how much it cost that person]

    *No sé cuánto costaba.* [no purchase implied]

**Llovía** un poco durante el partido. Todos los jugadores **eran** jóvenes; **tenían** 17 ó 18 años. ¡Y todos **esperaban** ganar!
*It rained a little bit during the game. All the players were young; they were 17 or 18 years old. And all of them hoped to win!*

## Changes in Meaning

Remember that, when used in the preterite, **saber, conocer, querer,** and **poder** have English equivalents different from that of the infinitives (see **Capítulo 8**). In the imperfect, the English equivalents of these verbs do not differ from the infinitive meanings.

Anoche **conocí** a Roberto.
*Last night I met Roberto.*

¿Anoche? Yo pensaba que ya lo **conocías.**
*Last night? I thought you already knew him.*

## Interrupting vs. Interrupted

The preterite and the imperfect frequently occur in the same sentence. In the first sentence the imperfect tells what was happening when another action—conveyed by the preterite—broke the continuity of the ongoing activity. In the second sentence, the preterite reports the action that took place because of a condition—described by the imperfect—that was in progress or in existence at that time.

Miguel **estudiaba** cuando **sonó** el teléfono.
*Miguel was studying when the phone rang.*

Olivia **comió** tanto porque **tenía** mucha hambre.
*Olivia ate so much because she was very hungry.*

**Suggestion**

Model sentences with the preterite and the imperfect of *saber, conocer, poder,* and *querer* and have students explain the differences in meaning.

## Action vs. the Stage (Background)/Conditions/Ongoing

The preterite and imperfect are also used together in the presentation of an event. The preterite narrates the action while the imperfect sets the stage, describes the conditions that caused the action, or emphasizes the continuing nature of a particular action.

Era un día hermoso. **Hacía** mucho sol pero no **hacía** mucho calor. Como no **tenía** que trabajar en la oficina, **compré** unas flores de primavera y **salí** vestida de camiseta y pantalones cortos para trabajar todo el día en el jardín.
*It was a beautiful day. It was very sunny but it wasn't very hot. Since I didn't have to work in the office, I bought some spring flowers and I went out dressed in a T-shirt and shorts to work in the garden all day.*

## ■ Práctica

**A. En el consultorio.** What did your doctor do the last time you had an appointment with him or her? Assume that you had the following conditions and match them with the appropriate procedure.

CONDICIONES: (yo / a mí)

1. __c__ Tenía mucho calor y temblaba.
2. __f, g__ Me dolía la garganta.
3. __d, g__ Tenía un poco de congestión en el pecho (*chest*).
4. __e__ Creía que estaba anémico/a.
5. __a__ No sabía lo que tenía.
6. __b__ Necesitaba medicinas.
7. __a, c–g__ Sólo necesitaba un chequeo (*checkup*) rutinario.

ACCIONES: El médico…

a. me hizo muchas preguntas.
b. me escribió una receta.
c. me tomó la temperatura.
d. me auscultó (*listened to*) los pulmones y el corazón.
e. me analizó la sangre (*blood*).
f. me hizo sacar la lengua.
g. me hizo toser.

## NOTA COMUNICATIVA

### Words and Expressions That Indicate the Use of Preterite and Imperfect

Certain words and expressions are frequently associated with the preterite, others with the imperfect.

Some words often associated with the preterite are:

> **ayer, anteayer** (*the day before yesterday*), **anoche** (*last night*)
> **una vez, dos veces** (*twice*)…
> **el año pasado, el lunes pasado…**
> **de repente** (*suddenly*)

Some words often associated with the imperfect are:

> **todos los días, todos los lunes…**
> **siempre, frecuentemente**
> **mientras**
> **de niño/a, de joven**

Some English equivalents also associated with the imperfect are:

> *was* _____ *-ing, were* _____ *-ing* (in English)
> *used to, would* (when *would* implies *used to* in English)

As you continue to practice preterite and imperfect, these expressions can help you determine which tense to use.

These words do not *automatically* cue either tense, however. The most important consideration is the meaning that the speaker wishes to convey.

| | |
|---|---|
| **Ayer cenamos** temprano. | *Yesterday we had dinner early.* |
| **Ayer cenábamos** cuando Juan llamó. | *Yesterday we were having dinner when Juan called.* |
| **Jugaba** al fútbol **de niño.** | *He played soccer as a child.* |
| **Empezó** a jugar al fútbol **de niño.** | *He began to play soccer as a child.* |

**B. Pequeñas historias.** Complete the following brief paragraphs with the appropriate phrases from the lists. Before you begin, it is a good idea to look at the drawing that accompanies each paragraph and to scan through the complete paragraph to get the gist of it, even though you may not understand everything the first time you read it.

**1.** estaba leyendo      había      salí      tenía
   estaban apagadas[a]   me levanté   se apagaron[b]

**E**ran las once de la noche cuando ¡de repente _____¹ todas las luces[c] de la casa! Puse el libro que _____² en la mesa y _____³ para investigar la causa del incidente. La verdad es que _____⁴ mucho miedo. _____⁵ a la calle y vi que _____⁶ las luces de todo el barrio.[d] En ese momento me di cuenta[e] que _____⁷ un problema con la electricidad en toda la ciudad.

[a]*out*   [b]*se… went out*   [c]*lights*   [d]*neighborhood*   [e]*me… I realized*

**2.** dio         estaba       intentaba[a] tomarle   puso
   esperaba    examinó      llegó                 se sintió

**L**a niña tosía mientras que la enfermera _____¹ la temperatura. La madre de la niña _____² pacientemente. Por fin _____³ la médica. Le _____⁴ la garganta a la niña, le _____⁵ una inyección y le _____⁶ a su madre una receta para un jarabe. La madre todavía _____⁷ muy preocupada, pero inmediatamente después que la médica le habló, _____⁸ más tranquila.

[a]*tried to*

**C. Rubén y Soledad.** Read the following paragraph at least once to familiarize yourself with the sequence of events, and look at the drawing. Then reread the paragraph, giving the proper form of the verbs in parentheses in the preterite or the imperfect, according to the needs of each sentence and the context of the paragraph as a whole.

**R**ubén estaba estudiando cuando Soledad entró en el cuarto. Le (preguntar¹) a Rubén si (querer²) ir al cine con ella. Rubén le (decir³) que sí porque se (sentir⁴) un poco aburrido con sus estudios. Los dos (salir⁵) en seguida[a] para el cine. (Ver⁶) una película cómica y (reírse⁷) mucho. Luego, como (hacer⁸) frío, (entrar⁹) en su café favorito, El Gato Negro, y (tomar¹⁰) un chocolate. (Ser¹¹) las dos de la mañana cuando por fin (regresar¹²) a casa. Soledad (acostarse¹³) inmediatamente porque (estar¹⁴) cansada, pero Rubén (empezar¹⁵) a estudiar otra vez.

[a]*en… right away*

**Comprensión.** Now answer the following questions based on the paragraph about Rubén and Soledad. **¡OJO!** A question is not always answered in the same tense as that in which it is asked. Remember this, especially when you are asked to explain why something happened.

**1.** ¿Qué hacía Rubén cuando Soledad entró?
**2.** ¿Qué le preguntó Soledad a Rubén?
**3.** ¿Por qué dijo Rubén que sí?
**4.** ¿Les gustó la película? ¿Por qué?
**5.** ¿Por qué tomaron un chocolate?
**6.** ¿Regresaron a casa a las tres?
**7.** ¿Qué hicieron cuando llegaron a casa?

## D. Caperucita Roja

PASO 1  Retell this familiar story, based on the drawings, sentences, and cues that accompany each drawing, using the imperfect or preterite of the verbs in parentheses. Add as many details as you can. Using context, try to guess the meaning of words that are glossed with ¿ ?.

1.    2.     3.

1. Érase una vez[a] una niña hermosa que (llamarse[1]) Caperucita Roja. Todos los animales del bosque[b] (ser[2]) sus amigos y Caperucita Roja los (querer[3]) mucho.
2. Un día su mamá le (decir[4]): —Lleva en seguida esta jarrita de miel[c] a casa de tu abuelita. Ten cuidado[d] con el lobo[e] feroz.
3. En el bosque, el lobo (salir[5]) a hablar con la niña. Le (preguntar[6]): —¿Adónde vas, Caperucita? Esta le (contestar[7]) dulcemente:[f] —Voy a casa de mi abuelita.

4.     5.     6.     7.

4. —Pues, si vas por este sendero,[g] vas a llegar antes, (decir[8]) el malvado[h] lobo. Él (irse[9]) por otro camino más corto.
5. El lobo (llegar[10]) primero a la casa de la abuelita y (entrar[11]) silenciosamente. La abuelita (tener[12]) mucho miedo. (*Ella:* Saltar[13]) de la cama y (correr[14]) a esconderse.
6. Caperucita Roja (llegar[15]) por fin a la casa de la abuelita. (*Ella:* Encontrar[16]) a su «abuelita», que (estar[17]) en la cama. Le (decir[18]): —¡Qué dientes tan largos tienes! —¡Son para comerte mejor!— (decir[19]) su «abuelita».
7. Una ardilla[i] del bosque (enterarse[20]) del peligro. Por eso (avisar[21]) a un cazador.[j]

[a]¿ ?   [b]¿ ?   [c]jarrita... *jar of honey*   [d]Ten... *Be careful*   [e]¿ ?   [f]*sweetly*   [g]*path*   [h]¿ ?   [i]¿ ?   [j]¿ ?

# PASO 2

### Más vocabulario útil

**atacar (qu)** (to attack)
**comérselo/la** (to eat something
  up)
**matar** (to kill)

**Need more practice?**

- Workbook/Laboratory Manual
- Interactive CD-ROM
- Online Learning Center
  (www.mhhe.com/quetal7)

**8.** El lobo (saltar[22]) de la cama y (abalanzarse[23]) sobre Caperucita. Ella (salir[24]) de la casa corriendo y pidiendo socorro[k] desesperadamente.

**9.** El cazador (ver[25]) lo que (ocurrir[26]). (*Él:* Dispararle[27]) al lobo y le (hacer[28]) huir.

**10.** Caperucita (regresar[29]) a la casa de su abuelita. La (*ella:* abrazar[30]) y le (prometer[31]) escuchar siempre los consejos de su mamá.

[k]*help*

PASO 2   Hay varias versiones del cuento de Caperucita Roja. La que Ud. acaba de leer termina felizmente, pero otras no. Con otros dos compañeros, vuelva a contar la historia, empezando por el dibujo número 7. Inventen un diálogo más largo entre Caperucita y el lobo y cambien por completo el final del cuento.

## ■ Conversación

**A. El primer día.**   Dé Ud. sus impresiones del primer día de clases en la universidad. Use estas preguntas como guía.

1. ¿Cuál fue la primera clase? ¿A qué hora era la clase y dónde era?
2. ¿Vino a clase con alguien? ¿Ya tenía su libro de texto o lo compró después?
3. ¿Qué hizo Ud. después de entrar en la sala de clase? ¿Qué hacía el profesor / la profesora?
4. ¿A quién conoció Ud. aquel día? ¿Ya conocía a algunos miembros de la clase? ¿A quiénes?
5. ¿Aprendió Ud. mucho durante la clase? ¿Ya sabía algo de esa materia?
6. ¿Le gustó el profesor / la profesora? ¿Por qué sí o por qué no? ¿Cómo era?
7. ¿Cómo se sentía durante la clase? ¿Nervioso/a? ¿aburrido/a? ¿cómodo/a?
8. ¿Les dio tarea el profesor / la profesora? ¿Pudo Ud. hacerla fácilmente?
9. Su primera impresión de la clase y del profesor / de la profesora, ¿fue válida o cambió con el tiempo? ¿Por qué?

**CAPÍTULO**

**10**

**Heritage Speakers**
Al hacer la Conversación B, es muy probable que los estudiantes hispanohablantes vayan a contestar las preguntas empleando el imperfecto del subjuntivo.

**PASO 2**

*Mis padres me dejaron que cruzara solo la calle cuando tenía 6 años.*

Si es necesario, explíqueles a los estudiantes de habla inglesa que aprenderán
ese tiempo verbal en el *Capítulo 17.*

## B. Entrevista. Unas preguntas sobre el pasado

PASO 1   Con un compañero / una compañera, haga y conteste las siguientes
preguntas.

¿Cuántos años tenías cuando… ?

1. aprendiste a pasear en bicicleta
2. hiciste tu primer viaje en avión
3. tuviste tu primera cita (*date*)
4. empezaste a afeitarte
5. conseguiste tu licencia de manejar (*driver's license*)
6. abriste una cuenta corriente (*checking account*)
7. dejaste de crecer (*grow*)

PASO 2   Con otro compañero / otra compañera, haga y conteste estas
preguntas.

¿Cuántos años tenías cuando tus padres… ?

1. te dejaron cruzar la calle (*street*) solo/a
2. te permitieron ir de compras a solas (*alone*)
3. te dejaron acostarte después de las nueve
4. te dejaron quedarte en casa sin niñero/a
5. te permitieron usar la estufa
6. te dejaron ver una película «R»
7. te dejaron conseguir un trabajo

PASO 3   Ahora, en grupos de cuatro, comparen sus respuestas. ¿Son muy
diferentes las respuestas que dieron? ¿Quién del grupo tiene los padres más
estrictos? ¿los menos estrictos?

**Con. B: Suggestions**
• Have students add three
questions of their own to
each list.
• Tell students to imagine that you are a
detective who has to write a report about
the theft of a rare book that disappeared
from the university library yesterday. You
need to know exactly where they were and
what they were doing from _____ to
_____ yesterday.

**En los Estados Unidos y el Canadá:
Suggestions**
• Have students describe movie and TV
roles Olmos has portrayed.
• Have students watch *American Me* or *Stand
and Deliver* and prepare a report on it.
• Have students name other actor-activists
and community leaders of Hispanic origin
(César Chávez, *Enfoque cultural* in *Capítulo 1;* Martin Sheen, *En los Estados
Unidos y el Canadá, Capítulo 2.*
• Encourage students to search the Internet
for more information about Edward James
Olmos and his humanitarian work. Have
them write a brief description of him as an
actor and community activist. Encourage
them to use the relative pronouns they
learned in this chapter.

## En los Estados Unidos y el Canadá

### Edward James Olmos: Actor y activista de la comunidad

El conocido **actor** de origen mexicano,
Edward James Olmos (Los Ángeles,
1947–), tiene en su historia profesional
papeles inolvidables[a] como el de Jaime
Escalante en *Stand and Deliver* y el de
policía en la famosa película cultista[b]
*Blade Runner.* Además es un reconocido[c]
**productor** y fue **director** y **guionista**[d] de
la película *American Me,* sobre las pandillas[e] de Los Ángeles. Ha recibido los
premios[f] Golden Globe y Emmy.

Pero el Sr. Olmos no es sólo un artista
sino también un destacado[g] **líder de la**

*Edward James Olmos*

**comunidad latina** en los Estados Unidos.
Su **trabajo humanitario** y **comunitario**
demuestra[h] un profundo compromiso[i] a
favor de **la juventud** y **la salud** y contra la
violencia de las pandillas y el racismo.
Entre los muchos cargos que ha desem-
peñado[j] están los de embajador[k] de los
Estados Unidos en UNICEF, portavoz[l] nacional de la Fundación Juvenil contra la
Diabetes, de la Fundación Alerta contra
el SIDA[m] y del Registro de Votantes. Además es miembro del comité de varios
hospitales para niños y también del Con-
cejo Nacional de Adopción.

[a]papeles… *unforgettable roles*   [b]*cult*   [c]*well-known*   [d]*scriptwriter*   [e]*gangs*   [f]Ha… *He has received the awards*   [g]*distinguished*   [h]*shows*   [i]*commitment*
[j]Entre… *Among the many positions he has held*   [k]*ambassador*   [l]*spokesperson*   [m]Fundación… *AIDS Awareness Foundation*

**En los Estados Unidos y el Canadá: Comprensión: ¿Cierto o falso?**
1. *Olmos nació en México.*
2. *Olmos trabaja mucho de voluntario con los jóvenes.*

# Voces de Venezuela

## LITERATURA: Rómulo Gallegos

**Rómulo Gallegos**
*(1884–1969)*

**Sobre el autor:** *Rómulo Gallegos nació en Caracas, Venezuela. En su novela más conocida,* Doña Bárbara, *el paisaje[a] de los llanos[b] venezolanos es el protagonista. Esto es un reflejo de la lucha[c] del hombre contra el enorme poder[d] de la naturaleza en América. El argumento[e] de la novela presenta la lucha entre la barbarie,[f] representada por doña Bárbara, y la civilización, representada por el personaje Santos Luzardo. El siguiente fragmento es de la novela* Doña Bárbara *(1ᵃ Parte Cap. VIII) (1929).*

La llanura[g] es bella y terrible a la vez; en ella caben[h] holgadamente,[i] hermosa vida y muerte[j] atroz; esta[k] acecha[l] por todas partes, pero allí nadie le teme.[m]

[a]landscape [b]plains [c]struggle [d]power [e]plot [f]barbarism [g]plain [h]fit [i]comfortably [j]death [k]she (the latter) [l]lies in wait [m]tiene miedo

## MÚSICA: El joropo

el arpa llanera

maracas

cuatro

la bandola llanera

El joropo es considerado como la música y baile nacionales de Venezuela. Originalmente, «el joropo» era un evento rural de baile, música de cuerdas[a] y canciones. Ahora este nombre puede referirse a la música, al baile o a una reunión[b] social celebrada con música y baile. El joropo se toca y se baila en varios festivales y celebraciones.

[a]música... *string music* [b]*get-together*

Los instrumentos principales del joropo son el arpa llanera,[c] la bandola llanera,[d] el cuatro[e] y las maracas. Son instrumentos tradicionales de los llaneros, que eran los «cowboys» venezolanos. Generalmente, tres músicos tocan estos instrumentos básicos del joropo y una cuarta[f] persona canta, siguiendo[g] la música del arpa.

[c]arpa... *plains harp (folk harp with 32 strings, descended from the Spanish harp and used in the plains regions of Venezuela and Colombia)* [d]*four-stringed guitar with a rounded body* [e]*four-stringed guitar* [f]*fourth* [g]*following*

El baile, que tiene muchos pasos y movimientos rápidos, es complicado y bastante[g] difícil de aprender. Se dice que la intención de esta danza es dramatizar el dominio del hombre sobre la mujer: él dirige,[h] y ella lo sigue en todo.

[g]*rather* [h]*leads*

**Paso 3: Gramática**
See the "Chapter-by-Chapter Supplementary Materials" in the IM for additional teaching suggestions, notes, activities, and other resources for *Paso 3*.

### ¿Recuerda Ud.?

Before learning how to express reciprocal actions, review the reflexive pronouns (**Gramática 13**), then provide the correct reflexive pronouns for the following sentences.

1. _____ levanté a las ocho y media.
2. Laura _____ puso el vestido.
3. Mis amigos y yo _____ sentamos en un café.
4. ¿Prefieres duchar_____ o bañar_____?

**Follow-Up**
Ask questions to expand the use of the art.

1. *Rosa y Casandra, ¿se entienden bien?*
2. *¿Cree Ud. que se ayudan con los problemas? ¿con la tarea?*

**Suggestion**
Emphasize that not all verbs can be made reciprocal, as not all verbs can be reflexive. Model some examples of intransitive verbs in exchanges with students.

*¿Adónde se van Uds. después de la clase?*
vs. *¿Uds. se ven después de la clase?*

## 30  Expressing *each other* Reciprocal Actions with Reflexive Pronouns

**Rosa y Casandra**

Rosa y Casandra *se conocen* bien. Son compañeras de cuarto. *Se ven* todos los días y *se encuentran* después de clase para hablar.
   ¿Qué hacen Rosa y Casandra en esta escena? *Se besan* en la mejilla.*

**¿Y Ud.?**
Cuando Ud. y sus amigos se encuentran, ¿cómo se saludan (*do you greet other*)?

The plural reflexive pronouns, **nos, os,** and **se,** can be used to express *reciprocal actions* (**las acciones recíprocas**). Reciprocal actions are usually expressed in English with *each other* or *one another.*

**Nos** queremos.

| | |
|---|---|
| **Nos** queremos. | *We love each other.* |
| ¿**Os** ayudáis? | *Do you help one another?* |
| **Se** miran. | *They're looking at each other.* |

### AUTOPRUEBA

Give the correct pronoun to express a reciprocal action.

1. _____ miramos        4. _____ conocen
2. _____ pelearon       5. _____ llamaban
3. _____ veíais         6. _____ saludamos

*Answers: 1. nos 2. se 3. os 4. se 5. se 6. nos*

---

*As in many cultures, in Spain and Latin America kissing on the cheek is a common form of greeting and leave-taking. In Hispanic cultures, women kiss each other on the cheek, and men and women kiss each other on the cheek. The number of kisses varies from country to country. In Spain, two kisses (one on each cheek) is common. In much of Latin America, only one kiss, usually on the right cheek, is the norm.*

**Rosa and Casandra** *Rosa and Casandra know each other well. They are roommates. They see each other every day and they meet each other after class to talk. What are Rosa and Casandra doing in this scene? They are kissing each other on the cheek.*

**Prác. A: Preliminary Exercise**
Have students restate the following sentences as reciprocal actions.

1. *Estela me mira a mí. Yo miro a Estela.*
2. *Eduardo habla con Pepita. Pepita habla con Eduardo.*
3. *El padre necesita a su hijo. El hijo necesita a su padre.*
4. *Tomás me conoce a mí. Yo conozco a Tomás.*
5. *Tú le escribes a Luisa. Luisa te escribe a ti.*
6. *La profesora escucha a los estudiantes. Los estudiantes escuchan a la profesora.*
7. *Ud. quiere a su esposo. Su esposo la quiere también a Ud.*
8. *Jorge le da la mano a Mario. Mario le da la mano a Jorge.*

**Prác. B: Suggestion**
Provide the following cues for students to construct a story about *La triste historia de amor de Orlando y Patricia.* Have students narrate the story in the preterite.

1. *verse en clase*
2. *mirarse*
3. *saludarse*
4. *empezar a llamarse por teléfono*
5. *escribirse durante las vacaciones*
6. *ayudarse con sus problemas*
7. *casarse* (translate)
8. *no llevarse bien* (translate)
9. *separarse*
10. *divorciarse*

## ■ Práctica

**Prác. A: Suggestion**
Have students repeat items using *ellos* as the subject, then *vosotros.*

**A. ¡Anticipemos! Buenos amigos.**   Indique las oraciones que describen lo que hacen Ud. y un buen amigo / una buena amiga para mantener su amistad (*friendship*).

1. ☐ Nos vemos con frecuencia.
2. ☐ Nos conocemos muy bien. No hay secretos entre nosotros.
3. ☐ Nos respetamos mucho.
4. ☐ Nos ayudamos con cualquier (*any*) problema.
5. ☐ Nos escribimos cuando no estamos en la misma ciudad.
6. ☐ Nos hablamos por teléfono con frecuencia.
7. ☐ Nos decimos la verdad siempre, sea esta (*be it*) bonita o fea.
8. ☐ Cuando estamos muy ocupados, no importa si no nos hablamos por mucho tiempo.

**B. ¿Qué se hacen?**   Describa las siguientes relaciones familiares o sociales, haciendo oraciones completas con una palabra o frase de cada grupo.

MODELO:   Los buenos amigos se conocen bien.

| | | |
|---|---|---|
| los buenos amigos<br>los parientes<br>los esposos<br>los padres y los niños<br>los amigos que no viven en la misma ciudad<br>los profesores y los estudiantes<br>los compañeros de cuarto/casa | **+** (no) **+** | verse con frecuencia<br>quererse, respetarse<br>ayudarse (con los quehaceres domésticos, con los problemas económicos, con los problemas personales)<br>hablarse (todos los días, con frecuencia, sinceramente)<br>llamarse por teléfono, escribirse (con frecuencia)<br>mirarse (en la clase, con cariño [*affection*])<br>necesitarse<br>conocerse bien<br>saludarse (en la clase, con cariño), darse la mano |

**Need more practice?**

- Workbook/Laboratory Manual
- Interactive CD-ROM
- Online Learning Center (www.mhhe.com/quetal7)

**Heritage Speakers**
Pídales a dos estudiantes que dramaticen algunas acciones recíprocas, por ejemplo, *verse el uno al otro, saludarse el uno al otro, hablarse el uno al otro.* Los demás estudiantes explican las acciones, por ejemplo, *Paco y Marta se saludan.*

## ■ Conversación

### Entrevista

1. ¿Con qué frecuencia se ven tú y tu novio/a (esposo/a, mejor amigo/a)? ¿Cuánto tiempo hace que (*How long has it been that*) se conocen? ¿Con qué frecuencia se dan regalos? ¿se escriben? ¿se telefonean? ¿Te gusta que se vean tanto (tan poco)?
2. ¿Con qué frecuencia se ven tú y tus abuelos/primos? ¿Por qué se ven Uds. tan poco (tanto)? ¿Cómo se mantienen en contacto? En la sociedad norteamericana, ¿los parientes se ven con frecuencia? En tu opinión, ¿es esto común entre los hispanos?

## UN POCO DE TODO

**Lengua y cultura: La leyenda del Lago de Maracaibo.**   Complete the following legend with the correct form of the word in parentheses, as suggested by the context. The verbs will be in the preterite or imperfect. When two possibilities are given, select the correct word.

En una tribu indígena de Venezuela, había una vez[a] un cacique[b] que se llamaba Zapara. Este[c] tenía una hija, Maruma, que (ser[1]) muy bonita. Al padre y a la hija (se/les[2]) (gustar[3]) pasar tiempo juntos andando por el bosque.[d]

Un día Zapara (comprender[4]) que su hija ya (ser[5]) una mujer y (se / le[6]) (decir[7]): «Debes escoger[e] esposo, pues ya tienes edad[f] para formar una familia. Pero (su / tu[8]) esposo debe ser guerrero,[g] como todos los hombres de nuestra familia.» Maruma (ponerse[9]) triste porque debía separarse de su padre para casarse.[h]

Un día, mientras su padre (estar[10]) ausente visitando otras tribus, Maruma (salir[11]) sola a cazar[i] en el bosque. Estaba a punto de dispararle a un ciervo,[j] cuando (un / —[12]) otro cazador[k] (matar[13])[l] al animal. El otro cazador era un joven guapo y simpático. Maruma (ponerse[14]) muy enojada[m] y le gritó:[n] «¿Quién te (dar[15]) permiso para cazar en este bosque?» El joven le contestó: «El ciervo es para (tú / ti[16]). Sólo quiero conocerte. Me llamo Tamaré.» A partir de ese día[o] los (joven[17]) (hacerse[18])[p] amigos. Pronto se enamoraron.[q]

Pero el joven no era guerrero y por eso el padre de Maruma (enojarse[19]) mucho cuando (saber[20]) que ella (querer[21]) casarse con él. Se enfadó tanto[r] que la naturaleza reaccionó y (haber[22]) grandes terremotos[s] e inundaciones:[t] las aguas cubrieron[u] las tierras del cacique Zapara y también a su hija con su amado,[v] formando así el Lago de Maracaibo. Zapara se convirtió en una de sus pequeñas islas.

[a]había... *once upon a time there was*  [b]*leader*  [c]*He*  [d]*forest*  [e]*choose*  [f]*ya... you're old enough*  [g]*a warrior*  [h]*get married*  [i]*hunt*  [j]Estaba... *She was about to shoot a deer*  [k]*hunter*  [l]*to kill*  [m]ponerse... *to become very angry*  [n]le... *she shouted at him*  [o]A... *From that day on*  [p]*to become*  [q]se... *they fell in love*  [r]Se... *He was so angry*  [s]*earthquakes*  [t]*floods*  [u]*covered*  [v]*beloved*

*Un residente del Lago de Maracaibo en su lancha (boat)*

**Suggestions**

• Review the contrastive uses of the preterite and imperfect before completing this activity.

*¿El pretérito o el imperfecto? ¿Cuál se usa... ?*

*...para indicar el comienzo o el final de una acción*

*...para hablar de una acción habitual del pasado*

*...para decir la hora*

*...para expresar características mentales*

**Resources for Review and Testing Preparation**

■ Workbook/Laboratory Manual
■ Interactive CD-ROM
■ Online Learning Center (www.mhhe.com/quetal7)

• This activity, like many in the text, is designed to help students develop conceptual knowledge of the differences in language concepts such as the preterite and imperfect, *ser* and *estar*, *saber* and *conocer*, direct and indirect objects, and relative pronouns. In addition, students will have to switch from present to past in order to complete the narration. A general rule of thumb that might help students is present follows present and past follows past.

**Comprensión: ¿Qué sabe Ud.?**   Conteste las siguientes preguntas en español.

1. ¿Quién era Zapara?
2. ¿Qué debía hacer su hija?
3. ¿De quién estaba enamorada (*in love*) Maruma?
4. ¿Por qué se enfadó Zapara?
5. ¿Cómo se formó el Lago de Maracaibo?

**Lengua y cultura: Answers**
1. *era* 2. *les* 3. *gustaba* 4. *comprendió* 5. *era* 6. *le* 7. *dijo* 8. *tu* 9. *se puso* 10. *estaba* 11. *salió* 12. —
13. *mató* 14. *se puso* 15. *dio* 16. *ti* 17. *jóvenes* 18. *se hicieron* 19. *se enojó* 20. *supo* 21. *quería*
22. *hubo* (*había*)   **Comprensión**   1. *Era el cacique de una tribu indígena.* 2. *Debía casarse con un guerrero.* 3. *Maruma estaba enamorada de Tamaré* 4. *Porque Tamaré no era guerrero.* 5. *Zapara estaba tan furioso que la naturaleza reaccionó y las aguas de las tormentas e inundaciones cubrieron la tierra.*

**Resources: Desenlace**
In the *Capítulo 10* segment of "Chapter-by-Chapter Supplementary Materials" in the IM, you will find a chapter-culminating activity. You can use this activity to consolidate and review the vocabulary and grammar skills students have acquired.

## VIDEOTECA

### Entrevista cultural: Venezuela

Sabina García es una estudiante venezolana. En esta entrevista, ella comenta sus estudios y sus hábitos personales. Sabina hace mucho para mantener un buen estado de salud. Antes de ver el vídeo, lea el siguiente fragmento de la entrevista.

ENTREVISTADORA: ¿Qué estudias?

SABINA: Estudio relaciones internacionales. Considero que actualmente[a] las relaciones internacionales son un campo muy importante en el mundo y se han desarrollado[b] con gran rapidez.

ENTREVISTADORA: ¿Cómo cuidas de tu salud?

SABINA: Trato de alimentarme sanamente, comiendo frutas, verduras, fibra principalmente y me acuesto temprano.

[a]*currently*   [b]*se... they have developed*

Ahora vea el vídeo y conteste las siguientes preguntas basándose en la entrevista.

1. ¿Qué estudia Sabina?
2. ¿Por qué estudia esta carrera?
3. ¿Qué come Sabina?
4. ¿Qué más hace Sabina para cuidarse?
5. ¿Qué hace para aliviarse el estrés?

### Entre amigos: ¡Yo sí hago ejercicio!

Tané, Karina, Rubén y Miguel visitan un mercado de pulgas (*flea market*) y hablan del ejercicio. En su opinión, ¿qué preguntas se van a hacer? Antes de mirar el vídeo, lea las preguntas a continuación. Mientras mire el vídeo, trate de entender la conversación en general y fíjese en la información sobre el ejercicio que hacen los amigos. Luego mire el vídeo una segunda vez, fijándose en la información que necesita para contestar las preguntas.

1. ¿Hace ejercicio Karina? ¿Qué tipo de ejercicio hace?
2. ¿Y Tané? ¿Qué tipo de ejercicio hace ella?
3. ¿Quiénes no tienen mucho tiempo para hacer ejercicio?
4. ¿Qué está haciendo Miguel mientras hablan del ejercicio?
5. ¿Cuántas veces por semana va Miguel al gimnasio?

## ENFOQUE CULTURAL

 **Venezuela**

**Notes**
• Christopher Columbus first sighted what is now Venezuela in 1498. It was the home of the Caribs and Arawaks, indigenous peoples who also populated the Antilles.

### Personas famosas: Simón Bolívar

Simón Bolívar (1783–1830) nació en Caracas. La fecha de su cumpleaños, el 24 de julio, es hoy día una fiesta nacional en Venezuela. Bolívar, llamado «el Libertador», ocupa un puesto[a] importante tanto en la historia de Venezuela como en la historia de Colombia, el Perú, el Ecuador y Bolivia por ser el personaje principal en las luchas[b] por la independencia de estos países. Bolívar, influenciado por las ideas de Jean Jacques Rousseau[c] y por la lucha de las colonias estadounidenses contra lnglaterra en el siglo XVIII, soñaba con[d] una América hispánica unida, sueño que nunca vio realizado.[e]

[a]*position* [b]*struggles* [c]*French writer and philosopher (1712–1778) whose ideas helped spark the French Revolution* [d]soñaba… *dreamed about* [e]*achieved*

*La estatua de Simón Bolívar en la Plaza Bolívar de Ciudad Bolívar*

### ¡Fíjese!

Por su variedad de climas, Venezuela le ofrece al turista atracciones diversas. El clima venezolano varía entre el clima templado de las regiones andinas y el clima tropical de los llanos[a] y la costa. De hecho, el clima es agradable la mayor parte del año. Entre las atracciones turísticas hay lo siguiente.

• las hermosas[b] playas tropicales de la Isla Margarita y la costa caribeña
• la famosa catarata[c] Salto Ángel que, siendo dieciséis veces más alta que las cataratas del Niágara, es considerada la más alta del mundo
• la belleza[d] colonial de Ciudad Bolívar y Coro
• la progresiva y cosmopolita ciudad de Caracas y las majestuosas montañas andinas

[a]*plains* [b]*beautiful* [c]*waterfall* [d]*beauty*

• The Genoese explorer sponsored by Spain named the country Venezuela, "little Venice," because the villages, built on pilings on Lake Maracaibo, reminded him of that European city. In 1567, Diego de Losada founded the city of Santiago de León de Caracas in the *tierra templada* more than half a mile above sea level—Santiago after the patron saint of Spain, León after the governor of that time, and Caracas after the indigenous group of the area. Colonization of the country continued rapidly in the next century, with Caracas as its urban center.

• Students can read an excerpt from the novel *Doña Bárbara* by Venezuela's Rómulo Gallegos in *Voces de Venezuela: Literatura*.
• Students can read about Venezuela's musical tradition *el joropo* in *Voces de Venezuela: Música*.
• See the Workbook/Laboratory Manual for focused practice with the material in *Enfoque cultural*.

**Multimedia: Internet**
• Have students look for the *Biblioteca Virtual* on the Internet. Here they can learn more about *Simón Bolívar* and other Latin American heroes and historical moments.
• Have students search the Internet for more information about Venezuela's government, educational system, geography, and economy. You might assign specific topics and have students give brief oral presentations based on their findings.

Learn more about Venezuela with the Video, the Interactive CD-ROM, and the Online Learning Center (www.mhhe.com/quetal7).

# PASO 4

**Note**

Remind students that the relationship between a pharmacist and a customer is generally a formal one. The pharmacist is considered a highly qualified medical professional who takes his or her responsibilities very seriously. This should be reflected in the language of the improvisation.

**Suggestions**

• Have students practice their scenes several times, then have volunteers present to the class.

• For writing practice, see the *Mi diario* activity in each chapter of the Workbook/Laboratory Manual.

### PASO FINAL

 **A CONVERSAR**

**En la farmacia**

Como Ud. leyó en la **Nota cultural** de este capítulo, en muchos países hispanos la gente puede consultar a un farmacéutico / una farmacéutica en vez de ir al médico. La persona enferma describe sus síntomas y el farmacéutico / la farmacéutica o (*either*) le receta un medicamento apropiado o le manda a ver al médico.

PASO 1   En una hoja de papel aparte, prepare un cuadro como el siguiente. En su cuadro, escriba los síntomas y los posibles tratamientos para las enfermedades en los espacios en blanco.

| enfermedad | una infección de garganta | un resfriado | una migraña |
|---|---|---|---|
| **síntomas** | | | |
| **tratamientos** | | | |

PASO 2   Con un compañero / una compañera, prepare una escena entre una persona enferma y un farmacéutico / una farmacéutica. Escojan el papel que quieren hacer e improvisen una escena basándose en los cuadros del **Paso 1.** Su escena debe incluir saludos, una descripción de los síntomas, las recomendaciones médicas y una despedida.

MODELO:   E1: Buenos días, Sr. Maldonado.
E2: Buenos días, Sra. Velázquez. ¿En qué le puedo servir?
E1: Me siento muy mal hoy. No sé qué me pasa.
E2: ¿Qué síntomas tiene?…

PASO 3   Cambien papeles e improvisen la escena otra vez.

**Suggestion**
Describe absurd creatures and have students draw them, for example, *Era una criatura inmensa. Tenía tres piernas y un brazo. En la cabeza tenía una oreja que extendía de la frente...*

## GRAMÁTICA

To review the grammar points presented in this chapter, refer to the indicated grammar presentations. You'll find further practice of these structures in the Workbook/Laboratory Manual, on the Interactive CD-ROM, and on the *¿Qué tal?* Online Learning Center (www.mhhe.com/quetal7).

**29** Narrating in the Past—Using the Preterite and the Imperfect

Do you know which tense to use to express habitual or repeated actions? Which tense should be used to express the beginning or end of an action?

**30** Expressing *each other*—Reciprocal Actions with Reflexive Pronouns

Which reflexive pronouns are used in reciprocal constructions?

## VOCABULARIO

Practice this vocabulary with digital flash cards on the Online Learning Center (www.mhhe.com/quetal7).

### Los verbos

| | |
|---|---|
| encontrarse (ue) (con) | to meet (*someone somewhere*) |
| saludarse | to greet each other |

### La salud y el bienestar

| | |
|---|---|
| el bienestar | well-being |
| la rueda de molino | treadmill |
| la salud | health |
| caminar | to walk |
| cuidarse | to take care of oneself |
| dejar de + *inf.* | to stop (*doing something*) |
| doler (ue) | to hurt, ache |
| encontrarse (ue) | to be, feel |
| examinar | to examine |
| guardar cama | to stay in bed |
| hacer (*irreg.*) ejercicios aeróbicos | to do aerobics |
| internarse (en) | to check into (*a hospital*) |
| llevar una vida sana/tranquila | to lead a healthy/calm life |
| ponerle (*irreg.*) una inyección | to give (someone) a shot, injection |
| resfriarse (me resfrío) | to get/catch a cold |
| respirar | to breathe |
| sacar (qu) | to extract |
| sacar la lengua | to stick out one's tongue |
| sacar una muela | to extract a tooth |

| | |
|---|---|
| tener (*irreg.*) dolor de | to have a pain in |
| tener dolor de cabeza | to have a headache |
| tener dolor de estómago | to have a stomachache |
| tener dolor de muela | to have a toothache |
| tomar(le) la temperatura | to take someone's temperature |
| toser | to cough |

**Repaso:** comer, correr, dormir (ue, u), enfermarse, hacer (*irreg.*) ejercicio, practicar (qu) deportes

### Algunas partes del cuerpo humano

| | |
|---|---|
| la boca | mouth |
| la cabeza | head |
| el cerebro | brain |
| el corazón | heart |
| el cuerpo | body |
| el diente | tooth |
| el estómago | stomach |
| la garganta | throat |
| la muela | tooth; molar |
| la nariz | nose |
| el oído | inner ear |
| el ojo | eye |
| la oreja | (outer) ear |
| los pulmones | lungs |
| la sangre | blood |

## Las enfermedades y los tratamientos

| | |
|---|---|
| el chequeo | checkup |
| el consultorio | (medical) office |
| el dolor (de) | pain, ache (in) |
| la farmacia | pharmacy |
| la fiebre | fever |
| las gafas | glasses |
| el jarabe | (cough) syrup |
| los lentes de contacto | contact lenses |
| la pastilla | pill |
| la receta | prescription |
| el resfriado | cold |
| el síntoma | symptom |
| la tos | cough |

Cognados: el antibiótico, la medicina
Repaso: llevar

## El personal médico

| | |
|---|---|
| el/la enfermero/a | nurse |
| el/la farmacéutico/a | pharmacist |
| el/la paciente | patient |

Cognado: el/la dentista
Repaso: el/la médico/a

## Otros sustantivos

| | |
|---|---|
| la desventaja | disadvantage |
| la ventaja | advantage |

## Los adjetivos

| | |
|---|---|
| congestionado/a | congested, stuffed up |
| mareado/a | dizzy; nauseated |
| mismo/a | same |
| pasado/a | past, last |

## Palabras adicionales

| | |
|---|---|
| anoche | last night |
| anteayer | the day before yesterday |
| de repente | suddenly |
| dos veces | twice |
| en seguida | right away |
| equilibradamente | in a balanced way |
| eso quiere decir… | that means . . . |
| lo bueno | the good thing, news |
| lo malo | the bad thing, news |
| lo suficiente | enough |

Repaso: ayer, de joven, de niño/a, mientras, siempre, una vez

**Suggestions**
- Ask students the following questions.

  1. ¿Con qué parte del cuerpo se asocian estas cosas?

     | | |
     |---|---|
     | la comida | las películas |
     | la música | el amor |
     | el oxígeno | el cálculo |

  2. ¿Se refiere a la médica o al paciente?

     Examina los ojos.
     Tiene fiebre.
     Saca la lengua.
     Escribe recetas.
     Le duele la garganta.
     Recomienda un jarabe.

- Read the following definitions and have students give the word for each.

  1. Es un sinónimo de «ponerse enfermo».
  2. Es un líquido que se toma contra la tos.
  3. Esto se hace con un termómetro.
  4. No se puede hacer esto sin los pulmones.
  5. Es el papelito que nos da el médico cuando nos manda a la farmacia.

- Read these sentences and have students tell whether or not the statements are cierto or falso for them based on their last dental visit.

  1. Me examinó los dientes.
  2. Me limpió los dientes.
  3. Me puso una inyección.
  4. Me sacó una muela.
  5. Me empastó (he/she filled) un diente.
  6. Me sacó unos rayos X.
  7. Me hizo muchas preguntas.
  8. Me preguntó si uso hilo dental (pantomime) con regularidad.

- Ask students the following questions.

  1. Una persona come hamburguesas y toma Coca-Cola con frecuencia. ¿Come bien o come mal? (Come mal.)
  2. Si se tiene problemas del corazón, ¿se debe caminar o correr para hacer ejercicio? (Se debe caminar.)
  3. Si se duerme siete horas y media cada noche, ¿duerme lo suficiente o necesita dormir más? (lo suficiente)

- Have students nominalize the following adjectives with lo. Encourage them to use them in model sentences: importante → lo importante → Lo importante en esta clase es practicar.

  | | |
  |---|---|
  | 1. divertido | 4. curioso |
  | 2. peor | 5. necesario |
  | 3. interesante | 6. bueno |

# Presiones de la vida° moderna

°life

Dos estudiantes en el campus de la Universidad de Puerto Rico, en Río Piedras

## CULTURA

- **Nota cultural:** Palabras y frases para momentos difíciles
- **En los Estados Unidos y el Canadá:** La impresionante variedad de la música latina
- **Voces** de Puerto Rico
    **Literatura:** Rosario Ferré
    **Música:** La bomba y la plena
- **Videoteca**
    **Entrevista cultural:** Puerto Rico
    **Entre amigos:** ¡Estoy superestresada!
- **Enfoque cultural:** Puerto Rico
- **A leer:** Divórciate del estrés

## VOCABULARIO

- Las presiones de la vida estudiantil
- ¡La profesora Martínez se levantó con el pie izquierdo!

## GRAMÁTICA

**31** Another Use of **se**

**32** ¿**Por** o **para**?

**Suggestions**
- Point out the chapter-opener photo. Have students talk about the campus and the students in the photo. Where are they going? How do they feel? Have them discuss their own situations as students, and their ideas about handling school-related stress. Encourage them to describe any stress they have had.

• Have students list their ideas about Puerto Rico, including information on geography, politics, economy, culture, music, and cuisine. When you finish the chapter, return to the lists and ask students what ideas they would change and/or add.

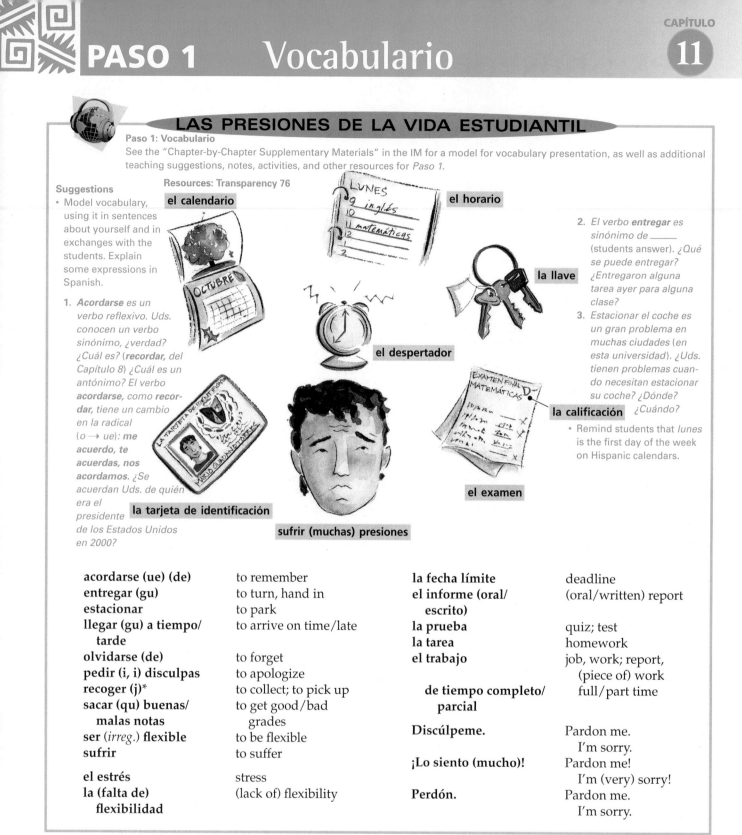

### LAS PRESIONES DE LA VIDA ESTUDIANTIL

**Paso 1: Vocabulario**
See the "Chapter-by-Chapter Supplementary Materials" in the IM for a model for vocabulary presentation, as well as additional teaching suggestions, notes, activities, and other resources for *Paso 1*.

**Suggestions**

• Model vocabulary, using it in sentences about yourself and in exchanges with the students. Explain some expressions in Spanish.

1. *Acordarse es un verbo reflexivo. Uds. conocen un verbo sinónimo, ¿verdad? ¿Cuál es? (recordar, del Capítulo 8) ¿Cuál es un antónimo? El verbo acordarse, como recordar, tiene un cambio en la radical (o → ue): me acuerdo, te acuerdas, nos acordamos. ¿Se acuerdan Uds. de quién era el presidente de los Estados Unidos en 2000?*

**Resources: Transparency 76**

el calendario

el horario

el despertador

la llave

la calificación

el examen

la tarjeta de identificación

sufrir (muchas) presiones

2. *El verbo entregar es sinónimo de _____ (students answer). ¿Qué se puede entregar? ¿Entregaron alguna tarea ayer para alguna clase?*

3. *Estacionar el coche es un gran problema en muchas ciudades (en esta universidad). ¿Uds. tienen problemas cuando necesitan estacionar su coche? ¿Dónde? ¿Cuándo?*

• Remind students that *lunes* is the first day of the week on Hispanic calendars.

| | | | |
|---|---|---|---|
| **acordarse (ue) (de)** | to remember | **la fecha límite** | deadline |
| **entregar (gu)** | to turn, hand in | **el informe (oral/ escrito)** | (oral/written) report |
| **estacionar** | to park | | |
| **llegar (gu) a tiempo/ tarde** | to arrive on time/late | **la prueba** | quiz; test |
| | | **la tarea** | homework |
| **olvidarse (de)** | to forget | **el trabajo** | job, work; report, (piece of) work |
| **pedir (i, i) disculpas** | to apologize | | |
| **recoger (j)*** | to collect; to pick up | **de tiempo completo/ parcial** | full/part time |
| **sacar (qu) buenas/ malas notas** | to get good/bad grades | | |
| **ser (*irreg.*) flexible** | to be flexible | **Discúlpeme.** | Pardon me. I'm sorry. |
| **sufrir** | to suffer | | |
| | | **¡Lo siento (mucho)!** | Pardon me! I'm (very) sorry! |
| **el estrés** | stress | | |
| **la (falta de) flexibilidad** | (lack of) flexibility | **Perdón.** | Pardon me. I'm sorry. |

**Multimedia: Audio**
Students can listen to and practice this chapter's vocabulary on the Online Learning Center (**www.mhhe.com/quetal7**), as well as on the Textbook Audio CD, part of the Laboratory Audio Program.

*Note the present indicative conjugation of **recoger: recojo, recoges, recoge, recogemos, recogéis, recogen.**

Preliminary Exercise

Ask students the following questions to personalize the vocabulary.

1. ¿Está Ud. contento/a con su horario de este semestre/trimestre? ¿Por qué? ¿Tiene Ud. que entregar algún informe esta semana? ¿Cuál es la fecha límite? ¿Tiene pruebas o exámenes? ¿Tuvo algún examen o informe importante la semana pasada?

2. ¿Viene Ud. en coche a la universidad? ¿Tiene problemas para estacionar? ¿Dónde estaciona?

3. ¿Saca Ud. buenas notas este semestre? ¿Son mejores o peores que las del semestre pasado?

4. ¿Le gusta el calendario de esta universidad (cuando empieza y termina el semestre [trimestre]/cuando hay vacaciones)? ¿Por qué?

5. Normalmente, ¿es Ud. una persona que llega tarde o temprano a las citas / las clases? ¿Necesita un despertador por la mañana o puede Ud. despertarse solo/a?

6. ¿Se acuerda Ud. de sus citas sin mirar la agenda? ¿Se acuerda Ud. de escribir sus citas en la agenda y de mirarla después?

# ■ Conversación

## A. Asociaciones

PASO 1  ¿Qué palabras asocia Ud. con estos verbos? Pueden ser sustantivos, antónimos o sinónimos.

1. estacionar
2. recoger
3. acordarse
4. entregar
5. sacar
6. sufrir
7. pedir
8. llegar a tiempo
9. abrir
10. perder
11. ser feliz
12. ser flexible

PASO 2  ¿Qué palabras y/o situaciones asocia Ud. con los siguientes sustantivos?

1. el calendario
2. el despertador
3. las calificaciones
4. el estrés
5. la fecha límite
6. el horario
7. los informes
8. la llave
9. la tarjeta de identificación
10. las disculpas
11. las presiones
12. la flexibilidad
13. la prueba
14. el trabajo

## B. Situaciones

PASO 1  La primera lista que Ud. va a leer consta de (*consists of*) preguntas o comentarios hechos por varias personas. La segunda lista incluye las respuestas de otras personas. Decida qué respuesta corresponde a cada comentario.

1. __b__ —Anoche no me acordé de poner el despertador.

2. __a__ —No puedes estacionar el coche aquí. No tienes permiso de estacionamiento para esta zona.

3. __d__ —¿Sacaste una buena nota en la prueba?

4. __e__ —Ramiro no tiene buen aspecto (*doesn't look right*). Creo que algo le causa mucho estrés.

5. __c__ —Aquí tiene mi trabajo escrito sobre el Mercado Común.

a. —Pues estoy cansado de buscar estacionamiento por todo el *campus*. Lo voy a dejar aquí.

b. —¿Lo olvidaste otra vez? ¿A qué hora llegaste a la oficina?

c. —Pero la fecha límite era ayer. Es la última vez que acepto un informe suyo (*of yours*) tarde.

d. —Muy buena, pero no la esperaba. No tuve tiempo de estudiar.

e. —Es porque tiene un trabajo de tiempo completo, y también toma tres cursos este semestre.

PASO 2  Ahora, con un compañero / una compañera, invente un contexto para cada diálogo. ¿Dónde están las personas que hablan? ¿En casa? ¿en una oficina? ¿en clase? ¿Quiénes son?

MODELO:  1. → Las personas que hablan están en el trabajo (la oficina). Probablemente están almorzando. Son compañeros de trabajo; no son buenos amigos…

Con. A: Answers

*Paso 1*  Possible answers:  1. el coche 2. los libros, la ropa 3. la fecha límite, la tarea 4. la tarea, el informe, el trabajo 5. la calificación, las notas 6. las presiones, el estrés 7. disculpas 8. las clases, el trabajo 9. la llave 10. la llave, la tarjeta de identificación 11. sacar buenas notas 12. el horario  *Paso 2* Possible answers:  1. la fecha límite 2. llegar a tiempo 3. los exámenes, sacar notas 4. los exámenes, la fecha límite 5. el informe, el trabajo 6. el calendario 7. la fecha límite, el trabajo 8. el coche, la casa 9. los estudiantes 10. la flexibilidad, la fecha límite 11. la fecha límite, el horario, examen 12. los profesores, el horario 13. la calificación, sacar notas 14. el horario, la flexibilidad

Con. A: Variation

Use a game format to get synonyms and antonyms. Divide the class into teams. Allow teams to work on each word for only one minute; the team with the most associations wins the round.

**Heritage Speakers**

• Por la influencia del inglés en algunos dialectos del español del suroeste de los Estados Unidos, se oye decir *grado* en vez de *calificación*. Las palabras aceptadas, sin embargo, son *nota* y *calificación*. Otra  expresión influida por el inglés es la palabra *notas* para expresar *apuntes*.

• Algunos hispanohablantes de los Estados Unidos usan la palabra *alarma* para referirse al *despertador*.

• El término *parquear* (*estacionar*) que se oye en México también se usa en algunos países latinoamericanos y en los Estados Unidos. Algunas derivaciones son *el parqueadero* (*estacionamiento*). En España, donde dicen *aparcar*, usan la palabra *aparcamiento*.

♻ **Suggestions**
- Review body parts presented in *Capítulo 10*.
- Point out that *dedos* can refer to fingers or toes. To distinguish the two, use *dedos del pie* and *dedos de la mano*.
- Have students give the corresponding word.

1. *Es sinónimo de no tener razón.*
2. *Tomo esto cuando me duele la cabeza.*
3. *Es sinónimo de hacerse daño.*
4. *Es un adjetivo que significa no estar atento a lo que pasa.*
5. *Es una persona que tiene muchos accidentes.*

**C. Los años estudiantiles, ¿una época** (*period, time*) **maravillosa?** Con frecuencia se oye a las personas mayores hablar de los años universitarios con nostalgia: años de libertad, sin responsabilidades, sin las tensiones propias de la vida laboral y familiar. ¿Ve Ud. así la época universitaria? Con un compañero / una compañera, comente este tema. Pueden usar las siguientes preguntas como guía (*guide*).

1. ¿Sufren muchas presiones los estudiantes universitarios? ¿Por qué? ¿Qué les causa estrés?
2. ¿Son más divertidos los años universitarios que los años de la escuela secundaria?
3. ¿Le preocupa a Ud. el costo de la matrícula? Para Ud. o para su familia, ¿es difícil pagarla?
4. ¿Piensa Ud. que la vida va a ser mejor después de graduarse en la universidad? ¿Por qué sí o por qué no?

con... *on the wrong side of the bed*

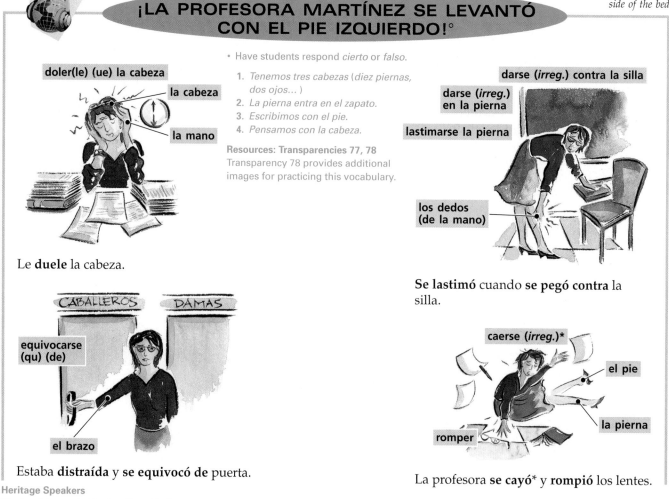

**¡LA PROFESORA MARTÍNEZ SE LEVANTÓ CON EL PIE IZQUIERDO!°**

- Have students respond *cierto* or *falso*.

1. *Tenemos tres cabezas (diez piernas, dos ojos... )*
2. *La pierna entra en el zapato.*
3. *Escribimos con el pie.*
4. *Pensamos con la cabeza.*

**Resources: Transparencies 77, 78**
Transparency 78 provides additional images for practicing this vocabulary.

**doler(le) (ue) la cabeza**

la cabeza

la mano

Le **duele** la cabeza.

**darse** (*irreg.*) **contra la silla**

**darse** (*irreg.*) **en la pierna**

**lastimarse la pierna**

**los dedos (de la mano)**

Se **lastimó** cuando **se pegó contra** la silla.

CABALLEROS   DAMAS

**equivocarse (qu) (de)**

el brazo

Estaba **distraída** y **se equivocó de** puerta.

**caerse** (*irreg.*)*

el pie

la pierna

**romper**

La profesora **se cayó*** y **rompió** los lentes.

**Heritage Speakers**
Muchos hispanohablantes dicen *Casi me caigo* o *Por poco me caigo*; es decir, usan el presente con *casi* o *por poco* para expresar *I almost fell* (el pasado).

*Note that the first person singular of **caer** is irregular: **caigo**. The present participle is **cayendo**.

## Accidentes

| | |
|---|---|
| **darse** (*irreg.*) **en/con/ contra** | to hit (*a part of one's body*); to run into / bump against |
| **doler (ue)** | to hurt, ache |
| **equivocarse (qu) (de)** | to be wrong, make a mistake (about) |
| **hacerse** (*irreg.*) **daño** | to hurt oneself |

| | |
|---|---|
| **pegarse (gu) en/con/ contra** | to run, bump into |
| **el dedo del pie** | toe |
| **Fue sin querer.** | It was unintentional. |
| **distraído/a** | absentminded |
| **torpe** | clumsy |
| **¡Qué torpe!** | How clumsy! |

## ■ Conversación

**Nota cultural: Suggestion**
Point out that in Spanish as in English, many expressions emerge and fade. An expression will often become associated with a specific time period.

### NOTA CULTURAL

#### Palabras y frases para momentos difíciles

**Nota cultural: Comprensión**
1. ¿Qué dice Ud. si un amigo está triste o deprimido?
2. ¿Qué dice Ud. si se hace daño a la mano?
3. ¿Qué puede decir si un amigo le cuenta algo increíble?

Hay muchas expresiones para **ocasiones de mala suerte**[a] **o de presión.** Varían mucho de región en región y de país en país. Estas son algunas de las más comunes.

Para expresar dolor, sorpresa o compasión

| | | | |
|---|---|---|---|
| **¡Ay!** | Ah! Ouch! | **¿Qué le vamos a hacer?** | What can you do? |
| **¡Uy!** | Oops! Oh! | **¡No me digas!** | You're kidding! (You don't say!) |
| **¡No puede ser!** | That can't be! | **¡Qué mala suerte!** | What bad luck! |
| **¡Cuánto lo siento!** | I'm so sorry! | | |

Para dar ánimo[b]

| | | | |
|---|---|---|---|
| **¡Venga!** | Come on! | **¡No es para tanto!** | It's not so bad! |
| **¡Órale!** (*Mex.*) | Come on! | **¡Anímate!** | Cheer up! |

[a]*luck*  [b]Para... *To cheer (someone up)*

**Heritage Speakers**
Pregúnteles a los hispanohablantes cuáles son algunas de las expresiones más corrientes en español para expresar dolor, sorpresa, compasión o para dar ánimo.

**A. Posibilidades.** ¿Qué puede Ud. hacer o decir —o qué le puede pasar— en cada situación?

MODELO: Ud. se da contra el escritorio de otro estudiante y se lastima el pie. →
—¡Ay! ¡Qué torpe soy!

**Con. A: Answers**
*Possible answers:* **1.** Tomo aspirinas. **2.** Digo: «Fue sin querer». **3.** Me pongo avergonzado/a. **4.** Me doy con una silla y me caigo. **5.** Me duele y digo: «¡Ay!». **6.** Le digo: «¡No es para tanto!».

1. A Ud. le duele mucho la cabeza.
2. Ud. le pega a otra persona sin querer.
3. Ud. se olvida del nombre de otra persona.
4. Ud. está muy distraído/a y no mira por dónde camina (*you're walking*).
5. Ud. se lastima la mano (el pie).
6. Su amigo está nervioso porque se dio contra la profesora antes de clase.

♻ **Reciclado**
• Recycle clothing vocabulary.

*¿Qué parte del cuerpo asocia Ud. con... ?*

| | |
|---|---|
| el reloj | la camisa |
| los pantalones | los zapatos |
| el sombrero | los guantes |

• Recycle the use of the preterite and imperfect. Have students work in pairs to tell each other about accidents they have had. Then have students report to the class their partner's accidents, including all information necessary to tell the story: when it happened, where, with whom, how the person felt, what he/she did afterward.

# PASO 1

**Adjetivos**

| | |
|---|---|
| **constante** | **posible** |
| **directo** | **puntual** |
| **fácil** | **rápido** |
| **inmediato** | **total** |
| **paciente** | **tranquilo** |

**Need more practice?**

■ Workbook/Laboratory Manual
■ Interactive CD-ROM
■ Online Learning Center (www.mhhe.com/quetal7) **Note**

**280** doscientos ochenta

---

**B. Accidentes y tropiezos** (*mishaps*). ¿Le pasaron a Ud. alguna vez las siguientes cosas? Complete las oraciones con información verdadera para Ud. Si nunca le pasó nada de esto, invente una situación que podría haber ocurrido (*could have happened*). Luego, con un compañero / una compañera, haga y conteste preguntas basadas en estas oraciones.

MODELO:   ¿Te caíste por las escaleras ayer? ¿Te hiciste daño?

1. Me caí por las escaleras (*stairs*) y _____.
2. No me acordé de hacer la tarea para la clase de _____.
3. Me equivoqué cuando _____.
4. El despertador sonó, pero _____.
5. No pude encontrar _____.
6. Me di con _____ y me lastimé _____.
7. Pasó la fecha límite para entregar un informe y _____.
8. Caminaba un poco distraído/a y _____.

## NOTA COMUNICATIVA

### More on Adverbs

You already know the most common Spanish adverbs: words like **bien/mal, mucho/poco, siempre/nunca...**

Adverbs that end in -*ly* in English usually end in **-mente** in Spanish. The suffix **-mente** is added to the feminine singular form of adjectives. Note that the accent mark on the stem word (if there is one) is retained.

| ADJECTIVE | ADVERB | ENGLISH |
|---|---|---|
| rápida | **rápida**mente | *rapidly* |
| fácil | **fácil**mente | *easily* |
| paciente | **paciente**mente | *patiently* |

**C. ¡Seamos** (*Let's be*) **lógicos!**   Complete estas oraciones lógicamente con adverbios basados en los siguientes adjetivos.

1. La familia está esperando _____ en la cola.   pacientemente
2. Hay examen mañana y tengo que empezar a estudiar _____.   inmediatamente
3. ¿Las enchiladas? Se preparan _____.   fácilmente
4. ¿Qué pasa? Estoy _____ confundido/a (*confused*).   totalmente
5. Cuando mira la tele, mi hermanito cambia el canal _____.   constantemente
6. Es necesario que las clases empiecen _____.   puntualmente

**D. Entrevista.**   Con un compañero / una compañera, haga y conteste las siguientes preguntas.

MODELO:   E1: ¿Qué haces pacientemente?
E2: Espero pacientemente a mi esposo cuando se viste para salir. ¡Lo hace muy lentamente (*slowly*)!

1. ¿Qué haces rápidamente?
2. ¿Qué te toca hacer inmediatamente?
3. ¿Qué hiciste (comiste,... ) solamente una vez que te gustó muchísimo (no te gustó nada)?
4. ¿Qué haces tú fácilmente que es difícil para otras personas?
5. ¿Qué hace constantemente tu compañero/a de casa (amigo/a, esposo/a,... ) que te molesta (*bothers*) muchísimo?

**Paso 2: Gramática**
See the "Chapter-by-Chapter Supplementary Materials" in the IM for additional teaching suggestions, notes, activities, and other resources for *Paso 2.*

## 31 Expressing Unplanned or Unexpected Events  Another Use of *se*

**Un día fatal**

Diego y Antonio son compañeros de cuarto. Hoy todo les salió mal.

A Diego *se le cayó* la taza de café.

También *se le perdió* la cartera.

A Antonio *se le olvidaron* sus libros y su trabajo cuando fue a clase.

También *se le perdieron* las llaves de su apartamento.

**¿Y Ud.?**

¿Le pasaron a Ud. las mismas cosas —o cosas parecidas (*similar*)— esta semana? Conteste, completando las oraciones.

1. *Se me perdieron / No se me perdieron* las llaves de mi coche/casa.
2. *Se me olvidó / No se me olvidó* una reunión importante.
3. *Se me cayó / No se me cayó* una taza de café.
4. *Se me rompió / No se me rompió* un objeto de valor (*value*) sentimental.

**Note**
Aim for partial control. This can include a few fixed or memorized sentences, such as *se me olvidó, se me perdió,* and so on.

**Extension**
Provide additional situations for *Un día fatal.*

5. (*No*) *Se me acabó el dinero cuando estaba de vacaciones.*
6. (*No*) *Se me olvidó hacer una tarea importante.*
7. (*No*) *Se me perdieron unos apuntes de clase.*
8. (*No*) *Se me rompió el brazo.*
9. (*No*) *Se me olvidó la cartera en casa.*
10. (*No*) *Se me quedaron los libros en la biblioteca.*
11. (*No*) *Se me perdió todo el dinero que tenía.*
12. (*No*) *Se me cayeron las gafas.*

**Suggestion**
Have students convert the following into *se* structures.

1. *Jaime perdió las llaves.*
2. *Carlos rompió la lámpara.*
3. *Susana y Roberto olvidaron sus libros.*

---

**A.** Unplanned or unexpected events (*I dropped . . . , We lost . . . , You forgot . . .*) are frequently expressed in Spanish with **se** and a third person form of the verb. In this structure, the occurrence is viewed as happening *to* someone—the unwitting "victim" of the action.

The chart on page 282 illustrates the different parts and word order of this structure. Note:

- The "victim" is indicated by an indirect object pronoun.
- As with the verb **gustar,** the **a** + *noun* phrase is required in sentences that express the "victim" as a noun. The **a** + *pronoun* phrase is often used to clarify or emphasize meaning when the "victim" is expressed as a pronoun.
- The subject of the verb is the thing that is dropped, broken, forgotten, and so on.
- The subject usually follows the verb in this structure.

**Se me** cayó el papel.
*I dropped the paper. (The paper was dropped by me.)*

**Se le** olvidaron las llaves.
*He forgot the keys. (The keys were forgotten by him.)*

**Se te** olvidó llamar a tu hija.
*You forgot to call your daughter. (Calling your daughter was forgotten by you.)*

**Emphasis A: Suggestions**
- Point out that the subject of the English sentence becomes the indirect object pronoun in the Spanish equivalent: I = *se **me**;* Antonio = *se **le.*** The structure is similar to that of *gustar.*
- Point out the option of emphasizing or clarifying the indirect object with the corresponding prepositional phrase: *a mí, a él,* and so on.
- Point out that the use of the singular vs. the plural verb depends on the direct object from the English sentence.

| a + Noun / (a + Pronoun) | se | Indirect Object Pronoun | Verb | Subject |
|---|---|---|---|---|
| (A mí) | Se | me | cayó | la taza de café. |
| ¿(A ti) | Se | te | perdió | la cartera? |
| A Antonio | se | le | olvidaron | los apuntes. |

The verb agrees with the grammatical subject of the Spanish sentence (**la taza, la cartera, los apuntes**), not with the indirect object pronoun. **No** immediately precedes **se**.

**A Diego** *se le* **perdió la cartera.**
*Diego lost his wallet. (Diego's wallet got lost on him.)*

**A Antonio** *no se le* **olvidaron los apuntes.**
*Antonio didn't forget his notes. (Antonio's notes were not forgotten by him.)*

**B.** Here are some verbs frequently used in this construction.

*Note:* In this structure **quedar** can mean *to have* (something left [over]) or *to leave* (something behind).

*Note:* Although all indirect object pronouns can be used in this construction, this section will focus on the first, second, and third person singular forms (**se me...**, **se te...**, **se le...** ).

**Emphasis B: Suggestion**
This section concentrates on the use of this structure with *me, te,* and *le.* You might expand the activities in this section to cover *nos, os,* and *les* if you want students to practice those forms.

| acabar | *to finish; to run out of* |
|---|---|
| olvidar | *to forget* |
| perder (ie) | *to lose* |

**caer**

**romper**

**quedar**

A Miguel no le queda mucha Coca-Cola. (*Miguel doesn't have much Coke left.*)

**C.** In general, this structure is used to emphasize the accidental nature of an event. When the speaker wishes to emphasize *who* committed the act, or that the act was intentional, that person becomes the subject of the verb and the **se** structure is not used. Compare the sentences at the right.

Se me rompió el plato.
*The plate broke on me.* (accidentally)

(Yo) Rompí el plato.
*I broke the plate.* (emphasizes either who broke the plate or the intentionality of the act)

**Heritage Speakers**
En algunas áreas rurales de Latinoamérica y de los Estados Unidos se oye decir *me se* y *te se* en vez de *se me* y *se te* en esta construcción. La construcción aceptada, sin embargo, es *se me* y *se te*.

**AUTOPRUEBA**

Match the following sentences.

1. _____ No encuentro las llaves.
2. _____ Tu calculadora no funciona.
3. _____ Paco no entregó la tarea.
4. _____ Necesito comprar leche.

a. Se te rompió.
b. Se me acabó.
c. Se me perdieron.
d. Se le olvidó.

*Answers: 1. c 2. a 3. d 4. b*

## ■ Práctica

**A. ¡Anticipemos! ¡Qué mala memoria!** Hortensia sufre muchas presiones en su vida. Por eso cuando se fue de vacaciones al Perú, estaba tan distraída que se le olvidó hacer muchas cosas importantes antes de salir. Empareje (*Match*) los lapsos de Hortensia con las consecuencias.

LAPSOS

1. __d__ Se le olvidó cerrar la puerta de su casa.
2. __c__ Se le olvidó pagar las cuentas (*bills*).
3. __e__ Se le olvidó pedirle a alguien que cuidara a (*to take care of*) su perro.
4. __g__ Se le olvidó cancelar el periódico.
5. __a__ Se le olvidó pedirle permiso a su jefa (*boss*).
6. __b__ Se le olvidó llevar el pasaporte.
7. __f__ Se le olvidó hacer reserva en un hotel.

CONSECUENCIAS

a. Va a perder el trabajo.
b. No la van a dejar entrar en el Perú.
c. Le van a suspender el servicio de la luz (*electricity*) y de gas... ¡y cancelar sus tarjetas de crédito!
d. Alguien le va a robar el televisor.
e. ¡«King» se va a morir de hambre!
f. No va a tener dónde alojarse (*to stay*).
g. Todos van a saber que no está en casa.

**B. ¡Desastres por todas partes (*everywhere*)!**

PASO 1 ¿Es Ud. una persona distraída o torpe? Indique las oraciones que se apliquen (*apply*) a Ud. Puede cambiar algunos de los detalles de las oraciones si es necesario.

1. ☐ Con frecuencia se me caen los libros (los platos,... ).
2. ☐ Se me pierden constantemente las llaves (los calcetines,... ).
3. ☐ A menudo (*Often*) se me olvida apagar (*to turn off*) la computadora (la luz,... ).
4. ☐ Siempre se me rompen las gafas (las lámparas,... ).
5. ☐ De vez en cuando (*From time to time*) se me quedan los libros (los cuadernos,... ) en la clase.
6. ☐ Se me olvida fácilmente mi horario (el teléfono de algún amigo,... ).

PASO 2 ¿Es Ud. igual ahora que cuando era más joven? Complete cada oración del **Paso 1** para describir cómo era de niño/a. No se olvide de usar el imperfecto en sus oraciones.

MODELO: De niño/a, (no) se me caían los libros con frecuencia.

PASO 3 Ahora compare sus respuestas con las de un compañero / una compañera. ¿Quién es más distraído/a o torpe ahora? ¿Quién lo era de niño/a?

**Prác. A: Preliminary Exercises**
• Ask students what indirect object pronoun they hear in the following sentences.

1. *Se me olvidó el bolígrafo.*
2. *Se le rompieron los platos.*
3. *Se te cayeron las flores.*
4. *Se te acabó la gasolina.*
5. *Se le quedaron en casa los boletos.*

• Give the following dictation.

1. *Se me cayeron las llaves.*
2. *Se te rompieron los vasos.*
3. *A Pepe se le rompió el despertador.*
4. *A María se le olvidaron las aspirinas.*

Follow up the dictation with questions to check comprehension or by having students provide the English equivalents.

• Have students do the following chain drill to practice the structure.

*¡Qué distraídos estuvimos todos ayer! Dé oraciones nuevas según las indicaciones.*

1. *A Pablo se le olvidó la cartera. (mí, Inés, ti, el chico)*
2. *Se te perdieron las llaves otra vez. (Ernesto, Ud. niña, mí)*
3. *María fue la más distraída de todos. Se le olvidó / olvidaron... (tomar el desayuno, las gafas, estudiar para el examen, los cheques, venir a clase)*

• Have students give the Spanish equivalents.

1. I dropped my glasses/plate/books.
2. Robert lost the book / keys / alarm clock.

**Prác. B: Follow-Up Paso 2**
• Ask students:

*¿Qué más le pasaba a Ud.? ¿Qué ha cambiado?*

• Have students give sentences with actions that used to happen to them but do not happen to them anymore.

*Antes se me perdían las gafas. Ahora se me pierden los suéteres.*

♻ • Note the review of the imperfect tense.

**Need more practice?**

■ Workbook/Laboratory Manual
■ Interactive CD-ROM
■ Online Learning Center (www.mhhe.com/quetal7)

## ■ Conversación

### Pablo tuvo una mañana fatal

PASO 1    Complete la siguiente descripción de lo que le pasó a Pablo ayer. Use expresiones con **se.**

Pablo tuvo una mañana fatal. Primero (olvidar[1]) poner el despertador. Se levantó tarde y se vistió rápidamente. No cerró bien su maletín;[a] por eso (caer[2]) unos papeles importantes. Recogió los papeles y subió al coche. Salió rápido pero después de cinco minutos, (acabar[3]) la gasolina y se le paró[b] el coche. Dejó el coche en la calle y decidió ir caminando. Llevaba el maletín en una mano y las llaves y un documento urgente en la otra. Desafortunadamente,[c] mientras caminaba, (perder[4]) el documento. Cuando llegó a la oficina, buscó a su jefe[d] para entregarle el documento pero no podía encontrar el documento entre sus papeles. Cansado y enojado, cerró el maletín sin cuidado y (romper[5]) los lentes.

[a]*briefcase*  [b]*se... (the car) stopped on him*  [c]*Unfortunately*  [d]*boss*

PASO 2    Ahora, con un compañero / una compañera, describa una mañana o un día fatal que Ud. tuvo. Trate de incluir expresiones con **se.**

MODELO:  El primer día de clases, se me olvidó poner el despertador, y llegué tarde a clase. Luego…

## En los Estados Unidos y el Canadá

### La impresionante variedad de la música latina

Es difícil hablar de «música latina» porque hay una inmensa **variedad.** La música de España y de toda Latinoamérica cuenta con[a] **diversos orígenes** que luego **se mezclan.**[b] La música de los españoles y portugueses llegó al Nuevo Mundo, pero pronto se mezcló con fuertes **tradiciones indígenas.** Cuando los conquistadores trajeron **esclavos**[c] **africanos** al Nuevo Mundo, estos trajeron consigo[d] sus propias tradiciones musicales, que influyeron en varios tipos de música que hoy consideramos música hispánica.

Hoy día, **los artistas hispanos** de los Estados Unidos **son cada vez más conocidos,** no sólo como representantes de la música latina, sino también en las áreas del rock, pop, hip hop y jazz. Como ejemplo, podemos nombrar, entre muchos, a los neoyorquinos de origen puertorri-

*Tito Puente (1923–2000)*

queño Jennifer López y Marc Anthony, al mexicoamericano Carlos Santana, a la colombiana Shakira, al español Enrique Iglesias y al pianista dominicano Michel Camilo.

**La salsa** es uno de los tipos de música hispana más reconocidos. Es una mezcla de **ritmos afrocaribeños** que fue creada en Nueva York por músicos hispanos en los años sesenta y setenta del siglo XX. La salsa es muy variada, pero siempre tiene una característica clara: es muy **bailable.** Uno de los nombres más asociados con la salsa es Tito Puente, el famoso percusionista. Carlos Santana grabó su versión de la composición de Puente, «Oye ¿cómo va?» e introdujo a Puente y un estilo de música hispánica no sólo a una nueva generación, sino también al público no hispano.

[a]*cuenta... has*  [b]*se... are combined*  [c]*slaves*  [d]*with them*

# Voces de Puerto Rico

**Literatura: Note**
Rosario Ferré was born into a family that was influential in business and politics. Her father, Luis Ferré, was a pro-statehood governor of the commonwealth from 1968 to 1972. Among Rosario Ferré's books is a biography of her father.

## LITERATURA: Rosario Ferré

**Sobre la autora:** *Rosario Ferré nació en Ponce, Puerto Rico. Además de biografías, crítica literaria y poesía, escribe también ficción en español y en inglés. Actualmente enseña en la Universidad de Puerto Rico y contribuye en el periódico* San Juan Star. *El siguiente fragmento es del ensayo:* «De cómo dejarse caer de la sartén al fuego[a]», Sitio a eros: Trece ensayos (1980).

**Rosario Ferré**
(1938– )

A lo largo del tiempo, las mujeres narradoras han escrito[b] por múltiples razones: Emily Brontë escribió para demostrar la naturaleza revolucionaria de la pasión; Virginia Woolf para exorcizar su terror a la locura y a la muerte; Joan Didion escribe para descubrir lo que piensa y cómo piensa; Clarisse Lispector descubre en su escritura una razón para amar y ser amada. En mi caso, escribir es una voluntad a la vez constructiva y destructiva; una posibilidad de crecimiento[c] y de cambio.[d]

[a]*de... from the frying pan into the fire*  [b]*han... have written*  [c]*growth*  [d]*change*

**Música: Notes**
• *La bomba*, the older of the "Afro-Rican" musical traditions, is a direct descendent of the Ashanti tribes of Ghana and is truer to its African roots than other dances that developed from the mixture of African, indigenous, and European cultures.
• Since the 1800s, *bomba* dances were held on Saturday and Sunday nights and holidays. The events generally lasted all night and took place outdoors, in the sugarcane fields or in the plazas of the town square.

## MÚSICA: La bomba y la plena

los tambores bomba

el güiro

las pleneras    las maracas

Los dos estilos de música puertorriqueña más conocidos son la bomba y la plena. Se asocian tanto que a veces se oye decir «bombayplena» como una sola palabra. Aunque[a] son diferentes, los dos estilos se derivan de tradiciones africanas. Su interpretación[b] incluye una danza y los dos son una especie de conversación entre los participantes. Los instrumentos principales de la bomba son dos tambores[c] bomba (el burlador y el subidor), la cuá[d] y las maracas. La plena se toca con tres pleneras[e] y un güiro.[f]

[a]*Although*  [b]*performance*  [c]*drums*  [d]*percussion instrument made of bamboo and played with two sticks*  [e]*percussion instruments, very similar to a tambourine, without the cymbals*  [f]*rasping percussion instrument often made from a gourd*

• *La plena* developed in the early 1900s on the southern coasts of Puerto Rico and functioned as a singing newspaper. Like *la bomba*, *la plena* is a call-and-response musical form, but the "conversation" is between two singers, not between the drummer and the dancer.

En la bomba, el músico que toca el burlador establece un ritmo constante. El músico que toca la otra bomba, el subidor, «dialoga» con la persona que baila e intenta interpretar el ritmo de sus pasos o su danza.

La plena es una «conversación» entre dos cantantes. El cantante principal echa una frase[g] y uno o dos de los otros cantantes contestan, todo al ritmo[h] de las pleneras. La plena se conoce también como el «periódico cantao[i]» porque es un comentario sobre eventos, elecciones y escándalos corrientes.[j]

[g]*echa... sings out a phrase*  [h]*al... to the rhythm*  [i]*abbreviated form of* cantado (sung), *past participle of the verb* cantar  [j]*recent*

• The main *plena* instruments are the *pleneras,* also called *panderetas.* They are hand-held drums that are similar to the tambourine. Originally, only two *pleneras* were used, but now there are three: the *seguidor* (lower-pitched), the *punteador* or *segundo* (middle-pitched), and the *requinto* (high-pitched). The *seguidor* and *punteador* establish the basic rhythm, and the *requinto* improvises.

**Follow-Up**

After completing *¿Qué se representa?*, read the following sentences and have students make drawings based on what they hear.

*Haga un dibujo que ilustre cada una de las siguientes oraciones.*

1. *Pedro trabaja para una familia muy rica.*
2. *Pedro va a trabajar por su compañero esta tarde.*
3. *Es una escultura* (write *escultura* on the board) *demasiado pequeña y fea para ese precio.*
4. *Teresa va a hacer algo especial mañana para el cumpleaños de su mejor amiga.*

To follow up, ask *¿Quién es el/la mejor dibujante de la clase?*

**Paso 3: Gramática**

See the "Chapter-by-Chapter Supplementary Materials" in the IM for additional teaching suggestions, notes, activities, and other resources for *Paso 3*.

---

### ¿Recuerda Ud.?

Before beginning **Gramática 32**, review what you have learned about prepositional pronouns. The first and second person singular pronouns differ from subject pronouns; the rest are identical to subject pronouns. Then give the prepositional pronouns that correspond to the following persons.

1. Pepe: de _____
2. Lisa y yo: después de _____
3. tú: para _____
4. yo: de _____
5. Ud.: con _____
6. Juan y Olga: para _____

**Note**

Students already know the most important uses of these prepositions.

---

## 32 ¿*Por* o *para*? A Summary of Their Uses

**¿Qué se representa?**

a.

b.

c.

d.

**Comprension:**

Empareje (*Match*) cada dibujo con la oración que le corresponde.

1. __d__ Caminamos *para* el parque.
2. __b__ Ayer compramos el regalo *por* la abuela.
3. __c__ Paseamos *por* el parque.
4. __a__ El regalo es *para* Eduardo.

**Refranes**

«No hay mal que por bien no venga.»
«Hay que sufrir para merecer.»
«Hoy por ti, mañana por mí.»

Point out that these are sayings for difficult moments. Have students give their interpretations of the sayings and brainstorm similar sayings in English (*Every cloud has a silver lining. No pain, no gain. You scratch my back, I'll scratch yours.*)

You have been using the prepositions **por** and **para** throughout your study of Spanish. Although most of the information in this section will be a review, you will also learn some new uses of **por** and **para.**

## Por

The preposition **por** has the following English equivalents.

| por | ↔ | para |
|---|---|---|
| reason | | destination |
| cause | | purpose |

**Suggestions**
• Have students say the following in Spanish (the numbers are coordinated with the presentation of the uses of *por*).

1. by train/plane; by phone/letter
2. through the campus/plaza; along the beach/river
3. in the afternoon/evening; at 2:00 in the afternoon (**¡OJO!** *de la tarde*)
4. because of the test/accident
5. Thanks for the book/pen/ money.
6. I'm doing it for you/him/us.
7. I studied for four hours / two days.

• *by, by means of*

Vamos **por** avión (tren, barco,… ).
*We're going by plane (train, ship, . . . ).*

Nos hablamos **por** teléfono mañana.
*We'll talk by (on the) phone tomorrow.*

• *through, along*

Me gusta pasear **por** el parque y **por** la playa.
*I like to stroll through the park and along the beach.*

• *during, in* (time of day)

Trabajo **por** la mañana.
*I work in the morning.*

• *because of, due to*

Estoy nervioso **por** la entrevista.
*I'm nervous because of the interview.*

• *for = in exchange for*

Piden 1.000 dólares **por** el coche.
*They're asking $1,000 for the car.*

Gracias **por** todo.
*Thanks for everything.*

• *for = for the sake of, on behalf of*

Lo hago **por** ti.
*I'm doing it for you (for your sake).*

• *for = duration* (often omitted)

Vivieron allí (**por**) un año.
*They lived there for a year.*

**Por** is also used in a number of fixed expressions.

• Point out that *in order to get* or *in search of* is expressed with *por: Van por pan.*
• Have students use fixed expressions with *por* to respond to these questions or comments.

1. *¿Es necesario estudiar treinta minutos cada día para la clase de español?*
2. *Parece que va a llover hoy. ¿Debo llevar impermeable?*
3. *¿Le paso la carne? ¿la ensalada?*
4. *Me dicen que Ud. toma ocho clases este semestre/trimestre.*
5. *Empecé a leer este libro el año pasado; lo terminé esta mañana.*
6. *¡Me robaron el coche anoche!*
7. *¿Le gusta viajar?*
8. *¿Por qué llegué tarde? Pues hay mil razones.*

| | |
|---|---|
| por Dios | for heaven's sake |
| por ejemplo | for example |
| por eso | that's why |
| por favor | please |
| por fin | finally |
| por lo general | generally, in general |
| por lo menos | at least |
| por primera/ última vez | for the first/ last time |
| por si acaso | just in case |
| ¡por supuesto! | of course! |
| por todas partes | everywhere |

## Para

Although **para** has many English equivalents, including *for,* it always has the underlying purpose of referring to a goal or destination.

- *in order to* + infinitive

**Suggestions**
- Emphasize that *para* is *for* with the concept of destination.
  a. Destined for whom? → *para su hijo*
  b. Destined for what point in time? → *para mañana*

Regresaron pronto **para** estudiar.
*They returned soon (in order) to study.*

Estudian **para** conseguir un buen trabajo.
*They're studying (in order) to get a good job.*

- *for = destined for, to be given to*

  c. Geographical destination, in space? → *Salieron para Lima.*
  d. Destined for what use? → *un vaso para agua.*
- Have students give the English equivalents (the numbers are coordinated with the order of presentation of the uses of *para*).

Todo esto es **para** ti.
*All this is for you.*

Le di un libro **para** su hijo.
*I gave her a book for her son.*

- *for = by* (deadline, specified future time)

  1. They came back to eat lunch / to rest.
  2. It's for her/me.
  3. The exercise is for Monday/ Friday.
  4. They left for Bolivia / Costa Rica.

**Para** mañana, estudien **por** y **para.**
*For tomorrow, study **por** and **para.***

La composición es **para** el lunes.
*The composition is for Monday.*

- *for = toward, in the direction of*

Salió **para** el Ecuador ayer.
*She left for Ecuador yesterday.*

- *for = to be used for*

**OJO** Compare the example at the right to **un vaso de agua** = *a glass (full) of water.*

El dinero es **para** la matrícula.
*The money is for tuition.*

Es un vaso **para** agua.
*It's a water glass.*

- *for = as compared with others, in relation to others*

  5. It's a wine/beer glass.
  6. For an American/German, he speaks French well.
  7. She works for Ramón / Mr. Jiménez. (¡**OJO**! *el Sr. Jiménez*)

**Para** mí, el español es fácil.
*For me, Spanish is easy.*

**Para** (ser) extranjera, habla muy bien el inglés.
*For (being) a foreigner, she speaks English very well.*

- *for = in the employ of*

Trabajan **para** el gobierno.
*They work for the government.*

**Bright Idea Suggestion**
Offer the following expressions as well.

*por ahora*     *por cierto*
*por casualidad*     *por desgracia*

**Heritage Speakers**
Una expresión con *para* es *estar para* (to be about to [do something]). En algunos dialectos, especialmente en México, se dice *estar por* en vez de *estar para*. Por ejemplo, *Carlota está por llegar* significa *Carlota está a punto de llegar.* También se oye *estar al* en algunos países caribeños. Pregúnteles a los hispanohablantes de la clase qué expresión prefieren usar.

**AUTOPRUEBA**

Indicate whether you would use **por** or **para.**

1. _____ to travel to a place
2. _____ to travel through a place
3. _____ to travel by plane
4. _____ to work for someone (a company)
5. _____ to work for someone (on behalf of)
6. _____ to last for a period of time
7. _____ to be due by a certain time

Answers: 1. para 2. por 3. por 4. por 5. para 6. por 7. para

## ■ Práctica

### A. Preguntas

PASO 1   Complete las siguientes preguntas con **por** y **para**.

1. ¿___Para___ quién trabaja Ud.? ¿Le pagan a Ud. bien?
2. ¿___Por___ dónde tiene que manejar (*drive*) para llegar a la universidad?
3. ¿Cuánto pagó Ud. ___por___ su carro/bicicleta?
4. ¿___Para___ qué es la llave grande que Ud. tiene?
5. ¿___Para___ qué profesión estudia Ud.? ¿___Por___ cuántos años tiene que estudiar?
6. ¿___Para___ cuándo necesita Ud. volver a casa hoy?

PASO 2   Ahora, conteste las preguntas del **Paso 1**. Invente la información necesaria.

### B. ¿Por o para?   Complete los siguientes diálogos y oraciones con **por** o **para**.

1. Los Sres. Arana salieron ___para___ el Perú ayer. Van ___por___ avión, claro, pero luego piensan viajar en coche ___por___ todo el país. Van a estar allí ___por___ dos meses. Va a ser una experiencia extraordinaria ___para___ toda la familia.

2. Mi prima Graciela quiere estudiar ___para___ (ser) doctora. ___Por___ eso trabaja ___para___ un médico ___por___ la mañana; tiene clases ___por___ la tarde.

3. —¿___Por___ qué están Uds. aquí todavía? Yo pensaba que iban a dar un paseo ___por___ el parque. —Íbamos a hacerlo, pero no fuimos, ___por___ la nieve.

4. Este cuadro fue pintado (*was painted*) por Picasso ___para___ expresar los desastres de la guerra (*war*). ___Para___ muchos críticos de arte, es la obra maestra (*masterpiece*) de este artista.

5. La «Asociación Todo ___Por___ Ellos» trabaja ___por___ las personas mayores, ___para___ ayudarlos cuando lo necesitan. ¿Trabaja Ud. ___para___ alguna asociación de voluntarios? ¿Qué tuvo que hacer ___para___ inscribirse (*sign up*)?

ASOCIACION
TODO ELLOS
POR

Trabajamos por las personas
mayores que están solas y con
escasos recursos económicos

**AYÚDANOS, NO ES POSIBLE SIN TI**

Para más información llama al teléfono
907 98 91 15, de 18.00 a 20.00 h.
tardes, martes y viernes

**CAJAMADRID, SUC. 1028
C/C 6000854579**

TODO POR ELLOS es una asociación
no gubernamental inscrita en el Registro
de Asociaciones del Ministerio del Interior
con el número 160.589

## ■ Conversación

**Entrevista.** Hágale preguntas a su profesor(a) para saber la siguiente información.

1. la tarea para mañana y para la semana que viene
2. lo que hay que estudiar para el próximo examen
3. si para él/ella son interesantes o aburridas las ciencias
4. la opinión que tiene de la pronunciación de Uds., para ser principiantes
5. qué deben hacer Uds. para mejorar su pronunciación del español
6. por cuánto tiempo deben Uds. practicar el español todos los días

## UN POCO DE TODO

*La estatua de Cristóbal Colón en la Plaza de Colón, en San Juan, Puerto Rico*

**Resources for Review and Testing Preparation**

- Workbook/Laboratory Manual
- Interactive CD-ROM
- Online Learning Center (www.mhhe.com/quetal7)

**Lengua y cultura: Un poco de historia de Puerto Rico.** Complete the following passages with the correct forms of the words in parentheses, as suggested by the context. When two possibilities are given in parentheses, select the correct word. **¡OJO!** As you conjugate verbs in this activity, use the present tense unless otherwise indicated in the parentheses. If you see *P/I*, you will choose between the preterite and the imperfect; *comm.* means to use an **Ud./Uds.** command; and *prog.* stands for the present/past progressive.

¿Qué saben Uds. de la historia de Puerto Rico? ¿Muy poco? Pues no (*comm. Uds.*: preocuparse[1]). Aquí tienen (algún / alguna[2]) información.

Originalmente, en Puerto Rico (*P/I,* vivir[3]) los indígenas[a] taínos y caribes, que (*P/I,* extenderse[4]) por gran parte de las costas caribeñas. En (esto/estas[5]) costas del Mar Caribe (ser/estar[6]) las islas Antillas, que se dividen en Antillas Mayores y Antillas Menores. Las Antillas Mayores (ser/estar[7]) las islas de Puerto Rico, Cuba, Jamaica y Española (la República Dominicana y Haití).

Cristóbal Colón (*P/I,* llegar[8]) a Puerto Rico en su segundo viaje a América. (Se/Le[9]) dice que el jefe[b] de los taínos, que (*P/I,* tener[10]) el título de cacique, (*P/I,* recibir[11]) a Colón con un collar de oro.[c] (Por/Para[12]) eso Colón pensó que (*P/I,* haber[13]) mucho oro en la isla, pero no (*P/I,* tener[14]) (razón/sueño[15]). De todas formas,[d] los españoles explotaron la isla intensamente. En poco tiempo, la población taína prácticamente (*P/I,* desaparecer[16]) debido a[e] tres factores: (el/la[17]) explotación de la tierra, las rebeliones de los nativos y las enfermedades que los españoles traían consigo[f] que (*P/I,* ser[18]) nuevas (por/para[19]) los taínos. La población africana, que los españoles importaron como esclavos,[g] (*P/I,* empezar[20]) a llegar en el siglo[h] XVI.

En el siglo XIX, mientras toda Latinoamérica (*P/I,* tener[21]) guerras[i] contra España y (*prog.,* obtener[22]) su independencia, las islas antillanas no (*P/I,* independizarse[23]). En 1898 Puerto Rico (*P/I,* convertirse[24]) en una colonia de los Estados Unidos, después de que España (*P/I,* perder[25]) la guerra que en los Estados Unidos (*P/I,* llamarse[26]) *the Spanish American War.*

En 1917, los puertorriqueños fueron declarados ciudadanos[j] (estadounidense[27]), y desde 1953 su país es un Estado Libre Asociado de los Estados Unidos. Esto quiere decir que aunque[k] no es independiente, tiene plena[l] autonomía interna.

[a]*Indians, indigenous peoples* [b]*chief* [c]*collar... gold necklace* [d]*De... In any case* [e]*debido... due to* [f]*with them* [g]*slaves* [h]*century* [i]*wars* [j]*citizens* [k]*although* [l]*full*

**Comprensión.** Conteste las preguntas en español.

1. ¿Dónde están las Antillas?
2. ¿Cuáles son las Antillas Mayores?
3. ¿Quiénes eran los habitantes originales de Puerto Rico?
4. ¿Qué otros grupos raciales había en la lsla?
5. ¿Desde cuándo es Puerto Rico territorio de los Estados Unidos?
6. ¿Cuál es la situación política actual (*current*) de Puerto Rico?

**Paso 4: Un paso más**
• The *Paso 4: Un paso más* sections are optional.
• See the "Chapter-by-Chapter Supplementary
  Materials" in the IM for additional teaching
  suggestions, notes, activities, and other resources for *Paso 4.*

**VIDEOTECA**

# Entrevista cultural: Puerto Rico

Antonio Solórzano es un estudiante puertorriqueño. Aquí describe su rutina diaria. También habla de las presiones que sufre y de lo que hace para disminuir el estrés. Antes de ver el vídeo, lea el siguiente fragmento de la entrevista.

ENTREVISTADORA: ¿Qué estudias?
ANTONIO: Estudio antropología.
ENTREVISTADORA: Antonio, ¿cómo es para ti un día típico?
ANTONIO: Pues un día típico para mí es despertarme temprano para ir a la universidad y,… este, estar allí casi todo el día. Y después en la tarde irme al trabajo como hasta las seis y media de la tarde, estudiar un rato cuando llego a mi casa y después irme en la noche a hacer ejercicio.

**Entrevista cultural: Preliminary Exercise**
Review with students different types of
situations that may induce stress and types
of activities designed to reduce stress.

**Entrevista cultural: Suggestions**
• Before showing the video, ask students
  questions about what typical days are like
  for them.

  *¿Cómo es para Ud. un día típico?*
  *¿Qué presiones sufre Ud.?*
  *¿Qué hace Ud. para aliviar el estrés?*

Ahora vea el vídeo y conteste las siguientes preguntas basándose en la entrevista.

1. ¿Dónde vive y estudia Antonio?
2. ¿Qué hace por la tarde, generalmente?
3. Según Antonio, ¿qué presiones sufren los estudiantes?
4. ¿Qué hace Antonio todos los días para aliviar el estrés?
5. Y los fines de semana, ¿qué hace?

• Show the video and allow students one to
  two minutes to work on the questions.
  Have volunteers answer the questions.
• Have volunteers role-play Antonio and his
  interviewer.

# Entre amigos: ¡Estoy superestresada!

Karina, Miguel, Tané y Rubén hablan del estrés y de las presiones de la vida diaria. En su opinión, ¿de qué van a hablar? Antes de mirar el vídeo, lea las preguntas a continuación. Mientras mire el vídeo, trate de entender la conversación en general y fíjese en la información sobre los exámenes, las clases y el trabajo. Luego mire el vídeo una segunda vez, fijándose en la información que necesita para contestar las preguntas.

**Entrevista cultural: Answers**
*Possible answers:* **1.** *Vive y estudia en Río
Piedras.* **2.** *Trabaja y estudia.* **3.** *Sufren estrés
por los exámenes, los proyectos y la familia.*
**4.** *Hace ejercicio por la noche.* **5.** *Sale con
sus amigos a bailar.*

1. ¿Cuántas horas por semana trabaja Rubén?
2. ¿Por qué está estresada Karina?
3. ¿Tiene Tané buenas o malas notas?
4. ¿Qué clase le da más dificultades a Tané?
5. ¿Qué tipo de ayuda le ofrece Miguel a Tané?

**Entre amigos: Answers**
*Possible answers:* **1.** *cincuenta a sesenta*
**2.** *Porque tiene exámenes en todas sus
clases.* **3.** *malas notas* **4.** *el inglés* **5.** *Le
ofrece ayuda con el inglés.*

**Entre amigos: Suggestions**
• Before viewing the video, review the
  questions with the students and ask them
  similar questions.

  *¿Sufre Ud. mucho estrés en sus estudios?*
  *¿en el trabajo?*
  *¿Qué clase le da más dificultades y estrés?*

  Have students answer or work in small
  groups to ask and answer these questions.
• After viewing the video, have volunteers
  read and answer the questions.
• Have students interview two or three
  classmates about the types of stress they
  feel and what they do to relieve it. After
  the interviews, have them report their
  findings to the class.

# PASO 4

## ENFOQUE CULTURAL

### Puerto Rico

Notes
• Sila María Calderón was elected in November 2000 as Puerto Rico's first woman governor. The mother of eight children and ex-mayor of the city of San Juan had been a prominent public figure for many years before her election to the post.

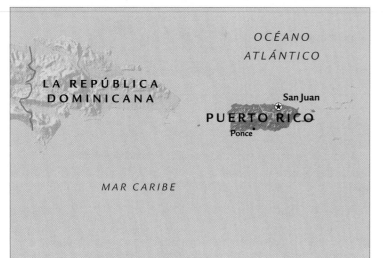

## ¡Fíjese!

- Puerto Rico ha estado relacionado[a] políticamente con los Estados Unidos desde la Guerra Hispano-norteamericana de 1898, año en que España perdió las ultimas colonias de su imperio. En 1952, Puerto Rico se convirtió en Estado Libre Asociado. Bajo[b] este sistema de gobierno, los puertorriqueños son ciudadanos[c] estado-unidenses. Sin embargo, los que viven en la Isla no pueden votar por el presidente de los Estados Unidos aunque deben servir en el ejército[d] de ese país en caso de guerra.
- Otro nombre de Puerto Rico es Borinquen y los puerto-rriqueños se conocen también como boricuas. Estas palabras originaron en el lenguaje de los indios taínos. Los taínos llegaron a la Isla en el siglo[e] XIII pero su cultura casi desapareció con la llegada de los españoles en 1493.
- El Parque Nacional del Yunque, ubicado[f] en una mon-taña de 1.065 metros de altura que está al noreste de la Isla, es pequeño cuando se compara a otros bosques[g] nacionales, pero es el único bosque *tropical* del sistema de Bosques Nacionales de los Estados Unidos.

[a]ha... *has been associated* [b]*Under* [c]*citizens* [d]*army* [e]*century* [f]*located* [g]*forests*

**Heritage Speakers**
Si hay hispanohablantes de Puerto Rico en su clase, anímelos a hablar de la Isla y comparar la vida de allí con la vida cotidiana de este país.

## Personas famosas: Alonso Ramírez

En 1690 se publicó en México la primera novela del Nuevo Mundo, *Infortunios[a] de Alonso Ramírez*. Aunque esta obra[b] se atribuyó al mexicano Carlos Sigüenza y Góngora, hoy se cree que el verdadero[c] autor fue el mismo Alonso Ramírez del título. También se cree que la obra no es ficticia, sino autobiográfica: la vida de un puertorriqueño que se cría[d] en la Isla, viaja a México y tiene aventuras en muchas partes del Mar Pacífico. Sus aventuras incluyen batallas contra piratas, una estadía[e] en una isla desierta y muchos otros eventos interesantísimos. Es una novela que vale la pena[f] leer.

[a]*Misfortunes* [b]*work* [c]*real* [d]se... *is brought up* [e]*stay* [f]que... *that is worthwhile*

*Una calle en el viejo San Juan*

• Doña Felisa Rincón de Gautier was another woman mayor of the capital city. A beloved figure, known for her extravagant hairdos as much as for her highly developed political sense, she ran San Juan from 1946 to 1968. Today a museum in the old city is dedicated to her life and work.

Learn more about Puerto Rico with the Video, the Interactive CD-ROM, and the Online Learning Center (www.mhhe.com/quetal7).

• Students can read an excerpt of the essay *"De cómo dejarse caer de la sartén al fuego"* by Puerto Rico's Rosario Ferré in *Voces de Puerto Rico: Literatura*.
• Students can read about Puerto Rico's *bomba* and *plena* music in *Voces de Puerto Rico: Música*.
• See the Workbook/Laboratory Manual for focused practice with the material in *Enfoque cultural*.

## PASO FINAL

### 📖 A LEER

**REPASO DE ESTRATEGIAS: Guessing the Content of a Passage**

In previous reading sections, you have learned several different strategies to improve your comprehension of a text. Whenever you can, it's a good idea to utilize as many of these strategies as possible. Of course, not all texts will lend themselves to the application of all strategies. For example, there might be limited visual cues such as photos to help you anticipate what the reading is about. In those instances, what else can you rely on to make predictions about the content? One strategy is to identify the source of the passage (see **Sobre la lectura**). And, of course, the title often reveals a great deal about the content of a passage. Take a look at the title of the reading that follows and the accompanying photo. What do you think this article is about?

1. Divorce rates in Spanish-speaking countries
2. The relationship between divorce and stress
3. Advice for reducing stress

If you picked number 3, you were right! The following article offers suggestions and techniques for reducing stress and enjoying a calmer life.

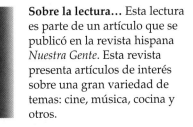

**Sobre la lectura...** Esta lectura es parte de un artículo que se publicó en la revista hispana *Nuestra Gente*. Esta revista presenta artículos de interés sobre una gran variedad de temas: cine, música, cocina y otros.

**Suggestions**

• Do the *Repaso de estrategias* section in class the day before you intend to cover the reading. Remind students to practice the strategies actively as they read, as part of their homework assignment. Remember to follow up on the underlined words the next day.

PREVIOUS STRATEGIES

1. guessing the meaning of unfamiliar words from context
2. using visuals and graphics to predict content
3. forming a general idea about content by using titles, subtitles, art, and comprehension questions
4. identifying the source of a passage
5. recognizing derivative adjectives

## *Divórciate del estrés*

<u>Convivimos</u> tanto con el estrés que hasta parece un miembro de la familia. Lo llevamos al trabajo, a las tiendas, a la lavandería,[a] a veces hasta nos acostamos y <u>amanecemos</u> con él. Pero es un compañero de muchos disfraces.[b] Nos mantiene en movimiento diario, pero aparece como dolor de cabeza, nudos[c] de músculos en el cuello,[d] ratos de <u>olvido</u>, cansancio o enojo.

### Cinco pasos hacia una vida más tranquila

#### ¡Córrele![e]

O hasta puedes decir «¡camínale!» si prefieres pues también te servirá.[f] Es decir, si notas que se te viene encima el maldito estrés, ponte los tenis, y ¡a la calle! Una simple <u>caminata</u> o <u>corrida</u> de veinte minutos diarios hace milagros.[g] Hasta los científicos han comprobado[h] que el ejercicio diario —aunque corto— sí reduce sustancialmente los niveles de estrés.

#### Respira profundamente

Uno de los mejores y más sencillos pasos a tomar para reducir el estrés es cuidar de tu respiración, según el Centro Médico Arnot Ogden de El-mira, Nueva York. Cuando te afecta el estrés, tu respiración <u>se acorta</u> y

*Correr o caminar veinte minutos todos los días reduce el estrés.*

• Have students work in small groups to create original titles in Spanish for each section of this article. Compare the titles and have the class vote on the best one for each passage.

---

[a]lugar público donde se puede lavar la ropa  [b]*disguises*  [c]*knots*  [d]*neck*  [e]*Run!*  [f]*te... it (walking) will work for you*  [g]*miracles, wonders*  [h]*han... have proven*

es poco <u>profunda</u> debido al efecto que producen los músculos tensos. Cada vez que te sientas tenso, concéntrate unos segundos en tu respiración y profundízala. Tu corazón te lo agradecerá.[i]

### Un <u>spa</u> en tu propia casa

Aunque sea un día a la semana —o al mes— aparta[j] una hora —o más— para ti mismo. <u>Prende</u> una vela[k] de aroma tranquilizante, llena la <u>tina del baño</u> con un delicioso jabón y tómate un té caliente de manzanilla,[l] vainilla o canela.[m]

### Come de manera saludable

Una buena dieta baja en <u>grasas</u>, alta en fibra y que incluye comer vegetales y frutas diariamente ayuda no sólo al cuerpo sino al estado mental. Cuando <u>ingerimos</u> en exceso comida grasosa y azucarada[n] —los famosos alimentos vacíos de

nutrición que suelen aparecer en nuestras cocinas— el cuerpo protesta de diversas formas. Las enfermedades que pueden aparecer a la larga[o] como la obesidad, el alto colesterol y enfermedades del corazón son aun otras y muy serias fuentes de estrés.

### Convierte estos pasos en una rutina diaria

Poco a poco —¡y sin estresarte!— incorpora estos pasos a la rutina de tus días y noches. No hay que hacerlo de un jalón.[p] Comienza al paso que puedas, <u>incrementando</u> gradualmente para que poco a poco se conviertan en algo cotidiano[q] y <u>esperado.</u> Verás[r] que dentro de poco tu cara sonriente y tranquila lo dirá todo:[s] ¿Estrés? ¿De qué hablas? ◾

[i]te... *will thank you for it*   [j]*set aside*   [k]*candle*   [l]*chamomile*   [m]*cinnamon*
[n]*sweetened, containing sugar*   [o]a... *over time*   [p]de... *all at once*   [q]*diario*
[r]*You'll see*   [s]lo... *will say it all*

## Comprensión

**A. Consejos.** De los siguientes consejos para reducir el estrés, ¿cuáles *no* se mencionan en el artículo?

1. comer bien
2. escuchar música
3. hacer ejercicio
4. controlar la respiración
5. practicar yoga
6. beber bastante agua

**B. Síntomas y soluciones**

PASO 1   Identifique tres síntomas del estrés, según la lectura.

1. _____ dolor de cabeza _____
2. _____ nudos de músculos _____
3. ratos de olvido / cansancio / enojo

PASO 2   Ahora haga una lista de posibles soluciones para el estrés. Indentifique las soluciones que Ud. prefiere o que cree que son más efectivos. ¿Puede añadir (*add*) otra solución no mencionada en el artículo?

 ## A ESCRIBIR

**Ud. y el estrés.** La lectura presenta varias sugerencias para reducir el estrés, pero claro que no es una lista definitiva. Seguro que hay otros métodos también. Cuando Ud. se siente estresado/a, ¿qué hace para bajar el nivel de estrés? ¿Tiene alguna técnica en particular? Escriba un breve ensayo de 100 palabras en el cual describa cómo responde Ud. al estrés y qué hace para aliviarlo (*alleviate it*).

## GRAMÁTICA

To review the grammar points presented in this chapter, refer to the indicated grammar presentations. You'll find further practice of these structures in the Workbook/Laboratory Manual, on the Interactive CD-ROM, and on the *¿Qué tal?* Online Learning Center (www.mhhe.com/quetal7).

**31** Expressing Unplanned or Unexpected Events—Another Use of **se**

Do you know how to use **se** to express unplanned or unexpected events?

**32** ¿**Por** o **para**?—A Summary of Their Uses

Do you know the difference between **por** and **para** and when to use one or the other?

## VOCABULARIO
Practice this vocabulary with digital flash cards on the Online Learning Center (www.mhhe.com/quetal7).

### Los verbos

| | |
|---|---|
| acabar | to finish; to run out of |
| apagar (gu) | to turn off |
| quedar | to remain, be left |

Repaso: olvidar, perder (ie)

### Presiones de la vida estudiantil

| | |
|---|---|
| la calificación | grade |
| el despertador | alarm clock |
| el estrés | stress |
| la (falta de) flexibilidad | (lack of) flexibility |
| la fecha límite | deadline |
| el horario | schedule |
| el informe (oral/escrito) | (oral/written) report |
| la llave | key |
| la nota | grade |
| la presión | pressure |
| la prueba | quiz; test |
| la tarjeta de identificación | identification card |
| el trabajo | job, work; report, (piece of) work |
| de tiempo completo/parcial | full time/part time |

Cognado: el calendario
Repaso: el examen, la tarea

| | |
|---|---|
| acordarse (ue) (de) | to remember |
| entregar (gu) | to turn, hand in |

| | |
|---|---|
| estacionar | to park |
| recoger (j) | to collect; to pick up |
| sacar (qu) | to get (*grades*) |
| sufrir | to suffer |
| (muchas) presiones | to be under (a lot of) pressure |

Repaso: llegar (gu) a tiempo / tarde, olvidarse de

### Más partes del cuerpo humano

| | |
|---|---|
| el brazo | arm |
| el dedo (de la mano) | finger |
| el dedo del pie | toe |
| la mano | hand |
| el pie | foot |
| la pierna | leg |

Repaso: la cabeza

### Accidentes

| | |
|---|---|
| caer (*irreg.*) | to fall |
| caerse | to fall down |
| darse (*irreg.*) en/con/contra | to run, bump into |
| equivocarse (qu) (de) | to be wrong, make a mistake (about) |
| hacerse (*irreg.*) daño | to hurt oneself |
| lastimarse | to injure oneself |
| levantarse con el pie izquierdo | to get up on the wrong side of the bed |
| pedir (i, i) disculpas | to apologize |

| | |
|---|---|
| pegarse (gu) en/con/contra | to hit (*a part of one's body*); to run into/bump against |
| romper | to break |

Repaso: doler (ue)

| | |
|---|---|
| Discúlpeme. | Pardon me. I'm sorry. |
| Fue sin querer. | It was unintentional. |
| ¡Lo siento (mucho)! | Pardon me! I'm (very) sorry! |
| ¡Qué mala suerte! | What bad luck! |

Repaso: perdón

## Los adjetivos

| | |
|---|---|
| distraído/a | absentminded |
| escrito/a | written |
| estudiantil | (of) student(s) |
| torpe | clumsy |
| universitario/a | (of the) university |

Cognado: flexible

## Otros sustantivos

| | |
|---|---|
| la época | era, time (*period*) |
| la luz (*pl.* luces) | light; electricity |

Repaso: la vida

## Palabras adicionales

| | |
|---|---|
| -mente | -ly (*adverbial suffix*) |
| por Dios | for heaven's sake |
| por ejemplo | for example |
| por primera/ última vez | for the first/last time |
| por si acaso | just in case |
| ¡por supuesto! | of course! |
| por todas partes | everywhere |
| ¡qué + *adj.*! | how + *adj.*! |

Repaso: gracias por, por eso, por favor, por fin, por la mañana/tarde/noche, por lo general, por lo menos

Suggestions
• Remind students that, in the preterite, the first person singular is *saqué*.
• Remind students that the plural of *luz* is *luces*.
• Have students use vocabulary words to narrate a round-robin *un día fatal*. As a class, they can establish the subject (an individual, real or imaginary). Each student gives a sentence that describes the subject's terrible day.
• Have students complete sentences, such as:

1. *Por primera vez en mi vida, yo...*
2. *Por supuesto, yo...*
3. *Por si acaso hay...*
4. *En esta clase, por lo menos...*

Encourage them to be creative and humorous in their responses. Ask them to compose new sentences that use the new *Palabras adicionales*.
• Remind students that the notation after *pedir* (*i, i*) indicates the *e → i* stem change in the present tense (except for *nosotros* and *vosotros*) and the *e → i* stem change in the third person singular and plural of the preterite and in the present participle.
• Have students give the opposite expressions for the following verbs.

| | | |
|---|---|---|
| *acabar* | *entregar* | *sacar* |
| *acordarse* | *quedar* | *ser flexible* |
| *caerse* | *recoger* | |

# La calidad de la vida

## CULTURA

- **Nota cultural:** Los barrios y las familias
- **En los Estados Unidos y el Canadá:** Las computadoras y la comunidad hispana
- **Voces** del Perú
    **Literatura:** Mario Vargas Llosa
    **Música:** El huayno
- **Videoteca**
    **Entrevista cultural:** El Perú
    **Entre amigos:** Me tiras un correo, ¿eh?
- **Enfoque cultural:** El Perú

## VOCABULARIO

- Tengo… Necesito… Quiero…
- La vivienda

## GRAMÁTICA

33 **Tú** (Informal) Commands

34 Present Subjunctive: An Introduction

35 Use of the Subjunctive: Influence

*Las terrazas de Machu Picchu, Perú*

Paso 1: Vocabulario
See the "Chapter-by-Chapter Supplementary Materials" in the

IM for a model for vocabulary presentation, as well as additional teaching suggestions, notes, activities, and other resources for *Paso 1*.

### TENGO... NECESITO... QUIERO...

Resources: Transparency 79

**Suggestions**
• Model vocabulary in sentences about yourself and communicative exchanges with the students.
• Have students give sentences about the kinds of vehicles or vehicle use they associate with the following circumstances or people.

1. *una persona muy deportista*
2. *un joven que vive en Miami*
3. *una tarde de verano*
4. *un hombre joven soltero que gana mucho dinero y vive en el sur de California*
5. *unos adolescentes urbanos*

**el equipo fotográfico**
**el lector de DVD**
**el monopatín**
**los patines**
**el televisor**
**el equipo estereofónico**
**la bicicleta (de montaña)**
**el radio (portátil)**
**la impresora**
**el ratón**
**la computadora / el ordenador (Sp.)**
**la moto(cicleta)**
**el carro / el coche (descapotable)**

♻ **Reciclado**
Review transportation words students have learned: *el coche = el carro, el tren, el autobús, el avión, el barco.*

### La electrónica

| | |
|---|---|
| **la cinta** | tape |
| **el contestador automático** | answering machine |
| **el correo electrónico** | e-mail |
| **el disco duro** | hard drive |
| **la grabadora** | (tape) recorder/player |
| **la Red** | Net |
| **navegar (gu) la Red** | to surf the Net |
| **la videocasetera** | videocassette recorder/player (VCR) |

**Cognados: la cámara (de vídeo), el CD-ROM, el control remoto, el disco compacto (el CD), el disco de computadora, el DVD, el fax, el *iPod*, la memoria, el módem, el teléfono (celular), el *walkman***

**Multimedia: Audio**
Students can listen to and practice this chapter's vocabulary on the Online Learning Center (**www.mhhe.com/quetal7**) as well as on the Textbook Audio CD, part of the Laboratory Audio Program.

### Verbos útiles

| | |
|---|---|
| **cambiar (de canal, de cuarto, de ropa... )** | to change (channels, rooms, clothing . . . ) |
| **conseguir (i, i) (g)** | to get, obtain |
| **copiar / hacer (*irreg.*) copia** | to copy |
| **fallar** | to "crash" (*of computers*) |
| **funcionar** | to work, function; to run (*machines*) |
| **grabar** | to record; to tape |
| **guardar** | to keep, to save (*documents*) |
| **imprimir** | to print |
| **manejar** | to drive; to operate (*a machine*) |
| **obtener** (*irreg.*) | to get, obtain |
| **sacar (qu) fotos** | to take photos |

### En el trabajo

| | |
|---|---|
| **el aumento** | raise |
| **el/la jefe/a** | boss |
| **el sueldo** | salary |

## ■ Conversación

### A. Ud. y los aparatos

PASO 1  ¿Qué se usa en estas situaciones? Con un compañero / una compañera, conteste las preguntas. Luego piense en cuatro situaciones similares. Uno/a de Uds. da la descripción y el otro / la otra identifica el aparato.

1. para mandar copias de documentos no originales que deben llegar inmediatamente
2. para grabar un programa de televisión cuando no podemos verlo a la hora de su emisión
3. para cambiar el programa de la tele sin levantarse del sillón
4. para recibir llamadas telefónicas cuando no estamos en casa
5. para escuchar música mientras hacemos ejercicio

PASO 2  Para Ud., ¿son ciertas o falsas las siguientes oraciones?

1. Entiendo cómo funcionan los aparatos.
2. Aprendí con facilidad a usar la computadora.
3. No me puedo imaginar la vida sin los aparatos electrónicos modernos.
4. Para mí, el vehículo es una expresión de la personalidad.
5. Una vez me falló la computadora y perdí unos documentos y archivos (*files*) muy importantes.
6. Uso la videocasetera para ver películas, pero no sé grabar.
7. Me gusta navegar la red porque encuentro mucha información.

### B. ¿Qué vehículos... ?  ¿Qué vehículo piensa Ud. que deben tener y usar las siguientes personas? ¿Qué vehículo(s) tiene Ud.? ¿Es lo más apropiado para su vida? ¿Por qué? ¿Qué vehículo le gustaría tener?

1. una persona joven que vive en Key West, una isla soleada e informal en el sur de Florida
2. una familia con tres hijos
3. un estudiante de artes liberales que vive en este *campus*
4. unos chicos que pasan gran parte de su tiempo libre en la playa y en el *boardwalk*
5. un matrimonio jubilado (*retired*) que vive en Nueva Inglaterra

### C. ¿Necesidad o lujo (*luxury*)?

PASO 1  ¿Considera Ud. que las siguientes posesiones son un lujo o una necesidad de la vida moderna? Indique si Ud. tiene este aparato o vehículo. Luego, dé tres cosas más que Ud. considera necesarias en la vida moderna.

MODELO:  un televisor → Para mí, un televisor es una necesidad. Tengo uno. (No tengo uno ahora.)

1. un contestador automático
2. una videocasetera
3. el equipo estereofónico
4. una computadora
5. un coche
6. una bicicleta
7. un *iPod*
8. un teléfono celular

PASO 2  Para terminar, entreviste a un compañero / una compañera para saber si está de acuerdo con Ud. y si tiene las mismas posesiones.

MODELO:  el televisor → E1: ¿El televisor?
E2: Yo lo considero un lujo y por eso no tengo uno.

---

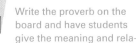
---

♻ **Reciclado**
Review place names from *Capítulo 3: el centro (comercial)*,
*el mercado, la tienda,* and so on.

La... *Housing*

## LA VIVIENDA°

**Resources: Transparencies 80, 81**
Transparency 81 provides additional
practice and vocabulary.

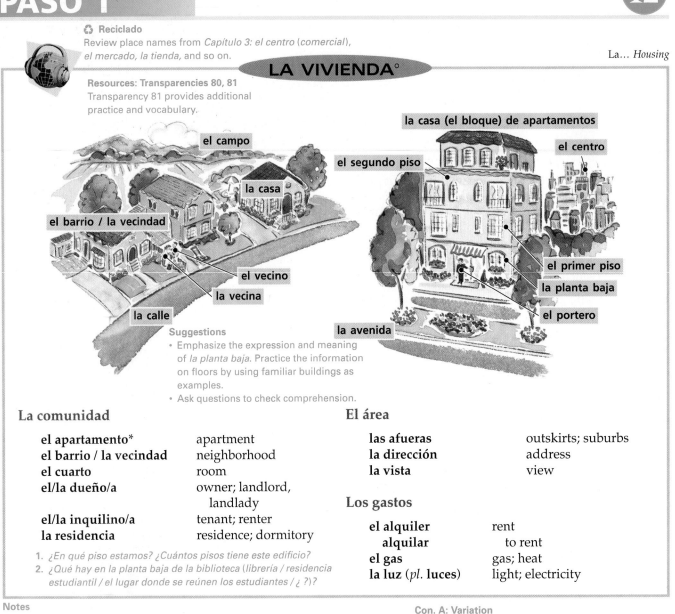

**Suggestions**
• Emphasize the expression and meaning
  of *la planta baja*. Practice the information
  on floors by using familiar buildings as
  examples.
• Ask questions to check comprehension.

### La comunidad

| | |
|---|---|
| **el apartamento*** | apartment |
| **el barrio / la vecindad** | neighborhood |
| **el cuarto** | room |
| **el/la dueño/a** | owner; landlord, landlady |
| **el/la inquilino/a** | tenant; renter |
| **la residencia** | residence; dormitory |

1. *¿En qué piso estamos? ¿Cuántos pisos tiene este edificio?*
2. *¿Qué hay en la planta baja de la biblioteca (librería / residencia estudiantil / el lugar donde se reúnen los estudiantes / ¿ ?)?*

### El área

| | |
|---|---|
| **las afueras** | outskirts; suburbs |
| **la dirección** | address |
| **la vista** | view |

### Los gastos

| | |
|---|---|
| **el alquiler** | rent |
| alquilar | to rent |
| **el gas** | gas; heat |
| **la luz** (*pl.* **luces**) | light; electricity |

**Notes**
• Ordinal numbers are formally presented in *Capítulo 13*. You may need to help students with ordinals as they talk about where they live.
• Point out that *suburbios* is a false cognate. It means "slums." *Afueras* is used to refer to suburbs.

---

**Frases útiles**

**Es una persona que…**
**Es un lugar donde…**
**Es una cosa que…**

---

**Con. A: Variation**
Play a Jeopardy game. Give or have students give a definition. The class (or teams) should respond with the corresponding question.

## ■ Conversación

**A. Definiciones.** Dé las definiciones de las siguientes palabras.

MODELO: la residencia → *Es un lugar donde viven muchos estudiantes. → ¿Qué es una residencia?*
Es un lugar donde viven muchos estudiantes. Por lo general está situada en el *campus* universitario.

| | | |
|---|---|---|
| 1. el inquilino | 6. la dueña | 11. la avenida |
| 2. el centro | 7. la dirección | 12. el campo |
| 3. el alquiler | 8. las afueras | 13. la planta baja |
| 4. el portero | 9. el barrio | 14. la vista |
| 5. la vecina | 10. la casa | 15. la luz |

---

*****El apartamento** *is used throughout Latin America and the Caribbean.* **El departamento** *is used in Mexico, Peru, and other Latin American countries, but* **el piso** *is the word most commonly used in Spain.*

CAPÍTULO
12
Nota cultural: Comprensión: ¿Cierto o falso?
1. En muchas familias extendidas del mundo hispánico, los tíos, primos, abuelos, etcétera, comen juntos con frecuencia.
2. En una casa de apartamentos, los vecinos no se comunican mucho si no son parientes.

PASO 1

## NOTA CULTURAL

### Los barrios y las familias

En los pueblos pequeños del mundo es común que **los parientes** de una familia **vivan en la misma calle,** o por lo menos, en el mismo barrio. También es común que la madre o la abuela de la familia prepare la comida para que **todos los familiares** que viven cerca **vengan a comer juntos.**[a]

Las personas que viven en apartamentos a veces mantienen **una relación muy unida** con **sus vecinos.** En una casa de apartamentos típica, muchos se consideran como una gran familia. Hay un ambiente familiar entre los vecinos aunque[b] no sean parientes.

A veces por necesidad o simplemente para seguir[c] una carrera,[d] unos **dejan su comunidad** y se mudan[e] a otra ciudad o a otro país.

*Una familia hispana durante una comida típica*

---

[a]*together*  [b]*although*  [c]*follow*  [d]*career, profession*  [e]*se... move*

## B. A buscar vivienda

PASO 1   Lea los tres anuncios de viviendas en el Perú y conteste las siguientes preguntas.

1. ¿Qué tipo de vivienda aparece (*appears*) en cada anuncio? ¿Son para comprar o alquilar?
2. ¿Cuántos dormitorios tiene cada vivienda?
3. ¿Cree Ud. que estas viviendas son para familias con mucho o poco dinero?

PASO 2   **Entrevista.** Con un  compañero / una compañera, hable sobre el tipo de vivienda que prefieren.

1. Como estudiante universitario, ¿prefieres vivir en el *campus* o fuera del *campus*? ¿en una residencia o en una casa o apartamento de alquiler con otras personas?
2. ¿Prefieres vivir en la planta baja o en los pisos más altos?
3. Si alquilas tu vivienda, ¿prefieres que el alquiler incluya (*include*) todos los gastos o prefieres pagar la luz y el gas por separado?
4. Si pudieras (*If you could*) escoger, ¿qué te gustaría más, tener un apartamento pequeño en un barrio elegante del centro o una casa grande en las afueras?
5. ¿Qué tipo de vecinos te gusta tener?

### CUZCO

**Alquilo casa. Barrio residencial. Semi-amueblada**[a] **con teléfono. Informes Teléf. Cuzco: 084-226752.   Lima: 774153 (horario 2 a 5 p.m.)**

[a]*Partially furnished*

## CHACARILLA DEL ESTANQUE

Departamentos exclusivos, diseño especial, 3 dormitorios, comedor de diario, área de servicio, totalmente equipados. Desde $41.500. Buenas facilidades.

**Av. Buena Vista N° 230
(a 2 Cdras. de Velasco Aslete)
Tels. 458107 – 357743**

## DEPARTAMENTOS MONTERRICO

**Finos departamentos de 3 dormitorios, 3½ baños, sala de estar,**[b] **1 ó 2 cocheras,**[c] **acabados de primera,**[d] **verlos todos los días en: Domingo de la Presa 165, espalda cuadra 12 Av. Primavera.**

[b]*sala... living room; sitting room*  [c]*1 ó 2... one- or two-car garage*  [d]*acabados... first-class finishing details*

**Con. B: Follow-Up**
• **Paso 1.** Have students explain which ad appeals to them the most and why.
• **Paso 2.** Have students tally their answers on the board, then have a class discussion about the similarities and differences.

**Need more practice?**
■ Workbook/Laboratory Manual
■ Interactive CD-ROM
■ Online Learning Center (www.mhhe.com/quetal7)

**Note**
See the Workbook/Laboratory Manual for presentation and practice of the letters *y* and *ll*.

**Paso 2: Gramática**
See the "Chapter-by-Chapter Supplementary Materials" in the IM for additional teaching suggestions, notes, activities, and other resources for *Paso 2*.

**Note**
If you have been using *tú* commands all along, start by having students list the ones they already know.

## ¿Recuerda Ud.?

In **Gramática 19** you learned about **Ud.** and **Uds.** (formal) commands. Remember that object pronouns (direct, indirect, reflexive) must follow and be attached to affirmative commands; they must precede negative commands.

AFFIRMATIVE: Háblele Ud.   Duérmase.   Dígaselo Ud.
NEGATIVE: No le hable Ud.   No se duerma.   No se lo diga Ud.

¿Cómo se dice en español?

1. Bring me the book. (**Uds.**)
2. Don't give it (*m.*) to her. (**Uds.**)
3. Sit here, please. (**Ud.**)
4. Don't sit in that chair! (**Ud.**)
5. Tell them the truth. (**Uds.**)
6. Tell it (*f.*) to them now! (**Uds.**)

7. Never tell it (*f.*) to her. (**Uds.**)
8. Take care of yourself. (**Ud.**)
9. Lead a healthy life. (**Ud.**)
10. Listen to me. (**Ud.**)
11. Wake up earlier. (**Ud.**)
12. Get dressed quickly. (**Uds.**)

13. Enjoy yourself with your friends. (**Ud.**)
14. Don't give it (*m.*) to them now. (**Uds.**)

---

**Suggestions**
- Have students give the infinitive form of each command in the *minidiálogo*.
- Have students write a paragraph about what they have in their rooms or homes, what they need, and what they would like to have some day. Then have students work in groups to read and compare their items.

## 33 Influencing Others *Tú* (Informal) Commands

**¡Marta, tu cuarto es un desastre!**

**Resources: Transparency 82**
Transparency 82 provides examples of *tú* commands.

**Suggestions**
- Point out to students that they already know all of the forms involved in this tense, and that the position of the object pronouns is identical to the pronoun position used in formal (*Ud.* and *Uds.*) commands.
- You may wish to treat the material in this section for passive recognition only. Have students learn only high-frequency irregular *tú* commands.
- Explain to students that the command system in Spanish (although easy to understand when someone gives you a command) is difficult to master in speaking. They should not be discouraged if complete control does not come easily.

El padre de Marta está enojado.

«¡Marta, qué desordenado está tu cuarto! Por favor, *arréglalo* antes de jugar con tus amigos. *Guarda* la ropa limpia en tu armario, *pon* la ropa sucia en el cesto, *haz* la cama, *recoge* los libros del piso y *ordénalos* en los estantes… Y no *dejes* los zapatos por todas partes… ¡Es muy peligroso!»

**Comprensión**

¿Quién diría (*would say*) lo siguiente, Marta o Manolo, su padre?

1. No te enojes… Ya voy a arreglarlo todo.   Marta
2. Hazlo inmediatamente… ¡antes de salir a jugar!   Manolo
3. Dime, ¿por qué tengo que hacerlo ahora mismo?   Marta
4. La próxima vez, ¡no dejes tu cuarto en estas condiciones!   Manolo

Informal commands (**los mandatos informales**) are used with persons whom you would address as **tú**.

| Past | PRESENT | Future |
|---|---|---|
| preterite | present indicative | |
| imperfect | present progressive | |
| | formal commands | |
| | informal commands | |

---

*Marta, your room is a disaster!*   Marta's father is angry. "Marta, what a messy room you have! Please straighten it up before you go out to play with your friends. Put your clean clothes away in the closet, put your dirty clothes in the hamper, make your bed, pick your books up off of the floor and arrange them on the shelves… And don't leave your shoes lying around everywhere… It's very dangerous!"

**Refrán**

«No vendas la piel del oso antes de haberlo muerto.»

Note the dialectal use of *muerto* in this saying. In some countries, *muerto* is used

## Negative *tú* Commands

synonymously with *matado*. For example: *Dos personas fueron muertas por los terroristas.* Have students give a common English equivalent (*Don't count your chickens before they've hatched.*).

**Preliminary Exercise**
Have students respond to statements with negative commands. Write the following example on the board, then give them additional statements.

| -*ar* verbs | | -*er*/-*ir* verbs | |
|---|---|---|---|
| **No hables.** | Don't speak. | **No comas.** | Don't eat. |
| **No cantes.** | Don't sing. | **No escribas.** | Don't write. |
| **No juegues.** | Don't play. | **No pidas.** | Don't order. |

**A.** Like Ud. commands (**Gramática 19**), the negative **tú** commands are expressed using the "opposite vowel": **no hable Ud., no hables (tú).** The pronoun **tú** is used only for emphasis.

No cantes **tú** tan fuerte.
*Don't **you** sing so loudly.*

*No quiero cantarlo.* → *Pues, no lo cantes.*

*No quiero comprarlo / mirarlo / leerlo / beberlo / escribirlo / decidirlo.*

**B.** As with negative Ud. commands, object pronouns—direct, indirect, and reflexive—precede negative **tú** commands.

| **No lo** mires. | **No les** escribas. | **No te** levantes. |
|---|---|---|
| *Don't look at him.* | *Don't write to them.* | *Don't get up.* |

## Affirmative *tú* Commands

| -*ar* verbs | | -*er*/-*ir* verbs | |
|---|---|---|---|
| **Habla.** | Speak. | **Come.** | Eat. |
| **Canta.** | Sing. | **Escribe.** | Write. |
| **Juega.** | Play. | **Pide.** | Order. |

**A.** Unlike the other command forms you have learned, most affirmative **tú** commands have the same form as the third person singular of the present indicative.* Some verbs have irregular affirmative **tú** command forms.

| decir: | **di** | salir: | **sal** |
|---|---|---|---|
| hacer: | **haz** | ser: | **sé** |
| ir: | **ve** | tener: | **ten** |
| poner: | **pon** | venir: | **ven** |

*Spelling Hint:* One-syllable words, like the affirmative **tú** commands of some verbs (**decir, ir, tener,**... ) do not need an accent mark: **di, ve, ten,**... Exceptions to this rule are those forms that could be mistaken for other words, like the command of **ser** (**sé**), which could be mistaken for the pronoun **se.**

**Sé** puntual pero **ten** cuidado.
*Be there on time, but be careful.*

**Note**
*Sé* from *ser* can also be mistaken for *sé* (first person singular of the present indicative), of the verb *saber*. Context will clarify the meaning.

**OJO** The affirmative **tú** commands for **ir** and **ver** are identical: **ve.** Context will clarify meaning.

¡**Ve** esa película!
*See that movie!*

**Ve** a casa ahora mismo.
*Go home right now.*

---

*As you know, there are two different moods in Spanish: the indicative mood (the one you have been using, which is used to state facts and ask questions) and the subjunctive mood (which is used to express more subjective actions or states). Beginning with **Gramática 34,** you will learn more about the subjunctive mood.*

**B.** As with affirmative **Ud.** commands, object and reflexive pronouns follow affirmative **tú** commands and are attached to them. Accent marks are necessary except when a single pronoun is added to a one-syllable command.

**Dile** la verdad.
*Tell him the truth.*

**Léela,** por favor.
*Read it, please.*

**Póntelos.**
*Put them on.*

---

**AUTOPRUEBA**

Choose the correct command form for each sentence.

1. \_\_\_\_\_me qué quieres.
2. No \_\_\_\_\_ al parque sola.
3. No le \_\_\_\_\_ nada de la fiesta.
4. \_\_\_\_\_te un abrigo.
5. \_\_\_\_\_ a la tienda.
6. No \_\_\_\_\_ eso en mi cama.

   **a.** di
   **b.** digas
   **c.** pon
   **d.** pongas
   **e.** vayas
   **f.** ve

Answers: 1. a, 2. e, 3. b, 4. c, 5. f, 6. d

---

**Nota comunicativa: Suggestions**
• Remind students that *vosotros/as* is primarily used in Spain.
• Model and practice the *vosotros/as* commands for the students, especially if you are a Spaniard, if you use *vosotros/as* forms, and/or if your students are likely to study in Spain.

## NOTA COMUNICATIVA

### *Vosotros* Commands

In **Capítulo 1,** you learned about the pronoun **vosotros/vosotras** that is used in Spain as the plural of **tú.** Here is information about forming **vosotros** commands, for recognition only.

• Affirmative **vosotros** commands are formed by substituting **-d** for the final **-r** of the infinitive. There are no irregular affirmative **vosotros** commands.

• Negative **vosotros** commands are expressed with the present subjunctive. (You will learn more about the present subjunctive in the next and subsequent grammar sections.)

• Placement of object pronouns is the same as for all other command forms.

hablar → hablad
comer → comed
escribir → escribid

no habléis
no comáis
no escribáis

Decídmelo.
No me lo digáis.

**Heritage Speakers**
Pregúnteles a los hispanohablantes de la clase si saben usar o si usan las formas de *vosotros/as*. También es posible que haya hispanohablantes en su clase que usen el *voseo*, que se oye en Colombia, el Ecuador, Costa Rica, la Argentina y el Uruguay. Revise con la clase los mandatos con *vos*.

  *Hablá vos.*    *No hablés vos.*
  *Acostate vos.*  *No te acostés vos.*

## ■ Práctica

♻ **Prác. A: Reciclado**
As continuing practice of preterite vs. imperfect, have students who heard each phrase as a teenager explain why their mother (or father) said that. *¿Te dijo tu madre eso una sola vez o te lo decía con frecuencia? ¿Por qué?*

### A. ¡Anticipemos! Recuerdos de la niñez

PASO 1  Indique los mandatos afirmativos que Ud. oía con frecuencia cuando era niño/a. Después de leerlos todos, indique los dos que oía más. ¿Hay entre estos algún mandato que Ud. no oyera (*heard*) nunca?

1. \_\_\_\_\_ Limpia tu cuarto.
2. \_\_\_\_\_ Cómete el desayuno.
3. \_\_\_\_\_ Haz la tarea.
4. \_\_\_\_\_ Cierra la puerta.
5. \_\_\_\_\_ Bébete la leche.
6. \_\_\_\_\_ Lávate las manos.
7. \_\_\_\_\_ Dime la verdad.
8. \_\_\_\_\_ Quítate el *walkman*.
9. \_\_\_\_\_ Guarda tu bicicleta en el garaje.

Note in **Práctica A** the use of the reflexive pronoun with the verbs **comer** and **beber**. This use of the reflexive means *to eat up* and *to drink up*, respectively.

**Cómete** las zanahorias.
*Eat up your carrots.*

No **te bebas** la leche tan rápido.
*Don't drink up your milk so fast.*

PASO 2   Ahora indique los mandatos negativos que escuchaba con frecuencia. Debe indicar también los dos que oía más. ¿Hay alguno que no oyera (*heard*) nunca?

1. _____ No cruces la calle solo/a.
2. _____ No juegues con cerillas (*matches*).
3. _____ No comas dulces antes de cenar.
4. _____ No me digas mentiras (*lies*).
5. _____ No les des tanta comida a los peces.
6. _____ No hables con personas desconocidas (*strangers*).
7. _____ No dejes el monopatín en el jardín.
8. _____ No cambies los canales tanto.
9. _____ No digas tonterías (*silly things*).

## B. Julita, la mal educada

PASO 1   Los Sres. Villarreal no están contentos con el comportamiento de su hija Julita. Continúe los comentarios de ellos con mandatos informales lógicos según cada situación. Siga los modelos.

MODELOS:   *Hablaste* demasiado (*too much*) ayer. → No *hables* tanto hoy, por favor.
*Dejaste* tu ropa en el suelo anoche. → No la *dejes* allí hoy, por favor.

1. También *dejaste* tus libros en el suelo (*floor*).
2. ¿Por qué *regresaste* tarde a casa hoy después de las clases?
3. ¿Por qué *vas* al parque todas las tardes?
4. No es bueno que *mires* la televisión constantemente. ¿Y por qué quieres *ver* todos esos programas de detectives?
5. ¿Por qué le *dices* mentiras (*lies*) a tu papá?
6. Siempre *te olvidas* de sacar la basura, que es tu único quehacer.
7. Ay, hija, no te comprendemos. ¡*Eres* tan insolente!

PASO 2   La pobre Julita también escucha muchos mandatos de su maestra en clase. Invente Ud. esos mandatos según las indicaciones.

1. llegar / a / escuela / puntualmente
2. quitarse / abrigo / y / sentarse
3. sacar / libro de matemáticas / y / abrirlo / en / página diez
4. leer / nuevo / palabras / y / aprenderlas / para mañana
5. venir / aquí / a / hablar conmigo / sobre / este / composición

## ■ Conversación

**A. Entre compañeros de casa.**   Con un compañero / una compañera, haga una lista de los cinco mandatos que se oyen con más frecuencia en su casa (apartamento, residencia). Piensen no sólo en los mandatos que Uds. escuchan sino (*but*) también en los que Uds. les dan a los demás (*others*).

### Frases útiles

| | | |
|---|---|---|
| **apagar (gu) la computadora** | **no ser** (*irreg.*)... | **prestarme dinero** |
| **contestar el teléfono** | **así** (like that), **bobo/a** (dumb), **impaciente,** | **poner** (*irreg.*) **la tele** |
| **lavar los platos** | **impulsivo/a, loco/a,** | **sacar (qu) la basura** |
| **no hacer** (*irreg.*) **ruido** | **pesado/a,** | **¿ ?** |
| | **precipitado/a** (hasty) | |

# PASO 2

**Con. B: Bright Idea Preliminary Exercise**
Have students indicate if they should use the formal or informal commands with the following people.

1. *su hermano/a*
2. *su profesor(a)*
3. *su médico/a*
4. *su jefe/a*
5. *su mejor amigo/a*
6. *un compañero / una compañera de clase*

**Con. B: Variation**
Have students write a letter to a columnist for a popular magazine for their age group. Have them present serious or complex problems in their letters. Have students complete the letters as homework, then have them read their letters to the class so that others can offer advice using *tú* commands.

**Con. B: Bright Idea Follow-Up**
*Consejos a una amiga. Roberta quiere mantenerse en buena salud. Conteste sus preguntas usando los mandatos informales.*

1. *¿Debo comer papas fritas tres veces a la semana?*
2. *¿Debo hacer ejercicio todos los días?*
3. *¿Debo fumar más?*
4. *¿Debo tomar más vino?*
5. *¿Debo pedir dos postres en los restaurantes?*
6. *¿Debo acostarme temprano por la noche?*

**En los Estados Unidos y el Canadá: Comprensión: ¿Cierto o falso?**
1. *La mayoría de los hispanos en los Estados Unidos usa computadora.*
2. *Los hispanos pueden leer los periódicos de toda Latinoamérica en el Internet.*

**B. Situaciones.** ¿Qué consejos les daría (*would you give*) a las siguientes personas si fueran (*they were*) sus amigos? Déles a todos consejos en forma de mandatos informales.

1. Celia siempre tiene mucha energía los viernes y le encanta ir al cine o salir a bailar. Pero a su novio no le gusta salir mucho los viernes porque está cansado después de una larga semana de trabajo.
2. Nati tiene 19 años. El próximo año quiere vivir en un apartamento ecónomico en un barrio estudiantil con cuatro amigos (dos de ellos son hombres). Pero los padres de Nati son muy tradicionales y no les va a gustar la situación.
3. Su abuelo va a comprarse su primera computadora y necesita su opinión y experiencia. Tiene muchas preguntas, desde qué tipo debe comprar hasta cómo usarla eficientemente. Él quiere una computadora para conectarse con unos amigos jubilados (*retired*) que ahora viven en otro estado, para navegar la Red y para realizar el sueño de su vida: escribir la historia de la llegada de sus padres a este país.
4. Mariana es una *yuppi*. Gana (*She makes*) muchísimo dinero pero trabaja demasiado. Duerme poco y bebe muchísimo café para seguir despierta (*awake*). No come bien y jamás hace ejercicio. Acaba de comprarse una agenda electrónica (*PDA*) para llevar su trabajo a todas partes.

## En los Estados Unidos y el Canadá

### Las computadoras y la comunidad hispana

**El acceso a las computadoras** entre la comunidad hispana es **mayor ahora** que hace diez años.[a] En un estudio del Departamento de Comercio de los Estados Unidos, con datos del año 2001, se ve que el 49 por ciento de los hispanos de este país usa una computadora. Sin embargo, este aumento es **una mejora**[b] **relativa,** pues la diferencia en cuanto al[c] uso de computadoras entre los hispanos y los no hispanos también creció.[d] Aún[e] más significativa es la diferencia en el porcentaje de hispanos **con acceso al Internet en sus hogares**[f] comparado con el de la población no hispana.

| | 1997 | 2001 |
|---|---|---|
| uso de computadoras | | |
| hispanos | 38% | 49% |
| no hispanos | 54% | 66% |
| uso del Internet | | |
| hispanos | 11% | 22% |
| no hispanos | 32% | 54% |

¿Por qué estas diferencias? Esencialmente por **razones económicas**. Es evidente que las personas que ganan más dinero pueden comprar más computadoras y tecnología, y por ahora hay muchos hispanos que no tienen suficientes

ingresos[g] para estar al día[h] con **los avances tecnológicos.**

En el futuro, será[i] necesario que las computadoras y el Internet se hagan accesibles[j] a más hispanos. Son herramientas[k] necesarias para **la educación, el trabajo, la comunicación** y sobre todo para **la información.** Casi todos los periódicos

*En Chicago, Illinois*

principales de los países hispanos se publican ahora en el Internet. A través de[l] las publicaciones ciberespaciales, los hispanos pueden leer las noticias en español y hasta[m] pueden leer las noticias de su país o ciudad natal. También pueden participar en comunicaciones con **la comunidad hispana** del Internet.

[a]*hace... ten years ago* [b]*improvement* [c]*en... regarding the* [d]*grew* [e]*Still* [f]*homes* [g]*income* [h]*al... up-to-date* [i]*it will be* [j]*available* [k]*tools* [l]*A... Through* [m]*even*

## 34 Expressing Subjective Actions or States Present Subjunctive: An Introduction

### Una decisión importante

José Miguel habla con Gustavo de cámaras digitales

JOSÉ MIGUEL: Quiero comprar una cámara digital. No tengo mucho dinero, pero *es posible que* un amigo me *preste* el dinero que necesito.

GUSTAVO: Pues yo acabo de comprar una cámara digital. Está muy bien y no era muy cara.

JOSÉ MIGUEL: *¿Me recomiendas que compre* alguna marca en particular?

GUSTAVO: Realmente, todas las marcas conocidas tienen buenos productos. *Yo te sugiero que mires* los anuncios en los periódicos y *que busques* las mejores ofertas.

JOSÉ MIGUEL: *Me alegro de que sepas* tanto de electrónica. *¿Me permites que vea* tu cámara?

GUSTAVO: Claro, voy por ella.

**Suggestion**

Have students pick out subjunctive and subjunctive cues in the *minidiálogo*. Ask them what the cues have in common (asking someone to do something, . . . ).

### Comprensión: ¿Cierto o falso?

1. José Miguel quiere que su mamá le preste dinero. falso
2. Gustavo le recomienda a José Miguel que compre una cámara de una marca específica. falso
3. Gustavo le sugiere a José Miguel que primero vaya a muchas tiendas. falso
4. José Miguel quiere que Gustavo le enseñe su cámara nueva. cierto

| Past | PRESENT | Future |
|------|---------|--------|
| preterite | present indicative | |
| imperfect | present progressive | |
| | formal commands | |
| | informal commands | |
| | present subjunctive | |

**Follow-Up**

After reviewing the *minidiálogo*, ask students:

*En el diálogo, ¿quién quiere comprar una cámara?*
*¿Quién sabe mucho de cámaras?*
*¿Quién le da consejos a quién?*
*¿Sugiere Gustavo que José Miguel compre una cámara inmediatamente?*

**Note**

The subjunctive is a difficult concept for native speakers of English, and most will need years of practice and immersion to master it. Aim at conceptual awareness and partial control at the elementary level. Partial control means that students are aware of the existence of the subjunctive and know the rules of use and the forms, but that, in general, they only produce it in well-guided contexts.

**Heritage Speakers**

Invite a dos estudiantes hispanohablantes a dramatizar el minidiálogo para la clase.

*An important decision* José Miguel is talking to Gustavo about digital cameras. JOSÉ MIGUEL: *I want to buy a digital camera. I don't have a lot of money, but it's possible that a friend will lend me the money I need.* GUSTAVO: *Well, I just bought a digital camera. It's very nice and it wasn't expensive.* JOSÉ MIGUEL: *Do you recommend that I buy a particular brand?* GUSTAVO: *To tell the truth, all of the well-known brands have good products. I suggest that you check out the ads in the newspapers and that you look for the best deals.* JOSÉ MIGUEL: *I'm glad you know so much about electronic equipment. Can I see your camera?* GUSTAVO: *Of course, I'll go get it.*

# PASO 2

**Emphasis A: Note**
Students were introduced to the subjunctive for passive recognition in *Capítulo 6,* along with formal commands.

## Present Subjunctive: An Introduction

**A.** Except for command forms, all the verb forms you have learned so far in *¿Qué tal?* are part of the *indicative mood* (**el modo indicativo**). In both English and Spanish, the indicative is used to state facts and to ask questions; it objectively expresses actions or states of being that are considered true by the speaker.

INDICATIVE:

¿**Vienes** a la fiesta?
*Are you coming to the party?*

**Prefiero** llegar temprano a casa.
*I prefer getting home early.*

**B.** Both English and Spanish have another verb system called the *subjunctive mood* (**el modo subjuntivo**). The subjunctive is used to express more subjective or conceptualized actions or states. These include things that the speaker wants to happen or wants others to do, events to which the speaker reacts emotionally, things that are as yet unknown, and so on.

SUBJUNCTIVE:

Espero que **vengas** a la fiesta.
*I hope (that) you are coming to the party.*

Prefiero que **llegues** temprano a casa.
*I prefer that you be home early.*

**C.** Sentences in English and Spanish may be simple or complex. A simple sentence is one that contains a single verb.

Complex sentences are comprised of two or more *clauses* (**las cláusulas**), each containing a conjugated verb. There are two types of clauses: main (independent) clause and subordinate (dependent) clause. *Independent clauses* (**las cláusulas principales**) contain a complete thought and can stand alone. *Dependent clauses* (**las cláusulas subordinadas**) contain an incomplete thought and cannot stand alone. Dependent clauses require an independent clause to form a complete sentence.

When the subjects of the clauses in a complex sentence are different, the subjunctive is often used in the subordinate clause in Spanish. Note that subordinate clauses are linked by the conjunction **que,** which is never optional (as it is in English).

SIMPLE SENTENCE:

**Vienes** a la fiesta.
*You are coming to the party.*

Alicia está en casa.
*Alicia is at home.*

COMPLEX SENTENCE:

INDICATIVE

| MAIN CLAUSE | | SUBORDINATE CLAUSE |
|---|---|---|
| Ella sabe *She knows* | **que** *(that)* | vienes a la fiesta. *you are coming to the party.* |
| Miguel piensa *Miguel thinks* | **que** *(that)* | Alicia está en casa. *Alicia is at home.* |

SUBJUNCTIVE

| MAIN CLAUSE | | SUBORDINATE CLAUSE |
|---|---|---|
| Quiere *She wants* | **que** *(for)* | **vengas** a la fiesta. *you to come to the party.* |
| Miguel espera *Miguel hopes* | **que** *(that)* | Alicia **esté** en casa. *Alicia is at home.* |
| Duda *She doubts* | **que** *(that)* | **vengas** a la fiesta. *you are coming to the party.* |

**Emphasis B: Suggestions**
• Point out that the subjunctive also exists in English.
  *God bless you.*
  *I suggest you be there at one.*
  *If I were a rich man, . . .*
• Point out that in English, the conjunction *that* is often optional, but *que* is required in Spanish.

**Emphasis C: Suggestions**
• Emphasize the syntactic requirements for the subjunctive.

  **1.** two clauses
  **2.** a different subject in each clause

• Provide a diagram to illustrate the sentence structure that points out the different subjects and their corresponding verbs in the indicative and subjunctive.

*Capítulo 12* • *La calidad de la vida*

When there is no change of subject in the sentence, the infinitive follows the conjugated verb and no conjunction is necessary. In this type of sentence, the infinitive functions as a direct object of the conjugated verb.

Quiero ir a la fiesta.
*I want to go to the party.*

D. Three of the most common uses of the subjunctive are to express influence, emotion, and doubt or denial. These are signaled in the previous examples by the verb forms **quiere, espera,** and **duda.**

*Yo quiero que Uds. trabajen mucho.*
*¿Quieren Uds. que yo trabaje mucho?*
*¿Quiero que John trabaje mucho?, and so on.*

*Que te vaya bien.*    *Que Dios te bendiga.*

# Forms of the Present Subjunctive

Many Spanish command forms that you have already learned are part of the subjunctive. The **Ud./Uds.** command forms are highlighted in the following box. What you have learned about forming these commands will help you learn the forms of the present subjunctive.

|  | **hablar** | **comer** | **escribir** | **volver** | **decir** |
|---|---|---|---|---|---|
| **Singular** | hable | coma | escriba | vuelva | diga |
|  | hables | comas | escribas | vuelvas | digas |
|  | hable | coma | escriba | vuelva | diga |
| **Plural** | hablemos | comamos | escribamos | volvamos | digamos |
|  | habléis | comáis | escribáis | volváis | digáis |
|  | hablen | coman | escriban | vuelvan | digan |

A. The personal endings of the present subjunctive are added to the first person singular of the present indicative minus its **-o** ending. **-Ar** verbs add endings with **-e,** and **-er/-ir** verbs add endings with **-a.**

-ar → -e
-er/-ir → -a

present indicative *yo* stem =
present subjunctive stem

B. **-Car, -gar,** and **-zar** verbs have a spelling change in all persons of the present subjunctive to preserve the **-c-, -g-,** and **-z-** sounds.

-car:  c → qu
-gar:  g → gu
-zar:  z → c

| **buscar** | | **pagar** | | **empezar** | |
|---|---|---|---|---|---|
| busque | busquemos | pague | paguemos | empiece | empecemos |
| busques | busquéis | pagues | paguéis | empieces | empecéis |
| busque | busquen | pague | paguen | empiece | empiecen |

# PASO 2

**C.** Verbs with irregular **yo** forms show the irregularity in all persons of the present subjunctive.

**Emphasis C: Suggestion**
Briefly model the subjunctive forms of irregular verbs in communicative exchanges with students, asking one or two questions using each verb. Continue to use only *Quiero que...* as the semantic cue or introduce *Ojalá que.*

| conocer: | **cono**zca,... | salir: | **sal**ga,... |
|---|---|---|---|
| decir: | **di**ga,... | tener: | **ten**ga,... |
| hacer: | **ha**ga,... | traer: | **trai**ga,... |
| oír: | **oi**ga,... | venir: | **ven**ga,... |
| poner: | **pon**ga,... | ver: | **ve**a,... |

**D.** A few verbs have irregular present subjunctive forms.

**Emphasis D: Suggestion**
Point out that the subjunctive of *hay* is *haya* and that, like *hay* and *había,* it is impersonal and does not change to the plural form before a plural noun.

*Ojalá que haya muchas personas en la fiesta.*

| dar: | **dé, des, dé, demos, deis, den** |
|---|---|
| estar: | **esté,...** |
| haber (hay): | **haya** |
| ir: | **vaya,...** |
| saber: | **sepa,...** |
| ser: | **sea,...** |

**E.** **-Ar** and **-er** stem-changing verbs follow the stem-changing pattern of the present indicative.

**Emphasis E: Suggestion**
Introduce the subjunctive forms of stem-changing verbs. Emphasize the second stem change and its connection to the preterite forms.

pensar (ie):

| p**ie**nse | pensemos |
|---|---|
| p**ie**nses | penséis |
| p**ie**nse | p**ie**nsen |

poder (ue):

| p**ue**da | podamos |
|---|---|
| p**ue**das | podáis |
| p**ue**da | p**ue**dan |

**F.** **-Ir** stem-changing verbs show a stem change in the four forms that have a change in the present indicative. In addition, however, they show a second stem change in the **nosotros** and **vosotros** forms, similar to the present progressive tense.

**-ir** stem-changing verbs (**nosotros, vosotros**):
o → u, e → i

dormir (ue, u):

| d**ue**rma | d**u**rmamos |
|---|---|
| d**ue**rmas | d**u**rmáis |
| d**ue**rma | d**ue**rman |

pedir (i, i):

| p**i**da | p**i**damos |
|---|---|
| p**i**das | p**i**dáis |
| p**i**da | p**i**dan |

preferir (ie, i):

| pref**ie**ra | pref**i**ramos |
|---|---|
| pref**ie**ras | pref**i**ráis |
| pref**ie**ra | pref**ie**ran |

**Heritage Speakers**
En el español estándar, la forma aceptada del presente del subjuntivo del verbo *haber* es *haya.* Sin embargo, algunos hispanohablantes dicen *haiga* en vez de *haya.* Este fenómeno es del habla cotidiana. No es una forma aceptada para el uso formal.

**AUTOPRUEBA**

Complete each verb form with the correct letters to form the subjunctive.

1. conocer: cono_____amos
2. decir: di_____an
3. sacar: sa_____es
4. entregar: entre_____en
5. conseguir: consi_____an
6. morir: m_____ramos

*Answers: 1. conozcamos 2. digan 3. saques 4. entreguen 5. consigan 6. muramos*

*Capítulo 12 • La calidad de la vida*

## ■ Práctica

**A. ¡Anticipemos! La vida tecnológica.**   Indique si está de acuerdo o no con las siguientes oraciones.

1. En la vida actual es absolutamente necesario tener una computadora.
2. Yo quiero comprarme una computadora nueva, pero no creo que pueda hacerlo inmediatamente.
3. Hoy día (*These days*) es posible comprar una buena computadora portátil por $1.000.
4. Es horrible que la tecnología cambie tan rápidamente; nadie puede aprender a este ritmo.
5. Prefiero que la gente no dependa tanto de la tecnología.
6. Es ridículo que tantas personas usen un teléfono celular.
7. Dudo que el precio de las llamadas de los teléfonos celulares baje más en los próximos dos años.
8. Espero que mi compañero/a de casa (esposo/a, hijo/a) cambie el mensaje del contestador automático.

**B. Su trabajo actual.**   Use frases de la lista a la derecha para completar las oraciones de modo (*in such a way*) que se refieran a su situación laboral actual. (Siempre hay más de una respuesta posible.) Si Ud. no trabaja ahora, no importa. ¡Invéntese una respuesta!

1. _____ El jefe quiere que _____.
2. _____ También espera que _____.
3. _____ Y duda que _____.
4. _____ Prohíbe (*He forbids*) que _____.
5. _____ En el trabajo, es importante que _____.
6. _____ Yo espero que _____.
7. _____ No quiero que _____.
8. _____ Es difícil que _____.

a. a veces trabajemos los fines de semana
b. todos lleguemos a tiempo
c. hablemos por teléfono con los amigos
d. me den un aumento de sueldo
e. nos paguen más a todos
f. no usemos el *fax* para asuntos (*matters*) personales
g. me den un trabajo de tiempo completo algún día
h. no perdamos mucho tiempo charlando (*chatting*) con los demás
i. fumemos en la oficina
j. tengamos muchas fechas límites
k. me den otro proyecto (*project*)
l. ¿ ?

**Prác. A: Preliminary Exercises**
• Read each verb form and have students tell whether it is in the present indicative or present subjunctive.

| *-ar:* | baile | hablemos |
| | cena | miramos |
| | lleguemos | buscan |
| | pago | te olvides |
| | recuerde | |
| *-er/-ir:* | aprende | recibo |
| | aprenda | beban |
| | lea | digo |
| | leemos | pongamos |
| | escribamos | traigan |
| | coma | sabe |
| | asisten | sepan |

• Use the following chain drill to practice the subjunctive forms:

*Dé oraciones nuevas según las indicaciones.*

1. *En clase: El profesor no quiere que Uds. fumen. (yo, nosotros, tú, los estudiantes, Lupe, vosotros)*
2. *En casa, el día antes de la fiesta, es necesario que alguien llame a nuestros amigos. (comprar los refrescos, buscar los discos compactos, invitar a María, traer la comida)*

**Prác. A, B: Note**
Both activities call for passive recognition of subjunctive forms and structures.

**Prác. B: Variation**
Change the context to *los estudiantes de la clase de español.* Have students make all other necessary changes, keeping the main clause verbs.

**Need more practice?**

■ Workbook/Laboratory Manual
■ Interactive CD-ROM
■ Online Learning Center (www.mhhe.com/quetal7)

## ■ Conversación

**A. ¿Puede Ud. substituir en la ausencia de su profesor(a)?** Demuéstrele a su profesor(a) que Ud. lo/la conoce bien, formando oraciones como las que dice él/ella en clase. (Sólo tiene que cambiar el infinitivo.)

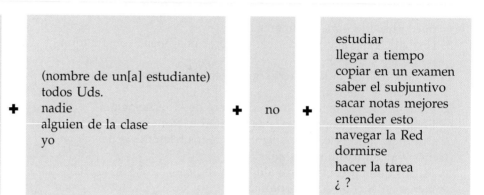

| | | |
|---|---|---|
| Quiero que | (nombre de un[a] estudiante) | estudiar |
| Espero que | todos Uds. | llegar a tiempo |
| Prohíbo que | nadie | copiar en un examen |
| Dudo que | alguien de la clase + no + | saber el subjuntivo |
| Es necesario que + | yo | sacar notas mejores |
| Me alegro de (*I'm glad*) que | | entender esto |
| No creo que | | navegar la Red |
| Recomiendo que | | dormirse |
| | | hacer la tarea |
| | | ¿ ? |

**B. Consejos para comprar y usar la tecnología de multimedia**

PASO 1   Complete las siguientes recomendaciones. Use el subjuntivo del verbo entre paréntesis y complete cada recomendación según su opinión y sus conocimientos (*knowledge*).

Recomiendo que…

> MODELO:   (encontrar) [un amigo / un experto / ¿ ?] para ayudarlo/la a montar (*set up*) la computadora →
> Recomiendo que *encuentre un experto* para ayudarlo/la a montar la computadora.

1. (ir) a [nombre de una tienda de computadoras] para comprar la computadora
2. (comprar) [marca y modelo de computadora]
3. (mirar) revistas especializadas, como [nombre de revista]
4. (no) (pagar) más de $ _____
5. (no) (usar) [marca o tipo de *software*]
6. (estar) seguro/a de que la computadora tenga [módem / impresora en colores / ¿ ?]
7. (poner) la computadora en [lugar]

PASO 2   Ahora, explique por qué hizo las recomendaciones del **Paso 1.**

> MODELO:   Recomiendo que encuentre un experto para ayudarlo/la a montar la computadora *porque es difícil hacerlo.*

PASO 3   Compare sus respuestas con las de algunos compañeros para ver si están de acuerdo. ¿Quién sabe más del tema en la clase?

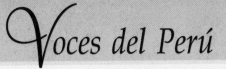

## LITERATURA: Mario Vargas Llosa

**Sobre el autor:** *Jorge Mario Pedro Vargas Llosa nació y estudió en el Perú, pero ha vivido[a] en varios países. En los años 90, se trasladó[b] a España, donde consiguió ciudadanía[c] española. Ha sido[d] profesor visitante en universidades de los Estados Unidos, Latinoamérica y Europa. El siguiente fragmento es de la novela:* La tía Julia y el escribidor *(1977).*

En ese tiempo remoto, yo era muy joven y vivía con mis abuelos en una quinta[e] de paredes blancas de la calle Ocharán, en Miraflores. Estudiaba en San Marcos, Derecho,[f] creo, resignado a ganarme más tarde la vida con una profesión liberal, aunque, en el fondo,[g] me hubiera gustado[h] más llegar a ser un escritor. Tenía un trabajo de título pomposo, sueldo modesto, apropiaciones ilícitas[i] y horario elástico: director de Informaciones de Radio Panamericana. Consistía en recortar las noticias interesantes que aparecían en los diarios[j] y maquillarlas[k] un poco para que se leyeran[l] en los boletines.

[a]*ha... he has lived* [b]*se... he moved* [c]*citizenship* [d]*Ha... He has been* [e]*casa* [f]*Law* [g]*en... deep down* [h]*me... I would have liked* [i]*apropiaciones... crooked deals* [j]*periódicos* [k]*editing them* [l]*para... so that they could be read*

**Mario Vargas Llosa**
(1936– )

**Literatura: Notes**

- Vargas Llosa is a novelist, playwright, journalist, essayist, and also literary critic. He uses "avant-garde" techniques to create a "double of the real world." Although he talks of many strong social and political themes in his work, he has emphasized that artistic aims should not be compromised for propaganda. Vargas Llosa writes regularly for *El País*, and has received numerous awards as a writer, including *El Príncipe de Asturias* prize, *el Premio Planeta*, the Max Schmidheiny Foundation Freedom Prize, the National Book Critics Award, the Ortega y Gasset Prize, the National Prize for the Novel in Peru, the Romulo Gallegos International prize for literature. He received a doctorate from *la Universidad Complutense* in Madrid, and holds honorary doctorates from Georgetown, Yale, Harvard, and other international universities.
- In 1990 Vargas Llosa was a candidate for the presidency of Peru, but after many electoral processes and battles, he lost the election. He currently lives in Spain.

## MÚSICA: El huayno

El huayno es una música tradicional del Perú y el baile andino más típico. Su sonido[a] es inconfundible,[b] como lo es[c] su baile, caracterizado por pequeños saltos.[d] El nombre «huayno» refleja el origen precolombino de esta forma musical; viene de la palabra quechua **wayna,** que significa «joven».

[a]*sound* [b]*unmistakable* [c]*como... as is* [d]*jumps, hops*

**Música: Notes**

- *Huayno* is also spelled *huaíño* or *wayno.*
- Music historians speculate that this dance derived from ancient Inca funeral rituals. Today, however, *el huayno* is purely festive, with bright costumes and lively rhythms.
- The *huayno* dance is performed by couples who execute a series of sharp turns, hops, and tap-like *zapateo* to mark time.

la quena

el charango

- Different regions have developed their own *huayno* styles, and in some areas, the *huayno* is performed by marching bands, which add brass instruments and/or accordions to the sound.

«Tres de mayo» es una canción huayno típica. La fecha, el tres de mayo, es una referencia a un festival nacional peruano.

### Tres de mayo

En una noche de tres de mayo
Tuve la suerte de conocerte[j]
Tuve la suerte de haberte querido.[k]

Cuando decías olvidaremos[l]
Olvidaremos todo lo pasado[m]
Huaycheña[n] todo lo pasado
Huaycheña todo lo pasado.

Originalmente, el huayno era una danza indígena rítmica acompañada de instrumentos precolombinos como la quena.[e] Con la llegada[f] de los españoles, el huayno se modificó para incluir instrumentos de cuerda.[g] La quena es un instrumento de viento[h] indígena del Perú, típica de la música de los Andes. Hoy el huayno también se toca con el charango (un instrumento andino de diez cuerdas), el arpa[i] y el violín.

[e]*Andean flute* [f]*arrival* [g]*instrumentos... stringed instruments* [h]*instrumento... wind instrument* [i]*harp*

[j]*Tuve... I was lucky to meet you* [k]*de... to have loved you* [l]*we will forget* [m]*lo... what has happened* [n]*Mujer joven*

**Follow-Up**
Ask students the following questions about the pairs of sentences that introduce this section.

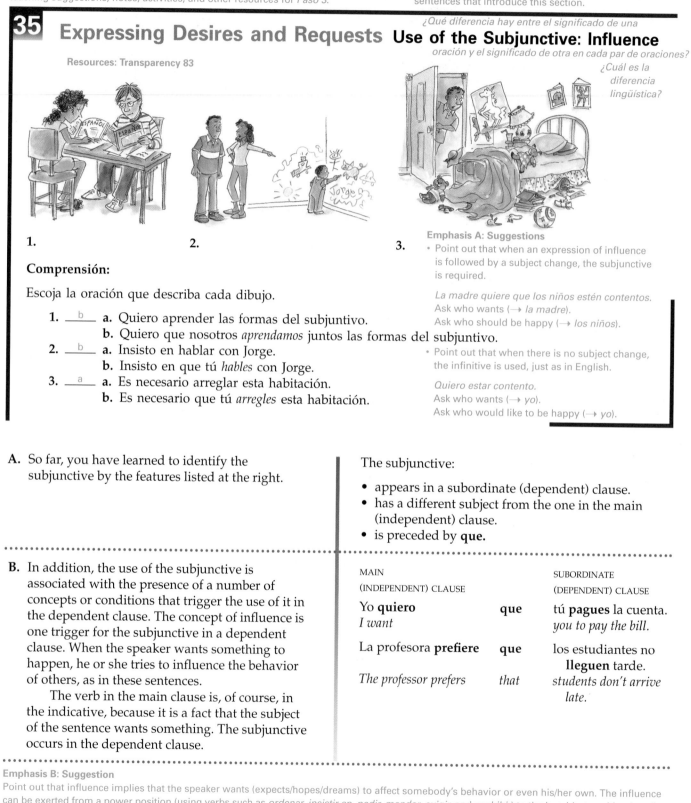

**35 Expressing Desires and Requests**

## Use of the Subjunctive: Influence

*¿Qué diferencia hay entre el significado de una oración y el significado de otra en cada par de oraciones?*

*¿Cuál es la diferencia lingüística?*

Resources: Transparency 83

1.

2.

3.

**Emphasis A: Suggestions**

• Point out that when an expression of influence is followed by a subject change, the subjunctive is required.

*La madre quiere que los niños estén contentos.*
Ask who wants (→ *la madre*).
Ask who should be happy (→ *los niños*).

• Point out that when there is no subject change, the infinitive is used, just as in English.

*Quiero estar contento.*
Ask who wants (→ *yo*).
Ask who would like to be happy (→ *yo*).

**Comprensión:**

Escoja la oración que describa cada dibujo.

1. __b__ **a.** Quiero aprender las formas del subjuntivo.
   **b.** Quiero que nosotros *aprendamos* juntos las formas del subjuntivo.
2. __b__ **a.** Insisto en hablar con Jorge.
   **b.** Insisto en que tú *hables* con Jorge.
3. __a__ **a.** Es necesario arreglar esta habitación.
   **b.** Es necesario que tú *arregles* esta habitación.

**A.** So far, you have learned to identify the subjunctive by the features listed at the right.

The subjunctive:

• appears in a subordinate (dependent) clause.
• has a different subject from the one in the main (independent) clause.
• is preceded by **que.**

**B.** In addition, the use of the subjunctive is associated with the presence of a number of concepts or conditions that trigger the use of it in the dependent clause. The concept of influence is one trigger for the subjunctive in a dependent clause. When the speaker wants something to happen, he or she tries to influence the behavior of others, as in these sentences.

The verb in the main clause is, of course, in the indicative, because it is a fact that the subject of the sentence wants something. The subjunctive occurs in the dependent clause.

| MAIN (INDEPENDENT) CLAUSE | | SUBORDINATE (DEPENDENT) CLAUSE |
|---|---|---|
| Yo **quiero** *I want* | que | tú **pagues** la cuenta. *you to pay the bill.* |
| La profesora **prefiere** *The professor prefers* | que *that* | los estudiantes no **lleguen** tarde. *students don't arrive late.* |

**Emphasis B: Suggestion**
Point out that influence implies that the speaker wants (expects/hopes/dreams) to affect somebody's behavior or even his/her own. The influence can be exerted from a power position (using verbs such as *ordenar, insistir en, pedir, mandar, exigir,* and *prohibir*) to the humblest position (*suplicar* [to beg] and *desear*).

*Capítulo 12 • La calidad de la vida*

**Emphasis C: Suggestion**
When the verbs are informative, they trigger the indicative in dependent clauses: *Carolina nos dice que llegan a las siete.* = Carolina tells (informs) us that they will arrive at 7:00. *Insisto en que son amigos.* = I insist (maintain) that they are friends (not enemies).

| | STRONG | SOFT |
|---|---|---|
| **C.** **Querer** and **preferir** are not the only verbs that can express the main subject's desire to influence what someone else thinks or does. There are many other verbs of influence, some very strong and direct, some very soft and polite. | insistir en<br>mandar (*to order*)<br>permitir (*to permit*)<br>prohibir (prohíbo) | desear<br>pedir (i, i)<br>recomendar (ie)<br>sugerir (ie, i) |
| **D.** An impersonal generalization of influence or volition can also be the main clause that triggers the subjunctive. Some examples of this appear at the right. | Es necesario que…<br>Es urgente que… | Es importante que…<br>Es mejor que… |

## ■ Práctica

**A. ¡Anticipemos! En la tienda de aparatos electrónicos.** Imagine que Ud. y un amigo están en una tienda de aparatos electrónicos. Ud. quiere comprarse un televisor pero no sabe cuál; por eso su amigo lo/la acompaña. ¿Quién dice las siguientes oraciones, Ud., su amigo o el vendedor (*salesperson*)?

1. Prefiero que busques un televisor en varias tiendas; así puedes comparar precios.   su amigo
2. Quiero que el televisor tenga pantalla plana (*flat screen*).   Ud.
3. Recomiendo que no le digas cuánto dinero quieres gastar.   su amigo
4. Insisto en que Ud. vea este modelo. ¡Es lo último!   el vendedor
5. Prefiero que me muestre otro modelo más barato.   Ud.
6. Es mejor que vayamos a buscar en otra tienda. Estos televisores son muy caros.   Ud., su amigo
7. Quiero que lo sepa: Este es uno de los mejores en el mercado.   el vendedor

**B. Expectativas de la educación**

PASO 1   ¿Qué expectativas de la educación tienen los profesores, los estudiantes y los padres de los estudiantes? Forme oraciones según las indicaciones y añada (*add*) palabras cuando sea necesario.

1. todos / profesores / querer / que / estudiantes / llegar / clase / a tiempo
2. profesor(a) de / español / preferir / que / (nosotros) ir / con frecuencia / laboratorio de lenguas
3. profesores / prohibir / que / estudiantes / traer / comida / y / bebidas / clase
4. padres / de / estudiantes / desear / que / hijos / asistir a / clases
5. estudiantes / pedir / que / profesores / no darles / mucho / trabajo
6. también / (ellos) querer / que / haber / más vacaciones
7. padres / insistir en / que / hijos / sacar / buenas / notas

PASO 2   Y Ud., ¿qué quiere que hagan los profesores? Invente tres oraciones más para indicar sus deseos.

• Give students each a command, and have them explain what you want them to do.

¡No fume Ud.! → Ud. no quiere que yo fume.

1. Grabe el programa.
2. No crea eso.
3. No cambie de canal.
4. Tráigame el control remoto.
5. No diga eso.
6. No me llame.
7. Escúchela.
8. Espérelo.
9. No nos busque.
10. Sírvalos.

🔃 **Prác. A: Follow-Up**
• Have students give formal commands for these situations. If it is a request, encourage them to use *por favor* and an appropriate tone.

**Need more practice?**
■ Workbook/Laboratory Manual
■ Interactive CD-ROM
■ Online Learning Center (www.mhhe.com/quetal7)

# PASO 3

**Con. A: Bright Idea Suggestion**
Have students give sentences that describe what you, the instructor, want / insist on / permit, and so on from them, and vice versa.

**Con. B: Follow-Up**
Have students share and compare their sentences. Write categories on the board that can be used to tally answers. Ask students if they see any patterns.

## ■ Conversación

**A. ¿Qué quieres?** Con un compañero/una compañera, hable de lo que Ud. quiere, prefiere, permite, etcétera, que otras personas hagan. Para formar las preguntas y oraciones, combinen palabras de las tres listas, o usen la imaginación. Luego, hablen de las cosas que otras personas quieren, prefieren, permiten, etcétera, que Uds. hagan.

MODELOS:   E1: ¿Qué quieres que haga tu padre?
           E2: Quiero que mi padre me compre una computadora.

           E1: ¿Qué quieren tus hijos que hagas?
           E2: Quieren que yo compre una computadora nueva.

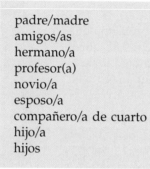

| querer<br>preferir<br>insistir en<br>mandar<br>permitir<br>prohibir<br>recomendar | **+** | padre/madre<br>amigos/as<br>hermano/a<br>profesor(a)<br>novio/a<br>esposo/a<br>compañero/a de cuarto<br>hijo/a<br>hijos | **+** | comprarme… (un televisor, rosas, ¿ ?)<br>visitarme… (mañana, el jueves, ¿ ?)<br>invitarme… (al cine, a cenar, ¿ ?)<br>(no) dar tarea… (hoy, mañana, ¿ ?)<br>ayudarme con… (los quehaceres, la tarea, ¿ ?)<br>salir con… (otra persona, mi amigo, ¿ ?)<br>llamarme… (todos los días, el viernes, ¿ ?)<br>explicarme… (la gramática, ¿ ?)<br>¿ ? |

**Lengua y cultura: Suggestions**
• Have students work in small groups. Each member will complete two of the following sentences. Remind them that *el presidente* refers to the president of a country. The president of a university is *el rector / la rectora*.

*Queremos que el presidente (primer ministro) / el rector (la rectora)…*
*Recomendamos que el presidente (primer ministro) / el rector (la rectora)…*
*Es importante que el presidente (primer ministro) / el rector (la rectora)…*
*Sugerimos que el presidente (primer ministro) / el rector (la rectora)…*

Have the groups select and then write their three best sentences on the board. Then have students work individually to select sentences from the board and use them to write a letter to the president or prime minister.

• Have volunteers read their letters.
• Have the class vote for the best letter.
• The final version can be assigned as homework. For the next day, have them exchange and correct each other's letters.

**B. Entrevista.** Complete las siguientes oraciones lógicamente… ¡y con sinceridad! Luego, entreviste a un compañero / una compañera para saber cómo él/ella completó las oraciones.

MODELO:   ¿En qué insisten tus padres?

1. Mis padres (hijos, abuelos,… ) insisten en que (yo) _____.
2. Mi mejor amigo/a (esposo/a, novio/a,… ) desea que (yo) _____.
3. Prefiero que mis amigos _____.
4. No quiero que mis amigos _____.
5. Es urgente que (yo) _____.
6. Es necesario que mi mejor amigo/a (esposo/a, novio/a,… ) _____.

## UN POCO DE TODO

**Lengua y cultura: Una visita a Lima.** Complete the following messages with the correct forms of the words in parentheses, as suggested by the context. When two possibilities are given in parentheses, select the correct word. ¡OJO! As you conjugate verbs in this activity, use the present tense unless otherwise indicated in parentheses. If you see *P/I*, you will choose between the preterite and the imperfect; *comm.* means to use a command; *prog.* stands for the present/past progressive, and *subj.* stands for the present subjunctive.

Marcia Hilbert, de Chicago, y su amiga limeña,ª Matilde O'Hara, se conocieron hace un mesᵇ por el Internet. (Escribirse¹) regularmente (por/para²) correo electrónico, y parece que cada día (descubrir³) una

ªde Lima, Perú    ᵇhace… *a year ago*

                                           *Capítulo 12* • *La calidad de la vida*

nueva cosa que (tener⁴) en común. Quieren conocerse en persona y Matilde (sugerir⁵) que Marcia (*subj.,* venir⁶) a Lima para (saber/conocer⁷) la capital del Perú. Los siguientes correos electrónicos son los últimos mensajes que se mandaron.

Querida Marci:
¿Cómo estás, amiga? Aquí todo (seguir⁸) más o menos igual. Es diciembre y (*yo:* alegrarse⁹) de que ya (*subj., nosotros:* ser/estar¹⁰) en verano. Ahora, la garúaᶜ que cubreᵈ (este¹¹) ciudad por muchos días del año (levantarse¹²), y (*nosotros:* ir¹³) a la playa casi todas las tardes. Muy pronto, todo el mundo (ir¹⁴) a (ser/estar¹⁵) ocupadísimo en (prepararse¹⁶) para las festividades del 18 de enero, aniversario de la fundación de Lima por Francisco Pizarro en 1535. Oye, (*yo:* tener¹⁷) una idea fabulosa. ¿Por qué no (*Uds.:* venir¹⁸) a Lima para entonces? Me gustaría mucho (verte¹⁹) y compartir contigo toda la gala del aniversario de esta ciudad. (*comm., Tú:* Preguntarles²⁰) a (tu²¹) padres, y (*comm.,* escribirme²²) pronto.
Un abrazo,
Tu amiga Mati

Querida Mati:
Chica, una noticia maravillosa. Ayer, mamá y yo (*prog.,* hablar²³) de tu correo electrónico. Mamá visitó Perú en 1980 y tiene (mucho²⁴) ganas de volver (a/de²⁵) Lima para el Aniversario. ¡Fíjateᵉ que (*nosotras:* ir²⁶) a vernos en poco más de un mes!
Muchos abrazos,
Marci

Hola Marci:
¡Qué suerte loca! ¿Sabes? Mis tíos viven en los Estados Unidos pero (tener²⁷) un apartamento aquí en Lima. Sólo (lo/la²⁸) usan cuando (venir²⁹) de visita. Mi tío le (*P/I:* decir³⁰) a papá que Uds. (poder³¹) quedarse en el apartamento en enero. ¡(*comm., Tú:* Escribirme³²) tu respuesta pronto!
Abrazos,
Mati

Hola Mati:
¡Qué buenas noticias! El ofrecimiento de quedarnos en el apartamento de los inquilinos es estupendo. Mamá y yo (lo/la³³) aceptamos con mucho gusto. ¡(*Nosotros:* Salir³⁴) (por/para³⁵) Lima en tres semanas!
Tu amiga loca de felicidad,
Marci

ᶜ*coastal fog*   ᵈ*covers*   ᵉ*Just think (figurative)*

**Comprensión: Una reorganización.**   The following series of events from the above e-mails is out of order. Rearrange the statements so they will be in chronological order.

1. Matilde invita a Marcia y a la familia de ella a visitar Lima.
2. Marcia y su mamá aceptan la oferta de quedarse en el apartamento.
3. Matilde y Marcia se conocen por correo electrónico.
4. La garúa de Lima se levanta, y todos van a la playa.
5. La madre de Marcia quiere hacer el viaje a Lima.

**Lengua y cultura: Answers**   1. *Se escriben* 2. *por* 3. *descubren* 4. *tienen* 5. *sugiere* 6. *venga* 7. *conocer* 8. *sigue* 9. *me alegro* 10. *estemos* 11. *esta* 12. *se levanta* 13. *vamos* 14. *va* 15. *estar* 16. *prepararse* 17. *tengo* 18. *vienen* 19. *verte* 20. *Pregúntales* 21. *tus* 22. *escríbeme* 23. *estábamos hablando* 24. *muchas* 25. *a* 26. *vamos* 27. *tienen* 28. *lo* 29. *vienen* 30. *dijo* 31. *pueden* 32. *Escríbeme* 33. *lo* 34. *Salimos* 35. *para*   **Comprensión** *Correct order of sentences:* 3, 4, 1, 5, 2.

**Resources: Desenlace**
In the *Capítulo 12* segment of "Chapter-by-Chapter Supplementary Materials" in the IM, you will find a chapter-culminating activity. You can use this activity to consolidate and review the vocabulary and grammar skills students have acquired.

*Una procesión durante las festividades del aniversario de la fundación de Lima*

**Resources for Review and Testing Preparation**

- Workbook/Laboratory Manual
- Interactive CD-ROM
- Online Learning Center (www.mhhe.com/quetal7)

**Paso 4: Un paso más**
• The *Paso 4: Un paso más* sections are optional.

• See the "Chapter-by-Chapter Supplementary Materials" in the IM for additional teaching suggestions, notes, activities, and other resources for *Paso 4.*

## VIDEOTECA

**Entrevista cultural: Suggestions**

• Before showing the video, ask students questions about working in department and electronic stores.

  *¿Trabaja Ud. en un almacén o una tienda de electrónica?*

  *¿Le gusta su trabajo? ¿Cómo es su jefe/a? ¿y sus compañeros de trabajo?*

  *¿Cuáles son algunas de sus responsabilidades en el trabajo?*

  *¿Qué se vende donde Ud. trabaja?*

  *¿Ud. gasta mucho dinero donde trabaja? ¿En qué?*

• Show the video and allow students one to two minutes to work on the questions. Have volunteers answer the questions.

• Have volunteers role-play Valdemar and his interviewer.

**Entrevista cultural: Answers**
*Possible answers:* **1.** *de Lima, Perú* **2.** *en una tienda de equipo electrónico* **3.** *los teléfonos celulares con cámara y otros aparatos para transmitir imágenes y datos* **4.** *Gasta todo su sueldo en la tienda.* **5.** *la computación*

**Entre amigos: Suggestions**

• Before viewing the video, review the questions with the students and ask them similar questions.

  *¿Tiene Ud. computadora? ¿Para qué la usa?*

  *¿Navega Ud. mucho el Internet?*

  *¿Qué otros aparatos electrónicos tiene Ud.?*

  *¿Cuáles son los más importantes para Ud.?*

Have students answer or work in small groups to ask and answer these questions.

• After viewing the video, have volunteers read and answer the questions.

### Entrevista cultural: El Perú

Valdemar de Icasa es un estudiante peruano que trabaja en una tienda. Habla con la entrevistadora de las cosas que se venden en la tienda y de los productos que son más populares. Antes de ver el vídeo, lea el siguiente fragmento de la entrevista.

ENTREVISTADORA:  …Y ¿te gusta tu trabajo?

VALDEMAR:  Sí, me gusta mucho, eh… digamos, lo único que no me gusta es que gasto mucho de mi… de mi sueldo, en… en comprar equipo de lo mismo que vendemos nosotros.[a] Por ejemplo la semana pasada me compré una cámara digital muy bonita. Pero bueno, salvo[b] eso, no… no pienso quedarme mucho tiempo en este trabajo.

[a]*equipo… the kind of equipment we sell here*   [b]*except for*

Ahora vea el vídeo y conteste las siguientes preguntas basándose en la entrevista.

  **1.** ¿De dónde es Valdemar?
  **2.** ¿Dónde trabaja Valdemar?
  **3.** Según él, ¿cuáles son los productos más populares ahora?
  **4.** ¿Qué problema menciona relativo al trabajo?
  **5.** ¿Qué estudia Valdemar?

### Entre amigos: Me tiras un correo, ¿eh?

Karina, Tané, Rubén y Miguel hablan de los aparatos electrónicos y de su uso. En su opinión, ¿qué preguntas se van a hacer? Antes de mirar el vídeo, lea las preguntas a continuación. Mientras mire el vídeo, trate de entender la conversación en general y fíjese en la información sobre las computadoras y otros aparatos electrónicos. Luego mire el vídeo una segunda vez, fijándose en la información que necesita para contestar las preguntas.

  **1.** ¿Qué hace Karina en la computadora?
  **2.** ¿Para qué usa Tané una computadora?
  **3.** ¿Cuál es la dirección electrónica de Tané?
  **4.** ¿Tiene Karina un sitio web?
  **5.** Según Rubén, ¿qué efecto tiene él en los aparatos electrónicos?

**Entre amigos: Answers**
*Possible answers:* **1.** *Mira las fotos que tomó en Cancún.* **2.** *para hacer su tarea* **3.** *tane@cubarte.com* **4.** *todavía no* **5.** *Cuando él llega, las máquinas o aparatos se descomponen.*

**CAPÍTULO**

**12**

Multimedia: Internet
Have students search the Internet for more information about Peru's government,
educational system, geography, and economy. They can also search for *la Red científica
peruana* online. This site, available in English and Spanish, contains information about
Peru and links to cultural, economic, and tourist information.

**PASO 4**

## ENFOQUE CULTURAL

**El Perú**

**Notes**
- The most important chronicler of the Incan presence in Peru, "El Inca" Garcilaso, was related to some of the outstanding literary figures of Spain, including the brilliant Spanish lyric poet, soldier, and courtier Garcilaso de la Vega, who died in 1536. Thus the need to use "El Inca" with his name, a distinction he was justly proud of, as his mother was descended from a brother of the Incan ruler, Huayna Capac, the last of the great Incan emperors (d. 1525).

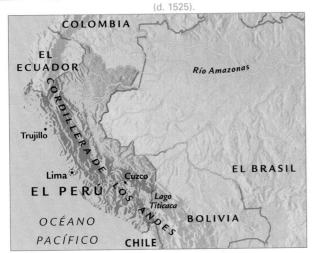

### ¡Fíjese!

- El Lago Titicaca, que queda entre Bolivia y el Perú, es el lago más grande de Sudamérica y es la ruta de transporte principal entre estos dos países.
- Cientos de años antes de la llegada[a] de los españoles, la agricultura de los indígenas del Perú ya era muy sofisticada. Hace más de 2.000 años,[b] los indígenas ya construían terrazas para sembrar en las faldas[c] de los Andes. Muchas de estas terrazas se usan todavía.
- Uno de los cultivos[d] más importantes de los incas es la papa, que originó en la región cerca del Lago Titicaca. La papa es una de las pocas plantas que puede subsistir[e] en altitudes de más de 13.000 pies y en regiones frías y áridas.

[a]*arrival* [b]*Hace… More than 2,000 years ago* [c]*para… so that they could plant on the slopes* [d]*crops* [e]*survive*

### Civilizaciones indígenas: La cultura inca

Cuando los españoles llegaron al Perú en 1532, los incas ya dominaban una gran zona de Sudamérica, desde Colombia hasta Chile, y desde el Pacífico hasta las selvas[a] del este. A partir del siglo XIII,[b] muchos otros pueblos indígenas de la inmensa región vivían bajo[c] el dominio de los incas. La capital del imperio era Cuzco.

La palabra *inca* significa *rey* o *príncipe*[d] en quechua, lengua que todavía se habla en el Perú. Bajo el inca, había un gobierno de poder[e] absoluto y un sistema burocrático y social muy complejo.

El imperio inca se destacó[f] por la arquitectura, la ingeniería[g] y las técnicas de cultivo. También estableció un sistema de correo[h] y un censo de la población. Tras la conquista[i] de los incas por los españoles Pizarro y Almagro, el Perú y su capital Lima se convirtieron en un centro fundamental de las colonias españolas en América. Lima fue fundada por Pizarro en 1535.

[a]*jungles* [b]*A… Beginning in the 13th century* [c]*under* [d]*rey… king or prince* [e]*power* [f]*se… distinguished itself* [g]*engineering* [h]*mail delivery* [i]*Tras… After the conquest*

*Cuzco, Perú*

- *Quechua* is an indigenous language spoken by approximately 13 million people in Bolivia, Peru, Ecuador, southern Colombia, northern Argentina, and northern Chile. It was the official language of *Tawantinsuyu,* the Incan Empire. Peruvian Spanish has hundreds of loan words from Quechua, many of which are the names of plants and animals. English also has words, such as the following, that are derived from Quechua.

| | | |
|---|---|---|
| coca | jerky | pampa |
| condor | lima bean | puma |
| guano | llama | quinine |

- Students can read an excerpt from the novel *La tía Julia y el escribidor* by Peru's Mario Vargas Llosa in *Voces del Perú: Literatura.*
- Students can read about Peru's *huayno* music in *Voces del Perú: Música.*
- See the Workbook/Laboratory Manual for focused practice with the material in *Enfoque cultural.*

Learn more about Peru with the Video, the Interactive CD-ROM, and the Online Learning Center (www.mhhe.com/quetal7).

## PASO FINAL

 **A CONVERSAR**

### Buscando apartamento

PASO 1   Lea los avisos (*ads*) de los apartmentos para alquilar y escoja el apartmento que Ud. prefiere.

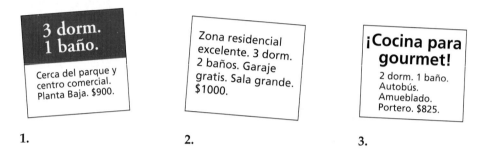

**3 dorm.
1 baño.**

Cerca del parque y centro comercial. Planta Baja. $900.

1.

Zona residencial excelente. 3 dorm. 2 baños. Garaje gratis. Sala grande. $1000.

2.

**¡Cocina para gourmet!**

2 dorm. 1 baño. Autobús. Amueblado. Portero. $825.

3.

PASO 2   En grupos de tres, imaginen que necesitan alquilar un apartamento juntos. Indiquen dónde prefieren vivir y por qué. Traten de comenzar sus oraciones con frases como **Prefiero que… , Recomiendo que… , Es mejor/ bueno que…** o **Es importante que…** Después, cada grupo debe escoger uno de los apartamentos.

> MODELO:   Recomiendo que alquilemos el apartamento número dos porque tiene una sala grande. También es bueno que haya dos baños.

PASO 3   Cada grupo debe inventar más información sobre el apartamento que escogió. La información puede incluir: dónde está el apartamento, cuánto es el alquiler, si se permiten animales, si está en una casa particular o en una casa de apartamentos, si se incluye la luz en el alquiler, etcétera.

> MODELO:   El alquiler es setecientos dólares al mes. La luz no está incluida.

PASO 4   Cada grupo debe improvisar una escena entre dos personas que buscan apartamento y el dueño / la dueña que lo alquila, basándose en los avisos y la información que inventaron.

> MODELO   E1: ¿Dónde está el apartamento?
> E2: Está en el centro, en una zona muy bonita.

## GRAMÁTICA

To review the grammar points presented in this chapter, refer to the indicated grammar presentations. You'll find further practice of these structures in the Workbook/Laboratory Manual, on the Interactive CD-ROM, and on the *¿Qué tal?* Online Learning Center (www.mhhe.com/quetal7).

**33** Influencing Others—**Tú** (Informal) Commands

Do you know how to give orders to friends and children in Spanish? How do you tell them what not to do?

**34** Expressing Subjective Actions or States—Present Subjunctive: An introduction

Do you understand how to form the present subjunctive?

**35** Expressing Desires and Requests—Use of the Subjunctive: Influence

You should be able to express what you want or need someone else to do without using a direct command.

## VOCABULARIO

Practice this vocabulary with digital flash cards on the Online Learning Center (www.mhhe.com/quetal7).

### Los verbos

| | |
|---|---|
| **alegrarse (de)** | to be happy (about) |
| **arreglar** | to straighten (up); to fix, repair |
| **dudar** | to doubt |
| **esperar** | to hope |
| **haber** (*infinitive form of* **hay**) | (there is, there are) |
| **insistir (en)** | to insist (on) |
| **mandar** | to order |
| **permitir** | to permit, allow |
| **prohibir (prohíbo)** | to prohibit, forbid |

**Repaso: conseguir (i, i) (g), desear, pedir (i, i), preferir (ie, i), querer (*irreg.*), recomendar (ie), sacar (qu) fotos, sugerir (ie, i)**

### Vehículos

| | |
|---|---|
| **la bicicleta (de montaña)** | (mountain) bike |
| **el carro (descapotable)** | (convertible) car |
| **el monopatín** | skateboard |
| **la moto(cicleta)** | motorcycle; moped |
| **los patines** | roller skates |
| **manejar** | to drive; to operate (*a machine*) |

**Repaso: el coche**

### La electrónica

| | |
|---|---|
| **el archivo** | (computer) file |
| **el canal** | channel |
| **el contestador automático** | answering machine |
| **el correo electrónico** | e-mail |
| **el disco duro** | hard drive |
| **el equipo estereofónico/ fotográfico** | stereo/photography equipment |
| **la grabadora** | (tape) recorder/player |
| **la impresora** | printer |
| **el lector de DVD** | DVD player |
| **el ordenador** (*Sp.*) | computer |
| **el ratón** | mouse |
| **la Red** | Net |
| **la videocasetera** | videocassette recorder/player (VCR) |
| **cambiar (de)** | to change |
| **copiar** | to copy |
| **fallar** | to "crash" (*of computers*) |
| **funcionar** | to work, function; to run (*machines*) |
| **grabar** | to record; to tape |
| **guardar** | to keep; to save (*documents*) |
| **hacer** (*irreg.*) **copia** | to copy |

1. *Además del teléfono tradicional, ¿qué otros tipos de teléfono hay?*
2. *Para mandar documentos, fotos, etcétera, ¿qué aparato resulta muy rápido?*
3. *¿Qué se necesita para comunicarse por correo electrónico?*

| imprimir | to print |
|---|---|
| navegar (gu) la Red | to surf the Net |
| obtener (*irreg.*) | to get, obtain |

**Cognados:** la cámara (de vídeo), el CD-ROM, la computadora, el control remoto, el disco compacto (el CD), el disco de computadora, el DVD, el fax, el *iPod*, la memoria, el módem, el radio (portátil) / la radio,* el teléfono celular, el *walkman*

**Repaso:** la cinta, el televisor

## En el trabajo

| el aumento | raise |
|---|---|
| el/la jefe/a | boss |
| el sueldo | salary |

## La vivienda

| las afueras | outskirts; suburbs |
|---|---|
| el alquiler | rent |
| la avenida | avenue |
| el barrio | neighborhood |
| el bloque de apartamentos | apartment building |
| la calle | street |
| el campo | countryside |
| el *campus* | (university) campus |
| la casa de apartamentos | apartment building |

| la comunidad | community |
|---|---|
| el/la dueño/a | landlord, landlady |
| el gas | gas; heat |
| el gasto | expense |
| el/la inquilino/a | tenant; renter |
| el piso | floor (*of a building*) |
| el primer piso | second floor |
| el segundo piso | third floor |
| la planta baja | ground floor |
| el/la portero/a | building manager; doorman |
| la vecindad | neighborhood |
| el/la vecino/a | neighbor |
| la vista | view |
| alquilar | to rent |

**Cognado:** el área (*but* las áreas)
**Repaso:** el apartamento, la casa, el centro, el cuarto, la dirección, el/la dueño/a (*owner*), la luz, la residencia

## Otros sustantivos

| el lujo | luxury |
|---|---|
| la mentira | lie |

## Palabras adicionales

| los/las demás | others |
|---|---|
| demasiado | too much |

---

*El radio *is the apparatus;* la radio *is the medium.*

# El arte y la cultura

# 13

## CAPÍTULO

*Unos residentes de Quito, Ecuador, que miran obras de arte en el Parque de la Alameda*

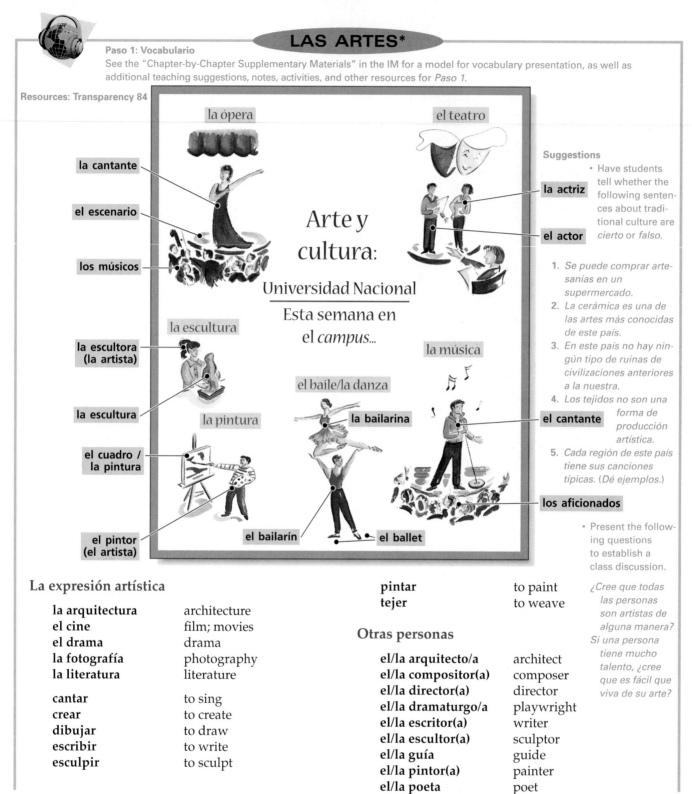

**LAS ARTES***

Paso 1: Vocabulario
See the "Chapter-by-Chapter Supplementary Materials" in the IM for a model for vocabulary presentation, as well as additional teaching suggestions, notes, activities, and other resources for *Paso 1*.

Resources: Transparency 84

**Suggestions**
- Have students tell whether the following sentences about traditional culture are *cierto* or *falso*.

1. *Se puede comprar artesanías en un supermercado.*
2. *La cerámica es una de las artes más conocidas de este país.*
3. *En este país no hay ningún tipo de ruinas de civilizaciones anteriores a la nuestra.*
4. *Los tejidos no son una forma de producción artística.*
5. *Cada región de este país tiene sus canciones típicas. (Dé ejemplos.)*

- Present the following questions to establish a class discussion.

*¿Cree que todas las personas son artistas de alguna manera? Si una persona tiene mucho talento, ¿cree que es fácil que viva de su arte?*

## La expresión artística

| | |
|---|---|
| la arquitectura | architecture |
| el cine | film; movies |
| el drama | drama |
| la fotografía | photography |
| la literatura | literature |
| | |
| cantar | to sing |
| crear | to create |
| dibujar | to draw |
| escribir | to write |
| esculpir | to sculpt |

| | |
|---|---|
| pintar | to paint |
| tejer | to weave |

## Otras personas

| | |
|---|---|
| el/la arquitecto/a | architect |
| el/la compositor(a) | composer |
| el/la director(a) | director |
| el/la dramaturgo/a | playwright |
| el/la escritor(a) | writer |
| el/la escultor(a) | sculptor |
| el/la guía | guide |
| el/la pintor(a) | painter |
| el/la poeta | poet |

**Multimedia: Audio**
Students can listen to and practice this chapter's vocabulary on the Online Learning Center (www.mhhe.com/quetal7) as well as on the Textbook Audio CD, part of the Laboratory Audio Program.

*The word **arte** is both masculine and feminine. The masculine articles and adjectives are normally used with **arte** in the singular while the feminine ones are used in the plural. Note that **las artes** often refers to "the arts" in general: Guillermo es estudiante **del arte moderno.** Me gustan mucho **las artes gráficas.**

| La tradición cultural | | Otras palabras útiles | |
| --- | --- | --- | --- |
| **la artesanía** | arts and crafts | **la canción** | song |
| **la cerámica** | pottery; ceramics | **el guión** | script |
| **las ruinas** | ruins | **la obra (de arte)** | work (of art) |
| **los tejidos** | woven goods | **la obra maestra** | masterpiece |

## ▓ Conversación

**A. Obras de arte.** Primero, diga qué tipo de arte representan las siguientes obras. Luego, dé otros ejemplos de obras en cada una de las categorías artísticas que Ud. mencionó.

1. la catedral de Notre Dame y la de Santiago de Compostela
2. los murales de Diego Rivera
3. las estatuas griegas y romanas
4. *El lago de los cisnes* (*Swan Lake*) y *El amor brujo* (*Love, the Magician*)
5. *El ciudadano Kane*
6. *La Bohème* y *La Traviata*
7. las pirámides (*pyramids*) aztecas y mayas
8. *Don Quijote*
9. la Torre Eiffel de París
10. la *Mona Lisa* de Leonardo da Vinci
11. «*El cuervo* (*The Raven*)» de Edgar Allen Poe
12. las imágenes de Ansel Adams
13. las canciones de Norah Jones
14. *El mago* (*The Wizard*) *de Oz* (¡**OJO!** Hay dos respuestas posibles.)

**B. ¿Qué hacen?**

PASO 1 Forme oraciones completas, emparejando palabras de cada columna. Hay más de una posibilidad en algunos casos.

MODELO: La compositora escribe canciones.

| | | |
| --- | --- | --- |
| la compositora<br>la artesana<br>la actriz<br>el director<br>el músico<br>el bailarín<br>el dramaturgo<br>la pintora<br>el escritor<br>la arquitecta<br>el poeta | **+** escribe<br>baila<br>esculpe<br>toca<br>compone (*composes*)<br>interpreta<br>diseña<br>pinta<br>mira<br>trabaja<br>dirige (*directs*)<br>teje | **+** novelas<br>canciones<br>en el ballet<br>cerámica<br>edificios y casas<br>papeles (*roles*) en la televisión<br>guiones<br>tejidos<br>con actores<br>obras de teatro<br>cuadros<br>instrumentos musicales<br>poesía |

PASO 2 Ahora, con dos o tres compañeros, dé nombres de artistas en cada categoría, ya sean (*whether they be*) hombres o mujeres. ¿Cuántos artistas hispanos pueden nombrar?

**Con. A: Suggestion**
Ask for works of art by Hispanic artists. This can be assigned as homework.

**Con. A: Note**
Students can read about Diego Rivera and other Mexican muralists in *Enfoque cultural: México*, p. 75.

**Con. A: Answers**
1. *la arquitectura* 2. *la pintura* 3. *la escultura* 4. *el ballet* (*el baile / la danza*) 5. *el cine* 6. *la ópera* 7. *las ruinas* (*la arquitectura*) 8. *la literatura* 9. *la arquitectura* 10. *la pintura* 11. *la literatura* 12. *la fotografía* 13. *la música* 14. *la literatura, el cine*

**Con. B: Suggestion**
Paso 2. Do this *paso* as a contest. Have each group write their answers on the board so that everyone can see what they came up with. Provide the following names after completing the activity.

*el cine:* Robert Rodríguez, Pedro Almodóvar, Antonio Banderas, Luis Buñuel, Salma Hayek
*la literatura:* Isabel Allende, Laura Esquivel, Gabriel García Márquez, Octavio Paz, Carlos Fuentes
*la música:* Manuel de Falla, Pablo Casals, Gloria Estefan, Julio Iglesias, Tito Puente, Carlos Santana, Los Lobos, Ricky Martin, Jennifer López
*la pintura:* Frida Kahlo, Diego Rivera, José Clemente Orozco, Salvador Dalí, Pablo Picasso
*la arquitectura:* Antoní Gaudí

## NOTA CULTURAL

### La Guinea Ecuatorial

Este país hispanohablante, el único del **continente africano,** se encuentra **en la costa atlántica.** La Guinea Ecuatorial, algo más grande que El Salvador, tiene un área de **28.051 kilómetros cuadrados** incluyendo sus **cinco islas habitadas** y **un clima tropical,** cálido[a] y lluvioso. Su historia colonial es evidente en su **variedad lingüística.** Las lenguas oficiales son el español y el francés, y además se hablan un inglés criollo, el fang, el bubi y el ibo, entre otras lenguas.

*Piruchi Apo Botupá (a la izquierda) y su sobrina Paloma Loribó (a la derecha), de* Las Hijas del Sol

La Guinea Ecuatorial **se independizó de España** en 1968 y poco después cayó bajo la represión de **una dictadura brutal.** Desde 1979 el país vive otra forma de dictadura, **una supuesta**[b] **democracia** en la cual el pueblo[c] vota, pero no se permiten partidos[d] de oposición. Sus reservas de gas natural y de petróleo no son suficientes para elevar el nivel de vida[e] de este **país en vías de desarrollo.**[f]

Pero la Guinea Ecuatorial tiene otro recurso natural que atrae la atención mundial, sobre todo entre los aficionados a la música internacional. **Las Hijas del Sol,** una tía y su sobrina, **cantantes** de la isla Bioko, saltaron a la fama[g] en 1992 al ganar un premio[h] en España por su música tradicional. Estas talentosas mujeres produjeron unos seis **discos** en diez años e hicieron numerosas **giras,**[i] cantando solas o con otros músicos como Rita Marley y Mano Negra. También han aparecido[j] en **películas.** Empezaron a cantar siempre **a capela,** sobre temas de su cultura, en su lengua natal—el bubi. Poco a poco incorporaron más **instrumentos musicales,** más español y temas más universales. Su cuarto disco lleva el título de *Pasaporte Mundial,* del cual ellas dicen: «Para vivir necesitas un pasaporte mundial, y para nosotras, ese pasaporte es el valor[k] que se necesita para enfrentarse a[l] todos los problemas».

---

[a]hot  [b]supposed  [c]people  [d](political) parties  [e]nivel... *standard of living*  [f]en... *developing*  [g]saltaron... *suddenly became famous*  [h]prize, award  [i]tours  [j]han... *they have appeared*  [k]bravery  [l]enfrentarse... *face*

**Nota cultural: Comprensión**
1. *¿Dónde está la Guinea Ecuatorial?*
2. *¿Cuáles son las lenguas oficiales de este país?*
3. *¿Quiénes son las Hijas del Sol?*

**Nota comunicativa: Suggestions**
- Offer the following optional word: *atraer → Me atrae el ballet moderno.*
- Point out that *apreciar* is like *odiar.* They both require direct objects.

## NOTA COMUNICATIVA

### Más sobre los gustos y preferencias

Here are some additional verbs to talk about what you like and don't like.

- The following two verbs are used like **gustar.**

  aburrir **Me aburre** el ballet moderno.
  *Modern ballet bores me.*

  agradar Pero **me agrada** el ballet folklórico.
  *But I like (I am pleased by) folkloric dances.*

- This verb functions as a transitive verb (one that can take a direct object).

  apreciar **Aprecio** mucho la arquitectura precolombina.
  *I really appreciate pre-Columbian architecture.*

## C. Preferencias personales

PASO 1   ¿Le gusta el arte? ¿Asiste a funciones culturales de vez en cuando (*from time to time*) o no asiste a esas funciones nunca? ¡Diga la verdad! (En otras actividades va a hablar de lo que prefiere en general.)

MODELO:   asistir a los ballets clásicos →
Me gusta mucho asistir a los ballets clásicos.
(No me agrada para nada asistir a los ballets clásicos. Es aburrido.)
(Me aburre asistir a los ballets clásicos. Prefiero ir a la ópera.)

| | |
|---|---|
| **1.** asistir a los ballets clásicos | **5.** ir a conciertos de música clásica |
| **2.** ir a los museos de arte moderno | **6.** asistir a lecturas de poesía en un café |
| **3.** asistir a funciones teatrales | **7.** ver películas extranjeras |
| **4.** ver obras maestras en los museos grandes | **8.** asistir a la ópera |

PASO 2   Ahora entreviste a un compañero / una compañera para saber cuáles son sus preferencias con respecto a este tema.

MODELO:   E1: ¿Te gusta ir a los museos de arte moderno?
E2: Sí, me gusta muchísimo. Voy siempre que puedo (*whenever I can*).

## D. Entrevista

1. ¿Tienes talento artístico? ¿Para qué? ¿Qué te gusta crear? ¿Cuándo empezaste a desarrollar (*develop*) esta actividad? ¿Tienes aspiraciones de dedicarte a esa actividad profesionalmente? ¿Cuáles son las ventajas y las desventajas de esa ocupación?

2. Si crees que no posees ningún talento artístico en particular, ¿sientes alguna atracción por el arte? ¿Qué tipo de arte en particular? ¿Por qué te gusta tanto?

3. ¿Te gusta ir a los mercados de artesanía? ¿Qué compras allí? Cuando vas de viaje, ¿te interesa saber cuáles son los trajes (*outfits*) y la música tradicionales del lugar que visitas? ¿Coleccionas obras de artesanía? ¿Qué coleccionas?

4. ¿Qué funciones teatrales te gustan? ¿Hay muchas oportunidades en esta ciudad / este pueblo (*town*) para asistir a interpretaciones (*performances*) de baile, música o drama? ¿Qué tipo de interpretaciones te gustan más?

5. ¿Tienes un pintor favorito / una pintora favorita? ¿Quién es? ¿Te gusta más la pintura abstracta o la figurativa?

6. Para ti, ¿qué es más importante, que un edificio sea elegante o práctico? ¿Qué tipo de arquitectura te gusta más? ¿Te gusta la arquitectura de esta universidad?

7. Para ti, ¿qué es más importante en una película, el guión, la dirección o la actuación? ¿Quiénes son tus actores favoritos? ¿Tienes algún director favorito o alguna directora favorita? ¿Quién es?

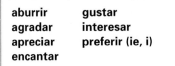

**Palabras útiles**

| | |
|---|---|
| aburrir | gustar |
| agradar | interesar |
| apreciar | preferir (ie, i) |
| encantar | |

**Con. C: Follow-Up**
Have each student write another cultural cue on a piece of paper. Collect all papers and write the cultural cues on the board so that students can answer them. Encourage both silly and serious cues.

**Refrán**

«Quien tiene arte va a toda parte.»

Have students brainstorm possible meanings for this *refrán*. (*He who has a trade/profession to offer, flourishes everywhere.*)

**Heritage Speakers**
Pregúnteles a sus estudiantes hispanohablantes si han visto una corrida de toros. ¿Qué opinan? ¿Es un arte o un acto violento?

**Suggestion**

○ Remind students that they have used *el primero* with dates, and in *Capítulo 12* they used a few ordinal numbers to refer to floors of a building.

## RANKING THINGS: ORDINALS

| | | | |
|---|---|---|---|
| **primer(o/a)** | first | **sexto/a** | sixth |
| **segundo/a** | second | **séptimo/a** | seventh |
| **tercer(o/a)** | third | **octavo/a** | eighth |
| **cuarto/a** | fourth | **noveno/a** | ninth |
| **quinto/a** | fifth | **décimo/a** | tenth |

- Ordinal numbers are adjectives and must agree in number and gender with the nouns they modify. Ordinals usually precede the noun: **la cuarta lección, el octavo ejercicio.**
- Like **bueno,** the ordinals **primero** and **tercero** shorten to **primer** and **tercer,** respectively, before masculine singular nouns: **el primer niño, el tercer mes.**
- Ordinal numbers are frequently abbreviated with superscript letters that show the adjective ending: **las 1$^{as}$ lecciones, el 1$^r$ grado, el 5° estudiante.**

○ **Reciclado**

Have students respond *cierto* or *falso* to the following sentences.

1. *El (lunes) es el (primer) día de la semana.* (Vary days, creating some incorrect items.)
2. *(Enero) es el (primer) mes del año.* (Vary months, creating some incorrect items.)
3. *Bob es el (quinto) estudiante en esta fila.*

**Refrán**

«Quien primero viene, primero muele.»

Have students guess the meaning of *muele.* Remind them that *la muela* means molar (*Capítulo 10*). Then have them brainstorm the English equivalent of this *refrán.* (First come, first served.)

**Need more practice?**

- Workbook/Laboratory Manual
- Interactive CD-ROM
- Online Learning Center (www.mhhe.com/quetal7)

**Note**

See the Workbook/Laboratory Manual for presentation and practice of the letters *x* and *n*.

## ▣ Conversación

### A. Mis actividades favoritas

PASO 1   Piense en lo que le gusta hacer en su tiempo libre en cuanto a (*regarding*) actividades culturales. Luego ponga en el orden de su preferencia (del 1 al 10) las siguientes actividades.

\_\_\_\_\_ ir al cine
\_\_\_\_\_ ir a ver películas extranjeras o clásicas
\_\_\_\_\_ ir a museos
\_\_\_\_\_ asistir a conciertos de música clásica/rock
\_\_\_\_\_ leer poesía
\_\_\_\_\_ bailar en una discoteca
\_\_\_\_\_ ver programas de televisión
\_\_\_\_\_ ver obras teatrales
\_\_\_\_\_ leer una novela
\_\_\_\_\_ ¿ ?

PASO 2   Ahora cuéntele a un compañero / una compañera sus cinco actividades favoritas. Use números ordinales.

MODELO:   Mi actividad favorita es ir a ver películas clásicas. Mi segunda actividad favorita es…

### B. Preguntas

1. ¿Es Ud. estudiante de cuarto año?
2. ¿Es este su segundo semestre/trimestre de español?
3. ¿A qué hora es su primera clase los lunes? ¿y su segunda clase?
4. ¿Vive Ud. en una casa de apartamentos o en una residencia? ¿En qué piso vive? Si vive en una casa, ¿en qué piso está su alcoba?

Paso 2: Gramática
See the "Chapter-by-Chapter Supplementary Materials" in the IM for additional
teaching suggestions, notes, activities, and other resources for *Paso 2*.

Multimedia: Internet
Have students search the Internet for music clips of *mariachi* music.
If possible, bring a video or CD of a *mariachi* performance to class.

## 36 Expressing Feelings Use of the Subjunctive: Emotion

**Diego y Lupe escuchan un grupo de mariachis**

DIEGO: Ay, ¡cómo me encanta esta música!

LUPE: *Me alegro de que te guste.*

DIEGO: Y yo *me alegro de que estemos* aquí. ¿Sabes el origen de la palabra **mariachi**?

LUPE: No... ¿Lo sabes tú?

DIEGO: Bueno, una teoría es que viene del siglo XIX, cuando los franceses ocuparon México. Ellos contrataban a grupos de músicos para tocar en las bodas. Y como los mexicanos no podían pronunciar bien la palabra francesa *mariage*, pues acabaron por decir **mariachi.** Y de allí viene el nombre de los grupos.

LUPE: ¡Qué fascinante! *Me sorprende que sepas* tantos datos interesantes de nuestra historia.

DIEGO: Pues, todo buen antropólogo debe saber un poco de historia también, ¿no?

**Note**
There is more than one theory regarding the origin of the word *mariachi*. Currently, the most favored theory among scholars is that the word has its origin in a Coca Indian word for *music maker*. The Coca were one of many indigenous groups that lived in parts of Mexico.

*México, D.F.*

**Comprensión**

1. Lupe se alegra de que _____ a Diego le guste la música _____.
2. Y Diego se alegra de que _____ estén allí _____.
3. A Lupe le sorprende que _____ Diego sepa tanto de la historia mexicana _____

**Suggestion**
Have students pick out the subjunctive and subjunctive cues in the *minidiálogo*. Ask: What do the cues have in common? (emotional responses)

**Heritage Speakers**
Anime a los hispanohablantes a describir a los mariachis. ¿Qué tipo de ropa llevan? ¿Dónde suelen cantar? ¿Qué temas predominan en sus canciones?

| MAIN (INDEPENDENT) CLAUSE | | SUBORDINATE (DEPENDENT) CLAUSE |
|---|---|---|
| first subject + *indicative* (expression of emotion) | **que** | second subject + *subjunctive* |

**A.** Expressions of emotion are those in which speakers express their feelings: *I'm glad you're here; It's good that they can come.* Such expressions of emotion are followed by the subjunctive mood in the subordinate (dependent) clause in Spanish.

**Follow-Up**
Ask students the following questions.

*¿Le sorprende a Ud. que la palabra **mariachi** venga del francés?*
*¿De qué cosas se alegra Ud.?*
*¿Qué le molesta que haga su compañero/a de cuarto/casa (esposo/a, etcétera)?*
*¿Qué le sorprende de la clase de español?*

**Esperamos** que Ud. **pueda** asistir.
*We hope (that) you'll be able to come.*

**Tengo miedo de** que mi abuelo **esté** muy enfermo.
*I'm afraid (that) my grandfather is very ill.*

**Es una lástima** que no **den** aumentos este año.
*It's a shame (that) they're not giving raises this year.*

**Emphasis A: Suggestions**
• Point out that a change of subject is required for the subjunctive with emotional statements, just as with expressions of influence.
• Emphasize the use of the infinitive, not the subjunctive, after expressions and generalizations of emotion when there is no change of subject.

*Siento estar tan cansado.* vs. *Siento que estés tan cansado.*
*Es mejor esperar.* vs. *Es mejor que esperen.*

***Diego and Lupe are listening to a mariachi group*** DIEGO: *Oh, how I love this music!* LUPE: *I'm glad you like it.* DIEGO: *And I'm glad we're here. Do you know the origin of the word **mariachi**?* LUPE: *No . . . Do you?* DIEGO: *Well, one theory is that it comes from the nineteenth century, when the French occupied Mexico. They used to hire musical groups to play at weddings. And because the Mexicans couldn't correctly pronounce the French word* mariage, *they ended up saying **mariachi**. And so that's where the name of the groups comes from.* LUPE: *How fascinating! I'm surprised you know so much interesting information about our history.* DIEGO: *Well, all good anthropologists should also know a little bit of history, shouldn't they?*

**B.** Some common expressions of emotion are found in the list and drawing at the right.

| | |
|---|---|
| **alegrarse (de)** | *to be happy (about)* |
| **esperar** | *to hope* |
| **sentir (ie, i)** | *to regret; to feel sorry* |
| **tener miedo (de)** | *to be afraid (of)* |

**temer: Temo** que María **se caiga** durante el baile.
*I'm afraid that María will fall during the dance.*

At the right are some common expressions of emotion used with indirect object pronouns. Not all Spanish expressions of emotion are given here. Remember that any expression of emotion is followed by the subjunctive in the dependent clause when there is a change in subject.

**Emphasis B, C: Note**
Many of these verbs and generalizations are also value judgments (*es bueno/malo/necesario/extraño*). They are reactions that imply a personal opinion, which may differ from one person to another.

**Heritage Speakers**
Note que los hispanohablantes a veces retienen la cláusula dependiente a pesar de que no haya cambio de sujeto.

*Espero que (yo) saque una buena nota en el examen.*
*Siento que (yo) lo haya ofendido.*

Anime a los hispanohablantes a describir la diferencia estructural o gramatical entre los siguientes pares de oraciones.

*Me alegro de que (yo) haya sacado una buena nota.*
*Me alegro de haber sacado una buena nota.*

*Espero que (yo) pueda asistir a la boda.*
*Espero poder asistir a la boda.*

| | |
|---|---|
| **me (te, le,… )** | I'm (you're, he's . . . ) |
| **gusta que** | glad that |

**Me molesta** que **fumen** en la galería.
*It bothers me that they smoke in the gallery.*

**Nos sorprende** que este cantante **tenga** tanto éxito.
*It surprises us that this singer is so successful.*

**C.** When a new subject is introduced after a generalization of emotion, it is followed by the subjunctive in the subordinate (dependent) clause. Here are some general expressions of emotion.

| | |
|---|---|
| **es extraño que…** | it's strange that . . . |
| **es increíble que…** | it's incredible that . . . |
| **es mejor/bueno/ malo que…** | it's better/good/ bad that . . . |
| **es ridículo que…** | it's ridiculous that . . . |
| **es terrible que…** | it's terrible that . . . |
| **es una lástima que…** | it's a shame that . . . |
| **es urgente que…** | it's urgent that . . . |
| **¡qué extraño que…!** | how strange that . . . ! |
| **¡qué lástima que…!** | what a shame that . . . ! |

---

**AUTOPRUEBA**

Identify the sentences that would require the subjunctive when expressed in Spanish.

1. ☐ I'm surprised you're here.
2. ☐ We're happy about the prize.
3. ☐ They're afraid of the director.
4. ☐ It's good that they want all of your paintings.
5. ☐ I hope to attend the concert.

Answers: 1, 4

---

**Prác. A: Preliminary Exercises**
• Use the following chain drill to practice forms.

1. *Espero que tú sepas el número correcto.* (Ud., ella, nosotros, Uds.)
2. *Los padres tienen miedo de que seamos malos estudiantes.* (yo, tú, ellos, Elvira)
3. *Es una lástima que no podamos ir al museo.* (yo, Uds., él, vosotras)

• Have students express the following ideas in Spanish.

1. I'm afraid that they're not coming / that he can't do it.
2. It surprises me that you can't do it / that he won't permit it.

**Prác. A: Follow-Up**
Have students give two opinions of their own. Use *Paso 1* as a model. Use *Paso 2* as a model for ensuing suggestions and wishes.

**Multimedia: Internet**
Have students search the Internet for Spanish language newspapers (*La Jornada*, for example). Based on current news events, students should prepare five statements expressing their emotions and using the subjunctive, for example: *Es increíble que haya tanto turismo en Costa Rica.*

**Nota comunicativa: Notes**
• ¡OJO! *Ojalá* is invariable in form and is always followed by the subjunctive. *Ojalá* itself is not conjugated.

## ▓ **Práctica**

**A. Opiniones sobre el cine**

PASO 1  **¡Anticipemos!** ¿Ciertas o falsas?

1. Me molesta que muchas películas sean tan violentas.
2. Es ridículo que algunos actores ganen (*earn*) tanto dinero.
3. Espero que salgan más actores asiáticos e hispanos en las películas.
4. Temo que muchas actrices no desempeñen (*play*) papeles inteligentes.
5. Es increíble que gasten millones de dólares en hacer películas.
6. Me sorprende que Julia Roberts sea tan famosa.

PASO 2   Ahora invente oraciones sobre lo que Ud. quiere o no quiere que pase con respecto al cine. Use las oraciones del **Paso 1** como base.

MODELO:   **1.** Quiero que las películas sean menos violentas.

---

## **NOTA COMUNICATIVA**

**Expressing Wishes with *ojalá***

• *Ojalá* comes from the Arabic expression that means *Allah* (*God*) *willing* or *may Allah want.* Point out that Arabs lived in most of what is today Spain and Portugal for eight centuries (8th–15th). Their influence was great in the Iberian Peninsula; their language, especially, influenced Spanish vocabulary. Other commonly used Spanish words that come from Arabic include *el álgebra, el aceite, la aceituna* (olive), *la almohada* (pillow).

The word **ojalá** is invariable in form and means *I wish* or *I hope*. It is used with the subjunctive to express wishes or hopes. The use of **que** with it is optional.

| | |
|---|---|
| **¡Ojalá (que)** yo **gane** la lotería algún día! | *I hope (that) I win the lottery some day!* |
| **¡Ojalá (que) haya** paz en el mundo algún día! | *I hope (that) there will be peace in the world some day!* |
| **Ojalá (que)** no **pierdan** tu equipaje. | *I hope (that) they don't lose your luggage.* |

**Ojalá** can also be used alone as an interjection in response to a question.

—¿Te va a ayudar Julio a estudiar para el examen?
—**¡Ojalá!**

---

**B. Una excursión a la ópera.** Imagine que Ud. y su amigo/a van a la ópera por primera vez en su vida. Piense en todas las expectativas que Ud. tiene y exprésalas usando **ojalá.**

MODELO:   las entradas (*tickets*) / no costar mucho →
          Ojalá que las entradas no cuesten mucho.

1. el escenario / ser / extravagante
2. haber / subtítulos / en inglés
3. el director (*conductor*) / estar / preparado
4. los cantantes / saber / sus papeles
5. nuestros asientos / no estar / lejos del escenario
6. (nosotros) llegar / a tiempo

## ■ Conversación

**A. Situaciones.** Las siguientes personas están pensando en otra persona o en algo que van a hacer. ¿Qué emociones sienten? ¿Qué temen? Con un compañero / una compañera, conteste las preguntas según los dibujos.

 ①

 ②

 ③

1. Jorge piensa en su amiga Estela. ¿Por qué piensa en ella? ¿Dónde está? ¿Qué siente Jorge? ¿Qué espera? ¿Qué espera Estela? ¿Espera que la visiten los amigos? ¿que le manden algo?

2. Fausto quiere comer fuera esta noche. ¿Quiere que alguien lo acompañe? ¿Dónde espera que cenen? ¿Qué teme Fausto? ¿Qué le parecen (*seem*) los precios del restaurante?

3. ¿Dónde quiere pasar las vacaciones Mariana? ¿Espera que alguien la acompañe? ¿Dónde espera que pasen los días? ¿Qué teme Mariana? ¿Qué espera?

**B. ¿Qué le molesta más?** The following phrases describe aspects of university life. React to them, using phrases such as: **Me gusta que…, Me molesta que…, Es terrible que…**

MODELO:   Gastan mucho/poco dinero en construir nuevos edificios. →
          Me molesta que gasten mucho dinero en construir nuevos edificios.

1. Se pone mucho énfasis en los deportes.
2. Pagamos mucho/poco por la matrícula.
3. Se ofrecen muchos/pocos cursos en mi especialización (*major*).
4. Es necesario estudiar ciencias/lenguas para graduarse.
5. Hay muchos/pocos requisitos (*requirements*) para graduarse.
6. En general, hay mucha/poca gente (*people*) en las clases.

# *Voces de Bolivia y el Ecuador*

## LITERATURA: Jorge Icaza

**Sobre el autor:** *Jorge Icaza nació en Icuña, Ecuador. Empezó su carrera como actor y dramaturgo, pero cuando las autoridades censuraron su drama,* El dictador, *abrió una librería y empezó a escribir novelas. Su novela* Huasipungo (1934) *es la novela ecuatoriana más famosa y una de las novelas indigenistas más importantes de Latinoamérica. El siguiente fragmento es de esa novela.*

—Nu han de robar[a] así nu más[b] a taita[c] Andrés Chiliquinga— concluyó el indio, rascándose[d] la cabeza, lleno de un despertar[e] de oscuras e indefinidas venganzas.[f] Ya le era imposible dudar de la verdad del atropello[g] que invadía el cerro.[h] Llegaban… Llegaban más pronto de lo que él pudo imaginarse. Echarían abajo su techo,[i] le quitarían la tierra.[j] Sin encontrar[k] una defensa posible, acorralado[l] como siempre, se puso pálido, con la boca semiabierta, con los ojos fijos,[m] con la garganta anudada.[n] ¡No!

[a]*Nu… They will not rob* [b]*nu… ever again* [c]*abuelo* [d]*scratching* [e]*lleno… overcome by an awakening* [f]*oscuras… dark and vague vengeance* [g]*attack, assault* [h]*hill* [i]*Echarían… They would tear down his roof (house)* [j]*le… they would take away his land* [k]*Sin… Without finding* [l]*corralled* [m]*fixed* [n]*con… with a lump in his throat*

**Jorge Icaza**
(*1906–1978*)

**Literatura: Notes**
- As a child, Jorge Icaza was deeply affected by a visit to his family's *hacienda*, where he was exposed to the suffering of the indigenous people who lived and worked there, essentially as slaves. Later, in his writings, he did not mince words. His texts use harsh, realistic terms to protest the exploitation of the indigenous people.
- Other novels include *En las calles* (1935), *Cholos* (1938), and *El chulla Romero y Flores* (1958). His short stories are collected in *Relatos* (1969).

## MÚSICA: Rumillajta

**Música: Notes**
- When Rumillajta tours, the band often supplements their concerts with educational activities. They have participated in many children's festivals.
- Although much of the music on Rumillajta's CDs comes from Bolivian folk music, they also perform music from the traditions of other Latin American countries, especially the Andean regions.

el bombo

el charango

las quenas

las zampoñas

Rumillajta es un conjunto[a] boliviano que interpreta[b] música y canciones andinas. Su nombre en quechua significa «ciudad de piedras[c]». Sus cinco músicos son de la ciudad de La Paz, donde viven y trabajan, aunque[d] hacen giras[e] internacionales. La meta[f] del conjunto, además de[g] crear música bella,[h] es promover[i] la cultura andina y sus valores sociales y espirituales de interdependencia y cooperación.

[a]*group* [b]*performs* [c]*stones* [d]*although* [e]*tours* [f]*goal* [g]*además… in addition to* [h]*beautiful* [i]*to promote*

Los músicos de Rumillajta fabrican sus propios[j] instrumentos tradicionales, como son las zampoñas,[k] quenas,[l] bombos[m] y charangos.[n] Los miembros del grupo dicen que su música tiene tres cualidades importantes: un vínculo[o] profundo con la naturaleza,[p] una melancolía que refleja la experiencia del pueblo[q] y una energía vital que llega al[r] corazón de los oyentes.[s]

[j]*own* [k]*panpipes* [l]*Andean flutes* [m]*large drums* [n]*type of guitar* [o]*link* [p]*nature* [q]*common people* [r]*llega… reaches* [s]*listeners*

# PASO 3  Gramática

## 37 Expressing Uncertainty Use of the Subjunctive: Doubt and Denial

Mire Ud. la pintura detenidamente (*carefully*) y luego complete las siguientes oraciones de acuerdo con su opinión.

**Familia andina**, *por Héctor Poleo*
(*venezolano, 1918–1989*)

| Vocabulario útil |
| --- |
| **la alegría** (happiness)
**la esperanza** (hope)
**los guardias** (guardsmen)
**el miedo** (fear)
**la tristeza** (sadness) |

**Suggestion**
Have students explain the uses of the subjunctive in the sentences.

**Follow-Up**
Show another painting and have students react to it with similar sentences.

### Comprensión

1. *Es posible que* los miembros de esta familia tengan (miedo / esperanza).
   Estoy seguro/a de que no tienen (miedo / esperanza).
2. Creo que los colores representan (la alegría / la tristeza).
   *Dudo que* representen (la alegría / la tristeza).
3. *Es probable que* los guardias estén (enojados / contentos).
   Estoy seguro/a de que no están (enojados / contentos).

| MAIN (INDEPENDENT) CLAUSE | | SUBORDINATE (DEPENDENT) CLAUSE |
| --- | --- | --- |
| first subject + *indicative*
(expression of doubt or denial) | **que** | second subject + *subjunctive* |

**Emphasis A:
Suggestion**
Point out the similarity of this pattern (two verbs, a second subject) to that of the subjunctive after expressions of influence/emotion.

**A.** Expressions of doubt and denial are those in which speakers express uncertainty or negation. Such expressions, however strong or weak, are followed by the subjunctive in the dependent clause in Spanish.

**No creo** que **sean** sus cuadros.
*I don't believe they're her paintings.*

**Es imposible** que ella **esté** en el escenario.
*It's impossible for her to be on the stage.*

**B.** Some expressions of doubt and denial appear at the right. Not all Spanish expressions of doubt are given here. Remember that any expression of doubt is followed by the subjunctive in the dependent clause.

| | |
| --- | --- |
| **no creer** | *to disbelieve* |
| **dudar** | *to doubt* |
| **negar (ie) (gu)** | *to deny* |
| **no estar seguro/a (de)** | *to be unsure (of)* |

**Bright Idea Suggestions**
• Point out to students that they should be able to do the following.

1. identify the independent clause
2. identify the dependent clause
3. locate expressions of influence, emotion, and feeling in the independent clause that require the use of the subjunctive in the dependent clause

• Have students provide expressions of influence, desire, request, emotion, and feeling that require the use of the subjunctive in the dependent clause.

**Emphasis B: Suggestions**
• Contrast and model *no creer* and *dudar* (subjunctive) with *creer*, which usually implies affirmation and is therefore followed by the indicative.

• In questions with *creer*, the use of the indicative or subjunctive in dependent clauses reflects the opinion of the person asking the question. Indicative: *¿Crees que los Ramírez son ricos?* (The speaker believes they are.) Subjunctive: *¿Crees que los Ramírez sean ricos?* (The speaker doubts that they are.)

**CAPÍTULO 13**
Emphasis B: Preliminary Exercises
Have students express the following ideas in Spanish.

**PASO 3**

1. I doubt that they are rich / that they are coming.
2. I don't believe that they are rich / that they are coming.
3. I believe that they are rich / that they are coming.

 **Creer** and **estar seguro/a** are usually followed by the indicative in affirmative statements because they do not express doubt, denial, or negation. Compare these examples.

**Estamos seguros de (Creemos)** que el concierto **es** hoy.
*We're sure (We believe) that the concert is today.*

**No estamos seguros de (No creemos)** que el concierto **sea** hoy.
*We're not sure (We don't believe) that the concert is today.*

**C.** When a new subject is introduced after a generalization of doubt, the subjunctive is used in the dependent clause. Some generalizations of doubt and denial are included at the right.

 Generalizations that express certainty are not followed by the subjunctive but by the indicative: **Es verdad que cocina bien. No hay duda de que Julio lo paga.**

*Emphasis C: Suggestion*
Emphasize and model the indicative used after *es verdad, es cierto,* and *es seguro.*

| | |
|---|---|
| es posible que… | it's possible that . . . |
| es imposible que… | it's impossible that . . . |
| es probable que… | it's probable (likely) that . . . |
| es improbable que… | it's improbable (unlikely) that . . . |
| no es cierto que… | it's not certain that . . . |
| no es seguro que… | it's not a sure thing that . . . |
| no es verdad que… | it's not true that . . . |

## ■ Práctica

**Opiniones distintas.** Imagine que Ud. y un amigo / una amiga están en un museo arqueológico. En este momento están mirando una figura. Desafortunadamente, no hay ningún letrero (*sign*) cerca de Uds. para indicar lo que representa la figura. Haga oraciones completas según las indicaciones. Añada palabras cuando sea necesario.

Habla Ud.:

1. creo / que / ser / figura / de / civilización / maya
2. es cierto / que / figura / estar / hecho (*made*) / de oro
3. es posible / que / representar / dios (*god, m.*) / importante
4. no estoy seguro/a de / que / figura / ser / auténtico

Habla su amigo/a:

5. no creo / que / ser / figura / de / civilización / maya
6. creo / que / ser / de / civilización / tolteca
7. estoy seguro/a de / que / estar / hecho / de bronce
8. creo / que / representar / víctima [*m.*] / de / sacrificio humano

*Prác: Preliminary Exercises*
• Have students indicate whether the following expressions would require the indicative or the subjunctive.
1. *Es cierto que…*
2. *No estamos seguros de que…*
3. *No es verdad que…*
4. *Dudo que…*
5. *No creo que…*
6. *Es imposible que…*
7. *Es probable que…*
8. *Estamos seguros que…*
9. *No es cierto que…*
10. *Es improbable que…*

• Have students tell whether the following sentences would require the indicative or the subjunctive in Spanish.
1. I'm sure she's right.
2. I doubt we'll get there on time.
3. I don't think they know.
4. It's impossible that he knows.
5. We believe she's at home.
6. I don't doubt that they will go.
7. It's true that Susan always arrives on time.
8. They don't believe I know how to cook.

**Need more practice?**
■ Workbook/Laboratory Manual
■ Interactive CD-ROM
■ Online Learning Center (www.mhhe.com/quetal7)

*Prác: Answers*
1. *Creo que es una figura de la civilización maya.* 2. *Es cierto que la figura está hecha de oro.* 3. *Es posible que represente a un dios importante.* 4. *No estoy seguro/a de que la figura sea auténtica.* 5. *No creo que sea una figura de la civilización maya.* 6. *Creo que es de la civilización tolteca.* 7. *Estoy seguro/a de que está hecha de bronce.* 8. *Creo que representa a la víctima de un sacrificio humano.*

## ■ Conversación

**A. ¿Una ganga?** Imagine que Ud. va a un mercado al aire libre. Encuentra algunos objetos de artesanía muy interesantes que parecen ser de origen azteca… ¡y son baratísimos! ¿Cómo reacciona Ud.?

Empiece sus oraciones con estas frases.

| **Vocabulario útil** |
| --- |
| **el calendario** (calendar) |
| **la joyería** (jewelry) |
| **la máscara** (mask) |
| |
| **auténtico/a** (authentic) |
| **falsificado/a** (forged) |

1. ¡Es imposible que… !
2. No creo que…
3. Dudo muchísimo que…
4. Estoy seguro/a de que…
5. Es improbable que…

## NOTA COMUNICATIVA

**Verbs that Require Prepositions**

You learned in earlier chapters that when two verbs occur in a series (one right after the other), the second verb is usually the infinitive.

**Prefiero** *cenar* a las siete.      *I prefer to eat at seven.*

Some Spanish verbs, however, require that a preposition or other word be placed before the second verb (still the infinitive). You have already used many of the important Spanish verbs that have this feature.

- The following verbs require the preposition **a** before an infinitive.

| aprender a | empezar (ie) (c) a | invitar a | venir (*irreg.*) a |
| --- | --- | --- | --- |
| ayudar a | enseñar a | ir (*irreg.*) a | volver (ue) a |

Mis padres me **enseñaron a bailar.**      *My parents taught me to dance.*

- These verbs or verb phrases require **de** before an infinitive.

| acabar de | dejar de | tener (*irreg.*) ganas de |
| --- | --- | --- |
| acordarse (ue) de | olvidarse de | tratar de (*to try to*) |

Siempre **tratamos de llegar** puntualmente.      *We always try to arrive on time.*

- **Insistir** requires **en** before an infinitive.

**Insisten en venir** esta noche.      *They insist on coming over tonight.*

- Two verbs require **que** before an infinitive: **haber que, tener que.**

**Hay que** ver el nuevo museo.      *It's necessary to see the new museum.*

## B. ¿Qué piensa Ud. del futuro?

PASO 1    Haga oraciones con frases de cada columna para expresar su opinión sobre lo que le puede ocurrir a Ud. en los próximos cinco años. ¡OJO! No se olvide de usar el subjuntivo después de expresiones de duda o negación.

En los próximos cinco años…

(no) creo que…
(no) dudo que…
es (im)posible que…
(no) estoy seguro/a de que…
(no) es cierto que…

**+**

(yo) { ir a
aprender a
empezar a
dejar de
tratar de
volver a

**+**

ser famoso/a
estar casado/a
ganar la lotería
jugar a la lotería
pintar cuadros
fumar
tener hijos
terminar mis estudios
esculpir
¿  ?

PASO 2    Compare sus respuestas con las de uno o dos compañeros. ¿Cuántas respuestas similares hay? ¿Cuántas diferentes?

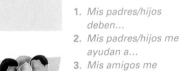

## En los Estados Unidos y el Canadá

### Carlos Santana y la Fundación Milagro[a]

El legendario **guitarrista** Carlos Santana nació en Autlán, México. Luego su familia se trasladó[b] de allí a Tijuana y más tarde a San Francisco, donde Carlos y su hermano Jorge empezaron a tener sus primeros seguidores.[c] Santana **se hizo famoso en el Festival de Woodstock** en 1969 con un increíble solo de guitarra. Después tuvo una serie de éxitos,[d] entre ellos su inolvidable **interpretación** en 1971 de **la canción** de Tito Puente, «Oye cómo va». En 1999, Santana creó una sensación con su **disco compacto** *Supernatural,* en el que tocó con una variedad de artistas norteamericanos e hispanos para crear una obra rica en

*Carlos Santana*

estilo y composición. Este esfuerzo de Santana le ganó varios *Grammys* en 2000.

Santana es una persona profundamente **dedicada a la comunidad,** especialmente **a los niños.** Junto con su esposa Deborah, Santana creó **la Fundación Milagro,** una organización educativa para niños y jóvenes. La Fundación Milagro contribuye con dinero a otras organizaciones comunitarias sin fines lucrativos[e] en San Francisco y sus alrededores.[f] El propósito es **ayudar a la juventud**[g] **del área** por medio de programas de salud, educación y arte. Puede encontrar más información sobre la Fundación en su página web en el Internet.

[a]*Miracle*  [b]*se… moved*  [c]*followers*  [d]*successes*  [e]*sin… nonprofit*  [f]*surrounding areas*  [g]*youth*

# PASO 3

## UN POCO DE TODO

### ♻ Reciclado
Reenter the no-fault *se* expressions. Have students express the following ideas in Spanish.

1. It's incredible that Miguel is so clumsy.
2. It's terrible that he breaks his glasses all the time.
3. I think he loses his keys every week.
4. I hope he doesn't run out of money this week!

### Multimedia: Internet
Have students search the Internet for more of Pablo Picasso's works, including *Guernica*. The *Museo Nacional Centro de Arte Reina Sofía* in Madrid has its own website and features some of his works. Have students look up this museum and research its relationship to *el Museo del Prado*.

### Lengua y cultura: Answers
1. *Pasen* 2. *dejen* 3. *delante* 4. *Es*
5. *representa* 6. *pintó* 7. *de la* 8. *durante*
9. *estuvo* 10. *se trasladó* 11. *este* 12. *sea*
13. *es* 14. *creo* 15. *tengan* 16. *ser* 17. *sirve*
18. *Por* 19. *puede*  **Comprensión** 1. *Ud.*
2. *el guía* 3. *su amigo* 4. *el guía*

### Follow-Up
Ask the following questions to personalize the activity.

*¿Qué expresa para Ud. el cuadro de Guernica?*

*¿Por qué (no) le gusta?*

*¿Cree Ud. que el arte se debe usar para transmitir un mensaje o sólo para producir un placer estético?*

### Resources: Desenlace
In the *Capítulo 13* segment of "Chapter-by-Chapter Supplementary Materials" in the IM, you will find a chapter-culminating activity. You can use this activity to consolidate and review the vocabulary and grammar skills students have acquired.

### Resources for Review and Testing Preparation

- Workbook/Laboratory Manual
- Interactive CD-ROM
- Online Learning Center (www.mhhe.com/quetal7)

**Lengua y cultura: El cuadro *Guernica* de Picasso.** En esta actividad hay información sobre el famoso cuadro del pintor español Picasso, *Guernica,* que está en el Museo Nacional Centro de Arte Reina Sofía, en Madrid, España. Un guía les habla sobre el cuadro. Complete el siguiente diálogo con la forma correcta de los verbos entre paréntesis. Cuando se den dos posibilidades, escoja la palabra correcta.

Guernica, *por Pablo Picasso (español, 1881–1973)*

GUÍA:   (Pasar[1]) Uds. por aquí, por favor. También les pido que (dejar[2]) suficiente espacio para todos. Y bien, aquí estamos (delante/detrás[3]) de *Guernica,* la obra maestra pintada por Picasso. (Ser[4]) obvio que el cuadro (representar[5]) los horrores de la guerra,[a] ¿no? En 1937 Picasso (pintar[6]) este cuadro como reacción al bombardeo[b] (del / de la[7]) ciudad de Guernica durante la Guerra Civil Española. Por razones políticas, (durante / encima de[8]) la dictadura[c] de Franco,[d] el cuadro (fue/estuvo[9]) muchos años en el Museo de Arte Moderno de Nueva York. Pero por deseo expreso del pintor, el cuadro (trasladarse[10])[e] a España después de la muerte de Franco…

UD.:   Yo dudo que (este/esto[11]) cuadro (ser[12]) una obra maestra. Creo que no (ser[13]) nada bonito. ¡No hay colores en él!

SU AMIGO:   Yo no (creer[14]) que todos los cuadros (tener[15]) que (ser[16]) bonitos. Para mí, la falta de color (servir[17]) para expresar el dolor y el desastre… (Por/Para[18]) eso, uno (poder[19]) sentir el mensaje de la destrucción de la guerra en la pintura.

[a]*war* [b]*bombing* [c]*dictatorship* [d]Francisco Franco (1892–1975), dictador de España desde 1939 hasta su muerte [e]*to be moved*

**Comprensión.** ¿Quién pudo haber dicho (*could have said*) lo siguiente, el guía, Ud. o su amigo?

1. Yo prefiero los cuadros en colores.
2. Ahora voy a mostrarles una obra maestra de la pintura española.
3. No me molesta que esta pintura esté pintada en blanco y negro.
4. Quiero que todos me sigan y que se pongan delante del cuadro.

# Un paso más    PASO 4

**Paso 4: Un paso más**
• The *Paso 4: Un paso más* sections are optional.
• See the "Chapter-by-Chapter Supplementary Materials" in the IM for additional teaching suggestions, notes, activities, and other resources for *Paso 4*.

**Entrevistas culturales: Suggestions**
• Before showing the video clips, ask students questions about what role art plays in their life.

## VIDEOTECA

*¿Le gusta a Ud. pintar o dibujar? ¿Le interesa la escultura?*

## Entrevista cultural: Bolivia

Juan Prudencio, un joven artista boliviano, habla de su trabajo artístico y de su familia. Antes de ver el vídeo, lea el siguiente fragmento de la entrevista.

ENTREVISTADORA:  Y ¿qué pintas?

JUAN:  Pinto cuadros abstractos. Pinto cosas que tienen que ver con mis emociones o con la manera en que yo veo las… la situación actual[a] en el mundo.

[a]*current*

Ahora vea el vídeo y conteste las siguientes preguntas basándose en la entrevista.

1. ¿Cómo son los cuadros que Juan pinta?
2. ¿Cómo reaccionan los padres de Juan a su trabajo artístico?
3. Y ¿cómo responden sus hermanos a sus obras?

*¿Ud. se considera artista? ¿Por qué sí o por qué no? ¿Qué museos y galerías hay en su ciudad o pueblo?*

• Show the video clips and allow students one to two minutes to work on the questions for each one. Have volunteers answer the questions.
• Have volunteers role-play Juan and Álvaro with their interviewers.

**Entrevista cultural (Bolivia): Answers**
*Possible answers:* 1. *abstractos* 2. *No los entienden.* 3. *Los entienden y los aprecian mucho.*

**Entrevista cultural (Ecuador): Answers**
*Possible answers:* 1. *Porque le gusta mucho el arte, especialmente la pintura.* 2. *Piensa abrir un museo o una galería.*

## Entrevista cultural: El Ecuador

Álvaro Montealbán, un estudiante ecuatoriano, habla del arte y de sus planes profesionales. Antes de ver el vídeo, lea el siguiente fragmento de la entrevista.

ENTREVISTADORA:  Álvaro, ¿qué planes tienes para el futuro?

ÁLVARO:  Para el futuro pienso desarrollarme profesionalmente y hacer un museo o una galería de arte. En un futuro más a largo plazo[a] trabajaré[b] …eh… por montarme[c] mi propia galería de arte.

[a]*más… more long term*   [b]*I will work*   [c]*establish, open*

Ahora vea el vídeo y conteste las siguientes preguntas basándose en la entrevista.

1. ¿Por qué estudia Álvaro la historia del arte?
2. ¿Qué quiere hacer Álvaro en el futuro?

**Entre amigos: Answers**
*Possible answers:* 1. *A Rubén le gusta Salvador Dalí. A Tané le gusta el arte contemporáneo. A Miguel le gusta el blues, el jazz y la música moderna.* 2. *Tané dice que es la fusión de la música y el teatro. Rubén dice que cuando una persona va a la ópera por primera vez, o le gusta mucho o la odia.*

## Entre amigos: ¿Y qué pintores te gustan?

Tané, Karina, Rubén y Miguel hablan del arte. En su opinión, ¿qué preguntas se van a hacer? Antes de mirar el vídeo, lea las preguntas a continuación. Mientras mire el vídeo, fíjese en la información sobre el arte y los artistas. Luego mire el vídeo una segunda vez, fijándose en la información que necesita para contestar las preguntas.

**Entre amigos: Suggestions**
• Before viewing the video, review the questions with the students and ask them similar questions.

*¿Qué artistas le gustan a Ud.? ¿Qué tipo de arte prefiere?*

1. ¿Qué pintor le gusta a Rubén? ¿Qué tipo de arte le gusta a Tané? Y a Miguel, ¿qué música le gusta?
2. ¿Cómo describe Tané la ópera? Y ¿qué dice Rubén de la ópera?

*¿Sabe Ud. cantar? ¿Qué tipo de música prefiere?*
*¿Asiste Ud. a conciertos de música clásica? ¿a óperas?*

Have students answer or work in small groups to ask and answer these questions.

*Paso 4   Videoteca*

• After viewing the video, have volunteers read and answer the questions.

trescientos treinta y nueve    **339**

## PASO 4

**Notes**
• Students can read an excerpt of the novel *Huasipungo* by Ecuador's Jorge Icaza in *Voces de Bolivia y el Ecuador: Literatura*.
• Students can read about Rumillajta, a band from Bolivia, in *Voces de Bolivia y el Ecuador: Música*.
• See the Workbook/Laboratory Manual for focused practice with the material in *Enfoque cultural*.

**CAPÍTULO**
**13**

## ENFOQUE CULTURAL

### Bolivia y el Ecuador

### Personas famosas: Oswaldo Guayasamín

Oswaldo Guayasamín (1919–1999) fue un pintor ecuatoriano cuyo[a] arte es un testimonio del sufrimiento[b] humano y de la vida difícil de los indios y los pobres de su país. Guayasamín se inspiró en los símbolos y motivos de los pueblos precolombinos y en el arte colonial del Ecuador.

[a]*whose*  [b]*suffering*

*Madre y niño*, por Oswaldo Guayasamín

### ¡Fíjese!

• Bolivia formó parte del antiguo imperio inca. Aproximadamente el 55 por ciento de la población boliviana actual es de origen indígena.
• Bolivia fue nombrada[a] en honor a Simón Bolívar, quien luchó por la independencia del país.
• A 12.000 pies de altura, La Paz es la capital más alta del mundo.
• Las Islas Galápagos pertenecen[b] al Ecuador y son de origen volcánico. Fueron descubiertas[c] en 1535, por el español Berlanga. Berlanga las llamó las Islas Encantadas[d] porque las fuertes corrientes[e] marinas confundían a los navegantes[f] como si fuera por[g] acto de magia. Trescientos años más tarde, el biólogo Charles Darwin llegó a las islas a bordo del barco *HMS Beagle*. De sus investigaciones de las plantas y animales de cuatro de las islas resultaron sus ideas sobre la evolución y su famoso libro, *El origen de las especies*. Darwin teorizó que los animales y las plantas cambian y se adaptan a su medio ambiente.[h]

[a]*fue… was named*  [b]*belong*  [c]*Fueron… They were discovered*  [d]*Enchanted*  [e]*currents*  [f]*sailors*  [g]*como… as if by*  [h]*medio… environment*

Learn more about Bolivia and Ecuador with the Video, the Interactive CD-ROM, and the Online Learning Center (www.mhhe.com/quetal7).

## PASO FINAL

### 📖 A LEER

#### REPASO DE ESTRATEGIAS: Guessing the Content of a Passage

Look at the photographs that accompany the reading. Read the title of the passage also. Based on these clues, what do you think the article is going to be about? How do you know? What important information do the photos and the title provide? Remember to always look for these types of visual and textual clues as a useful strategy to facilitate comprehension when reading in a second language (or even in your first language).

**Sobre la lectura…** Este artículo es de la revista hispana *Cristina*, que publica la famosa cubanoamericana Cristina Saralegui. Frecuentemente comparada con Oprah Winfrey, Saralegui también tiene un *talk show* en español y un sitio web. Su sitio web es cristinaonline.com.

**Suggestions**
- Do the *Estrategia* in class and assign the reading as homework for discussion during the next class meeting.
- Have students share predictions about the passage. Then ask what strategies they used to make predictions.

## El arte de la Talavera

La cerámica que hoy conocemos como Talavera proviene[a] del pueblo español de Talavera de la Reina, situado en la provincia de Toledo. Los árabes se establecieron en la Península Ibérica en el siglo[b] VI, y trajeron consigo[c] sus técnicas artísticas para <u>moldear</u> la cerámica. Pintar <u>adornos</u> azules en cerámicas blancas, un distintivo[d] de Talavera, se debe a la influencia árabe en este arte.

*Cerámica mexicana Talavera auténtica*

Un grupo de artesanos de Talavera de la Reina trajo la técnica de Talavera con sus raíces árabes a Puebla, México, ciudad que se ha convertido en[e] el centro de este arte. Inicialmente, el propósito fue crear lozas[f] y murales en las iglesias y monasterios católicos, para adornar los templos religiosos.

La cerámica de Talavera se convirtió en una verdadera pieza de colección, porque recibe múltiples influencias. Además de la árabe y española, les debe[g] a italianos y chinos, convirtiéndose así en una de las más famosas del mundo.

El arte y sus técnicas iban trasladándose[h] de un lugar a otro. Así llega también a México la influencia que ejerció la técnica italiana del artista Francisco Niculoso en la cerámica Talavera, conocida también como cerámica italiana Majólica. De ahí es que <u>surge</u> el uso del verde, negro y amarillo intenso. En las piezas de la cerámica mexicana Talavera de finales del siglo XVII se aprecia este baño de nuevos colores, lo que hace preciosos[i] los adornos.

En México, la Talavera también se enriqueció de lo oriental, por el arte chino que se recibió a través de Filipinas. Algunas piezas orientales fueron copiadas por los artesanos mexicanos. De esta forma, surgen las figuras orientales, las cerámicas de animales y los diseños florales.

La Talavera mexicana es una técnica que, aunque[j] llegó de España en el siglo XVI, se depuró[k] en el siglo XVIII. Se <u>agregaron</u> otros colores como el morado, que junto al azul convencional, el amarillo y el verde, le impartieron muchísima personalidad.

La Talavera se puso[l] tan de moda que fue necesaria una ordenanza con los requisitos[m] estéticos y de manufactura. En México una pieza siempre debe incluir el color azul y estar firmada[n] por el artesano para evitar[o] la falsificación. Este tipo de cerámica también se subdivide en [categorías:] fina, semifina y para el uso diario.

[a]viene   [b]*century*   [c]*with them*   [d]característica   [e]*se… has become*
[f]porcelana   [g]*les… it owes a debt*   [h]*moving*   [i]*valuable*   [j]*although*
[k]*se… se refinó*   [l]*se… became*   [m]estipulaciones   [n]*signed*   [o]*avoid*

Es importante que, al comprar[P] una pieza, le preguntes al artesano si es posible darle un uso práctico, como usarla de vajilla,[q] lavar en lavadora de platos automática y poner en el microondas, porque algunas piezas son sólo decorativas. ■

[P]al... *upon purchasing*   [q]de... *as dishes*

## Comprensión

**A. Preguntas.**   Conteste las siguientes preguntas.

1. ¿En que país tiene su origen la cerámica Talavera?
2. ¿Qué culturas influyen en el arte de la Talavera?
3. ¿Cuáles son algunos de los colores tradicionales de la cerámica Talavera, y cuál es el color esencial?

**B. ¿Cierto o falso?**   Conteste según la lectura y corrija las oraciones falsas.

1. La cerámica Talavera puede usarse tanto para ocasiones formales como informales.
2. La Talavera siempre tiene diseños geográficos.
3. El arte de la Talavera llegó a América cuando los árabes conquistaron México.

## A ESCRIBIR

**La expresión artística.**   Muchas personas se expresan mediante (*by means of*) el arte en sus varias formas. Es decir, el arte no se limita solamente a la pintura y la escultura. El arte puede tomar varias formas: la música, la escritura, el diseño de ropa o muebles, etcétera. ¿Qué «arte» usa Ud. para expresar su personalidad? Escriba un breve ensayo para explicar cómo se expresa Ud. por medio del arte. Ideas para considerar:

- el medio artístico (la música, etcétera)
- cómo el arte expresa sus emociones y personalidad
- si sus preferencias con respecto a la expresión artística están cambiando o si son siempre las mismas

Cuando termine su ensayo, entrégueselo a su profesor(a). El profesor / La profesora se lo va a presentar al resto de la clase para ver si entre todos pueden adivinar quién es el autor / la autora.

4. En este lugar se representan obras de teatro.
5. Gloria Estefan y Julio Iglesias tienen esta profesión.
6. El sinónimo de crear una escultura.
7. Los artistas hacen esto antes de pintar un cuadro, generalmente.

## GRAMÁTICA

To review the grammar points presented in this chapter, refer to the indicated grammar presentations. You'll find further practice of these structures in the Workbook/Laboratory Manual, on the Interactive CD-ROM, and on the *¿Qué tal?* Online Learning Center (www.mhhe.com/quetal7).

 **Expressing Feelings—Use of the Subjunctive: Emotion**

You should know how and when to use the subjunctive in a dependent clause when the main clause of a sentence expresses emotion.

 **Expressing Uncertainty—Use of the Subjunctive: Doubt and Denial**

You should know how and when to use the subjunctive in a dependent clause when the main clause of a sentence expresses doubt or denial.

## VOCABULARIO

Practice this vocabulary with digital flash cards on the Online Learning Center (www.mhhe.com/quetal7).

### Los verbos

| | |
|---|---|
| aburrir | to bore |
| agradar | to please |
| apreciar | to appreciate |
| negar (ie) (gu) | to deny |
| parecer (zc) | to seem |
| representar | to represent |
| sentir (ie, i) | to regret; to feel sorry |
| temer | to fear |
| tratar de + *inf.* | to try to (*do something*) |

**Repaso: alegrarse (de), creer, dudar, esperar, gustar, tener (*irreg.*) miedo de**

### La expresión artística

| | |
|---|---|
| el baile | dance |
| el cuadro | painting (*piece of art*) |
| la danza | dance |
| la escultura | sculpture |
| la fotografía | photography |
| la pintura | painting (*general; piece of art; the art form*) |

**Cognados: la arquitectura, el arte (*but* las artes), el ballet, el drama, la música, la ópera**
**Repaso: el cine, la foto(grafía) (photo[graph]), la literatura, el teatro**

| | |
|---|---|
| crear | to create |
| desempeñar | to play, perform (*a part*) |

| | |
|---|---|
| dibujar | to draw |
| esculpir | to sculpt |
| tejer | to weave |

**Repaso: cantar, escribir, pintar**

### Los artistas

| | |
|---|---|
| el actor / la actriz | actor, actress |
| el bailarín / la bailarina | dancer |
| el/la cantante | singer |
| el/la compositor(a) | composer |
| el/la director(a) | director; conductor |
| el/la dramaturgo/a | playwright |
| el/la escritor(a) | writer |
| el/la escultor(a) | sculptor |
| el/la músico | musician |
| el/la pintor(a) | painter |

**Cognados: el/la arquitecto/a, el/la artista, el/la poeta**
**Repaso: el/la aficionado/a**

### La tradición cultural

| | |
|---|---|
| la artesanía | arts and crafts |
| la cerámica | pottery; ceramics |
| los tejidos | woven goods |

**Cognado: las ruinas**

## Otros sustantivos

| | |
|---|---|
| **la canción** | song |
| **el escenario** | stage |
| **la gente** | people |
| **el/la guía** | guide |
| **el guión** | script |
| **la obra (de arte)** | work (of art) |
| **la obra maestra** | masterpiece |
| **el papel** | role |

## Los adjetivos

| | |
|---|---|
| **clásico/a** | classic(al) |
| **folklórico/a** | folkloric |
| **moderno/a** | modern |

## Los números ordinales

**primer(o/a)**
**segundo/a**
**tercer(o/a)**
**cuarto/a**
**quinto/a**
**sexto/a**
**séptimo/a**
**octavo/a**
**noveno/a**
**décimo/a**

**Suggestions**

- Bring or have students bring images of fine and performing arts. Use the images to elicit descriptions and ask/answer questions.
- Make statements about the images displayed in class or about aspects of university life on your campus to which students can react with the following expressions: *No, no creo... , No, dudo que... , No, niego que...*
- Write the expressions from *Palabras adicionales* on the board. Make statements about people in the class, university, state, or national events, or other people and events that students should know about. Have them respond to each statement using one of the expressions.

*Muchos estudiantes estudian el arte.* → *Me sorprende que tantos estudiantes estudien el arte.*

## Palabras adicionales

| | |
|---|---|
| **es extraño que** | it's strange that |
| **¡qué extraño que… !** | how strange that . . . ! |
| **es…** | it's . . . |
| **cierto que** | certain that |
| **imposible que** | impossible that |
| **(im)probable que** | (un)likely, (im)probable that |
| **increíble que** | incredible that |
| **ridículo que** | ridiculous that |
| **seguro que** | a sure thing that |
| **terrible que** | terrible that |
| **urgente que** | urgent that |
| **es una lástima que** | it's a shame that |
| **¡qué lástima que… !** | what a shame that . . . ! |
| **hay que** + *inf.* | it is necessary to (*do something*) |
| **me (te, le,… ) molesta que** | it bothers me (you, him, . . . ) that |
| **me (te, le,… ) sorprende que** | it surprises me (you, him, . . . ) that |
| **ojalá (que)** | I hope, wish (that) |

**Repaso: es posible que, es mejor/bueno/malo que, es verdad que, estar seguro/a (de) que**

# La naturaleza y el medio ambiente°

°**La...** *Nature and the environment*

**Suggestions**
• Point out the chapter-opener photo. According to legend, the falls were created by the rage of an angry god of the river, who lived in what is called *la Garganta del Diablo* (the Devil's Throat),

one of the most spectacular parts of the waterfall system. The borders of Argentina, Paraguay, and Brazil converge at these falls. The falls are made up of approximately 275 cataracts that plunge 269 feet over a cliff more than two miles wide. The average discharge of about 60,000 cubic feet per second increases to more than 400,000 in times of flood. In 1986 Iguazú Falls were declared a Natural Heritage of Mankind by UNESCO. Encourage students to research and compare this waterfall to other famous waterfalls.

*Las cataratas del Iguazú, en la Argentina*

• Have students list their ideas about Argentina, including information on geography, politics, economy, culture, music, and cuisine. When you finish the chapter, return to the lists and ask students what ideas they would change and/or add.

## LA NATURALEZA Y EL MEDIO AMBIENTE

Paso 1: Vocabulario
See the "Chapter-by-Chapter Supplementary Materials" in the IM for a model for vocabulary presentation, as well as additional teaching suggestions, notes, activities, and other resources for *Paso 1*.

Resources: Transparency 87

la contaminación (del aire)
el aire puro
la montaña
el árbol
el rascacielos
la fábrica
el caballo
la agricultora
el agricultor
el río
la finca
la vaca
el lago
el toro
el pez (*pl.* peces)

| | | | |
|---|---|---|---|
| el animal doméstico | domesticated animal; pet | la falta | lack; absence |
| el animal salvaje | wild animal | el gobierno | government |
| la ballena | whale | la población | population |
| el bosque | forest | los recursos naturales | natural resources |
| el/la campesino/a | farm worker; peasant | | |
| el campo | countryside; field | Cognados: el elefante, el gorila | |
| la ciudad | city | | |
| la energía | energy | acabar | to finish; run out (of) (use up completely) |
| eléctrica | electric | | |
| nuclear | nuclear | conservar | to save, conserve |
| solar | solar | construir (y)* | to build |
| la escasez | lack; shortage | contaminar | to pollute |
| (*pl.* escaseces) | | desarrollar | to develop |
| la especie (en peligro de extinción) | (endangered) species | destruir (y)* | to destroy |
| | | proteger (j) | to protect |

**Multimedia: Audio**
Students can listen to and practice this chapter's vocabulary on the Online Learning Center (**www.mhhe.com/quetal7**), as well as on the Textbook Audio CD, part of the Laboratory Audio Program.

*Note the present indicative conjugation of **construir**: construyo, construyes, construye, construímos, construís, construyen. **Destruir** is conjugated like **construir**.

## Más vocabulario

| | | | |
|---|---|---|---|
| **el delito** | crime | **el transporte público** | public transportation |
| **el ritmo (acelerado) de la vida** | (fast) pace of life | **la violencia** | violence |
| **los servicios públicos** | public services | **bello/a** | beautiful |
| | | **denso/a** | dense |

## ■ Conversación

### A. ¿La ciudad o el campo?

Possible answers

1. El aire es más puro y hay menos contaminación.   el campo
2. La naturaleza es más bella.   el campo
3. El ritmo de la vida es más acelerado.   la ciudad
4. Hay más delitos.   la ciudad
5. Los servicios financieros y legales son más asequibles (*available*).   la ciudad
6. Hay pocos medios de transporte públicos.   el campo
7. La población es menos densa.   el campo
8. Hay escasez de viviendas.   la ciudad

## NOTA CULTURAL

### Programas medioambientales

Muchos países del mundo se encuentran en la posición de **equilibrar**[a] la **protección** del medio ambiente con los objetivos del **desarrollo económico.** En muchos casos, **la explotación de recursos naturales** es la **mayor fuente de ingreso**[b] para la economía de un país. Pero los gobiernos latinoamericanos están conscientes de la necesidad de **proteger** el medio ambiente y de **conservar** los recursos naturales, y están haciendo lo posible por hacerlo. Los siguientes son algunos de los muchos **programas medioambientales** que se encuentran en los países hispanohablantes.

- En la Ciudad de México, existe un programa permanente de **restricción vehicular** que se llama Hoy no circula.[c] Los coches no deben circular un día por semana. El día está determinado por el **último número de la placa.**[d] El propósito de este programa es controlar **la emisión de contaminantes.** Programas semejantes a Hoy no circula existen también en otros países como Chile y la Argentina.
- En México, España y otros países existen programas de **separación de basura.** Se depositan materiales distintos en recipientes[e] de colores diferentes, desde el papel y el cartón, el vidrio,[f] el metal y el plástico, hasta la materia orgánica y los desechos[g] sanitarios.

*Madrid, España*

---

[a]*needing to balance*   [b]*fuente… source of income*   [c]*Hoy… Today (these) don't drive.*
[d]*license plate*   [e]*containers*   [f]*glass*   [g]*waste*

Con. B: Bright Idea Preliminary Exercise
Ask students the following questions.

CAPÍTULO

14

# PASO 1

*¿Qué hacen para conservar la energía?*
*¿Qué productos destruyen la capa de ozono (ozone layer)?*
*¿Usa Ud. mucha agua y energía en su casa?*
*¿Qué cosas recicla Ud.? ¿periódicos? ¿botellas? ¿latas?*
*¿Echa Ud. (Do you throw) basura a la calle?*

**Con. B: Suggestion**
Create a chart on the board to tally the number of students for and against each item.

**Con. B: Bright Idea Follow-Up**
Have students create a poster in Spanish to motivate others to conserve energy and to reduce pollution. Give them the following suggestions.

## Expresiones útiles

**Es / Me/Nos parece…**
 **fundamental que…**
 **importantísimo que…**
 **ridículo que…**
 **¿ ?**
**Me opongo / Nos oponemos a que (*I am / We are against*)…**
**No creo/creemos que…**

*la conservación de la energía*
*la contaminación del agua/aire*
*la promoción de energías alternativas*
*el reciclaje*

Have students present their posters in class.

**B. Problemas del mundo en que vivimos.** Con un compañero / una compañera, dé sus reacciones a las siguientes opiniones. Puede usar las expresiones útiles para aclarar (*clarify*) su posición con respecto a cada tema. **¡OJO!** Todas las expresiones requieren el uso del subjuntivo, porque expresan deseos e influencia.

1. Para conservar energía debemos reciclar todo lo posible.
2. Es mejor calentar las casas con estufas de leña (*wood stoves*) que con gas o electricidad.
3. Se debe crear más parques urbanos, estatales y nacionales.
4. La protección del medio ambiente no debe impedir la explotación de los recursos naturales.
5. Para evitar (*avoid*) la contaminación urbana, debemos limitar el uso de los coches y no usarlos algunos días de la semana, como se hace en otros países.
6. El gobierno debe ponerles multas (*fines*) muy graves a las compañías e individuos que causan la contaminación.
7. El desarrollo de las tecnologías promueve (*promotes*) el ritmo tan acelerado de nuestra vida.
8. Los países desarrollados están destruyendo los recursos naturales de los países más pobres.

## C. Un recurso natural importante

PASO 1  Lea este anuncio de una empresa (compañía) colombiana y conteste las preguntas.

1. ¿Qué tipo de negocio cree Ud. que es Ecopetrol? ¿Qué produce?
2. ¿Qué asuntos (*matters*) son de mayor interés para esta empresa? ¿El tránsito? ¿la deforestación? ¿las poblaciones humanas? ¿otros asuntos?
3. ¿Le parece que la foto que han elegido (*they chose*) para el anuncio es buena para la imagen de la empresa? ¿Por qué?
4. El sustantivo **convivencia** se relaciona con el verbo **vivir** y contiene la preposición **con**. ¿Qué cree Ud. que significa **convivencia**?
5. ¿Sabe Ud. cuáles son algunos de los países que producen lo mismo que Ecopetrol?

En ECOPETROL tenemos conciencia ambiental y social. Nuestra planeación incluye siempre los estudios de localización e impacto ambiental, buscando no perturbar la naturaleza y la vida de las poblaciones vecinas a nuestras futuras operaciones. En esta planeación el trabajo con la comunidad es indispensable.

### Nuestro propósito: Una mejor convivencia

EMPRESA COLOMBIANA DE PETROLEOS
**ECOPETROL**

## Vocabulario útil

**la energía eólica** (wind energy)
**la energía hidráulica** (hydraulic energy)

**Con. C: Suggestion**
Have students look through Spanish-language magazines and newspapers to locate ads with environmental statements or themes. Are there many? What kinds of messages do they convey?

**Con. C: Answers**
*Paso 1  Possible answers:* **1.** Es un negocio petrolero que produce petróleo o gasolina.
**2.** los asuntos ambientales y sociales
**3.** Answers will vary. **4.** coexistence; living together **5.** *México, Venezuela*

PASO 2  Hay varias formas de energía. ¿Las conoce Ud. bien? Diga a qué tipo de energía corresponde cada descripción.

1. Es la energía más usada en los hogares (*homes*).
2. Según los expertos, es la forma de energía más limpia; es decir, es la que menos contaminación produce.
3. Puede ser la forma de energía más eficiente, pero también la más peligrosa (*dangerous*).
4. Esta energía viene del viento; por eso sólo se puede desarrollar en lugares específicos.
5. Para producir esta forma de energía son necesarios los ríos y las cataratas (*waterfalls*).

**Heritage Speakers**
Invite a un estudiante hispanohablante a leer el anuncio en voz alta.

**Suggestion**
Ask students what vocabulary words they associate with the following.

*¿Con qué asocia Ud.... ?*

1. *¿los colores rojo, amarillo y verde?*
2. *¿los mecánicos?*
3. *¿la contaminación?*
4. *¿parar?*
5. *¿una llanta?*
6. *¿arrancar?*
7. *¿la carretera?*
8. *¿doblar?*

## LOS COCHES

En la gasolinera Gómez

**Resources:** Transparencies 88, 89
Transparency 89 provides additional images and vocabulary.

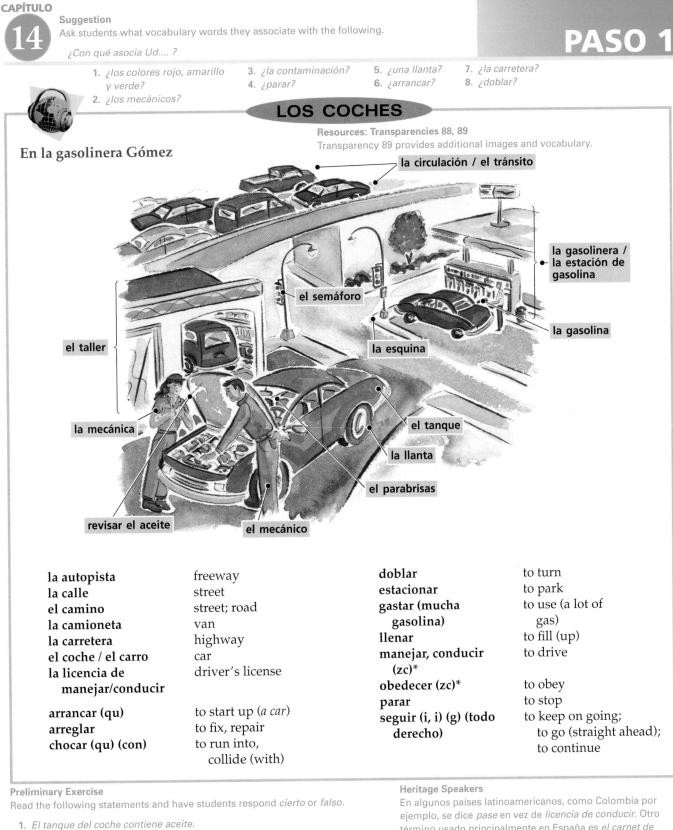

- la circulación / el tránsito
- la gasolinera / la estación de gasolina
- la gasolina
- el semáforo
- la esquina
- el taller
- el tanque
- la llanta
- la mecánica
- el parabrisas
- revisar el aceite
- el mecánico

| | | | |
|---|---|---|---|
| **la autopista** | freeway | **doblar** | to turn |
| **la calle** | street | **estacionar** | to park |
| **el camino** | street; road | **gastar (mucha gasolina)** | to use (a lot of gas) |
| **la camioneta** | van | | |
| **la carretera** | highway | **llenar** | to fill (up) |
| **el coche / el carro** | car | **manejar, conducir (zc)\*** | to drive |
| **la licencia de manejar/conducir** | driver's license | **obedecer (zc)\*** | to obey |
| | | **parar** | to stop |
| **arrancar (qu)** | to start up (*a car*) | **seguir (i, i) (g) (todo derecho)** | to keep on going; to go (straight ahead); to continue |
| **arreglar** | to fix, repair | | |
| **chocar (qu) (con)** | to run into, collide (with) | | |

**Preliminary Exercise**
Read the following statements and have students respond *cierto* or *falso*.

1. *El tanque del coche contiene aceite.*
2. *Si el semáforo está rojo, es necesario parar.*
3. *Un Cadillac gasta poca gasolina.*
4. *Es necesario tener una licencia para conducir.*
5. *Si Ud. no dobla, Ud. sigue todo derecho.*

**Heritage Speakers**
En algunos países latinoamericanos, como Colombia por ejemplo, se dice *pase* en vez de *licencia de conducir*. Otro término usado principalmente en España es *el carnet de chófer / de conducir*. También hay varios términos para expresar *to park: estacionar(se), aparcar (Esp.) y parquear (Méx.).* Para referirse a *parking lot* o *parking place*, se puede decir *estacionamiento* o *parqueadero*. Pregúnteles a los hispanohablantes de la clase qué palabras usan y por qué.

---

\*Like the verb **conocer, conducir** and **obedecer** *have a spelling change in the* **yo** *form of the present indicative:* **conozco, conduzco, obedezco.** *This spelling change is also used in all forms of the present subjunctive.*

**Preliminary Exercise**
Ask students the following questions.

1. *En esta clase, ¿cuántos tienen coche? ¿Es viejo o nuevo su coche? ¿grande o pequeño? ¿Gasta mucha o poca gasolina? ¿mucho o poco aceite? ¿Cuánto le cuesta llenar el tanque?*
2. *En general, ¿funciona bien su coche? Cuando no funciona, ¿lo arregla Ud. o se lo arregla un mecánico? ¿un amigo? ¿Es vieja o nueva la batería? ¿Le es difícil hacer arrancar el coche por la mañana? ¿Le es difícil arrancar cuando hace frío?*
3. *¿Tuvo Ud. alguna vez una llanta desinflada (pantomime)? ¿Dónde y cómo ocurrió? ¿Quién la cambió? ¿Tuvo Ud. que llamar para pedir ayuda? ¿Siempre lleva Ud. una llanta de repuesto (llanta de recambio/una quinta llanta) (pantomime)?*
4. *¿Maneja Ud. para venir al campus? ¿Es fácil estacionarse aquí? ¿Es necesario pagar para poder estacionarse en el campus? ¿Cuánto? ¿Quiénes encuentran un estacionamiento con más facilidad, los profesores o los estudiantes?*
5. *¿Sabe Ud. manejar? ¿Cuándo aprendió a manejar? ¿Cuántos años tenía? ¿Quién le enseñó a manejar? ¿Tuvo Ud. algún accidente mientras aprendía? ¿Qué es lo mejor de manejar? ¿y lo peor?*

**Con. B: Suggestions**
• Have students rank question items in order of importance.
• Ask students the following questions.

*¿Es símbolo de mucho prestigio social tener un Ferrari? ¿un Volkswagen? ¿un Hyundai? ¿un BMW? ¿un Toyota? ¿una camioneta? ¿un pickup?*

*¿Cómo es el típico dueño / la típica dueña de cada uno de estos coches?*

**Con. A: Answers**
*Paso 2  Possible answers:*
*1. Son las luces que controlan la circulación. Son de color rojo, amarillo y verde. 2. Son los vehículos que están en la carretera o en la calle. 3. Es poner el coche en un lugar para dejarlo allí. 4. Es lo que hace el coche para poder funcionar. 5. Es el lugar donde se compra gasolina para el coche. 6. Es una carretera grande sin semáforos, donde los coches pueden circular a gran velocidad.*

**Need more practice?**

- Workbook/Laboratory Manual
- Interactive CD-ROM
- Online Learning Center (www.mhhe.com/quetal7)

**Note**
See the Workbook/Laboratory Manual for review and practice of cognates.

## ■ Conversación

### A. Definiciones

PASO 1  Busque Ud. la definición de las palabras de la columna de la derecha.

1. __g__ Se pone en el tanque.
2. __h__ Se llenan de aire.
3. __i__ Lubrica el motor.
4. __d__ Es necesaria para arrancar el motor.
5. __b__ Cuando se llega a una esquina, hay que hacer esto o seguir todo derecho.
6. __f__ No contiene aire suficiente y por eso es necesario cambiarla.
7. __c__ Es un camino público ancho (*wide*) donde los coches circulan rápidamente.
8. __a__ Se usan para parar el coche.
9. __j__ El policía nos la pide cuando nos para en el camino.
10. __e__ Allí se revisan y se arreglan los coches.

a. los frenos (*brakes*)
b. doblar
c. la carretera
d. la batería
e. el taller
f. una llanta desinflada (*flat*)
g. la gasolina
h. las llantas
i. el aceite
j. la licencia

**Con. A: Variation**
Have students work in pairs, one covering the first column and the other the second.

PASO 2  Ahora, siguiendo el modelo de las definiciones anteriores, ¿puede Ud. dar una definición de las siguientes palabras?

1. el semáforo
2. la circulación
3. estacionar
4. gastar gasolina
5. la gasolinera
6. la autopista

### B. Entrevista: Un conductor (*driver*) responsable

PASO 1  Entreviste a un compañero / una compañera de clase para determinar con qué frecuencia hace las siguientes cosas.

1. dejar la licencia en casa cuando va a manejar
2. acelerar (*to speed up*) cuando ve a un policía
3. manejar después de tomar bebidas alcohólicas
4. respetar o exceder el límite de velocidad
5. estacionar el coche donde dice «Prohibido estacionar»
6. revisar el nivel (*level*) del aceite y la batería
7. seguir todo derecho a toda velocidad cuando no sabe llegar a su destino
8. rebasar (*to pass*) tres carros a la vez (*at the same time*)

PASO 2  Ahora, con el mismo compañero / la misma compañera, haga una lista de diez cosas que hace —o no hace— un conductor responsable. Pueden usar frases del **Paso 1**, si quieren.

PASO 3  Ahora, analice Ud. sus propias (*own*) costumbres y cualidades como conductor(a). ¡Diga la verdad! ¿Es Ud. un conductor / una conductora responsable? ¿Cuál de los dos es el mejor conductor / la mejor conductora?

**Paso 2: Gramática**

See the "Chapter-by-Chapter Supplementary Materials" in the IM for additional teaching suggestions, notes, activities, and other resources for *Paso 2.*

**Follow-Up**
• After reviewing the *refranes*, ask students the following questions.

1. *¿Es mejor no decir nada? ¿Qué le puede pasar a uno cuando tiene la boca abierta?*

## 38 *Más descripciones* Past Participle Used as an Adjective

2. *¿Llevan una vida muy interesante las ostras? ¿Por qué? ¿Sufren muchas presiones?*
3. *¿Todos los que cometen delitos son criminales? ¿Es posible que una persona honrada llegue a cometer un crimen? ¿Cree que las personas sufrimos demasiadas tentaciones en el mundo moderno?*

### Algunos refranes y dichos en español

♻ **Reciclado**
Review past participles students have been using, especially with *estar*, since the early chapters.

| casado | aburrido | abierto |
|--------|----------|---------|
| cansado | preocupado | cerrado |
| ocupado | | |

**a.** En boca *cerrada* no entran moscas.

**b.** Estoy tan *aburrido* como una ostra.

**c.** Cuando está *abierto* el cajón, el más *honrado* es ladrón.

### Comprensión

Empareje estas oraciones con el refrán o dicho que explican.

1. __c__ Es posible que una persona honrada caiga en la tentación de hacer algo malo si la oportunidad se le presenta.
2. __a__ Hay que ser prudente. A veces es mejor no decir nada para evitar (*avoid*) problemas.
3. __b__ Las ostras ejemplifican el aburrimiento (*boredom*) porque llevan una vida tranquila… siempre igual.

## Forms of the Past Participle

**A.** The past participle of most English verbs ends in *-ed.*

*to walk* → *walked*    *to close* → *closed*

Many, however, are irregular.

*to sing* → **sung**    *to write* → **written**

In Spanish, the *past participle* (**el participio pasado**) is formed by adding **-ado** to the stem of **-ar** verbs, and **-ido** to the stem of **-er** and **-ir** verbs. An accent mark is used on the past participle of **-er/-ir** verbs with stems ending in **-a, -e,** or **-o.**

**Heritage Speakers**
*Aburrido como una ostra* se presenta aquí con el verbo *estar* y expresa la idea *as bored as an oyster.* Sin embargo, algunos hispanohablantes prefieren la idea *as boring as an oyster.* Para esta versión, el verbo *ser* sería necesario. Pregúnteles a los hispanohablantes de la clase qué dirían: *Está tan aburrido/a como una ostra* o *Es tan aburrido/a como una ostra.* Pídales que compartan otros refranes que se dicen en su familia con la clase.

> **past participle** = the form of a verb used with **haber** in Spanish and *to have* in English to form perfect tenses

| hablar | comer | vivir |
|--------|-------|-------|
| hablado | comido | vivido |
| (*spoken*) | (*eaten*) | (*lived*) |

| | |
|---|---|
| caer → **caído** | oír → **oído** |
| creer → **creído** | (son)reír → **(son)reído** |
| leer → **leído** | traer → **traído** |

*A few Spanish proverbs and sayings*   **1.** *Into a closed mouth no flies enter.* **2.** *I am as bored as an oyster.*
**3.** *When the (cash) drawer is open, the most honest person is (can become) a thief.*

**Refranes**

«Del dicho al hecho hay un gran trecho.»
«A lo hecho, pecho.»

*Pronunciation hint:* The Spanish **d** between vowels, as found in past participle endings, is pronounced as the fricative [đ] (see **Pronunciación** in **Capítulo 6**, Workbook/Laboratory Manual).

Write the *refranes* on the board. Have students find the meaning of *trecho* and *pecho*. If they cannot come up with the English equivalents of these sayings, give them the following three English proverbs and have them match the Spanish (one of the Spanish sayings matches two of the English.)

Grin and bear it.
Easier said than done.
What's done is done.

**B.** The Spanish verbs at the right have irregular past participles.

**Emphasis B: Suggestions**

- Model the pronunciation of irregular past participles. Say the participle and have students give the corresponding infinitive. Then, reverse the procedure.
- Have students express the following in Spanish.

| | | |
|---|---|---|
| broken | returned | made |
| seen | written | done |
| covered | said | open(ed) |
| discovered | dead | put |

| | | | |
|---|---|---|---|
| abrir: | **abierto** | morir: | **muerto** |
| cubrir (*to cover*): | **cubierto** | poner: | **puesto** |
| | | resolver: | **resuelto** |
| decir: | **dicho** | romper: | **roto** |
| descubrir: | **descubierto** | ver: | **visto** |
| escribir: | **escrito** | volver: | **vuelto** |
| hacer: | **hecho** | | |

## The Past Participle Used as an Adjective

**A.** In both English and Spanish, the past participle can be used as an adjective to modify a noun. Like other Spanish adjectives, the past participle must agree in number and gender with the noun modified.

Viven en una casa **construida** en 1920.
*They live in a house built in 1920.*

El español es una de las lenguas **habladas** en los Estados Unidos y en el Canadá.
*Spanish is one of the languages spoken in the United States and in Canada.*

**B.** The past participle is frequently used with **estar** to describe conditions that are the result of a previous action.

El lago **está contaminado**.
*The lake is polluted.*

Todos los peces **estaban cubiertos** de crudo.
*All the fish were covered with crude oil.*

**OJO**

English past participles often have the same form as the past tense.

*I **closed** the book.*

*The thief stood behind the **closed** door.*

The Spanish past participle is never identical in form or use to a past tense. Compare the sentences at the right.

**Cerré** la puerta. Ahora la puerta está **cerrada**.
*I **closed** the door. Now the door is **closed**.*

**Resolvieron** el problema. Ahora el problema está **resuelto**.
*They **solved** the problem. Now the problem is **solved**.*

**Emphasis B: Suggestions**

♻ • Emphasize the use of the past participle with *estar* to describe resulting conditions. Point out that students learned many *-ado/-ido* adjectives in *Capítulo 5* with *estar*.

- Point out that compound verbs that have an irregular root verb, with few exceptions, have the same irregularity as the root verb in the past participle.

decir → pre**decir**: pre**dicho**
poner → com**poner**: com**puesto**
hacer → satis**facer**: satis**fecho**

**AUTOPRUEBA**

Give the infinitive of the past participles.

1. estudiadas    4. dicha
2. leído    5. abiertas
3. vistos    6. bebido

Answers: 1. estudiar 2. leer 3. ver 4. decir 5. abrir 6. beber

(Some words that now have the letter *h* at one time were written with *f*.)

- Have students give the past participle for the following verbs and also give their English equivalent.

| | | |
|---|---|---|
| revolver | deponer | describir |
| exponer | reponer | envolver |
| prescribir | oponer | rever |
| prever | presuponer | redecir |
| recubrir | encubrir | subscribir |
| imponer | rehacer | suponer |

*Capítulo 14 • La naturaleza y el medio ambiente*

# CAPÍTULO 14

**Prác. A: Preliminary Exercise**
Have students express the
following ideas in Spanish.

¿Cómo se dice en español?
1. a game won
2. the lost luggage
3. a repeated sentence
4. the tired child
5. dead flies
6. the broken plate

## ■ Práctica

**A. En este momento…**

♻ Reciclado
Note review of parts of the house.

PASO 1 **¡Anticipemos!** En este momento, ¿son ciertas o falsas las siguientes oraciones con relación a su sala de clase?

1. La puerta está abierta.
2. Las luces están apagadas.
3. Las ventanas están cerradas.
4. Algunos libros están abiertos.
5. Los estudiantes están sentados.
6. Hay algo escrito en la pizarra.
7. Una silla está rota.
8. Hay carteles y anuncios colgados en la pared.
9. Un aparato está enchufado.
10. Las persianas (*blinds*) están bajadas.

> **Palabras útiles**
>
> **colgar (ue) (gu)** (to hang)
> **enchufar** (to plug in)
> **prender** (to turn on [*lights or an appliance*])

PASO 2 Ahora describa el estado de las siguientes cosas en su casa (cuarto, apartamento).

1. las luces
2. la cama
3. el televisor
4. las ventanas
5. la puerta
6. las cortinas (*curtains*)

**B. Situaciones.** ¿Cuál es la situación en este momento? Conteste según el modelo.

MODELO: Natalia les tiene que *escribir* una *tarjeta* (*card*) a sus abuelos. →
La *tarjeta* no está *escrita* todavía.

1. Los Sres. García deben *abrir* la *tienda* más temprano. ¡Ya son las nueve!
2. Pablo tiene que *cerrar* las *ventanas*; entra un aire frío.
3. Los niños siempre esperan que la *tierra* se *cubra* de nieve para la Navidad.
4. Delia debe *poner* la *mesa.* Los invitados llegan a las nueve y ya son las ocho.
5. Claro está que la contaminación va a contribuir a la *destrucción* de la *capa de ozono.*
6. Es posible que los ingenieros *descubran* el *error* en la construcción del reactor nuclear.
7. Se debe *resolver* pronto el *problema* de la escasez de energía.

**Prác. A: Suggestions**
• Point out that *prender* is a synonym of *encender* and *poner* in some contexts (to turn on, light).
• Have students invent additional sentences to describe the classroom. Others respond *cierto* or *falso.* Write on the board the verbs that are useful for describing the classroom.

**Prác. B: Variations**
• Point out that *de* is used to express *with* in covered **with** (snow): cubierta **de** (nieve).
• Have students give sentences with *tener* + past participle.

La carta no está escrita todavía. → Natalia no tiene la carta escrita todavía.

**Need more practice?**
■ Workbook/Laboratory Manual
■ Interactive CD-ROM
■ Online Learning Center (www.mhhe.com/quetal7)

## ■ Conversación

Resources: Transparency 90

**¡Ojo alerta!** Hay por lo menos cinco cosas que difieren (*are different*) entre un dibujo y el otro. Con un compañero / una compañera, encuéntralos todas. Use participios pasados como adjetivos cuando pueda.

Ⓐ

Ⓑ

**Con: Answers**
*Possible answers:*
1. *En el dibujo A, el niño está dormido. En el dibujo B, el niño está despierto.* 2. *En el dibujo A, la lámpara está apagada. En el dibujo B, la lámpara está encendida.*
3. *En el dibujo A, el perro está dormido. En el dibujo B, el perro está despierto.* 4. *En el dibujo A, las personas están sentadas en el sofá. En el dibujo B, tres personas están sentadas a la mesa.* 5. *En el dibujo A, la mesa no está puesta. En el dibujo B, la mesa está puesta.* 6. *En el dibujo A, el gato está sentado en el sofá. En el dibujo B, el gato está jugando.*

En los Estados Unidos y el Canadá: Comprensión

1. *¿Qué estados tienen muchas ciudades con nombres hispanos?*
2. *En California, ¿el nombre de qué ciudad es el nombre de un árbol?*

## En los Estados Unidos y el Canadá

## Lugares con nombres españoles

La **geografía de Norteamérica** está llena de **nombres que dejaron los españoles,** los primeros europeos que exploraron y se establecieron en estas tierras. Varios **estados** de los Estados Unidos tienen nombres españoles, por ejemplo: Colorado (*de color rojo*), Nevada (*cubierta de nieve*), Montana (*de la palabra «montaña»*), Florida (*con flores*) y Nuevo México. Numerosas **ciudades** estadounidenses también llevan nombres de origen español.

**St. Augustine:** Esta ciudad de Florida, establecida en 1564, lleva el nombre de la **misión** San Agustín. Es la ciudad más antigua de Norteamérica fuera de[a] México.

**Santa Fe:** El nombre original y completo de la capital de Nuevo México es la **Villa Real de la Santa Fe** de San Francisco de Asís. Santa Fe, el nombre usado hoy, significa *Holy Faith*. Es la capital más antigua de los Estados Unidos (establecida en 1607).

**Sarasota:** Esta ciudad fue nombrada en honor de la **hija del gobernador de Florida,** Sara de Soto.

**Las Vegas:** El nombre de esta ciudad en Nevada significa *fertile plains*.

**Los Angeles:** En 1781 los españoles fundaron el Pueblo de Nuestra Señora la Reina de Los Ángeles de Porciúncula, en California. Hoy es la segunda ciudad más grande de los Estados Unidos.

**Fresno:** Esta ciudad de California fue nombrada por sus **árboles,** los fresnos.[b]

Los españoles también exploraron la **costa pacífica** hasta Alaska, donde hay muchos nombres de influencia española: el Cabo[c] Blanco, en Oregón; el Cabo de Álava, en Washington; las ciudades de Valdez y Córdova y el Glaciar Malaspina, en Alaska. En Canadá están los estrechos[d] de Juan de Fuca y de Laredo, y las islas Quadra, Saturna, Galiano, Gabriola, Aristazábal y Flores, todos en la costa de la Columbia Británica.

[a]fuera... *outside of* [b]*ash trees* [c]*Cape* [d]*straits*

# Voces de la Argentina

## LITERATURA: Alfonsina Storni

**Sobre la autora:** *Alfonsina Storni nació en Sala Capriasca, Suiza, pero vivió en la Argentina casi toda la vida, una vida llena de desilusiones y obstáculos. Storni era —y sufría los problemas de— una mujer intelectual a principios del siglo XX. El poema «Cuadrados[a] y ángulos» es de la colección* El dulce daño *(1918).*

Casas enfiladas,[b] casas enfiladas,
casas enfiladas.
Cuadrados, cuadrados, cuadrados.
Casas enfiladas.
Las gentes ya tienen el alma[c] cuadrada,
Ideas en fila[d]
y ángulos en la espalda.
Yo misma he vertido[e] ayer una lágrima,[f]
Dios mío, cuadrada.

[a]*Squares* [b]*in a straight row* [c]*soul* [d]*en... in single file* [e]*he... have shed* [f]*tear*

**Alfonsina Storni**
*(1892–1938)*

**Literatura: Note**
Storni battled cancer in her 40s, and when she found out she was losing the fight, she turned in her last poem to an Argentine newspaper. As the poem circulated in the newspapers, she drowned herself in the ocean.

**Literatura: Suggestion**
Play for students the song "*Alfonsina y el mar,*" by Ariel Ramírez and Félix Luna. This song was made famous by the Argentine singer Mercedes Sosa.

**Música: Suggestions**
• Give students background information about Astor Piazzola (1921–1986). This Argentine musician and composer, influenced by Carlos Gardel and trained in Paris by Nadia Boulanger, used the tango as the inspiration for his classical compositions. Play some Gardel tangos and some Piazzola pieces for students and ask them to compare the two.
• Show Carlos Saura's 1999 film *Tango* in class. You may wish to show the 1933 film of the same name, which stars Argentine actress Libertad Lamarque as the tango singer, as a comparison.

## MÚSICA: El tango

El tango es uno de los bailes más populares de la Argentina, pero su historia no está muy clara. Muchos creen que se originó en la Argentina entre los negros que habían sido importados[a] como esclavos. Estos[b] llamaban «tangó» al tambor,[c] al baile y al espacio en que se bailaba. El tango evolucionó y llegó a su forma moderna en los barrios pobres de Buenos Aires. Originalmente, el baile representaba la lucha[d] entre una prostituta y su chulo,[e] y por muchos años tuvo mala fama[f] y hasta[g] se consideraba escandaloso.

[a]habían... *had been imported* [b]*They (The slaves)* [c]*drum* [d]*struggle* [e]*pimp* [f]mala... *a bad reputation* [g]*even*

Para tocar el tango, se usan muchos instrumentos, pero el principal,[h] introducido durante la «italianización[*]» del tango, es el bandoneón, un tipo de acordeón.

[h]el... *the main one (instrument)*

El cantante de tango más famoso fue Carlos Gardel (1890–1935), quien se hizo estrella[i] de cine en Hollywood cantando tangos en varias películas. Murió trágicamente en un accidente de avión con otro grande del tango, el compositor Alfredo Lepera.

[i]se... *became a star*

[*]*This term refers to the late nineteenth century and early twentieth century, during which many Italians immigrated to Argentina, especially to Buenos Aires. The addition of the mandolin and the* **bandoneón** *(accordion) to the instrumentation of the tango reflects the Italian influence.*

## 39 ¿Qué has hecho? Perfect Forms: Present Perfect Indicative and Present Perfect Subjunctive

**Una llanta desinflada**

Paso 3: Gramática
See the "Chapter-by-Chapter Supplementary Materials" in the IM for additional teaching suggestions, notes, activities, and other resources for *Paso 3.*

MANOLO: ¡Ay, qué mala suerte!

LOLA: ¿Qué pasa?

MANOLO: Parece que el coche tiene una llanta desinflada. Y como no hay ningún taller por aquí, tengo que cambiarla yo mismo.

LOLA: *¿Has cambiado* una llanta alguna vez?

MANOLO: No. Siempre *he llevado* el coche a un taller cuando hay problemas.

LOLA: Pues, yo nunca *he cambiado* una llanta tampoco. Pero te puedo ayudar, si quieres.

MANOLO: Gracias. ¡Espero que la llanta de recambio* no esté desinflada también! Follow-Up

**¿Y Ud.? ¿Ha... ?**

1. cambiado una llanta desinflada
2. revisado el nivel del aceite de su coche
3. arreglado otras cosas del coche
4. tenido un accidente con el coche
5. excedido el límite de velocidad en la autopista

Ask the following questions after completing the *minidiálogo.*

1. *Si Ud. tiene una llanta desinflada, ¿le pide a alguien que lo/la ayude a cambiarla?*
2. *¿Le dice Ud. al mecánico que le revise el nivel del aceite o lo hace Ud. mismo/a?*
3. *¿Puede Ud. arreglar algunas fallas* (write "problemas" on board) *o necesita siempre que se lo haga un mecánico?*

## Present Perfect Indicative

**Suggestions**
- Read the following phrases and have students give the corresponding subject pronoun: *he corrido, hemos caminado, han perdido, has dormido, habéis dicho, ha visto.*
- Have students express the following ideas in Spanish.

*¿Cómo se dice en español?*

1. I have studied / eaten / read / gotten up.
2. He/She has answered/promised/ lived/opened.
3. We have called/lost/written.
4. They have traveled/run/discovered.

**Heritage Speakers**
Explíqueles a los estudiantes que en España se usa consistentemente el presente perfecto en lugar del pretérito para hablar de eventos muy recientes: *¿A qué hora has desayunado?* en vez de *¿A qué hora desayunaste?*

| PAST ------------------- Present ------------------- Future |
|---|
| preterite · present indicative |
| imperfect · present progressive |
| present perfect · formal commands |
| present perfect subjunctive · informal commands |
| present subjunctive |

he hablado — *I have spoken*   hemos hablado — *we have spoken*

has hablado — *you have spoken*   habéis hablado — *you (pl.) have spoken*

ha hablado — *you have spoken, he/she has spoken*   han hablado — *you (pl.) / they have spoken*

*A flat tire*   MANOLO: *Aw, what bad luck!*   LOLA: *What's wrong?*   MANOLO: *It seems the car has a flat tire. And, since there aren't any repair shops around here, I have to change it myself.*   LOLA: *Have you ever changed a flat tire before?*   MANOLO: *No. I've always taken the car to a repair shop when there are problems.*   LOLA: *Well, I've never changed a tire either. But I can help you, if you want.*   MANOLO: *Thanks. I hope that the spare tire isn't flat, too!*

*Other terms for spare tire in Spanish are **la llanta de respuesto** and **la quinta llanta.***

**Note**
Students will often try to use the present perfect indicative instead of the *hace* + time + *que* construction, due to interference from English. For example, instead of *Hace un año que estudio español*, students might say *\*He estudiado español por un año*. Although the *hace* + time + *que*

**A.** In English, the present perfect is a compound tense consisting of the present tense form of the verb *to have* plus the past participle: *I have written, you have spoken,* and so on.

In the Spanish *present perfect indicative* (**el presente perfecto del indicativo**), the past participle is used with present tense forms of **haber,** the equivalent of English *to have* in this construction.

In general, the use of the Spanish present perfect parallels that of the English present perfect.

No **hemos estado** aquí antes.
*We haven't been here before.*

**Me he divertido** mucho.
*I've had a very good time.*

Ya le **han escrito** la carta.
*They've already written her the letter.*

 **Haber,** an auxiliary verb, is not interchangeable with **tener.**

construction appears in readings and activities with English glossing, this structure is not presented in *¿Qué tal?* and students are not required to produce it.

**B.** The form of the past participle never changes with **haber,** regardless of the gender or number of the subject. The past participle always appears immediately after the appropriate form of **haber** and is never separated from it. Object pronouns and **no** are always placed directly before the form of **haber.**
[Práctica A–B]

Ella **ha cambiado** una llanta desinflada varias veces.
*She's changed a flat tire several times.*

Todavía **no le** han revisado el aceite al coche.
*They still haven't checked the car's oil.*

**Suggestions**
♻ Review the basic concept and uses of the subjunctive before beginning.

**C.** The present perfect form of **hay** is **ha habido** (*there has/have been*).

 Remember that **acabar** + **de** + *infinitive*—not the present perfect tense—is used to state that something *has just occurred.*

**Ha habido** un accidente.
*There's been an accident.*

**Acabo de mandar** la carta.
*I've just mailed the letter.*

1. influence
2. emotion
3. doubt

• Review the subjunctive forms of *haber.*
• Emphasize that these forms are the subjunctive counterparts of the present indicative (*he hablado, has hablado, ha hablado,* and so on).

## Present Perfect Subjunctive

The *present perfect subjunctive* (**el perfecto del subjuntivo**) is formed with the present subjunctive of **haber** plus the past participle. It is used to express *I have spoken* (*written,* and so on) when the subjunctive is required. Although its most frequent equivalent is *I have* plus the past participle, its exact equivalent in English depends on the context in which it occurs.

Note in the model sentences at the right that the English equivalent of the present perfect subjunctive can be expressed as a simple or as a compound tense: *did/have done; came/have come; built/have built.*
[Práctica C]

| | |
|---|---|
| **haya** hablado | **hayamos** hablado |
| **hayas** hablado | **hayáis** hablado |
| **haya** hablado | **hayan** hablado |

Es posible que lo **haya hecho.**
*It's possible (that) he may have done (he did) it.*

Me alegro de que **hayas venido.**
*I'm glad (that) you've come (you came).*

Es bueno que lo **hayan construido.**
*It's good (that) they built (have built) it.*

• Point out that the first and third person forms (*yo, Ud./él/ella*) are the same.
• Read the following phrases and have students give the corresponding subject pronouns.

*haya dicho*
*hayamos perdido*
*hayan escuchado*
*hayáis llamado*

**AUTOPRUEBA**

Give the correct form of **haber.**

INDICATIVE    **1.** yo _____    **2.** Uds. _____    **3.** nosotros _____
SUBJUNCTIVE    **4.** tú _____    **5.** Ud. _____    **6.** ellos _____

*Answers: 1. he 2. han 3. hemos 4. hayas 5. haya 6. hayan*

# PASO 3

**Prác. A: Follow-Up**
Ask students the following questions to personalize the activity. Extend all of the questions with: *¿Qué más ha hecho Ud. hoy / esta semana / este mes?*

1. *¿Qué ha hecho Ud. hoy? ¿Ha hablado con un amigo / una amiga? ¿Ha estudiado? ¿Ha comido?*
2. *¿Qué ha hecho Ud. esta semana? ¿Ha ido a una fiesta? ¿Ha bailado? ¿Ha cantado? ¿Ha tomado Coca-Cola / cerveza / vino? ¿Ha visto una película?*
3. *¿Ha escrito una carta este mes? ¿Ha visitado un museo? ¿Ha salido de la ciudad? ¿Se ha levantado antes de las seis? ¿antes de las cinco? ¿Por qué tan temprano?*
4. *¿Ha depositado dinero en el banco? ¿Ha vendido/comprado algo?*

**Prác. B: Answers**
1. *Le ha pedido ayuda a su padre.* 2. *Ha hecho preguntas acerca de los diferentes coches.* 3. *Ha visto uno bastante barato.* 4. *Ha revisado las llantas.* 5. *Lo ha conducido como prueba.* 6. *Ha regresado a la agencia.* 7. *Ha decidido comprarlo.* 8. *Lo ha comprado.* 9. *Ha vuelto a casa.* 10. *Ha llevado a sus amigas al cine en su coche.*

**Prác. C: Preliminary Exercises**
• Read the following sentences and have students tell whether the present perfect indicative or the present perfect subjunctive is used.

1. *Dice que ha hablado con ella.*
2. *Es posible que haya hablado con ella.*
3. *No, no han repetido las palabras.*
4. *No creo que hayan repetido las palabras.*
5. *Me alegro de que me hayas escrito.*
6. *No vengas a menos que me hayas escrito antes.*

• Have students give the subjunctive equivalents.

| | |
|---|---|
| *he hablado* | *ha venido* |
| *he repetido* | *hemos podido* |
| *has comido* | *hemos alquilado* |
| *has manejado* | *han comprendido* |
| *ha mandado* | *se han acostado* |

### Vocabulario útil

**escalar** (to climb)
**hacer** (*irreg.*) **autostop** (to hitchhike)
**el paracaidismo** (skydiving)

## ■ Práctica

**Prác. A: Suggestion**
Have students report what they have done or not done by saying *ya lo he hecho* or *no lo he hecho todavía.*

### A. El pasado y el futuro

PASO 1 **¡Anticipemos!** Indique las actividades que Ud. ha hecho en el pasado.

1. _____ He hecho un viaje a Europa.
2. _____ He montado a camello (*camel*).
3. _____ He tomado una clase de informática.
4. _____ He buceado (*gone scuba diving*).
5. _____ He ido de safari a África.
6. _____ He comprado un coche.
7. _____ He preparado una comida italiana.
8. _____ He ocupado un puesto (*position*) político.
9. _____ He tenido una mascota.
10. _____ He escrito un poema.
11. _____ He visto una película de Almodóvar.
12. _____ He leído un periódico en español.
13. _____ Me he puesto un sombrero para ir a clase.
14. _____ Me he roto el brazo o la pierna.

PASO 2 Ahora, entre las cosas que Ud. no ha hecho, ¿cuáles le gustaría hacer? Conteste, siguiendo los modelos.

MODELOS: Nunca he montado a camello, pero me gustaría hacerlo.
(Nunca he montado a camello y no me interesa hacerlo.)

### B. El coche de Carmina.
Carmina acaba de comprarse un coche usado. Describa lo que le ha pasado a Carmina, según el modelo.

MODELO: ir a la agencia de compra-venta de coches →
Ha ido a la agencia de compra-venta de coches.

1. pedirle ayuda a su padre
2. hacer preguntas acerca de (*about*) los diferentes coches
3. ver uno bastante barato
4. revisar las llantas
5. conducirlo como prueba
6. regresar a la agencia
7. decidir comprarlo
8. comprarlo
9. volver a casa
10. llevar a sus amigas al cine en su coche

### C. ¡No lo creo!
¿Tienen espíritu aventurero sus compañeros de clase? ¿Llevan una vida interesante? ¿O están tan aburridos como una ostra? ¡A ver!

PASO 1 **¡Anticipemos!** De cada par de oraciones, indique la que (*the one that*) expresa su opinión acerca de los estudiantes de esta clase.

1. ☐ Creo que alguien en esta clase ha visto las pirámides de Egipto.
   ☐ Es dudoso que alguien haya visto las pirámides de Egipto.
2. ☐ Estoy seguro/a de que por lo menos uno de mis compañeros ha escalado una montaña alta.
   ☐ No creo que nadie haya escalado una montaña alta.
3. ☐ Creo que alguien ha viajado haciendo autostop.
   ☐ Dudo que alguien haya hecho autostop en un viaje.
4. ☐ Creo que alguien ha practicado el paracaidismo.
   ☐ Es improbable que alguien haya practicado el paracaidismo.

Prác. C: Follow-Up
Have students suggest other things that they think no one in class has ever
done, for example, *No creo que nadie haya... ; Creo que nadie ha...*

5. ☐ Estoy seguro/a de que alguien ha tomado el metro en Nueva York
a medianoche.
☐ No creo que nadie haya tomado el metro neoyorquino a
medianoche.

PASO 2  Ahora escuche mientras el profesor / la profesora pregunta si
alguien ha hecho estas actividades. ¿Tenía Ud. razón en el **Paso 1**?

**Need more practice?**

- Workbook/Laboratory Manual
- Interactive CD-ROM
- Online Learning Center
  (www.mhhe.com/quetal7)

### ■ Conversación

**A. ¿Verdad o mentira?**

PASO 1  Invente Ud. tres oraciones sobre cosas que ha hecho y no ha hecho
en su vida. Dos oraciones deben ser verdaderas y una debe ser una mentira.

MODELO:  *He hecho* un viaje a Sudamérica.
Nunca *he conocido* a mis primos.
*He visto* muchas películas en español.

PASO 2  Lea sus oraciones a unos compañeros o a la clase entera. Ellos van a
tratar de encontrar la mentira.

MODELO:  Creo que *has hecho* un viaje a Sudamérica y que *has visto*
muchas películas en español. Dudo que no *hayas conocido* a
tus primos.

Con. A: Suggestions
• Model one or two series of sentences about yourself.
• Model some possible reactions to the sentences: (*No*)
*Dudo que..., Es imposible que..., Estoy seguro de
que..., Es obvio que...*

Con. A: Follow-Up
Ask the following questions after completing
the activity.

*¿Qué es posible que hayan hecho las
siguientes personas?*

1. *Un hombre que lleva máscara sale
corriendo de un banco, con una bolsa en
la mano.*
2. *Un joven está saliendo de una lavandería
con un montón de ropa limpia.*

3. *Un sábado de otoño, a
las cuatro y media de la
tarde, muchas personas
están saliendo de un
estadio.*

4. *Unos turistas están hablando ansiosamente
con un policía. La mujer no lleva bolsa.*
5. *Una familia está saliendo de McDonald's.*

---

### NOTA COMUNICATIVA

#### Talking About What You Had Done

Use the past participle with the imperfect form of **haber** (**había, habías,...** ) to talk about what you had—or
had not—done before a given time in the past. This form is called the *past perfect* (**el pluscuamperfecto**).

Antes de graduarme en la escuela secundaria,
no **había estudiado** español.

*Before graduating from high school, I hadn't
studied Spanish.*

Antes de 1985, siempre **habíamos vivido** en Kansas.

*Before 1985, we had always lived in Kansas.*

---

**B. Entrevista.**  Use the following cues to interview a classmate about his
or her activities before coming to this campus.

MODELO:  ¿qué? / no haber aprendido a hacer antes del año pasado →
E1: ¿Qué no *habías aprendido* a hacer antes del año pasado?
E2: Pues... no *había aprendido* a nadar. Aprendí a nadar este año
en mi clase de natación.

1. ¿qué? / no haber aprendido a hacer antes del año pasado
2. ¿qué materia? / no haber estudiado antes del año pasado
3. ¿qué deporte? / haber practicado mucho
4. ¿qué viaje? / haber hecho varias veces
5. ¿qué libro importante? / no haber leído
6. ¿qué decisión? / no haber tomado
7. ¿ ?

Con. B: Follow-Up
Have students describe what they
had already done or not done by
the time they turned 18 years old:
*Antes de cumplir 18 años, ¿qué ha-
bía hecho? ¿Qué no había hecho?*

Nota comunicativa: Suggestion
The past perfect is presented here and practiced
in *Conversación B*. Use
additional activities, such as the following,
if you prefer to stress this tense.

*Jaime es un acusón (tattletale). Siempre le
dice a su madre las cosas que ha hecho
Laura, su hermana mayor. ¿Qué le dijo a
su madre ayer?*
*Jaimito le dijo que Laura **había dicho una
mentira.***

*mirar la televisión toda la tarde
no estudiar
perder sus libros
romper un plato
faltar a clase
comer todo el pastel
pegarlo
¿ ?*

**C. Dos dibujos, un punto de vista.** Un español hizo el dibujo de la izquierda; un argentino, el de la derecha. Pero los dos comentan el mismo tema.

| Palabras útiles | | | |
| --- | --- | --- | --- |
| el arado (plow) | la flor | la mecanización | el tractor |
| la deshumanización | la gente | la mula | |

SÍ, CLARO, MÁS MODERNO, PERO...
¿CON QUIÉN COMENTAS TU VIDA?

© Joaquín Salvador,
Lavado (QUINO),
*Esto no es todo,*
Ediciones de la
Flor, © 2001.

PASO 1  Conteste estas preguntas sobre el dibujo de la izquierda.

1. Describa la ciudad que se ve en el dibujo.
2. ¿Qué ha descubierto la gente? ¿Por qué mira con tanto interés?
3. Para construir esta ciudad, ¿qué han hecho? ¿Qué han destruido?

PASO 2  Conteste estas preguntas sobre el dibujo de la derecha.

1. ¿Qué se ha comprado el agricultor de la izquierda? ¿Qué ha vendido?
2. ¿Qué es «más moderno», según el otro agricultor?
3. ¿Qué desventaja tiene el tractor?

PASO 3  Ahora explique su reacción personal a estos dos dibujos. ¿Son chistosos (*funny*)? ¿serios?

## UN POCO DE TODO

**Lengua y cultura: ¿Glaciares en la Argentina?** Complete the following dialogue and article with the correct forms of the words in parentheses, as suggested by the context. When two possibilities are given in parentheses, select the correct word. **¡OJO!** When **haber** appears in parentheses followed by an infinitive, you will decide whether to use present perfect indicative or subjunctive. You will also need to decide between using present tense indicative or subjunctive with several other infinitives.

En la clase de Geografía mundial, todos los estudiantes se han reunido en grupos de tres para investigar la geografía de uno de los países de Sudamérica. Luego deben hacer una presentación «PowerPoint» con la intención de mostrar(les/los[1]) a sus compañeros de clase lo que el grupo (haber descubrir[2]) del país que seleccionaron. Milton, Marisol y Petra están (tratado/tratando[3]) de terminar su informe sobre la Argentina.

**Multimedia: Internet**
Have students search the Web for information about *la Patagonia, la Pampa,* and *los gauchos.* Then have them present a written or oral report on one of the topics.

MARISOL: Bueno, ya tenemos muchos datos sobre las ciudades argentinas y las famosas Pampas.[a] Es suficiente, ¿no creen Uds.?

MILTON: Creo que sí. Y (yo/me[4]) encanta que (*tú:* haber encontrar[5]) esos artículos que (comparar[6]) históricamente la figura del gaucho con la del «cowboy» del oeste de los Estados Unidos. Y a (tú/ti[7]), ¿qué te (parecer[8]), Petra?

PETRA: Pues, yo no (encontrarse[9]) totalmente satisfecha[b] con la presentación. Sí, sí, estoy de acuerdo en que está muy bien (escrito[10]), pero esa información no tiene (algo/nada[11]) de nuevo. Yo (haber oír[12]) hablar de las Pampas, de los gauchos y de la ciudad de Buenos Aires desde que estaba en la escuela primaria. Quiero que (*nosotros:* presentar[13]) algo diferente, algo menos común…

MARISOL: ¿Qué (*tú:* sugerir[14]), entonces?

PETRA: Miren este párrafo breve que tengo. Es un resumen de un artículo que encontré en el Internet. Sugiero que lo (*nosotros:* poner[15]) al final de la presentación.

MILTON: De acuerdo. Pero quiero que (*nosotros:* entregar[16]) el informe hoy. A ver… ¿qué dice tu párrafo?

*El párrafo:*

Y, finalmente, atención ecoturistas extremistas:

Vengan (a / —[17]) ver el Parque Nacional Los Glaciares, en la Patagonia, en el sur de la Argentina. El gobierno argentino (*P/I,* crear[18]) este parque en 1937, y en 1982 el parque (*P/I,* ser[19]) designado Patrimonio Natural de la Humanidad por la UNESCO. Allí, en las 600.000 hectáreas[c] del parque, pueden explorar unos glaciares (impresionante[20]). Se calcula que aproximadamente 200 de esos glaciares (salir[21]) de los campos de hielo[d] que dominan este parque. Con (alguno[22]) precauciones, es posible que los ecoturistas aventureros (escalar[23])[e] unas montañas de hielo precipitosas como el Cerro Torre, un desafío[f] para los mejores alpinistas profesionales. Es fascinante encontrar una geografía tan variada dentro de un solo país.

[a]*grassy plains of Argentina*  [b]*satisfied*  [c]*hectares (2.47 acres)*  [d]*campos… ice fields*  [e]*to climb*  [f]*challenge*

## Comprensión: ¿Cierto o falso? Corrija las oraciones falsas.

1. Todos los estudiantes de la clase de Geografía mundial van a preparar un informe sobre la Argentina.
2. Milton, Marisol y Petra necesitan empezar su informe sobre la Argentina.
3. Marisol ha encontrado unos artículos sobre el gaucho y el «cowboy».
4. Petra no está contenta porque dice que la información es incorrecta.
5. Petra les trae un párrafo que ella ha escrito con información que encontró en el Internet.
6. El Parque Nacional Los Glaciares es un pequeño parque al sur de Buenos Aires.

*Un turista en el Parque Nacional Los Glaciares, Argentina*

**Lengua y cultura: Answers**
1. *les* 2. *ha descubierto* 3. *tratando* 4. *me*
5. *hayas encontrado* 6. *comparan* 7. *ti*
8. *parece* 9. *me encuentro* 10. *escrita*
11. *nada* 12. *he oído* 13. *presentemos*
14. *sugieres* 15. *pongamos* 16. *entreguemos*
17. *a* 18. *creó* 19. *fue* 20. *impresionantes*
21. *salen* 22. *algunas* 23. *escalen*
*Comprensión* 1. *falso: Los estudiantes de la clase de Geografía mundial van a preparar un informe sobre el país que seleccionaron.* 2. *falso: Milton, Marisol y Petra están terminando su informe sobre la Argentina.* 3. *cierto* 4. *falso: Petra no está contenta porque dice que la información no tiene nada de nuevo.* 5. *cierto* 6. *falso: El Parque Nacional Los Glaciares es un parque muy grande en el sur de la Argentina.*

**Resources: Desenlace**
In the *Capítulo 14* segment of "Chapter-by-Chapter Supplementary Materials" in the IM, you will find a chapter-culminating activity. You can use this activity to consolidate and review the vocabulary and grammar skills students have acquired.

**Resources for Review and Testing Preparation**

- Workbook/Laboratory Manual
- Interactive CD-ROM
- Online Learning Center (www.mhhe.com/quetal7)

**Paso 4: Un paso más**
- The *Paso 4: Un paso más* sections are optional.
- See the "Chapter-by-Chapter Supplementary Materials" in the IM for additional teaching suggestions, notes, activities, and other resources for *Paso 4.*

**Entrevista cultural: Suggestions**
- Before showing the video, ask students questions about organizations they support or belong to.

  *¿Es Ud. miembro/a de alguna asociación u organización en la universidad? ¿Cómo se llama y por qué existe?*

  *¿Tienen el grupo algún proyecto filantrópico?*

  *¿Cuándo se reúnen los miembros del grupo?*

  *¿Participa Ud. en alguna asociación o actividad ecológica? ¿Qué hace? ¿Cuántas personas participan?*

  *¿Qué hace Ud. individualmente para preservar la ecología y los recursos naturales?*

- Show the video and allow students one to two minutes to work on the questions. Have volunteers answer the questions.
- Have volunteers role-play Natalia and her interviewer.

**Entrevista cultural: Answers**
*Possible answers:*
1. *en Buenos Aires* 2. *en ciencias biológicas* 3. *Se preocupan mucho.* 4. *Pueden participar en una organización o programa.* 5. *Es una zona extensa pero poco poblada en el sur de la Argentina.*

**Entre amigos: Suggestions**
- Before viewing the video, review the questions with the students and ask them similar questions.

  *¿Tiene Ud. coche? ¿Qué tipo de coche es? ¿Es grande o pequeño?*

  *Si Ud. no tiene coche, ¿cómo llega a clase y/o al trabajo?*

  *¿Maneja Ud. el coche todos los días? ¿Cuándo usa el transporte público?*

  Have students answer or work in small groups to ask and answer these questions.

- After viewing the video, have volunteers read and answer the questions.

## VIDEOTECA

### Entrevista cultural: La Argentina

Natalia D'Ángelo es una estudiante de la Argentina. Habla de sus estudios, pero se enfoca en el medio ambiente. Antes de ver el vídeo, lea el siguiente fragmento de la entrevista.

ENTREVISTADORA: ¿Perteneces tú[a] a alguna asociación?

NATALIA: En la universidad estamos trabajando en una asociación para proteger la biodiversidad de una zona de la Argentina que se llama la Patagonia.

ENTREVISTADORA: ¿Nos puedes hablar un poco más sobre la Patagonia?

NATALIA: Sí, la Patagonia es un territorio muy extenso que es todo el sur de Argentina y es una zona muy poco poblada, con actividades que están centradas principalmente en la pesca[b] y en el turismo.

[a]Perteneces… *Do you belong*  [b]*fishing*

Ahora vea el vídeo y conteste las siguientes preguntas, basándose en la entrevista.

1. ¿Dónde estudia Natalia?
2. ¿En qué se especializa?
3. Según Natalia, ¿se preocupan mucho o poco los estudiantes por los problemas ecológicos?
4. ¿Cómo pueden participar los estudiantes en actividades ecológicas?
5. ¿Qué es la Patagonia?

### Entre amigos: Nuestro pequeño grano de arena (*grain of sand*)

Miguel, Tané, Rubén y Karina hablan del medio ambiente. En su opinión, ¿qué preguntas se van a hacer? Antes de mirar el vídeo, lea las preguntas a continuación. Mientras mire el vídeo, trate de entender la conversación en general y fíjese en la información sobre la ecología, la naturaleza y el medio ambiente. Luego mire el vídeo una segunda vez, fijándose en la información que necesita para contestar las preguntas.

1. ¿Qué tipo de coche está manejando Miguel?
2. ¿Por qué no tiene Miguel su propio (*own*) coche?
3. ¿Qué tipo de coche tiene Karina?
4. ¿Cómo sugiere Karina cuidar el medio ambiente?
5. ¿Qué opinión tiene Rubén de las fábricas?

**Entre amigos: Answers**
*Possible answers:* 1. *un coche de pedales* 2. *No quiere contaminar la ciudad.* 3. *una camioneta* 4. *no tirar la basura al piso* (*suelo*) 5. *Tiran desperdicios al medio ambiente.*

## ENFOQUE CULTURAL

### La Argentina

Notes
• Sosa has a beautiful and deep contralto voice that enhances the dramatic effect of her music.
• Sosa's nickname is *La Negra*, a name given to her due to her jet black hair.
• Sosa was searched and arrested on stage at a concert in La Plata in 1979. The crowd attending the concert was also arrested. Sosa lived in exile in Paris and Madrid until 1982.

### ¡Fíjese!

• La inmigración de europeos en el siglo XIX ha tenido un papel decisivo en la formación de la población de la Argentina (así como en la del Uruguay). En 1856 la población argentina era de 1.200.000 habitantes; para 1930, 10.500.000 extranjeros habían entrado en la Argentina por el puerto[a] de Buenos Aires. La mitad[b] estaba formada por italianos, una tercera parte por españoles, y el resto estaba formado principal-mente por alemanes y eslavos. Muchos de los que llegaron fueron trabajadores temporales que, tarde o temprano, regresaron a Europa. El resto, sin embargo, se estableció permanente-mente, porque el gobierno quería estimular la inmigración para poblar la Pampa. Pero mu-chos, acostumbrados a la vida urbana, se que-daron en Buenos Aires.

• Buenos Aires es una ciudad con una población de más de 13.000.000 de habitantes, lo cual supone[c] el 30 por ciento de la población del país. Es el centro cultural, comercial, industrial y financiero, así como el puerto principal de la Argentina. A las personas de Buenos Aires se les llama «porteños», derivado de la palabra «puerto».

[a]*port*  [b]*half*  [c]*lo… which constitutes*

### Personas famosas: Mercedes Sosa

Mercedes Sosa (1935– ) es probablemente la cantante argentina más conocida del mundo. Es también una de las figuras más prominentes del canto nuevo, una forma de música de protesta que surgió[a] en la Argentina en los años 60 y se hizo muy popular en otras partes de Latinoamérica. Hace unos cuarenta años que[b] Sosa canta,[c] sola y con otros artistas, en su país y en todos los continentes. Ha grabado[d] más de treinta discos y sus conciertos son muy concurridos.[e] Sosa tiene una voz fuerte y dramática y su repertorio incluye canciones folklóricas de la Argentina y toda Latinoamérica. Las canciones pueden ser alegres o trágicas, pero siempre son bellas y conmovedoras.[f] De 1979 a 1982, años de un régimen dictatorial en la Argentina, Sosa vivió en el exilio, porque el gobierno argentino no la permitía cantar en la Argentina. Pero volvió, triunfante, en 1982.

[a]*sprang up*  [b]*Hace… For some forty years*  [c]*has been singing*  [d]*recorded*
[e]*well attended*  [f]*moving*

*La Plaza de Mayo, que data de 1580, año de la fundación de Buenos Aires*

• Students can read an excerpt of the poem *"Cuadrados y ángulos"* by Argentina's Alfonsina Storni in *Voces de la Argentina: Literatura.*
• Students can read about Argentina's *tango* in *Voces de la Argentina: Música.*
• Students can read more about *el canto nuevo* in *Capítulo 15, Voces de Chile: Música.*
• See the Workbook/Laboratory Manual for focused practice with the material in *Enfoque cultural.*

Learn more about Argentina with the Video, the Interactive CD-ROM, and the Online Learning Center (www.mhhe.com/quetal7).

## PASO FINAL

## A CONVERSAR

### ¿Somos buenos o malos conductores?

PASO 1   Con un compañero / una compañera, haga y conteste preguntas basadas en el siguiente cuadro. Utilice el presente perfecto en sus preguntas y respuestas y marque el cuadro según las respuestas de su compañero/a. También añada (*add*) al cuadro otro problema relacionado con los coches.

> MODELO:   E1: ¿Has superado (*Have you exceeded*) el límite de velocidad recientemente?
>
> E2: Sí, (No, no) he superado el límite de velocidad recientemente.

|  | sí | no |
|---|---|---|
| **chocar con otro coche** | | |
| **superar el límite de velocidad** | | |
| **pasarse (*to run*) un semáforo en rojo** | | |
| **desobedecerle a un policía** | | |
| **¿ ?** | | |

PASO 2   Ahora, entre todos, hablen de sus compañeros/as. En general, ¿son Uds. buenos o malos conductores? Deben marcar la información en un cuadro como el del **Paso 1.** Incluyan los problemas que añadieron al cuadro.

> MODELOS:   ¿Quiénes han chocado con otro coche recientemente? →
> Tom ha chocado con otro coche este mes.

PASO 3   Calculen el porcentaje de personas que contestaron **sí** a cada pregunta del **Paso 1.** Reaccionen a los porcentajes con las siguientes frases. **¡OJO!** Las frases requieren el uso del subjuntivo.

> Es bueno/malo que…
> Me alegra / No me alegra que…
> Me sorprende que / No me sorprende que…

> MODELO:   Siete de veintiún estudiantes han superado recientemente el límite de velocidad. → El 33 por ciento de la clase ha superado recientemente el límite de velocidad.
>
> E1: No me sorprende que el 33 por ciento de la clase haya superado el límite de velocidad.

**Suggestions**
• Bring or have students bring magazine clippings of images related to the vocabulary words. Use the images for quick comprehension checks (*¿Qué es eso?* → *Es una llanta desinflada.*) and as a springboard for questions and short discussions.

• Remind students that *conducir* and *obedecer* are conjugated like *conocer*, with a *-zc-* in the first person singular: *conduzco, obedezco.* They should also remember the spelling changes for *construir* (*y*), *destruir* (*y*), *proteger* (*j*), *arrancar* (*qu*), *chocar* (*qu*), and *seguir* (*g*).

## GRAMÁTICA

To review the grammar points presented in this chapter, refer to the indicated grammar presentations. You'll find further practice of these structures in the Workbook/Laboratory Manual, on the Interactive CD-ROM, and on the *¿Qué tal?* Online Learning Center (www.mhhe.com/quetal7).

**38** **Más descripciones**—Past Participle Used As an Adjective

Do you know how to form past participles? You should remember that past participles that are used as adjectives agree with the noun they describe.

**39** **¿Qué has hecho?**—Perfect Forms: Present Perfect Indicative and Present Perfect Subjunctive

How do you express that you have done something? Do you know how to say that you're happy or sad that someone else did or has done something?

## VOCABULARIO

Practice this vocabulary with digital flash cards on the Online Learning Center (www.mhhe.com/quetal7).

### Los verbos

| | |
|---|---|
| cubrir | to cover |
| descubrir | to discover |
| evitar | to avoid |
| resolver (ue) | to solve, resolve |

### El medio ambiente

| | |
|---|---|
| la escasez (*pl.* escaseces) | lack; shortage |
| la fábrica | factory |
| el gobierno | government |
| el medio ambiente | environment (*natural*) |
| la naturaleza | nature |
| la población | population |
| los recursos naturales | natural resources |

Cognados: el aire, la energía eléctrica (nuclear, solar)
Repaso: la contaminación, la falta

| | |
|---|---|
| acabar | to run out (of), use up completely |
| conservar | to save, conserve |
| construir (y) | to build |
| contaminar | to pollute |
| desarrollar | to develop |
| destruir (y) | to destroy |
| proteger (j) | to protect |
| reciclar | to recycle |

### ¿La ciudad o el campo?

| | |
|---|---|
| el/la agricultor(a) | farmer |
| el/la campesino/a | farm worker; peasant |
| el campo | countryside; field |
| el delito | crime |
| la finca | farm |
| el rascacielos | skyscraper |
| el ritmo | rhythm, pace |
| el transporte | (means of) transportation |

Cognados: el servicio, la violencia
Repaso: la ciudad, la vida

### Los animales

| | |
|---|---|
| el animal doméstico | domesticated animal; pet |
| el animal salvaje | wild animal |
| la ballena | whale |
| el caballo | horse |
| la especie (en peligro de extinción) | (endangered) species |
| el pez (*pl.* peces) | fish |
| el toro | bull |
| la vaca | cow |

Cognados: el elefante, el gorila

## El paisaje

| | |
|---|---|
| el árbol | tree |
| el bosque | forest |
| el lago | lake |
| el paisaje | countryside |
| el río | river |

Repaso: la montaña

## Los coches

| | |
|---|---|
| el aceite | oil |
| la estación de gasolina | gas station |
| los frenos | brakes |
| la gasolinera | gas station |
| la llanta (desinflada) | (flat) tire |
| el/la mecánico/a | mechanic |
| el nivel | level |
| el parabrisas | windshield |
| el taller | (repair) shop |
| el tanque | tank |

Cognados: la batería, la gasolina
Repaso: la camioneta, el carro, el coche

| | |
|---|---|
| arrancar (qu) | to start up (*a car*) |
| gastar | to use (*gas*) |
| llenar | to fill (up) |
| revisar | to check |

Repaso: arreglar

## En el camino

| | |
|---|---|
| la autopista | freeway |
| el camino | street; road |

| | |
|---|---|
| la carretera | highway |
| la circulación | traffic |
| el/la conductor(a) | driver |
| la esquina | (street) corner |
| la licencia de manejar/conducir | driver's license |
| el límite de velocidad | speed limit |
| el/la policía | police officer |
| el semáforo | traffic signal |
| el tránsito | traffic |

Repaso: la calle

| | |
|---|---|
| chocar (qu) (con) | to run into, collide (with) |
| conducir (zc) | to drive |
| doblar | to turn |
| obedecer (zc) | to obey |
| parar | to stop |
| seguir (i, i) (g) | to keep on going; to go; to continue |

Repaso: estacionar, manejar

| | |
|---|---|
| todo derecho | straight ahead |

## Los adjetivos

| | |
|---|---|
| acelerado/a | fast, accelerated |
| bello/a | beautiful |
| puro/a | clean; pure |

Cognados: denso/a, público/a

# La vida social y la vida afectiva°

°emotional

*Unos novios en el Parque Forestal de Santiago, Chile*

**Suggestions**
- Point out the chapter-opener photo. Have students talk about places that young couples meet in this country. Do they go to parks together? If not, where? Have students describe the park in the photo. What might draw couples to the park?

• Have students list their ideas about Chile, including information on geography, politics, economy, culture, music, and cuisine. When you finish the chapter, return to the lists and ask students what ideas they would change and/or add.

**Paso 1: Vocabulario**
See the "Chapter-by-Chapter Supplementary Materials" in the IM for a model for vocabulary presentation, as well as additional teaching suggestions, notes, activities, and other resources for *Paso 1*.

## LAS RELACIONES SENTIMENTALES

**Resources: Transparencies 91, 92, 14**
Transparency 92 provides additional images and vocabulary. Use Transparency 14 from Capítulo 2 (family tree) to practice new vocabulary.

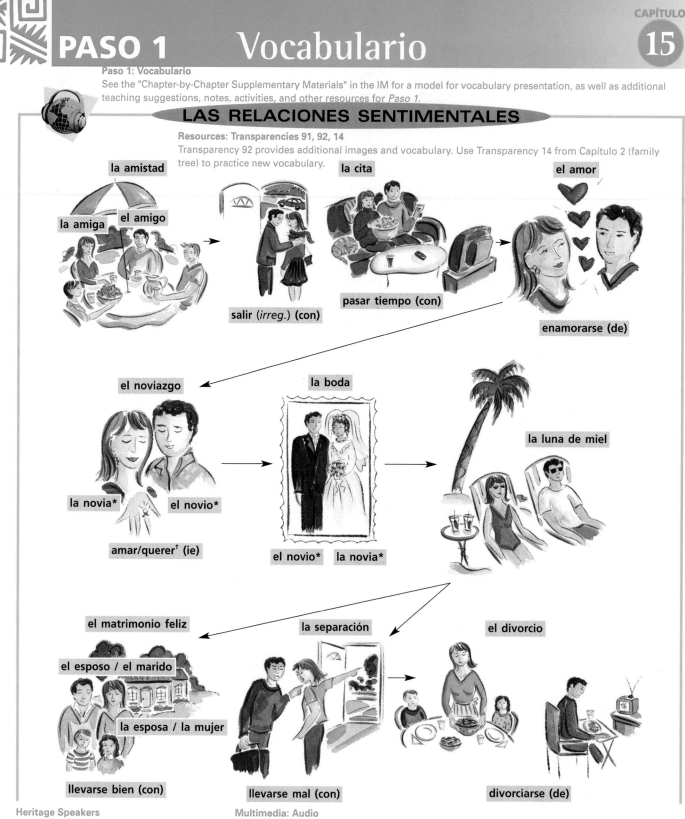

la amistad

la amiga el amigo

la cita

el amor

salir (*irreg.*) (con)

pasar tiempo (con)

enamorarse (de)

el noviazgo

la boda

la luna de miel

la novia* el novio*

amar/querer† (ie)

el novio* la novia*

el matrimonio feliz

la separación

el divorcio

el esposo / el marido

la esposa / la mujer

llevarse bien (con)

llevarse mal (con)

divorciarse (de)

**Heritage Speakers**
Pídales a los hispanohablantes que hablen de la importancia de las relaciones entre familiares y amigos y las diferencias y semejanzas entre los hispanos y los no hispanos en cuanto a la familia.

**Multimedia: Audio**
Students can listen to and practice this chapter's vocabulary on the Online Learning Center (**www.mhhe.com/quetal7**), as well as on the Textbook Audio CD, part of the Laboratory Audio Program.

---

*El novio / La novia *can mean* boyfriend/girlfriend, fiancé(e), *or* groom/bride.
†Amar *and* querer *both mean* to love, *but* amar *can imply more passion in some dialects.*

| | | | |
|---|---|---|---|
| **la pareja** | (married) couple; partner | **amistoso/a** | friendly |
| **el/la viudo/a** | widower/widow | **cariñoso/a** | affectionate |
| | | **casado/a\* (con)** | married (to) |
| **casarse (con)** | to marry | **divorciado/a (de)** | divorced (from) |
| **pelear (con)** | to fight (with) | **enamorado/a† (de)** | in love (with) |
| **romper (con)** | to break up (with) | **recién casado/a (con)** | newlywed (to) |
| **separarse (de)** | to separate (from) | **soltero/a\*** | single, not married |

## ■ Conversación

**A. Definiciones.** Empareje las palabras con sus definiciones. Luego, para cada palabra definida, dé un verbo y también el nombre de una persona asociada con esa relación social. Hay más de una respuesta posible en cada caso.

1. __e__ el matrimonio
2. __c__ el amor
3. __b__ el divorcio
4. __d__ la boda
5. __a__ la amistad

**a.** Es una relación cariñosa entre dos personas. Se llevan bien y se hablan con frecuencia.

**b.** Es el posible resultado de un matrimonio, cuando los esposos no se llevan bien.

**c.** Es una relación sentimental, apasionada, muy especial, entre dos personas. Puede llevar al (*lead to*) matrimonio.

**d.** Es una ceremonia religiosa o civil en la que (*which*) la novia a veces lleva un vestido blanco.

**e.** Es una relación legal entre dos personas que viven juntas (*together*) y que a veces tienen hijos.

**B. ¡Seamos lógicos!** Complete las oraciones lógicamente.

1. Mi abuelo es el __esposo__ de mi abuela.
2. Muchos novios tienen un largo __noviazgo__ antes de la boda.
3. María y Julio tienen una __cita__ el viernes para comer en un restaurante. Luego van a bailar.
4. La __boda__ de Juan y Pati es el domingo a las dos de la tarde, en la iglesia (*church*) de San Martín.
5. En una __cita__, ¿quién debe comprar los boletos, el hombre o la mujer?
6. La __amistad__ entre los ex esposos es imposible. No pueden ser amigos.
7. ¡El __amor__ es ciego (*blind*)!
8. Para algunas personas, el __matrimonio__ es un concepto anticuado. Prefieren vivir juntos, sin casarse.
9. Algunas parejas modernas no quieren gastar su dinero en una __luna de miel__.
10. ¿Cree Ud. que es posible el __amor__ a primera vista (*at first sight*)?

**Suggestions**

- Remind students that the first person singular of *salir* is *salgo*.
- Remind students that *to have a good time* cannot be translated directly from English to Spanish. The correct verb is *divertirse*.
- Ask students the following questions to check comprehension and personalize the vocabulary.

1. *¿Qué palabras asocia Ud. con la amistad? ¿el amor? ¿una boda? ¿la luna de miel? ¿el novio? ¿la esposa?*

♻ 2. *¿Cómo es el novio / la novia ideal? ¿Es rubio/a o moreno/a? ¿joven o viejo/a? ¿alto/a o bajo/a? ¿guapo/a o feo/a? ¿trabajador(a) o perezoso/a? ¿romántico/a (cariñoso/a) o frío/a?*

3. *¿Pasa Ud. mucho tiempo con sus amigos? ¿Qué hacen? ¿Siempre se llevan bien?*

4. *¿Sus amigos tienen los mismos intereses que Ud.?*

5. *¿Cree que un matrimonio debe tener intereses parecidos? ¿Es importante que los esposos sean amigos?*

6. *¿Cuál es la edad ideal para casarse?*

**Con. A: Follow-Up**

Have students react to the following statements using *estoy de acuerdo* and *no estoy de acuerdo*.

1. *El matrimonio (La luna de miel) es un concepto muy anticuado.*
2. *Si el noviazgo es corto, el matrimonio va a ser corto también.*
3. *Las mujeres son más románticas que los hombres.*
4. *El noviazgo debe ser largo y formal.*
5. *El matrimonio es una obligación social necesaria.*

---

\*In the activities of **Capítulo 2,** *you began to use* **ser casado/a.** *A variation of this phrase is* **estar casado/a.** **Estar casado/a** *means* to be married; **ser casado/a** *means* to be a married person. **Ser soltero/a** *is used exclusively to describe an unmarried person.*

†**(Mi) Enamorado/a** *can also mean* (my) boyfriend/girlfriend.

# PASO 1

**Refrán**

«La vida es la novia de la muerte.»

Have students talk about this *refrán*. Is there any English equivalent? (*Life and death are but two sides of the same coin.*) What are some other English sayings about life and death? (*Nothing is certain but death and taxes. The best things in life are free.*)

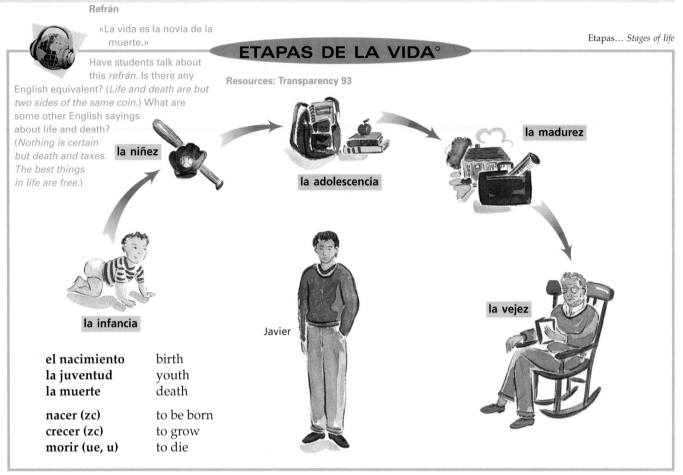

## ETAPAS DE LA VIDA°

Etapas... *Stages of life*

Resources: Transparency 93

la niñez

la adolescencia

la madurez

la infancia

Javier

la vejez

| | |
|---|---|
| **el nacimiento** | birth |
| **la juventud** | youth |
| **la muerte** | death |
| **nacer (zc)** | to be born |
| **crecer (zc)** | to grow |
| **morir (ue, u)** | to die |

## NOTA CULTURAL

### ¿Amigos, novios, prometidos… ?

Dos palabras españolas que no tienen equivalente exacto en inglés son **amigo** y **novio.** En el mundo hispánico la palabra «amigo» se usa casi exclusivamente para indicar una relación de amistad fraternal. Normalmente no tiene ninguna connotación romántica. Palabras como **mi pareja, mi enamorado/a** y **mi chico/a** denotan una relación romántica entre dos personas y, por lo tanto, son equivalentes a *boyfriend/girlfriend.* En la mayoría de los países sólo se usan las palabras **novio/a** y **prometido/a** después de formalizarse las relaciones y hacer planes para contraer matrimonio.

*Unos novios en Chile*

| *friend* | *girlfriend/boyfriend* | *fiancée/fiancé* | *bride/groom* |
|---|---|---|---|

amiga / amigo

novia / novio

**Nota cultural: Comprensión**
1. *¿Qué palabra indica relaciones más serias, amigo o boyfriend?*
2. *¿Qué palabras se usan después de un noviazgo?*

**Nota cultural: Suggestions**
• Provide some common terms of endearment such as *mi amor(cito/a), mi vida,*

*cielo, viejo/a, gordo/a* (Sp.) and *negro/a* (Venezuela). Remind students that terms like the last three have nothing to do with a person's age, weight, or skin color.
• Point out that a common word to refer to a live-in significant other is *compañero/a.*

**Heritage Speakers**
Pídales a los hispanohablantes que den otras expresiones de cariño que usan. Pregúnteles con quién(es) las usan y en qué circunstancias.

*Capítulo 15 • La vida social y la vida afectiva*

## ■ Conversación

**A. Etapas de la vida.** Relacione las siguientes palabras y frases con las distintas etapas de la vida de una persona. **¡OJO!** Hay más de una posible relación en algunos casos.

1. el amor
2. los nietos
3. los juguetes (*toys*)
4. no poder comer sin ayuda
5. los hijos en la universidad
6. los granos (*pimples*)
7. la universidad
8. la boda

**B. Entrevista**

1. ¿Son bastante (*rather*) importantes en tu vida los amigos? ¿Quién es tu mejor amigo/a? ¿En qué año lo/la conociste? ¿Crecieron Uds. juntos/as? Es decir, ¿se han conocido desde la niñez? ¿desde la adolescencia? ¿Por qué te llevas bien con esa persona?

2. ¿Quieres casarte algún día? (¿Ya te casaste?) ¿Te gusta la idea de tener una boda grande? (¿Tuviste una boda grande?) ¿Piensas hacer un viaje de luna de miel? (¿Hiciste un viaje de luna de miel?) ¿Adónde?

3. ¿Qué es lo bueno de estar casado? ¿y lo malo? ¿Qué es lo bueno de ser soltero? ¿y lo malo?

4. ¿En qué década del siglo (*century*) pasado naciste? ¿Has visto muchos cambios desde entonces (*then*)? ¿Cuáles son? ¿Cómo piensas pasar tu vejez? (Si ya eres una persona madura, ¿cómo pasas tu tiempo?)

5. ¿Has sido afectado/a personalmente por la muerte de alguien? ¿Quién murió? ¿Cómo te sentiste? ¿Tienes buenos recuerdos (*memories*) de esa persona? ¿Cuáles son?

**C. Una receta para unas buenas relaciones.** Piense en su propio (*own*) matrimonio o en el de sus padres / unos amigos. O, si lo prefiere, piense en sus relaciones con su mejor amigo/a o en las de un par de amigos que Ud. tiene. En su opinión, ¿cuáles son los ingredientes necesarios para un buen matrimonio o una buena amistad?

PASO 1  Haga una lista de los cinco ingredientes más esenciales. Los ingredientes pueden expresarse con una palabra o una frase.

PASO 2  Compare su lista con las de otros tres estudiantes. ¿Coinciden en la selección de algunos ingredientes? Hablen de todos los ingredientes y hagan una lista de los cinco más importantes.

PASO 3  Ahora comparen los resultados de todos los grupos. ¿Han contestado todos más o menos de la misma manera?

**Con. A: Extension**
  9. *dos coches y un perro*
 10. *pasarlo bien*
 11. *los amigos íntimos*
 12. *un coche con cuatro puertas*

**Con. B: Suggestions**
• If done as a whole-class activity, have volunteers answer or offer opinions. Some students may find these questions too personal.
• For item 5, introduce and discuss the concept of *el luto* (mourning), observed by older Hispanics.

**Con. A: Answers**
*Possible answers:*  **1.** *la adolescencia, la juventud* **2.** *la vejez* **3.** *la niñez* **4.** *la infancia, la vejez* **5.** *la madurez* **6.** *la adolescencia, la juventud* **7.** *la juventud* **8.** *la juventud, la madurez*

**Need more practice?**

■ Workbook/Laboratory Manual
■ Interactive CD-ROM
■ Online Learning Center
  (www.mhhe.com/quetal7)

**Note**
See the Workbook/Laboratory Manual for review and practice of cognates.

Paso 2: Gramática
See the "Chapter-by-Chapter Supplementary Materials" in the IM for additional
teaching suggestions, notes, activities, and other resources for *Paso 2*.

## ¿Recuerda Ud.?

Before studying **Gramática 40,** review the indefinite and negative words that you learned in **Capítulo 6.**
Remember that **alguien** and **nadie** take the personal **a** when they are used as direct objects.

Busco **a alguien** de la familia.     *I'm looking for someone from the family.*
**No** veo **a nadie** en el salón de baile.     *I don't see anyone in the dance hall.*

Give the opposite of the following words. **1.** nada **2.** algunos **3.** alguien

## 40   ¿Hay alguien que... ? ¿Hay un lugar donde... ? Subjunctive
### After Nonexistent and Indefinite Antecedents

Follow-Up       2. *Un padre / Una madre ideal es una persona que...*
• Have students complete the following sentences.
**Un buen lunes**       • Ask the following questions.
      1. *Mi padre/madre es una persona que...*

*Los lunes por la mañana, ¿hay algo
que lo/la haga feliz? ¿que lo/la haga
sonreír?*
*¿Y los viernes por la mañana? ¿los
domingos por la mañana?*

Help students with negative answers.

*No, no hay nada que me haga sonreír.*
© Joaquín Salvador Lavado
(QUINO), *Toda Mafalda,*
Ediciones de la Flor © 1993

ªeres

Mafalda tiene un padre que la quiere, la protege y que pasa mucho tiempo con ella. Por eso, Mafalda ve a
su padre como un hombre que ahora es más guapo que cuando era joven. Todos los niños *necesitan padres
que los quieran, los cuiden y que pasen* tiempo con ellos.

### Comprensión

¿Quién lo dice o piensa, el padre de Mafalda u otro pasajero en el autobús?    Suggestion
Review noun clauses and the use of

  **1.** No hay nadie en este autobús que sea más feliz que yo.    el padre    the subjunctive in them before introducing adjective clauses.
  **2.** Tengo una hija que es una maravilla, ¿verdad?    el padre
  **3.** En camino al trabajo no hay nada que me haga sonreír.    otro pasajero

Emphasis A: Suggestion
Emphasize and model the relationship between adjectives and

**A.** In English and Spanish, statements or questions
that give or ask for information about a person,
place, thing, or idea often contain two clauses.

    Each of the example sentences contains a
main clause (*I have a car; Is there a house for sale*).
In addition, each sentence also has a subordinate
clause (*that gets good mileage; that is closer to the
city*) that modifies a noun in the main clause: *car,
house.*

adjective clauses (to modify a noun), for example, *Veo una casa
blanca / que tiene ventanas.* Draw parallels with noun clauses and
their relationship to nouns.

I have a **car** *that gets good mileage.*
Is there a **house** for sale *that is closer to the city?*

    *A good Monday*    *Mafalda has a father who loves her, protects her, and spends a lot of time with her. That's
why Mafalda sees her father as a man who is now more handsome than when he was young. All children
need parents who love them, take care of them, and spend time with them.*

The noun (or pronoun) modified is called the *antecedent* (**el antecedente**) of the subordinate clause, and the clause itself is called an adjective clause because—like an adjective—it modifies a noun (or pronoun).

**Bright Idea Suggestions**
• As a class, briefly review the formation and uses of the subjunctive.

**B.** Sometimes the antecedent of an adjective clause is something that, in the speaker's mind, does not exist or whose existence is indefinite or uncertain.

• At this point, students should be able to identify independent and dependent clauses, as well as expressions of (1) influence, (2) emotion and feeling, and (3) doubt and denial, which require the use of the subjunctive in the dependent clause.

In these cases, the subjunctive must be used in the adjective (subordinate) clause in Spanish.

Note in the examples that adjective clauses that describe a place can be introduced with **donde...** as well as with **que...**

**Emphasis B: Suggestions**
• Give students the following formulas and models to help them conceptualize the use of subjunctive with adjective clauses.

  1. experience = knowledge of the existence of the object qualified
  2. + subjunctive = − experience: *Quiero salir con un muchacho que tenga interés en la política internacional.* (*No lo conozco todavía.*)
  3. − subjunctive = + experience: *Quiero salir con un muchacho que tiene interés en la política internacional.* (*Ya lo conozco.*)

• Relate the uses of the subjunctive in adjective clauses to the general use of the subjunctive to express conceptualized states/actions.
• Emphasize and model the use of *donde* to introduce the adjective clause: *Queremos trabajar en una ciudad donde haya una comunidad intercultural. Viven en un barrio donde los niños pueden jugar en la calle.*

**OJO**
The dependent adjective clause structure is often used in questions to find out about someone or something the speaker does not know much about. Note, however, that the indicative is used to answer the question if the antecedent is known to the person who answers.

**OJO**
The personal **a** is not used with direct object nouns that refer to hypothetical persons. Compare the use of the indicative and the subjunctive in the sentences at the right.

• Model, in brief exchanges with students, more examples of the question/answer series noted in the first ¡**OJO**! box.

*¿Hay estudiantes en esta clase que tengan hijos?* →
*No, no hay ningún estudiante en esta clase que tenga hijos.*
*Sí, hay un (dos) estudiante(s) en esta clase que tienen hijos.*
*¿Hay profesores en esta universidad que vivan en residencias estudiantiles?* →

---

**antecedent** = the word, noun, or phrase referred to by a pronoun or clause

NONEXISTENT ANTECEDENT

There is *nothing* that you can do.

INDEFINITE ANTECEDENT

We need *a car* that will last us for years. (We don't have one yet.)

EXISTENT ANTECEDENT

**Hay algo** aquí que me **interesa.**
*There is something here that interests me.*

NONEXISTENT ANTECEDENT

**No veo nada** que me **interese.**
*I don't see anything that interests me.*

DEFINITE ANTECEDENT

**Hay muchos restaurantes** donde **sirven** comida mexicana auténtica.
*There are a lot of restaurants where they serve authentic Mexican food.*

INDEFINITE ANTECEDENT

**Buscamos un restaurante** donde **sirvan** comida chilena auténtica.
*We're looking for a restaurant where they serve authentic Chilean food.*

INDEFINITE ANTECEDENT

**¿Hay algo** aquí que te **guste?**
*Is there anything here that you like?*

DEFINITE ANTECEDENT

Sí, **hay varias bolsas** que me **gustan.**
*Yes, there are several purses that I like.*

NONEXISTENT ANTECEDENT

Busco **un señor** que **sepa** francés.
*I'm looking for a man who knows French.*

EXISTENT ANTECEDENT

Busco **al señor** que **sabe** francés.
*I'm looking for the man who knows French.*

*No, no hay ningún profesor en esta universidad que viva en una residencia estudiantil.*
*Sí, hay profesores en esta universidad que viven en residencias estudiantiles.*

---

*Paso 2   Gramática*

# PASO 2

**Prác. A: Extension**

• Ask students: *¿Tiene parientes que hagan algo «especial»? Descríbalos.*

• Give students one minute to form a question about some unusual activity they like, then have them ask the class if anyone else shares their hobby.

**Refranes**

«No hay mal que cien años dure ni médico que lo cure.»
«No hay mal que por bien no venga.»

Write the *refranes* on the board and review the possible English equivalents (*Every cloud has a silver lining.*). Then point out that there are still more renditions of this saying, such as «*No hay mal que dure cien años, ni hombre que lo aguante*» and «*No hay mal que dure cien años, ni médico que lo cure, ni medicina en botica*». Ask students if they can think of sayings in English that have several different versions.

**Need more practice?**

■ Workbook/Laboratory Manual
■ Interactive CD-ROM
■ Online Learning Center (www.mhhe.com/quetal7)

## ■ Práctica

**A. ¡Anticipemos! Hablando de gente que conocemos.** En su familia, ¿hay personas que tengan las siguientes características? Indique la oración apropiada en cada par de oraciones.

TENGO UN PARIENTE…

1. ☐ que habla alemán.
2. ☐ que vive en el extranjero.
3. ☐ que es dueño de un restaurante.
4. ☐ que sabe tocar el piano.
5. ☐ que es médico/a.
6. ☐ que se lleva mal conmigo.
7. ☐ que está divorciado/a.
8. ☐ que trabaja en la televisión.
9. ☐ que es viudo/a.
10. ☐ que se casa este año.

NO TENGO NINGÚN PARIENTE…

☐ que hable alemán.
☐ que viva en el extranjero.
☐ que sea dueño de un restaurante.
☐ que sepa tocar el piano.
☐ que sea médico/a.
☐ que se lleve mal conmigo.
☐ que esté divorciado/a.
☐ que trabaje en la televisión.
☐ que sea viudo/a.
☐ que se case este año.

**B. Las preguntas de Carmen**

PASO 1 Carmen acaba de llegar aquí de otro estado. Necesita tener información sobre la universidad y la ciudad. Haga las preguntas de Carmen según el modelo.

MODELO: restaurantes / sirven comida latinoamericana →
¿Hay restaurantes que *sirvan* (donde *sirvan*) comida latinoamericana?

1. librerías / venden libros usados
2. tiendas / se puede comprar revistas de Latinoamérica
3. cafés cerca de la universidad / se reúnen muchos estudiantes
4. apartamentos cerca de la universidad / son buenos y baratos
5. cines / pasan (*they show*) películas en español
6. un gimnasio en la universidad / se juega al ráquetbol
7. parques / la gente corre o da paseos
8. museos / hacen exposiciones de arte latinoamericano

PASO 2 ¿Cierto o falso?

1. A Carmen no le interesa la cultura hispánica.
2. Carmen es deportista.
3. Es posible que sea estudiante.
4. Este año piensa vivir con unos amigos de sus padres.

PASO 3 Ahora conteste las preguntas de Carmen con información verdadera sobre la ciudad donde Ud. vive y su universidad.

**Prác. B: Answers**
*Paso 1* **1.** ¿Hay librerías que (donde) vendan libros usados? **2.** ¿Hay tiendas donde se pueda comprar revistas de Latinoamérica? **3.** ¿Hay cafés cerca de la universidad donde se reúnan muchos estudiantes? **4.** ¿Hay apartamentos cerca de la universidad que sean buenos y baratos? **5.** ¿Hay cines donde pasen películas en español? **6.** ¿Hay un gimnasio en la universidad donde se juegue al ráquetbol? **7.** ¿Hay parques donde la gente corra o dé paseos? **8.** ¿Hay museos donde hagan exposiciones de arte latinoamericano? *Paso 2* **1.** falso **2.** cierto **3.** cierto **4.** falso

**Con. B: Suggestion**
Encourage students to use conversation-extending techniques to elicit more information.

## Conversación

**A. Una encuesta.** ¿Qué sabe Ud. de los compañeros de su clase de español? Pregúnteles a los miembros de la clase si saben hacer lo siguiente o a quién le ocurre lo siguiente. Deben levantar la mano sólo los que puedan contestar afirmativamente. Luego la persona que hizo la pregunta debe hacer un comentario apropiado. Siga el modelo.

MODELO: hablar chino →
En esta clase, ¿hay alguien que hable chino?
(*Nadie levanta la mano.*) No hay nadie que hable chino.
(*Alguien levanta la mano.*) Hay una persona que habla chino.

1. hablar ruso
2. saber tocar la viola
3. conocer a un actor / una actriz
4. saber preparar comida vietnamita
5. tener su cumpleaños hoy
6. escribir poemas
7. vivir en las afueras
8. ¿ ?

**B. Entrevista.** With another student, ask and answer the following questions. Then report any interesting details to the class.

1. ¿Hay alguien en tu vida que te quiera locamente?
2. ¿Hay algo que te importe más que los estudios universitarios?
3. ¿Con qué tipo de persona te gusta salir / pasar tiempo?
4. Para el semestre/trimestre que viene, ¿qué clases buscas? ¿Una que empiece a las ocho de la mañana?
5. ¿Tienes algún amigo o alguna amiga de la escuela secundaria que esté casado/a? ¿que tenga hijos? ¿que esté divorciado/a?
6. ¡OJO! Unas preguntas indiscretas: ¿Has conocido recientemente a alguien que te haya gustado mucho? ¿de quien te hayas enamorado? ¿Hay algún pariente con quien te lleves muy mal? ¿o muy, muy bien?

**Con. B: Extension**
Write these sentences on the board. Have students supply their own details to form questions to use in an interview situation.

7. ¿Tienes algún amigo que... ?
8. ¿Tienes alguna clase que... ?
9. En mi opinión, no hay nada/nadie que...

**En los Estados Unidos y el Canadá: Comprensión**

1. ¿Dónde nació Isabel Allende?
2. ¿Qué relación tiene con Salvador Allende?
3. ¿Qué tragedia familiar sufrió Isabel?
4. ¿Cuál es el título de una novela famosa de la escritora?
5. ¿Ha leído Ud. alguna de sus novelas?

**En los Estados Unidos y el Canadá: Suggestion**
Encourage students to find Allende's home page on the Internet. They can also read translated contemporary fiction by Spanish and Latin  American writers such as Gabriel García Márquez, Mario Vargas Llosa, Carlos Fuentes, and Elena Poniatowska, and bilingual editions of poetry by authors such as Federico García Lorca, Pablo Neruda, Octavio Paz, and César Vallejo.

**Heritage Speakers**
Pídales a los hispanohablantes que nombren a otros escritores latinoamericanos y españoles cuyas obras conozcan o hayan leído. Puede sugerirles que describan brevemente al resto de la clase los temas y las demás características propias de la obra de esos escritores.

## En los Estados Unidos y el Canadá

### Isabel Allende: Novelista chilena

Es posible que la chilena Isabel Allende (1942– ) sea **la escritora hispánica más conocida de Norteamérica.** Sobrina del presidente de Chile, Salvador Allende, quien fue derrocado[a] violentamente y murió en 1973, Isabel viene de **una familia que tiene un pasado muy interesante.** Este pasado, con su mezcla[b] de lo familiar y lo político, aparece como uno de los elementos más salientes[c] de sus novelas. Estas se caracterizan también por el uso del «realismo mágico», técnica literaria en que elementos fantásticos se entretejen[d] con aspectos de la vida diaria. Su primera novela, *La casa de los espíritus,* apareció en 1982. Otras incluyen *De amor y de sombra* (1984), *Eva Luna* (1985), *El plan infinito* (1991) y *Retrato en Sepia* (2000).

*Isabel Allende*

La vida de Allende no ha sido fácil. Después de los eventos políticos en que murió su tío, tuvo que **abandonar su país** con sus hijos pequeños. Vivió por un tiempo en Venezuela y hoy **reside en los Estados Unidos con su segundo esposo. Perdió a su segunda hija,** Paula, después de una larga y trágica enfermedad, cuando esta tenía 28 años. A ella le dedicó un libro en el que[e] cuenta la historia de la familia a la vez que narra los cambios que sufre la escritora a consecuencia del trauma de la enfermedad de su hija. Pero los contratiempos[f] no parecen detener a la incansable Isabel Allende.

[a]*overthrown* [b]*mixture* [c]*prominent* [d]*se... are interwoven* [e]*en... in which* [f]*mishaps, disappointments*

## LITERATURA: Gabriela Mistral

**Gabriela Mistral**
*(1889–1957)*

**Sobra la autora:** *Gabriela Mistral nació en Vicuña, Chile. Publicó sus primeros versos a los 15 años. Fue maestra y cónsul de Chile en varios países. Participó en la asamblea de las Naciones Unidas y publicó varias colecciones de poesía. En 1945 le otorgaron el Premio Nóbel de Literatura por sus versos líricos. Murió en Nueva York. Los siguientes versos son del poema, «Puertas», Lagar (1954).*

Entre los gestos[a] del mundo
recibí el que dan las puertas.
En la luz yo las he visto
o selladas[b] o entreabiertas[c]
y volviendo sus espaldas[d]
del color de la vulpeja.[e]
¿Por qué fue que las hicimos
para ser sus prisioneras?

[a]*gestures*  [b]*cerradas*  [c]*half-open, ajar*  [d]*volviendo… turning a cold shoulder*  [e]*vixen (female fox)*

**Literatura: Notes**
- Mistral's given name was Lucila Godoy Alcayaga.
- Although her father abandoned the family when she was only 3 years old, Mistral seems to have inherited her father's passion for verse.
- Students can read Gabriela Mistral's acceptance speech at the Nobel Foundation's official website. Encourage them to look for it, and to find more information and images related to Mistral. You might assign specific topics about Chile and Gabriela Mistral and have students give brief oral presentations on their findings.

**Música: Notes**
- Many regard Victor Jara's life as a reflection of the tumultuous politics and struggles of Chile during the late 60s and 70s. He became one of the best-known and most influential figures of Latin America.
- Sergio Ortega also collaborated with Víctor Jara and Quilapayún. Ortega was a key figure of *el canto nuevo*. He composed a wide range of music, from chamber pieces to operas. His best known pieces, however, are *canto nuevo* songs that he wrote for the Chilean socialist movement: Allende's election theme, *"Venceremos"* and *"El pueblo unido."*

## MÚSICA: El canto nuevo y Víctor Jara

Víctor Jara (1932–1973) fue uno de los compositores más representativos del canto nuevo chileno, un movimiento musical que surgió[a] en Chile y la Argentina en los años 60 y 70. El canto nuevo (o la nueva canción) expresa la lucha[b] de los latinoamericanos por la libertad y contra la opresión. Jara fue el Embajador Cultural de Chile durante la breve presidencia del socialista Salvador Allende, quien celebró su victoria en las elecciones bajo una bandera[c] que decía: «No puede haber revolución sin canciones».

[a]*emerged*  [b]*struggle*  [c]*flag*

**Música: Suggestions**
- Remind students that the *Enfoque cultural of Capítulo 14* features an Argentine *nuevo canto* artist, Mercedes Sosa.

Víctor Jara también colaboró con Quilapayún, el conjunto[d] que le dio impulso popular y comercial al nuevo canto. El nombre Quilapayún es una palabra mapuche[e] que significa «tres barbas[f]».

[d]*band*  [e]*grupo indígena de Chile*  [f]*beards*

Durante el golpe de estado[g] en el cual[h] murió Salvador Allende, se oía al pueblo[i] cantar los versos de la canción «El pueblo unido»,* de Sergio Ortega (1938–2003), un compositor importante del canto nuevo. «El pueblo unido» se considera como el himno[j] de la resistencia del pueblo chileno.

Y ahora el pueblo
que se alza[k] en la lucha
con voz[l] de gigante

gritando: ¡Adelante![m]
¡El pueblo unido
jamás será[n] vencido[o]!

*(de «El pueblo unido», de Sergio Ortega)*

[g]*golpe… coup d'etat*  [h]*el… which*  [i]*people*  [j]*hymn*  [k]*se… rises up*  [l]*voice*  [m]*Onward!*  [n]*will be*  [o]*overcome*

- There are many outstanding Chilean folk musicians who dedicated an important part of their creative work to *el canto nuevo*. Their songs speak out against social injustice and

*During this military coup, Víctor Jara was arrested, tortured, and murdered. El canto nuevo, which had been the voice of the people protesting bad government, became even more representative of the struggle of the Chilean people for justice and liberty.*

exploitation. Have students also look up information on Violeta Parra, Patricio Manns, Rolando Alarcón, Charo Jofre, Payo Grondona, Tito Fernández, Quelentaro, Héctor Pávez, and Isabel and Ángel Parra, as well as the groups Inti-Illimani and Illapu.

Paso 3: Gramática
See the "Chapter-by-Chapter Supplementary Materials" in the IM for additional
teaching suggestions, notes, activities, and other resources for *Paso 3.*

**Follow-Up**
• Ask students the following question.

¿*Han estado Uds. en situaciones similares a las de los dibujos?*

**41** *Lo hago para que tú...* Subjunctive After Conjunctions of
Contingency and Purpose

Encourage students to give details.
• Have students complete the following sentences with their own ideas.

1. *En una fiesta, nunca bailo a menos que...*
2. *Cuando salgo con mis amigos, siempre tengo mi licencia de conducir en caso de que...*
3. *No me voy a casar a menos que...*
4. *Tengo planes hechos en caso de que...*
5. *Voy a estudiar _____ para que...*

**Maneras de amar**

Resources: Transparency 94

a.                              b.                              c.

**Emphasis A: Suggestions**
• Present the following initial pattern to help students remember the five conjunctions that are always followed by the subjunctive.

A PACE:
*A menos que*
*Para que*
*Antes (de) que*
*Con tal (de) que*
*En caso de que*

• Include the lower frequency *sin que* in your presentation of the always subjunctive conjunctions (A SPACE).
• Some teachers prefer using the acronym ESCAPA to help students remember adverbial conjunctions that always require the subjunctive.
• Emphasize and model the relationship of the adverbial clauses to adverbs (they function as an adverb): *Llega mañana / antes de que salgamos.*
• In *Capítulo 16,* students will be introduced to temporal adverbial conjunctions (*cuando, tan pronto como, hasta que,* and so on). The subjunctive is used only when they introduce future, incomplete actions or states.

¿A qué dibujo corresponde cada una de las siguientes oraciones? ¿Quién las dice?

1. __b__ Aquí tienes la tarjeta de crédito, pero úsala sólo *en caso de que haya una emergencia,* ¿eh?    el padre
2. __a__ Escúchame bien. No vas a salir *antes de que termines* la tarea.    la madre
3. __c__ Quiero casarme contigo *para que estemos* siempre juntos *y no salgas más* con Raúl.    el chico

Comprensión: Answers

**Comprensión**    *Possible answers:* 1. *no hace la tarea/le diga que la haga* 2. *va a la universidad/nervioso* 3. *está enamorado/esté enamorada/casarse*

1. En el dibujo **a,** es obvio que el chico _____. Es normal que la madre _____.
2. En el dibujo **b,** está claro que la chica _____. Por eso el padre se siente _____ (adjetivo).
3. En el dibujo **c,** creo que el chico _____. No estoy seguro/a de que la chica _____. Pienso que esta pareja es muy joven para _____.

**A.** When one action or condition is related to another—*x* will happen provided that *y* occurs; we'll do *z* unless *a* happens—a relationship of *contingency* is said to exist: one thing is contingent, or depends, on another.

The Spanish *conjunctions* (**las conjunciones**) at the right express relationships of contingency or purpose. The subjunctive always occurs in subordinate clauses introduced by these conjunctions.

| a menos que | unless |
| antes (de) que | before |
| con tal (de) que | provided (that) |
| en caso de que | in case |
| para que | so that |

**conjunction** = a word or phrase that connects words, phrases, or clauses

**B.** Note that these conjunctions introduce subordinate clauses in which the events have not yet materialized; the events are conceptualized, not real-world, events.

Voy **con tal de que** ellos me **acompañen.**
*I'm going, provided (that) they go with me.*

**En caso de que llegue** Juan, dile que ya salí.
*In case Juan arrives, tell him that I already left.*

**Emphasis C: Suggestion**
Emphasize the difference between the preposition + infinitive structure (*Nota comunicativa, Capítulo 13*) and the conjunction + subjunctive structure. The latter has a second subject (*Van al cine antes de que llegue Raúl.*), and the former does not (*Van al cine antes de cenar.*).

**C.** When there is no change of subject in the sentence, Spanish more frequently uses the prepositions **antes de** and **para,** plus an infinitive, instead of the corresponding conjunctions plus the subjunctive. Compare the sentences at the right.

| | |
|---|---|
| PREPOSITION (one subject) | Estoy aquí **para aprender.** *I'm here to (in order to) learn.* |
| CONJUNCTION (two subjects) | Estoy aquí **para que Uds. aprendan.** *I'm here so that you will learn.* |
| PREPOSITION (one subject) | Voy a comer **antes de salir.** *I'm going to eat before leaving.* |
| CONJUNCTION (two subjects) | Voy a comer **antes de que salgamos.** *I'm going to eat before we leave.* |

**AUTOPRUEBA**

Match each conjunction with its correct meaning in English.

1. _____ para que
2. _____ antes de que
3. _____ con tal de que
4. _____ a menos que
5. _____ en caso de que

a. unless
b. before
c. provided that
d. in case
e. so that

*Answers: 1. e 2. b 3. c 4. a 5. d*

**Prác. B: Follow-Up**

• ¿Cierto, falso o no lo dice?

1. *Manolo y Lola acaban de casarse.* (falso)
2. *Casi siempre van de vacaciones con su hija.* (falso)
3. *Los dos son excelentes esquiadores.* (falso)
4. *Van a dejar a la niña con los abuelos.* (cierto)

• Write the conjunctions on the board. Have students use them as appropriate to complete the following sentences.

1. *El cielo está muy nublado hoy. Voy a llevar impermeable…*
2. *Es fácil recibir una buena nota en esta clase…*
3. *Nunca pienso casarme/divorciarme…*
4. *Vamos a las montañas este fin de semana…*

• Have students complete the following sentences with information about themselves.

1. *Voy a graduarme en… a menos que…*
2. *Este verano voy a… a menos que…*
3. *Voy a seguir viviendo en esta ciudad con tal que…*
4. *Voy a comprar… en caso de que…*

**Prác. B: Answers**
1. *No voy a menos que dejemos a la niña con los abuelos.* 2. *Vamos solos a las montañas para que pasemos un fin de semana romántico.* 3. *Esta vez voy a aprender a esquiar con tal de que tú me enseñes.* 4. *Vamos a salir temprano por la mañana a menos que nos acostemos tarde la noche anterior.* 5. *Es importante que lleguemos a la estación de esquí antes de que empiece a nevar.* 6. *Deja la dirección y el teléfono del hotel en caso de que tus padres nos necesiten.* 7. *No vamos a regresar antes de que nos hayamos cansado de esquiar.*

**Need more practice?**
■ Workbook/Laboratory Manual
■ Interactive CD-ROM
■ Online Learning Center (www.mhhe.com/quetal7)

## ■ Práctica

**Prác. A: Suggestion**
Have students add at least two more characteristics of a good (or bad) friend.

**A.** **¡Anticipemos! ¿Es Ud. un buen amigo / una buena amiga?** La amistad es una de las relaciones más importantes de la vida. Indique si las siguientes oraciones son ciertas o falsas para Ud. con respecto a sus amigos. **¡OJO!** No todas las características son buenas. Hay que leer con cuidado.

| | C | F |
|---|---|---|
| 1. Les hago muchos favores a mis amigos, con tal que ellos después me ayuden a mí. | ☐ | ☐ |
| 2. Les ofrezco consejos a mis amigos para que tomen buenas decisiones. | ☐ | ☐ |
| 3. Les presto dinero a menos que yo sepa que no me lo pueden devolver. | ☐ | ☐ |
| 4. Les traduzco el menú en los restaurantes mexicanos en caso de que no sepan leer español. | ☐ | ☐ |
| 5. Los llevo a casa cuando beben, para que no tengan accidentes de coche. | ☐ | ☐ |

**B.** **Un fin de semana en las montañas.** Hablan Manolo y Lola. Use la conjunción entre paréntesis para unir las oraciones, haciendo todos los cambios necesarios.

1. No voy. Dejamos a la niña con los abuelos. (a menos que)
2. Vamos solos a las montañas. Pasamos un fin de semana romántico. (para que)
3. Esta vez voy a aprender a esquiar. Tú me enseñas. (con tal de que)
4. Vamos a salir temprano por la mañana. Nos acostamos tarde la noche anterior. (a menos que)
5. Es importante que lleguemos a la estación (*resort*) de esquí. Empieza a nevar. (antes de que)
6. Deja la dirección y el teléfono del hotel. Tus padres nos necesitan. (en caso de que)
7. No vamos a regresar. Nos hemos cansado de esquiar. (antes de que)

*Capítulo 15 • La vida social y la vida afectiva*

Con. A: Extension
8. *Estudiamos para (que)...*
9. *Reciclamos para (que)...*
10. *Votamos para (que)...*

## ■ Conversación

Con. A: Variation

Write the conjunctions on the board. Have students share their plans for the future, using these phrases.

*Voy a graduarme en...*

*Este verano voy a...*
*No quiero enamorarme/casarme/ divorciarme...*
*Quiero tener hijos/nietos...*
*Voy a llevarme bien con...*

Provide a model: *Voy a graduarme en diciembre con tal de que salga bien en esta clase.*

**A. Situaciones.** Cualquier acción puede justificarse. Con un compañero / una compañera o con un grupo de estudiantes, dé una explicación para las siguientes situaciones. Luego comparen sus explicaciones con las de otro grupo.

1. Los padres trabajan mucho para (que)…
2. Los profesores les dan tarea a los estudiantes para (que)…
3. Los dueños de los equipos deportivos profesionales les pagan mucho a algunos jugadores para (que)…
4. Las películas extranjeras se doblan (*are dubbed*) para (que)…
5. Los padres castigan (*punish*) a los niños para (que)…
6. Las parejas se divorcian para (que)…
7. Los jóvenes forman pandillas (*gangs*) para (que)…

## NOTA COMUNICATIVA

Nota comunicativa: Suggestion
Have students review the uses of *por* and *para* in *Gramática 32.* Remind them that a general rule of thumb is that *por* looks "back" at causes and *para* looks "forward" at purpose and goal.

**¿Para qué... ? / ¿Por qué... ? and *para que / porque***

English usage offers a general guideline for knowing when to use **¿Para qué... ?** versus **¿Por qué... ?** and **para que** versus **porque. ¿Por qué... ?** asks *Why . . . ?*, in the general sense, but if the question is specifically asking *For what reason / purpose?* something is for, use **¿Para qué... ?**

| | |
|---|---|
| **¿Por qué** te casaste con él? | *Why did you marry him?* |
| **¿Para qué** te casaste con él? | *For what reason did you marry him?* |
| **¿Para qué** es el anillo? | *What (purpose) is the ring for?* |

The conjunction **porque** means *because* in English, when *because* serves as a conjunction between two clauses. The adverbial conjunction **para que**, on the other hand, means *in order that* or *so that*.

| | |
|---|---|
| Me casé con él **porque** lo quiero. | *I married him because I love him.* |
| Me voy a casar con él **para que** mis padres nos acepten. | *I'm going to marry him so that my parents accept us.* |

**B. La boda.** Julia y Salvador se casan este año y quieren una gran boda. Todos los parientes tienen preguntas. Con un compañero / una compañera, haga y conteste las siguientes preguntas, imaginando que uno/a de Uds. es Julia o Salvador. Si quieren, pueden usar las sugerencias entre paréntesis.

Con. B: Bright Idea Follow-Up
Bring magazine clippings or printed images from the Internet. Display the images and encourage students to ask appropriate questions using *¿Por qué?* and *¿Para qué?* For example, for a pain relief advertisement, students might ask: *¿Para qué es ese producto?* (What is that product used for?) and *¿Por qué necesita el señor tomar ese producto?* (Why does the man need to take that product?).

MODELO: ¿Por qué se casan en enero? (el invierno) →
Nos casamos en enero porque nos gusta el invierno.

1. ¿Para qué son las velas (*candles*)? (la ceremonia)
2. ¿Por qué quieren mandar trescientas invitaciones? (todos nuestros amigos y parientes / asistir)
3. ¿Por qué van a mandar las invitaciones con cuatro meses de anticipación (*ahead*)? (todos los invitados / poder hacer planes para asistir)
4. ¿Por qué buscan un salón tan grande para la recepción después de la boda? (haber música y baile)
5. ¿Por qué quieren contratar un grupo latino de música? (todos / bailar)

# PASO 3

*Cuatro muchachas chilenas que pasan un rato juntas en un parque, en Valparaíso, Chile*

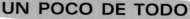

## UN POCO DE TODO

**Lengua y cultura: ¿Cómo se divierten los hispanos?** Complete the following passages with the correct forms of the words in parentheses, as suggested by the context. When two possibilities are given in parentheses, select the correct word. **¡OJO!** As you conjugate verbs in this activity, you will decide whether to use the subjunctive mood (the present or present perfect tense) or the indicative mood (the present, the present perfect, the preterite, or the imperfect tense). The context of the passages will give clues to help you choose, and occasionally clues in italics will guide you in choosing a tense or mood.

Como Ud. sabe, hay semejanzas y diferencias entre las culturas hispana y norteamericana. En cuanto a[a] las diversiones, la verdad es (que / lo que[1]), en general, no hay (mucho[2]) diferencia entre la manera de divertirse de los (joven[3]) hispanos y los norteamericanos. Es normal que los muchachos y muchachas—chicos y chicas en España, gallos y gallas en Chile, patojos y patojas en Guatemala, (por / para[4]) ejemplo—(ir[5]) a bailar por la noche a las discotecas y clubes y que (bailar[6]) casi hasta el amanecer.[b] La música (ser / estar[7]) una de las grandes aficiones de todos, y (a / —[8]) los muchachos especialmente les (gusta / gustan[9]) también mirar los partidos deportivos. En años recientes, el concepto de los centros comerciales (llegar[10]) a las ciudades hispánicas. En estos centros (haber[11]) tiendas y restaurantes que (le / les[12]) (interesar[13]) a la gente joven. Con frecuencia también hay cines y hasta (grande[14]) supermercados.

Pero hay algo que sí es diferente entre las dos culturas, y es la costumbre del paseo. Consiste en andar por distracción[c] o por hacer ejercicio, particularmente al aire libre. Para dar un paseo, tradicionalmente la gente de todas las edades (ir[15]) a una plaza o a otro lugar céntrico a pasar un rato. Allí (por / para[16]) la tarde, (relajarse[17]) y (encontrarse[18]) con amigos y familiares. Hoy día, como[d] las ciudades son más grandes, el paseo no (concentrarse[19]) en un solo[e] lugar, pero la costumbre (seguir[20]) existiendo de igual forma.

Hay que recordar que el paseo no (se / —[21]) considera como una actividad deportiva sino[f] social. El paseo *no se compara con el* hiking norteamericano. Para expresar esa idea, se (poder[22]) decir «dar / hacer una caminata por el bosque o la montaña». Pero (ese[23]) actividad no es muy típico de la cultura hispana, a menos que los que[g] la practican (ser[24]) jóvenes con tendencia al naturismo.[h]

[a]En... *As far as . . . are concerned* [b]el... *dawn* [c]*amusement* [d]*since* [e]*single* [f]*but rather* [g]los... *those who* [h]*actividades recreativas en la naturaleza*

**Comprensión.** Conteste las preguntas en español.

1. Según la información en los párrafos, ¿cuáles son algunas de las diferencias y semejanzas entre la forma de divertirse de los jóvenes en las culturas hispánicas y en la norteamericana?
2. ¿Qué palabras se usan para expresar «muchachos y muchachas» en varios países hispánicos?
3. ¿Qué ventajas ve Ud. en la costumbre hispana del paseo? ¿Y qué desventajas ve? ¿En qué sentido puede un hispano sentirse incómodo en una ciudad norteamericana en cuanto a las formas de divertirse de este país?

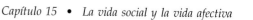

**Paso 4: Un paso más**
• The *Paso 4: Un paso más* sections are optional.
• See the "Chapter-by-Chapter Supplementary Materials" in the IM for additional teaching suggestions, notes, activities, and other resources for *Paso 4*.

**VIDEOTECA**

## Entrevista cultural: Chile

*Entrevista cultural: Suggestions*
• Before showing the video, ask students questions about events such as weddings. Ask students to name some of the professions related to weddings.

Jorge Balmaceda es chileno. Habla de su trabajo y de sus clientes. ¡Le encanta su profesión! Antes de ver el vídeo, lea el siguiente fragmento de la entrevista.

JORGE: Me encanta mi trabajo, sobre todo sacar fotos en bodas. Me encanta fotografiar a la novia, al novio, a los padrinos, amigos y familiares. Es una fiesta bastante feliz. Me encanta retratarla.[a]

ENTREVISTADORA: Y ¿es siempre agradable, o de vez en cuando encuentras dificultades o problemas?

JORGE: Porque [la novia] no se siente bien, porque no le quedó bien[b] el vestido o porque el peinado[c] no le gusta como le quedó.

*¿Qué profesiones se asocian con las bodas?*

• Have them use Spanish if possible, and give them the Spanish for words they don't know. Which of these professions would interest them and why?

*la costurera / el sastre*
*el fotógrafo / la fotógrafa*
*el peluquero / la peluquera*
*un profesional religioso (el cura, el pastor / la pastora protestante, el rabino / la rabina, el sacerdote)*
*el servicio de banquetes*

• Have them talk about photographers.

*¿Para qué tipo de reuniones y celebraciones familiares se necesitan fotógrafos?*

• Show the video and allow students one to two minutes to work on the questions. Have volunteers answer the questions.

[a]*portraying it in photos* [b]*no... didn't fit well* [c]*hairdo*

Ahora vea el vídeo y conteste las siguientes preguntas basándose en la entrevista. *Entrevista cultural: Answers*
*Possible answers: 1. Es fotógrafo. 2. a las bodas 3. A veces hay problemas con el vestido o el peinado. 4. los aniversarios de bodas 5. Porque generalmente retrata ocasiones felices.*

1. ¿Cuál es la profesión de Jorge?
2. ¿A qué eventos sociales debe asistir?
3. ¿Qué problemas ocurren en su trabajo?
4. ¿Cuáles de las celebraciones le parecen más felices a Jorge?
5. ¿Por qué le gusta su trabajo?

## Entre amigos: Es muy lindo estar enamorado

Miguel, Tané, Rubén y Karina hablan de las relaciones sentimentales. En su opinión, ¿qué preguntas se van a hacer? Antes de mirar el vídeo, lea las preguntas a continuación. Mientras mire el vídeo, trate de entender la conversación en general y fíjese en la información sobre los novios y las relaciones. Luego mire el vídeo una segunda vez, fijándose en la información que necesita para contestar las preguntas.

1. ¿Cuándo rompieron Miguel y su novia? (Hace... [. . . *ago*.])
2. Según Karina, ¿qué es importante en una relación amorosa?
3. ¿Dónde vive el novio de Tané?
4. ¿Qué planes tienen Tané y su novio para el futuro?
5. ¿Sabe Tané cuántos hijos quiere tener?

• Have volunteers role-play Jorge and his interviewer.

*Entre amigos: Suggestions*
• Before viewing the video, review the questions with the students and ask them similar questions.

*¿Tiene Ud. novio/a? ¿Está casado/a?*
*¿Rompió Ud. con un novio / una novia alguna vez? ¿Cuánto tiempo hace (new expression)?*
*¿Qué expectativas tiene Ud. para el matrimonio? Si ya está casado/a, ¿qué expectativas tenía antes de casarse?*

Have students answer or work in small groups to ask and answer these questions.

• After viewing the video, have volunteers read and answer the questions.

**Heritage Speakers**
Anime a los hispanohablantes a hablar de cómo son las relaciones íntimas en su país.

*¿Cómo son los noviazgos en los países latinoamericanos y en España?*
*¿Todavía existe la práctica de cortejar a una persona?*
*¿Qué papel desempeñan los otros miembros de la familia?*
*Antes, la novia no podía salir sin chaperón o chaperona. ¿Todavía es así?*

**Entre amigos: Answers**
*Possible answers: 1. Hace casi dos meses. 2. la comunicación 3. en Cuba 4. Van a casarse y tener hijos. 5. no*

# PASO 4

**Notes**
• The tradition of wine began in Chile with the sacramental wines used by the Spanish missions. Little care and art went into the preparations of those wines, and the Spanish crown limited the amount of wine that Chile could produce in order to protect its own exports. In 1870 Chilean wine growers decided to import *vinifera* vine stocks from France and other wine regions from Europe to improve wine quality and production. This coincided with the years when phylloxera, a tiny insect that is a serious pest for commercial grapevines, began its devastating plagues in Europe and North America. Chilean grapes were not affected by the plague. As Europe struggled to recover from it, they studied the Chilean vines and took grafts of plague-resistant plants back to Europe. Today, the only place where ungrafted European vines still flourish is Chile.
• Students can read an excerpt of the poem *"Puertas"* by Chile's Gabriela Mistral in *Voces de Chile: Literatura.*
• Students can read about Chile's *el canto nuevo* in *Voces de Chile: Música.*
• See the Workbook/Laboratory Manual for focused practice with the material in *Enfoque cultural.*

**CAPÍTULO 15**

## ENFOQUE CULTURAL

**Chile**

## Lugares famosos: La geografía chilena

Se puede dividir Chile en tres regiones principales. El norte de Chile principalmente consiste en 600 millas (1.000 kilómetros) del desierto Atacama. Aunque el desierto tiene un clima moderado, es uno de los lugares más áridos del mundo. En algunas partes del desierto, no hay evidencia ninguna de pluviosidad.[a]

El centro de Chile se extiende unas mil millas (1.600 kilómetros). Mucho del centro consiste en el Valle de Chile entre los Andes y la Cordillera de la Costa. Es la región más poblada de Chile y el centro agrícola del país.

El sur de Chile es una región escabrosa.[b] Aquí los Andes descienden al océano para formar fiordos e islas y se encuentran los glaciares de la Tierra del Fuego, que Chile comparte con la Argentina.

[a]*rainfall*  [b]*rugged*

**Multimedia: Internet** Have students search the Internet for more information about Chile's government, educational system, geography, and economy. Assign specific topics and have students prepare brief oral presentations for the class based on their findings.

*Un viñedo* (vineyard) *chileno, con los Andes al fondo* (in the background)

## ¡Fíjese!

- El nombre de Chile se deriva de la palabra indígena *chilli*, que significa «lugar donde termina la tierra».
- Chile es uno de los países más modernos e industrializados de Sudamérica. Durante la colonización de Sudamérica, los españoles no tenían mucho interés en Chile. Los Andes dificultaban los viajes al país y, como no habían encontrado allí oro como en el Perú, los colonizadores pensaban que la tierra de Chile tenía poco valor. Esto es irónico porque hoy la minería del cobre[a] es la industria más importante del país, y Chile es uno de los mayores exportadores de cobre del mundo.
- Aunque Chile sufrió una crisis económica en los años 70, a finales del siglo XX muchos lo llamaban «el jaguar económico de Latinoamérica». La calidad de la vida en Chile es una de las mejores entre los países hispánicos. La natalidad[b] ha bajado drásticamente y la esperanza de vida al nacer es de aproximadamente 80 años. Con una tasa de alfabetización[c] de casi el 95 por ciento, Chile tiene un estable sistema de escuelas y universidades.

[a]*copper*  [b]*birthrate*  [c]*tasa... literacy rate*

Learn more about Chile with the Video, the Interactive CD-ROM, and the Online Learning Center (www.mhhe.com/quetal7).

## PASO FINAL

### A LEER

**ESTRATEGIA: Using Graphics to Get Information**

Reading graphics such as tables and pie charts requires as much concentration as, if not more than, any other reading since a lot information is often summarized in a compact space. Paying attention to the head of a section as well as to the categories within the graphic can help you to focus on important parts of the information presented.

The following chart provides a summary of statistical information regarding how males and females in Spain spend their time each day. As you read and analyze the information in the chart, remember to rely on all of the visual clues that you can to facilitate your comprehension.

**Sobre la lectura...** La lectura, o mejor dicho, el gráfico, es del periódico *El País*, de España. Es parte de un artículo más largo que da los resultados de una encuesta (*survey*), entre más de 23.000 personas a partir de (*older than*) 10 años de edad, que estudia las actividades a que dedican su tiempo los españoles.

## *Una encuesta revela que las mujeres españolas dedican el triple de tiempo que los varones al hogar y la familia*

**Encuesta sobre el empleo del tlempo**

PORCENTAJE DE PERSONAS QUE REALIZAN LA ACTIVIDAD EN EL TRANSCURSO DEL DÍA Y  PROMEDIO DE TIEMPO DIARIO DEDICADO A LA ACTIVIDAD POR DICHAS PERSONAS

| Actividades principales | Ambos sexos | | Varones | | Mujeres | |
|---|---|---|---|---|---|---|
| | % de personas | Duración media diaria | % de personas | Duración media diaria | % de personas | Duración media diaria |
| Cuidados personales | 100,0 | 11:22 | 100,0 | 11:24 | 100,0 | 11:20 |
| Trabajo | 34,3 | 7:43 | 43,5 | 8:18 | 26,0 | 6:51 |
| Estudios | 15,0 | 5:25 | 14,9 | 5:32 | 15,2 | 5:19 |
| Hogar y familia | 82,0 | 3:44 | 70,1 | 2:06 | 92,7 | 4:50 |
| Trabajo voluntario y reuniones | 12,7 | 1:45 | 9,9 | 1:51 | 15,2 | 1:42 |
| Vida social y diversión | 64,4 | 2:03 | 64,3 | 2:08 | 64,5 | 1:58 |
| Deportes y actividades al aire libre | 37,8 | 1:54 | 40,6 | 2:11 | 35,4 | 1:36 |
| Aflclones y juegos | 17,3 | 1:45 | 22,5 | 1:55 | 12,7 | 1:30 |
| Medios de comunicación | 87,7 | 2:42 | 88,0 | 2:54 | 87,5 | 2:31 |
| Trayectos y tlempo no especificado | 84,6 | 1:24 | 87,3 | 1:27 | 82,2 | 1:21 |

DISTRIBUCIÓN DE ACTIVIDADES EN UN DÍA PROMEDIO (por sexo)

| | Varones | Mujeres |
|---|---|---|
| Cuidados personales (Incluye comer y dormir) | 11:24 | 11:20 |
| Trabajo y estudios | 4:26 | 2:35 |
| Hogar y familia | 1:29 | 4:29 |
| Trabajo voluntario y reuniones | 0:11 | 0:16 |
| Tiempo libre | 6:16 | 4:13 |
| Trayectos y tlempo no especificado | 1:16 | 1:07 |

Fuente:INE

EL PAÍS

## Comprensión

**A. ¿Cierto o falso?**   Conteste según el gráfico. Corrija las oraciones falsas.

1. Hay un alto nivel de voluntarismo entre los dos sexos en España.
2. Los hombres y las mujeres dedican más o menos el mismo tiempo a las tareas domésticas, al cuidado (*care*) de los niños y a otras responsabilidades de hogar.
3. Parece que el tiempo libre es más importante para las mujeres que para los hombres.
4. Ambos (*Both*) sexos dedican la mayoría de su tiempo al trabajo y los estudios.

*Una madre que acompaña a sus hijas a la escuela, en Lima, Perú*

**B. Preguntas.**   Conteste según el gráfico.

1. ¿Cuánto tiempo dedican cada día los hombres y las mujeres, respectivamente, a los deportes y otras actividades físicas?
2. ¿Cuántos minutos de diferencia hay entre el tiempo dedicado a los estudios por los hombres y el tiempo dedicado por las mujeres?
3. Apunte las tres actividades a las que las mujeres, típicamente, dedican más tiempo. ¿Y los hombres?
4. ¿Cree Ud. que un gráfico que compara las actividades de los hombres con las de las mujeres en este país sería (*would be*) muy diferente? Explique.

 **A ESCRIBIR**

**A. Una encuesta entre amigos.**   Ud. va a hacer una encuesta entre ocho amigos (cuatro hombres y cuatro mujeres) para determinar cuánto tiempo dedican cada día a cinco actividades: el cuidado personal, el trabajo, los estudios, la vida social y los deportes. Organice los resultados en un gráfico. Luego prepare un breve informe para resumir la información y también para comparar su estudio con el estudio español.

**B. ¿Y Ud.?**   Ahora, analice las actividades a las que Ud. dedica el tiempo. Puede usar las diez categorías del gráfico de la lectura o puede usar las cinco actividades de **Actividad A** en **A escribir.** Haga un gráfico para analizar la información. Luego, escriba un breve informe para comparar sus resultados con los de la lectura y/o de la **Actividad A.**

*Comiendo tapas* (appetizers), *en San Sebastián, España*

# En resumen

**Suggestions**
- Point out the first person singular of *crecer* (*crezco*) and *nacer* (*nazco*).
- Have students describe a relationship in their family, for example, that of their parents, and tell when and how they met, how long they dated, and so on. Model a description for them.
- Write the stages of life in Spanish on the board. Have students write at least two sentences for each stage of life. Have them write sentences describing a typical activity for the stages of life, for example:

  *Llora a menos que esté cerca de su mamá* (*infancia*).

## GRAMÁTICA

To review the grammar points presented in this chapter, refer to the indicated grammar presentations. You'll find further practice of these structures in the Workbook/Laboratory Manual, on the Interactive CD-ROM, and on the *¿Qué tal?* Online Learning Center (www.mhhe.com/quetal7).

**40** **¿Hay alguien que… ? ¿Hay un lugar donde… ?** —Subjunctive After Nonexistent and Indefinite Antecedents

You should know how to use the subjunctive in two-clause sentences when the antecedent is nonexistent or indefinite.

**41** **Lo hago para que tú…** —Subjunctive After Conjunctions of Contingency and Purpose

You should know how and when to use the subjunctive after certain conjunctions of contingency and purpose.

*Está muy solo y deprimido porque ya no trabaja y sus hijos están muy ocupados con familias.* (*vejez*)
*Está muy contento porque por fin tiene tiempo para viajar y trabajar en el jardín* (*vejez*).

## VOCABULARIO

Practice this vocabulary with digital flash cards on the Online Learning Center (www.mhhe.com/quetal7).

Have students read sentences to the class. The class should identify the stage of life.

### Las relaciones sentimentales

| | |
|---|---|
| la amistad | friendship |
| el amor | love |
| la boda | wedding (ceremony) |
| la cita | date |
| la luna de miel | honeymoon |
| el marido | husband |
| el matrimonio | marriage; married couple |
| la mujer | wife |
| la novia | fiancée; bride |
| el noviazgo | engagement |
| el novio | fiancé; groom |
| la pareja | (married) couple; partner |
| el/la viudo/a | widower/widow |

**Cognados: el divorcio, la separación**
**Repaso: el/la amigo/a, el/la esposo/a, el/la novio/a (boy/girlfriend)**

| | |
|---|---|
| amar | to love |
| casarse (con) | to marry |
| divorciarse (de) | to get divorced (from) |
| enamorarse (de) | to fall in love (with) |
| llevarse bien/mal (con) | to get along well/poorly (with) |
| pasar tiempo (con) | to spend time (with) |
| querer (ie) | to love |
| romper (con) | to break up (with) |
| separarse (de) | to separate (from) |

**Repaso: pelear (con), salir (*irreg.*) con**

| | |
|---|---|
| amistoso/a | friendly |
| divorciado/a (de) | divorced (from) |
| enamorado/a (de) | in love (with) |
| recién casado/a (con) | newlywed (to) |

**Repaso: cariñoso/a, casado/a (con), feliz, soltero/a**

### Etapas de la vida

| | |
|---|---|
| la etapa | stage (*period of time*) |
| la juventud | youth |
| la madurez | middle age |
| la muerte | death |
| el nacimiento | birth |
| la vejez | old age |

**Cognados: la adolescencia, la infancia**
**Repaso: la niñez**

| | |
|---|---|
| crecer (zc) | to grow |
| nacer (zc) | to be born |

**Repaso: morir (ue, u)**

### Conjunciones

| | |
|---|---|
| a menos que | unless |
| antes (de) que | before |
| con tal (de) que | provided (that) |
| en caso de que | in case |
| para que | so that |

### Palabras adicionales

| | |
|---|---|
| a primera vista | at first sight |
| bastante | rather, sufficiently; enough |
| juntos/as | together |
| propio/a | own |

**Multimedia: Internet** Have students search the web for more information on weddings in Latin America and Spain. There are several websites in Spanish that describe different ways of planning civil and religious weddings. Encourage students to talk about differences and similarities between weddings in Spain and/or Latin America and weddings in the United States and/or Canada.

# ¿Trabajar para vivir o vivir para trabajar?

*Mujeres profesionales que caminan por la Puerta de la Ciudadela, en Montevideo, Uruguay*

## CULTURA

- **Nota cultural:** Los nombres de las profesiones
- **En los Estados Unidos y el Canadá:** El creciente mercado hispánico
- **Voces** del Uruguay y del Paraguay
    - **Literatura:** Horacio Quiroga
    - **Música:** El candombe y el arpa paraguaya
- **Videoteca**
    - **Entrevista cultural:** El Uruguay y el Paraguay
    - **Entre amigos:** ¿A qué hora es la entrevista?
- **Enfoque cultural:** El Uruguay y el Paraguay

## VOCABULARIO

- Profesiones y oficios
- El mundo del trabajo
- Una cuestión de dinero

## GRAMÁTICA

**42** Future Verb Forms

**43** Subjunctive and Indicative After Conjunctions of Time

**Suggestions**

- Point out the chapter-opener photo. Have students talk about this business area and the people in it. What kind of professionals do they think the two women in the foreground are? What kinds of offices would they expect to find in these buildings? Also, have students compare the architecture in this area. Ask if they see contrasting architectural periods in many cities in this country.

- Have students list their ideas about Uruguay and Paraguay, including information on geography, politics, economy, culture, music, and cuisine. When you finish the chapter, return to the lists and ask students what ideas they would change and/or add.

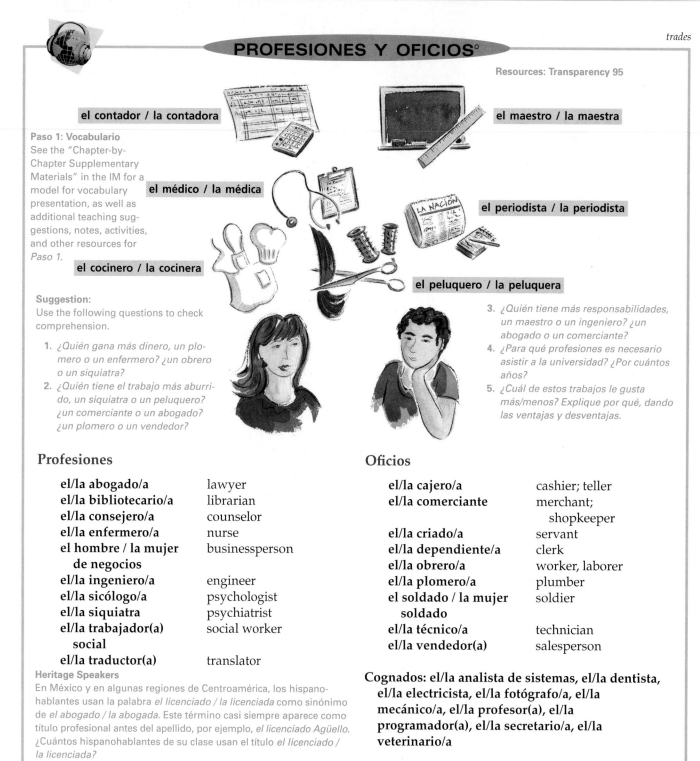

**PROFESIONES Y OFICIOS°**

*trades*

Resources: Transparency 95

el contador / la contadora

el maestro / la maestra

el médico / la médica

el periodista / la periodista

el cocinero / la cocinera

el peluquero / la peluquera

**Paso 1: Vocabulario**
See the "Chapter-by-Chapter Supplementary Materials" in the IM for a model for vocabulary presentation, as well as additional teaching suggestions, notes, activities, and other resources for *Paso 1.*

**Suggestion:**
Use the following questions to check comprehension.

1. *¿Quién gana más dinero, un plomero o un enfermero? ¿un obrero o un siquiatra?*
2. *¿Quién tiene el trabajo más aburrido, un siquiatra o un peluquero? ¿un comerciante o un abogado? ¿un plomero o un vendedor?*

3. *¿Quién tiene más responsabilidades, un maestro o un ingeniero? ¿un abogado o un comerciante?*
4. *¿Para qué profesiones es necesario asistir a la universidad? ¿Por cuántos años?*
5. *¿Cuál de estos trabajos le gusta más/menos? Explique por qué, dando las ventajas y desventajas.*

## Profesiones

| | |
|---|---|
| el/la abogado/a | lawyer |
| el/la bibliotecario/a | librarian |
| el/la consejero/a | counselor |
| el/la enfermero/a | nurse |
| el hombre / la mujer de negocios | businessperson |
| el/la ingeniero/a | engineer |
| el/la sicólogo/a | psychologist |
| el/la siquiatra | psychiatrist |
| el/la trabajador(a) social | social worker |
| el/la traductor(a) | translator |

## Oficios

| | |
|---|---|
| el/la cajero/a | cashier; teller |
| el/la comerciante | merchant; shopkeeper |
| el/la criado/a | servant |
| el/la dependiente/a | clerk |
| el/la obrero/a | worker, laborer |
| el/la plomero/a | plumber |
| el soldado / la mujer soldado | soldier |
| el/la técnico/a | technician |
| el/la vendedor(a) | salesperson |

**Cognados: el/la analista de sistemas, el/la dentista, el/la electricista, el/la fotógrafo/a, el/la mecánico/a, el/la profesor(a), el/la programador(a), el/la secretario/a, el/la veterinario/a**

**Heritage Speakers**
En México y en algunas regiones de Centroamérica, los hispanohablantes usan la palabra *el licenciado / la licenciada* como sinónimo de *el abogado / la abogada.* Este término casi siempre aparece como título profesional antes del apellido, por ejemplo, *el licenciado Agüello.* ¿Cuántos hispanohablantes de su clase usan el título *el licenciado / la licenciada?*

**Multimedia: Audio**
Students can listen to and practice this chapter's vocabulary on the Online Learning Center (**www.mhhe.com/quetal7**), as well as on the Textbook Audio CD, part of the Laboratory Audio Program.

In the preceding chapters of *¿Qué tal?* you learned to use a number of the words for professions and trades that are listed here. You will practice all of these words in the following activities. However, you may also want to learn new terms that are particularly important or interesting to you. If the vocabulary needed to describe your career goal is not listed here, look it up in a dictionary or ask your instructor.

Con. A: Suggestion
Do *Conversación A* as a listening comprehension activity

## ■ Conversación

**A. ¿A quién necesita Ud.?**   ¿A quién debe llamar o con quién debe consultar en estas situaciones? Hay más de una respuesta posible en algunos casos.

1. La tubería (*plumbing*) de la cocina no funciona bien.
2. Ud. acaba de tener un accidente automovilístico; el otro conductor dice que Ud. tuvo la culpa (*blame*).
3. Por las muchas tensiones y presiones de su vida profesional y personal, Ud. tiene serios problemas afectivos (*emotional*).
4. Ud. quiere que alguien lo/la ayude con los quehaceres domésticos porque no tiene mucho tiempo para hacerlos.
5. Ud. quiere que alguien le construya un muro (*wall*) en el jardín.
6. Ud. conoce todos los detalles de un escándalo en el gobierno de su ciudad y quiere divulgarlos.

Con. A: Answers
*Possible answers:* **1.** *el plomero / la plomera* **2.** *el abogado / la abogada* **3.** *el/la siquiatra* **4.** *el criado / la criada* **5.** *el obrero / la obrera* **6.** *el/la periodista*

Con. A: Bright Idea Extension
7. *Ud. y su pareja están invitados a una boda el sábado por la noche, pero no tienen a nadie que les cuide a sus hijos.*
8. *Ud. tiene una muela o un diente que le duele.*
9. *Ud. está en un avión que está volando a Miami y tiene sed.*
10. *Ud. no está contento/a con las decisiones del gobierno federal y quiere enviar un correo electrónico con sus quejas.*

Con. B: Suggestion
Have students keep a list of their first association for each item, then report back to the class. Tally first associations for all students on the board. Do patterns emerge? Discuss them as a whole class activity.

**B. Asociaciones.**   ¿Qué profesiones u oficios asocia Ud. con estas frases? Con un compañero / una compañera, consulte la lista de profesiones y oficios y use las siguientes palabras también. Hagan asociaciones rápidas. ¡No lo piensen demasiado!

Con. B: Variation
Have students give definitions of professions following the models given.

1. creativo/rutinario
2. muchos/pocos años de preparación
3. mucho/poco salario
4. mucha/poca responsabilidad
5. mucho/poco prestigio
6. flexibilidad/«de nueve a cinco»
7. mucho/poco tiempo libre
8. peligroso (*dangerous*)/seguro
9. en el pasado, sólo para hombres/mujeres
10. todavía, sólo para hombres/mujeres

| **Profesiones y oficios** | |
| --- | --- |
| **el actor / la actriz** | **el/la detective** |
| **el/la arquitecto/a** | **el/la niñero/a** |
| **el/la asistente de vuelo** | **el/la pintor(a)** |
| **el *barman*** | **el/la poeta** |
| **el/la camarero/a** | **el policía /** |
| **el/la carpintero/a** | **la mujer policía** |
| **el/la chófer** | **el/la político/a** |
| **el/la consejero/a** | **el/la presidente/a** |
| **el cura** (*priest*) **/ el/la** | **el/la senador(a)** |
| **pastor(a) protestante /** | |
| **el/la rabino/a** | |

**C. ¿Qué preparación se necesita para ser... ?**   Imagine que Ud. es consejero universitario / consejera universitaria. Explíquele a un(a) estudiante qué cursos debe tomar para prepararse para las siguientes carreras. Use el **Vocabulario útil** y la lista de cursos académicos del **Capítulo 1.** Piense también en el tipo de experiencia que debe obtener.

1. traductor(a) en la ONU (Organización de las Naciones Unidas)
2. reportero/a en la televisión, especializado/a en los deportes
3. contador(a) para un grupo de abogados
4. periodista para una revista de ecología
5. trabajador(a) social, especializado/a en los problemas de los ancianos
6. maestro/a de primaria, especializado/a en la educación bilingüe

| **Vocabulario útil** |
| --- |
| **las comunicaciones** |
| **la contabilidad** (accounting) |
| **el derecho** (law) |
| **la gerontología** |
| **la ingeniería** |
| **el *marketing*/mercadeo** |
| **la organización administrativa** |
| **la pedagogía/enseñanza** |
| **la retórica** (speech) |
| **la sociología** |

Con. C: Suggestions
• Model several recommendations before allowing students to begin the activity. Demonstrate the use of the subjunctive syntax in your model.
• Have students work in pairs to role-play an advisor and a student who is seeking advice about his/her future. Have students discuss a variety of topics including summer jobs, time management, experience, preferences, and money. Have students report their findings to the class.

**Suggestions**
- Have students respond *cierto* or *falso* to the following sentences.

1. *Una persona que busca un puesto se llama un aspirante.*
2. *Si a Ud. no le gusta su trabajo, debe despedirlo.*
3. *Si a Ud. le gustaría renunciar su trabajo, debe conseguir una solicitud.*
4. *Para llenar una solicitud, es necesario tener bolígrafo o lápiz.*

Have students correct the false statements.
- Point out that *compañía* is frequently used in company names, but *empresa* is the general word for *corporation* and

**D. Entrevista.** Con un compañero / una compañera, haga y conteste preguntas para averiguar (*find out*) la siguiente información.

1. lo que hacían sus abuelos
2. la profesión u oficio de sus padres
3. si tiene un amigo o pariente que tenga una profesión extraordinaria o interesante y el nombre de esa profesión
4. lo que sus padres (su esposo/a) quiere(n) que Ud. sea (lo que Ud. quiere que sean sus hijos)
5. lo que Ud. quiere ser (lo que sus hijos quieren ser)
6. la carrera para la cual (*which*) se preparan muchos de sus amigos (los hijos de sus amigos)

## EL MUNDO DEL TRABAJO

Resources: Transparencies 96, 97
Transparency 97 provides model sentences using work vocabulary.

| | | | |
|---|---|---|---|
| **el/la aspirante** | candidate; applicant | **el/la gerente** | manager |
| **el currículum** | résumé | **el puesto** | job; position |
| **la dirección de personal** | personnel office, employment office | **el salario / el sueldo** | salary |
| **el/la director(a) de personal** | personnel director | **caerle** (*irreg.*) **bien/ mal a alguien** | to make a good/bad impression on someone |
| **la empresa** | corporation; business | **dejar** | to quit |
| **el/la entrevistador(a)** | interviewer | **renunciar (a)** | to resign (from) |

*company. Caerle bien/mal* is used like *gustar* to refer to people. *Renunciar* and *dimitir* mean *to resign from a job. Resignar* is a false cognate and is never used to express *to resign from a job.*

**Heritage Speakers**
Algunos hispanohablantes usan la palabra *aplicación* en vez de *solicitud*. Esta forma es un anglicismo, y es preferible usar *solicitud*, especialmente en situaciones formales. Pregúnteles a los hispanohablantes de la clase qué término usan. Pídales que nombren otros anglicismos comunes entre los hispanohablantes que viven en este país.

## ■ Conversación

**A. Definiciones.** Dé definiciones de las siguientes palabras y frases.

MODELO: la empresa →
una compañía grande, como la IBM o Ford

1. el currículum
2. dejar un puesto
3. la aspirante
4. el gerente
5. el sueldo
6. llenar una solicitud

**Con. B: Suggestion**
Encourage students to read all items before beginning the activity.

**Con. B: Follow-Up**
Have students work in groups to write brief dialogues that illustrate the different parts of the sequence. Then have them present their sections to the class.

**B. En busca de un puesto.** Imagine que Ud. solicitó un puesto el mes pasado. Usando los números del 1 al 7 para cada sección, indique en qué orden ocurrió lo siguiente. El número 1 ya está indicado.

ANTES DE LA ENTREVISTA

a. __2__ Fue a la biblioteca para informarse sobre la empresa: su historia, dónde tiene sucursales (*branches*), etcétera.

b. __5__ Ud. llenó la solicitud tan pronto como la recibió y se la mandó, con el currículum, a la empresa.

c. __1__ En la oficina de empleos de su universidad, Ud. leyó un anuncio para un puesto en su especialización.

d. __4__ Le dijo que le iba a mandar una solicitud para que la llenara (*you could fill it out*) y también le pidió que mandara (*you send*) su currículum.

e. __3__ Llamó al teléfono que se dio el anuncio y habló con un secretario en la dirección de personal.

f. __7__ La mañana de la entrevista, Ud. se levantó temprano, se vistió con cuidado y salió temprano para la empresa para llegar puntualmente.

g. __6__ En una semana lo/la llamaron para arreglar una entrevista.

EL DÍA DE LA ENTREVISTA Y EN ADELANTE (*ON*)

a. __6__ Se despidió de Ud. cordialmente, diciendo que lo/la iba a llamar en una semana.

b. __2__ Por fin, el secretario le dijo que Ud. se iba a entrevistar con (*were going to be interviewed by*) la directora de personal.

c. __7__ Cuando por fin lo/la llamó la directora, ¡fue para ofrecerle el puesto!

d. __1__ Mientras esperaba en la dirección de personal, Ud. estaba nerviosísimo/a.

e. __4__ La directora le hizo una serie de preguntas: cuándo se iba a graduar, qué cursos había tomado, etcétera.

f. __3__ Al entrar en la oficina de la directora, Ud. la saludó con cortesía, tratando de caerle bien desde el principio.

g. __5__ También le pidió que hablara (*you speak*) un poco en español, ya que la empresa tiene una sucursal en Santiago, Chile.

## NOTA CULTURAL

### Los nombres de las profesiones

En el mundo de habla española **hay poco acuerdo** sobre las palabras que deben usarse para **referirse a las mujeres que ejercen ciertas profesiones.** En gran parte, eso se debe al hecho de que, en muchos de estos países, **las mujeres acaban de empezar a ejercer esas profesiones;** por eso el idioma todavía está cambiando para acomodarse a esa nueva realidad. **En la actualidad se emplean,** entre otras, **las siguientes formas.**

- Se usa el artículo **la** con los sustantivos que terminan en **-ista.**

  el dentista → **la** den**tista**

- En otros casos se usa una forma femenina.

  el médico → **la** médi**ca**          el trabajador → **la** trabajado**ra**

- Se usa la palabra **mujer** con el nombre de la profesión.

  el policía → **la mujer** policía          el soldado → **la mujer** soldado

Escuche lo que dice cualquier[a] persona con quien Ud. habla español para saber las formas que él o ella usa. No se trata de[b] formas correctas o incorrectas, sólo de usos y costumbres locales.

*Una científica en su laboratorio*

---

[a]*any*   [b]*No… It's not a question of*

**Nota cultural: Comprensión: ¿Cierto o falso?**
1. *Las mujeres todavía no ejercen profesiones como médica o policía en los países hispánicos.*
2. *El uso de formas femeninas para los nombres de las profesiones todavía depende de usos y costumbres, no de reglas lingüísticas.*

**UNA CUESTIÓN DE DINERO**

Resources: Transparency 98

**Refrán**

«Dinero ahorrado, dos veces ganado.»

Have students give a similar saying in English. (*A penny saved is a penny earned.*)

| | |
|---|---|
| la caja | cashier window |
| la chequera | checkbook |
| la cuenta corriente | checking account |
| la cuenta de ahorros | savings account |
| la identificación | ID |
| el interés | interest |
| el préstamo | loan |
| el presupuesto | budget |
| | |
| ahorrar | to save (*money*) |
| cargar (gu) (a la cuenta de uno) | to charge (to someone's account) |
| cobrar | to cash (*a check*); to charge (*someone for an item or service*) |
| depositar/sacar (qu) | to deposit/withdraw, take out |
| devolver (ue) | to return (*something*) |
| economizar (c) | to economize |
| ganar | to earn |
| gastar | to spend (*money*) |

el banco

la factura / la cuenta

BANCO POPULAR

el cajero automático

la tarjeta de crédito

el cheque

el efectivo

| | |
|---|---|
| pagar (gu) a plazos / con cheque | to pay in installments / by check |
| pagar (gu) en efectivo / al contado | to pay in cash |
| pedir (i, i) prestado/a | to borrow |
| prestar | to lend |

**Suggestions**

- Point out that *cobrar un cheque* means *to cash a check,* but for cashing traveler's checks *cambiar un cheque de viajero* is used. Explain and model the differences between *ahorrar* (to save money or time), *guardar* (to save, keep something), and *salvar* (to save, rescue someone). Contrast and model the difference between *gastar* (to spend money) and *pasar* (to spend time).
- Explain that vocabulary for financial and banking transactions varies a good deal in the Spanish-speaking world. Introduce other terms you might prefer or hear, for example, *depositar* vs. *ingresar* and *libreta* (*de ahorros*) vs. *cartilla.*
- Offer the following optional vocabulary.

*los ingresos* (income)
*hacer una transferencia / un giro*

## ■ Conversación

**A. El mes pasado.** Piense en sus finanzas personales del mes pasado. ¿Fue un mes típico? ¿Tuvo dificultades al final del mes o todo le salió bien?

PASO 1 Indique las respuestas apropiadas para Ud.

| | ¡CLARO QUE SÍ! | ¡CLARO QUE NO! |
|---|---|---|
| 1. Hice un presupuesto al principio del mes. | ☐ | ☐ |
| 2. Deposité más dinero en el banco del que (*than what*) saqué. | ☐ | ☐ |
| 3. Saqué dinero del cajero automático sin apuntar (*writing down*) la cantidad en mi chequera. | ☐ | ☐ |
| 4. Pagué todas mis cuentas a tiempo. | ☐ | ☐ |
| 5. Saqué un préstamo (Le pedí dinero prestado al banco) para pagar mis cuentas. | ☐ | ☐ |
| 6. Tomé el autobús en vez de (*instead of*) usar el coche, para economizar un poco. | ☐ | ☐ |
| 7. Gasté mucho dinero en diversiones. | ☐ | ☐ |
| 8. Saqué el saldo (*I balanced*) de mi chequera sin dificultades. | ☐ | ☐ |

<table>
</table>

|  | ¡CLARO QUE SÍ! | ¡CLARO QUE NO! |
|---|---|---|
| 9. Le presté dinero a un amigo. | ☐ | ☐ |
| 10. Usé mis tarjetas de crédito sólo en casos de urgencia. | ☐ | ☐ |

Con. A: Suggestion
• Have students complete this as a pair activity, turning the items into questions.
• **Paso 2.** Have students complete this as written homework.

PASO 2 Vuelva a mirar sus respuestas. ¿Fue el mes pasado un mes típico? Pensando todavía en sus respuestas, sugiera tres cosas que Ud. debe hacer para mejorar su situación económica.

MODELO: Debo hacer un presupuesto mensual.

## B. Diálogos

PASO 1 Empareje las preguntas de la izquierda con las respuestas de la derecha.

1. __f__ ¿Cómo prefiere Ud. pagar?
2. __d__ ¿Hay algún problema?
3. __e__ Me da su identificación, por favor. Necesito verla para que pueda cobrar su cheque.
4. __c__ ¿Quisiera (*Would you like*) usar su tarjeta de crédito?
5. __a__ ¿Va a depositar este cheque en su cuenta corriente o en su cuenta de ahorros?
6. __b__ ¿Adónde quiere Ud. que mandemos la factura?

a. En la cuenta de ahorros, por favor.
b. Me la manda a la oficina, por favor.
c. No, prefiero pagar al contado.
d. Sí, señorita. Ud. me cobró demasiado por el jarabe.
e. Aquí la tiene Ud. Me la va a devolver pronto, ¿verdad?
f. Cárguelo a mi cuenta, por favor.

Con. B: Suggestion
Have students role-play this activity. You or a native speaker can take the role of the Spanish-speaking clerk (left-hand column).

Con. C: Variation
Have students do this as a written activity.

**Need more practice?**

■ Workbook/Laboratory Manual
■ Interactive CD-ROM
■ Online Learning Center (www.mhhe.com/quetal7)

PASO 2 Ahora, con un compañero / una compañera, invente un contexto posible para cada diálogo. ¿Dónde están las personas que hablan? ¿En un banco? ¿en una tienda? ¿Quiénes son? ¿Clientes? ¿cajeros? ¿dependientes?

## C. Situaciones.
Con un compañero / una compañera, describa lo que pasa en los siguientes dibujos. Usen las preguntas a continuación como guía.

¿Quiénes son estas personas?
¿Dónde están?
¿Qué van a comprar?

¿Cómo van a pagar?
¿Qué van a hacer después?

**Resources: Transparency 99**

1.     2.     3.     4.

**Note**
See the Workbook/Laboratory Manual for review and practice of stress and the written accent.

**Paso 2: Gramática**
See the "Chapter-by-Chapter Supplementary Materials" in the IM for additional teaching suggestions, notes, activities, and other resources for *Paso 2*.

**Suggestion**
Use items to introduce *Ud.* forms of the future by asking follow-up questions.

**1.** *¿En qué ciudad vivirá Ud.?*

Then introduce the *tú* form by giving students the *-ás* ending and allowing them to ask follow-up questions of other students.

**1.** *¿En qué país vivirás?*

**Note**
The future perfect is presented only in the footnote on page 395. Active production is not required in the activities.

**Heritage Speakers**
En español las palabras *a* y *ha* se confunden fácilmente porque se pronuncian de la misma manera. Por lo tanto, los hispanos pueden tener dificultades en distinguir entre *va a haber / va a ver* y *va a ser / va a hacer.* El uso del futuro evita la confusión: *habrá, verá, será* y *hará* respectivamente. Anime a los hispanohablantes a explicar la diferencia entre estas cuatro formas y a usarlas en oraciones.

**Multimedia: Internet**
Have students search the Internet for a Spanish language horoscope site. Students should print out and bring in their horoscope to share with the class. Have students rewrite their horoscope in the future tense if it is not already in the future.

---

### ¿Recuerda Ud.?

Before studying the future tense in **Gramática 42,** review **Gramática 3 (Capítulo 1)** and **Gramática 10 (Capítulo 3),** where you learned ways of expressing future actions. Then indicate which of the following sentences can be used to express a future action.

1. Trabajé hasta las dos.
2. Trabajo a las dos.
3. Voy a trabajar a las dos.
4. Trabajaba a las dos.
5. Estoy trabajando.
6. He trabajado a las dos.

---

## 42 Talking About the Future Future Verb Forms

¿Cómo va a ser su vida dentro de diez años? ¿Está de acuerdo con las primeras cinco oraciones? Conteste sí o no. Luego, complete las últimas dos con información verdadera —¡o por lo menos deseable!

1. *Viviré* en otra ciudad / otro país.
2. *Estaré* casado/a.
3. *Tendré* uno o más hijos (nietos).
4. *Seré* dueño/a de mi propia casa.
5. *Llevaré* una vida más tranquila.
6. *Trabajaré* como _____ (nombre de profesión).
7. *Ganaré* por lo menos _____ dólares al año.

The future tense expresses things or events that *will* or *are going* to happen.

| Past | Present | FUTURE |
|---|---|---|
| preterite | present indicative | future |
| imperfect | present progressive | |
| present perfect | formal commands | |
| present perfect subjunctive | informal commands | |
| | present subjunctive | |

**A.** In English, the future is formed with the auxiliary verbs *will* or *shall*. *I **will**/**shall*** *speak.*

In Spanish, the *future* (**el futuro**) is a simple verb form (only one word). It is formed by adding future endings to the infinitive. No auxiliary verbs are needed.

Future verb endings.

| | |
|---|---|
| -é | -emos |
| -ás | -éis |
| -á | -án |

| hablar | | comer | | vivir | |
|---|---|---|---|---|---|
| hablaré | hablaremos | comeré | comeremos | viviré | viviremos |
| hablarás | hablaréis | comerás | comeréis | vivirás | viviréis |
| hablará | hablarán | comerá | comerán | vivirá | vivirán |

**B.** The verbs on the right are the most common Spanish verbs that are irregular in the future. The future endings are attached to their irregular stems.

**decir:** diré, dirás, dirá, diremos, diréis, dirán

| | | |
|---|---|---|
| decir: | **dir-** | |
| haber (hay): | **habr-** | |
| hacer: | **har-** | **-é** |
| poder: | **podr-** | **-ás** |
| poner: | **pondr-** | **-á** |
| querer: | **querr-** | **-emos** |
| saber: | **sabr-** | **-éis** |
| salir: | **saldr-** | **-án** |
| tener: | **tendr-** | |
| venir: | **vendr-** | |

> Note that the future of **hay (haber)** is **habrá** (*there will be*).*

**C.** Compare the use of the indicative and subjunctive present tense forms to express the immediate future.

**Llegaré** a tiempo.
*I'll arrive on time.*

**Llego** a las ocho mañana. ¿Vienes a buscarme?
*I'll arrive at 8:00 tomorrow. Will you come to pick me up?*

No creo que Pepe **llegue** a tiempo.
*I don't think Pepe will arrive on time.*

¿**Quieres** cerrar la puerta, por favor?
*Will you please close the door?*

**OJO** When the English *will* refers not to future time but to the willingness of someone to do something, Spanish uses the verb **querer**, not the future.

---

*The future forms of the verb **haber** are used to form the future perfect tense (**el futuro perfecto**), which expresses what* will have *occurred at some point in the future.*

Para mañana, ya **habré hablado** con Miguel.    *By tomorrow, I will have spoken with Miguel.*

*You will find a more detailed presentation of these forms in Appendix 3, Additional Perfect Forms (Indicative and Subjunctive).*

# PASO 2

## ■ Práctica

**AUTOPRUEBA**

Complete the verbs with the correct future endings.

1. yo vivir_____
2. ella dir_____
3. ellos saldr_____
4. Uds. vendr_____
5. nosotros comer_____
6. tú querr_____

*Answers: 1. viviré 2. dirá 3. saldrán 4. vendrán 5. comeremos 6. querrás*

**A. ¡Anticipemos! Mis compañeros de clase.** ¿Cree Ud. que conoce bien a sus compañeros de clase? ¿Sabe lo que les va a pasar en el futuro? Vamos a ver.

PASO 1   Indique si las siguientes oraciones serán ciertas para Ud. algún día.

|  | SÍ | NO |
|---|---|---|
| 1. Seré profesor(a) de idiomas. | ☐ | ☐ |
| 2. Me casaré (Me divorciaré) dentro de tres años. | ☐ | ☐ |
| 3. Me mudaré (*I will move*) a otro país. | ☐ | ☐ |
| 4. Compraré un coche deportivo. | ☐ | ☐ |
| 5. Tendré una familia muy grande (mucho más grande). | ☐ | ☐ |
| 6. Asistiré a una escuela de estudios graduados. | ☐ | ☐ |
| 7. Visitaré Latinoamérica. | ☐ | ☐ |
| 8. Estaré en bancarrota (*bankruptcy*). | ☐ | ☐ |
| 9. Estaré jubilado/a (*retired*). | ☐ | ☐ |
| 10. No tendré que trabajar porque seré rico/a. | ☐ | ☐ |

PASO 2   Ahora, para cada oración del **Paso 1**, indique el nombre de una persona de la clase para quien Ud. cree que la oración es cierta. Puede ser un compañero / una compañera de clase o su profesor(a).

PASO 3   Ahora compare sus predicciones con las respuestas de estas personas. ¿Hizo Ud. predicciones correctas?

**B. ¿Qué harán en los próximos diez años?**   Haga oraciones sobre lo que harán las siguientes personas en los próximos diez años, usando frases de cada grupo.

| yo<br>tú<br>nosotros (los estudiantes de esta clase)<br>el/la profesor(a)<br>mi padre/madre / mis padres/hijos<br>mi mejor amigo/a<br>¿ ? | **+** | (no) | **+** | tener uno o dos hijos<br>jubilarse (*to retire*)<br>querer cambiar de trabajo<br>ganar mucho/poco dinero<br>saber hablar español perfectamente<br>venir a esta universidad<br>poder hacer lo que quiera<br>dar clases de...<br>decir que...<br>trabajar en...<br>poner mucho dinero mensualmente en la cuenta del banco<br>ser dueño/a de...<br>ir/viajar a...<br>¿ ? |

Prác. C: Suggestion
Have students name the following.

1. *tres cosas que harán hoy*
2. *tres cosas que harán mañana*
3. *tres cosas que harán este fin de semana*
4. *tres cosas que harán durante las vacaciones*
5. *tres cosas que harán después de graduarse*

## C. Mi amigo Gregorio

PASO 1   Describa Ud. las siguientes cosas que hará su compañero Gregorio. Luego indique si Ud. hará lo mismo (**Yo también… Yo tampoco…** ) u otra cosa.

MODELO:   no / gastar / menos / mes →
Gregorio no *gastará* menos este mes. Yo tampoco *gastaré* menos. (Yo sí *gastaré* menos este mes. ¡Tengo que ahorrar!)

1. pagar / tarde / todo / cuentas
2. tratar / adaptarse a / presupuesto
3. volver / hacer / presupuesto / próximo mes
4. no / depositar / nada / en / cuenta de ahorros
5. quejarse / porque / no / tener / suficiente dinero
6. seguir / usando / tarjetas / crédito
7. pedirles / dinero / a / padres
8. buscar / trabajo / de tiempo parcial

PASO 2   ¿Cuál de las siguientes oraciones describe mejor a su amigo?

- Gregorio es muy responsable en cuanto a (*regarding*) asuntos de dinero. Es un buen modelo para imitar.
- Gregorio tiene que aprender a ser más responsable con su dinero.

## ■ Conversación

A. **Ventajas y desventajas.**   What can you do to get extra cash or to save money? The first three possibilities are shown in the following drawings. What are the advantages and disadvantages of each suggestion?

MODELO:   dejar de tomar tanto café →
Si dejo de tomar tanto café, ahorraré sólo un poco de dinero. Estaré menos nervioso/a, pero creo que será más difícil despertarme por la mañana.

Resources: Transparency 100

1. pedirles dinero a mis amigos o parientes
2. cometer un robo
3. alquilar unos cuartos de mi casa a otras personas
4. dejar de fumar / beber cerveza / tomar tanto café
5. buscar un trabajo de tiempo parcial
6. vender mi coche / televisor
7. comprar muchos billetes de lotería
8. estudiar más
9. invertir mis ahorros en bonos y acciones (*stocks and bonds*)

Prác. C: Answers
*Paso 1*  **1.** *Gregorio pagará tarde todas sus cuentas.* **2.** *Tratará de adaptarse a un presupuesto.* **3.** *Volverá a hacer un presupuesto el próximo mes.* **4.** *No depositará nada en su cuenta de ahorros.* **5.** *Se quejará porque no tendrá suficiente dinero.* **6.** *Seguirá usando sus tarjetas de crédito.* **7.** *Les pedirá dinero a sus padres.* **8.** *Buscará un trabajo de tiempo parcial.*   *Possible answers:*  **1.** *Yo también pagaré tarde todas mis cuentas.* **2.** *Yo también trataré de adaptarme a un presupuesto.* **3.** *Yo también volveré a hacer un presupuesto el próximo mes.* **4.** *Yo sí depositaré algo en mi cuenta de ahorros.* **5.** *Yo*

**Need more practice?**

- Workbook/Laboratory Manual
- Interactive CD-ROM
- Online Learning Center (www.mhhe.com/quetal7)

*no me quejaré porque tendré suficiente dinero.* **6.** *Yo no seguiré usando mis tarjetas de crédito.* **7.** *Yo no les pediré dinero a mis padres.* **8.** *Yo también buscaré un trabajo de tiempo parcial.*   *Paso 2*  **2.** *Gregorio tiene que aprender a ser más responsable con su dinero.*

**Nota comunicativa: Suggestions**
- Use visuals with the future of probability to speculate about the individuals in the drawings.

  *¿Quién será la mujer que espera?*
  *¿Dónde estará esperando?*
  *¿Para quién estará esperando?*

- Emphasize that this use of the future is frequent in Spanish, possibly even more frequent than the use of the standard future (the future of intention).
- Point out that the future of probability in English can also be expressed with *must* and *will: Cecilia must (will) be on her way by now.*
- Point out that another word for *lío* is *embotellamiento.*

**Heritage Speakers**
Note que en español, cuando el futuro se usa para expresar probabilidad en el presente, equivale a *to wonder* y *probably* en inglés. Anime a los hispanohablantes a dar la forma del futuro de probabilidad para las oraciones a continuación.

  *¿Qué está en la puerta?*
  *¿Cuántos años tiene esa señora?*

También pídales que expliquen en sus propias palabras el significado de cada oración.

♻ **Reciclado**
Have students change the following sentences to express probability and conjecture with the future. The first set of sentences reenters travel and money vocabulary, the second set reenters health vocabulary.

DE VIAJE
1. *Cobran mucho en aquella tienda, ¿no crees?*
2. *¿Cuánto es el precio de aquella estatua?*
3. *Podemos usar las tarjetas de crédito aunque estamos en el extranjero.*
4. *¡Las facturas llegan a casa antes de que lleguemos nosotros!*
5. *¿Tengo suficiente dinero para pagarlas?*

LA SALUD
1. *Julito está enfermo.*
2. *¿Cuántos grados de temperatura tiene?*
3. *La doctora viene más tarde.*
4. *Le da un antibiótico.*
5. *Le pone una inyección.*

**B. El mundo en el año 2500.** ¿Cómo será el mundo del futuro? Haga una lista de temas o cosas que Ud. cree que van a ser diferentes en el año 2500. Por ejemplo: el transporte, la comida, la vivienda… Piense también en temas globales: la política, los problemas que presenta la capa de ozono…

Ahora, a base de su lista, haga una serie de predicciones para el futuro.

MODELO: La gente comerá (Comeremos) comidas sintéticas.

---

### Vocabulario útil

| | |
|---|---|
| la colonización | el transbordador espacial (space |
| la energía nuclear/solar | shuttle) |
| el espacio | la vida artificial |
| los OVNIs (Objetos Volantes No | |
| Identificados) | diseñar (to design) |
| el planeta | eliminar |
| la pobreza (poverty) | |
| el robot | intergaláctico/a |
| el satélite | interplanetario/a |
| | sintético/a |

---

## NOTA COMUNICATIVA

### Expressing Conjecture

Estela, en el aeropuerto

¿Dónde **estará** Cecilia?

¿Qué le **pasará**?

**Estará** en un lío de tráfico.

Cecilia, en la carretera

*I wonder where Cecilia is. (Where can Cecilia be?)*

*I wonder what's up with her. (What can be wrong?)*

*She's probably (must be) in a traffic jam. (I bet she's in a traffic jam.)*

The future can also be used in Spanish to express probability or conjecture about what is happening now. This use of the future is called the *future of probability* (**el futuro de probabilidad**). Note in the preceding examples that the English cues for expressing probability (*probably, I bet, must be, I wonder . . . , Where can . . .* , and so on) are not directly expressed in Spanish. Their sense is conveyed in Spanish by the use of the future form of the verb.

## C. Predicciones.

¿Quiénes serán las siguientes personas? ¿Qué estarán haciendo? ¿Dónde estarán? Invente todos los detalles que pueda sobre los siguientes dibujos.

Resources: Transparency 101

Con. C: Preliminary Exercise
Have students express the following ideas in Spanish using the future of probability.

1. He's probably a teacher, and she must be a doctor.
2. I wonder where she works.

3. I wonder which one earns more money.
4. They're probably from a big city.
5. They probably have a lot of kids.
6. They must be asking questions about (*acerca de*) us, too!

1.

2.

3.

4.

## En los Estados Unidos y el Canadá

### El creciente mercado hispánico

¿Qué tienen en común Ford, Chevrolet, Sprint, Dockers, United Health y Toys "Я" Us? Pues, como muchas compañías norteamericanas, **tienen activas campañas publicitarias para atraer al mercado hispánico nacional.** Con más de 40 millones de hispanos, según el censo estadounidense del año 2004, los Estados Unidos ocupa **el cuarto puesto**[a] entre las naciones que tienen una población hispanohablante (se calcula que podría[b] ser **la segunda** o **tercera nación** en los próximos quince años, por delante de España). La población hispana de los Estados Unidos se traduce en[c] **un mercado de más de 600.000 millones de**[d] **dólares.**

*CNN en español, HBO Latino* y *People en español* se dirigen a[e] la variada comunidad hispana de los Estados

Unidos. Muchos programas y publicaciones se originan en la Florida, entre ellos *Latin Trade,* una **revista mensual**[f] de **negocios** y **economía** referente a Norteamérica en relación con todos los países hispánicos. El ámbito de lectores[g] de *Latin Trade* incluye a hispanos de todo el mundo, un grupo de más de 400 millones de personas.

Desgraciadamente,[h] **la importancia numérica de los hispanos,** más del 12 por ciento de la población de los Estados Unidos, **no se ve reflejada**[i] **en el mundo de la comunicación, de la política ni de los negocios.** Es este el gran reto[j] para los hispanos de este país.

[a]*position* [b]*it could* [c]*se… translates into* [d]*600.000… seiscientos millones de (600 billion)* [e]*se… target* [f]*monthly* [g]*ámbito… readership* [h]*Unfortunately* [i]*no… is not reflected* [j]*challenge*

**En los Estados Unidos y el Canadá: Comprensión**
1. ¿Cuántos dólares al año, más o menos, gastan los hispanos en los Estados Unidos?
2. ¿Cuáles son algunas de las publicaciones estadounidenses para lectores hispanos?

# Voces del Uruguay y del Paraguay

## LITERATURA: Horacio Quiroga

**Horacio Quiroga**
*(1878– 1937)*

**Sobre el autor:** *Horacio Silvestre Quiroga nació en Salto, Uruguay. En 1899 fundó la* Revista de Salto, *y en 1900 viajó a París con otros jóvenes intelectuales. Volvió al Uruguay pero, después de matar[a] accidentalmente a un amigo, se trasladó a la Argentina. En 1935 publicó* Más allá, *su último libro de cuentos antes de morir. El siguiente fragmento es del cuento* «El hijo», Más allá *(1935).*

Es un poderoso[b] día de verano en Misiones, con todo el sol, el calor y la calma que puede deparar[c] la estación. La naturaleza plenamente[d] abierta, se siente satisfecha de sí. Como el sol, el calor y la calma ambiente, el padre abre también su corazón a la naturaleza.

—Ten cuidado, chiquito —dice a su hijo; abreviando[e] en esa frase todas las observaciones del caso y que su hijo comprende perfectamente.

—Sí, papá —responde la criatura[f] mientras coge la escopeta[g] y carga de cartuchos[h] los bolsillos de su camisa, que cierra con cuidado.

[a]*killing* [b]*powerful* [c]*traer* [d]*completely, fully* [e]*abbreviating* [f]*niño* [g]*shotgun* [h]*carga... fills with cartridges*

## MÚSICA: El candombe y el arpa paraguaya

El candombe es una música basada en los ritmos de tambores.[a] Fue creado[b] por los afro-uruguayos de Montevideo en el siglo[c] XVIII y con gran influencia del tamborileo[d] bantú de África. La música y el baile candombe son esenciales en la celebración del Carnaval en Montevideo y son una de las principales atracciones turísticas del país. Este carnaval tiene mucho en común con otras celebraciones carnavalescas, como las de Río de Janeiro y Nueva Orleáns. La comparsa[e] se prepara todo el año para perfeccionar su traje, sus ritmos y su baile.

[a]*drums* [b]*created* [c]*century* [d]*drumming* [e]*dance troupe*

Aunque[f] la mayoría de los paraguayos son mestizos y de fuerte ascendencia indígena, la música del Paraguay es de carácter europeo. El instrumento nacional del Paraguay es el arpa, que los jesuitas* hicieron popular en la cuenca[g] del Paraná.

[f]*Although* [g]*river basin*

*\*Beginning in the late sixteenth century, the Jesuits established missions in Paraguay along the Paraná River to convert the Guaraní people. Some of the priests brought musical instruments, such as the harp. Paraguay continues to be an internationally recognized center for making harps.*

**Suggestions**
• Point out the chapter opener photo from the 2004 presidential elections in the Dominican Republic. Ask students what political campaigns and elections are like in this country. Explain that the Dominican Republic is a democracy with three branches of government: executive, legislative, and judicial. The presidential and vice presidential candidates run together under the same ticket, and the elections for

# En la actualidad

president are held every four years. The three primary political parties are the *Partido de la Liberación Dominicana* (*PLD*), the *Partido Revolucionario Dominicano* (*PRD*), and the *Partido Reformista Social Cristiano* (*PRSC*). In the 2004 elections, Eduardo Estrella and the presidential incumbent, Hipólito Mejía (*PRD*), lost to Leonel Fernández (*PLD*), who won 57% of the votes.

• Have students list their ideas about the Dominican Republic, including information on geography, politics, economy, culture, music, and cuisine. When you finish the chapter, return to the lists and ask students what ideas they would change and/or add.

*Partidaria (Supporter) de Eduardo Estrella, el candidato del Partido Reformista Social Cristiano, para la presidencia de la República Dominicana en 2004*

Paso 1: Vocabulario
See the "Chapter-by-Chapter Supplementary Materials" in the IM for a model for vocabulary presentation, as well as additional teaching suggestions, notes, activities, and other resources for *Paso 1*.

## LAS NOTICIAS

Resources: Transparency 103

**el reportero**

**Multimedia: Audio**
Students can listen to and practice this chapter's vocabulary on the Online Learning Center (www.mhhe.com/quetal7), as well as on the Textbook Audio CD, part of the Laboratory Audio Program.

Y ahora, **el canal** 45 les ofrece a Uds. el NOTICIERO 45, con los últimos **eventos** del **mundo**...

**El asesinato** de **un dictador**

**La huelga** de obreros

**La guerra** en el Oriente Medio

**La erupción** de un volcán en Centroamérica

**Bombas** en un avión

**El choque** de trenes

| | |
|---|---|
| el acontecimiento | event, happening |
| el desastre | disaster |
| la esperanza | hope, wish |
| el medio de comunicación | means of communication |
| la paz (*pl.* **paces**) | peace |
| la prensa | press; news media |
| el/la testigo | witness |

| | |
|---|---|
| comunicarse (qu) (con) | to communicate (with) |
| enterarse (de) | to find out, learn (about) |
| informar | to inform |
| mantener (*irreg.*) **la paz** | to maintain, keep peace |
| ofrecer (zc) | to offer |
| vivir en paz | to live in peace |

**Cognados: el ataque (terrorista), el terrorismo, el/la terrorista, la víctima**

**Suggestions**
- Remind students that the first person singular of *ofrecer* is *ofrezco*.
- Read the following definitions and have students give the corresponding words from the vocabulary.

1. *cuando una persona asesina a alguien*
2. *cuando un grupo de obreros o empleados deja de trabajar, como un acto de protesta*
3. *cuando se sabe algo por primera vez*
4. *las formas en que se da la información al mundo*
5. *antónimo de la guerra*

## ■ Conversación

**A. ¿Cómo se entera Ud.?** El público utiliza diferentes medios para enterarse de los acontecimientos locales, nacionales e internacionales. ¿Cómo se entera Ud. de las noticias?

PASO 1 Indique con qué frecuencia utiliza los siguientes medios.

| | TODOS LOS DÍAS | DE 3 A 5 VECES POR SEMANA | DE 1 A 2 VECES POR SEMANA | CASI NUNCA |
|---|---|---|---|---|
| 1. Leo un periódico local. | ☐ | ☐ | ☐ | ☐ |
| 2. Leo un periódico nacional. | ☐ | ☐ | ☐ | ☐ |
| 3. Leo una revista. | ☐ | ☐ | ☐ | ☐ |
| 4. Leo las noticias en el Internet. | ☐ | ☐ | ☐ | ☐ |
| 5. Miro el noticiero local. | ☐ | ☐ | ☐ | ☐ |
| 6. Miro el noticiero nacional. | ☐ | ☐ | ☐ | ☐ |
| 7. Miro CNN. | ☐ | ☐ | ☐ | ☐ |
| 8. Escucho la radio. | ☐ | ☐ | ☐ | ☐ |

PASO 2 Compare sus respuestas con las de sus compañeros. ¿Cuál es el medio preferido por la mayoría de Uds. para informarse?

**B. Definiciones.** ¿Qué palabra se asocia con cada definición?

1. __a__ un programa que nos informa de lo que pasa en nuestro mundo
2. __f__ una persona que está presente durante un acontecimiento y lo ve todo
3. __i__ un medio importantísimo de comunicación
4. __g__ una persona que nos informa de los acontecimientos
5. __d__ una persona que gobierna un país de una forma absoluta
6. __c__ una persona que emplea la violencia para cambiar el mundo según sus deseos
7. __h__ cuando los obreros se niegan a (*refuse*) trabajar
8. __e__ la frecuencia en que se transmiten y se reciben los programas de televisión
9. __b__ la confrontación armada entre dos o más países

a. el noticiero
b. la guerra
c. el/la terrorista
d. el/la dictador(a)
e. el canal
f. el/la testigo
g. el/la reportero/a
h. la huelga
i. la prensa

**C. Uds. y la televisión.** Con un compañero / una compañera, diga si está de acuerdo con las siguientes opiniones. Si no están de acuerdo, hagan los cambios necesarios para expresar su opinión. En cualquier caso, intenten dar un ejemplo que justifique su punto de vista.

1. Los reporteros de la televisión nos informan imparcialmente de los acontecimientos.
2. Por lo general ofrecen los programas más interesantes en el canal de televisión pública.
3. En este país la prensa es irresponsable. Nos da sólo los detalles que apoyan (*support*) sus ideas políticas.
4. Las telenovelas (*soap operas*) reflejan la vida tal (*just*) como es.
5. Los anuncios son sumamente (*extremely*) informativos y más interesantes que muchos programas.
6. Me gusta que los reporteros y meteorólogos cuenten chistes (*jokes*) durante el noticiero.

## EL GOBIERNO Y LA RESPONSABILIDAD CÍVICA

el rey

la reina

el dictador

el político

la ciudadana

votar

el ciudadano

el ejército

| | | | |
|---|---|---|---|
| **el deber** | responsibility; obligation | **la ley** | law |
| **los/las demás** | others, other people | **la política** | politics |
| **el derecho** | right | **el servicio militar** | military service |
| **la (des)igualdad** | (in)equality | | |
| **la dictadura** | dictatorship | **durar** | to last |
| **la discriminación** | discrimination | **obedecer (zc)** | to obey |

## ■ Conversación

**A. ¡Peligro!** (*Jeopardy!*)   ¿Cuánto sabe Ud. de la historia y la política? Conteste rápidamente con la información necesaria y en forma de pregunta. Use las preguntas a la derecha.

¿Quién/Qué es… ?

1. __g__ Fue un dictador argentino que tenía una esposa famosa.
2. __b__ Se llama Elizabeth y vive en Buckingham Palace.
3. __e__ Es una famosa película de Orson Welles, y su protagonista se llama Kane.
4. __h__ Fue un presidente estadounidense que se opuso a (*opposed*) la esclavitud de los negros.
5. __a__ En algunos países, es un deber de los hombres de cierta edad. Generalmente, tienen que entrar en el ejército por dos años, más o menos.
6. __d__ Es la forma de gobierno que existe en España.
7. __f__ Existe cuando muchas personas no tienen los mismos derechos que los demás.
8. __c__ Es un deber de los ciudadanos en una democracia.

a. el servicio militar
b. la reina de Inglaterra
c. votar
d. la monarquía parlamentaria
e. *El ciudadano Kane* (*Citizen Kane*)
f. la discriminación
g. Juan Perón
h. Abraham Lincoln

## NOTA CULTURAL

### La mayoría de edad en los países hispánicos

En el mundo hispánico los jóvenes se consideran legalmente adultos, es decir, **alcanzan**[a] **la mayoría de edad, a los 18 años.** Al cumplir los 18 años, los jóvenes hispanos pueden **participar en la política y pueden votar.** En varios países los hombres de 18 años también tienen la responsabilidad de inscribirse[b] en **el servicio militar.** En Colombia, los jóvenes pueden inscribirse en el servicio militar a los 16 años. La selección de los conscriptos[c] generalmente se hace mediante[d] una lotería. Recientemente, las mujeres mexicanas y argentinas también pueden inscribirse en el servicio militar, un hecho[e] sin precedentes en Latinoamérica.

*Una licencia de conducir argentina*

A los 18 años, los jóvenes hispanos pueden obtener su **licencia de manejar.** Sin embargo, algunos jóvenes en ciertos países no esperan hasta los 18 años. A los 16 años solicitan un **permiso especial para menores de edad** para operar un vehículo.

Otro aspecto importante al llegar a la mayoría de edad es el consumo de alcohol. **La edad límite para tomar bebidas alcohólicas** varía entre los 18 y 21 años. En Ecuador, por ejemplo, la edad límite es de 21 años. En algunos países hay menos restricciones sociales sobre el alcohol.

*Nota cultural: Comprensión ¿Cierto o falso?*

*1. Los menores de 18 años no pueden manejar un coche en los países hispánicos.*

[a] *they reach*    [b] *de... of registering*    [c] *draftees*    [d] *by means of*    [e] *evento*

*2. Todos los hispanos de 18 años tienen que hacer su servicio militar.*

---

**B. Asociaciones.** ¿Qué cosas, personas o ideas asocia Ud. con las siguientes palabras?

| | | |
|---|---|---|
| **1.** el deber | **3.** la política | **5.** la monarquía |
| **2.** el ejército | **4.** la ley | **6.** la dictadura |

**C. Opiniones.** ¿Qué piensan Uds. de las siguientes ideas? Den su opinión, empezando con una de las **Expresiones útiles.**

1. En este país consumimos demasiada energía.
2. La paz mundial completa es (im)posible.
3. En este país, la igualdad de todos los ciudadanos es una realidad, no sólo una esperanza.
4. Los policías, los bomberos (*firefighters*) y los médicos no tienen derecho a declararse en huelga.
5. El servicio militar obligatorio es necesario para formar un ejército.
6. El mundo de la política está lleno de gente (des)honesta.
7. La edad permitida para tomar bebidas alcohólicas debe ser la misma que la edad para votar.
8. Hay muchos países que tienen dictadores.

> **Expresiones útiles**
>
> Dudo que...
> (No) Creo que...
> Es probable que...
> Es bueno/malo que...
> Es una lástima que...
> Es increíble que...
> Me parece terrible/buena idea que...

**Need more practice?**

- Workbook/Laboratory Manual
- Interactive CD-ROM
- Online Learning Center (www.mhhe.com/quetal7)

**Con. C: Follow-Up**
- Have students report their opinions back to the class. Have one student tally the responses on the board.
- Use this activity as a written assignment.

**Note**
See the Workbook/Laboratory Manual for presentation and practice of intonation, punctuation, and rhythm.

♻ **¿Recuerda Ud.?: Bright Idea Suggestion**
Review with students the formation of the preterite, starting with regular *-ar, -er,* and *-ir* forms, followed by the irregular verbs. Special attention should be given to *-ir* stem-changing verbs that require an additional change in the third person singular and plural.

## ¿Recuerda Ud.?

In **Gramática 44,** you will learn about and begin to use the forms of the past subjunctive. As you learn this new tense, you will be continually using the past tense forms you have already learned along with the new material, so this section presents many opportunities for review.

To learn the forms of the past subjunctive, you will need to know the forms of the preterite well, especially the third person plural.

- Regular **-ar** verbs end in **-aron** and regular **-er/-ir** verbs in **-ieron** in the third person plural of the preterite.
- Stem-changing **-ir** verbs show the second change in the third person.

  **servir (i, i)** → **si**r**vieron   dormir (ue, u)** → **du**r**mieron**

- Verbs with a stem ending in a vowel change the **i** to **y.**

  **le**y**eron, ca**y**eron, constru**y**eron**

- Many common verbs have irregular stems in the preterite.

  **quisieron, hicieron, dijeron,** and so on

- Four common verbs are totally irregular in this tense.

  **ser/ir** → **fueron   dar** → **dieron   ver** → **vieron**

The following brief exercises will help you get started.

**A.** Give the third person plural of the preterite for these infinitives.

| | | | | |
|---|---|---|---|---|
| **1.** hablar | **5.** perder | **9.** estar | **13.** traer | **17.** decir |
| **2.** comer | **6.** dormir | **10.** tener | **14.** dar | **18.** creer |
| **3.** vivir | **7.** reír | **11.** destruir | **15.** saber | **19.** ir |
| **4.** jugar | **8.** leer | **12.** mantener | **16.** vestirse | **20.** poder |

**B.** You will often use the imperfect indicative in structures that trigger the past subjunctive. The forms of the imperfect indicative are relatively regular. Only three verbs have irregular imperfect forms: **ir, ser,** and **ver.** Give their first person singular and plural forms.

## 44 *¡No queríamos que fuera así!* Past Subjunctive

**¡Qué pena que no *nos lleváramos* bien!**

Elisa habla con su madre sobre su niñez.

MARÍA:   ¿No recuerdas? ¡Qué mala memoria!
ELISA:   Pero, mamá, ¿tú permitías que yo *hablara* así? ¡Qué falta de respeto hacia ti!

---

*It's a shame we didn't get along!* Elisa talks to her mother about her childhood. MARÍA: *You don't remember? What a bad memory!* ELISA: *But, Mom, did you let me talk that way? What a lack of respect for you!*

MARÍA: Eras muy cabezuda. No había nadie que *pudiera* contigo. ¡Cómo discutíamos! Tú creías que siempre tenías razón. Era imposible que *te equivocaras.* Tampoco querías que te *dijeran* lo que debías hacer.

ELISA: Bueno, por lo menos ahora no soy así. Digo, no tanto…

MARÍA: Sí, pero de todos modos, es necesario que una buena periodista sea un poco terca.

ELISA: Estoy de acuerdo. Es probable que, sin esa cualidad mía, yo no hubiera obtenido ese puesto.

## ¿Y Ud.?

Hace diez años (*Ten years ago*)…

1. ¿era difícil que Ud. hablara con sus padres sobre algún tema? ¿Cuál?
2. ¿con quién era imposible que Ud. se pusiera de acuerdo?
3. ¿con quién era imposible que Ud. se comunicara?
4. ¿contra qué orden de sus padres era común que Ud. protestara?

Cuando Ud. era niño/a…

5. ¿era probable que discutiera con alguien en la escuela primaria o en el barrio? ¿Con quién?
6. ¿dónde le prohibían sus padres que jugara?
7. ¿qué era obligatorio que comiera o bebiera?
8. ¿de qué temía que sus padres se enteraran?

Although Spanish has two simple indicative past tenses (preterite and imperfect), it has only one simple subjunctive past tense, the *past subjunctive* (**el imperfecto del subjuntivo**). Generally speaking, this tense is used in the same situations as the present subjunctive but, of course, when talking about past events. The exact English equivalent depends on the context in which it is used.

| PAST | Present | Future |
|---|---|---|
| preterite | present indicative | future |
| imperfect | present progressive | |
| present perfect | formal commands | |
| present perfect subjunctive | informal commands | |
| past subjunctive | present subjunctive | |

MARÍA: *You were very stubborn. No one could change your mind. How we used to argue! You thought you were always right. It was impossible that you could ever make a mistake. Nor did you want anyone to tell you what to do.* ELISA: *Well, at least I'm not like that now. I mean, not as much . . .* MARÍA: *Yes, but, in any case, it's necessary for a good journalist to be a little bit stubborn.* ELISA: *I agree. It's likely that, without that quality of mine, I wouldn't have gotten that job.*

**Emphasis A: Suggestions**
• Present the formation of the past subjunctive and emphasize that all forms, without exception, are based on the third person plural of the preterite.
• Model the past subjunctive in sentences about yourself or communicative exchanges. Use the verbs *trabajar, volver,* and *abrir.*

## Forms of the Past Subjunctive

**A.** The past subjunctive endings **-a, -as, -a, -amos, -ais, -an** are identical for **-ar, -er,** and **-ir** verbs. These endings are added to the third person plural of the preterite, minus its **-on** ending. For this reason, the forms of the past subjunctive reflect the irregularities of the preterite.

| PAST SUBJUNCTIVE ENDINGS | |
|---|---|
| -a | -amos |
| -as | -ais |
| -a | -an |

• Have students give the third person plural preterite forms.

| caminar | nadar | leer |
| terminar | ofrecer | creer |
| usar | resolver | abrir |
| pensar | correr | escribir |
| esperar | prometer | subir |
| cerrar | volver | admitir |

### Past Subjunctive of Regular Verbs*

| **hablar: hablar~~on~~** | | **comer: comier~~on~~** | | **vivir: vivier~~on~~** | |
|---|---|---|---|---|---|
| hablara | habláramos | comiera | comiéramos | viviera | viviéramos |
| hablaras | hablarais | comieras | comierais | vivieras | vivierais |
| hablara | hablaran | comiera | comieran | viviera | vivieran |

**B.** Stem-changing verbs

**-Ar** and **-er** verbs: no change

**-Ir** verbs: all persons of the past subjunctive reflect the vowel change in the third person plural of the preterite.

empezar (ie): empezar~~on~~ → **empezara, empezaras,...**
volver (ue): volvier~~on~~ → **volviera, volvieras,...**
dormir (ue, u): durmier~~on~~ → **durmiera, durmieras,...**
pedir (i, i): pidier~~on~~ → **pidiera, pidieras,...**

**C.** Spelling changes

All persons of the past subjunctive reflect the change from **i** to **y** between two vowels.

i → y (caer, construir, creer, destruir, leer, oír)

creer: creyer~~on~~ →
| creyera | creyéramos |
| creyeras | creyerais |
| creyera | creyeran |

**D.** Verbs with irregular preterites

dar: dier~~on~~ →
| diera | diéramos |
| dieras | dierais |
| diera | dieran |

**Emphasis D: Suggestions**
• Have students give the third person plural preterite forms.

| dar | poder | venir |
| hacer | poner | divertirse |
| ser | querer | servir |
| ir | saber | dormir |
| decir | tener | jugar |
| estar | traer | pedir |

decir: dijer~~on~~ → **dijera**
estar: estuvier~~on~~ → **estuviera**
haber: hubier~~on~~ → **hubiera**
hacer: hicier~~on~~ → **hiciera**
ir: fuer~~on~~ → **fuera**
poder: pudier~~on~~ → **pudiera**

poner: pusier~~on~~ → **pusiera**
querer: quisier~~on~~ → **quisiera**
saber: supier~~on~~ → **supiera**
ser: fuer~~on~~ → **fuera**
tener: tuvier~~on~~ → **tuviera**
venir: vinier~~on~~ → **viniera**

• Model the past subjunctive forms of *servir, sentir, dar, decir, hacer, ir,* and *venir* in sentences about yourself and communicative exchanges with the students.

**Heritage Speakers**
Pregúnteles a los hispanohablantes de la clase si usan o no las terminaciones en *-se, -ses, -se, -semos, -seis, -sen* del pasado de subjuntivo. Si las usan, pregúnteles cuándo y por qué.

*An alternative form of the past subjunctive (used primarily in Spain) ends in **-se:** hablase, hablases, hablase, hablásemos, hablaseis, hablasen. This form will not be practiced in ¿Qué tal?*

# Uses of the Past Subjunctive

**A.** The past subjunctive usually has the same applications as the present subjunctive, but it is used for past events. Compare these pairs of sentences.

Emphasis A: Suggestions
- Point out that the past subjunctive is used to describe past events in grammatical contexts that require the subjunctive.
- Emphasize that when a verb in the main clause is in the past, the past (never the present) subjunctive is used in the subordinate clause (past → past).
- Remind students that when the verb in the main clause is in the present, the verb in the dependent can be in the past: *Siento que no pudieran estar allí. Sé que no estaban allí.* Help students develop simple logic about time sequence (I'm sorry now about something that happened yesterday).

**Quiero** que **se enteren** esta tarde.
*I want them to find out this afternoon.*

**Quería** que **se enteraran** por la tarde.
*I wanted them to find out in the afternoon.*

**Siente** que no **estén** allí esta noche.
*He's sorry (that) they aren't there tonight.*

**Sintió** que no **estuvieran** allí anoche.
*He was sorry (that) they weren't there last night.*

**Dudamos** que **mantengan** la paz.
*We doubt that they will keep the peace.*

**Dudábamos** que **mantuvieran** la paz.
*We doubted that they would keep the peace.*

**B.** Remember that the subjunctive is used after
   (1) expressions of *influence, emotion,* and *doubt;*
   (2) *nonexistent* and *indefinite antecedents;* and
   (3) *conjunctions* of *contingency and purpose,* as well as those of *time.*

Emphasis C: Suggestions
- Emphasize that this tense is used to form polite requests. This is similar to the English *really should* and *would like you to* softened requests.
- Point out that the verbs *deber* and *poder* are used by some Spanish speakers in softened requests: *Debieras estudiar más. ¿Pudieras darme el libro?*
- Remind students of the importance of tone whenever requests of any kind are made. The most polite words if said in a harsh way can be offensive.

(1) **¿Era necesario** que **regatearas**?
*Was it necessary for you to bargain?*

(1) **Sentí** que no **tuvieran** tiempo para ver Granada.
*I was sorry that they didn't have time to see Granada.*

(2) **No había nadie** que **pudiera** resolverlo.
*There wasn't anyone who could (might have been able to) resolve it.*

(3) Los padres **trabajaron para que** sus hijos **asistieran** a la universidad.
*The parents worked so that their children could (might) go to the university.*

(3) Anoche, **íbamos** a salir **en cuanto llegara** Felipe.
*Last night, we were going to leave as soon as Felipe arrived.*

**C.** The past subjunctive of the verb **querer** is often used to make a request sound more polite.

**Quisiéramos** hablar con Ud. en seguida.
*We would like to speak with you immediately.*

**Quisiera** un café, por favor.
*I would like a cup of coffee, please.*

---

**AUTOPRUEBA**

Change the following verbs from the present subjunctive to the past subjunctive.

1. quiera
2. tengamos
3. salgan
4. sepas
5. esté
6. traigas

Answers: 1. quisiera 2. tuviéramos 3. salieran 4. supieras 5. estuviera 6. trajeras

## ■ Práctica

**A. ¡Anticipemos! Si pudiera volver...** ¿Le gusta la idea de volver a la escuela secundaria? ¿O prefiere la vida de la universidad?

PASO 1 Lea las siguientes oraciones e indique las que son verdaderas para Ud. Cambie las oraciones falsas para que expresen su propia experiencia.

En la escuela secundaria...

1. ☐ era obligatorio que yo asistiera a todas mis clases.
2. ☐ mis padres insistían en que yo estudiara mucho.
3. ☐ era necesario que yo trabajara para que pudiera asistir a la universidad algún día.
4. ☐ no había ninguna clase que me interesara.
5. ☐ sacaba buenas notas para que mis padres me dieran dinero.
6. ☐ era necesario que volviera a casa a una hora determinada, aun (*even*) en los fines de semana.
7. ☐ mis padres me exigían que limpiara mi cuarto cada semana.
8. ☐ mis padres no permitían que saliera con alguna persona o con los miembros de ciertos grupos.

PASO 2 Ahora considere sus respuestas. ¿Realmente era mejor la vida en la escuela secundaria? ¿Le gustaría regresar a esa época? Explique.

**B. Escenas históricas**

PASO 1 La gente emigra por varias razones. Complete las siguientes oraciones con la forma correcta del infinitivo. Luego, si puede, nombre un grupo que emigró por la razón citada.

1. Las leyes de su país de origen no permitían que este grupo (practicar) libremente su religión.
2. Algunas personas esperaban que (haber) oro y plata en América.
3. El rey no quería que estos criminales (seguir) viviendo en su país.
4. Estos inmigrantes buscaban un país donde (haber) paz y esperanza.
5. Este grupo buscaba un país donde no (tener) que pasar hambre.

PASO 2 Dé una breve descripción del pasado histórico de los Estados Unidos, haciendo oraciones según las indicaciones. Empiece en el pasado. Desde el número 8, las oraciones se refieren al presente.

1. indios / temer / que / colonos / quitarles / toda la tierra
2. colonos / no / gustar / que / ser necesario / pagarle / impuestos / rey
3. parecía imposible / que / joven república / tener éxito (*success*)
4. los del sur / no / gustar / que / gobernarlos / los del norte
5. abolicionistas / no / gustar / que / algunos / no / tener / mismo / libertades
6. era necesario / que / declararse / en huelga / obreros / para / obtener / alguno / derechos
7. era terrible / que / haber / dos / guerra / mundial
8. para que / nosotros / vivir / en paz / es cuestión de / aprender / comunicarse
9. también / es necesario / que / haber / leyes / que / garantizar / derechos

**Prác. A, C: Suggestion**
If you have a multigenerational class, compare the answers of students of different generations.

**C. Y ahora, la niñez.** ¿Qué quería Ud. de la vida cuando era niño/a? ¿Y qué querían los demás que Ud. hiciera? Conteste, haciendo oraciones con una frase de cada grupo.

**Prác. C: Extension**
Have students describe a friend from their youth.

  *Yo tenía un amigo / una amiga que...*

**¡OJO!** Students will need the indicative in this initial sentence.

1. Mis padres (no) querían que yo...
2. Mis maestros me pedían que...
3. Yo buscaba amigos que...
4. Me gustaba mucho que nosotros...

**+**

ir a la iglesia / al templo con ellos
portarse bien, ser bueno/a
estudiar mucho, hacer la tarea todas las noches, sacar buenas notas
ponerse ropa vieja para jugar, jugar en la calle, pelear con mis amigos
mirar mucho la televisión, leer muchas tiras cómicas, comer muchos dulces
vivir en nuestro barrio, asistir a la misma escuela, tener muchos juguetes, ser aventureros
ir de vacaciones en verano, pasar todos juntos los días feriados, tener un árbol de Navidad muy alto

**D. El noticiero de las seis.** En las noticias los reporteros nos informan de los acontecimientos del día, pero a veces también ofrecen sus propias opiniones. Lea las siguientes oraciones y cámbielas al pasado. Debe usar el imperfecto del primer verbo en cada oración y luego el imperfecto del subjuntivo en la segunda parte.

1. «Los obreros quieren que les den un aumento de sueldo.»
2. «Es posible que los trabajadores sigan en huelga hasta el verano.»
3. «Es necesario que las víctimas reciban atención médica en la Clínica del Sagrado Corazón.»
4. «Los terroristas piden que los oficiales no los persigan.»
5. «Es necesario que el gobierno informe a todos los ciudadanos del desastre.»
6. «El presidente y los directores prefieren que la nueva fábrica se construya en México.»
7. «Temo que el número de votantes sea muy bajo en las próximas elecciones.»

**Prác. C: Follow-Up**
Include the following questions as well.

1. *¿Qué no le gustaba nada?*
2. *¿Qué quería Ud. que sus padres (sus hermanos) hicieran?*
3. *¿Qué quería que sus abuelos le regalaran para su cumpleaños?*
4. *¿Adónde quería Ud. que sus padres lo/la llevaran de vacaciones cuando era más joven?*

5. *¿Sus padres permitían que Ud. bebiera alcohol cuando tenía 15 años?*

**Need more practice?**

- Workbook/Laboratory Manual
- Interactive CD-ROM
- Online Learning Center (www.mhhe.com/quetal7)

■ **Conversación**

**A. Entrevista**

**Heritage Speakers**
Los hispanohablantes también usan el imperfecto de subjuntivo de los verbos *poder* y *deber* (*pudieras, debieras*) para ser más corteses al pedirle o sugerirle algo a alguien. Pregúnteles a los hispanohablantes en qué situaciones usarían las formas más corteses de *poder* y *deber*. También anímelos a hacerles pedidos corteses a sus compañeros de clase usando las formas *pudieras, debieras* y *yo quisiera que...*

1. ¿A qué le tenías miedo cuando eras pequeño/a? ¿Era probable que ocurrieran las cosas que temías? ¿Temías a veces que tus padres te castigaran (*punish*)? ¿Lo merecías a veces? ¿Era necesario que siempre los obedecieras? ¿Qué te prohibían que hicieras?
2. ¿Qué tipo de clases buscabas para este semestre/trimestre? ¿Clases que fueran fáciles? ¿interesantes? ¿Las encontraste? ¿Han sido las clases tal como las esperabas? ¿Qué tipo de clases vas a buscar para el semestre/trimestre que viene?
3. ¿Qué buscaban los primeros inmigrantes que vinieron a los Estados Unidos? ¿Buscaban un lugar donde pudieran practicar su religión? ¿un lugar donde hubiera abundancia de recursos naturales? ¿menos restricciones? ¿más libertad política y personal? ¿más respeto por los derechos humanos? ¿menos gente? ¿más espacio?

**Con. A: Suggestion**
Encourage students to use clauses with *para que, con tal que,* and so on.

# PASO 2

—Verás, quisiera un vaso de agua. Pero no te molestes, porque ya no tengo sed. Sólo quisiera saber si, en el caso de que tuviese otra vez sed, podría (*I could*) venir a pedirte un vaso de agua.

**Con. B: Suggestion**
Practice comprehension of the past subjunctive using the following context.

*Imagine que su abuela, quien asistió a la universidad en los años cincuenta, le ha explicado a Ud. las normas de conducta de esa época. ¿Qué es diferente hoy día? ¿Hay algunas normas antiguas que a Ud. le parezcan mejores que las modernas? ¿Por qué?*

1. *Era obligatorio que los hombres y las mujeres vivieran en residencias apartes.*
2. *Todos cenaban a la misma hora. Para entrar en el comedor, era necesario que los hombres llevaran corbata y las mujeres, falda.*
3. *Había «hora de visita» en las residencias. Los hombres sólo podían visitar a sus amigas durante esas horas y viceversa.*
4. *Era necesario que las mujeres estuvieran en su residencia a una hora determinada de la noche. Pero no había ninguna restricción semejante para los hombres.*

**Con. B: Follow-Up**
Have students tell what they would say in the following situations, using the past subjunctive whenever possible.

*¿Qué diría Ud. en las siguientes situaciones?*

1. *Ud. ha llamado a un amigo a las diez de la noche para invitarlo a salir, pero ya estaba dormido y Ud. lo ha despertado.*
2. *Ud. llega a casa muy enfermo/a, con tos y fiebre. El médico le ha aconsejado guardar cama para descansar. Pero su compañero/a de cuarto (esposo/a, etcétera) le ha preparado una fiesta sorpresa de cumpleaños. Todos los amigos lo/la saludan cuando entra.*

**B. Situaciones.** El niño del dibujo sabe que está molestando a sus padres cuando los despierta pidiendo ahora un vaso de agua que no quiere pero que podría (*he might*) querer más tarde. Por eso les habla de una forma muy cortés: «quisiera un vaso de agua… quisiera saber… ». Con un compañero / una compañera, explique cómo podrían Uds. pedir de una forma muy cortés lo que necesitan en las siguientes situaciones. ¿Qué dirían para conseguirlo?

1. Ud. quiere tener el número de teléfono de un chico / una chica que acaba de conocer. Habla con un amigo de él / una amiga de ella.
2. En un restaurante, el camarero no lo/la atiende como debe. Ud. no quiere perder la paciencia con él, pero quiere el café que le pidió hace diez minutos (*ten minutes ago*)… y la cuenta.
3. Uds. quieren saber cuándo es el examen final en esta clase y qué va a incluir.
4. Ud. necesita una extensión para el próximo examen de español.
5. Ud. piensa que va a necesitar una extensión para el próximo proyecto.
6. Ud. necesita una carta de recomendación del profesor / de la profesora.
7. Ud. quiere hablar con el rector / la rectora de la universidad para invitarlo/la a cenar en su residencia con motivo de pedirle algo especial.

## NOTA COMUNICATIVA

**I wish I could . . . I wish they would . . .**

There are many ways to express wishes in Spanish. As you know, one of the most common is **ojalá (que)**. Used alone, **¡Ojalá!** means *I hope so!* It can also be used with the present or past subjunctive to mean *I hope . . . !* or *I wish . . .*

| | |
|---|---|
| **¡Ojala (que)** la guerra **acabe** pronto! | *I hope (that) the war will be over soon!* |

The past subjunctive following **ojalá** is one of the most frequent uses of those verb forms. Here **ojalá** expresses *I wish.*

| | |
|---|---|
| **Ojalá (que) pudiera** acompañarlos, pero no es posible. | *I wish (that) I could go with you, but it's not possible.* |

**C. ¡Ojalá!** Complete las oraciones lógicamente.

1. Ojalá que (yo) tuviera _____.
2. Ojalá que pudiera _____.
3. Ojalá inventaran una máquina que _____.
4. Ojalá solucionaran el problema de _____.
5. Ojalá que en esta universidad fuera posible _____.

**Nota comunicativa: Suggestions**
• Remind students that *ojalá* + present subjunctive means *I hope* (*something will happen*). *Ojalá* + past subjunctive means *I wish.* Wishes with the past subjunctive are unlikely or impossible to happen.
• Remind students that the use of *que* after *ojalá* is optional.

# Voces de la República Dominicana

## LITERATURA: Manuel del Cabral

**Sobre el autor:** *Manuel del Cabral nació en Santiago de los Caballeros, República Dominicana. Estudió derecho,[a] pero prefirió escribir. También sirvió de diplomático de la República Dominicana en Nueva York y en varios países latinoamericanos. En su poesía aparece el tema del negro caribeño. Murió en Santo Domingo en 1999. El siguiente poema, «Sobre el agua», es de la colección* Color de agua *(1932).*

**Manuel del Cabral**
(1907–1999)

Agua tan pura que casi
no se ve en el vaso de agua.

Del otro lado está el mundo.
De este lado, casi nada...

Un agua pura, tan limpia
que da trabajo mirarla.

### AGUA

La del río, ¡qué blanda![b]
Pero qué dura[c] es ésta:
¡La que cae de los párpados[d]
es un agua que piensa!

[a]*law*  [b]*soft*  [c]*hard*  [d]*eyelids*

**Literatura: Notes**
- Cabral traveled extensively and often lived in Buenos Aires, Argentina, where he published many of his works.
- Cabral was a defender of human rights, and his sociopolitical concerns were often reflected in his poetry. A theme in many poems was the Afro-Caribbean experience and situation.
- In addition to his extensive volumes of poetry, Cabral wrote novels and short stories.

**Música: Notes**
- The origin of *el merengue* is popularly explained in two different stories. According to one story, the dance originated with slaves who were chained together. These slaves dragged one leg as they worked cutting cane to the beat of drums. In the other story, a war hero returns from battle with a leg injury. He is welcomed home with a victory celebration, and, out of sympathy, everyone dances with a limp, dragging one foot.
- Originally *el merengue* was a circle dance. The couples faced each other and held hands at arm's length. Unlike today's version of the dance in which couples hold each other closely and use a great deal of hip movement, the original movements were only the shoulder shaking and swift foot movement.
- Students can read more about *el merengue* and the *Festival del Merengue* in *Enfoque cultural*.
- Haiti has a similar dance called the *méringue*. Sung in Creole, it has a slower, more nostalgic sound, based on guitar music.

## MÚSICA: El merengue

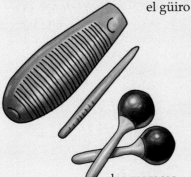

El merengue es la música y danza nacional de la República Dominicana. El festival del Merengue se celebra en Santo Domingo las dos últimas semanas de julio.

el güiro

las maracas

Dos de los instrumentos típicos del merengue son las maracas y el güiro.[a] El acordeón o el saxofón típicamente acompaña el ritmo animado del merengue.

[a]*rasping percussion instrument, often made from a gourd*

Juan Luis Guerra es un compositor y cantante del merengue. Promueve[b] las tradiciones musicales de su país y también usa su música para hacer crítica social. Su canción «El costo de la vida» es una protesta contra la pobreza[c] de los países latinoamericanos. Ha ganado muchos premios, incluso[d] tres Grammy Latinos en 2000 por su álbum *Ni es lo mismo ni es igual*.

[b]*He promotes*  [c]*poverty*  [d]*including*

**Paso 3: Gramática**
See the "Chapter-by-Chapter Supplementary Materials" in the IM for additional teaching suggestions, notes, activities, and other resources for *Paso 3*.

## En los Estados Unidos y el Canadá

### Los medios de comunicación en español

A la creciente[a] población hispánica (más de 40 millones) en los Estados Unidos se le ofrece[b] cada vez **más variedad en los mundos del entretenimiento[c] y la información.** Hoy día se puede comprar la revista *People en español* en cualquier lugar del país donde haya población hispanohablante. *Latin Trade*, una revista de economía y comercio que cubre los intereses de toda Latinoamérica, también tiene un ámbito[d] nacional.

*Unas publicaciones hispánicas en Nueva York*

Las ciudades con una gran concentración de hispanos tienen sus **propios periódicos en español.** Algunos de los muchos son el *Diario de las Américas* y el *Nuevo Herald* de Miami, *LA Opinión* de Los Ángeles, *La Prensa* de Minnesota, *La Semana* de Boston, *La Raza* de Chicago y *El Canillita* de Connecticut. Muchas ciudades tienen hasta varias[e] estaciones de radio y televisión, como WSKQ-FM, WPAT-FM y WXTV-TV en Nueva York y KLEY-FM y KWEX-TV en San Antonio. El grupo Televisa es **la empresa más grande de medios de comunicación,** con participación en programas de televisión, revistas, servicios de televisión por satélite y por cable, radio, etcétera. **La cadena[f] de televisión** Univisión es **la más popular en los Estados Unidos,** con una difusión del 97 por ciento de los hogares[g] hispanos.

Últimamente,[h] **la televisión satelital** ha añadido aun[i] más opciones a la oferta de entretenimientos para los hispanohablantes. A través de ella[j] no sólo se pueden ver las cadenas más famosas de México y los Estados Unidos, como Univisión, Telefutura y CNN en español, sino que se ven canales de toda Hispanoamérica y España.

[a]*growing* [b]*se… is offered* [c]*entertainment* [d]*market* [e]*hasta… as many as several* [f]*channel* [g]*residences* [h]*Lately* [i]*even* [j]*A… Through it*

**En los Estados Unidos y el Canadá: Comprensión**
1. ¿Qué revistas se publican en los Estados Unidos para los hispanohablantes?
2. ¿Qué ciudades tienen periódicos en español?
3. ¿Qué ofrece Televisa? ¿Y Univisión?

## UN POCO DE TODO

**Lengua y cultura: Preliminary Exercise**
To help students review the past tense structures, have them complete the following sentences.

1. *ayer / (yo) ver / mi / nota / en / último / examen*
2. *no / poder / creer / que / nota / ser / tan / bajo*
3. *no / ser / posible / que / yo / hacer / examen / tan / mal*
4. *por eso / (yo) hablar / con / profesor / para que / (él) explicarme / causa / de / nota*
5. *(él) decirme / que / haber / errores / importante / pero / que / haber / partes / bueno / también*
6. *(él) pedirme / que / leer / examen / otro / vez*
7. *ser / verdad / que / haber / errores / en / examen*
8. *pero / ¡no / ser / justo / que / profesor / darme / nota / tan / bajo!*

Follow up with questions to personalize the sentences.

1. ¿Le ha ocurrido algo similar?
2. ¿Qué hizo Ud.? ¿Le cambió la nota su profesor(a) o no?
3. ¿Piensa Ud. que muchos profesores son injustos? ¿Por qué sí o por qué no?

**Lengua y cultura: Maneras de practicar el español fuera** (*outside of*) **de clase**

Complete the following dialogue with the correct form of the words in parentheses, as suggested by the context. When two possibilities are given in parentheses, select the correct word.

**¡OJO!** When you conjugate verbs in this activity, you will often have to decide whether to use the subjunctive mood (present, present perfect, or past) or the indicative mood (present, present perfect, future, preterite, or imperfect). The context of the passage will guide you in choosing among the indicative verb tenses, and you will also occasionally see clues in italics to show you which tense to use. Start in the present tense.

Claro está que Ud. habla español en clase. También es probable que lo (hablar[1]) con su profesor(a) cada vez que lo/la (ver[2]) en el *campus*. Pero (por/para[3]) hablar español con soltura[a] Ud. tiene que practicar (tanto/más[4]).

«¡Ojalá que (*yo: poder*[5]) practicar español fuera de clase!» ¿(*pres. perf., Decir*[6]) Ud. eso alguna vez? Pues hay muchas maneras de hacerlo. Por ejemplo, los compañeros y compañeras de una misma clase de español siempre pueden hablar español cuando (verse[7]) para no (perder[8]) (ninguno[9]) oportunidad de (practicar[10]).

Pero hablar con los compañeros de estudio no es lo (único/unica[11]) que un estudiante puede hacer fuera de clase. Es buena idea que (*Ud.: mirar*[12]) la televisión o (escuchar[13]) la radio en español. ¿(Qué/Cuál[14]) programa? Realmente (ese/eso[15]) no importa: se puede mirar una telenovela[b] o escuchar (un/una[16]) programa de noticias. Lo importante es (dedicar[17]) un rato[c] a escuchar español auténtico con frecuencia. Muchas personas (encontrar[18]) muy frustrante esta actividad (por qué/porque[19]) no pueden comprenderlo todo. Hay que recordar que no es necesario (entender[20]) cada palabra que se oye. Para los estudiantes principiantes[d] es suficiente identificar el tema y (alguno[21]) palabras o expresiones. Si Ud. escucha español habitualmente en los medios de comunicación, seguro que (*fut., aprender*[22]) mucho… y rápidamente.

Otra actividad útil es leer el periódico o una revista de actualidad en español. Puesto que[e] hay muchos hispanohablantes en este país, es relativamente fácil (seguir/conseguir[23]) algo que leer en español en muchos lugares. Y si esto no es fácil en el lugar donde Ud. vive, (*comm., Ud.: buscar*[24]) en el Internet; en (el/la[25]) Red hay miles de páginas con información de todo tipo en español. Por ejemplo, si le gusta viajar, (*comm., Ud.: consultar*[26]) las páginas relacionadas con el turismo en los países donde se habla español.

Finalmente, (*comm., Ud.: recordar*[27]) su propia comunidad. Es muy posible que Ud. (vivir[28]) en una ciudad o estado en que (hay/haya[29]) una comunidad hispana. Si hay una comunidad hispana, entonces[f] (*fut., tener*[30]) restaurantes y tiendas. ¿(Porque/Por qué[31]) no visita una de esas tienda o supermercados hispanos para que (*Ud.: ver*[32]) las cosas que se venden allí? ¡Leer una lista de ingredientes en cualquier producto es ya[g] un ejercicio de lectura!

[a]hablar… *speak Spanish fluently* [b]*soap opera* [c]*un… a bit of time* [d]*beginning* [e]*Puesto… Since* [f]*then* [g]*actually*

**Comprensión.** Conteste las preguntas en español.

1. Además de hablar español con sus compañeros en clase, ¿qué otras opciones tiene Ud. para practicar el idioma fuera de la clase?
2. ¿Es buena o mala la idea de mirar la televisión en español? ¿Qué tipo de programas se recomienda ver?
3. ¿Es necesario que un estudiante entienda cada palabra de lo que oye o mira en los medios de comunicación en español?
4. ¿Qué tipo de lecturas puede Ud. conseguir en español para practicar más?
5. ¿Qué posibilidades de hablar español existen en la mayoría de las comunidades? ¿Existen en la de Ud. (*yours*)?

*Paso 3 Gramática*

*El noticiero de un canal de televisión en San Antonio, Texas*

**Multimedia: Internet**
Have students look up the program *Finalmente* on the Internet as well as other television and radio programming in the Dominican Republic. Students can read about the program, the anchors, and so on, as well as read "articles" that were presented on the program.

**Resources for Review and Testing Preparation**

- Workbook/Laboratory Manual
- Interactive CD-ROM
- Online Learning Center (www.mhhe.com/quetal7)

**Paso 4: Un paso más**

- The *Paso 4: Un paso más* sections are optional.
- See the "Chapter-by-Chapter Supplementary Materials" in the IM for additional teaching suggestions, notes, activities, and other resources for *Paso 4*.

**Entrevista cultural: Suggestions**

- Before showing the video, ask students questions about professional ambitions.

  *¿Para qué estudia Ud.? ¿Le interesa ahora o le ha interesado en el pasado una carrera en comunicaciones?*

  *¿Cómo se informa Ud.? ¿Prefiere ver las noticias en la televisión, escucharlas en la radio o leerlas en el periódico o el Internet?*

  *¿Cuáles son los problemas más graves del mundo contemporáneo? ¿El cáncer? ¿las guerras? ¿el SIDA? ¿las armas nucleares? ¿la contaminación del medioambiente?*

- Show the video and allow students one to two minutes to work on the questions for each one. Have volunteers answer the questions.
- Have volunteers role-play Milstry and her interviewer.
- Provide a brief introduction to the video. What do students know about the Dominican Republic? Do they think Milstry would agree with their assessment of serious problems facing the contemporary world?

**Entre amigos: Suggestions**

- Before viewing the video, review the questions with the students and ask them similar questions.

  *¿Qué asuntos le importan a Ud.? ¿Ha protestado en una manifestación (new word) alguna vez?*

  *¿Para qué causas o contra qué asuntos participaría en una manifestación?*

  Have students answer or work in small groups to ask and answer these questions.

- After viewing the video, have volunteers read and answer the questions.

## VIDEOTECA

### Entrevista cultural: La República Dominicana

Una estudiante dominicana, Milstry del Orbe, habla de la carrera profesional que quiere seguir. Además, comenta los problemas del mundo contemporáneo que ella considera más graves. Antes de ver el vídeo, lea el siguiente fragmento de la entrevista.

ENTREVISTADORA: ¿Por qué te interesa esa carrera?

MILSTRY: Creo que es muy importante poder informar a la gente, a la juventud,[a] de lo que acontece[b] en otros… en otros países en el momento y en el lugar exacto de donde… de donde ocurre.

ENTREVISTADORA: ¿Cuáles son los problemas mundiales más graves hoy en día?

MILSTRY: Pues hoy en día considero que hay muchísimos problemas graves, entre ellos problemas de enfermedades como el SIDA,[c] que todavía no se le ha podido encontrar cura. Problemas de terrorismo, problemas de medio ambiente, destrucción del medio ambiente.

[a]*young people*   [b]*happens*   [c]*AIDS*

Ahora vea el vídeo y conteste las siguientes preguntas basándose en la entrevista.

**Entrevista cultural: Answers**
*Possible answers:* **1.** *el periodismo* **2.** *Porque cree que es importante informar a la gente.* **3.** *las enfermedades como el SIDA y el terrorismo*

1. ¿Qué estudia Milstry?
2. ¿Por qué ha escogido esta profesión?
3. Según Milstry, ¿cuál es uno de los problemas graves en el mundo de hoy? ¿Y otro de los problemas?

### Entre amigos: ¡Por eso sí protestaría!

Tané, Karina, Rubén y Miguel hablan de las manifestaciones y las protestas. En su opinión, ¿qué van a decir sobre estos temas? Antes de mirar el vídeo, lea las preguntas a continuación. Mientras mire el vídeo, trate de entender la conversación en general y fíjese en la información sobre las manifestaciones y protestas. Luego mire el vídeo una segunda vez, fijándose en la información que necesita para contestar las preguntas.

1. ¿De dónde viene Miguel con la pancarta (*banner*)?
2. ¿Por qué va a protestar Tané?
3. ¿Por qué no va a protestar Karina?
4. ¿Por qué protestaría (*would protest*) Rubén?
5. Al final, ¿qué sugiere hacer Tané?

**Entre amigos: Answers**
*Possible answers:* **1.** *Viene de una manifestación.* **2.** *por el aumento en la matrícula* **3.** *No está de acuerdo porque puede pagar la matrícula y tiene buenas notas.* **4.** *por el aumento de inseguridad en la ciudad* **5.** *comunicarse con los medios de comunicación para que sepan que hay estudiantes que se preocupan por los problemas*

# PASO 4

• Have students find recipes from the Dominican Republic online and bring them to class. You may wish to make or have students make some of these for students to taste.

• Invite a student or member of the community from the Dominican Republic to come to class and talk to the students about his or her country.

## ENFOQUE CULTURAL

### La República Dominicana

• Have students research Taino art and culture and prepare short written reports for extra credit.

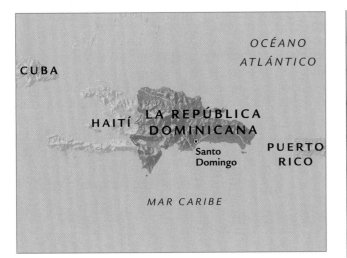

## ¡Fíjese!

• España le cedió[a] a Francia, en 1697, el tercio occidental[b] de La Española. Por esta razón, este territorio, el actual país de Haití, tiene una cultura y un idioma diferentes a los de la República Dominicana.

• El merengue es el baile nacional de la República Dominicana. Hay dos leyendas sobre el origen del baile. Según la primera leyenda, el baile se originó entre los esclavos que tenían que arrastrar[c] una pierna porque la tenían encadenada[d] con la pierna de otro esclavo. La segunda leyenda atribuye el baile a un héroe que regresó de una batalla con una pierna herida. El pueblo, para mostrar su empatía, bailó durante las celebraciones cojeando[e] y arrastrando un pie. En Santo Domingo se celebra el Festival del Merengue, diez días de música, bailes, espectáculos, ferias y festejos en las calles.

*El Convento Dominico en Santo Domingo*

[a]*ceded* [b]*tercio... western third* [c]*drag* [d]*chained* [e]*limping*

## Lugares famosos: Santo Domingo

La ciudad de Santo Domingo fue fundada en 1496 por Bartolomé Colón, hermano de Cristóbal Colón. Esta capital, establecida a orillas del río Ozama y el mar Caribe, es la primera ciudad europea del Hemisferio Occidental. La zona original de Santo Domingo se conoce como la Ciudad Colonial y está rodeada[a] de antiguos muros.[b] La UNESCO designó a Santo Domingo como la cuna[c] de la civilización europea en América, porque es aquí donde se encuentra la primera catedral del Nuevo Mundo, así como el primer monasterio, el primer hospital, la primera universidad, los primeros palacios de estilo europeo y la primera corte de justicia. A Santo Domingo también se le llamaba la Atenas[d] del Nuevo Mundo por la actividad intelectual que había en la universidad y otras instituciones.

En 1992, la UNESCO designó la Ciudad Colonial Patrimonio de la Humanidad[e] por sus riquezas arquitectónicas e históricas que datan del siglo XVI. Las imponentes casas e iglesias de piedra fueron cuidadosamente colocadas[f] en forma octogonal. El plan de la ciudad fue diseñado y trazado[g] en 1502 y sirvió de patrón[h] para otras ciudades establecidas por los españoles en el Nuevo Mundo. Hoy por muchas de las calles de la Ciudad Colonial se encuentran pintorescos cafés y bares, pequeños hoteles y conocidos restaurantes, discotecas y tiendas.

[a]*surrounded* [b]*walls* [c]*cradle, birthplace* [d]*Athens* [e]*Patrimonio... World Heritage Site* [f]*placed* [g]*laid out* [h]*model*

**Notes**
• When Santo Domingo was founded, the island was called *La Española*.
• Students can read an excerpt of the poem *"Sobre el agua"* by the Dominican Republic's Manuel del Cabral in *Voces de la República Dominicana: Literatura*.
• Students can read about the Dominican Republic's *merengue* in *Voces de la República Dominicana: Música*.
• See the Workbook/Laboratory Manual for focused practice with the material in *Enfoque cultural*.

Learn more about the Dominican Republic with the Video, the Interactive CD-ROM, and the Online Learning Center (www.mhhe.com/quetal7).

**Sobre el autor...** Gustavo Pérez Firmat (1949– ) nació en La Habana, Cuba, y se crió en Miami, Florida. Su poesía tiene una variedad de temas, entre los que se incluyen las relaciones de familia y la experiencia cubanoamericana en los Estados Unidos. Pérez Firmat recibió un doctorado de la Universidad de Michigan y ahora enseña en la Universidad de Columbia. El poema que aquí se presenta, «Cubanita descubanizada», es de una colección que se titula *Bilingual Blues*.

**A leer: Suggestions**
- Do the *Estrategia* in class before assigning the poem.
- Have volunteers read the poem out loud for the class.

**A leer: Notes**
- Pérez Firmat's autobiographical book *Next Year in Cuba: A Cubano's Coming of Age in America* was nominated for a Pulitzer Prize in 1995.
- Pérez Firmat has two collections of poems in English and Spanish in addition to *Bilingual Blues: Carolina Cuban* (1987) and *Equivocaciones*.
- Pérez Firmat's works include books about literature and culture, such as *Idle Fiction* (1982), *The Cuban Condition* (1989), and *Life on the Hyphen* (1994).
- *Newsweek* magazine included Pérez Firmat among the "100 Americans to Watch in the Next Century," and *Hispanic Business* magazine listed him among "100 Most Influential" Hispanics in the United States.

 **A LEER**

**ESTRATEGIA: Using Language Cues to Understand Poetry**

Part of the meaning of a poem can be conveyed through grammatical structures. The particular grammatical forms in a poem can convey information or contribute to its unique mood. For example, a poem written primarily in the imperfect may convey a sense of timelessness or of things recurring in the poet's personal history. The use of the preterite may give you the feeling that the moment was fleeting, perhaps all too fleeting.

As you read the following poem, note the instances of the past subjunctive that you have learned in this chapter. Why do you think the poet chose this form? What or how does it make you feel? Do you think the poem would be different if the poet had chosen a different grammatical form?

## *Cubanita descubanizada*

Cubanita descubanizada
quién te pudiera recubanizar.
Quién supiera devolverte
el ron[a] y la palma,[b]
el alma y el son.[c]

Cubanita descubanizada,
tú que pronuncias todas las eses*
y dices ómnibus[d] y autobús
quién te pudiera
quién te supiera
si te quisieras recubanizar.

[a]*rum* [b]*palm tree* [c]*el... the soul and the sound* (*the* son *is also a popular Cuban dance*) [d]*synonym for* autobús (*the author is referring to the rich lexical variety that exists in Cuban Spanish, but that in this case signals a departure from its local, rural roots*)

**Heritage Speakers**
- En muchos dialectos del español, especialmente en Cuba, Puerto Rico y la República Dominicana, a veces la pronunciación de la *s* al final de una sílaba es parecida a la *h* en inglés. Así que la palabra *esperar* se pronunciaría como *ehperar* y *desde* como *dehde*. Anime a los hispanohablantes a imitar esta pronunciación.
- Si hay un estudiante hispanohablante de ascendencia cubana en la clase, invítele a leer en voz alta el poema para que los demás estudiantes oigan la pronunciación cubana.

---

*\*In general, Cuban Spanish is characterized by a lack of pronunciation of the letter **s** when found in certain positions within a word.*

## Comprensión

**A. Definiciones.**  El autor toma libertades poéticas en su poema e inventa palabras que sirven para expresar sus ideas. Con un compañero / una compañera, trate de definir las siguientes palabras inventadas por Pérez Firmat. Comparen sus definiciones con las de otra persona en la clase.

- descubanizada
- recubanizar

**B. Interpretación.**  ¿Cuál cree Ud. que es el punto de vista del narrador del poema? ¿Tiene una actitud positiva hacia la vida en el extranjero? ¿Qué mensaje intenta expresar? ¿Qué elementos de la poesía comunican este mensaje?

## A ESCRIBIR

**A. ¿El bilingüismo o no?**  El tema de la inmigración es uno que provoca mucha reacción en este país. A continuación hay dos puntos de vista contrarios. Escoja una de estas posturas y escriba un breve informe en el que presenta y apoya su opinión.

1. El bilingüismo y el biculturalismo enriquecen la vida de este país.
2. Los inmigrantes a este país deben asimilarse por completo a la lengua, a la vida y a la cultura.

**B. Una experiencia personal.**  Escriba una breve composición sobre la experiencia de inmigrar a los Estados Unidos o al Canadá. Puede escribir desde el punto de vista de un(a) pariente o un amigo / una amiga, o puede tomar la perspectiva de una persona imaginaria. Explique cuándo se inmigró, por qué y con quién. También incluya información sobre el lugar al que llegó, cómo se sentía en aquel entonces (*back then*) y cómo se siente ahora.

**Comprensión: Suggestion**
Have students talk about the image that Pérez Firmat presents of Cuba. Ask questions such as the following.

1. *¿Por qué se mencionan el ron y el son en el poema? ¿y la palma?*
2. *Según el poeta, ¿qué implica* (write on board) *el hecho de que la cubanita haya perdido el alma?*
3. *¿Qué perdió la cubanita exactamente?*
4. *¿Qué otros elementos no mencionados en el poema creen Uds. que son típicamente cubanos?*

**Multimedia: Internet**
- Encourage students to look for online bookstores that sell works by Cuban and Cuban-American authors. These websites often include biographical and literary information on the authors they feature.
- Have students search the Internet for information on the popular Cuban dance *el son.*

**A escribir: Suggestion**
For additional writing practice, see the *Mi diario* activity in each chapter of the Workbook/Laboratory Manual.

**A escribir: Variation**
Have students find or hand out other poems from *Bilingual Blues* and have students write several paragraphs comparing one of the poems to *Cubanita descubanizada.*

# En resumen

## GRAMÁTICA

To review the grammar points presented in this chapter, refer to the indicated grammar presentation. You'll find further practice of these structures in the Workbook/Laboratory Manual, on the Interactive CD-ROM, and on the *¿Qué tal?* Online Learning Center (www.mhhe.com/quetal7).

**44** **¡No queríamos que fuera así!**—Past Subjunctive

You should know the forms of the past subjunctive and when to use it.

## VOCABULARIO

Practice this vocabulary with digital flash cards on the Online Learning Center (www.mhhe.com/quetal7).

### Las noticias

| | |
|---|---|
| el acontecimiento | event, happening |
| el asesinato | assassination |
| el choque | collision |
| el desastre | disaster |
| la esperanza | hope, wish |
| la guerra | war |
| la huelga | strike (*labor*) |
| el medio de comunicación | means of communication |
| las noticias | (evening) news |
| el noticiero | newscast |
| la paz (*pl.* paces) | peace |
| la prensa | press; news media |
| el/la testigo | witness |

Cognados: el ataque (terrorista), la bomba, la erupción, el evento, el/la reportero/a, el terrorismo, el/la terrorista, la víctima
Repaso: el canal, el mundo, el/la obrero/a

| | |
|---|---|
| comunicarse (qu) (con) | to communicate (with) |
| enterarse (de) | to find out, learn (about) |
| informar | to inform |
| mantener (*irreg.*) | to maintain, keep |

Repaso: ofrecer (zc), vivir

**Suggestions**
• Have students write in Spanish definitions for the words in the list. Then have them create crossword puzzles and use their definitions as cues. Have them exchange and solve each other's puzzles.
• Have students choose one word from the list and use this as the title for a brief composition.
• Ask students the following questions to review the vocabulary.

1. ¿Cómo se entera Ud. de las noticias? ¿Lee el periódico o mira el noticiero en la tele o escucha las noticias en la radio?
2. ¿Cree todo lo que lee en la prensa? ¿Cree que los medios de información informan bien al público, por lo general?

### El gobierno y la responsabilidad cívica

| | |
|---|---|
| el/la ciudadano/a | citizen |
| el deber | responsibility; obligation |
| el derecho | right |
| la (des)igualdad | (in)equality |
| el/la dictador(a) | dictator |
| la dictadura | dictatorship |
| la discriminación | discrimination |
| el ejército | army |
| la ley | law |
| la libertad | liberty, freedom |
| la política | politics |
| el/la político/a | politician |
| el rey / la reina | king/queen |
| el servicio militar | military service |

Repaso: los/las demás, el gobierno

| | |
|---|---|
| apoyar | to support |
| castigar (gu) | to punish |
| durar | to last |
| gobernar (ie) | to govern, rule |
| votar | to vote |

Repaso: obedecer (zc)

**Bright Idea Suggestion**
Have students give words based on the following definitions.

1. *una persona que nace o que es residente permanente de un país*
2. *lo que forman los obreros cuando no están contentos con las condiciones de trabajo*
3. *lo que deben hacer los ciudadanos cuando hay elecciones*
4. *una pelea armada entre dos o más países*
5. *un sinónimo de* responsabilidad *u* obligación
6. *una palabra que refiere a la radio, la televisión y los periódicos*
7. *las otras personas de nuestra comunidad*
8. *la acción de aceptar una ley, una regla o un mandato*
9. *una persona que representa a un país de forma hereditaria, no por votación*
10. *el grupo de personas que defiende a un país en caso de guerra*

**Suggestions**
• Point out the chapter-opener photo. *La Giralda,* considered a symbol of the city of Seville, was originally part of that city's main mosque during the Moorish occupation. The mosque and original tower were built in the 12th century. Later the building was repurposed to serve as a Catholic cathedral. The shape of the tower has been altered in different stages of reconstruction and repair. *La Giralda* was the first tower in Spain to have a clock. Ask students if they have visited any

# En el extranjero°

°**En...** *Abroad*

architectural treasures in this or other countries. What kinds of buildings, monuments, bridges, and so on, do they find most interesting? Are there any particular attractions that they would like to visit one day?

## CAPÍTULO 18

## CULTURA

- **Nota cultural:** De compras en el extranjero
- **En los Estados Unidos y el Canadá:** Churrísimo
- **Voces** de España
  - **Literatura:** Juan Ramón Jiménez
  - **Música:** Los romances
- **Videoteca**
  - **Entrevista cultural:** España
  - **Entre amigos:** Tengo mi pasaje a San Francisco
- **Enfoque cultural:** España

## VOCABULARIO

- Lugares y cosas en el extranjero
- En un viaje al extranjero

## GRAMÁTICA

**45** Conditional Verb Forms

• Have students list their ideas about Spain, including information on geography, politics, economy, culture, music, and cuisine. When you finish the chapter, return to the lists and ask students what ideas they would change and/or add.

*La Giralda de Sevilla, España, una torre campanaria* (bell tower) *construida en 1184 como parte de una mezquita* (mosque) *musulmana*

Paso 1: Vocabulario
See the "Chapter-by-Chapter Supplementary Materials" in the IM for a model for vocabulary presentation, as well as additional teaching suggestions, notes, activities, and other resources for *Paso 1*.

## LUGARES Y COSAS EN EL EXTRANJERO

Resources: Transparencies 104–106
Transparencies 105 and 106 provide additional vocabulary and sentences about travel.

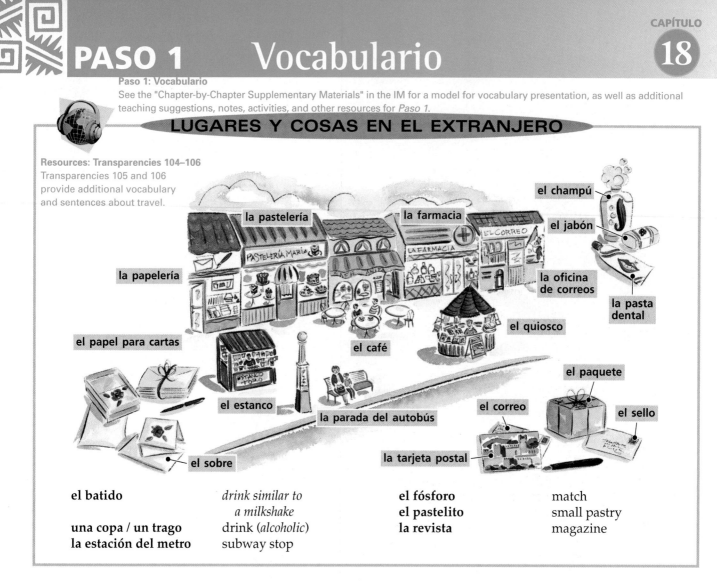

| | | | |
|---|---|---|---|
| **el batido** | drink similar to a milkshake | **el fósforo** | match |
| **una copa / un trago** | drink (alcoholic) | **el pastelito** | small pastry |
| **la estación del metro** | subway stop | **la revista** | magazine |

## Suggestions

- Have students identify the places where the following activities take place.

  1. *Se compran y se venden medicamentos allí.*
  2. *Allí se puede tomar algo de beber y mirar pasar a la gente.*
  3. *Allí se esperan los autobuses.*
  4. *Se compran cigarrillos y fósforos allí.*
  5. *Se compran sellos y se mandan cartas y paquetes allí.*
  6. *Si se tiene ganas de comer un pastel, se puede ir a ese sitio.*

- Point out that *el correo* means mail or post office, but the plural *los correos* means postal service. Tell students there are several words for stamps: *el sello, el timbre, la estampilla.*

## Multimedia: Audio

Students can listen to and practice this chapter's vocabulary on the Online Learning Center (**www.mhhe.com/quetal7**), as well as on the Textbook Audio CD, part of the Laboratory Audio Program.

## ■ Conversación

**A. ¿Cierto o falso?** Corrija las oraciones falsas. (Sugerencia: Lea primero la **Nota cultural** en la página 436.)

1. Se puede comprar batidos y pastelitos en una pastelería.
2. Si yo quisiera tomar una copa, iría (*I would go*) a un quiosco.
3. Se va a una papelería para mandar paquetes.
4. Es más rápido ir a pie que tomar el metro.
5. Se va a un café a comprar champú.
6. Si yo necesitara pasta dental, iría a la oficina de correos.
7. Se puede comprar fósforos en un estanco.
8. Un batido se hace con vino.

**B. En el extranjero.** Con un compañero / una compañera, conteste con oraciones completas.

1. ¿Dónde se compra el champú? ¿el jabón?
2. ¿Cuál es la diferencia entre una farmacia de este país y una farmacia en el extranjero?
3. ¿Dónde se puede comprar sellos? (dos lugares)
4. Si se necesitan cigarrillos o fósforos, ¿adónde se va?
5. ¿Qué es un quiosco? ¿Qué cosas se venden allí?
6. ¿Qué venden en una papelería?

Suggestion
Have students use the *alojamiento* vocabulary to describe their last stay in a (luxury) hotel or motel. They should give as many details as possible, using new vocabulary whenever possible. Ask questions such as: *¿Era un hotel de tres, cuatro o cinco estrellas?*

## EN UN VIAJE AL EXTRANJERO

Resources: Transparency 107

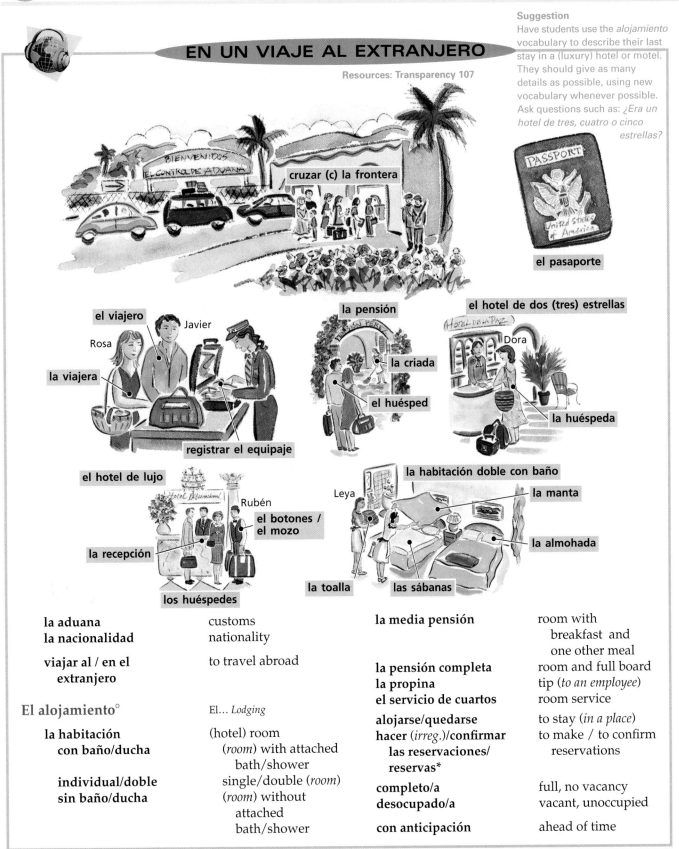

cruzar (c) la frontera

el pasaporte

el viajero — Javier

Rosa

la viajera

registrar el equipaje

la pensión

la criada

el huésped

el hotel de dos (tres) estrellas

Dora

la huéspeda

el hotel de lujo

Rubén

el botones / el mozo

la recepción

los huéspedes

la habitación doble con baño

Leya

la manta

la almohada

la toalla     las sábanas

| | | | |
|---|---|---|---|
| la aduana | customs | la media pensión | room with breakfast and one other meal |
| la nacionalidad | nationality | | |
| viajar al / en el extranjero | to travel abroad | la pensión completa | room and full board |
| | | la propina | tip (*to an employee*) |
| **El alojamiento°** | El... *Lodging* | el servicio de cuartos | room service |
| la habitación | (hotel) room | alojarse/quedarse | to stay (*in a place*) |
| con baño/ducha | (*room*) with attached bath/shower | hacer (*irreg.*)/confirmar las reservaciones/ reservas* | to make / to confirm reservations |
| individual/doble | single/double (*room*) | | |
| sin baño/ducha | (*room*) without attached bath/shower | completo/a | full, no vacancy |
| | | desocupado/a | vacant, unoccupied |
| | | con anticipación | ahead of time |

*La reserva *is used in Spain for a reservation (for accommodations).* La reservación *is widely used in other parts of the Spanish-speaking world.*

Heritage Speakers
Anime a los hispanohablantes a hablar de la última vez que pasaron por la aduana. ¿Tuvieron que mostrar el pasaporte? ¿Tenían algo que declarar?

## NOTA CULTURAL

### De compras en el extranjero

Aunque[a] **los nombres** de muchos lugares y tiendas del mundo hispánico **se parecen** a los de este país, **no siempre son iguales los productos** que en ellos se venden. Tome en cuenta sobre todo las siguientes diferencias.

- En **las farmacias** no venden la variedad de cosas —dulces, tarjetas postales, etcétera— que se venden en las farmacias de los EE.UU.* y el Canadá. Por lo general, sólo se venden medicinas y productos para **la higiene personal** como jabón, pasta dental, champú…
- En **los estancos,** además de productos tabacaleros, se venden **sellos,** así que[b] uno no tiene que ir a una oficina de correos para comprarlos. También se venden **sobres** y **tarjetas postales** en los estancos.
- En **los quioscos** se vende una **gran variedad** de cosas: periódicos, revistas, libros, etcétera, pero también lápices, papel para cartas…

*Un quiosco en Madrid, España*

---

[a]*Although*   [b]*así… so*

## ■ Conversación

### A. Definiciones

PASO 1   Empareje las personas con la descripción apropiada.

1. __b__ el huésped
2. __f__ el recepcionista
3. __a__ el botones
4. __d__ la turista
5. __e__ la inspectora de aduanas
6. __c__ el viajero

a. la persona que nos ayuda con el equipaje en un hotel
b. la persona que se aloja en un hotel o una pensión
c. una persona que va de un lugar a otro
d. alguien que viaja para ver otros lugares
e. la persona que nos registra las maletas y toma la declaración en la aduana
f. la persona que nos atiende en la recepción de un hotel

PASO 2   Defina las siguientes palabras en español.

1. la aduana
2. el pasaporte
3. la pensión completa
4. la frontera
5. la propina
6. el formulario de inmigración

---

*EE.UU. is one way to abbreviate **Estados Unidos**. **E.U.** and **USA** are also used.*

**B. En la aduana.** ¿Ha viajado Ud. al extranjero? ¿Sabe Ud. lo que pasa en la aduana? Aunque (*Although*) no lo haya hecho, va a poder contestar las preguntas de esta actividad, pues se trata de (*it's a question of*) utilizar el sentido común. De las siguientes acciones, ¿cuáles pueden causar problemas en la aduana?

1. ☐ ser cortés con el inspector
2. ☑ no tener el pasaporte (o el visado necesario)
3. ☐ tener toallas de su hotel en las maletas
4. ☑ esconder (*hiding*) artículos de contrabando en su equipaje, con la esperanza que el inspector no los encuentre
5. ☑ quejarse del gobierno del país del inspector
6. ☑ intentar cruzar la frontera con un pasaporte falsificado
7. ☑ traficar en drogas
8. ☑ tratar de distraer al inspector mientras este (*he*) registra sus maletas

**C. Cuando Ud. viaja…**

PASO 1  Lea la lista de acciones típicas de los viajeros. ¿Hace Ud. lo mismo cuando viaja? Indique las acciones que son verdaderas para Ud.

1. ☐ Hago una reserva en un hotel con un mes de anticipación.
2. ☐ Confirmo la reserva antes de salir de viaje.
3. ☐ Voy al banco a conseguir cheques de viajero (*traveler's checks*).
4. ☐ Alquilo un coche.
5. ☐ Me alojo en un hotel de lujo.
6. ☐ Pido que el mozo me suba las maletas.
7. ☐ Llamo al servicio de cuartos en vez de comer en el restaurante.
8. ☐ Le dejo una propina a la criada el último día de mi estancia (*stay*).

PASO 2  Ahora piense en su último viaje. ¿Hizo Ud. las cosas de la lista del **Paso 1**? Conteste según el modelo y cambie los detalles de esas oraciones por los que en realidad ocurrieron en su viaje.

MODELO:  La última vez que hice un viaje… →
Hice una reserva en un hotel, pero con sólo dos días de anticipación.

**D. Situaciones.**  Con un compañero / una compañera, haga el papel de un viajero / una viajera o del / de la recepcionista de un hotel.

PASO 1  El/La recepcionista le pregunta al viajero / a la viajera que acaba de llegar:

- si tiene una reserva
- cuánto tiempo piensa quedarse
- el tipo de habitación reservada o deseada
- la forma de pago

PASO 2  El huésped / La huéspeda pide los siguientes servicios:

- el desayuno en su cuarto
- más toallas/jabón
- información sobre lugares turísticos de interés

PASO 3  Por fin, el huésped / la huéspeda pasa por la recepción para pagar la cuenta. Encuentra los siguientes errores en su cuenta.

- Le cobraron por un desayuno que no tomó.
- Le cobraron por cuatro noches en vez de tres.
- Le cobraron por una llamada a larga distancia que nunca hizo.

**Con. B: Preliminary Exercise**
Ask students the following questions.

1. *¿Ha viajado Ud. por el extranjero? ¿Qué país(es) ha visitado? ¿Cuánto tiempo estuvo en… ? ¿Tiene ganas de volver? ¿Qué hizo allí? ¿Trabajó? ¿Estudió? ¿Visitó a sus parientes o a sus amigos?*

2. *En esta clase, ¿cuántos tienen pasaporte? ¿Les fue difícil conseguirlo? ¿Qué hizo Ud. para conseguirlo? ¿Tuvo que pagar algo? ¿Salió Ud. bien en la foto o no le gusta como salió?*

3. *¿Ha cruzado Ud. alguna vez la frontera entre el Canadá y los Estados Unidos? ¿la frontera entre México y los Estados Unidos? ¿Tuvo problemas al cruzar? ¿Qué le pidió el inspector? ¿El pasaporte? ¿una visa? ¿Qué te preguntó? ¿Estaba Ud. nervioso/a? ¿Tenía algo que declarar que no declaraba antes?*

4. *¿Siempre declara la gente lo que tiene cuando pasa por la aduana?*

**Con. B: Variation**
Have students give their opinions about the statements in the activity, beginning with phrases such as *Es bueno… , Es buena idea… ,* and so on.

**Con. B: Follow-Up**
Have students explain why particular actions could cause problems.

**Con. D: Suggestion**
Role-play each *Paso* with at least one student before letting students do the role play on their own.

**Con. D: Bright Idea Suggestion**
Role-play the *recepcionista* and have several sets of students check into your hotel.

**Heritage Speakers**
Pídales a dos estudiantes hispanohablantes que representen los papeles y el diálogo primero para que los demás estudiantes vean un modelo.

 **Note**
See the Workbook/ Laboratory Manual for review and practice of the names of Hispanic nationalities, as well as general pronunciation practice.

**Need more practice?**

- Workbook/Laboratory Manual
- Interactive CD-ROM
- Online Learning Center (www.mhhe.com/quetal7)

**Paso 2: Gramática**
See the "Chapter-by-Chapter Supplementary Materials" in the IM for additional
teaching suggestions, notes, activities, and other resources for *Paso 2*.

**Suggestions**
- Before beginning *Gramática 45*, lead into the *minidiálogo* with *le gustaría* + infinitive questions, which have been active since *Capítulo 7*.
- Preview this section by asking the following kinds of questions.

  *Si Ud. tuviera un millón de dólares, ¿qué haría?*

  *Si Ud. pudiera hacerle una sola pregunta al presidente de los Estados Unidos / al primer ministro del Canadá, ¿qué le preguntaría?*

  *Si pudiera cambiar cualquier cosa en el mundo, ¿qué cambiaría?*

---

## ¿Recuerda Ud.?

In **Gramática 42** you learned the forms and uses of the future tense. Can you provide the correct future forms of the following verbs?

1. (yo) viajar
2. (ellos) beber
3. (tú) ir
4. (Ud.) venir
5. (nosotros) hacer
6. (ella) poner

Review all of the future forms before studying the conditional tense in **Gramática 45**. Also note that you learned a conditional expression in **Capítulo 7: me gustaría(n)**. What is the English equivalent of the following sentence?

**Me gustaría** visitar el museo esta tarde.

---

## 45 Expressing What You Would Do Conditional Verb Forms

### La fantasía de Yolanda Torres-Luján

Yolanda es una mujer de negocios muy ocupada. Sufre muchas presiones y está muy cansada. Le *gustaría* ir de vacaciones.

«Con tres días de vacaciones, simplemente *dormiría* todo el día. No *haría* más que comer y dormir. Con una semana de vacaciones, *iría* a la playa, *tomaría* el sol todo el día y *tomaría* copas tropicales en bares elegantes. Con un mes de vacaciones… *descansaría* una semana en casa y luego *viajaría* por Europa.»

- Using the conditional, ask students what their ideal vacation would be.

¿Irían a la playa? ¿a las montañas?
¿A qué país visitarían?
¿Preferirían alojarse en un hotel de lujo o en un hotel menos caro?
¿Qué harían durante sus vacaciones ideales?

### ¿Y Ud.?

¿Sufre muchas presiones? ¿Le gustaría ir de vacaciones? ¿Qué haría en las vacaciones? Haga oraciones con las siguientes indicaciones. Use **no** cuando sea necesario.

MODELO: dormir todo el día → *Dormiría* todo el día.

1. ir a la playa
2. tomar el sol
3. tomar copas tropicales en bares elegantes
4. descansar una semana
5. viajar por Europa
6. ¿ ?

- Point out that *vacaciones* is rarely used in the singular form in Spanish.

**Refrán**

«La gente joven dice lo que hace, la gente vieja dice lo que hizo y los tontos lo que les gustaría hacer.»

Have students discuss the meaning of this *refrán*. What do they think this saying "teaches"?

---

*The fantasy of Yolanda Torres-Luján* Yolanda is a very busy businesswoman. She's under a lot of pressure, and she's very tired. She would like to go on vacation. "With three days of vacation, I would simply sleep all day. I wouldn't do anything but eat and sleep. With a week of vacation, I would go to the beach, sunbathe all day, and have tropical drinks in elegant bars. With a month of vacation . . . I would rest at home a week and then I would travel through Europe."

The phrase **me gustaría...** expresses what you *would like to* (do, say, and so on). **Gustaría** is a conditional verb form, part of a system that will allow you to talk about what you and others *would* (do, say, buy, and so on) in a given situation.

| Past | Present | FUTURE |
|---|---|---|
| preterite | present indicative | future |
| imperfect | present progressive | conditional |
| present perfect | formal commands | |
| present perfect subjunctive | informal commands | |
| past subjunctive | present subjunctive | |

**A.** Like the English future, the English conditional is formed with an auxiliary verb: *I **would** speak, I **would** write.*

The Spanish *conditional* (**el condicional**), like the Spanish future, is a simple verb form (only one word). It is formed by adding conditional endings to the infinitive. No auxiliary verbs are needed.

CONDITIONAL ENDINGS

| | |
|---|---|
| **-ía** | **-íamos** |
| **-ías** | **-íais** |
| **-ía** | **-ían** |

| hablar | | comer | | vivir | |
|---|---|---|---|---|---|
| hablaría | hablaríamos | comería | comeríamos | viviría | viviríamos |
| hablarías | hablaríais | comerías | comeríais | vivirías | viviríais |
| hablaría | hablarían | comería | comerían | viviría | vivirían |

**B.** Verbs that form the future on an irregular stem use the same stem to form the conditional.

Note that the conditional of **hay (haber)** is **habría** (*there would be*).*

decir: diría, dirías, diría, diríamos, diríais, dirían

| | |
|---|---|
| decir: | **dir-** |
| haber (hay): | **habr-** |
| hacer: | **har-** |
| poder: | **podr-** |
| poner: | **pondr-** |
| querer: | **querr-** |
| saber: | **sabr-** |
| salir: | **saldr-** |
| tener: | **tendr-** |
| venir: | **vendr-** |

-ía
-ías
-ía
-íamos
-íais
-ían

*The conditional forms of the verb **haber** are used to form the conditional perfect tense (**el condicional perfecto**), which expresses what* would have *occurred at some point in the past.*

**Habríamos tenido** que buscarla en el aeropuerto.

*We **would have had** to pick her up at the airport.*

*You will find a more detailed presentation of these forms in Appendix 3, Additional Perfect Forms (Indicative and Subjunctive).*

**C.** The conditional expresses what you would do in a particular situation, given a particular set of circumstances.

 When *would* implies *used to* in English, use the imperfect in Spanish.

—**¿Hablarías** español en el Brasil?
*Would you speak Spanish in Brazil?*

—No. **Hablaría** portugués.
*No. I would speak Portuguese.*

**Íbamos** a la playa todos los veranos.
*We would go (used to go) to the beach every summer.*

## ■ Práctica

**A. ¡Anticipemos! ¿Qué haría Ud.?**

PASO 1  Imagine que hace un viaje a España. Complete las siguientes oraciones de manera que (*so that*) correspondan a la realidad y a lo que a Ud. le gustaría hacer. ¡Es una gran oportunidad de demostrarles a sus compañeros y a su profesor(a) su conocimiento (*knowledge*) sobre la vida y la cultura españolas!

1. Hablaría _____.
2. Comería _____ y bebería _____.
3. Iría a _____ y allí vería _____.
4. No podría irme sin antes visitar _____.
5. Me compraría _____.
6. Me divertiría mucho _____ (**Sugerencia:** Se puede usar un gerundio: **-iendo** o **-ando**.)

PASO 2  Claro que durante un viaje no sólo se hacen actividades culturales. Las oraciones a continuación muestran actividades típicas durante un viaje, pero Ud. debe completarlas con algunos detalles.

1. Yo haría el viaje a España con _____.
2. Tendría que sacar muchas fotos para mostrárselas a _____.
3. Le(s) mandaría tarjetas postales a _____.
4. Querría _____ durante el viaje, pero probablemente no lo haría.
5. Conocería a _____.

PASO 3  Ahora con un compañero / una compañera, haga una lista similar a las del **Paso 1** y el **Paso 2,** pero sobre otro país hispánico.

**B. ¿Es posible escapar?**  Cuente Ud. la fantasía de esta trabajadora social, dando la forma condicional de los verbos.

Necesito salir de todo esto… Creo que me (gustar[1]) ir a Puerto Rico o a algún otro lugar exótico del Caribe… No (trabajar[2])… (Poder[3]) nadar todos los días… (Tomar[4]) el sol en la playa… (Comer[5]) platos exóticos… (Ver[6]) bellos lugares naturales… El viaje (ser[7]) ideal…

Pero… , tarde o temprano, (tener[8]) que volver a lo de siempre… a los rascacielos de la ciudad… al tráfico… al medio ambiente contaminado… al mundo del trabajo… (Poder[9]) usar mi tarjeta de crédito, como dice el anuncio —pero ¡(tener[10]) que pagar después!

**Comprensión: ¿Cierto, falso o no lo dice?** Corrija las oraciones falsas.

1. Esta persona trabaja en una ciudad grande.
2. No le interesan los deportes acuáticos.
3. Puede pagar este viaje de sueños (*dreams*) al contado.
4. Tiene un novio con quien quisiera hacer el viaje.

**C. ¿Qué harías si pudieras?**

PASO 1 Con un compañero / una compañera, haga y conteste preguntas según el modelo. Pueden cambiar los detalles, si quieren.

> MODELO: estudiar árabe / japonés →
> E1: ¿Estudiarías *árabe*?
> E2: No. Estudiaría *japonés*.

1. estudiar italiano / chino
2. renunciar a un puesto sin avisar / con dos semanas de anticipación
3. hacer un viaje a España / la Argentina
4. salir de casa sin apagar el estéreo / las luces
5. seguir un presupuesto rígido / flexible
6. gastar menos en ropa / libros
7. poner el aire acondicionado en invierno / verano
8. alquilar un coche de lujo / económico

PASO 2 Ahora sigan con el mismo modelo, pero inventen las respuestas.

1. dejar de estudiar / ¿ ?
2. vivir en otra ciudad / ¿ ?
3. ser presidente/a de los Estados Unidos / primer ministro (primera ministra) del Canadá / ¿ ?
4. gustarle conocer a una persona famosa / ¿ ?

---

## ■ Conversación

**A. Entrevista.** ¿Cómo será su futuro? ¿Qué hará? ¿Qué haría? Con otro/a estudiante, haga y conteste las siguientes preguntas.

> MODELO: E1: ¿Dejarás de fumar algún día? →
> E2: No. No dejaré de fumar nunca. No puedo.
> (Creo que sí. Dejaré de fumar algún día.)

PREGUNTAS CON EL FUTURO

1. ¿Te graduarás en esta universidad (o en otra)?
2. ¿Vivirás en esta ciudad después de graduarte?
3. ¿Buscarás un puesto aquí?
4. ¿Cuántos niños (nietos) crees que tendrás algún día?

PREGUNTAS CON EL CONDICIONAL

1. ¿Te casarías con una persona de otro país?
2. ¿Podrías estar contento/a sin la televisión?
3. ¿Serías capaz de (*capable of*) ahorrar el 10 por ciento de tu salario?
4. ¿Podrías vivir sin las tarjetas de crédito?

---

**Prác. C: Suggestions**

• Have students complete the items in the future. Contrast the difference in meaning when the future is used.

• Have students add two questions of their own to each group.

**Prác. C: Answers**

*Paso 1* 1. —¿Estudiarías italiano? —No, estudiaría chino. 2. —¿Renunciarías a un puesto sin avisar? —No, avisaría con dos semanas de anticipación. 3. —¿Harías un viaje a España? —No, haría un viaje a la Argentina. 4. —¿Saldrías de casa sin apagar el estéreo? —No, saldría sin apagar las luces. 5. —¿Seguirías un presupuesto rígido? —No, seguiría un presupuesto flexible (uno flexible). 6. —¿Gastarías menos en ropa? —No, gastaría menos en libros. 7. —¿Pondrías el aire acondicionado en invierno? —No, lo pondría en verano. 8. —¿Alquilarías un coche de lujo? —No, alquilaría un coche económico (uno económico).

**Need more practice?**

■ Workbook/Laboratory Manual
■ Interactive CD-ROM
■ Online Learning Center (www.mhhe.com/quetal7)

**Con. A: Bright Idea Suggestion**

This activity recycles the future and prepares students for the next section. Review and compare future and conditional forms. You can also model responding with the conditional.

*Sí, ya te dije que dejaría de fumar pronto. No, ya te dije que nunca dejaré de fumar.*

**Con. A: Follow-Up**

Have students write two questions that use the future tense and two that use the conditional. Have them ask their classmates these questions.

**Con. A: Bright Idea Extension**

*¿Qué harías con mil dólares?* (Saving is not an option.)
*¿Qué no harías por un millón de dólares?* (Refer to reality television programming.)

---

**Note**
- Point out that, like *if* in English, *si* can mean *cuando* if it is a recurrent situation: *Si mi mejor amiga me llama por teléfono, cierro la puerta para que nadie me oiga.*
- Stress similarity between English and Spanish. Point out that past tense form after *if,* as in *If I had a million dollars . . .* , does not necessarily mean past action. It is the equivalent to the meaning of the imperfect subjunctive in Spanish.

**Con. B: Suggestion**
Assign as homework.

**Resources: Transparency 108**
Transparency 108 provides images that can be used to make speculations with *si* clauses.

**Heritage Speakers**
En algunos países y regiones hispanohablantes, es muy común oír que se usa el condicional cuando, por lo general, se recomienda el uso del imperfecto de subjuntivo en cláusulas condicionales con *si*. Por ejemplo, es posible oír *Si yo tendría el dinero, iría a Francia* en vez de *Si yo tuviera el dinero, iría a Francia*. A pesar del  uso popular del condicional en cláusulas con *si*, se recomienda usar el imperfecto de subjuntivo. Anime a los hispanohablantes a indicar qué tiempo verbal prefieren usar con cláusulas con *si*.

**Con. B: Follow-Up**
Have students report back to the class information about their partners. Have them use the *nosotros* forms to explain what they have in common with their partners.

## NOTA COMUNICATIVA

### If I were you, I would . . .

Both English and Spanish use clauses to speculate about likely or unlikely situations. These are called *if* or **si** clauses.

- The present indicative after **si** presents a situation that is likely to occur. It is followed or preceded by a clause in the indicative or by a command.

  LIKELY

  Si **ahorro** suficiente dinero, **iré** de vacaciones a España.
  *If I save enough money, I will go to Spain on vacation.*

- The imperfect subjunctive after **si** introduces an unlikely event. The preceding or following clause includes a verb in the conditional.

  UNLIKELY

  Si **tuviera** dinero suficiente, le **daría** la vuelta al mundo.
  *If I had enough money, I would go around the world.*

**B. Circunstancias.** Con un compañero / una compañera, haga y conteste preguntas según los modelos.

PASO 1 ¿Qué haces si... ?

MODELO: ¿Qué haces si... ? / haces tu maleta para un viaje pero no toda la ropa que deseas llevar cabe (*fits*) en la maleta →
  E1: ¿Qué haces si haces tu maleta para un viaje pero no toda la ropa que deseas llevar cabe en la maleta?
  E2: Si hago mi maleta pero no toda la ropa cabe en la maleta, trato de llevar menos ropa / busco una maleta más grande.

¿Qué haces si... ?

1. tu primera clase es a las nueve de la mañana y te despiertas a las 8:50
2. tu mejor amigo/a (novio/a, esposo/a, hijo/a) tiene un resfriado muy fuerte
3. es viernes por la noche y no tienes ningún plan para divertirte esa noche
4. se te pierde la llave de tu cuarto/casa

PASO 2 ¿Qué harías si... ?

MODELO: ¿Qué harías si... ? / en una lotería ganaras un viaje al extranjero a cualquier (*any*) país del mundo →
  E1: ¿Qué harías si en una lotería ganaras un viaje al extranjero a cualquier país del mundo?
  E2: Si en una lotería ganara un viaje al extranjero a cualquier país del mundo, tendría que decidirme entre España y el Perú. Primero, buscaría información en el Internet.

¿Qué harías si... ?

1. alguien te dejara una herencia (*inheritance*) de dos millones de dólares
2. pudieras hacer lo que quisieras en este momento
3. tuvieras un solo (*single*) deseo para todo el mundo
4. pudieras dar la fiesta de tus sueños (*dreams*)

## LITERATURA: Juan Ramón Jiménez

**Sobre el autor:** *Juan Ramón Jiménez nació en Moguer, en la provincia de Andalucía, España. Estudió derecho,[a] pero se interesó más en la poesía y la pintura. Llegó a ser un poeta prolífico, y escribió varios libros. Le otorgaron[b] el Premio Nóbel de Literatura en 1956. El siguiente poema, «El viaje definitivo», es del libro de poesías* Canción *(1936).*

**Juan Ramón Jiménez**
*(1881–1958)*
**y su esposa Zenobia**

**Literatura: Notes**
• Juan Ramón Jiménez's family produced and exported wines.
• *Platero y yo* (1914) is one of Jiménez's most famous books. It tells the story of a donkey and a writer.
• Jiménez opposed the Franco regime and lived in exile in Cuba and Puerto Rico from 1939 until he died in 1958.

### El viaje definitivo

Y yo me iré. Y se quedarán los pájaros
cantando;
y se quedará mi huerto,[c] con su verde árbol,
y con su pozo[d] blanco.

Todas las tardes, el cielo será azul y plácido;
y tocarán, como esta tarde están tocando,
las campanas del campanario.[e]

Se morirán aquellos que me amaron;
y el pueblo se hará nuevo cada año;
y en el rincón[f] aquel de mi huerto florido y encalado,[g]
mi espíritu errará,[h] nostálgico…

Y yo me iré; y estaré solo, sin hogar,[i] sin árbol
verde, sin pozo blanco,
sin cielo azul y plácido…
Y se quedarán los pájaros cantando.

[a]*law* [b]*they awarded* [c]*jardín* [d]*well* [e]*campanas… bells of the bell tower* [f]*corner* [g]*whitewashed* [h]*will wander* [i]*home*

## MÚSICA: Los romances

El romance es una canción narrativa que trata aventuras, amores y lamentaciones líricas. Esta forma oral de la Edad Media[a] se cantaba en todas partes de España, para propagar[b] noticias, recordar la historia, celebrar eventos y entretener.[c]

**Música: Notes**
• In Spain the tradition of *los romances* or epic poems often revolved around the tales *el mío Cid*. Similar verses and songs circulated about heroes from other European countries, such as Roland of France and Arthur of England.

El Quarteto Medieval de Urueña se dedica a la interpretación de la música antigua de España.

### El prisionero

Que por mayo era, por mayo,
cuando hace la calor,
cuando los trigos encañan[d]
y están los campos en flor,

cuando canta la calandria[e]
y responde el ruiseñor,[f]
cuando los enamorados
van a servir al amor;

sino yo,[g] triste, cuitado,[h]
que vivo en esta prisión;
que no sé cuándo es de día
ni cuándo las noches son,

sino[i] por una avecilla[j]
que me canta al albor.[k]
Matómela un ballestero;[l]
déle Dios mal galardón.[m]

[a]*Edad… Middle Ages (roughly spanning from the fifth through the fifteenth centuries)* [b]*spread* [c]*entertain* [d]*cuando… when the wheat forms stalks* [e]*lark (bird)* [f]*nightingale* [g]*sino… but not I* [h]*forlorn* [i]*except* [j]*little bird* [k]*dawn* [l]*Matómela… A crossbowman shot it* [m]*reward*

• Ureña is a town in the province of Valladolid.
• Ziryab, a gifted musician and talented singer, was forced to move from Baghdad to Spain because he surpassed his teacher in talent and skill. He settled in Córdoba where he revolutionized music. He founded a school of music and added a fifth string (G bass) to the lute (*laúd*), one of the main changes made to that instrument in the modern era.

Ziryab fue innovador de instrumentos como el laúd, un ancestro de la guitarra española. Nació en lo que hoy es Irak, se trasladó[n] a España en el siglo[o] IX y llegó a ser[p] una figura muy importante en la fusión de varios aspectos de las culturas ibérica y árabe, incluyendo la música.

[n]*se… moved* [o]*century* [p]*llegó… became*

# PASO 3 Gramática

**Paso 3: Gramática**
See the "Chapter-by-Chapter Supplementary Materials" in the IM for additional teaching suggestions, notes, activities, and other resources for *Paso 3*.

**En los Estados Unidos y el Canadá: Comprensión**
1. ¿Qué son los churros?
2. ¿Por qué son una comida ideal para los canadienses?

## En los Estados Unidos y el Canadá

### Churrísimo

¿Sabe Ud. qué son **los churros**? Son **pedacitos de masa**[a] **frita** que se comen solos con azúcar o mojados[b] en el café o el chocolate caliente. Son originarios **de España**, pero se encuentran **por toda Latinoamérica**. Y ahora también se pueden conseguir en el Canadá, gracias a la cadena[c] Churrísimo.

**El dueño** de la cadena es Moses Bendayan, un venezolano-canadiense de origen sefardí. **Los sefardíes** son descendientes de los judíos que vivieron en España hasta el siglo[d] XVI. En la cultura sefardí todavía se conservan las tradiciones culinarias de la época de su vida

*Churros y chocolate*

española, y su lengua es una mezcla de hebreo con español.

Según el Sr. Bendayan, los churros son **exitosos**[e] en el Canadá por dos **razones principales**: a los canadienses les gustan mucho **las meriendas y comidas entre horas**, y **el chocolate caliente** —el compañero por excelencia de los churros— **es ideal en su clima frío**. Además,[f] el Sr. Bendayan señala[g] que el mercado norteamericano anglosajón es un público con curiosidad por los gustos[h] nuevos, y tiene en la actualidad[i] un interés especial en todo lo hispano. ¡Que los disfruten![j]

[a]pedacitos... *little pieces of dough*  [b]*dunked*
[c]*(restaurant) chain*  [d]*century*  [e]*successful*  [f]*In addition*
[g]*notes*  [h]*tastes*  [i]*en... currently*  [j]¡Que... *Enjoy them!*

## UN POCO DE TODO

**Lengua y cultura: Un viaje por España.**   Complete the following passages with the correct forms of the words in parentheses, as suggested by the context. When two possibilities are given in parentheses, select the correct word. **¡OJO!** As you conjugate verbs in this activity, sometimes you will have to decide which mood (subjunctive or indicative) and tense to use according to context.

Seguro que a Ud. le interesa conocer España algún día. Cuando (ir[1]) Ud. a España por primera vez, ¿qué (*cond.*, deber[2]) visitar? Una pregunta difícil de contestar, porque (es/hay[3]) una inmensa cantidad de lugares recomendables. Todo depende de lo que le guste (a/—[4]) Ud. y del tiempo que (tener[5]).

(Por/Para[6]) empezar, España es tan grande (que/como[7]) Texas, y eso quiere decir que las distancias de un punto a otro del país (ser/estar[8]) considerables. Recuerde que en España hay muestras[a] de su rica y antiquísima[b] historia de más de 2.000 años (por/para[9]) todas partes del país. Finalmente, a causa de la diversidad cultural y geográfica del país, cada región parece (ser[10]) un país diferente. España tiene las montañas más altas (de/que[11]) Europa, después de los Alpes; islas en el Mediterráneo y en la costa africana; una región celta; una gran zona que muestra la larga influencia musulmana[c] en el pasado; una zona desértica; zonas de (gran/grande[12]) actividad agrícola y miles de kilómetros de costa de todo tipo. ¡Es imposible que alguien no (encontrar[13]) (algo/algún[14]) de su interés!

[a]*examples*  [b]*very old*  [c]*Islamic*

El otro día (le/se[15]) pedimos a una (español/española[16]), Patricia, que nos (recomendar[17]) un itinerario para un (primer/primero[18]) viaje a España. Nos (*ella:* sugerir[19]) que antes de todo (*nosotros:* escoger[20])[d] el clima que preferimos (fresco o caluroso), el tipo de paisaje (más o menos urbano, en las montañas o donde hay playa). Despúes nos aseguró que no (*ella:* conocer/saber[21]) a (nadie/alguien[22]) que no (pensar[23]) que España es un país interesante y (muy/mucho[24]) bello. Otro español, Jesús, (nos/—[25]) (decir[26]) que, (por/para[27]) él, es importante (pasar[28]) tiempo suficiente en los lugares que se visitan; cree que no (ser[29]) bueno ver demasiados lugares en poco tiempo. Por eso, él nos recomienda que no (*nosotros:* tratar[30]) (a/de[31]) ver media España en una semana o diez días, sino que[e] (escoger[32]) una zona del país para conocer(lo/la[33]) bien.

¿Tiene Ud. ahora una idea de lo que le (gustar[34]) ver en España?

[d]*to choose*  [e]*sino... but rather that*

*Un puerto en Palma de Mallorca, en las Islas Baleares*

**Comprensión.**   Las siguientes oraciones son falsas. Corríjalas.

1. En España, hay pocos lugares recomendables para los turistas.
2. España es un país recién fundado.
3. Todas las regiones de España se parecen; no hay diferencia entre ellas.
4. Los árabes vivieron en España, pero sin gran impacto cultural.
5. España casi no tiene costas.
6. A las personas que conoce Patricia, les parece que España es un país muy aburrido.
7. Jesús recomienda verlo todo... ¡y muy rápidamente!

**Multimedia: Internet**
Have students search the Internet for more information about Spain. You may assign specific topics for them to research and to present to their classmates. Some topics may include tourist sites, customs, and languages (*el catalán* in Barcelona).

**Resources: Desenlace**
In the *Capítulo 18* segment of "Chapter-by-Chapter Supplementary Materials" in the IM, you will find a chapter-culminating activity. You can use this activity to consolidate and review the vocabulary and grammar skills students have acquired.

**Resources for Review and Testing Preparation**

- Workbook/Laboratory Manual
- Interactive CD-ROM
- Online Learning Center (www.mhhe.com/quetal7)

# PASO 4    Un paso más

**Paso 4: Un paso más**
- The *Paso 4: Un paso más* sections are optional.
- See the "Chapter-by-Chapter Supplementary Materials" in the IM for additional teaching suggestions, notes, activities, and other resources for *Paso 4*.

**Entrevista cultural: Suggestions**
- Before showing the video, ask students questions about traveling and hotel stays.

  *Cuando viaja, ¿qué tipo de hotel prefiere? ¿Busca un hotel económico? ¿un hotel cerca del centro o cerca de las atracciones que le interesen? ¿Qué tipo de habitación prefiere? ¿Le importa si la habitación tiene vista?*

- Show the video and allow students one to two minutes to work on the questions. Have volunteers answer the questions.
- Have volunteers role-play Margarita and her interviewer.

**Entrevista cultural: Answers**
*Possible answers:* **1.** *de Gijón, Asturias, España* **2.** *un hotel* **3.** *Sus padres trabajan en la recepción, su hermano maneja el restaurante y Margarita se dedica a la administración.* **4.** *turistas internacionales* **5.** *Es una experiencia extraordinaria porque siempre conoce a gente de otros países.*

**Entre amigos: Suggestions**
- Before viewing the video, review the questions with the students and ask them similar questions.

  *¿Adónde piensa Ud. ir para las próximas vacaciones? ¿Piensa hacer un viaje? ¿Cómo se prepara Ud. para un viaje? ¿Busca información en una agencia de viajes o en el Internet?*

Have students answer or work in small groups to ask and answer these questions in Spanish.

- After viewing the video, have volunteers read and answer the questions.

**Multimedia: Internet**
Have students search the Internet for more information about the government, educational system, geography, and economy of Spain. You might assign specific topics and have students give brief oral presentations based on their findings.

---

## VIDEOTECA

### Entrevista cultural: España

Margarita Durán es una española que trabaja en el negocio de su familia. En esta entrevista, habla del negocio y de los clientes. Antes de ver el vídeo, lea el siguiente fragmento de la entrevista.

ENTREVISTADORA: ¿De dónde vienen sus huéspedes?

MARGARITA: Por lo general nuestros huéspedes vienen de muchas partes del mundo. Generalmente predominan los alemanes; también tenemos ingleses, franceses y muchos norteamericanos. Eh, las parejas jóvenes son nuestros huéspedes más frecuentes, y eh, normalmente ellos nos solicitan habitaciones que den a[a] la ciudad, que tengan una vista bonita pero que al mismo tiempo sean tranquilas, y esto para nosotros es una contradicción, porque todas las habitaciones que dan a la calle siempre van a tener algún ruido.

[a]den... *open to, overlook*

Ahora vea el vídeo y conteste las siguientes preguntas basándose en la entrevista.

1. ¿De dónde es Margarita?
2. ¿Cuál es el negocio de su familia?
3. ¿Cuáles son las responsabilidades de los miembros de la familia?
4. ¿Quiénes son los clientes, generalmente?
5. ¿Qué opinión tiene Margarita de su trabajo? ¿Por qué?

---

### Entre amigos: Tengo mi pasaje a San Francisco.

Miguel, Karina, Rubén y Tané hablan de las vacaciones. En su opinión, ¿qué van a decir sobre este tema? Antes de mirar el vídeo, lea las preguntas a continuación. Mientras mire el vídeo, trate de entender la conversación en general y fíjese en la información sobre las vacaciones y los arreglos (*arrangements*). Luego mire el vídeo una segunda vez, fijándose en la información que necesita para contestar las preguntas.

1. ¿Para qué necesita Rubén folletos (*brochures*) de viaje?
2. ¿Adónde piensa ir de vacaciones Miguel? ¿Ha decidido?
3. ¿Qué sugiere Karina que busquen en un hotel? Y Rubén, ¿qué sugiere?
4. ¿Qué ha comprado Tané?
5. ¿Qué le sugiere Miguel a Tané?

**Entre amigos: Answers**
*Possible answers:* **1.** *para preparar sus vacaciones* **2.** *Va al Canadá pero todavía no sabe a qué parte.* **3.** *Karina sugiere un hotel con el desayuno incluido y Rubén, un hotel con aire acondicionado.* **4.** *Ha comprado su pasaje a San Francisco.* **5.** *Dice que su amigo le puede conseguir a buen precio una habitación en un hotel muy bueno en San Francisco.*

## ENFOQUE CULTURAL

### España

### ¡Fíjese!

- España es un país donde muchas culturas se han encontrado a través de[a] la historia. Sin embargo fueron los romanos los que marcaron el principio de la historia de la España que hoy conocemos, pues ellos introdujeron el latín a la península durante su dominio (desde el año 200 a.C.[b] hasta la invasión de los visigodos, un pueblo germánico, en el 419 d.C.[c]).
- El latín es la lengua madre del español y también del catalán, el gallego y el portugués. La otra lengua que se habla en la península, el vasco, es una lengua ancestral de origen desconocido: ni siquiera es[d] una lengua indoeuropea.
- España no fue siempre un solo país. De hecho,[e] España se unificó en el siglo XV cuando los Reyes Católicos, Isabel y Fernando, monarcas de dos reinos[f] independientes, se casaron. Su campaña[g] de unificación terminó en 1492 con la conquista del reino musulmán[h] de Granada.
- Los árabes vivieron en España durante ocho siglos, hasta su expulsión, junto con los judíos, en el año 1492.

[a]*... throughout*  [b]*a.C.... antes de Cristo*  [c]*d.C.... después de Cristo*
[d]*ni... it is not even*  [e]*De... In fact*  [f]*kingdoms*  [g]*campaign*  [h]*Moslem*

**Notes**
- Students can read the poem "*El viaje definitivo*" by Spain's Juan Ramón Jiménez in *Voces de España: Literatura.*
- Students can read about Spain's *romance* in *Voces de España: Música.*
- See the Workbook/Laboratory Manual for focused practice with the material in *Enfoque cultural.*

### Personas famosas: Pedro Almodóvar

Las películas del cineasta[a] Pedro Almodóvar (1951– ) han tenido y siguen teniendo un éxito enorme dentro y fuera de España, y Almodóvar es el director de cine español más conocido de las últimas décadas. Con temas que satirizan actitudes tradicionales respecto a la familia, la religión, el machismo y la moralidad convencional, sus películas presentan una sociedad española moderna y cambiante.[b]

Muchas de sus películas se pueden conseguir en las bibliotecas públicas y universitarias, así como en los videoclubs de este país: *Mujeres al borde de un ataque de nervios, La ley del deseo, ¿Qué he hecho yo para merecer esto?, ¡Átame!,[c] Kika, La flor de mi secreto, Todo sobre mi madre* y *Hable con ella.* Las útimas dos fueron ganadoras del Óscar: *Todo sobre mi madre* para la mejor película extranjera (1999) y *Hable con ella* para el mejor guión[d] original (2002).

[a]*director de cine*  [b]*changing*  [c]*Tie Me Up! Tie Me Down!*  [d]*screenplay*

*El escudo (shield) de Fernando e Isabel*

**Suggestions**
- Have students research and report to the class about famous Spanish historic and literary figures, such as *el Cid Campeador, el Lazarillo de Tormes, Isabel la Católica* and *Fernando de Aragón, Don Quijote* and *Sancho Panza, la Celestina,* and *don Juan Tenorio.* You may wish to invite students to dress up as these characters at an end-of-class party.
- If the class is composed of mature students, show Almodóvar's *Todo sobre mi madre* as an end-of-term activity.

Learn more about Spain with the Video, the Interactive CD-ROM, and the Online Learning Center (www.mhhe.com/quetal7).

**PASO FINAL**

 **A CONVERSAR**

**Improvisación turística**

Si Ud. viaja a un país hispanohablante algún día, tendrá la oportunidad de hablar español. Imagine que Ud. es turista en un país hispanohablante. ¿Qué diría en las siguientes situaciones?

PASO 1   Formen grupos de tres o cuatro personas. Escojan una de las siguientes situaciones para improvisar. Lean la situación y escriban en una hoja de papel aparte un esquema (*outline*) de la improvisación.

MODELO:   en el aeropuerto → saludarse; pedir los pasaportes; preguntar y contestar por qué vienen a este país...

| Lugar | Situación | Personajes (*Characters*) |
|---|---|---|
| **En el aeropuerto** | pasar por el control de pasaportes y por la aduana | uno o dos turistas, el/la agente que revisa los pasaportes, el/la agente de aduana |
| **En el hotel** | pedir una habitación y pedirle al botones que lleve las maletas a la habitación | uno o dos turistas, el/la recepcionista del hotel, el botones |
| **En la calle** | pedirles direcciones a algunas personas | uno o dos turistas, las personas del grupo |

PASO 2   Cada miembro del grupo debe escoger un personaje y prepararse para la improvisación, haciendo apuntes sobre las posibles preguntas que necesitará hacer y contestar.

MODELO:   agente de aduana → preguntarles si tienen algo que declarar; preguntarles si llevan plantas o productos orgánicos...

PASO 3   Improvisen la escena varias veces, modificándola si es necesario. Luego, presenten su escena improvisada a la clase.

MODELO:   E1: Sus pasaportes, por favor. Gracias. ¿De dónde vienen?
E2: Venimos de los Estados Unidos.
E1: ¿Y por qué vienen a México?
E3: Estamos de vacaciones. Vamos a ir a la playa...

**Suggestion**
Ask students the following questions to review the vocabulary.

1. *¿Adónde va Ud. si quiere tomar una copa / un trago con los amigos? ¿Le gustan los batidos? ¿Dónde se toma un buen batido en esta ciudad? En general, ¿es necesario preparar los batidos con puro helado o se puede sustituir los ingredientes artificiales?*

## GRAMÁTICA

To review the grammar points presented in this chapter, refer to the indicated grammar presentation. You'll find further practice of these structures in the Workbook/Laboratory Manual, on the Interactive CD-ROM, and on the *¿Qué tal?* Online Learning Center (www.mhhe.com/quetal7).

2. *¿Está bien situado el lugar donde Ud. vive? ¿Hay un correo cerca? ¿una parada de autobús? ¿Adónde va Ud. para comprar artículos de uso personal (el champú, la pasta dental, etcétera)? ¿Hay una tienda de comestibles cerca de donde Ud. vive?*

**45** Expressing What You Would Do—Conditional Verb Forms

Do you know how to form the conditional tense? When would you use the conditional in Spanish?

3. *¿Hay quioscos en este país? ¿Qué cosa espera Ud. comprar en un quiosco?*

4. *¿Cuánto vale un sello para mandar una carta de primera clase? ¿Se puede usar un sello de primera clase para mandar una carta a México? ¿a España? ¿a Puerto Rico?*

## VOCABULARIO

Practice this vocabulary with digital flash cards on the Online Learning Center (www.mhhe.com/quetal7).

### Lugares y cosas en el extranjero

| | |
|---|---|
| el batido | *drink similar to a milkshake* |
| el champú | shampoo |
| una copa | drink (*alcoholic*) |
| el correo | mail |
| la oficina de correos | post office |
| la estación del metro | subway stop |
| el estanco | tobacco stand/shop |
| el fósforo | match |
| el jabón | soap |
| el papel para cartas | stationery |
| la papelería | stationery store |
| el paquete | package |
| la parada del autobús | bus stop |
| la pasta dental | toothpaste |
| la pastelería | pastry shop |
| el pastelito | small pastry |
| el quiosco | kiosk |
| el sello | (postage) stamp |
| el sobre | envelope |
| un trago | drink (*alcoholic*) |

**Cognado:** el café
**Repaso:** la farmacia, la revista, la tarjeta postal

### En un viaje al extranjero

| | |
|---|---|
| la aduana | customs |
| el cheque de viajero | traveler's check |
| el extranjero | abroad |
| el formulario | form (*to fill out*) |
| la frontera | border |
| el/la viajero/a | traveler |

**Cognados:** la nacionalidad, el pasaporte
**Repaso:** el equipaje

| | |
|---|---|
| cruzar (c) | to cross |
| registrar | to search, examine |

**Repaso:** viajar

### El alojamiento

| | |
|---|---|
| la almohada | pillow |
| el alojamiento | lodging |
| el botones | bellhop |
| la criada | maid |
| la estancia | stay (*in a place*) |
| la habitación | (hotel) room |
| con baño/ducha | (*room*) with attached bath/shower |
| individual/doble | single/double (*room*) |
| sin baño/ducha | (*room*) without attached bath/shower |
| el hotel (de lujo) | (luxury) hotel |
| el hotel de dos (tres) estrellas | two (three) star hotel |
| el/la huésped(a) | (hotel) guest |
| la manta | blanket |
| el mozo | bellhop |
| la pensión | boardinghouse |
| pensión completa | room and full board |
| media pensión | room with breakfast and one other meal |
| la propina | tip (*to an employee*) |
| la recepción | front desk |
| las reservas | reservations |
| las sábanas | sheets |
| el servicio de cuartos | room service |
| la toalla | towel |

**Cognado:** las reservaciones

| | |
|---|---|
| alojarse | to stay (*in a place*) |
| confirmar | to confirm |

**Repaso:** quedarse

| | |
|---|---|
| completo/a | full, no vacancy |
| desocupado/a | vacant, unoccupied |

| | |
|---|---|
| con anticipación | ahead of time |

♻ **Reciclado**
Remind students of accent mark rules, drawing special attention to words like the following.

habitación / habitaciones
reservación / reservaciones
autobús / autobuses

# Glossary of Grammatical Terms

**ADJECTIVE**   A word that describes a noun or pronoun.

una casa **grande**
*a **big** house*

Ella es **inteligente**.
*She is **smart**.*

**Demonstrative adjective**   An adjective that points out a particular noun.

**este** chico, **esos** libros, **aquellas** personas
***this** boy, **those** books, **those** people (over there)*

**Interrogative adjective**   An adjective used to form questions.

¿**Qué** cuaderno?
***Which** notebook?*

¿**Cuáles** son los carteles que buscas?
***What (Which)** posters are you looking for?*

**Possessive adjective (unstressed)**   An adjective that indicates possession or a special relationship.

**sus** coches
***their** cars*

**mi** hermana
***my** sister*

**Possessive adjective (stressed)**   An adjective that more emphatically describes possession.

Es **una** amiga **mía**.
*She's **my** friend. | She's a friend **of mine**.*

Es **un** coche **suyo**.
*It's **her** car. | It's a car **of hers**.*

**ADVERB**   A word that describes an adjective, a verb, or another adverb.

Él es **muy** alto.
*He is **very** tall.*

Ella escribe **bien**.
*She writes **well**.*

Van **demasiado** rápido.
*They are going **too** quickly.*

**ARTICLE**   A determiner that sets off a noun.

**Definite article**   An article that indicates a specific noun.

**el** país
***the** country*

**la** silla
***the** chair*

**las** mujeres
***the** women*

**Indefinite article**   An article that indicates an unspecified noun.

**un** chico
***a** boy*

**una** ciudad
***a** city*

**unas** zanahorias
*(**some**) carrots*

**CLAUSE** A construction that contains a subject and a verb.

**Main (Independent) clause** A clause that can stand on its own because it expresses a complete thought.

**Busco una muchacha.**
*I'm looking for a girl.*

Si yo fuera rica, **me compraría una casa.**
*If I were rich, **I would buy a house.***

**Subordinate (Dependent) clause** A clause that cannot stand on its own because it does not express a complete thought.

Busco a la muchacha **que juega al tenis.**
*I'm looking for the girl **who plays tennis.***

**Si yo fuera rica,** me compraría una casa.
*If I were rich, I would buy a house.*

**COMPARATIVE** The form of adjectives and adverbs used to compare two nouns or actions.

Luis es **menos hablador** que Julián.
*Luis is **less talkative** than Julián.*

Él corre **más rápido** que Julián.
*He runs **faster** than Julián.*

**CONJUGATION** The different forms of a verb for a particular tense or mood. This is a present indicative conjugation.

| | |
|---|---|
| (yo) hablo | (nosotros/as) hablamos |
| (tú) hablas | (vosotros/as) habláis |
| (Ud.) habla | (Uds.) hablan |
| (él/ella) habla | (ellos/as) hablan |

| | |
|---|---|
| *I speak* | *we speak* |
| *you (fam. sing.) speak* | *you (fam. pl.) speak* |
| *you (form. sing.) speak* | *you (form. pl.) speak* |
| *he/she speaks* | *they speak* |

**CONJUNCTION** An expression that connects words, phrases, or clauses.

Cristóbal **y** Diana
*Cristóbal **and** Diana*

Hace frío, **pero** hace buen tiempo.
*It's cold, **but** it's nice out.*

**DIRECT OBJECT** The noun or pronoun that receives the action of a verb.

Veo **la caja.**
*I see **the box.***

**La** veo.
*I see **it.***

**GENDER** A grammatical category of words. In Spanish, there are two genders: masculine and feminine.

| | Masculine | Feminine |
|---|---|---|
| Articles and Nouns: | **el** disco compacto | **la** cinta |
| Pronouns: | **él** | **ella** |
| Adjectives: | bonit**o**, list**o** | bonit**a**, list**a** |
| Past Participles: | El informe | La composición |
| | está **escrito.** | está **escrita.** |

**IMPERATIVE** *See* Mood.

**IMPERFECT (*IMPERFECTO*)** In Spanish, a verb tense that expresses a past action with no specific beginning or ending.

**Nadábamos** con frecuencia.
*We **used to swim** often.*

**IMPERSONAL CONSTRUCTION** One that contains a third person singular verb but no specific subject in Spanish. The subject of English impersonal constructions is generally *it*.

**Es importante** que...
*It is important that . . .*

**Es necesario** que...
*It is necessary that . . .*

**INDICATIVE** *See* Mood.

**INDIRECT OBJECT** The noun or pronoun that indicates for whom or to whom an action is performed. In Spanish, the indirect object pronoun must always be included, even when the indirect object pronoun is explicitly stated.

Marcos **le** da el suéter a **Raquel.** / Marcos **le** da el suéter.
*Marcos gives the sweater **to Raquel.** / Marcos gives **her** the sweater.*

**INFINITIVE** The form of a verb introduced in English by *to: to play, to sell, to come.* In Spanish dictionaries, the infinitive form of the verb appears as the main entry.

Luisa va a **comprar** un periódico.
*Luisa is going **to buy** a newspaper.*

**MOOD** A set of categories for verbs indicating the attitude of the speaker toward what he or she is saying.

**Imperative mood** A verb form expressing a command.

¡**Ten** cuidado!
*Be careful!*

**Indicative mood** A verb form denoting actions or states considered facts.

**Voy** a la biblioteca.
*I'm going to the library.*

**Subjunctive mood** A verb form, uncommon in English, used primarily in subordinate clauses after expressions of desire, doubt, or emotion. Spanish constructions with the subjunctive have many possible English equivalents.

Quiero que **vayas** inmediatamente.
*I want you **to go** immediately.*

**NOUN** A word that denotes a person, place, thing, or idea. Proper nouns are capitalized names.

**abogado, ciudad, periódico, libertad, Luisa**
*lawyer, city, newspaper, freedom, Luisa*

**NUMBER**

**Cardinal number** A number that expresses an amount.

**una** silla, **tres** estudiantes
*one chair, three students*

**Ordinal number** A number that indicates position in a series.

la **primera** silla, el **tercer** estudiante
*the **first** chair, the **third** student*

**PAST PARTICIPLE** The form of a verb used in compound tenses (*see* Perfect Tenses). Used with forms of *to have* or *to be* in English and with **ser, estar,** or **haber** in Spanish.

**comido, terminado, perdido**
*eaten, finished, lost*

**PERFECT TENSES** Compound tenses that combine the auxiliary verb **haber** with a past participle.

**Present perfect indicative** This form uses a present indicative form of **haber.** The use of the Spanish present perfect generally parallels that of the English present perfect.

No **he viajado** nunca a México.
*I've never **traveled** to Mexico.*

**Past perfect indicative** This form uses **haber** in the imperfect tense to talk about something that had or had not been done before a given time in the past.

Antes de 2004, **no había estudiado** español.
*Before 2004, **I hadn't studied** Spanish.*

**Present perfect subjunctive** This form uses the present subjunctive of **haber** to express a present perfect action when the subjunctive is required.

¡Ojalá que Marisa **haya llegado** a su destino!
*I hope Marisa **has arrived** at her destination!*

**PERSON** The form of a pronoun or verb that indicates the person involved in an action.

|  | Singular | Plural |
|---|---|---|
| First Person | *I* / yo | *we* / nosotros/as |
| Second Person | *you* / tú, Ud. | *you* / vosotros/as, Uds. |
| Third Person | *he, she* / él, ella | *they* / ellos, ellas |

**PREPOSITION** A word or phrase that specifies the relationship of one word (usually a noun or pronoun) to another. The relationship is usually spatial or temporal.

**a** la escuela
*to school*

**cerca de** la biblioteca
*near the library*

**con** él
*with him*

**antes de** la medianoche
*before midnight*

**PRETERITE (*PRETÉRITO*)** In Spanish, a verb tense that expresses a past action with a specific beginning and ending.

**Salí** para Roma el jueves.
*I left for Rome on Thursday.*

**PRONOUN** A word that refers to a person (I, you) or that is used in place of one or more nouns.

**Demonstrative pronoun** A pronoun that singles out a particular person, place, thing, or idea.

Aquí hay dos libros. **Este** es interesante, pero **ese** es aburrido.
*Here are two books. **This one** is interesting, but **that one** is boring.*

**Interrogative pronoun** A pronoun used to ask a question.

¿**Quién** es él?      ¿**Qué** prefieres?
*Who is he?*      *What do you prefer?*

**Object pronoun** A pronoun that replaces a direct object noun or an indirect object noun. Both direct and indirect object pronouns can be used together in the same sentence. However, when the pronouns **le** or **les** are used with **lo, la, los,** or **las,** they change to **se.**

Si **me** llamas más tarde, **te** doy el número de David.
*If you call **me** later, I'll give **you** David's (phone) number.*

Veo a **Alejandro. Lo** veo.
*I see **Alejandro.** I see **him.***

**Le** doy el libro **a Juana.**
*I give the book **to Juana.***

**Se lo** doy **(a ella).**
*I give **it** to **her.***

| | |
|---|---|
| **Reflexive pronoun** A pronoun that represents the same person as the subject of the verb. | **Me** miro en el espejo.<br>*I look at **myself** in the mirror.* |
| **Relative pronoun** A pronoun that introduces a dependent clause and denotes a noun already mentioned. | El hombre con **quien** hablaba era mi vecino.<br>*The man with **whom** I was talking was my neighbor.*<br><br>Aquí está el bolígrafo **que** buscas.<br>*Here is the pen (**that**) you are looking for.* |
| **Subject pronoun** A pronoun representing the person thing, or idea performing the action of a verb. | **Lucas y Julia** juegan al tenis.<br>***Lucas and Julia** are playing tennis.*<br><br>**Ellos** juegan al tenis.<br>***They**'re playing tennis.* |
| **SUBJECT** The word(s) denoting the person, place, thing, or idea performing an action or existing in a state. | **Sara** trabaja aquí.<br>***Sara** works here.*<br><br>¡**Buenos Aires** es una ciudad magnífica!<br>***Buenos Aires** is a great city!*<br><br>Mis **libros** y mi **computadora** están allí.<br>*My **books** and my **computer** are over there.* |
| **SUBJUNCTIVE** *See* Mood. | |
| **SUPERLATIVE** The form of adjectives or adverbs used to compare three or more nouns or actions. In English, the superlative is marked by *most, least,* or *-est.* | Escogí el vestido **más caro**.<br>*I chose **the most expensive** dress.*<br><br>Ana es la persona **menos habladora** que conozco.<br>*Ana is **the least talkative** person I know.* |
| **TENSE** The form of a verb indicating time: present, past, or future. | Raúl **era, es** y siempre **será** mi mejor amigo.<br>*Raúl **was, is,** and always **will be** my best friend.* |
| **VERB** A word that reports an action or state. | Ella **llegó**.<br>*She **arrived**.*<br><br>Ella **estaba** cansada.<br>*She **was** tired.* |
| **Auxiliary verb** A verb in conjuction with a participle to convey distinctions of tense and mood. In Spanish, one auxiliary verb is **haber.** | **Han** viajado por todas partes del mundo.<br>*They **have** traveled everywhere in the world.* |
| **Reflexive verb** A verb whose subject and object are the same. | Él **se corta** la cara cuando **se afeita**.<br>*He **cuts himself** when he shaves (**himself**).* |

## Using Adjectives as Nouns

*Nominalization* means using an adjective as a noun. In Spanish, adjectives can be nominalized in a number of ways, all of which involve dropping the noun that accompanies the adjective, then using the adjective in combination with an article or other word. One kind of adjective, the demonstrative, can simply be used alone. In most cases, these usages parallel those of English, although the English equivalent may be phrased differently from the Spanish.

### Article + Adjective

Simply omit the noun from an *article + noun + adjective* phrase.

el **libro** azul → **el azul** (*the blue one*)
la **hermana** casada → **la casada** (*the married one*)
el **señor** mexicano → **el mexicano** (*the Mexican one*)
los **pantalones** baratos → **los baratos** (*the inexpensive ones*)

You can also drop the first noun in an *article + noun + de + noun* phrase.

la **casa** de Julio → **la de Julio** (*Julio's*)
los **coches** del Sr. Martínez → **los del Sr. Martínez** (*Mr. Martínez's*)

In both cases, the construction is used to refer to a noun that has already been mentioned. The English equivalent uses *one* or *ones*, or a possessive without the noun.

—¿Necesitas el libro grande?
—No. Necesito **el pequeño.**
*Do you need the big book?*
*No. I need the small one.*

—¿Usamos el coche de Ernesto?
—No. Usemos **el de Ana.**
*Shall we use Ernesto's car?*
*No. Let's use Ana's.*

Note that in the preceding examples the noun is mentioned in the first part of the exchange (**libro, coche**) but not in the response or rejoinder.

Note also that a demonstrative can be used to nominalize an adjective: **este rojo** (*this red one*), **esos azules** (*those blue ones*).

### Lo + Adjective

As seen in **Capítulo 10, lo** combines with the masculine singular form of an adjective to describe general qualities or characteristics. The English equivalent is expressed with words like *part* or *thing*.

lo mejor    *the best thing (part), what's best*
lo mismo    *the same thing*
lo cómico   *the funny thing (part), what's funny*

### Article + Stressed Possessive Adjective

The stressed possessive adjectives—but not the unstressed possessives—can be used as possessive pronouns: **la maleta suya → la suya.** The article and the possessive form agree in gender and number with the noun to which they refer.

Este es mi **banco.** ¿Dónde está **el suyo?**
*This is my bank. Where is yours?*

Sus **bebidas** están preparadas; **las nuestras,** no.
*Their drinks are ready; ours aren't.*

No es **la maleta** de Juan; es **la mía.**
*It isn't Juan's suitcase; it's mine.*

Note that the definite article is frequently omitted after forms of **ser: ¿Esa maleta? Es suya.**

### Demonstrative Pronouns

When the demonstrative adjective is used alone, without a noun, it is a demonstrative pronoun. An accent mark can be added to the demonstrative pronoun to distinguish it from the demonstrative adjectives (**éste, ése, aquél**).

Necesito este diccionario y **ese (ése).**
*I need this dictionary and that one.*

Estas señoras y **aquellas (aquéllas)** son las hermanas de Sara, ¿no?
*These women and those (over there) are Sara's sisters, aren't they?*

It is acceptable in modern Spanish, per the **Real Academia Española,** to omit the accent on demonstrative pronouns when context makes the meaning clear and no ambiguity is possible.

## Additional Perfect Forms (Indicative and Subjunctive)

Some indicative verb tenses have corresponding perfect forms in the indicative and subjunctive moods. Here is the present tense system.

| | |
|---|---|
| el presente: | yo hablo, como, pongo |
| el presente perfecto: | yo he hablado, comido, puesto |
| el presente perfecto de subjuntivo: | yo haya hablado, comido, puesto |

Other indicative forms that you have learned also have corresponding perfect indicative and subjunctive forms. Here are the most important ones, along with examples of their use. In each case, the tense or mood is formed with the appropriate form of **haber.**

### El pluscuamperfecto del subjuntivo

| | |
|---|---|
| yo: | hubiera hablado, comido, puesto |
| tú: | hubieras hablado, comido, puesto |
| Ud./él/ella: | hubiera hablado, comido, puesto |
| nosotros: | hubiéramos hablado, comido, puesto |
| vosotros: | hubierais hablado, comido, puesto |
| Uds./ellos/ellas: | hubieran hablado, comido, puesto |

These forms correspond to **el presente perfecto del indicativo (Capítulo 14)**. These forms are most frequently used in **si** clause sentences, along with the conditional perfect. See examples below in the *Si clause* section.

### El futuro perfecto

| | |
|---|---|
| yo: | habré hablado, comido, puesto |
| tú: | habrás hablado, comido, puesto |
| Ud./él/ella: | habrá hablado, comido, puesto |
| nosotros: | habremos hablado, comido, puesto |
| vosotros: | habréis hablado, comido, puesto |
| Uds./ellos/ellas: | habrán hablado, comido, puesto |

These forms correspond to **el futuro (Capítulo 16)** and are most frequently used to tell what *will have already happened* at some point in the future. (In contrast, the future is used to tell what *will happen*.)

Mañana **hablaré** con Miguel.
*I'll speak with Miguel tomorrow.*

Para las tres, ya **habré hablado** con Miguel.
*By 3:00, I'll already have spoken to Miguel.*

El año que viene **visitaremos** a los nietos.
*We'll visit our grandchildren next year.*

Para las Navidades, ya **habremos visitado** a los nietos.
*We'll already have visited our grandchildren by Christmas.*

### El condicional perfecto

| | |
|---|---|
| yo: | habría hablado, comido, puesto |
| tú: | habrías hablado, comido, puesto |
| Ud./él/ella: | habría hablado, comido, puesto |
| nosotros: | habríamos hablado, comido, puesto |
| vosotros: | habríais hablado, comido, puesto |
| Uds./ellos/ellas: | habrían hablado, comido, puesto |

These forms correspond to **el condicional (Capítulo 18)**. These forms are frequently used to tell what *would have happened* at some point in the past. (In contrast, the conditional tells what one *would do*.)

Yo **hablaría** con Miguel.
*I would speak with Miguel (if I were you, at some point in the future).*

Yo **habría hablado** con Miguel.
*I would have spoken with Miguel (if I had been you, at some point in the past).*

### *Si* Clause: Sentences About the Past

You have learned (**Capítulo 18**) to use the past subjunctive and conditional to speculate about the present in **si** clause sentences: what *would happen* if a particular event *were* (or *were not*) to occur.

> Si **tuviera** el tiempo, **aprendería** francés.
> *If I had the time, I would learn French* (in the present or at some point in the future).

The perfect forms of the past subjunctive and the conditional are used to speculate about the past: what *would have happened* if a particular event *had* (or *had not*) occurred.

> En la escuela superior, si **hubiera tenido** el tiempo, **habría aprendido** francés.
> *In high school, if I had had the time, I would have learned French.*

## Verbs

### A. Regular Verbs: Simple Tenses

| INFINITIVE PRESENT PARTICIPLE PAST PARTICIPLE | INDICATIVE | | | | | SUBJUNCTIVE | | IMPERATIVE |
|---|---|---|---|---|---|---|---|---|
| | Present | Imperfect | Preterite | Future | Conditional | Present | Imperfect | |
| hablar hablando hablado | hablo hablas habla hablamos habláis hablan | hablaba hablabas hablaba hablábamos hablabais hablaban | hablé hablaste habló hablamos hablasteis hablaron | hablaré hablarás hablará hablaremos hablaréis hablarán | hablaría hablarías hablaría hablaríamos hablaríais hablarían | hable hables hable hablemos habléis hablen | hablara hablaras hablara habláramos hablarais hablaran | habla tú, no hables hable Ud. hablemos hablen |
| comer comiendo comido | como comes come comemos coméis comen | comía comías comía comíamos comíais comían | comí comiste comió comimos comisteis comieron | comeré comerás comerá comeremos comeréis comerán | comería comerías comería comeríamos comeríais comerían | coma comas coma comamos comáis coman | comiera comieras comiera comiéramos comierais comieran | come tú, no comas coma Ud. comamos coman |
| vivir viviendo vivido | vivo vives vive vivimos vivís viven | vivía vivías vivía vivíamos vivíais vivían | viví viviste vivió vivimos vivisteis vivieron | viviré vivirás vivirá viviremos viviréis vivirán | viviría vivirías viviría viviríamos viviríais vivirían | viva vivas viva vivamos viváis vivan | viviera vivieras viviera viviéramos vivierais vivieran | vive tú, no vivas viva Ud. vivamos vivan |

## B. Regular Verbs: Perfect Tenses

| INDICATIVE | | | | | SUBJUNCTIVE | |
|---|---|---|---|---|---|---|
| Present Perfect | Past Perfect | Preterite Perfect | Future Perfect | Conditional Perfect | Present Perfect | Past Perfect |
| he<br>has<br>ha<br>hemos<br>habéis<br>han { hablado comido vivido | había<br>habías<br>había<br>habíamos<br>habíais<br>habían { hablado comido vivido | hube<br>hubiste<br>hubo<br>hubimos<br>hubisteis<br>hubieron { hablado comido vivido | habré<br>habrás<br>habrá<br>habremos<br>habréis<br>habrán { hablado comido vivido | habría<br>habrías<br>habría<br>habríamos<br>habríais<br>habrían { hablado comido vivido | haya<br>hayas<br>haya<br>hayamos<br>hayáis<br>hayan { hablado comido vivido | hubiera<br>hubieras<br>hubiera<br>hubiéramos<br>hubierais<br>hubieran { hablado comido vivido |

## C. Irregular Verbs

| INFINITIVE<br>PRESENT PARTICIPLE<br>PAST PARTICIPLE | INDICATIVE | | | | | SUBJUNCTIVE | | IMPERATIVE |
|---|---|---|---|---|---|---|---|---|
| | Present | Imperfect | Preterite | Future | Conditional | Present | Imperfect | |
| andar<br>andando<br>andado | ando<br>andas<br>anda<br>andamos<br>andáis<br>andan | andaba<br>andabas<br>andaba<br>andábamos<br>andabais<br>andaban | anduve<br>anduviste<br>anduvo<br>anduvimos<br>anduvisteis<br>anduvieron | andaré<br>andarás<br>andará<br>andaremos<br>andaréis<br>andarán | andaría<br>andarías<br>andaría<br>andaríamos<br>andaríais<br>andarían | ande<br>andes<br>ande<br>andemos<br>andéis<br>anden | anduviera<br>anduvieras<br>anduviera<br>anduviéramos<br>anduvierais<br>anduvieran | anda tú, no<br>andes<br>ande Ud.<br>andemos<br>anden |
| caer<br>cayendo<br>caído | caigo<br>caes<br>cae<br>caemos<br>caéis<br>caen | caía<br>caías<br>caía<br>caíamos<br>caíais<br>caían | caí<br>caíste<br>cayó<br>caímos<br>caísteis<br>cayeron | caeré<br>caerás<br>caerá<br>caeremos<br>caeréis<br>caerán | caería<br>caerías<br>caería<br>caeríamos<br>caeríais<br>caerían | caiga<br>caigas<br>caiga<br>caigamos<br>caigáis<br>caigan | cayera<br>cayeras<br>cayera<br>cayéramos<br>cayerais<br>cayeran | cae tú, no<br>caigas<br>caiga Ud.<br>caigamos<br>caigan |

| INFINITIVE PRESENT PARTICIPLE PAST PARTICIPLE | INDICATIVE | | | | | SUBJUNCTIVE | | IMPERATIVE |
|---|---|---|---|---|---|---|---|---|
| | Present | Imperfect | Preterite | Future | Conditional | Present | Imperfect | |
| dar dando dado | doy das da damos dais dan | daba dabas daba dábamos dabais daban | di diste dio dimos disteis dieron | daré darás dará daremos daréis darán | daría darías daría daríamos daríais darían | dé des dé demos deis den | diera dieras diera diéramos dierais dieran | da tú, no des dé Ud. demos den |
| decir diciendo dicho | digo dices dice decimos decís dicen | decía decías decía decíamos decíais decían | dije dijiste dijo dijimos dijisteis dijeron | diré dirás dirá diremos diréis dirán | diría dirías diría diríamos diríais dirían | diga digas diga digamos digáis digan | dijera dijeras dijera dijéramos dijerais dijeran | di tú, no digas diga Ud. digamos digan |
| estar estando estado | estoy estás está estamos estáis están | estaba estabas estaba estábamos estabais estaban | estuve estuviste estuvo estuvimos estuvisteis estuvieron | estaré estarás estará estaremos estaréis estarán | estaría estarías estaría estaríamos estaríais estarían | esté estés esté estemos estéis estén | estuviera estuvieras estuviera estuviéramos estuvierais estuviera | está tú, no estés esté Ud. estemos estén |
| haber habiendo habido | he has ha hemos habéis han | había habías había habíamos habíais habían | hube hubiste hubo hubimos hubisteis hubieron | habré habrás habrá habremos habréis habrán | habría habrías habría habríamos habríais habrían | haya hayas haya hayamos hayáis hayan | hubiera hubieras hubiera hubiéramos hubierais hubieran | |

## C. Irregular Verbs (*continued*)

| INFINITIVE PRESENT PARTICIPLE PAST PARTICIPLE | INDICATIVE | | | | | SUBJUNCTIVE | | IMPERATIVE |
|---|---|---|---|---|---|---|---|---|
| | Present | Imperfect | Preterite | Future | Conditional | Present | Imperfect | |
| hacer haciendo hecho | hago haces hace hacemos hacéis hacen | hacía hacías hacía hacíamos hacíais hacían | hice hiciste hizo hicimos hicisteis hicieron | haré harás hará haremos haréis harán | haría harías haría haríamos haríais harían | haga hagas haga hagamos hagáis hagan | hiciera hicieras hiciera hiciéramos hicierais hicieran | haz tú, no hagas haga Ud. hagamos hagan |
| ir yendo ido | voy vas va vamos vais van | iba ibas iba íbamos ibais iban | fui fuiste fue fuimos fuisteis fueron | iré irás irá iremos iréis irán | iría irías iría iríamos iríais irían | vaya vayas vaya vayamos vayáis vayan | fuera fueras fuera fuéramos fuerais fueran | ve tú, no vayas vaya Ud. vayamos vayan |
| oír oyendo oído | oigo oyes oye oímos oís oyen | oía oías oía oíamos oíais oían | oí oíste oyó oímos oísteis oyeron | oiré oirás oirá oiremos oiréis oirán | oiría oirías oiría oiríamos oiríais oirían | oiga oigas oiga oigamos oigáis oigan | oyera oyeras oyera oyéramos oyerais oyeran | oye tú, no oigas oiga Ud. oigamos oigan |
| poder pudiendo podido | puedo puedes puede podemos podéis pueden | podía podías podía podíamos podíais podían | pude pudiste pudo pudimos pudisteis pudieron | podré podrás podrá podremos podréis podrán | podría podrías podría podríamos podríais podrían | pueda puedas pueda podamos podáis puedan | pudiera pudieras pudiera pudiéramos pudierais pudieran | |

## C. Irregular Verbs (*continued*)

| INFINITIVE PRESENT PARTICIPLE PAST PARTICIPLE | INDICATIVE | | | | | | SUBJUNCTIVE | | IMPERATIVE |
|---|---|---|---|---|---|---|---|---|---|
| | Present | Imperfect | Preterite | Future | Conditional | | Present | Imperfect | |
| poner poniendo puesto | pongo pones pone ponemos ponéis ponen | ponía ponías ponía poníamos poníais ponían | puse pusiste puso pusimos pusisteis pusieron | pondré pondrás pondrá pondremos pondréis pondrán | pondría pondrías pondría pondríamos pondríais pondrían | | ponga pongas ponga pongamos pongáis pongan | pusiera pusieras pusiera pusiéramos pusierais pusieran | pon tú, no pongas ponga Ud. pongamos pongan |
| querer queriendo querido | quiero quieres quiere queremos queréis quieren | quería querías quería queríamos queríais querían | quise quisiste quiso quisimos quisisteis quisieron | querré querrás querrá querremos querréis querrán | querría querrías querría querríamos querríais querrían | | quiera quieras quiera queramos queráis quieran | quisiera quisieras quisiera quisiéramos quisierais quisieran | quiere tú, no quieras quiera Ud. queramos quieran |
| saber sabiendo sabido | sé sabes sabe sabemos sabéis saben | sabía sabías sabía sabíamos sabíais sabían | supe supiste supo supimos supisteis supieron | sabré sabrás sabrá sabremos sabréis sabrán | sabría sabrías sabría sabríamos sabríais sabrían | | sepa sepas sepa sepamos sepáis sepan | supiera supieras supiera supiéramos supierais supieran | sabe tú, no sepas sepa Ud. sepamos sepan |
| salir saliendo salido | salgo sales sale salimos salís salen | salía salías salía salíamos salíais salían | salí saliste salió salimos salisteis salieron | saldré saldrás saldrá saldremos saldréis saldrán | saldría saldrías saldría saldríamos saldríais saldrían | | salga salgas salga salgamos salgáis salgan | saliera salieras saliera saliéramos salierais salieran | sal tú, no salgas salga Ud. salgamos salgan |

## C. Irregular Verbs (*continued*)

| INFINITIVE PRESENT PARTICIPLE PAST PARTICIPLE | INDICATIVE | | | | | SUBJUNCTIVE | | IMPERATIVE |
|---|---|---|---|---|---|---|---|---|
| | Present | Imperfect | Preterite | Future | Conditional | Present | Imperfect | |
| ser<br>siendo<br>sido | soy<br>eres<br>es<br>somos<br>sois<br>son | era<br>eras<br>era<br>éramos<br>erais<br>eran | fui<br>fuiste<br>fue<br>fuimos<br>fuisteis<br>fueron | seré<br>serás<br>será<br>seremos<br>seréis<br>serán | sería<br>serías<br>sería<br>seríamos<br>seríais<br>serían | sea<br>seas<br>sea<br>seamos<br>seáis<br>sean | fuera<br>fueras<br>fuera<br>fuéramos<br>fuerais<br>fueran | sé tú, no seas<br>sea Ud.<br>seamos<br>sean |
| tener<br>teniendo<br>tenido | tengo<br>tienes<br>tiene<br>tenemos<br>tenéis<br>tienen | tenía<br>tenías<br>tenía<br>teníamos<br>teníais<br>tenían | tuve<br>tuviste<br>tuvo<br>tuvimos<br>tuvisteis<br>tuvieron | tendré<br>tendrás<br>tendrá<br>tendremos<br>tendréis<br>tendrán | tendría<br>tendrías<br>tendría<br>tendríamos<br>tendríais<br>tendrían | tenga<br>tengas<br>tenga<br>tengamos<br>tengáis<br>tengan | tuviera<br>tuvieras<br>tuviera<br>tuviéramos<br>tuvierais<br>tuvieran | ten tú, no<br>tengas<br>tenga Ud.<br>tengamos<br>tengan |
| traer<br>trayendo<br>traído | traigo<br>traes<br>trae<br>traemos<br>traéis<br>traen | traía<br>traías<br>traía<br>traíamos<br>traíais<br>traían | traje<br>trajiste<br>trajo<br>trajimos<br>trajisteis<br>trajeron | traeré<br>traerás<br>traerá<br>traeremos<br>traeréis<br>traerán | traería<br>traerías<br>traería<br>traeríamos<br>traeríais<br>traerían | traiga<br>traigas<br>traiga<br>traigamos<br>traigáis<br>traigan | trajera<br>trajeras<br>trajera<br>trajéramos<br>trajerais<br>trajeran | trae tú, no<br>traigas<br>traiga Ud.<br>traigamos<br>traigan |
| venir<br>viniendo<br>venido | vengo<br>vienes<br>viene<br>venimos<br>venís<br>vienen | venía<br>venías<br>venía<br>veníamos<br>veníais<br>venían | vine<br>viniste<br>vino<br>vinimos<br>vinisteis<br>vinieron | vendré<br>vendrás<br>vendrá<br>vendremos<br>vendréis<br>vendrán | vendría<br>vendrías<br>vendría<br>vendríamos<br>vendríais<br>vendrían | venga<br>vengas<br>venga<br>vengamos<br>vengáis<br>vengan | viniera<br>vinieras<br>viniera<br>viniéramos<br>vinierais<br>vinieran | ven tú, no<br>vengas<br>venga Ud.<br>vengamos<br>vengan |

## C. Irregular Verbs (continued)

| INFINITIVE PRESENT PARTICIPLE PAST PARTICIPLE | INDICATIVE | | | | | SUBJUNCTIVE | | IMPERATIVE |
|---|---|---|---|---|---|---|---|---|
| | Present | Imperfect | Preterite | Future | Conditional | Present | Imperfect | |
| ver<br>viendo<br>visto | veo<br>ves<br>ve<br>vemos<br>veis<br>ven | veía<br>veías<br>veía<br>veíamos<br>veíais<br>veían | vi<br>viste<br>vio<br>vimos<br>visteis<br>vieron | veré<br>verás<br>verá<br>veremos<br>veréis<br>verán | vería<br>verías<br>vería<br>veríamos<br>veríais<br>verían | vea<br>veas<br>vea<br>veamos<br>veáis<br>vean | viera<br>vieras<br>viera<br>viéramos<br>vierais<br>vieran | ve tú, no veas<br>vea Ud.<br>veamos<br>vean |

## D. Stem-Changing and Spelling Change Verbs

| INFINITIVE PRESENT PARTICIPLE PAST PARTICIPLE | INDICATIVE | | | | | SUBJUNCTIVE | | IMPERATIVE |
|---|---|---|---|---|---|---|---|---|
| | Present | Imperfect | Preterite | Future | Conditional | Present | Imperfect | |
| pensar (ie)<br>pensando<br>pensado | pienso<br>piensas<br>piensa<br>pensamos<br>pensáis<br>piensan | pensaba<br>pensabas<br>pensaba<br>pensábamos<br>pensabais<br>pensaban | pensé<br>pensaste<br>pensó<br>pensamos<br>pensasteis<br>pensaron | pensaré<br>pensarás<br>pensará<br>pensaremos<br>pensaréis<br>pensarán | pensaría<br>pensarías<br>pensaría<br>pensaríamos<br>pensaríais<br>pensarían | piense<br>pienses<br>piense<br>pensemos<br>penséis<br>piensen | pensara<br>pensaras<br>pensara<br>pensáramos<br>pensarais<br>pensaran | piensa tú, no<br>pienses<br>piense Ud.<br>pensemos<br>piensen |
| volver (ue)<br>volviendo<br>vuelto | vuelvo<br>vuelves<br>vuelve<br>volvemos<br>volvéis<br>vuelven | volvía<br>volvías<br>volvía<br>volvíamos<br>volvíais<br>volvían | volví<br>volviste<br>volvió<br>volvimos<br>volvisteis<br>volvieron | volveré<br>volverás<br>volverá<br>volveremos<br>volveréis<br>volverán | volvería<br>volverías<br>volvería<br>volveríamos<br>volveríais<br>volverían | vuelva<br>vuelvas<br>vuelva<br>volvamos<br>volváis<br>vuelvan | volviera<br>volvieras<br>volviera<br>volviéramos<br>volvierais<br>volvieran | vuelve tú, no<br>vuelvas<br>vuelva Ud.<br>volvamos<br>vuelvan |

## D. Stem-Changing and Spelling Change Verbs (*continued*)

| INFINITIVE PRESENT PARTICIPLE PAST PARTICIPLE | INDICATIVE | | | | | | SUBJUNCTIVE | | IMPERATIVE |
|---|---|---|---|---|---|---|---|---|---|
| | Present | Imperfect | Preterite | Future | Conditional | Present | Imperfect | |
| dormir (ue, u) dormiendo dormido | duermo duermes duerme dormimos dormís duermen | dormía dormías dormía dormíamos dormíais dormían | dormí dormiste durmió dormimos dormisteis durmieron | dormiré dormirás dormirá dormiremos dormiréis dormirán | dormiría dormirías dormiría dormiríamos dormiríais dormirían | duerma duermas duerma durmamos durmáis duerman | durmiera durmieras durmiera durmiéramos durmierais durmieran | duerme tú, no duermas duerma Ud. durmamos duerman |
| sentir (ie, i) sintiendo sentido | siento sientes siente sentimos sentís sienten | sentía sentías sentía sentíamos sentíais sentían | sentí sentiste sintió sentimos sentisteis sintieron | sentiré sentirás sentirá sentiremos sentiréis sentirán | sentiría sentirías sentiría sentiríamos sentiríais sentirían | sienta sientas sienta sintamos sintáis sientan | sintiera sintieras sintiera sintiéramos sintierais sintieran | siente tú, no sientas sienta Ud. sintamos sientan |
| pedir (i, i) pidiendo pedido | pido pides pide pedimos pedís piden | pedía pedías pedía pedíamos pedíais pedían | pedí pediste pidió pedimos pedisteis pidieron | pediré pedirás pedirá pediremos pediréis pedirán | pediría pedirías pediría pediríamos pediríais pedirían | pida pidas pida pidamos pidáis pidan | pidiera pidieras pidiera pidiéramos pidierais pidieran | pide tú, no pidas pida Ud. pidamos pidan |
| reír (i, i) riendo reído | río ríes ríe reímos reís ríen | reía reías reía reíamos reíais reían | reí reíste rio reímos reísteis rieron | reiré reirás reirá reiremos reiréis reirán | reiría reirías reiría reiríamos reiríais reirían | ría rías ría riamos riáis rían | riera rieras riera riéramos rierais rieran | ríe tú, no rías ría Ud. riamos rían |

## D. Stem-Changing and Spelling Change Verbs (*continued*)

| INFINITIVE PRESENT PARTICIPLE PAST PARTICIPLE | INDICATIVE | | | | | | SUBJUNCTIVE | | IMPERATIVE |
|---|---|---|---|---|---|---|---|---|---|
| | Present | Imperfect | Preterite | Future | Conditional | | Present | Imperfect | |
| seguir (i, i) (g) siguiendo seguido | sigo sigues sigue seguimos seguís siguen | seguía seguías seguía seguíamos seguíais seguían | seguí seguiste siguió seguimos seguisteis siguieron | seguiré seguirás seguirá seguiremos seguiréis seguirán | seguiría seguirías seguiría seguiríamos seguiríais seguirían | | siga sigas siga sigamos sigáis sigan | siguiera siguieras siguiera siguiéramos siguierais siguieran | sigue tú, no sigas siga Ud. sigamos sigan |
| construir (y) construyendo construido | construyo construyes construye construimos construís construyen | construía construías construía construíamos construíais construían | construí construiste construyó construimos construisteis construyeron | construiré construirás construirá construiremos construiréis construirán | construiría construirías construiría construiríamos construiríais construirían | | construya construyas construya construyamos construyáis construyan | construyera construyeras construyera construyéramos construyerais construyeran | construye tú, no construyas construya Ud. construyamos construyan |
| producir (zc) produciendo producido | produzco produces produce producimos producís producen | producía producías producía producíamos producíais producían | produje produjiste produjo produjimos produjisteis produjeron | produciré producirás producirá produciremos produciréis producirán | produciría producirías produciría produciríamos produciríais producirían | | produzca produzcas produzca produzcamos produzcáis produzcan | produjera produjeras produjera produjéramos produjerais produjeran | produce tú, no produzcas produzca Ud. produzcamos produzcan |

This **Spanish-English Vocabulary** contains all the words that appear in the text, with the following exceptions: (1) most close or identical cognates that do not appear in the chapter vocabulary lists; (2) most conjugated verb forms; (3) diminutives ending in **-ito/a;** (4) absolute superlatives in **-ísimo/a;** and (5) most adverbs in **-mente.** Active vocabulary is indicated by the number of the chapter in which a word or given meaning is first listed (**P=Preliminar**); vocabulary that is glossed in the text is not considered to be active vocabulary and is not numbered. Only meanings that are used in the text are given. The **English-Spanish Vocabulary** is based on the chapter lists of active vocabulary.

The gender of nouns is indicated, except for masculine nouns ending in **-o** and feminine nouns ending in **-a.** Stem changes and spelling changes are indicated for verbs: **dormir (ue, u); llegar (gu).** Because **ch** and **ll** are no longer considered separate letters, words beginning with **ch** and **ll** are found as they would be found in English. The letter **ñ** follows the letter **n: añadir** follows **anuncio,** for example. The following abbreviations are used:

| | | | | | |
|---|---|---|---|---|---|
| *adj.* | adjective | *ind. art.* | indefinite article | *pl.* | plural |
| *adv.* | adverb | *inf.* | infinitive | *poss.* | possessive |
| *Arg.* | Argentina | *interj.* | interjection | *p.p.* | past participle |
| *C.A.* | Central America | *inv.* | invariable form | *prep.* | preposition |
| *coll.* | colloquial | *i.o.* | indirect object | *pron.* | pronoun |
| *conj.* | conjunction | *irreg.* | irregular | *refl. pron.* | reflexive pronoun |
| *d.o.* | direct object | *L.A.* | Latin America | *s.* | singular |
| *def. art.* | definite article | *m.* | masculine | *sl.* | slang |
| *f.* | feminine | *Mex.* | Mexico | *Sp.* | Spain |
| *fam.* | familiar | *n.* | noun | *sub. pron.* | subject pronoun |
| *form.* | formal | *obj. (of prep.)* | object (of a | *Uru.* | Uruguay |
| *gram.* | grammatical term | | preposition) | | |

## Spanish–English Vocabulary

# A

**a** to (P); at (*with time*) (P); **a base de** based on; **a bordo** on board; **a consecuencia de** as a consequence of; **a continuación** following, below; **a diferencia de** unlike; **a favor de** in favor of; with the aid of; **a finales de** at the end of; **a la(s)...** at ... (*hour*) (P); **a la derecha (de)** to the right (of) (5); **a la izquierda (de)** to the left (of) (5); **a la plancha** grilled; **a la vez** at the same time; **a larga distancia** long-distance; **a largo plazo** long-term; **a lo largo de** along; throughout; **a menos que** *conj.* unless (15); **a menudo** often; **a partir de** as of; from (*this moment, date on*); **a pesar de** in spite of; **a pie** on foot; **a plazos** in installments (16); **a primera vista** at first sight (15); **a principios de** at the

beginning of; **¿a qué hora?** at what time? (P); **a raíz de** as a result of; because of; **a sus órdenes** at your service; **a tiempo** on time (7); **a veces** sometimes, at times (2); **a ver** let's see
**abajo** below, underneath
**abalanzarse (c) (sobre)** to pounce (on)
**abandonar** to abandon; to leave
**abanicar (qu)** to fan
**abarcar (qu)** to comprise; to encompass
**abecedario** alphabet
**abierto/a** (*p.p. of* **abrir**) open (5); opened
**abogado/a** lawyer (16)
**abolicionista** *n. m., f.* abolitionist
**abrazar (c)** to embrace, hug
**abreviar** to abbreviate
**abrigo** coat (3)
**abril** *m.* April (5)
**abrir** (*p.p.* **abierto**) to open (2)

**absoluto/a** absolute; **en absoluto** at all
**abstracto/a** abstract
**abuelo/a** grandfather/grandmother (2)
**abuelos** *m. pl.* grandparents (2)
**abundancia** abundance
**aburrido/a** bored (5); **ser** (*irreg.*) **aburrido/a** to be boring (9)
**aburrir** to bore (13); **aburrirse** to get bored (9)
**abuso** abuse
**acabar** to finish (11); to run out of (11); to use up completely (14); **acabar de +** *inf.* to have just (*done something*) (6); **acabar por +** *inf.* to end up by (*doing something*)
**academia: Real Academia Española** Royal Spanish Academy
**académico/a** *adj.* academic
**acaso: por si acaso** just in case (11)

**accesible** accessible
**acceso** access
**accidentalmente** accidentally
**accidente** *m.* accident
**acción** *f.* action; **Día** (*m.*) **de Acción de Gracias** Thanksgiving
**acecho/a: estar** (*irreg.*) **acecho/a** to be lying in wait; to watch, be on the lookout
**aceite** *m.* oil (14); **aceite de oliva** olive oil; **revisar el aceite** to check the oil (14)
**aceituna** olive
**acelerado/a** fast (14), accelerated (14)
**acelerar** to speed up
**acento** accent
**aceptar** to accept
**acerca de** *prep.* about, concerning
**aclaración** *f.* clarification
**aclarar** to clarify
**acogedor(a)** welcoming
**acomodarse (a)** to adapt oneself (to)
**acompañar** to accompany; to go with
**acondicionado/a: aire** (*m.*) **acondicionado** air conditioning
**aconsejable** advisable
**aconsejar** to advise
**acontecimiento** event (17), happening *n.* (17)
**acordarse (ue) (de)** to remember (11)
**acordeón** *m.* accordion
**acorralado/a** corralled; frightened
**acortarse** to become, get shorter
**acostarse (ue)** to go to bed (4)
**acostumbrarse a** to become accustomed to, get used to
**acreedor(a)** worthy, deserving
**acrílico** acrylic
**actitud** *f.* attitude
**actividad** *f.* activity
**activista** *n. m., f.* activist
**activo/a** active
**acto** act
**actor** *m.* actor (13)
**actriz** *f.* (*pl.* **actrices**) actress (13)
**actual** *adj.* current, present-day
**actualidad** *f.* present time
**actuar (actúo)** to act
**acuario** aquarium; **Acuario** Aquarius
**acuático/a: deportes** (*m. pl.*) **acuáticos** water sports
**acuerdo** agreement; **de acuerdo** agreed; **de acuerdo con** in accordance with; **(no) estoy de acuerdo** I (don't) agree (2); **ponerse** (*irreg.*) **de acuerdo** to reach an agreement
**adaptación** *f.* adaptation

**adaptar** to adapt; **adaptarse (a)** to adapt oneself (to)
**adarga** leather shield
**adecuado/a** appropriate
**adelante** let's go; **de ahora en adelante** from now on
**adelanto** advance
**adelgazar (c)** to lose weight
**además** *adv.* moreover; **además de** *prep.* besides
**adicional** additional
**adiós** bye (P), good-bye (P)
**adivinanza** riddle
**adivinar** to guess
**adjetivo** adjective
**administración** *f.* administration; **administración de empresas** business administration (1)
**administrado/a** administered
**administrativo/a** administrative
**admirar** to admire
**admitir** to admit; to accept
**adolescencia** adolescence (15)
**¿adónde?** where (to)? (3)
**adopción** *f.* adoption
**adoquinado/a** cobblestoned
**adorado/a** adored
**adorno** decoration
**adquirir (ie)** to acquire
**adquisitivo/a** purchasing, buying
**aduana** *s.* customs (18); **inspector(a) de aduanas** customs inspector
**adulto/a** adult
**adverbio** adverb
**aeróbico/a: hacer** (*irreg.*) **ejercicios aeróbicos** to do aerobics (10)
**aeropuerto** airport (7)
**afectar** to affect
**afectivo/a** emotional
**afectuoso/a** affectionate
**afeitadora** razor
**afeitarse** to shave oneself (4)
**afición** *f.* pastime (9), fun activity (9), hobby (9)
**aficionado/a** fan; **ser** (*irreg.*) **aficionado/a (a)** to be a fan (of) (9)
**afirmación** *f.* statement
**afirmar** to affirm, state
**africano/a** *n., adj.* African
**afrocaribeño/a** *adj.* Afro-Caribbean
**afrocubano/a** *adj.* Afro-Cuban
**afuera** *adv.* outside, outdoors (5)
**afueras** *n. f. pl.* suburbs (12), outskirts (12)
**agencia** agency; **agencia de viajes** travel agency (7)

**agenda** agenda; date book; **agenda de teléfonos** address/telephone book; **agenda digital/electrónica** electronic calendar, date book
**agente** (*m., f.*): **agente de viajes** travel agent (7)
**ágil** agile
**agosto** August (5)
**agotar** to use up
**agradable** pleasant
**agradar** to please (13)
**agradecer (zc)** to thank; to be grateful
**agradecido/a** grateful
**agravar** to make worse
**agregar (gu)** to add
**agresividad** *f.* aggressiveness
**agresivo/a** aggressive
**agrícola** *adj. m., f.* agricultural; **trabajador(a) agrícola** farm worker
**agricultor(a)** farmer (14)
**agricultura** agriculture
**agroturismo** agrotourism (*farm stays*)
**agroturista** *n. m., f.* agrotourist
**agua** *f.* (*but* **el agua**) water (6); **agua dulce** fresh water; **agua mineral** mineral water (6); **cama de agua** waterbed (4); **huevo pasado por agua** poached egg
**aguacate** *m.* avocado
**aguantar** to stand, tolerate
**aguar (agüe)** to spoil (*a party*)
**agudo/a** sharp
**ahí** there
**ahora** now (1); **ahora mismo** right now; at once; **de ahora en adelante** from now on
**ahorrar** to save (*money*) (16)
**ahorros** (*m. pl.*): **cuenta de ahorros** savings account (16)
**aire** *m.* air; (14); **aire acondicionado** air conditioning; **aire puro** clean air (14); **al aire libre** outdoors; **contaminación** (*f.*) **del aire** air pollution (14)
**ajedrez** *m.* chess (4)
**ajillo: al ajillo** in garlic sauce
**ajo** garlic; **diente** (*m.*) **de ajo** garlic clove
**al** (*contraction of* **a** + **el**) to the (3); **al** + *inf.* upon, while, when + *verb form*; **al aire libre** outdoors; **al ajillo** in garlic sauce; **al alza** on the rise; **al borde de** on the verge of; **al contado** in cash (16); **al contrario** on the contrary; **al este/norte/oeste/sur** to the east/north/west/south (5); **al fondo** in the background; **al lado de** *prep.* alongside of (5); beside; next to; **al principio (de)** at the beginning of (16); **al revés** backward

**ala** *f.* (*but* **el ala**) wing
**alarma** alarm
**albor** *m.* dawn
**álbum** *m.* album
**alcance** *m.* reach
**alcanzar (c)** to reach
**alce** *m.* elk, moose
**alcoba** bedroom (4)
**alcohol** *m.* alcohol
**alcohólico/a** *adj.* alcoholic
**aldea** village
**alegrarse (de)** to be happy (about) (12)
**alegre** happy (5)
**alemán** *m.* German (*language*) (1)
**alemán, alemana** *n., adj.* German (2);
  **perro pastor alemán** German Shepherd
**Alemania** Germany
**alergia** allergy; **tener** (*irreg.*) **alergia a** to
  be allergic to
**alérgico/a: ser** (*irreg.*) **alérgico/a a** to be
  allergic to
**alerta: ojo alerta** eagle eye; **Fundación**
  (*f.*) **Alerta contra el SIDA** AIDS
  Awareness Foundation
**alertar** to warn
**alfabetización** *f.* literacy
**alfabetizado/a** alphabetized
**alfabeto** alphabet
**alfombra** rug (4)
**alfombrado/a** carpeted
**algo** something (3), anything (3)
**algodón** *m.* cotton (3); **es de algodón** it's
  made of cotton (3)
**alguien** someone (6), anyone (6)
**algún, alguno/a(s)** some (6); any (6); **algún**
  **día** some day; **alguna vez** once; ever
**alimentar** to feed
**aliviar** to relieve, alleviate
**alivio** relief
**allá** over there; **más allá** further, farther;
  **más allá de** beyond, farther than
**allí** (over) there (3)
**alma** *f.* (*but* **el alma**) soul
**almacén** *m.* department store (3)
**almacenamiento** storage
**almendra** almond
**almohada** pillow (18)
**almorzar (ue) (c)** to have lunch (4)
**almuerzo** lunch (6)
**aló** hello
**alojamiento** lodging (18)
**alojarse** to stay (*in a place*) (18)
**alpinismo: hacer** (*irreg.*) **alpinismo** to
  mountain climb
**alquilar** to rent (12)

**alquiler** *m.* rent (12)
**alrededor de** *prep.* around; about
**alrededores** *m. pl.* surroundings
**alteración** *f.* irregularity
**alternativa** *n.* alternative
**altitud** *f.* altitude
**alto/a** tall (2); high; **clase** (*f.*) **alta** upper
  class
**altura** height, altitude; **ponerse** (*irreg.*) **a**
  **la altura de** to compete on the same
  level as
**alza: al alza** on the rise
**alzarse (c)** to rise up
**ama** (*f.* [*but* **el ama**]) **de casa** homemaker
**amable** kind (2), nice (2)
**amado/a** *adj.* beloved
**amanecer (zc)** to wake up
**amar** to love (15)
**amarillo/a** yellow (3)
**Amazonas** *m. s.* Amazon
**Amazonia** Amazon (Basin)
**amazónico/a** *adj.* Amazonian
**ambiental** environmental (*pertaining to*
  *surroundings*)
**ambiente** *m.* atmosphere, environment;
  **medio ambiente** environment
  (*nature*) (14)
**ámbito** scope
**amenazador(a)** threatening
**América Central** Central America
**americano/a** *n., adj.* American; **fútbol**
  (*m.*) **americano** football (9)
**amigo/a** friend (1)
**amistad** *f.* friendship (15)
**amistoso/a** friendly (15)
**amor** *m.* love (15)
**amplio/a** large, spacious
**amueblado/a** furnished
**analfabetismo** illiteracy
**análisis** *m. inv.* analysis
**analista** (*m., f.*) **de sistemas** systems
  analyst (16)
**analizar (c)** to analyze
**anaranjado/a** orange *adj.* (3)
**ancho/a** wide; **de ancho** in width
**anciano/a** *n.* old person; *adj.* old; ancient
**andar** (*irreg.*) to walk; **andar en bicicleta**
  to ride a bicycle; **rueda de andar**
  treadmill
**andino/a** *adj.* Andean
**anémico/a** anemic
**anfitrión, anfitriona** host(ess) (8)
**anglohablante** *m., f.* English-speaker
**angula** eel
**ángulo** angle

**animado/a** lively; animated; **dibujos** (*m.*
  *pl.*) **animados** cartoons
**animal** *m.* animal (14); **animal doméstico**
  domesticated animal (14), pet (14);
  **animal salvaje** wild animal (14)
**ánimo: dar** (*irreg.*) **ánimo** to cheer; **estado**
  **de ánimo** state of mind
**aniversario** anniversary
**anoche** *adv.* last night (10)
**anotar** to jot down
**ansiedad** *f.* fatigue; restlessness; worry;
  nervousness
**Antártida** Antarctica
**ante** *prep.* before; in front of; **ante todo**
  above all; first of all
**anteayer** *adv.* the day before yesterday (10)
**antecedente** *m.* antecedent
**antemano: de antemano** beforehand
**anterior** previous, preceding
**antes** *adv.* before; **antes de** *prep.* before
  (4); **antes de Cristo (a.C.)** before Christ
  (B.C.); **antes (de) que** *conj.* before (15)
**antibiótico** antibiotic (10)
**anticipación** (*f.*): **con anticipación** in
  advance (18), ahead of time (18); **de**
  **anticipación** ahead
**anticipar** to anticipate
**anticuado/a** antiquated, old-fashioned
**antigüedad** *f.* antiquity; advanced age; *pl.*
  antiques
**antiguo/a** old; ancient; former
**antipático/a** unpleasant (2)
**antirrevolucionario/a** *n.*
  counterrevolutionary
**antónimo** antonym
**antropología** anthropology
**antropólogo/a** anthropologist
**anual** annual, yearly
**anudado/a** knotted
**anunciar** to announce (7)
**anuncio** announcement; advertisement
**añadidura: de añadidura** on the side
**añadir** to add
**año** year (5); **cumplir años** to have a
  birthday (8); **de los últimos años** in
  recent years; **Día** (*m.*) **del Año Nuevo**
  New Year's Day; **el año pasado** last
  year; **Feliz Año Nuevo** Happy New
  Year; **los años sesenta, ochenta,…** the
  sixties, eighties, . . .; **pasar… años** to be
  more than . . . years old; **tener** (*irreg.*)**…**
  **años** to be . . . years old (2)
**apagado/a** out; turned off (*lights*)
**apagar (gu)** to turn off (11); **apagarse** to
  go out (*lights*)

**aparato** appliance; **aparato doméstico** home appliance (9); **aparato electrónico** electronic device

**aparcar (qu)** to park

**aparecer (zc)** to appear

**aparentemente** apparently

**apariencia** appearance

**apartamento** apartment (1); **casa/ bloque** (*m.*) **de apartamentos** apartment building (12)

**apartar** to separate

**aparte** *adv.* apart, separately

**apasionado/a** passionate

**apellido** last name, surname

**apenas** hardly

**apendicitis** *f. inv.* appendicitis

**aperitivo** aperitif; appetizer

**apilado/a** piled up

**apinado/a** tightly arranged

**apio** celery

**aplicar (qu)** to apply

**apoyar** to support (17)

**apoyo** support; **fondos** (*m. pl.*) **de apoyo** economic assistance

**apreciar** to appreciate (13)

**aprender** to learn (2); **aprender a** + *inf.* to learn how to (*do something*)

**apretado/a** tight

**apropiado/a** appropriate

**aprovechar (de)** to make use (of), avail oneself (of); **que aproveche** enjoy your meal

**aproximadamente** approximately

**apuntar** to write down

**apuntes** *m. pl.* notes

**apurarse** to hurry (up)

**aquel, aquella** *dem. adj.* that (*over there*) (3); *dem. pron.* that one (*over there*) (3)

**aquello** *dem. pron.* that (3); that thing

**aquellos/as** *dem. adj.* those (*over there*) (3); *dem. pron.* those (ones) (*over there*) (3)

**aquí** here (1)

**árabe** *m.* Arabic (*language*)

**árabe** *n., adj. m., f.* Arab

**arado** plow

**árbol** *m.* tree (14)

**archipiélago** archipelago

**archivo** (computer) file (12)

**ardilla** squirrel

**área** *f.* (*but* **el área**) area (12)

**arena** sand

**arete** *m.* earring (3)

**argentino/a** *n., adj.* Argentine

**argumento** argument; plot (*of a play, book*)

**árido/a** dry, arid

**arma** *f.* (*but* **el arma**) weapon

**armado/a** armed

**armario** closet (4)

**arpa** *f.* (*but* **el arpa**) harp

**arqueológico/a** archeological

**arquitecto/a** architect (13)

**arquitectónico/a** *adj.* architectural

**arquitectura** architecture (13)

**arrancar (qu)** to start up (*a car*) (14); to pull out, wrench

**arrastrar** to drag

**arreglar** to fix (12); to repair (12); to straighten (up) (12)

**arriba** *adv.* above; up

**arrogante** arrogant

**arroz** *m.* (*pl.* **arroces**) rice (6)

**arte** *f.* (*but* **el arte**) art (1); **obra de arte** work of art (13)

**artesanía** *s.* arts and crafts (13)

**artículo** article

**artificial: fuegos** (*m. pl.*) **artificiales** fireworks

**artista** *m., f.* artist (13)

**artístico/a** artistic

**arvejas** *f. pl.* green peas (6)

**arzobispo** archbishop

**asado/a** roasted (6); **pollo asado** roast chicken (6)

**asamblea** assembly

**ascensor** *m.* elevator

**asco: dar** (*irreg.*) **asco** to make sick

**asegurar** to assure; **asegurarse** to make sure

**asequible** available

**asesinado/a** murdered

**asesinato** assassination (17); murder

**asesoramiento** advice

**así** thus, so; **así como** as well as; **así que** therefore, consequently, so

**asiático/a** *adj.* Asian

**asiento** seat (7)

**asimilarse** to assimilate

**asistente** *m., f.* assistant; **asistente de vuelo** flight attendant (7); **asistente del profesor** teaching assistant

**asistir (a)** to attend (*a class, function*) (2), to go to (*a class, function*) (2)

**asma** *f.* (*but* **el asma**) asthma

**asociación** *f.* association

**asociado/a: estado libre asociado** commonwealth

**asociar** to associate

**aspecto** aspect; appearance; **no tener** (*irreg.*) **buen aspecto** to not look right

**aspiración** *f.* aspiration

**aspiradora** vacuum cleaner (9); **pasar la aspiradora** to vacuum (9)

**aspirante** *m., f.* candidate (16), applicant (16)

**aspirina** aspirin

**astronauta** *m., f.* astronaut

**astronomía** astronomy

**asumir** to assume

**asunto** question, matter

**atacar (qu)** to attack

**ataque** *m.* attack (17); **ataque de nervios** nervous breakdown; **ataque terrorista** terrorist attack (17)

**atar** to tie

**atención** *f.* attention; **atención médica** healthcare

**atender (ie)** to attend to; to serve

**ateo/a** *adj.* atheist

**atlántico/a: Océano Atlántico** Atlantic Ocean

**atleta** *m., f.* athlete

**atlético/a** athletic

**átono/a** *gram.* unstressed

**atracción** *f.* attraction; **parque** (*m.*) **de atracciones** amusement park

**atractivo/a** attractive

**atraer** (*like* **traer**) to attract

**atrapado/a** trapped

**atrás** *adv.* back, backward; behind

**atrasado/a: estar** (*irreg.*) **atrasado/a** to be late (7)

**atrevido/a** daring

**atribuir (y)** to attribute

**atropello** assault, attack; abuse, outrage

**atroz** (*pl.* **atroces**) atrocious, brutal

**atún** *m.* tuna (6)

**auditivo/a: comprensión** (*f.*) **auditiva** listening comprehension

**aumentar** to increase

**aumento** increase; raise (12); **aumento de sueldo** raise (*in salary*) (16)

**aun** *adv.* even

**aún** *adv.* still, yet

**aunque** although

**auscultar** to listen (*with a stethoscope*)

**ausencia** absence

**ausente** absent

**autenticidad** *f.* authenticity

**auténtico/a** authentic

**auto** car; **auto chocador de choque** bumper car

**autobiografía** autobiography

**autobiográfico/a** autobiographical

**autobús** *m.* bus (7); **estación** (*f.*) **de autobuses** bus station (7); **ir** (*irreg.*) **en autobús** to go/travel by bus (7); **parada del autobús** bus stop (18)

**autoestima** self-esteem

**automático/a: cajero automático** automatic teller machine (16); **contestador** (*m.*) **automático** answering machine (12)

**automovilístico/a** *adj.* automobile

**autónomo/a** autonomous

**autopista** freeway (14)

**autoprueba** self-test

**autor(a)** author

**autoridad** *f.* authority

**autostop** (*m.*): **hacer** (*irreg.*) **autostop** to hitchhike

**avanzado/a** advanced

**avenida** avenue (12)

**aventura** adventure

**aventurero/a** adventurous

**aventurismo** adventure tourism

**aventurista** *m., f.* adventure tourist

**avergonzado/a** embarrassed (8)

**avergonzarse (me avergüenzo) (c)** to be ashamed

**averiguar (averiguo)** to find out

**aves** *f. pl.* fowl

**avestruz** *m.* (*pl.* **avestruces**) ostrich

**avión** *m.* airplane (7); **ir** (*irreg.*) **en avión** to go/travel by plane (7)

**avisar** to warn

**aviso** warning

**¡ay!** *interj.* ah!; ouch!

**ayer** yesterday (4)

**ayuda** help

**ayudante** *m., f.* assistant

**ayudar** to help (6)

**azafrán** *m.* saffron

**azteca** *n., adj. m., f.* Aztec

**azúcar** *m.* sugar

**azucarado/a** sweetened; containing sugar

**azul** blue (3)

# B

**bailable** danceable

**bailar** to dance (1)

**bailarín, bailarina** dancer (13)

**baile** *m.* dance (13)

**bajado/a** lowered

**bajar** to carry down; to lower; to go down; **bajar de** to get down from (*a vehicle*) (7); to get off (*a vehicle*) (7)

**bajo** *n.* bass (*music*)

**bajo** *prep.* under

**bajo/a** *adj.* low; short (*in height*) (2); **planta baja** ground floor (12)

**balance** *m.* balance

**balboa** Panamanian monetary unit

**balcón** *m.* balcony

**ballena** whale (14)

**ballestero** crossbowman

**ballet** *m.* ballet (13)

**banana** banana (6)

**bancarrota** bankruptcy

**banco** bank (16)

**banda** band

**banderilla** *Sp.* appetizer

**bandoneón** *m.* large concertina

**banquero/a** banker

**bañar** to bathe; **bañarse** to take a bath (4)

**bañera** bathtub (4)

**baño** bathroom (4); **habitación** (*f.*) **con/sin baño** room with(out) attached bath (18); **traje** (*m.*) **de baño** swimsuit (3)

**bar** *m.* bar (9); club; **ir** (*irreg.*) **a un bar** to go to a bar (9)

**barato/a** inexpensive (3)

**barbacoa** barbecue

**barca** small boat

**barcaza** barge

**barco** boat (7), ship (7); **ir** (*irreg.*) **en barco** to go/travel by boat (7)

**barra** bar, railing

**barrer (el piso)** to sweep (the floor) (9)

**barrera** barrier

**barriga** belly

**barril** *m.* barrel

**barrio** neighborhood (12)

**barro** clay

**basar** to base, support (*an opinion*); **basarse en** to base one's ideas, opinions on

**base** *f.* base, foundation; basis; **a base de** based on

**básico/a** basic

**basílica** basilica

**basquetbol** *m.* basketball (9)

**bastante** *adv.* enough (15); rather (15), sufficiently (15)

**bastar** to be enough

**basura** trash; **sacar (qu) la basura** to take out the trash (9)

**basurero** wastebasket

**bata** robe

**batá: tambores** (*m. pl.*) **batá** *set of drums used in Cuban music*

**batalla** battle

**batería** battery (14)

**batido** *drink similar to a milkshake* (17)

**bautismo** baptism

**bebé** *m., f.* baby

**beber** to drink (2)

**bebida** drink (6), beverage (6)

**beca** scholarship

**béisbol** *m.* baseball (9)

**belleza** beauty

**bello/a** beautiful (14); **Bella Durmiente** Sleeping Beauty

**besar** to kiss

**beso** kiss

**biblioteca** library (1)

**bibliotecario/a** librarian (1)

**bicicleta (de montaña)** (mountain) bike (12); **andar** (*irreg.*)**/montar en bicicleta** to ride a bicycle; **montañismo en bicicleta** mountain biking; **pasear en bicicleta** to ride a bicycle (9)

**biculturalismo** biculturalism

**bidón** (*m.*) *drum made of an oil drum*

**bien** *adv.* well (P); **caerle** (*irreg.*) **bien a alguien** to make a good impression on someone (16); **estar** (*irreg.*) **bien** to be comfortable (*temperature*) (5); **llevarse bien (con)** to get along well (with) (15); **muy bien** fine (P), very well (P); **pasarlo bien** to have a good time (8); **quedarle bien** to fit well; **salir** (*irreg.*) **bien** to turn out well

**bienestar** *m.* well-being (10)

**bienvenido/a** welcome

**bilingüe** bilingual

**bilingüismo** bilingualism

**billete** *m.* ticket (7); **billete de ida** one-way ticket (7); **billete de ida y vuelta** round-trip ticket (7)

**biodiversidad** *f.* biodiversity

**biografía** biography

**biología** biology

**biólogo/a** biologist

**bisonte** *m.* bison, buffalo

**bistec** *m.* steak (6)

**blanco/a** white (3); **espacio en blanco** blank space; **vino blanco** white wine (6)

**blancura** whiteness

**bloque** (*m.*) **de apartamentos** apartment building (12)

**blusa** blouse (3)

**bobo/a** dumb, stupid

**boca** mouth (10)

**boda** wedding (ceremony) (15); **lista de bodas** bride's registry

**bodegón** *m.* inexpensive restaurant, tavern

**boicoteo** boycott

**boleto** ticket (7); **boleto de ida** one-way ticket (7); **boleto de ida y vuelta** round-trip ticket (7)

**bolígrafo** pen (1)

**bolívar** *m.* Venezuelan monetary unit

**boliviano/a** *n., adj.* Bolivian

**bolsa** purse (3)

**bolsillo** pocket

**bomba** bomb (17); *traditional music from Puerto Rico*

**bombardeo** bombing

**bombero/a** firefighter

**bombilla** lightbulb

**bonito/a** pretty (2)

**borde: al borde de** on the verge of

**bordo: a bordo** on board

**boricua** *n., adj. m., f.* Puerto Rican

**Borinquén** *f. indigenous name for Puerto Rico*

**bosque** *m.* forest (14); **bosque primario** old-growth forest

**bota** boot (3)

**botella** bottle

**botones** *m. inv.* bellhop (18)

**brasileño/a** *n., adj.* Brazilian

**bravura** fierceness; bravery

**brazo** arm (11)

**breve** *adj.* brief

**brindar** to offer

**británico/a** *adj.* British

**bronce** *m.* bronze

**bronquitis** *f. inv.* bronchitis

**bruja** witch

**brujo** warlock; magician

**bucanero/a** buccaneer, pirate

**bucear** to scuba dive; to snorkle

**buen, bueno/a** *adj.* good (2); **buenas noches** good evening (P); good night (P); **buenas tardes** good afternoon (P); **buenos días** good morning (P); **hace buen tiempo** it's good weather (5); **lo bueno** the good thing, news (10); **muy buenas** good afternoon/evening (P)

**bueno...** *interj.* well . . . (2)

**buque** (*m.*) **petrolero** oil tanker

**burbuja** bubble

**burlador** *m.* one of two *bomba* drums

**burocrático/a** bureaucratic

**busca: en busca de** in search of

**buscar (qu)** to look for (1)

**butaca** seat (*in a theater*)

## C

**caballero** knight; gentleman

**caballo** horse (14); **montar a caballo** to ride a horse (9)

**caber** *irreg.* to fit

**cabeza** head (10); **doler(le) (ue) la cabeza** to have a headache (11); **dolor** (*m.*) **de cabeza** headache (10)

**cabezudo/a** stubborn

**cabina** cabin (*on a ship*) (7)

**cabo** cape (*geography*)

**cacique** *m.* chief

**cada** *inv.* each (4), every (4); **cada vez más** increasingly

**cadena** channel (*television*); chain

**cadera** hip

**caer** *irreg.* to fall (11); **caerle bien/mal a alguien** to make a good/bad impression on someone (16); **caerse** to fall down (11)

**café** *m.* café (18); coffee (1); **(de) color café** brown (3)

**cafeína** caffeine

**cafetera** coffee pot, coffeemaker (9)

**cafetería** cafeteria (1)

**caída** fall (*accident*)

**caja** box; cashier window (16); *type of drum*

**cajero automático** ATM (16); automatic teller machine (16)

**cajero/a** cashier (16); teller (16)

**calabaza** gourd

**calamar** *m.* squid

**calandria** lark (*bird*)

**calcetín** *m.* (*pl.* **calcetines**) sock (3)

**calculadora** calculator (1)

**calcular** to calculate

**cálculo** calculus; calculation

**calendario** calendar (11)

**calentar (ie)** to heat

**calidad** *f.* quality

**cálido/a** hot

**caliente** hot

**calificación** *f.* grade (11)

**calle** *f.* street (12)

**callos** (*m. pl.*) **a la madrileña** tripe Madrid–style

**calma** calm

**calor** *m.* heat; **hace calor** it's hot (5); **tener** (*irreg.*) **(mucho) calor** to be (very) warm, hot (5)

**caloría** calorie

**calzas** *f. pl.* stockings

**cama (de agua)** (water)bed (4); **guardar cama** to stay in bed (10); **hacer** (*irreg.*) **la cama** to make the bed (9); **tender (ie) la cama** to make the bed

**cámara** camera (12); **cámara de vídeo** video camera (12)

**camarero/a** waiter, waitress (6)

**camarógrafo/a** cameraman/woman

**camarones** *m. pl.* shrimp (6)

**cambiante** changing

**cambiar** to change; **cambiar (de canal/cuarto/ropa)** to change (channels/rooms/clothes) (12)

**cambio** change; **en cambio** on the other hand, on the contrary

**camello** camel

**caminar** to walk (10)

**caminata** walk

**camino** way; road (14), street (14); **camino de** on the way (to); **Camino Real** Royal Highway

**camión** *m.* truck

**camioneta** station wagon (7)

**camisa** shirt (3)

**camiseta** T-shirt (3)

**campana** bell

**campanada** stroke, ringing of a bell

**campanario** bell tower

**campaña** campaign; **tienda de campaña** tent (7)

**campeón, campeona** champion

**campeonato** championship

**campesino/a** farm worker (14), peasant (14)

*camping* *m.* campground (7); **hacer** (*irreg.*) *camping* to go camping (7)

**campo** field (14); countryside (12); **mozo de campo y plaza** farmhand

*campus* *m. inv.* (university) campus (12)

**canadiense** *n., adj. m., f.* Canadian

**canal** *m.* canal; channel (12); **cambiar de canal** to change channels (12)

**cancelar** to cancel

**cáncer** *m.* cancer

**cancha** court (*sports*)

**canción** *f.* song (13)

**candidato/a** candidate

**canela** cinnamon

**cansado/a** tired (5)

**cansancio** fatigue, weariness

**cansarse** to get tired

**cantante** *m., f.* singer (13)

**cantar** *m.* song

**cantar** to sing (1)

**cantidad** *f.* quantity

**canto** song

**capa de ozono** ozone layer

**capacidad** *f.* ability

**capacitación** *f.* training

**capacitado/a** trained

**capaz** (*pl.* **capaces**) able
**Caperucita Roja** Little Red Ridinghood
**capital** *f.* capital city (5)
**capítulo** chapter
**Capricornio** Capricorn
**capturado/a** captured
**cara** face; **plantar cara a** to confront
**característica** *n.* characteristic
**caracterizar (c)** to characterize
**caramelo** candy
**carcajadas** (*f. pl.*): **reírse (i, i) (me río) a carcajadas** to laugh one's head off
**cardinal: punto cardinal** cardinal direction (5)
**carga** charge; payload (*ammunition*)
**cargar (gu)** to charge (*to an account*) (16); to carry
**cargo** position, post; **estar** (*irreg.*) **a cargo** to be in control of
**Caribe** *m.* Caribbean
**caribeño/a** *n., adj.* Caribbean
**cariño** affection
**cariñoso/a** affectionate (5)
**carne** *f.* meat (6); flesh
**carnero** mutton
**carnet** *m.* identity card
**caro/a** expensive (3)
**carpintero/a** carpenter
**carrera** career; major (*academic*)
**carreta** wooden cart
**carretera** highway (14)
**carro (descapotable)** (convertible) car (12)
**carta** letter (2); **jugar (ue) (gu) a las cartas** to play cards (9); **papel** (*m.*) **de cartas** stationery (18)
**cartel** *m.* poster
**cartera** wallet (3); handbag (3)
**cartón** *m.* cardboard
**cartucho** cartridge
**casa** house (2), home (2); **ama** (*f.* [*but* **el ama**]) **de casa** homemaker; **casa de apartamentos** apartment building (12); **en casa** at home (1); **limpiar la casa (entera)** to clean the (whole) house (9); **regresar a casa** to go home (1)
**casado/a** married (2); **recién casado/a (con)** newlywed (to) (15)
**casarse (con)** to marry (15)
**cascada** waterfall
**cascanueces** *m. inv.* nutcracker
**casero/a** *adj.* home
**casi** almost (2); **casi nunca** almost never (2)
**caso** case; **caso de urgencia** emergency; **en caso de que** *conj.* in case (15)
**castigar (gu)** to punish (17)

**catalán** *m.* Catalan (*language*)
**catálogo** catalogue
**catarata** waterfall
**catastrófico/a** catastrophic
**catedral** *f.* cathedral
**categoría** category
**católico/a** *n., adj.* Catholic
**catorce** fourteen (P)
**causa** cause
**causar** to cause
**caza** hunting
**cazador(a)** hunter
**cazuelita** bowl
**CD** CD (12), compact disc (12)
**CD-ROM** *m.* CD-ROM (12)
**ceder** to cede
**celebración** *f.* celebration
**celebrar** to celebrate (5)
**celular: teléfono celular** cellular phone (12)
**cementerio** cemetery
**cena** dinner (6), supper (6)
**cenar** to have (eat) dinner, supper (6)
**Cenicienta** Cinderella
**censo** census
**censurar** to censure
**centavo** cent
**centrado/a** centered
**central** central; **América Central** Central America
**céntrico/a** central
**centro** center; downtown (3); **centro comercial** shopping mall (3)
**Centroamérica** Central America
**centroamericano/a** *n., adj.* Central American
**ceño** frown
**cepillarse los dientes** to brush one's teeth (4)
**cerámica** *s.* pottery (13); ceramics (13)
**cerca** *adv.* near, nearby, close; **cerca de** *prep.* close to (5); **de cerca** up close
**cercanía** closeness
**cercano/a** *adj.* close, near
**cerdo** pork; **chuleta de cerdo** pork chop (6)
**cereal** *m.* cereal (6)
**cerebro** brain (10)
**ceremonia** ceremony
**cerilla** *Sp.* match (*for lighting things*)
**cero** zero (P)
**cerrado/a** closed (5)
**cerrar (ie)** to close (4)
**cerro** hill
**cervantino/a** Cervantine (*pertaining to Miguel de Cervantes*)

**cervecería** beer hall
**cerveza** beer (1)
**césped** *m.* grass
**cesto** basket
**ceviche** *m. raw fish dish*
**champán** *m.* champagne
**champanería** champagne bar
**champiñón** *m.* mushroom (6)
**champú** *m.* shampoo (18)
**chaperón, chaperona** chaperone
**chaqueta** jacket (3)
**charango** *ten-string guitar-like instrument*
**charlar** to chat
**chau** good-bye
**cheque** *m.* check (16); **cheque de viajero** traveler's check (18); **pagar (gu) con cheque** pay by check (16); **talonario de cheques** *Sp.* checkbook
**chequeo** checkup (10)
**chequera** checkbook (16)
**chicharrón** *m.* pork flavorings
**chico/a** boy, girl
**chileno/a** *n., adj.* Chilean
**chimenea** chimney
**chimpancé** *m.* chimpanzee
**chino** Chinese (*language*)
**chino/a** *n., adj.* Chinese
**chirimía** *clarinet-type wind instrument*
**chiste** *m.* joke (8)
**chistoso/a** funny, amusing
**chocador(a): auto chocador** bumper car
**chocar (qu) (con)** to run into (14), to collide (with) (14)
**chocolate** *m.* chocolate; hot chocolate
**chofer** *m., f.* driver
**choque** *m.* collision (17); **auto de choque** bumper car; **choque** (*m.*) **de trenes** train wreck
**chorizo** sausage
**chuleta** rib steak; **chuleta de cerdo** pork chop (6)
**chulo** pimp
**ciberespacial** *adj.* cyberspace
**ciberespacio** *n.* cyberspace
**ciclismo** bicycling (9)
**ciclo** cycle
**ciego/a** blind
**cielo** heaven; sky
**cien, ciento** one hundred (2); **por ciento** percent
**ciencia** science; *pl.* (*academic discipline*) science (1); **ciencia ficción** science fiction; **ciencias políticas** *f. pl.* political science
**científico/a** *n.* scientist; *adj.* scientific

**cierto/a** true; certain, **en cierta medida** in some measure; **es cierto que** it's certain that (13)

**cigarrillo** cigarette

**cilantro** cilantro, fresh coriander

**cinco** five (P); **Cinco de Mayo** Mexican awareness celebration

**cincuenta** fifty (2)

**cine** *m.* movies (4); movie theater (4); **ir** (*irreg.*) **al cine** to go to the movies (9)

**cineasta** *m., f.* film director

**cinta** tape (3)

**cinturón** *m.* belt (3)

**circuito** circuit

**circulación** *f.* traffic (14)

**circular** to circulate; to move

**círculo** circle, ring

**circunstancia** circumstance

**cisne** *m.* swan

**cita** appointment; date (15)

**citado/a** quoted

**ciudad** *f.* city (2)

**ciudadanía** citizenship

**ciudadano/a** citizen (17)

**ciudadela** citadel

**cívico/a** civic (17)

**civil: estado civil** marital status

**civilización** *f.* civilization

**claro** *interj.* of course

**claro/a** clear

**clase** *f.* class(room) (1); **clase alta** upper class; **clase turística** tourist class (7); **compañero/a de clase** classmate (1); **primera clase** first class (7); **sala de clase** classroom

**clásico/a** classic(al) (13)

**claúsula** *gram.* clause; **cláusula nominal** noun clause

**clave** *adj. inv.* key

**clave** *m.* percussion stick (*used in Caribbean music*)

**cliente** *m., f.* client (1); customer

**clima** *m.* climate (5)

**climatología** climatology

**clínica** clinic

**club** *m.* club

**coágulo** clot

**cobrar** to cash (*a check*) (16); to charge (*someone for an item or service*) (16)

**cobre** *m.* copper; brass instrument

**coche** *m.* car (2); **coche deportivo** sports car; **coche descapotable** convertible car (12)

**cochera** garage

**cocido/a: huevo cocido** hard-boiled egg

**cocina** kitchen (4)

**cocinar** to cook (6)

**cocinero/a** cook (16), chef (16)

**coco** coconut

**cóctel** *m.* cocktail

**coger (j)** to catch; to seize, grab

**cognado** cognate

**coherente** coherent

**coincidir** to coincide; to agree

**cojear** to limp

**cola** line; **hacer** (*irreg.*) **cola** to stand in line (7)

**colección** *f.* collection

**coleccionar** to collect

**colega** *m., f.* colleague

**colegiatura** *s.* fees (*academic*)

**colegio** secondary school

**colesterol** *m.* cholesterol

**colgar (ue) (gu)** to hang

**colocar (qu)** to place

**colombiano/a** *n., adj.* Colombian

**colón** *m.* monetary unit of Costa Rica and El Salvador

**colonia** colony

**colonialismo** colonialism

**colonizador(a)** colonist

**colonizar (c)** to colonize

**colono/a** settler

**color** *m.* color (3); **(de) color café** brown (3); **¿de qué color es?** what color is it?

**colorado/a** red

**columna** column

**comandante** *m., f.* commander

**combatir** to fight, combat

**combinación** *f.* combination

**combinar** to combine

**comedor** *m.* dining room (4)

**comentar** to comment on; to discuss

**comentario** commentary

**comenzar (ie) (c)** to begin

**comer** to eat (2); **comer equilibradamente** to eat in a balanced way (10); **comérselo/la** to eat (*something*) up

**comercial: centro comercial** shopping mall (3)

**comerciante** *m., f.* merchant (16); shopkeeper (16)

**cometer** to commit

**cómico/a** funny; **tira cómica** comic strip

**comida** food (6); meal (6)

**comisión** *f.* commission

**como** like, as; **así como** as well as; **tal como** just as; **tan... como** as . . . as (5);

**tan pronto como** as soon as (16); **tanto como** as much as (5); **tanto/a(s)... como** as much/many . . . as (5)

**¿cómo?** how? (P); what? (P); **¿cómo es usted?** what are you (*form. s.*) like? (P); **¿cómo está(s)?** how are you? (P); **¿cómo se llama usted?** what's your (*form. s.*) name? (P); **¿cómo te llamas?** what's your (*fam. s.*) name? (P)

**cómoda** bureau (4), dresser (4)

**cómodo/a** comfortable (4)

**compacto/a: disco compacto** CD (12); compact disc (12)

**compañero/a** companion, friend; **compañero/a de clase** classmate (1); **compañero/a de cuarto** roommate (1)

**compañía** company

**comparación** *f.* comparison

**comparar** to compare

**comparativo** *gram.* comparative

**comparsa** dance troupe

**compartir** to share

**compasión** *f.* compassion

**compatabilizar (c)** to make compatible

**compensar** to compensate, make up for

**competencia** competition

**competición** *f.* competition

**complacer (zc)** to please

**complejo/a** complex

**complementar** to complement

**complementario/a** complementary

**complemento** *gram.* object; **complemento directo** direct object; **complemento indirecto** indirect object

**completar** to complete

**completo/a** complete; full (18), no vacancy (18), **pensión** (*f.*) **completa** room and full board (18); **por completo** completely; **trabajo de tiempo completo** full time work (11)

**complexión** *f.* body type/build

**complicado/a** complicated

**complicar (qu)** to complicate

**componer** (*like* **poner**) to compose

**comportamiento** behavior

**composición** *f.* composition

**compositor(a)** composer (13)

**comprar** to buy (1)

**compras: de compras** shopping (3); **ir** (*irreg.*) **de compras** to go shopping (3)

**comprender** to understand (2)

**comprensión** *f.* comprehension; **comprensión auditiva** listening comprehension

**comprensivo/a** understanding
**comprobar** (*like* **probar**) to prove
**compromiso** commitment
**computación** *f.* computer science (1)
**computadora** computer (12);
   **computadora portátil** laptop
   computer; **disco de computadora**
   computer disc (12); **escribir** (*p.p.*
   **escrito**) **en la computadora** to key in,
   type (16)
**común** common, usual, ordinary
**comunicación** *f.* communication; *pl.*
   communications (1); **medio de**
   **comunicación** means of
   communication (17); **medios** (*m. pl.*)
   **de comunicación** media
**comunicarse** (**qu**) (**con**) to communicate
   (with) (17)
**comunicativo/a** communicative
**comunidad** *f.* community (12)
**comunitario/a** *adj.* community
**con** with (1); **con anticipación** in advance
   (18), ahead of time (18); **con cheque** by
   check (16); **con cuidado** carefully; **con**
   **frecuencia** frequently (1); **con permiso**
   excuse me (P); pardon me (P); **con**
   **respecto a** with regard to, with respect
   to; **con tal (de) que** *conj.* provided
   that (15)
**concentrarse** to concentrate
**concepción** *f.* conception, idea
**concepto** concept, idea
**concertar** (**ie**) to arrange; to agree upon
**conciencia** conscience, moral awareness
**concierto** concert; **ir** (*irreg.*) **a un**
   **concierto** to go to a concert (9)
**concluir** (**y**) to conclude
**conclusión** *f.* conclusion
**concordar** (**ue**) (**con**) to correspond (to)
**concurso** contest
**condición** *f.* condition
**condicional** *m. gram.* conditional
**conducir** *irreg.* to drive (14); to conduct;
   **conducir a** to lead to; **licencia de**
   **conducir** driver's license (14)
**conductor(a)** driver (14)
**conectar** to connect
**conexión** *f.* connection
**confección** *f.* confection
**conferencia** lecture
**conferenciante** *m., f.* lecturer
**confianza** trust
**confiar** (**confío**) to trust
**configurado/a** configured
**confirmación** *f.* confirmation

**confirmar** to confirm (18)
**confluencia** coming together
**confrontación** *f.* confrontation
**confundido/a** confused
**congelado/a** frozen (5); very cold (5)
**congelador** *m.* freezer (9)
**congestionado/a** congested (10), stuffed
   up (10)
**congreso** congress
**conjugar** (**gu**) *gram.* to conjugate
**conjunción** *f. gram.* conjunction
**conjunto** group; band
**conmemorar** to commemorate
**conmigo** with me (5)
**conocer** (**zc**) to know (6), to be
   acquainted with (6); to meet
**conocido/a** known, famous
**conocimiento** knowledge
**conquista** conquest
**conquistador(a)** conqueror
**consciente** conscious, aware
**conscripto** draftee
**consecuencia** consequence; **a**
   **consecuencia de** as a consequence of
**conseguir** (*like* **seguir**) to get (8), to
   obtain (8); **conseguir** + *inf.* to succeed
   in (*doing something*) (8)
**consejero/a** advisor (1)
**consejo** (piece of) advice (6); council
**conservación** *f.* conservation
**conservador(a)** *n., adj.* conservative
**conservar** to save (14), to conserve (14)
**considerar** to consider
**consigo** with them
**consistir en** to consist of
**constante** *adj.* constant
**constar de** to consist of
**constitución** *f.* constitution
**constitucional** constitutional
**constituir** (**y**) to constitute; to be
**construcción** *f.* construction
**constructivo/a** constructive
**construir** (**y**) to build (14)
**cónsul** *m.* consul
**consulta** consultation
**consultar** to consult
**consultorio** (medical) office (10)
**consumidor(a)** consumer
**consumir** to consume
**consumo** consumption; use
**contabilidad** *f.* accounting
**contable** *m., f.* accountant
**contacto** contact; **lentes** (*m. pl.*) **de**
   **contacto** contact lenses (10); **llevar**
   **lentes de contacto** to wear contact

lenses (10); **mantenerse** (*like* **tener**) **en**
   **contacto** to keep in touch
**contado: pagar** (**gu**) **al contado** to pay in
   cash (16)
**contador(a)** accountant (16)
**contaminación** (*f.*) (**del aire**) (air) pollution
   (14); **hay** (**mucha**) **contaminación**
   there's (lots of) pollution (5)
**contaminar** to pollute (14)
**contar** (**ue**) to tell (7); **contar con** to count on
**contemplar** to contemplate
**contemporáneo/a** contemporary
**contenido** *s.* contents
**contento/a** content (5), happy (5)
**contestador** (*m.*) **automático** answering
   machine (12)
**contestar el teléfono** to answer the
   phone (16)
**contexto** context
**contigo** with you (5)
**continente** *m.* continent
**continuación** (*f.*)**: a continuación**
   following, below
**continuar** (**continúo**) to continue
**contra** against; **en contra** opposed;
   **Fundación** (*f.*) **Alerta contra el SIDA**
   AIDS Awareness Foundation
**contrabajo** double bass (*instrument*)
**contrabando** contraband
**contradicción** *f.* contradiction
**contraer** (*like* **traer**) **matrimonio** to get
   married
**contrario/a** opposite; **al contrario** on the
   contrary; **lo contrario** the opposite
**contrastar** to contrast
**contratar** to contract
**contratiempos** *m. pl.* mishaps;
   disappointments
**contrato** contract
**contribución** *f.* contribution
**contribuir** (**y**) to contribute
**control** (*m.*) **de aduana** customs
   checkpoint; **control remoto** remote
   control (12); **pasar por el control de**
   **la seguridad** to go/pass through
   security (7)
**controlar** to control
**convencer** (**convenzo**) to convince
**convencional** conventional
**conveniencia** convenience
**conveniente** convenient
**conversación** *f.* conversation
**conversar** to talk, converse
**convertir** (**ie, i**) to change, convert;
   **convertirse en** to turn into

**convivencia** living together, cohabitation

**convivir** to live together

**cónyuge** *m., f.* spouse

**cooperativo/a** cooperative

**copa** glass; drink (*alcoholic*) (18); upper branches in a tree; **Copa Mundial** World Cup; **tomar una copa** to have a drink

**copia: hacer** (*irreg.*) **copia** to copy (12)

**copiar** to copy (12)

**coquí** *m.* frog (*found in the Caribbean*)

**coraje** *m.* courage

**corazón** *m.* heart (10)

**corbata** tie (3)

**corcho** cork

**cordillera** mountain range

**córdoba** *m.* monetary unit of Nicaragua

**coro** chorus

**corona** wreath

**coronel** *m.* colonel

**correcto/a** correct, right

**corredor(a)** *adj.* running

**corregir (i, i) (j)** to correct

**correo** mail (18); **correo electrónico** e-mail (12); **oficina de correos** post office (18)

**correr** to run (9); to jog (9); to flow (*water*)

**corresponder** to correspond

**correspondiente** corresponding

**corresponsal** *m., f.* (news) correspondent

**corrida de toros** bullfight

**corrido** *traditional song from Mexico, associated with the Mexican Revolution*

**corriente** (*adj.*): **cuenta corriente** checking account (16)

**corriente** *f.* current

**cortar** to cut

**corte** *m.* cut; *f.* court (of law)

**cortés** *m., f.* courteous

**cortesía** courtesy

**cortina** curtain

**corto/a** short (*in length*) (2); **pantalones** (*m. pl.*) **cortos** shorts

**cosa** thing (1)

**cosechar** to harvest

**cosmopolita** *adj. m., f.* cosmopolitan

**costa** coast

**costar (ue)** to cost; **¿cuánto cuesta?** how much does it cost? (3)

**costarricense** *n., adj. m., f.* Costa Rican

**costero/a** coastal

**costilla** rib

**costo** cost

**costumbre** *f.* custom (9); habit (9); **por costumbre** customarily

**cotidiano/a** everyday, daily

**crear** to create (13)

**creatividad** *f.* creativity

**creativo/a** creative

**crecer (zc)** to grow (15)

**creciente** growing

**crecimiento** growth

**crédito** credit; **tarjeta de crédito** credit card (6)

**creencia** belief

**creer (y) (en)** to think (2); to believe (in) (2)

**criada** maid (18)

**criado/a** servant (16)

**criar (crío)** to raise (*children*)

**criatura** child

**crimen** *m.* crime

**criminal** *n., adj. m., f.* criminal

**criollo/a** creole

**crisis** *f. inv.* crisis

**cristal** *m.* crystal

**Cristo: antes de Cristo (a.C.)** before Christ (B.C.); **después de Cristo (d.C.)** after Christ (A.D.)

**crítica** criticism

**crítico/a** *n.* critic; *adj.* critical

**cronológico/a** chronological

**crudo** *n.* crude (oil)

**cruzar (c)** to cross (18)

**cuá** *m. percussion instrument made of bamboo and played with two sticks*

**cuaderno** notebook (1)

**cuadrado** *n.* square

**cuadrado/a** *adj.* square(d)

**cuadro** chart; painting (*piece of art*) (13); square; **de cuadros** plaid

**¿cuál(es)?** what? (1); which? (1); **¿cuál es la fecha de hoy?** what's today's date? (5)

**cualidad** *f.* quality

**cualquier** *adj.* any

**cualquiera** *pron.* anyone; either

**¿cuán?** *adv.* how?

**cuando** when; **de vez en cuando** once in a while

**¿cuándo?** when? (1)

**cuanto: en cuanto** *conj.* as soon as (16); **en cuanto a** *prep.* regarding

**¿cuánto/a?** how much? (1); **¿cuánto cuesta?** how much does it cost? (3); **¿cuánto es?** how much is it? (3)

**¿cuántos/as?** how many? (1)

**cuarenta** forty (2)

**cuarto** *n.* room (1); one-fourth; quarter (of an hour); **cambiar de cuarto** to change rooms (12); **compañero/a de cuarto** roommate (1); **servicio de cuarto** room service (18); **y/menos cuarto** a quarter (fifteen minutes) after/to (*the hour*) (P)

**cuarto/a** *adj.* fourth (13)

**cuatro** four (P)

**cuatro** four-stringed guitar

**cuatrocientos/as** four hundred (3)

**cubano/a** *n., adj.* Cuban

**cubanoamericano/a** *adj.* Cuban American

**cubierto/a** (*p.p. of* **cubrir**) covered

**cubito** ice cube

**cubo** cube

**cubrir** (*p.p.* **cubierto**) to cover (14)

**cuchara** spoon

**cucharada** spoonful

**cucharadita** teaspoon

**cuchillo** knife

**cuello** neck

**cuenca** basin

**cuenta** account (16); (*for service*) bill (6), check (6); **cuenta corriente** checking account (16); **cuenta de ahorros** savings account (16); **darse** (*irreg.*) **cuenta (de)** to realize; **estado de cuentas** bank statement; **tomar en cuenta** to take into account

**cuento** story

**cuerda** string

**cuero** leather

**cuerpo** body (10)

**cuesta: ¿cuánto cuesta?** how much does it cost? (3)

**cuestión** *f.* question, matter

**cuidado** care; *interj.* careful; **con cuidado** carefully; **tener** (*irreg.*) **cuidado** to be careful

**cuidadosamente** carefully

**cuidar(se)** to take care of (oneself) (10); **¡hay que cuidarse!** you must take care of yourself!

**cuitado/a** forlorn

**culinario/a** culinary

**culpa: tener** (*irreg.*) **la culpa** to be guilty

**cultista** *adj. m., f.* cult member

**cultivo** cultivation, raising (*of crops*)

**cultura** culture

**cumpleaños** *m. inv.* birthday (5); **feliz cumpleaños** happy birthday; **pastel** (*m.*) **de cumpleaños** birthday cake (8)

**cumplir años** to have a birthday (8)

**cuna** cradle; birthplace

**cuñado/a** brother-in-law, sister-in-law
**cupo** quota, share
**cura** *m.* priest
**curador(a)** curator
**curar(se)** to heal, cure (oneself); **curarse de** to be cured of
**currículum** *m.* (*pl.* **currículos**) résumé (16)
**cursar** to study (*at a university*)
**cursivo/a: letra cursiva** *s.* italics
**curso** course
**cuyo/a** whose

# D
**dados** *m. pl.* dice
**dama** woman
**danza** dance (13)
**daño** damage; **hacerse** (*irreg.*) **daño** to hurt oneself (11)
**dar** *irreg.* to give (7); **dar ánimo** to cheer; **dar asco** to make sick; **dar un paseo** to take a walk (9); **dar una fiesta** to give a party (8); **darle la gana** to feel like; **darse** to occur; **darse cuenta (de)** to realize; **darse en/contra/con** to run, bump into (11); **darse la mano** to shake hands; **darse la vuelta** to turn oneself around
**datar (de)** to date (from)
**datos** *m. pl.* information; facts
**dé** give (*form. command*)
**de** *prep.* of (P); from (P); **de acuerdo** agreed; **de acuerdo con** in accordance with; **de ahora en adelante** from now on; **de ancho** in width; **de antemano** beforehand; **de anticipación** ahead; **de añadidura** on the side; **de cerca** up close; **(de) color café** brown (3); **de compras** shopping (3); **de cuadros** plaid; **de desnudismo** nudist; **¿de dónde eres?** where are you (*fam. s.*) from? (P) **¿de dónde es usted?** where are you (*form. s.*) from? (P); **de guardia** on-call; **de hecho** in fact; **de ida** one-way (7); **de ida y vuelta** round-trip (7); **de joven** as a youth (9); **de la mañana/ tarde/noche** in the morning/afternoon/ evening (P); **de la noche** at night (P); **de largo** in length; **de los últimos años** in recent years; **de lujo** luxury (*adj.*) (18); **de lunares** polka-dotted; **de manera que** *conj.* so that, in such a way that; **de moda** in style; **de modo** in such a way; **de nada** you're welcome (P); **de niño/a** as a child (9); **de noche** at night; **de paso** passing through; **de**

**primera** first-class; **¿de qué color es?** what color is it?; **¿de quién?** whose? (2); **de rayas** striped; **de repente** suddenly (10); **de tiempo completo/parcial** full time/part time (11); **de todas maneras** by all means; whatever happens; **de todo** everything (3); **de todos modos** anyway; **de última moda** the latest style (3); **de un jalón** all at once; **de vacaciones** on vacation (7); **de vez en cuando** once in a while; **de viaje** on a trip (7)
**debajo de** *prep.* below (5)
**deber** *n. m.* responsibility (17), obligation (17); *v.* **deber** (+ *inf.*) should, must, ought to (*do something*) (2); **deberse a** to be due to
**debido a** due to, because
**débil** weak
**debilitamiento** weakening, debilitation
**década** decade
**decidir** to decide
**décimo/a** tenth (13)
**decir** *irreg.* (*p.p.* **dicho**) to say (7); to tell (7); **es decir** that is to say; **eso quiere decir...** that means . . . (10)
**decisión** *f.* decision
**decisivo/a** decisive
**declaración** *f.* declaration
**declarar** to declare
**decoración** *f.* decoration
**decorar** to decorate
**dedicarse (qu) a** to dedicate oneself to
**dedo (de la mano)** finger (11); **dedo del pie** toe (11)
**deducir** *irreg.* to deduct
**defecto** defect
**defender (ie)** to defend
**defensa** defense
**definición** *f.* definition
**definir** to define
**definitivo/a** definitive
**deforestación** *f.* deforestation
**deforestado/a** deforested
**deformación** *f.* deformation
**degustar** to taste; to try, sample
**dejar (en)** to quit (16); **dejar** + *inf.* to allow, let (*something happen*); **dejar (en)** to leave (behind) (in [*a place*]) (9); **dejar de** + *inf.* to stop (*doing something*) (10)
**del** (*contraction of* **de** + **el**) of the (2); from the (2)
**delante** *adv.* before, in front, ahead; **delante de** *prep.* in front of (5)
**delegación** *f.* delegation

**delegado/a** delegate
**deleitarse** to take delight; to enjoy
**deletrear** to spell
**delgado/a** thin (2), slender (2)
**delicioso/a** delicious
**delincuente** delinquent
**delito** crime (14)
**demanda** demand
**demás: los/las demás** the others (12), the rest
**demasiado** *adv.* too, too much (12)
**demasiado/a** *adj.* too much; *pl.* too many
**democracia** democracy
**demócrata** *m., f.* Democrat
**demográfico/a** demographic
**demonio** devil, demon
**demora** delay (7)
**demostración** *f.* demonstration
**demostrar** (*like* **mostrar**) to show, demonstrate
**demostrativo/a** *gram.* demonstrative
**denso/a** dense (14)
**dental: pasta dental** toothpaste (18)
**dentista** *m., f.* dentist (10)
**dentro** *adv.* in, within, inside; **dentro de** *prep.* within; **dentro de poco** in a little while
**denuncia** accusation
**deparar** to supply
**departamento** department; *Sp.* apartment
**depender (de)** to depend (on)
**dependiente/a** clerk (1)
**deporte** *m.* sport (9); **deportes acuáticos** water sports; **practicar (qu) deportes** to practice, play sports (10)
**deportista** *m., f.* sports player
**deportivo/a** sports *adj.* (9), sporting *adj.* (9), sports-loving (9); **coche** (*m.*) **deportivo** sports car
**depositar** to deposit (16)
**depósito** deposit
**deprimente** depressing
**depurar** to refine
**derecha** *n.* right; right hand; **a la derecha (de)** to the right (of) (5)
**derecho** *n.* right (*legal*) (17); **todo derecho** straight ahead (14)
**derivarse (de)** to derive (from)
**dermatológico/a** dermatologic, skin
**derretido/a** melted
**derrocado/a** overthrown
**derrotado/a** defeated
**desafortunadamente** unfortunately
**desagradable** unpleasant

**desaparecer** (*like* **parecer**) to disappear
**desarraigado/a** uprooted
**desarrollar** to develop (14)
**desarrollo** development
**desastre** *m.* disaster (17)
**desastroso/a** disastrous
**desayunar** to have (eat) breakfast (6)
**desayuno** breakfast (4)
**descansar** to rest (4)
**descanso** rest
**descapotable: carro/coche** (*m.*) **descapotable** convertible car (12)
**descender (ie)** to descend
**descendiente** *m., f.* descendent
**desconocido/a** unknown
**descortésmente** discourteously, impolitely
**describir** (*like* **escribir**) to describe
**descripción** *f.* description
**descubanizado/a** less Cuban
**descubierto/a** (*p.p. of* **descubrir**) discovered
**descubrimiento** discovery
**descubrir** (*like* **cubrir**) to discover (14)
**descuidado/a** careless
**desde** *prep.* from (7); since; **desde entonces** from then on; **desde que** *conj.* since
**deseable** desirable
**desear** to want (1), to desire
**desecho** waste (product)
**desempeñar** to play (*a part*) (13), to perform (*a part*) (13); to hold, carry out (*a responsibility*)
**deseo** wish (8)
**desequilibrio** imbalance
**desertización** *f.* process of becoming a desert
**desesperadamente** desperately
**desfile** *m.* parade
**desgracia** disgrace
**desgraciadamente** unfortunately
**deshumanización** *f.* dehumanization
**desierto** *n.* desert
**desierto/a** *adj.* deserted
**designar** to designate
**desigualdad** *f.* inequality (17)
**desilusión** *f.* disillusion
**desinflado/a** flat; **llanta desinflada** flat tire (14)
**desintegrarse** to break up
**desnudismo: de desnudismo** nudist
**desnudo/a** nude, naked
**desocupado/a** vacant (18), unoccupied (18)
**desordenado/a** messy (5)

**desorientar** to disorient, confuse
**despacio** *adv.* slowly
**despedirse** (*like* **pedir**) **(de)** to say good-bye (to) (8); to take leave (of) (8)
**despegar (gu)** to take off (*airplane*)
**desperdiciar** to waste
**despertador** *m.* alarm clock (11)
**despertarse (ie)** (*p.p.* **despierto**) to wake up (4)
**despierto/a** (*p.p. of* **despertar**) awake
**desplazamiento** journey; move
**desplegar(se) (ie) (gu)** to unfold
**después** *adv.* after, afterwards; later; **después de** *prep.* after (4); **después de Cristo (d.C.)** after Christ (A.D.); **después (de) que** *conj.* after (16)
**destacado/a** distinguished
**destacar (qu)** to emphasize; to stand out; **destacarse** to distinguish oneself
**desterrado/a** exiled
**destinar** to designate, assign
**destino** destination
**destreza** skill
**destrucción** *f.* destruction
**destructivo/a** destructive
**destructor(a)** destructive
**destruir (y)** to destroy (14)
**desventaja** disadvantage (10)
**detalle** *m.* detail (6)
**detective** *m., f.* detective
**detener** (*like* **tener**) to detain
**detenidamente** carefully
**determinar** to determine
**detestar** to detest, hate
**detrás de** *prep.* behind (5)
**devolver** (*like* **volver**) to return (*something*) (16)
**día** *m.* day (1); **algún día** some day; **buenos días** good morning (P); **Día de Acción de Gracias** Thanksgiving; **Día de la Independencia** Independence Day; **Día de la Raza** Columbus Day (Hispanic Awareness Day); **día de la semana** weekday (4); **Día de los Enamorados** Valentine's Day; **Día de los Inocentes** April Fool's Day; **Día de los Reyes Magos** Day of the Magi (Three Kings); **Día de San Patricio** St. Patrick's Day; **Día del Año Nuevo** New Year's Day; **día del santo** saint's day; **día festivo** holiday (8); **Día Internacional de los Trabajadores** International Labor Day; **hoy (en) día** nowadays,

these days; **ponerse** (*irreg.*) **al día** to get up-to-date; **¿qué día es hoy?** what day is today? (4); **todos los días** every day (1)
**diabetes** *f. inv.* diabetes
**diablo** devil
**diáfano/a** transparent
**diagrama** *m.* diagram
**dialecto** dialect
**diálogo** dialogue
**diamante** *m.* diamond
**diario/a** daily; **rutina diaria** daily routine (4)
**diarrea** diarrhea
**dibujar** to draw (13)
**dibujo** drawing; **dibujos animados** cartoons
**diccionario** dictionary (1)
**dicho/a** (*p.p. of* **decir**) said
**diciembre** *m.* December (5)
**dictador(a)** dictator (17)
**dictadura** dictatorship (17)
**dictar** to dictate
**diecinueve** nineteen (P)
**dieciocho** eighteen (P)
**dieciséis** sixteen (P)
**diecisiete** seventeen (P)
**diente** *m.* tooth (10); **cepillarse los dientes** to brush one's teeth (4); **diente de ajo** garlic clove
**dieta** diet; **estar** (*irreg.*) **a dieta** to be on a diet (6)
**dietético/a** *adj.* diet
**diez** ten (P)
**diferencia** difference; **a diferencia de** unlike
**diferente** different
**diferir (ie, i)** to differ
**difícil** difficult (5); hard (5)
**dificultad** *f.* difficulty
**dificultar** to make difficult
**difundir** to spread
**difusión** *f.* broadcasting
**diga** *interj.* hello (*on the telephone, Sp.*)
**digestión** *f.* digestion
**digital: agenda digital** electronic date book
**dimensión** *f.* dimension
**Dinamarca** Denmark
**dinero** money (1)
**Dios** *m. s.* God; **por Dios** for heaven's sake (11); *pl.* gods
**diosa** goddess
**diplomático/a** diplomatic
**diptongo** *gram.* diphthong

**dirección** *f.* address (9); **dirección de personal** personnel office (16), employment office (16)

**directo/a** direct; **complemento directo** *gram.* direct object pronoun

**director(a)** director (13); conductor (13); **director(a) de personal** personnel director (16)

**dirigir (j)** to direct; to target

**disco** disk; **disco compacto** CD (12), compact disc (12); **disco de computadora** computer disc (12); **disco duro** hard drive (12)

**discoteca** discotheque; **ir** (*irreg.*) **a una discoteca** to go to a disco (9)

**discriminación** *f.* discrimination (17)

**disculpa** apology, excuse; **pedir (i, i) disculpas** to apologize (11)

**disculpar** to excuse, pardon

**discúlpeme** pardon me (11); I'm sorry (11)

**discutir (sobre) (con)** to argue (with) (about) (8)

**diseñador(a)** designer

**diseñar** to design

**diseño** design

**disfraz** *m.* (*pl.* **disfraces**) disguise, costume; **fiesta de disfraz** costume party

**disfrutar (de)** to enjoy

**disminuir (y)** to lessen, diminish

**disparar** to shoot, fire

**disparate** *m.* silly thing; crazy idea

**disponible** available

**disputa** dispute, argument

**distancia** distance; **a/por larga distancia** long-distance

**distante** distant, far

**distinguir (g)** to distinguish

**distinto/a** different, distinct

**distraer** (*like* **traer**) to distract

**distraído/a** absentminded (11)

**distribución** *f.* distribution

**distrito** district

**diversidad** *f.* diversity

**diversificar (qu)** to diversify

**diversión** *f.* entertainment (9), amusement (9)

**diverso/a** diverse; various

**divertido/a** fun; **ser** (*irreg.*) **divertido/a** to be fun (9)

**divertir (ie, i)** to entertain; **divertirse** to have a good time (4), to enjoy oneself (4)

**dividir** to divide

**divorciado/a (de)** divorced (from) (15)

**divorciarse (de)** to get divorced (from) (15)

**divorcio** divorce (15)

**divulgar (gu)** to make known

**doblar** to turn (14); to dub (*movies*)

**doble** double; **habitación** (*f.*) **doble** double room (*in a hotel*) (18)

**doce** twelve (P)

**dócil** tame, docile

**doctor(a)** doctor

**doctorado** doctorate, Ph.D.

**documentar** to document

**documento** document

**dólar** *m.* dollar

**doler (ue)** to hurt (10), ache (10); **doler(le) la cabeza** to have a headache (11)

**dolor** *m.* pain, ache (10); **tener** (*irreg.*) **dolor de cabeza/estómago/muela** to have a headache/stomachache/toothache (10)

**doméstico/a** domestic; household; **animal** (*m.*) **doméstico** domesticated animal (14); pet (14); **aparato doméstico** home appliance (9); **quehacer** (*m.*) **doméstico** household chore (9)

**domicilio** home, residence

**dominación** *f.* domination

**dominar** to dominate

**domingo** Sunday (4)

**dominicano/a** *n., adj.* Dominican

**dominio** mastery

**don** *m. title of respect used with a man's first name*

**donde** where

**¿dónde?** where? (P); **¿de dónde eres?** where are you (*fam. s.*) from? (P); **¿de dónde es usted?** where are you (*form. s.*) from? (P)

**doña** *f. title of respect used with a woman's first name*

**dorado/a** golden

**dormir (ue, u)** to sleep (4); **dormir la siesta** to take a nap (4); **dormir lo suficiente** to sleep enough (10); **dormirse** to fall asleep (4)

**dormitorio** bedroom

**dos** two (P); **dos veces** twice (10); **hotel** (*m.*) **de dos estrellas** two-star hotel (18)

**doscientos/as** two hundred (3)

**dosis** *f. inv.* dose

**drama** *m.* drama (13)

**dramático/a** dramatic

**dramaturgo/a** playwright (13)

**drásticamente** drastically

**droga** drug; **traficar (qu) en drogas** to traffic in/deal drugs

**dromedario** dromedary (*camel*)

**dualidad** *f.* duality

**ducha** shower; **habitación** (*f.*) **con/sin ducha** room with/without attached shower (18)

**ducharse** to take a shower (4)

**duda** doubt; **no hay duda** there is no doubt; **sin duda** without a doubt

**dudar** to doubt (12)

**dudoso/a** doubtful

**duende** *m.* ghost; spirit

**dueño/a** owner (6); landlord, landlady (12)

**dulce** *adj.* sweet; **agua dulce** fresh water; **dulces** *n. m. pl.* sweets (6); candy (6)

**dulzura** sweetness

**durante** during (4)

**durar** to last (17)

**durmiente: Bella Durmiente** Sleeping Beauty

**duro/a** hard, firm; **disco duro** hard drive (12)

**DVD** *m.* DVD (12); **lector** (*m.*) **de DVD** DVD player (12)

# E

**e** and (*used instead of* **y** *before words beginning with stressed* **i** *or* **hi,** *except* **hie-**)

**echar** to throw

**ecología** ecology

**ecológico/a** ecological

**economía** economy; *s.* economics (1)

**económico/a** economic

**economizar (c)** to economize (16)

**ecosistema** *m.* ecosystem

**ecoturismo** ecotourism

**ecoturista** *m., f.* ecotourist

**ecuador** *m.* equator

**ecuatoriano/a** *n., adj.* Ecuadorian

**edad** *f.* age; **Edad Media** Middle Ages

**edificio** building (1)

**editor(a)** editor

**educación** *f.* education

**educado/a** educated; polite; **mal educado/a** rude, bad-mannered

**educativo/a** educational

**efectivo** cash (16); **pagar (gu) en efectivo** to pay in cash (16)

**efecto** effect

**eficiencia** efficiency

**eficiente** efficient

**Egipto** Egypt

**egoísta** *m., f.* selfish

**ejecutivo/a** executive

**ejemplar** *m.* issue (*magazine*)

**ejemplo** example; **por ejemplo** for example (11)

**ejercer (z)** to practice (*a profession*)

**ejercicio** exercise (3); **hacer** (*irreg.*) **ejercicio** to exercise, get exercise (4); **hacer ejercicios aeróbicos** to do aerobics (10)

**ejército** army (17)

**él** *sub. pron.* he (1); *obj.* (*of prep.*) him

**el** *def. art. m. s.* the; **el primero de** the first of (*month*) (5)

**elaborar** to elaborate

**elección** *f.* election

**electricidad** *f.* electricity

**electricista** *m., f.* electrician (16)

**eléctrico/a: energía eléctrica** electric energy (14)

**electrónica** *s.* electronics

**electrónico/a** electronic; **agenda electrónica** electronic calendar; **aparato electrónico** electronic device; **correo electrónico** e-mail (12); **mensaje** (*m.*) **electrónico** e-mail message

**electrostático/a** electrostatic

**elefante** *m.* elephant (14)

**elegancia** elegance

**elegante** elegant

**elegir (i, i) (j)** to choose; to elect

**elemento** element

**elevar** to raise, elevate

**eliminar** to eliminate

**ella** *sub. pron.* she (1); *obj.* (*of prep.*) her

**ellos/as** *sub. pron.* they (1); *obj.* (*of prep.*) them

**embajada** embassy

**embajador(a)** ambassador

**embarazada** *n.* pregnant woman

**embargo: sin embargo** however (5), nevertheless

**embotellamiento de tráfico** traffic jam

**embriagado/a** drunk

**emergencia** emergency; **sala de emergencias** emergency room

**emigrante** *m., f.* emigrant

**emigrar** to emigrate

**emisión** *f.* emission; broadcast

**emoción** *f.* emotion (8)

**emocional** emotional

**emocionante** exciting

**empanado/a** breaded

**empapelado/a** (wall)papered

**emparejar** to match

**emperador** emperor

**empezar (ie) (c)** to begin (4); **empezar a** + *inf.* to begin to (*do something*) (4)

**empleado/a** employee

**emplear** to use; to employ

**empleo** employment

**empresa** company, corporation (16), business (16); **administración** (*f.*) **de empresas** business administration (1)

**empresario/a** businessman/woman

**empuje** *m.* push

**en** in (P); on (P); at (P); **en absoluto** at all; **en busca de** in search of; **en cambio** on the other hand, on the contrary; **en casa** at home (1); **en caso de que** *conj.* in case (15); **en cierta medida** in some measure; **en contra** opposed; **en cuanto** *conj.* as soon as (16); **en cuanto a** *prep.* regarding; **en efectivo** in cash (16); **en este momento** right now; **en exceso** to excess, excessively; **en fila** in single file; **en fin** in short; **en punto** exactly (*time*) (P); on the dot (*time*) (P); sharp (*time*) (P); **en realidad** in fact; **en resumen** in short; **en seguida** right away (10); **en vez de** instead of (16)

**enamorado/a (de)** in love (with) (15); **Día** (*m.*) **de los Enamorados** Valentine's Day

**enamorarse (de)** to fall in love (with) (15)

**encabezado/a por** headed by

**encadenado/a** chained

**encalado/a** whitewashed

**encantado/a** enchanted; delighted; nice/pleased to meet you (P)

**encantador(a)** enchanting; delightful

**encantamiento** enchantment

**encantar** to like very much (7), to love (7)

**encañar** to form stalks

**encarar** to confront, face up to

**encargado/a** person in charge

**encargarse (gu) de** to be in charge of

**encender (ie)** to turn on; to light

**encendido/a** lit up

**encerado/a** waxed

**enchufar** to plug in

**encima de** *prep.* on top of (5); in addition to

**encontrar (ue)** to find (8); **encontrarse** to be (10), to feel (10); **encontrarse con** to meet (*someone* [*somewhere*]) (10)

**encuesta** survey

**energía** energy (14); **energía eléctrica (nuclear, solar)** electric (nuclear, solar) energy (14)

**enero** January (5)

**énfasis** *m. inv.* emphasis

**enfático/a** emphatic

**enfermarse** to get sick (8)

**enfermedad** *f.* illness, sickness

**enfermero/a** nurse (10)

**enfermo/a** sick (5); **ponerse** (*irreg.*) **enfermo/a** to get sick

**enfilado/a** in a row

**enfisema** *m.* emphysema

**enfocarse (qu) (en)** to focus (on)

**enfoque** *m.* focus

**enlace** *m.* link

**enlatado/a** canned

**enojado/a** angry

**enojarse (con)** to get angry (at) (8)

**enorme** enormous

**enriquecer (zc)** to enrich

**enrollado/a** rolled up; in a roll

**ensalada** salad (6)

**ensayo** essay

**enseñanza** teaching

**enseñar** to teach (1)

**entender (ie)** to understand (4)

**enterado/a** informed

**enterarse (de)** to find out (17), to learn (about) (17)

**entero/a** entire; whole; **limpiar la casa entera** to clean the whole house (9)

**entonces** then, next; **desde entonces** from then on

**entrada** entrance; ticket

**entrar** to enter

**entre** between (5); among (5)

**entreabierto/a** half-open, ajar

**entregar (gu)** to turn in (11), to hand in (11)

**entremeses** *m. pl.* hors d'œuvres (8)

**entrenamiento** training

**entrenar** to practice (9), to train (9)

**entretejer** to interweave

**entretener** (*like* **tener**) to entertain

**entretenimiento** entertainment

**entrevista** interview (16); **tener** (*irreg.*) **una entrevista** to have an interview (16)

**entrevistador(a)** interviewer (16)

**entrevistar** to interview (16); **entrevistarse** to be interviewed

**envase** *m.* container

**enviar (envío)** to send

**envidia** envy

**envuelto/a** (*p.p. of* **envolver**) wrapped

**eólico/a** *adj.* wind

**epifanía** epiphany

**episodio** episode

**época** era, time (*period*) (11)

**equilibradamente: comer equilibradamente** to eat in a balanced way (10)

**equilibrado/a** balanced

**equilibrar** to balance

**equilibrio** balance
**equipaje** *m.* baggage (7), luggage (7); **facturar el equipaje** to check baggage (7)
**equipo** team; equipment; **equipo estereofónico/fotográfico** stereo/photography equipment (12)
**equivalente** *n. m.* equivalence; *adj.* equivalent
**equivaler** (*like* **valer**) to equal
**equivocarse (qu) (de)** to be wrong (about) (11), to make a mistake (about) (11)
**érase una vez** once upon a time
**eres** you (*fam. s.*) are (P)
**errante** wandering
**error** *m.* mistake, error
**erupción** *f.* eruption (17)
**es** he/she/it is (P); you (*form. s.*) are (P); **¿cómo es usted?** what are you (*form. s.*) like? (P); **¿cuánto es?** how much is it? (3); **es cierto/extraño/imposible/ increíble/ridículo/seguro/terrible/una lástima/urgente que** it's certain, strange/impossible/incredible/ ridiculous/a sure thing/terrible/a shame/urgent that (13); **es de...** it is made of . . . (3); **¡es de última moda!** it's the latest style! (3); **es decir** that is to say; **es (im)probable que** it's (un)likely, (im)probable that (13); **es la...** it's (*time*) (P)
**escabroso/a** rugged
**escala** stop; **hacer** (*irreg.*) **escalas** to make stops (7); **vuelo sin escalas** nonstop flight
**escalar** to climb
**escaleras** *f. pl.* stairs; **escaleras mecánicas** escalator
**escalón** *m.* step
**escalopín** *m.* breaded cutlet
**escándalo** scandal
**escapar** to escape
**escaparate** *m.* store (display) window
**escasez** *f.* (*pl.* **escaseces**) lack (14), shortage (14)
**escaso/a** scarce
**escena** scene
**escenario** stage (13)
**esclavitud** *f.* slavery
**esclavo/a** slave
**escoger (j)** to choose
**esconder(se)** to hide
**escondido/a** hidden
**escopeta** shotgun

**escorpión** *m.* scorpion
**escribir** (*p.p.* **escrito**) to write (2); **escribir en la computadora** to key in (16), to type (16); **máquina de escribir** typewriter
**escrito/a** (*p.p. of* **escribir**) written (11); **informe** (*m.*) **escrito** written report (11)
**escritor(a)** writer (13)
**escritorio** desk (1)
**escritura** writing
**escuchar** to listen (to) (1)
**escudo** shield
**escuela** school (9)
**esculpir** to sculpt (13)
**esculsa** canal lock
**escultor(a)** sculptor (13)
**escultura** sculpture (*general*) (13); (piece of) sculpture (13)
**ese/a** *dem. adj.* that (3); *dem. pron.* that one (3)
**esencial** essential
**esfuerzo** effort
**eslavo/a** *n.* Slav
**esmeralda** emerald
**eso** *dem. pron.* that (3); **eso quiere decir...** that means . . . (10); **por eso** therefore (1)
**esos/as** *dem. adj.* those (3); *dem. pron.* those (*ones*) (3)
**espacial** *adj.* space; **transbordador** (*m.*) **espacial** space shuttle
**espacio** *n.* space; **espacio en blanco** blank space
**espacioso/a** spacious
**espalda** back
**espantoso/a** frightening
**España** Spain
**español** *m.* Spanish (*language*) (1)
**español(a)** *n.* Spaniard; *adj.* Spanish (2); **de habla española** Spanish-speaking; **Real Academia Española** Royal Spanish Academy
**espárragos** *m. pl.* asparagus (6)
**especial** special
**especialidad** *f.* specialty
**especialista** *m., f.* specialist
**especialización** *f.* specialization
**especializado/a en** majoring in
**especializarse (c) (en)** to major (in)
**especie** (*f. s.*) **(en peligro de extinción)** (endangered) species (14)
**específico/a** specific
**espectáculo** spectacle; show
**espectador(a)** spectator
**espera: sala de espera** waiting room (7); **llamada en espera** call-waiting

**esperanza** hope (17), wish (17); **esperanza de vida** life expectancy
**esperar** to wait (for) (6); to expect (6); to hope (12)
**espíritu** *m.* spirit
**espléndido/a** splendid
**esposo/a** husband/wife (2); spouse
**esqueleto** skeleton
**esquí** *m.* skiing; **estación** (*f.*) **de esquí** ski resort
**esquiar (esquío)** to ski (9)
**esquina** (street) corner (14)
**está (muy) nublado** it's (very) cloudy (5), it's (very) overcast (5); **¿cómo está?** how are you (*form. s.*)? (P)
**estable** *adj.* stable
**establecer (zc)** to establish, set up; **establecerse** to settle, establish oneself
**estación** *f.* season (5); **estación de autobúses / del tren** bus/train station (7); **estación de esquí** ski resort; **estación de gasolina** gas station (14); **estación de metro** subway stop (18)
**estacionamiento** parking
**estacionar** to park (11)
**estadía** stay
**estadística** statistic
**estado** state (2); **estado civil** marital status; **estado de ánimo** state of mind; **estado de cuentas** bank statement; **estado libre asociado** commonwealth; **golpe de estado** coup d'etat
**Estados** (*m. pl.*) **Unidos** United States
**estadounidense** *adj. m., f.* U.S. (2)
**estancia** stay (*in a place*) (18)
**estanco** tobacco stand/shop (18)
**estanque** *m.* pond; reservoir
**estante** *m.* bookshelf (4)
**estar** *irreg.* to be (1); **¿cómo esta(s)?** how are you? (P); **estar a cargo (de)** to be in control (of); **estar a dieta** to be on a diet (6); **estar acecho/a** to be lying in wait; to watch, be on the lookout; **estar atrasado/a** to be late (7); **estar bien** to be comfortable (*temperature*) (5); **estar de mal humor** to be in a bad mood; **estar de vacaciones** to be on vacation (7); **estar en manos de** to belong to; **(no) estar de acuerdo** to (dis)agree; **no estar seguro/a (de)** to be (un)sure (of); **(no) estoy de acuerdo** I (don't) agree (2); **sala de estar** living room; sitting room
**estás: ¿cómo estás?** how are you (*fam. s.*) (P)

**estatal** *adj.* state (*pertaining to the government*)

**estatua** statue

**este** *n. m.* east (5)

**este/a** *dem. adj.* this (2); **esta noche** tonight (5); *dem. pron.* this one (3)

**estéreo** stereo

**estereofónico/a: equipo estereofónico** stereo equipment (12)

**estereotipado/a** stereotyped

**estereotipo** stereotype

**estilo** style

**estimado/a** esteemed

**estimulante** *m.* stimulant

**estimular** to stimulate

**esto** *dem. pron.* this (2)

**estofado/a** stewed

**estómago** stomach (10); **dolor** (*m.*) **de estómago** stomachache (10)

**estos/as** *dem. adj.* these (2); *dem. pron.* these (ones) (3)

**estoy: (no) estoy de acuerdo** I (don't) agree (2)

**estrategia** strategy

**estrechar las manos** to shake hands

**estrecho/a** close; tight; narrow

**estrechos** *m. pl.* straits (*geography*)

**estrella** star; **hotel** (*m.*) **de dos (tres) estrellas** two (three) star hotel (18)

**estrés** *m. s.* stress (11)

**estresado/a** stressed

**estresarse** to become stressed

**estricto/a** strict

**estructura** structure

**estudiante** *m., f.* student (1)

**estudiantil** *adj.* student (11), of students (11); **residencia estudiantil** dormitory (1)

**estudiar** to study (1)

**estudio** study

**estudioso/a** studious

**estufa** stove (9); **estufa de leña** wood stove

**estupendo/a** stupendous

**etapa** stage (*period of time*) (15)

**etnia** ethnic group

**étnico/a** ethnic

**euro** monetary unit of many European countries

**europeo/a** *n., adj.* European

**evaluar (evalúo)** to evaluate

**evento** event (17)

**evidencia** evidence

**evidente** evident

**evitar** to avoid (14)

**evolución** *f.* evolution

**exacto/a** exact

**examen** *m.* exam (3), test (3)

**examinar** to examine (10)

**exceder** to exceed

**excelente** excellent

**excepto** except

**exceso** excess; **en exceso** to excess, excessively; **tener** (*irreg.*) **exceso de peso** to be overweight

**exclusivo/a** exclusive

**excursión** *f.* excursion

**excusa** excuse

**exhibición** *f.* exhibition

**exigente** demanding

**exigir (j)** to demand

**exiliarse** to be exiled

**existencia** existence

**existir** to exist

**éxito** success; **tener** (*irreg.*) **éxito** to be successful

**exitoso/a** successful

**éxodo** exodus

**exorcizar (c)** to exorcize

**exótico/a** exotic

**expectativa** expectation

**expendedor(a)** *adj.* dispensing

**experiencia** experience

**experimentar** to experience

**experimento** experiment

**experto** expert

**explicación** *f.* explanation

**explicar (qu)** to explain (7)

**exploración** *f.* exploration

**explorar** to explore

**explosión** *f.* explosion

**explosivo/a** explosive

**explotación** *f.* exploitation; use

**explotado/a** exploited; used

**exportación** *f.* export

**exportador(a)** exporter

**exposición** *f.* show, exhibition

**expresar** to express

**expresión** *f.* expression

**expreso/a** express, exact

**expuesto/a** (*p.p. of* **exponer**) exposed; on display

**expulsar** to expel

**expulsión** *f.* expulsion

**extender (ie)** to extend

**extenso/a** extensive

**exterior** *adj.* outside

**extinción** (*f.*): **especie** (*f. s.*) **en peligro de extinción** endangered species (14)

**extracción** *f.* extraction

**extraer** (*like* **traer**) to extract

**extranjero/a** *n.* foreigner; *adj.* foreign (1); **lenguas** (*f. pl.*) **extranjeras** foreign languages (1)

**extranjero** *n.* abroad, overseas (18); **viajar al/en el extranjero** to travel abroad (18)

**extraño** strange; **es extraño que** it's strange that (13); **¡qué extraño que… !** how strange that . . . ! (13)

**extraordinario/a** extraordinary

**extravagante** extravagant

**extremo/a** extreme

**extroversión** *f.* extroversion

**extrovertido/a** extrovert

**exuberancia** exuberance

**exuberante** exuberant

# F

**fábrica** factory (14)

**fabricación** *f.* making

**fabricar (qu)** to manufacture

**fabuloso/a** fabulous

**fachada** facade

**fácil** easy (5)

**facilidad** *f.* ease; facility; ability

**facilitar** to facilitate

**factible** feasible

**factor** *m.* factor

**factura** bill (16)

**facturar** to check (*baggage*) (7)

**facultad** *f.* department (*in a university*)

**falda** skirt (3)

**fallar** to "crash" (*of computers*) (12)

**falsificado/a** forged

**falso/a** false

**falta** lack (11); absence; **falta de flexibilidad** lack of flexibility (11)

**faltar** to be lacking; to be absent; **faltar (a)** to be absent (from) (8), to not attend (8)

**familia** family (2)

**familiar** *n. m.* relation, member of the family; *adj.* pertaining to a family

**famoso/a** famous

**fantasía** fantasy

**fantástico/a** fantastic

**farmacéutico/a** pharmacist (10)

**farmacia** pharmacy (10)

**farmacología** pharmacology

**faro** lighthouse

**fascinante** fascinating

**fatal** bad; unlucky

**fatiga** fatigue

**favor** *m.* favor; **a favor de** in favor of; with the aid of; **favor de** + *inf.* please (*do something*); **por favor** please (P); **si me hace el favor** if you would do me the favor

**favorecer (zc)** to favor

**favorito/a** favorite

**fax** *m.* fax (12)

**fe** *f.* faith

**febrero** February (5)

**fecha** date (*calendar*) (5); **¿cuál es la fecha de hoy?** what's today's date? (5); **fecha límite** deadline (11)

**felicitaciones** *f. pl. interj.* congratulations (8)

**feliz** (*pl.* **felices**) happy (8); **Feliz Año Nuevo** Happy New Year; **feliz cumpleaños** (*m. pl.*) happy birthday; **Feliz Navidad** (*f.*) Merry Christmas

**femenino/a** feminine

**feminidad** *f.* femininity

**Fénix** *m.* Phoenix

**fenomenal** phenomenal

**fenómeno** phenomenon

**feo/a** ugly (2)

**feria** fair, festival; **rueda de feria** Ferris wheel

**feriado/a: día** (*m.*) **feriado** holiday

**feroz** (*pl.* **feroces**) fierce

**ferrocarril** *m.* railroad

**fértil** fertile

**festejos** *m. pl.* public festivities

**festival** *m.* festival

**festividad** *f.* festivity

**festivo/a: día** (*m.*) **festivo** holiday (8)

**fibra** fiber

**ficción** *f.* fiction; **ciencia ficción** science fiction

**fiebre** *f.* fever (10); **tener** (*irreg.*) **fiebre** to have a fever (10)

**fiel** faithful (2)

**fiesta** party (1); **dar** (*irreg.*)/**hacer** (*irreg.*) **una fiesta** to give/have a party (8); **fiesta de disfraz** costume party; **fiesta de sorpresa** surprise party

**figura** figure

**fijarse (en)** to take note (of), pay attention (to)

**fijo/a** set; fixed; **precio fijo** fixed price (3)

**fila** line, row; **en fila** in single file

**filete** *m.* fillet

**filmar** to film

**filosofía** philosophy (1)

**filtro** filter

**fin** *m.* end; **en fin** in short; **fin de semana** weekend (1); **por fin** at last, finally (4);

**sin fines de lucro** not-for-profit; **sin fines lucrativos** nonprofit

**final** *n. m.* end; *adj.* final; **a finales de** at the end of

**financiamiento** financing

**financiero/a** financial

**finanza** finance

**finca** farm (14)

**fino/a** fine

**fiordo** fjord

**firmar** to sign

**física** *s.* physics (1)

**físico/a** physical

**flaco/a** skinny

**flan** *m.* (baked) custard (6)

**flexibilidad** *f.* flexibility (11); **falta de flexibilidad** lack of flexibility (11)

**flexible** flexible; **ser** (*irreg.*) **flexible** to be flexible (11)

**flor** *f.* flower (7)

**florecer (zc)** to flourish

**florido/a: Pascua Florida** Easter (8)

**flota** fleet

**folklore** *m.* folklore

**folklórico/a** folkloric (13)

**folleto** pamphlet

**fondo** fund; **al fondo** in the background; **fondos** (*m. pl.*) **de apoyo** economic assistance

**fontanero/a** *Sp.* plumber

**forestal** pertaining to forests or forestry

**forma** form; shape; **de todas formas** anyway

**formación** *f.* background

**formar** to form; **formar parte de** to be part of, a member of

**formular** to formulate

**formulario** form (*to fill out*) (18)

**fortaleza** fort

**fósforo** match (*for lighting things*) (18)

**foto(grafía)** photo(graph) (7); photography (13); **sacar (qu) fotos** to take photos (7)

**fotografía** photography (13)

**fotográfico/a** photographic; **equipo fotográfico** photography equipment (12)

**fotógrafo/a** photographer (16)

**frágil** fragile

**fragmento** fragment

**francés** *m.* French (*language*) (1)

**francés, francesa** *n., adj.* French (2)

**franco/a** free, open

**frase** *f.* phrase

**frecuencia** frequency; **con frecuencia** frequently (1)

**frecuente** frequent

**fregar (ie) (gu) los platos** to wash the dishes

**frenar** to brake

**freno** brake (14)

**frente a** facing, opposite

**fresco/a** fresh (6); cool (*weather*); **hace fresco** it's cool (*weather*) (5)

**fresno** ash tree

**frialdad** *f.* coldness

**frigidez** *f.* frigidity

**frigorífico** refrigerator

**frijoles** *m. pl.* beans (6)

**frío** *n.* cold(ness); *adj.* cold; **hace (mucho) frío** it's (very) cold (*weather*) (5); **tener** (*irreg.*) **(mucho) frío** to be (very) cold (5)

**frito/a** fried (6); **patata frita** French fried potato

**frontera** border (*political, geographical*) (18)

**frugalidad** *f.* frugality

**fruncir (z)** to knit (*brows*)

**fruta** fruit (6); **jugo de fruta** fruit juice (6)

**frutal** *adj.* fruit

**fruto seco** nut

**fue sin querer** it was unintentional (11)

**fuego** fire; **fuegos artificiales** fireworks

**fuente** *f.* source

**fuera** *adv.* outside

**fuerte** strong (6); heavy (*meal*) (6)

**fuerza** strength; force

**fulano/a** so-and-so (*person*)

**fumador(a)** smoker

**fumar** to smoke (7); **sección** (*f.*) **de (no) fumar** (non)smoking section (7)

**función** *f.* function

**funcionar** to work (12), to function (12); to run (*machines*) (12)

**fundación** *f.* foundation; **Fundación Alerta contra EL SIDA** AIDS Awareness Foundation

**fundar** to found

**furioso/a** furious, angry (5)

**fusilamiento** shooting, execution; **pelotón** (*m.*) **de fusilamiento** firing squad

**fútbol** *m.* soccer (9); **fútbol americano** football (9)

**futbolista** *m., f.* soccer player

**futuro** *n.* future

**futuro/a** *adj.* future

# G

**gabrielino/a** person from the San Gabriel mission

**gafas** *f. pl.* glasses (10); **llevar gafas** to wear glasses (10)

**gajo** branch (*of a tree*)
**galante** gallant
**galardón** *m.* reward
**galería** gallery
**gallego/a** *n.* Galician
**galleta** cookie (6)
**gallina** hen, chicken
**gallinero** chicken coop
**gallo: misa del gallo** Midnight Mass; **gallo/a** guy, gal (*sl., Chile*)
**gamba** *Sp.* shrimp
**gana** desire, wish; **darle** (*irreg.*) **la gana** to feel like; **tener** (*irreg.*) **ganas de** + *inf.* to feel like (*doing something*) (3)
**ganar** to earn (16); to win (9); **ganarse la vida** to earn a living
**ganga** bargain (3); **¡qué ganga!** what a bargain!
**garaje** *m.* garage (4)
**garantizar (c)** to guarantee
**garawón** *m. traditional drum of Central America*
**garganta** throat (10)
**garífuna** *m. s., pl. ethnic group from Nicaragua*
**garúa** coastal fog
**gas** *m.* gas (12); heat (12)
**gasolina** gasoline (14); **estación** (*f.*) **de gasolina** gas station (14)
**gasolinera** gas station (14)
**gastar** to spend (*money*) (8); to use (*gas*) (14); to expend
**gasto** expense (12)
**gastronómico/a** gastronomic
**gato/a** cat (2)
**gazpacho** *cold, tomato-based soup (Sp.)*
**generación** *f.* generation
**general** general; **por lo general** generally (4)
**generalizar (c)** to generalize
**género** genre
**generoso/a** generous
**génesis** *m. inv.* beginning
**genio/a** genius
**gente** *f. s.* people (13)
**geografía** geography
**geográfico/a** geographic
**geoturismo** geotourism
**gerente** *m., f.* manager (16)
**germánico/a** Germanic
**gerontología** gerontology
**gerundio** *gram.* gerund
**gesto** gesture
**gigante** *adj.* giant
**gimnasio** gymnasium

**gira** tour
**glaciación** *f.* glaciation
**glaciar** *m.* glacier
**globo** balloon
**gobernador(a)** governor
**gobernar (ie)** to govern (17), to rule (17)
**gobierno** government (14)
**golf** *m.* golf (9)
**golpe** (*m.*) **de estado** coup d'etat
**gordo/a** fat (2)
**gorila** *m.* gorilla (14)
**gorra** cap (3)
**gozar (c)** to enjoy
**gozo** joy
**grabadora** (tape) recorder / player (12)
**grabar** to record (12), to tape (12)
**gracias** thank you (P); **Día** (*m.*) **de Acción de Gracias** Thanksgiving; **gracias por** thanks for (8); **muchas gracias** thank you very much (P)
**grado** grade (*in school*) (9), year (*in school*) (9)
**graduado/a** *adj.* graduate
**graduarse (me gradúo) (en)** to graduate (from) (16)
**gráfico** *n.* graph, diagram
**gráfico/a** *adj.* graphic
**gramática** grammar
**gran, grande** big (2), large (2); great (2)
**granada** pomegranate
**grandeza** majesty, grandeur; greatness
**granito** granite
**granja** farm
**grano** pimple
**grasa** fat
**grasoso/a** fatty; greasy
**gratuito/a** free (of charge)
**grave** serious
**Grecia** Greece
**griego/a** *n., adj.* Greek
**gripe** *f.* flu
**gris** gray (3)
**gritar** to shout, yell
**grotesco/a** grotesque
**gruñir** to grunt; to growl
**grupo** group
**guacamole** *m.* avocado dip or side-dish
**guacharaca** *wooden percussion stick*
**guanacaste: punto guanacaste** *national dance of Costa Rica*
**guapo/a** handsome (2); good-looking (2)
**guaraní** *m.* Guarani (*L.A. indigenous language*)
**guardar** to save (*a place*) (7); to keep (12); to save (*documents*) (12); **guardar cama** to stay in bed (10)

**guardia** *m.* guard, guardsman; **de guardia** on-call
**guatemalteco/a** *n., adj.* Guatemalan
**guerra** war (17); **Segunda Guerra Mundial** World War II
**guerrero/a** warrior
**gueto** ghetto
**guía** *f.* guide(book); *m., f.* guide (*person*) (13)
**guiado/a** guided
**guión** *m.* script (13)
**guionista** *m., f.* scriptwriter
**guisante** *m.* green pea
**guitarra** guitar
**guitarrista** *m., f.* guitarist
**gusta: ¿le gusta… ?** do you (*form. s.*) like . . . ? (P); **sí, (no, no) me gusta…** yes, I do (no, I don't) like . . . (P); **¿te gusta… ?** do you (*fam. s.*) like . . . ? (P)
**gustar** to be pleasing (7)
**me gustaría…** I would (really) like (7)
**gusto** like, preference, taste; **mucho gusto** nice / pleased to meet you (P)

# H

**haber** *irreg.* (*inf. of* **hay** there is, there are) have *auxilary with past participle* (12); **hay que** + *inf.* it's necessary to (*do something*) (13)
**habilidad** *f.* ability, skill
**habilidoso/a** skillful, clever
**habitable** habitable
**habitación** *f.* room; **habitación con/sin baño/ducha** room with(out) attached bath/shower (18); **habitación individual/doble** single/double room (*in a hotel*) (18); **servicio de habitación** *Sp.* room service
**habitante** *m., f.* inhabitant
**habitar** to live, reside
**hábito** habit, custom
**hablante** *m. f.* speaker
**hablar** to speak (1); to talk (1); **de habla española** Spanish-speaking; **hablar por teléfono** to talk on the phone (1)
**hacer** *irreg.* (*p.p.* **hecho**) to do (4); to make (4); **hace** + *period of time* + **que** + *present tense* to have been (*doing something*) for (*a period of time*); **hace** + *time* time ago; **hace (muy) buen/mal tiempo** it's (very) good/bad weather (5); **hace fresco** it's cool (*weather*) (5); **hace (mucho) frío/calor** it's (very) cold/hot (weather) (5); **hace (mucho) sol** it's (very) sunny (5); **hace (mucho) viento** it's (very) windy (5); **hacer**

**hacer** (*continued*)

**alpinismo** to mountain climb; **hacer autostop** to hitchhike; **hacer** *camping* to go camping (7); **hacer cola** to stand in line (7); **hacer copia** to copy (12); **hacer ejercicio** to exercise (4), to get exercise; **hacer ejercicios aeróbicos** to do aerobics (10); **hacer escalas/paradas** to make stops (7); **hacer la cama** to make the bed (9); **hacer la(s) maleta(s)** to pack one's suitcase(s) (7); **hacer las cuentas** to pretend; **hacer planes para** + *inf.* to make plans to (*do something*) (9); **hacer preguntas** to ask questions; **hacer un** *picnic* to have a picnic (9); **hacer un viaje** to take a trip (4); **hacer una fiesta** to have/give a party (8); **hacer una pregunta** to ask a question (4); **hacer visitas** to visit; **hacerse** to become; **hacerse daño** to hurt oneself (11); **¿qué tiempo hace hoy?** what's the weather like today? (5); **si me hace el favor** if you would do me the favor

**hacia** toward

**hacienda** farm, ranch; country estate

**hallar** to find

**hambre** *f.* (*but* **el hambre**) hunger; **pasar hambre** to go hungry; **tener** (*irreg.*) **(mucha) hambre** to be (very) hungry (6)

**hamburguesa** hamburger (6)

**harto/a** fed up

**hasta** *adv.* even; *prep.* until (4); **hasta luego** see you later (P); **hasta mañana** see you tomorrow (P); **hasta pronto** see you soon; **hasta que** *conj.* until (16)

**hay: (no) hay** there is (not) (P); there are (not) (P); **hay (mucha) contaminación** there's (lots of) pollution (5); **hay que** + *inf.* it's necessary to (*do something*) (13); **¡hay que cuidarse!** you must take care of yourself!; **no hay de qué** you're welcome (P); **no hay duda** there is no doubt

**hebreo/a** *n.* Hebrew; **Pascua (de los hebreos)** Passover

**hecho** *n.* fact (8); deed; event (8); **de hecho** in fact

**hecho/a** (*p.p. of* **hacer**) made; done; taken

**helado** *n.* ice cream (6)

**helado/a** *adj.* frozen

**hemisferio** hemisphere

**heredar** to inherit

**herido/a** wounded

**hermanastro/a** stepbrother, stepsister

**hermano/a** brother/sister (2); **medio hermano/media hermana** half-brother / half-sister

**hermoso/a** beautiful

**héroe** *m.* hero

**herramienta** tool

**hervir** (**ie, i**) to boil

**hidalgo** nobleman; gentleman

**hidráulico/a** hydraulic

**hidroeléctrico/a** hydroelectric

**hidrógeno** hydrogen

**hielo** ice

**hígado** liver

**higiénico/a** hygienic, sanitary

**hijastro/a** stepson, stepdaughter

**hijo/a** son/daughter (2)

**hijos** *m. pl.* children (2)

**himno** hymn

**hipopótamo** hippopotamus

**hipoteca** mortgage

**hispánico/a** *adj.* Hispanic

**hispano/a** *n., adj.* Hispanic

**hispanoamericano/a** *n., adj.* Hispanic-American

**hispanocanadiense** *n., adj. m., f.* Hispanic-Canadian

**hispanohablante** *adj. m., f.* Spanish-speaking

**historia** story; history (1)

**historiador(a)** historian

**histórico/a** historic

**hockey** *m.* hockey (9)

**hogar** *m.* home; household

**hoja** leaf

**hola** hello (P)

**Holanda** Holland

**holgadamente** comfortably, easily

**hombre** *m.* man (1); **hombre de negocios** businessman (16)

**homeopatía** homeopathy

**homeópato/a** homeopathic

**hondureño/a** *n., adj.* Honduran

**honesto/a** honest

**honor** *n. m.* honor

**honrar** to honor

**hora** hour; time; **¿a qué hora?** at what time? (P); **¿qué hora es?** what time is it? (P)

**horario** schedule (11)

**horneado/a** baked

**horno** oven; **horno de microondas** microwave oven (9)

**horóscopo** horoscope

**horror** *m.* horror

**hospedarse** to stay (as a guest)

**hospicio** hospice

**hospital** *m.* hospital

**hotel** (*m.*) **(de lujo)** (luxury) hotel (18); **hotel de dos (tres) estrellas** two (three) star hotel (18)

**hoy** today (P); **¿cuál es la fecha de hoy?** what's today's date? (5); **hoy (en) día** nowadays, these days

**huayno** *traditional music and dance from Peru*

**huelga** strike (*labor*) (17)

**huella** footprint

**huerto** orchard; garden

**hueso** bone

**huésped(a)** (hotel) guest (18)

**huevo** egg (6); **huevo cocido** hard-boiled egg; **huevo tibio/pasado por agua** poached egg; **huevos revueltos** scrambled eggs

**huir** (**y**) to flee

**humanidad** *f.* humanity; *pl.* humanities (1)

**humanitario/a** humanitarian

**humano/a** *adj.* human; **ser** (*m.*) **humano** human being

**humedad** *f.* humidity

**humilde** humble

**humo** smoke

**humor** *m.* humor; mood; **estar** (*irreg.*) **de mal humor** to be in a bad mood

**huracán** *m.* hurricane

# I

**ibérico/a** *adj.* Iberian

**ida: de ida** one-way (7); **de ida y vuelta** round-trip (7)

**idealista** *adj. m., f.* idealistic

**idéntico/a** identical

**identidad** *f.* identity; **tarjeta de identidad** identification card

**identificación** *f.* ID (16); **tarjeta de identificación** identification card (11)

**identificado/a: objeto volante no identificado (OVNI)** unidentified flying object (UFO)

**identificar** (**qu**) to identify

**idioma** *m.* language

**iglesia** church

**ignorante** ignorant

**igual** equal, same

**igualdad** *f.* equality (17)

**igualmente** likewise (P), same here (P)

**ilegal** illegal

**iluminación** *f.* lighting

**imagen** *f.* image

**imaginación** *f.* imagination

**imaginar(se)** to imagine
**imaginario/a** imaginary
**imán** *m.* magnet
**imitar** to imitate
**impaciente** impatient
**impacto** impact
**impar** uneven, odd (*with numbers*)
**imparcialmente** impartially
**impedir** (*like* **pedir**) to impede, hinder
**imperfecto** *gram.* imperfect (*past tense*)
**imperio** empire
**impermeable** *m.* raincoat (3)
**imponente** imposing; majestic
**importación** *f.* import
**importancia** importance
**importante** important
**importar** to matter, be important; **no me importa un pito** I don't care one bit
**imposible** impossible; **es imposible que** it's impossible that (13)
**imprescindible** essential, indispensable
**impresión** *f.* impression
**impresionante** impressive
**impresora** printer (12)
**imprimir** to print (12)
**improbable** unlikely; **es improbable que** it's improbable, unlikely that (13)
**impuesto** tax
**impulsivo/a** impulsive
**inadecuado/a** inadequate
**inaugurar** to inaugurate
**inca** *n. m., f.* Inca; *adj. m., f.* Incan
**incidente** *m.* incident
**incluir (y)** to include
**inclusive** *adj.* including
**incluso** *adv.* even; including
**incomodar** to make uncomfortable
**inconcebible** inconceivable
**inconfundible** unmistakeable
**inconveniente** *m.* drawback, difficulty
**incorporar** to incorporate
**incorrecto/a** incorrect
**increíble** incredible; **es increíble que** it's incredible that (13)
**incrementar** to increase
**indefinido/a: artículo indefinido** *gram.* indefinite article
**independencia** independence; **Día** (*m.*) **de la Independencia** Independence Day
**independiente** independent
**indicación** *f.* instruction; direction
**indicar (qu)** to indicate
**indicativo** *gram.* indicative
**indiferencia** indifference

**indiferenciado/a** undifferentiated
**indígena** *n. m., f.* indigenous person; *adj. m., f.* indigenous
**indigenista** pertaining to indigenous topics and themes
**indio/a** *n., adj.* Indian
**indirecto/a: complemento indirecto** *gram.* indirect object pronoun
**indiscreto/a** indiscreet
**individual: habitación** (*f.*) **individual** single room (*in a hotel*) (18)
**individuo** *n.* individual
**indoeuropeo/a** *adj.* Indo-European
**industria** industry
**industrializado/a** industrialized
**inequívoco/a** unmistakable, certain
**infancia** infancy (15)
**infantil** *adj.* child, children's
**infección** *f.* infection
**inferior** lower
**infinitivo** *gram.* infinitive
**infinito/a** infinite
**influencia** influence
**influenciado/a** influenced
**influente** influential
**influir (y)** to influence
**infográfico** graph (with information)
**información** *f.* information
**informar** to inform (17); **informarse (de)** to find out (about)
**informática** *s.* computer studies
**informativo/a** informative
**informe** *m.* **(oral/escrito)** (written/oral) report (11)
**infortunio** misfortune
**infraestructura** infrastructure
**ingeniería** engineering
**ingeniero/a** engineer (16)
**ingenioso/a** ingenious, clever
**ingerir (ie, i)** to ingest
**Inglaterra** England
**inglés** *m.* English (*language*) (1)
**inglés, inglesa** *n.* Englishman, Englishwoman; *adj.* English (2)
**ingrediente** *m.* ingredient
**ingreso** income
**iniciar** to begin, initiate
**inicio** beginning
**injusticia** injustice
**inmediato/a** immediate
**inmenso/a** huge, immense
**inmigración** *f.* immigration
**inmigrante** *m., f.* immigrant
**inmigrar(se)** to immigrate
**inmortalizar (c)** to immortalize

**innecesario/a** unnecessary
**innumerable** countless
**inocente** innocent; **Día** (*m.*) **de los Inocentes** April Fool's Day
**inolvidable** unforgettable
**inquietante** worrisome
**inquilino/a** tenant (12), renter (12)
**insano/a** insane; unhealthy
**inscribirse** (*p.p.* **inscrito**) to sign up, register
**inscrito/a** (*p.p. of* **inscribir**) registered
**insistir (en)** + *inf.* to insist (on) (12)
**insolente** insolent
**insomnio** insomnia
**inspector(a)** inspector; **inspector(a) de aduanas** customs inspector
**inspiración** *f.* inspiration
**inspirarse en** to be inspired by
**instalación** *f.* equipment
**institución** *f.* institution
**instituto** institute
**instrumento** instrument
**intacto/a** intact
**integral** *adj.* whole grain
**integrar** to integrate; to form, make up
**integridad** *f.* integrity
**intelectual** intellectual
**inteligente** intelligent (2)
**intención** *f.* intention
**intensivo/a** intensive
**intentar** to try
**interactivo/a** interactive
**interés** *m.* interest (16)
**interesante** interesting
**interesar** to interest; to be interesting (7)
**intergaláctico/a** intergalactic
**interior** *n.* interior; *adj.* inside, inner; interior; **ropa interior** underwear (3)
**internacional** international; **Día** (*m.*) **Internacional de los Trabajadores** International Labor Day
**internarse (en)** to check into (*a hospital*) (10)
**Internet** *m.* Internet
**interno/a** internal
**interplanetario/a** interplanetary
**interpretación** *f.* interpretation
**interpretar** to interpret; to perform
**intérprete** *m., f.* interpreter
**interrogativo/a** *gram.* interrogative
**interrumpir** to interrupt
**intervención** *f.* intervention
**íntimamente** intimately
**intranquilidad** *f.* uneasiness, restlessness
**introducción** *f.* introduction
**introducir** *irreg.* to introduce

**intromisión** *f.* intrusion
**introversión** *f.* introversion
**introvertido/a** introverted
**inútilmente** uselessly
**invadir** to invade
**invasión** *f.* invasion
**invención** *f.* invention
**inventar** to invent
**investigación** *f.* investigation
**investigar (gu)** to investigate
**invierno** winter (5)
**invitación** *f.* invitation
**invitado/a** guest (8)
**invitar** to invite (6)
**involucrado/a** involved
**inyección** (*f.*): **ponerle** (*irreg.*) **una inyección** to give (someone) a shot, injection (10)
*iPod* *m.* iPod (12)
**ir** *irreg.* to go (3); **ir a** + *inf.* to be going to (*do something*) (3); **ir a una discoteca / un bar / un concierto** to go to a disco/bar/concert (9); **ir a ver una película** to go to see a movie (9); **ir al cine** to go to the movies (9); **ir al teatro** to go to the theater (9); **ir de compras** to go shopping (3); **ir de vacaciones** to go on vacation (7); **ir en autobús/avión/barco/tren** to go/travel by bus/plane/boat, ship/train (7); **irse** to leave
**Irlanda** Ireland
**irónico/a** ironic
**irresponsable** irresponsible
**irritación** *f.* irritation
**isla** island (5)
**Islandia** Iceland
**isleta** isle
**istmo** isthmus
**Italia** Italy
**italiano** Italian (*language*) (1)
**italiano/a** *n., adj.* Italian
**itólele** *m. one of three batá drums*
**iyá** *m. one of three batá drums*
**izquierda** *n.* left-hand side; **a la izquierda (de)** to the left (of) (5)
**izquierdo/a** *adj.* left (*direction*); **levantarse con el pie izquierdo** to get up on the wrong side of the bed (11)

## J

**jabón** *m.* soap (18)
**jalón** (*m.*): **de un jalón** all at once
**jamás** never (6), not ever
**jamón** *m.* ham (6)
**Japón** *m.* Japan

**japonés** *m.* Japanese (*language*)
**japonés, japonesa** *n., adj.* Japanese
**jarabe** *m.* (cough) syrup (10)
**jardín** *m.* yard (4)
**jarrita** jar
*jeans* *m. pl.* jeans (3)
**jefe/a** boss (12)
**jerez** *m.* (*pl.* **jereces**) sherry
**jeroglífico/a** *adj.* hieroglyphic
**jipijapa** Panama hat, straw hat
**jirafa** giraffe
**joropo** *traditional music and dance from Venezuela*
**joven** *n. m., f.* youth; *adj.* young (2); **de joven** as a youth (9)
**joya** jewel
**joyería** jewelry store
**jubilado/a** retired
**jubilarse** to retire (16)
**judío/a** Jewish person
**juego** game; **Juegos Olímpicos** Olympic Games
**jueves** *m. inv.* Thursday (4)
**jugador(a)** player (9)
**jugar (ue) (gu) (al)** to play (*a game, sport*) (4); **jugar a las cartas** to play cards (9); **jugar al ajedrez** to play chess
**jugo (de fruta)** (fruit) juice (6)
**jugoso/a** juicy
**juguete** *m.* toy
**juicio: perder (ie) el juicio** to go crazy
**julio** July (5)
**jungla** jungle
**junio** June (5)
**juntarse** to get together
**junto a** near, next to; **junto con** along with, together with
**juntos/as** *adj.* together (15)
**justificar (qu)** to justify
**justo/a** fair
**juvenil** *adj.* juvenile
**juventud** *f.* youth (15)
**juzgado** court
**juzgar (gu)** to judge

## K

**kilogramo** kilogram
**kilómetro** kilometer
**kiosco** kiosk

## L

**la** *def. art. f. s.* the (1); *d.o. f. s.* you (*form.*); her, it
**labor** *f.* work
**laborable: día** (*m.*) **laborable** workday

**laboral** *adj.* pertaining to work or labor
**laboratorio** laboratory
**lado** side; **al lado de** *prep.* alongside of (5); beside; next to; **por otro lado** on the other hand; **por un lado** on the one hand
**ladrar** to bark
**lago** lake (14)
**lágrima** tear
**lámpara** lamp (4)
**lana** wool (3); **es de lana** it's made of wool (3); **perro de lanas** poodle
**langosta** lobster (6)
**lanza** spear, lance
**lápiz** *m.* (*pl.* **lápices**) pencil (1)
**largo** (*n.*): **de largo** in length
**largo/a** *adj.* long (2); **a largo plazo** long-term; **a lo largo de** along; throughout; **llamada a larga distancia** long-distance call
**las** *def. art. f. pl.* the; *d.o. f. pl.* you (*form.*); them; **a las...** at . . . (*hour*) (P); **las demás** others (12)
**lástima** shame; **es una lástima que** it's a shame that (13) **¡qué lástima que... !** what a shame that . . . ! (13)
**lastimarse** to injure oneself (11)
**lata: ser** (*irreg.*) **una lata** to be a pain, drag
**latín** *m.* Latin (*language*)
**latino/a** *adj.* Latin
**Latinoamérica** Latin America
**latinoamericano/a** *n., adj.* Latin American
**latinocanadiense** *adj. m., f.* Latin-Canadian
**lavabo** (bathroom) sink (4)
**lavadora** washing machine (9)
**lavandería** laundromat
**lavaplatos** *m. inv.* dishwasher (9)
**lavar** to wash; **lavar (las ventanas, los platos, la ropa)** to wash (the windows, the dishes, the clothes) (9)
**le** *i.o. s.* to/for you (*form.*), him, her, it; **¿le gusta... ?** do you (*form. s.*) like . . . ? (P); **le molesta/sorprende que** it bothers/surprises you (*form. s.*)/him/her that (13)
**lección** *f.* lesson
**leche** *f.* milk (6)
**lecho** bed
**lechuga** lettuce (6)
**lector** (*m.*) **de DVD** DVD player (12)
**lector(a)** reader
**lectura** reading

**leer (y)** to read (2)
**legalizar (c)** to legalize
**legendario/a** legendary
**legislación** *f.* legislation
**lejos de** *prep.* far from (5)
**lempira** *m.* monetary unit of Honduras
**lengua** language (1); tongue; **lenguas extranjeras** foreign languages (1); **sacar (qu) la lengua** to stick out one's tongue (10)
**lenguado** flounder
**lenguaje** *m.* language
**lentamente** slowly
**lentes** (*m. pl.*) **de contacto** contact lenses (10); **llevar lentes de contacto** to wear contact lenses (10)
**leña: estufa de leña** wood stove
**les** *i.o. pl.* to/for you (*form. pl.*); them
**letanía** litany
**letra** letter (*alphabet*); lyrics; **letra cursiva** *s.* italics
**letrero** sign
**levantar** to raise, lift; **levantar pesas** to lift weights; **levantarse** to get up (4); to stand up (4); **levantarse con el pie izquierdo** to get up on the wrong side of the bed (11)
**leve** light, slight
**ley** *f.* law (17)
**leyenda** legend
**liberación** *f.* liberation
**libertad** *f.* liberty (17), freedom (17)
**libertador(a)** liberator
**libra** pound
**libre** free; **al aire libre** outdoors; **estado libre asociado** commonwealth; **ratos** (*m. pl.*) **libres** spare (free) time (9)
**librería** bookstore (1)
**libro** book (1); **libro de texto** textbook (1)
**licencia** license; **licencia de conducir/ manejar** driver's license (14)
**líder** *m.* leader
**liga** league
**ligero/a** light(weight); light (6); not heavy (6)
**limeño/a** person from Lima, Peru
**limitación** *f.* limitation
**limitar** to limit
**límite** *m.* limit; **fecha límite** deadline (11); **límite de velocidad** speed limit (14)
**limón** *m.* lemon
**limonada** lemonade
**limpiaparabrisas** *m. inv.* windshield wiper

**limpiar la casa (entera)** to clean the (whole) house (9)
**limpio/a** clean (5)
**lindo/a** pretty, lovely
**línea** line; **patinar en línea** to rollerblade (9)
**lingüístico/a** linguistic
**lío de tráfico** traffic jam
**líquido** *n.* liquid
**lírico/a** lyrical
**lista** list; **lista de bodas** bride's registry
**listo/a** smart (2); clever (2); ready
**literario/a** literary
**literatura** literature (1)
**llamada** (telephone) call; **llamada a larga distancia** long-distance call; **llamada en espera** call-waiting
**llamar** to call (6); **¿cómo se llama usted?** what is your (*form. s.*) name? (P); **¿cómo te llamas?** what is your (*fam. s.*) name? (P); **llamarse** to be called (4); **me llamo…** my name is . . . (P)
**llanero/a** pertaining to the plains
**llanta** tire (14); **llanta de recambio** spare tire; **llanta desinflada** flat tire (14)
**llanura** *n.* plain
**llave** *f.* key (11)
**llegada** arrival (7)
**llegar (gu)** to arrive (6); **llegar a ser** to become; **llegar a tiempo** to arrive on time
**llenar** to fill (up) (14); **llenar la solicitud** to fill out the application (16)
**lleno/a** full
**llevar** to wear (3); to carry (3); to take (3); to lead; **llevar gafas/lentes de contacto** to wear glasses/contact lenses (10); **llevar puesto/a** to have on; **llevar una vida sana/tranquila** to lead a healthy/calm life (10); **llevarse bien/mal (con)** to get along well/poorly (with) (15)
**llorar** to cry (8)
**llover (ue)** to rain (5)
**llueve** it's raining (5)
**lluvia** rain
**lluvioso/a** rainy
**lo** *d.o. m. s.* you (*form.*); him, it; **lo bueno / lo malo** the good/bad thing, news (10); **lo contrario** the opposite; **lo mismo** the same thing; **lo que** what (4), that which; **¡lo siento (mucho)!** pardon me! (11), I'm (very) sorry! (11); **lo suficiente** enough (10)
**lobo** wolf

**local** *n. m.* stall (market); *adj.* local
**localidad** *f.* ticket (*to a movie, play*)
**localización** *f.* location
**localizar (c)** to locate
**loco/a** crazy (5)
**locura** madness, craziness
**lógico/a** logical
**lograr** to achieve
**loma** hill
**Londres** London
**los** *def. art. m. pl.* the; *d.o. m. pl.* you (*form.*); them; **los años sesenta, ochenta, …** the sixties, eighties, . . . ; **los demás** others (12); **los lunes, martes…** on Mondays, Tuesdays, . . . (4)
**lotería** lottery
**loza** porcelain
**lubricar (qu)** to lubricate
**lucha** struggle; fight
**luchar** to fight; to struggle
**lucrativo/a: sin fines lucrativos** nonprofit
**lucro: sin fines de lucro** not-for-profit
**lúdico/a** entertaining
**luego** *adv.* then (4); afterwards (4); **hasta luego** see you later (P)
**lugar** *m.* place (1); **ningún lugar** nowhere; **tener** (*irreg.*) **lugar** to take place
**lujo** luxury (12); **hotel** (*m.*) **de lujo** luxury hotel (18)
**lujoso/a** luxurious
**luna** moon; **luna de miel** honeymoon (15)
**lunar** (*m.*)**: de lunares** polka-dotted
**lunes** *m. inv.* Monday (4); **los lunes** on Mondays (4)
**lustroso/a** shiny
**Luxemburgo** Luxembourg
**luz** *f.* (*pl.* **luces**) light (11); electricity (11)

# M

**machista** *adj. m., f.* male; chauvinistic
**madera** wood
**madrastra** stepmother
**madre** *f.* mother (2)
**madrileño/a: callos** (*m. pl.*) **a la madrileña** tripe Madrid–style
**madrugada** dawn
**madurez** *f.* maturity (15)
**maduro/a** mature
**maestro/a** school teacher (16); **obra maestra** masterpiece (13)
**magia** magic
**mágico/a** magic
**magnético/a** magnetic

**magnífico/a** magnificent

**mago** wizard; **Día** (*m.*) **de los Reyes Magos** Day of the Magi (Three Kings)

**maíz** *m.* (*pl.* **maíces**) corn

**majestuoso/a** majestic

**mal** *n. m.* evil; illness, sickness; *adv.* badly; poorly (1); **caerle** (*irreg.*) **mal a alguien** to make a bad impression on someone (16); **llevarse mal (con)** to get along poorly (with) (15); **mal educado/a** rude, bad-mannered; **pasarlo mal** to have a bad time (8); **salir** (*irreg.*) **mal** to turn/come out badly

**mal, malo/a** *adj.* bad (2); **hace mal tiempo** it's bad weather (5); **lo malo** the bad thing, news (10); **¡qué mala suerte!** what bad luck! (11); **sacar (qu) malas notas** to get bad grades (11)

**maldito/a** accursed, awful

**maleta** suitcase (7); **hacer** (*irreg.*) **la(s) maleta(s)** to pack one's suitcase(s) (7)

**maletero** porter (7)

**maletín** *m.* briefcase

**malvado/a** wicked

**mamá** mother (2), mom (2)

**mamífero** mammal

**manchego: queso manchego** hard, white cheese (*from La Mancha, Spain*)

**mandar** to send (7); to order (*someone to do something*) (12)

**mandato** command

**manejar** to drive (12); to operate (*a machine*) (12); to manage; **licencia de manejar** driver's license (14)

**manera** way, manner; **de manera que** *conj.* so that, in such a way that; **de todas maneras** by all means; whatever happens

**manifestación** *f.* manifestation; demonstration

**manjar** *m.* delicacy

**mano** *f.* hand (11); **darse** (*irreg.*) **la mano** to shake hands; **dedo de la mano** finger (11); **estar** (*irreg.*) **en manos de** to belong to; **¡manos a la obra!** let's get to work!

**manta** blanket (18)

**mantener** (*like* **tener**) to maintain; to keep; **mantener la paz** to maintain, keep the peace (17); **mantenerse en contacto** to keep/stay in touch

**mantequilla** butter (6)

**manzana** apple (6)

**manzanilla** chamomile

**mañana** *n.* morning; *adv.* tomorrow (P); (*an hour*) **de la mañana** in the morning (P); **hasta mañana** see you tomorrow (P); **pasado mañana** day after tomorrow (4); **por la mañana** in the morning (1)

**mapa** *m.* map

**mapuche** *m.* Araucan (*indigenous language of S.A.*)

**máquina** machine; **máquina de escribir** typewriter

**mar** *m.* sea (7)

**maratón** *m.* marathon

**maravilla** wonder, marvel

**maravilloso/a** marvelous, wondrous

**marca** brand name

**marcar (qu)** to strike (*clock*); to mark

**mareado/a** dizzy (10); nauseated (10)

**mareo** dizziness

**marido** husband (15)

**marihuana** marijuana

**marinado/a** marinated

**marino/a** *adj.* sea

**mariposa** butterfly

**mariscos** *m. pl.* seafood; shellfish (6)

**marítimo/a** maritime; sea, marine

**Marruecos** *m.* Morocco

**martes** *m. inv.* Tuesday (4); **los martes** on Tuesdays (4)

**marzo** March (5)

**más** more (1); **cada vez más** increasingly; **más allá** further, farther; **más allá de** beyond, farther than; **más... que** more . . . than (5)

**masa** dough

**máscara** mask

**mascota** pet (2)

**masculino/a** masculine

**masoquista** *n. m., f.* masochist

**matar** to kill

**matemáticas** *f. pl.* mathematics (1)

**materia** (school) subject (1)

**material** *m.* material (3)

**materialista** *m., f.* materialistic

**matrícula** tuition (1)

**matrimonio** marriage (15); married couple (15); **contraer** (*like* **traer**) **matrimonio** to get married

**máximo/a** maximum

**maya** *n., adj. m., f.* Mayan

**mayo** May (5); **Cinco de Mayo** *Mexican awareness celebration*

**mayor** older (5); oldest; greater; greatest; **la mayor parte** most

**mayoría** majority

**me** *d.o.* me; *i.o.* to/for me; *refl. pron.* myself; **me gustaría...** I would (really) like . . . (7); **me llamo...** my name is . . . (P); **me molesta/sorprende que** it bothers/surprises me that (13); **sí, (no, no) me gusta(n)...** yes, I do (no, I don't) like . . . (P)

**mecánico/a** *n.* mechanic (14); *adj.* mechanical; **escaleras** (*f. pl.*) **mecánicas** escalator

**mecanización** *f.* mechanization

**media: media pensión** *f.* room with breakfast and one other meal (18); **y media** half-past/30 minutes past (*the hour*) (P)

**mediano/a** medium; average

**medianoche** *f.* midnight (8)

**mediante** *prep.* by means of, through

**medias** *f. pl.* stockings (3)

**medicina** medicine (10)

**médico/a** *n.* (medical) doctor (2); *adj.* medical; **atención** (*f.*) **médica** healthcare

**medida** measure; **en cierta medida** in some measure

**medio** *n.* medium; means; **medio ambiente** environment (*nature*) (14); **medio de comunicación** means of communication (17); **medios de comunicación** media; **por medio de** by means of

**medio/a** *adj.* half; middle; average; **Edad** (*f.*) **Media** Middle Ages; **media hermana** half-sister; **media pensión** *f.* room with breakfast and one other meal (18); **medio hermano** half-brother; **Oriente** (*m.*) **Medio** Middle East

**medioambiental** environmental

**mediodía** *m.* noon

**mediterráneo/a** *adj.* Mediterranean

**mejor** better (5); best (5)

**mejorar** to improve

**membrana** membrane

**memoria** memory (12)

**mencionar** to mention

**menor** *m.* minor; *adj.* younger (5); youngest; less; least

**menos** less; least; minus; **a menos que** *conj.* unless (15); **menos cuarto (quince)** a quarter (fifteen minutes) to (*the hour*) (P); **menos... que** less . . . than (5); **por lo menos** at least (8)

**mensaje** *m.* message; **mensaje electrónico** e-mail message

**mensual** monthly

**mensualidad** *f.* monthly installment

**menta** mint

**-mente** *suffix* -ly (11)
**mentira** lie (12)
**menú** *m.* menu (6)
**menudo: a menudo** often
**mercadeo** marketing
**mercado** market(place) (3)
**merecer (zc)** to deserve
**merengue** *m. traditional music and dance from the Dominican Republic*
**merienda** snack
**mes** *m.* month (5)
**mesa** table (1); **poner** (*irreg.*) **la mesa** to set the table (9); **quitar la mesa** to clear the table (9); **uva de mesa** table grape
**meseta** plateau (*geography*)
**mesita** end table (4)
**mesón** *m.* tavern
**mestizo/a** mixed-race person
**meta** goal
**metáfora** metaphor
**metereólogo/a** meteorologist
**método** method
**metro** subway; meter; **estación** (*f.*) **de metro** subway stop (18)
**metrópoli** *f.* metropolis; capital city
**mexicano/a** *n., adj.* Mexican (2)
**México** Mexico
**mexicoamericano/a** *n., adj.* Mexican American
**mezcla** mixture
**mezclar** to mix
**mí** *obj.* (*of prep.*) me (5)
**mi(s)** *poss. adj.* my (2)
**microondas** (*f. pl.*): **horno de microondas** microwave oven (9)
**miedo** fear; **tener** (*irreg.*) **miedo (de)** to be afraid (of) (3)
**miel** *f.* honey; **luna de miel** honeymoon (15)
**miembro** member
**mientras** while (9); **mientras que** *conj.* while
**miércoles** *m. inv.* Wednesday (4)
**migrante** *adj.* migrant
**mil** *m.* thousand, one thousand (3); **dos mil** two thousand (3); **mil millón** (*m.*) billion
**milagro** miracle
**milanesa** cutlet
**milenio** millennium
**miligramo** milligram
**militar: servicio militar** military service (17)
**milla** mile

**millón** *m.* million, **un millón (de)** million (3); **dos millones** two million (3); **mil millón** billion
**millonario/a** millionaire
**mineral: agua** (*f.* [*but* **el agua**]) **mineral** mineral water (6)
**minería** mining
**minero/a** miner
**minidiálogo** minidialogue
**minidrama** *m.* minidrama
**minifalda** miniskirt
**mínimo/a** minimum
**ministerio** ministry
**ministro/a: primer(a) ministro/a** prime minister
**minoría** minority
**minuto** minute
**mío/a(s)** *poss. adj.* my; *poss. pron.* (of) mine
**mirar** to look at (2), to watch (2); **mirar la televisión** to watch television (2)
**misa** mass; **misa del gallo** Midnight Mass; **oficiar una misa** to celebrate a mass
**misión** *f.* mission
**mismo** *adv.* same (10); **ahora mismo** right now; at once
**mismo/a** *adj.* same; self; **lo mismo** the same thing
**misterioso/a** mysterious
**mitad** *f.* half
**mito** myth
**mitología** mythology
**mixteca** *m.* Mixtec (*indigenous language*)
**mixteca** *n., adj. m., f.* Mixtec
**mochila** backpack (1)
**moda** fashion; style; **de moda** in style; **¡es de última moda!** it's the latest style! (3)
**modelo** model
**módem** *m.* modem (12)
**moderación** *f.* moderation
**moderado/a** moderate
**modernismo** modernism
**moderno/a** modern (13)
**modificación** *f.* modification
**modificar (qu)** to modify
**modismo** idiom
**modo** way, manner; mode; *gram.* mood; **de modo** in such a way; **de todos modos** anyway; **modo (de transporte)** means (of transportation) (7)
**molestar** to bother, annoy; **me (te, le...) molesta que** it bothers me (you, him . . .) that (13)

**molestia** bother, annoyance
**molido/a** *adj.* ground (up)
**molino: rueda de molino** treadmill (10)
**momento** moment; **en este momento** right now
**monarca** *m., f.* monarch
**monarquía** monarchy
**monasterio** monastery
**moneda** currency; coin
**monoparental** *adj.* single-parent
**monopatín** *m..* skateboard (12)
**monstruo** monster
**montaña** mountain (7); **bicicleta de montaña** mountain bike (12); **montaña rusa** roller coaster
**montañismo en bicicleta** mountain biking
**montar** to set up; to ride; **montar a caballo** to ride a horse (9); **montar en bicicleta** to ride a bicycle
**montón** (*m.*): **un montón** a bunch
**monumento** monument
**morado/a** purple (3)
**moralidad** *f.* morality
**morcilla** blood sausage
**moreno/a** brunet(te) (2)
**morirse (ue, u)** (*p.p.* **muerto**) to die (8)
**moro/a** *n.* Moor; *adj.* Moorish
**mostaza** mustard
**mostrar (ue)** to show (7)
**motivo** reason, motive; motif
**moto(cicleta)** *f.* motorcycle (12); moped (12)
**motor** *m.* motor, engine
**movimiento** movement
**mozo** bellhop (18); **mozo de campo y plaza** farmhand
**muchacho/a** boy, girl (4)
**muchísimo** *adv.* an awful lot (7)
**mucho** *adv.* a lot, much (1); **¡lo siento mucho!** I'm very sorry!
**mucho/a** *adj.* a lot (of) (2); *pl.* many (2); **muchas gracias** thank you very much (P); **mucho gusto** pleased to meet you (P)
**mucoso/a** *adj.* mucous
**mudanza** *n.* move; moving
**mudarse** to move (*residence*) (16)
**muebles** *m. pl.* furniture (4); **sacudir los muebles** to dust the furniture (9)
**muela** tooth (10); molar (10), **sacar (qu) una muela** to extract a tooth (10); **tener** (*irreg.*) **dolor de muela** toothache (10)
**muerte** *f.* death (15)
**muerto/a** (*p.p. of* **morir**) dead; **muerto/a de risa** dying of laughter

**mujer** *f.* woman (1); wife (15); **mujer de negocios** businesswoman (16); **mujer soldado** female soldier (16)

**mula** mule

**mulato/a** mulatto

**multa** *n.* fine

**multimillonario/a** multimillionaire; billionaire

**multinacional** *f.* multinational company

**mundial** *adj.* world; **Copa Mundial** World Cup; **Segunda Guerra Mundial** World War II

**mundo** *n.* world (7)

**muralismo** muralism

**murciélago** bat

**murmurar** to murmur, whisper

**muro** wall

**músculo** muscle

**museo** museum; **visitar un museo** to visit a museum (9)

**música** music (13)

**músico/a** musician (13)

**musulmán, musulmana** *adj.* Moslem

**muy** very (1); **muy bien** fine (P), very well (P); **muy buenas** good afternoon/evening (P)

# N

**nacer (zc)** to be born (15)

**nacido/a** born; **recién nacido/a** newborn

**nacimiento** birth (15)

**nación** *f.* nation; **Naciones** (*f. pl.*) **Unidas** United Nations

**nacional** national

**nacionalidad** *f.* nationality (18)

**nada** nothing (6), not anything (6); **de nada** you're welcome (P)

**nadar** to swim (7)

**nadie** no one (6), nobody (6), not anybody (6)

**náhuatl** *m. indigenous language of Central America*

**naranja** *n.* orange (6)

**nariz** *f.* nose (10); *pl.* **narices** nostrils

**narración** *f.* narration

**narrador(a)** narrator

**narrar** to narrate

**natación** *f.* swimming (9)

**natal** *adj.* native

**natalidad** *f.* birth

**nativo/a** *n.* native

**natural: recursos** (*m. pl.*) **naturales** natural resources (14)

**naturaleza** nature (14)

**náuseas** *f. pl.* nausea

**navegación** *f.* navigation; sailing

**navegar (gu)** to sail; to navigate; **navegar la Red** to surf the Net (12)

**Navidad** *f.* Christmas (8); **Feliz Navidad** Merry Christmas

**navideño/a** *adj.* Christmas; **tarjeta navideña** Christmas card

**necesario/a** necessary (2)

**necesidad** *f.* necessity

**necesitar** to need (1)

**negación** *f.* negation

**negar (ie) (gu)** to deny (13); **negarse a +** *inf.* to refuse to (*do something*)

**negativa** *n. gram.* negative

**negativo/a** *adj.* negative

**negocio** business; **hombre** (*m.*)/**mujer** (*f.*) **de negocios** businessperson (16)

**negro/a** *n.* black (person); *adj.* black (3)

**neoyorquino/a** *adj.* pertaining to New York

**nervio: ataque** (*m.*) **de nervios** nervous breakdown

**nervioso/a** nervous (5)

**neutro/a** neutral

**nevado/a** snow-covered

**nevar (ie)** to snow (5)

**nevera** refrigerator

**ni** neither; nor; not even; **ni... ni...** neither . . . nor . . .; **ni siquiera** not even

**nicaragüense** *n., adj. m., f.* Nicaraguan

**nido** nest

**nieto/a** grandson/granddaughter (2)

**nietos** *m. pl.* grandchildren (2)

**nieva** it's snowing (5)

**nieve** *f.* snow

**ningún, ninguno/a** no (6), none (6), not any (6); **ningún lugar** nowhere

**niñero/a** baby-sitter (9)

**niñez** *f.* (*pl.* **niñeces**) childhood (9)

**niño/a** small child; boy/girl; **de niño/a** as a child (9)

**nitrógeno** nitrogen

**nivel** *m.* level (14)

**no** no (P); not; **¿no?** right?, don't they (you, *and so on*) (3); **no estoy de acuerdo** I don't agree (2); **no hay** there is not/are not (P); **no hay de qué** you're welcome (P); **no hay duda** there is no doubt; **no, no me gusta(n)...** no, I don't like . . . (P); **no tener** (*irreg.*) **razón** to be wrong (3); **ya no** no longer

**noche** *f.* night; **buenas noches** good evening (P); good night (P); **de noche** at night; (*an hour*) **de la noche** in the evening (P); at night (P); **esta noche** tonight (5); **Noche Vieja** New Year's Eve (8); **por la noche** in the evening (1); at night (1)

**Nochebuena** Christmas Eve (8)

**nombrar** to name

**nombre** *m.* name

**nominación** *f.* nomination

**nominado/a** nominated

**nominal: cláusula nominal** *gram.* noun clause

**noreste** *m.* northeast

**noria** Ferris wheel

**norma** norm; standard

**normalidad** *f.* normality

**norte** *n., adj. m.* north (5)

**Norteamérica** North America

**norteamericano/a** *n., adj.* North American

**nos** *d.o. pron.* us; *i.o. pron.* to/for us; *refl. pron.* ourselves; **nos vemos** see you around (P)

**nosotros/as** *sub. pron.* we (1); *obj.* (*of prep.*) us

**nota** grade (11); note

**notar** to notice, note

**noticia** piece of news (8); *pl.* news (17)

**noticiero** newscast (17)

**novecientos/as** nine hundred (3)

**novedades** *f. pl.* news

**novela** novel

**novelista** *m., f.* novelist

**noveno/a** ninth (13)

**noventa** ninety (2)

**noviazgo** engagement (15)

**noviembre** *m.* November (5)

**novio/a** boyfriend/girlfriend (5); fiancé(e) (15); groom/bride (15); **vestido de novia** wedding gown

**nublado/a** cloudy; **está (muy) nublado** it's (very) cloudy (5)

**nuclear: energía nuclear** nuclear energy (14)

**nudo** knot

**nuera** daughter-in-law

**nuestro/a(s)** *poss. adj.* our (2); *poss. pron.* ours, of ours

**nueve** nine (P)

**nuevo/a** new (2); **Día** (*m.*) **del Año Nuevo** New Year's Day; **Feliz Año Nuevo** Happy New Year

**numérico/a** numerical

**número** number (2)

**numeroso/a** numerous

**nunca** never (2), not ever; **casi nunca** almost never (2)

**nutrición** *f.* nutrition

# O

**o** or (P)

**ó** or (*between two numbers* [*digits*])

**obedecer (zc)** to obey (14)

**obelisco** obelisk

**obesidad** *f.* obesity

**objetivo** objective

**objeto** object; **objeto volante no identificado (OVNI)** unidentified flying object (UFO)

**obligación** *f.* obligation

**obligatorio/a** compulsory

**obra (de arte)** work (of art) (13); **¡manos a la obra!** let's get to work!; **obra maestra** masterpiece (13)

**obrero/a** worker (16), laborer (16)

**observación** *f.* observation

**observar** to observe

**obstáculo** obstacle

**obtener** (*like* **tener**) to get (12), to obtain (12)

**obvio/a** obvious

**ocarina** *potato-shaped wind instrument*

**ocasión** *f.* occasion

**ocasionar** to bring about

**occidental** western

**océano** ocean (7); **Océano Atlántico** Atlantic Ocean

**ochenta** eighty (2)

**ocho** eight (P)

**ochocientos/as** eight hundred (3)

**ocio** leisure time

**ocioso/a** leisurely

**octavo/a** eighth (13)

**octubre** *m.* October (5)

**ocular** *adj.* eye, pertaining to the eye

**ocupación** *f.* occupation

**ocupado/a** busy (5)

**ocupar** to occupy

**ocurrir** to occur, happen

**odiar** to hate (7)

**oeste** *m.* west (5)

**oferta** offer; sale, special

**oficial** *n., adj. m., f.* official

**oficiar una misa** to celebrate a mass

**oficina** office (1); **oficina de correos** post office (18); **oficina de personal** personnel office

**oficio** trade (*profession*) (16)

**ofrecer (zc)** to offer (7)

**oído** inner ear (10)

**oír** *irreg.* to hear (4)

**ojalá (que)** I wish (that) (13), I hope (that) (13)

**ojo** eye (10); **¡ojo!** watch out!; **ojo alerta** eagle eye

**okónkolo** *one of three* **batá** *drums*

**olímpico/a: Juegos** (*m. pl.*) **Olímpicos** Olympic Games

**oliva** olive; **aceite** (*m.*) **de oliva** olive oil

**olla** pot

**olmeca** *n., adj. m., f.* Olmec

**olvidadizo/a** forgetful

**olvidar(se) (de)** to forget (about) (8)

**olvido** forgetfulness; oblivion

**ómnibus** *m.* bus

**once** eleven (P)

**onda** wave; **¿qué onda?** *sl.* what's new?, what's happening?

**ONU** *f.* (**Organización de Naciones Unidas**) U.N. (United Nations)

**opción** *f.* option

**ópera** opera (13)

**operación** *f.* operation

**operar** to operate

**opinar** to think; to have, express an opinion

**oponerse** (*like* **poner**) to oppose

**oportunidad** *f.* opportunity

**oposición** *f.* opposition

**optimista** *adj. m., f.* optimist

**opuesto/a** (*p.p. of* **oponer**) opposite

**oración** *f.* sentence

**oral: informe** (*m.*) **oral** oral report (11)

**órale** *sl. Mex.* come on

**orden** *m.* order (*chronological*); *f.* order, command; **a sus órdenes** at your service

**ordenado/a** neat (5)

**ordenador** *m. Sp.* computer (12); **ordenador portátil** laptop computer

**ordenar** to put in order

**oreja** (outer) ear (10)

**orgánico/a** organic

**organismo** organism

**organización** *f.* organization

**organizar (c)** to organize

**oriental** eastern

**Oriente** (*m.*) **Medio** Middle East

**origen** *m.* origin

**originar(se)** to originate

**originario/a** originating; native

**orilla** shore; bank (*of a river*)

**oriundo/a (de)** native (of)

**oro** gold; **Ricitos de Oro** Goldilocks

**orquesta** orchestra

**ortiga** nettle

**ortográfico/a** *adj.* spelling, orthographic

**os** *d.o. pron.* you (*fam. pl.*); *i.o. pron.* to/for you (*fam. pl.*)

**oscuro/a** dark

**oso** bear; **oso pardo** grizzly bear

**ostra** oyster

**otoño** autumn (5), fall (5)

**otorgar (gu)** to grant

**otro/a** other (2), another (2); **otra vez** again; **por otra parte/otro lado** on the other hand

**OVNI** *m.* (**objeto volante no identificado**) UFO (unidentified flying object)

**oxígeno** oxygen

**oye** *interj.* listen; hey

**oyente** *m., f.* listener

**ozono: capa de ozono** ozone layer

# P

**paciencia** patience

**paciente** *n. m., f.* patient (10); *adj.* patient

**Pacífico/a** Pacific (Ocean, Coast)

**padecer (zc)** to suffer

**padrastro** stepfather

**padre** *m.* father (2)

**padres** *m. pl.* parents (2)

**padrino** godfather

**padrinos** *m. pl.* godparents

**paella** *dish made with rice, shellfish, and often chicken, and flavored with saffron*

**pagar (gu)** to pay (1); **pagar a plazos** to pay in installments (16); **pagar al contado/en efectivo** to pay in cash (16); **pagar con cheque** to pay by check (16)

**página** page

**país** *m.* country (2)

**paisaje** *m.* countryside (14); landscape

**pájaro** bird (2)

**palabra** word (P)

**palacio** palace

**pálido/a** pale

**palma** palm tree

**palo** stick

**palomino** young dove

**palomitas** *f. pl.* popcorn

**pampa** plain (*geography, Arg.*)

**pan** *m.* bread (6); **pan tostado** toast (6)

**panameño/a** *n., adj.* Panamanian

**pantalones** *m. pl.* pants (3); **pantalones cortos** shorts

**papá** *m.* father (2), dad (2); **Papá Noel** Santa Claus

**papa** potato (6)

**papel** *m.* paper (1); role (*in a play*) (13); **papel para cartas** stationery (18)

**papelería** stationery store (18)

**paquete** *m.* package (18)

**par** *m.* pair (3)

**para** *prep.* (intended) for (2); in order to (2); **para** + *inf.* in order to (*do something*); **para que** *conj.* so that (15)

**parabrisas** *m. inv.* windshield (14)

**paracaidismo** skydiving

**parada** stop; **hacer** (*irreg.*) **paradas** to make stops (7); **parada de autobús** bus stop (18)

**paraguas** *m. inv.* umbrella

**paraguayo/a** *n., adj.* Paraguayan

**parar** to stop (14)

**parcial: de tiempo parcial** part time (11)

**pardo/a** brown; **oso pardo** grizzly bear

**parecer (zc)** to seem (13)

**parecido/a** similar

**pared** *f.* wall (4); **pintar las paredes** to paint the walls (9)

**pareja** (married) couple (15); partner (15)

**paréntesis** *m. inv.* parentheses

**pariente** *m., f.* relative (2)

**parlamentario/a** parliamentary

**párpado** eyelid

**parque** *m.* park (5); **parque de atracciones** amusement park

**párrafo** paragraph

**parrandero/a** party-loving

**parroquiano/a** client

**parte** *f.* part; **la mayor parte** most; **formar parte de** to be part of, a member of; **por otra parte** on the other hand; **por parte de** by; **por todas partes** everywhere (11)

**participante** *m., f.* participant

**participar** to participate

**participativo/a** participatory

**participio** *gram.* participle

**partícula** particle

**particular** particular; private

**partida: punto de partida** starting point

**partido** game (9), match (*sports*) (9)

**partir: a partir de** as of; from (*this moment, date on*)

**párvulo** tot

**pasado** *n.* past

**pasado/a** *adj.* last (10); past (10); **el año pasado** last year; **huevo pasado por agua** poached egg; **pasado mañana** day after tomorrow (4)

**pasaje** *m.* passage (7); ticket (7)

**pasajero/a** passenger (7)

**pasaporte** *m.* passport (18)

**pasar** to happen (5); to pass; to spend (*time*) (5); **pasar... años** to be more than . . . years old; **pasar hambre** to go hungry; **pasar la aspiradora** to vacuum (9); **pasar películas** to show movies; **pasar por el control de la seguridad** to go/pass through security (7); **pasar tiempo (con)** to spend time (with) (15); **pasarlo bien/mal** to have a good/bad time (8)

**pasatiempo** pastime (9), hobby (9)

**Pascua (Florida)** Easter (8); **Pascua (de los hebreos)** Passover

**pasear** to take a walk, stroll; to go for a ride; **pasear en bicicleta** to ride a bicycle (9)

**paseo** walk, stroll; **dar** (*irreg.*) **un paseo** to take a walk (9)

**pasión** *f.* passion

**pasional** passionate

**pasivo/a** passive

**paso** step; **de paso** passing through

**pasta dental** toothpaste (18)

**pastel** *m.* cake (6); pie (6); **pastel de cumpleaños** birthday cake (8)

**pastelería** pastry shop (18)

**pastelito** small pastry (18)

**pastilla** pill (10)

**pastor(a)** shepherd; **perro pastor alemán** German Shepherd

**pata** paw

**patata** potato *Sp.* (6); **patata frita** French fried potato (6)

**patinar** to skate (9); **patinar en línea** to rollerblade (9)

**patines** *n. m. pl.* roller skates (12)

**patio** patio (4); yard (4)

**pato** duck

**patria** homeland

**patrón** *m.* pattern

**patrona: santa patrona** patron saint

**pavo** turkey (6); **pavo real** peacock

**paz** *f.* (*pl.* **paces**) peace (17); **mantener** (*like* **tener**) **la paz** to maintain, keep the peace (17); **vivir en paz** to live in peace (17)

**pecho** chest

**pechuga** breast

**pedagogía** pedagogy

**pedir (i, i)** to ask for (4); to order (4); **pedir disculpas** to apologize (11); **pedir prestado/a** to borrow (16)

**pegar (gu)** to hit (9), strike; **pegarse en/con/contra** to hit (*a part of one's body*) (11); to run into (11), to bump against (11)

**peinado** hairdo

**peinarse** to comb one's hair (4)

**pelado/a** peeled

**pelear** to fight (9)

**película** movie (4), film; **ir** (*irreg.*) **a ver una película** to go to see a movie (9); **pasar películas** to show movies

**peligro** danger; jeopardy; **especie** (*f. s.*) **en peligro de extinción** endangered species (14)

**peligroso/a** dangerous

**pelo** hair; **tomarle el pelo** to pull someone's leg

**pelota** ball

**pelotón** (*m.*) **de fusilamiento** firing squad

**peluquero/a** hairstylist (16)

**pena: ¡qué pena!** what a shame!; **valer** (*irreg.*) **la pena** to be worthwhile, worth the trouble

**pendencia** quarrel, fight

**péndulo** pendulum

**pensar (ie)** to intend (4), to plan to (4); **pensar (en)** to think (about) (4)

**pensión** *f.* boardinghouse (18); **media pensión** room with breakfast and one other meal (18); **pensión completa** room and full board (18)

**peor** worse (5); worst

**pepino** cucumber

**pequeño/a** small (2)

**percibido/a** perceived

**percusionista** *m., f.* percussionist

**perder (ie)** to lose (4); to miss (*a function*) (4); **perder el juicio** to go crazy

**pérdida** loss

**perdón** pardon me (P), excuse me (P)

**perezoso/a** lazy (2)

**perfecto/a** perfect

**periódico** newspaper (2)

**periodista** *m., f.* journalist (16)

**periodístico/a** *adj.* journalistic

**perjudicar (qu)** to damage, hurt

**permanente** permanent

**permiso** permission; permit; **con permiso** excuse me (P)

**permitir** to permit (12), to allow (12)

**pero** but (P)

**perpetuo/a** perpetual

**perro** dog (2); **perro de lanas** poodle; **perro pastor alemán** German Shepherd

**persa** *adj. m., f.* Persian
**perseguir** (*like* **seguir**) to pursue
**persona** person (1)
**personaje** *m.* character (*in literature*)
**personal** (*m.*): **dirección** (*f.*) **de personal** personnel office (16); employment office (16); **director(a) de personal** personnel director (16); **oficina de personal** personnel office
**personalidad** *f.* personality
**perspectiva** perspective
**persuadir** to persuade
**pertenecer (zc) a** to belong to
**perturbar** to disturb
**peruano/a** *n., adj.* Peruvian
**pesado/a** boring (9); difficult (9); heavy
**pesar** to weigh; **a pesar de** in spite of
**pesas: levantar pesas** to lift weights
**pesca** fishing
**pescado** fish (*cooked*) (6)
**peseta** former monetary unit of Spain
**pesimista** *adj. m., f.* pessimist
**peso** weight; **tener** (*irreg.*) **exceso de peso** to be overweight
**pesticida** pesticide
**petróleo** petroleum, oil
**petrolero/a** *adj.* petroleum, oil; **buque** (*m.*) **petrolero** oil tanker
**petrolífero/a** *adj.* oil-bearing, oil
**pez** *m.* (*pl.* **peces**) fish (*animal*) (14)
**pianista** *m., f.* pianist
**picnic: hacer** (*irreg.*) **un** *picnic* to have a picnic (9)
**pico** beak
**pie** *m.* foot (11); **a pie** on foot; **dedo del pie** toe (11); **levantarse con el pie izquierdo** to get up on the wrong side of the bed (11); **poner** (*irreg.*) **pie en** to set foot on
**piedra** stone
**piel** *f.* skin
**pierna** leg (11)
**pieza** piece
**píldora** pill
**piloto/a** pilot
**pimienta** pepper
**pingüino** penguin
**pintar (las paredes)** to paint (the walls) (9)
**pintor(a)** painter (13)
**pintoresco/a** picturesque
**pintura** painting (*art form*) (13); (*general*) (13); (*piece of art*) (13); paint
**pirámide** *f.* pyramid
**pirata** *m., f.* pirate
**Pirineos** *m. pl.* Pyrenees

**pisar** to tread on, step on
**piscina** swimming pool (4)
**piso** floor; apartment (*Sp.*); **barrer el piso** to sweep the floor (9); **primer/segundo piso** second/third floor (first/second floor above ground floor) (12)
**pistacho** pistachio
**pitar** to whistle
**pito: no me importa un pito** I don't care one bit
**pizarra** chalkboard (1)
**pizzería** pizza parlor
**placa** license plate
**placer** *m.* pleasure
**plan** *m.* plan; **hacer** (*irreg.*) **planes para** + *inf.* to make plans to (*do something*) (9)
**plancha: a la plancha** grilled
**planchar la ropa** to iron clothing (9)
**planeación** *f.* plan
**planear** to plan
**planeta** *m.* planet
**plano/a** flat
**planta** plant; **planta baja** ground floor (12)
**plantación** *f.* plantation
**plantar cara a** to confront
**plástico** *n.* plastic
**plata** silver
**plátano** banana
**platino** platinum
**plato** dish (*of a meal*) (6); course (*of a meal*) (6); **platos** dishes, plates (4); **fregar (ie) (gu) los platos** to wash the dishes; **lavar los platos** to wash the dishes (9); **plato principal** entrée
**playa** beach (5)
**plaza: plaza de toros** bullring
**plazo** period, term; **a largo plazo** long-term; **pagar (gu) a plazos** to pay in installments (16)
**plegaria** prayer
**plena** *traditional music from Puerto Rico*
**plenamente** fully, completely
**plenera** *tambourine-like instrument*
**plomero/a** plumber (16)
**pluralismo** pluralism
**pluviosidad** *f.* rainfall
**población** *f.* population (14)
**poblado/a** populated
**poblar** to settle
**pobre** *n. m., f.* poor person; *adj.* poor (2)
**pobreza** poverty
**poco** *adv.* little (1); **dentro de poco** in a little while; **poco a poco** little by little; **un poco (de)** a little bit (of)
**poco/a** *adj.* little (3); *pl.* few

**poder** *v. irreg.* to be able to (3), can (3)
**poder** *n. m.* power
**poderoso/a** powerful
**poema** *m.* poem
**poesía** poetry
**poeta** *m., f.* poet (13)
**poético/a** poetic
**policía** *m., f.* police officer (14); *f.* police (force)
**poliomielitis** *f.* poliomyelitis (polio)
**política** *s.* politics (17)
**político/a** *n.* politician (17); *adj.* political; **ciencias** (*f. pl.*) **políticas** political science
**pollo (asado)** (roast) chicken (6)
**pololo/a** *sl.* (*Chile*) boyfriend/girlfriend
**polvo: quitar el polvo** to dust
**poner** *irreg.* (*p.p.* **puesto**) to put (4), to place (4); to turn on (*appliances*) (4); **poner la mesa** to set the table (9); **poner pie en** to set foot on; **ponerle** + *adj.* to make someone (*feel a certain way*); **ponerle una inyección** to give (someone) a shot, injection (10); **ponerse** to put on (*clothing*) (4); **ponerse** + *adj.* to become, get + *adj.* (8); **ponerse a la altura de** to compete on the same level as; **ponerse al día** to get up-to-date; **ponerse de acuerdo** to reach an agreement; **ponerse enfermo/a** to get sick
**popularidad** *f.* popularity
**popularizar (c)** to popularize
**por** *prep.* by; for (4); through; in (1); during (4); along; by way of; **por ciento** percent; **por completo** completely; **por costumbre** customarily; **por Dios** for heaven's sake (11); **por ejemplo** for example (11); **por eso** therefore (1); **por favor** please (P); **por fin** at last, finally (4); **por la mañana/tarde/noche** in/during the morning/afternoon/evening (1); **por la noche** at night (1); **por lo general** generally (4); **por lo menos** at least (8); **por medio de** by means of; **por otra parte/por otro lado** on the other hand; **por parte de** by; **por primera/última vez** for the first/last time (11); **¿por qué?** why? (2); **por si acaso** just in case (11); **¡por supuesto!** of course! (11); **por todas partes** everywhere (11); **por último** finally; **por un lado** on the one hand
**¿por qué?** why? (2)

**porcentaje** *m.* percentage
**pordiosero/a** beggar
**porque** because (2)
**portarse** to behave (8)
**portátil:** portable; **computadora/ ordenador** (*m.*) (*Sp.*) **portátil** laptop computer; **radio portátil** portable radio (12)
**porteño/a** person from Buenos Aires
**portero/a** building manager; doorman (12)
**portugués** *m.* Portuguese (*language*)
**portugués, portuguesa** *n., adj.* Portuguese
**porvenir** *m.* future
**posada** boarding house; inn
**posesión** *f.* possession
**posesivo/a** possessive
**posgraduado/a** *adj.* graduate; postgraduate
**posibilidad** *f.* possibility
**posible** possible (2)
**posición** *f.* position
**postal: tarjeta postal** postcard (7)
**postre** *m.* dessert (6)
**postura** stance
**potencia** power
**potente** strong
**pozo** well
**práctica** practice
**practicar (qu)** to practice (1); to participate (*in a sport*) (9); **practicar deportes** to practice, play sports (10)
**práctico/a** practical
**precedente** *m.* precedent
**precio** price (3); **precio fijo** fixed price (3), set price (3)
**precioso/a** precious
**precipitado/a** hasty
**precipitarse** to rush headlong
**preciso/a** exact, precise
**precolombino/a** pre-Columbian
**predicción** *f.* prediction
**predominar** to dominate
**preferencia** preference
**preferible** preferable
**preferir (ie, i)** to prefer (3)
**pregunta** question; **hacer** (*irreg.*) **preguntas** to ask questions; **hacer una pregunta** to ask a question (4)
**preguntar** to ask (a question) (6)
**prehistórico/a** prehistoric
**prejuicio** prejudice
**prematuro/a** premature
**premio** prize
**prender** to turn on (*lights, appliance*)

**prensa** press (17), news media (17)
**prensado/a** crushed
**preocupación** *f.* worry, concern
**preocupado/a** worried (5)
**preocupante** worrisome
**preocuparse (por)** to worry (about)
**preparación** *f.* preparation
**preparar** to prepare (6)
**preparativo** preparation
**preposición** *f. gram.* preposition
**presa** seizure; **ser** (*irreg.*) **presa de** to be a victim of
**presea** treasure
**presencia** presence
**presentación** *f.* presentation
**presentar** to present, introduce
**presente** *n. m.* present (*time*); *gram.* present tense
**preservación** *f.* preservation
**presidencia** presidency
**presidencial** presidential
**presidente/a** president
**presidio** fort
**presión** *f.* pressure; **sufrir (muchas) presiones** to be under (a lot of) pressure (11)
**prestado/a: pedir (i, i) prestado/a** to borrow (16)
**préstamo** loan (16)
**prestar** to lend (7)
**prestigio** prestige
**prestigioso/a** prestigious
**presupuesto** budget (16)
**pretérito** *gram.* preterite (*past tense*)
**primario/a** primary; **bosque** (*m.*) **primario** old-growth forest
**primavera** spring (5); **vacaciones** (*f. pl.*) **de primavera** spring break
**primer, primero/a** *adj.* first (13); **a primera vista** at first sight (15); **de primera** first-class; **el primero de** the first of (*month*) (5); **por primera vez** for the first time (11); **primer(a) ministro/a** prime minister; **primer piso** second floor (12); **primera clase** first class (7)
**primero** *adv.* first (4)
**primo/a** cousin (2)
**principal** main, principle; **plato principal** entrée
**príncipe** *m.* prince
**principiante** *m., f.* beginner
**principio** beginning; **a principios de** at the beginning of; **al principio de** at the beginning of (16)

**prisa** hurry *n.;* **tener** (*irreg.*) **prisa** to be in a hurry (3)
**prisionero/a** prisoner
**privado/a** private
**privilegio** privilege
**probabilidad** *f.* probability
**probable: es probable que** it's probable, likely that (13)
**probar (ue)** to try; to taste
**problema** *m.* problem
**procesamiento** processing
**proceso** process
**producción** *f.* production
**producir** *irreg.* to produce
**producto** product
**productor(a)** producer
**profesión** *f.* profession (16)
**profesional** professional
**profesor(a)** professor (1); **asistente** (*m., f.*) **del profesor** teaching assistant
**profundidad** *f.* depth
**profundo/a** deep
**programa** *m.* program
**programador(a)** programmer (16)
**progresista** *adj. m., f.* progressive
**progresivo/a** progressive
**progreso** progress
**prohibición** *f.* prohibition
**prohibir (prohíbo)** to forbid (12), to prohibit (12)
**proliferación** *f.* proliferation
**promedio** *n.* average
**prometer** to promise (7)
**promover (ue)** to promote
**pronombre** *m. gram.* pronoun
**pronto** soon; **hasta pronto** see you soon; **tan pronto como** as soon as (16)
**pronunciación** *f.* pronunciation
**pronunciar** to pronounce
**propagar (gu)** to spread (*news*)
**propiedad** *f.* property
**propina** tip (18)
**propio/a** *adj.* own (15)
**proponer** (*like* **poner**) to propose
**proporcionar** to provide
**propósito** purpose
**protagonista** *m., f.* protagonist
**protección** *f.* protection
**proteger (j)** to protect (14)
**protestar** to protest
**proveer** (*like* **ver**) to provide
**provenir** (*like* **venir**) to come from
**proverbio** proverb
**providencia** providence
**provincia** province

**provocar (qu)** to provoke, cause
**proximidad** *f.* closeness
**próximo/a** next (4)
**proyecto** project
**prueba** test (11); quiz (11)
**psicología** psychology
**psicológico/a** psychological
**psiquiatra** *m., f.* psychiatrist
**psíquico/a** *adj.* psychic
**publicación** *f.* publication
**publicar (qu)** to publish
**publicidad** *f.* publicity; advertising
**público** *n.* audience; public
**público/a** *adj.* public (14); **servicios** (*m. pl.*)
  **públicos** public services (14); **transporte**
  (*m.*) **público** public transportation (14)
**pueblo** town; people
**puerta** door (1)
**puerto** port (7)
**puertorriqueño/a** *n., adj.* Puerto Rican
**pues** *conj.* since, because, for; *adv.* then,
  well, all right
**puesto** *n.* job (16); position; place (*in line*)
  (7); **guardar un puesto** to save a place
  (7); **renunciar el puesto** to resign from
  a job, position (16)
**puesto/a** (*p.p. of* **poner**): **llevar puesto/a**
  to have on
**pulgada** inch
**pulido/a** polished
**pulmón** *m.* lung (10); **a todo pulmón** at
  the top of one's lungs
**punto** point; **en punto** exactly (*time*) (P);
  on the dot (*time*) (P); sharp (*time*) (P);
  **punto cardinal** cardinal direction;
  **punto de partida** starting point, point
  of departure; **punto de vista** point of
  view; **punto guanacaste** *national dance*
  *of Costa Rica*
**puntual** punctual
**puro** *n.* cigar
**puro/a** pure (14); clean (14); **aire** (*m.*)
  **puro** clean air (14)

# Q

**que** that (2); which; who (2); **así que**
  therefore, consequently, so; **hasta que**
  *conj.* until (16); **hay que** + *inf.* it's
  necessary to (*do something*) (13); **lo que**
  what (4); that which; **más... que**
  more . . . than (5); **menos... que** less . . .
  than (5); **que aproveche** enjoy your
  meal; **ya que** since
**¿qué?** what? (P); which?; **¿a qué hora?**
  what time? (P); **¿de qué color es?** what

color is it?; **¿por qué?** why?; **¿qué**
  **día es hoy?** what day is today?; **¿qué**
  **hora es?** what time is it? (P); **¿qué tal?**
  how are you doing? (P); **¿qué tiempo**
  **hace hoy?** what's the weather like
  today? (5)
**¡qué** + *adj.***!** how + *adj.***!** (11); **¡qué** +
  *noun***!** what (a) + *noun***!**; **¡qué extraño**
  **qué…!** how strange that . . . ! (13); **¡qué**
  **ganga!** what a bargain!; **¡qué lástima**
  **que…!** what a shame that . . . ! (13);
  **¡qué mala suerte!** what bad luck! (11);
  **¡qué pena!** what a shame!; **¡qué torpe!**
  how clumsy! (11)
**quebranto** misfortune
**quechua** *m.* Quechua (*indigenous language*)
**quedar** to remain (11); to be left (11); to
  be situated; **quedarle bien** to fit well;
  to look good (*on someone*); **quedarse** to
  stay, remain (*in a place*) (5)
**quehacer** *m.* chore; **quehacer doméstico**
  household chore (9)
**quejarse (de)** to complain (about) (8)
**quemar** to burn (up)
**quena** Andean flute
**querella** fight
**querer** *irreg.* to want (3); to love (15); **eso**
  **quiere decir…** that means . . . (10); **fue**
  **sin querer** it was unintentional (11)
**querido/a** dear (5)
**queso** cheese (6); **queso manchego** hard,
  white cheese (*from La Mancha, Spain*)
**quetzal** *m.* monetary unit of Guatemala
**quiché** *m.* Quiché (*indigenous language*
  *from Central America*)
**quien** who, whom
**¿quién(es)?** who? (1), whom? (1); **¿de**
  **quién?** whose? (2)
**quiere: eso quiere decir…** that means (10)
**quieto/a** still (*movement*)
**quijongo** *single-string bow with gourd*
  *resonator*
**química** chemistry (1)
**quince** fifteen (P); **y/menos quince** a
  quarter (fifteen minutes) after / to (*the*
  *hour*) (P)
**quinceañera** *young woman's fifteenth*
  *birthday party*
**quinientos/as** five hundred (3)
**quinto/a** fifth (13)
**quiosco** kiosk (18)
**quitar** to remove; **quitar la mesa** to clear
  the table (9); **quitar el polvo** to dust;
  **quitarse** to take off (*clothing*) (4)
**quizás** perhaps

# R

**rabino/a** rabbi
**racismo** racism
**radical** *m. gram.* stem
**radio** *m.* (**portátil**) (portable) radio
  (*apparatus*) (12); *f.* radio (*medium*) (12)
**radioyente** *m., f.* radio listener; *m., pl.*
  radio audience
**raíz** *f.* (*pl.* **raíces**) root; **a raíz de** as a
  result of; because of
**rama** branch
**rancho** ranch
**rapidez** *f.* speed
**rápido/a** fast (6)
**ráquetbol** *m.* racketball
**raro/a** strange (8)
**rascacielos** *m. inv.* skyscraper (14)
**rato** *n.* while, short time; **ratos** (*m. pl.*)
  **libres** spare (free) time (9)
**ratón** *m.* mouse (12)
**raya: de rayas** striped
**raza** race; **Día** (*m.*) **de la Raza** Columbus
  Day (Hispanic Awareness Day)
**razón** *f.* reason; **no tener** (*irreg.*) **razón** to
  be wrong (3); **tener** (*irreg.*) **razón** to be
  right (3)
**reacción** *f.* reaction
**reaccionar** to react (8)
**real** real; royal; **Camino Real** Royal
  Highway; **pavo real** peacock; **Real**
  **Academia Española** Royal Spanish
  Academy
**realidad** *f.* reality; **en realidad** in fact
**realismo** realism
**realista** *adj. m., f.* realistic
**realizar (c)** to achieve, attain
**rebajas** *f. pl.* sales (3), reductions (3)
**rebelde** *n. m., f.* rebel; *adj.* rebellious
**rebozo** shawl
**recado** message
**recambio: llanta de recambio** spare tire
**recepción** *f.* front desk (18)
**recepcionista** *m., f.* receptionist
**receta** recipe; prescription (10)
**recetar** to prescribe (*medicine*)
**rechazar (c)** to reject
**recibir** to receive (2)
**reciclaje** *m.* recycling
**reciclar** to recycle (14)
**recién** *adv.* newly, recently; **recién**
  **casado/a (con)** newlywed (to) (15);
  **recién nacido/a** newborn
**reciente** recent
**recinto** enclosure, space
**recipiente** *m.* container

**reciprocidad** *f.* reciprocity
**recíproco/a** reciprocal
**recoger (j)** to collect (11); to pick up (11)
**recomendación** *f.* recommendation
**recomendar (ie)** to recommend (7)
**reconocer (zc)** to recognize
**reconocido/a** recognized, well-known
**recopilado/a** compiled
**recordar (ue)** to remember (8)
**recorrer** to travel through
**recorte** *m.* clipping (*newspaper*)
**recreativo/a** recreational
**recreo** recreation
**recto/a** straight
**rector(a)** university president
**recubanizar (c)** to become Cuban again
**recuerdo** souvenir; memory
**recuperación** *f.* recovery, recuperation
**recurso** resource; **recursos naturales** natural resources (14)
**Red** *f.* Net (12); Internet; **navegar (gu) la Red** to surf the Net (12)
**redacción** *f.* editorial staff
**redecorado/a** redecorated
**redondo/a** round
**reducción** *f.* reduction
**reducir** *irreg.* to reduce
**reemplazar (c)** to replace
**reencarnación** *f.* reincarnation
**referencia** reference
**referente (a)** referring, relating (to)
**referirse (ie, i) (a)** to refer (to)
**refinado/a** refined
**reflejar** to reflect
**reflejo** reflection
**reflexivo/a** reflexive
**reformar** to reform
**refresco** soft drink (6)
**refrigerador** *m.* refrigerator (9)
**refugiarse** to take refuge
**refugio** refuge
**regalar** to give (*as a gift*) (7)
**regalo** gift (2), present (2)
**regatear** to haggle (3), to bargain (3)
**régimen** *m.* regime
**región** *f.* region
**registrar** to search (18), to examine (18)
**registro** register; registration
**regla** rule
**regresar** to return (*to a place*) (1); **regresar a casa** to go home (1)
**regulador** (*m.*) **termómetro** thermostat
**regular** so-so (P), OK (P)
**reina** queen (17)
**reino** kingdom

**reír(se) (i, i) (me río)** to laugh (8); **reírse a carcajadas** to laugh one's head off
**relación** *f.* relation; *pl.* relationship
**relacionarse con** to be related to
**relajante** relaxing
**relajarse** to relax
**relativo/a** relative
**religión** *f.* religion
**religioso/a** religious
**reloj** *m.* clock; watch (3)
**remar** to row
**remedio** remedy
**remodelado/a** remodeled
**remoto/a** remote; **control** (*m.*) **remoto** remote control (12)
**renovar (ue)** to renovate
**renunciar (a)** to resign (from) (16)
**reparar** to fix, repair
**repasar** to review
**repaso** review
**repente: de repente** suddenly (10)
**repertorio** repertory
**repetición** *f.* repetition
**repetir (i, i)** to repeat
**repetitivo/a** repetitive
**reportaje** *m.* article; report
**reportar** to report
**reportero/a** reporter (17)
**represa** dam
**representante** *n. m., f.* representative
**representar** to represent (13)
**república** republic
**requerir (ie, i)** to require
**requisito** requirement
**resaltar** to emphasize
**reserva** reservation (18); **hacer** (*irreg.*)/**confirmar las reservas** to make/confirm reservations (18)
**reservación** *f.* reservation (18); **hacer** (*irreg.*)/**confirmar las reservaciones** to make/confirm reservations (18)
**reservar** to reserve
**resfriado** cold (*illness*) (10)
**resfriarse (me resfrío)** to get/catch a cold (10)
**residencia** dormitory (1)
**residencial** residential
**residente** *m., f.* resident
**resolver (ue)** (*p.p.* **resuelto**) to solve (14); to resolve (14)
**respectivamente** respectively
**respecto: (con) respecto a** with regard to, with respect to
**respetar** to respect
**respeto** respect

**respiración** *f.* breathing
**respirar** to breathe (10)
**respiratorio/a** respiratory
**resplandor** *m.* brilliance, radiance
**responder** to answer
**responsabilidad** *f.* responsibility (17)
**responsabilizar (c)** to make responsible
**respuesta** answer (5)
**restaurante** *m.* restaurant (6)
**resto** rest
**restricción** *f.* restriction
**restringido/a** restrained
**resuelto/a** (*p.p. of* **resolver**) solved, resolved
**resultado** result
**resultar** to turn out
**resumen** *m.* summary; **en resumen** in short
**retener** (*like* **tener**) to retain
**reto** challenge
**retórico/a** rhetorical
**retrasado/a** late
**retratar** to paint a portrait of
**retrato** portrait
**reunión** *f.* meeting; gathering
**reunirse (me reúno) (con)** to get together (with) (8)
**revelar** to reveal
**revés: al revés** backward
**revisar (el aceite)** to check (the oil) (14)
**revista** magazine (2)
**revolución** *f.* revolution
**revolucionario/a** revolutionary
**revolver (ue)** (*p.p.* **revuelto**) to scramble
**revuelto/a** (*p.p. of* **revolver**): **huevos** (*m. pl.*) **revueltos** scrambled eggs
**rey** *m.* king (17); **Día** (*m.*) **de los Reyes Magos** Day of the Magi (Three Kings)
**rezar (c)** to pray
**Ricitos de Oro** Goldilocks
**rico/a** rich (2)
**ridículo/a** ridiculous; **es ridículo que** it's ridiculous that (13)
**riesgo** risk
**riesgoso/a** risky
**rígido/a** rigid
**rima** rhyme
**rincón** *m.* corner
**rinoceronte** *m.* rhinoceros
**riñón** *m.* kidney
**río** river (14)
**riqueza** wealth
**risa** laughter; **muerto/a de risa** dying of laughter
**ritmo** rhythm (14), pace (14)

**rito** ritual
**róbalo** sea bass
**robar** to steal
**robo** robbery, theft
**roca** rock
**rodaje** *m.* shooting, filming
**rodeado/a** surrounded
**rodilla** knee
**rojo/a** red (3); **Caperucita Roja** Little Red Ridinghood
**romance** *m.* song
**romano/a** *n., adj.* Roman
**romántico/a** romantic
**rompecabezas** *m. inv.* puzzle
**romper** (*p.p.* **roto**) to break (11); **romper (con)** to break up (with) (15)
**ron** *m.* rum
**ropa** clothes (3), clothing (3); **cambiar de ropa** to change clothes (12); **lavar la ropa** to wash the clothes (9); **planchar la ropa** to iron clothing (9); **ropa interior** underwear (3)
**rosa** rose
**rosado/a** pink (3)
**rostro** face
**roto/a** (*p.p. of* **romper**) broken; torn
**rubio/a** blond(e) (2)
**rueda de feria** Ferris wheel; **rueda de andar** treadmill; **rueda de molino** treadmill (10)
**ruido** noise (4)
**ruidoso/a** noisy
**ruinas** *f. pl.* ruins (13)
**ruiseñor** *m.* nightingale
**ruptura** rupture, break
**ruso** *n.* Russian (*language*)
**ruso/a** *n., adj.* Russian; **montaña rusa** roller coaster
**ruta** route
**rutina diaria** daily routine (4)
**rutinario/a** *adj.* routine

# S

**sábado** Saturday (4)
**sábanas** *f. pl.* sheets (*bed*) (18)
**saber** *irreg.* to know (6); **saber** + *inf.* to know how to (*do something*) (6)
**sabiduría** wisdom
**sabor** *m.* taste; flavor
**sabroso/a** tasty
**sacar (qu)** to extract (10); to take out, withdraw (*money*) (16); to get (*grades*) (11); **sacar el saldo** to balance a checkbook (16); **sacar fotos** to take photos (7); **sacar la basura** to take out the trash (9); **sacar la lengua** to stick out one's tongue (10); **sacar una muela** to extract a tooth (10)
**sacrificio** sacrifice
**sacudir los muebles** to dust the furniture (9)
**Sagitario** Sagitarius
**sagrado/a** sacred
**sal** *f.* salt
**sala** room; living room (4); **sala de clase** classroom; **sala de emergencias/urgencia** emergency room; **sala de espera** waiting room (7); **sala de estar** living room; sitting room
**salario** salary (16)
**salchicha** sausage (6); hot dog (6)
**saldo** balance (*bank*); **sacar (qu) el saldo** to balance a checkbook (16)
**salida** departure (7)
**saliente** prominent
**salir** *irreg.* (**de**) to leave (from) (*a place*) (4); to go out (4); **salir (para)** to leave (*for/to a place*); **salir (con)** to go out (with) (4); **salir bien/mal** to turn/come out well/badly
**salmón** *m.* salmon (6)
**salpicón** *m. cold fish dish*
**salsa** sauce; salsa (*music*); **salsa de tomate** catsup; tomato sauce
**saltar** to jump
**salteado/a** sautéed
**salto** waterfall; jump
**salud** *f.* health (10)
**saludable** healthy
**saludarse** to greet each other (10)
**saludo** greeting
**salvadoreño/a** *n., adj.* Salvadoran
**salvaje: animal** (*m.*) **salvaje** wild animal (14)
**salvo** except
**san, santo/a** *n.* saint; **Día** (*m.*) **de San Patricio** St. Patrick's Day; **Día de Todos los Santos** All Saints' Day; **día del santo** saint's day; **santa patrona** patron saint
**sancocho** *stew prepared with meat or fish and other ingredients such as yucca, corn, and plaintains*
**sandalia** sandal (3)
**sándwich** *m.* sandwich (6)
**sangre** *f.* blood (10)
**sanitario/a** sanitary
**sano/a** healthy; **llevar una vida sana** to lead a healthy life (10)
**santo/a** *adj.* holy

**santuario** sanctuary
**sardina** sardine
**sartén** *f.* frying pan
**satélite** *m.* satellite
**satirizar (c)** to satirize
**satisfacción** *f.* satisfaction
**satisfacer** *irreg.* (*p.p.* **satisfecho**) to satisfy
**satisfecho/a** (*p.p. of* **satisfacer**) satisfied
**se** *refl. pron.* yourself (*form.*); himself, herself, itself, yourselves (*form.*); themselves; **se trata de** it's a question of
**secadora** clothes dryer (9)
**sección** *f.* section; **sección de (no) fumar** (non)smoking section (7)
**seco/a** dry; **fruto seco** nut
**secretario/a** secretary (1)
**secreto** *n.* secret
**secuencia** sequence
**secundario/a** secondary
**sed** *f.* thirst; **tener** (*irreg.*) **(mucha) sed** to be (very) thirsty (6)
**seda** silk (3); **es de seda** it's made of silk (3)
**sede** *f.* seat; headquarters
**seguida: en seguida** right away (10)
**seguidor(a)** follower
**seguir (i, i) (g)** to keep on going; to go; to continue (14); **seguir todo derecho** to go straight ahead (14)
**según** according to (2)
**segundo** *n.* second (*time*)
**segundo/a** second (13); **Segunda Guerra Mundial** World War II; **segundo piso** third floor (12)
**seguridad** *f.* security; **pasar por el control de la seguridad** to go/pass through security (7)
**seguro** *n.* insurance; **seguro social** social security
**seguro/a** *adj.* sure (5), certain (5); **es seguro que** it's a sure thing that (13); **no estar seguro/a (de)** to be (un)sure (of)
**seis** six (P)
**seiscientos/as** six hundred (3)
**selección** *f.* selection
**seleccionar** to choose
**sellado/a** sealed; stamped; closed
**sello** (postage) stamp (18)
**selva** jungle
**semáforo** traffic signal (14)
**semana** week; **día** (*m.*) **de la semana** weekday (4); **fin** (*m.*) **de semana** weekend (1); **semana que viene** next week (4); **una vez a la semana** once a week (2)
**sembrar (ie)** to plant

**semejante** similar
**semejanza** similarity
**semestre** *m.* semester
**semiabierto/a** partially open
**semilla** seed
**senado** senate
**senador(a)** senator
**sencillo/a** simple
**senda** path
**sendero** path
**sensación** *f.* sensation
**sensible** sensitive
**sentarse (ie)** to sit down (4)
**sentencia** judgment, verdict, sentence
**sentido** meaning; sense
**sentimental** sentimental
**sentimiento** feeling
**sentir (ie, i)** to regret (13); to feel sorry (13); **¡lo siento (mucho)!** I'm (very) sorry! (11); pardon me! (11); **sentirse** to feel *(an emotion)* (8)
**señor (Sr.)** *m.* man; Mr. (P); sir (P)
**señora (Sra.)** woman; Mrs. (P); ma'am (P)
**señorita (Srta.)** young woman; Miss (P)
**separación** *f.* separation (15)
**separado/a** separate
**separar** to separate; **separarse (de)** to separate (from) (15)
**septiembre** *m.* September (5)
**séptimo/a** seventh (13)
**ser (***m.***) humano** human being
**ser** *irreg.* to be (2); **llegar (gu) a ser** to become; **ser aburrido/a** to be boring (9); **ser aficionado/a (a)** to be a fan (of) (9); **ser alérgico/a (a)** to be allergic (to); **ser divertido/a** to be fun (9); **ser en** + *place* to take place at/in *(place)* (8); **ser flexible** to be flexible (11); **ser una lata** to be a pain, drag
**serie** *f. s.* series
**serio/a** serious
**serpenteante** winding
**serpentino/a** serpentine
**serpiente** *f.* snake
**servicio** service (14); **servicio de cuartos** room service (18); **servicio de habitación** *Sp.* room service; **servicio militar** military service (17); **servicios públicos** public services (14)
**servido/a** served
**servilleta** napkin
**servir (i, i)** to serve (4)
**sesenta** sixty (2)
**sesión** *f.* session

**setecientos/as** seven hundred (3)
**setenta** seventy (2)
**severo/a** severe
**sevillano/a** *n.* person from Seville; *adj.* of/from Seville
**sexo** sex
**sexto/a** sixth (13)
**si** if (2); **por si acaso** just in case (11); **si me hace el favor** if you would do me the favor
**sí** yes (P); **sí, me gusta…** yes, I like . . . (P)
**siamés, siamesa** *adj.* Siamese
**sicoanálisis** *m. inv.* psychoanalysis
**sicología** psychology (1)
**sicólogo/a** psychologist (16)
SIDA AIDS; **Fundación (***f.***) Alerta contra el SIDA** AIDS Awareness Foundation
**siembra** harvest
**siempre** always (2)
**siento: ¡lo siento (mucho)** I'm (very) sorry (11); pardon me! (11)
**sierra** mountain
**siesta** nap; **dormir (ue, u) la siesta** to take a nap (4)
**siete** seven (P)
**siglo** century
**significado** meaning
**significar (qu)** to mean
**signo** sign
**siguiente** *adj.* following (4)
**sílaba** syllable
**silencio** silence
**silenciosamente** silently
**silla** chair (1)
**sillón** *m.* armchair (4)
**simbólico/a** symbolic
**simbolizar (c)** to symbolize
**símbolo** symbol
**simpatía** affection; pleasantness
**simpático/a** nice (2); likeable (2)
**simulador** *m.* simulator
**sin** without (4); **fue sin querer** it was unintentional (11) **sin duda** without a doubt; **sin embargo** however (5); nevertheless; **sin fines de lucro** not-for-profit; **sin fines lucrativos** nonprofit
**sinceridad** *f.* sincerity
**sincero/a** sincere
**sindical** *adj.* pertaining to a labor union
**sindicato** *n.* (labor) union
**sino** but (rather); **sino que** *conj.* but (rather)
**sinónimo** synonym
**sintético/a** synthetic

**síntoma** *m.* symptom (10)
**siquiatra** *m., f.* psychiatrist (16)
**siquiera: ni siquiera** not even
**sistema** *m.* system; **analista (***m., f.***) de sistemas** systems analyst (16)
**sitio** place, location; room *(space)*
**situación** *f.* situation
**situado/a** situated
**sobre** *n. m.* envelope (18); *prep.* on; on top of; over; about; **sobre todo** especially; above all
**sobredosis** *f. inv.* overdose
**sobrepasar** to surpass
**sobrepoblación** *f.* overpopulation
**sobrino/a** nephew/niece (2)
**social: seguro social** social security; **trabajador(a) social** social worker (16)
**socialista** *adj. m., f.* socialist
**socializar (c)** to socialize
**sociedad** *f.* society
**socioeconómico/a** socioeconomic
**sociología** sociology (1)
**socorro** help, aid
**sofá** *m.* sofa (4)
**sofisticado/a** sophisticated
**sofrito/a** sautéed
**sol** *m.* sun; **hace (mucho) sol** it's (very) sunny (5); **tomar el sol** to sunbathe (7)
**solar: energía solar** solar energy (14)
**soldado** soldier (16); **mujer (***f.***) soldado** (female) soldier (16)
**soleado/a** sunny
**soledad** *f.* solitude
**soler (ue)** to be in the habit of, accustomed to
**solicitante** *m., f.* applicant
**solicitar** to request
**solicitud** *f.* application (form) (16); **llenar la solicitud** to fill out the application (16)
**solista** *m., f.* soloist
**solitario/a** solitary
**sólo** *adv.* only (1)
**solo/a** *adj.* alone (7); single
**soltero/a** single (2), unmarried
**solución** *f.* solution
**solucionar** to solve
**sombra** shadow
**sombrero** hat (3)
**son** *n.m. traditional music from Cuba*
**son las…** it's . . . *(hour)* (P)
**sonar (ue)** to ring (9); to sound (9)
**sonido** sound
**sonreír(se)** (*like* **reír**) to smile (8)
**soñar (ue) (con)** to dream (about)

**sopa** soup (6)

**sorprendente** surprising

**sorprender** to surprise; **me (te, le…) sorprende** it surprises me (you, him, . . .) (13)

**sorpresa** surprise (8); **fiesta de sorpresa** surprise party

**soviético/a** *adj.* Soviet

**soy** I am (P); **soy de…** I'm from . . . (P)

**su(s)** *poss. adj.* his, her, its, your (*form. s.*) (2); their, your (*form. pl.*) (2)

**suaca** *traditional music and dance from El Salvador*

**suave** soft

**suavizar (c)** to soften

**subidor** *m. one of two* **bomba** *drums*

**subir (a)** to climb; to go up (7); to get on (*a vehicle*) (7); to take, carry up

**subjuntivo** *gram.* subjunctive

**submarino** submarine

**subordinado/a** *gram.* subordinate

**subrayar** to underline

**subsistir** to survive

**substituir (y)** to substitute

**subtítulo** subtitle

**sucio/a** dirty (5)

**sucre** *m.* former monetary unit of Ecuador

**sucursal** *f.* branch (office) (16)

**Sudáfrica** South Africa

**Sudamérica** South America

**sudamericano/a** *n., adj.* South American

**Suecia** Sweden

**suegro/a** father-in-law/mother-in-law

**sueldo** salary (12); **aumento de sueldo** raise (*in salary*) (16)

**suelo** floor

**suelto/a** loose; free

**sueño** dream; **tener** (*irreg.*) **sueño** to be sleepy (3)

**suerte** *f.* luck; **¡qué mala suerte!** what bad luck! (11); **tener** (*irreg.*) **suerte** to be lucky

**suéter** *m.* sweater (3)

**suficiente** enough, sufficient; **dormir (ue, u) lo suficiente** to sleep enough (10)

**sufijo** *gram.* suffix

**sufrir** to suffer (11); **sufrir (muchas) presiones** to be under (a lot of) pressure (11)

**sugerencia** suggestion

**sugerir (ie, i)** to suggest (8)

**Suiza** Switzerland

**sumamente** extremely

**superado/a** exceeded

**supercarretera** superhighway

**superlativo** *n. gram.* superlative

**supermercado** supermarket

**supervisar** to supervise

**supervisor(a)** supervisor

**supuesto/a** (*p.p. of* **suponer**): **por supuesto** of course (11)

**sur** *m.* south (5)

**surgir (j)** to arise

**suroeste** southwest

**surrealista** *adj. m., f.* surrealistic

**suspender** to suspend

**sustancialmente** substantially

**sustantivo** *gram.* noun

**sustituir (y)** to substitute

**sustituto** substitute

**suyo/a(s)** *poss. adj.* your (*form.*); his, her, its, their; *poss. pron.* (of) yours (*form.*); (of) his, hers; (of) theirs

# T

**tabacalero/a** *adj.* pertaining to tobacco

**taberna** tavern, open-air pub

**tabla** table, chart

**tal** such, such a; **con tal (de) que** *conj.* provided (that) (15); **¿qué tal?** how are you (doing)?; (P); **tal como** just as; **tal vez** perhaps

**talento** talent

**talentoso/a** talented

**taller** *m.* (repair) shop (14)

**talonario de cheques** *Sp.* checkbook

**tamaño** size

**también** too, also (P)

**tambor** *m.* drum

**tamborileo** drumming

**tampoco** neither (6), not either (6)

**tan** *adv.* so; as; **tan… como** as . . . as (5); **tan pronto como** as soon as (16)

**tanque** *m.* tank (14)

**tanto** *adv.* so much; **tanto como** as much as (5)

**tanto/a** *adj.* as much; so much; such a; *pl.* so many; as many; **tanto/a(s)… como** as much/many . . . as (5)

**tapa** *Sp.* appetizer

**tarde** *n. f.* afternoon; **buenas tardes** good afternoon (P); (*an hour*) **de la tarde** in the afternoon (P); **por la tarde** in the afternoon; *adv.* late (1)

**tarea** homework (4); chore

**tarjeta** card (7); **tarjeta de crédito** credit card (6); **tarjeta de identidad** identification card; **tarjeta de identificación** identification card (11);

**tarjeta navideña** Christmas card; **tarjeta postal** postcard (7)

**tasa** rate

**tasca** bar

**Tauro** Taurus

**taxi** *m.* taxi

**taza** cup

**te** *d.o. pron. s.* you (*fam.*); *i.o. pron. s.* to/for you (*fam.*); *refl. pron. s.* yourself (*fam.*); **¿te gusta… ?** do you (*fam. s.*) like . . .? (P); **te molesta/sorprende que** it bothers/surprises you (*fam. s.*) that (13)

**té** *m.* tea (6)

**teatral** theatrical

**teatro** theater; **ir** (*irreg.*) **al teatro** to go to the theater (9)

**techo** roof

**teclado** keyboard

**técnica** technique

**técnico/a** *n.* technician (16); *adj.* technical

**tecnología** technology

**tejano** *traditional Mexican-American music*

**tejer** to weave (13)

**tejidos** *m. pl.* woven goods (13)

**tele** *f.* T.V.

**telediario** newscast

**telefonear** to call on the telephone

**telefónico/a** *adj.* telephone

**teléfono (celular)** (cellular) phone (12); **agenda de teléfonos** address/telephone book; **contestar el teléfono** to answer the phone (6); **hablar por teléfono** to talk on the phone (1)

**telegrama** *m.* telegram

**telenovela** soap opera

**televidente** *m., f.* (television) viewer

**televisión** *f.* television; **mirar la televisión** to watch television (2)

**televisor** *m.* television (set) (4)

**tema** *m.* subject, topic

**temático/a: parque** (*m.*) **temático** theme park

**temblar** to tremble

**temer** to fear (13)

**temperatura** temperature; **tomarle la temperatura** to take someone's temperature (10)

**templado/a** temperate

**templo** temple

**temporada** season

**temporal** seasonal; temporary

**temprano** *adv.* early (1)

**temprano/a** *adj.* early

**tender (ie) a** to tend to, be inclined to; **tender la cama** to make the bed

**tener** *irreg.* to have (3); **no tener buen aspecto** to not look right; **tener alergia a** to be allergic to; **tener... años** to be . . . years old (2); **tener (mucho) calor/frío** to be (very) warm, hot/cold (5); **tener cuidado** to be careful; **tener dolor de cabeza/estómago/muela** to have a headache/stomachache/toothache (10); **tener exceso de peso** to be overweight; **tener éxito** to be successful; **tener fiebre** to have a fever (10); **tener ganas de** + *inf.* to feel like (*doing something*) (3); **tener (mucha) hambre/sed** to be (very) hungry/thirsty (6); **tener la culpa** to be guilty; **tener lugar** to take place; **tener miedo (de)** to be afraid (of) (3); **tener prisa** to be in a hurry (3); **tener que** + *inf.* to have to (*do something*) (3); **(no) tener razón** to be right (wrong) (3); **tener sueño** to be sleepy (3); **tener suerte** to be lucky; **tener una entrevista** to have an interview (16)
**tenis** *m. inv.* tennis (9); **zapato de tenis** tennis shoe (3)
**tensión** *f.* tension
**tenso/a** tense
**teoría** theory
**teorizar (c)** theorize
**tepui** *m.* flat mountain top
**tequila** tequilla
**terapia** therapy
**tercer, tercero/a** *adj.* third (13); **tercer piso** second floor (12)
**tercio** *n.* third
**terco/a** stubborn
**térmico/a** thermal
**terminación** *f.* ending
**terminar** to end
**término** term
**termómetro: regulador** (*m.*) **termómetro** thermostat
**termostato** thermostat
**terraza** terrace
**terremoto** earthquake
**terreno** field (*sports*)
**terrestre** terrestrial
**terrible: es terrible que** it's terrible that (13)
**territorio** territory
**terrorismo** terrorism (17)
**terrorista** *n., adj. m., f.* terrorist (17); **ataque** (*m.*) **terrorista** terrorist attack (17)
**tertulia** *regular meeting of people for informal discussion of topics of interest*

**testigo** *m., f.* witness (17)
**testimonio** testimony
**texto** text; **libro de texto** textbook (1)
**ti** *obj.* (*of prep.*) you (*fam. s.*) (5)
**tibio/a: huevo tibio** poached egg
**tiburón** *m.* shark
**tiempo** time; *gram.* tense; weather (5); **a tiempo** on time (7); **de tiempo completo/parcial** full time/part time (11); **hace buen/mal tiempo** it's good/bad weather (5); **llegar (gu) a tiempo** to arrive on time; **pasar tiempo (con)** to spend time (with) (15); **¿qué tiempo hace hoy?** what's the weather like today? (5)
**tienda** shop (3), store (3); **tienda (de campaña)** tent (7)
**tierra** land; Earth (*planet*); soil
**tigre** *m.* tiger
**tímido/a** shy
**tinta** ink
**tinto/a: vino tinto** red wine (6)
**tío/a** uncle/aunt (2)
**tiovivo** merry-go-round
**típico/a** typical
**tipo** type
**tipo/a** *coll.* character, person
**tira cómica** comic strip
**tirar** to throw
**titular** to (en)title
**título** title
**toalla** towel (18)
**tocar (qu)** to touch; to play (*a musical instrument*) (1); **tocarle a uno** to be someone's turn (9)
**todavía** yet; still (5)
**todo** *adv.* entirely, completely
**todo/a** *n.* whole; all, everything; *adj.* all (2); every (2), each; *pl.* everybody, all; **a toda velocidad** at full speed; **ante todo** above all; first of all; **de todas formas** anyway; **de todas maneras** by all means; whatever happens; **de todo** everything (3); **de todos modos** anyway; **Día** (*m.*) **de Todos los Santos** All Saints' Day; **por todas partes** everywhere (11); **sobre todo** especially; above all; **todo derecho** straight ahead (14); **todos los días** every day (1); **venden de todo** they sell everything (3)
**tolerante** tolerant
**tolteca** *n., adj. m., f.* Toltec
**tomar** to take (1); to drink (1); **tomar el sol** to sunbathe (7); **tomar en cuenta** to

take into account; **tomar una copa** to have a drink; **tomarle el pelo** to pull someone's leg; **tomarl(e) la temperatura** to take someone's temperature (10)
**tomate** *m.* tomato (6); **salsa de tomate** catsup; tomato sauce
**tónico/a** *gram.* stressed
**tonto/a** silly (2), foolish (2)
**torcido/a** twisted
**toreo** bullfighting
**torero/a** bullfighter, matador
**torno: en torno a** around
**toro** bull (14); **corrida de toros** bullfight; **plaza de toros** bullring
**torpe** clumsy (11); **¡qué torpe!** how clumsy! (11)
**torre** *f.* tower
**tortilla** potato omelet (*Sp.*); *thin unleavened cornmeal or flour pancake (Mex.)*
**tos** *f. s.* cough (10)
**toser** to cough (10)
**tostado/a** toasted; **pan** (*m.*) **tostado** toast (6)
**tostadora** toaster (9)
**tóxico/a** toxic
**trabajador(a)** *n.* worker (2); **Día** (*m.*) **Internacional de los Trabajadores** International Labor Day; **trabajador(a) agrícola** farm worker; **trabajador(a) social** social worker (16); *adj.* hard-working (2)
**trabajar** to work (1)
**trabajo** (piece of) work (11); job (11); report (11); **trabajo de tiempo completo/parcial** full time/part time job (11)
**trabalenguas** *m. inv.* tongue twister
**tradición** *f.* tradition
**tradicional** traditional
**traducir** *irreg.* to translate
**traductor(a)** translator (16)
**traer** *irreg.* to bring (4)
**traficar (qu) en drogas** to traffic in/ deal drugs
**tráfico** traffic; **lío/embotellamiento de tráfico** traffic jam
**tragedia** tragedy
**trágico/a** tragic
**tragicómico/a** tragicomic
**trago** drink (*alcoholic*) (18)
**traje** *m.* suit (3); **traje de baño** swimsuit (3)
**tranquilidad** *f.* quiet, calm
**tranquilizante** calming, quieting
**tranquilizar (c)** to calm
**tranquilo/a** calm, quiet; **llevar una vida tranquila** to lead a calm life (10)

**transbordador** (*m.*) **espacial** space shuttle

**transcurrir** to take place

**transferir (ie, i)** to transfer

**tránsito** traffic (14)

**transmisión** *f.* transmission

**transmitir** to transmit

**transportación** *f.* transportation

**transporte** *m.* (means of) transportation (14); **modo de transporte** means of transportation (7); **transporte público** public transportation (14)

**tras** *prep.* after

**trasladarse** to move

**tratamiento** treatment

**tratar** to treat; to deal with (*a subject*); **se trata de** it's a question of; **tratar de** + *inf.* to try to (*do something*) (13)

**trauma** *m.* trauma

**través: a través de** across; through; throughout

**travieso/a** mischievous

**trazado/a** laid out

**trece** thirteen (P)

**treinta** thirty (P); **y treinta** half-past/30 minutes past (*the hour*) (P)

**tremendo/a** tremendous

**tren** *m.* train; **choque** (*m.*) **de trenes** train wreck; **estación** (*f.*) **del tren** train station (7); **ir** (*irreg.*) **en tren** to go by train (7)

**tres** *m.* type of guitar

**tres** three (P); **hotel** (*m.*) **de tres estrellas** three star hotel (18)

**trescientos/as** three hundred (3)

**trimestre** *m.* trimester

**triste** sad (5)

**tristeza** sadness

**triunfar** to triumph

**trofeo** trophy

**trópicos** tropics

**tropiezo** mishap

**trozo** piece

**trucha** trout

**tú** *sub. pron.* you (*fam. s.*) (1); **¿y tú?** and you? (P)

**tu(s)** *poss. adj.* your (*fam.*) (2)

**tubería** plumbing

**turbulento/a** turbulent

**turismo** tourism

**turista** *n. m., f.* tourist

**turístico/a** *adj.* tourist; **clase** (*f.*) **turística** tourist class (7)

**turno** turn

**Turquía** Turkey

**tuyo/a(s)** *poss. adj.* your (*fam. s.*); *poss. pron.* of yours (*fam. s.*)

## U

**u** or (*used instead of **o** before words beginning with **o** or **ho***)

**ubicar (qu)** to locate

**último/a** last; latest; **de los últimos años** in recent years; **¡es de última moda!** it's the latest style! (3); **por última vez** for the last time (11); **por último** finally

**un, uno/a** one (P); *ind. art.* a, an; **un millón** (*m.*) **(de)** one million (3); **una vez** once; **una vez a la semana** once a week (2)

**único/a** *adj.* only; unique

**unidad** *f.* unit

**unido/a** united; **Estados** (*m. pl.*) **Unidos** United States; **Naciones** (*f. pl.*) **Unidas** United Nations

**unificación** *f.* unification

**unificarse (qu)** to unify

**unión** *f.* union

**unir** to join (together); to unite

**universidad** *f.* university (1)

**universitario/a** university *adj.* (11), of the university (11)

**unívoco/a** univocal, of one voice; unambiguous

**unos/as** *ind. art.* some, a few

**urbano/a** urban

**urgencia: caso de urgencia** emergency; **sala de urgencia** emergency room

**urgente: es urgente que** it's urgent that (13)

**uruguayo/a** *n., adj.* Uruguayan

**usar** to use (3); to wear (3)

**uso** use

**usted (Ud.)** *sub. pron.* you (*form. s.*) (1); *obj.* (*of prep.*) you (*form. s.*); **¿cómo es usted?** what are you like? (P); **¿cómo se llama usted?** what is your name? (P); **¿de dónde es usted?** where are you from? (P); **¿y usted?** and you? (P)

**ustedes (Uds.)** *sub. pron.* you (*form. pl.*) (1); *obj.* (*of prep.*) you

**usualmente** usually

**útil** useful

**utilización** *f.* use, utilization

**utilizar (c)** to use, utilize

**uva** grape; **uva de mesa** table grape

**¡uy!** *interj.* oops!

## V

**vaca** cow (14)

**vacaciones** *f. pl.* vacation; **de vacaciones** on vacation (7); **estar** (*irreg.*) **de vacaciones** to be on vacation (7); **ir** (*irreg.*) **de vacaciones** to go on vacation (7); **vacaciones de primavera** spring break

**vacilante** hesitant

**vacío** *n.* emptiness; void

**vacío/a** *adj.* empty

**vacuna** vaccine

**vahído** blackout (fainting)

**vainilla** vanilla

**valenciano/a** of/from Valencia, Spain

**valentía** bravery

**valer** (*irreg.*) **la pena** to be worthwhile, worth the trouble

**válido/a** valid

**valiente** brave

**valle** *m.* valley

**vallenato** *traditional music from Colombia*

**valor** *m.* value; courage, bravery

**vals** *m. inv.* waltz

**variación** *f.* variation

**variar (varío)** to vary

**variedad** *f.* variety

**varios/as** several

**vasco** Basque (*language*)

**vasco/a** *n., adj.* Basque

**vaso** glass

**vecindad** *f.* neighborhood (12)

**vecino/a** *n.* neighbor (12); *adj.* neighboring

**vegetal** *adj.* vegetable

**vegetariano/a** vegetarian

**vehículo** vehicle (12)

**veinte** twenty (P)

**veinticinco** twenty-five

**veinticuatro** twenty-four

**veintidós** twenty-two

**veintinueve** twenty-nine

**veintiocho** twenty-eight

**veintiséis** twenty-six

**veintisiete** twenty-seven

**veintitrés** twenty-three

**veintiún, veintiuno/a** twenty-one

**vejez** *f.* old age (15)

**vela** candle

**velludo/a** hairy

**velocidad** *f.* speed; **a toda velocidad** at full speed; **límite** (*m.*) **de velocidad** speed limit (14)

**vemos: nos vemos** see you around (P)

**vencido/a** overcome

**vendedor(a)** salesperson (16)

**vender** to sell (2); **venden de todo** they sell everything (3)

**venezolano/a** *n., adj.* Venezuelan

**venga** *interj.* come on

venganza revenge

venir *irreg.* to come (3); **la semana que viene** next week (4); **venga** *interj.* come on

venta sale

ventaja advantage (10)

ventana window (1); **lavar las ventanas** to wash the windows (9)

ventilación *f.* ventilation

ver *irreg.* (*p.p.* **visto**) to see (4); **a ver** let's see; **ir** (*irreg.*) **a ver una película** to go to see a movie (9); **nos vemos** see you around (P)

veranear to spend summer vacation

verano summer (5)

verbo *gram.* verb

verdad *f.* truth; **¿verdad?** right?, don't they (you, *and so on*)? (3)

verdadero/a true; real

verde green (3)

verduras *f. pl.* vegetables (6)

verificar (qu) to verify

versión *f.* version

verso verse; line of a poem

verter (ie) to spill; to shed (*a tear*)

vestíbulo vestibule

vestido dress (3); **vestido de novia** wedding gown

vestir (i, i) to dress; **vestirse** to get dressed (4)

veterinario/a veterinarian (16)

vez *f.* (*pl.* **veces**) time; **a la vez** at the same time; **a veces** sometimes (2), at times (2); **alguna vez** once; ever; **cada vez más** increasingly; **de vez en cuando** once in a while; **dos veces** twice (10); **en vez de** instead of (16); **érase una vez** once upon a time; **otra vez** again; **por primera/última vez** for the first/last time (11); **tal vez** perhaps; **una vez** once; **una vez a la semana** once a week (2)

viajar to travel (7); **viajar al/en el extranjero** to travel abroad (18)

viaje *m.* trip (7); **agencia de viajes** travel agency (7); **agente** (*m., f.*) **de viajes** travel agent (7); **de viaje** on a trip (7); **hacer** (*irreg.*) **un viaje** to take a trip (4)

viajero/a traveler (18); **cheque** (*m.*) **de viajero** traveler's check (18)

vicepresidente/a vice president

víctima victim (17)

vida life; **esperanza de vida** life expectancy; **ganarse la vida** to earn a living; **llevar una vida sana/tranquila** to lead a healthy/calm life (10)

vídeo video; **cámara de vídeo** video camera (12)

videocasetera videocassette recorder (VCR) (12)

videoclub *m.* video club

videoteca video library

vidrio glass

viejo/a *n.* old person; *adj.* old (2); **Noche** (*f.*) **Vieja** New Year's Eve (8)

viene: la semana que viene next week (4)

viento wind; **hace (mucho) viento** it's (very) windy (5)

viernes *m. inv.* Friday (4)

vietnamita *n., adj. m., f.* Vietnamese

villancico Christmas carol

vinícola *adj. m., f.* pertaining to wine

vino (blanco, tinto) (white, red) wine (6)

viñedo vineyard

violencia violence (14)

violento/a violent

violeta violet

violín *m.* violin

virgen *n. f.* virgin

visado visa

visigodo/a *n.* Visigoth

visión *f.* vision

visita visit; **hacer** (*irreg.*) **visitas** to visit

visitante *m., f.* visitor

visitar to visit; **visitar un museo** to visit a museum (9)

víspera eve

vista view (12); sight; **a primera vista** at first sight (15); **punto de vista** point of view

vistazo glimpse

visto/a (*p.p. of* **ver**) seen

vitamina vitamin

viudo/a widower/widow (15)

vivienda housing

vivir to live (2); **vivir en paz** to live in peace (17)

vivo/a lively

vocabulario vocabulary

vocación *f.* vocation

vocal *n. f.* vowel

volante: objeto volante no identificado **(OVNI)** unidentified flying object (UFO)

volcán *m.* volcano

volcánico/a volcanic

vólibol *m.* volleyball (9)

volumen *m.* volume

voluntad *f.* will; choice, decision

voluntario/a *n.* volunteer

volver (ue) (*p.p.* **vuelto**) to return (*to a place*) (4); **volver a** + *inf.* to (*do something*) again (4)

vos *sub. pron.* you (*fam. s. Arg., Uru., C.A.*); *obj.* (*of prep.*) you (*fam. s. Arg. Uru., C.A.*)

vosotros/as *sub. pron.* you (*fam. pl. Sp.*) (1); *obj.* (*of prep.*) you (*fam. pl. Sp.*)

votante *m., f.* voter

votar to vote (17)

vuelo flight (7); **asistente** (*m., f.*) **de vuelo** flight attendant (7); **vuelo sin escalas** nonstop flight

vuelta: billete (*m.*)/boleto de ida y vuelta round-trip ticket (7); **darse** (*irreg.*) **la vuelta** to turn oneself around; **de vuelta** returned

vuestro/a(s) *poss. adj.* your (*fam. pl. Sp.*) (2); *poss. pron.* yours, of yours (*fam. pl. Sp.*)

vulpeja vixen

# W

walkman *m.* Walkman (12)

# Y

y and (P); **y cuarto (quince)** a quarter (fifteen minutes) after (*the hour*) (P); **y media (treinta)** half-past/30 minutes past (*the hour*) (P); **¿y tú?** and you? (*fam. s.*) (P); **¿y usted?** and you? (*form. s.*) (P)

ya already (8); **ya no** no longer; **ya que** since

yacimiento deposit (*mineral*)

yerno son-in-law

yo *sub. pron.* I (1)

yogur *m.* yogurt (6)

# Z

zampoña pan-flute (*Andean*)

zanahoria carrot (6)

zapatería shoe store

zapato shoe (3); **zapato de tenis** tennis shoe (3)

zona zone

# English-Spanish Vocabulary

## A

a lot **mucho** (1)
able: to be able **poder** (*irreg.*) (3)
abroad **extranjero** *n.* (18)
absent: to be absent (from) **faltar (a)** (8)
absentminded **distraído/a** (11)
accelerated **acelerado/a** (14)
according to **según** (2)
account **cuenta** (16); checking account **cuenta corriente** (16); savings account **cuenta de ahorros** (16)
accountant **contador(a)** (16)
ache *v.* **doler (ue)** (10); *n.* **dolor** *m.*
acquainted: to be acquainted with **conocer (zc)** (6)
actor **actor** *m.* (13)
actress **actriz** *f.* (*pl.* **actrices**) (13)
address **dirección** *f.* (9)
administration: business administration **administración** (*f.*) **de empresas** (1)
adolescence **adolescencia** (15)
advantage **ventaja** (10)
advice (piece of) **consejo** (6)
advisor **consejero/a** (1)
aerobic: to do aerobics **hacer** (*irreg.*) (*p.p.* **hecho**) **ejercicios aeróbicos** (10)
affectionate **cariñoso/a** (5)
afraid: to be afraid (of) **tener** (*irreg.*) **miedo (de)** (3)
after *prep.* **después de** (4); *conj.* **después (de) que** (16)
afternoon **tarde** *n. f.* (1); good afternoon **buenas tardes** (P); **(muy) buenas** (P); (*an hour*) in the afternoon **de la tarde** (P); in the afternoon **por la tarde** (1)
afterwards **luego** (4)
again: to do (*something*) again **volver (ue)** (*p.p.* **vuelto**) **a** + *inf.* (4)
age: middle age **madurez** *f.* (15) old age **vejez** *f.* (15)
agency: travel agency **agencia de viajes** (7)
agent: travel agent **agente** (*m., f.*) **de viajes** (7)
agree: I (don't) agree **(no) estoy de acuerdo** (2)
ahead of time **con anticipación** (18); straight ahead **todo derecho** (14)
air **aire** *m.* (14); air pollution **contaminación** (*f.*) **del aire** (14); clean air **aire puro** (14)
airplane **avión** *m.* (7)
airport **aeropuerto** (7)
alarm clock **despertador** *m.* (11)

all **todo/a(s)** *adj.* (2)
allow **permitir** (12)
almost **casi** (2); almost never **casi nunca** (2)
alone **solo/a** *adj.* (7)
along: to get along well/poorly (with) **llevarse bien/mal (con)** (15)
alongside of **al lado de** *prep.* (5)
already **ya** (8)
also **también** (P)
always **siempre** (2)
among **entre** *prep.* (5)
amusement **diversión** *f.* (9)
analyst: systems analyst **analista** (*m., f.*) **de sistemas** (16)
and **y** (P); and you? (*fam. s.*) **¿y tú?** (P); (*form. s.*) **¿y usted?** (P)
angry **furioso/a** (5); to get angry (at) **enojarse (con)** (8)
animal **animal** *m.* (14); domesticated animal **animal doméstico** (14); wild animal **animal salvaje** (14)
announce **anunciar** (7)
another **otro/a** (2)
answer *n.* **respuesta** (5); to answer the phone **contestar el teléfono** (16)
answering machine **contestador** (*m.*) **automático** (12)
antibiotic **antibiótico** (10)
any **algún, alguno/a** (6); not any **ningún ninguno/a** (6)
anybody **alguien** (6); not anybody **nadie** (6)
anything **algo** (3)
apartment **apartamento** (1); apartment building **bloque** (*m.*)**/casa de apartamentos** (12)
apologize **pedir (i, i) disculpas** (11)
apple **manzana** (6)
appliance: home appliance **aparato doméstico** (9)
applicant **aspirante** *m., f.* (16)
application (form) **solicitud** *f.* (16)
appreciate **apreciar** (13)
April **abril** *m.* (5)
architect **arquitecto/a** (13)
architecture **arquitectura** (13)
area **área** *f.* (*but* **el área**) (12)
argue (about) (with) **discutir (sobre) (con)** (8)
arm **brazo** (11)
armchair **sillón** *m.* (4)
army **ejército** (17)
around: see you around **nos vemos** (P)

arrival **llegada** (7)
arrive **llegar (gu)** (6)
art **arte** *f.* (*but* **el arte**) (1); work of art **obra de arte** (13)
artist **artista** *m., f.* (13)
arts and crafts **artesanía** *s.* (13)
as: as . . . as **tan... como** (5); as a child **de niño/a (a)** (9); as a youth **de joven** (9); as much as **tanto como** (5); as much/ many as **tanto/a(s)... como** (5); as soon as **tan pronto como** *conj.* (16); **en cuanto** *conj.* (16)
ask: to ask a question **hacer** (*irreg.*) (*p.p.* **hecho**) **una pregunta** (4); **preguntas** (6); to ask for **pedir (i, i)** (4)
asleep: to fall asleep **dormirse (ue, u)** (4)
asparagus **espárragos** *m. pl.* (6)
assassination **asesinato** (17)
at **en** (P); **a** (*with time*) (P); at . . . (hour) **a la(s)...** (P); at first sight **a primera vista** (15); at home **en casa** (1); at least **por lo menos** (8); (*an hour*) at night **de la noche** (P); at night **por la noche** (1); at the beginning of **al principio de** (16); at times **a veces** (2); at what time? **¿a qué hora?** (P)
ATM **cajero automático** (16)
attack: terrorist attack **ataque** (*m.*) **terrorista** (17)
attend (*a class, function*) **asistir (a)** (2); to not attend **faltar (a)** (8)
attendant: flight attendant **asistente** (*m., f.*) **de vuelo** (7)
August **agosto** (5)
aunt **tía** (2)
automatic teller machine **cajero automático** (16)
autumn **otoño** (5)
avenue **avenida** (12)
avoid **evitar** (14)
away: right away **en seguida** (10)
awful: an awful lot **muchísimo** (7)

## B

baby-sitter **niñero/a** (9)
backpack **mochila** (1)
bad **mal, malo/a** *adj.* (2); it's (very) bad weather **hace (muy) mal tiempo** (5); the bad thing, news **lo malo** (10); to have a bad time **pasarlo mal** (8); to make a bad impression on someone **caerle** (*irreg.*) **mal a alguien** (16); what bad luck! **¡qué mala suerte!** (11)

baked custard **flan** *m.* (6)

baggage **equipaje** *m.* (7)

balance: in a balanced way **equilibradamente** (10); to balance a checkbook **sacar (qu) el saldo** (16)

ballet **ballet** *m.* (13)

banana **banana** (6)

bank **banco** (16)

bar **bar** *m.* (9); to go to a bar **ir** (*irreg.*) **a un bar** (9)

bargain **ganga** (3)

baseball **béisbol** *m.* (9)

basketball **basquetbol** *m.* (9)

bath: room with(out) attached bath **habitación** (*f.*) **con/sin baño** (18) to take a bath **bañarse** (4)

bathroom **baño** (4); bathroom sink **lavabo** (4)

bathtub **bañera** (4)

battery **batería** (14)

be **estar** (*irreg.*) (1); **ser** (*irreg.*) (2); **encontrarse (ue)** (10); to be a fan (of) **ser aficionado/a (a)** (9); to be able **poder** (*irreg.*) (3); to be absent (from) **faltar (a)** (8); to be acquainted with **conocer (zc)** (6); to be afraid (of) **tener** (*irreg.*) **miedo de** (3); to be boring **ser aburrido/a** (9); to be born **nacer (zc)** (15); to be called **llamarse** (4); to be (very) cold **tener (mucho) frío** (5); to be comfortable (*temperature*) **estar bien** (5); to be flexible **ser flexible** (11); to be fun **ser divertido/a** (9); to be going to (*do something*) **ir** (*irreg.*) **a** + *inf.* (3); to be happy (about) **alegrarse (de)** (12); to be (very) hungry **tener (mucha) hambre** (6); to be in a hurry **tener prisa** (3); to be interesting **interesar** (7); to be late **estar atrasado/a** (7); to be left **quedar** (11); to be on a diet **estar a dieta** (6); to be on vacation **estar de vacaciones** (7); to be pleasing **gustar** (7); to be right **tener razón** (3); to be sleepy **tener sueño** (3); to be someone's turn **tocarle (qu) a uno** (9); to be (very) thirsty **tener (mucha) sed** (6); to be under (a lot of) pressure **sufrir (muchas) presiones** (11); to be (very) warm, hot **tener (mucho) calor** (5); to be wrong **no tener razón** (3); to be wrong (about) **equivocarse (qu) (de)** (11); to be . . . years old **tener… años** (2)

beach **playa** (5)

beans **frijoles** *m. pl.* (6)

beautiful **bello/a** (14)

because **porque** (2)

become + *adj.* **ponerse** (*irreg.*) (*p.p.* **puesto**) + *adj.* (8)

bed **cama** (4); to get up on the wrong side of the bed **levantarse con el pie izquierdo** (11); to go to bed **acostarse (ue)** (4); to make the bed **hacer** (*irreg.*) (*p.p.* **hecho**) **la cama** (9); to stay in bed **guardar cama** (10)

bedroom **alcoba** (4)

beer **cerveza** (1)

before *conj.* **antes (de) que** (15); *prep.* **antes de** (4)

begin **empezar (ie) (c)** (4); to begin to (*do something*) **empezar a** + *inf.* (4)

beginning: at the beginning of **al principio de** (16)

behave **portarse** (8)

behind **detrás de** *prep.* (5)

believe (in) **creer (y) (en)** (2)

bellhop **botones** *m. inv.* (18), **mozo** (18)

below **debajo de** *prep.* (5)

belt **cinturón** *m.* (3)

best **mejor** (5)

better **mejor** (5)

between **entre** *prep.* (5)

beverage **bebida** (6)

bicycle: to ride a bicycle **pasear en bicicleta** (9)

bicycling **ciclismo** (9)

big **gran, grande** (2)

bike **bicicleta** (12); mountain bike **bicicleta de montaña** (12)

bill (*for service*) **cuenta** (6); **factura** (16)

bird **pájaro** (2)

birth **nacimiento** (15)

birthday **cumpleaños** *m. inv.* (5); birthday cake **pastel** (*m.*) **de cumpleaños** (8); to have a birthday **cumplir años** (8)

black **negro/a** (3)

blanket **manta** (18)

blond(e) **rubio/a** *n., adj.* (2)

blood **sangre** *f.* (10)

blouse **blusa** (3)

blue **azul** (3)

board: room and full board **pensión** (*f.*) **completa** (18)

boardinghouse **pensión** *f.* (18)

boat **barco** (7); to go/travel by boat **ir** (*irreg.*) **en barco** (7)

body **cuerpo** (10)

bomb **bomba** (17)

book **libro** (1)

bookshelf **estante** *m.* (4)

bookstore **librería** (1)

boot **bota** (3)

border **frontera** (18)

bore **aburrir** (13)

bored **aburrido/a** (5); to get bored **aburrirse** (9)

boring **pesado** (9); to be boring **ser** (*irreg.*) **aburrido/a** (9)

born: to be born **nacer (zc)** (15)

borrow **pedir (i, i) prestado/a** (16)

boss **jefe/a** (12)

bother: it bothers me (you, him, . . .) that **me (te, le, …) molesta que** (13)

boy **muchacho** (4); **niño** (2)

boyfriend **novio** (5)

brain **cerebro** (10)

brakes **frenos** *m. pl.* (14)

branch (office) **sucursal** *f.* (16)

bread **pan** *m.* (6)

break **romper** (*p.p.* **roto**) (11); to break up (with) **romper (con)** (15)

breakfast **desayuno** (4); room with breakfast and one other meal **media pensión** *f.* (18); to have breakfast **desayunar** (6)

breathe **respirar** (10)

bride **novia** (15)

bring **traer** (*irreg.*) (4)

brother **hermano** (2)

brown **(de) color café** (3)

brunet(te) **moreno/a** *n., adj.* (2)

brush one's teeth **cepillarse los dientes** (4)

budget **presupuesto** (16)

build **construir (y)** (14)

building **edificio** *n.* (1); apartment building **bloque** (*m.*)/**casa de apartamentos** (12); building manager **portero/a** (12)

bull **toro** (14)

bump into **darse** (*irreg.*) **en/con/contra** (11); to bump against **pegarse (gu) en/con/contra** (11)

bureau (*furniture*) **cómoda** (4)

bus **autobús** *m.* (7); bus station **estación** (*f.*) **de autobuses** (7); bus stop **parada del autobús** (18); to go/travel by bus **ir** (*irreg.*) **en autobús** (7)

business **empresa** (16); business administration **administración** (*f.*) **de empresas** (1)

businessperson **hombre** (*m.*)/**mujer** (*f.*) **de negocios** (16)

busy **ocupado/a** (5)

but **pero** *conj.* (P)

butter **mantequilla** (6)

buy **comprar** (1)

by check **con cheque** (16)
bye **adiós** (P)

# C

cabin **cabina** (*on a ship*) (7)
café **café** *m.* (18)
cafeteria **cafetería** (1)
cake **pastel** *m.* (6); birthday cake **pastel de cumpleaños** (8)
calculator **calculadora** (1)
calendar **calendario** (11)
call *v.* **llamar** (6); to be called **llamarse** (4)
calm: to lead a calm life **llevar una vida tranquila** (10)
campground *camping* *m.* (7)
camping: to go camping **hacer** (*irreg.*) (*p.p.* **hecho**) *camping* (7)
campus *campus* *m. inv.* (12); university campus *campus* (12)
can **poder** *v.* (*irreg.*) (3)
candidate **aspirante** *m., f.* (16)
candy **dulces** *m. pl.* (6)
cap **gorra** (3)
capital city **capital** *f.* (5)
car **coche** *m.* (2); **carro** (12); convertible car **carro/coche descapotable** (12)
card **tarjeta** (7); credit card **tarjeta de crédito** (6); identification card **tarjeta de identificación** (11); to play cards **jugar (ue) (gu) a las cartas** (9)
carrot **zanahoria** (6)
carry **llevar** (3)
case: in case **en caso de que** (15); just in case **por si acaso** (11)
cash **efectivo** (16); in cash **al contado/en efectivo** (16); to cash (*a check*) **cobrar** (16); to pay in cash **pagar (gu) al contado / en efectivo** (16)
cashier **cajero/a** (16); cashier window **caja** (16)
cat **gato/a** (2)
catch a cold **resfriarse (me resfrío)** (10)
CD **disco compacto, CD** *m.* (12)
CD-ROM **CD-ROM** *m.* (12)
celebrate **celebrar** (5)
cellular phone **teléfono cellular** (12)
ceramics **cerámica** *s.* (13)
ceremony: wedding ceremony **boda** (15)
cereal **cereal** *m.* (6)
certain **seguro/a** *adj.* (5); it's certain that **es cierto que** (13)
chair **silla** (1)
chalkboard **pizarra** (1)
change *v.* (channels, clothes, rooms) **cambiar (de canal, ropa, cuarto)** (12)

channel **canal** *m.* (12); to change channels **cambiar de canal** (12)
charge (*to an account*) **cargar (gu)** (16); (*someone for an item or service*) **cobrar** (16)
check (*bank*) **cheque** *m.* (16); (*for service*) **cuenta** (6); by check **con cheque** (16); traveler's check **cheque de viajero** (18); to check (the oil) **revisar (el aceite)** (14); to check into (*a hospital*) **internarse (en)** (10); to check (*baggage*) **facturar** (7); to go/pass through security check **pasar por el control de la seguridad** (7)
checkbook **chequera** (16); to balance a checkbook **sacar (qu) el saldo** (16)
checking account **cuenta corriente** (16)
checkup **chequeo** (10)
cheese **queso** (6)
chef **cocinero/a** (16)
chemistry **química** (1)
chess **ajedrez** *m.* (4)
chicken **pollo** (6); roast chicken **pollo asado** (6)
chief **jefe/a** (12)
child: as a child **de niño/a** (9); small child **niño/a** (2)
childhood **niñez** *f.* (*pl.* **niñeces**) (9)
children **hijos** *m. pl.* (2)
chop **chuleta** (6); pork chop **chuleta de cerdo** (6)
chore: household chore **quehacer** (*m.*) **doméstico**
Christmas **Navidad** *f.* (8); Christmas Eve **Nochebuena** (8)
citizen **ciudadano/a** (17)
city **ciudad** *f.* (2)
civic **cívico** (17)
class **clase** *f.* (1); first class **primera clase** (7); tourist class **clase turística** (7)
classroom **clase** *f.* (1)
classic **clasico/a** (13)
classical **clásico/a** (13)
classmate **compañero/a de clase** (1)
clean *adj.* **limpio/a** (5); **puro/a** (14); clean air **aire** (*m.*) **puro** (14); to clean the (whole) house **limpiar la casa (entera)** (9)
clear the table **quitar la mesa** (9)
clerk **dependiente/a** (1)
clever **listo/a** (2)
client **cliente** *m., f.* (1)
climate **clima** *m.* (5)
close *v.* **cerrar (ie)** (4)
close to *prep.* **cerca de** (5)
closed **cerrado/a** (5)
closet **armario** (4)

clothes **ropa** (3); clothes dryer **secadora** (9); to change clothes **cambiar de ropa** (12); to wash the clothes **lavar la ropa** (9)
clothing **ropa** (3)
cloudy: it's (very) cloudy **está (muy) nublado** (5)
clumsy **torpe** (11)
coat **abrigo** (3)
coffee **café** *m.* (1)
coffeemaker **cafetera** (9)
cold (*illness*) **resfriado** (10); it's (very) cold (*weather*) **hace (mucho) frío** (5); to be (very) cold **tener** (*irreg.*) **(mucho) frío** (5); to get/catch a cold **resfriarse (me resfrío)** (10); very cold **congelado/a** (5)
collect **recoger (j)** (11)
collide (with) **chocar (qu) (con)** (14)
collision **choque** *m.* (17)
color **color** *m.* (3)
comb one's hair **peinarse** (4)
come **venir** (*irreg.*) (3)
comfortable **cómodo/a** (4); to be comfortable (*temperature*) **estar** (*irreg.*) **bien** (5)
communicate (with) **comunicarse (qu) (con)** (17)
communication (*major*) **comunicación** *f.* (1); means of communication **medio de comunicación** (17)
community **comunidad** *f.* (12)
compact disc **disco compacto** (12); **CD** *m.* (12)
complain (about) **quejarse (de)** (8)
composer **compositor(a)** (13)
computer **computadora** (12); **ordenador** *m.* (*Sp.*) (12); computer disc **disco de computadora** (12); computer file **archivo** (12); computer science **computación** *f.* (1)
concert: to go to a concert **ir** (*irreg.*) **a un concierto** (9)
conductor **director(a)** (13)
confirm **confirmar** (18)
congested **congestionado/a** (10)
congratulations **felicitaciones** *f. pl.* (8)
conserve **conservar** (14)
contact lenses **lentes** (*m. pl.*) **de contacto** (10); to wear contact lenses **llevar lentes de contacto** (10)
content *adj.* **contento/a** (5)
continue **seguir (i, i) (g)** (14)
control: remote control **control** (*m.*) **remoto** (12)
convertible car **carro/coche** (*m.*) **descapotable** (12)

cook *v.* **cocinar** (6); *n.* **cocinero/a** (16)
cookie **galleta** (6)
cool: it's cool (*weather*) **hace fresco** (5)
copy *v.* **copiar** (12); **hacer** (*irreg.*) (*p.p.* **hecho**) **copia** (12)
corner (street) **esquina** (14)
corporation **empresa** (16)
cotton **algodón** *m.* (3); it's made of cotton **es de algodón** (3)
cough **tos** *f.* (10); to cough **toser** (10); cough syrup **jarabe** *m.* (10)
country **país** *m.* (2)
countryside **campo** (12); **paisaje** *m.* (12)
couple **pareja** (15); married couple **pareja** (15)
course (*of a meal*) **plato** (6)
cousin **primo/a** (2)
cover *v.* **cubrir** (*p.p.* **cubierto**) (14)
cow **vaca** (14)
crafts: arts and crafts **artesanía** *s.* (13)
"crash" (*of computers*) **fallar** (12)
crazy **loco/a** (5)
create **crear** (13)
credit card **tarjeta de crédito** (6)
crime **delito** (14)
cross **cruzar (c)** (18)
cry **llorar** (8)
custard, baked custard **flan** *m.* (6)
custom **costumbre** *f.* (9)
customs **aduana** *s.* (18)

# D

dad **papá** *m.* (2)
daily routine **rutina diaria** (4)
dance **baile** *m.* (13); **danza** (13); to dance **bailar** (1)
dancer **bailarín, bailarina** (13)
date (*calendar*) **fecha** (5); (*social*) **cita** (15)
daughter **hija** (2)
day **día** *m.* (1); the day after tomorrow **pasado mañana** (4); the day before yesterday **anteayer** (10); every day **todos los días** (1)
deadline **fecha límite** (11)
dear **querido/a** *n., adj.* (5)
death **muerte** *f.* (15)
December **diciembre** *m.* (5)
delay *n.* **demora** (7)
dense **denso/a** (14)
dentist **dentista** *m., f.* (10)
deny **negar (ie) (gu)** (13)
department store **almacén** *m.* (3)
departure **salida** (7)
deposit **depositar** (16)
desk **escritorio** (1)

dessert **postre** *m.* (6)
destroy **destruir (y)** (14)
detail **detalle** *m.* (6)
develop **desarrollar** (14)
dictator **dictador(a)** (17)
dictatorship **dictadura** (17)
dictionary **diccionario** (1)
die **morirse (ue, u)** (*p.p.* **muerto**) (8)
diet: to be on a diet **estar** (*irreg.*) **a dieta** (6)
difficult **difícil** (5); **pesado/a** (9)
dining room **comedor** *m.* (4)
dinner **cena** (6); to have dinner **cenar** (6)
director **director(a)** (13); personnel director **director(a) de personal** (16)
dirty **sucio/a** (5)
disadvantage **desventaja** (10)
disaster **desastre** *m.* (17)
disc: compact disc **disco compacto, CD** *m.* (12); computer disc **disco de computadora** (12)
disco: to go to a disco **ir** (*irreg.*) **a una discoteca** (9)
discover **descubrir** (*p.p.* **descubierto**) (14)
discrimination **discriminación** *f.* (17)
dish (*course of a meal*) **plato** (6); dishes **platos** *m. pl.* (4); to wash dishes **lavar los platos** (9)
dishwasher **lavaplatos** *m. inv.* (9)
divorce **divorcio** (15)
divorced (from) **divorciado/a (de)** (15); to get divorced (from) **divorciarse (de)** (15)
dizzy **mareado/a** (10)
do **hacer** (*irreg.*) (*p.p.* **hecho**) (4); do you (*fam. s.*) like . . . ? **¿te gusta… ?** (P) do you (*form. s.*) like . . . ? **¿le gusta… ?** (P); to do aerobics **hacer ejercicios aeróbicos** (10)
doctor (medical) **médico/a** (2)
dog **perro/a** (2)
domesticated animal **animal** (*m.*) **doméstico** (14)
door **puerta** (1)
doorman **portero/a** (12)
dormitory **residencia** (1)
double (*hotel*) room (18) **habitación** (*f.*) **doble**
doubt **dudar** (12)
down: to fall down **caerse** (*irreg.*) (11)
downtown **centro** (3)
drama **drama** *m.* (13)
draw **dibujar** (13)
dress **vestido** (3)
dressed: to get dressed **vestirse (i, i)** (4)

dresser **cómoda** (4)
drink **bebida** (6); (*alcoholic*) **copa, trago** (18); *drink similar to a milkshake* **batido** (18); to drink **beber** (2); **tomar** (1)
drive **conducir** (*irreg.*) (14); **manejar** (12); hard drive **disco duro** (12)
driver **conductor(a)** (14); driver's license **licencia de manejar/conducir** (14)
during **durante** (4); **por** (4)
dust the furniture **sacudir los muebles** (9)
DVD **DVD** *m.* (12)
DVD player **lector** (*m.*) **de DVD** (12)

# E

e-mail **correo electrónico** (12)
each **cada** *inv.* (4)
ear: inner ear **oído** (10); (outer) ear **oreja** (10)
early **temprano** *adv.* (1)
earn **ganar** (16)
earring **arete** *m.* (3)
east **este** *m.* (5)
Easter **Pascua (Florida)** (8)
easy **fácil** (5)
eat **comer** (2); eat breakfast **desayunar** (6); eat dinner, supper **cenar** (6)
economics **economía** *s.* (1)
economize **economizar (c)** (16)
egg **huevo** (6)
eight **ocho** (P)
eight hundred **ochocientos/as** (3)
eighteen **dieciocho** (P)
eighth **octavo/a** *adj.* (13)
eighty **ochenta** (2)
electric **eléctrico/a** (14); electric energy **energía eléctrica** (14)
electrician **electricista** *m., f.* (16)
electricity **luz** *f.* (*pl.* **luces**) (11)
elephant **elefante** *m.* (14)
eleven **once** (P)
embarrassed **avergonzado/a** (8)
emotion **emoción** *f.* (8)
employment office **dirección** (*f.*) **de personal** (16)
end table **mesita** (4)
endangered species **especie** (*f. s.*) **en peligro de extinción** (14)
energy **energía** (14); electric (nuclear, solar) energy **energía eléctrica (nuclear, solar)** (14)
engagement **noviazgo** (15)
engineer **ingeniero/a** (16)
English (*language*) **inglés** *m.* (1); *n., adj.* **inglés, inglesa** (2)

enjoy oneself **divertirse (ie, i)** (4)

enough **bastante** *adv.* (15); **lo suficiente** (10)

entertainment **diversión** *f.* (9)

envelope **sobre** *m.* (18)

environment (*nature*) **medio ambiente** (14)

equality **igualdad** *f.* (17)

equipment: photography equipment **equipo fotográfico** (12); stereo equipment **equipo estereofónico** (12)

era **época** (11)

eruption **erupción** *f.* (17)

evening **noche** *f.* (1); good evening **(muy) buenas** (P); **buenas noches** (P); (*an hour*) in the evening **de la noche** (P); in the evening **por la noche** (1)

event **acontecimiento** (17); **evento** (17); **hecho** (8)

every **cada** *inv.* (4); **todo/a(s)** *adj.* (2); every day **todos los días** (1)

everything **de todo**

everywhere **por todas partes** (11)

exactly (*time*) **en punto** (P)

exam **examen** *m.* (3)

examine **examinar** (10); **registrar** (18)

example: for example **por ejemplo** (11)

excuse me **con permiso** (P); **perdón** (P)

exercise **ejercicio** (3); to exercise **hacer** (*irreg.*) (*p.p.* **hecho**) **ejercicio** (4)

expect **esperar** (6)

expense **gasto** (12)

expensive **caro/a** (3)

explain **explicar (qu)** (7)

extract **sacar (qu)** (10); to extract a tooth **sacar una muela** (10)

eye **ojo** (10)

# F

fact **hecho** *n.* (8)

factory **fábrica** (14)

faithful **fiel** (2)

fall (*season*) **otoño** (5); to fall **caer** (*irreg.*) (11); to fall asleep **dormirse (ue, u)** (4); to fall down **caerse** (11); to fall in love (with) **enamorarse (de)** (15)

family **familia** (2)

fan: to be a fan (of) **ser** (*irreg.*) **aficionado/a (a)** (9)

far from **lejos de** *prep.* (5)

farm **finca** (14); farm worker **campesino/a** (14)

farmer **agricultor(a)** (14)

fast *adj.* **rápido/a** (6); **acelerado/a** (14)

fat **gordo/a** (2)

father **padre** *m.* (2); **papá** *m.* (2)

fax **fax** *m.* (12)

fear: to fear **temer** (13)

February **febrero** (5)

feel **encontrarse (ue)** (10); to feel (*an emotion*) **sentirse (ie, i)** (8); to feel like (*doing something*) **tener** (*irreg.*) **ganas de + inf.** (3); to feel sorry **sentir (ie, i)** (13)

fever **fiebre** *f.* (10); to have a fever **tener** (*irreg.*) **fiebre** (10)

fiancé(e) **novio/a** (15)

field **campo** (14)

fifteen **quince** (P); fifteen minutes past (*the hour*) **y quince (cuarto)** (P); fifteen minutes to (*the hour*) **menos quince (cuarto)**

fifth **quinto/a** *adj.* (13)

fifty **cincuenta** (2)

fight **pelear** (9)

file **archivo** (12); computer file **archivo** (12)

fill (up) **llenar** (14); to fill out (*a form*) **llenar** (16)

finally **por fin** (4)

find **encontrar (ue)** (8); to find out (about) **enterarse (de)** (17)

fine **muy bien** (P)

finger **dedo (de la mano)** (11)

finish **acabar** (11)

first *adj.* **primer, primero/a** (13); *adv.* **primero** (4); at first site **a primera vista** (15); first class **primera clase** *f.* (7) first floor of a building **segundo piso** (12); the first of (*month*) **el primero de** (5)

fish (*cooked*) **pescado** (6); (*animal*) **pez** *m.* (*pl.* **peces**) (14)

five **cinco** (P)

five hundred **quinientos/as** (3)

fix **arreglar** (12)

fixed price **precio fijo** (3)

flat tire **llanta desinflada** (14)

flexibility **flexibilidad** *f.* (11); lack of flexibility **falta de flexibilidad** (11)

flexible **flexible** (11)

flight **vuelo** (7); flight attendant **asistente** (*m., f.*) **de vuelo** (7)

floor (*of a building*) **piso** (12); first floor **segundo piso** (12); ground floor **planta baja** (12); second floor **tercer piso** (12); to sweep the floor **barrer el piso** (9)

flower **flor** *f.* (7)

folkloric **folklórico/a** (13)

following *adj.* **siguiente** (4)

food **comida** (6)

foolish **tonto/a** (2)

foot **pie** *m.* (11)

football **fútbol** (*m.*) **americano** (9)

for **por** *prep.* (4); (intended) for **para** *prep.* (2); for example **por ejemplo** (11); for heaven's sake **por Dios** (11); for the first/last time **por primera/última vez** (11)

forbid **prohibir (prohíbo)** (12)

foreign languages **lenguas** (*f. pl.*) **extranjeras** (1)

foreigner **extranjero/a** (1)

forest **bosque** *m.* (14)

forget (about) **olvidarse (de)** (8)

form (*to fill out*) **formulario** (18)

forty **cuarenta** (2)

four **cuatro** (P)

four hundred **cuatrocientos/as** (3)

fourteen **catorce** (P)

fourth **cuarto/a** *adj.* (13)

free time **ratos** (*m. pl.*) **libres** (9)

freedom **libertad** *f.* (17)

freeway **autopista** (14)

freezer **congelador** *m.* (9)

French (*language*) **francés** *n. m.* (1); **francés, francesa** *n., adj.* (2); French fried potato **patata frita**

frequently **con frecuencia** (1)

fresh **fresco/a** (6)

Friday **viernes** *m. inv.* (4)

fried **frito/a** (6); **patata frita** French fried potato

friend **amigo/a** (1)

friendly **amistoso/a** (15)

friendship **amistad** *f.* (15)

from **de** (P); **desde** (7); from the **del** (*contraction of* **de** + **el**) (2)

front: front desk **recepción** *f.* (18); in front of **delante de** *prep.* (5)

frozen **congelado/a** (5)

fruit **fruta** (6); **jugo de fruta** fruit juice (6)

full **completo/a** (18); full time **de tiempo completo** (11); full time job **trabajo de tiempo completo** (11)

fun: fun activity **afición** *f.* (9); to be fun **ser** (*irreg.*) **divertido/a** (9)

function *v.* **funcionar** (12)

furious **furioso/a** (5)

furniture **muebles** *m. pl.* (4); to dust the furniture **sacudir los muebles** (9)

# G

game **partido** (9)

garage **garaje** *m.* (4)

gas **gas** *m. s.* (12); gas station **estación** (*f.*) **de gasolina** (14); **gasolinera** (14)

gasoline **gasolina** (14)

generally **por lo general** (4)

German (*language*) **alemán** *m.* (1); **alemán, alemana** *n., adj.* (2)

get **conseguir** (*like* **seguir**) (8); **obtener** (*like* **tener**) (12); to get + *adj.* **ponerse** (*irreg.*) (*p.p.* **puesto**) (8); to get (*grades*) **sacar** (**qu**) (11); to get a cold **resfriarse (me resfrío)** (10); to get along well/poorly (with) **llevarse bien/mal (con)** (15); to get angry (at) **enojarse (con)** (8); to get bored **aburrirse** (9); to get divorced (from) **divorciarse (de)** (15); to get down (from) (*a vehicle*) **bajar (de)** (7); to get dressed **vestirse (i, i)** (4); to get off (of) (*a vehicle*) **bajar (de)** (7); to get on (*a vehicle*) **subir (a)** (7); to get sick **enfermarse** (8); to get together (with) **reunirse (me reúno) (con)** (8); to get up **levantarse** (4); to get up on the wrong side of the bed **levantarse con el pie izquierdo** (11)

gift **regalo** (2)

girl **muchacha** (4); **niña** (2)

girlfriend **novia** (5)

give **dar** (*irreg.*) (7); to give (*as a gift*) **regalar** (7); to give (someone) a shot, injection **poner(le)** (*irreg.*) (*p.p.* **puesto**) **una inyección** (10); give a party **dar** (*irreg.*)/ **hacer** (*irreg.*) (*p.p.* **hecho**) **una fiesta** (8)

glasses **gafas** *f. pl.* (10); to wear glasses **llevar gafas** (10)

go **ir** (*irreg.*) (3); **seguir (i, i) (g)** (14); to go to a bar / concert / disco **ir a un bar / un concierto / una discoteca** (9); to go by bus / plane / boat, ship / train **ir en autobús / avión / barco / tren** (7); to go camping **hacer** (*irreg.*) (*p.p.* **hecho**) *camping* (7); to go home **regresar a casa** (1); to go out (with) **salir** (*irreg.*) **(con)**; (4); to go shopping **ir de compras** (3); to go to (*a class, function*) **asistir (a)** (2); to go to bed **acostarse (ue)** (4); to go to see a movie **ir a ver una película** (9); to go to the movies / theater **ir al cine / teatro** (9); to go through security check **pasar por el control de la seguridad** (7); to go up **subir a** (7)

going: to be going (*to do something*) **ir** (*irreg.*) **a** + *inf.* (3)

golf **golf** *m.* (9)

good **buen, bueno/a** *adj.* (2); good afternoon **buenas tardes** (P); **(muy) buenas** (P); good evening **buenas tardes** (P); **(muy) buenas** (P); good morning **buenos días** (P); good night

buenas noches (P); it's (very) good weather **hace muy buen tiempo** (5); the good thing, news **lo bueno** (10); to have a good time **divertirse (ie, i)** (4); **pasarlo bien** (8); to make a good impression on someone **caerle** (*irreg.*) **bien a alguien** (16)

good-bye **adiós** (P); to say good-bye (to) **despedirse** (*like* **pedir**) **(de)** (8)

good-looking **guapo/a** (2)

gorilla **gorila** *m.* (14)

govern **gobernar (ie)** (17)

government **gobierno** (14)

grade **calificación** *f.* (11); **nota** (11); **grado** (9)

graduate (from) **graduarse (me gradúo) (en)** (16)

grandchildren **nietos** *m. pl.* (2)

granddaughter **nieta** (2)

grandfather **abuelo** (2)

grandmother **abuela** (2)

grandparents **abuelos** *m. pl.* (2)

grandson **nieto** (2)

gray **gris** (3)

great **gran, grande** (2)

green **verde** (3)

greet each other **saludarse** (10)

groom **novio** (15)

ground floor **planta baja** (12)

grow **crecer (zc)** (15)

guest **invitado/a** *n.* (8); **huésped(a)** (18)

guide **guía** *m., f.* (13)

# H

habit **costumbre** *f.* (9)

haggle **regatear** (3)

hairstylist **peluquero/a** (16)

half-past (*the hour*) **y media** (P)

ham **jamón** *m.* (6)

hamburger **hamburguesa** (6)

hand **mano** *f.* (11); to hand in **entregar (gu)** (11)

handbag **cartera** (3)

handsome **guapo/a** (2)

happen **pasar** (5)

happening *n.* **acontecimiento** (17)

happy **alegre** (5); **contento/a** (5); **feliz** (*pl.* **felices**) (8); to be happy (about) **alegrarse (de)** (12)

hard **difícil** (5); hard drive **disco duro** (12)

hat **sombrero** (3)

hate **odiar** (7)

have **tener** (*irreg.*) (3); *auxiliary with past participle* **haber** (*inf. form of* **hay** there is, there are) (12); to have a birthday

cumplir años (8); to have a fever **tener fiebre** (10); to have a good time **divertirse (ie, i)** (4); to have a good/bad time **pasarlo bien/mal** (8); to have a headache / stomachache / toothache **tener dolor de cabeza / estómago / muela** (10); to have a pain in **tener dolor de** (10); to have a party **dar** (*irreg.*) / **hacer** (*irreg.*) (*p.p.* **hecho**) **una fiesta** (8); to have a picnic **hacer un picnic** (9); to have breakfast **desayunar** (6); to have dinner, supper **cenar** (6); to have just (*done something*) **acabar de** + *inf.* (6); to have lunch **almorzar (ue)** (4); to have to (*do something*) **tener que** + *inf.* (3)

he *subj. pron.* **él** (1); he is **es** (P)

head **cabeza** (10)

headache **dolor** (*m.*) **de cabeza** (10); to have a headache **tener** (*irreg.*) **dolor de cabeza** (10)

health **salud** *f.* (10)

healthy: to lead a healthy life **llevar una vida sana** (10)

hear **oír** (*irreg.*) (4)

heart **corazón** *m.* (10)

heat **gas** *m.* (12)

heaven: for heaven's sake **por Dios** (11)

heavy (*meal, food*) **fuerte** (6); not heavy **ligero/a** (6)

hello **hola** (P)

help **ayudar** (6)

her *poss. adj.* **su(s)** (2)

here **aquí** (1)

highway **carretera** (14)

his *poss. adj.* **su(s)** (2)

history **historia** (1)

hit **pegar (gu)** (9); to hit (*a part of one's body*) **pegarse (gu) en/con/contra** (11)

hobby **afición** *f.* (9); **pasatiempo** (9)

hockey **hockey** *m.* (9)

holiday **día** (*m.*) **festivo** (8)

home **casa** (2); at home **en casa** (1); home appliance **aparato doméstico** (9); to go home **regresar a casa** (1)

homework **tarea** (4)

honeymoon **luna de miel** (15)

hope **esperanza** (17); to hope **esperar** (12); I hope (that) **ojalá (que)** (13)

hors d'oeuvres **entremeses** *m. pl.* (8)

horse **caballo** (14); to ride a horse **montar a caballo** (9)

host **anfitrión** *m.* (8)

hostess **anfitriona** (8)

hot dog **salchicha** (6)

hot: to be (feel) (very) hot **tener** (*irreg.*) **(mucho) calor** (5); it's (very) hot **hace (mucho) calor** (5)

hotel **hotel** *m.* (18); hotel guest **huésped(a)** (18); luxury hotel **hotel de lujo** (18); two (three) star hotel **hotel de dos (tres) estrellas** (18)

house **casa** (2)

household chore **quehacer** (*m.*) **doméstico**

how? **¿cómo?** (P); how are you doing? **¿qué tal?** (P); how are you? **¿cómo está(s)?** (P); how many? **¿cuántos/as?** (1); how much? **¿cuánto/a?** (1); how much does it cost? **¿cuánto cuesta?** (3); how much is it **¿cuánto es?** (3)

how + *adj.*! **¡qué + *adj.*!** (11); how clumsy! **¡qué torpe!** (11); how strange that . . . ! **¡qué extraño que… !** (13); to know how to (*do something*) **saber + *inf.*** (6)

however **sin embargo** (5)

humanities **humanidades** *f. pl.* (1)

hundred **cien, ciento** (2)

hungry: to be (very) hungry **tener** (*irreg.*) **(mucha) hambre** (6)

hurry: to be in a hurry **tener** (*irreg.*) **prisa** (3)

hurt **doler (ue)** (10)

hurt oneself **hacerse** (*irreg.*) (*p.p.* **hecho**) **daño** (11)

husband **esposo** (2); **marido** (15)

# I

I *subj. pron.* **yo** (1); I am **soy** (P); I (don't) agree **(no) estoy de acuerdo** (2); I hope, wish (that) **ojalá (que)** (13); I'm from . . . **soy de…** (P); I'm sorry **discúlpeme** (11); I'm (very) sorry! **¡lo siento (mucho)!** (11); I would (really) like **me gustaría** (7); yes, I (no, I don't) like . . . **sí, (no, no) me gusta…** (P)

ice cream **helado** (6)

ID **identificación** *f.* (16)

identification card **tarjeta de identificación** (11)

if **si** (2)

impossible: it's impossible that **es imposible que** (13)

improbable: it's improbable that **es improbable que** (13)

in **en** (P); in a balanced way **equilibradamente** (10); in advance **con anticipación** (18); in case **en caso de que** (15); in cash **al contado** (16); **en efectivo** (16); in front of **delante de** (5); in installments **a plazos** (16); in love

(with) **enamorado/a (de)** (15); in order to **para** (2); in the morning (afternoon, evening) **por la mañana (tarde, noche)** (1); (*an hour*) in the morning (afternoon, evening) **de la mañana (tarde, noche)** (P)

incredible: it's incredible that **es increíble que** (13)

inequality **desigualdad** *f.* (17)

inexpensive **barato/a** (3)

infancy **infancia** (15)

inform **informar** (17)

injection: to give (someone) an injection **ponerle** (*irreg.*) (*p.p.* **puesto**) **una inyección** *f.* (10)

injure oneself **lastimarse** (11)

inner ear **oído** (10)

insist (on) **insistir (en)** (12)

installment: to pay in installments **pagar (gu) a plazos** (16)

instead of **en vez de** (16)

intelligent **inteligente** (2)

intend **pensar (ie)** (4)

intended for **para** (2)

interest *n.* **interés** *m.* (16)

interesting: to be interesting **interesar** (7)

interview *n.* **entrevista** (16); *v.* **entrevistar** (16)

interviewer **entrevistador(a)** (16)

invite **invitar** (6)

iPod *iPod m.* (12)

iron clothing **planchar la ropa** (9)

island **isla** (5)

Italian (*language*) **italiano** *m.* (1)

its *poss. adj.* **su(s)** (2)

# J

jacket **chaqueta** (3)

January **enero** (5)

jeans *jeans m. pl.* (3)

job **trabajo** (11); **puesto** (16); full time/part time job **trabajo de tiempo completo/parcial** (11)

jog **correr** (9)

joke **chiste** *m.* (8)

journalist **periodista** *m., f.* (16)

juice (6); fruit juice **jugo de fruta** (6)

July **julio** (5)

June **junio** (5)

just in case **por si acaso** (11)

# K

keep **guardar** (12); to keep on going **seguir (i, i) (g)** (14); to keep peace **mantener** (*like* **tener**) **la paz** (17)

key *n.* **llave** *f.* (11); to key in **escribir** (*p.p.* **escrito**) **en la computadora** (16)

kind *adj.* **amable** (2)

king **rey** *m.* (17)

kiosk **quiosco** (118)

kitchen **cocina** (4)

know **conocer (zc)** (6); **saber** (*irreg.*) (6); to know how to (*do something*) **saber + *inf.*** (6)

# L

laborer **obrero/a** (16)

lack **escasez** *f.* (*pl.* **escaseces**) (14); lack of flexibility **falta de flexibilidad** (11)

lake **lago** (14)

lamp **lámpara** (4)

landlady **dueña** (12)

landlord **dueño** (12)

language: foreign languages **lenguas** (*f. pl.*) **extranjeras** (1)

large **gran, grande** (2)

last *adj.* **pasado/a** (10); for the last time **por última vez** (11); last night **anoche** (10); to last **durar** (17)

late **tarde** *adv.* (1); to be late **estar** (*irreg.*) **atrasado/a** (7)

later: see you later **hasta luego** (P)

latest: the latest style **de última moda** (3)

laugh **reírse (i, i) (me río)** (8)

law **ley** *f.* (17)

lawyer **abogado/a** (16)

lazy **perezoso/a** (2)

lead a healthy/calm life **llevar una vida sana/tranquila** (10)

learn **aprender** (2); to learn (about) **enterarse (de)** (17)

least: at least **por lo menos** (8)

leave (*a place*) **salir** (*irreg.*) (4); to leave (behind) (in [*a place*]) **dejar (en)** (9); to leave (for, to) (*a place*) **salir (para)** (4); to leave (from) (*a place*) **salir (de)**

left: to be left **quedar(se)** (11); to the left (of) **a la izquierda (de)** (5)

leg **pierna** (11)

lend **prestar** (7)

lenses: contact lenses **lentes** (*m. pl.*) **de contacto** (10); to wear contact lenses **llevar lentes de contacto** (10)

less: less . . . than **menos… que** (5)

letter **carta** (2)

lettuce **lechuga** (6)

level **nivel** *m.* (14)

liberty **libertad** *f.* (17)

librarian **bibliotecario/a** (1)

library **biblioteca** (1)

license: driver's license **licencia de manejar/conducir** (14)

lie **mentira** (12)

life: to lead a healthy/calm life **llevar una vida sana/tranquila** (10)

light *adj.* **ligero/a** (6); *n.* **luz** *f.* (*pl.* **luces**) (11)

like: do you (*fam. s.*) like . . . ? **¿te gusta... ?** (9); do you (*form. s.*) like. . . ? **¿le gusta... ?** (9); I would (really) like . . . **me gustaría...** (7); to feel like (*doing something*) **tener** (*irreg.*) **ganas de** + *inf.* (3); to like very much **encantar** (7); yes, I (no, I don't) like . . . **sí, (no, no) me gusta...** (9); what are you like? **¿cómo es usted?** (9)

likeable **simpático/a** (2)

likely: it's likely that **es probable que** (13)

likewise **igualmente** (P)

limit: speed limit **límite** (*m.*) **de velocidad** (14)

line: to stand in line **hacer** (*irreg.*) (*p.p.* **hecho**) **cola** (7)

listen (to) **escuchar** (1)

literature **literatura** (1)

little *adj.* **poco/a** (3); *adv.* **poco** (1)

live **vivir** (2); to live in peace **vivir en paz** (17)

living room **sala** (4)

loan **préstamo** (16)

lobster **langosta** (6)

lodging **alojamiento** (18)

long **largo/a** (2)

look at **mirar** (2); to look for **buscar (qu)** (1)

lose **perder (ie)** (4)

lot: a lot (of) **mucho/a** (2); an awful lot **muchísimo** (7)

love **amar** (15); **encantar** (7); **querer** (*irreg.*) (15); *n.* **amor** *m.* (15); in love (with) **enamorado/a (de)** (15); to fall in love (with) **enamorarse (de)** (15)

luggage **equipaje** *m.* (7)

lunch **almuerzo** (6); to have lunch **almorzar (ue) (c)** (4)

lung **pulmón** *m.* (10)

luxury *n.* **lujo** (12); luxury hotel **hotel** (*m.*) **de lujo** (18)

–ly *adverbial suffix* **–mente** (11)

# M

ma'am **señora (Sra.)** (P)

machine: answering machine **contestador** (*m.*) **automático** (12); automatic teller machine **cajero automático** (16)

magazine **revista** (2)

maid **criada** (18)

mail **correo** (18)

maintain **mantener** (*like* **tener**) (17); to maintain peace **mantener la paz** (17)

make **hacer** (*irreg.*) (*p.p.* **hecho**) (4); to make a good/bad impression on someone **caerle** (*irreg.*) **bien/mal a alguien** (16); to make a mistake (about) **equivocarse (qu) (de)** (11); to make plans to (*do something*) **hacer planes para** + *inf.* (9); to make stops **hacer escalas/paradas** (7); to make the bed **hacer la cama** (9)

mall: shopping mall **centro commercial** (3)

man **hombre** *m.* (1)

manager **gerente** *m., f.* (16)

many **muchos/as** (2); as many . . . as **tantos/as... como** (5); how many? **¿cuántos/as?** (1)

March **marzo** (5)

market(place) **mercado** (3)

marriage **matrimonio** (15)

married **casado/a** (2); married couple **matrimonio** (15); **pareja** (15)

marry **casarse (con)** (15)

masterpiece **obra maestra** (13)

match (*for lighting things*) **fósforo** (18); (*sport*) **partido** (9)

material **material** *n. m.* (3)

mathematics **matemáticas** *f. pl.* (1)

May **mayo** (5)

me *obj.* (*of prep.*) **mí** (5); with me **conmigo** (5)

meal **comida** (6)

means: means of communication **medio** (*s.*) **de comunicación** (17); means (of transportation) **modo** (*s.*) **(de transporte)** (7); **transporte** *m.* (14)

meat **carne** *f.* (6)

mechanic **mecánico/a** (14)

medical: medical doctor **médico/a** (2); medical office **consultorio** (10)

medicine **medicina** (10)

meet (*someone somewhere*) **encontrarse (ue) (con)** (10)

memory **memoria** (12)

menu **menú** *m.* (6)

merchant **comerciante** *m., f.* (16)

messy **desordenado/a** (5)

Mexican **mexicano/a** *n., adj.* (2)

microwave oven **horno de microondas** (9)

middle age **madurez** *f.* (15)

midnight **medianoche** *f.* (8)

military service **servicio militar** (17)

milk **leche** *f.* (6)

million **un millón** (*m.*) **de** (3)

mineral water **agua** *f.* (*but* **el agua**) **mineral** (6)

miss (*a function*) **perder (ie)** (4)

Miss **señorita (Srta.)** (P)

mistake: to make a mistake (about) **equivocarse (qu) (de)** (11)

modem **módem** *m.* (12)

modern **moderno/a** (13)

molar **muela** (10)

mom **mamá** (2)

Monday **lunes** *m. inv.* (4)

money **dinero** (1)

month **mes** *m.* (5)

moped **moto(cicleta)** *f.* (12)

more **más** *adv.* (1); more . . . than **más... que** (5)

morning: (*an hour*) in the morning **de la mañana** (P); in the morning **por la mañana** (1); good morning **buenos días** (P)

mother **mamá** *f.* (2); **madre** *f.* (2)

motorcycle **moto(cicleta)** *f.* (12)

mountain **montaña** (7)

mouse **ratón** *m.* (12)

mouth **boca** (10)

move (*residence*) **mudarse** (16)

movie **película** (4); movie theater **cine** *m.* (4); movies **cine** (4); to go to see a movie **ir** (*irreg.*) **a ver una película** (9); to go to the movies **ir al cine** (9)

Mr. **señor (Sr.)** *m.* (P)

Mrs. **señora (Sra.)** (P)

Ms. **señorita (Srta.)** (P)

much **mucho** *adv.* (1); as much as **tanto como** (5); as much . . . as **tanto... como** (5); how much **¿cuánto/a?** (1); how much does it cost? **¿cuánto cuesta?** (3); how much is it? **¿cuánto es?** (3); to like very much **encantar** (7); too much **demasiado** *adv.* (12)

museum: to visit a museum **visitar un museo** (9)

mushroom **champiñón** *m.* (6)

music **música** (13)

musician **músico/a** *n. m., f.* (13)

must (*do something*) **deber** (+ *inf.*) (2)

my *poss. adj.* **mi(s)** (2): my name is . . . **me llamo...** (P)

# N

name: my name is . . . **me llamo...** (P); what's your (*fam. s.*) name **¿cómo te llamas?** (P); what's your (*form. s.*) name? **¿cómo se llama usted?** (P) nap: to take a nap **dormir (ue, u) la siesta** (4)

nationality **nacionalidad** *f.* (18)

natural resources **recursos** (*m. pl.*) **naturales** (14)

nature **naturaleza** (14)

nauseated **mareado/a** (10)

neat **ordenado/a** (5)

necessary **necesario/a** (2); it is necessary to (*do something*) **hay que** + *inf.* (13)

need *v.* **necesitar** (1)

neighbor **vecino/a** (12)

neighborhood **barrio** (12), **vecindad** *f.* (12)

neither **tampoco** (6)

nephew **sobrino** (2)

nervous **nervioso/a** (5)

Net **Red** *f.* (12); to surf the Net **navegar (gu) la Red** (12)

never **jamás** (6); **nunca** (2); almost never **casi nunca** (2)

new **nuevo/a** (2); New Year's Eve **Noche** (*f.*) **Vieja** (8)

newlywed (to) **recién casado/a (con)** (15)

news **noticias** *f. pl.* (17); news media **prensa** (17); piece of news **noticia** (8)

newscast **noticiero** (17)

newspaper **periódico** (2)

next **próximo/a** (4); next week **la semana que viene** (4)

nice **amable** (2), **simpático/a** (2); nice to meet you **encantado/a** (P)

niece **sobrina** (2)

night: at night **por la noche** (1); (*an hour*) at night **de la noche** (P); good night **buenas noches** (P); last night **anoche** (10)

nine **nueve** (P)

nine hundred **novecientos/as** (3)

nineteen **diecinueve** (P)

ninety **noventa** (2)

ninth **noveno/a** (13)

no **no** (P); **ningún, ninguno** (6); no one **nadie** (6); no vacancy **completo/a** (18)

nobody **nadie** (6)

noise **ruido** (4)

none **ningún, ninguno/a** (6)

nonsmoking section **sección** (*f.*) **de no fumar** (7)

north **norte** *m.* (5)

nose **nariz** (*pl.* **narices**) (10)

not any **ningún, ninguno/a** (6); not anybody **nadie** (6); not anything **nada** (6); not either **tampoco** (6); not heavy **ligero/a** (6); there is not / are not **no hay** (P); to not attend **faltar (a)** (8)

notebook **cuaderno** (1)

nothing **nada** (6)

November **noviembre** *m.* (5)

now **ahora** (1)

nuclear **nuclear** (14); nuclear energy **energía nuclear** (14)

number **número** (2)

nurse **enfermero/a** (10)

# O

obey **obedecer (zc)** (14)

obligation **deber** *m.* (17)

obtain **conseguir** (*like* **seguir**) (8); **obtener** (*like* **tener**) (12)

ocean **océano** (7)

October **octubre** *m.* (5)

of *prep.* **de** (P); of course! **¡por supuesto!** (11); of the **del** (*contraction of* **de** + **el**) (2); of the university **universitario/a** (11)

off: to get off (of) (*a vehicle*) **bajar (de)** (7); to take off (*clothing*) **quitarse** (4); to turn off **apagar (gu)** (11)

offer *v.* **ofrecer (zc)** (7)

office **oficina** (1); employment office **direccion** (*f.*) **de personal** (16); (*medical*) office **consultorio** (10); personnel office **dirección** (*f.*) **de personal** (16)

oil **aceite** *m.* (14); to check the oil **revisar el aceite** (14)

OK **regular** *adj.* (P)

old **viejo/a** *adj.* (2); old age **vejez** *f.* (15); to be . . . years old **tener** (*irreg.*) . . . **años** (2)

older **mayor** (5)

on **en** (P); on a trip **de viaje** (7); on Mondays (Tuesdays, . . . ) **los lunes (martes,... )** (4); on the dot (*time*) **en punto** (P); on time **a tiempo** (7); on top of **encima de** (5); to be on a diet **estar** (*irreg.*) **a dieta** (6); to be on vacation **estar de vacaciones** (7); to get on (*a vehicle*) **subir (a)** (7); to go on vacation **ir** (*irreg.*) **de vacaciones** (7); to put on (*clothing*) **ponerse** (*irreg.*) (*p.p.* **puesto**) (4); to talk on the phone **hablar por teléfono** (1); to turn on (*appliances*) **poner** (4)

once a week **una vez a la semana** (2)

one **un, uno/a** (P)

one hundred **cien, ciento** (2)

one-way (*ticket*) **de ida** (7)

oneself: to enjoy oneself **divertirse (ie, i)** (4); to hurt oneself **hacerse** (*irreg.*) (*p.p.* **hecho**) **daño** (11); to injure oneself **lastimarse** (11); to take care of oneself **cuidarse** (10)

only **sólo** *adv.* (1)

open **abierto/a** (5); to open **abrir** (*p.p.* **abierto**) (2)

opera **ópera** (13)

operate (*a machine*) **manejar** (12)

or **o** (P)

oral report **informe** (*m.*) **oral** (11)

orange (*color*) *adj.* **anaranjado/a** (3); orange (*fruit*) **naranja** (6)

order (*in a restaurant*) **pedir (i, i)** (4); (*someone to do something*) **mandar** (12); in order to **para** (2)

other **otro/a** (2); others **los/las demás** (12)

ought to (*do something*) **deber** (+ *inf.*) (2)

our *poss. adj.* **nuestro/a(s)** (2)

outdoors **afuera** *adv.* (5)

outskirts **afueras** *n. f. pl.* (12)

oven: microwave oven **horno de microondas** (9)

over there **allí** (3)

own *adj.* **propio/a** (15)

owner **dueño/a** (6)

# P

pace **ritmo** (14)

pack one's suitcase(s) **hacer** (*irreg.*) (*p.p.* **hecho**) **la(s) maleta(s)** (7)

package **paquete** *m.* (18)

pain (in) **dolor** (*m.*) **(de)** (10); to have a pain in **tener** (*irreg.*) **dolor de** (10)

paint (the walls) **pintar (las paredes)** (9)

painter **pintor(a)** (13)

painting (*piece of art*) **cuadro,** (*general, art form, and piece of art*) **pintura** (13)

pair **par** *m.* (3)

pants **pantalones** *m. pl.* (3)

paper **papel** *m.* (1)

pardon me **con permiso** (P), **discúlpeme** (11); **lo siento** (11); **perdón** (P)

parents **padres** *m. pl.* (2)

park *n.* **parque** *m.* (5); to park *v.* **estacionar** (11)

part time **de tiempo parcial** (11); part time job **trabajo de tiempo parcial** (11)

participate (*in a sport*) **practicar (qu)** (9)

party **fiesta** (1); to give/have a party **dar** (*irreg.*)/**hacer** (*irreg.*) (*p.p.* **hecho**) **una fiesta** (8)

pass through security (check) **pasar por el control de la seguridad** (7)

passage **pasaje** *m.* (7)

passenger **pasajero/a** *n.* (7)

passport **pasaporte** *m.* (18)

past *adj.* **pasado/a** (10)

pastime **afición** *f.* (9); **pasatiempo** (9)

pastry (small) **pastelito** (18); pastry shop **pastelería** (18)

patient **paciente** *n., m., f.* (10)

patio **patio** (4)

pay (for) **pagar (gu)** (1); to pay cash **pagar al contado/en efectivo** (16); to pay in installments **pagar a plazos** (16)

peace **paz** *f.* (*pl.* **paces**) (17); to live in peace **vivir en paz** (17); to maintain, keep peace **mantener** (*like* **tener**) **la paz** (17)

peas **arvejas** *f. pl.* (6)

peasant **campesino/a** (14)

pen **bolígrafo** (1)

pencil **lápiz** *m.* (*pl.* **lápices**) (1)

people **gente** *f. s.* (13)

perform (*a part*) **desempeñar** (13)

permit **permitir** (12)

person **persona** (1)

personnel director **director(a) de personal** (16); personnel office **dirección** (*f.*) **de personal** (16)

pet; animal (*m.*) **doméstico** (14); **mascota** (2)

pharmacist **farmacéutico/a** (10)

pharmacy **farmacia** (10)

philosophy **filosofía** (1)

phone: cellular phone **teléfono celular** (12) to talk on the phone **hablar por teléfono** (1)

photo(graph) **foto(grafía)** *f.* (7)

photographer **fotógrafo/a** (16)

photography **fotografía** (13); photography equipment **equipo fotográfico** (12)

photos: to take photos **sacar (qu) fotos** (7)

physics **física** *s.* (1)

pick up **recoger (j)** (11)

picnic: to have a picnic **hacer** (*irreg.*) (*p.p.* **hecho**) **un** *picnic* (9)

pie **pastel** *m.* (6)

piece: piece of advice **consejo** (6); piece of news **noticia** (8); piece of work **trabajo** (11)

pill **pastilla** (10)

pillow **almohada** (18)

pink **rosado/a** (3)

place **lugar** *m.* (1); (*in line*) **puesto** (7); to place **poner** (*irreg.*) (*p.p.* **puesto**) (4); to take place in/at (*place*) **ser** (*irreg.*) **en** + *place* (8)

plan to **pensar (ie)** (4); to make plans to (*do something*) **hacer** (*irreg.*) (*p.p.* **hecho**) **planes para** + *inf.* (9)

plane: to go/travel by plane **ir** (*irreg.*) **en avión** (7)

plates **platos** *m. pl.* (4)

play (*a game, sport*) **jugar (ue) (al)** (4); to play (*a musical instrument*) **tocar (qu)** (1); to play (*a part*) **desempeñar** (13); to play cards **jugar a las cartas** (9); to play chess **jugar ajedrez** (4); to play sports **practicar (qu) deportes** (10)

player **jugador(a)** (9); (tape) player **grabadora** (12)

playwright **dramaturgo/a** (13)

please **por favor** (P); to please **agradar** (13)

pleased to meet you **encantado/a, mucho gusto** (P)

pleasing: to be pleasing **gustar** (7)

plumber **plomero/a** (16)

poet **poeta** *m., f.* (13)

police officer **policía** *m., f.* (14)

politician **político/a** (17)

politics **política** *s.* (17)

pollute **contaminar** (14)

pollution: air pollution **contaminación** (*f.*) **del aire** (14) there's (lots of) pollution **hay (mucha) contaminación** *f.* (5)

poor **pobre** (2)

poorly **mal** *adv.* (1)

population **población** *f.* (14)

pork chop **chuleta de cerdo** (6)

port **puerto** (7)

porter **maletero** (7)

position **puesto** (16)

possible **posible** (2)

post office **correo; oficina de correos** (18)

postage stamp **sello** (18)

postcard **tarjeta postal** (7)

potato **papa** (6); **patata** *Sp.* (6); French fried potato **patata frita** (6)

pottery **cerámica** (13)

practice **entrenar** (9); **practicar (qu)** (1); to practice sports **practicar (qu) deportes** (10)

prefer **preferir (ie, i)** (3)

prepare **preparar** (6)

prescription **receta** (10)

present (*gift*) **regalo** *n.* (2)

press *n.* **prensa** (17)

pressure: to be under (a lot of) pressure **sufrir (muchas) presiones** (11)

pretty **bonito/a** (2)

price **precio** (3); fixed, set price **precio fijo** (3)

print **imprimir** (12)

printer **impresora** (12)

probable: it's probable that **es probable que** (13)

profession **profesión** *f.* (16)

professor **profesor(a)** (1)

programmer **programador(a)** (16)

prohibit **prohibir (prohíbo)** (12)

promise *v.* **prometer** (7)

protect **proteger (j)** (14)

provided (that) **con tal (de) que** (15)

psychiatrist **siquiatra** *m., f.* (16)

psychologist **sicólogo/a** (16)

psychology **sicología** (1)

public **público/a** *adj.* (14)

punish **castigar (gu)** (17)

pure **puro/a** (14)

purple **morado/a** (3)

purse **bolsa** (3)

put **poner** (*irreg.*) (*p.p.* **puesto**) (4); to put on (*clothing*) **ponerse** (*irreg.*) (4)

# Q

quarter after/to (the *hour*) **y/menos cuarto** (P)

queen **reina** (17)

question: to ask (a question) **hacer** (*irreg.*) (*p.p.* **hecho**) **una pregunta** (4); **preguntar** (6)

quit **dejar** (16); (*doing something*) **dejar de** + *inf.* (10)

quiz **prueba** (11)

# R

radio (*apparatus*) **radio** *m.* (12); (*medium*) **radio** *f.* (12); portable radio **radio portátil** (12)

rain **llover (ue)** (5); it's raining **llueve** (5)

raincoat **impermeable** *m.* (3)

raise **aumento** (12); (in salary) **aumento de sueldo** (16)

rather **bastante** *adv.* (15)

react **reaccionar** (8)

read **leer (y)** (2)

receive **recibir** (2)

recommend **recomendar (ie)** (7)

record **grabar** (12)

recorder (tape) **grabadora** (12)

recycle **reciclar** (14)

red **rojo/a** (3); red wine **vino tinto** (6)

reductions **rebajas** *f. pl.* (3)

refrigerator **refrigerador** *m.* (9)

regret **sentir (ie, i)** (13)

relative **pariente** *m., f.* (2)

remain **quedar** (11); to remain (*in a place*) **quedarse** (5)

remember **acordarse (ue) (de)** (11); **recordar (ue)** (8)

remote control **control** (*m.*) **remoto** (12)

rent *n.* **alquiler** *m.* (12); to rent *v.* **alquilar** (12) renter **inquilino/a** (12)

repair **arreglar** (12); repair shop **taller** *m.* (14)

report **informe** *m.* (11), **trabajo** (11), oral/written report **informe oral/escrito** (11)

reporter **reportero/a** (17)

represent **representar** (13)

reservations **reservaciones** *f. pl.* (18); **reservas** *f. pl.* (18)

resign (from) **renunciar (a)** (16)

resolve **resolver (ue)** (*p.p.* **resuelto**) (14)

resource **recurso**; natural resources **recursos** (*m. pl.*) **naturales** (14)

responsibility **deber** *m.* (17); **responsabilidad** *f.* (17)

rest *v.* **descansar** (4)

restaurant **restaurante** *m.* (6)

résumé **currículum** *m.* (*pl.* **currículos**) (16)

retire **jubilarse** (16)

return (*something*) **devolver** (*like* **volver**) (16); (*to a place*) **regresar** (1); **volver (ue)** (*p.p.* **vuelto**) (4)

rhythm **ritmo** (14)

rice **arroz** *m.* (*pl.* **arroces**) (6)

rich **rico/a** (2)

ride: to ride a bicycle **pasear en bicicleta** (9); to ride a horse **montar a caballo** (9)

ridiculous: it's ridiculous that **es ridículo que** (13)

right (*legal*) **derecho** *n.* (17); right? **¿no?**, (3), **¿verdad?** (3); right away **en seguida** (10); to be right **tener** (*irreg.*) **razón** (3); to the right of **a la derecha de** (5)

ring **sonar (ue)** (9)

river **río** (14)

road **camino** (14)

roast chicken **pollo asado** (6)

role (*in a play*) **papel** *m.* (13)

roller skates **patines** *m. pl.* (12)

rollerblade *v.* **patinar en línea** (9)

room **cuarto** (1); room (*in a hotel*) **habitación** *f.* (18); double room **habitación doble** (18); living room **sala** (4); room and full board (all meals) **pensión** (*f.*) **completa** (18); room service **servicio de cuartos** (18); room with(out) attached bath/shower **habitación con/sin baño/ducha** (18); room with breakfast and one other meal **media pensión** (18); single room **habitación individual** (18); to change rooms **cambiar de cuarto** (12); waiting room **sala de espera** (7)

roommate **compañero/a de cuarto** (1)

round-trip ticket **billete** (*m.*)/**boleto de ida y vuelta** (7)

routine: daily routine **rutina diaria** (4)

rug **alfombra** (4)

ruins *n.* **ruinas** *f. pl.* (13)

rule **gobernar (ie)** (17)

run **correr** (9); (*machines*) **funcionar** (12); to run (into) (*vehicles*) **chocar (gu) (con)** (14); to run into **darse** (*irreg.*) **en/con/contra** (11); **pegarse (gu) en/con/contra** (11); to run out (of) **acabar** (11)

# S

sad **triste** (5)

salad **ensalada** (6)

salary **salario** (16); **sueldo** (12)

sales **rebajas** *f. pl.* (3)

salesperson **vendedor(a)** (16)

salmon **salmón** *m.* (6)

same **mismo/a** (10); same here **igualmente** (P)

sandal **sandalia** (3)

sandwich **sándwich** *m.* (6)

Saturday **sábado** (4)

sausage **salchicha** (6)

save (*a place*) **guardar** (7); (*documents*) **guardar** (12); (*energy*) **conservar** (14); (money) **ahorrar** (16)

savings account **cuenta de ahorros** (16)

say **decir** (*irreg.*) (*p.p.* **dicho**) (7); to say good-bye (to) **despedirse** (*like* **pedir**) **(de)** (8)

schedule **horario** (11)

school **escuela** (9); school subject **materia** (1)

schoolteacher **maestro/a** (16)

science **ciencias** *f. pl.* (*academic discipline*) (1); computer science **computación** *f.* (1)

script **guión** *m.* (13)

sculpt **esculpir** (13)

sculptor **escultor(a)** (13)

sculpture **escultura** (13)

sea **mar** *m.* (7)

search **registrar** (18)

season **estación** *f.* (5)

seat **asiento** (7)

second **segundo/a** *adj.* (13); second floor **primer piso** (12)

secretary **secretario/a** (1)

section: (non) smoking section **sección** *f.* **de (no) fumar** (7)

security: to go/pass through security check **pasar por el control de la seguridad** (7)

see **ver** (*irreg.*) (*p.p.* **visto**) (4); see you around **nos vemos** (P); see you later **hasta luego** (P); see you tomorrow **hasta mañana** (P)

seem **parecer (zc)** (13)

sell **vender** (2)

send **mandar** (7)

separate (from) *v.* **separarse (de)** (15)

separation **separación** *f.* (15)

September **septiembre** *m.* (5)

servant **criado/a** (16)

serve **servir (i, i)** (4)

service **servicio** (14); military service **servicio militar** (17); room service **servicio de cuartos** (18)

set: set price **precio fijo** (3); to set the table **poner** (*irreg.*) (*p.p.* **puesto**) **la mesa** (9)

seven **siete** (P)

seven hundred **setecientos/as** (3)

seventeen **diecisiete** (P)

seventh **séptimo/a** *adj.* (13)

seventy **setenta** (2)

shame: it's a shame that **es una lástima que** (13); what a shame that . . . ! **¡qué lástima que… !** (13)

shampoo **champú** *m.* (18)

shave oneself **afeitarse** (4)

*sharp* (*time*) **en punto** (P)

she *subj. pron.* **ella** (1); she is **es** (P)

sheets **sábanas** *f. pl.* (18)

shellfish **mariscos** *m. pl.* (6)

ship **barco** (7); to go/travel by ship **ir** (*irreg.*) **en barco** (7)

shirt **camisa** (3)

shoe **zapato** (3); tennis shoe **zapato de tenis** (3)

shop **tienda** (3); (repair) shop **taller** *m.* (14); tobacco shop **estanco** (18)

shopkeeper **comerciante** *m., f.* (16)

shopping **de compras** (3); shopping mall **centro comercial** (3); to go shopping **ir** (*irreg.*) **de compras** (3)

short (*in height*) **bajo/a** (2); (*in length*) **corto/a** (2)

shortage **escasez** *f.* (*pl.* **escaseces**) (14)

shot: to give (someone) a shot **ponerle** (*irreg.*) (*p.p.* **puesto**) **una inyección** *f.* (10)

should (*do something*) **deber** (+ *inf.*) (2)

show **mostrar (ue)** (7)

shower: room with attached shower **habitación** (*f.*) **con ducha** (18); to take a shower **ducharse** (4)

shrimp **camarones** *m. pl.* (6)

sick **enfermo/a** *adj.* (5); to get sick **enfermarse** (8) sight: at first sight **a primera vista** (15)

silk **seda** (3); it's made of silk **es de seda** (3)

silly **tonto/a** (2)

sing **cantar** (1)

singer **cantante** *m., f.* (13)

single (*not married*) **soltero/a** (2); single room **habitación** (*f.*) **individual** (18)

sink; bathroom sink **lavabo** (4)

sir **señor (Sr.)** *m.* (P)

sister **hermana** (2)

sit down **sentarse (ie)** (4)

six **seis** (P)

six hundred **seiscientos/as** (3)

sixteen **dieciséis** (P)

sixth **sexto/a** *adj.* (13)

sixty **sesenta** (2)

skate **patinar** (9)

skateboard **monopatín** *m.* (12)

ski **esquiar (esquío)** (9)

skirt **falda** (3)

skyscraper **rascacielos** *m. inv.* (14)

sleep **dormir (ue, u)** (4)

sleepy: to be sleepy **tener** (*irreg.*) **sueño** (3)

slender **delgado/a** (2)

small **pequeño/a** (2); small child **niño/a** (2); small pastry **pastelito** (18)

smart **listo/a** (2)

smile **sonreír(se)** (*like* **reír**) (8)

smoke **fumar** (7)

smoking section **sección** (*f.*) **de fumar** (7)

snow **nevar (ie)** (5); it's snowing **nieva** (5)

so: so-so **regular** (P); so that **para que** (15)

soap **jabón** *m.* (18)

soccer **fútbol** *m.* (9)

social worker **trabajador(a) social** (16)

sociology **sociología** (1)

sock **calcetín** *m.* (*pl.* **calcetines**) (3)

sofa **sofá** *m.* (4)

soft drink **refresco** (6)

solar **solar** *adj.* (14); solar energy **energía solar** (14)

soldier **soldado, mujer** (*f.*) **soldado** (16)

solve **resolver (ue)** (*p.p.* **resuelto**) (14)

some **algún, alguno/a/os/as** (6)

someone **alguien** (6)

something **algo** (3)

sometimes **a veces** (2)

son **hijo** (2)

song **canción** *f.* (13)

soon: as soon as *conj.* **en cuanto** (16); *conj.* **tan pronto como** (16)

sorry: I'm sorry **discúlpeme** (11); I'm (very) sorry! **¡lo siento (mucho)!** (11); to feel sorry **sentir (ie, i)** (13)

sound *v.* **sonar (ue)** (9)

soup **sopa** (6)

south **sur** *m.* (5)

Spanish (*language*) **español** *m.* (1); **español(a)** *n., adj.* (2)

spare time **ratos** (*m. pl.*) **libres** (9)

speak **hablar** (1)

species **especie** *f. s.* (14); endangered species **especie en peligro de extinción** (14)

speed limit **límite** (*m.*) **de velocidad** (14)

spend (*money*) **gastar** (8); (*time*) **pasar** (5); to spend time (with) **pasar tiempo (con)** (15)

sport **deporte** *m.* (9); to practice, play sports **practicar (qu) deportes** (10)

sporting *adj.* **deportivo/a** (9)

sports *adj.* **deportivo/a** (9)

sports-loving **deportivo/a** (9)

spring **primavera** (5)

stage **escenario** (13); (*period of time*) **etapa** (15)

stamp, postage stamp **sello** (18)

stand: stand in line **hacer** (*irreg.*) (*p.p.* **hecho**) **cola** (7); to stand up **levantarse** (4); tobacco stand **estanco** (18)

start up (*a car*) **arrancar (qu)** (14)

state **estado** (2)

station **estación** *f.* (7); bus station **estación de autobuses** (7); gas station **estación de gasolina** (14), **gasolinera** (14); station wagon **camioneta** (7) train station **estación del tren** (7)

stationery **papel** (*m.*) **para cartas** (18); stationery store **papelería** (18)

stay *n.* (*in a place*) **estancia** (18); to stay (*in a place*) **alojarse** (18); **quedar(se)** (5); to stay in bed **guardar cama** (10)

steak **bistec** *m.* (6)

stereo equipment **equipo estereofónico** (12)

stick out one's tongue **sacar (qu) la lengua** (10)

still **todavía** (5)

stockings **medias** *f. pl.* (3)

stomach **estómago** (10)

stomachache **dolor** (*m.*) **de estómago** (10); to have a stomachache **tener** (*irreg.*) **dolor de estómago** (10)

stop *v.* **parar** (14); (*doing something*) **dejar de + inf.** (10); bus stop **parada de autobús** (7); subway stop **estación** (*f.*) **de metro** (18); to make stops **hacer** (*irreg.*) (*p.p.* **hecho**) **escalas/paradas** (7)

store **tienda** (3)

stove **estufa** (9)

straight ahead **todo derecho** (14)

straighten (up) **arreglar** (12)

strange **raro/a** (8); how strange that . . . ! **¡qué extraño que… !** (13); it's strange that **es extraño que** (13)

street **calle** *f.* (12); **camino** (14)

stress **estrés** *m. inv.* (11); **tensión** *f.*

strike (*labor*) **huelga** (17)

strong **fuerte** (6)

student *n.* **estudiante** *m., f.* (1); *adj.* **estudiantil** (11); of students **estudiantil** (11)

study **estudiar** (1)

stuffed up **congestionado/a** (10)

style: it's latest style **es de última moda** (3)

subject (school) **materia** (1)

suburbs **afueras** *f. pl.* (12)

subway stop **estación** (*f.*) **de metro** (18)

succeed in (*doing something*) **conseguir** (*like* **seguir**) **+inf.** (8)

suddenly **de repente** (10)

suffer **sufrir** (11)

sufficiently **bastante** *adv.* (15)

suggest **sugerir (ie, i)** (8)

suit **traje** *m.* (3)

suitcase **maleta** (7); to pack one's suitcase(s) **hacer** (*irreg.*) (*p.p.* **hecho**) **las maleta(s)** (7)

summer **verano** (5)

sunbathe **tomar el sol** (7)

Sunday **domingo** (4)

sunny: it's (very) sunny **hace (mucho) sol** (5)

supper **cena** (6); to have/eat supper **cenar** (6)

support **apoyar** (17)

sure **seguro/a** *adj.* (5); it's a sure thing that **es seguro que** (13)

surf the Net **navegar (gu) la Red** (12)

surprise **sorpresa** (8); it surprises me (you, him, . . .) that **me (te, le, …) sorprende que** (13)

sweater **suéter** *m.* (3)

sweep (the floor) **barrer (el piso)** (9)

sweets **dulces** *m. pl.* (6)

swim **nadar** (7)

swimming **natación** *f.* (9); swimming pool **piscina** (4)

swimsuit **traje** (*m.*) **de baño** (3)

symptom **síntoma** *m.* (10)

systems analyst **analista** (*m., f.*) **de sistemas** (16)

# T

T-shirt **camiseta** (3)

table **mesa** (1); end table **mesita** (4); to clear the table **quitar la mesa** (9); to set the table **poner** (*irreg.*) (*p.p.* **puesto**) **la mesa** (9)

take **llevar** (3); to take **tomar** (1); to take (photos) **sacar (qu) (fotos)** (7); to take a bath **bañarse** (4); to take a nap **dormir (ue, u) la siesta** (4); to take a shower **ducharse** (4); to take a trip **hacer** (*irreg.*) (*p.p.* **hecho**) **un viaje** (4); to take a walk **dar** (*irreg.*) **un paseo** (9); to take care of oneself **cuidarse** (10); to take leave (of) **despedirse** (*like* **pedir**) **(de)** (8); to take off (*clothing*) **quitarse** (4); to take out (*money*) **sacar** (16); to take out the trash **sacar la basura** (9); to take place at/in (*place*) **ser** (*irreg.*) **en** + *place* (8); to take someone's temperature **tomar(le) la temperatura** (10)

talk **hablar** (1); to talk on the phone **hablar por teléfono** (1)

tall **alto/a** (2)

tank **tanque** *m.* (14)

tape **cinta** (3) tape recorder/player **grabadora** (12); to tape **grabar** (12)

tea **té** *m.* (6)

teach **enseñar** (1)

technician **técnico/a** *n.* (16)

teeth: to brush one's teeth **cepillarse los dientes** (4)

television set **televisor** *m.* (4); to watch television **mirar la televisión** (2)

tell **decir** (*irreg.*) (*p.p.* **dicho**) (7); **contar (ue)** (7)

teller **cajero/a** (16); automatic teller machine **cajero automático** (16)

temperature **temperatura** (10); to take someone's temperature **tomarle la temperatura** (10)

ten **diez** (P)

tenant **inquilino/a** (12)

tennis **tenis** *m. inv.* (9); tennis shoe **zapato de tenis** (3)

tent **tienda (de campaña)** (7)

tenth **décimo/a** (13)

terrible: it's terrible that **es terrible que** (13)

terrorism **terrorismo** (17)

terrorist **terrorista** *m., f.* (17); terrorist attack **ataque** (*m.*) **terrorista** (17)

test **examen** *m.* (3); **prueba** (11)

textbook **libro de texto** (1)

thank you **gracias** (P); thank you very much **muchas gracias** (P); thanks for **gracias por** (8)

that *dem. adj.* **ese/a** (3); that *dem. pron.* **eso** (3); that (*over there*) *dem. adj.* **aquel, aquello/a** (3); that (*over there*) *dem. pron.* **aquello** (3); that one *dem. adj.* **ese/a** (3); that one (*over there*) *dem. pron.* **aquel, aquello/a** (3); that *conj.* **que** (2); that means . . . **eso quiere decir...** (10)

theater: to go to the theater **ir** (*irreg.*) **al teatro** (9)

their *poss. adj.* **su(s)** (2)

then **luego** (4)

there is (not), there are (not) **(no) hay** (P); there's (lots of) pollution **hay (mucha) contaminación** (5)

there: (over) there **allí** (3)

therefore **por eso** (1)

these *dem. adj.* **estos/as** (2); *dem. pron.* these (ones) **estos/as** (2)

they *subj. pron.* **ellos/as** (1)

thin **delgado/a** (2)

thing **cosa** (1); it's a sure thing **es seguro que** (13); the bad thing **lo malo** (10); the good thing **lo bueno** (10)

think **creer (y) (en)** (2); to think (about) **pensar (ie) (en)** (4)

third **tercer, tercero/a** *adj.* (13); third floor **segundo piso** (12)

thirsty: to be (very) thirsty **tener** (*irreg.*) **(mucha) sed** (6)

thirteen **trece** (P)

thirty **treinta** (P); thirty past (*the hour*) **y media** (P), **y treinta** (P)

this *dem. adj.* **este/a** (2); *dem. pron.* **esto** (2); this one *dem. pron.* **este/a** (2)

those *dem. adj.* **esos/as** (3); those (ones) *dem. pron.* **esos/as** (3); those (over there) *dem. adj.* **aquellos/as** (3); those (ones) (*dem. pron.*) (*over there*) **aquellos/as** (3)

thousand **mil** *m.* (3)

three **tres** (P); three star hotel **hotel** (*m.*) **de tres estrellas** (18)

three hundred **trescientos/as** (3)

throat **garganta** (10)

Thursday **jueves** *m. inv.* (4)

ticket **billete** *m.* (7); **boleto** (7); **pasaje** *m.* (7); one-way ticket **billete/boleto de ida** (7); round-trip ticket **billete/boleto de ida y vuelta** (7)

tie **corbata** (3)

time (*period*) **época** (11); ahead of time **con anticipación** (18); at what time? **¿a qué hora?** (P); for the first/last time **por primera / última vez** (11); free time **ratos** (*m. pl.*) **libres** (9); full time **de tiempo completo** (11); on time **a tiempo** (7); part time **de tiempo parcial** (11); to have a good time **divertirse (ie, i)** (4); to have a good/bad time **pasarlo bien/mal** (8); to spend time (with) **pasar tiempo (con)** (15); what time is it? **¿qué hora es?** (P)

tip (*money given to an employee*) **propina** (18)

tire *n.* **llanta** (14)

tired **cansado/a** (5)

to **a** (P); according to **según** (2); close to *prep.* **cerca de** (5); in order to **para** (2); (*minutes*) to (*the hour*) **menos** (P); newlywed to **recién casado/a con** (15); to the **al** (*contraction of* **a** + **el**) (3); to the north / south / east / west **al norte / sur / este / oeste** (5); to the right/left of **a la derecha/izquierda de** (5)

toast **pan** (*m.*) **tostado** (6)

toaster **tostadora** (9)

tobacco stand/shop **estanco** (18)

today **hoy** (P); what's today's date? **¿cuál es la fecha de hoy?** (5)

toe **dedo del pie** (11)

together **juntos/as** (15)

tomato **tomate** *m.* (6)

tomorrow **mañana** *adv.* (P); day after tomorrow **pasado mañana** (4); see you tomorrow **hasta mañana** (P)

tongue: to stick out one's tongue **sacar (qu) la lengua** (10)

tonight **esta noche** (5)

too much **demasiado** *adv.* (12)

tooth **diente** *m.* (10); **muela** (10); to extract a tooth **sacar (qu) una muela** (10)

toothache **dolor** (*m.*) **de muela** (10)

toothpaste **pasta dental** (18)

tourist: tourist class **clase** (*f.*) **turística** (7)

towel **toalla** (18)

trade **oficio** (16)

traffic **tránsito** (14), **circulación** *f.* (14); traffic signal **semáforo** (14)

train **tren** *m.* (7); train station **estación** (*f.*) **del tren** (7); to go/travel by train **ir** (*irreg.*) **en tren** (7); to train **entrenar** (9)

translator **traductor(a)** (16)

transportation **transporte** *m.* (14); means of transportation **modo de transporte** (7)

trash: to take out the trash **sacar (qu) la basura** (9)

travel **viajar** (7); travel agency **agencia de viajes** (7); travel agent **agente** (*m., f.*) **de viajes** (7); to travel by boat/ship **ir** (*irreg.*) **en barco** (7); to travel by bus/plane/train **ir en autobús/avión/tren** (7)

traveler **viajero/a** (18); traveler's check **cheque** (*m.*) **de viajero** (18)

treadmill **rueda de molino** (10)

treatment **tratamiento** (10)

tree **árbol** *m.* (14)

trip **viaje** *m.* (7); on a trip **de viaje** (7); round-trip ticket **billete** (*m.*)/**boleto de ida y vuelta** (7); to take a trip **hacer** (*irreg.*) (*p.p.* **hecho**) **un viaje** (4)

try to (*do something*) **tratar de** + *inf.* (13)

Tuesday **martes** *m. inv.* (4)

tuition **matrícula** (1)

tuna **atún** *m.* (6)

turkey **pavo** (6)

turn **doblar** (14); to turn in **entregar (gu)** (11); to turn off **apagar (gu)** (11); to turn on (*appliances*) **poner** (*irreg.*) (*p.p.* **puesto**) (4); to be someone's turn **tocarle (qu) a uno** (9)

twelve **doce** (P)

twenty **veinte** (P)

twice **dos veces** (10)

two **dos** (P); two star hotel **hotel** (*m.*) **de dos estrellas** (18)

two hundred **doscientos/as** (3)

type **escribir** (*p.p.* **escrito**) **en la computadora** (16)

## U

U.S. *adj.* **estadounidense** *m., f.* (2)

ugly **feo/a** (2)

uncle **tío** (2)

understand **comprender** (2); **entender (ie)** (4)

underwear **ropa interior** (3)

unintentional: it was unintentional **fue sin querer** (11)

university **universidad** *f.* (1); *adj.*, of the university **universitario/a** (11); university campus *campus m. inv.* (12)

unless **a menos que** (15)

unlikely: it's unlikely that **es improbable que** (13)

unoccupied **desocupado/a** (18)

unpleasant **antipático/a** (2)

until *prep.* **hasta** (4); *conj.* **hasta que** (16)

urgent: it's urgent that **es urgente que** (13)

use **usar** (3); to use (*gas*) **gastar** (14); to use up completely **acabar** (14)

## V

vacancy: no vacancy **completo/a** (18)

vacant **desocupado/a** (18)

vacation: to be on vacation **estar** (*irreg.*) **de vacaciones** (7); to go on vacation **ir** (*irreg.*) **de vacaciones** (7)

vacuum *v.* **pasar la aspiradora** (9); vacuum cleaner **aspiradora** (9)

VCR **videocasetera** (12)

vegetables **verduras** *f. pl.* (6)

vehicle **vehículo** (12)

very **muy** (1); very cold **congelado/a** (5); very well **muy bien** (P)

veterinarian **veterinario/a** (16)

victim **víctima** (17)

video camera **camara de vídeo** (12)

videocassette recorder (VCR) **videocasetera** (12)

view **vista** (12)

violence **violencia** (14)

visit a museum **visitar un museo** (9)

volleyball **vólibol** *m.* (9)

vote *v.* **votar** (17)

## W

wait (for) **esperar** (6)

waiter **camarero** (6)

waiting room **sala de espera** (7)

waitress **camarera** (6)

wake up **despertarse (ie)** (*p.p.* **despierto**) (4)

walk **caminar** (10); to take a walk **dar** (*irreg.*) **un paseo** (9)

Walkman *walkman m.* (12)

wall **pared** *f.* (4); to paint the walls **pintar las paredes** (9)

wallet **cartera** (3)

want **desear** (1); **querer** (*irreg.*) (3)

war **guerra** (17)

warm: to be (very) warm, hot **tener (mucho)** (*irreg.*) **calor** (5)

wash *v.* wash (the clothes, the dishes, the windows) **lavar (la ropa, los platos, las ventanas)** (9)

washing machine **lavadora** (9)

watch **reloj** *m.* (3); to watch **mirar** (2); to watch television **mirar la televisión** (2)

water **agua** *f.* (*but* **el agua**) (6); mineral water **agua mineral** (6)

waterbed **cama de agua** (4)

we **nosotros/as** (1)

wear (*clothing*) **llevar** (3), **usar** (3); to wear contact lenses/glasses **llevar lentes de contacto/gafas** (10)

weather **tiempo** (5); it's (very) good/bad weather **hace (muy) buen/mal tiempo** (5); what's the weather like? **¿qué tiempo hace?** (5)

weave **tejer** (13)

wedding (ceremony) **boda** (15)

Wednesday **miércoles** *m. inv.* (4)

week: next week **la semana que viene** (4); once a week **una vez a la semana** (2)

weekday **día** (*m.*) **de la semana** (4)

weekend **fin** (*m.*) **de semana** (1)

welcome: you're welcome **de nada** (P), **no hay de qué** (P)

well **bien** *adv.* (P); well . . . *interj.* **bueno...** (2)

well-being **bienestar** *m.* (10)

west **oeste** *m.* (5)

whale **ballena** (14)

what **lo que** (4); what a shame that . . . ! **¡qué lástima que... !** (13); what bad luck! **¡qué mala suerte!** (11)

what? **¿qué?** (P); what? **¿cuál(es)?** (1); at what time? **¿a qué hora?** (P); what are you (*form. s.*) like? **¿cómo es usted?** (P); what time is it? **¿qué hora es?** (P); what's the weather like? **¿qué tiempo hace?** (5); what's today's date? **¿cuál es la fecha de hoy?** (5); what's your (*form. s.*) name? **¿cómo se llama usted?** (P); what's your (*fam. s.*) name? **¿cómo te llamas?** (P)

when? **¿cuándo?** (1)

where? **¿dónde?** (P); where (to)? **¿adónde?** (3); where are you (*fam. s.*) from? **¿de dónde eres?** (P); where are you (*form. s.*) from? **¿de dónde es usted?** (P)

which? **¿cuál(es)?** (1)

while **mientras** *conj.* (9)

white **blanco/a** (3); white wine **vino blanco** (6)

who **que** (2)

who? **¿quién(es)?** (1)

whole: to clean the whole house **limpiar la casa entera** (9)

whom? **¿quién(es)?** (1)

whose? **¿de quién?** (2)

why? **¿por qué?** (2)

widow **viuda** (15)

widower **viudo** (15)

wife **esposa** (2); **mujer** *f.* (15)

wild animal **animal** (*m.*) **salvaje** (14)

win **ganar** (9)

window **ventana** (1); to wash the windows **lavar las ventanas** (9)

windshield **parabrisas** *m. inv.* (14)

windy: it's (very) windy **hace (mucho) viento** (5)

wine (white, red) **vino (blanco, tinto)** (6)

winter **invierno** (5)

wish **deseo** (8); **esperanza** (17); I wish (that) **ojalá (que)** (13)

with **con** (1); with me **conmigo** (5); with you *fam. s.* **contigo** (5)

withdraw (*money*) **sacar (qu)** (16)

without **sin** (4)

witness **testigo** *m., f.* (17)

woman **mujer** *f.* (1)

wool **lana** (3); it's made of wool **es de lana** (3)

word **palabra** (P)

work *n.* **trabajo** (11); (of art) **obra (de arte)** (13); piece of work **trabajo** (11); to work **trabajar** (1); (*machine*) **funcionar** (12)

worker **obrero/a** (16); **trabajador(a)** (2); social worker **trabajador(a) social** (16)

world **mundo** (7)

worried **preocupado/a** (5)

worse **peor** (5)

would: I would (really) like . . . **me gustaría...** (7)

woven goods **tejidos** *m. pl.* (13)

write **escribir** (*p.p.* **escrito**) (2)

writer **escritor(a)** (13)

written **escrito/a** (*p.p.* of **escribir**) (11); written report **informe** (*m.*) **escrito** (11)

wrong: to be wrong **no tener** (*irreg.*) **razón** (3); to be wrong (about) **equivocarse (qu) (de)** (11) to get up on the wrong side of the bed **levantarse con el pie izquierdo** (11)

## Y

yard **jardín** *m.* (4); **patio** (4)

year **año** (5); (*in school*) **grado** (9); to be . . . years old **tener** (*irreg.*)... **años** (2)

yellow **amarillo/a** (3)

yes **sí** (P); yes, I like . . . **sí, me gusta...** (P)

yesterday **ayer** (4); the day before yesterday **anteayer** (10)

yogurt **yogur** *m.* (6)

you *sub. pron.* **tú** *fam. s.* (1); **usted (Ud.)** *form. s.* (1); **ustedes (Uds.)** *form. pl.* (1); **vosotos/as** *fam. pl.* (1); *obj. of prep.* **ti** *fam. s.* (5); and you? *fam.s.* **¿y tú?** (P); *form. s.* **¿y usted?** (P); you (*fam. s.*) are **eres** (P); you (*form. s.*) are **es** (P)

you're welcome **de nada** (P), **no hay de qué** (P)

young **joven** *m., f.* (2)

younger **menor** (5)

your *poss. adj.* **tú(s)** *fam.* (2); **su(s)** *form.* (2); **vuestro/a(s)** *fam. pl. Sp.* (2)

youth **juventud** *f.* (15); as a youth **de joven** (9)

## Z

zero **cero** (P)

## Photos

Page 1 left: © Ulrike Welsch; p. 1 right: © Ulrike Welsch; p. 10: © Stuart Cohen; p. 13: SuperStock; p. 17 bottom: SuperStock; p. 17 top: PICTOR/ImageState; p. 18 bottom: © Peter Menzel; p. 18 top left: Antonio Mendoza/Stock Boston; p. 18 top right: © Ulrike Welsch; p. 21: PhotoDisc; p. 24: © Ken Welsh/age fotostock; p. 33 bottom: © Tim Mosenfelder/Getty Images; p. 33 middle: AP Wide World Photos; p. 33 top: AP Wide World Photos; p. 40: AP Wide World Photos; p. 41: Photography by Marsha Miller, Courtesy of University of Texas at Austin; p. 43: US Postal Service; p. 44: © Ulrike Welsch; p. 49: © Jimmy Dorantes/LatinFocus.com; p. 56: PICTOR/ImageState; p. 65 bottom: Vince Bucci/AFP/Getty Images; p. 65 top: © Mike Ramirez/LatinFocus.com; p. 66: Museo del Prado, Madrid, Spain/Giraudon, Paris/SuperStock; p. 73 bottom: © Fernando Botero, courtesy, Marlborough Gallery, New York; p. 73 top: © Trapper Frank/Corbis Sygma; p. 75: Commissioned by the Trustees of Dartmouth College, © Clemente Orozco Valladares; p. 76: © 1987 Carmen Lomas Garza Photo credit: Wolfgang Dietze; Collection of Leonila Ramirez, Don Ramon's Restaurant, San Francisco, California; p. 79: © Tomas Stargardter/Latin Focus.com; p. 82: © Reuters NewMedia Inc./Corbis; p. 83: © Gonzalo Endara Crow; p. 94 bottom: German Miranda/LA PRENSA; p. 94 middle: AP/Wide World Photos; p. 94 top: HO/AFP/Getty Images; p. 97: Topham/The Image Works; p. 98: © Robert Frerck, Odyssey Productions, Chicago; p. 100: John Mitchell/DDB Stock Photography; p. 105: © Beryl Goldberg; p. 108: © Ric Ergenbright; p. 116 bottom: John Dominis/Time Life Pictures/Getty Images; p. 116 middle: © Dave G. Houser/Corbis; p. 116 top: Ardis L. Nelson; p. 120: © Robert Holmes/Corbis; p. 121: © Victor Englebert; p. 123: © Bill Gentile/Corbis; p. 127: © Moises Castillo/LatinFocus.com; p. 131: AP Wide World Photos; p. 142 top & bottom: "A logo for America" by Alfredo Jaar; p. 143 bottom: AP Wide World Photos; p. 143 top: Pierre Boulat/Time Life Pictures/Getty Images; p. 144 bottom: © Ulrike Welsch; p. 144 top: PICTOR/ImageState; p. 148 © J.J. Halber/DDB Stock Photo; p. 150: © Rob Crandall/The Image Works; p. 151: Frans Lanting; p. 152: PhotoDisc/Getty Images; p. 155: © John Neubauer; p. 158 left: © FoodPix; p. 158 right: © Peter Guttman/Corbis; p. 168 middle: © Don Tremain/Alamy; p. 168 right: Rosario de Mou; p. 168 top: Courtesy of Prof. Carlos "Cubena" Guillermo Wilson, Ph.D.; p. 174: © Jimmy Dorantes/LatinFocus.com; p. 176: Courtesy of Oswaldo & Alice Arana; p. 181: © Chris Sharp/DDB Stock: p. 185 bottom: Michael J. Doolittle/The Image Works; p. 185 top: © Stuart Cohen; p. 194 middle: Yolocamba I Ta; p. 194 top: Clementina c. 1940; p. 200 bottom: © PhotoDisc/Getty Images; p. 200 top: © Corbis; p. 202: © Stephen and Donna O'Meara/Photo Researchers, Inc.; p. 203: © Alfredo Maiquez/Lonely Planet Images; p. 207: © A. Garcia/LatinFocus.com; p. 210: © Jack Kurtz/The Image Works; p. 219 middle left: © Peter Turnley/Corbis; p. 219 middle right: J. J. Orts/Courtesy of Nebenegra; p. 219 top: Bettman/Corbis; p. 222: Bob Riha Jr./Getty Images; p. 223: © Lorenzo Armendariz/LatinFocus.com; p. 225: Prensa Latina/Getty Images; p. 229: EPA/Miguel Mendez V./Landov Ê; p. 231: Reuters/Bettmann/Corbis; p. 239 left: Stephane Cardinale/Corbis Sygma; p. 239 middle: © Reuters NewMedia/Inc./Corbis; p. 239 right: AP Wide World Photos; p. 241: © Michael Kim/Corbis; p. 242 bottom: The Grosby Group; p. 242 middle: © Jeremy Horner/Corbis; p. 242 top: AP Wide World

**Marty Knorre** was formerly Associate Professor of Romance Languages and Coordinator of basic Spanish courses at the University of Cincinnati, where she taught undergraduate and graduate courses in language, linguistics, and methodology. She received her Ph.D. in foreign language education from The Ohio State University in 1975. Dr. Knorre is coauthor of *Cara a cara* and *Reflejos* and has taught at several NEH Institutes for Language Instructors. She received a Master of Divinity at McCormick Theological Seminary in 1991.

**Thalia Dorwick** recently retired as McGraw-Hill's Editor-in-Chief for Humanities, Social Sciences, and Languages. For many years she was also in charge of McGraw-Hill's World Languages college list in Spanish, French, Italian, German, Japanese, and Russian. She has taught at Allegheny College, California State University (Sacramento), and Case Western Reserve University, where she received her Ph.D. in Spanish in 1973. She was recognized as an Outstanding Foreign Language Teacher by the California Foreign Language Teachers Association in 1978. Dr. Dorwick is the coauthor of several textbooks and the author of several articles on language teaching issues. She is a frequent guest speaker on topics related to language learning, and she was also an invited speaker at the *II Congreso Internacional de la Lengua Española,* in Valladolid, Spain, in October 2001. In retirement, she consults for McGraw-Hill, especially in the area of world languages, which are of personal interest to her. She also serves on the Board of Trustees of Case Western Reserve University and on the Board of Directors of the Berkeley Repertory Theater.

**Ana María Pérez-Gironés** is an Adjunct Associate Professor of Spanish at Wesleyan University, Middletown, Connecticut, where she teaches and coordinates Spanish language courses. She received a *Licenciatura en Filología Anglogermánica* from the *Universidad de Sevilla* in 1985, and her M.A. in General Linguistics from Cornell University in 1988. Professor Pérez-Gironés' professional interests include second language acquisition and the use of technology in language learning. She is a coauthor of the *Student Manuals for Intermediate Grammar Review* and *Intensive and High Beginner Courses* that accompany *Nuevos Destinos.*

**William R. Glass** is the Publisher for World Languages and Health and Human Performance at McGraw-Hill Higher Education. He received his Ph.D. from the University of Illinois at Urbana-Champaign in Spanish Applied Linguistics with a concentration in Second Language Acquisition and Teacher Education (SLATE). He was previously Assistant Professor of Spanish at The Pennsylvania State University where he was also Director of the Language Program in Spanish. He has published numerous articles and edited books on issues related to second language instruction and acquisition.

**Hildebrando Villarreal** is Professor of Spanish at California State University, Los Angeles, where he teaches undergraduate and graduate courses in language and linguistics. He received his Ph.D. in Spanish with an emphasis in Applied Linguistics from UCLA in 1976. Professor Villarreal is the author of several reviews and articles on language, language teaching, and

Spanish for Native Speakers of Spanish. He is the author of *¡A leer! Un paso más*, an intermediate textbook that focuses on reading skills.

**A. Raymond Elliott** is Associate Professor of Spanish and Chair of the Department of Modern Languages at the University of Texas, Arlington. He received his Ph.D. from Indiana University-Bloomington in 1993. His areas of specialization are Spanish applied linguistics, second language acquisition, the acquisition of second language phonological skills, and the historical development of Spanish. Dr. Elliott has published several articles, book chapters, reviews in *The Modern Language Journal, Hispania,* and with Georgetown University Press. He served as a panelist in the McGraw-Hill Annual Teleconference on Authentic Materials, and as a member of the Academic Advisory Board for the package to accompany *Nuevos Destinos.* He is the author of *Nuevos Destinos: Español para hispanohablantes.*

In this index, communication strategies, cultural topics, reading strategies, and vocabulary topic groups are listed by individual topic as well as under those headings. References to pages A-1 through A-17 are references to the appendixes that appear after chapter 18.

-ir verbs, regular, 69, A-9–10. *See also* **vivir.**
   stem-changing, A-16–17. *See also* stem-changing verbs.
**ir** (*irreg.*), A-12
   formal command forms, 170
   imperfect, 235
   informal command forms, 303
   **ir** + **a** + infinitive, 95, 336
   past subjunctive, 420
   present indicative, 95
   present subjunctive, 310
   preterite, 197
irregular verbs, A-10–15
**-ísimo/a/os/as,** 211, 239
**-ista,** for names of professions, 391

# J

**j,** pronunciation of, 5, 6
Jaar, Alfredo, 142
Jara, Víctor, 376
Jiménez, Juan Ramón, 443
jobs and professions (*vocabulary*), 47, 274, 388, 389, 390, 391, 411
**joropo,** 266
Juanes, 247
**jugar (ue) (gu) (a),** 114, 114n, 303

# K

kissing on the cheek, 267n
*know,* expressing (*vocabulary*), 159

# L

**la,** 28–29, 31, 106, A-4
   with feminine names for professions, 391
language cues to understand poetry, using, 430
Latin music in the United States, 284
**le,** 187
   becomes **se,** 220, A-4
   for **lo,** 162n
**Lectura.** *See* reading strategies.
**leer (y),** past participle, 351
   past subjunctive, 420
   present indicative, 69
   preterite, 196
legal majority (adulthood), 417
leisure activities (*vocabulary*), 40, 107, 112, 115, 251, 358
life stages, coming of age, 417 (*vocabulary*), 370, 386
likes and dislikes, expressing, 190–191, 193, 326
   (*vocabulary*), 13

linking, 27
**ll,** pronunciation of, 5n, 6, 128
**lo,** 162, A-4
   **lo bueno / lo malo,** 257
   with singular masculine adjective, 257, A-6
location, with **en,** 185, 192
   with **estar** (*irreg.*), 139
Lonely Boys, 33
**los / las.** *See* definite article.

# M

main clause. *See* independent clause.
**mal(o/a),** 58, 166
   **lo malo,** 257
marimba, 116, 143
Martí, José, 219
**más (de),** 145
   in superlative, 239
**más… que,** 144–146
masculine. *See also* agreement and forms of adjectives; gender.
   nouns, 28–29, 31, 57
**mayor,** 145
meals (*vocabulary*), 156–157
meaning from context, guessing, 17, 44
media, the (*vocabulary*), 414, 432
medicine in Spanish-speaking countries, 255
**mejor,** 145, 146, 239
   **lo mejor,** 257
Menchú, Rigoberta, 150
**menor,** 145
**menos (de),** 145
**menos… que,** 144–146
**-mente,** 280
**merengue,** 425
Mexico, 17, 65, 75, 341, 347
**mí,** 132
**mientras,** with the imperfect, 236, 259
**mil, millón,** 84, 130
**mirar,** 160
missions of California, 120
Mistral, Gabriela, 376
money (*vocabulary*), 392
months of the year (*vocabulary*), 130
mood, 172, 308, A-3. *See also* commands; conditional; indicative mood; subjunctive mood.
**morir(se) (ue, u),** 217, 352
Mou, Julio, 168
**mucho,** 92, 193
   in weather expressions, 128
   **muchísimo,** 211

**mujer,** in names for professions, 391
muralists, Mexican, 75
music and dance, **arpa paraguaya,** 400
   **bomba,** 285
   **calipso,** 168
   **candombe,** 400
   **canto nuevo,** 376
   **corrido,** 65
   **huayno,** 313
   **joropo,** 266
   Juanes, 247
   marimba, 116, 143
   **merengue,** 425
   **música latina,** 284
   **plena,** 285
   **punta,** 94
   **punto guanacaste,** 116
   **romances,** 443
   Rumillajta, 333
   salsa, 284
   **son,** 219
   tango, 355
   **tejano,** 33
   **vallenato,** 242
   Yolocamba I Ta, 194

# N

**nada,** 193
naming systems, 52
Naranjo, Carmen, 116
narrating in the past. *See* imperfect indicative; preterite.
nationality, adjectives of, 57, 59, 139
natural world (*vocabulary*), 346–347
near future, 95
**necesitar** (+ infinitive), 36, 233
negation, 165–166
   and the subjunctive, 334–335
   in the accidental **se** construction, 282
   in **tú** commands, 303
   in **vosotros** commands, 304
   of **querer** and **poder,** in the preterite, 214
   placement of direct object pronouns in negative sentences, 162, 170, 303
   placement of indirect object pronouns in negative sentences, 187, 303
   placement of **no,** 37, 357
   placement of reflexive pronouns in negative sentences, 119, 170, 303
neighborhoods, 301
news, the (*vocabulary*), 414, 432
Nicaragua, 94, 100